Books by His Divine Grace
A. C. Bhaktivedanta Swami Prabhupāda:

Bhagavad-gītā As It Is
Śrīmad-Bhāgavatam (1st to 10th Cantos)
Śrī Caitanya-Caritāmṛta (9 vols.)
Kṛṣṇa, The Supreme Personality of Godhead
Teachings of Lord Caitanya
The Nectar of Devotion
The Nectar of Instruction
Śrī Īśopaniṣad
Light of the Bhāgavata
Easy Journey to Other Planets
The Science of Self-Realization
Kṛṣṇa Consciousness: The Topmost Yoga System
Perfect Questions, Perfect Answers
Teachings of Lord Kapila, the Son of Devahuti
Transcendental Teachings of Prahlāda Mahārāja
Teachings of Queen Kuntī
Kṛṣṇa, the Reservoir of Pleasure
The Path of Perfection
Life Comes from Life
Message of Godhead
The Perfection of Yoga
Beyond Birth and Death
On the Way to Kṛṣṇa
Rāja-vidyā: The King of Knowledge
Elevation to Kṛṣṇa Consciousness
Kṛṣṇa Consciousness: The Matchless Gift
Selected Verses from the Vedic Scriptures
Back to Godhead magazine (founder)

ALL GLORY TO ŚRĪ GURU AND GAURĀṄGA

ŚRĪMAD BHĀGAVATAM

of

KṚṢṆA - DVAIPĀYANA VYĀSA

ऋषभ उवाच
नायं देहो देहभाजां नृलोके
कष्टान् कामानर्हते विड्भुजां ये ।
तपो दिव्यं पुत्रका येन सत्त्वं
शुद्ध्येद्यस्माद् ब्रह्मसौख्यं त्वनन्तम् ॥१॥

ṛṣabha uvāca
nāyaṁ deho deha-bhājāṁ nṛloke
kaṣṭān kāmān arhate viḍ-bhujāṁ ye
tapo divyaṁ putrakā yena sattvaṁ
śuddhyed yasmād brahma-saukhyaṁ tv anantaṁ
(*Śrīmad-Bhāgavatam* - 5.5

ŚRĪMAD BHĀGAVATAM

Fifth Canto
"The Creative Impetus "

With the Original Sanskrit Text,
Its Roman Transliteration, Synonyms,
Translation and Elaborate Purports

by

His Divine Grace
A.C.Bhaktivedanta Swami Prabhupāda
Founder - *Ācārya* of the International Society for Krishna Consciousness

THE BHAKTIVEDANTA BOOK TRUST

Readers interested in the subject matter of this book are invited by The Bhaktivedanta Book Trust to correspond with its secretary at the following address:

The Bhaktivedanta Book Trust
Hare Krishna Land,
Juhu, Mumbai 400 049, India.

Website / E-mail :
www.indiabbt.com
admin@indiabbt.com

Śrīmad Bhāgavatam Fifth Canto (English)

First printing in India : 2,000 copies
Second to Eighteenth printings : 59,500 copies
Nineteenth printing, July 2020 : 5,000 copies

ISBN : 978-93-84564-07-0 (v. 7)
ISBN : 978-93-84564-00-1 (18-volume set)

Published and Printed by
The Bhaktivedanta Book Trust.

SJ1K

Table of Contents

CHAPTER FOUR

The Characteristics of Ṛṣabhadeva, the
Supreme Personality of Godhead   **119**

CHAPTER FIVE

Lord Ṛṣabhadeva's Teachings to His Sons   **141**

CHAPTER SIX

The Activities of Lord Ṛṣabhadeva   **191**

Preface

We must know the present need of human society. And what is that need? Human society is no longer bounded by geographical limits to particular countries or communities. Human society is broader than in the Middle Ages, and the world tendency is toward one state or one human society. The ideals of spiritual communism, according to *Śrīmad-Bhāgavatam,* are based more or less on the oneness of the entire human society, nay, of the entire energy of living beings. The need is felt by great thinkers to make this a successful ideology. *Śrīmad-Bhāgavatam* will fill this need in human society. It begins, therefore, with an aphorism of Vedānta philosophy, *janmādy asya yataḥ,* to establish the ideal of a common cause.

Human society, at the present moment, is not in the darkness of oblivion. It has made rapid progress in the fields of material comforts, education and economic development throughout the entire world. But there is a pinprick somewhere in the social body at large, and therefore there are large-scale quarrels, even over less important issues. There is need of a clue as to how humanity can become one in peace, friendship and prosperity with a common cause. *Śrīmad-Bhāgavatam* will fill this need, for it is a cultural presentation for the respiritualization of the entire human society.

Śrīmad-Bhāgavatam should be introduced also in the schools and colleges, for it is recommended by the great student-devotee Prahlāda Mahārāja in order to change the demoniac face of society.

kaumāra ācaret prājño
dharmān bhāgavatān iha
durlabhaṁ mānuṣaṁ janma
tad apy adhruvam artha-dam
(Bhāg. 7.6.1)

Disparity in human society is due to lack of principles in a godless civilization. There is God, or the Almighty One, from whom everything emanates, by whom everything is maintained and in whom everything is merged to rest. Material science has tried to find the ultimate source of creation very insufficiently, but it is a fact that there is one ultimate source of everything that be. This ultimate source is explained rationally and authoritatively in the beautiful *Bhāgavatam,* or *Śrīmad-Bhāgavatam.*

Śrīmad-Bhāgavatam is the transcendental science not only for knowing the ultimate source of everything but also for knowing our relation with Him and our duty toward perfection of the human society on the basis of this perfect knowledge. It is powerful reading matter in the Sanskrit language, and it is now rendered into English elaborately so that simply by a careful reading one will know God perfectly well, so much so that the reader will be sufficiently educated to defend himself from the onslaught of atheists. Over and above this, the reader will be able to convert others to accepting God as a concrete principle.

Śrīmad-Bhāgavatam begins with the definition of the ultimate source. It is a bona fide commentary on the *Vedānta-sūtra* by the same author, Śrīla Vyāsadeva, and gradually it develops into nine cantos up to the highest state of God realization. The only qualification one needs to study this great book of transcendental knowledge is to proceed step by step cautiously and not jump forward haphazardly as with an ordinary book. It should be gone through chapter by chapter, one after another. The reading matter is so arranged with the original Sanskrit text, its English transliteration, synonyms, translation and purports so that one is sure to become a God-realized soul at the end of finishing the first nine cantos.

The Tenth Canto is distinct from the first nine cantos because it deals directly with the transcendental activities of the Personality of Godhead, Śrī Kṛṣṇa. One will be unable to capture the effects of the Tenth Canto without going through the first nine cantos. The book is complete in twelve cantos, each independent, but it is good for all to read them in small installments one after another.

I must admit my frailties in presenting *Śrīmad-Bhāgavatam,* but still I am hopeful of its good reception by the thinkers and leaders of society on the strength of the following statement of *Śrīmad-Bhāgavatam* (1.5.11):

tad-vāg-visargo janatāgha-viplavo
yasmin prati-ślokam abaddhavaty api
nāmāny anantasya yaśo 'ṅkitāni yac
chṛṇvanti gāyanti gṛṇanti sādhavaḥ

"On the other hand, that literature which is full of descriptions of the transcendental glories of the name, fame, form and pastimes of the unlimited Supreme Lord is a transcendental creation meant for bringing about a revolution in the impious life of a misdirected civilization. Such transcendental literature, even though irregularly composed, is heard, sung and accepted by purified men who are thoroughly honest."

Oṁ tat sat

A. C. Bhaktivedanta Swami

Introduction

"This *Bhāgavata Purāṇa* is as brilliant as the sun, and it has arisen just after the departure of Lord Kṛṣṇa to His own abode, accompanied by religion, knowledge, etc. Persons who have lost their vision due to the dense darkness of ignorance in the age of Kali shall get light from this *Purāṇa.*" (*Śrīmad-Bhāgavatam* 1.3.43)

The timeless wisdom of India is expressed in the *Vedas,* ancient Sanskrit texts that touch upon all fields of human knowledge. Originally preserved through oral tradition, the *Vedas* were first put into writing five thousand years ago by Śrīla Vyāsadeva, the "literary incarnation of God." After compiling the *Vedas,* Vyāsadeva set forth their essence in the aphorisms known as *Vedānta-sūtras. Śrīmad-Bhāgavatam* (*Bhāgavata Purāṇa*) is Vyāsadeva's commentary on his own *Vedānta-sūtras.* It was written in the maturity of his spiritual life under the direction of Nārada Muni, his spiritual master. Referred to as "the ripened fruit of the tree of Vedic literature," *Śrīmad-Bhāgavatam* is the most complete and authoritative exposition of Vedic knowledge.

After compiling the *Bhāgavatam,* Vyāsa imparted the synopsis of it to his son, the sage Śukadeva Gosvāmī. Śukadeva Gosvāmī subsequently recited the entire *Bhāgavatam* to Mahārāja Parīkṣit in an assembly of learned saints on the bank of the Ganges at Hastināpura (now Delhi). Mahārāja Parīkṣit was the emperor of the world and was a great *rājarṣi* (saintly king). Having received a warning that he would die within a week, he renounced his entire kingdom and retired to the bank of the Ganges to fast until death and receive spiritual enlightenment. The *Bhāgavatam* begins with Emperor Parīkṣit's sober inquiry to Śukadeva Gosvāmī: "You are the spiritual master of great saints and devotees. I am therefore begging you to show the way of perfection for all persons, and especially for one who is about to die. Please let me know what a man should hear, chant, remember and worship, and also what he should not do. Please explain all this to me."

Śukadeva Gosvāmī's answer to this question, and numerous other questions posed by Mahārāja Parīkṣit, concerning everything from the nature of the self to the origin of the universe, held the assembled sages in rapt attention continuously for the seven days leading up to the king's death. The sage Sūta Gosvāmī, who was present in that assembly when Śukadeva Gosvāmī first recited *Śrīmad-Bhāgavatam,* later repeated the *Bhāgavatam* before a gathering of sages in the forest of Naimiṣāraṇya. Those sages, concerned about the spiritual welfare of the people in general, had gathered to perform a long, continuous chain of sacrifices to counteract the degrading influence of the incipient age of Kali. In response to the sages' request that he speak the essence of Vedic wisdom, Sūta Gosvāmī repeated from memory the entire eighteen thousand verses of *Śrīmad-Bhāgavatam,* as spoken by Śukadeva Gosvāmī to Mahārāja Parīkṣit.

The reader of *Śrīmad-Bhāgavatam* hears Sūta Gosvāmī relate the questions of Mahārāja Parīkṣit and the answers of Śukadeva Gosvāmī. Also, Sūta Gosvāmī sometimes responds directly to questions put by Śaunaka Ṛṣi, the spokesman for the sages gathered at Naimiṣāraṇya. One therefore simultaneously hears two dialogues: one between Mahārāja Parīkṣit and Śukadeva Gosvāmī on the bank of the Ganges, and another at Naimiṣāraṇya between Sūta Gosvāmī and the sages at Naimiṣāraṇya forest, headed by Śaunaka Ṛṣi. Futhermore, while instructing King Parīkṣit, Śukadeva Gosvāmī often relates historical episodes and gives accounts of lengthy philosophical discussions between such great souls as Nārada Muni and Vasudeva. With this understanding of the history of the *Bhāgavatam,* the reader will easily be able to follow its intermingling of dialogues and events from various sources. Since philosophical wisdom, not chronological order , is most important in the text, one need only be attentive to the subject matter of *Śrīmad-Bhāgavatam* to appreciate fully its profound message.

The translators of this edition compare the *Bhāgavatam* to sugar candy—wherever you taste it, you will find it equally sweet and relishable. Therefore, to taste the sweetness of the *Bhāgavatam,* one may begin by reading any of its volumes. After such an introductory taste, however, the serious reader is best advised to go back to the First Canto and then proceed through the *Bhāgavatam,* canto after canto, in its natural order.

This edition of the *Bhāgavatam* is the first complete English translation of this important text with an elaborate commentary, and it is the first widely available to the English-speaking public. The first twelve volumes (Canto One through Canto Ten, Part One) are the product of the scholarly and devotional effort of His Divine Grace A. C. Bhaktivedanta Swami Prabhupāda, the founder-*ācārya* of the International Society for Krishna Consciousness and the world's most distinguished teacher of Indian religious and Philosophical thought. His consummate Sanskrit scholarship and intimate familiarity with Vedic culture and thought as well as the modern way of life combine to reveal to the West a magnificent exposition of this important classic. After the departure of Śrīla

Prabhupāda from this world in 1977, his monumental work of translating and annotating *Śrīmad-Bhāgavatam* has been continued by his disciples Hridayananda dāsa Goswami and Gopīparāṇadhana dāsa.

Readers will find this work of value for many reasons. For those interested in the classical roots of Indian civilization, it serves as a vast reservoir of detailed information on virtually every one of its aspects. For students of comparative philosophy and religion, the *Bhāgavatam* offers a penetrating view into the meaning of India's profound spiritual heritage. To sociologists and anthropologists, the *Bhāgavatam* reveals the practical workings of a peaceful and scientifically organized Vedic culture, whose institutions were integrated on the basis of a highly developed spiritual world view. Students of literature will discover the *Bhāgavatam* to be a masterpiece of majestic poetry. For students of psychology, the text provides important perspectives on the nature of consciousness, human behavior and the philosophical study of identity. Finally, to those seeking spiritual insight, the *Bhāgavatam* offers simple and practical guidance for attainment of the highest self-knowledge and realization of the Absolute Truth. The entire multivolume text, presented by the Bhaktivedanta Book Trust, promises to occupy a significant place in the intellectual, cultural and spiritual life of modern man for a long time to come.

—The Publishers

CHAPTER ONE

The Activities of Mahārāja Priyavrata

This chapter describes how King Priyavrata enjoyed royal opulence and majesty and then returned to full knowledge. King Priyavrata was detached from worldly opulence, and then he became attached to his kingdom, but finally he again became detached from material enjoyment and thus achieved liberation. When King Parīkṣit heard about this, he was struck with wonder, but he was somewhat bewildered as to how a devotee with no attachment for material enjoyment could later become attached to it. Thus in astonishment he questioned Śukadeva Gosvāmī about this.

In response to the King's inquiries, Śukadeva Gosvāmī said that devotional service, being transcendental, cannot be deviated by any material influences. Priyavrata had received transcendental knowledge from the instructions of Nārada, and therefore he did not want to enter a materialistic life of enjoyment in a kingdom. He accepted the kingdom, however, at the request of such superior demigods as Lord Brahmā and Lord Indra, the King of heaven.

Everything is under the control of the Supreme Personality of Godhead, the supreme controller, and everyone must work accordingly. Just as a bull is controlled by a rope tied to its nose, so all conditioned souls are forced to work under the spells of the modes of nature. A civilized man, therefore, works according to the institution of *varṇa* and *āśrama.* Even in materialistic life, however, no one is free to act. Everyone is compelled to accept a certain type of body offered by the Supreme Lord and thus be allotted different grades of happiness and distress. Therefore even if one artificially leaves home and goes to the forest, he again becomes attached to materialistic life. Family life is compared to a fortress for practicing sense control. When the senses are controlled, one may live either at home or in the forest; there is no difference.

When Mahārāja Priyavrata, following the instruction of Lord Brahmā, accepted the royal throne, his father, Manu, left home for the forest. Mahārāja Priyavrata then married Barhiṣmatī, the daughter of Viśvakarmā. In the womb of Barhiṣmatī he begot ten sons, named Āgnīdhra, Idhmajihva, Yajñabāhu, Mahāvīra, Hiraṇyaretā, Ghṛtapṛṣṭha, Savana, Medhātithi, Vītihotra and Kavi. He also begot one daughter, whose name was Ūrjasvatī. Mahārāja Priyavrata lived with his wife and family for many thousands of years. The impressions from the rims of Mahārāja Priyavrata's chariot wheels created seven oceans and seven islands. Of the ten sons of Priyavrata, three sons named Kavi, Mahāvīra and Savana accepted *sannyāsa,* the fourth order of life, and the remaining seven sons became the rulers of the seven islands. Mahārāja Priyavrata also had a second wife, in whom he begot three sons named Uttama, Raivata and Tāmasa. All of them were elevated to the post of Manu. Śukadeva Gosvāmī thus described how Mahārāja Priyavrata achieved liberation.

TEXT 1

राजोवाच
प्रियव्रतो भागवत आत्मारामः कथं मुने ।
गृहेऽरमत यन्मूलः कर्मबन्धः पराभवः ॥१॥

rājovāca
priyavrato bhāgavata
ātmārāmaḥ kathaṁ mune
gṛhe'ramata yan-mūlaḥ
karma-bandhaḥ parābhavaḥ

rājā uvāca—King Parīkṣit said; *priya-vrataḥ*—King Priyavrata; *bhāgavataḥ*—the great devotee; *ātma-ārāmaḥ*—who takes pleasure in self-realization; *katham*—why; *mune*—O great sage; *gṛhe*—at home; *aramata*—enjoyed; *yat-mūlaḥ*—having which as the root cause; *karma-bandhaḥ*—the bondage of fruitive activities; *parābhavaḥ*—the defeat of one's human mission.

TRANSLATION

King Parīkṣit inquired from Śukadeva Gosvāmī: O great sage, why did King Priyavrata, who was a great, self-realized devotee of the Lord, remain in household life, which is the root cause of the bondage of karma [fruitive activities] and which defeats the mission of human life?

PURPORT

In the Fourth Canto, Śrīla Śukadeva Gosvāmī explains that Nārada Muni perfectly instructed King Priyavrata about the mission of human life. The mission of human life is to realize one's self and then gradually to go back home, back to Godhead. Since Nārada Muni instructed the King fully on this subject, why did he again enter household life, which is the main cause of material bondage? Mahārāja Parīkṣit was greatly astonished that King

Priyavrata remained in household life, especially since he was not only a self-realized soul but also a first-class devotee of the Lord. A devotee actually has no attraction for household life, but surprisingly, King Priyavrata enjoyed household life very much. One may argue, "Why is it wrong to enjoy household life?" The reply is that in household life one becomes bound by the results of fruitive activities. The essence of household life is sense enjoyment, and as long as one engrosses his mind in working hard for sense enjoyment, one becomes bound by the reactions of fruitive activities. This ignorance of self-realization is the greatest defeat in human life. The human form of life is especially meant for getting out of the bondage of fruitive activities, but as long as one is forgetful of his life's mission and acts like an ordinary animal—eating, sleeping, mating and defending—he must continue his conditioned life of material existence. Such a life is called *svarūpa-vismṛti,* forgetfulness of one's real constitutional position. Therefore in Vedic civilization one is trained in the very beginning of life as a *brahmacārī.* A *brahmacārī* must execute austerities and refrain from sex indulgence. Therefore if one is completely trained in the principles of *brahmacarya,* he generally does not enter household life. He is then called a *naiṣṭhika-brahmacārī,* which indicates total celibacy. King Parīkṣit was thus astonished that the great King Priyavrata, although trained in the principles of *naiṣṭhika-brahmacarya,* entered household life.

The words *bhāgavata ātmārāmaḥ* are very significant in this verse. If one is self-satisfied as is the Supreme Personality of Godhead, he is called *bhāgavata ātmārāmaḥ.* There are different types of satisfaction. *Karmīs* are satisfied in their fruitive activities, *jñānīs* are satisfied to merge into the effulgence of Brahman, and devotees are satisfied to engage in the Lord's service. The Lord is self-satisfied because He is fully opulent, and one who is satisfied by serving Him is called *bhāgavata ātmārāmaḥ. Manuṣyāṇāṁ sahasreṣu:* out of many thousands of persons, one may endeavor for liberation, and of many thousands of persons attempting to become liberated, one may achieve liberation from the anxieties of material existence and become self-satisfied. Even that satisfaction, however, is not the ultimate satisfaction. The *jñānīs* and the *karmīs* have desires, as do the *yogīs,* but devotees have no desires. Satisfaction in the service of the Lord is called *akāma,* freedom from desire, and this is the ultimate satisfaction. Therefore Mahārāja Parīkṣit inquired, "How could one who was fully satisfied on the highest platform be satisfied with family life?"

The word *parābhavaḥ* in this verse is also significant. When one is satisfied in family life, he is doomed because he must already have forgotten his relationship with the Lord. Prahlāda Mahārāja describes how the activities of family life implicate one more and more. *Ātma-pātaṁ gṛham andha-kūpam:* household life is like a dark well. If one falls into this well, his spiritual death is assured. How Priyavrata Mahārāja remained a liberated *paramahaṁsa* even within family life is described in the next verse.

TEXT 2

न नूनं मुक्तसङ्गानां तादृशानां द्विजर्षभ ।
गृहेष्वभिनिवेशोऽयं पुंसां भवितुमर्हति ॥२॥

na nūnaṁ mukta-saṅgānāṁ
tādṛśānāṁ dvijarṣabha
gṛheṣv abhiniveśo'yaṁ
puṁsāṁ bhavitum arhati

na—not; *nūnam*—certainly; *mukta-saṅgānām*—who are free from attachment; *tādṛśānām*—such; *dvija-ṛṣabha*—O greatest of the *brāhmaṇas; gṛheṣu*—to family life; *abhiniveśaḥ*—excessive attachment; *ayam*—this; *puṁsām*—of persons; *bhavitum*—to be; *arhati*—is possible.

TRANSLATION

Devotees are certainly liberated persons. Therefore, O greatest of the brāhmaṇas, they cannot possibly be absorbed in family affairs.

PURPORT

In *Bhakti-rasāmṛta-sindhu* it is said that by executing devotional service to the Lord, one can understand the transcendental position of the living being and the Supreme Personality of Godhead. The Supreme Personality of Godhead cannot be understood by any means except *bhakti.* The Lord confirms this in *Śrīmad-Bhāgavatam* (11.14.21). *Bhaktyāham ekayā grāhyaḥ:* "Only by executing devotional service can one appreciate Me." Similarly, in *Bhagavad-gītā* (18.55) Lord Kṛṣṇa says, *bhaktyā mām abhijānāti:* "Simply by discharging devotional service, one can understand Me." Thus for a *bhakta* to become attached to family affairs is impossible, since a *bhakta* and his associates are liberated. Everyone is searching after *ānanda,* or bliss, but in the material world there can never be any bliss. It is only possible in devotional service. Attachment for family affairs and devotional service are incompatible. Therefore Mahārāja Parīkṣit was somewhat surprised to hear that Mahārāja Priyavrata was simultaneously attached to devotional service and to family life.

TEXT 3

महतां खलु विप्रर्षे उत्तमश्लोकपादयोः ।
छायानिर्वृतचित्तानां न कुटुम्बे स्पृहामतिः ॥३॥

mahatāṁ khalu viprarṣe
uttamaśloka-pādayoḥ
chāyā-nirvṛta-cittānāṁ
na kuṭumbe spṛhā-matiḥ

mahatām—of great devotees; *khalu*—certainly; *vipra-ṛṣe*—O great sage among the *brāhmaṇas; uttama-śloka-pādayoḥ*—of the lotus feet of the Supreme Personality of Godhead; *chāyā*—by the shade; *nirvṛta*—satiated; *cittānām*—whose consciousness; *na*—never; *kuṭumbe*—to family members; *spṛhā-matiḥ*—consciousness with attachment.

TRANSLATION

Elevated mahātmās who have taken shelter of the lotus feet of the Supreme Personality of Godhead are fully satiated by the shade of those lotus feet. Their consciousness cannot possibly become attached to family members.

PURPORT

Śrīla Narottama dāsa Ṭhākura has sung, *nitāi pada-kamala, koṭī-candra suśītala, ye chāyāya jagat juḍāya.* He describes the shade of the lotus feet of Lord Nityānanda as being so nice and cooling that all materialists, who are always in the blazing fire of material activities, may come under the shade of His lotus feet and be fully relieved and satiated. The distinction between family life and spiritual life can be experienced by any person who has undergone the tribulations of living with a family. One who comes under the shelter of the lotus feet of the Lord never becomes attracted by the activities of family life. As stated in *Bhagavad-gītā* (2.59), *paraṁ dṛṣṭvā nivartate:* one gives up lower engagements when he experiences a higher taste. Thus one becomes detached from family life as soon as he comes under the shelter of the lotus feet of the Lord.

TEXT 4

संशयोऽयं महान् ब्रह्मन्दारागारसुतादिषु ।
सक्तस्य यत्सिद्धिरभूत्कृष्णे च मतिरच्युता ॥४॥

saṁśayo'yaṁ mahān brahman
dārāgāra-sutādiṣu
saktasya yat siddhir abhūt
kṛṣṇe ca matir acyutā

saṁśayaḥ—doubt; *ayam*—this; *mahān*—great; *brahman*—O *brāhmaṇa; dāra*—to the wife; *āgāra*—home; *suta*—children; *ādiṣu*—and so on; *saktasya*—of a person attached; *yat*—because; *siddhiḥ*—perfection; *abhūt*—became; *kṛṣṇe*—unto Kṛṣṇa; *ca*—also; *matiḥ*—attachment; *acyutā*—infallible.

TRANSLATION

The King continued: O great brāhmaṇa, this is my great doubt. How was it possible for a person like King Priyavrata, who was so attached to wife, children and home, to achieve the topmost infallible perfection in Kṛṣṇa consciousness?

PURPORT

King Parīkṣit wondered how a person so attached to wife, children and home could become so perfectly Kṛṣṇa conscious. Prahlāda Mahārāja has said:

matir na kṛṣṇe parataḥ svato vā
mitho'bhipadyeta gṛha-vratānām

A *gṛhavrata,* one who has taken a vow to execute family duties, has no chance to become Kṛṣṇa conscious. This is because most *gṛhavratas* are guided by sense gratification and therefore gradually glide down to the darkest regions of material existence (*adānta-gobhir viśatāṁ tamisram*). How can they possibly become perfect in Kṛṣṇa consciousness? Mahārāja Parīkṣit asked Śukadeva Gosvāmī to resolve this great doubt.

TEXT 5

श्रीशुक उवाच

बाढमुक्तं भगवत उत्तमश्लोकस्य श्रीमच्चरणारविन्दमकरन्दरस आवेशितचेतसो भागवतपरमहंस दयितकथां किञ्चिदन्तरायविहतां स्वां शिवतमां पदवीं न प्रायेण हिन्वन्ति ॥५॥

śrī-śuka uvāca
bāḍham uktaṁ bhagavata uttamaślokasya śrīmac-
caraṇāravinda-makaranda-rasa āveśita-cetaso bhāgavata-
paramahaṁsa-dayita-kathāṁ kiñcid antarāya-vihatāṁ
svāṁ śivatamāṁ padavīṁ na prāyeṇa hinvanti.

śrī-śukaḥ uvāca—Śrī Śukadeva Gosvāmī said; *bāḍham*—correct; *uktam*—what you have said; *bhagavataḥ*—of the Personality of Godhead; *uttama-ślokasya*—who is praised with excellent verses; *śrīmat-caraṇa-aravinda*—of the feet, which are just like the most beautiful fragrant lotus flowers; *makaranda*—honey; *rase*—in the nectar; *āveśita*—absorbed; *cetasaḥ*—whose hearts; *bhāgavata*—to the devotees; *paramahaṁsa*—liberated persons; *dayita*—pleasing; *kathām*—glorification; *kiñcit*—sometimes; *antarāya*—by impediments; *vihatām*—checked; *svām*—own; *śiva-tamām*—most exalted; *padavīm*—position; *na*—do not; *prāyeṇa*—almost always; *hinvanti*—give up.

TRANSLATION

Śrī Śukadeva Gosvāmī said: What you have said is correct. The glories of the Supreme Personality of Godhead, who is praised in eloquent, transcendental verses by such exalted personalities as Brahmā, are very pleasing to great devotees and liberated persons. One who is attached to the nectarean honey of the Lord's lotus feet, and whose mind is always absorbed in His glories, may sometimes be checked by some impediment, but he still never gives up the exalted position he has acquired.

PURPORT

Śrī Śukadeva Gosvāmī accepted both of the King's propositions—that a person who is advanced in Kṛṣṇa consciousness cannot embrace materialistic life again and that one who has embraced materialistic life cannot take up Kṛṣṇa consciousness at any stage of his existence. Although accepting both these statements, Śukadeva Gosvāmī qualified them by saying that a person who has once absorbed his mind in the glories of the Supreme Personality of Godhead may sometimes be influenced by impediments, but he still does not give up his exalted devotional position.

According to Śrīla Viśvanātha Cakravartī Ṭhākura, there are two kinds of impediments to devotional service. The first is an offense at the lotus feet of a Vaiṣṇava. This is called *vaiṣṇava-aparādha.* Śrī Caitanya Mahāprabhu warned

His devotees not to commit *vaiṣṇava-aparādha,* which He described as the mad elephant offense. When a mad elephant enters a beautiful garden, it destroys everything, leaving a barren field. Similarly, the power of *vaiṣṇava-aparādha* is so great that even an advanced devotee becomes almost devoid of his spiritual assets if he commits it. Since Kṛṣṇa consciousness is eternal, it cannot be destroyed altogether, but advancement may be checked for the time being. Thus *vaiṣṇava-aparādha* is one kind of impediment to devotional service. Sometimes, however, the Supreme Personality of Godhead or His devotee desires to impede one's devotional service. For example, Hiraṇyakaśipu and Hiraṇyākṣa were formerly Jaya and Vijaya, the gatekeepers in Vaikuṇṭha, but by the desire of the Lord, they became His enemies for three lives. Thus the desire of the Lord is another kind of impediment. But in both cases, the pure devotee, once advanced in Kṛṣṇa consciousness, cannot be lost. Following the orders of his superiors (Svāyambhuva and Lord Brahmā), Priyavrata accepted family life, but this did not mean he lost his position in devotional service. Kṛṣṇa consciousness is perfect and eternal, and therefore it cannot be lost under any circumstances. Because the material world is full of obstructions to advancement in Kṛṣṇa consciousness, there may appear to be many impediments, yet Kṛṣṇa, the Supreme Personality of Godhead, declares in *Bhagavad-gītā* (9.31), *kaunteya pratijānīhi na me bhaktaḥ praṇaśyati:* once one has taken shelter at the lotus feet of the Lord, he cannot be lost.

In this verse, the word *śivatamām* is very significant. *Śivatamām* means "the most auspicious." The devotional path is so auspicious that a devotee cannot be lost under any circumstances. This is described in the *Śrīmad Bhagavad-gītā* by the Lord Himself. *Pārtha naiveha nāmutra vināśas tasya vidyate:* "My dear Arjuna, for a devotee there is no question of being lost, either in this life or in the next." (Bg. 6.40) In *Bhagavad-gītā* (6.43) the Lord clearly explains how this is so.

tatra taṁ buddhi-saṁyogaṁ
labhate paurva-dehikam
yatate ca tato bhūyaḥ
saṁsiddhau kuru-nandana

By the order of the Lord, a perfect devotee sometimes comes to this material world like an ordinary human being. Because of his previous practice, such a perfect devotee naturally becomes attached to devotional service, apparently without cause. Despite all kinds of impediments due to surrounding circumstances, he automatically perseveres in devotional service and gradually advances until he once again becomes perfect. Bilvamaṅgala Ṭhākura had been an advanced devotee in his previous life, but in his next life he became greatly fallen and was attached to a prostitute. Suddenly, however, his entire behavior was changed by the words of the very prostitute who had so much attracted him, and he became a great devotee. In the lives of exalted devotees, there are many such instances, proving that once one has taken to the shelter of the lotus feet of the Lord, he cannot be lost (*kaunteya pratijānīhi na me bhaktaḥ praṇaśyati*).

The fact is, however, that one becomes a devotee when he is completely freed from all reactions to sinful life. As Kṛṣṇa states in *Bhagavad-gītā* (7.28):

yeṣāṁ tv anta-gataṁ pāpaṁ
janānāṁ puṇya-karmaṇām
te dvanda-moha-nirmuktā
bhajante māṁ dṛḍha-vratāḥ

"Persons who have acted piously in previous lives and in this life, whose sinful actions are completely eradicated and who are freed from the duality of illusion, engage themselves in My service with determination." On the other hand, as Prahlāda Mahārāja said:

matir na kṛṣṇe parataḥ svato vā
mitho'bhipadyeta gṛha-vratānām

A person who is too attached to materialistic family life—home, family, wife, children and so on—cannot develop Kṛṣṇa consciousness.

These apparent contradictions are resolved in the life of a devotee by the grace of the Supreme Lord, and therefore a devotee is never bereft of his position on the path of liberation, which is described in this verse as *śivatamāṁ padavīm.*

TEXT 6

यर्हि वाव ह राजन् स राजपुत्रः प्रियव्रतः परमभागवतोनारदस्य
चरणोपसेवयाञ्जसावगतपरमार्थसतत्त्वो ब्रह्मसत्रेण दीक्षिष्यमाणो
ऽवनितलपरिपालनायाम्नातप्रवरगुणगणैकान्तभाजनतया स्वपित्रोपामन्त्रितो
भगवति वासुदेव एवाव्यवधानसमाधियोगेन समावेशितसकलकारकक्रिया
कलापो नैवाभ्यनन्दद्यद्यपि तदप्रत्याम्नातव्यं तदधिकरण आत्मनोऽन्यस्माद
सतोऽपि पराभवमन्वीक्षमाणः ॥६॥

yarhi vāva ha rājan sa rāja-putraḥ priyavrataḥ parama-bhāgavato nāradasya caraṇopasevayāñjasāvagata-paramārtha-satattvo brahma-satreṇa dīkṣiṣyamāṇo'vani-tala-paripālanāyāmnāta -pravara- guṇa-gaṇaikānta-bhājanatayā sva-pitropāmantrito bhagavati vāsudeva evāvyavadhāna-samādhi-yogena samāveśita-sakala-kāraka-kriyā-kalāpo naivābhyanandad yadyapi tad apratyāmnātavyaṁ tad-adhikaraṇa ātmano'nyasmād asato'pi parābhavam anvīkṣamāṇaḥ.

yarhi—because; *vāva ha*—indeed; *rājan*—O King; *saḥ*—he; *rāja-putraḥ*—the Prince; *priyavrataḥ*—Priyavrata; *parama*—supreme; *bhāgavataḥ*—devotee; *nāradasya*—of Nārada; *caraṇa*—the lotus feet; *upasevayā*—by serving; *añjasā*—quickly; *avagata*—became aware of; *parama-artha*—transcendental subject matter; *sa-tattvaḥ*—with all knowable facts; *brahma-satreṇa*—by continuous discussion of the Supreme; *dīkṣiṣyamāṇaḥ*—desiring to fully dedicate himself; *avani-tala*—the surface of the globe; *paripālanāya*—to rule over; *āmnāta*—directed in the revealed scriptures; *pravara*—highest; *guṇa*—of qualities; *gaṇa*—the sum total; *ekānta*—without deviation; *bhājanatayā*—because of his possessing; *sva-pitrā*—by his father; *upāmantritaḥ*—being asked; *bhagavati*—in the Supreme Personality of Godhead; *vāsudeve*—the all-pervading Lord; *eva*—certainly; *avyavadhāna*—without cessation; *samādhi-yogena*—by practicing *yoga* in complete absorption; *samāveśita*—completely dedicated; *sakala*—all; *kāraka*—senses; *kriyā-kalāpaḥ*—whose total activities; *na*—not; *eva*—thus; *abhyanandat*—welcomed; *yadyapi*—although; *tat*—that; *apratyāmnātavyam*—not to be rejected for any reason; *tat-adhikaraṇe*—in occupying that post; *ātmanaḥ*—of himself; *anyasmāt*—by other engagements; *asataḥ*—material; *api*—certainly; *parābhavam*—deterioration; *anvīkṣamāṇaḥ*—foreseeing.

TRANSLATION

Śukadeva Gosvāmī continued: My dear King, Prince Priyavrata was a great devotee because he sought the lotus feet of Nārada, his spiritual master, and thus achieved the highest perfection in transcendental knowledge. With advanced knowledge, he always engaged in discussing spiritual subjects and did not divert his attention to anything else. The Prince's father then asked him to take charge of ruling the world. He tried to convince Priyavrata that this was his duty as indicated in the revealed scriptures. Prince Priyavrata, however, was continuously practicing bhakti-yoga by constantly remembering the Supreme Personality of Godhead,

thus engaging all his senses in the service of the Lord. Therefore, although the order of his father could not be rejected, the Prince did not welcome it. Thus he very conscientiously raised the question of whether he might be diverted from devotional service by accepting the responsibility of ruling over the world.

PURPORT

Śrīla Narottama dāsa Ṭhākura has sung, *chāḍiyā vaiṣṇava-sevā nistāra pāyeche kebā:* "Without serving the lotus feet of a pure Vaiṣṇava or spiritual master, no one has ever attained perfect liberation from material bondage." Prince Priyavrata regularly served the lotus feet of Nārada, and thus the Prince perfectly understood transcendental subjects in truth (*sa-tattvaḥ*). The word *sa-tattvaḥ* means that Priyavrata knew all the facts about the spirit soul, the Supreme Personality of Godhead, and the relationship between the spirit soul and the Supreme Personality of Godhead, and he also knew all about this material world and the relationship of the spirit soul and the Supreme Lord within the material world. Thus the Prince decided to engage himself only in rendering service to the Lord.

When Priyavrata's father, Svāyambhuva Manu, requested him to accept the responsibility of ruling over the world, he did not welcome the suggestion. This is the symptom of a great, liberated devotee. Even though engaged in worldly affairs, he does not take pleasure in them, but remains always absorbed in the Lord's service. While thus serving the Lord, he deals externally with worldly affairs without being affected. For example, although he has no attraction for his children, he cares for them and educates them to become devotees. Similarly, he speaks to his wife with affectionate words, but he is not attached to her. By rendering devotional service, a devotee acquires all the good qualities of the Supreme Lord. Lord Kṛṣṇa had sixteen thousand wives, all of them very beautiful, and although He dealt with each of them as a beloved husband, He was not attracted or attached to any of them. In the same way, although a devotee may enter family life and act very affectionately toward his wife and children, he is never attached to these activities.

This verse states that by serving the lotus feet of his spiritual master, Prince Priyavrata very soon attained the perfectional stage of Kṛṣṇa consciousness. This is the only way to advance in spiritual life. As stated in the *Vedas:*

yasya deve parā bhaktir
yathā deve tathā gurau

tasyaite kathitā hy arthāḥ
prakāśante mahātmanaḥ

"If one has unflinching faith in the Supreme Lord and the spiritual master, the essence of all Vedic knowledge is revealed to him." (*Śvetāśvatara Upaniṣad* 6.23) A devotee always thinks of the Lord continuously. While chanting the Hare Kṛṣṇa *mantra,* the words Kṛṣṇa and Hare immediately remind him of all the Lord's activities. Since his entire life is engaged in the service of the Lord, a devotee cannot forget the Lord at any time. Just as an ordinary man always engages his mind in material activities, a devotee always engages his mind in spiritual activities. This is called *brahma-satra,* or meditating upon the Supreme Lord always. Prince Priyavrata was perfectly initiated into this practice by Śrī Nārada.

TEXT 7

अथ ह भगवानादिदेव एतस्य गुणविसर्गस्य परिबृंहणानुध्यानव्यवसित सकलजगदभिप्राय आत्मयोनिरखिलनिगमनिजगणपरिवेष्टितः स्वभवनाद-वततार ॥७॥

atha ha bhagavān ādi-deva etasya guṇa-visargasya
paribṛṁhaṇānudhyāna-vyavasita-sakala-jagad-abhiprāya ātma-yonir
akhila-nigama-nija-gaṇa-pariveṣṭitaḥ sva-bhavanād avatatāra.

atha—thus; *ha*—indeed; *bhagavān*—the most powerful; *ādi-devaḥ*—the first demigod; *etasya*—of this universe; *guṇa-visargasya*—the creation of the three modes of material nature; *paribṛṁhaṇa*—the welfare; *anudhyāna*—always thinking of; *vyavasita*—known; *sakala*—whole; *jagat*—of the universe; *abhiprāyaḥ*—by whom the ultimate purpose; *ātma*—the Supreme Self; *yoniḥ*—whose source of birth; *akhila*—all; *nigama*—by the *Vedas; nija-gaṇa*—by personal associates; *pariveṣṭitaḥ*—being surrounded; *sva-bhavanāt*—from his own abode; *avatatāra*—descended.

TRANSLATION

Śrī Śukadeva Gosvāmī continued: The first created being and most powerful demigod in this universe is Lord Brahmā, who is always responsible for developing universal affairs. Born directly from the Supreme Personality of Godhead, he dedicates his activities to the welfare of the entire universe, for he knows the purpose of the universal creation.

His Divine Grace
A. C. Bhaktivedanta Swami Prabhupāda
Founder-Ācārya of ISKCON and greatest exponent of Kṛṣṇa consciousness in the modern world

While ruling the universe, King Priyavrata became dissatisfied with the circumambulation of the powerful sun-god. As the sun-god circles Sumeru Hill on his chariot, he illuminates all the surrounding planetary systems. However, when the sun is on the northern side of the hill, the south receives less light, and when the sun is in the south, the north

receives less. King Priyavrata disliked this situation and therefore decided to make daylight in the part of the universe where there was night. He followed the orbit of the sun-god on a brilliant chariot and thus fulfilled his desire. (5.1.30)

As soon as Nārada saw the great swan, he understood that Lord Brahmā had arrived. Therefore Nārada immediately stood up, along with Svāyambhuva Manu and his son Priyavrata. (5.1.9)

Seeing the Lord arrive on His carrier Garuḍa, King Nābhi and his priests and associates felt like paupers who had suddenly attained great wealth. They received the Lord with great respect and adoration. (5.3.3)

The Supreme Lord, Ṛṣabhadeva, instructed his devoted and well-behaved sons in transcendental science so that in the future they could rule the world perfectly. (5.4.19)

After accepting the feature of an *avadhūta*, a great saintly person without material cares, Lord Ṛṣabhadeva traversed human society like a blind, deaf and dumb man, or a madman. (5.5.29–30)

Attached to raising the deer, Mahārāja Bharata forgot the rules and regulations for the advancement of spiritual life, and gradually he forgot to worship the Supreme Lord. (5.8.8)

Bhadra Kālī burst out of her deity form, leapt from the altar and immediately decapitated all the rogues and thieves who had intended to kill Jaḍa Bharata. (5.9.14–18)

In Ilāvṛta-varṣa, as he meditates in trance upon Lord Saṅkarṣaṇa, Lord Śiva is encircled by ten billion of Durgā's maidservants, who minister to him.(5.17.16)

Ignorance personified once stole all the *Vedas* and took them down to the planet of Rasātala. But Lord Hayagrīva retrieved the *Vedas* and returned them to Lord Brahmā when he begged for them. (5.18.1)

It was ordained that Rāvaṇa, the ten-headed chief of the Rākṣasas, could be killed only by a man, and thus Lord Rāmacandra appeared in the form of a human being to kill him. The furious battle between Rāma and Rāvaṇa lasted for days without letup. The earth, seas and heavens

were disturbed by the sheer force of their combat, and various astronomical events portended the demon's imminent defeat. Finally the Lord released an arrow from His bow that struck Rāvaṇa's heart like a nuclear bomb. (5.19.5)

In the abode of Yamarāja are thousands of hellish planets. All impious people must enter these various planets and suffer according to their impiety. Any *brāhmaṇa* who drinks liquor is taken to Ayaḥpāna, where the agents of Yamarāja force him to drink molten iron. A man who indulges in sex with another man's wife is forced to embrace a red-hot

form of a woman after death. Thieves are taken to a hell known as Sandaṁśa, where their skin is torn and separated by red-hot tongs. And for those who cook poor animals alive, there is a hell known as Kumbhīpāka, where the Yamadūtas cook such sinners in boiling oil. (5.26.14–29)

At the time of universal devastation, Rudra appears. An embodiment of eleven incarnations of Lord Śiva, Rudra devastates the entire creation. (5.25.3)

This supremely powerful Lord Brahmā, accompanied by his associates and the personified Vedas, left his own abode in the highest planetary system and descended to the place of Prince Priyavrata's meditation.

PURPORT

Lord Viṣṇu, the Supreme Self (*ātmā*), is the source of everything, as explained in the *Vedānta-sūtra: janmādy asya yataḥ.* Because Brahmā was born directly from Lord Viṣṇu, he is called *ātma-yoni.* He is also called *bhagavān,* although generally *bhagavān* refers to the Supreme Personality of Godhead (Viṣṇu or Lord Kṛṣṇa). Sometimes great personalities—such as demigods like Lord Brahmā, Nārada or Lord Śiva—are also addressed as *bhagavān* because they carry out the purpose of the Supreme Personality of Godhead. Lord Brahmā is called *bhagavān* because he is the secondary creator of this universe. He is always thinking of how to improve the situation of the conditioned souls who have come to the material world to enjoy material activities. For this reason, he disseminates the Vedic knowledge throughout the universe for everyone's guidance.

Vedic knowledge is divided into two parts: *pravṛtti-mārga* and *nivṛtti-mārga. Nivṛtti-mārga* is the path of negating sense enjoyment, and *pravṛtti-mārga* is the path by which the living entities are given a chance to enjoy and at the same time are directed in such a way that they can go back home, back to Godhead. Because ruling over this universe is a great responsibility, Brahmā must force many Manus in different ages to take charge of universal affairs. Under each Manu there are different kings who also execute the purpose of Lord Brahmā. It is understood from previous explanations that the father of Dhruva Mahārāja, King Uttānapāda, ruled over the universe because his elder brother, Priyavrata, practiced austerity from the very beginning of his life. Thus up to the point of the Pracetās, the kings of the universe were all descendants of Uttānapāda Mahārāja. Since there were no suitable kings after the Pracetās, Svāyambhuva Manu went to the Gandhamādana Hill to bring back his eldest son, Priyavrata, who was meditating there. Svāyambhuva Manu requested Priyavrata to rule over the universe. When he refused, Lord Brahmā descended from the supreme planetary system, known as Satyaloka, to request Priyavrata to accept the order. Lord Brahmā did not come alone. He came with other great sages like Marīci, Ātreya and Vasiṣṭha. To convince Priyavrata that it was necessary for him to follow the Vedic injunctions and accept the responsibility of ruling over the world, Lord Brahmā also brought with him the personified *Vedas,* his constant associates.

A significant word in this verse is *sva-bhavanāt,* indicating that Lord Brahmā descended from his own abode. Every demigod has his own abode. Indra, the King of the demigods, has his own abode, as do Candra, the lord of the moon planet, and Sūrya, the predominating deity of the sun planet. There are many millions of demigods, and the stars and planets are their respective homes. This is confirmed in *Bhagavad-gītā. Yānti deva-vratā devān:* "Those who worship the demigods go to their different planetary systems." Lord Brahmā's abode. the highest planetary system, is called Satyaloka or sometimes Brahmaloka. Brahmaloka usually refers to the spiritual world. The abode of Lord Brahmā is Satyaloka, but because Lord Brahmā resides there, it is also sometimes called Brahmaloka.

TEXT 8

**स तत्र तत्र गगनतल उडुपतिरिव विमा नावलिभिरनुपथममरपरिवृढैरभि-
पूज्यमानः पथि पथि च वरूथशः सिद्धगन्धर्वसाध्यचारणमुनिगणैरुपगीय मानो
गन्धमादनद्रोणीमवभासयन्नुपससर्प ॥८॥**

*sa tatra tatra gagana-tala uḍu-patir iva vimānāvalibhir anupatham
amara-parivṛḍhair abhipūjyamānaḥ pathi pathi ca varūthaśaḥ siddha-
gandharva-sādhya-cāraṇa-muni-gaṇair upagīyamāno gandha-
mādana-droṇīm avabhāsayann upasasarpa.*

saḥ—he (Lord Brahmā); *tatra tatra*—here and there; *gagana-tale*—under the canopy of the sky; *uḍu-patiḥ*—the moon; *iva*—like; *vimāna-āvalibhiḥ*—in their different airplanes; *anupatham*—along the path; *amara*—of the demigods; *parivṛḍhaiḥ*—by the leaders; *abhipūjyamānaḥ*—being worshiped; *pathi pathi*—on the way, one after another; *ca*—also; *varūthaśaḥ*—in groups; *siddha*—by the residents of Siddhaloka; *gandharva*—by the residents of Gandharvaloka; *sādhya*—by the residents of Sādhyaloka; *cāraṇa*—by the residents of Cāraṇaloka; *muni-gaṇaiḥ*—and by great sages; *upagīyamānaḥ*—being worshiped; *gandha-mādana*—of the planet where the Gandhamādana Hill is found; *droṇīm*—the border; *avabhāsayan*—illuminating; *upasasarpa*—he approached.

TRANSLATION

As Lord Brahmā descended on his carrier, the great swan, all the residents of the planets named Siddhaloka, Gandharvaloka, Sādhyaloka and Cāraṇaloka, as well as great sages and demigods flying in their

different airplanes, assembled within the canopy of the sky to receive Lord Brahmā and worship him. As he received respect and adoration from the residents of the various planets, Lord Brahmā appeared just like the full moon surrounded by illuminating stars. Lord Brahmā's great swan then arrived at the border of Gandhamādana Hill and approached Prince Priyavrata, who was sitting there.

PURPORT

It appears from this description that there is regular interplanetary travel between the planets of the demigods. Another significant point is that there is a planet covered mostly by great mountains, one of which is Gandhamādana Hill. Three great personalities—Priyavrata, Nārada and Svāyambhuva Manu—were sitting on this hill. According to *Brahmā-saṁhitā,* each universe is filled with different planetary systems, and every system has a unique opulence. For example, on Siddhaloka, all the residents are very advanced in the powers of mystic *yoga.* They can fly from one planet to another without airplanes or other flying machines. Similarly, the residents of Gandharvaloka are expert in musical science, and those on Sādhyaloka are all great saints. The interplanetary system undoubtedly exists, and residents of different planets may go from one to another. On this earth, however, we have not invented any machine that can go directly from one planet to another, although an unsuccessful attempt has been made to go directly to the moon.

TEXT 9

तत्र ह वा एनं देवर्षिर्हंसयानेन पितरं भगवन्तं हिरण्यगर्भमुपलभमानः
सहसैवोत्थायार्हणेन सह पितापुत्राभ्यामवहिताञ्जलिरुपतस्थे ॥९॥

tatra ha vā enaṁ devarṣir haṁsa-yānena pitaraṁ bhagavantaṁ
hiraṇya-garbham upalabhamānaḥ sahasaivotthāyārhaṇena saha pitā-
putrābhyām avahitāñjalir upatasthe.

tatra—there; *ha vā*—certainly; *enam*—him; *deva-ṛṣiḥ*—the great saint Nārada; *haṁsa-yānena*—by the swan carrier; *pitaram*—his father; *bhagavantam*—most powerful; *hiraṇya-garbham*—Lord Brahmā; *upalabhamānaḥ*—understanding; *sahasā eva*—immediately; *utthāya*—having stood up; *arhaṇena*—with paraphernalia for worship; *saha*—accompanied; *pitā-putrābhyām*—by Priyavrata and his father, Svāyambhuva Manu; *avahita-añjaliḥ*—with respect and folded hands; *upatasthe*—worshiped.

TRANSLATION

Lord Brahmā, the father of Nārada Muni, is the supreme person within this universe. As soon as Nārada saw the great swan, he could understand that Lord Brahmā had arrived. Therefore he immediately stood up, along with Svāyambhuva Manu and his son Priyavrata, whom Nārada was instructing. Then they folded their hands and began to worship Lord Brahmā with great respect.

PURPORT

As stated in the previous verse, Lord Brahmā was accompanied by other demigods, but his specific carrier was the great swan. Therefore as soon as Nārada Muni saw the swan, he could understand that his father, Lord Brahmā, who is also known as Hiraṇyagarbha, was arriving. Thus he immediately stood up with Svāyambhuva Manu and his son Priyavrata to receive Lord Brahmā and offer him respect.

TEXT 10

भगवानपि भारत तदुपनीतार्हणः सूक्तवाकेनातितरामुदितगुणगणावतार - सुजय : प्रियव्रतमादि पुरुषस्तं सदयहासावलोक इति होवाच ॥१०॥

bhagavān api bhārata tad-upanītārhaṇaḥ sūkta-vākenātitarām udita-guṇa-gaṇāvatāra-sujayaḥ priyavratam ādi-puruṣas taṁ sadaya-hāsāvaloka iti hovāca.

bhagavān—Lord Brahmā; *api*—moreover; *bhārata*—O King Parīkṣit; *tat*—by them; *upanīta*—brought forward; *arhaṇaḥ*—worshipable paraphernalia; *sūkta*—according to Vedic etiquette; *vākena*—by language; *atitarām*—highly; *udita*—praised; *guṇa-gaṇa*—qualities; *avatāra*—because of the descent; *su-jayaḥ*—whose glories; *priyavratam*—unto Priyavrata; *ādi-puruṣaḥ*—the original person; *tam*—unto him; *sa-daya*—with compassion; *hāsa*—smiling; *avalokaḥ*—whose looking; *iti*—thus; *ha*—certainly; *uvāca*—said.

TRANSLATION

My dear King Parīkṣit, because Lord Brahmā had finally descended from Satyaloka to Bhūloka, Nārada Muni, Prince Priyavrata and Svāyambhuva Manu came forward to offer him objects of worship and to praise him in highly qualified language, according to Vedic etiquette. At that time, Lord Brahmā, the original person of this universe, felt compassion for Priyavrata and, looking upon him with a smiling face, spoke to him as follows.

PURPORT

That Lord Brahmā descended from Satyaloka to see Priyavrata indicates that the matter was very serious. Nārada Muni had come to advise Priyavrata about the value of spiritual life, knowledge, renunciation and *bhakti,* and Lord Brahmā knew that Nārada's instructions were very impressive. Therefore unless Lord Brahmā personally went to Gandhamādana Hill to request Priyavrata, Lord Brahmā knew that Prince Priyavrata would not accept his father's order. Brahmā's purpose was to break Priyavrata's determination. Therefore Brahmā first looked upon Priyavrata with compassion. His smile and compassionate features also indicated that although Brahmā would request Priyavrata to accept household life, Priyavrata would not be out of touch with devotional service. By the blessings of a Vaiṣṇava, everything is possible. This is described in *Bhakti-rasāmṛta-sindhu* as *kṛpā-siddhi,* or perfection attained simply by the blessings of a superior person. One usually becomes liberated and perfect by executing the regulative principles set down in the *śāstras.* Nonetheless, many persons have achieved perfection simply by the blessings of a spiritual master or superior.

Priyavrata was the grandson of Lord Brahmā, and as joking competition sometimes takes place between grandson and grandfather, in this case also Priyavrata was determined to remain in meditation, whereas Brahmā was determined that he rule the universe. Thus Lord Brahmā's affectionate smile and glance meant, "My dear Priyavrata, you have decided not to accept household life, but I have decided to convince you that you must accept it." Actually, Brahmā had come to praise Priyavrata for his high standard of renunciation, austerity, penance and devotion so that he would not be deviated from devotional service, even though he would accept household life.

In this verse, one important word is *sūkta-vākena* (by Vedic hymns). In the *Vedas,* there is the following prayer to Lord Brahmā: *hiraṇyagarbhaḥ samavartatāgre bhūtasya jātaḥ patir eka āsīt.* Brahmā was received with the appropriate Vedic hymns, and because he was welcomed according to the Vedic etiquette, he was very pleased.

TEXT 11

श्रीभगवानुवाच

निबोध तातेदमृतं ब्रवीमि

मासूयितुं देवमर्हस्यप्रमेयम् ।

वयं भवस्ते तत एष महर्षि-
र्वहाम सर्वे विवशा यस्य दिष्टम् ॥११॥

śrī-bhagavān uvāca
nibodha tatedam ṛtaṁ bravīmi
māsūyituṁ devam arhasy aprameyam
vayaṁ bhavas te tata eṣa maharṣir
vahāma sarve vivaśā yasya diṣṭam

śrī-bhagavān uvāca—the supreme person, Lord Brahmā, said; *nibodha*—kindly hear with attention; *tata*—my dear son; *idam*—this; *ṛtam*—true; *bravīmi*—I am speaking; *mā*—not; *asūyitum*—to be jealous of; *devam*—the Supreme Personality of Godhead; *arhasi*—you ought; *aprameyam*—who is beyond our experimental knowledge; *vayam*—we; *bhavaḥ*—Lord Śiva; *te*—your; *tataḥ*—father; *eṣaḥ*—this; *mahā-ṛṣiḥ*—Nārada; *vahāmaḥ*—carry out; *sarve*—all; *vivaśāḥ*—unable to deviate; *yasya*—of whom; *diṣṭam*—the order.

TRANSLATION

Lord Brahmā, the supreme person within this universe, said: My dear Priyavrata, kindly hear attentively what I shall say to you. Do not be jealous of the Supreme Lord, who is beyond our experimental measurements. All of us, including Lord Śiva, your father and the great sage Mahārṣi Nārada, must carry out the order of the Supreme. We cannot deviate from His order.

PURPORT

Of the twelve great authorities in devotional service, four—Lord Brahmā himself, his son Nārada, Svāyambhuva Manu and Lord Śiva—were present before Priyavrata. They were accompanied by many other authoritative sages. Brahmā first wanted to impress upon Priyavrata that although these great personalities are all authorities, they cannot possibly disobey the orders of the Supreme Personality of Godhead, who is described in this verse as *deva,* which means "always glorious." The power, glory and potencies of the Supreme Personality of Godhead can never be diminished. In the *Īśopaniṣad,* the Lord is described as *apāpa-viddha,* which indicates that He is never affected by anything materially considered sinful. Similarly, *Śrīmad-Bhāgavatam* describes the Supreme Personality of Godhead as being so powerful that nothing we might consider abominable can affect Him. An example sometimes given to explain the position of the Supreme Lord is that of the sun, which evaporates urine from the earth but is never affected by contamination. The Supreme Lord can never be accused of doing anything wrong.

When Lord Brahmā went to induce Priyavrata to accept the responsibility for ruling the universe, he did not go whimsically; he was following the dictations of the Supreme Lord. Indeed, Brahmā and other genuine authorities never do anything without His permission. The Supreme Lord is situated in everyone's heart. In the beginning of *Śrīmad-Bhāgavatam* it is said, *tene brahma hṛdā ya ādi-kavaye:* the Lord dictated Vedic knowledge to Brahmā through his heart. The more a living entity is purified by devotional service, the more he comes in direct contact with the Supreme Personality of Godhead, as confirmed in *Śrīmad Bhagavad-gītā:*

teṣāṁ satata-yuktānāṁ
bhajatāṁ prīti-pūrvakam
dadāmi buddhi-yogaṁ taṁ
yena mām upayānti te

"To those who are constantly devoted and worship Me with love, I give the understanding by which they can come to Me." (Bg. 10.10) Lord Brahmā, therefore, had not come to Priyavrata by his own whims: rather, it is understood that he had been ordered to persuade Priyavrata by the Supreme Personality of Godhead, whose activities cannot be understood by material senses and who is therefore described herein as *aprameya.* Thus Lord Brahmā first advised Priyavrata to hear his words with attention and without envy.

Why one is induced to perform certain acts despite his desire to do something else is indicated herein. One cannot disobey the orders of the Supreme Lord, even if one is as powerful as Lord Śiva, Lord Brahmā, Manu or the great sage Nārada. All these authorities are certainly very powerful, but they do not have the power to disobey the orders of the Supreme Personality of Godhead. Since Lord Brahmā had come to Priyavrata in accordance with the orders of the Supreme Lord, he first wanted to dispel any suspicions that he might be acting as Priyavrata's enemy. Lord Brahmā was following the orders of the Supreme Lord, and therefore it would be worthwhile for Priyavrata to accept Lord Brahmā's order, as the Lord desired.

TEXT 12

न तस्य कश्चित्तपसा विद्यया वा
न योगवीर्येण मनीषया वा ।

नैवार्थधर्मैः परतः स्वतो वा
कृतं विहन्तुं तनुभृद्विभूयात् ॥१२॥

na tasya kaścit tapasā vidyayā vā
na yoga-vīryeṇa manīṣayā vā
naivārtha-dharmaiḥ parataḥ svato vā
kṛtaṁ vihantuṁ tanu-bhṛd vibhūyāt

na—never; *tasya*—His; *kaścit*—anyone; *tapasā*—by austerity; *vidyayā*—by education; *vā*—or; *na*—never; *yoga*—by power of mystic *yoga; vīryeṇa*—by personal strength; *manīṣayā*—by intelligence; *vā*—or; *na*—never; *eva*—certainly; *artha*—by material opulence; *dharmaiḥ*—by the power of religion; *parataḥ*—by any external power; *svataḥ*—by personal endeavor; *vā*—or; *kṛtam*—the order; *vihantum*—to avoid; *tanu-bhṛt*—a living entity who has accepted a material body; *vibhūyāt*—is able.

TRANSLATION

One cannot avoid the order of the Supreme Personality of Godhead, not by the strength of severe austerities, an exalted Vedic education, or the power of mystic yoga, physical prowess or intellectual activities. Nor can one use his power of religion, his material opulence or any other means, either by himself or with the help of others, to defy the orders of the Supreme Lord. That is not possible for any living being, from Brahmā down to the ant.

PURPORT

In the *Garga Upanisad*, Gargamuni says to his wife, *etasya vā ak-ṣarasya praśāsane gargi sūryā-candramasau vidhṛtau tiṣṭhataḥ: :* "My dear Gargī, everything is under the control of the Supreme Personality of Godhead. Even the sun, the moon and other controllers and demigods like Lord Brahmā and King Indra are all under His control." An ordinary human being or animal who has accepted a material body cannot go beyond the jurisdiction of the Supreme Personality of Godhead's control. A material body includes senses. However, the sense activities of so-called scientists who try to be free from God's law or the laws of nature are useless. This is also confirmed in *Bhagavad-gītā* (7.14). *Mama māyā duratyayā:* it is impossible to surpass the control of material nature, for the Supreme Personality of Godhead is working behind it. Sometimes we are proud of our austerities, penances and mystic yogic powers, but it is clearly stated herein that one cannot surpass the laws and directions of the Supreme Personality of Godhead, either by dint of mystic power, a scientific education, or austerities and penances. It is impossible.

The word *manīṣayā* ("by intelligence") is of special significance. Priyavrata might argue that Lord Brahmā was requesting him to accept family life and the responsibility for ruling a kingdom, although Nārada Muni had advised him not to enter household life and be entangled in material affairs. Whom to accept would be a puzzle for Priyavrata because both Lord Brahmā and Nārada Muni are authorities. Under the circumstances, the use of the word *manīṣayā* is very appropriate, for it indicates that since both Nārada Muni and Lord Brahmā are authorized to give instruction, Priyavrata should neglect neither of them but should use his intelligence to follow the advice of both. To solve such dilemmas, Śrīla Rūpa Gosvāmī has given a very clear conception of intelligence. He says:

anāsaktasya viṣayān
yathārham upayuñjataḥ
nirbandhaḥ kṛṣṇa-sambandhe
yuktaṁ vairāgyam ucyate

Viṣayān, material affairs, should be accepted without attachment, and everything should be dovetailed with the service of the Lord. That is real intelligence (*manīṣā*). Becoming a family man or king in the material world is not harmful if one accepts everything for Kṛṣṇa's service. That necessitates clear intelligence. Māyāvādī philosophers say, *brahma satyaṁ jagan mithyā:* this material world is false, and only the Absolute Truth is real. However, an intelligent devotee in the line of Lord Brahmā and the great sage Nārada—or, in other words, in the Brahma-*sampradāya*—does not consider this world false. That which is created by the Supreme Personality of Godhead cannot be false, but using it for enjoyment is. Everything is meant to be enjoyed by the Supreme Personality of Godhead, as confirmed in *Bhagavad-gītā* (5.29). *Bhoktāraṁ yajña-tapasāṁ sarva-loka-maheśvaram:* the Supreme Personality of Godhead is the supreme proprietor and enjoyer, and therefore everything should be dovetailed for His enjoyment and service. Regardless of one's circumstances, favorable or unfavorable, one should use everything to serve the Supreme Lord. That is the perfect way to use one's intelligence.

TEXT 13

भवाय नाशाय च कर्म कर्तुं
शोकाय मोहाय सदा भयाय ।

सुखाय दुःखाय च देहयोग-
मव्यक्तदिष्टं जनताङ्ग धत्ते ॥१३॥

bhavāya nāśāya ca karma kartuṁ
śokāya mohāya sadā bhayāya
sukhāya duḥkhāya ca deha-yogam
avyakta-diṣṭaṁ janatāṅga dhatte

bhavāya—for birth; *nāśāya*—for death; *ca*—also; *karma*—activity; *kartum*—to do; *śokāya*—for bereavement; *mohāya*—for illusion; *sadā*—always; *bhayāya*—for fear; *sukhāya*—for happiness; *duḥkhāya*—for distress; *ca*—also; *deha-yogam*—connection with a material body; *avyakta*—by the Supreme Personality of Godhead; *diṣṭam*—directed; *janatā*—the living entities; *aṅga*—O Priyavrata; *dhatte*—accept.

TRANSLATION

My dear Priyavrata, by the order of the Supreme Personality of Godhead, all living entities accept different types of bodies for birth and death, activity, lamentation, illusion, fear of future dangers, and happiness and distress.

PURPORT

Every living entity who has come to this material world has come here for material enjoyment, but according to his own *karma,* activities, he must accept a certain type of body given to him by material nature under the order of the Supreme Personality of Godhead. As stated in *Bhagavad-gītā* (3.27), *prakṛteḥ kriyamāṇāni guṇaiḥ karmāṇi sarvaśaḥ:* everything is being done by *prakṛti,* material nature, under the direction of the Supreme Lord. Modern scientists do not know why there are varieties of bodies in 8,400,000 forms. The fact is that all these bodies are ordained for the living entities by the Supreme Personality of Godhead according to the living entities' desires. He gives the living entities freedom to act as they like, but on the other hand they must accept a body according to the reactions of their activities. Thus there are different types of bodies. Some living entities have short durations of life, whereas others live for fantastic durations. Every one of them, however, from Brahmā down to the ant, acts according to the direction of the Supreme Personality of Godhead, who is sitting in everyone's heart. As confirmed in *Bhagavad-gītā* (15.15):

sarvasya cāhaṁ hṛdi sanniviṣṭo
mattaḥ smṛtir jñānam apohanaṁ ca

"I am seated in everyone's heart, and from Me come remembrance, knowledge and forgetfulness." It is not a fact, however, that the Supreme Personality of Godhead gives direction to certain living entities in one way and other living entities in another way. The truth is that every living entity has a certain desire, and the Supreme Lord gives him a chance to fulfill it. The best course, therefore, is to surrender unto the Supreme Personality of Godhead and act according to His desire. One who does so is liberated.

TEXT 14

यद्वाचि तन्त्यां गुणकर्मदामभिः
सुदुस्तरैर्वत्स वयं सुयोजिताः ।
सर्वे वहामो बलिमीश्वराय
प्रोता नसीव द्विपदे चतुष्पदः ॥१४॥

yad-vāci tantyāṁ guṇa-karma-dāmabhiḥ
sudustarair vatsa vayaṁ suyojitāḥ
sarve vahāmo balim īśvarāya
protā nasīva dvi-pade catuṣ-padaḥ

yat—of whom; *vāci*—in the form of Vedic instruction; *tantyām*—to a long rope; *guṇa*—of quality; *karma*—and work; *dāmabhiḥ*—by the ropes; *su-dustaraiḥ*—very difficult to avoid; *vatsa*—my dear boy; *vayam*—we; *su-yojitāḥ*—are engaged; *sarve*—all; *vahāmaḥ*—carry out; *balim*—orders to please Him; *īśvarāya*—unto the Supreme Personality of Godhead; *protāḥ*—being bound; *nasi*—in the nose; *iva*—like; *dvi-pade*—to the two-legged (driver); *catuḥ-padaḥ*—the four-legged (bulls).

TRANSLATION

My dear boy, all of us are bound by the Vedic injunctions to the divisions of varṇāśrama according to our qualities and work. These divisions are difficult to avoid because they are scientifically arranged. We must therefore carry out our duties of varṇāśrama-dharma, like bulls obliged to move according to the direction of a driver pulling on ropes knotted to their noses.

PURPORT

In this verse, the words *tantyāṁ guṇa-karma-dāmabhiḥ* are very important. We each get a body according to our association with the *guṇas,* the qualities or modes of material nature, and we act accordingly. As stated in *Bhagavad-gītā,* the four orders of the social system—namely *brāhmaṇa, kṣatriya, vaiśya* and *śūdra*—are arranged according to *guṇa* and *karma,* their qualities and work. There is some controversy about this, however, because some say that since one receives a body according to the *guṇa* and *karma* of his past life, it is one's birth that determines his social status. Others say, however, that one's birth according to the *guṇa* and *karma* of his past life is not the essential consideration, since one can change his *guṇa* and *karma* even in this life. Thus they say that the four divisions of the social order—*brāhmaṇa, kṣatriya, vaiśya* and *śūdra*—should be arranged according to the *guṇa* and *karma* of this life. This version is confirmed in *Śrīmad-Bhāgavatam* by Nārada Muni. While instructing Mahārāja Yudhiṣṭhira about the symptoms of *guṇa* and *karma,* Nārada Muni said that these symptoms must govern the division of society. In other words, if a person born in the family of a *brāhmaṇa* has the symptoms of a *śūdra,* he should be designated as a *śūdra.* Similarly, if a *śūdra* has brahminical qualities, he should be designated a *brāhmaṇa.*

The *varṇāśrama* system is scientific. Therefore if we accept the divisions of *varṇa* and *āśrama* according to the Vedic instructions, our lives will be successful. Unless human society is thus divided and arranged, it cannot be perfect. As stated in the *Viṣṇu Purāṇa* (3.8.9):

varṇāśramācāravatā
puruṣeṇa paraḥ pumān
viṣṇur ārādhyate panthā
nānyat tat-toṣa-kāraṇam

"The Supreme Personality of Godhead, Lord Viṣṇu, is worshiped by the proper execution of prescribed duties in the system of *varṇa* and *āśrama.* There is no other way to satisfy the Supreme Personality of Godhead. One must be situated in the institution of the four *varṇas* and *āśramas.*" All of human society is meant to worship Lord Viṣṇu. At the present moment, however, human society does not know that this is the ultimate goal or perfection of life. Therefore instead of worshiping Lord Viṣṇu, people have been educated to worship matter. According to the direction of modern society, men think they can advance in civilization by manipulating matter to build skyscrapers, big roads, automobiles and so on. Such a civilization must certainly be called materialistic because its people do not know the goal of life. The goal of life is to reach Viṣṇu, but instead of reaching Viṣṇu, people are bewildered by the external manifestation of the material energy. Therefore progress in material advancement is blind, and the leaders of such material advancement are also blind. They are leading their followers in the wrong way.

It is best, therefore, to accept the injunctions of the *Vedas,* which are mentioned in this verse as *yad-vāci.* In accordance with those injunctions, everyone should find out whether he is a *brāhmaṇa, kṣatriya, vaiśya* or *śūdra* and should thus be educated accordingly. Then his life will be successful. Otherwise, all of human society will be confused. If human society is divided scientifically according to *varṇa* and *āśrama,* and if the Vedic directions are followed, one's life, regardless of his position, will be successful. It is not that *brāhmaṇas* will be elevated to the transcendental platform but not the *śūdras.* If the Vedic injunctions are followed, all of them—*brāhmaṇas, kṣatriyas, vaiśyas* and *śūdras*—will be elevated to the transcendental platform, and their lives will be successful. The injunctions in the *Vedas* are explicit directions from the Supreme Personality of Godhead. The example cited in this verse is that bulls tied by ropes in their nostrils move according to the direction of the driver. Similarly, if we move according to the instructions of the *Vedas,* the perfect paths for our lives will be set. Otherwise, if we do not move in that way but act according to our whimsical ideas, our lives will be spoiled by confusion and will end in despair. Actually, because people at the present moment are not following the instructions of the *Vedas,* they are all confused. We must therefore accept this instruction by Lord Brahmā to Priyavrata as the factual scientific direction leading to the success of life. This is also confirmed in *Bhagavad-gītā* (16.23):

yaḥ śāstra-vidhim utsṛjya
vartate kāma-kārataḥ
na sa siddhim avāpnoti
na sukhaṁ na parāṁ gatim

If we do not live according to the injunctions of the *śāstras,* the *Vedas,* we shall never achieve success in life, to say nothing of happiness or elevation to higher statuses of living.

TEXT 15

ईशाभिसृष्टं ह्यवरुन्ध्महेऽङ्ग
दुःखं सुखं वा गुणकर्मसङ्गात् ।
आस्थाय तत्तद्यदयुङ्क्त नाथ-
श्चक्षुष्मतान्धा इव नीयमानाः ॥१५॥

īśābhisṛṣṭaṁ hy avarundhmahe'ṅga
duḥkhaṁ sukhaṁ vā guṇa-karma-saṅgāt
āsthāya tat tad yad ayuṅkta nāthaś
cakṣuṣmatāndhā iva nīyamānāḥ

īśa-abhisṛṣṭam—created or given by the Lord; *hi*—certainly; *avarundhmahe*—we have to accept; *aṅga*—my dear Priyavrata; *duḥkham*—distress; *sukham*—happiness; *vā*—or; *guṇa-karma*—with quality and work; *saṅgāt*—by association; *āsthāya*—being situated in; *tat tat*—that condition; *yat*—which body; *ayuṅkta*—He gave; *nāthaḥ*—the Supreme Lord; *cakṣuṣmatā*—by a person having eyes; *andhāḥ*—blind men; *iva*—like; *nīyamānāḥ*—being conducted.

TRANSLATION

My dear Priyavrata, according to our association with different modes of material nature, the Supreme Personality of Godhead gives us our specific bodies and the happiness and distress we achieve. One must therefore remain situated as he is and be conducted by the Supreme Personality of Godhead, exactly as a blind man is led by a person who has eyes with which to see.

PURPORT

By material means, one cannot avoid the happiness and distress unique to his particular body. There are 8,400,000 bodily forms, each destined to enjoy and suffer a certain amount of happiness and distress. This we cannot change, for the happiness and distress are ordained by the Supreme Personality of Godhead, in accordance with whose decision we have received our bodies. Since we cannot avoid the plan of the Supreme Godhead, we must agree to be directed by Him, just as a blind man is led by a person who has eyes. Under any circumstances, if we remain in the condition allotted to us by the Supreme Lord and follow His instructions, we will become perfect. The main purpose of life is to follow the instructions of the Supreme Personality of Godhead. It is such instructions that constitute one's religion or occupational duty.

In *Bhagavad-gītā,* therefore, Lord Kṛṣṇa says, *sarva-dharmān parityajya mām ekaṁ śaraṇaṁ vraja:* "Give up all other engagements. Simply surrender unto Me and follow Me." (Bg. 18.66) This process of surrendering by following the instructions of the Supreme Personality of Godhead is not meant for any particular caste or creed. A *brāhmaṇa* can surrender, and so can a *kṣatriya, vaiśya* or *śūdra.* Everyone can adopt this process. As stated in this verse, *cakṣuṣmatāndhā iva nīyamānāḥ:* one should follow the Lord the way a blind man follows a person who has eyes. If we follow the Supreme Personality of Godhead by following the directions He gives in the *Vedas* and *Bhagavad-gītā,* our lives will be successful. The Lord therefore says:

man-manā bhava mad-bhakto
mad-yājī māṁ namaskuru
mām evaiṣyasi satyaṁ te
pratijāne priyo'si me

"Always think of Me, become My devotee, and offer respect and obeisances unto Me. Then you will certainly come back home, back to Godhead. I promise you this because you are My very dear friend." (Bg. 18.65) This instruction is meant for everyone—*brāhmaṇa, kṣatriya, vaiśya* or *śūdra.* If anyone, from any division of life, surrenders to the Supreme Personality of Godhead and follows His instructions, his life will be successful.

The previous verse has given the analogy of bulls moving under the direction of the driver of a bullock cart. The bulls, being completely surrendered to the driver, remain wherever he wants to place them and eat whatever he wants them to eat. Similarly, being completely surrendered to the Supreme Personality of Godhead, we should not aspire for happiness, or regret distress; we must be satisfied with the position allotted to us by the Lord. We should follow the path of devotional service and not be dissatisfied with the happiness and distress He has given. People in the material modes of passion and ignorance generally cannot understand the plan of the Supreme Personality of Godhead with its 8,400,000 forms of life, but the human form affords one the special privilege to understand this plan, engage in devotional service and elevate oneself to the highest position of perfection by following the Lord's instructions. The entire world is working under the influence of the modes of material nature, especially ignorance and passion, but if people engage in hearing and chanting about the glories of the Supreme Lord, their lives can be successful, and they can be elevated to the highest perfection. In the *Bṛhan-nāradīya Purāṇa,* therefore, it is said:

harer nāma harer nāma
harer nāmaiva kevalam
kalau nāsty eva nāsty eva
nāsty eva gatir anyathā

"In this age of Kali, there is no other way, no other way, no other way for spiritual perfection than the holy name, the holy name, the holy name of the Lord." Everyone should be given the chance to hear the holy names of the Supreme Personality of Godhead, for thus one will gradually come to understand his real position in life and be elevated to the transcendental position above the mode of goodness. Thus all impediments to his progress will be cut to pieces. In conclusion, therefore, we must be satisfied in whatever position we have been put into by the Supreme Personality of Godhead, and we should try to engage ourselves in His devotional service. Then our lives will be successful.

TEXT 16

मुक्तोऽपि तावद्बिभृयात्स्वदेह-
मारब्धमश्नन्नभिमानशून्यः ।
यथानुभूतं प्रतियातनिद्रः
किं त्वन्यदेहाय गुणान्न वृङ्क्ते ॥१६॥

mukto'pi tāvad bibhṛyāt sva-deham
ārabdham aśnann abhimāna-śūnyaḥ
yathānubhūtaṁ pratiyāta-nidraḥ
kiṁ tv anya-dehāya guṇān na vṛṅkte

muktaḥ—a liberated person; *api*—even; *tāvat*—so long; *bibhṛyāt*—must maintain; *sva-deham*—his own body; *ārabdham*—obtained as a result of past activity; *aśnan*—accepting; *abhimāna-śūnyaḥ*—without erroneous conceptions; *yathā*—as; *anubhūtam*—what was perceived; *pratiyāta-nidraḥ*—one who has awakened from sleep; *kim tu*—but; *anya-dehāya*—for another material body; *guṇān*—the material qualities; *na*—never; *vṛṅkte*—enjoys.

TRANSLATION

Even if one is liberated, he nevertheless accepts the body he has received according to his past karma. Without misconceptions, however, he regards his enjoyment and suffering due to that karma the way an awakened person regards a dream he had while sleeping. He thus remains steadfast and never works to achieve another material body under the influence of the three modes of material nature.

PURPORT

The difference between a liberated and conditioned soul is that the conditioned soul is under the concept of bodily life, whereas a liberated person knows that he is not the body but a spirit, different from the body. Priyavrata might have thought that although a conditioned soul is forced to act according to the laws of nature, why should he, who was far advanced in spiritual understanding, accept the same kind of bondage and impediments to spiritual advancement? To answer this doubt, Lord Brahmā informed him that even those who are liberated do not resent accepting, in the present body, the results of their past activities. While sleeping, one dreams many unreal things, but when he awakens he disregards them and makes progress in factual life. Similarly, a liberated person—one who has completely understood that he is not the body but a spirit soul—disregards past activities performed in ignorance and performs his present activities in such a way that they produce no reactions. This is described in *Bhagavad-gītā* (3.9). *Yajñārthāt karmaṇo'nyatra loko'yaṁ karma-bandhanaḥ:* if one performs activities for the satisfaction of the Supreme Personality, the *yajña-puruṣa,* his work does not produce reactions, whereas *karmīs,* who act for themselves, are bound by the reactions of their work. A liberated person, therefore, does not think about whatever he has ignorantly done in the past; instead, he acts in such a way that he will not produce another body by fruitive activities. As clearly mentioned in *Bhagavad-gītā:*

māṁ ca yo'vyabhicāreṇa
bhakti-yogena sevate
sa guṇān samatītyaitān
brahma-bhūyāya kalpate

"One who engages in full devotional service, who does not fall down in any circumstance, at once transcends the modes of material nature and thus comes to the level of Brahman." (Bg. 14.26) Regardless of what we have done in our past lives, if we engage ourselves in unalloyed devotional service to the Lord in this life, we will always be situated in the *brahma-bhūta* (liberated) state, free from reactions, and will not be obliged to accept another material body. *Tyaktvā dehaṁ punar janma naiti mām eti so'rjuna* (Bg. 4.9). After giving up the body, one who has acted in that way does not accept another material body, but instead goes back home, back to Godhead.

TEXT 17

भयं प्रमत्तस्य वनेष्वपि स्याद्
यतः स आस्ते सहषट्सपत्नः ।
जितेन्द्रियस्यात्मरतेर्बुधस्य
गृहाश्रमः किं नु करोत्यवद्यम् ॥१७॥

bhayaṁ pramattasya vaneṣv api syād
yataḥ sa āste saha-ṣaṭ-sapatnaḥ
jitendriyasyātma-rater budhasya
gṛhāśramaḥ kiṁ nu karoty avadyam

bhayam—fear; *pramattasya*—of one who is bewildered; *vaneṣu*—in forests; *api*—even; *syāt*—there must be; *yataḥ*—because; *saḥ*—he (one who is not self-controlled); *āste*—is existing; *saha*—with; *ṣaṭ-sapatnaḥ*—six co-wives; *jita-indriyasya*—for one who has already conquered the senses; *ātma-rateḥ*—self-satisfied; *budhasya*—for such a learned man; *gṛha-āśramaḥ*—household life; *kim*—what; *nu*—indeed; *karoti*—can do; *avadyam*—harm.

TRANSLATION

Even if he goes from forest to forest, one who is not self-controlled must always fear material bondage because he is living with six co-wives—the mind and knowledge-acquiring senses. Even householder life, however, cannot harm a self-satisfied, learned man who has conquered his senses.

PURPORT

Śrīla Narottama dāsa Ṭhākura has sung, *gṛhe vā vanete thāke, 'hā gaurāṅga' bale ḍāke:* whether one is situated in the forest or at home, if he is engaged in the devotional service of Lord Caitanya, he is a liberated person. Here this is also repeated. For one who has not controlled his senses, going to the forest to become a so-called *yogī* is meaningless. Because his uncontrolled mind and senses are going with him, he cannot achieve anything, even by giving up household life and staying in the forest. Formerly many mercantile men from the up-country of India used to go to Bengal, and thus there is a familiar saying, "If you go to Bengal, your fortune will go with you." Our first concern, therefore, should be to control the senses, and since the senses cannot be controlled unless engaged in the devotional service of the Lord, our most important duty is to engage the senses in devotional service. *Hṛṣīkeṇa hṛṣīkeśa-sevanaṁ bhaktir ucyate: bhakti* means engagement of the purified senses in the service of the Lord.

Herein Lord Brahmā indicates that instead of going to the forest with uncontrolled senses, it is better and more secure to engage the senses in the service of the Lord. Even household life can do no harm to a self-controlled person acting in this way; it cannot force him into material bondage. Śrīla Rūpa Gosvāmī has further enunciated this position:

īhā yasya harer dāsye
karmaṇā manasā girā
nikhilāsv apy avasthāsu
jīvan-muktaḥ sa ucyate

"Regardless of one's circumstances, if one fully engages his activities, mind and words in the devotional service of the Lord, he should be understood to be a liberated person." Śrīla Bhaktivinoda Ṭhākura was a responsible officer and a householder, yet his service to the cause of expanding the mission of Lord Caitanya Mahāprabhu is unique. Śrīla Prabodhānanda Sarasvatī Ṭhākura says, *durdāntendriya-kāla-sarpa-paṭalī protkhāta-daṁṣṭrāyate.* The sense organs are certainly our greatest enemies, and they are therefore compared to venomous serpents. However, if a venomous serpent is bereft of its poison fangs, it is no longer fearful.Similarly, if the senses are engaged in the service of the Lord, there is no need to fear their activities. The devotees in the Kṛṣṇa consciousness movement move within this material world, but because their senses are fully engaged in the service of the Lord, they are always aloof from the material world. They are always living in a transcendental position.

TEXT 18

यः षट् सपत्नान् विजिगीषमाणो
गृहेषु निर्विश्य यतेत पूर्वम् ।

अत्येति दुर्गाश्रित ऊर्जितारीन्
क्षीणेषु कामं विचरेद्विपश्चित् ॥१८॥

yaḥ ṣaṭ sapatnān vijigīṣamāṇo
gṛheṣu nirviśya yateta pūrvam
atyeti durgāśrita ūrjitārīn
kṣīṇeṣu kāmaṁ vicared vipaścit

yaḥ—anyone who; *ṣaṭ*—six; *sapatnān*—adversaries; *vijigīṣamāṇaḥ*—desiring to conquer; *gṛheṣu*—in household life; *nirviśya*—having entered; *yateta*—must try; *pūrvam*—first; *atyeti*—conquers; *durga-āśritaḥ*—being in a fortified place; *ūrjita-arīn*—very strong enemies; *kṣīṇeṣu*—decreased; *kāmam*—lusty desires; *vicaret*—can go; *vipaścit*—the most experienced, learned.

TRANSLATION

One who is situated in household life and who systematically conquers his mind and five sense organs is like a king in his fortress who conquers his powerful enemies. After one has been trained in household life and his lusty desires have decreased, he can move anywhere without danger.

PURPORT

The Vedic system of four *varṇas* and four *āśramas* is very scientific, and its entire purpose is to enable one to control the senses. Before entering household life (*gṛhastha-āśrama*), a student is fully trained to become *jitendriya,* a conqueror of the senses. Such a mature student is allowed to become a householder, and because he was first trained in conquering his senses, he retires from household life and becomes *vānaprastha* as soon as the strong waves of youthful life are past and he reaches the verge of old age at fifty years or slightly more. Then, after being further trained, he accepts *sannyāsa.* He is then a fully learned and renounced person who can move anywhere and everywhere without fear of being captivated by material desires. The senses are considered very powerful enemies. As a king in a strong fortress can conquer powerful enemies, so a householder in *gṛhastha-āśrama,* household life, can conquer the lusty desires of youth and be very secure when he takes *vānaprastha* and *sannyāsa.*

TEXT 19

त्वं त्वब्जनाभाङ्घ्रिसरोजकोश-
दुर्गाश्रितो निर्जितषट्सपत्नः ।
भुङ्क्ष्वेह भोगान् पुरुषातिदिष्टान्
विमुक्तसङ्गः प्रकृतिं भजस्व ॥१९॥

tvaṁ tv abja-nābhāṅghri-saroja-kośa-
durgāśrito nirjita-ṣaṭ-sapatnaḥ
bhuṅkṣveha bhogān puruṣātidiṣṭān
vimukta-saṅgaḥ prakṛtiṁ bhajasva

tvam—yourself; *tu*—then; *abja-nābha*—of the Supreme Personality of Godhead, whose navel is like a lotus flower; *aṅghri*—feet; *saroja*—lotus; *kośa*—hole; *durga*—the stronghold; *āśritaḥ*—taken shelter of; *nirjita*—conquered; *ṣaṭ-sapatnaḥ*—the six enemies (the mind and five senses); *bhuṅkṣva*—enjoy; *iha*—in this material world; *bhogān*—enjoyable things; *puruṣa*—by the Supreme Person; *atidiṣṭān*—extraordinarily ordered; *vimukta*—liberated; *saṅgaḥ*—from material association; *prakṛtim*—constitutional position; *bhajasva*—enjoy.

TRANSLATION

Lord Brahmā continued: My dear Priyavrata, seek shelter inside the opening in the lotus of the feet of the Lord, whose navel is also like a lotus. Thus conquer the six sense organs [the mind and knowledge-acquiring senses]. Accept material enjoyment because the Lord, extraordinarily, has ordered you to do this. You will thus always be liberated from material association and be able to carry out the Lord's orders in your constitutional position.

PURPORT

There are three kinds of men within this material world. Those who are trying to enjoy the senses to the utmost are called *karmīs,* above them are the *jñānīs,* who try to conquer the urges of the senses, and above them are the *yogīs,* who have already conquered the senses. None of them, however, are situated in a transcendental position. Only devotees, who belong to none of the above-mentioned groups, are transcendental. As explained in *Bhagavad-gītā* (14.26):

māṁ ca yo'vyabhicāreṇa
bhakti-yogena sevate
sa guṇān samatītyaitān
brahma-bhūyāya kalpate

"One who engages in full devotional service, who does not fall down in any circumstance, at once transcends the modes of material nature and thus comes to the level of Brahman." Lord Brahmā herein advises Priyavrata to remain transcendental in the fortress not of family life but of the lotus feet of the Lord (*abja-nābhāṅghri-saroja*). When a bumblebee enters the opening of a lotus flower and drinks its honey, it is fully protected by the petals of the lotus. The bee is undisturbed by sunshine and other external influences. Similarly, one who always seeks shelter at the lotus feet of the Personality of Godhead is protected from all dangers. It is therefore said in *Śrīmad-Bhāgavatam* (10.14.58):

samāśritā ye pada-pallava-plavaṁ
mahat-padaṁ puṇya-yaśo murāreḥ
bhavāmbudhir vatsa-padaṁ paraṁ padaṁ
padaṁ padaṁ yad vipadāṁ na teṣām

For one who has taken shelter of the lotus feet of the Lord, everything becomes easier. Indeed, even crossing the great ocean of nescience (*bhavāmbudhi*) is exactly like crossing the hoofprint created by a calf (*vatsa-padam*). For such a devotee, there is no question of remaining in a place where every step is dangerous.

Our actual duty is to carry out the supreme order of the Personality of Godhead. If we are fixed in our determination to carry out the supreme order of the Lord, we are always secure, regardless of where we are situated, whether in hell or in heaven. Herein the words *prakṛtiṁ bhajasva* are very significant. *Prakṛtim* refers to one's constitutional position. Every living entity has the constitutional position of being an eternal servant of God. Therefore Lord Brahmā advised Priyavrata, "Be situated in your original position as an eternal servant of the Lord. If you carry out His orders, you will never fall, even in the midst of material enjoyment." Material enjoyment achieved by dint of one's fruitive activities differs from material enjoyment given by the Supreme Personality of Godhead. A devotee sometimes appears to be in a very opulent position, but he accepts that position to follow the orders of the Supreme Personality of Godhead. Therefore a devotee is never affected by material influences. The devotees in the Kṛṣṇa consciousness movement are preaching all over the world in accordance with the order of Śrī Caitanya Mahāprabhu. They have to meet many *karmīs,* but by the mercy of Śrī Caitanya Mahāprabhu, they are unaffected by material influences. He has blessed them, as described in the *Caitanya-caritāmṛta* (*Madhya* 7.129):

kabhu nā bādhibe tomāra viṣaya-taraṅga
punarapi ei ṭhāñi pābe mora saṅge

A sincere devotee who engages in the service of Lord Śrī Caitanya Mahāprabhu by preaching His cult all over the world will never be affected by *viṣaya-taraṅga,* material influences. On the contrary, in due course of time he will return to the shelter of the lotus feet of Lord Śrī Caitanya Mahāprabhu and will thus have perpetual association with Him.

TEXT 20

श्रीशुक उवाच
इति समभिहितो महाभागवतो भगवतस्त्रिभुवनगुरोरनुशासनमात्मनो लघुतयावनतशिरोधरो बाढमिति सबहुमानमुवाह ॥२०॥

śrī-śuka uvāca
iti samabhihito mahā-bhāgavato bhagavatas tri-bhuvana-guror anuśāsanam ātmano laghutayāvanata-śirodharo bāḍham iti sabahu-mānam uvāha.

śrī-śukaḥ uvāca—Śrī Śukadeva Gosvāmī said; *iti*—thus; *samabhihitaḥ*—completely instructed; *mahā-bhāgavataḥ*—the great devotee; *bhagavataḥ*—of the most powerful Lord Brahmā; *tri-bhuvana*—of the three worlds; *guroḥ*—the spiritual master; *anuśāsanam*—the order; *ātmanaḥ*—of himself; *laghutayā*—because of inferiority; *avanata*—bowed down; *śirodharaḥ*—his head; *bāḍham*—yes, sir; *iti*—thus; *sa-bahu-mānam*—with great respect; *uvāha*—carried out.

TRANSLATION

Śrī Śukadeva Gosvāmī continued: After thus being fully instructed by Lord Brahmā, who is the spiritual master of the three worlds, Priyavrata, his own position being inferior, offered obeisances, accepted the order and carried it out with great respect.

PURPORT

Śrī Priyavrata was the grandson of Lord Brahmā. Therefore according to social etiquette, his position was inferior. It is the duty of the inferior to carry out the order of the superior with great respect. Priyavrata therefore immediately said, "Yes, sir. I shall carry out your order." Priyavrata is described as a *mahā-bhāgavata,* a great devotee. The duty of a great devotee is to carry out the order of the spiritual master, or the spiritual master of the spiritual master in the *paramparā* system. As described in *Bhagavad-gītā* (4.2), *evaṁ paramparā prāptam:* one has to receive the instructions of the Supreme Lord through the disciplic chain of spiritual masters. A devotee of the Lord always considers himself a servant of the servant of the servant of the Lord.

TEXT 21

भगवानपि मनुना यथावदुपकल्पितापचितिः प्रियव्रतनारद योरविषमम-
भिसमीक्षमाणयोरात्मसमवस्थानमवाङ्मनसं क्षयमव्यवहृतं प्रवर्तयन्नगमत् ॥२१॥

bhagavān api manunā yathāvad upakalpitāpacitiḥ priyavrata-
nāradayor aviṣamam abhisamīkṣamāṇayor ātmasam avasthānam avāṅ-
manasaṁ kṣayam avyavahṛtaṁ pravartayann agamat.

bhagavān—the most powerful Lord Brahmā; *api*—also; *manunā*—by Manu; *yathāvat*—as deserved; *upakalpita-apacitiḥ*—being worshiped; *priyavrata-nāradayoḥ*—in the presence of Priyavrata and Nārada; *aviṣamam*—without aversion; *abhisamīkṣamāṇayoḥ*—looking on; *ātmasam*—just suitable for his position; *avasthānam*—to his abode; *avāk-manasam*—beyond the description of mind and words; *kṣayam*—the planet; *avyavahṛtam*—extraordinarily situated; *pravartayan*—departing; *agamat*—returned.

TRANSLATION

Lord Brahmā was then worshiped by Manu, who respectfully satisfied him as well as he could. Priyavrata and Nārada also looked upon Brahmā with no tinges of resentment. Having engaged Priyavrata in accepting his father's request, Lord Brahmā returned to his abode, Satyaloka, which is indescribable by the endeavor of mundane mind or words.

PURPORT

Manu was certainly very satisfied that Lord Brahmā had persuaded his son Priyavrata to take the responsibility for ruling the world. Priyavrata and Nārada were also very satisfied. Although Brahmā had forced Priyavrata to accept the management of worldly affairs, thus breaking his vow to remain *brahmacārī* and completely engage in devotional service, Nārada and Priyavrata did not look upon Brahmā with resentment. Nārada was not at all sorry that he had been frustrated in making Priyavrata a disciple. Both Priyavrata and Nārada were exalted personalities who knew how to respect Lord Brahmā. Therefore instead of looking upon Brahmā with resentment, they very feelingly offered him their respect. Lord Brahmā then returned to his celestial abode, known as Satyaloka, which is described here as being impeccable and being unapproachable by words.

It is stated in this verse that Lord Brahmā returned to his residence, which is as important as his own personality. Lord Brahmā is the creator of this universe and the most exalted personality within it. His lifetime is described in *Bhagavad-gītā* (8.17). *Sahasra-yuga-paryantam ahar yad brahmaṇo viduḥ.* The total duration of the four yugas is 4,300,000 years, and when that is multiplied a thousand times, it equals twelve hours in the life of Brahmā. Therefore we cannot factually comprehend even twelve hours of Brahmā's life, to say nothing of the one hundred years that constitute his entire lifetime. How, then, can we understand his abode? The Vedic literatures describe that in Satyaloka there is no birth, death, old age or disease. In other words, since Satyaloka is situated next to Brahmaloka, or the Brahman effulgence, it is almost as good as Vaikuṇṭhaloka. Lord Brahmā's abode is practically indescribable from our present status. Therefore it has been described as *avāṅ-manasa-gocara,* or beyond the description of our words and the imagination of our minds. The Vedic literatures thus describe the abode of Lord Brahmā: *yad vai parārdhyaṁ tad upārameṣṭhyaṁ na yatra śoko na jarā na mṛtyur nārtir na codvegaḥ.* "In Satyaloka, which is situated many millions and billions of years away, there is no lamentation, nor is there old age, death, anxiety or the influence of enemies."

TEXT 22

मनुरपि परेणैवं प्रतिसन्धितमनोरथः सुरर्षिवरानुमतेनात्मजम खिलधरामण्डल-
स्थितिगुप्तय आस्थाप्य स्वयमतिविषमविषयविषजलाशयाशाया उपरराम ॥२२॥

manur api pareṇaivaṁ pratisandhita-manorathaḥ surarṣi-
varānumatenātmajam akhila-dharā-maṇḍala-sthiti-guptaya āsthāpya
svayam ati-viṣama-viṣaya-viṣa-jalāśayāśāyā upararāma.

manuḥ—Svāyambhuva Manu; *api*—also; *pareṇa*—by Lord Brahmā; *evam*—thus; *pratisandhita*—executed; *manaḥ-rathaḥ*—his mental aspiration; *sura-ṛṣi-vara*—of the great sage Nārada; *anumatena*—by the permission; *ātma-jam*—his son; *akhila*—of the entire universe; *dharā-maṇḍala*—of planets; *sthiti*—maintenance; *guptaye*—for the protection; *āsthāpya*—establishing; *svayam*—personally; *ati-viṣama*—very dangerous; *viṣaya*—material affairs; *viṣa*—of poison; *jala-āśaya*—ocean; *āśāyāḥ*—from desires; *upararāma*—got relief.

TRANSLATION

Svāyambhuva Manu, with the assistance of Lord Brahmā, thus fulfilled his desires. With the permission of the great sage Nārada, he delivered to his son the governmental responsibility for maintaining and protecting all the planets of the universe. He thus achieved relief from the most dangerous, poisonous ocean of material desires.

PURPORT

Svāyambhuva Manu was practically hopeless because such a great personality as Nārada was instructing his son Priyavrata not to accept household life. Now he was very pleased that Lord Brahmā had interfered by inducing his son to accept the responsibility for ruling the government of the universe. From *Bhagavad-gītā* we get information that Vaivasvata Manu was the son of the sun-god and that his son, Mahārāja Ikṣvāku, ruled this planet earth. Svāyambhuva Manu, however, appears to have been in charge of the entire universe, and he entrusted to his son, Mahārāja Priyavrata, the responsibility for maintaining and protecting all the planetary systems. *Dharā-maṇḍala* means "planet." This earth, for instance, is called *dharā-maṇḍala. Akhila,* however, means "all" or "universal." It is therefore difficult to understand where Mahārāja Priyavrata was situated, but from this literature his position certainly appears greater than that of Vaivasvata Manu, for he was entrusted with all the planetary systems of the entire universe.

Another significant statement is that Svāyambhuva Manu took great satisfaction from abnegating the responsibility for ruling all the planetary systems of the universe. At present, politicians are very eager to take charge of the government, and they engage their men in canvassing from door to door to get votes to win the post of president or a similar exalted office. On the contrary, however, herein we find that King Priyavrata had to be persuaded by Lord Brahmā to accept the post of emperor of the entire universe. Similarly, his father, Svāyambhuva Manu, felt relieved to entrust the universal government to Priyavrata. Thus it is evident that the kings and executive heads of government in the Vedic age never accepted their positions for sense enjoyment. Such exalted kings, who were known as *rājarṣis,* ruled only to maintain and protect the kingdom for the welfare of the citizens. The history of Priyavrata and Svāyambhuva Manu describes how exemplary, responsible monarchs performed the duties of government with disinterest, keeping themselves always aloof from the contamination of material attachment.

Material affairs have herein been compared to an ocean of poison. They have been described in a similar way by Śrīla Narottama dāsa Ṭhākura in one of his songs:

saṁsāra-viṣānale, divā-niśi hiyā jvale,
juḍāite nā kainu upāya

"My heart is always burning in the fire of material existence, and I have made no provisions for getting out of it."

golokera prema-dhana, hari-nāma-saṅkīrtana,
rati nā janmila kene tāya

"The only remedy is *hari-nāma-saṅkīrtana,* the chanting of the Hare Kṛṣṇa *mahā-mantra,* which is imported from the spiritual world, Goloka Vṛndāvana. How unfortunate I am that I have no attraction for this." Manu wanted to seek shelter at the lotus feet of the Lord, and therefore when his son Priyavrata took charge of his worldly affairs, Manu was very relieved. That is the system of Vedic civilization. At the end of life, one must free himself from worldly affairs and completely engage in the service of the Lord.

The word *surarṣi-vara-anumatena* is also significant. Manu entrusted the government to his son with the permission of the great saint Nārada. This is particularly mentioned because although Nārada wanted Priyavrata to become free from all material affairs, when Priyavrata took charge of the universe by the request of Lord Brahmā and Manu, Nārada was also very pleased.

TEXT 23

इति ह वाव स जगतीपतिरीश्वरेच्छयाधिनिवेशितकर्माधिकारोऽखिलजगद्बन्ध
ध्वंसनपरानुभावस्य भगवत आदिपुरुषस्याङ्घ्रियुगलानवरतध्यानानुभावेन
परिरन्धितकषायाशयोऽवदातोऽपि मानवर्धनो महतां महीतलमनुशशास ॥२३॥

iti ha vāva sa jagatī-patir īśvarecchayādhiniveśita-karmādhikāro 'khila-jagad-bandha-dhvaṁsana-parānubhāvasya bhagavata ādi-puruṣasyāṅghri-yugalānavarata-dhyānānubhāvena parirandhita-kaṣāyāśayo'vadāto'pi māna-vardhano mahatāṁ mahītalam anuśaśāsa.

iti—thus; *ha vāva*—indeed; *saḥ*—he; *jagatī-patiḥ*—the emperor of the whole universe; *īśvara-icchayā*—by the order of the Supreme Personality of Godhead; *adhiniveśita*—completely engaged; *karma-adhikāraḥ*—in material affairs; *akhila-jagat*—of the entire universe; *bandha*—bondage; *dhvaṁsana*—destroying; *para*—transcendental; *anubhāvasya*—whose influence; *bhagavataḥ*—of the Supreme Personality of Godhead; *ādi-puruṣasya*—the original person; *aṅghri*—on the lotus feet; *yugala*—two; *anavarata*—constant; *dhyāna-anubhāvena*—by meditation; *parirandhita*—destroyed; *kaṣāya*—all the dirty things; *āśayaḥ*—in his heart; *avadātaḥ*—completely pure; *api*—although; *māna-vardhanaḥ*—just to give honor; *mahatām*—to superiors; *mahītalam*—the material world; *anuśaśāsa*—ruled.

TRANSLATION

Following the order of the Supreme Personality of Godhead, Mahārāja Priyavrata fully engaged in worldly affairs, yet he always thought of the lotus feet of the Lord, which are the cause of liberation from all material attachment. Although Priyavrata Mahārāja was completely freed from all material contamination, he ruled the material world just to honor the orders of his superiors.

PURPORT

The words *māna-vardhano mahatām* ("just to show honor to superiors") are very significant. Although Mahārāja Priyavrata was already a liberated person and had no attraction for material things, he engaged himself fully in governmental affairs just to show respect to Lord Brahmā. Arjuna had also acted in the same way. Arjuna had no desire to participate in political affairs or the fighting at Kurukṣetra, but when ordered to do so by the Supreme Lord, Kṛṣṇa, he executed those duties very nicely. One who always thinks of the lotus feet of the Lord is certainly above all the contamination of the material world. As stated in *Bhagavad-gītā:*

yoginām api sarveṣāṁ
mad-gatenāntarātmanā
śraddhāvān bhajate yo māṁ
sa me yuktatamo mataḥ

"Of all *yogīs,* he who always abides in Me with great faith, worshiping Me in transcendental loving service, is most intimately united with Me in *yoga* and is the highest of all." (Bg. 6.47) Mahārāja Priyavrata, therefore, was a liberated person and was among the highest of *yogīs,* yet superficially he became the emperor of the universe in accordance with the order of Lord Brahmā. Showing respect to his superior in this way was another of his extraordinary qualifications. As stated in *Śrīmad-Bhāgavatam* (6.17.28):

nārāyaṇa-parāḥ sarve
na kutaścana bibhyati
svargāpavarga-narakeṣv
api tulyārtha-darśinaḥ

A devotee who is actually advanced is not afraid of anything, provided he has the opportunity to execute the order of the Supreme Personality of Godhead. This is the proper explanation of why Priyavrata engaged in worldly affairs although he was a liberated person. Also, only because of this principle does a *mahā-bhāgavata,* who has nothing to do with the material world, come down to the second platform of devotional service to preach the glories of the Lord all over the world.

TEXT 24

अथ च दुहितरं प्रजापतेर्विश्वकर्मण उपयेमे बर्हिष्मतीं नाम तस्यामु ह वाव आत्मजानात्मसमानशीलगुणकर्मरूपवीर्योदारान्दश भावयाम्बभूव कन्यां च यवीयसीमूर्जस्वतीं नाम ॥२४॥

atha ca duhitaraṁ prajāpater viśvakarmaṇa upayeme barhiṣmatīṁ nāma tasyām u ha vāva ātmajān ātma-samāna-śīla-guṇa-karma-rūpa-vīryodārān daśa bhāvayām babhūva kanyāṁ ca yavīyasīṁ ūrjasvatīṁ nāma.

atha—thereafter; *ca*—also; *duhitaram*—the daughter; *prajāpateḥ*—of one of the *prajāpatis* entrusted with increasing population; *viśvakarmaṇaḥ*—named Viśvakarmā; *upayeme*—married; *barhiṣmatīm*—Barhiṣmatī; *nāma*—named; *tasyām*—in her; *u ha*—as it is celebrated; *vāva*—wonderful; *ātmajān*—sons; *ātma-samāna*—exactly equal to him; *śīla*—character; *guṇa*—quality; *karma*—activities; *rūpa*—beauty; *vīrya*—prowess; *udārān*—whose magnanimity; *daśa*—ten; *bhāvayām babhūva*—he begot; *kanyām*—daughter; *ca*—also; *yavīyasīm*—the youngest of all; *ūrjasvatīm*—Ūrjasvatī; *nāma*—named.

TRANSLATION

Thereafter, Mahārāja Priyavrata married Barhiṣmatī, the daughter of the prajāpati named Viśvakarmā. In her he begot ten sons equal to him in beauty, character, magnanimity and other qualities. He also begot a daughter, the youngest of all, named Ūrjasvatī.

PURPORT

Mahārāja Priyavrata not only carried out the order of Lord Brahmā by accepting the duties of government, but also married Barhiṣmatī, the daughter of Viśvakarmā, one of the *prajāpatis.* Since Mahārāja Priyavrata was fully trained in transcendental knowledge, he could have returned home and conducted the business of government as a *brahmacārī.* Instead, however, when he returned to household life, he accepted a wife also. The principle is that when one becomes a *gṛhastha,* he must live perfectly in that order, which means he must live peacefully with a wife and children. When Caitanya Mahāprabhu's first wife died, His mother requested Him to marry for a second time. He was twenty years old and was going to take *sannyāsa* at the age of twenty-four, yet by the request of His mother, He married. "As long as I am in household life," He told His mother, "I must have a wife, for household life does not mean staying in a house. Real household life means living in a house with a wife."

Three words in this verse are very significant—*u ha vāva.* These words are used to express wonder. Priyavrata Mahārāja had taken a vow of renunciation, but accepting a wife and begetting children have nothing to do with the path of renunciation; these are activities on the path of enjoyment. It was a source of great wonder, therefore, that Priyavrata Mahārāja, who had followed the path of renunciation, had now accepted the path of enjoyment.

Sometimes we are criticized because although I am a *sannyāsī,* I have taken part in the marriage ceremonies of my disciples. It must be explained, however, that since we have started a Kṛṣṇa conscious society and since a human society must also have ideal marriages, to correctly establish an ideal society we must take part in marrying some of its members, although we have taken to the path of renunciation. This may be astonishing to persons who are not very interested in establishing *daiva-varṇāśrama,* the transcendental system of four social orders and four spiritual orders. Śrīla Bhaktisiddhānta Sarasvatī Ṭhākura, however, wanted to reestablish *daiva-varṇāśrama.* In *daiva-varṇāśrama* there cannot be acknowledgement of social status according to birthright because in *Bhagavad-gītā* it is said that the determining considerations are *guṇa* and *karma,* one's qualities and work. It is this *daiva-*

varṇāśrama that should be established all over the world to continue a perfect society for Kṛṣṇa consciousness. This may be astonishing to foolish critics, but it is one of the functions of a Kṛṣṇa conscious society.

TEXT 25

आग्नीध्रेध्मजिह्वयज्ञबाहुमहावीरहिरण्यरेतोघृतपृष्ठ सवनमेधातिथिवीतिहोत्रकवय इति सर्व एवाग्निनामानः ॥२५॥

āgnīdhredhmajihva-yajñabāhu-mahāvīra-hiraṇyareto-ghṛtapṛṣṭha-savana-medhātithi-vītihotra-kavaya iti sarva evāgni-nāmānaḥ.

āgnīdhra—Āgnīdhra; *idhma-jihva*—Idhmajihva; *yajña-bāhu*—Yajñabāhu; *mahā-vīra*—Mahāvīra; *hiraṇya-retaḥ*—Hiraṇyaretā; *ghṛtapṛṣṭha*—Ghṛtapṛṣṭha; *savana*—Savana; *medhā-tithi*—Medhātithi; *vītihotra*—Vītihotra; *kavayaḥ*—and Kavi; *iti*—thus; *sarve*—all these; *eva*—certainly; *agni*—of the demigod controlling fire; *nāmānaḥ*—names.

TRANSLATION

The ten sons of Mahārāja Priyavrata were named Āgnīdhra, Idhmajihva, Yajñabāhu, Mahāvīra, Hiraṇyaretā, Ghṛtapṛṣṭha, Savana, Medhātithi, Vītihotra and Kavi. These are also names of Agni, the fire-god.

TEXT 26

एतेषां कविर्महावीरः सवन इति त्रय आसन्नूर्ध्वरेतसस्त आत्मविद्यायामर्भ - भावादारभ्य कृतपरिचयाः पारमहंस्यमेवाश्रममभजन् ॥२६॥

eteṣāṁ kavir mahāvīraḥ savana iti traya āsann ūrdhva-retasas ta ātma-vidyāyām arbha-bhāvād ārabhya kṛta-paricayāḥ pāramahaṁsyam evāśramam abhajan.

eteṣām—of these; *kaviḥ*—Kavi; *mahāvīraḥ*—Mahāvīra; *savanaḥ*—Savana; *iti*—thus; *trayaḥ*—three; *āsan*—were; *ūrdhva-retasaḥ*—completely celibate; *te*—they; *ātma-vidyāyām*—in transcendental knowledge; *arbha-bhāvāt*—from childhood; *ārabhya*—beginning; *kṛta-paricayāḥ*—very well versed; *pāramahaṁsyam*—of the highest spiritual perfection of human life; *eva*—certainly; *āśramam*—the order; *abhajan*—executed.

TRANSLATION

Three among these ten—namely Kavi, Mahāvīra and Savana—lived in complete celibacy. Thus trained in brahmacārī life from the beginning of

childhood, they were very conversant with the highest perfection, known as the paramahaṁsa-āśrama.

PURPORT

The word *ūrdhva-retasaḥ* in this verse is very significant. *Ūrdhva-retaḥ* refers to one who can control sex life and who instead of wasting semen by discharging it, can use this most important substance accumulated in the body to enrich the brain. One who can completely control sex life is able to work wonderfully with his brain, especially in remembering. Thus students who simply hear Vedic instructions once from their teacher could remember them verbatim without needing to read books, which therefore did not exist in former times.

Another significant word is *arbha-bhāvāt,* which means "from very childhood." Another meaning is "from being very affectionate to children." In other words, *paramahaṁsa* life is dedicated for the benefit of others. Just as a father sacrifices many things out of affection for his son, great saintly persons sacrifice all kinds of bodily comforts for the benefit of human society. In this connection there is a verse concerning the six Gosvāmīs:

tyaktvā tūrṇam aśeṣa-maṇḍala-pati-śreṇīṁ sadā tucchavat
bhūtvā dīna-gaṇeśakau karuṇayā kaupīna-kanthāśritau

Because of their compassion for the poor fallen souls, the six Gosvāmīs gave up their exalted positions as ministers and took vows as mendicants. Thus minimizing their bodily wants as far as possible, they each accepted only a loincloth and a begging bowl. Thus they remained in Vṛndāvana to execute the orders of Śrī Caitanya Mahāprabhu by compiling and publishing various Vaiṣṇava literatures.

TEXT 27

तस्मिन्नु ह वा उपशमशीलाः परमर्षयः सकलजीवनिकायावासस्य भगवतो वासुदेवस्य भीतानां शरणभूतस्य श्रीमच्चरणारविन्दाविरतस्मरणाविगलितपरम-भक्तियोगानुभावेन परिभावितान्तर्हृदयाधिगते भगवति सर्वेषां भूतानामात्मभूते प्रत्यगात्मन्येवात्मनस्तादात्म्यमविशेषेण समीयुः ॥२७॥

tasminn u ha vā upaśama-śīlāḥ paramarṣayaḥ sakala-jīva-
nikāyāvāsasya bhagavato vāsudevasya bhītānāṁ śaraṇa-bhūtasya
śrīmac-caraṇāravindāvirata-smaraṇāvigalita-parama-bhakti-yogānu-

bhāvena paribhāvitāntar-hṛdayādhigate bhagavati sarveṣāṁ bhūtānām ātma-bhūte pratyag-ātmany evātmanas tādātmyam aviśeṣeṇa samīyuḥ.

tasmin—in that *paramahaṁsa-āśrama; u*—certainly; *ha*—so celebrated; *vā*—indeed; *upaśama-śīlāḥ*—in the renounced order of life; *parama-ṛṣayaḥ*—the great sages; *sakala*—all; *jīva*—of living entities; *nikāya*—in total; *āvāsasya*—the residence; *bhagavataḥ*—of the Supreme Personality of Godhead; *vāsudevasya*—Lord Vāsudeva; *bhītānām*—of those afraid of material existence; *śaraṇa-bhūtasya*—the one who is the only shelter; *śrīmat*—of the Supreme Personality of Godhead; *caraṇa-aravinda*—the lotus feet; *avirata*—constantly; *smaraṇa*—remembering; *avigalita*—completely uncontaminated; *parama*—supreme; *bhakti-yoga*—of mystic devotional service; *anubhāvena*—by the prowess; *paribhāvita*—purified; *antaḥ*—within; *hṛdaya*—the heart; *adhigate*—perceived; *bhagavati*—the Supreme Personality of Godhead; *sarveṣām*—of all; *bhūtānām*—living entities; *ātma-bhūte*—situated within the body; *pratyak*—directly; *ātmani*—with the Supreme Supersoul; *eva*—certainly; *ātmanaḥ*—of the self; *tādātmyam*—qualitative equality; *aviśeṣeṇa*—without differences; *samīyuḥ*—realized.

TRANSLATION

Thus situated in the renounced order from the beginning of their lives, all three of them completely controlled the activities of their senses and thus became great saints. They concentrated their minds always upon the lotus feet of the Supreme Personality of Godhead, who is the resting place of the totality of living entities and who is therefore celebrated as Vāsudeva. Lord Vāsudeva is the only shelter of those who are actually afraid of material existence. By constantly thinking of His lotus feet, these three sons of Mahārāja Priyavrata became advanced in pure devotional service. By the prowess of their devotional service, they could directly perceive the Supreme Personality of Godhead, who is situated in everyone's heart as the Supersoul, and realize that there was qualitatively no difference between themselves and Him.

PURPORT

The *paramahaṁsa* stage is the topmost position in renounced life. In *sannyāsa,* the renounced order, there are four stages—*kuṭīcaka, bahūdaka, parivrājakācārya* and *paramahaṁsa.* According to the Vedic system, when one accepts the renounced order, he stays outside his village in a cottage, and his necessities, especially his food, are supplied from home. This is called the *kuṭīcaka* stage. When a *sannyāsī* advances further, he no longer accepts anything from home: instead, he collects his necessities, especially his food, from many places. This system is called *mādhukarī,* which literally means "the profession of the bumblebees." As bumblebees collect honey from many flowers, a little from each, so a *sannyāsī* should beg from door to door but not accept very much food from any particular house; he should collect a little bit from every house. This is called the *bahūdaka* stage. When a *sannyāsī* is still more experienced, he travels all over the world to preach the glories of Lord Vāsudeva. He is then known as *parivrājakācārya.* The *sannyāsī* reaches the *paramahaṁsa* stage when he finishes his preaching work and sits down in one place, strictly for the sake of advancing in spiritual life. An actual *paramahaṁsa* is one who completely controls his senses and engages in the unalloyed service of the Lord. Therefore all three of these sons of Priyavrata, namely Kavi, Mahāvīra and Savana, were situated in the *paramahaṁsa* stage from the very beginning. Their senses could not disturb them, for their senses were completely engaged in serving the Lord. Therefore the three brothers are described in this verse as *upaśama-śīlāḥ. Upaśama* means "completely subdued." Because they completely subdued their senses, they are understood to have been great sages and saints.

After subduing their senses, the three brothers concentrated their minds upon the lotus feet of Vāsudeva, Lord Kṛṣṇa. As stated in *Bhagavad-gītā* (7.19), *vāsudevaḥ sarvam iti.* The lotus feet of Vāsudeva are everything. Lord Vāsudeva is the reservoir of all living entities. When this cosmic manifestation is dissolved, all living entities enter the supreme body of the Lord, Garbhodakaśāyī Viṣṇu, who merges within the body of Mahā-Viṣṇu. Both of these *viṣṇu-tattvas* are *vāsudeva-tattvas,* and therefore the great sages Kavi, Mahāvīra and Savana concentrated always upon the lotus feet of Lord Vāsudeva, Kṛṣṇa. In this way they could understand that the Supersoul within the heart is the Supreme Personality of Godhead, and they could recognize their identity with Him. The complete description of this realization is that simply by discharging the unalloyed form of devotional service, one can realize his self completely. The *parama-bhakti-yoga* mentioned in this verse means that a living entity, by dint of unalloyed devotional service, has no other interest than the service of the Lord, as described in *Bhagavad-gītā* (*vāsudevaḥ sarvam iti*). By *parama-bhakti-yoga,* by elevating oneself to the highest platform of loving service, one can automatically be relieved from the bodily concept of life and see the Supreme Personality of Godhead face to face. As confirmed in *Brahma-saṁhitā:*

premāñjana-cchurita-bhakti-vilocanena
santaḥ sadaiva hṛdayeṣu vilokayanti
yaṁ śyāmasundaram acintya-guṇa-svarūpaṁ
govindam ādi-puruṣaṁ tam ahaṁ bhajāmi

An advanced devotee, who is known as a *sat,* or saint, can always see within his heart the Supreme Personality of Godhead, face to face. Kṛṣṇa, Śyāmasundara, expands Himself by His plenary portion, and thus a devotee can always see Him within his heart.

TEXT 28

अन्यस्यामपि जायायां त्रयः पुत्रा आसन्नुत्तमस्तामसो रैवत इति मन्वन्तरा-
धिपतयः ॥२८॥

anyasyām api jāyāyāṁ trayaḥ putrā āsann uttamas tāmaso raivata iti manvantarādhipatayaḥ.

anyasyām—other; *api*—also; *jāyāyām*—in the wife; *trayaḥ*—three; *putrāḥ*—sons; *āsan*—there were; *uttamaḥ tāmasaḥ raivataḥ*—Uttama, Tāmasa and Raivata; *iti*—thus; *manu-antara*—of the *manvantara* millennium; *adhipatayaḥ*—rulers.

TRANSLATION

In his other wife, Mahārāja Priyavrata begot three sons, named Uttama, Tāmasa and Raivata. All of them later took charge of manvantara millenniums.

PURPORT

In every day of Brahmā there are fourteen *manvantaras.* The duration of one *manvantara,* the life span of one Manu, is seventy-one *yugas,* and each *yuga* is 4,320,000 years. Almost all the Manus selected to rule the *manvantaras* came from the family of Mahārāja Priyavrata. Three of them are particularly mentioned herein, namely Uttama, Tāmasa and Raivata.

TEXT 29

एवमुपशमायनेषु स्वतनयेष्वथ जगतीपतिर्जगतीमर्बुदान्येकादश परिवत्स
राणामव्याहताखिलपुरुषकारसारसम्भृतदोर्दण्डयुगलापीडितमौर्वीगुणस्तनितविरमि
तधर्मप्रतिपक्षो बर्हिष्मत्याश्चानुदिनमेधमानप्रमोदप्रसरणयौषिण्यव्रीडा-

प्रमुषितहासावलोक रुचिरक्ष्वेल्यादिभिः पराभूयमानविवेक इवानव- बुध्यमान इव महामना बुभुजे ॥२९॥

evam upaśamāyaneṣu sva-tanayeṣv atha jagatī-patir jagatīm arbudāny ekādaśa parivatsarāṇām avyāhatākhila-puruṣa-kāra-sāra-sambhṛta-dor-daṇḍa-yugalāpīḍita-maurvī-guṇa-stanita-viramita-dharma-pratipakṣo barhiṣmatyāś cānudinam edhamāna-pramoda-prasaraṇa-yauṣiṇya-vrīḍā-pramuṣita-hāsāvaloka-rucira-kṣvely-ādibhiḥ parābhūyamāna-viveka ivānavabudhyamāna iva mahāmanā bubhuje.

evam—thus; *upaśama-ayaneṣu*—all well qualified; *sva-tanayeṣu*—his own sons; *atha*—thereafter; *jagatī-patiḥ*—the master of the universe; *jagatīm*—the universe; *arbudāni*—*arbudas* (one *arbuda* equals 100,000,000); *ekādaśa*—eleven; *parivatsarāṇām*—of years; *avyāhata*—without being interrupted; *akhila*—universal; *puruṣa-kāra*—prowess; *sāra*—strength; *sambhṛta*—endowed with; *doḥ-daṇḍaḥ*—of powerful arms; *yugala*—by the pair; *āpīḍita*—being drawn; *maurvī-guṇa*—of the bowstring; *stanita*—by the loud sound; *viramita*—defeated; *dharma*—religious principles; *pratipakṣaḥ*—those who are against; *barhiṣmatyāḥ*—of his wife Barhiṣmatī; *ca*—and; *anudinam*—daily; *edhamāna*—increasing; *pramoda*—pleasing intercourse; *prasaraṇa*—amiability; *yauṣiṇya*—feminine behavior; *vrīḍā*—by shyness; *pramuṣita*—held back; *hāsa*—laughing; *avaloka*—glancing; *rucira*—pleasing; *kṣveli-ādibhiḥ*—by exchanges of loving propensities; *parābhūyamāna*—being defeated; *vivekaḥ*—his true knowledge; *iva*—like; *anavabudhyamānaḥ*—a less intelligent person; *iva*—like; *mahā-manāḥ*—the great soul; *bubhuje*—ruled.

TRANSLATION

After Kavi, Mahāvīra and Savana were completely trained in the paramahaṁsa stage of life, Mahārāja Priyavrata ruled the universe for eleven arbudas of years. Whenever he was determined to fix his arrow upon his bowstring with his two powerful arms, all opponents of the regulative principles of religious life would flee from his presence in fear of the unparalleled prowess he displayed in ruling the universe. He greatly loved his wife Barhiṣmatī, and with the increase of days, their exchange of nuptial love also increased. By her feminine behavior as she dressed herself, walked, got up, smiled, laughed, and glanced about, Queen Barhiṣmatī increased his energy. Thus although he was a great soul, he

appeared lost in the feminine conduct of his wife. He behaved with her just like an ordinary man, but actually he was a great soul.

PURPORT

In this verse, the word *dharma-pratipakṣaḥ* ("opponents of religious principles") refers not to a particular faith, but to *varṇāśrama-dharma,* the division of society, socially and spiritually, into four *varṇas* (*brāhmaṇa, kṣatriya, vaiśya* and *śūdra*) and four *āśramas* (*brahmacarya, gṛhastha, vānaprastha* and *sannyāsa*). To maintain proper social order and help the citizens gradually progress toward the goal of life—namely spiritual understanding—the principles of *varṇāśrama-dharma* must be accepted. From this verse, Mahārāja Priyavrata appears to have been so strict in maintaining this institution of *varṇāśrama-dharma* that anyone neglecting it would immediately flee from his presence as soon as the King warned him by fighting or administering light punishment. Indeed, Mahārāja Priyavrata would not have to fight, for simply because of his strong determination, they dared not disobey the rules and regulations of *varṇāśrama-dharma.* It is said that unless human society is regulated by *varṇāśrama-dharma,* it is no better than a bestial society of cats and dogs. Mahārāja Priyavrata, therefore, strictly maintained *varṇāśrama-dharma* by his extraordinary, unparalleled prowess.

To maintain such a life of strict vigilance, one needs encouragement from his wife. In the *varṇāśrama-dharma* system, certain classes, such as the *brāhmaṇas* and *sannyāsīs,* do not need encouragement from the opposite sex. *Kṣatriyas* and *gṛhasthas,* however, actually need the encouragement of their wives in order to execute their duties. Indeed, a *gṛhastha* or *kṣatriya* cannot properly execute his responsibilities without the association of his wife. Śrī Caitanya Mahāprabhu personally admitted that a *gṛhastha* must live with a wife. *Kṣatriyas* were even allowed to have many wives to encourage them in discharging the duties of government. The association of a good wife is necessary in a life of *karma* and political affairs. To execute his duties properly, therefore, Mahārāja Priyavrata took advantage of his good wife Barhiṣmatī, who was always very expert in pleasing her great husband by properly dressing herself, smiling, and exhibiting her feminine bodily features. Queen Barhiṣmatī always kept Mahārāja Priyavrata very encouraged, and thus he executed his governmental duty very properly. In this verse *iva* has twice been used to indicate that Mahārāja Priyavrata acted exactly like a henpecked husband and thereby seemed to have lost his sense of human responsibility. Actually, however, he was fully conscious of his position as a spirit soul, although he seemingly behaved like an acquiescent *karmī* husband. Mahārāja Priyavrata thus ruled the universe for eleven *arbudas* of years. One *arbuda* consists of 100,000,000 years, and Mahārāja Priyavrata ruled the universe for eleven such *arbudas.*

TEXT 30

यावदवभासयति सुरगिरिमनुपरिक्रामन् भगवानादित्यो वसुधातलमर्धेनैव प्रतपत्यर्धेनावच्छादयति तदा हि भगवदुपासनोपचितातिपुरुषप्रभावस्तदनभिनन्दन् समजवेन रथेन ज्योतिर्मयेन रजनीमपि दिनं करिष्यामीति सप्तकृत्वस्तरणिमनुपर्यक्रामद् द्वितीय इव पतङ्गः ॥३०॥

yāvad avabhāsayati sura-girim anuparikrāman bhagavān ādityo vasudhā-talam ardhenaiva pratapaty ardhenāvacchādayati tadā hi bhagavad-upāsanopacitāti-puruṣa-prabhāvas tad anabhinandan samajavena rathena jyotirmayena rajanīm api dinaṁ kariṣyāmīti sapta-kṛt vastaraṇim anuparyakrāmad dvitīya iva pataṅgaḥ.

yāvat—so long; *avabhāsayati*—illuminates; *sura-girim*—the Sumeru Hill; *anuparikrāman*—by circumambulating; *bhagavān*—the most powerful; *ādityaḥ*——sun-god; *vasudhā-talam*—the lower planetary system; *ardhena*—by half; *eva*—certainly; *pratapati*—makes dazzling; *ardhena*—by half; *avacchādayati*—covers with darkness; *tadā*—at that time; *hi*—certainly; *bhagavat-upāsanā*—by worshiping the Supreme Personality of Godhead; *upacita*—by satisfying Him perfectly; *ati-puruṣa*—superhuman; *prabhāvaḥ*—influence; *tat*—that; *anabhinandan*—without appreciating; *samajavena*—by equally powerful; *rathena*—on a chariot; *jyotiḥ-mayena*—dazzling; *rajanīm*—night; *api*—also; *dinam*—day; *kariṣyāmi*—I shall make it; *iti*—thus; *sapta-kṛt*—seven times; *vastaraṇim*—exactly following the orbit of the sun; *anuparyakrāmat*—circumambulated; *dvitīyaḥ*—second; *iva*—like; *pataṅgaḥ*—sun.

TRANSLATION

While so excellently ruling the universe, King Priyavrata once became dissatisfied with the circumambulation of the most powerful sun-god. Encircling Sumeru Hill on his chariot, the sun-god illuminates all the surrounding planetary systems. However, when the sun is on the northern side of the hill, the south receives less light, and when the sun is in the south, the north receives less. King Priyavrata disliked this situation and

therefore decided to make daylight in the part of the universe where there was night. He followed the orbit of the sun-god on a brilliant chariot and thus fulfilled his desire. He could perform such wonderful activities because of the power he had achieved by worshiping the Supreme Personality of Godhead.

PURPORT

There is a Bengali saying which describes that someone is so powerful that he can make the night day and the day night. That saying is current because of the prowess of Priyavrata. His activities demonstrate how powerful he became by worshiping the Supreme Personality of Godhead. Lord Kṛṣṇa is known as Yogeśvara, the master of all mystic powers. In *Bhagavad-gītā* (18.78) it is said wherever there is the master of all mystic powers (*yatra yogeśvaraḥ kṛṣṇaḥ*), victory, fortune and all other opulences are present. Devotional service is so powerful. When a devotee achieves what he wants to accomplish, it is not by his own mystic power but by the grace of the master of mystic power, Lord Kṛṣṇa: by His grace, a devotee can accomplish wonderful things unimaginable even to the most powerful scientist.

From the description in this verse, it appears that the sun moves. According to modern astronomers, the sun is fixed in one place, surrounded by the solar system, but here we find that the sun is not stationary: it is rotating in a prescribed orbit. This fact is corroborated by *Brahma-saṁhitā* (5.52). *Yasyājñayā bhramati saṁbhṛta-kāla-cakraḥ:* the sun is rotating in its fixed orbit in accordance with the order of the Supreme Personality of Godhead. According to *Jyotir Veda,* the science of astronomy in the Vedic literature, the sun moves for six months on the northern side of the Sumeru Hill and for six months on the southern side. We have practical experience on this planet that when there is summer in the north there is winter in the south and vice versa. Modern materialistic scientists sometimes present themselves as knowing all the ingredients of the sun, yet they are unable to offer a second sun like Mahārāja Priyavrata's.

Although Mahārāja Priyavrata devised a very powerful chariot as brilliant as the sun, he had no desire to compete with the sun-god, for a Vaiṣṇava never wants to supersede another Vaiṣṇava. His purpose was to give abundant benefits in material existence. Śrīla Viśvanātha Cakravartī Ṭhākura remarks that in the months of April and May the rays of Mahārāja Priyavrata's brilliant sun were as pleasing as the rays of the moon, and in October and November, both morning and evening, that sun provided more warmth than the sunshine. In short, Mahārāja Priyavrata was extremely powerful, and his actions extended his power in all directions.

TEXT 31

ये वा उ ह तद्रथचरणनेमिकृतपरिखातास्ते सप्त सिन्धव आसन् यत एव कृताः सप्त भुवो द्वीपाः ॥३१॥

ye vā u ha tad-ratha-caraṇa-nemi-kṛta-parikhātās te sapta sindhava āsan yata eva kṛtāḥ sapta bhuvo dvīpāḥ.

ye—that; *vā u ha*—certainly; *tat-ratha*—of his chariot; *caraṇa*—of the wheels; *nemi*—by the rims; *kṛta*—made; *parikhātāḥ*—trenches; *te*—those; *sapta*—seven; *sindhavaḥ*—oceans; *āsan*—became; *yataḥ*—because of which; *eva*—certainly; *kṛtāḥ*—were made; *sapta*—seven; *bhuvaḥ*—of the Bhū-maṇḍala; *dvīpāḥ*—islands.

TRANSLATION

When Priyavrata drove his chariot behind the sun, the rims of his chariot wheels created impressions that later became seven oceans, dividing the planetary system known as Bhū-maṇḍala into seven islands.

PURPORT

Sometimes the planets in outer space are called islands. We have experience of various types of islands in the ocean, and similarly the various planets, divided into fourteen *lokas,* are islands in the ocean of space. As Priyavrata drove his chariot behind the sun, he created seven different types of oceans and planetary systems, which altogether are known as Bhū-maṇḍala, or Bhūloka. In the Gāyatrī *mantra,* we chant, oṁ *bhūr bhuvaḥ svaḥ tat savitur vareṇyam.* Above the Bhūloka planetary system is Bhuvarloka, and above that is Svargaloka, the heavenly planetary system. All these planetary systems are controlled by Savitā, the sun-god. By chanting the Gāyatrī *mantra* just after rising early in the morning, one worships the sun-god.

TEXT 32

जम्बूप्लक्षशाल्मलिकुशक्रौञ्चशाकपुष्करसंज्ञास्तेषां परिमाणं पूर्वस्मात्पूर्वस्मादुत्तर उत्तरो यथासंख्यं द्विगुणमानेन बहिः समन्तत उपक्लृप्ताः ॥३२॥

jambū-plakṣa-śālmali-kuśa-krauñca-śāka-puṣkara-saṁjñās teṣāṁ parimāṇaṁ pūrvasmāt pūrvasmād uttara uttaro yathā-saṅkhyaṁ dvi-guṇa-mānena bahiḥ samantata upakḷptāḥ.

jambū—Jambū; *plakṣa*—Plakṣa; *śālmali*—Śālmali; *kuśa*—Kuśa; *krauñca*—Krauñca; *śāka*—Śāka; *puṣkara*—Puṣkara; *saṁjñāḥ*—known as; *teṣām*—of them; *parimāṇam*—dimensions ; *pūrvasmāt pūrvasmāt*—from the former; *uttaraḥ uttaraḥ*—the following; *yathā*—according to; *saṅkhyam*—number; *dvi-guṇa*—twice as much; *mānena*—with a measure; *bahiḥ*—outside; *samantataḥ*—all around; *upakḷptāḥ*—produced.

TRANSLATION

The names of the islands are Jambū, Plakṣa, Śālmali, Kuśa, Krauñca, Śāka and Puṣkara. Each island is twice as large as the one preceding it, and each is surrounded by a liquid substance, beyond which is the next island.

PURPORT

The ocean in each planetary system has a different type of liquid. How they are situated is explained in the next verse.

TEXT 33

क्षारोदेक्षुरसोदसुरोदघृतोदक्षीरोददधिमण्डोदशुद्धोदाः सप्त जलधयः सप्त द्वीपपरिखा इवाभ्यन्तरद्वीपसमाना एकैकश्येन यथानुपूर्वं सप्तस्वपि बहिर्द्वीपेषु पृथक्परित उपकल्पितास्तेषु जम्ब्वादिषु बर्हिष्मतीपतिरनुव्रतानात्मजाना - ग्नीध्रेध्मजिह्वयज्ञबाहुहिरण्यरेतोघृतपृष्ठमेधातिथिवीतिहोत्रसंज्ञान् यथासंख्ये-नैकैकस्मिन्नेकमेवाधिपतिं विदधे ॥ ३३ ॥

kṣārodekṣu-rasoda-suroda-ghṛtoda-kṣīroda-dadhi-maṇḍoda-śuddhodāḥ sapta jaladhayaḥ sapta dvīpa-parikhā ivābhyantara-dvīpa-samānā ekaikaśyena yathānupūrvaṁ saptasv api bahir dvīpeṣu pṛthak parita upakalpitās teṣu jambv-ādiṣu barhiṣmatī-patir anuvratānātmajān āgnīdhredhmajihva-yajñabāhu-hiraṇyareto-ghṛtapṛṣṭha-medhātithi-vītihotra-saṁjñān yathā-saṅkhyenaikaikasminn ekam evādhi-patiṁ vidadhe.

kṣāra—salt; *uda*—water; *ikṣu-rasa*—the liquid extract from sugarcane; *uda*—water; *surā*—liquor; *uda*—water; *ghṛta*—clarified butter; *uda*—water; *kṣīra*—milk; *uda*—water; *dadhi-maṇḍa*—emulsified yogurt; *uda*—water;

śuddha-udāḥ—and drinking water; *sapta*—seven; *jala-dhayaḥ*—oceans; *sapta*—seven; *dvīpa*—islands; *parikhāḥ*—trenches; *iva*—like; *abhyantara*—internal; *dvīpa*—islands; *samānāḥ*—equal to; *eka-ekaśyena*—one after another; *yathā-anupūrvam*—in chronological order; *saptasu*—seven; *api*—although; *bahiḥ*—outside; *dvīpeṣu*—in islands; *pṛthak*—separate; *paritaḥ*—all around; *upakalpitāḥ*—situated; *teṣu*—within them; *jambū-ādiṣu*—beginning with Jambū; *barhiṣmatī*—of Barhiṣmatī; *patiḥ*—the husband; *anuvratān*—who were actually followers of the father's principles; *ātma-jān*—sons; *āgnīdhra-idhmajihva-yajñabāhu-hiraṇyaretaḥ-ghṛtapṛṣṭha-medhātithi-vītihotra-saṁjñān*—named Āgnīḍhra, Idhmajihva, Yajñabāhu, Hiraṇyaretā, Ghṛtapṛṣṭha, Medhātithi and Vītihotra; *yathā-saṅkhyena*—by the same number; *eka-ekasmin*—in each island; *ekam*—one; *eva*—certainly; *adhi-patim*—king; *vidadhe*—he made.

TRANSLATION

The seven oceans respectively contain salt water, sugarcane juice, liquor, clarified butter, milk, emulsified yogurt, and sweet drinking water. All the islands are completely surrounded by these oceans, and each ocean is equal in breadth to the island it surrounds. Mahārāja Priyavrata, the husband of Queen Barhiṣmatī, gave sovereignty over these islands to his respective sons, namely Āgnīdhra, Idhmajihva, Yajñabāhu, Hiraṇyaretā, Ghṛtapṛṣṭha, Medhātithi and Vītihotra. Thus they all became kings by the order of their father.

PURPORT

It is to be understood that all the *dvīpas,* or islands, are surrounded by different types of oceans, and it is said herein that the breadth of each ocean is the same as that of the island it surrounds. The length of the oceans, however, cannot equal the length of the islands. According to Vīrarāghava Ācārya, the breadth of the first island is 100,000 *yojanas.* One *yojana* equals eight miles, and therefore the breadth of the first island is calculated to be 800,000 miles. The water surrounding it must have the same breadth, but its length must be different.

TEXT 34

दुहितरं चोर्जस्वतीं नामोशनसे प्रायच्छद्यस्या मासीद् देवयानी नाम काव्यसुता ॥३४॥

duhitaraṁ corjasvatīṁ nāmośanase prāyacchad yasyām āsīd devayānī nāma kāvya-sutā.

duhitaram—the daughter; *ca*—also; *ūrjasvatīm*—Ūrjasvatī; *nāma*—named; *uśanase*—unto the great sage Uśanā (Śukrācārya); *prāyacchat*—he gave; *yasyām*—unto whom; *āsīt*—there was; *devayānī*—Devayānī; *nāma*—named; *kāvya-sutā*—the daughter of Śukrācārya.

TRANSLATION

King Priyavrata then gave his daughter, Ūrjasvatī, in marriage to Śukrācārya, who begot in her a daughter named Devayānī.

TEXT 35

नैवंविधः पुरुषकार उरुक्रमस्य
पुंसां तदङ्घ्रिरजसा जितषड्गुणानाम् ।
चित्रं विदूरविगतः सकृदाददीत
यन्नामधेयमधुना स जहाति बन्धम् ॥३५॥

naivaṁ-vidhaḥ puruṣa-kāra urukramasya
puṁsāṁ tad-aṅghri-rajasā jita-ṣaḍ-guṇānām
citraṁ vidūra-vigataḥ sakṛd ādadīta
yan-nāmadheyam adhunā sa jahāti bandham

na—not; *evam-vidhaḥ*—like that; *puruṣa-kāraḥ*—personal influence; *uru-kramasya*—of the Supreme Personality of Godhead; *puṁsām*—of the devotees; *tat-aṅghri*—of His lotus feet; *rajasā*—by the dust; *jita-ṣaṭ-guṇānām*—who have conquered the influence of the six kinds of material whips; *citram*—wonderful; *vidūra-vigataḥ*—the fifth-grade person, or the untouchable; *sakṛt*—only once; *ādadīta*—if he utters; *yat*—whose; *nāmadheyam*—holy name; *adhunā*—immediately; *saḥ*—he; *jahāti*—gives up; *bandham*—material bondage.

TRANSLATION

My dear King, a devotee who has taken shelter of the dust from the lotus feet of the Lord can transcend the influence of the six material whips—namely hunger, thirst, lamentation, illusion, old age and death—and he can conquer the mind and five senses. However, this is not very wonderful for a pure devotee of the Lord because even a person beyond

the jurisdiction of the four castes—in other words, an untouchable—is immediately relieved of bondage to material existence if he utters the holy name of the Lord even once.

PURPORT

Śukadeva Gosvāmī was speaking to Mahārāja Parīkṣit about the activities of King Priyavrata, and since the King might have had doubts about these wonderful, uncommon activities, Śukadeva Gosvāmī reassured him. "My dear King," he said, "don't be doubtful about the wonderful activities of Priyavrata. For a devotee of the Supreme Personality of Godhead, everything is possible because the Lord is also known as Urukrama." Urukrama is a name for Lord Vāmanadeva, who performed the wonderful act of occupying the three worlds with three footsteps. Lord Vāmanadeva requested three paces of land from Mahārāja Bali, and when Mahārāja Bali agreed to grant them, the Lord immediately covered the entire world with two footsteps, and for His third step He placed His foot upon Bali Mahārāja's head. Śrī Jayadeva Gosvāmī says:

chalayasi vikramaṇe balim adbhuta-vāmana
pada-nakha-nīra-janita-jana-pāvana
keśava dhṛta-vamāna-rūpa jaya jagadīśa hare

"All glories to Lord Keśava, who assumed the form of a dwarf. O Lord of the universe, who takes away everything inauspicious for the devotees! O wonderful Vāmanadeva! You tricked the great demon Bali Mahārāja by Your steps. The water that touched the nails of Your lotus feet when You pierced through the covering of the universe purifies all living entities in the form of the River Ganges."

Since the Supreme Lord is all-powerful, He can do things that seem wonderful for a common man. Similarly, a devotee who has taken shelter at the lotus feet of the Lord can also do wonderful things, unimaginable to a common man, by the grace of the dust of those lotus feet. Caitanya Mahāprabhu therefore teaches us to take shelter of the Lord's lotus feet:

ayi nanda-tanuja kiṅkaraṁ
patitaṁ māṁ viṣame bhavāmbudhau
kṛpayā tava pāda-paṅkaja-
sthita-dhūlī-sadṛśaṁ vicintaya

"O son of Nanda Mahārāja, I am Your eternal servant, yet somehow or other I have fallen into the ocean of birth and death. Please pick me up from this ocean of death and place me as one of the atoms of Your lotus feet." Lord Caitanya teaches us to come in touch with the dust of the Lord's lotus feet, for then there will undoubtedly be all success.

Because of the material body, every living entity in material existence is always disturbed by *ṣaḍ-guṇa,* six whips—hunger, thirst, lamentation, illusion, invalidity and death. Furthermore, another *ṣaḍ-guṇa* are the mind and five sense organs. Not to speak of a sanctified devotee, even a *caṇḍāla,* an outcaste, who is untouchable, is immediately freed from material bondage if he utters the holy name of the Lord even once. Sometimes caste *brāhmaṇas* argue that unless one changes his body he cannot be accepted as a *brāhmaṇa,* for since the present body is obtained as a result of past actions, one who has in the past acted as a *brāhmaṇa* takes birth in a *brāhmaṇa* family. Therefore, they contend, without such a brahminical body, one cannot be accepted as a *brāhmaṇa.* Herein it is said, however, that even *vidūra-vigata,* a *caṇḍāla*—a fifth-class untouchable—is freed if he utters the holy name even once. Being freed means that he immediately changes his body. Sanātana Gosvāmī confirms this:

yathā kāñcanatāṁ yāti
kāṁsyaṁ rasa-vidhānataḥ
tathā dīkṣā-vidhānena
dvijatvaṁ jāyate nṛṇām

When a person, even though a *caṇḍāla,* is initiated by a pure devotee into chanting the holy name of the Lord, his body changes as he follows the instructions of the spiritual master. Although one cannot see how his body has changed, we must accept, on the grounds of the authoritative statements of the *śāstras,* that he changes his body. This is to be understood without arguments. This verse clearly says, *sa jahāti bandham:* "He gives up his material bondage." The body is a symbolic representation of material bondage according to one's *karma.* Although sometimes we cannot see the gross body changing, chanting the holy name of the Supreme Lord immediately changes the subtle body, and because the subtle body changes, the living entity is immediately freed from material bondage. After all, changes of the gross body are conducted by the subtle body. After the destruction of the gross body, the subtle body takes the living entity from his present gross body to another. In the subtle body, the mind is predominant, and therefore if one's mind is always absorbed in remembering the activities or the lotus feet of the Lord, he is to be understood to have already changed his present body and become purified.

Therefore it is irrefutable that a *caṇḍāla,* or any fallen or lowborn person, can become a *brāhmaṇa* simply by the method of bona fide initiation.

TEXT 36

स एवमपरिमितबलपराक्रम एकदा तु देवर्षिचरणानुशयनानुपतितगुण -
विसर्गसंसर्गेणानिर्वृतमिवात्मानं मन्यमान आत्मनिर्वेद इदमाह ॥३६॥

sa evam aparimita-bala-parākrama ekadā tu devarṣi-
caraṇānuśayanānu-patita-guṇa-visarga-saṁsargeṇānirvṛtam
ivātmānaṁ manyamāna ātma-nirveda idam āha.

saḥ—he (Mahārāja Priyavrata); *evam*—thus; *aparimita*—unparalleled; *bala*—strength; *parākramaḥ*—whose influence; *ekadā*—once upon a time; *tu*—then; *deva-ṛṣi*—of the great saint Nārada; *caraṇa-anuśayana*—surrendering unto the lotus feet; *anu*—thereafter; *patita*—fallen down; *guṇa-visarga*—with material affairs (created by the three material modes of nature); *saṁsargeṇa*—by connection; *anirvṛtam*—not satisfied; *iva*—like; *ātmānam*—himself; *manyamānaḥ*—thinking like that; *ātma*—self; *nirvedaḥ* —possessing renunciation; *idam*—this; *āha*—said.

TRANSLATION

While enjoying his material opulences with full strength and influence, Mahārāja Priyavrata once began to consider that although he had fully surrendered to the great saint Nārada and was actually on the path of Kṛṣṇa consciousness, he had somehow become again entangled in material activities. Thus his mind now became restless, and he began to speak in a spirit of renunciation.

PURPORT

In *Śrīmad-Bhāgavatam* (1.5.17) it is said:

tyaktvā sva-dharmaṁ caraṇāmbujaṁ harer
bhajann apakvo'tha patet tato yadi
yatra kva vābhadram abhūd amuṣya kiṁ
ko vārtha āpto'bhajatāṁ sva-dharmataḥ

"One who has forsaken his material occupations to engage in the devotional service of the Lord may sometimes fall down while in an immature stage, yet there is no danger of his being unsuccessful. On the other hand, a nondevotee, though fully engaged in occupational duties, does not gain anything." If one somehow or other comes to the shelter of a great Vaiṣṇava, takes to Kṛṣṇa consciousness because of sentiment or realization, but in course of time falls down because of immature understanding, he is not actually fallen, for his having engaged in Kṛṣṇa consciousness is a permanent asset. If one falls down, therefore, his progress might be checked for a certain time, but it will again become manifest at an opportune moment. Although Priyavrata Mahārāja was serving according to the instructions of Nārada Muni meant for going back home, back to Godhead, he returned to material affairs at the request of his father. In due course of time, however, his consciousness for serving Kṛṣṇa reawakened by the grace of his spiritual master, Nārada.

As stated in *Bhagavad-gītā* (6.41), *śucīnāṁ śrīmatāṁ gehe yoga-bhraṣṭo'bhijāyate.* One who falls down from the process of *bhakti-yoga* is again offered the opulence of the demigods, and after enjoying such material opulence, he is given a chance to take birth in a noble family of a pure *brāhmaṇa,* or in a rich family, to be given the chance to revive his Kṛṣṇa consciousness. This actually happened in the life of Priyavrata: he is a most glorious example of this truth. In due course of time, he no longer wanted to enjoy his material opulences and his wife, kingdom and sons; instead, he wanted to renounce them all. Therefore, after having described the material opulences of Mahārāja Priyavrata, Śukadeva Gosvāmī, in this verse, describes his tendency for renunciation.

The words *devarṣi-caraṇānuśayana* indicate that Mahārāja Priyavrata, having fully surrendered to the great sage Devarṣi Nārada, was strictly following all the devotional processes and regulative principles under his direction. In regard to strictly following the regulative principles, Śrīla Viśvanātha Cakravartī Ṭhākura says; *daṇḍavat-praṇāmās tān anupatitaḥ.* By immediately offering obeisances (*daṇḍavat*) unto the spiritual master and by strictly following his directions, the student becomes advanced. Mahārāja Priyavrata was doing all these things regularly.

As long as one is in the material world, he has to be under the influence of the modes of material nature (*guṇa-visarga*). It is not that Mahārāja Priyavrata was freed from material influence because he possessed all material opulences. In this material world, both the very poor man and the very rich man are under material influences, for both wealth and poverty are creations of the modes of material nature. As stated in *Bhagavad-gītā* (3.27), *prakṛteḥ kriyamāṇāni guṇaiḥ karmāṇi sarvaśaḥ.* According to the modes of material nature we acquire, the material nature gives us facility for material enjoyment.

TEXT 37

अहो असाध्वनुष्ठितं यदभिनिवेशितोऽहमिन्द्रियैरविद्यारचितविषमविषयान्धकूपे तदलममलममुष्या वनिताया विनोदमृगं मां धिग्धिगिति गर्हयाञ्चकार ॥३७॥

aho asādhv anuṣṭhitaṁ yad abhiniveśito'ham indriyair avidyā-racita-
viṣama-viṣayāndha-kūpe tad alam alam amuṣyā vanitāyā vinoda-
mṛgaṁ māṁ dhig dhig iti garhayāṁ cakāra.

aho—alas; *asādhu*—not good; *anuṣṭhitam*—executed; *yat*—because; *abhiniveśitaḥ*—being completely absorbed; *aham*—I; *indriyaiḥ*—for sense gratification; *avidyā*—by nescience; *racita*—made; *viṣama*—causing distress; *viṣaya*—sense gratification; *andha-kūpe*—in the dark well; *tat*—that; *alam*—insignificant; *alam*—of no importance; *amuṣyāḥ*—of that; *vanitāyāḥ*—wife; *vinoda-mṛgam*—just like a dancing monkey; *mām*—unto me; *dhik*—all condemnation; *dhik*—all condemnation; *iti*—thus; *garhayām*—criticism; *cakāra*—he did.

TRANSLATION

The King thus began criticizing himself: Alas, how condemned I have become because of my sense gratification! I have now fallen into material enjoyment, which is exactly like a covered well. I have had enough! I am not going to enjoy any more. Just see how I have become like a dancing monkey in the hands of my wife. Because of this, I am condemned.

PURPORT

How condemned is the advancement of material knowledge can be understood from the behavior of Mahārāja Priyavrata. He performed such wonderful acts as creating another sun, which shined during the night, and creating a chariot so great that its wheels formed vast oceans. These activities are so great that modern scientists cannot even imagine how such things can be done. Mahārāja Priyavrata acted very wonderfully in the material field of activities, but because he was dealing in sense gratification—ruling his kingdom and dancing to the indications of his beautiful wife—he personally condemned himself. When we think about this example of Mahārāja Priyavrata, we can just consider how degraded is the modern civilization of materialistic advancement. Modern so-called scientists and other materialists are very satisfied because they can construct great bridges, roads and machines, but such activities are nothing comparable to those of Mahārāja

Priyavrata. If Mahārāja Priyavrata could condemn himself in spite of his wonderful activities, how condemned we are in our so-called advancement of material civilization. We can conclude that such advancement has nothing to do with the problems of the living entity entangled within this material world. Unfortunately, modern man does not understand his entanglement and how condemned he is, nor does he know what kind of body he is going to have in the next life. From a spiritual point of view, a great kingdom, beautiful wife and wonderful material activities are all impediments to spiritual advancement. Mahārāja Priyavrata had served the great sage Nārada sincerely. Therefore even though he had accepted material opulences, he could not be deviated from his own task. He again became Kṛṣṇa conscious. As confirmed in *Bhagavad-gītā:*

nehābhikrama-nāśo'sti
pratyavāyo na vidyate
svalpam apy asya dharmasya
trāyate mahato bhayāt

"In devotional service there is no loss or diminution, and even a small service rendered in devotional life is sufficient to save one from the greatest danger." (Bg. 2.40) Such renunciation as Mahārāja Priyavrata's is possible only by the grace of the Supreme Personality of Godhead. Generally when people are powerful or when they have a beautiful wife, a beautiful home and material popularity, they become more and more entangled. Priyavrata Mahārāja, however, having been completely trained by the great sage Nārada, revived his Kṛṣṇa consciousness in spite of all impediments.

TEXT 38

परदेवताप्रसादाधिगतात्मप्रत्यवमर्शेनानुप्रवृत्तेभ्यः पुत्रेभ्य इमां यथादायं विभज्य भुक्तभोगां च महिषीं मृतकमिव सहमहाविभूतिमपहाय स्वयं निहितनिर्वेदो हृदि गृहीतहरिविहारानुभावो भगवतो नारदस्य पदवीं पुनरेवानुससार ॥३८॥

para-devatā-prasādādhigatātma-pratyavamarśenānupravṛttebhyaḥ putrebhya imāṁ yathā-dāyaṁ vibhajya bhukta-bhogāṁ ca mahiṣīṁ mṛtakam iva saha mahā-vibhūtim apahāya svayaṁ nihita-nirvedo hṛdi gṛhīta-hari-vihārānubhāvo bhagavato nāradasya padavīṁ punar evānusasāra.

para-devatā—of the Supreme Personality of Godhead; *prasāda*—by the mercy; *adhigata*—obtained; *ātma-pratyavamarśena*—by self-realization; *anupravṛttebhyaḥ*—who exactly follow his path; *putrebhyaḥ*—unto his sons; *imām*—this earth; *yathā-dāyam*—exactly according to the inheritance; *vibhajya*—dividing; *bhukta-bhogām*—whom he enjoyed in so many ways; *ca*—also; *mahiṣīm*—the Queen; *mṛtakam iva*—exactly like a dead body; *saha*—with; *mahā-vibhūtim*—great opulence; *apahāya*—giving up; *svayam*—himself; *nihita*—perfectly taken to; *nirvedaḥ*—renunciation; *hṛdi*—in the heart; *gṛhīta*—accepted; *hari*—of the Supreme Personality of Godhead; *vihāra*—pastimes; *anubhāvaḥ*—in such an attitude; *bhagavataḥ*—of the great saintly person; *nāradasya*—of Saint Nārada; *padavīm*—position; *punaḥ*—again; *eva*—certainly; *anusasāra*—began to follow.

TRANSLATION

By the grace of the Supreme Personality of Godhead, Mahārāja Priyavrata reawakened to his senses. He divided all his earthly possessions among his obedient sons. He gave up everything, including his wife, with whom he had enjoyed so much sense gratification, and his great and opulent kingdom, and he completely renounced all attachment. His heart, having been cleansed, became a place of pastimes for the Supreme Personality of Godhead. Thus he was able to return to the path of Kṛṣṇa consciousness, spiritual life, and resume the position he had attained by the grace of the great saint Nārada.

PURPORT

As enunciated by Śrī Caitanya Mahāprabhu in His *Śikṣāṣṭaka, ceto-darpaṇa-mārjanaṁ bhava-mahā-dāvāgni-nirvāpaṇam:* as soon as one's heart is cleansed, the blazing fire of material existence is immediately extinguished. Our hearts are meant for the pastimes of the Supreme Personality of Godhead. This means that one should be fully Kṛṣṇa conscious, thinking of Kṛṣṇa, as He Himself advises (*man-manā bhava mad-bhakto mad-yājī māṁ namaskuru*). This should be our only business. One whose heart is not clean cannot think of the transcendental pastimes of the Supreme Lord, but if one can once again place the Supreme Personality of Godhead in his heart, he very easily becomes qualified to renounce material attachment. Māyāvādī philosophers, *yogīs* and *jñānīs* try to give up this material world simply by saying, *brahma satyaṁ jagan mithyā:* "This world is false. There is no use of it. Let us take to Brahman." Such theoretical knowledge will not help us. If we believe that Brahman is the real truth, we have to place within our hearts the lotus feet of Śrī Kṛṣṇa, as Mahārāja Ambarīṣa did (*sa vai manaḥ kṛṣṇa-padāravindayoḥ*). One has to fix the lotus feet of the Lord within his heart. Then he gets the strength to be freed from material entanglement.

Mahārāja Priyavrata was able to give up his opulent kingdom, and he also gave up the association of his beautiful wife as if she were a dead body. However beautiful one's wife and however attractive her bodily features, one is no longer interested in her when her body is dead. We praise a beautiful woman for her body, but that same body, when bereft of a spirit soul, is no longer interesting to any lusty man. Mahārāja Priyavrata was so strong, by the grace of the Lord, that even though his beautiful wife was alive, he could give up her association exactly like one who is forced to give up the association of a dead wife. Śrī Caitanya Mahāprabhu said:

na dhanaṁ na janaṁ na sundarīṁ
kavitāṁ vā jagadīśa kāmaye
mama janmani janmanīśvare
bhavatād bhaktir ahaitukī tvayi

"O almighty Lord, I have no desire to accumulate wealth, nor do I desire beautiful women, nor do I want any number of followers. I only want Your causeless devotional service birth after birth." For one who desires to advance in spiritual life, attachment to material opulence and attachment to a beautiful wife are two great impediments. Such attachments are condemned even more than suicide. Therefore anyone desiring to cross beyond material nescience must, by the grace of Kṛṣṇa, be freed from attachment to women and money. When Mahārāja Priyavrata became completely free from these attachments, he could again peacefully follow the principles instructed by the great sage Nārada.

TEXT 39

तस्य ह वा एते श्लोकाः —
प्रियव्रतकृतं कर्म को नु कुर्याद्विनेश्वरम् ।
यो नेमिनिम्नैरकरोच्छायां घ्नन् सप्त वारिधीन् ॥३९॥

tasya ha vā ete ślokāḥ —
priyavrata-kṛtaṁ karma
ko nu kuryād vineśvaram
yo nemi-nimnair akaroc
chāyāṁ ghnan sapta vāridhīn

tasya—his; *ha vā*—certainly; *ete*—all these; *ślokāḥ*—verses; *priyavrata*—by King Priyavrata; *kṛtam*—done; *karma*—activities; *kaḥ*—who; *nu*—then; *kuryāt*—can execute; *vinā*—without; *īśvaram*—the Supreme Personality of Godhead; *yaḥ*—one who; *nemi*—of the rim of the wheels of his chariot; *nimnaiḥ*—by the depressions; *akarot*—made; *chāyām*—darkness; *ghnan*—dissipating; *sapta*—seven; *vāridhīn*—oceans.

TRANSLATION

There are many famous verses regarding Mahārāja Priyavrata's activities:

"No one but the Supreme Personality of Godhead could do what Mahārāja Priyavrata has done. Mahārāja Priyavrata dissipated the darkness of night, and with the rims of his great chariot, he excavated seven oceans."

PURPORT

There are many excellent verses, famous all over the world, concerning the activities of Mahārāja Priyavrata. He is so celebrated that his activities are compared to those of the Supreme Personality of Godhead. Sometimes a sincere servant and devotee of the Lord is also called *bhagavān.* Śrī Nārada is called *bhagavān,* and Lord Śiva and Vyāsadeva are also sometimes called *bhagavān.* This designation, *bhagavān,* is sometimes conferred upon a pure devotee by the grace of the Lord so that he will be very highly esteemed. Mahārāja Priyavrata was such a devotee.

TEXT 40

भूसंस्थानं कृतं येन सरिद्गिरिवनादिभिः ।
सीमा च भूतनिर्वृत्यै द्वीपे द्वीपे विभागशः ॥४०॥

bhū-saṁsthānaṁ kṛtaṁ yena
sarid-giri-vanādibhiḥ
sīmā ca bhūta-nirvṛtyai
dvīpe dvīpe vibhāgaśaḥ

bhū-saṁsthānam—the situation of the earth; *kṛtam*—done; *yena*—by whom; *sarit*—by rivers; *giri*—by hills and mountains; *vana-ādibhiḥ*—by forests and so on; *sīmā*—boundaries; *ca*—also; *bhūta*—of different nations; *nirvṛtyai*—to stop fighting; *dvīpe dvīpe*—on the various islands; *vibhāgaśaḥ*—separately.

TRANSLATION

"To stop the quarreling among different peoples, Mahārāja Priyavrata marked boundaries at rivers and at the edges of mountains and forests so that no one would trespass upon another's property."

PURPORT

The example set by Mahārāja Priyavrata in marking off different states is still followed. As indicated here, different classes of men are destined to live in different areas, and therefore the boundaries of various tracts of land, which are described here as islands, should be defined by different rivers, forests and hills. This is also mentioned in relation to Mahārāja Pṛthu, who was born from the dead body of his father by the manipulation of great sages. Mahārāja Pṛthu's father was very sinful, and therefore a black man called Niṣāda was first born from his dead body. The Naiṣāda race was given a place in the forest because by nature they are thieves and rogues. As animals are given places in various forests and hills, men who are like animals are also destined to live there. One cannot be promoted to civilized life unless one comes to Kṛṣṇa consciousness, for by nature one is destined to live in a particular situation according to one's *karma* and association with the modes of nature. If men want to live in harmony and peace, they must take to Kṛṣṇa consciousness, for they cannot achieve the highest standard while absorbed in the bodily concept of life. Mahārāja Priyavrata divided the surface of the globe into different islands so that each class of men would live peacefully and not clash with the others. The modern idea of nationhood has gradually developed from the divisions made by Mahārāja Priyavrata.

TEXT 41

भौमं दिव्यं मानुषं च महित्वं कर्मयोगजम् ।
यश्चक्रे निरयौपम्यं पुरुषानुजनप्रियः ॥४१॥

bhaumaṁ divyaṁ mānuṣaṁ ca
mahitvaṁ karma-yogajam
yaś cakre nirayaupamyaṁ
puruṣānujana-priyaḥ

bhaumam—of the lower planets; *divyam*—heavenly; *mānuṣam*—of human beings; *ca*—also; *mahitvam*—all opulences; *karma*—by fruitive activities; *yoga*—by mystic power; *jam*—born; *yaḥ*—one who; *cakre*—did;

niraya—with hell; *aupamyam*—comparison or equality; *puruṣa*—of the Supreme Personality of Godhead; *anujana*—to the devotee; *priyaḥ*—most dear.

TRANSLATION

"As a great follower and devotee of the sage Nārada, Mahārāja Priyavrata considered hellish the opulences he had achieved by dint of fruitive activities and mystic power, whether in the lower or heavenly planetary systems or in human society."

PURPORT

Śrīla Rūpa Gosvāmī has said that the position of a devotee is so superexcellent that a devotee does not consider any material opulence worth having. There are different types of opulences on earth, in the heavenly planets and even in the lower planetary system, known as Pātāla. A devotee, however, knows that they are all material, and consequently he is not at all interested in them. As stated in *Bhagavad-gītā, paraṁ dṛṣṭvā nivartate.* Sometimes *yogīs* and *jñānīs* voluntarily give up all material opulences to practice their system of liberation and taste spiritual bliss. However, they frequently fall down because artificial renunciation of material opulences cannot endure. One must have a superior taste in spiritual life; then he can give up material opulence. Mahārāja Priyavrata had already tasted spiritual bliss, and therefore he had no interest in any of the material achievements available in the lower, higher or middle planetary systems.

Thus end the Bhaktivedanta purports to the Fifth Canto, First Chapter, of Śrīmad-Bhāgavatam, *entitled "The Activities of Mahārāja Priyavrata."*

CHAPTER TWO

The Activities of Mahārāja Āgnīdhra

In this chapter, the character of Mahārāja Āgnīdhra is described. When Mahārāja Priyavrata went off for spiritual realization, his son Āgnīdhra became the ruler of Jambūdvīpa, in accordance with Mahārāja Priyavrata's instructions, and maintained its residents with the same affection a father feels for his sons. Once Mahārāja Āgnīdhra desired to have a son, and therefore he entered a cave of Mandara Mountain to practice austerity. Understanding his desire, Lord Brahmā sent a celestial girl named Pūrvacitti to Āgnīdhra's hermitage. After dressing herself very attractively, she presented herself before him with various feminine movements, and Āgnīdhra was naturally attracted to her. The girl's actions, expressions, smile, sweet words and moving eyes were fascinating to him. Āgnīdhra was expert in flattery. Thus he attracted the celestial girl, who was pleased to accept him as her husband because of his mellifluous words. She enjoyed royal happiness with Āgnīdhra for many years before returning to her abode in the heavenly planets. In her womb Āgnīdhra begot nine sons—Nābhi, Kiṁpuruṣa, Harivarṣa, Ilāvṛta, Ramyaka, Hiraṇmaya, Kuru, Bhadrāśva and Ketumāla. He gave them nine islands with names corresponding to theirs. Āgnīdhra, however, his senses unsatisfied, was always thinking of his celestial wife, and therefore in his next life he was born in her celestial planet. After the death of Āgnīdhra, his nine sons married nine daughters of Meru named Merudevī, Pratirūpā, Ugradaṁṣṭrī, Latā, Ramyā, Śyāmā, Nārī, Bhadrā and Devavīti.

TEXT 1

श्रीशुक उवाच

एवं पितरि सम्प्रवृत्ते तदनुशासने वर्तमान आग्नीध्रो जम्बूद्वीपौकसः प्रजा औरसवद्धर्मावेक्षमाणः पर्यगोपायत् ॥१॥

śrī-śuka uvāca

evaṁ pitari sampravṛtte tad-anuśāsane vartamāna āgnīdhro jambūdvīpaukasaḥ prajā aurasavad dharmāvekṣamāṇaḥ paryagopāyat.

śrī-śukaḥ—Śrī Śukadeva Gosvāmī; *uvāca*—said; *evam*—thus; *pitari*—when his father; *sampravṛtte*—took to the path of liberation; *tat-anuśāsane*

—according to his order; *vartamānaḥ*—situated; *āgnīdhraḥ*—King Āgnīdhra; *jambū-dvīpa-okasaḥ*—the inhabitants of Jambūdvīpa; *prajāḥ*—citizens; *aurasa-vat*—as if they were his sons; *dharma*—religious principles; *avekṣamāṇaḥ*—strictly observing; *paryagopāyat*—completely protected.

TRANSLATION

Śrī Śukadeva Gosvāmī continued: After his father, Mahārāja Priyavrata, departed to follow the path of spiritual life by undergoing austerities, King Āgnīdhra completely obeyed his order. Strictly observing the principles of religion, he gave full protection to the inhabitants of Jambūdvīpa as if they were his own begotten sons.

PURPORT

Following the instruction of his father, Mahārāja Priyavrata, Mahārāja Āgnīdhra ruled the inhabitants of Jambūdvīpa according to religious principles. These principles are exactly contrary to the modern principles of faithlessness. As clearly stated here, the King protected the citizens the way a father protects his begotten children. How he ruled the citizens is also described here—*dharmāvekṣamāṇaḥ,* strictly according to religious principles. It is the duty of the executive head of a state to see that the citizens strictly follow religious principles. The Vedic religious principles begin with *varṇāśrama-dharma,* the duties of the four *varṇas* and four *āśramas. Dharma* refers to principles given by the Supreme Personality of Godhead. The first principle of *dharma,* or religion, is to observe the duties of the four orders as enjoined by the Supreme Personality of Godhead. According to people's qualities and activities, society should be divided into *brāhmaṇas, kṣatriyas, vaiśyas* and *śūdras* and then again into *brahmacārīs, gṛhasthas, vānaprasthas* and *sannyāsīs.* These are religious principles, and it is the duty of the head of state to see that his citizens strictly follow them. He should not merely act officially; he should be like a father who is always a well-wisher of his sons. Such a father strictly observes whether his sons are performing their duties, and sometimes he also punishes them.

Just contrary to the principles mentioned here, the presidents and chief executives in the age of Kali are simply tax collectors who do not care whether religious principles are observed. Indeed, the chief executives of the present day introduce all kinds of sinful activity, especially illicit sex, intoxication, animal killing and gambling. These sinful activities are now very prominently manifested in India. Although a hundred years ago these four principles of sinful life were strictly prohibited in the families of India, they have now been introduced into every Indian family; therefore they cannot follow religious principles. In contrast to the principles of the kings of old, the modern state is concerned only with propaganda for levying taxes and is no longer responsible for the spiritual welfare of the citizens. The state is now callous to religious principles. *Śrīmad-Bhāgavatam* predicts that in Kali-yuga the government will be entrusted with *dasyu-dharma,* which means the occupational duty of rogues and thieves. Modern heads of state are rogues and thieves who plunder the citizens instead of giving them protection. Rogues and thieves plunder without regard for law, but in this age of Kali, as stated in *Śrīmad-Bhāgavatam,* the lawmakers themselves plunder the citizens. The next prediction to be fulfilled, which is already coming to pass, is that because of the sinful activities of the citizens and the government, rain will become increasingly scarce. Gradually there will be complete drought and no production of food grains. People will be reduced to eating flesh and seeds, and many good, spiritually inclined people will have to forsake their homes because they will be too harassed by drought, taxation and famine. The Kṛṣṇa consciousness movement is the only hope to save the world from such devastation. It is the most scientific and authorized movement for the actual welfare of the whole human society.

TEXT 2

स च कदाचित्पितृलोककामः सुरवरवनिताक्रीडाचलद्रोण्यां भगवन्तं विश्वसृजां पतिमाभृतपरिचर्योपकरण आत्मैकाग्र्येण तपस्व्याराधयाम्बभूव ॥२॥

sa ca kadācit pitṛloka-kāmaḥ sura-vara-vanitākrīḍācala-droṇyāṁ
bhagavantaṁ viśva-sṛjāṁ patim ābhṛta-paricaryopakaraṇa ātmaikāgryeṇa
tapasvy ārādhayāṁ babhūva.

saḥ—he (King Āgnīdhra); *ca*—also; *kadācit*—once upon a time; *pitṛloka*—the Pitṛloka planet; *kāmaḥ*—desiring; *sura-vara*—of the great demigods; *vanitā*—the women; *ākrīḍā*—the place of pastimes; *acala-droṇyām*—in one valley of the Mandara Hill; *bhagavantam*—unto the most powerful (Lord Brahmā); *viśva-sṛjām*—of personalities who have created this universe; *patim*—the master; *ābhṛta*—having collected; *paricaryā-upakaraṇaḥ*—ingredients for worship; *ātma*—of the mind; *eka-agryeṇa*—with full attention; *tapasvī*—one who executes austerity; *ārādhayām babhūva*—became engaged in worshiping.

TRANSLATION

Desiring to get a perfect son and become an inhabitant of Pitṛloka, Mahārāja Āgnīdhra once worshiped Lord Brahmā, the master of those in charge of material creation. He went to a valley of Mandara Hill, where the damsels of the heavenly planets come down to stroll. There he collected garden flowers and other necessary paraphernalia and then engaged in severe austerities and worship.

PURPORT

The King became *pitṛloka-kāma,* or desirous of being transferred to the planet named Pitṛloka. Pitṛloka is mentioned in *Bhagavad-gītā* (*yānti deva-vratā devān pitṝn yānti pitṛ-vratāḥ*). To go to this planet, one needs very good sons who can make offerings to Lord Viṣṇu and then offer the remnants to their forefathers. The purpose of the *śrāddha* ceremony is to please the Supreme Personality of Godhead, Lord Viṣṇu, so that after pleasing Him one may offer *prasāda* to one's forefathers and in this way make them happy. The inhabitants of Pitṛloka are generally men of the *karma-kāṇḍīya,* or fruitive activities category, who have been transferred there because of their pious activities. They can stay there as long as their descendants offer them *viṣṇu-prasāda.* Everyone in heavenly planets such as Pitṛloka, however, must return to earth after exhausting the effects of his pious acts. As confirmed in *Bhagavad-gītā* (9.21), *kṣīṇe puṇye martya-lokaṁ viśanti:* persons who perform pious acts are transferred to higher planets, but when the effects of their pious acts are over, they are again transferred to earth.

Since Mahārāja Priyavrata was a great devotee, how could he have begotten a son who desired to be transferred to Pitṛloka? Lord Kṛṣṇa says, *pitṝn yānti pitṛ-vratāḥ:* persons who desire to go to Pitṛloka are transferred there. Similarly, *yānti mad-yājino'pi mām:* persons who desire to be transferred to the spiritual planets, Vaikuṇṭhalokas, can also go there. Since Mahārāja Āgnīdhra was the son of a Vaiṣṇava, he should have desired to be transferred to the spiritual world, Vaikuṇṭhaloka. Why, then, did he desire to be transferred to Pitṛloka? In answer to this, Gosvāmī Giridhara, one of the *Bhāgavatam* commentators, remarks that Āgnīdhra was born when Mahārāja Priyavrata was infatuated by lusty desires. This may be accepted as a fact because sons are begotten with different mentalities according to the time of their conception. According to the Vedic system, therefore, before a child is conceived, the *garbhādhāna-saṁskāra* is performed. This ceremony molds the mentality of the father in such a way that when he plants his seed in the womb of his wife, he will beget a child whose mind will be completely saturated with a devotional attitude. At the present moment, however, there are no such *garbhādhāna-saṁskāras,* and therefore people generally have a lusty attitude when they beget children. Especially in this age of Kali, there are no *garbhādhāna* ceremonies; everyone enjoys sex with his wife like a cat or dog. Therefore according to śāstric injunctions, almost all the people of this age belong to the *śūdra* category. Of course, although Mahārāja Āgnīdhra had a desire to be transferred to Pitṛloka, this does not mean that his mentality was that of a *śūdra;* he was a *kṣatriya.*

Mahārāja Āgnīdhra desired to be transferred to Pitṛloka, and therefore he needed a wife because anyone desiring to be transferred to Pitṛloka must leave behind a good son to offer yearly *piṇḍa,* or *prasāda* from Lord Viṣṇu. To have a good son, Mahārāja Āgnīdhra wanted a wife from a family of demigods. Therefore he went to Mandara Hill, where the women of the demigods generally come, to worship Lord Brahmā. In *Bhagavad-gītā* (4.12) it is said, *kāṅkṣantaḥ karmaṇāṁ siddhiṁ yajanta iha devatāḥ:* materialists who want quick results in the material world worship demigods. This is also confirmed in *Śrīmad-Bhāgavatam. Śrī-aiśvarya-prajepsavaḥ:* those who desire beautiful wives, substantial wealth and many sons worship the demigods, but an intelligent devotee, instead of being entangled by the happiness of this material world in the form of a beautiful wife, material opulence and children, desires to be immediately transferred back home, back to Godhead. Thus he worships the Supreme Personality of Godhead, Viṣṇu.

TEXT 3

तदुपलभ्य भगवानादिपुरुषः सदसि गायन्तीं पूर्वचित्तिं नामाप्सरसम - भियापयामास ॥३॥

tad upalabhya bhagavān ādi-puruṣaḥ sadasi gāyantīṁ pūrvacittiṁ
nāmāpsarasam abhiyāpayām āsa.

tat—that; *upalabhya*—understanding; *bhagavān*—the most powerful; *ādi-puruṣaḥ*—the first created being within this universe; *sadasi*—in his assembly; *gāyantīm*—dancing girl; *pūrvacittim*—Pūrvacitti; *nāma*—named; *apsarasam*—the heavenly dancing girl; *abhiyāpayām āsa*—sent down.

TRANSLATION

Understanding King Āgnīdhra's desire, the first and most powerful created being of this universe, Lord Brahmā, selected the best of the

dancing girls in his assembly, whose name was Pūrvacitti, and sent her to the King.

PURPORT

In this verse, the words *bhagavān ādi-puruṣaḥ* are significant. *Bhagavān ādi-puruṣaḥ* is Lord Kṛṣṇa. *Govindam ādi-puruṣaṁ tam ahaṁ bhajāmi.* Lord Kṛṣṇa is the original person. In *Bhagavad-gītā,* He is also addressed by Arjuna as *puruṣam ādyam,* the original person, and He is called Bhagavān. In this verse, however, we see that Lord Brahmā is described as *bhagavān ādi-puruṣaḥ.* The reason he is called *bhagavān* is that he fully represents the Supreme Personality of Godhead and is the first-born creature in this universe. Lord Brahmā could understand Mahārāja Āgnīdhra's desire because he is as powerful as Lord Viṣṇu. As Lord Viṣṇu, situated as Paramātmā, can understand the desire of the living entity, so Lord Brahmā can also understand the living entity's desire, for Viṣṇu, as a via medium, informs him. As stated in *Śrīmad-Bhāgavatam* (1.1.1), *tene brahma hṛdā ya ādi-kavaye:* Lord Viṣṇu informs Lord Brahmā of everything from within his heart. Because Mahārāja Āgnīdhra specifically worshiped Lord Brahmā, Lord Brahmā was pleased, and he sent Pūrvacitti, the Apsarā, to satisfy him.

TEXT 4

सा च तदाश्रमोपवनमतिरमणीयं विविधनिबिडविटपिविटपनिकरसंश्लिष्टपुर-
टलतारूढस्थलविहङ्गममिथुनैः प्रोच्यमानश्रुतिभिः प्रतिबोध्यमानसलिलकुक्कुट-
कारण्डवकलहंसादिभिर्विचित्रमुपकूजितामलजलाशयकमलाकरमुप बभ्राम ॥४॥

sā ca tad-āśramopavanam ati-ramaṇīyaṁ vividha-nibiḍa-viṭapi-viṭapa-
nikara-saṁśliṣṭa-puraṭa-latārūḍha-sthala-vihaṅgama-mithunaiḥ
procyamāna-śrutibhiḥ pratibodhyamāna-salila-kukkuṭa-kāraṇḍava-
kalahaṁsādibhir vicitram upakūjitāmala-jalāśaya-kamalākaram
upababhrāma.

sā—she (Pūrvacitti); *ca*—also; *tat*—of Mahārāja Āgnīdhra; *āśrama*—of the place of meditation; *upavanam*—the park; *ati*—very; *ramaṇīyam*—beautiful; *vividha*—varieties of; *nibiḍa*—dense; *viṭapi*—trees; *viṭapa*—of branches and twigs; *nikara*—masses; *saṁśliṣṭa*—attached; *puraṭa*—golden; *latā*—with creepers; *ārūḍha*—going high; *sthala-vihaṅgama*—of land birds; *mithunaiḥ*—with pairs; *procyamāna*—vibrating; *śrutibhiḥ*—pleasing sounds; *pratibodhyamāna*—responding; *salila-kukkuṭa*—water fowl; *kāraṇḍava*—

ducks; *kala-haṁsa*—with various kinds of swans; *ādibhiḥ*—and so on; *vicitram*—variegated; *upakūjita*—resounding with the vibration; *amala*—clear; *jala-āśaya*—in the lake; *kamala-ākaram*—the source of lotus flowers; *upababhrāma*—began to walk in.

TRANSLATION

The Apsarā sent by Lord Brahmā began strolling in a beautiful park near the place where the King was meditating and worshiping. The park was beautiful because of its dense green foliage and golden creepers. There were pairs of varied birds such as peacocks, and in a lake there were ducks and swans, all vibrating very sweet sounds. Thus the park was magnificently beautiful because of the foliage, the clear water, the lotus flowers and the sweet singing of various kinds of birds.

TEXT 5

तस्याः सुललितगमनपदविन्यासगतिविलासायाश्चानुपदं खणखणायमान -
रुचिरचरणाभरणस्वनमुपाकर्ण्य नरदेवकुमारः समाधियोगेनामीलितन -
यननलिनमुकुलयुगलमीषद्विकचय्य व्यचष्ट ॥५॥

tasyāḥ sulalita-gamana-pada-vinyāsa-gati-vilāsāyāś cānupadaṁ
khaṇa-khaṇāyamāna-rucira-caraṇābharaṇa-svanam upākarṇya
naradeva-kumāraḥ samādhi-yogenāmīlita-nayana-nalina-mukula-
yugalam īṣad vikacayya vyacaṣṭa.

tasyāḥ—of her (Pūrvacitti); *sulalita*—in a very beautiful; *gamana*—movements; *pada-vinyāsa*—with styles of walking; *gati*—in the progression; *vilāsāyāḥ*—whose pastime; *ca*—also; *anupadam*—with every step; *khaṇa-khaṇāyamāna*—making a tinkling sound; *rucira*—very pleasing; *caraṇa-ābharaṇa*—of the ornaments on the feet; *svanam*—the sound; *upākarṇya*—hearing; *naradeva-kumāraḥ*—the Prince; *samādhi*—in ecstasy; *yogena*—by controlling the senses; *āmīlita*—half-open; *nayana*—eyes; *nalina*—of lotus; *mukula*—buds; *yugalam*—like a pair; *īṣat*—slightly; *vikacayya*—opening; *vyacaṣṭa*—saw.

TRANSLATION

As Pūrvacitti passed by on the road in a very beautiful style and mood of her own, the pleasing ornaments on her ankles tinkled with her every step. Although Prince Āgnīdhra was controlling his senses, practicing yoga

with half-open eyes, he could see her with his lotuslike eyes, and when he heard the sweet tinkling of her bangles, he opened his eyes slightly more and could see that she was just nearby.

PURPORT

It is said that *yogīs* always think of the Supreme Personality of Godhead within their hearts. *Dhyānāvasthita-tad-gatena manasā paśyanti yaṁ yoginaḥ* (*Bhāg.* 12.13.1). The Supreme Personality of Godhead is always observed by *yogīs* who practice controlling the venomous senses. As recommended in *Bhagavad-gītā, yogīs* should practice *samprekṣya nāsikāgram,* keeping their eyes half- open. If the eyes are closed completely, there will be a tendency to sleep. So-called *yogīs* sometimes practice a fashionable form of *yoga* by closing their eyes and meditating, but we have actually seen such so-called *yogīs* sleeping and snoring while meditating. This is not the practice of *yoga.* To actually practice *yoga,* one should keep his eyes half open and gaze at the tip of his nose.

Although Āgnīdhra, the son of Priyavrata, was practicing mystic *yoga* and trying to control his senses, the tinkling sound of Pūrvacitti's ankle bells disturbed his practice. *Yoga indriya-saṁyamaḥ:* actual *yoga* practice means controlling the senses. One must practice mystic *yoga,* to control the senses, but the sense control of a devotee who fully engages in the service of the Lord with his purified senses (*hṛṣīkeṇa hṛṣīkeśa-sevanam*) can never be disturbed. Śrīla Prabodhānanda Sarasvatī therefore stated, *durdāntendriya-kāla-sarpa-paṭalī protkhāta-daṁṣṭra-yate* (*Caitanya-candrāmṛta* 5). The practice of *yoga* is undoubtedly good because it controls the senses, which are like venomous serpents. When one engages in devotional service, however, completely employing all the activities of the senses in the service of the Lord, the venomous quality of the senses is completely nullified. It is explained that a serpent is to be feared because of its poison fangs, but if those fangs are broken, the serpent, although it seems fearsome, is not at all dangerous. Devotees, therefore, may see hundreds and thousands of beautiful women with fascinating bodily movements and gestures but not be allured, whereas such women would make ordinary *yogīs* fall. Even the advanced *yogī* Viśvāmitra broke his mystic practice to unite with Menakā and beget a child known as Śakuntalā. The practice of mystic *yoga,* therefore, is not sufficiently strong to control the senses. Another example is Prince Āgnīdhra, whose attention was drawn to the movements of Pūrvacitti, the Apsarā, simply because he heard the tinkling of her ankle bells. In the same way that

Viśvāmitra Muni was attracted by the tinkling bangles of Menakā, Prince Āgnīdhra, upon hearing the tinkling bangles of Pūrvacitti, immediately opened his eyes to see her beautiful movements as she walked. The prince was also very handsome. As described herein, his eyes were just like the buds of lotus flowers. As he opened his lotuslike eyes, he could immediately see that the Apsarā was present by his side.

TEXT 6

तामेवाविदूरे मधुकरीमिव सुमनस उपजिघ्रन्तीं दिविजमनुजमनोनयनाह्लाद - दुघैर्गति विहारव्रीडाविनयावलोकसुस्वराक्षरावयवैर्मनसि नृणां कुसुमायुधस्य विदधतीं विवरं निजमुखविगलितामृतासवसहासभाषणामोदमदान्धमधुकर-निकरोपरोधेन द्रुतपदविन्यासेन वल्गुस्पन्दनस्तनकलशकबरभाररशनां देवीं तदवलोकनेन विवृतावसरस्य भगवतो मकरध्वजस्य वशमुपनीतो जडवदिति होवाच ॥६॥

tām evāvidūre madhukarīm iva sumanasa upajighrantīṁ divija-manuja-mano-nayanāhlāda-dughair gati-vihāra-vrīḍā-vinayāvaloka-susvarākṣarāvayavair manasi nṛṇāṁ kusumāyudhasya vidadhatīṁ vivaraṁ nija-mukha-vigalitāmṛtāsava-sahāsa-bhāṣaṇāmoda-madāndha-madhukara-nikaroparodhena druta-pada-vinyāsena valgu-spandana-stana-kalaśa-kabara-bhāra-raśanāṁ devīṁ tad-avalokanena vivṛtāvasarasya bhagavato makara-dhvajasya vaśam upanīto jaḍavad iti hovāca.

tām—to her; *eva*—indeed; *avidūre*—nearby; *madhukarīm iva*—like a honeybee; *sumanasaḥ*—beautiful flowers; *upajighrantīm*—smelling; *divi-ja*—of those born in the heavenly planets; *manu-ja*—of those born in human society; *manaḥ*—mind; *nayana*—for the eyes; *āhlāda*—pleasure; *dughaiḥ*—producing; *gati*—by her movement; *vihāra*—by pastimes; *vrīḍā*—by shyness; *vinaya*—by humility; *avaloka*—by glancing; *su-svara-akṣara*—by her sweet voice; *avayavaiḥ*—and by the limbs of the body; *manasi*—in the mind; *nṛṇām*—of men; *kusuma-āyudhasya*—of Cupid, who has a flower arrow in his hand; *vidadhatīm*—making; *vivaram*—aural reception; *nija-mukha*—from her own mouth; *vigalita*—pouring out; *amṛta-āsava*—nectar like honey; *sa-hāsa*—in her smiling; *bhāṣaṇa*—and talking; *āmoda*—by the pleasure; *mada-andha*—blinded by intoxication; *madhukara*—of bees; *nikara*—by groups; *uparodhena*—because of being surrounded; *druta*—hasty; *pada*—of feet;

vinyāsena—by stylish stepping; *valgu*—a little; *spandana*—moving; *stana*—breasts; *kalaśa*—like waterpots; *kabara*—of her braids of hair; *bhāra*—weight; *raśanām*—the belt upon the hips; *devīm*—the goddess; *tat-avalokanena*—simply by seeing her; *vivṛta-avasarasya*—taking the opportunity of; *bhagavataḥ*—of the greatly powerful; *makara-dhvajasya*—of Cupid; *vaśam*—under the control; *upanītaḥ*—being brought in; *jaḍa-vat*—as if stunned; *iti*—thus; *ha*—certainly; *uvāca*—he said.

TRANSLATION

Like a honeybee, the Apsarā smelled the beautiful and attractive flowers. She could attract the minds and vision of both humans and demigods by her playful movements, her shyness and humility, her glances, the very pleasing sounds that poured from her mouth as she spoke, and the motion of her limbs. By all these qualities, she opened for Cupid, who bears an arrow of flowers, a path of aural reception into the minds of men. When she spoke, nectar seemed to flow from her mouth. As she breathed, the bees, mad for the taste of her breath, tried to hover about her beautiful lotuslike eyes. Disturbed by the bees, she tried to move hastily, but as she raised her feet to walk quickly, her hair, the belt on her hips, and her breasts, which were like water jugs, also moved in a way that made her extremely beautiful and attractive. Indeed, she seemed to be making a path for the entrance of Cupid, who is most powerful. Therefore the prince, completely subdued by seeing her, spoke to her as follows.

PURPORT

How a beautiful woman's movements and gestures, her hair and the structure of her breasts, hips and other bodily features attract the minds not only of men but of demigods also is very finely described in this statement. The words *divija* and *manuja* specifically emphasize that the attraction of feminine gestures is powerful everywhere within this material world, both on this planet and in the higher planetary systems. It is said that the standard of living in the higher planetary systems is thousands and thousands of times higher than the standard of living on this planet. Therefore the beautiful bodily features of the women there are also thousands and thousands of times more attractive than the features of the women on earth. The creator has constructed women in such a way that their beautiful voices and movements and the beautiful features of their hips, their breasts, and the other parts of their bodies attract the members of the opposite sex, both on earth and on other planets, and awaken their lusty desires. When one is controlled by Cupid or the beauty of women, he becomes stunned like matter such as stone. Captivated by the material movements of women, he wants to remain in this material world. Thus one's promotion to the spiritual world is checked simply by seeing the beautiful bodily structure and movements of women. Śrī Caitanya Mahāprabhu has therefore warned all devotees to beware of the attraction of beautiful women and materialistic civilization. Śrī Caitanya Mahāprabhu even refused to see Pratāparudra Mahārāja because he was a very opulent person in the material world. Lord Caitanya said in this connection, *niṣkiñcanasya bhagavad-bhajanonmukhasya:* those who are engaged in the devotional service of the Lord because they are very serious about going back home, back to Godhead, should be very careful to avoid seeing the beautiful gestures of women and should also avoid seeing persons who are very rich.

niṣkiñcanasya bhagavad-bhajanonmukhasya
pāraṁ paraṁ jigamiṣor bhava-sāgarasya
sandarśanaṁ viṣayiṇām atha yoṣitāṁ ca
hā hanta hanta viṣa-bhakṣaṇato 'py asādhu

"Alas, for a person who is seriously desiring to cross the material ocean and engage in the transcendental loving service of the Lord without material motives, seeing a materialist engaged in sense gratification or seeing a woman who is similarly interested is more abominable than drinking poison willingly." (*Caitanya-caritāmṛta, Madhya* 11.8) One who is serious about going back home, back to Godhead, should not contemplate the attractive features of women and the opulence of rich men. Such contemplation will check one's advancement in spiritual life. Once a devotee is fixed in Kṛṣṇa consciousness, however, these attractions will not agitate his mind.

TEXT 7

का त्वं चिकीर्षसि च किं मुनिवर्य शैले
मायासि कापि भगवत्परदेवतायाः ।
विज्ये बिभर्षि धनुषी सुहृदात्मनोऽर्थे
किं वा मृगान्मृगयसे विपिने प्रमत्तान् ॥७॥

kā tvaṁ cikīrṣasi ca kiṁ muni-varya śaile
māyāsi kāpi bhagavat-para-devatāyāḥ

vijye bibharṣi dhanuṣī suhṛd-ātmano'rthe
kiṁ vā mṛgān mṛgayase vipine pramattān

kā—who; *tvam*—are you; *cikīrṣasi*—are you trying to do; *ca*—also; *kim*—what; *muni-varya*—O best of *munis; śaile*—on this hill; *māyā*—illusory potency; *asi*—are you; *kāpi*—some; *bhagavat*—the Supreme Personality of Godhead; *para-devatāyāḥ*—of the transcendental Lord; *vijye*—without strings; *bibharṣi*—you are carrying; *dhanuṣī*—two bows; *suhṛt*—of a friend; *ātmanaḥ*—of yourself; *arthe*—for the sake; *kim vā*—or; *mṛgān*—forest animals; *mṛgayase*—are you trying to hunt; *vipine*—in this forest; *pramattān*—who are materially maddened.

TRANSLATION

The Prince mistakenly addressed the Apsarā: O best of saintly persons, who are you? Why are you on this hill, and what do you want to do? Are you one of the illusory potencies of the Supreme Personality of Godhead? You seem to be carrying two bows without strings. What is the reason you carry these bows? Is it for some purpose of your own or for the sake of a friend? Perhaps you carry them to kill the mad animals in this forest.

PURPORT

While undergoing severe penances in the forest, Āgnīdhra was captivated by the movements of Pūrvacitti, the girl sent by Lord Brahmā. As stated in *Bhagavad-gītā, kāmais tais tair hṛta jñānāḥ:* when one becomes lusty, he loses his intelligence. Therefore Āgnīdhra, having lost his intelligence, could not distinguish whether Pūrvacitti was male or female. He mistook her for a *muni-putra,* the son of a saintly person in the forest, and addressed her as *muni-varya.* Because of her personal beauty, however, he could not believe her to be a boy. He therefore began studying her features. First he saw her two eyebrows, which were so expressive that he wondered whether he or she might be the *māyā* of the Supreme Personality of Godhead. The words used in this connection are *bhagavat-para-devatāyāḥ. Devatāḥ,* the demigods, all belong to this material world, whereas Bhagavān, the Supreme Personality of Godhead, Kṛṣṇa, is always beyond this material world and is therefore known as *para-devatā.* The material world is certainly created by *māyā,* but it is created under the direction of *para-devatā,* the Supreme Personality of Godhead. As confirmed in *Bhagavad-gītā* (*mayādhyakṣeṇa prakṛtiḥ sūyate sa-carācaram*), *māyā* is not the ultimate authority for the creation of this material world. *Māyā* acts on behalf of Kṛṣṇa.

Pūrvacitti's eyebrows were so beautiful that Āgnīdhra compared them to bows without strings. He therefore asked her whether they were to be used for her own purposes or for the sake of someone else. Her eyebrows were like bows meant to kill animals in the forest. This material world is like a great forest, and its inhabitants are like forest animals such as deer and tigers meant to be killed. The killers are the eyebrows of beautiful women. Captivated by the beauty of the fair sex, all the men of the world are killed by bows without strings, but cannot see how they are killed by *māyā.* It is a fact, however, that they are being killed (*bhūtvā bhūtvā pralīyate*). By dint of his *tapasya,* Āgnīdhra could understand how *māyā* acts under the direction of the Supreme Personality of Godhead.

The word *pramattān* is also significant. *Pramatta* refers to one who cannot control his senses. The entire material world is being exploited by people who are *pramatta,* or *vimūḍha.* Prahlāda Mahārāja therefore said:

śoce tato vimukha-cetasa indriyārtha-
māyā-sukhāya bharam udvahato vimūḍhān

"They are rotting in material activities for transient material pleasure and spoiling their lives toiling all day and night simply for sense gratification, with no attachment for love of Godhead. I am simply lamenting for them and devising various plans to deliver them from the clutches of *māyā.*" (*Bhāg.* 7.9.43) *Karmīs* who act very seriously for sense gratification are always referred to in the *śāstras* by such terms as *pramatta, vimukha* and *vimūḍha.* They are killed by *māyā.* However, one who is *apramatta,* a sane, sober person, a *dhīra,* knows very well that a human being's primary duty is to render service to the Supreme Person. *Māyā* is always ready to kill those who are *pramatta* with her invisible bows and arrows. Āgnīdhra questioned Pūrvacitti about this.

TEXT 8

बाणाविमौ भगवतः शतपत्रपत्रौ
शान्तावपुङ्खरुचिरावतितिग्मदन्तौ ।
कस्मै युयुङ्क्षसि वने विचरन्न विद्मः
क्षेमाय नो जडधियां तव विक्रमोऽस्तु ॥८॥

bāṇāv imau bhagavataḥ śata-patra-patrau
śāntāv apuṅkha-rucirāv ati-tigma-dantau
kasmai yuyuṅkṣasi vane vicaran na vidmaḥ
kṣemāya no jaḍa-dhiyāṁ tava vikramo'stu

bāṇau—two arrows; *imau*—these; *bhagavataḥ*—of you, the most powerful; *śata-patra-patrau*—having feathers like the petals of a lotus flower; *śāntau*—peaceful; *apuṅkha*—without a shaft; *rucirau*—very beautiful; *ati-tigma-dantau*—having a very sharp point; *kasmai*—whom; *yuyuṅkṣasi*—you want to pierce; *vane*—in the forest; *vicaran*—loitering; *na vidmaḥ*—we cannot understand; *kṣemāya*—for welfare; *naḥ*—of us; *jaḍa-dhiyām*—who are dull-headed; *tava*—your; *vikramaḥ*—prowess; *astu*—may be.

TRANSLATION

Then Āgnīdhra observed the glancing eyes of Pūrvacitti and said: My dear friend, you have two very powerful arrows, namely your glancing eyes. Those arrows have feathers like the petals of a lotus flower. Although they have no shafts, they are very beautiful, and they have very sharp, piercing points. They appear very peaceful, and thus it seems that they will not be shot at anyone. You must be loitering in this forest to shoot those arrows at someone, but I cannot understand whom. My intelligence is dull, and I cannot combat you. Indeed, no one can equal you in prowess, and therefore I pray that your prowess will be for my good fortune.

PURPORT

Āgnīdhra thus began appreciating Pūrvacitti's powerful glance upon him. He compared her glancing eyes to very sharp arrows. Although her eyes were as beautiful as lotuses, they were simultaneously like shaftless arrows, and Āgnīdhra was therefore afraid of them. He hoped that her glances upon him would be favorable because he was already captivated, and the more captivated he became, the more impossible it would be for him to remain without her. Āgnīdhra therefore prayed to Pūrvacitti that her glances at him would be auspicious, not futile. In other words, he prayed that she would become his wife.

TEXT 9

शिष्या इमे भगवतः परितः पठन्ति
गायन्ति साम सरहस्यमजस्रमीशम् ।
युष्मच्छिखाविलुलिताः सुमनोऽभिवृष्टीः
सर्वे भजन्त्यृषिगणा इव वेदशाखाः ॥९॥

śiṣyā ime bhagavataḥ paritaḥ paṭhanti
gāyanti sāma sarahasyam ajasram īśam

yuṣmac-chikhā-vilulitāḥ sumano'bhivṛṣṭīḥ
sarve bhajanty ṛṣi-gaṇā iva veda-śākhāḥ

śiṣyāḥ—disciples, followers; *ime*—these; *bhagavataḥ*—of your worshipable self; *paritaḥ*—surrounding; *paṭhanti*—are reciting; *gāyanti*—are singing; *sāma*—the *Sāma Veda; sa-rahasyam*—with the confidential portion; *ajasram*—incessantly; *īśam*—unto the Lord; *yuṣmat*—your; *śikhā*—from bunches of hair; *vilulitāḥ*—fallen; *sumanaḥ*—of flowers; *abhivṛṣṭīḥ*—showers; *sarve*—all; *bhajanti*—enjoy, resort to; *ṛṣi-gaṇāḥ*—sages; *iva*—like; *veda-śākhāḥ*—branches of Vedic literature.

TRANSLATION

Seeing the bumblebees following Pūrvacitti, Mahārāja Āgnīdhra said: My dear Lord, the bumblebees surrounding your body are like disciples surrounding your worshipable self. They are incessantly chanting the mantras of the Sāma Veda and the Upaniṣads, thus offering prayers to you. Just as great sages resort to the branches of Vedic literatures, the bumblebees are enjoying the showers of flowers falling from your hair.

TEXT 10

वाचं परं चरणपञ्जरतित्तिरीणां
ब्रह्मन्नरूपमुखरां शृणवाम तुभ्यम् ।
लब्धा कदम्बरुचिरङ्कविटङ्कबिम्बे
यस्यामलातपरिधिः क्व च वल्कलं ते ॥१०॥

vācaṁ paraṁ caraṇa-pañjara-tittirīṇāṁ
brahmann arūpa-mukharāṁ śṛṇavāma tubhyam
labdhā kadamba-rucir aṅka-viṭaṅka-bimbe
yasyām alāta-paridhiḥ kva ca valkalaṁ te

vācam—the resounding vibration; *param*—only; *caraṇa-pañjara*—of the ankle bells; *tittirīṇām*—of the *tittiri* birds; *brahman*—O *brāhmaṇa; arūpa*—without form; *mukharām*—able to be very distinctly heard; *śṛṇavāma*—I hear; *tubhyam*—your; *labdhā*—gotten; *kadamba*—like the *kadamba* flower; *ruciḥ*—lovely color; *aṅka-viṭaṅka-bimbe*—on the beautiful circular hips; *yasyām*—on which; *alāta-paridhiḥ*—encirclement of burning cinders; *kva*—where; *ca*—also; *valkalam*—covering cloth; *te*—your.

TRANSLATION

O brāhmaṇa, I can simply hear the tinkling of your ankle bells. Within those bells, tittiri birds seem to be chirping among themselves. Although I do not see their forms, I can hear how they are chirping. When I look at your beautiful circular hips, I see they are the lovely color of kadamba flowers, and your waist is encircled by a belt of burning cinders. Indeed, you seem to have forgotten to dress yourself.

PURPORT

With lusty desires to see Pūrvacitti, Āgnīdhra especially gazed upon the girl's attractive hips and waist. When a man looks upon a woman with such lusty desires, he is captivated by her face, her breasts and her waist, for a woman first attracts a man to fulfill his sexual desires by the beautiful features of her face, by the beautiful slope of her breasts and also by her waist. Pūrvacitti was dressed in fine yellow silk, and therefore her hips looked like *kadamba* flowers. Because of her belt, her waist seemed to be encircled by burning cinders. She was fully dressed, but Āgnīdhra had become so lusty that he asked, "Why have you come naked?"

TEXT 11

किं सम्भृतं रुचिरयोर्द्विज शृङ्गयोस्ते
मध्ये कृशो वहसि यत्र दृशिः श्रिता मे ।
पङ्कोऽरुणः सुरभिरात्मविषाण ईदृग्
येनाश्रमं सुभग मे सुरभीकरोषि ॥११॥

kiṁ sambhṛtaṁ rucirayor dvija śṛṅgayos te
madhye kṛśo vahasi yatra dṛśiḥ śritā me
paṅko'ruṇaḥ surabhīr ātma-viṣāṇa īdṛg
yenāśramaṁ subhaga me surabhī-karoṣi

kim—what; *sambhṛtam*—filled; *rucirayoḥ*—very beautiful; *dvija*—O *brāhmaṇa; śṛṅgayoḥ*—within two horns; *te*—your; *madhye*—in the middle; *kṛśaḥ*—thin; *vahasi*—you are carrying; *yatra*—wherein; *dṛśiḥ*—eyes; *śritā*—attached; *me*—my; *paṅkaḥ*—powder; *aruṇaḥ*—red; *surabhiḥ*—fragrant; *ātma-viṣāṇe*—on the two horns; *īdṛk*—such; *yena*—by which; *āśramam*—place of residence; *su-bhaga*—O most fortunate one; *me*—my; *surabhī-karoṣi*—you are perfuming.

TRANSLATION

Āgnīdhra then praised Pūrvacitti's raised breasts. He said: My dear brāhmaṇa your waist is very thin, yet with great difficulty you are carefully carrying two horns, to which my eyes have become attracted. What is filling those two beautiful horns? You seem to have spread fragrant red powder upon them, powder that is like the rising morning sun. O most fortunate one, I beg to inquire where you have gotten this fragrant powder that is perfuming my āśrama, my place of residence.

PURPORT

Āgnīdhra appreciated Pūrvacitti's raised breasts. After seeing the girl's breasts, he became almost mad. Nevertheless, he could not recognize whether Pūrvacitti was a boy or a girl, for as a result of his austerity, he saw no distinction between the two. He therefore addressed her with the word *dvija,* "O *brāhmaṇa.*" Yet why should a *dvija,* a *brāhmaṇa* boy, have horns on his chest? Because the boy's waist was thin, Āgnīdhra thought, he was carrying the horns with great difficulty, and therefore they must be filled with something very valuable. Otherwise why would he carry them? When a woman's waist is thin and her breasts are full, she looks very attractive. Āgnīdhra, his eyes attracted, contemplated the heavy breasts on the girl's thin body and imagined how her back must sustain them. Āgnīdhra imagined that her raised breasts were two horns she had covered with cloth so that others would not see the valuables within them. Āgnīdhra, however, was very anxious to see them. Therefore he requested, "Please uncover them so that I can see what you are carrying. Rest assured that I shall not take it away. If you feel an inconvenience in removing the covering, I can help you; I myself can uncover them to see what valuable things those raised horns contain." He was also surprised to see the red dust of perfumed *kuṅkuma* spread over her breasts. Nevertheless, still considering Pūrvacitti a boy, Āgnīdhra addressed her as *subhaga,* most fortunate *muni.* The boy must have been fortunate; otherwise how simply by standing there could he perfume Āgnīdhra's entire *āśrama?*

TEXT 12

लोकं प्रदर्शय सुहृत्तम तावकं मे
यत्रत्य इत्थमुरसावयवावपूर्वौ ।
अस्मद्विधस्य मनउन्नयनौ बिभर्ति
बह्वद्भुतं सरसराससुधादि वक्त्रे ॥१२॥

lokaṁ pradarśaya suhṛttama tāvakaṁ me
yatratya ittham urasāvayavāv apūrvau
asmad-vidhasya mana-unnayanau bibharti
bahv adbhutaṁ sarasa-rāsa-sudhādi vaktre

lokam—residential place; *pradarśaya*—please show; *suhṛt-tama*—O best of friends; *tāvakam*—your; *me*—unto me; *yatratyaḥ*—a person born wherein; *ittham*—like this; *urasā*—by the chest; *avayavau*—two limbs (breasts); *apūrvau*—wonderful; *asmat-vidhasya*—of a person like me; *manaḥ-unnayanau*—very agitating to the mind; *bibharti*—sustains; *bahu*—many; *adbhutam*—wonderful; *sarasa*—sweet words; *rāsa*—amorous gestures like smiling; *sudhā-ādi*—such as nectar; *vaktre*—in the mouth.

TRANSLATION

O best friend, will you kindly show me the place where you reside? I cannot imagine how the residents of that place have gotten such wonderful bodily features as your raised breasts, which agitate the mind and eyes of a person like me who sees them. Judging by the sweet speech and kind smiles of those residents, I think that their mouths must contain nectar.

PURPORT

Still bewildered, Āgnīdhra wanted to see the place from which the *brāhmaṇa* boy had come, where the men had such raised breasts. Such attractive features, he thought, must be due to the severe austerities performed there. Āgnīdhra addressed the girl as *suhṛttama,* the best friend, so that she would not refuse to take him there. Not only was Āgnīdhra captivated by the girl's raised breasts; he was also attracted by her sweet speech. Nectar seemed to emanate from her mouth, and therefore he was increasingly surprised.

TEXT 13

का वाऽऽत्मवृत्तिरदनाद्धविरङ्ग वाति
विष्णोः कलास्यनिमिषोन्मकरौ च कर्णौ ।
उद्विग्नमीनयुगलं द्विजपङ्क्तिशोचि-
रासन्नभृङ्गनिकरं सर इन्मुखं ते ॥१३॥

kā vātma-vṛttir adanād dhavir aṅga vāti
viṣṇoḥ kalāsy animiṣonmakarau ca karṇau

udvigna-mīna-yugalaṁ dvija-paṅkti-śocir
āsanna-bhṛṅga-nikaraṁ sara in mukhaṁ te

kā—what; *vā*—and; *ātma-vṛttiḥ*—food for maintenance of the body; *adanāt*—by the chewing (of betel); *haviḥ*—pure sacrificial ingredients; *aṅga*—my dear friend; *vāti*—emanate; *viṣṇoḥ*—of Lord Viṣṇu; *kalā*—expansion of the body; *asi*—you are; *animiṣa*—without blinking; *unmakarau*—two brilliant sharks; *ca*—also; *karṇau*—two ears; *udvigna*—restless; *mīna-yugalam*—possessing two fish; *dvija-paṅkti*—of lines of teeth; *śociḥ*—beauty; *āsanna*—nearby; *bhṛṅga-nikaram*—possessing swarms of bumblebees; *saraḥ it*—like a lake; *mukham*—face; *te*—your.

TRANSLATION

My dear friend, what do you eat to maintain your body? Because you are chewing betel, a pleasing scent is emanating from your mouth. This proves that you always eat the remnants of food offered to Viṣṇu. Indeed, you must also be an expansion of Lord Viṣṇu's body. Your face is as beautiful as a pleasing lake. Your jeweled earrings resemble two brilliant sharks with unblinking eyes like those of Viṣṇu, and your own eyes resemble two restless fish. Simultaneously, therefore, two sharks and two restless fish are swimming in the lake of your face. Besides them, the white rows of your teeth seem like rows of very beautiful swans in the water, and your scattered hair resembles swarms of bumblebees following the beauty of your face.

PURPORT

The devotees of Lord Viṣṇu are also His expansions. They are called *vibhinnāṁśa.* Lord Viṣṇu is offered all kinds of sacrificial ingredients, and because devotees always eat *prasāda,* the remnants of His food, the scent of sacrificial ingredients emanates not only from Viṣṇu but also from the devotees who eat the remnants of His food or the food of His devotees. Āgnīdhra considered Pūrvacitti an expansion of Lord Viṣṇu because of the pleasing scent of her body. Aside from that, because of her jeweled earrings, shaped like sharks, because of her scattered hair, resembling bumblebees mad after the scent of her body, and because of the white rows of her teeth, which resembled swans, Āgnīdhra compared Pūrvacitti's face to a beautiful lake decorated with lotus flowers, fish, swans and bumblebees.

TEXT 14

योऽसौ त्वया करसरोजहतः पतङ्गो
दिक्षु भ्रमन् भ्रमत एजयतेऽक्षिणी मे ।
मुक्तं न ते स्मरसि वक्रजटावरूथं
कष्टोऽनिलो हरति लम्पट एष नीवीम् ॥१४॥

yo'sau tvayā kara-saroja-hataḥ pataṅgo
dikṣu bhraman bhramata ejayate'kṣiṇī me
muktaṁ na te smarasi vakra-jaṭā-varūthaṁ
kaṣṭo'nilo harati lampaṭa eṣa nīvīm

yaḥ—which; *asau*—that; *tvayā*—by you; *kara-saroja*—with the lotus palm; *hataḥ*—struck; *pataṅgaḥ*—the ball; *dikṣu*—in all directions; *bhraman*—moving; *bhramataḥ*—restless; *ejayate*—disturbs; *akṣiṇī*—eyes; *me*—of me; *muktam*—scattered; *na*—not; *te*—your; *smarasi*—are you mindful of; *vakra*—curling; *jaṭā*—of hair; *varūtham*—bunches; *kaṣṭaḥ*—giving trouble; *anilaḥ*—wind; *harati*—takes away; *lampaṭaḥ*—like a man attached to women; *eṣaḥ*—this; *nīvīm*—lower garment.

TRANSLATION

My mind is already restless, and by playing with a ball, moving it all about with your lotuslike palm, you are also agitating my eyes. Your curling black hair is now scattered, but you are not attentive to arranging it. Are you not going to arrange it? Like a man attached to women, the most cunning wind is trying to take off your lower garment. Are you not mindful of it?

PURPORT

The girl Pūrvacitti was playing with a ball in her hand, and the ball seemed like nothing but another lotus flower captured by her lotuslike palm. Because of her movements, her hair was loose, and the belt holding her cloth was giving way, as if the cunning wind were trying to make her naked. Yet she paid no attention to arranging her hair or fixing her dress. As Āgnīdhra tried to see the girl's naked beauty, his eyes were very agitated by her movements.

TEXT 15

रूपं तपोधन तपश्चरतां तपोघ्नं
ह्येतत्तु केन तपसा भवतोपलब्धम् ।

चर्तुं तपोऽर्हसि मया सह मित्र मह्यं
किं वा प्रसीदति स वै भवभावनो मे ॥१५॥

rūpaṁ tapodhana tapaś caratāṁ tapoghnaṁ
hy etat tu kena tapasā bhavatopalabdham
cartuṁ tapo'rhasi mayā saha mitra mahyaṁ
kiṁ vā prasīdati sa vai bhava-bhāvano me

rūpam—beauty; *tapaḥ-dhana*—O best of the sages performing austerity; *tapaḥ caratām*—of persons engaged in executing austerities and penances; *tapaḥ-ghnam*—which dismantles the austerities; *hi*—certainly; *etat*—this; *tu*—indeed; *kena*—by what; *tapasā*—austerity; *bhavatā*—by you; *upalabdham*—achieved; *cartum*—to execute; *tapaḥ*—austerity; *arhasi*—you ought; *mayā saha*—with me; *mitra*—my dear friend; *mahyam*—unto me; *kim vā*—or maybe; *prasīdati*—is pleased; *saḥ*—he; *vai*—certainly; *bhava-bhāvanaḥ*—the creator of this universe; *me*—with me.

TRANSLATION

O best among those performing austerities, where did you get this wonderful beauty that dismantles the austerities performed by others? Where have you learned this art? What austerity have you undergone to achieve this beauty, my dear friend? I desire that you join me to perform austerity and penance, for it may be that the creator of the universe, Lord Brahmā, being pleased with me, has sent you to become my wife.

PURPORT

Āgnīdhra appreciated the wonderful beauty of Pūrvacitti. Indeed, he was surprised to see such exceptional beauty, which must have been the result of past austerities and penances. He therefore asked the girl whether she had achieved such beauty just to break the penances and austerities of others. He thought that Lord Brahmā, the creator of the universe, might have been pleased with him and might therefore have sent her to become his wife. He requested Pūrvacitti to become his wife so that together they could perform austerities and penances in family life. In other words, a suitable wife helps her husband perform penances and austerities in household life if both of them are on the same elevated platform of spiritual understanding. Without spiritual understanding, husband and wife cannot be equally situated. Lord Brahmā, the creator of the universe, is interested in good progeny. Therefore unless he is pleased, one cannot get a suitable wife. In fact, Lord Brahmā is worshiped in marriage ceremonies. In India even today, wedding invitations are still issued with a picture of Lord Brahmā on the face of the card.

TEXT 16

न त्वां त्यजामि दयितं द्विजदेवदत्तं
यस्मिन्मनो दृगपि नो न वियाति लग्नम् ।
मां चारुशृङ्ग्यर्हसि नेतुमनुव्रतं ते
चित्तं यतः प्रतिसरन्तु शिवाः सचिव्यः ॥१६॥

na tvāṁ tyajāmi dayitaṁ dvija-deva-dattaṁ
yasmin mano dṛg api no na viyāti lagnam
māṁ cāru-śṛṅgy arhasi netum anuvrataṁ te
cittaṁ yataḥ pratisarantu śivāḥ sacivyaḥ

na—not; *tvām*—you; *tyajāmi*—I shall give up; *dayitam*—very dear; *dvija-deva*—by Lord Brahmā, the demigod worshiped by the *brāhmaṇas; dattam*—given; *yasmin*—unto whom; *manaḥ*—mind; *dṛk*—eyes; *api*—also; *naḥ*—my; *na viyāti*—do not go away; *lagnam*—tightly attached; *mām*—me; *cāru-śṛṅgi*—O woman with beautiful raised breasts; *arhasi*—you ought; *netum*—to lead; *anuvratam*—follower; *te*—your; *cittam*—desire; *yataḥ*—wherever; *pratisarantu*—may follow; *śivāḥ*—favorable; *sacivyaḥ*—friends.

TRANSLATION

Lord Brahmā, who is worshiped by the brāhmaṇas, has very mercifully given you to me, and that is why I have met you. I do not want to give up your company, for my mind and eyes are fixed upon you and cannot be drawn away. O woman with beautiful raised breasts, I am your follower. You may take me wherever you like, and your friends may also follow me.

PURPORT

Now Āgnīdhra frankly admits his weakness. He was attracted to Pūrvacitti, and therefore before she could say, "But I have no business with you," he expressed his desire to be united with her. He was so attracted that he was ready to go anywhere, hell or heaven, in her company. When one is absorbed in lust and the influence of sex, one surrenders to the feet of a woman without reservations. Śrīla Madhvācārya remarks in this connection that when one engages in joking and talking like a crazy person, one may say anything and everything, but his words will be meaningless.

TEXT 17

श्रीशुक उवाच

इति ललनानुनयातिविशारदो ग्राम्यवैदग्ध्यया परिभाषया तां विबुधवधूं विबुधमतिरधिसभाजयामास ॥१७॥

śrī-śuka uvāca
iti lalanānunayāti-viśārado grāmya-vaidagdhyayā paribhāṣayā tāṁ vibudha-vadhūṁ vibudha-matir adhisabhājayām āsa.

śrī-śukaḥ uvāca—Śukadeva Gosvāmī said; *iti*—thus; *lalanā*—women; *anunaya*—in winning over; *ati-viśāradaḥ*—very expert; *grāmya-vaidagdhyayā*—expert in fulfilling one's material desires; *paribhāṣayā*—by selected words; *tām*—her; *vibudha-vadhūm*—the celestial girl; *vibudha-matiḥ*—Āgnīdhra, who possessed intelligence like that of the demigods; *adhisabhājayām āsa*—gained the favor of.

TRANSLATION

Śukadeva Gosvāmī continued: Mahārāja Āgnīdhra, whose intelligence was like that of a demigod, knew the art of flattering women to win them to his side. He therefore pleased that celestial girl with his lusty words and gained her favor.

PURPORT

Since King Āgnīdhra was a devotee, he actually had no attraction for material enjoyment, but because he wanted a wife for progeny and Lord Brahmā had sent Pūrvacitti for this purpose, he expertly pleased her with flattering words. Women are attracted by a man's flattering words. One who is expert in this art of flattery is called *vidagdha.*

TEXT 18

सा च ततस्तस्य वीरयूथपतेर्बुद्धिशीलरूपवयःश्रियौदार्येण पराक्षिप्तमनास्तेन सहायुतायुतपरिवत्सरोपलक्षणं कालं जम्बूद्वीपपतिना भौमस्वर्गभोगान् बुभुजे ॥१८॥

sā ca tatas tasya vīra-yūtha-pater buddhi-śīla-rūpa-vayaḥ-
śriyaudāryeṇa parākṣipta-manās tena sahāyutāyuta-
parivatsaropalakṣaṇaṁ kālaṁ jambūdvīpa-patinā bhauma-svarga-
bhogān bubhuje.

sā—she; *ca*—also; *tataḥ*—thereafter; *tasya*—of him; *vīra-yūtha-pateḥ*—the master of heroes; *buddhi*—by the intelligence; *śīla*—behavior; *rūpa*—beauty; *vayaḥ*—youth; *śriyā*—opulence; *audāryeṇa*—and by the magnanimity; *parākṣipta*—attracted; *manāḥ*—her mind; *tena saha*—with him; *ayuta*—ten thousand; *ayuta*—ten thousand; *parivatsara*—years; *upalakṣaṇam*—extending; *kālam*—time; *jambūdvīpa-patinā*—with the King of Jambūdvīpa; *bhauma*—earthly; *svarga*—heavenly; *bhogān*—pleasures; *bubhuje*—enjoyed.

TRANSLATION

Attracted by the intelligence, learning, youth, beauty, behavior, opulence and magnanimity of Āgnīdhra, the King of Jambūdvīpa and master of all heroes, Pūrvacitti lived with him for many thousands of years and luxuriously enjoyed both worldly and heavenly happiness.

PURPORT

By the grace of Lord Brahmā, King Āgnīdhra and the heavenly girl Pūrvacitti, found their union quite suitable. Thus they enjoyed worldly and heavenly happiness for many thousands of years.

TEXT 19

तस्यामु ह वा आत्मजान् स राजवर आग्नीध्रो नाभिकिम्पुरुषहरिवर्षेलावृत - रम्यकहिरण्मयकुरुभद्राश्वकेतुमालसंज्ञान्नव पुत्रानजनयत् ॥१९॥

tasyām u ha vā ātmajān sa rāja-vara āgnīdhro nābhi-kimpuruṣa-
harivarṣelāvṛta-ramyaka-hiraṇmaya-kuru-bhadrāśva-ketumāla-
saṁjñān nava putrān ajanayat.

tasyām—in her; *u ha vā*—certainly; *ātma-jān*—sons; *saḥ*—he; *rāja-varaḥ*—the best of kings; *āgnīdhraḥ*—Āgnīdhra; *nābhi*—Nābhi; *kiṁpuruṣa*—Kiṁpuruṣa; *hari-varṣa*—Harivarṣa; *ilāvṛta*—Ilāvṛta; *ramyaka*—Ramyaka; *hiraṇmaya*—Hiraṇmaya; *kuru*—Kuru; *bhadrāśva*—Bhadrāśva; *ketu-māla*—Ketumāla; *saṁjñān*—named; *nava*—nine; *putrān*—sons; *ajanayat*—begot.

TRANSLATION

In the womb of Pūrvacitti, Mahārāja Āgnīdhra, the best of kings, begot nine sons, named Nābhi, Kiṁpuruṣa, Harivarṣa, Ilāvṛta, Ramyaka, Hiraṇmaya, Kuru, Bhadrāśva and Ketumāla.

TEXT 20

सा सूत्वाथ सुतान्नवानुवत्सरं गृह एवापहाय पूर्वचित्तिर्भूय एवाजं देवमुपतस्थे ॥२०॥

sā sūtvātha sutān navānuvatsaraṁ gṛha evāpahāya pūrvacittir bhūya evājaṁ devam upatasthe.

sā—she; *sūtvā*—after giving birth to; *atha*—thereafter; *sutān*—sons; *nava*—nine; *anuvatsaram*—year after year; *gṛhe*—at home; *eva*—certainly; *apahāya*—leaving; *pūrvacittiḥ*—Pūrvacitti; *bhūyaḥ*—again; *eva*—certainly; *ajam*—Lord Brahmā; *devam*—the demigod; *upatasthe*—approached.

TRANSLATION

Pūrvacitti gave birth to these nine sons, one each year, but after they grew up, she left them at home and again approached Lord Brahmā to worship him.

PURPORT

There are many instances in which Apsarās, heavenly angels, have descended to this earth by the order of a superior demigod like Lord Brahmā or Lord Indra, have followed the demigod's order by marrying someone and giving birth to children, and have then returned to their celestial homes. For example, after Menakā, the celestial woman who had come to delude Viśvāmitra Muni, gave birth to the child Śakuntalā, she left both the child and her husband and returned to the heavenly planets. Pūrvacitti did not remain permanently with Mahārāja Āgnīdhra. After cooperating in his household affairs, she left Mahārāja Āgnīdhra and all nine sons and returned to Brahmā to worship him.

TEXT 21

आग्नीध्रसुतास्ते मातुरनुग्रहादौत्पत्तिकेनैव संहननबलोपेताः पित्रा विभक्ता आत्मतुल्यनामानि यथाभागं जम्बूद्वीपवर्षाणि बुभुजुः ॥२१॥

āgnīdhra-sutās te mātur anugrahād autpattikenaiva saṁhanana-balopetāḥ pitrā vibhaktā ātma-tulya-nāmāni yathā-bhāgaṁ jambūdvīpa-varṣāṇi bubhujuḥ.

āgnīdhra-sutāḥ—the sons of Mahārāja Āgnīdhra; *te*—they; *mātuḥ*—of the mother; *anugrahāt*—by the mercy or by drinking the breast milk; *autpattikena*—naturally; *eva*—certainly; *saṁhanana*—well-built body; *bala*—strength; *upetāḥ*—obtained; *pitrā*—by the father; *vibhaktāḥ*—divided; *ātma-tulya*—following their own; *nāmāni*—possessing names; *yathā-bhāgam*—divided properly; *jambūdvīpa-varṣāṇi*—different parts of Jambūdvīpa (probably Asia and Europe combined together); *bubhujuḥ*—ruled.

TRANSLATION

Because of drinking the breast milk of their mother, the nine sons of Āgnīdhra naturally had strong, well-built bodies. Their father gave them each a kingdom in a different part of Jambūdvīpa. The kingdoms were named according to the names of the sons. Thus the sons of Āgnīdhra ruled the kingdoms they received from their father.

PURPORT

The *ācāryas* specifically mention that in this verse the words *mātuḥ anugrahāt* ("by the mercy of their mother") refer to the breast milk of their mother. In India it is a common belief that if a baby is fed his mother's milk for at least six months, his body will be very strong. Besides that, it is mentioned herein that all the sons of Āgnīdhra were endowed with the nature of their mother. *Bhagavad-gītā* (1.40) also declares, *strīṣu duṣṭāsu vārṣṇeya jāyate varṇa-saṅkaraḥ:* when women are polluted, *varṇa-saṅkara,* unqualified children, are generated, and when the *varṇa-saṅkara* population increases, the entire world becomes hellish. Therefore, according to *Manu-saṁhitā,* a woman needs a great deal of protection in order to remain pure and chaste so that her children can be fully engaged for the benefit of human society.

TEXT 22

आग्नीध्रो राजातृप्तः कामानामप्सरसमेवानुदिनमधिमन्यमानस्तस्याः सलोकतां श्रुतिभिरवारुन्ध यत्र पितरो मादयन्ते ॥२२॥

āgnīdhro rājātṛptaḥ kāmānām apsarasam evānudinam adhi-
manyamānas tasyāḥ salokatāṁ śrutibhir avārundha yatra pitaro
mādayante.

āgnīdhraḥ—Āgnīdhra; *rājā*—the King; *atṛptaḥ*—not satisfied; *kāmānām*—with sense gratification; *apsarasam*—the celestial woman (Pūrvacitti); *eva*

—certainly; *anudinam*—day after day; *adhi*—exceedingly; *manyamānaḥ*—thinking of; *tasyāḥ*—of her; *sa-lokatām*—promotion to the same planet; *śrutibhiḥ*—by the *Vedas; avārundha*—got; *yatra*—where; *pitaraḥ*—the forefathers; *mādayante*—take pleasure.

TRANSLATION

After Pūrvacitti's departure, King Āgnīdhra, his lusty desires not at all satisfied, always thought of her. Therefore, in accordance with the Vedic injunctions, the King, after his death, was promoted to the same planet as his celestial wife. That planet, which is called Pitṛloka, is where the pitās, the forefathers, live in great delight.

PURPORT

If one always thinks of something, he certainly gets a related body after death. Mahārāja Āgnīdhra was always thinking of Pitṛloka, the place where his wife had returned. Therefore after his death he achieved that same planet, probably to live with her again. *Bhagavad-gītā* also says:

yaṁ yaṁ vāpi smaran bhāvaṁ
tyajaty ante kalevaram
taṁ tam evaiti kaunteya
sadā tad-bhāva-bhāvitaḥ

"Whatever state of being one remembers when he quits his body, that state he will attain without fail." (Bg. 8.6) We can naturally conclude that if we always think of Kṛṣṇa or become fully Kṛṣṇa conscious, we can be promoted to the planet of Goloka Vṛndāvana, where Kṛṣṇa eternally lives.

TEXT 23

सम्परेते पितरि नव भ्रातरो मेरुदुहितॄर्मेरुदेवीं प्रतिरूपामुग्रदंष्ट्रीं लतां रम्यां श्यामां नारीं भद्रां देववीतिमितिसंज्ञा नवोदवहन् ॥२३॥

samparete pitari nava bhrātaro meru-duhitṝr merudevīṁ pratirūpām ugradaṁṣṭrīṁ latāṁ ramyāṁ śyāmāṁ nārīṁ bhadrāṁ devavītim iti saṁjñā navodavahan.

samparete pitari—after the departure of their father; *nava*—nine; *bhrātaraḥ*—brothers; *meru-duhitṝḥ*—the daughters of Meru; *merudevīm*—Merudevī; *prati-rūpām*—Pratirūpā; *ugra-daṁṣṭrīm*—Ugradaṁṣṭrī; *latām*

—Latā; *ramyām*—Ramyā; *śyāmām*—Śyāmā; *nārīm*—Nārī; *bhadrām*—Bhadrā; *deva-vītim*—Devavīti; *iti*—thus; *saṁjñāḥ*—the names; *nava*—nine; *udavahan*—married.

TRANSLATION

After the departure of their father, the nine brothers married the nine daughters of Meru named Merudevī, Pratirūpā, Ugradaṁṣṭrī, Latā, Ramyā, Śyāmā, Nārī, Bhadrā and Devavīti.

Thus end the Bhaktivedanta purports of the Fifth Canto, Second Chapter, of the Śrīmad-Bhāgavatam, *entitled "The Activities of Mahārāja Āgnīdhra."*

CHAPTER THREE

Ṛṣabhadeva's Appearance in the Womb of Merudevī, the Wife of King Nābhi

In this chapter the spotless character of King Nābhi, the oldest son of Āgnīdhra, is described. Wanting to have sons, Mahārāja Nābhi underwent severe austerities and penances. He performed many sacrifices along with his wife and worshiped Lord Viṣṇu, master of all sacrifices. Being very kind to His devotees, the Supreme Personality of Godhead was very pleased with the austerities of Mahārāja Nābhi. He personally appeared before the King in His four-handed feature, and the priests, who were performing the sacrifices, began to offer their prayers unto Him. They prayed for a son like the Lord, and Lord Viṣṇu agreed to take birth in the womb of Merudevī, the wife of King Nābhi, and incarnate as King Ṛṣabhadeva.

TEXT 1

श्रीशुक उवाच

नाभिरपत्यकामोऽप्रजया मेरुदेव्या भगवन्तं यज्ञपुरुषमवहितात्मायजत ॥१॥

śrī-śuka uvāca

nābhir apatya-kāmo'prajayā merudevyā bhagavantaṁ yajña-puruṣam avahitātmāyajata.

śrī-śukaḥ uvāca—Śukadeva Gosvāmī said; *nābhiḥ*—the son of Mahārāja Āgnīdhra; *apatya-kāmaḥ*—desiring to have sons; *aprajayā*—who had not given birth to any children; *merudevyā*—with Merudevī; *bhagavantam*—the Supreme Personality of Godhead; *yajña-puruṣam*—Lord Viṣṇu, the master and enjoyer of all performances of sacrifice; *avahita-ātmā*—with great attention; *ayajata*—offered prayers and worshiped.

TRANSLATION

Śukadeva Gosvāmī continued to speak: Mahārāja Nābhi, the son of Āgnīdhra, wished to have sons, and therefore he attentively began to offer prayers and worship the Supreme Personality of Godhead, Lord Viṣṇu, the

master and enjoyer of all sacrifices. Mahārāja Nābhi's wife, Merudevī, who had not given birth to any children at that time, also worshiped Lord Viṣṇu along with her husband.

TEXT 2

तस्य ह वाव श्रद्धया विशुद्धभावेन यजतः प्रवर्ग्येषु प्रचरत्सु द्रव्यदेशकाल -
मन्त्रर्त्विग्दक्षिणाविधानयोगोपपत्त्या दुरधिगमोऽपि भगवान् भागवतवात्सल्यतया
सुप्रतीक आत्मानमपराजितं निजजनाभिप्रेतार्थविधित्सया गृहीतहृदयो हृदयङ्गमं
मनोनयनानन्दनावयवाभिराममाविश्चकार ॥२॥

tasya ha vāva śraddhayā viśuddha-bhāvena yajataḥ pravargyeṣu
pracaratsu dravya-deśa-kāla-mantrartvig-dakṣiṇā-vidhāna-
yogopapattyā duradhigamo'pi bhagavān bhāgavata-vātsalyatayā
supratīka ātmānam aparājitaṁ nija-janābhipretārtha-vidhitsayā
gṛhīta-hṛdayo hṛdayaṅgamaṁ mano-nayanānandanāvayavābhirāmam
āviścakāra.

tasya—when he (Nābhi); *ha vāva*—certainly; *śraddhayā*—with great faith and devotion; *viśuddha-bhāvena*—with a pure, uncontaminated mind; *yajataḥ*—was worshiping; *pravargyeṣu*—while the fruitive activities called *pravargya; pracaratsu*—were being performed; *dravya*—the ingredients; *deśa*—place; *kāla*—time; *mantra*—hymns; *ṛtvik*—priests conducting the ceremony; *dakṣiṇā*—gifts to the priests; *vidhāna*—regulative principles; *yoga*—and of the means; *upapattyā*—by the performance; *duradhigamaḥ*—not obtainable; *api*—although; *bhagavān*—the Supreme Personality of Godhead; *bhāgavata-vātsalyatayā*—because of His being very affectionate to His devotee; *su-pratīkaḥ*—possessing a very beautiful form; *ātmānam*—Himself; *aparājitam*—not to be conquered by anyone; *nija-jana*—of His devotee; *abhipreta-artha*—the desire; *vidhitsayā*—to fulfill; *gṛhīta-hṛdayaḥ*—His heart being attracted; *hṛdayaṅgamam*—captivating; *manaḥ-nayana-ānandana*—pleasing to the mind and eyes; *avayava*—by the limbs; *abhirāmam*—beautiful; *āviścakāra*—manifested.

TRANSLATION

In the performance of a sacrifice, there are seven transcendental means to obtain the mercy of the Supreme Personality of Godhead: (1) by sacrificing valuable things or eatables, (2) by acting in terms of place, (3) by acting in terms of time, (4) by offering hymns, (5) by going through

the priest, (6) by offering gifts to the priests and (7) by observing the regulative principles. However, one cannot always obtain the Supreme Lord through this paraphernalia. Nonetheless, the Lord is affectionate to His devotee; therefore when Mahārāja Nābhi, who was a devotee, worshiped and offered prayers to the Lord with great faith and devotion and with a pure uncontaminated mind, superficially performing some yajña in the line of pravargya, the kind Supreme Personality of Godhead, due to His affection for His devotees, appeared before King Nābhi in His unconquerable and captivating form with four hands. In this way, to fulfill the desire of His devotee, the Supreme Personality of Godhead manifested Himself in His beautiful body before His devotee. This body pleases the mind and eyes of the devotees.

PURPORT

In *Bhagavad-gītā* it is clearly said:

bhaktyā mām abhijānāti
yāvān yaś cāsmi tattvataḥ
tato māṁ tattvato jñātvā
viśate tad-anantaram

"One can understand the Supreme Personality as He is only by devotional service. And when one is in full consciousness of the Supreme Lord by such devotion, he can enter into the kingdom of God." (Bg. 18.55)

One can understand and see the Supreme Personality of Godhead through the process of devotional service, and not in any other way. Although Mahārāja Nābhi performed prescribed duties and sacrifices, it should still be considered that the Lord appeared before him not due to his sacrifices but because of his devotional service. It was for this reason that the Lord agreed to appear before him in His beautiful bodily features. As stated in *Brahma-saṁhitā* (5.30), the Supreme Lord in His original nature is very beautiful. *Veṇuṁ kvaṇantam aravinda-dalāyatākṣaṁ barhāvataṁsam asitāmbuda-sundarāṅgam:* the Supreme Personality of Godhead, although blackish, is very, very beautiful.

TEXT 3

अथ ह तमाविष्कृतभुजयुगलद्वयं हिरणमयं पुरुषविशेषं कपिशकौशेयाम्बर -
धरमुरसि विलसच्छ्री वत्सललामं दरवरवनरुहवनमालाच्छूर्यमृतमणिगदादि -
भिरुपलक्षितं स्फुटकिरणप्रवरमुकुटकुण्डलकटककटिसूत्रहारकेयूरनूपुरा

द्यङ्गभूषणविभूषितमृत्विक् सदस्यगृहपतयोऽधना इवोत्तमधनमुपलभ्य सबहुमानमर्हणेनावनतशीर्षाण उपतस्थुः ॥ ३ ॥

atha ha tam āviṣkṛta-bhuja-yugala-dvayaṁ hiraṇmayaṁ puruṣa-viśeṣaṁ kapiśa-kauśeyāmbara-dharam urasi vilasac-chrīvatsa-lalāmaṁ daravara-vanaruha-vana-mālācchūry-amṛta-maṇi-gadādibhir upalakṣitaṁ sphuṭa-kiraṇa-pravara-mukuṭa-kuṇḍala-kaṭaka-kaṭi-sūtra-hāra-keyūra-nūpurādy-aṅga-bhūṣaṇa-vibhūṣitam ṛtvik-sadasya-gṛha-patayo'dhanā ivottama-dhanam upalabhya sabahu-mānam arhaṇenāvanata-śīrṣāṇa upatasthuḥ.

atha—thereafter; *ha*—certainly; *tam*—Him; *āviṣkṛta-bhuja-yugala-dvayam*—who manifested Himself with four arms; *hiraṇmayam*—very bright; *puruṣa-viśeṣam*—the topmost of all living beings, Puruṣottama; *kapiśa-kauśeya-ambara-dharam*—wearing a yellow silk garment; *urasi*—on the chest; *vilasat*—beautiful; *śrīvatsa*—called Śrīvatsa; *lalāmam*—possessing the mark; *dara-vara*—by a conchshell; *vana-ruha*—lotus flower; *vana-mālā*—garland of forest flowers; *acchūri*—disc; *amṛta-maṇi*—the Kaustubha gem; *gadā-ādibhiḥ*—and by a club and other symbols; *upalakṣitam*—symptomized; *sphuṭa-kiraṇa*—radiant; *pravara*—excellent; *mukuṭa*—helmet; *kuṇḍala*—earrings; *kaṭaka*—bracelets; *kaṭi-sūtra*—girdle; *hāra*—necklace; *keyūra*—armlets; *nūpura*—ankle bells; *ādi*—and so on; *aṅga*—of the body; *bhūṣaṇa*—with ornaments; *vibhūṣitam*—decorated; *ṛtvik*—the priests; *sadasya*—associates; *gṛha-patayaḥ*—and King Nābhi; *adhanāḥ*—poor persons; *iva*—like; *uttama-dhanam*—a great treasure; *upalabhya*—having achieved; *sa-bahu-mānam*—with great regard; *arhaṇena*—with ingredients for worship; *avanata*—bent; *śīrṣāṇaḥ*—their heads; *upatasthuḥ*—worshiped.

TRANSLATION

Lord Viṣṇu appeared before King Nābhi with four arms. He was very bright, and He appeared to be the best of all personalities. Around the lower portion of His body, He wore a yellow silken garment. On His chest was the mark of Śrīvatsa, which always displays beauty. He carried a conchshell, lotus flower, disc and club, and He wore a garland of forest flowers and the Kaustubha gem. He was beautifully decorated with a helmet, earrings, bangles, belt, pearl necklace, armlets, ankle bells and other bodily ornaments bedecked with radiant jewels. Seeing the Lord

present before them, King Nābhi and his priests and associates felt just like poor people who have suddenly attained great riches. They received the Lord and respectfully bent their heads and offered Him things in worship.

PURPORT

It is distinctly mentioned here that the Supreme Personality of Godhead did not appear as an ordinary human being. He appeared before King Nābhi and his associates as the best of all personalities (Puruṣottama). As stated in the *Vedas: Nityo nityānāṁ cetanaś cetanānām.* The Supreme Personality of Godhead is also a living being, but He is the supreme living being. In *Bhagavad-gītā (7.7),* Lord Kṛṣṇa Himself says, *mattaḥ parataraṁ nānyat kiñcid asti dhanañjaya:* "O conqueror of wealth [Arjuna], there is no truth superior to Me." No one is more attractive or more authoritative than Lord Kṛṣṇa. That is one of the differences between God and an ordinary living being. According to this description of the transcendental body of Lord Viṣṇu, the Lord can easily be distinguished from all other living beings. Consequently Mahārāja Nābhi and his priests and associates all offered the Lord obeisances and began to worship Him with various things. As stated in *Bhagavad-gītā* (6.22), *yaṁ labdhvā cāparaṁ lābhaṁ manyate nādhikaṁ tataḥ.* That is, "Upon gaining this, one thinks that there is no greater gain." When one realizes God and sees the Lord face to face, one certainly thinks that he has gained the best of all things. *Raso'py asya paraṁ dṛṣṭvā nivartate:* when one experiences a higher taste, his consciousness is fixed. After seeing the Supreme Personality of Godhead, one ceases to be attracted by anything material. One then remains steady in his worship of the Supreme Personality of Godhead.

TEXTS 4–5

ऋत्विज ऊचुः

अर्हसि मुहुरर्हत्तमार्हणमस्माकमनुपथानां नमो नम इत्येतावत्सदुपशिक्षितं -
को ऽर्हति पुमान् प्रकृतिगुणव्यतिकरमतिरनीश ईश्वरस्य परस्य प्रकृतिपुरुष -
योरर्वाक्तनाभिर्नामरूपाकृतिभी रूपनिरूपणम् ॥४॥ सकलजननिकाय-
वृजिननिरसनशिवतमप्रवरगुणगणैकदेशकथनादृते ॥५॥

ṛtvija ūcuḥ

arhasi muhur arhattamārhaṇam asmākam anupathānāṁ namo nama ity etāvat sad-upaśikṣitaṁ ko'rhati pumān prakṛti-guṇa-vyatikara-matir anīśa īśvarasya parasya prakṛti-puruṣayor arvāktanābhir nāma-rūpākṛtibhī rūpa-nirūpaṇam; sakala-jana-

nikāya-vṛjina-nirasana-śivatama-pravara-guṇa-gaṇaika-deśa-kathanād ṛte.

ṛtvijaḥ ūcuḥ—the priests said; *arhasi*—please (accept); *muhuḥ*—again and again; *arhat-tama*—O most exalted, worshipable person; *arhaṇam*—offering of worship; *asmākam*—of us; *anupathānām*—who are Your servants; *namaḥ*—respectful obeisances; *namaḥ*—respectful obeisances; *iti*—thus; *etāvat*—so far; *sat*—by exalted personalities; *upaśikṣitam*—instructed; *kaḥ*—what; *arhati*—is able (to make); *pumān*—man; *prakṛti*—of material nature; *guṇa*—of the modes; *vyatikara*—in the transformations; *matiḥ*—whose mind (is absorbed); *anīśaḥ*—who is most incapable; *īśvarasya*—of the Supreme Personality of Godhead; *parasya*—beyond; *prakṛti-puruṣayoḥ*—the jurisdiction of the three modes of material nature; *arvāktanābhiḥ*—which do not reach up to, or which are of this material world; *nāma-rūpa-ākṛtibhiḥ*—by names, forms and qualities; *rūpa*—of Your nature or position; *nirūpaṇam*—ascertainment, perception; *sakala*—all; *jana-nikāya*—of mankind; *vṛjina*—sinful actions; *nirasana*—which wipe out; *śivatama*—most auspicious; *pravara*—excellent; *guṇa-gaṇa*—of the transcendental qualities; *eka-deśa*—one part; *kathanāt*—by speaking; *ṛte*—except.

TRANSLATION

The priests began to offer prayers to the Lord, saying: O most worshipable one, we are simply Your servants. Although You are full in Yourself, please, out of Your causeless mercy, accept a little service from us, Your eternal servants. We are not actually aware of Your transcendental form, but we can simply offer our respectful obeisances again and again, as instructed by the Vedic literatures and authorized ācāryas. Materialistic living entities are very much attracted to the modes of material nature, and therefore they are never perfect, but You are above the jurisdiction of all material conceptions. Your name, form and qualities are all transcendental and beyond the conception of experimental knowledge. Indeed, who can conceive of You? In the material world we can perceive only material names and qualities. We have no other power than to offer our respectful obeisances and prayers unto You, the transcendental person. The chanting of Your auspicious transcendental qualities will wipe out the sins of all mankind. That is the most auspicious activity for us, and we can thus partially understand Your supernatural position.

PURPORT

The Supreme Personality of Godhead has nothing to do with material perception. Even the impersonalist Śaṅkarācārya says, *nārāyaṇaḥ paro'vyaktāt:* "Nārāyaṇa, the Supreme Personality of Godhead, is beyond the material conception." We cannot concoct the form and attributes of the Supreme Personality of Godhead. We must simply accept the description given in Vedic literatures about the Lord's form and activities. As stated in *Brahma-saṁhitā* (5.29):

cintāmaṇi-prakara-sadmasu kalpa-vṛkṣa-
lakṣāvṛteṣu surabhīr abhipālayantam
lakṣmī-sahasra-śata-sambhrama-sevyamānaṁ
govindam ādi-puruṣaṁ tam ahaṁ bhajāmi

"I worship Govinda, the primeval Lord, the first progenitor, who is tending the cows, yielding all desires, in abodes built with spiritual gems and surrounded by millions of purpose trees. He is always served with great reverence and affection by hundreds and thousands of goddesses of fortune." We can have some conception of the Absolute Truth, His form and His attributes simply by reading the descriptions given in Vedic literatures and authoritative statements given by exalted personalities like Brahmā, Nārada, Śukadeva Gosvāmī and others. Śrīla Rūpa Gosvāmī says, *ataḥ śrī-kṛṣṇa-nāmādi na bhaved grāhyam indriyaiḥ:* "We cannot conceive the name, form and qualities of Śrī Kṛṣṇa through our material senses." Because of this, other names for the Lord are *adhokṣaja* and *aprākṛta,* which indicate that He is beyond any material senses. Out of His causeless mercy upon His devotees, the Lord appeared before Mahārāja Nābhi. Similarly, when we are engaged in the Lord's devotional service, the Lord reveals Himself to us. *Sevonmukhe hi jihvādau svayam eva sphuraty adaḥ.* This is the only way to understand the Supreme Personality of Godhead. As confirmed in *Bhagavad-gītā, bhaktyā mām abhijānāti yāvān yaś cāsmi tattvataḥ:* one can understand the Supreme Personality of Godhead through devotional service. There is no other way. We have to hear from the authorities and from the *śāstras* and consider the Supreme Lord in terms of their statements. We cannot imagine or concoct forms and attributes of the Lord.

TEXT 6

परिजनानुरागविरचितशबलसंशब्दसलिलसितकिसलयतुलसिकादूर्वाङ्कुरैरपि
सम्भृतया सपर्यया किल परम परितुष्यसि ॥६॥

parijanānurāga-viracita-śabala-saṁśabda-salila-sita-kisalaya-tulasikā-dūrvāṅkurair api sambhṛtayā saparyayā kila parama parituṣyasi.

parijana—by Your servants; *anurāga*—in great ecstasy; *viracita*—executed; *śabala*—with a faltering voice; *saṁśabda*—with prayers; *salila*—water; *sita-kisalaya*—twigs bearing new leaves; *tulasikā*—*tulasī* leaves; *dūrvā-aṅkuraiḥ*—and with newly grown grass; *api*—also; *sambhṛtayā*—performed; *saparyayā*—by worship; *kila*—indeed; *parama*—O Supreme Lord; *parituṣyasi*—You become satisfied.

TRANSLATION

O Supreme Lord, You are full in every respect. You are certainly very satisfied when Your devotees offer You prayers with faltering voices and in ecstasy bring You tulasī leaves, water, twigs bearing new leaves, and newly grown grass. This surely makes You satisfied.

PURPORT

One does not need great wealth, education or opulence to satisfy the Supreme Personality of Godhead. If one is fully absorbed in love and ecstasy, he need offer only a flower and a little water. As stated in *Bhagavad-gītā, patraṁ puṣpaṁ phalaṁ toyaṁ yo me bhaktyā prayacchati:* "If one offers Me with love and devotion a leaf, a flower, fruit or water, I will accept it." (Bg. 9.26)

The Supreme Lord can be pleased only by devotional service: therefore it is said here that the Lord is surely satisfied by devotion and nothing else. Quoting from the *Gautamīya-tantra,* the *Hari-bhakti-vilāsa* states:

tulasī-dala-mātreṇa
jalasya culukena vā
vikrīṇīte svam ātmānaṁ
bhaktebhyo bhakta-vatsalaḥ

"Śrī Kṛṣṇa, who is very affectionate toward His devotees, sells Himself to a devotee who offers merely a *tulasī* leaf and a palmful of water." The Supreme Lord is causelessly merciful upon His devotee, so much so that even the poorest of men can offer Him a little water and a flower in devotion and thus please Him. This is due to His affectionate dealings with His devotees.

TEXT 7

अथानयापि न भवत इज्ययोरुभारभरया समुचितमर्थमिहोपलभामहे ॥७॥

athānayāpi na bhavata ijyayoru-bhāra-bharayā samucitam artham ihopalabhāmahe.

atha—otherwise; *anayā*—this; *api*—even; *na*—not; *bhavataḥ*—of Your exalted personality; *ijyayā*—by performance of sacrifice; *urubhāra-bharayā*—encumbered by much paraphernalia; *samucitam*—required; *artham*—use; *iha*—here; *upalabhāmahe*—we can see.

TRANSLATION

We have engaged in Your worship with many things and have offered sacrifices unto You, but we think that there is no need for so many arrangements to please Your Lordship.

PURPORT

Śrīla Rūpa Gosvāmī says that if one is offered varied foods but has no appetite, the offering has no value. In a big sacrificial ceremony there may be many things accumulated to satisfy the Supreme Personality of Godhead, but if there is no devotion, attachment or love for the Lord, the arrangement is useless. The Lord is complete in Himself, and He does not need anything from us. However, if we offer Him a little water, a flower and a *tulasi* leaf, He will accept them. *Bhakti,* devotional service, is the main way to satisfy the Supreme Personality of Godhead. It is not a question of arranging huge sacrifices. The priests were regretful, thinking that they were not on the path of devotional service and that their sacrifice was not pleasing to the Lord.

TEXT 8

आत्मन एवानुसवनमञ्जसाव्यतिरेकेण बोभूयमानाशेषपुरुषार्थस्वरूपस्य किन्तु नाथाशिष आशासानानामेतदभिसंराधनमात्रं भवितुमर्हति ॥८॥

ātmana evānusavanam añjasāvyatirekeṇa bobhūyamānāśeṣa-puruṣārtha-svarūpasya kintu nāthāśiṣa āśāsānānām etad abhisaṁrādhana-mātraṁ bhavitum arhati.

ātmanaḥ—self-sufficiently; *eva*—certainly; *anusavanam*—at every moment; *añjasā*—directly; *avyatirekeṇa*—without stopping; *bobhūyamāna*—increasing; *aśeṣa*—unlimitedly; *puruṣa-artha*—the goals of life; *sva-rūpasya*—Your actual identity; *kintu*—but; *nātha*—O Lord; *āśiṣaḥ*—benedictions for material enjoyment; *āśāsānānām*—of us, who are always desiring; *etat*—this; *abhisaṁrādhana*—for getting Your mercy; *mātram*—only; *bhavitum arhati*—can be.

TRANSLATION

All of life's goals and opulences are directly, self-sufficiently, unceasingly and unlimitedly increasing in You at every moment. Indeed, You are unlimited enjoyment and blissful existence itself. As far as we are concerned, O Lord, we are always after material enjoyment. You do not need all these sacrificial arrangements, but they are meant for us so that we may be benedicted by Your Lordship. All these sacrifices are performed for our fruitive results, and they are not actually needed by You.

PURPORT

Being self-sufficient, the Supreme Lord does not need huge sacrifices. Fruitive activity for a more opulent life is for those who desire such material opulence for their interest. *Yajñārthāt karmaṇo'nyatra loko'yaṁ karma-bandhanaḥ:* if we do not act to satisfy the Supreme Lord, we engage in *māyā's* activities. We may construct a gorgeous temple and spend thousands of dollars, but such a temple is not required by the Lord. The Lord has many millions of temples for His residence, and He does not need our attempt. He does not require opulent activity at all. Such engagement is meant for our benefit. If we engage our money in constructing a gorgeous temple, we are freed from the reactions of our endeavors. This is for our benefit. In addition, if we attempt to do something nice for the Supreme Lord, He is pleased with us and gives us His benediction. In conclusion, the gorgeous arrangements are not for the Lord's sake but for our own. If we somehow or other receive blessings and benedictions from the Lord, our consciousness can be purified and we can become eligible to return home, back to Godhead.

TEXT 9

तद्यथा बालिशानां स्वयमात्मनः श्रेयः परमविदुषां परमपरमपुरुष प्रकर्षकरुणया स्वमहिमानं चापवर्गाख्यमुपकल्पयिष्यन् स्वयं नापचित एवेतरवदिहोपलक्षितः ॥९॥

tad yathā bāliśānāṁ svayam ātmanaḥ śreyaḥ param aviduṣāṁ parama-parama-puruṣa prakarṣa-karuṇayā sva-mahimānaṁ cāpavargākhyam upakalpayiṣyan svayaṁ nāpacita evetaravad ihopalakṣitaḥ.

tat—that; *yathā*—as; *bāliśānām*—of the fools; *svayam*—by Yourself; *ātmanaḥ*—own; *śreyaḥ*—welfare; *param*—ultimate; *aviduṣām*—of persons who do not know; *parama-parama-puruṣa*—O Lord of lords; *prakarṣa-karuṇayā*—by abundant causeless mercy; *sva-mahimānam*—Your personal glory; *ca*—and; *apavarga-ākhyam*—called *apavarga* (liberation); *upakalpayiṣyan*—desiring to give; *svayam*—personally; *na apacitaḥ*—not properly worshiped; *eva*—although; *itara-vat*—like an ordinary person; *iha*—here; *upalakṣitaḥ*—(You are) present and seen (by us).

TRANSLATION

O Lord of lords, we are completely ignorant of the execution of dharma, artha, kāma and mokṣa, the process of liberation, because we do not actually know the goal of life. You have appeared personally before us like a person soliciting worship, but actually You are present here just so we can see You. You have come out of Your abundant and causeless mercy in order to serve our purpose, our interest, and give us the benefit of Your personal glory called apavarga, liberation. You have come, although You are not properly worshiped by us due to our ignorance.

PURPORT

Lord Viṣṇu was personally present at the sacrificial arena, but this does not mean that He had any interest in His own personal benefit. Similarly, the *arcā-vigraha,* the Deity in the temple, is present for the same purpose. Out of His causeless mercy, the Supreme Personality of Godhead presents Himself before us so that we can see Him. Since we have no transcendental vision, we cannot see the spiritual *sac-cid-ānanda-vigraha* of the Lord; therefore, out of His causeless mercy He comes in a form we can see. We can only see material things like stone and wood, and therefore He accepts a form of stone and wood and thus accepts our service in the temple. This is an exhibition of the Lord's causeless mercy. Although He has no interest in such things, in order to receive our loving service, He agrees to act as He does. We cannot actually offer suitable paraphernalia for the Lord's worship because we are completely ignorant. It was out of His causeless mercy that the Lord appeared in the sacrificial arena of Mahārāja Nābhi.

TEXT 10

अथायमेव वरो ह्यर्हत्तम यर्हि बर्हिषि राजर्षेर्वरदर्षभो भवान्निजपुरुषेक्षणविषय आसीत् ॥१०॥

athāyam eva varo hy arhattama yarhi barhiṣi rājarṣer varadarṣabho bhavān nija-puruṣekṣaṇa-viṣaya āsīt.

atha—then; *ayam*—this; *eva*—certainly; *varaḥ*—benediction; *hi*—indeed; *arhat-tama*—O most worshipable of the worshipable; *yarhi*—because; *barhiṣi*—in the sacrifice; *rāja-ṛṣeḥ*—of King Nābhi; *varada-ṛṣabhaḥ*—the best of the benefactors; *bhavān*—Your Lordship; *nija-puruṣa*—of Your devotees; *īkṣaṇa-viṣayaḥ*—the object of the sight; *āsīt*—has become.

TRANSLATION

O most worshipable of all, You are the best of all benefactors, and Your appearance at saintly King Nābhi's sacrificial arena is meant for our benediction. Because You have been seen by us, You have bestowed upon us the most valuable benediction.

PURPORT

Nija-puruṣa-īkṣaṇa-viṣaya. In *Bhagavad-gītā* (9.29) Kṛṣṇa says, *samo 'haṁ sarva-bhūteṣu:* "I envy no one, nor am I partial to anyone. I am equal to all. But whoever renders service unto Me in devotion is a friend, is in Me, and I am also a friend to him."

The Supreme Personality of Godhead is equal to everyone. In that sense, He has no enemies and no friends. Everyone is enjoying the fruitive reactions of his own work, and the Lord, within everyone's heart, is observing and giving everyone the desired result. However, just as the devotees are always anxious to see the Supreme Lord satisfied in every way, similarly the Supreme Lord is very anxious to present Himself before His devotees. Śrī Kṛṣṇa says in *Bhagavad-gītā* (4.8):

paritrāṇāya sādhūnāṁ
vināśāya ca duṣkṛtām
dharma-saṁsthāpanārthāya
sambhavāmi yuge yuge

"To deliver the pious and to annihilate the miscreants, as well as to reestablish the principles of religion, I advent Myself millennium after millennium."

Thus Kṛṣṇa's appearance is for the deliverance and satisfaction of His devotees. Actually He does not advent Himself simply to kill the demons, for that can be done by His agents. Lord Viṣṇu's appearance at the sacrificial arena of Mahārāja Nābhi was just to please the King and his assistants. Otherwise there was no reason for His being present there.

TEXT 11

असङ्गनिशितज्ञानानलविधूताशेषमलानां भवत्स्वभावानामात्मारामाणां मुनीना-
मनवरतपरिगुणितगुणगण परममङ्गलायनगुणगणकथनोऽसि ॥११॥

asaṅga-niśita-jñānānala-vidhūtāśeṣa-malānāṁ bhavat-svabhāvānām ātmārāmāṇāṁ munīnām anavarata-pariguṇita-guṇa-gaṇa parama-maṅgalāyana-guṇa-gaṇa-kathano'si.

asaṅga—by detachment; *niśita*—strengthened; *jñāna*—of knowledge; *anala*—by the fire; *vidhūta*—removed; *aśeṣa*—unlimited; *malānām*—whose dirty things; *bhavat-svabhāvānām*—who have attained Your qualities; *ātma-ārāmāṇām*—who are self-satisfied; *munīnām*—of great sages; *anavarata*—incessantly; *pariguṇita*—recounted; *guṇa-gaṇa*—O Lord, whose spiritual qualities; *parama-maṅgala*—supreme bliss; *āyana*—produces; *guṇa-gaṇa-kathanaḥ*—He, the chanting of whose attributes; *asi*—You are.

TRANSLATION

Dear Lord, all the great sages who are thoughtful and saintly persons incessantly recount Your spiritual qualities. These sages have already burned up all the unlimited dirty things and, by the fire of knowledge, strengthened their detachment from the material world. Thus they have attained Your qualities and are self-satisfied. Yet even for those who feel spiritual bliss in chanting Your attributes, Your personal presence is very rare.

PURPORT

The priests in Mahārāja Nābhi's sacrificial arena appreciated the personal presence of the Supreme Lord Viṣṇu, and they considered themselves very much obliged. The Lord's appearance is rare even for great saintly persons who have become completely detached from this material world and whose hearts are clean due to constantly chanting the glories of the Lord. Such people are satisfied by chanting the transcendental qualities of the Lord. The Lord's personal presence is not actually required. The priests are pointing out that the Lord's personal presence is very rare even for such elevated sages but that He was so kind to them that now He was personally present. Therefore the priests were very much obliged.

TEXT 12

अथ कथञ्चित्स्खलनक्षुत्पतनजृम्भणदुरवस्थानादिषु विवशानां नः स्मरणाय ज्वरमरणदशायामपि सकलकश्मलनिरसनानि तव गुणकृतनामधेयानि वचनगोचराणि भवन्तु ॥१२॥

atha kathañcit skhalana-kṣut-patana-jṛmbhaṇa-duravasthānādiṣu ivaśānāṁ naḥ smaraṇāya jvara-maraṇa-daśāyām api sakala-kaśmala-nirasanāni tava guṇa-kṛta-nāmadheyāni vacana-gocarāṇi bhavantu.

atha—still; *kathañcit*—somehow or other; *skhalana*—stumbling; *kṣut*—hunger; *patana*—falling down; *jṛmbhaṇa*—yawning; *duravasthāna*—because of being placed in an undesirable position; *ādiṣu*—and so on; *vivaśānām*—unable; *naḥ*—of ourselves; *smaraṇāya*—to remember; *jvara-maraṇa-daśāyām*—in the case of having a high fever at the time of death; *api*—also; *sakala*—all; *kaśmala*—sins; *nirasanāni*—which can dispel; *tava*—Your; *guṇa*—attributes; *kṛta*—activities; *nāmadheyāni*—names; *vacana-gocarāṇi*—possible to be uttered; *bhavantu*—let them become.

TRANSLATION

Dear Lord, we may not be able to remember Your name, form and qualities due to stumbling, hunger, falling down, yawning or being in a miserable diseased condition at the time of death when there is a high fever. We therefore pray unto You, O Lord, for You are very affectionate to Your devotees. Please help us remember You and utter Your holy names, attributes and activities, which can dispel all the reactions of our sinful lives.

PURPORT

The real success in life is *ante nārāyaṇa-smṛti*—remembering the holy name, attributes, activities and form of the Lord at the time of death. Although we may be engaged in the Lord's devotional service in the temple, material conditions are so tough and inevitable that we may forget the Lord at the time of death due to a diseased condition or mental derangement. Therefore we should pray to the Lord to be able to remember His lotus feet without fail at the time of death, when we are in such a precarious condition. In this regard, one may also see *Śrīmad-Bhāgavatam* (6.2.9–10 and 14–15).

TEXT 13

किञ्चायं राजर्षिरपत्यकामः प्रजां भवादृशीमाशासान ईश्वरमाशिषां स्वर्गापवर्गयोरपि भवन्तमुपधावति प्रजायामर्थप्रत्ययो धनदमिवाधनः फलीकरणम् ॥१३॥

kiñcāyaṁ rājarṣir apatya-kāmaḥ prajāṁ bhavādṛśīm āśāsāna īśvaram āśiṣāṁ svargāpavargayor api bhavantam upadhāvati prajāyām artha-pratyayo dhanadam ivādhanaḥ phalīkaraṇam.

kiñca—moreover; *ayam*—this; *rāja-ṛṣiḥ*—pious King (Nābhi); *apatya-kāmaḥ*—desiring offspring; *prajām*—a son; *bhavādṛśīm*—exactly like You; *āśāsānaḥ*—hoping for; *īśvaram*—the supreme controller; *āśiṣām*—of benedictions; *svarga-apavargayoḥ*—of the heavenly planets and liberation; *api*—although; *bhavantam*—You; *upadhāvati*—worships; *prajāyām*—children; *artha-pratyayaḥ*—regarding as the ultimate goal of life; *dhana-dam*—unto a person who can give immense wealth as charity; *iva*—like; *adhanaḥ*—a poor man; *phalīkaraṇam*—a little husk.

TRANSLATION

Dear Lord, here is the great King Nābhi, whose ultimate goal in life is to have a son like You. Your Lordship, his position is like that of a person approaching a very rich man and begging for a little grain. Mahārāja Nābhi is so desirous of having a son that he is worshiping You for a son, although You can offer him any exalted position, including elevation to the heavenly planets or liberation back to Godhead.

PURPORT

The priests were a little ashamed that King Nābhi was performing a great sacrifice just to ask the Lord's benediction for a son. The Lord could offer him promotion to the heavenly planets or the Vaikuṇṭha planets. Śrī Caitanya Mahāprabhu has taught us how to approach the Supreme Lord and ask Him for the ultimate benediction. He said: *na dhanaṁ na janaṁ na sundarīṁ kavitāṁ vā jagad-īśa kāmaye.* He did not want to ask the Supreme Lord for anything material. Material opulence means riches, a nice family, a good wife and many followers, but an intelligent devotee doesn't ask the Supreme Lord for anything material. His only prayer is: *mama janmani janmanīśvare bhavatād bhaktir ahaitukī tvayi.* He wants to be engaged perpetually in the loving service of the Lord. He does not want promotion to the heavenly planets or *mukti,* liberation from material bondage. If this were the case, Śrī Caitanya

Mahāprabhu would not have said, *mama janmani janmani.* It doesn't matter to a devotee whether or not he takes birth life after life, as long as he remains a devotee. Actually eternal liberty means returning home, back to Godhead. A devotee is never concerned about anything material. Although Nābhi Mahārāja wanted a son like Viṣṇu, wanting a son like God is also a form of sense gratification. A pure devotee wants only to engage in the Lord's loving service.

TEXT 14

को वा इह तेऽपराजितोऽपराजितया माययानवसितपदव्यानावृतमतिर्विषय -
विषरयानावृतप्रकृतिरनुपासितमहच्चरणः ॥१४॥

ko vā iha te'parājito'parājitayā māyayānavasita-padavyānāvṛta-matir
viṣaya-viṣa-rayānāvṛta-prakṛtir anupāsita-mahac-caraṇaḥ.

kaḥ vā—who is that person; *iha*—within this material world; *te*—of Your Lordship; *aparājitaḥ*—not conquered; *aparājitayā*—by the unconquerable; *māyayā*—illusory energy; *anavasita-padavya*—whose path cannot be ascertained; *anāvṛta-matiḥ*—whose intelligence is not bewildered; *viṣaya-viṣa*—of material enjoyment, which is like poison; *raya*—by the course; *anāvṛta*—not covered; *prakṛtiḥ*—whose nature; *anupāsita*—without worshiping; *mahat-caraṇaḥ*—the lotus feet of great devotees.

TRANSLATION

Dear Lord, unless one worships the lotus feet of great devotees, one will be conquered by the illusory energy, and his intelligence will be bewildered. Indeed, who has not been carried away by the waves of material enjoyment, which are like poison? Your illusory energy is unconquerable. No one can see the path of this material energy or tell how it is working.

PURPORT

Mahārāja Nābhi was inclined to performing great sacrifices for begetting a son. The son might be as good as the Supreme Personality of Godhead, but such a material desire—be it great or insignificant—is brought about by the influence of *māyā.* A devotee does not at all desire anything for sense gratification. Devotion is therefore explained as devoid of material desires (*anyābhilāṣitā-śūnya*). Everyone is subjected to the influence of *māyā* and entangled in all kinds of material desire, and Mahārāja Nābhi was no exception. Freedom from *māyā's* influence is possible when one engages in the service of the great devotees (*mahac-caraṇa-sevā*). Without worshiping the lotus feet of a great devotee, one cannot be freed from *māyā's* influence. Śrīla Narottama dāsa Ṭhākura therefore says, *chāḍiyā vaiṣṇava-sevā nistāra pāyeche kebā:* "Who has been freed from *māyā's* clutches without serving the lotus feet of a Vaiṣṇava?" *Māyā* is *aparājita,* and her influence is also *aparājita.* As confirmed in *Bhagavad-gītā* (7.14):

daivī hy eṣā guṇa-mayī
mama māyā duratyayā

"This divine energy of Mine, consisting of the three modes of material nature, is difficult to overcome."

Only a devotee can surpass *māyā's* great influence. It was no fault on Mahārāja Nābhi's part that he wanted a son. He wanted a son like the Supreme Personality of Godhead, who is the best of all sons. By the association of the Lord's devotee, one no longer desires material opulence. This is confirmed in *Caitanya-caritāmṛta* (*Madhya* 22.54):

'sādhu-saṅga', 'sādhu-saṅga' sarva-śāstre kaya
lava-mātra sādhu-saṅge sarva-siddhi haya

and *Madhya* 22.51:

mahat-kṛpā vinā kona karme 'bhakti' naya
kṛṣṇa-bhakti dūre rahu, saṁsāra nahe kṣaya

If one is serious about escaping *māyā's* influence and returning home, back to Godhead, one must associate with a *sādhu* (devotee). That is the verdict of all scriptures. By the slight association of a devotee, one can be freed from the clutches of *māyā.* Without the mercy of the pure devotee, one cannot get freedom by any means. Certainly a pure devotee's association is necessary in order to obtain the loving service of the Lord. One cannot be freed from *māyā's* clutches without *sādhu-saṅga,* the benediction of a great devotee. In *Śrīmad-Bhāgavatam* (7.5.32) Prahlāda Mahārāja says:

naiṣāṁ matis tāvad urukramāṅghriṁ
spṛśaty anarthāpagamo yad arthaḥ
mahīyasāṁ pāda-rajo-'bhiṣekaṁ
niṣkiñcanānāṁ na vṛṇīta yāvat

One cannot become the Lord's pure devotee without taking the dust of a great devotee on his head (*pāda-rajo-'bhiṣekam*). A pure devotee is *niṣkiñcana;* he has no material desire to enjoy the material world. One has to take shelter of such a pure devotee in order to attain his qualities. The pure devotee is always free from the clutches of *māyā* and her influence.

TEXT 15

यदु ह वाव तव पुनरदभ्रकर्तरिह समाहूतस्तत्रार्थधियां मन्दानां नस्तद्यद्देवहेलनं देवदेवार्हसि साम्येन सर्वान् प्रतिवोढुमविदुषाम् ॥१५॥

yad u ha vāva tava punar adabhra-kartar iha samāhūtas tatrārtha-dhiyāṁ mandānāṁ nas tad yad deva-helanaṁ deva-devārhasi sāmyena sarvān prativoḍhum aviduṣām.

yat—because; *u ha vāva*—indeed; *tava*—Your; *punaḥ*—again; *adabhra-kartaḥ*—O Lord, who performs many activities; *iha*—here, in this arena of sacrifice; *samāhūtaḥ*—invited; *tatra*—therefore; *artha-dhiyām*—who aspire to fulfill material desires; *mandānām*—not very intelligent; *naḥ*—of us; *tat*—that; *yat*—which; *deva-helanam*—disrespect of the Supreme Personality of Godhead; *deva-deva*—Lord of lords; *arhasi*—please; *sāmyena*—because of Your equipoised position; *sarvān*—everything; *prativoḍhum*—tolerate; *aviduṣām*—of us, who are all ignorant.

TRANSLATION

O Lord, You perform many wonderful activities. Our only aim was to acquire a son by performing this great sacrifice; therefore our intelligence is not very sharp. We are not experienced in ascertaining life's goal. By inviting You to this negligible sacrifice for some material motive, we have certainly committed a great offense at Your lotus feet. Therefore, O Lord of lords, please excuse our offense because of Your causeless mercy and equal mind.

PURPORT

The priests were certainly unhappy to have called the Supreme Lord from Vaikuṇṭha for such an insignificant reason. A pure devotee never wants to see the Lord unnecessarily. The Lord is engaged in various activities, and the pure devotee does not want to see Him whimsically, for his own sense gratification. The pure devotee simply depends on the Lord's mercy, and when the Lord is pleased, he can see Him face to face. The Lord is unseen even by demigods like

Lord Brahmā and Lord Śiva. By calling on the Supreme Lord, the priests of Nābhi Mahārāja proved themselves unintelligent; nonetheless, the Lord came out of His causeless mercy. All of them therefore wanted to be excused by the Lord.

Worship of the Supreme Lord for material gain is not approved by authorities. As stated in *Bhagavad-gītā* (7.16):

catur-vidhā bhajante māṁ
janāḥ sukṛtino'rjuna
ārto jijñāsur arthārthī
jñānī ca bharatarṣabha

"O best among the Bharatas [Arjuna], four kinds of pious men render devotional service unto Me—the distressed, the desirer of wealth, the inquisitive, and he who is searching for knowledge of the Absolute."

Initiation into *bhakti* begins when one is in a distressed condition or in want of money, or when one is inquisitive to understand the Absolute Truth. Nonetheless, people who approach the Supreme Lord in this way are not actually devotees. They are accepted as pious (*sukṛtinaḥ*) due to their inquiring about the Absolute Truth, the Supreme Personality of Godhead. Not knowing the various activities and engagements of the Lord, such people unnecessarily disturb the Lord for material gain. However, the Lord is so kind that even though disturbed, He fulfills the desires of such beggars. The pure devotee is *anyābhilāṣitā-śūnya;* he has no motive behind his worship. He is not conducted by the influence of *māyā* in the form of *karma* or *jñāna.* The pure devotee is always prepared to execute the order of the Lord without personal consideration. The *ṛtvijaḥ,* the priests at the sacrifice, knew very well the distinction between *karma* and *bhakti,* and because they considered themselves under the influence of *karma,* fruitive activity, they begged the Lord's pardon. They knew that the Lord had been invited to come for some paltry reason.

TEXT 16

श्रीशुक उवाच
इति निगदेनाभिष्टूयमानो भगवाननिमिषर्षभो वर्षधराभिवादिताभिवन्दित चरणः सदयमिदमाह ॥१६॥

śrī-śuka uvāca
iti nigadenābhiṣṭūyamāno bhagavān animiṣarṣabho varṣa-dharābhivāditābhivandita-caraṇaḥ sadayam idam āha.

śrī-śukaḥ uvāca—Śrī Śukadeva Gosvāmī said; *iti*—thus; *nigadena*—by prayers in prose; *abhiṣṭūyamānaḥ*—being worshiped; *bhagavān*—the Supreme Personality of Godhead; *animiṣa-ṛṣabhaḥ*—the chief of all the demigods; *varṣa-dhara*—by King Nābhi, the Emperor of Bhārata-varṣa; *abhivādita*—worshiped; *abhivandita*—were bowed down to; *caraṇaḥ*—whose feet; *sadayam*—kindly; *idam*—this; *āha*—said.

TRANSLATION

Śrī Śukadeva Gosvāmī said: The priests, who were even worshiped by King Nābhi, the Emperor of Bhārata-varṣa, offered prayers in prose [generally they were in poetry] and bowed down at the Lord's lotus feet. The Lord of lords, the ruler of the demigods, was very pleased with them, and He began to speak as follows.

TEXT 17

श्री भगवानुवाच

अहो बताहमृषयो भवद्भिरवितथगीर्भिर्वरमसुलभमभियाचितो यदमुष्यात्मजो मया सदृशो भूयादिति ममाहमेवाभिरूपः कैवल्यादथापि ब्रह्मवादो न मृषा भवितुमर्हति ममैव हि मुखं यद् द्विजदेवकुलम् ॥१७॥

śrī-bhagavān uvāca
aho batāham ṛṣayo bhavadbhir avitatha-gīrbhir varam asulabham
abhiyācito yad amuṣyātmajo mayā sadṛśo bhūyād iti mamāham
evābhirūpaḥ kaivalyād athāpi brahma-vādo na mṛṣā bhavitum arhati
mamaiva hi mukhaṁ yad dvija-deva-kulam.

śrī-bhagavān uvāca—the Supreme Personality of Godhead said; *aho*—alas; *bata*—certainly I am pleased; *aham*—I; *ṛṣayaḥ*—O great sages; *bhavadbhiḥ*—by you; *avitatha-gīrbhiḥ*—whose words are all true; *varam*—for a benediction; *asulabham*—very difficult to achieve; *abhiyācitaḥ*—have been requested; *yat*—that; *amuṣya*—of King Nābhi; *ātma-jaḥ*—a son; *mayā sadṛśaḥ*—like Me; *bhūyāt*—there may be; *iti*—thus; *mama*—My; *aham*—I; *eva*—only; *abhirūpaḥ*—equal; *kaivalyāt*—because of being without a second; *athāpi*—nevertheless; *brahma-vādaḥ*—the words spoken by exalted *brāhmaṇas; na*—not; *mṛṣā*—false; *bhavitum*—to become; *arhati*—ought; *mama*—My; *eva*—certainly; *hi*—because; *mukham*—mouth; *yat*—that; *dvija-deva-kulam*—the class of pure *brāhmaṇas.*

TRANSLATION

The Supreme Personality of Godhead replied: O great sages, I am certainly very pleased with your prayers. You are all truthful. You have prayed for the benediction of a son like Me for King Nābhi, but this is very difficult to obtain. Since I am the Supreme Person without a second and since no one is equal to Me, another personality like Me is not possible to find. In any case, because you are all qualified brāhmaṇas, your vibrations should not prove untrue. I consider the brāhmaṇas who are well qualified with brahminical qualities to be as good as My own mouth.

PURPORT

The word *avitatha-gīrbhiḥ* means "they whose spoken vibrations cannot be nullified." The *brāhmaṇas* (*dvija,* the twice-born), are given a chance by the śāstric regulations to become almost as powerful as the Supreme Lord. Whatever a *brāhmaṇa* speaks cannot be nullified or changed in any circumstance. According to the Vedic injunctions, a *brāhmaṇa* is the mouth of the Supreme Personality of Godhead; therefore in all rituals a *brāhmaṇa* is offered food (*brāhmaṇa-bhojana*) because when a *brāhmaṇa* eats, it is considered that the Supreme Lord Himself eats. Similarly, whatever a *brāhmaṇa* speaks cannot be changed. It must act. The learned sages who were priests at Mahārāja Nābhi's sacrifice were not only *brāhmaṇas* but were so qualified that they were like *devas,* demigods, or God Himself. If this were not the case, how could they invite Lord Viṣṇu to come to the sacrificial arena? God is one, and God does not belong to this or that religion. In Kali-yuga, different religious sects consider their God to be different from the God of others, but that is not possible. God is one, and He is appreciated according to different angles of vision. In this verse the word *kaivalyāt* means that God has no competitor. There is only one God. In the *Śvetāśvatara Upaniṣad* (6.8) it is said, *na tat-samaś cābhyadhikaś ca dṛśyate:* "No one is found to be equal to Him or greater than Him." That is the definition of God.

TEXT 18

तत आग्नीध्रीयेंऽशकलयावतरिष्याम्यात्मतुल्यमनुपलभमानः ॥१८॥

tata āgnīdhrīye'ṁśa-kalayāvatariṣyāmy ātma-tulyam anupalabhamānaḥ.

tataḥ—therefore; *āgnīdhrīye*—in the wife of Nābhi, the son of Āgnīdhra; *aṁśa-kalayā*—by an expansion of My personal form; *avatariṣyāmi*—I shall advent Myself; *ātma-tulyam*—My equal; *anupalabhamānaḥ*—not finding.

TRANSLATION

Since I cannot find anyone equal to Me, I shall personally expand Myself into a plenary portion and thus advent Myself in the womb of Merudevī, the wife of Mahārāja Nābhi, the son of Āgnīdhra.

PURPORT

This is an example of the omnipotence of the Supreme Personality of Godhead. Although He is one without a second, He expands Himself by *svāṁśa,* His personal expansion, and sometimes by *vibhinnāṁśa,* or His separated expansion. Lord Viṣṇu herein agrees to send His personal expansion as the son of Merudevī, the wife of Mahārāja Nābhi, who is the son of Āgnīdhra. The *ṛtvijaḥ,* the priests, knew that God is one, yet they prayed for the Supreme Lord to become the son of Mahārāja Nābhi to let the world know that the Absolute Truth, the Supreme Personality of Godhead, is one without a second. When He incarnates, He expands Himself in different potencies.

TEXT 19

श्रीशुक उवाच
इति निशामयन्त्या मेरुदेव्याः पतिमभिधायान्तर्दधे भगवान् ॥१९॥

śrī-śuka uvāca
iti niśāmayantyā merudevyāḥ patim abhidhāyāntardadhe bhagavān.

śrī-śukaḥ uvāca—Śrī Śukadeva Gosvāmī said; *iti*—thus; *niśāmayantyāḥ*—who was listening; *merudevyāḥ*—in the presence of Merudevī; *patim*—unto her husband; *abhidhāya*—having spoken; *antardadhe*—disappeared; *bhagavān*—the Supreme Personality of Godhead.

TRANSLATION

Śukadeva Gosvāmī continued: After saying this, the Lord disappeared. The wife of King Nābhi, Queen Merudevī, was sitting by the side of her husband, and consequently she could hear everything the Supreme Lord had spoken.

PURPORT

According to the Vedic injunctions, one should perform sacrifices in the company of one's own wife. *Sapatnīko dharmam ācaret:* religious rituals should be performed with one's wife; therefore Mahārāja Nābhi conducted his great sacrifice with his wife by his side.

TEXT 20

बर्हिषि तस्मिन्नेव विष्णुदत्त भगवान् परमर्षिभिः प्रसादितो नाभेः प्रियचिकीर्षया तदवरोधायने मेरुदेव्यां धर्मान्दर्शयितुकामो वातरशनानां श्रमणाना - मृषीणामूर्ध्वमन्थिनां शुक्लया तनुवावततार ॥२०॥

barhiṣi tasminn eva viṣṇudatta bhagavān paramarṣibhiḥ prasādito
nābheḥ priya-cikīrṣayā tad-avarodhāyane merudevyāṁ dharmān
darśayitu-kāmo vāta-raśanānāṁ śramaṇānām ṛṣīṇām ūrdhva-
manthināṁ śuklayā tanuvāvatatāra.

barhiṣi—in the arena of sacrifice; *tasmin*—that; *eva*—in this way; *viṣṇu-datta*—O Mahārāja Parīkṣit; *bhagavān*—the Supreme Personality of Godhead; *parama-ṛṣibhiḥ*—by the great *ṛṣis; prasāditaḥ*—being pleased; *nābheḥ priya-cikīrṣayā*—to please King Nābhi; *tat-avarodhāyane*—in his wife; *merudevyām*—Merudevī; *dharmān*—the principles of religion; *darśayitu-kāmaḥ*—desiring to exhibit how to perform; *vāta-raśanānām*—of the *sannyāsīs* (who have almost no cloth); *śramaṇānām*—of the *vānaprasthas; ṛṣīṇām*—of the great sages; *ūrdhva-manthinām*—of the *brahmacārīs; śuklayā tanuvā*—in His original spiritual form, which is above the modes of material nature; *avatatāra*—appeared as an incarnation.

TRANSLATION

O Viṣṇudatta, Parīkṣit Mahārāja, the Supreme Personality of Godhead was pleased by the great sages at that sacrifice. Consequently the Lord decided to personally exhibit the method of executing religious principles [as observed by brahmacārīs, sannyāsīs, vānaprasthas and gṛhasthas engaged in rituals] and also satisfy Mahārāja Nābhi's desire. Consequently He appeared as the son of Merudevī in His original spiritual form, which is above the modes of material nature.

PURPORT

When the Supreme Lord appears or descends as an incarnation within this material world, He does not accept a body made of the three modes of material nature (*sattva-guṇa, rajo-guṇa* and *tamo-guṇa*). Māyāvādī philosophers say that the impersonal God appears in this material world by accepting a body in the *sattva-guṇa.* Śrīla Viśvanātha Cakravartī states that the word *śukla* means "consisting of *śuddha-sattva.*" Lord Viṣṇu descends in His *śuddha-sattva* form. *Śuddha-sattva* refers to the *sattva-guṇa* which is never contaminated. In this material world, even the mode of goodness (*sattva-guṇa*) is contaminated by tinges of *rajo-guṇa* and *tamo-guṇa.* When *sattva-guṇa* is never contaminated by *rajo-guṇa* and *tamo-guṇa,* it is called *śuddha-sattva. Sattvaṁ viśuddhaṁ vasudeva-śabditam* (*Bhāg.* 4.3.23). That is the platform of *vasudeva,* whereby the Supreme Personality of Godhead, Vāsudeva, can be experienced. In *Bhagavad-gītā* (4.7) Śrī Kṛṣṇa Himself says:

yadā yadā hi dharmasya
glānir bhavati bhārata
abhyutthānam adharmasya
tadātmānaṁ sṛjāmy aham

"Whenever and wherever there is a decline in religious practice, O descendant of Bharata, and a predominant rise of irreligion—at that time I descend Myself."

Unlike ordinary living entities, the Supreme Lord is not forced by the modes of material nature to appear. He appears *dharmān darśayitu-kāma*—to show how to execute the functions of a human being. The word *dharma* is meant for human beings and is never used in connection with beings inferior to human beings, such as animals. Unfortunately, without being guided by the Supreme Lord, human beings sometimes manufacture a process of *dharma* by concoction. Actually *dharma* cannot be made by man. *Dharmaṁ tu sākṣād bhagavat-praṇītam.* (*Bhāg.* 6.3.19) *Dharma* is given by the Supreme Personality of Godhead, just as the law is given by the state government. Man-made *dharma* has no meaning. *Śrīmad-Bhāgavatam* refers to man-made *dharma* as *kaitava-dharma,* cheating religion. The Supreme Lord sends an *avatāra* (incarnation) to teach human society the proper way to execute religious principles. Such religious principles are *bhakti-mārga.* As the Supreme Lord Himself says in *Bhagavad-gītā: sarva-dharmān parityajya mām ekaṁ śaraṇaṁ vraja.* The son of Mahārāja Nābhi, Ṛṣabhadeva, appeared on this earth to preach the principles of religion. That will be explained in the Fifth Chapter of this Fifth Canto.

Thus end the Bhaktivedanta purports of the Fifth Canto, Third Chapter, of the Śrīmad-Bhāgavatam, *entitled "Ṛṣabhadeva's Appearance in the Womb of Merudevī, the wife of King Nābhi."*

CHAPTER FOUR

The Characteristics of Ṛṣabhadeva, the Supreme Personality of Godhead

In this chapter, Ṛṣabhadeva, the son of Mahārāja Nābhi, begot a hundred sons, and during the reign of those sons the world was very happy in all respects. When Ṛṣabhadeva appeared as the son of Mahārāja Nābhi, He was appreciated by the people as the most exalted and beautiful personality of that age. His poise, influence, strength, enthusiasm, bodily luster and other transcendental qualities were beyond compare. The word *ṛṣabha* refers to the best, or the supreme. Due to the superexcellent attributes of the son of Mahārāja Nābhi, the King named his son Ṛṣabha, or "the best." His influence was incomparable. Although there was a scarcity of rain, Ṛṣabhadeva did not care for Indra, the King of heaven, who is in charge of supplying rain. Through His own potency, Ṛṣabhadeva sumptuously covered Ajanābha with ample rain. Upon receiving Ṛṣabhadeva, who is the Supreme Personality of Godhead, as his son, King Nābhi began to raise Him very carefully. After that, he entrusted the ruling power to Him and, retiring from family life, lived at Badarikāśrama completely engaged in the worship of Vāsudeva, the Supreme Lord. To follow social customs, Lord Ṛṣabhadeva for a while became a student in the *gurukula,* and after returning, He followed the orders of His *guru* and accepted a wife named Jayantī, who had been given to Him by the King of heaven, Indra. He begot a hundred sons in the womb of Jayantī. Of these hundred sons, the eldest was known as Bharata. Since the reign of Mahārāja Bharata, this planet has been called Bhārata-varṣa. Ṛṣabhadeva's other sons were headed by Kuśāvarta, Ilāvarta, Brahmāvarta, Malaya, Ketu, Bhadrasena, Indraspṛk, Vidarbha and Kīkaṭa. There were also other sons named Kavi, Havi, Antarikṣa, Prabuddha, Pippalāyana, Āvirhotra, Drumila, Camasa and Karabhājana. Instead of ruling the kingdom, these nine became mendicant preachers of Kṛṣṇa consciousness, following the religious precepts of the *Bhāgavatam.* Their characteristics and activities are described in the Eleventh Canto of *Śrīmad-Bhāgavatam* during the talks between Vasudeva and Nārada at Kurukṣetra. To teach the general populace, King Ṛṣabhadeva performed many sacrifices and taught His sons how to rule the citizens.

TEXT 1

श्रीशुक उवाच

अथ ह तमुत्पत्त्यैवाभिव्यज्यमानभगवल्लक्षणं साम्योपशमवैराग्यैश्वर्यमहा - विभूतिभिरनुदिनमेध मानानुभावं प्रकृतयः प्रजा ब्राह्मणा देवताश्चावनितल- समवनायातितरां जगृधुः ॥१॥

śrī-śuka uvāca
atha ha tam utpattyaivābhivyajyamāna-bhagaval-lakṣaṇaṁ
sāmyopaśama-vairāgyaiśvarya-mahā-vibhūtibhir anudinam
edhamānānubhāvaṁ prakṛtayaḥ prajā brāhmaṇā devatāś cāvani-tala-
samavanāyātitarāṁ jagṛdhuḥ.

śrī-śukaḥ uvāca—Śrī Śukadeva Gosvāmī said; *atha ha*—thus (after the Supreme Personality of Godhead appeared); *tam*—Him; *utpattyā*—from the beginning of His appearance; *eva*—even; *abhivyajyamāna*—distinctly manifested; *bhagavat-lakṣaṇam*—possessing the symptoms of the Supreme Personality of Godhead; *sāmya*—equal to everyone; *upaśama*—completely peaceful, in control of the senses and mind; *vairāgya*—renunciation; *aiśvarya*—opulences; *mahā-vibhūtibhiḥ*—with great attributes; *anudinam*—day after day; *edhamāna*—increasing; *anubhāvam*—His power; *prakṛtayaḥ*—the ministers; *prajāḥ*—the citizens; *brāhmaṇāḥ*—the learned scholars in full knowledge of Brahman; *devatāḥ*—the demigods; *ca*—and; *avani-tala*—the surface of the globe; *samavanāya*—to rule; *atitarām*—greatly; *jagṛdhuḥ*—desired.

TRANSLATION

Śrī Śukadeva Gosvāmī said: As soon as the Lord was born as the son of Mahārāja Nābhi, He manifested symptoms of the Supreme Lord, such as marks on the bottoms of His feet [the flag, thunderbolt, etc.]. This son was equal to everyone and very peaceful. He could control His senses and His mind, and, possessing all opulence, He did not hanker for material enjoyment. Endowed with all these attributes, the son of Mahārāja Nābhi became more powerful day after day. Due to this, the citizens, learned brāhmaṇas, demigods and ministers wanted Ṛṣabhadeva to be appointed ruler of the earth.

PURPORT

In these days of cheap incarnations, it is very interesting to note the bodily symptoms found in an incarnation. From the very beginning of His birth, it was observed that Ṛṣabhadeva's feet were marked with the transcendental signs (a flag, thunderbolt, lotus flower, etc.). In addition to this, as the Lord began to grow, He became very prominent. He was equal to everyone. He did not favor one person and neglect another. An incarnation of God must have the six opulences—wealth, strength, knowledge, beauty, fame and renunciation. It is said that although Ṛṣabhadeva was endowed with all opulences, He was not at all attached to material enjoyment. He was self-controlled and therefore liked by everyone. Due to His superexcellent qualities, everyone wanted Him to rule the earth. An incarnation of God has to be accepted by experienced people and by the symptoms described in the *śāstras.* An incarnation is not accepted simply by the adulation of foolish people.

TEXT 2

तस्य ह वा इत्थं वर्ष्मणा वरीयसा बृहच्छ्लोकेन चौजसा बलेन श्रिया यशसा वीर्यशौर्याभ्यां च पिता ऋषभ इतीदं नाम चकार ॥२॥

tasya ha vā itthaṁ varṣmaṇā varīyasā bṛhac-chlokena caujasā balena
śriyā yaśasā vīrya-śauryābhyāṁ ca pitā ṛṣabha itīdaṁ nāma cakāra.

tasya—of Him; *ha vā*—certainly; *ittham*—thus; *varṣmaṇā*—by the bodily features; *varīyasā*—most exalted; *bṛhat-ślokena*—decorated with all the high qualities described by poets; *ca*—also; *ojasā*—by prowess; *balena*—by strength; *śriyā*—by beauty; *yaśasā*—by fame; *vīrya-śauryābhyām*—by influence and heroism; *ca*—and; *pitā*—the father (Mahārāja Nābhi); *ṛṣabhaḥ*—the best; *iti*—thus; *idam*—this; *nāma*—name; *cakāra*—gave.

TRANSLATION

When the son of Mahārāja Nābhi became visible, He evinced all good qualities described by the great poets—namely, a well-built body with all the symptoms of the Godhead, prowess, strength, beauty, name, fame, influence and enthusiasm. When the father, Mahārāja Nābhi, saw all these qualities, he thought his son to be the best of human beings or the supreme being. Therefore he gave Him the name Ṛṣabha.

PURPORT

To accept someone as God or an incarnation of God, one must observe the symptoms of God in his body. All the symptoms were found in the body of Mahārāja Nābhi's extraordinarily powerful son. His body was well structured, and He displayed all the transcendental qualities. He showed great influence, and He could control His mind and senses. Consequently He was named Ṛṣabha, which indicates that He was the supreme living being.

TEXT 3

यस्य हीन्द्रः स्पर्धमानो भगवान् वर्षे न ववर्ष तदवधार्य भगवानृषभदेवो योगेश्वरः प्रहस्यात्मयोगमायया स्ववर्षमजनाभं नामाभ्यवर्षत् ॥ ३ ॥

yasya hīndraḥ spardhamāno bhagavān varṣe na vavarṣa tad
avadhārya bhagavān ṛṣabhadevo yogeśvaraḥ prahasyātma-
yogamāyayā sva-varṣam ajanābhaṁ nāmābhyavarṣat.

yasya—of whom; *hi*—indeed; *indraḥ*—King Indra of heaven; *spardhamānaḥ*—being envious; *bhagavān*—very opulent; *varṣe*—on Bhārata-varṣa; *na vavarṣa*—did not pour water; *tat*—that; *avadhārya*—knowing; *bhagavān*—the Supreme Personality of Godhead; *ṛṣabha-devaḥ*—Ṛṣabha-deva; *yoga-īśvaraḥ*—the master of all mystic power; *prahasya*—smiling; *ātma-yoga-māyayā*—by His own spiritual potency; *sva-varṣam*—on His place; *ajanābham*—Ajanābha; *nāma*—named; *abhyavarṣat*—He poured water.

TRANSLATION

Indra, the King of heaven, who is very materially opulent, became envious of King Ṛṣabhadeva. Consequently he stopped pouring water on the planet known as Bhārata-varṣa. At that time the Supreme Lord, Ṛṣabhadeva, the master of all mystic power, understood King Indra's purpose and smiled a little. Then, by His own prowess, through yoga-māyā [His internal potency], He profusely poured water upon His own place, which was known as Ajanābha.

PURPORT

We find the word *bhagavān* used twice in this verse. Both King Indra and Ṛṣabhadeva, the incarnation of the Supreme Lord, are described as *bhagavān.* Sometimes Nārada and Lord Brahmā are also addressed as *bhagavān.* The word *bhagavān* means that one is a very opulent and powerful person like Lord Brahmā, Lord Śiva, Nārada or Indra. They are all addressed as *bhagavān* due to their extraordinary opulence. King Ṛṣabhadeva is an incarnation of the Supreme Lord, and therefore He was the original Bhagavān. Consequently He is described herein as *yogeśvara,* which indicates that He has the most powerful spiritual potency. He is not dependent on King Indra for water. He can supply water Himself, and He did so in this case. In *Bhagavad-gītā,* it is stated: *yajñād bhavati parjanyaḥ.* Due to the performance of *yajña,* clouds of water are manifest in the sky. Clouds and rainfall are under the management of Indra, the heavenly King, but when Indra is neglectful, the Supreme Lord Himself, who is also known as *yajña* or *yajña-pati,* takes the task upon Himself. Consequently there was sufficient rainfall in the place named Ajanābha. When *yajña-pati* wants to, He can do anything without the help of any subordinate. Therefore the Supreme Lord is known as almighty. In the present age of Kali there will eventually be a great scarcity of water (*anāvṛṣṭi*), for the general populace, due to ignorance and the scarcity of yajñic ingredients, will neglect to perform *yajñas. Śrīmad-Bhāgavatam* therefore advises: *yajñaiḥ saṅkīrtana-prāyaiḥ yajanti hi sumedhasaḥ.* After all, *yajña* is meant to satisfy the Supreme Personality of Godhead. In this age of Kali, there is great scarcity and ignorance; nonetheless, everyone can perform *saṅkīrtana-yajña.* Every family in every society can conduct *saṅkīrtana-yajña* at least every evening. In this way there will be no disturbance or scarcity of rain. It is essential for the people in this age to perform the *saṅkīrtana-yajña* in order to be materially happy and to advance spiritually.

TEXT 4

नाभिस्तु यथाभिलषितं सुप्रजस्त्वमवरुध्यातिप्रमोदभरविह्वलो गद्गदाक्षरया गिरा स्वैरं गृहीत नरलोकसधर्मं भगवन्तं पुराणपुरुषं मायाविलसितमतिर्वत्स तातेति सानुरागमुपलालयन् परां निर्वृतिमुपगतः ॥४॥

nābhis tu yathābhilaṣitaṁ suprajastvam avarudhyāti-pramoda-bhara-
vihvalo gadgadākṣarayā girā svairaṁ gṛhīta-naraloka-sadharmaṁ
bhagavantaṁ purāṇa-puruṣaṁ māyā-vilasita-matir vatsa tāteti
sānurāgam upalālayan parāṁ nirvṛtim upagataḥ.

nābhiḥ—King Nābhi; *tu*—certainly; *yathā-abhilaṣitam*—according to his desire; *su-prajastvam*—the most beautiful son; *avarudhya*—getting; *ati-pramoda*—of great jubilation; *bhara*—by an excess; *vihvalaḥ*—being overwhelmed; *gadgada-akṣarayā*—faltering in ecstasy; *girā*—with a voice; *svairam*—by His independent will; *gṛhīta*—accepted; *nara-loka-sadharmam*—acting as if a human being; *bhagavantam*—the Supreme Personality of Godhead; *purāṇa-puruṣam*—the oldest among living beings; *māyā*—by *yoga-māyā; vilasita*—bewildered; *matiḥ*—his mentality; *vatsa*—my dear son;

tāta—my darling; *iti*—thus; *sa-anurāgam*—with great affection; *upalālayan*—raising; *parām*—transcendental; *nirvṛtim*—bliss; *upagataḥ*—achieved.

TRANSLATION

Due to getting a perfect son according to his desire, King Nābhi was always overwhelmed with transcendental bliss and was very affectionate to his son. It was with ecstasy and a faltering voice that he addressed Him, "My dear son, my darling." This mentality was brought about by yoga-māyā, whereby he accepted the Supreme Lord, the supreme father, as his own son. Out of His supreme good will, the Lord became his son and dealt with everyone as if He were an ordinary human being. Thus King Nābhi began to raise his transcendental son with great affection, and he was overwhelmed with transcendental bliss, joy and devotion.

PURPORT

The word *māyā* is used in the sense of illusion. Considering the Supreme Personality of Godhead to be his own son, Mahārāja Nābhi was certainly in illusion, but this was transcendental illusion. This illusion is required; otherwise how can one accept the supreme father as his own son? The Supreme Lord appears as the son of one of His devotees, just as Lord Kṛṣṇa appeared as the son of Yaśodā and Nanda Mahārāja. These devotees could never think of their son as the Supreme Personality of Godhead, for such appreciation would hamper their relationship of paternal love.

TEXT 5

विदितानुरागमापौरप्रकृति जनपदो राजा नाभिरात्मजं समयसेतु-
रक्षायामभिषिच्य ब्राह्मणेषूपनिधाय सह मेरुदेव्या विशालायां प्रसन्ननिपुणेन तपसा
समाधियोगेन नरनारायणाख्यं भगवन्तं वासुदेवमुपासीनः कालेन तन्महिमा-
नमवाप ॥ ५ ॥

viditānurāgam āpaura-prakṛti jana-pado rājā nābhir ātmajaṁ
samaya-setu-rakṣāyām abhiṣicya brāhmaṇeṣūpanidhāya saha
merudevyā viśālāyāṁ prasanna-nipuṇena tapasā samādhi-yogena
nara-nārāyaṇākhyaṁ bhagavantaṁ vāsudevam upāsīnaḥ kālena tan-
mahimānam avāpa.

vidita—known very well; *anurāgam*—popularity; *āpaura-prakṛti*—among all the citizens and government officers; *jana-padaḥ*—desiring to serve the people in general; *rājā*—the King; *nābhiḥ*—Nābhi; *ātmajam*—his son; *samaya-setu-rakṣāyām*—to protect the people strictly according to the Vedic principles of religious life; *abhiṣicya*—enthroning; *brāhmaṇeṣu*—to the learned *brāhmaṇas; upanidhāya*—entrusting; *saha*—with; *merudevyā*—his wife, Merudevī; *viśālāyām*—in Badarikāśrama; *prasanna-nipuṇena*—performed with great satisfaction and expertise; *tapasā*—by austerities and penances; *samādhi-yogena*—by full *samādhi; nara-nārāyaṇa-ākhyam*—named Nara-Nārāyaṇa; *bhagavantam*—the Supreme Personality of Godhead; *vāsudevam*—Kṛṣṇa; *upāsīnaḥ*—worshiping; *kālena*—in due course of time; *tat-mahimānam*—His glorious abode, the spiritual world, Vaikuṇṭha; *avāpa*—achieved.

TRANSLATION

King Nābhi understood that his son, Ṛṣabhadeva, was very popular among the citizens and among government officers and ministers. Understanding the popularity of his son, Mahārāja Nābhi enthroned Him as the emperor of the world to give protection to the general populace in terms of the Vedic religious system. To do this, he entrusted Him into the hands of learned brāhmaṇas, who would guide Him in administrating the government. Then Mahārāja Nābhi and his wife, Merudevī, went to Badarikāśrama in the Himalaya Mountains, where the King engaged Himself very expertly in austerities and penances with great jubilation. In full samādhi he worshiped the Supreme Personality of Godhead, Nara-Nārāyaṇa, who is Kṛṣṇa in His plenary expansion. By doing so, in course of time Mahārāja Nābhi was elevated to the spiritual world known as Vaikuṇṭha.

PURPORT

When Mahārāja Nābhi saw that his son Ṛṣabhadeva was popular with the general populace and the governmental servants, he chose to install Him on the imperial throne. In addition, he wanted to entrust his son into the hands of the learned *brāhmaṇas.* This means that a monarch was supposed to govern strictly according to Vedic principles under the guidance of learned *brāhmaṇas,* who could advise Him according to the standard Vedic scriptures like *Manu-smṛti* and similar *śāstras.* It is the duty of the king to rule the citizens according to Vedic principles. According to Vedic principles, society is divided into four categories—*brāhmaṇa, kṣatriya, vaiśya* and *śūdra. Cātur-varṇyaṁ mayā sṛṣṭaṁ guṇa-karma-vibhāgaśaḥ.* After dividing society in this way, it is the king's duty to see that everyone executes Vedic principles according to his caste. A *brāhmaṇa* must perform the duty of a *brāhmaṇa* without cheating the public. It is not that one attains the name of a *brāhmaṇa* without the qualifications. It is the king's duty to see that everyone engages in his occupational duty according to Vedic principles. In addition, retirement at the end of life is compulsory. Mahārāja Nābhi, although still a king, retired from family life and went with his wife to a place called Badarikāśrama in the Himalayas, where the Deity Nara-Nārāyaṇa is worshiped. The words *prasanna-nipuṇena tapasā* indicate that the King accepted all kinds of austerity very expertly and jubilantly. He did not at all mind leaving his comfortable life at home, although he was the emperor. Despite undergoing severe austerities and penances, he felt very pleased at Badarikāśrama, and he did everything there expertly. In this way, being fully absorbed in Kṛṣṇa consciousness (*samādhi-yoga*), always thinking of Kṛṣṇa, Vāsudeva, Mahārāja Nābhi attained success at the end of his life and was promoted to the spiritual world, Vaikuṇṭhaloka.

This is the way of Vedic life. One must stop the process of repeated birth and death and return home, back to Godhead. The words *tan-mahimānam avāpa* are significant in this regard. Śrīla Śrīdhara Svāmī says that *mahimā* means liberation in this life. We should act in such a way in this life that after giving up this body, we will become liberated from the bondage of repeated birth and death. This is called *jīvan-mukti.* Śrīla Vīrarāghava Ācārya states that in the *Chāndogya Upaniṣad* there are eight symptoms of a *jīvan-mukta,* a person who is already liberated even when living in this body. The first symptom of one so liberated is that he is freed from all sinful activity (*apahata-pāpa*). As long as one is under the clutches of *māyā* in the material energy, one has to engage in sinful activity. *Bhagavad-gītā* describes such people as *duṣkṛtinaḥ,* which indicates that they are always engaged in sinful activity. One who is liberated in this life does not commit any sinful activities. Sinful activity involves illicit sex, meat-eating, intoxication and gambling. Another symptom of a liberated person is *vijara,* which indicates that he is not subjected to the miseries of old age. Another symptom is *vimṛtyu.* A liberated person prepares himself in such a way that he does not take on any more material bodies, which are destined to die. In other words, he does not fall down again to repeat birth and death. Another symptom is *viśoka,* which indicates that he is callous to material distress and happiness. Another is *vijighatsa,* which indicates that he no longer desires material enjoyment. Another symptom is *apipātā,* which means that he has no desire other than to engage in the devotional service of Kṛṣṇa, his dearmost pursuable Lord. A further symptom is *satya-kāma,* which indicates that all his desires are directed to the Supreme Truth, Kṛṣṇa. He does not want anything else. He is *satya-saṅkalpa.* Whatever he desires is fulfilled by the grace of Kṛṣṇa. First of all, he does not desire anything for his material benefit, and secondly if he desires anything at all, he simply desires to serve the Supreme Lord. That desire is fulfilled by the Lord's grace. That is called *satya-saṅkalpa.* Śrīla Viśvanātha Cakravartī points out that the word *mahimā* means returning to the spiritual world, back home, back to Vaikuṇṭha. Śrī Śukadeva says that the word *mahimā* means that the devotee attains the qualities of the Supreme Personality of Godhead. This is called *sadharma,* or "the same quality." Just as Kṛṣṇa is never born and never dies, His devotees who return to Godhead never die and never take birth within the material world.

TEXT 6

यस्य ह पाण्डवेय श्लोकावुदाहरन्ति —
को नु तत्कर्म राजर्षेर्नाभेरन्वाचरेत्पुमान् ।
अपत्यतामगाद्यस्य हरिः शुद्धेन कर्मणा ॥६॥

yasya ha pāṇḍaveya ślokāv udāharanti—
ko nu tat karma rājarṣer
nābher anv ācaret pumān
apatyatām agād yasya
hariḥ śuddhena karmaṇā

yasya—of whom; *ha*—indeed; *pāṇḍaveya*—O Mahārāja Parīkṣit; *ślokau*—two verses; *udāharanti*—recite; *kaḥ*—who; *nu*—then; *tat*—that; *karma*—work; *rāja-ṛṣeḥ*—of the pious King; *nābheḥ*—Nābhi; *anu*—following; *ācaret*—could execute; *pumān*—a man; *apatyatām*—sonhood; *agāt*—accepted; *yasya*—whose; *hariḥ*—the Supreme Personality of Godhead; *śuddhena*—pure, executed in devotional service; *karmaṇā*—by activities.

TRANSLATION

O Mahārāja Parīkṣit, to glorify Mahārāja Nābhi, the old sages composed two verses. One of them is this: "Who can attain the perfection of Mahārāja Nābhi? Who can attain his activities? Because of his devotional service, the Supreme Personality of Godhead agreed to become his son."

PURPORT

The words *śuddhena karmaṇā* are significant in this verse. If work is not carried out in devotional service, it is contaminated by the modes of material nature. That is explained in *Bhagavad-gītā: yajñārthāt karmaṇo'nyatra loko'yaṁ karma-bandhanaḥ.* Activities performed only for the satisfaction of the Supreme Lord are pure and are not contaminated by the modes of material nature. All other activities are contaminated by the modes of ignorance and passion, as well as goodness. All material activities meant for satisfying the senses are contaminated, and Mahārāja Nābhi did not perform anything contaminated. He simply executed his transcendental activities even when performing *yajña.* Consequently he obtained the Supreme Lord as his son.

TEXT 7

ब्रह्मण्योऽन्यः कुतो नाभेर्विप्रा मङ्गलपूजिताः ।
यस्य बर्हिषि यज्ञेशं दर्शयामासुरोजसा ॥ ७ ॥

brahmaṇyo'nyaḥ kuto nābher
viprā maṅgala-pūjitāḥ
yasya barhiṣi yajñeśaṁ
darśayām āsur ojasā

brahmaṇyaḥ—a devotee of the *brāhmaṇas; anyaḥ*—any other; *kutaḥ*—where is; *nābheḥ*—besides Mahārāja Nābhi; *viprāḥ*—the *brāhmaṇas; maṅgala-pūjitāḥ*—well worshiped and satisfied; *yasya*—of whom; *barhiṣi*—in the sacrificial arena; *yajña-īśam*—the Supreme Personality of Godhead, the enjoyer of all sacrificial ceremonies; *darśayām āsuḥ*—showed; *ojasā*—by their brahminical prowess.

TRANSLATION

[The second prayer is this.] "Who is a better worshiper of brāhmaṇas than Mahārāja Nābhi? Because he worshiped the qualified brāhmaṇas to their full satisfaction, the brāhmaṇas, by their brahminical prowess, showed Mahārāja Nābhi the Supreme Personality of Godhead, Nārāyaṇa, in person."

PURPORT

The *brāhmaṇas* engaged as priests in the sacrificial ceremony were not ordinary *brāhmaṇas.* They were so powerful that they could bring forth the

Supreme Personality of Godhead by their prayers. Thus Mahārāja Nābhi was able to see the Lord face to face. Unless one is a Vaiṣṇava, he cannot call forth the Supreme Personality of Godhead. The Lord does not accept an invitation unless one is a Vaiṣṇava. Therefore it is said in *Padma Purāṇa:*

ṣaṭ-karma-nipuṇo vipro
mantra-tantra-viśāradaḥ
avaiṣṇavo gurur na syād
vaiṣṇavaḥ śva-paco guruḥ

"A scholarly *brāhmaṇa* expert in all subjects of Vedic knowledge is unfit to become a spiritual master without being a Vaiṣṇava, but a person born in a family of a lower caste can become a spiritual master if he is a Vaiṣṇava." These *brāhmaṇas* were certainly very expert in chanting the Vedic *mantras.* They were competent in the performance of the Vedic rituals, and over and above this they were Vaiṣṇavas. Therefore by their spiritual powers they could call on the Supreme Personality of Godhead and enable their disciple, Mahārāja Nābhi, to see the Lord face to face. Śrīla Viśvanātha Cakravartī Ṭhākura comments that the word *ojasā* means "by dint of devotional service."

TEXT 8

अथ ह भगवानृषभदेवः स्ववर्षं कर्मक्षेत्रमनुमन्यमानः प्रदर्शितगुरुकुलवासो लब्धवरैर्गुरुभिरनुज्ञातो गृहमेधिनां धर्माननुशिक्षमाणो जयन्त्यामिन्द्रदत्तायामुभयलक्षणं कर्म समाम्नायाम्नातमभियुञ्जन्नात्मजानामात्मसमानानां शतं जनयामास ॥ ८ ॥

atha ha bhagavān ṛṣabhadevaḥ sva-varṣaṁ karma-kṣetram anumanyamānaḥ pradarśita-gurukula-vāso labdha-varair gurubhir anujñāto gṛhamedhināṁ dharmān anuśikṣamāṇo jayantyām indra-dattāyām ubhaya-lakṣaṇaṁ karma samāmnāyāmnātam abhiyuñjann ātmajānām ātma-samānānāṁ śataṁ janayām āsa.

atha—thereupon (after the departure of his father); *ha*—indeed; *bhagavān*—the Supreme Personality of Godhead; *ṛṣabha-devaḥ*—Ṛṣabhadeva; *sva*—His own; *varṣam*—kingdom; *karma-kṣetram*—the field of activities; *anumanyamānaḥ*—accepting as; *pradarśita*—shown as an example; *gurukula-vāsaḥ*—lived at the *gurukula; labdha*—having achieved; *varaiḥ*—gifts; *gurubhiḥ*—by the spiritual masters; *anujñātaḥ*—being ordered; *gṛha-medhinām*—of the householders; *dharmān*—duties; *anuśikṣamāṇaḥ*—teaching by example; *jayantyām*—in His wife, Jayantī; *indra-dattāyām*—offered by Lord Indra; *ubhaya-lakṣaṇam*—of both types; *karma*—activities; *samāmnāyāmnātam*—mentioned in the scriptures; *abhiyuñjan*—performing; *ātmajānām*—sons; *ātma-samānānām*—exactly like Himself; *śatam*—one hundred; *janayām āsa*—begot.

TRANSLATION

After Nābhi Mahārāja departed for Badarikāśrama, the Supreme Lord, Ṛṣabhadeva, understood that His kingdom was His field of activities. He therefore showed Himself as an example and taught the duties of a householder by first accepting brahmacarya under the direction of spiritual masters. He also went to live at the spiritual masters' place, gurukula. After His education was finished, He gave gifts (guru-dakṣiṇā) to His spiritual masters and then accepted the life of a householder. He took a wife named Jayantī and begot one hundred sons who were as powerful and qualified as He Himself. His wife Jayantī had been offered to Him by Indra, the King of heaven. Ṛṣabhadeva and Jayantī performed householder life in an exemplary way, carrying out ritualistic activities ordained by the śruti and smṛti śāstra.

PURPORT

Being an incarnation of the Supreme Personality of Godhead, Ṛṣabhadeva had nothing to do with material affairs. As stated in *Bhagavad-gītā, paritrāṇāya sādhūnāṁ vināśāya ca duṣkṛtām:* the purpose of an incarnation is to liberate His devotees and to stop the demoniac activities of nondevotees. These are the two functions of the Supreme Lord when He incarnates. Śrī Caitanya Mahāprabhu has said that in order to preach, one must live a practical life and show people how to do things. *Āpani ācari' bhakti śikhāimu sabāre.* One cannot teach others unless he behaves the same way himself. Ṛṣabhadeva was an ideal king, and He took His education in the *gurukula,* although He was already educated because the Supreme Lord is omniscient. Although Ṛṣabhadeva had nothing to learn from *gurukula,* He went there just to teach the people in general how to take an education from the right source, from Vedic teachers. He then entered householder life and lived according to the principles of Vedic knowledge —*śruti* and *smṛti.* In his *Bhakti-rasāmṛta-sindhu* (1.2.10) Śrīla Rūpa Gosvāmī, quoting the *Skanda Purāṇa,* states:

śruti-smṛti-purāṇādi-
pañcarātra-vidhiṁ vinā
aikāntikī harer bhaktir
utpātāyaiva kalpate

Human society must follow the instructions received from *śruti* and *smṛti,* Vedic literature. Practically applied in life this is worship of the Supreme Personality of Godhead according to the *pāñcarātrika-vidhi.* Every human being must advance his spiritual life and at the end return home, back to Godhead. Mahārāja Ṛṣabhadeva strictly followed all these principles. He remained an ideal *gṛhastha* and taught His sons how to become perfect in spiritual life. These are some examples of how He ruled the earth and completed His mission as an incarnation.

TEXT 9

येषां खलु महायोगी भरतो ज्येष्ठः श्रेष्ठगुण आसीद्येनेदं वर्षं भारतमिति व्यपदिशन्ति ॥९॥

yeṣāṁ khalu mahā-yogī bharato jyeṣṭhaḥ śreṣṭha-guṇa āsīd yenedaṁ varṣaṁ bhāratam iti vyapadiśanti.

yeṣām—of whom; *khalu*—indeed; *mahā-yogī*—a very highly exalted devotee of the Lord; *bharataḥ*—Bharata; *jyeṣṭhaḥ*—the eldest; *śreṣṭha-guṇaḥ*—qualified with the best attributes; *āsīt*—was; *yena*—by whom; *idam*—this; *varṣam*—planet; *bhāratam*—Bhārata; *iti*—thus; *vyapadiśanti*—people call.

TRANSLATION

Of Ṛṣabhadeva's one hundred sons, the eldest, named Bharata, was a great, exalted devotee qualified with the best attributes. In his honor, this planet has become known as Bhārata-varṣa.

PURPORT

This planet known as Bhārata-varṣa is also called *puṇya-bhūmi,* the pious land. At the present moment Bhārata-bhūmi, or Bhārata-varṣa, is a small piece of land extending from the Himalaya Mountains to Cape Comorin. Sometimes this peninsula is called *puṇya-bhūmi.* Śrī Caitanya Mahāprabhu has given special importance to the people of this land.

bhārata-bhūmite haila manuṣya-janma yāra
janma sārthaka kari' kara para-upakāra

"One who has taken his birth as a human being in the land of India (Bhārata-varṣa) should make his life successful and work for the benefit of all other people." (*Cc. Ādi* 9.41) The inhabitants of this piece of land are very fortunate. They can purify their existence by accepting this Kṛṣṇa consciousness movement and go outside Bhārata-bhūmi (India) and preach this cult to benefit the whole world.

TEXT 10

तमनु कुशावर्त इलावर्तो ब्रह्मावर्तो मलयः केतुर्भद्रसेन इन्द्रस्पृग्विदर्भः कीकट इति नव नवति प्रधानाः ॥१०॥

tam anu kuśāvarta ilāvarto brahmāvarto malayaḥ ketur bhadrasena indraspṛg vidarbhaḥ kīkaṭa iti nava navati pradhānāḥ.

tam—him; *anu*—following; *kuśāvarta*—Kuśāvarta; *ilāvartaḥ*—Ilāvarta; *brahmāvartaḥ*—Brahmāvarta; *malayaḥ*—Malaya; *ketuḥ*—Ketu; *bhadra-senaḥ*—Bhadrasena; *indra-spṛk*—Indraspṛk; *vidarbhaḥ*—Vidarbha; *kīkaṭaḥ*—Kīkaṭa; *iti*—thus; *nava*—nine; *navati*—ninety; *pradhānāḥ*—older than.

TRANSLATION

Following Bharata, there were ninety-nine other sons. Among these were nine elderly sons, named Kuśāvarta, Ilāvarta, Brahmāvarta, Malaya, Ketu, Bhadrasena, Indraspṛk, Vidarbha and Kīkaṭa.

TEXTS 11–12

कविर्हविरन्तरिक्षः प्रबुद्धः पिप्पलायनः ।
आविर्होत्रोऽथ द्रुमिलश्चमसः करभाजनः ॥११॥

इति भागवतधर्मदर्शना नव महाभागवतास्तेषां सुचरितं भगवन्महिमोपबृंहितं वसुदेवनारदसंवादमुपशमायनमुपरिष्टाद्वर्णयिष्यामः ॥१२॥

kavir havir antarikṣaḥ
prabuddhaḥ pippalāyanaḥ
āvirhotro'tha drumilaś
camasaḥ karabhājanaḥ

iti bhāgavata-dharma-darśanā nava mahā-bhāgavatās teṣāṁ sucaritaṁ bhagavan-mahimopabṛṁhitaṁ vasudeva-nārada-saṁvādam upaśamāyanam upariṣṭād varṇayiṣyāmaḥ.

kaviḥ—Kavi; *haviḥ*—Havi; *antarikṣaḥ*—Antarikṣa; *prabuddhaḥ*—Prabuddha; *pippalāyanaḥ*—Pippalāyana; *āvirhotraḥ*—Āvirhotra; *atha*—also; *drumilaḥ*—Drumila; *camasaḥ*—Camasa; *karabhājanaḥ*—Karabhājana; *iti*—thus; *bhāgavata-dharma-darśanāḥ*—authorized preachers of *Śrīmad-Bhāgavatam; nava*—nine; *mahā-bhāgavatāḥ*—highly advanced devotees; *teṣām*—of them; *sucaritam*—good characteristics; *bhagavat-mahimā-upabṛṁhitam*—accompanied by the glories of the Supreme Lord; *vasudeva-nārada-saṁvādam*—within the conversation between Vasudeva and Nārada; *upaśamāyanam*—which gives full satisfaction to the mind; *upariṣṭāt*—hereafter (in the Eleventh Canto); *varṇayiṣyāmaḥ*—I shall vividly explain.

TRANSLATION

In addition to these sons were Kavi, Havi, Antarikṣa, Prabuddha, Pippalāyana, Āvirhotra, Drumila, Camasa and Karabhājana. These were all very exalted, advanced devotees and authorized preachers of Śrīmad-Bhāgavatam. These devotees were glorified due to their strong devotion to Vāsudeva, the Supreme Personality of Godhead. Therefore they were very exalted. To satisfy the mind perfectly, I [Śukadeva Gosvāmī] shall hereafter describe the characteristics of these nine devotees when I discuss the conversation between Nārada and Vasudeva.

TEXT 13

यवीयांस एकाशीतिर्जायन्तेयाः पितुरादेशकरा महाशालीना महाश्रोत्रिया यज्ञशीलाः कर्मविशुद्धा ब्राह्मणा बभूवुः ॥१३॥

yavīyāṁsa ekāśītir jāyanteyāḥ pitur ādeśakarā mahā-śālīnā mahā-
śrotriyā yajña-śīlāḥ karma-viśuddhā brāhmaṇā babhūvuḥ.

yavīyāṁsaḥ—younger; *ekāśītiḥ*—numbering eighty-one; *jāyanteyāḥ*—the sons of Jayantī, the wife of Ṛṣabhadeva; *pituḥ*—of their father; *ādeśakarāḥ*—following the order; *mahā-śālīnāḥ*—well-behaved, well cultured; *mahā-śrotriyāḥ*—extremely learned in Vedic knowledge; *yajña-śīlāḥ*—expert in performing ritualistic ceremonies; *karma-viśuddhāḥ*—very pure in their activities; *brāhmaṇāḥ*—qualified *brāhmaṇas; babhūvuḥ*—became.

TRANSLATION

In addition to these nineteen sons mentioned above, there were eighty-one younger ones, all born of Ṛṣabhadeva and Jayantī. According to the

order of their father, they became well cultured, well behaved, very pure in their activities and expert in Vedic knowledge and the performance of Vedic rituals. Thus they all became perfectly qualified brāhmaṇas.

PURPORT

From this verse we have good information of how the castes are qualified according to quality and work. Ṛṣabhadeva, a king, was certainly a *kṣatriya.* He had a hundred sons, and out of these, ten were engaged as *kṣatriyas* and ruled the planet. Nine sons became good preachers of *Śrīmad-Bhāgavatam* (*mahā-bhāgavatas*), and this indicates that they were above the position of *brāhmaṇas.* The other eighty-one sons became highly qualified *brāhmaṇas.* These are some practical examples of how one can become fit for a certain type of activity by qualification, not by birth. All the sons of Mahārāja Ṛṣabhadeva were *kṣatriyas* by birth, but by quality some of them became *kṣatriyas,* and some became *brāhmaṇas.* Nine became preachers of *Śrīmad-Bhāgavatam* (*bhāgavata-dharma-darśanāḥ*), which means that they were above the categories of *kṣatriya* and *brāhmaṇa.*

TEXT 14

भगवानृषभसंज्ञ आत्मतन्त्रः स्वयं नित्यनिवृत्तानर्थपरम्परः केवलानन्दानुभव ईश्वर एव विपरीतवत्कर्माण्यारभमाणः कालेनानुगतं धर्ममाचरणेनोपशि-क्षयन्नतद्विदां सम उपशान्तो मैत्रः कारुणिको धर्मार्थयशःप्रजानन्दामृतावरोधेन गृहेषु लोकं नियमयत् ॥१४॥

bhagavān ṛṣabha-saṁjña ātma-tantraḥ svayaṁ nitya-nivṛttānartha-paramparaḥ kevalānandānubhava īśvara eva viparītavat karmāṇy ārabhamāṇaḥ kālenānugataṁ dharmam ācaraṇenopaśikṣayann atad-vidāṁ sama upaśānto maitraḥ kāruṇiko dharmārtha- yaśaḥ- prajānan-dāmṛtāvarodhena gṛheṣu lokaṁ niyamayat.

bhagavān—the Supreme Personality of Godhead; *ṛṣabha*—Ṛṣabha; *saṁjñaḥ*—named; *ātma-tantraḥ*—fully independent; *svayam*—personally; *nitya*—eternally; *nivṛtta*—free from; *anartha*—of things not wanted (birth, old age, disease and death); *paramparaḥ*—the continual succession, one after another; *kevala*—only; *ānanda-anubhavaḥ*—full of transcendental bliss; *īśvaraḥ*—the Supreme Lord, the controller; *eva*—indeed; *viparīta-vat*—just like the opposite; *karmāṇi*—material activities; *ārabhamāṇaḥ*—performing; *kālena*—in course of time; *anugatam*—neglected; *dharmam*—the *varṇāśrama-dharma;*

ācaraṇena—by executing; *upaśikṣayan*—teaching; *a-tat-vidām*—persons who are in ignorance; *samaḥ*—equipoised; *upaśāntaḥ*—undisturbed by the material senses; *maitraḥ*—very friendly to everyone; *kāruṇikaḥ*—very merciful to all; *dharma*—religious principles; *artha*—economic development; *yaśaḥ*—reputation; *prajā*—sons and daughters; *ānanda*—material pleasure; *amṛta*—eternal life; *avarodhena*—for achieving; *gṛheṣu*—in household life; *lokam*—the people in general; *niyamayat*—He regulated.

TRANSLATION

Being an incarnation of the Supreme Personality of Godhead, Lord Ṛṣabhadeva was fully independent because His form was spiritual, eternal and full of transcendental bliss. He eternally had nothing to do with the four principles of material misery [birth, death, old age and disease]. Nor was He materially attached. He was always equipoised, and He saw everyone on the same level. He was unhappy to see others unhappy, and He was the well-wisher of all living entities. Although He was a perfect personality, the Supreme Lord and controller of all, He nonetheless acted as if He were an ordinary conditioned soul. Therefore He strictly followed the principles of varṇāśrama-dharma and acted accordingly. In due course of time, the principles of varṇāśrama-dharma had become neglected; therefore through His personal characteristics and behavior, He taught the ignorant public how to perform duties within the varṇāśrama-dharma. In this way He regulated the general populace in householder life, enabling them to develop religion and economic well-being and to attain reputations, sons and daughters, material pleasure and finally eternal life. By His instructions, He showed how people could remain householders and at the same time become perfect by following the principles of varṇāśrama-dharma.

PURPORT

The *varṇāśrama-dharma* is meant for imperfect, conditioned souls. It trains them to become spiritually advanced in order to return home, back to Godhead. A civilization that does not know the highest aim of life is no better than an animal society. As stated in *Śrīmad-Bhāgavatam: na te viduḥ svārtha-gatiṁ hi viṣṇum.* A human society is meant for elevation to spiritual knowledge so that all of the people can be freed from the clutches of birth, death, old age and disease. The *varṇāśrama-dharma* enables human society to become perfectly fit for getting out of the clutches of *māyā,* and by following the regulative principles of *varṇāśrama-dharma,* one can become successful. In this regard, see *Bhagavad-gītā* (3.21–24).

TEXT 15

यद्यच्छीर्षण्याचरितं तत्तदनुवर्तते लोकः ॥१५॥

yad yac chīrṣaṇyācaritaṁ tat tad anuvartate lokaḥ.

yat yat—whatever; *śīrṣaṇya*—by the leading personalities; *ācaritam*—performed; *tat tat*—that; *anuvartate*—follow; *lokaḥ*—the people in general.

TRANSLATION

Whatever action is performed by a great man, common men follow.

PURPORT

A similar verse is also found in *Bhagavad-gītā* (3.21). It is essential for human society to have a section of men perfectly trained as qualified *brāhmaṇas* according to the instructions of Vedic knowledge. Those below the brahminical qualification—administrators, merchants and workers—should take instructions from those ideal people who are considered to be intellectuals. In this way, everyone can be elevated to the highest transcendental position and be freed from material attachment. The material world is described by Lord Kṛṣṇa Himself as *duḥkhālayam aśāśvatam,* a temporary place of misery. No one can stay here, even if he makes a compromise with misery. One has to give up this body and accept another, which may not even be a human body. As soon as one gets a material body, he becomes *deha-bhṛt,* or *dehī.* In other words, he is subjected to all the material conditions. The leaders of society must be so ideal that by following them one can be relieved from the clutches of material existence.

TEXT 16

यद्यपि स्वविदितं सकलधर्मं ब्राह्मं गुह्यं ब्राह्मणैर्दर्शितमार्गेण सामादिभि-रुपायैर्जनतामनुशशास ॥१६॥

yadyapi sva-viditaṁ sakala-dharmaṁ brāhmaṁ guhyaṁ brāhmaṇair darśita-mārgeṇa sāmādibhir upāyair janatām anuśaśāsa.

yadyapi—although; *sva-viditam*—known by Him; *sakala-dharmam*—which includes all different types of occupational duties; *brāhmam*—Vedic instruction; *guhyam*—very confidential; *brāhmaṇaiḥ*—by the *brāhmaṇas; darśita-mārgeṇa*—by the path showed; *sāma-ādibhiḥ*—*sāma, dama, titikṣā* (controlling the mind, controlling the senses, practicing tolerance) and so on; *upāyaiḥ*—by the means; *janatām*—the people in general; *anuśaśāsa*—he ruled over.

TRANSLATION

Although Lord Ṛṣabhadeva knew everything about confidential Vedic knowledge, which includes information about all types of occupational duties, He still maintained Himself as a kṣatriya and followed the instructions of the brāhmaṇas as they related to mind control, sense control, tolerance and so forth. Thus He ruled the people according to the system of varṇāśrama-dharma, which enjoins that the brāhmaṇas instruct the kṣatriyas and the kṣatriyas administer to the state through the vaiśyas and śūdras.

PURPORT

Although Ṛṣabhadeva knew all the Vedic instructions perfectly well, He nonetheless followed the instructions of the *brāhmaṇas* in order to perfectly maintain the social order. The *brāhmaṇas* would give advice according to the *śāstras,* and all the other castes would follow. The word *brahma* means "perfect knowledge of all activities," and this knowledge is very confidentially described in the Vedic literatures. Men trained perfectly as *brāhmaṇas* should know all Vedic literature, and the benefit derived from this literature should be distributed to the general populace. The general populace should follow the perfect *brāhmaṇa.* In this way, one can learn how to control the mind and senses and thus gradually advance to spiritual perfection.

TEXT 17

द्रव्यदेशकालवय:श्रद्धर्त्विग्विविधोद्देशोपचितैः सर्वैरपि क्रतुभिर्यथोपदेशं शतकृत्व इयाज ॥१७॥

dravya-deśa-kāla-vayaḥ-śraddhartvig-vividhoddeśopacitaiḥ sarvair api kratubhir yathopadeśaṁ śata-kṛtva iyāja.

dravya—the ingredients for performing *yajña; deśa*—the particular place, a holy place or a temple; *kāla*—the suitable time, such as springtime; *vayaḥ*—the age, especially youth; *śraddhā*—faith in goodness, not in passion and ignorance; *ṛtvik*—the priests; *vividha-uddeśa*—worshiping different demigods for different purposes; *upacitaiḥ*—enriched by; *sarvaiḥ*—all kinds of; *api*—certainly; *kratubhiḥ*—by sacrificial ceremonies; *yathā-upadeśam*—according to the instruction; *śata-kṛtvaḥ*—one hundred times; *iyāja*—He worshiped.

TRANSLATION

Lord Ṛṣabhadeva performed all kinds of sacrifices one hundred times according to the instructions of the Vedic literatures. Thus He satisfied Lord Viṣṇu in every respect. All the rituals were enriched by first-class ingredients. They were executed in holy places according to the proper time by priests who were all young and faithful. In this way Lord Viṣṇu was worshiped, and the prasāda was offered to all the demigods. Thus the functions and festivals were all successful.

PURPORT

It is said, *kaumāra ācaret prājño dharmān bhāgavatān iha* (*Bhāg.* 7.6.1). A ritual should be performed by young men, even boys, at a tender age in order for the ritual to be performed successfully. From childhood, people should be trained in Vedic culture, especially in devotional service. In this way, one can perfect one's life. A Vaiṣṇava does not disrespect the demigods, but on the other hand he is not so foolish that he accepts each and every demigod as the Supreme Lord. The Supreme Lord is master of all demigods; therefore the demigods are His servants. The Vaiṣṇava accepts them as servants of the Supreme Lord, and he worships them directly. In the *Brahma-saṁhitā,* the important demigods—Lord Śiva, Lord Brahmā and even the incarnations and expansions of Lord Kṛṣṇa like Mahā-Viṣṇu, Garbhodakaśāyī Viṣṇu and all the other *viṣṇu-tattvas,* as well as the *śakti-tattvas* like Durgādevī—are all worshiped by the process of worshiping Govinda with the words *govindam ādi-puruṣaṁ tam ahaṁ bhajāmi.* A Vaiṣṇava worships the demigods in relation to Govinda, not independently. Vaiṣṇavas are not so foolish that they consider the demigods independent of the Supreme Personality of Godhead. This is confirmed in *Caitanya-caritāmṛta. Ekale īśvara kṛṣṇa, āra saba bhṛtya:* the supreme master is Kṛṣṇa, and all others are His servants.

TEXT 18

भगवतर्षभेण परिरक्ष्यमाण एतस्मिन् वर्षे न कश्चन पुरुषो वाञ्छत्यविद्यमा-
नमिवात्मनोऽन्यस्मात्कथञ्चन किमपि कर्हिचिदवेक्षते भर्तर्यनुसवनं विजृम्भि-
तस्नेहातिशयमन्तरेण ॥१८॥

bhagavatarṣabheṇa parirakṣyamāṇa etasmin varṣe na kaścana puruṣo vāñchaty avidyamānam ivātmano'nyasmāt kathañcana kimapi karhicid avekṣate bhartary anusavanaṁ vijṛmbhita-snehātiśayam antareṇa.

bhagavatā—by the Supreme Personality of Godhead; *ṛṣabheṇa*—King Ṛṣabha; *parirakṣyamāṇe*—being protected; *etasmin*—on this; *varṣe*—planet; *na*—not; *kaścana*—anyone; *puruṣaḥ*—even a common man; *vāñchati*—desires; *avidyamānam*—not existing in reality; *iva*—as if; *ātmanaḥ*—for himself; *anyasmāt*—from anyone else; *kathañcana*—by any means; *kimapi*—anything; *karhicit*—at any time; *avekṣate*—does care to see; *bhartari*—toward the master; *anusavanam*—always; *vijṛmbhita*—expanding; *sneha-atiśayam*—very great affection; *antareṇa*—within one's self.

TRANSLATION

No one likes to possess anything that is like a will-o'-the-wisp or a flower in the sky, for everyone knows very well that such things do not exist. When Lord Ṛṣabhadeva ruled this planet of Bhāratavarṣa, even common men did not want to ask for anything, at any time or by any means. No one ever asks for a will-o'-the-wisp. In other words, everyone was completely satisfied, and therefore there was no chance of anyone's asking for anything. The people were absorbed in great affection for the King. Since this affection was always expanding, they were not inclined to ask for anything.

PURPORT

In Bengal the word *ghoḍā-ḍimba* is used, which means "the egg of a horse." Since a horse never lays an egg, the word *ghoḍā-ḍimba* actually has no meaning. In Sanskrit there is a word *kha-puṣpa,* which means "the flower in the sky." No flower grows in the sky; therefore no one is interested in asking for *kha-puṣpa* or *ghoḍā-ḍimba.* During the reign of Mahārāja Ṛṣabhadeva, people were so well equipped that they did not want to ask for anything. They were immensely supplied with all necessities for life due to King Ṛṣabhadeva's good government. Consequently everyone felt full satisfaction and did not want anything. This is the perfection of government. If the citizens are unhappy due to bad government, the heads of government are condemned. During these democratic days, monarchy is disliked by the people, but here is an example of how an emperor of the whole world kept all the citizens fully satisfied by supplying the necessities of life and following the Vedic principles. Thus everyone was happy during the reign of Mahārāja Ṛṣabhadeva, the Supreme Personality of Godhead.

TEXT 19

स कदाचिदटमानो भगवानृषभो ब्रह्मावर्तगतो ब्रह्मर्षिप्रवरसभायां प्रजानां निशामयन्तीनामात्मजानवहितात्मनः प्रश्रयप्रणयभरसुयन्त्रितानप्युपशिक्ष-यन्निति होवाच ॥१९॥

sa kadācid aṭamāno bhagavān ṛṣabho brahmāvarta-gato brahmarṣi-pravara-sabhāyāṁ prajānāṁ niśāmayantīnām ātmajān avahitātmanaḥ praśraya-praṇaya-bhara-suyantritān apy upaśikṣayann iti hovāca.

saḥ—He; *kadācit*—once; *aṭamānaḥ*—while on tour; *bhagavān*—the Supreme Personality of Godhead; *ṛṣabhaḥ*—Lord Ṛṣabha; *brahmāvarta-gataḥ*—when He reached the place known as Brahmāvarta (identified by some as Burma and by others as a place near Kanpura, Uttar Pradesh); *brahma-ṛṣi-pravara-sabhāyām*—in a meeting of first-class *brāhmaṇas; prajānām*—while the citizens; *niśāmayantīnām*—were hearing; *ātmajān*—His sons; *avahita-ātmanaḥ*—attentive; *praśraya*—of good behavior; *praṇaya*—of devotion; *bhara*—by an abundance; *su-yantritān*—well controlled; *api*—although; *upaśikṣayan*—teaching; *iti*—thus; *ha*—certainly; *uvāca*—said.

TRANSLATION

Once while touring the world, Lord Ṛṣabhadeva, the Supreme Lord, reached a place known as Brahmāvarta. There was a great conference of learned brāhmaṇas at that place, and all the King's sons attentively heard the instructions of the brāhmaṇas there. At that assembly, within the hearing of the citizens, Ṛṣabhadeva instructed His sons, although they were already very well-behaved, devoted and qualified. He instructed them so that in the future they could rule the world very perfectly. Thus he spoke as follows.

PURPORT

The instructions of Lord Ṛṣabhadeva to His sons are very valuable if one wants to live peacefully within this world, which is full of miseries. In the next chapter, Lord Ṛṣabhadeva gives His sons these valuable instructions.

Thus end the Bhaktivedanta purports of the Fifth Canto, Fourth Chapter, of the Śrīmad-Bhāgavatam, *entitled "The Characteristics of Ṛṣabhadeva, the Supreme Personality of Godhead."*

CHAPTER FIVE

Lord Ṛṣabhadeva's Teachings to His Sons

In this chapter there is a description of *bhāgavata-dharma,* religious principles in devotional service that transcend religious principles for liberation and the mitigation of material misery. It is stated in this chapter that a human being should not work hard like dogs and hogs for sense gratification. The human life is especially meant for the revival of our relationship with the Supreme Lord, and to this end all kinds of austerities and penances should be accepted. By austere activities, one's heart can be cleansed of material contamination, and as a result one can be situated on the spiritual platform. To attain this perfection, one has to take shelter of a devotee and serve him. Then the door of liberation will be open. Those who are materially attached to women and sense gratification gradually become entangled in material consciousness and suffer the miseries of birth, old age, disease and death. Those who are engaged in the general welfare of all and who are not attached to children and family are called *mahātmās.* Those who are engaged in sense gratification, who act piously or impiously, cannot understand the purpose of the soul. Therefore they should approach a highly elevated devotee and accept him as a spiritual master. By his association, one will be able to understand the purpose of life. Under the instructions of such a spiritual master, one can attain devotional service to the Lord, detachment from material things, and tolerance of material misery and distress. One can then see all living entities equally, and one becomes very eager to know about transcendental subject matters. Endeavoring persistently for the satisfaction of Kṛṣṇa, one becomes detached from wife, children and home. He is not interested in wasting time. In this way one becomes self-realized. A person advanced in spiritual knowledge does not engage anyone in material activity. And one who cannot deliver another person by instructing him in devotional service should not become a spiritual master, father, mother, demigod or husband. Instructing His one hundred sons, Lord Ṛṣabhadeva advised them to accept their eldest brother, Bharata, as their guide and lord, and thereby serve him. Of all living entities, the *brāhmaṇas* are the best, and above the *brāhmaṇas* the Vaiṣṇavas are situated in an even better position. Serving a Vaiṣṇava means serving the Supreme

Personality of Godhead. Thus Śukadeva Gosvāmī describes the characteristics of Bharata Mahārāja and the sacrificial performance executed by Lord Ṛṣabhadeva for the instruction of the general populace.

TEXT 1

ऋषभ उवाच
नायं देहो देहभाजां नृलोके
कष्टान् कामानर्हते विड्भुजां ये ।
तपो दिव्यं पुत्रका येन सत्त्वं
शुद्ध्येद्यस्माद् ब्रह्मसौख्यं त्वनन्तम् ॥१॥

ṛṣabha uvāca
nāyaṁ deho deha-bhājāṁ nṛloke
kaṣṭān kāmān arhate viḍ-bhujāṁ ye
tapo divyaṁ putrakā yena sattvaṁ
śuddhyed yasmād brahma-saukhyaṁ tv anantam

ṛṣabhaḥ uvāca—Lord Ṛṣabhadeva said; *na*—not; *ayam*—this; *dehaḥ*—body; *deha-bhājām*—of all living entities who have accepted material bodies; *nṛ-loke*—in this world; *kaṣṭān*—troublesome; *kāmān*—sense gratification; *arhate*—deserves; *viṭ-bhujām*—of stool-eaters; *ye*—which; *tapaḥ*—austerities and penances; *divyam*—divine; *putrakāḥ*—My dear sons; *yena*—by which; *sattvam*—the heart; *śuddhyet*—becomes purified; *yasmāt*—from which; *brahma-saukhyam*—spiritual happiness; *tu*—certainly; *anantam*—unending.

TRANSLATION

Lord Ṛṣabhadeva told His sons: My dear boys, of all the living entities who have accepted material bodies in this world, one who has been awarded this human form should not work hard day and night simply for sense gratification, which is available even for dogs and hogs that eat stool. One should engage in penance and austerity to attain the divine position of devotional service. By such activity, one's heart is purified, and when one attains this position, he attains eternal, blissful life, which is transcendental to material happiness and which continues forever.

PURPORT

In this verse Lord Ṛṣabhadeva tells His sons about the importance of human life. The word *deha-bhāk* refers to anyone who accepts a material body, but the living entity who is awarded the human form must act differently from animals. Animals like dogs and hogs enjoy sense gratification by eating stool. After undergoing severe hardships all day, human beings are trying to enjoy themselves at night by eating, drinking, having sex and sleeping. At the same time, they have to properly defend themselves. However, this is not human civilization. Human life means voluntarily practicing suffering for the advancement of spiritual life. There is, of course, suffering in the lives of animals and plants, which are suffering due to their past misdeeds. However, human beings should voluntarily accept suffering in the form of austerities and penances in order to attain the divine life. After attaining the divine life, one can enjoy happiness eternally. After all, every living entity is trying to enjoy happiness, but as long as one is encaged in the material body, he has to suffer different kinds of misery. A higher sense is present in the human form. We should act according to superior advice in order to attain eternal happiness and go back to Godhead.

It is significant in this verse that the government and the natural guardian, the father, should educate subordinates and raise them to Kṛṣṇa consciousness. Devoid of Kṛṣṇa consciousness, every living being suffers in this cycle of birth and death perpetually. To relieve them from this bondage and enable them to become blissful and happy, *bhakti-yoga* should be taught. A foolish civilization neglects to teach people how to rise to the platform of *bhakti-yoga.* Without Kṛṣṇa consciousness a person is no better than a hog or dog. The instructions of Ṛṣabhadeva are very essential at the present moment. People are being educated and trained to work very hard for sense gratification, and there is no sublime aim in life. A man travels to earn his livelihood, leaving home early in the morning, catching a local train and being packed in a compartment. He has to stand for an hour or two in order to reach his place of business. Then again he takes a bus to get to the office. At the office he works hard from nine to five; then he takes two or three hours to return home. After eating, he has sex and goes to sleep. For all this hardship, his only happiness is a little sex. *Yan maithunādi-gṛhamedhi-sukhaṁ hi tuccham.* Ṛṣabhadeva clearly states that human life is not meant for this kind of existence, which is enjoyed even by dogs and hogs. Indeed, dogs and hogs do not have to work so hard for sex. A human being should try to live in a different way and should not try to imitate dogs and hogs. The alternative is mentioned. Human life is meant for *tapasya,* austerity and penance. By *tapasya,* one can get out of the material clutches. When one is situated in Kṛṣṇa consciousness, devotional service, his happiness is guaranteed eternally. By taking to *bhakti-*

yoga, devotional service, one's existence is purified. The living entity is seeking happiness life after life, but he can make a solution to all his problems simply by practicing *bhakti-yoga.* Then he immediately becomes eligible to return home, back to Godhead. As confirmed in *Bhagavad-gītā* (4.9):

janma karma ca me divyam
evaṁ yo vetti tattvataḥ
tyaktvā dehaṁ punar janma
naiti mām eti so'rjuna

"One who knows the transcendental nature of My appearance and activities does not, upon leaving the body, take his birth again in this material world, but attains My eternal abode, O Arjuna."

TEXT 2

महत्सेवां द्वारमाहुर्विमुक्ते-
स्तमोद्वारं योषितां सङ्गिसङ्गम् ।
महान्तस्ते समचित्ताः प्रशान्ता
विमन्यवः सुहृदः साधवो ये ॥२॥

mahat-sevāṁ dvāram āhur vimuktes
tamo-dvāraṁ yoṣitāṁ saṅgi-saṅgam
mahāntas te sama-cittāḥ praśāntā
vimanyavaḥ suhṛdaḥ sādhavo ye

mahat-sevām—service to the spiritually advanced persons called *mahātmās; dvāram*—the way; *āhuḥ*—they say; *vimukteḥ*—of liberation; *tamaḥ-dvāram*—the way to the dungeon of a dark, hellish condition of life; *yoṣitām*—of women; *saṅgi*—of associates; *saṅgam*—association; *mahāntaḥ*—highly advanced in spiritual understanding; *te*—they; *sama-cittāḥ*—persons who see everyone in a spiritual identity; *praśāntāḥ*—very peaceful, situated in Brahman or Bhagavān; *vimanyavaḥ*—without anger (one must distribute Kṛṣṇa consciousness to persons who are hostile without becoming angry at them); *suhṛdaḥ*—well-wishers of everyone; *sādhavaḥ*—qualified devotees, without abominable behavior; *ye*—they who.

TRANSLATION

One can attain the path of liberation from material bondage only by rendering service to highly advanced spiritual personalities. These

personalities are impersonalists and devotees. Whether one wants to merge into the Lord's existence or wants to associate with the Personality of Godhead, one should render service to the mahātmās. For those who are not interested in such activities, who associate with people fond of women and sex, the path to hell is wide open. The mahātmās are equipoised. They do not see any difference between one living entity and another. They are very peaceful and are fully engaged in devotional service. They are devoid of anger, and they work for the benefit of everyone. They do not behave in any abominable way. Such people are known as mahātmās.

PURPORT

The human body is like a junction. One may either take the path of liberation or the path leading to a hellish condition. How one can take these paths is described herein. On the path of liberation, one associates with *mahātmās,* and on the path of bondage one associates with those attached to sense gratification and women. There are two types of *mahātmās*—the impersonalist and the devotee. Although their ultimate goal is different, the process of emancipation is almost the same. Both want eternal happiness. One seeks happiness in impersonal Brahman, and the other seeks happiness in the association of the Supreme Personality of Godhead. As described in the first verse: *brahma-saukhyam.* Brahman means spiritual or eternal; both the impersonalist and the devotee seek eternal blissful life. In any case, it is advised that one become perfect. In the words of *Caitanya-caritāmṛta* (*Madhya* 22.87):

asat-saṅga-tyāga,—ei vaiṣṇava-ācāra
'strī-saṅgī'—eka asādhu, 'kṛṣṇābhakta' āra

To remain unattached to the modes of material nature, one should avoid associating with those who are *asat,* materialistic. There are two kinds of materialists. One is attached to women and sense gratification, and the other is simply a nondevotee. On the positive side is association with *mahātmās,* and on the negative side is the avoidance of nondevotees and women-hunters.

TEXT 3

ये वा मयीशे कृतसौहृदार्था
जनेषु देहम्भरवार्तिकेषु ।

गृहेषु जायात्मजरातिमत्सु
न प्रीतियुक्ता यावदर्थाश्च लोके ॥३॥

ye vā mayīśe kṛta-sauhṛdārthā
janeṣu dehambhara-vārtikeṣu
gṛheṣu jāyātmaja-rātimatsu
na prīti-yuktā yāvad-arthāś ca loke

ye—those who; *vā*—or; *mayi*—unto Me; *īśe*—the Supreme Personality of Godhead; *kṛta-sauhṛda-arthāḥ*—very eager to develop love (in a relationship of *dāsya, sakhya, vātsalya* or *mādhurya*); *janeṣu*—to people; *dehambhara-vārtikeṣu*—who are interested only in maintaining the body, not in spiritual salvation; *gṛheṣu*—to the home; *jāyā*—wife; *ātma-ja*—children; *rāti*—wealth or friends; *matsu*—consisting of; *na*—not; *prīti-yuktāḥ*—very attached; *yāvat-arthāḥ*—who live by collecting only as much as required; *ca*—and; *loke*—in the material world.

TRANSLATION

Those who are interested in reviving Kṛṣṇa consciousness and increasing their love of Godhead do not like to do anything that is not related to Kṛṣṇa. They are not interested in mingling with people who are busy maintaining their bodies, eating, sleeping, mating and defending. They are not attached to their homes, although they may be householders. Nor are they attached to wives, children, friends or wealth. At the same time, they are not indifferent to the execution of their duties. Such people are interested in collecting only enough money to keep the body and soul together.

PURPORT

Whether he is an impersonalist or a devotee, one who is actually interested in advancing spiritually should not mingle with those who are simply interested in maintaining the body by means of the so-called advancement of civilization. Those who are interested in spiritual life should not be attached to homely comforts in the company of wife, children, friends and so forth. Even if one is a *gṛhastha* and has to earn his livelihood, he should be satisfied by collecting only enough money to maintain body and soul together. One should not have more than that nor less than that. As indicated herein, a householder should endeavor to earn money for the execution of *bhakti-yoga—śravaṇaṁ kīrtanaṁ viṣṇoḥ smaraṇaṁ pāda-sevanam/ arcanaṁ vandanaṁ dāsyaṁ sakhyam ātma-nivedanam.* A householder should lead such a life that he gets full opportunity to hear and chant. He should worship the Deity at home, observe festivals, invite friends in and give them *prasāda.* A householder should earn money for this purpose, not for sense gratification.

TEXT 4

नूनं प्रमत्तः कुरुते विकर्म
यदिन्द्रियप्रीतय आपृणोति ।
न साधु मन्ये यत आत्मनोऽय-
मसन्नपि क्लेशद आस देहः ॥ ४ ॥

nūnaṁ pramattaḥ kurute vikarma
yad indriya-prītaya āpṛṇoti
na sādhu manye yata ātmano'yam
asann api kleśada āsa dehaḥ

nūnam—indeed; *pramattaḥ*—mad; *kurute*—performs; *vikarma*—sinful activities forbidden in the scriptures; *yat*—when; *indriya-prītaye*—for sense gratification; *āpṛṇoti*—engages; *na*—not; *sādhu*—befitting; *manye*—I think; *yataḥ*—by which; *ātmanaḥ*—of the soul; *ayam*—this; *asan*—being temporary; *api*—although; *kleśa-daḥ*—giving misery; *āsa*—became possible; *dehaḥ*—the body.

TRANSLATION

When a person considers sense gratification the aim of life, he certainly becomes mad after materialistic living and engages in all kinds of sinful activity. He does not know that due to his past misdeeds he has already received a body which, although temporary, is the cause of his misery. Actually the living entity should not have taken on a material body, but he has been awarded the material body for sense gratification. Therefore I think it not befitting an intelligent man to involve himself again in the activities of sense gratification by which he perpetually gets material bodies one after another.

PURPORT

Begging, borrowing and stealing to live for sense gratification is condemned in this verse because such consciousness leads one to a dark, hellish condition. The four sinful activities are illicit sex, meat-eating, intoxication and gambling. These are the means by which one gets another material body that is full of miseries. In the *Vedas* it is said: *asaṅgo hy ayaṁ puruṣaḥ.* The living entity is not really connected with this material world, but due to his tendency to enjoy the material senses, he is put into the material condition. One should perfect his life by associating with devotees. He should not become further implicated in the material body.

TEXT 5

पराभवस्तावदबोधजातो
यावन्न जिज्ञासत आत्मतत्त्वम् ।
यावत्क्रियास्तावदिदं मनो वै
कर्मात्मकं येन शरीरबन्धः ॥५॥

parābhavas tāvad abodha-jāto
yāvan na jijñāsata ātma-tattvam
yāvat kriyās tāvad idaṁ mano vai
karmātmakaṁ yena śarīra-bandhaḥ

parābhavaḥ—defeat, misery; *tāvat*—so long; *abodha-jātaḥ*—produced from ignorance; *yāvat*—as long as; *na*—not; *jijñāsate*—inquires about; *ātma-tattvam*—the truth of the self; *yāvat*—as long as; *kriyāḥ*—fruitive activities; *tāvat*—so long; *idam*—this; *manaḥ*—mind; *vai*—indeed; *karma-ātmakam*—absorbed in material activities; *yena*—by which; *śarīra-bandhaḥ*—bondage in this material body.

TRANSLATION

As long as one does not inquire about the spiritual values of life, one is defeated and subjected to miseries arising from ignorance. Be it sinful or pious, karma has its resultant actions. If a person is engaged in any kind of karma, his mind is called karmātmaka, colored with fruitive activity. As long as the mind is impure, consciousness is unclear, and as long as one is absorbed in fruitive activity, he has to accept a material body.

PURPORT

Generally people think that one should act very piously in order to be relieved from misery, but this is not a fact. Even though one engages in pious activity and speculation, he is nonetheless defeated. His only aim should be emancipation from the clutches of *māyā* and all material activities. Speculative knowledge and pious activity do not solve the problems of material life. One should be inquisitive to understand his spiritual position. As stated in *Bhagavad-gītā* (4.37):

yathaidhāṁsi samiddho'gnir
bhasmasāt kurute'rjuna
jñānāgniḥ sarva-karmāṇi
bhasmasāt kurute tathā

"As a blazing fire turns firewood to ashes, O Arjuna, so does the fire of knowledge burn to ashes all reactions to material activities."

Unless one understands the self and its activities, one has to be considered in material bondage. In *Śrīmad-Bhāgavatam* (10.2.32) it is also said: *ye'nye'ravindākṣa vimukta-māninas tvayy asta-bhāvād aviśuddha-buddhayaḥ.* A person who doesn't have knowledge of devotional service may think himself liberated, but actually he is not. *Āruhya kṛcchreṇa paraṁ padaṁ tataḥ patanty adho'nādṛta-yuṣmad-aṅghrayaḥ:* such people may approach the impersonal Brahman effulgence, but they fall down again into material enjoyment because they have no knowledge of devotional service. As long as one is interested in *karma* and *jñāna,* he continues enduring the miseries of material life—birth, old age, disease and death. *Karmīs* certainly take on one body after another. As far as *jñānīs* are concerned, unless they are promoted to the topmost understanding, they must return to the material world. As explained in *Bhagavad-gītā* (7.19): *bahūnāṁ janmanām ante jñānavān māṁ prapadyate.* The point is to know Kṛṣṇa, Vāsudeva, as everything and surrender unto Him. *Karmīs* do not know this, but a devotee who is one hundred percent engaged in the devotional service of the Lord knows fully what is *karma* and *jñāna;* therefore a pure devotee is no longer interested in *karma* or *jñāna. Anyābhilāṣitā-śūnyaṁ jñāna-karmādy-anāvṛtam.* The real *bhakta* is untouched by any tinge of *karma* and *jñāna.* His only purpose in life is to serve the Lord.

TEXT 6

एवं मनः कर्मवशं प्रयुङ्क्ते
अविद्ययाऽऽत्मन्युपधीयमाने ।
प्रीतिर्न यावन्मयि वासुदेवे
न मुच्यते देहयोगेन तावत् ॥६॥

evaṁ manaḥ karma-vaśaṁ prayuṅkte
avidyayātmany upadhīyamāne
prītir na yāvan mayi vāsudeve
na mucyate deha-yogena tāvat

evam—thus; *manaḥ*—the mind; *karma-vaśam*—subjugated by fruitive activities; *prayuṅkte*—acts; *avidyayā*—by ignorance; *ātmani*—when the living entity; *upadhīyamāne*—is covered; *prītiḥ*—love; *na*—not; *yāvat*—as long as; *mayi*—unto Me; *vāsudeve*—Vāsudeva, Kṛṣṇa; *na*—not; *mucyate*—is delivered; *deha-yogena*—from contact with the material body; *tāvat*—so long.

TRANSLATION

When the living entity is covered by the mode of ignorance, he does not understand the individual living being and the supreme living being, and his mind is subjugated to fruitive activity. Therefore, until one has love for Lord Vāsudeva, who is none other than Myself, he is certainly not delivered from having to accept a material body again and again.

PURPORT

When the mind is polluted by fruitive activity, the living entity wants to be elevated from one material position to another. Generally everyone is involved in working hard day and night to improve his economic condition. Even when one understands the Vedic rituals, he becomes interested in promotion to heavenly planets, not knowing that one's real interest lies in returning home, back to Godhead. By acting on the platform of fruitive activity, one wanders throughout the universe in different species and forms. Unless he comes in contact with a devotee of the Lord, a *guru,* he does not become attached to the service of Lord Vāsudeva. Knowledge of Vāsudeva requires many births to understand. As confirmed in *Bhagavad-gītā* (7.19): *vāsudevaḥ sarvam iti sa mahātmā sudurlabhaḥ.* After struggling for existence for many births one may take shelter at the lotus feet of Vāsudeva, Kṛṣṇa. When this happens, one actually becomes wise and surrenders unto Him. That is the only way to stop the repetition of birth and death. This is confirmed in *Caitanya-caritāmṛta* (*Madhya* 19.151) in the instructions given by Śrī Caitanya Mahāprabhu to Śrīla Rūpa Gosvāmī at Daśāśvamedha-ghāṭa.

brahmāṇḍa bhramite kona bhāgyavān jīva
guru-kṛṣṇa-prasāde pāya bhakti-latā-bīja

The living entity wanders throughout different planets in different forms and bodies, but if by chance he comes in contact with a bona fide spiritual master, by the grace of the spiritual master he receives Lord Kṛṣṇa's shelter, and his devotional life begins.

TEXT 7

यदा न पश्यत्ययथा गुणेहां
स्वार्थे प्रमत्तः सहसा विपश्चित् ।
गतस्मृतिर्विन्दति तत्र तापा-
नासाद्य मैथुन्यमगारमज्ञः ॥७॥

yadā na paśyaty ayathā guṇehāṁ
svārthe pramattaḥ sahasā vipaścit
gata-smṛtir vindati tatra tāpān
āsādya maithunyam agāram ajñaḥ

yadā—when; *na*—not; *paśyati*—sees; *ayathā*—unnecessary; *guṇa-īhām*—endeavor to satisfy the senses; *sva-arthe*—in self-interest; *pramattaḥ*—mad; *sahasā*—very soon; *vipaścit*—even one advanced in knowledge; *gata-smṛtiḥ*—being forgetful; *vindati*—gets; *tatra*—there; *tāpān*—material miseries; *āsādya*—getting; *maithunyam*—based on sexual intercourse; *agāram*—a home; *ajñaḥ*—being foolish.

TRANSLATION

Even though one may be very learned and wise, he is mad if he does not understand that the endeavor for sense gratification is a useless waste of time. Being forgetful of his own interest, he tries to be happy in the material world, centering his interests around his home, which is based on sexual intercourse and which brings him all kinds of material miseries. In this way one is no better than a foolish animal.

PURPORT

In the lowest stage of devotional life, one is not an unalloyed devotee. *Anyābhilāṣitā-śūnyaṁ jñāna-karmādy-anāvṛtam:* to be an unalloyed devotee, one must be freed from all material desires and untouched by fruitive activity and speculative knowledge. On the lower platform, one may sometimes be interested in philosophical speculation with a tinge of devotion. However, at that stage one is still interested in sense gratification and is contaminated by the modes of material nature. The influence of *māyā* is so strong that even a person advanced in knowledge actually forgets that he is Kṛṣṇa's eternal servant. Therefore he remains satisfied in his householder life, which is centered around sexual intercourse. Conceding to a life of sex, he agrees to suffer all kinds of material miseries. Due to ignorance, one is thus bound by the chain of material laws.

TEXT 8

पुंसः स्त्रिया मिथुनीभावमेतं
तयोर्मिथो हृदयग्रन्थिमाहुः ।
अतो गृहक्षेत्रसुताप्तवित्तै-
र्जनस्य मोहोऽयमहं ममेति ॥८॥

puṁsaḥ striyā mithunī-bhāvam etaṁ
tayor mitho hṛdaya-granthim āhuḥ
ato gṛha-kṣetra-sutāpta-vittair
janasya moho'yam ahaṁ mameti

puṁsaḥ—of a male; *striyāḥ*—of a female; *mithunī-bhāvam*—attraction for sexual life; *etam*—this; *tayoḥ*—of both of them; *mithaḥ*—between one another; *hṛdaya-granthim*—the knot of the hearts; *āhuḥ*—they call; *ataḥ*—thereafter; *gṛha*—by home; *kṣetra*—field; *suta*—children; *āpta*—relatives; *vittaiḥ*—and by wealth; *janasya*—of the living being; *mohaḥ*—illusion; *ayam*—this; *aham*—I; *mama*—mine; *iti*—thus.

TRANSLATION

The attraction between male and female is the basic principle of material existence. On the basis of this misconception, which ties together the hearts of the male and female, one becomes attracted to his body, home, property, children, relatives and wealth. In this way one increases life's illusions and thinks in terms of "I and mine."

PURPORT

Sex serves as the natural attraction between man and woman, and when they are married, their relationship becomes more involved. Due to the entangling relationship between man and woman, there is a sense of illusion whereby one thinks, "This man is my husband," or "This woman is my wife." This is called *hṛdaya-granthi,* "the hard knot in the heart." This knot is very difficult to undo, even though a man and woman separate either for the principles of *varṇāśrama* or simply to get a divorce. In any case, the man always thinks of the woman, and the woman always thinks of the man. Thus a person becomes materially attached to family, property and children, although all of these are temporary. The possessor unfortunately identifies with his property and wealth. Sometimes, even after renunciation, one becomes attached to a temple or to the few things that constitute the property of a *sannyāsī,* but such attachment is not as strong as family attachment. The attachment to the family is the strongest illusion. In the *Satya-saṁhitā,* it is stated:

brahmādyā yājñavalkādyā
mucyante strī-sahāyinaḥ
bodhyante kecanaiteṣāṁ
viśeṣam ca vido viduḥ

Sometimes it is found among exalted personalities like Lord Brahmā that the wife and children are not a cause of bondage. On the contrary, the wife actually helps further spiritual life and liberation. Nonetheless, most people are bound by the knots of the marital relationship, and consequently they forget their relationship with Kṛṣṇa.

TEXT 9

यदा मनोहृदयग्रन्थिरस्य
कर्मानुबद्धो दृढ आश्लथेत ।
तदा जनः सम्परिवर्ततेऽस्माद्
मुक्तः परं यात्यतिहाय हेतुम् ॥९॥

yadā mano-hṛdaya-granthir asya
karmānubaddho dṛḍha āślatheta
tadā janaḥ samparivartate'smād
muktaḥ paraṁ yāty atihāya hetum

yadā—when; *manaḥ*—the mind; *hṛdaya-granthiḥ*—the knot in the heart; *asya*—of this person; *karma-anubaddhaḥ*—bound by the results of his past deeds; *dṛḍhaḥ*—very strong; *āślatheta*—becomes slackened; *tadā*—at that time; *janaḥ*—the conditioned soul; *samparivartate*—turns away; *asmāt*—from this attachment for sex life; *muktaḥ*—liberated; *param*—to the transcendental world; *yāti*—goes; *atihāya*—giving up; *hetum*—the original cause.

TRANSLATION

When the strong knot in the heart of a person implicated in material life due to the results of past action is slackened, one turns away from his attachment to home, wife and children. In this way, one gives up the basic principle of illusion [I and mine] and becomes liberated. Thus one goes to the transcendental world.

PURPORT

When, by associating with *sādhus* and engaging in devotional service, one is gradually freed from the material conception due to knowledge, practice and detachment, the knot of attachment in the heart is slackened. Thus one can get freed from conditional life and become eligible to return home, back to Godhead.

TEXTS 10–13

हंसे गुरौ मयि भक्त्यानुवृत्या
वितृष्णया द्वन्द्वतितिक्षया च ।
सर्वत्र जन्तोर्व्यसनावगत्या
जिज्ञासया तपसेहानिवृत्त्या ॥१०॥
मत्कर्मभिर्मत्कथया च नित्यं
मद्देवसङ्गाद् गुणकीर्तनान्मे ।
निर्वैरसाम्योपशमेन पुत्रा
जिहासया देहगेहात्मबुद्धेः ॥११॥
अध्यात्मयोगेन विविक्तसेवया
प्राणेन्द्रियात्माभिजयेन सध्र्यक् ।
सच्छ्रद्धया ब्रह्मचर्येण शश्वद्
असम्प्रमादेन यमेन वाचाम् ॥१२॥
सर्वत्र मद्भावविचक्षणेन
ज्ञानेन विज्ञानविराजितेन ।
योगेन धृत्युद्यमसत्त्वयुक्तो
लिङ्गं व्यपोहेत्कुशलोऽहमाख्यम् ॥१३॥

haṁse gurau mayi bhaktyānuvṛtyā
vitṛṣṇayā dvandva-titikṣayā ca

sarvatra jantor vyasanāvagatyā
jijñāsayā tapasehā-nivṛttyā

mat-karmabhir mat-kathayā ca nityaṁ
mad-deva-saṅgād guṇa-kīrtanān me
nirvaira-sāmyopaśamena putrā
jihāsayā deha-gehātma-buddheḥ

adhyātma-yogena vivikta-sevayā
prāṇendriyātmābhijayena sadhryak
sac-chraddhayā brahmacaryeṇa śaśvad
asampramādena yamena vācām

sarvatra mad-bhāva-vicakṣaṇena
jñānena vijñāna-virājitena
yogena dhṛty-udyama-sattva-yukto
liṅgaṁ vyapohet kuśalo'ham-ākhyam

haṁse—who is a *paramahaṁsa,* or the most exalted, spiritually advanced person; *gurau*—to the spiritual master; *mayi*—unto Me, the Supreme Personality of Godhead; *bhaktyā*—by devotional service; *anuvṛtyā*—by following; *vitṛṣṇayā*—by detachment from sense gratification; *dvandva*—of the dualities of the material world; *titikṣayā*—by tolerance; *ca*—also; *sarvatra* —everywhere; *jantoḥ*—of the living entity; *vyasana*—the miserable condition of life; *avagatyā*—by realizing; *jijñāsayā*—by inquiring about the truth; *tapasā* —by practicing austerities and penances; *īhā-nivṛttyā*—by giving up the endeavor for sense enjoyment; *mat-karmabhiḥ*—by working for Me; *mat-kathayā*—by hearing topics about Me; *ca*—also; *nityam*—always; *mat-deva-saṅgāt*—by association with My devotees; *guṇa-kīrtanāt me*—by chanting and glorifying My transcendental qualities; *nirvaira*—being without enmity; *sāmya*—seeing everyone equally by spiritual understanding; *upaśamena*—by subduing anger, lamentation and so on; *putrāḥ*—O sons; *jihāsayā*—by desiring to give up; *deha*—with the body; *geha*—with the home; *ātma-buddheḥ*—identification of the self; *adhyātma-yogena*—by study of the revealed scriptures; *vivikta-sevayā*—by living in a solitary place; *prāṇa*—the life air; *indriya*—the senses; *ātma*—the mind; *abhijayena*—by controlling; *sadhryak*—completely; *sat-śraddhayā*—by developing faith in the scriptures; *brahmacaryeṇa*—by observing celibacy; *śaśvat*—always; *asampramādena*—by not being bewildered; *yamena*—by restraint; *vācām*

—of words; *sarvatra*—everywhere; *mat-bhāva*—thinking of Me; *vicakṣaṇena* —by observing; *jñānena*—by development of knowledge; *vijñāna*—by practical application of knowledge; *virājitena*—illumined; *yogena*—by practice of *bhakti-yoga; dhṛti*—patience; *udyama*—enthusiasm; *sattva*—discretion; *yuktaḥ*—endowed with; *liṅgam*—the cause of material bondage; *vyapohet*—one can give up; *kuśalaḥ*—in full auspiciousness; *aham-ākhyam* —false ego, false identification with the material world.

TRANSLATION

O My sons, you should accept a highly elevated paramahaṁsa, a spiritually advanced spiritual master. In this way, you should place your faith and love in Me, the Supreme Personality of Godhead. You should detest sense gratification and tolerate the duality of pleasure and pain, which are like the seasonal changes of summer and winter. Try to realize the miserable condition of living entities, who are miserable even in the higher planetary systems. Philosophically inquire about the truth. Then undergo all kinds of austerities and penances for the sake of devotional service. Give up the endeavor for sense enjoyment and engage in the service of the Lord. Listen to discussions about the Supreme Personality of Godhead, and always associate with devotees. Chant about and glorify the Supreme Lord, and look upon everyone equally on the spiritual platform. Give up enmity and subdue anger and lamentation. Abandon identifying the self with the body and the home, and practice reading the revealed scriptures. Live in a secluded place and practice the process by which you can completely control your life air, mind and senses. Have full faith in the revealed scriptures, the Vedic literatures, and always observe celibacy. Perform your prescribed duties and avoid unnecessary talks. Always thinking of the Supreme Personality of Godhead, acquire knowledge from the right source. Thus practicing bhakti-yoga, you will patiently and enthusiastically be elevated in knowledge and will be able to give up the false ego.

PURPORT

In these four verses, Ṛṣabhadeva tells His sons how they can be freed from the false identification arising from false ego and material conditional life. One gradually becomes liberated by practicing as mentioned above. All these prescribed methods enable one to give up the material body (*liṅgaṁ vyapohet*) and be situated in his original spiritual body. First of all one has to accept a bona fide spiritual master. This is advocated by Śrīla Rūpa Gosvāmī in his *Bhakti-rasāmṛta-sindhu: śrī-guru-pādāśrayaḥ.* To be freed from the entanglement of the material world, one has to approach a spiritual master. *Tad-vijñānārthaṁ sa gurum evābhigacchet.* By questioning the spiritual master and by serving him, one can advance in spiritual life. When one engages in devotional service, naturally the attraction for personal comfort—for eating, sleeping and dressing—is reduced. By associating with the devotee, a spiritual standard is maintained. The word *mad-deva-saṅgāt* is very important. There are many so-called religions devoted to the worship of various demigods, but here good association means association with one who simply accepts Kṛṣṇa as his worshipable Deity.

Another important item is *dvandva-titikṣā.* As long as one is situated in the material world, there must be pleasure and pain arising from the material body. As Kṛṣṇa advises in *Bhagavad-gītā, tāṁs titikṣasva bhārata.* One has to learn how to tolerate the temporary pains and pleasures of this material world. One must also be detached from his family and practice celibacy. Sex with one's wife according to the scriptural injunctions is also accepted as *brahmacarya* (celibacy), but illicit sex is opposed to religious principles, and it hampers advancement in spiritual consciousness. Another important word is *vijñāna-virājita.* Everything should be done very scientifically and consciously. One should be a realized soul. In this way, one can give up the entanglement of material bondage.

As Śrī Madhvācārya points out, the sum and substance of these four *ślokas* is that one should refrain from acting out of a desire for sense gratification and should instead always engage in the Lord's loving service. In other words, *bhakti-yoga* is the acknowledged path of liberation. Śrīla Madhvācārya quotes from the *Adhyātma:*

ātmano'vihitaṁ karma
varjayitvānya-karmaṇaḥ
kāmasya ca parityāgo
nirīhety āhur uttamāḥ

One should perform activities only for the benefit of the soul; any other activity should be given up. When a person is situated in this way, he is said to be desireless. Actually a living entity cannot be totally desireless, but when he desires the benefit of the soul and nothing else, he is said to be desireless.

Spiritual knowledge is *jñāna-vijñāna-samanvitam.* When one is fully equipped with *jñāna* and *vijñāna,* he is perfect. *Jñāna* means that one understands the Supreme Personality of Godhead, Viṣṇu, to be the Supreme Being. *Vijñāna* refers to the activities that liberate one from the ignorance of material existence. As stated in *Śrīmad-Bhāgavatam* (2.9.31): *jñānaṁ parama-guhyaṁ me yad vijñāna-samanvitam.* Knowledge of the Supreme Lord is very confidential, and the supreme knowledge by which one understands Him furthers the liberation of all living entities. This knowledge is *vijñāna.* As confirmed in *Bhagavad-gītā* (4.9):

janma karma ca me divyam
evaṁ yo vetti tattvataḥ
tyaktvā dehaṁ punar janma
naiti mām eti so'rjuna

"One who knows the transcendental nature of My appearance and activities does not, upon leaving the body, take his birth again in this material world, but attains My eternal abode, O Arjuna."

TEXT 14

कर्माशयं हृदयग्रन्थिबन्ध-
मविद्ययाऽऽसादितमप्रमत्तः ।
अनेन योगेन यथोपदेशं
सम्यग्व्यपोह्योपरमेत योगात् ॥१४॥

karmāśayaṁ hṛdaya-granthi-bandham
avidyayāsāditam apramattaḥ
anena yogena yathopadeśaṁ
samyag vyapohyoparameta yogāt

karma-āśayam—the desire for fruitive activities; *hṛdaya-granthi*—the knot in the heart; *bandham*—bondage; *avidyayā*—because of ignorance; *āsāditam*—brought about; *apramattaḥ*—not being covered by ignorance or illusion, very careful; *anena*—by this; *yogena*—practice of *yoga; yathā-upadeśam*—as advised; *samyak*—completely; *vyapohya*—becoming free from; *uparameta*—one should desist; *yogāt*—from the practice of *yoga,* the means of liberation.

TRANSLATION

As I have advised you, My dear sons, you should act accordingly. Be very careful. By these means you will be freed from the ignorance of the desire

for fruitive activity, and the knot of bondage in the heart will be completely severed. For further advancement, you should also give up the means. That is, you should not become attached to the process of liberation itself.

PURPORT

The process of liberation is *brahma jijñāsā,* the search for the Absolute Truth. Generally *brahma jijñāsā* is called *neti neti,* the process by which one analyzes existence to search out the Absolute Truth. This method continues as long as one is not situated in his spiritual life. Spiritual life is *brahma-bhūta,* the self-realized state. In the words of *Bhagavad-gītā* (18.54):

brahma-bhūtaḥ prasannātmā
na śocati na kāṅkṣati
samaḥ sarveṣu bhūteṣu
mad-bhaktiṁ labhate parām

"One who is thus transcendentally situated at once realizes the Supreme Brahman and becomes fully joyful. He never laments nor desires to have anything; he is equally disposed to every living entity. In that state, he attains pure devotional service unto Me."

The idea is to enter into the *parā bhakti,* the transcendental devotional service of the Supreme Lord. To attain this, one must analyze one's existence, but when one is actually engaged in devotional service, he should not bother seeking out knowledge. By simply engaging in devotional service undeviatingly, one will always remain in the liberated condition.

māṁ ca yo'vyabhicāreṇa
bhakti-yogena sevate
sa guṇān samatītyaitān
brahma-bhūyāya kalpate
(Bg. 14.26)

The unflinching execution of devotional service is in itself *brahma-bhūta.* Another important feature in this connection is *anena yogena yathopadeśam.* The instructions received from the spiritual master must be followed immediately. One should not deviate from or surpass the instructions of the spiritual master. One should not be simply intent on consulting books but should simultaneously execute the spiritual master's order (*yathopadeśam*). Mystic power should be achieved to enable one to give up the material conception, but when one actually engages in devotional service, one does not need to practice the mystic *yoga* system. The point is that one can give up the practice of *yoga*, but devotional service cannot be given up. As stated in *Śrīmad-Bhāgavatam* (1.7.10):

ātmārāmāś ca munayo
nirgranthā apy urukrame
kurvanty ahaitukīṁ bhaktim
ittham-bhūta-guṇo hariḥ

Even those who are liberated (*ātmārāma*) must always engage in devotional service. One may give up the practice of *yoga* when one is self-realized, but at no stage can one give up devotional service. All other activities for self-realization, including *yoga* and philosophical speculation, may be given up, but devotional service must be retained at all times.

TEXT 15

पुत्रांश्च शिष्यांश्च नृपो गुरुर्वा
मल्लोककामो मदनुग्रहार्थः ।
इत्थं विमन्युरनुशिष्यादतज्ज्ञान्
न योजयेत्कर्मसु कर्ममूढान् ।
कं योजयन्मनुजोऽर्थं लभेत
निपातयन्नष्टदृशं हि गर्ते ॥१५॥

putrāṁś ca śiṣyāṁś ca nṛpo gurur vā
mal-loka-kāmo mad-anugrahārthaḥ
itthaṁ vimanyur anuśiṣyād ataj-jñān
na yojayet karmasu karma-mūḍhān
kaṁ yojayan manujo'rthaṁ labheta
nipātayan naṣṭa-dṛśaṁ hi garte

putrān—the sons; *ca*—and; *śiṣyān*—the disciples; *ca*—and; *nṛpaḥ*—the king; *guruḥ*—the spiritual master; *vā*—or; *mat-loka-kāmaḥ*—desiring to go to My abode; *mat-anugraha-arthaḥ*—thinking that to achieve My mercy is the aim of life; *ittham*—in this manner; *vimanyuḥ*—free from anger; *anuśiṣyāt*—should instruct; *a-tat-jñān*—bereft of spiritual knowledge; *na*—not; *yojayet*—should engage; *karmasu*—in fruitive activities; *karma-mūḍhān*—simply engaged in pious or impious activities; *kam*—what; *yojayan*—engaging; *manu-jaḥ*—a man; *artham*—benefit; *labheta*—can achieve; *nipātayan*—

causing to fall; *naṣṭa-dṛśam*—one who is already bereft of his transcendental sight; *hi*—indeed; *garte*—in the hole.

TRANSLATION

If one is serious about going back home, back to Godhead, he must consider the mercy of the Supreme Personality of Godhead the summum bonum and chief aim of life. If he is a father instructing his sons, a spiritual master instructing his disciples, or a king instructing his citizens, he must instruct them as I have advised. Without being angry, he should continue giving instructions, even if his disciple, son or citizen is sometimes unable to follow his order. Ignorant people who engage in pious and impious activities should be engaged in devotional service by all means. They should always avoid fruitive activity. If one puts into the bondage of karmic activity his disciple, son or citizen who is bereft of transcendental vision, how will one profit? It is like leading a blind man to a dark well and causing him to fall in.

PURPORT

It is stated in *Bhagavad-gītā* (3.26):

na buddhi-bhedaṁ janayed
ajñānāṁ karma-saṅginām
joṣayet sarva-karmāṇi
vidvān yuktaḥ samācaran

"Let not the wise disrupt the minds of the ignorant who are attached to fruitive action. They should be encouraged not to refrain from work, but to work in the spirit of devotion."

TEXT 16

लोकः स्वयं श्रेयसि नष्टदृष्टि-
योऽर्थान् समीहेत निकामकामः ।
अन्योन्यवैरः सुखलेशहेतो-
रनन्तदुःखं च न वेद मूढः ॥१६॥

lokaḥ svayaṁ śreyasi naṣṭa-dṛṣṭir
yo'rthān samīheta nikāma-kāmaḥ
anyonya-vairaḥ sukha-leśa-hetor
ananta-duḥkhaṁ ca na veda mūḍhaḥ

lokaḥ—people; *svayam*—personally; *śreyasi*—of the path of auspiciousness; *naṣṭa-dṛṣṭiḥ*—who have lost sight; *yaḥ*—who; *arthān*—things meant for sense gratification; *samīheta*—desire; *nikāma-kāmaḥ*—having too many lusty desires for sense enjoyment; *anyonya-vairaḥ*—being envious of one another; *sukha-leśa-hetoḥ*—simply for temporary material happiness; *ananta-duḥkham*—unlimited sufferings; *ca*—also; *na*—do not; *veda*—know; *mūḍhaḥ*—foolish.

TRANSLATION

Due to ignorance, the materialistic person does not know anything about his real self-interest, the auspicious path in life. He is simply bound to material enjoyment by lusty desires, and all his plans are made for this purpose. For temporary sense gratification, such a person creates a society of envy, and due to this mentality, he plunges into the ocean of suffering. Such a foolish person does not even know about this.

PURPORT

The word *naṣṭa-dṛṣṭiḥ,* meaning "one who has no eyes to see the future," is very significant in this verse. Life goes on from one body to another, and the activities performed in this life are enjoyed or suffered in the next life, if not later in this life. One who is unintelligent, who has no eyes to see the future, simply creates enmity and fights with others for sense gratification. As a result, one suffers in the next life, but due to being like a blind man, he continues to act in such a way that he suffers unlimitedly. Such a person is a *mūḍha,* one who simply wastes his time and does not understand the Lord's devotional service. As stated in *Bhagavad-gītā* (7.25):

nāhaṁ prakāśaḥ sarvasya
yoga-māyā-samāvṛtaḥ
mūḍho'yaṁ nābhijānāti
loko mām ajam avyayam

"I am never manifest to the foolish and unintelligent. For them I am covered by My eternal creative potency [*yoga-māyā*]; and so the deluded world knows Me not, who am unborn and infallible."

In the *Kaṭha Upaniṣad* it is also said: *avidyāyām antare vartamānāḥ svayaṁ dhīrāḥ paṇḍitaṁ manyamānāḥ.* Although ignorant, people still go to other blind men for leadership. As a result, both are subjected to miserable conditions. The blind lead the blind into the ditch.

TEXT 17

कस्तं स्वयं तदभिज्ञो विपश्चिद्
अविद्यायामन्तरे वर्तमानम् ।
दृष्ट्वा पुनस्तं सघृणः कुबुद्धिं
प्रयोजयेदुत्पथगं यथान्धम् ॥१७॥

kas taṁ svayaṁ tad-abhijño vipaścid
avidyāyām antare vartamānam
dṛṣṭvā punas taṁ saghṛṇaḥ kubuddhiṁ
prayojayed utpathagaṁ yathāndham

kaḥ—who is that person; *tam*—him; *svayam*—personally; *tat-abhijñaḥ*—knowing spiritual knowledge; *vipaścit*—a learned scholar; *avidyāyām antare*—in ignorance; *vartamānam*—existing; *dṛṣṭvā*—seeing; *punaḥ*—again; *tam*—him; *sa-ghṛṇaḥ*—very merciful; *ku-buddhim*—who is addicted to the path of *saṁsāra; prayojayet*—would engage; *utpatha-gam*—who is proceeding on the wrong path; *yathā*—like; *andham*—a blind man.

TRANSLATION

If someone is ignorant and addicted to the path of saṁsāra, how can one who is actually learned, merciful and advanced in spiritual knowledge engage him in fruitive activity and thus further entangle him in material existence? If a blind man is walking down the wrong path, how can a gentleman allow him to continue on his way to danger? How can he approve this method? No wise or kind man can allow this.

TEXT 18

गुरुर्न स स्यात्स्वजनो न स स्यात्
पिता न स स्याज्जननी न सा स्यात् ।
दैवं न तत्स्यान्न पतिश्च स स्या-
न्न मोचयेद्यः समुपेतमृत्युम् ॥१८॥

gurur na sa syāt sva-jano na sa syāt
pitā na sa syāj jananī na sā syāt
daivaṁ na tat syān na patiś ca sa syān
na mocayed yaḥ samupeta-mṛtyum

guruḥ—a spiritual master; *na*—not; *saḥ*—he; *syāt*—should become; *sva-janaḥ*—a relative; *na*—not; *saḥ*—such a person; *syāt*—should become; *pitā*—a father; *na*—not; *saḥ*—he; *syāt*—should become; *jananī*—a mother; *na*—not; *sā*—she; *syāt*—should become; *daivam*—the worshipable deity; *na*—not; *tat*—that; *syāt*—should become; *na*—not; *patiḥ*—a husband; *ca*—also; *saḥ*—he; *syāt*—should become; *na*—not; *mocayet*—can deliver; *yaḥ*—who; *samupeta-mṛtyum*—one who is on the path of repeated birth and death.

TRANSLATION

One who cannot deliver his dependents from the path of repeated birth and death should never become a spiritual master, a father, a husband, a mother or a worshipable demigod.

PURPORT

There are many spiritual masters, but Ṛṣabhadeva advises that one should not become a spiritual master if he is unable to save his disciple from the path of birth and death. Unless one is a pure devotee of Kṛṣṇa, he cannot save himself from the path of repeated birth and death. *Tyaktvā dehaṁ punar janma naiti mām eti so 'rjuna.* One can stop birth and death only by returning home, back to Godhead. However, who can go back to Godhead unless he understands the Supreme Lord in truth? *Janma karma ca me divyam evaṁ yo vetti tattvataḥ.*

We have many instances in history illustrating Ṛṣabhadeva's instructions. Śukrācārya was rejected by Bali Mahārāja due to his inability to save Bali Mahārāja from the path of repeated birth and death. Śukrācārya was not a pure devotee, he was more or less inclined to fruitive activity, and he objected when Bali Mahārāja promised to give everything to Lord Viṣṇu. Actually one is supposed to give everything to the Lord because everything belongs to the Lord. Consequently, the Supreme Lord advises in *Bhagavad-gītā* (9.27):

yat karoṣi yad aśnāsi
yaj juhoṣi dadāsi yat
yat tapasyasi kaunteya
tat kuruṣva mad-arpaṇam

"O son of Kuntī, all that you do, all that you eat, all that you offer and give away, as well as all austerities that you may perform, should be done as an offering unto Me." This is *bhakti.* Unless one is devoted, he cannot give everything to the Supreme Lord. Unless one can do so, he cannot become a spiritual master, husband, father or mother. Similarly, the wives of the *brāhmaṇas* who were performing sacrifices gave up their relatives just to satisfy Kṛṣṇa. This is an example of a wife rejecting a husband who cannot deliver her from the impending dangers of birth and death. Similarly, Prahlāda Mahārāja rejected his father, and Bharata Mahārāja rejected his mother (*jananī na sā syāt*). The word *daivam* indicates a demigod or one who accepts worship from a dependent. Ordinarily, the spiritual master, husband, father, mother or superior relative accepts worship from an inferior relative, but here Ṛṣabhadeva forbids this. First the father, spiritual master or husband must be able to release the dependent from repeated birth and death. If he cannot do this, he plunges himself into the ocean of reproachment for his unlawful activities. Everyone should be very responsible and take charge of his dependents just as a spiritual master takes charge of his disciple or a father takes charge of his son. All these responsibilities cannot be discharged honestly unless one can save the dependent from repeated birth and death.

TEXT 19

इदं शरीरं मम दुर्विभाव्यं
सत्त्वं हि मे हृदयं यत्र धर्मः ।
पृष्ठे कृतो मे यदधर्म आराद्
अतो हि मामृषभं प्राहुरार्याः ॥१९॥

idaṁ śarīraṁ mama durvibhāvyaṁ
sattvaṁ hi me hṛdayaṁ yatra dharmaḥ
pṛṣṭhe kṛto me yad adharma ārād
ato hi māṁ ṛṣabhaṁ prāhur āryāḥ

idam—this; *śarīram*—transcendental body, *sac-cid-ānanda-vigraha; mama*—My; *durvibhāvyam*—inconceivable; *sattvam*—with no tinge of the material modes of nature; *hi*—indeed; *me*—My; *hṛdayam*—heart; *yatra*—wherein; *dharmaḥ*—the real platform of religion, *bhakti-yoga; pṛṣṭhe*—on the back; *kṛtaḥ*—made; *me*—by Me; *yat*—because; *adharmaḥ*—irreligion; *ārāt*—far away; *ataḥ*—therefore; *hi*—indeed; *mām*—Me; *ṛṣabham*—the best of the living beings; *prāhuḥ*—call; *āryāḥ*—those who are advanced in spiritual life, or the respectable superiors.

TRANSLATION

My transcendental body [sac-cid-ānanda-vigraha] looks exactly like a human form, but it is not a material human body. It is inconceivable. I am not forced by nature to accept a particular type of body; I take on a body by My own sweet will. My heart is also spiritual, and I always think of the welfare of My devotees. Therefore within My heart can be found the process of devotional service, which is meant for the devotees. Far from My heart have I abandoned irreligion [adharma] and nondevotional activities. They do not appeal to Me. Due to all these transcendental qualities, people generally pray to Me as Ṛṣabhadeva, the Supreme Personality of Godhead, the best of all living entities.

PURPORT

In this verse the words *idaṁ śarīraṁ mama durvibhāvyam* are very significant. Generally we experience two energies—material energy and spiritual energy. We have some experience of the material energy (earth, water, air, fire, ether, mind, intelligence and ego) because in the material world everyone's body is composed of these elements. Within the material body is the spirit soul, but we cannot see it with the material eyes. When we see a body full of spiritual energy, it is very difficult for us to understand how the spiritual energy can have a body. It is said that Lord Ṛṣabhadeva's body is completely spiritual; therefore for a materialistic person, it is very difficult to understand. For a materialistic person, the completely spiritual body is inconceivable. We have to accept the version of the *Vedas* when our experimental perception cannot understand a subject. As stated in *Brahma-saṁhitā: īśvaraḥ paramaḥ kṛṣṇaḥ sac-cid-ānanda-vigrahaḥ.* The Supreme Lord has a body with form, but that body is not composed of material elements. It is made of spiritual bliss, eternity and living force. By the inconceivable energy of the Supreme Personality of Godhead, the Lord can appear before us in His original spiritual body, but because we have no experience of the spiritual body, we are sometimes bewildered and see the form of the Lord as material. The Māyāvādī philosophers are completely unable to conceive of a spiritual body. They say that the spirit is always impersonal, and whenever they see something personal, they take it for granted that it is material. In *Bhagavad-gītā* (9.11) it is said:

avajānanti māṁ mūḍhā
mānuṣīṁ tanum āśritam

paraṁ bhāvam ajānanto
mama bhūta-maheśvaram

"Fools deride Me when I descend in the human form. They do not know My transcendental nature and My supreme dominion over all that be."

Unintelligent people think that the Supreme Lord accepts a body composed of the material energy. We can easily understand the material body, but we cannot understand the spiritual body. Therefore Ṛṣabhadeva says: *idaṁ śarīraṁ mama durvibhāvyam.* In the spiritual world, everyone has a spiritual body. There is no conception of material existence there. In the spiritual world there is only service and the receiving of service. There is only *sevya, sevā* and *sevaka*—the person served, the process of service and the servant. These three items are completely spiritual, and therefore the spiritual world is called absolute. There is no tinge of material contamination there. Being completely transcendental to the material conception, Lord Ṛṣabhadeva states that His heart is composed of *dharma. Dharma* is explained in *Bhagavad-gītā* (18.66): *sarva-dharmān parityajya mām ekaṁ śaraṇaṁ vraja.* In the spiritual world, every living entity is surrendered to the Supreme Lord and is completely on the spiritual platform. Although there are servitors, the served and service, all are spiritual and variegated. At the present moment, due to our material conception, everything is *durvibhāvya,* inconceivable. Being the Supreme, the Lord is called Ṛṣabha, the best. In terms of the Vedic language, *nityo nityānām.* We are also spiritual. but we are subordinate. Kṛṣṇa, the Supreme Lord, is the foremost living entity. The word *ṛṣabha* means "the chief," or "the supreme," and indicates the Supreme Being, or God Himself.

TEXT 20

तस्माद्भवन्तो हृदयेन जाताः
सर्वे महीयांसममुं सनाभम् ।
अक्लिष्टबुद्ध्या भरतं भजध्वं
शुश्रूषणं तद्भरणं प्रजानाम् ॥२०॥

tasmād bhavanto hṛdayena jātāḥ
sarve mahīyāṁsam amuṁ sanābham
akliṣṭa-buddhyā bharataṁ bhajadhvaṁ
śuśrūṣaṇaṁ tad bharaṇaṁ prajānām

tasmāt—therefore (because I am the Supreme); *bhavantaḥ*—you; *hṛdayena*—from My heart; *jātāḥ*—born; *sarve*—all; *mahīyāṁsam*—the best; *amum*—that; *sa-nābham*—brother; *akliṣṭa-buddhyā*—with your intelligence, without material contamination; *bharatam*—Bharata; *bhajadhvam*—just try to serve; *śuśrūṣaṇam*—service; *tat*—that; *bharaṇam prajānām*—ruling over the citizens.

TRANSLATION

My dear boys, you are all born of My heart, which is the seat of all spiritual qualities. Therefore you should not be like materialistic and envious men. You should accept your eldest brother, Bharata, who is exalted in devotional service. If you engage yourselves in Bharata's service, your service to him will include My service, and you will rule the citizens automatically.

PURPORT

In this verse the word *hṛdaya* indicates the heart, which is also called *uraḥ,* the chest. The heart is situated within the chest, and although instrumentally the son is born with the aid of the genitals, he is actually born from within the heart. According to the heart's situation, the semen takes the form of a body. Therefore according to the Vedic system, when one begets a child his heart should be purified through the ritualistic ceremony known as *garbhādhāna.* Ṛṣabhadeva's heart was always uncontaminated and spiritual. Consequently all the sons born from the heart of Ṛṣabhadeva were spiritually inclined. Nonetheless, Ṛṣabhadeva suggested that His eldest son was superior, and He advised the others to serve him. All the brothers of Bharata Mahārāja were advised by Ṛṣabhadeva to adhere to Bharata's service. The question may be asked why one should be attached to family members, for in the beginning it was advised that one should not be attached to home and family. However, it is also advised, *mahīyasām pāda-rajo-'bhiṣeka*—one has to serve the *mahīyān,* one who is very spiritually advanced. *Mahat-sevāṁ dvāram āhur vimukteḥ:* by serving the *mahat,* the exalted devotee, one's path for liberation is open. The family of Ṛṣabhadeva should not be compared to an ordinary materialistic family. Bharata Mahārāja, Ṛṣabhadeva's eldest son, was specifically very exalted. For this reason the other sons were advised to serve him for his pleasure. That was to be their duty.

The Supreme Lord was advising Bharata Mahārāja to be the chief ruler of the planet. This is the real plan of the Supreme Lord. In the Battle of Kurukṣetra, we find that Lord Kṛṣṇa wanted Mahārāja Yudhiṣṭhira to be the supreme emperor of this planet. He never wanted Duryodhana to take the post. As stated in the previous verse, Lord Ṛṣabhadeva's heart is *hṛdayaṁ yatra dharmaḥ.* The characteristic *dharma* is also explained in *Bhagavad-gītā:* surrender unto the Supreme Personality of Godhead. To protect *dharma* (*paritrāṇāya sādhūnām*), the Lord always wants the ruler of the earth to be a devotee. Then everything goes on nicely for the benefit of everyone. As soon as a demon rules the earth, everything becomes chaotic. At the present moment, the world is inclined toward the democratic process, but the people in general are all contaminated by the modes of passion and ignorance. Consequently they cannot select the right person to head the government. The president is selected by the votes of ignorant *śūdras;* therefore another *śūdra* is elected, and immediately the entire government becomes polluted. If people strictly followed the principles of *Bhagavad-gītā,* they would elect a person who is the Lord's devotee. Then automatically there would be good government. Ṛṣabhadeva therefore recommended Bharata Mahārāja as the emperor of this planet. Serving a devotee means serving the Supreme Lord, for a devotee always represents the Lord. When a devotee is in charge, the government is always congenial and beneficial for everyone.

TEXTS 21–22

भूतेषु वीरुद्भ्य उदुत्तमा ये
सरीसृपास्तेषु सबोधनिष्ठाः ।
ततो मनुष्याः प्रमथास्ततोऽपि
गन्धर्वसिद्धा विबुधानुगा ये ॥२१॥

देवासुरेभ्यो मघवत्प्रधाना
दक्षादयो ब्रह्मसुतास्तु तेषाम् ।
भवः परः सोऽथ विरिञ्चवीर्यः
स मत्परोऽहं द्विजदेवदेवः ॥२२॥

bhūteṣu vīrudbhya uduttamā ye
sarīsṛpās teṣu sabodha-niṣṭhāḥ
tato manuṣyāḥ pramathās tato'pi
gandharva-siddhā vibudhānugā ye

devāsurebhyo maghavat-pradhānā
dakṣādayo brahma-sutās tu teṣām

bhavaḥ paraḥ so'tha viriñca-vīryaḥ
sa mat-paro'haṁ dvija-deva-devaḥ

bhūteṣu—among things generated (with and without symptoms of life); *vīrudbhyaḥ*—than the plants; *uduttamāḥ*—far superior; *ye*—those who; *sarīsṛpāḥ*—moving entities like worms and snakes; *teṣu*—of them; *sa-bodha-niṣṭhāḥ*—those who have developed intelligence; *tataḥ*—than them; *manuṣyāḥ*—the human beings; *pramathāḥ*—the ghostly spirits; *tataḥ api*—better than them; *gandharva*—the inhabitants of Gandharvaloka (appointed singers in the planets of the demigods); *siddhāḥ*—the inhabitants of Siddhaloka, who have all mystic powers; *vibudha-anugāḥ*—the Kinnaras; *ye*—those who; *deva*—the demigods; *asurebhyaḥ*—than the *asuras; maghavat-pradhānāḥ*—headed by Indra; *dakṣa-ādayaḥ*—beginning with Dakṣa; *brahma-sutāḥ*—the direct sons of Brahmā; *tu*—then; *teṣām*—of them; *bhavaḥ*—Lord Śiva; *paraḥ*—the best; *saḥ*—he (Lord Śiva); *atha*—moreover; *viriñca-vīryaḥ*—producing from Lord Brahmā; *saḥ*—he (Brahmā); *mat-paraḥ*—My devotee; *aham*—I; *dvija-deva-devaḥ*—a worshiper of the *brāhmaṇas,* or the Lord of the *brāhmaṇas.*

TRANSLATION

Of the two energies manifest [spirit and dull matter], beings possessing living force [vegetables, grass, trees and plants] are superior to dull matter [stone, earth, etc.]. Superior to nonmoving plants and vegetables are worms and snakes, which can move. Superior to worms and snakes are animals that have developed intelligence. Superior to animals are human beings, and superior to human beings are ghosts because they have no material bodies. Superior to ghosts are the Gandharvas, and superior to them are the Siddhas. Superior to the Siddhas are the Kinnaras, and superior to them are the asuras. Superior to the asuras are the demigods, and of the demigods, Indra, the King of heaven, is supreme. Superior to Indra are the direct sons of Lord Brahmā, sons like King Dakṣa, and supreme among Brahmā's sons is Lord Śiva. Since Lord Śiva is the son of Lord Brahmā, Brahmā is considered superior, but Brahmā is also subordinate to Me, the Supreme Personality of Godhead. Because I am inclined to the brāhmaṇas, the brāhmaṇas are best of all.

PURPORT

In this verse the *brāhmaṇas* are given a position superior to that of the Supreme Lord. The idea is that the government should be conducted under the guidance of the *brāhmaṇas.* Although Ṛṣabhadeva recommended His eldest son, Bharata, as emperor of the earth, he still had to follow the instructions of the *brāhmaṇas* in order to govern the world perfectly. The Lord is worshiped as *brahmaṇya-deva.* The Lord is very fond of devotees, or *brāhmaṇas.* This does not refer to so-called caste *brāhmaṇas,* but to qualified *brāhmaṇas.* A *brāhmaṇa* should be qualified with the eight qualities mentioned in text 24, such as *śama, dama, satya* and *titikṣā.* The *brāhmaṇas* should always be worshiped, and under their guidance the ruler should discharge his duty and rule the citizens. Unfortunately, in this age of Kali, the executive is not selected by very intelligent people, nor is he guided by qualified *brāhmaṇas.* Consequently, chaos results. The mass of people should be educated in Kṛṣṇa consciousness so that according to the democratic process they can select a first-class devotee like Bharata Mahārāja to head the government. If the head of the state is headed by qualified *brāhmaṇas,* everything is completely perfect.

In this verse, the evolutionary process is indirectly mentioned. The modern theory that life evolves from matter is to some extent supported in this verse because it is stated, *bhūteṣu vīrudbhyaḥ.* That is, the living entities evolve from vegetables, grass, plants and trees, which are superior to dull matter. In other words, matter also has the potency to manifest living entities in the form of vegetables. In this sense, life comes out of matter, but matter also comes out of life. As Kṛṣṇa says in *Bhagavad-gītā* (10.8), *ahaṁ sarvasya prabhavo mattaḥ sarvaṁ pravartate:* "I am the source of all spiritual and material worlds. Everything emanates from Me."

There are two energies—material and spiritual—and both originally come from Kṛṣṇa. Kṛṣṇa is the supreme living being. Although it may be said that in the material world a living force is generated from matter, it must be admitted that originally matter is generated from the supreme living being. *Nityo nityānāṁ cetanaś cetanānām.* The conclusion is that everything, both material and spiritual, is generated from the Supreme Being. From the evolutionary point of view, perfection is reached when the living entity attains the platform of a *brāhmaṇa. A brāhmaṇa* is a worshiper of the Supreme Brahman, and the Supreme Brahman worships the *brāhmaṇa.* In other words, the devotee is subordinate to the Supreme Lord, and the Lord is inclined to see to the satisfaction of His devotee. A *brāhmaṇa* is called *dvija-deva,* and the Lord is called *dvija-deva-deva.* He is the Lord of *brāhmaṇas.*

The evolutionary process is also explained in *Caitanya-caritāmṛta* (*Madhya,* Chapter Nineteen), wherein it is said that there are two types of living entities

—moving and nonmoving. Among moving entities, there are birds, beasts, aquatics, human beings and so on. Of these, the human beings are supposed to be the best, but they are few. Of these small numbers of human beings, there are many low-class human beings like *mlecchas,* Pulindas, *bauddhas* and *śabaras.* The human being elevated enough to accept the Vedic principles is superior. Among those who accept the Vedic principles generally known as *varṇāśrama* (presently known as the Hindu system), few actually follow these principles. Of those who actually follow the Vedic principles, most perform fruitive activity or pious activity for elevation to a high position. *Manuṣyāṇāṁ sahasreṣu kaścid yatati siddhaye:* out of many attached to fruitive activity, one may be a *jñānī*—that is, one philosophically inclined and superior to the *karmīs. Yatatām api siddhānāṁ kaścin māṁ vetti tattvataḥ:* out of many *jñānīs,* one may be liberated from material bondage, and out of many millions of liberated *jñānīs,* one may become a devotee of Kṛṣṇa.

TEXT 23

न ब्राह्मणैस्तुलये भूतमन्यत्
पश्यामि विप्राः किमतः परं तु ।
यस्मिन्नृभिः प्रहुतं श्रद्धयाह-
मश्नामि कामं न तथाग्निहोत्रे ॥२३॥

na brāhmaṇais tulaye bhūtam anyat
paśyāmi viprāḥ kim ataḥ paraṁ tu
yasmin nṛbhiḥ prahutaṁ śraddhayāham
aśnāmi kāmaṁ na tathāgni-hotre

na—not; *brāhmaṇaiḥ*—with the *brāhmaṇas; tulaye*—I count as equal; *bhūtam*—entity; *anyat*—other; *paśyāmi*—I can see; *viprāḥ*—O assembled *brāhmaṇas; kim*—anything; *ataḥ*—to the *brāhmaṇas; param*—superior; *tu*—certainly; *yasmin*—through whom; *nṛbhiḥ*—by people; *prahutam*—food offered after ritualistic ceremonies are properly performed; *śraddhayā*—with faith and love; *aham*—I; *aśnāmi*—eat; *kāmam*—with full satisfaction; *na*—not; *tathā*—in that way; *agni-hotre*—in the fire sacrifice.

TRANSLATION

O respectful brāhmaṇas, as far as I am concerned, no one is equal or superior to the brāhmaṇas in this world. I do not find anyone comparable to them. When people know My motive, after performing rituals according

to the Vedic principles, they offer food to Me with faith and love through the mouth of a brāhmaṇa. When food is thus offered unto Me, I eat it with full satisfaction. Indeed, I derive more pleasure from food offered in that way than from the food offered in the sacrificial fire.

PURPORT

According to the Vedic system, after the sacrificial ceremony the *brāhmaṇas* are invited to eat the remnants of the offered food. When the *brāhmaṇas* eat the food, it is to be considered directly eaten by the Supreme Lord. Thus no one can be compared to qualified *brāhmaṇas.* The perfection of evolution is to be situated on the brahminical platform. Any civilization not based on brahminical culture or guided by *brāhmaṇas* is certainly a condemned civilization. Presently human civilization is based on sense gratification, and consequently more and more people are becoming addicted to different types of things. No one respects brahminical culture. Demoniac civilization is attached to *ugra-karma,* horrible activities, and big industries are created to satisfy unfathomable lusty desires. Consequently the people are greatly harassed by governmental taxation. The people are irreligious and do not perform the sacrifices recommended in *Bhagavad-gītā. Yajñād bhavati parjanyaḥ:* by the performance of sacrifice, clouds form and rain falls. Due to sufficient rainfall, there is sufficient production of food. Guided by the *brāhmaṇas,* society should follow the principles of *Bhagavad-gītā.* Then people will become very happy. *Annād bhavanti bhūtāni:* when animals and man are sufficiently fed with grains, they become stronger, their hearts become tranquil and their brains peaceful. They can then advance in spiritual life, life's ultimate destination.

TEXT 24

धृता तनूरुशती मे पुराणी
येनेह सत्त्वं परमं पवित्रम् ।
शमो दमः सत्यमनुग्रहश्च
तपस्तितिक्षानुभवश्च यत्र ॥२४॥

dhṛtā tanūr uśatī me purāṇī
yeneha sattvaṁ paramaṁ pavitram
śamo damaḥ satyam anugrahaś ca
tapas titikṣānubhavaś ca yatra

dhṛtā—maintained by transcendental education; *tanūḥ*—body; *uśatī*—free from material contamination; *me*—My; *purāṇī*—eternal; *yena*—by whom; *iha*—in this material world; *sattvam*—the mode of goodness; *paramam*—supreme; *pavitram*—purified; *śamaḥ*—control of the mind; *damaḥ*—control of the senses; *satyam*—truthfulness; *anugrahaḥ*—mercy; *ca*—and; *tapaḥ*—austerity; *titikṣā*—tolerance; *anubhavaḥ*—realization of God and the living entity; *ca*—and; *yatra*—wherein.

TRANSLATION

The Vedas are My eternal transcendental sound incarnation. Therefore the Vedas are śabda-brahma. In this world, the brāhmaṇas thoroughly study all the Vedas, and because they assimilate the Vedic conclusions, they are also to be considered the Vedas personified. The brāhmaṇas are situated in the supreme transcendental mode of nature—sattva-guṇa. Because of this, they are fixed in mind control [śama], sense control [dama], and truthfulness [satya]. They describe the Vedas in their original sense, and out of mercy [anugraha] they preach the purpose of the Vedas to all conditioned souls. They practice penance [tapasya] and tolerance [titikṣā], and they realize the position of the living entity and the Supreme Lord [anubhava]. These are the eight qualifications of the brāhmaṇas. Therefore among all living entities, no one is superior to the brāhmaṇas.

PURPORT

This is a true description of a *brāhmaṇa. A brāhmaṇa* is one who has assimilated the Vedic conclusions by practicing mind and sense control. He speaks the true version of all the *Vedas.* As confirmed in the *Bhagavad-gītā* (15.15): *vedaiś ca sarvair aham eva vedyaḥ.* By studying all the *Vedas,* one should come to understand the transcendental position of Lord Śrī Kṛṣṇa. One who actually assimilated the essence of the *Vedas* can preach the truth. He is compassionate to conditioned souls who are suffering the threefold miseries of this conditional world due to their not being Kṛṣṇa conscious. A *brāhmaṇa* should take pity on the people and preach Kṛṣṇa consciousness in order to elevate them. Śrī Kṛṣṇa Himself, the Supreme Personality of Godhead, personally descends into this universe from the spiritual kingdom to teach conditioned souls about the values of spiritual life. He tries to induce them to surrender unto Him. Similarly, the *brāhmaṇas* do the same thing. After assimilating the Vedic instructions, they assist the Supreme Lord in His endeavor to deliver conditioned souls. The *brāhmaṇas* are very dear to the

Supreme Lord due to their high *sattva-guṇa* qualities, and they also engage in welfare activities for all conditioned souls in the material world.

TEXT 25

मत्तोऽप्यनन्तात्परतः परस्मात्
स्वर्गापवर्गाधिपतेर्न किञ्चित् ।
येषां किमु स्यादितरेण तेषा-
मकिञ्चनानां मयि भक्तिभाजाम् ॥२५॥

matto 'py anantāt parataḥ parasmāt
svargāpavargādhipater na kiñcit
yeṣāṁ kim u syād itareṇa teṣām
akiñcanānāṁ mayi bhakti-bhājām

mattaḥ—from Me; *api*—even; *anantāt*—unlimited in strength and opulence; *parataḥ parasmāt*—higher than the highest; *svarga-apavarga-adhipateḥ*—able to bestow happiness obtainable by living in the heavenly kingdom, by liberation, or by enjoyment of material comfort and then liberation; *na*—not; *kiñcit*—anything; *yeṣām*—of whom; *kim*—what need; *u*—oh; *syāt*—can there be; *itareṇa*—with any other; *teṣām*—of them; *akiñcanānām*—without needs or without possessions; *mayi*—unto Me; *bhakti-bhājām*—executing devotional service.

TRANSLATION

I am fully opulent, almighty and superior to Lord Brahmā and Indra, the King of the heavenly planets. I am also the bestower of all happiness obtained in the heavenly kingdom and by liberation. Nonetheless, the brāhmaṇas do not seek material comforts from Me. They are very pure and do not want to possess anything. They simply engage in My devotional service. What is the need of their asking for material benefits from anyone else?

PURPORT

The perfect brahminical qualification is stated herein: *akiñcanānāṁ mayi bhakti-bhājām.* The *brāhmaṇas* are always engaged in the devotional service of the Lord: consequently they have no material wants, nor do they possess material things. In *Caitanya-caritāmṛta* (*Madhya* 11.8), Caitanya Mahāprabhu explains the position of pure Vaiṣṇavas who are anxious to return home, back to Godhead. *Niṣkiñcanasya bhagavad-bhajanonmukhasya.* Those who actually want to return back to Godhead are *niṣkiñcana*—that is, they have no desire for material comfort. Śrī Caitanya Mahāprabhu advises, *sandarśanaṁ viṣayiṇām atha yoṣitāṁ ca hā hanta hanta viṣa-bhakṣaṇato'py asādhu:* material opulence and sense gratification through the association of women are more dangerous than poison. *Brāhmaṇas* who are pure Vaiṣṇavas always engage in the Lord's service and are devoid of any desire for material gain. The *brāhmaṇas* do not worship demigods like Lord Brahmā, Indra or Lord Śiva for any material comfort. They do not even ask the Supreme Lord for material profit; therefore it is concluded that the *brāhmaṇas* are the supreme living entities of this world. Śrī Kapiladeva also confirms this in *Śrīmad-Bhāgavatam* (3.29.33):

tasmān mayy arpitāśeṣa-
kriyārthātmā nirantaraḥ
mayy arpitātmanaḥ puṁso
mayi sannyasta-karmaṇaḥ
na paśyāmi paraṁ bhūtam
akartuḥ sama-darśanāt

The *brāhmaṇas* are always dedicated to the Lord's service with their bodies, words and mind. There is no better person than a *brāhmaṇa* who thus engages himself and dedicates himself to the Supreme Lord.

TEXT 26

सर्वाणि मद्धिष्ण्यतया भवद्भि-
श्चराणि भूतानि सुता ध्रुवाणि ।
सम्भावितव्यानि पदे पदे वो
विविक्तदृग्भिस्तदु हार्हणं मे ॥२६॥

sarvāṇi mad-dhiṣṇyatayā bhavadbhiś
carāṇi bhūtāni sutā dhruvāṇi
sambhāvitavyāni pade pade vo
vivikta-dṛgbhis tad u hārhaṇaṁ me

sarvāṇi—all; *mat-dhiṣṇyatayā*—because of being My sitting place; *bhavadbhiḥ*—by you; *carāṇi*—that move; *bhūtāni*—living entities; *sutāḥ*—My dear sons; *dhruvāṇi*—that do not move; *sambhāvitavyāni*—to be respected; *pade pade*—at every moment; *vaḥ*—by you; *vivikta-dṛgbhiḥ*—possessing clear vision and understanding (that the Supreme Personality of Godhead in His Paramātmā feature is situated everywhere); *tat u*—that indirectly; *ha*—certainly; *arhaṇam*—offering respect; *me*—unto Me.

TRANSLATION

My dear sons, you should not envy any living entity—be he moving or nonmoving. Knowing that I am situated in them, you should offer respect to all of them at every moment. In this way, you offer respect to Me.

PURPORT

In this verse the word *vivikta-dṛgbhiḥ,* meaning without envy, is used. All living entities are the abode of the Supreme Personality of Godhead in His Paramātmā feature. As confirmed in *Brahma-saṁhitā: aṇḍāntara-sthaṁ paramāṇu-cayāntara-stham.* The Lord is situated in this universe as Garbhodakaśāyī Viṣṇu and Kṣīrodakaśāyī Viṣṇu. He is also situated within every atom. According to the Vedic statement: *īśāvāsyam idaṁ sarvam.* The Supreme Lord is situated everywhere, and wherever He is situated is His temple. We even offer respects to a temple from a distant place, and all living entities should similarly be offered respect. This is different from the theory of pantheism, which holds that everything is God. Everything has a relationship with God because God is situated everywhere. We should not make any particular distinction between the poor and the rich like the foolish worshipers of *daridra-nārāyaṇa.* Nārāyaṇa is present in the rich as well as the poor. One should not simply think Nārāyaṇa is situated among the poor. He is everywhere. An advanced devotee will offer respects to everyone—even to cats and dogs.

vidyā-vinaya-sampanne
brāhmaṇe gavi hastini
śuni caiva śva-pāke ca
paṇḍitāḥ sama-darśinaḥ

"The humble sage, by virtue of true knowledge, sees with equal vision a learned and gentle *brāhmaṇa,* a cow, an elephant, a dog and a dog-eater [outcaste]." (Bg. 5.18) This *sama-darśinaḥ,* equal vision, should not be mistaken to mean that the individual is the same as the Supreme Lord. They are always distinct. Every individual person is different from the Supreme Lord. It is a mistake to equate the individual living entity with the Supreme Lord on the plea of *vivikta-dṛk, sama-dṛk.* The Lord is always in an exalted position, even though He agrees to live everywhere. Śrīla Madhvācārya, quoting *Padma Purāṇa,* states: *vivikta-dṛṣṭi jīvānāṁ dhiṣṇyatayā parameśvarasya bheda-dṛṣṭiḥ.* "One who has clear vision and who is devoid of envy can see that the Supreme Lord is separate from all living entities, although He is situated in every living entity." Madhvācārya further quotes from *Padma Purāṇa:*

upapādayet parātmānaṁ
jīvebhyo yaḥ pade pade
bhedenaiva na caitasmāt
priyo viṣṇos tu kaścana

"One who sees the living entity and the Supreme Lord as always distinct is very dear to the Lord." *Padma Purāṇa* also states, *yo hareś caiva jīvānāṁ bheda-vaktā hareḥ priyaḥ:* "One who preaches that the living entities are separate from the Supreme Lord is very dear to Lord Viṣṇu."

TEXT 27

मनोवचोदृक्करणेहितस्य
साक्षात्कृतं मे परिबर्हणं हि ।
विना पुमान् येन महाविमोहात्
कृतान्तपाशान्न विमोक्तुमीशेत् ॥२७॥

mano-vaco-dṛk-karaṇehitasya
sākṣāt-kṛtaṁ me paribarhaṇaṁ hi
vinā pumān yena mahā-vimohāt
kṛtānta-pāśān na vimoktum īśet

manaḥ—mind; *vacaḥ*—words; *dṛk*—sight; *karaṇa*—of the senses; *īhitasya*—of all activities (for maintenance of body, society, friendship and so on); *sākṣāt-kṛtam*—directly offered; *me*—of Me; *paribarhaṇam*—worship; *hi*—because; *vinā*—without; *pumān*—any person; *yena*—which; *mahā-vimohāt*—from the great illusion; *kṛtānta-pāśāt*—exactly like the stringent rope of Yamarāja; *na*—not; *vimoktum*—to become free; *īśet*—becomes able.

TRANSLATION

The true activity of the sense organs—mind, sight, words and all the knowledge-gathering and working senses—is to engage fully in My

service. Unless his senses are thus engaged, a living entity cannot think of getting out of the great entanglement of material existence, which is exactly like Yamarāja's stringent rope.

PURPORT

As stated in the *Nārada-pañcarātra*:

sarvopādhi-vinirmuktaṁ
tat-paratvena nirmalam
hṛṣīkeṇa hṛṣīkeśa-
sevanaṁ bhaktir ucyate

This is the conclusion of *bhakti.* All the time, Lord Ṛṣabhadeva has been stressing devotional service, and now He is concluding by saying that all the senses should be engaged in the Lord's service. There are five senses by which we gather knowledge and five senses with which we work. These ten senses and the mind should be fully engaged in the Lord's service. Without engaging them in this way, one cannot get out of the clutches of *māyā.*

TEXT 28

श्रीशुक उवाच

एवमनुशास्यात्मजान् स्वयमनुशिष्टानपि लोकानुशासनार्थं महानुभावः परम-सुहृद्भगवानृषभापदेश उपशमशीलानामुपरतकर्मणां महामुनीनां भक्तिज्ञान-वैराग्यलक्षणं पारमहंस्यधर्ममुपशिक्षमाणः स्वतनयशतज्येष्ठं परमभागवतं भगवज्जनपरायणं भरतं धरणिपालनायाभिषिच्य स्वयं भवन एवोर्वरितशरीर-मात्रपरिग्रह उन्मत्त इव गगनपरिधानः प्रकीर्णकेश आत्मन्यारोपिताहवनीयो ब्रह्मावर्तात्प्रवव्राज ॥२८॥

śrī-śuka uvāca

evam anuśāsyātmajān svayam anuśiṣṭān api lokānuśāsanārthaṁ mahānubhāvaḥ parama-suhṛd bhagavān ṛṣabhāpadeśa upaśama-śīlānām uparata-karmaṇāṁ mahā-munīnāṁ bhakti-jñāna-vairāgya-lakṣaṇaṁ pāramahaṁsya-dharmam upaśikṣamāṇaḥ sva-tanaya-śata-jyeṣṭhaṁ parama-bhāgavataṁ bhagavaj-jana-parāyaṇaṁ bharataṁ dharaṇi-pālanāyābhiṣicya svayaṁ bhavana evorvarita-śarīra-mātra-parigraha unmatta iva gagana-paridhānaḥ prakīrṇa-keśa ātmany āropitāhavanīyo brahmāvartāt pravavrāja.

śrī-śukaḥ uvāca—Śrī Śukadeva Gosvāmī said; *evam*—in this way; *anuśāsya*—after instructing; *ātma-jān*—His sons; *svayam*—personally; *anuśiṣṭān*—highly educated in culture; *api*—although; *loka-anuśāsana-artham*—just to instruct the people; *mahā-anubhāvaḥ*—the great personality; *parama-suhṛt*—everyone's sublime well-wisher; *bhagavān*—the Supreme Personality of Godhead; *ṛṣabha-apadeśaḥ*—who is celebrated and known as Ṛṣabhadeva; *upaśama-śīlānām*—of persons who have no desire for material enjoyment; *uparata-karmaṇām*—who are no longer interested in fruitive activities; *mahā-munīnām*—who are *sannyāsīs; bhakti*—devotional service; *jñāna*—perfect knowledge; *vairāgya*—detachment; *lakṣaṇam*—characterized by; *pāramahaṁsya*—of the best of human beings; *dharmam*—the duties; *upaśikṣamāṇaḥ*—instructing; *sva-tanaya*—of His sons; *śata*—hundred; *jyeṣṭham*—the eldest; *parama-bhāgavatam*—a topmost devotee of the Lord; *bhagavat-jana-parāyaṇam*—a follower of the devotees of the Lord, *brāhmaṇas* and Vaiṣṇavas; *bharatam*—Bharata Mahārāja; *dharaṇi-pālanāya*—with a view to ruling the world; *abhiṣicya*—placing on the throne; *svayam*—personally; *bhavane*—at home; *eva*—although; *urvarita*—remaining; *śarīra-mātra*—the body only; *parigrahaḥ*—accepting; *unmattaḥ*—a madman; *iva*—exactly like; *gagana-paridhānaḥ*—taking the sky as His dress; *prakīrṇa-keśaḥ*—having scattered hair; *ātmani*—in Himself; *āropita*—keeping; *āhavanīyaḥ*—the Vedic fire; *brahmāvartāt*—from the place known as Brahmāvarta; *pravavrāja*—began to travel all over the world.

TRANSLATION

Śukadeva Gosvāmī said: Thus the great well-wisher of everyone, the Supreme Lord Ṛṣabhadeva, instructed His own sons. Although they were perfectly educated and cultured, He instructed them just to set an example of how a father should instruct his sons before retiring from family life. Sannyāsīs, who are no longer bound by fruitive activity and who have taken to devotional service after all their material desires have been vanquished, also learn by these instructions. Lord Ṛṣabhadeva instructed His one hundred sons, of whom the eldest, Bharata, was a very advanced devotee and a follower of Vaiṣṇavas. In order to rule the whole world, the Lord enthroned His eldest son on the royal seat. Thereafter, although still at home, Lord Ṛṣabhadeva lived like a madman, naked and with disheveled hair. Then the Lord took the sacrificial fire within Himself, and He left Brahmāvarta to tour the whole world.

PURPORT

Actually the instructions given to Lord Ṛṣabhadeva's sons were not exactly meant for His sons because they were already educated and highly advanced in knowledge. Rather, these instructions were meant for *sannyāsīs* who intend to become advanced devotees. *Sannyāsīs* must abide by Lord Ṛṣabhadeva's instructions while on the path of devotional service. Lord Ṛṣabhadeva retired from family life and lived like a naked madman even while still with His family.

TEXT 29

जडान्धमूकबधिरपिशाचोन्मादकवदवधूतवेषोऽभिभाष्यमाणोऽपि जनानां गृहीतमौनव्रतस्तूष्णीं बभूव ॥२९॥

jaḍāndha-mūka-badhira-piśāconmādakavad-avadhūta-veṣo
'bhibhāṣyamāṇo'pi janānāṁ gṛhīta-mauna-vratas tūṣṇīṁ babhūva.

jaḍa—idle; *andha*—blind; *mūka*—dumb; *badhira*—deaf; *piśāca*—ghost; *unmādaka*—a madman; *vat*—like; *avadhūta-veṣaḥ*—appearing like an *avadhūta* (having no concern with the material world); *abhibhāṣyamāṇaḥ*—being thus addressed (as deaf, dumb and blind); *api*—although; *janānām*—by the people; *gṛhīta*—took; *mauna*—of silence; *vrataḥ*—the vow; *tūṣṇīm babhūva*—He remained silent.

TRANSLATION

After accepting the feature of avadhūta, a great saintly person without material cares, Lord Ṛṣabhadeva passed through human society like a blind, deaf and dumb man, an idle stone, a ghost or a madman. Although people called Him such names, He remained silent and did not speak to anyone.

PURPORT

The word *avadhūta* refers to one who does not care for social conventions, particularly the *varṇāśrama-dharma.* However, such a person may be situated fully within himself and be satisfied with the Supreme Personality of Godhead, on whom he meditates. In other words, one who has surpassed the rules and regulations of *varṇāśrama-dharma* is called *avadhūta.* Such a person has already surpassed the clutches of *māyā,* and he lives completely separate and independent.

TEXT 30

तत्र तत्र पुरग्रामाकरखेटवाटखर्वटशिबिरव्रजघोषसार्थगिरिवनाश्रमादिष्वनुपथमवनिचरापसदैः परिभूयमानो मक्षिकाभिरिव वनगजस्तर्जनताडनावमेहनष्ठीवनग्रावशकृद्रजःप्रक्षेपपूतिवातदुरुक्तैस्तदविगणयन्नेवासत्संस्थान एतस्मिन् देहोपलक्षणे सदपदेश उभयानुभवस्वरूपेण स्वमहिमावस्थानेनासमारोपिताहंममाभिमानत्वादविखण्डितमनाः पृथिवीमेकचरः परिबभ्राम ॥३०॥

tatra tatra pura-grāmākara-kheṭa-vāṭa-kharvaṭa-śibira-vraja-ghoṣa-sārtha-giri-vanāśramādiṣv anupatham avanicarāpasadaiḥ paribhūyamāno makṣikābhir iva vana-gajas tarjana-tāḍanāvamehana-ṣṭhīvana-grāva-śakṛd-rajaḥ-prakṣepa-pūti-vāta-duruktais tad aviganayann evāsat-saṁsthāna etasmin dehopalakṣaṇe sad-apadeśa ubhayānubhava-svarūpeṇa sva-mahimāvasthānenāsamāropitāhaṁ-mamābhimānatvād avikhaṇḍita-manāḥ pṛthivīm eka-caraḥ paribabhrāma.

tatra tatra—here and there; *pura*—cities; *grāma*—villages; *ākara*—mines; *kheṭa*—agricultural places; *vāṭa*—gardens; *kharvaṭa*—villages in valleys; *śibira*—military encampments; *vraja*—cow pens; *ghoṣa*—residential places of cowherd men; *sārtha*—resting places for pilgrims; *giri*—hills; *vana*—forests; *āśrama*—in the residential places of hermits; *ādiṣu*—and so on; *anupatham*—as He passed through; *avanicara-apasadaiḥ*—by undesirable elements, wicked persons; *paribhūyamānaḥ*—being surrounded; *makṣikābhiḥ*—by flies; *iva*—like; *vana-gajaḥ*—an elephant coming from the forest; *tarjana*—by threats; *tāḍana*—beating; *avamehana*—passing urine on the body; *ṣṭhīvana*—spitting on the body; *grāva-śakṛt*—stones and stool; *rajaḥ*—dust; *prakṣepa*—throwing; *pūti-vāta*—passing air over the body; *duruktaiḥ*—and by bad words; *tat*—that; *avigaṇayan*—without caring about; *eva*—thus; *asat-saṁsthāne*—habitat not fit for a gentleman; *etasmin*—in this; *deha-upalakṣaṇe*—in the shape of the material body; *sat-apadeśe*—called real; *ubhaya-anubhava-svarūpeṇa*—by understanding the proper situation of the body and the soul; *sva-mahima*—in His personal glory; *avasthānena*—by being situated; *asamāropita-aham-mama-abhimānatvāt*—from not accepting the misconception of "I and mine"; *avikhaṇḍita-manāḥ*—undisturbed in mind; *pṛthivīm*—all over the world; *eka-caraḥ*—alone; *paribabhrāma*—He wandered.

TRANSLATION

Ṛṣabhadeva began to tour through cities, villages, mines, countrysides, valleys, gardens, military camps, cow pens, the homes of cowherd men, transient hotels, hills, forests and hermitages. Wherever He traveled, all bad elements surrounded Him, just as flies surround the body of an elephant coming from a forest. He was always being threatened, beaten, urinated upon and spat upon. Sometimes people threw stones, stool and dust at Him, and sometimes people passed foul air before Him. Thus people called Him many bad names and gave Him a great deal of trouble, but He did not care about this, for He understood that the body is simply meant for such an end. He was situated on the spiritual platform, and, being in His spiritual glory, He did not care for all these material insults. In other words, He completely understood that matter and spirit are separate, and He had no bodily conception. Thus, without being angry at anyone, He walked through the whole world alone.

PURPORT

Narottama dāsa Ṭhākura says: *deha-smṛti nāhi yāra, saṁsāra bandhana kāhāṅ tāra.* When a person fully realizes that the material body and world are temporary, he is not concerned with pain and pleasures of the body. As Śrī Kṛṣṇa advises in *Bhagavad-gītā* (2.14):

mātrā-sparśās tu kaunteya
śītoṣṇa-sukha-duḥkha-dāḥ
āgamāpāyino'nityās
tāṁs titikṣasva bhārata

"O son of Kuntī, the nonpermanent appearance of happiness and distress, and their disappearance in due course, are like the appearance and disappearance of winter and summer seasons. They arise from sense perception, O scion of Bharata, and one must learn to tolerate them without being disturbed."

As far as Ṛṣabhadeva is concerned, it has already been explained: *idaṁ śarīraṁ mama durvibhāvyam.* He did not at all possess a material body; and therefore He was tolerant of all the trouble offered to Him by the bad elements in society. Consequently He could tolerate people's throwing stool and dust upon Him and beating Him. His body was transcendental and consequently did not at all suffer pain. He was always situated in His spiritual bliss. As stated in *Bhagavad-gītā* (18.61):

īśvaraḥ sarva-bhūtānāṁ
hṛd-deśe'rjuna tiṣṭhati
bhrāmayan sarva-bhūtāni
yantrārūḍhāni māyayā

"The Supreme Lord is situated in everyone's heart, O Arjuna, and is directing the wanderings of all living entities, who are seated as on a machine, made of the material energy."

Since the Lord is situated in everyone's heart, He is in the heart of hogs and dogs also. If hogs and dogs in their material bodies live in filthy places, one should not think that the Supreme Personality of Godhead in His Paramātmā feature also lives in a filthy place. Although Lord Ṛṣabhadeva was maltreated by the bad elements of the world, He was not at all affected. Therefore it is stated here, *sva-mahima-avasthānena:* "He was situated in His own glory." He was never saddened due to being insulted in the many ways described above.

TEXT 31

अतिसुकुमारकरचरणोरःस्थलविपुलबाह्वंसगलवदनाद्यवयवविन्यासः प्रकृतिसुन्दरस्वभावहाससुमुखो नवनलिनदलायमानशिशिरतारारुणायतनयनरुचिरः सदृशसुभगकपोलकर्णकण्ठनासो विगूढस्मितवदनमहोत्सवेन पुरवनितानां मनसि कुसुमशरासनमुपदधानः परागवलम्बमानकुटिलजटिलकपिशकेशभूरिभारोऽवधूतमलिननिजशरीरेण ग्रहगृहीत इवादृश्यत ॥३१॥

ati-sukumāra-kara-caraṇoraḥ-sthala-vipula-bāhv-aṁsa-gala-vadanādy-avayava-vinyāsaḥ prakṛti-sundara-svabhāva-hāsa-sumukho nava-nalina-dalāyamāna-śiśira-tārāruṇāyata-nayana-ruciraḥ sadṛśa-subhaga-kapola-karṇa-kaṇṭha-nāso vigūḍha-smita-vadana-mahotsavena pura-vanitānāṁ manasi kusuma-śarāsanam upadadhānaḥ parāg-avalambamāna-kuṭila-jaṭila-kapiśa-keśa-bhūri-bhāro'vadhūta-malina-nija-śarīreṇa graha-gṛhīta ivādṛśyata.

ati-su-kumāra—very delicate; *kara*—hands; *caraṇa*—feet; *uraḥ-sthala*—chest; *vipula*—long; *bāhu*—arms; *aṁsa*—shoulders; *gala*—neck; *vadana*—face; *ādi*—and so on; *avayava*—limbs; *vinyāsaḥ*—properly situated; *prakṛti*—by nature; *sundara*—lovely; *sva-bhāva*—natural; *hāsa*—with smiling; *su-mukhaḥ*—His beautiful mouth; *nava-nalina-dalāyamāna*—appearing like the petals of a new lotus flower; *śiśira*—taking away all miseries; *tāra*—the irises; *aruṇa*—reddish; *āyata*—spread wide; *nayana*—with eyes; *ruciraḥ*—lovely;

sadṛśa—such; *subhaga*—beauty; *kapola*—forehead; *karṇa*—ears; *kaṇṭha*—neck; *nāsaḥ*—His nose; *vigūḍha-smita*—by deep smiling; *vadana*—by His face; *mahā-utsavena*—appearing like a festival; *pura-vanitānām*—of women within household life; *manasi*—in the heart; *kusuma-śarāsanam*—Cupid; *upadadhānaḥ*—awakening; *parāk*—all around; *avalambamāna*—spread; *kuṭila*—curly; *jaṭila*—matted; *kapiśa*—brown; *keśa*—of hair; *bhūri-bhāraḥ*—possessing a great abundance; *avadhūta*—neglected; *malina*—dirty; *nija-śarīreṇa*—by His body; *graha-gṛhītaḥ*—haunted by a ghost; *iva*—as if; *adṛśyata*—He appeared.

TRANSLATION

Lord Ṛṣabhadeva's hands, feet and chest were very long.His shoulders, face and limbs were all very delicate and symmetrically proportioned.His mouth was beautifully decorated with His natural smile, and He appeared all the more lovely with His reddish eyes spread wide like the petals of a newly grown lotus flower covered with dew in the early morning. The irises of His eyes were so pleasing that they removed all the troubles of everyone who saw Him. His forehead, ears, neck, nose and all His other features were very beautiful. His gentle smile always made His face beautiful, so much so that He even attracted the hearts of married women. It was as though they had been pierced by arrows of Cupid. About His head was an abundance of curly, matted brown hair. His hair was disheveled because His body was dirty and not taken care of. He appeared as if He were haunted by a ghost.

PURPORT

Although Lord Ṛṣabhadeva's body was very much neglected, His transcendental features were so attractive that even married women were attracted to Him. His beauty and dirtiness combined to make His beautiful body appear as though it were haunted by a ghost.

TEXT 32

यर्हि वाव स भगवान् लोकमिमं योगस्याद्धा प्रतीपमिवाचक्षाणस्त-
त्प्रतिक्रियाकर्म बीभत्सितमिति व्रतमाजगरमास्थितः शयान एवाश्नाति पिबति
खादत्यवमेहति हदति स्म चेष्टमान उच्चरित आदिग्धोद्देशः ॥३२॥

yarhi vāva sa bhagavān lokam imaṁ yogasyāddhā pratīpam
ivācakṣāṇas tat-pratikriyā-karma bībhatsitam iti vratam ājagaram

āsthitaḥ śayāna evāśnāti pibati khādaty avamehati hadati sma ceṣṭamāna uccarita ādigdhoddeśaḥ.

yarhi vāva—when; *saḥ*—He; *bhagavān*—the Personality of Godhead; *lokam*—the people in general; *imam*—this; *yogasya*—to the performance of *yoga; addhā*—directly; *pratīpam*—antagonistic; *iva*—like; *ācakṣāṇaḥ*—observed; *tat*—of that; *pratikriyā*—for counteraction; *karma*—activity; *bībhatsitam*—abominable; *iti*—thus; *vratam*—the behavior; *ājagaram*—of a python (to stay in one place); *āsthitaḥ*—accepting; *śayānaḥ*—lying down; *eva*—indeed; *aśnāti*—eats; *pibati*—drinks; *khādati*—chews; *avamehati*—passes urine; *hadati*—passes stool; *sma*—thus; *ceṣṭamānaḥ*—rolling; *uccarite*—in the stool and urine; *ādigdha-uddeśaḥ*—His body thus smeared.

TRANSLATION

When Lord Ṛṣabhadeva saw that the general populace was very antagonistic to His execution of mystic yoga, He accepted the behavior of a python in order to counteract their opposition. Thus He stayed in one place and lay down. While lying down, He ate and drank, and He passed stool and urine and rolled in it. Indeed, He smeared His whole body with His own stool and urine so that opposing elements might not come and disturb Him.

PURPORT

According to one's destiny, one enjoys allotted happiness and distress, even though one keeps himself in one place. This is the injunction of the *śāstras.* When one is spiritually situated, he may stay in one place, and all his necessities will be supplied by the arrangement of the supreme controller. Unless one is a preacher, there is no need to travel all over the world. A person can stay in one place and execute devotional service suitably according to time and circumstance. When Ṛṣabhadeva saw that He was simply being disturbed by traveling throughout the world, He decided to lie down in one place like a python. Thus He ate, drank, and He passed stool and urine and smeared His body with them so that people would not disturb Him.

TEXT 33

तस्य ह यः पुरीषसुरभिसौगन्ध्यवायुस्तं देशं दशयोजनं समन्तात् सुरभिं चकार ॥३३॥

tasya ha yaḥ purīṣa-surabhi-saugandhya-vāyus taṁ deśaṁ daśa-yojanaṁ samantāt surabhiṁ cakāra.

tasya—His; *ha*—indeed; *yaḥ*—which; *purīṣa*—of the stool; *surabhi*—by the aroma; *saugandhya*—possessing a good fragrance; *vāyuḥ*—the air; *tam*—that; *deśam*—country; *daśa*—up to ten; *yojanam*—*yojanas* (one *yojana* equals eight miles); *samantāt*—all around; *surabhim*—aromatic; *cakāra*—made.

TRANSLATION

Because Lord Ṛṣabhadeva remained in that condition, the public did not disturb Him, but no bad aroma emanated from His stool and urine. Quite the contrary, His stool and urine were so aromatic that they filled eighty miles of the countryside with a pleasant fragrance.

PURPORT

From this we can certainly assume that Lord Ṛṣabhadeva was transcendentally blissful. His stool and urine were so completely different from material stool and urine that they were aromatic. Even in the material world, cow dung is accepted as purified and antiseptic. A person can keep stacks of cow dung in one place, and it will not create a bad odor to disturb anyone. We can take it for granted that in the spiritual world, stool and urine are also pleasantly scented. Indeed, the entire atmosphere became very pleasant due to Lord Ṛṣabhadeva's stool and urine.

TEXT 34

एवं गोमृगकाकचर्यया व्रजंस्तिष्ठन्नासीनः शयानः काकमृगगोचरितः पिबति खादत्यवमेहति स्म ॥३४॥

evaṁ go-mṛga-kāka-caryayā vrajaṁs tiṣṭhann āsīnaḥ śayānaḥ kāka-mṛga-go-caritaḥ pibati khādaty avamehati sma.

evam—thus; *go*—of cows; *mṛga*—deer; *kāka*—crows; *caryayā*—by the activities; *vrajan*—moving; *tiṣṭhan*—standing; *āsīnaḥ*—sitting; *śayānaḥ*—lying down; *kāka-mṛga-go-caritaḥ*—behaving exactly like the crows, deer and cows; *pibati*—drinks; *khādati*—eats; *avamehati*—passes urine; *sma*—He did so.

TRANSLATION

In this way Lord Ṛṣabhadeva followed the behavior of cows, deer and crows. Sometimes He moved or walked, and sometimes He sat down in

one place. Sometimes He lay down, behaving exactly like cows, deer and crows. In that way, He ate, drank, passed stool and urine and cheated the people in this way.

PURPORT

Being the Supreme Personality of Godhead, Lord Ṛṣabhadeva possessed a transcendental, spiritual body. Since the general public could not appreciate His behavior and mystic *yoga* practice, they began to disturb Him. To cheat them, He behaved like crows, cows and deer.

TEXT 35

इति नानायोगचर्याचरणो भगवान् कैवल्यपतिर्ऋषभोऽविरतपरममहानन्दानुभव आत्मनि सर्वेषां भूतानामात्मभूते भगवति वासुदेव आत्मनोऽव्यवधानानन्तरोदरभावेन सिद्धसमस्तार्थपरिपूर्णो योगैश्वर्याणि वैहायसमनोजवान्तर्धानपरकाय-प्रवेशदूरग्रहणादीनि यदृच्छयोपगतानि नाञ्जसा नृप हृदयेनाभ्यनन्दत् ॥३५॥

iti nānā-yoga-caryācaraṇo bhagavān kaivalya-patir ṛṣabho'virata-parama-mahānandānubhava ātmani sarveṣāṁ bhūtānām ātma-bhūte bhagavati vāsudeva ātmano'vyavadhānānanta-rodara-bhāvena siddha-samastārtha-paripūrṇo yogaiśvaryāṇi vaihāyasa-mano-javāntardhāna-parakāya-praveśa-dūra-grahaṇādīni yadṛcchayopagatāni nāñjasā nṛpa hṛdayenābhyanandat.

iti—thus; *nānā*—various; *yoga*—of mystic *yoga; caryā*—performances; *ācaraṇaḥ*—practicing; *bhagavān*—the Supreme Personality of Godhead; *kaivalya-patiḥ*—the master of *kaivalya,* oneness, or the giver of *sāyujya-mukti; ṛṣabhaḥ*—Lord Ṛṣabha; *avirata*—incessantly; *parama*—supreme; *mahā*—great; *ānanda-anubhavaḥ*—feeling transcendental bliss; *ātmani*—in the Supreme Soul; *sarveṣām*—of all; *bhūtānām*—living entities; *ātma-bhūte*—situated in the heart; *bhagavati*—unto the Supreme Personality of Godhead; *vāsudeve*—Kṛṣṇa, the son of Vasudeva; *ātmanaḥ*—of Himself; *avyavadhāna*—by the nondifference of constitution; *ananta*—unlimited; *rodara*—like crying, laughing and shivering; *bhāvena*—by the symptoms of love; *siddha*—completely perfect; *samasta*—all; *artha*—with desirable opulences; *paripūrṇaḥ*—full; *yoga-aiśvaryāṇi*—the mystic powers; *vaihāyasa*—flying in the sky; *manaḥ-java*—traveling at the speed of mind; *antardhāna*—the ability to disappear; *parakāya-praveśa*—the ability to enter another's body; *dūra-grahaṇa*—the ability to perceive things far, far away; *ādīni*—and others;

yadṛcchayā—without difficulty, automatically; *upagatāni*—achieved; *na*—not; *añjasā*—directly; *nṛpa*—O King Parīkṣit; *hṛdayena*—within the heart; *abhyanandat*—accepted.

TRANSLATION

O King Parīkṣit, just to show all the yogīs the mystic process, Lord Ṛṣabhadeva, the partial expansion of Lord Kṛṣṇa, performed wonderful activities. Actually He was the master of liberation and was fully absorbed in transcendental bliss, which increased a thousandfold. Lord Kṛṣṇa, Vāsudeva, the son of Vasudeva, is the original source of Lord Ṛṣabhadeva. There is no difference in Their constitution, and consequently Lord Ṛṣabhadeva awakened the loving symptoms of crying, laughing and shivering. He was always absorbed in transcendental love. Due to this, all mystic powers automatically approached Him, such as the ability to travel in outer space at the speed of mind, to appear and disappear, to enter the bodies of others, and to see things far, far away. Although He could do all this, He did not exercise these powers.

PURPORT

In the *Caitanya-caritāmṛta* (*Madhya* 19.149) it is said:

kṛṣṇa-bhakta—niṣkāma, ataeva 'śānta'
bhukti-mukti-siddhi-kāmī—sakali 'aśānta'

The word *śānta* means completely peaceful. Unless all one's desires are fulfilled, one cannot be peaceful. Everyone is trying to fulfill his aspirations and desires, be they material or spiritual. Those in the material world are *aśānta* (without peace) because they have so many desires to fulfill. The pure devotee, however, is without desire. *Anyābhilāṣitā-śūnya:* a pure devotee is completely free from all kinds of material desire. *Karmīs,* on the other hand, are simply full of desires because they try to enjoy sense gratification. They are not peaceful in this life, nor the next, during the past, present or future. Similarly, *jñānīs* are always aspiring after liberation and trying to become one with the Supreme. *Yogīs* are aspiring after many *siddhis* (powers)—*aṇimā, laghimā, prāpti,* etc. However, a devotee is not at all interested in these things because he is fully dependent on the mercy of Kṛṣṇa. Kṛṣṇa is *yogeśvara,* the possessor of all mystic powers (*siddhis*), and He is *ātmārāma,* fully self-satisfied. The *yoga-siddhis* are described in this verse. One can fly in outer space without the aid of a machine, and he can travel at the speed of mind.

This means that as soon as a *yogī* desires to go somewhere within this universe or even beyond this universe, he can do so immediately. One cannot estimate the speed of mind, for within a second the mind can go many millions of miles. Sometimes *yogīs* enter into the bodies of other people and act as they desire when their bodies are not working properly. When the body becomes old, a perfect *yogī* can find a young, able body. Giving up his old body, the *yogī* can enter into the young body and act as he pleases. Being a plenary expansion of Lord Vāsudeva, Lord Ṛṣabhadeva possessed all these mystic *yoga* powers, but He was satisfied with His devotional love of Kṛṣṇa, which was evinced by the ecstatic symptoms, such as crying, laughing and shivering.

Thus end the Bhaktivedanta purports of the Fifth Canto, Fifth Chapter, of the Śrīmad-Bhāgavatam, *entitled "Lord Ṛṣabhadeva's Teachings to His Sons."*

CHAPTER SIX

The Activities of Lord Ṛṣabhadeva

This chapter tells how Lord Ṛṣabhadeva left His body. He was not attached to His body even when it was being burned up in a forest fire. When the seed of fruitive activity is burned by the fire of knowledge, the spiritual properties and mystic powers are automatically manifest, yet *bhakti-yoga* is not affected by these mystic powers. An ordinary *yogī* is captivated by mystic powers and his progress checked; therefore a perfect *yogī* does not welcome them. Because the mind is restless and undependable, it must remain always under control. Even the mind of the advanced *yogī* Saubhari created such a disturbance that he lost his yogic mystic powers. Due to a restless mind, even a very advanced *yogī* can fall down. The mind is so restless that it induces even a perfect *yogī* to be controlled by the senses. Therefore Lord Ṛṣabhadeva, for the instruction of all *yogīs,* showed the process of quitting the body. While traveling in South India, through the provinces of Karṇāṭa, Koṅka, Veṅka and Kuṭaka, Lord Ṛṣabhadeva arrived in the neighborhood of Kuṭakācala. Suddenly there was a forest fire that burned the forest and Lord Ṛṣabhadeva's body to ashes. The pastimes of Lord Ṛṣabhadeva as a liberated soul were known by the King of Koṅka, Veṅka and Kuṭaka. This King's name was Arhat. He later became captivated by the illusory energy, and in this condition he set forth the basic principles of Jainism. Lord Ṛṣabhadeva set forth the principles of religion that can free one from material bondage, and He put an end to all kinds of atheistic activities. On this earth, the place known as Bhārata-varṣa was a very pious land because the Supreme Lord appeared there when He wanted to incarnate.

Lord Ṛṣabhadeva neglected all the mystic powers for which the so-called *yogīs* hanker. Because of the beauty of devotional service, devotees are not at all interested in so-called mystic power. The master of all yogic power, Lord Kṛṣṇa, can exhibit all powers on behalf of His devotee. Devotional service is more valuable than yogic mystic powers. Devotees who are sometimes misled aspire for liberation and mystic powers. The Supreme Lord gives these devotees whatever they desire, but they cannot attain the most important function of devotional service. Devotional service to the Lord is guaranteed for those who do not desire liberation and mystic power.

TEXT 1

राजोवाच

न नूनं भगव आत्मारामाणां योगसमीरितज्ञानावभर्जितकर्मबीजानामैश्वर्याणि पुनः क्लेशदानि भवितुमर्हन्ति यदृच्छयोपगतानि ॥१॥

rājovāca
na nūnaṁ bhagava ātmārāmāṇāṁ yoga-samīrita-jñānāvabharjita-karma-bījānām aiśvaryāṇi punaḥ kleśadāni bhavitum arhanti yadṛc-chayopagatāni.

rājā uvāca—King Parīkṣit inquired; *na*—not; *nūnam*—indeed; *bhagavaḥ*—O most powerful Śukadeva Gosvāmī; *ātmārāmāṇām*—of pure devotees simply engaged in devotional service; *yoga-samīrita*—achieved by practice of *yoga; jñāna*—by knowledge; *avabharjita*—burned; *karma-bījānām*—of those whose seeds of fruitive activities; *aiśvaryāṇi*—the mystic powers; *punaḥ*—again; *kleśadāni*—sources of distress; *bhavitum*—to become; *arhanti*—are able; *yadṛcchayā*—automatically; *upagatāni*—achieved.

TRANSLATION

King Parīkṣit asked Śukadeva Gosvāmī: My dear Lord, for those who are completely pure in heart, knowledge is attained by the practice of bhakti-yoga, and attachment for fruitive activity is completely burned to ashes. For such people, the powers of mystic yoga automatically arise. They do not cause distress. Why, then, did Ṛṣabhadeva neglect them?

PURPORT

A pure devotee is constantly engaged in the service of the Supreme Personality of Godhead. Whatever is necessary for the discharge of devotional service is automatically attained, though it may appear to be the result of mystic *yoga* power. Sometimes a *yogī* displays a little yogic power by manufacturing gold. A little quantity of gold captivates foolish people, and thus the *yogī* gets many followers, who are willing to accept such a tiny person as the Supreme Personality of Godhead. Such a *yogī* may also advertise himself as Bhagavān. However, a devotee does not have to exhibit such magical wonders. Without practicing the mystic yogic process, he achieves even greater opulence all over the world. Under the circumstances, Lord Ṛṣabhadeva refused to manifest mystic yogic perfections, and Mahārāja Parīkṣit asked why He did not accept them, since, for a devotee, they are not at all disturbing. A devotee is never distressed or satisfied by material opulence. His concern is how to please the Supreme Personality of Godhead. If, by the grace of the Supreme Lord, a devotee achieves extraordinary opulence, he utilizes the opportunity for the Lord's service. He is not disturbed by the opulence.

TEXT 2

ऋषिरुवाच
सत्यमुक्तं किन्त्विह वा एके न मनसोऽद्धा विश्रम्भमनवस्थानस्य शठकिरात इव सङ्गच्छन्ते ॥२॥

ṛṣir uvāca
satyam uktaṁ kintv iha vā eke na manaso'ddhā viśrambham anavasthānasya śaṭha-kirāta iva saṅgacchante.

ṛṣiḥ uvāca—Śukadeva Gosvāmī said; *satyam*—the correct thing; *uktam*—have said; *kintu*—but; *iha*—in this material world; *vā*—either; *eke*—some; *na*—not; *manasaḥ*—of the mind; *addhā*—directly; *viśrambham*—faithful; *anavasthānasya*—being unsteady; *śaṭha*—very cunning; *kirātaḥ*—a hunter; *iva*—like; *saṅgacchante*—become.

TRANSLATION

Śrīla Śukadeva Gosvāmī replied: My dear King, you have spoken correctly. However, after capturing animals, a cunning hunter does not put faith in them, for they might run away. Similarly, those who are advanced in spiritual life do not put faith in the mind. Indeed, they always remain vigilant and watch the mind's action.

PURPORT

In *Bhagavad-gītā* (18.5) Lord Kṛṣṇa says:

yajña-dāna-tapaḥ-karma
na tyājyaṁ kāryam eva tat
yajño dānaṁ tapaś caiva
pāvanāni manīṣiṇām

"Acts of sacrifice, charity and penance are not to be given up but should be performed. Indeed, sacrifice, charity and penance purify even the great souls."

Even one who has renounced the world and has taken *sannyāsa* should not renounce chanting the Hare Kṛṣṇa *mahā-mantra.* Renunciation does not mean that one has to renounce *saṅkīrtana-yajña.* Similarly, one should not renounce charity or *tapasya.* The *yoga* system for control of the mind and senses must be strictly followed. Lord Ṛṣabhadeva showed how severe types of *tapasya* could be performed, and He set an example for all others.

TEXT 3

तथा चोक्तम् —
न कुर्यात्कर्हिचित्सख्यं मनसि ह्यनवस्थिते ।
यद्विश्रम्भाच्चिराच्चीर्णं चस्कन्द तप ऐश्वरम् ॥३॥

tathā coktam —
na kuryāt karhicit sakhyaṁ
manasi hy anavasthite
yad-viśrambhāc cirāc cīrṇaṁ
caskanda tapa aiśvaram

tathā—so; *ca*—and; *uktam*—it is said; *na*—never; *kuryāt*—should do; *karhicit*—at any time or with anyone; *sakhyam*—friendship; *manasi*—in the mind; *hi*—certainly; *anavasthite*—which is very restless; *yat*—in which; *viśrambhāt*—from placing too much faith; *cirāt*—for a long time; *cīrṇam*—practiced; *caskanda*—became disturbed; *tapaḥ*—the austerity; *aiśvaram*—of great personalities like Lord Śiva and the great sage Saubhari.

TRANSLATION

All the learned scholars have given their opinion. The mind is by nature very restless, and one should not make friends with it. If we place full confidence in the mind, it may cheat us at any moment. Even Lord Śiva became agitated upon seeing the Mohinī form of Lord Kṛṣṇa, and Saubhari Muni also fell down from the mature stage of yogic perfection.

PURPORT

The first business of one trying to advance in spiritual life is to control the mind and senses. As Śrī Kṛṣṇa says in *Bhagavad-gītā* (15.7):

mamaivāṁśo jīva-loke
jīva-bhūtaḥ sanātanaḥ
manaḥ ṣaṣṭhānīndriyāṇi
prakṛti-sthāni karṣati

Although the living entities are part and parcel of the Supreme Lord and are therefore in a transcendental position, they are still suffering in this material world and struggling for existence due to the mind and the senses. To get out of this false struggle for existence and become happy in the material world, one has to control the mind and senses and be detached from material conditions. One should never neglect austerities and penances; one should always perform them. Lord Ṛṣabhadeva personally showed us how to do this. In the *Śrīmad-Bhāgavatam* (9.19.17) it is specifically stated:

mātrā svasrā duhitrā vā
nāviviktāsano bhavet
balavān indriya-grāmo
vidvāṁsam api karṣati

A *gṛhastha, vānaprastha, sannyāsī* and *brahmacārī* should be very careful when associating with women. One is forbidden to sit down in a solitary place even with one's mother, sister or daughter. In our Kṛṣṇa consciousness movement it has been very difficult to disassociate ourselves from women in our society, especially in Western countries. We are therefore sometimes criticized, but nonetheless we are trying to give everyone a chance to chant the Hare Kṛṣṇa *mahā-mantra* and thus advance spiritually. If we stick to the principle of chanting the Hare Kṛṣṇa *mahā-mantra* offenselessly, then, by the grace of Śrīla Haridāsa Ṭhākura, we may be saved from the allurement of women. However, if we are not very strict in chanting the Hare Kṛṣṇa *mahā-mantra,* we may at any time fall victim to women.

TEXT 4

नित्यं ददाति कामस्यच्छिद्रं तमनु येऽरयः ।
योगिनः कृतमैत्रस्य पत्युर्जायेव पुंश्चली ॥४॥

nityaṁ dadāti kāmasya
cchidraṁ tam anu ye 'rayaḥ
yoginaḥ kṛta-maitrasya
patyur jāyeva puṁścalī

nityam—always; *dadāti*—gives; *kāmasya*—of lust; *chidram*—facility; *tam*—that (lust); *anu*—following; *ye*—those; *arayaḥ*—enemies; *yoginaḥ*—of the *yogīs* or persons trying to advance in spiritual life; *kṛta-maitrasya*—having put faith in the mind; *patyuḥ*—of the husband; *jāyā iva*—like the wife; *puṁścalī*—who is unchaste or easily carried away by other men.

TRANSLATION

An unchaste woman is very easily carried away by paramours, and it sometimes happens that her husband is violently killed by her paramours. If the yogī gives his mind a chance and does not restrain it, his mind will give facility to enemies like lust, anger and greed, and they will doubtlessly kill the yogī.

PURPORT

In this verse the word *puṁścalī* refers to a woman who is easily carried away by men. Such a woman is never to be trusted. Unfortunately, in the present age, women are never controlled. According to the directions of the *śāstras,* women are never to be given freedom. When a child, a woman must be strictly controlled by her father. When she is young, she must be strictly controlled by her husband, and when she is old, she must be controlled by her elderly sons. If she is given independence and allowed to mingle unrestrictedly with men, she will be spoiled. A spoiled woman, being manipulated by paramours, might even kill her husband. This example is given here because a *yogī* desiring to get free from material conditions must always keep his mind under control. Śrīla Bhaktisiddhānta Sarasvatī Ṭhākura used to say that in the morning our first business should be to beat the mind with shoes a hundred times, and, before going to bed, to beat the mind a hundred times with a broomstick. In this way one's mind can be kept under control. An uncontrolled mind and an unchaste wife are the same. An unchaste wife can kill her husband at any time, and an uncontrolled mind, followed by lust, anger, greed, madness, envy and illusion, can certainly kill the *yogī.* When the *yogī* is controlled by the mind, he falls down into the material condition. One should be very careful of the mind, just as a husband should be careful of an unchaste wife.

TEXT 5

कामो मन्युर्मदो लोभः शोकमोहभयादयः ।
कर्मबन्धश्च यन्मूलः स्वीकुर्यात्को नु तद् बुधः ॥ ५ ॥

kāmo manyur mado lobhaḥ
śoka-moha-bhayādayaḥ
karma-bandhaś ca yan-mūlaḥ
svīkuryāt ko nu tad budhaḥ

kāmaḥ—lust; *manyuḥ*—anger; *madaḥ*—pride; *lobhaḥ*—greed; *śoka*—lamentation; *moha*—illusion; *bhaya*—fear; *ādayaḥ*—all these together; *karma-bandhaḥ*—bondage to fruitive activities; *ca*—and; *yat-mūlaḥ*—the origin of which; *svīkuryāt*—would accept; *kaḥ*—who; *nu*—indeed; *tat*—that mind; *budhaḥ*—if one is learned.

TRANSLATION

The mind is the root cause of lust, anger, pride, greed, lamentation, illusion and fear. Combined, these constitute bondage to fruitive activity. What learned man would put faith in the mind?

PURPORT

The mind is the original cause of material bondage. It is followed by many enemies, such as anger, pride, greed, lamentation, illusion and fear. The best way to control the mind is to engage it always in Kṛṣṇa consciousness (*sa vai manaḥ kṛṣṇa-padāravindayoḥ*). Since the followers of the mind bring about material bondage, we should be very careful not to trust the mind.

TEXT 6

अथैवमखिललोकपालललामोऽपि विलक्षणैर्जडवदवधूतवेषभाषाचरितैर-विलक्षितभगवत्प्रभावो योगिनां साम्परायविधिमनुशिक्षयन् स्वकलेवरं जिहासुरात्मन्यात्मानमसंव्यवहितमनर्थान्तरभावेनान्वीक्षमाण उपरतानुवृत्तिरुपरराम ॥६॥

athaivam akhila-loka-pāla-lalāmo'pi vilakṣaṇair jaḍavad avadhūta-veṣa-bhāṣā-caritair avilakṣita-bhagavat-prabhāvo yogināṁ sāmparāya-vidhim anuśikṣayan sva-kalevaraṁ jihāsur ātmany ātmānam asaṁvyavahitam anarthāntara-bhāvenānvīkṣamāṇa uparatānuvṛttir upararāma.

atha—thereafter; *evam*—in this way; *akhila-loka-pāla-lalāmaḥ*—the head of all kings and monarchs of the universe; *api*—although; *vilakṣaṇaiḥ*—various; *jaḍa-vat*—as if stupid; *avadhūta-veṣa-bhāṣā-caritaiḥ*—by the dress, language and characteristics of an *avadhūta; avilakṣita-bhagavat-prabhāvaḥ*—hiding the opulence of the Supreme Personality of Godhead (keeping Himself like an ordinary human being); *yoginām*—of the *yogīs; sāmparāya-vidhim*—the method of giving up this material body; *anuśikṣayan*—teaching; *sva-kalevaram*—His own personal body, which is not at all material; *jihāsuḥ*—desiring to give up like an ordinary human being; *ātmani*—unto Vāsudeva, the original person;

ātmānam—Himself, Lord Ṛṣabhadeva, being an *āveśa-avatāra* of Lord Viṣṇu; *asaṁvyavahitam*—without intervention by the illusory energy; *anartha-antara-bhāvena*—Himself in the status of Viṣṇu; *anvīkṣamāṇaḥ*—always seeing; *uparata-anuvṛttiḥ*—who was acting as if giving up His material body; *upararāma*—ceased His pastimes as the King of this planet.

TRANSLATION

Lord Ṛṣabhadeva was the head of all kings and emperors within this universe, but assuming the dress and language of an avadhūta, He acted as if dull and materially bound. Consequently no one could observe His divine opulence. He adopted this behavior just to teach yogīs how to give up the body. Nonetheless, He maintained His original position as a plenary expansion of Lord Vāsudeva, Kṛṣṇa. Remaining always in that state, He gave up His pastimes as Lord Ṛṣabhadeva within the material world. If, following in the footsteps of Lord Ṛṣabhadeva, one can give up his subtle body, there is no chance that one will accept a material body again.

PURPORT

As Lord Kṛṣṇa says in *Bhagavad-gītā* (4.9):

janma karma ca me divyam
evaṁ yo vetti tattvataḥ
tyaktvā dehaṁ punar janma
naiti mām eti so'rjuna

"One who knows the transcendental nature of My appearance and activities does not, upon leaving the body, take his birth again in this material world, but attains My eternal abode, O Arjuna."

This is possible simply by keeping oneself an eternal servant of the Supreme Lord. One must understand his constitutional position and the constitutional position of the Supreme Lord as well. Both have the same spiritual identity. Maintaining oneself as a servant of the Supreme Lord, one should avoid rebirth in this material world. If one keeps himself spiritually fit and thinks of himself as an eternal servant of the Supreme Lord, he will be successful at the time he has to give up the material body.

TEXT 7

तस्य ह वा एवं मुक्तलिङ्गस्य भगवत ऋषभस्य योगमायावासनया देह इमां जगतीमभिमानाभासेन संक्रममाणः कोङ्कवेङ्ककुटकान्दक्षिणकर्णाटका-

न्देशान् यदृच्छयोपगतः कुटकाचलोपवन आस्यकृताश्मकवल उन्माद इव मुक्तमूर्धजोऽसंवीत एव विचचार ॥७॥

tasya ha vā evaṁ mukta-liṅgasya bhagavata ṛṣabhasya yogamāyā-vāsanayā deha imāṁ jagatīm abhimānābhāsena saṅkramamāṇaḥ koṅka-veṅka-kuṭakān dakṣiṇa-karṇāṭakān deśān yadṛcchayopagataḥ kuṭakācalopavana āsya kṛtāśma-kavala unmāda iva mukta-mūrdhajo' saṁvīta eva vicacāra.

tasya—of Him (Lord Ṛṣabhadeva); *ha vā*—as it were; *evam*—thus; *mukta-liṅgasya*—who had no identification with the gross and subtle body; *bhagavataḥ*—of the Supreme Personality of Godhead; *ṛṣabhasya*—of Lord Ṛṣabhadeva; *yoga-māyā-vāsanayā*—by the accomplishment of *yoga-māyā* for the purpose of the Lord's pastimes; *dehaḥ*—body; *imām*—this; *jagatīm*—earth; *abhimāna-ābhāsena*—with the apparent conception of having a body of material elements; *saṅkramamāṇaḥ*—traveling; *koṅka-veṅka-kuṭakān*—Koṅka, Veṅka and Kuṭaka; *dakṣiṇa*—in South India; *karṇāṭakān*—in the province of Karṇāṭa; *deśān*—all the countries; *yadṛcchayā*—of His own accord; *upagataḥ*—reached; *kuṭakācala-upavane*—a forest near Kuṭakācala; *āsya*—within the mouth; *kṛta-aśma-kavalaḥ*—having put a mouthful of stone; *unmādaḥ iva*—just like a madman; *mukta-mūrdhajaḥ*—having scattered hair; *asaṁvītaḥ*—naked; *eva*—just; *vicacāra*—traveled.

TRANSLATION

Actually Lord Ṛṣabhadeva had no material body, but due to yoga-māyā, He considered His body material, and therefore, because He played like an ordinary human being, He gave up the mentality of identifying with it. Following this principle, He began to wander all over the world. While traveling, He came to the province of Karṇāṭa in South India and passed through Koṅka, Veṅka and Kuṭaka. He had no plan to travel this way, but He arrived near Kuṭakācala and entered a forest there. He placed stones within His mouth and began to wander through the forest, naked and with His hair disheveled like a madman.

TEXT 8

अथ समीरवेगविधूतवेणुविकर्षणजातोग्रदावानलस्तद्वनमालेलिहानः सह तेन ददाह ॥८॥

atha samīra-vega-vidhūta-veṇu-vikarṣaṇa-jātogra-dāvānalas tad vanam ālelihānaḥ saha tena dadāha.

atha—thereafter; *samīra-vega*—by the force of the wind; *vidhūta*—tossed about; *veṇu*—of bamboos; *vikarṣaṇa*—by the rubbing; *jāta*—produced; *ugra*—fierce; *dāva-analaḥ*—a forest fire; *tat*—that; *vanam*—forest near Kuṭakācala; *ālelihānaḥ*—devouring all around; *saha*—with; *tena*—that body; *dadāha*—burned to ashes.

TRANSLATION

While He was wandering about, a wild forest fire began. This fire was caused by the friction of bamboos, which were being blown by the wind. In that fire, the entire forest near Kuṭakācala and the body of Lord Ṛṣabhadeva were burnt to ashes.

PURPORT

Such a forest fire can burn the external bodies of animals, but Lord Ṛṣabhadeva was not burned, although He apparently seemed so. Lord Ṛṣabhadeva is the Supersoul of all living entities within the forest, and His soul is never burned by fire. As stated in *Bhagavad-gītā, adāhyo'yam*—the soul is never burned by fire. Due to Lord Ṛṣabhadeva's presence, all the animals in the forest were also liberated from material encagement.

TEXT 9

यस्य किलानुचरितमुपाकर्ण्य कोङ्कवेङ्ककुटकानां राजार्हन्नामोपशिक्ष्य कलावधर्म उत्कृष्यमाणे भवितव्येन विमोहितः स्वधर्मपथमकुतोभयमपहाय कुपथपाखण्डमसमञ्जसं निजमनीषया मन्दः सम्प्रवर्तयिष्यते ॥ ९ ॥

yasya kilānucaritam upākarṇya koṅka-veṅka-kuṭakānāṁ rājārhan-
nāmopaśikṣya kalāv adharma utkṛṣyamāṇe bhavitavyena vimohitaḥ
sva-dharma-patham akuto-bhayam apahāya kupatha-pākhaṇḍam
asamañjasaṁ nija-manīṣayā mandaḥ sampravartayiṣyate.

yasya—of whom (Lord Ṛṣabhadeva); *kila anucaritam*—pastimes as a *paramahaṁsa,* above all regulative *varṇāśrama* principles; *upākarṇya*—hearing; *koṅka-veṅka-kuṭakānām*—of Koṅka, Veṅka and Kuṭaka; *rājā*—the King; *arhat-nāma*—whose name was Arhat (now known as the Jain); *upaśikṣya*—imitating the activities of Lord Ṛṣabhadeva in His *paramahaṁsa* feature; *kalau*—in this age of Kali; *adharme utkṛṣyamāṇe*—because of increasing irreligious life; *bhavitavyena*—by that which was about to happen; *vimohitaḥ*—bewildered; *sva-dharma-patham*—the path of religion; *akutaḥ-bhayam*—which is free from all kinds of fearful danger; *apahāya*—giving up (such practices as cleanliness, truthfulness, control of the senses and mind, simplicity, the principles of religion, and practical application of knowledge); *ku-patha-pākhaṇḍam*—the wrong path of atheism; *asamañjasam*—improper or against the Vedic literature; *nija-manīṣayā*—by his own fertile brain; *mandaḥ*—most foolish; *sampravartayiṣyate*—will introduce.

TRANSLATION

Śukadeva Gosvāmī continued speaking to Mahārāja Parīkṣit: My dear King, the King of Koṅka, Veṅka and Kuṭaka whose name was Arhat, heard of the activities of Ṛṣabhadeva and, imitating Ṛṣabhadeva's principles, introduced a new system of religion. Taking advantage of Kali-yuga, the age of sinful activity, King Arhat, being bewildered, gave up the Vedic principles, which are free from risk, and concocted a new system of religion opposed to the Vedas. That was the beginning of the Jain dharma. Many other so-called religions followed this atheistic system.

PURPORT

When Lord Śrī Kṛṣṇa was present on this planet, a person named Pauṇḍraka imitated the four-handed Nārāyaṇa and declared himself the Supreme Personality of Godhead. He desired to compete with Kṛṣṇa. Similarly, during the time of Lord Ṛṣabhadeva, the King of Koṅka and Veṅka acted like a *paramahaṁsa* and imitated Lord Ṛṣabhadeva. He introduced a system of religion and took advantage of the fallen condition of the people in this age of Kali. It is said in Vedic literatures that people in this age will be more inclined to accept anyone as the Supreme Lord and accept any religious system opposed to Vedic principles. The people in this age are described as *mandāḥ sumanda-matayaḥ.* Generally they have no spiritual culture, and therefore they are very fallen. Due to this, they will accept any religious system. Due to their misfortune. they forget the Vedic principles. Following non-Vedic principles in this age, they think themselves the Supreme Lord and thus spread the cult of atheism all over the world.

TEXT 10

येन ह वाव कलौ मनुजापसदा देवमायामोहिताः स्वविधिनियोगशौच-
चारित्रविहीना देवहेलनान्यपव्रतानि निजनिजेच्छया गृह्णाना
अस्नानानाचमनाशौचकेशोल्लुञ्चनादीनि कलिनाधर्मबहुलेनोपहतधियो
ब्रह्मब्राह्मणयज्ञपुरुषलोकविदूषकाः प्रायेण भविष्यन्ति ॥१०॥

yena ha vāva kalau manujāpasadā deva-māyā-mohitāḥ sva-vidhi-niyoga-śauca-cāritra-vihīnā deva-helanāny apavratāni nija-nijecchayā gṛhṇānā asnānānācamanāśauca-keśolluñcanādīni kalinādharma-bahulenopahata-dhiyo brahma-brāhmaṇa-yajña-puruṣa-loka-vidūṣakāḥ prāyeṇa bhaviṣyanti.

yena—by which pseudo religious system; *ha vāva*—certainly; *kalau*—in this age of Kali; *manuja-apasadāḥ*—the most condemned men; *deva-māyā-mohitāḥ*—bewildered by the external energy, or illusory energy, of the Supreme Personality of Godhead; *sva-vidhi-niyoga-śauca-cāritra-vihīnāḥ*—without character, cleanliness, and the rules and regulations given according to one's own duty in life; *deva-helanāni*—negligent of the Supreme Personality of Godhead; *apavratāni*—impious vows; *nija-nija-icchayā*—by their own desires; *gṛhṇānāḥ*—accepting; *asnāna-anācamana-aśauca-keśa-ulluñcana-ādīni*—concocted religious principles such as no bathing, no washing of the mouth, being unclean and plucking out the hair; *kalinā*—by the age of Kali; *adharma-bahulena*—with an abundance of irreligion; *upahata-dhiyaḥ*—whose pure consciousness is destroyed; *brahma-brāhmaṇa-yajña-puruṣa-loka-vidūṣakāḥ*—blasphemous toward the *Vedas,* the strict *brāhmaṇas,* ritualistic ceremonies such as sacrifice, and toward the Supreme Personality of Godhead and the devotees; *prāyeṇa*—almost entirely; *bhaviṣyanti*—will become.

TRANSLATION

People who are lowest among men and bewildered by the illusory energy of the Supreme Lord will give up the original varṇāśrama-dharma and its rules and regulations. They will abandon bathing three times daily and worshiping the Lord. Abandoning cleanliness and neglecting the Supreme Lord, they will accept nonsensical principles. Not regularly bathing or washing their mouths regularly, they will always remain unclean, and they will pluck out their hair. Following a concocted religion, they will flourish. During this age of Kali, people are more inclined to irreligious systems. Consequently these people will naturally deride Vedic authority, the followers of Vedic authority, the brāhmaṇas, the Supreme Personality of Godhead and the devotees.

PURPORT

Presently the hippies in the Western countries fit this description. They are irresponsible and unregulated. They do not bathe, and they deride standard Vedic knowledge. They concoct new lifestyles and religions. There are many hippie groups at the present moment, but they all originated from King Arhat, who imitated the activities of Lord Ṛṣabhadeva, who was situated on the *paramahaṁsa* stage. King Arhat did not care for the fact that although Lord Ṛṣabhadeva acted like a madman, His stool and urine were nonetheless aromatic, so much so that they nicely scented the countryside for miles around. The followers of King Arhat went under the name Jains, and they were later followed by many others, particularly by the hippies, who are more or less offshoots of Māyāvāda philosophy because they think themselves the Supreme Personality of Godhead. Such people do not respect the real followers of Vedic principles, the ideal *brāhmaṇas.* Nor do they have respect for the Supreme Personality of Godhead, the Supreme Brahman. Due to the influence of this age of Kali, they are apt to concoct false religious systems.

TEXT 11

ते च ह्यर्वाक्तनया निजलोकयात्रयान्धपरम्परयाऽऽश्वस्तास्तमस्यन्धे स्वयमेव प्रपतिष्यन्ति ॥११॥

te ca hy arvāktanayā nija-loka-yātrayāndha-paramparayāśvastās
tamasy andhe svayam eva prapatiṣyanti.

te—those people not following the Vedic principles; *ca*—and; *hi*—certainly; *arvāktanayā*—deviating from the eternal principles of Vedic religion; *nija-loka-yātrayā*—by a practice arrived at by their own mental concoction; *andha-paramparayā*—by a disciplic succession of blind, ignorant people; *āśvastāḥ*—being encouraged; *tamasi*—into the darkness of ignorance; *andhe*—blindness; *svayam eva*—themselves; *prapatiṣyanti*—will fall down.

TRANSLATION

Low-class people, due to their gross ignorance, introduce a system of religion that deviates from the Vedic principles. Following their own mental concoctions, they automatically fall down into the darkest regions of existence.

PURPORT

In this connection, one may see *Bhagavad-gītā,* Chapter Sixteen, where there is a description of the downfall of the *asuras* (16.16 and 16.23).

TEXT 12

अयमवतारो रजसोपप्लुतकैवल्योपशिक्षणार्थः ॥१२॥

ayam avatāro rajasopapluta-kaivalyopaśikṣaṇārthaḥ.

ayam avatāraḥ—this incarnation (Lord Ṛṣabhadeva); *rajasā*—by the mode of passion; *upapluta*—overwhelmed; *kaivalya-upaśikṣaṇa-arthaḥ*—to teach people the path of liberation.

TRANSLATION

In this age of Kali, people are overwhelmed by the modes of passion and ignorance. Lord Ṛṣabhadeva incarnated Himself to deliver them from the clutches of māyā.

PURPORT

The symptoms of Kali-yuga are predicted in the Twelfth Canto, Third Chapter, of *Śrīmad-Bhāgavatam. Lāvaṇyaṁ keśa-dhāraṇam.* It is predicted how fallen souls will behave. They will keep their hair long and consider themselves very beautiful, or they will pluck out their hair as the Jains do. They will keep themselves unclean and will not wash their mouths. Jains refer to Lord Ṛṣabhadeva as their original preceptor. If such people are serious followers of Ṛṣabhadeva, they must also take His instructions. In the Fifth Chapter of this canto, Ṛṣabhadeva gave His one hundred sons instructions whereby they could become free from the clutches of *māyā.* If one actually follows Ṛṣabhadeva, he will certainly be delivered from the clutches of *māyā* and return home, back to Godhead. If one strictly follows the instructions of Ṛṣabhadeva given in the Fifth Chapter, he will certainly be liberated. Lord Ṛṣabhadeva incarnated specifically to deliver these fallen souls.

TEXT 13

तस्यानुगुणान् श्लोकान् गायन्ति —
अहो भुवः सप्तसमुद्रवत्या
द्वीपेषु वर्षेष्वधिपुण्यमेतत् ।
गायन्ति यत्रत्यजना मुरारेः
कर्माणि भद्राण्यवतारवन्ति ॥१३॥

tasyānuguṇān ślokān gāyanti—
aho bhuvaḥ sapta-samudravatyā
dvīpeṣu varṣeṣv adhipuṇyam etat
gāyanti yatratya-janā murāreḥ
karmāṇi bhadrāṇy avatāravanti

tasya—of Him (Lord Ṛṣabhadeva); *anuguṇān*—conforming to the instructions for liberation; *ślokān*—verses; *gāyanti*—chant; *aho*—oh; *bhuvaḥ*—of this earthly planet; *sapta-samudra-vatyāḥ*—possessing seven seas; *dvīpeṣu*—among the islands; *varṣeṣu*—among the lands; *adhipuṇyam*—more pious than any other island; *etat*—this (Bhārata-varṣa); *gāyanti*—sing about; *yatratya-janāḥ*—the people of this tract of land; *murāreḥ*—of Murāri, the Supreme Personality of Godhead; *karmāṇi*—the activities; *bhadrāṇi*—all-auspicious; *avatāravanti*—in many incarnations such as Lord Ṛṣabhadeva.

TRANSLATION

Learned scholars chant about the transcendental qualities of Lord Ṛṣabhadeva in this way: "Oh, this earthly planet contains seven seas and many islands and lands, of which Bhārata-varṣa is considered the most pious. People of Bhārata-varṣa are accustomed to glorifying the activities of the Supreme Personality of Godhead in His incarnations as Lord Ṛṣabhadeva and others. All these activities are very auspicious for the welfare of humanity."

PURPORT

Śrī Caitanya Mahāprabhu said:

bhārata-bhūmite haila manuṣya-janma yāra
janma sārthaka kari' kara para-upakāra

As stated in this verse, Bhārata-varṣa is a most pious land. The followers of Vedic literature understand the Supreme Personality of Godhead in His different incarnations, and they are privileged to glorify the Lord by following the directions of Vedic literature. After realizing the glories of human life, such people should take up the mission to spread the importance of human life throughout the whole world. This is the mission of Śrī Caitanya Mahāprabhu. The word *adhipuṇyam* indicates that there are certainly many other pious men throughout the world, but the people of Bhārata-varṣa are even more pious. Therefore they are fit to spread Kṛṣṇa Consciousness throughout the world for the benefit of all human society. Śrīla Madhvācārya also recognizes the land of Bhārata-varṣa: *viśeṣād bhārate puṇyam.* Throughout the world, there is no question of *bhagavad-bhakti* or devotional service, but the people of Bhārata-varṣa can easily understand the devotional service of the Lord. Thus every inhabitant of Bhārata-varṣa can perfect his life by discharging *bhagavad-bhakti* and then preaching this cult throughout the world for the benefit of everyone.

TEXT 14

अहो नु वंशो यशसावदातः
प्रैयव्रतो यत्र पुमान् पुराणः ।
कृतावतारः पुरुषः स आद्य-
श्चचार धर्मं यदकर्महेतुम् ॥१४॥

aho nu vaṁśo yaśasāvadātaḥ
praiyavrato yatra pumān purāṇaḥ
kṛtāvatāraḥ puruṣaḥ sa ādyaś
cacāra dharmaṁ yad akarma-hetum

aho—oh; *nu*—indeed; *vaṁśaḥ*—the dynasty; *yaśasā*—with widespread fame; *avadātaḥ*—fully pure; *praiyavrataḥ*—related to King Priyavrata; *yatra*—wherein; *pumān*—the Supreme Person; *purāṇaḥ*—the original; *kṛta-avatāraḥ*—descended as an incarnation; *puruṣaḥ*—the Supreme Personality of Godhead; *saḥ*—He; *ādyaḥ*—the original person; *cacāra*—executed; *dharmam*—religious principles; *yat*—from which; *akarma-hetum*—the cause of the end of fruitive activities.

TRANSLATION

"Oh, what shall I say of the dynasty of Priyavrata, which is pure and very much celebrated. In that dynasty, the Supreme Person, the original Personality of Godhead, descended as an incarnation and executed religious principles that could free one from the results of fruitive activity."

PURPORT

There are many dynasties in human society wherein the Supreme Lord descends as an incarnation. Lord Kṛṣṇa appeared in the Yadu dynasty, and Lord Rāmacandra appeared in the Ikṣvāku, or Raghu, dynasty. Similarly, Lord

Ṛṣabhadeva appeared in the dynasty of King Priyavrata. All these dynasties are very famous, and of them the dynasty of Priyavrata is most famous.

TEXT 15

को न्वस्य काष्ठामपरोऽनुगच्छे-
न्मनोरथेनाप्यभवस्य योगी ।
यो योगमायाः स्पृहयत्युदस्ता
ह्यसत्तया येन कृतप्रयत्नाः ॥१५॥

ko nv asya kāṣṭhām aparo'nugacchen
mano-rathenāpy abhavasya yogī
yo yoga-māyāḥ spṛhayaty udastā
hy asattayā yena kṛta-prayatnāḥ

kaḥ—who; *nu*—indeed; *asya*—of Lord Ṛṣabhadeva; *kāṣṭhām*—the example; *aparaḥ*—else; *anugacchet*—can follow; *manaḥ-rathena*—by the mind; *api*—even; *abhavasya*—of the unborn; *yogī*—the mystic; *yaḥ*—who; *yoga-māyāḥ*—the mystic perfections of *yoga; spṛhayati*—desires; *udastāḥ*—rejected by Ṛṣabhadeva; *hi*—certainly; *asattayā*—by the quality of being insubstantial; *yena*—by whom, Ṛṣabhadeva; *kṛta-prayatnāḥ*—although eager to serve.

TRANSLATION

"Who is that mystic yogī who can follow the examples of Lord Ṛṣabhadeva even with his mind? Lord Ṛṣabhadeva rejected all kinds of yogic perfection, which other yogīs hanker to attain. Who is that yogī who can compare to Lord Ṛṣabhadeva?"

PURPORT

Generally *yogīs* desire the yogic perfections of *aṇimā, laghimā, mahimā, prākāmya, prāpti, īśitva, vaśitva* and *kāmāvasāyitā.* Lord Ṛṣabhadeva, however, never aspired for all these material things. Such *siddhis* (perfections) are presented by the illusory energy of the Lord. The real purpose of the *yoga* system is to achieve the favor and shelter of the lotus feet of the Supreme Personality of Godhead, but this purpose is covered by the illusory energy of *yoga-māyā.* So-called *yogīs* are therefore allured by the superficial material perfections of *aṇimā, laghimā, prāpti* and so forth.

Consequently ordinary *yogīs* cannot compare to Lord Ṛṣabhadeva, the Supreme Personality of Godhead.

TEXT 16

इति ह स्म सकलवेदलोकदेवब्राह्मणगवां परमगुरोर्भगवत ऋषभाख्यस्य विशुद्धाचरितमीरितं पुंसां समस्तदुश्चरिताभिहरणं परममहामङ्गलायनमिदमनुश्रद्धयोपचितयानुशृणोत्याश्रावयति वावहितो भगवति तस्मिन् वासुदेव एकान्ततो भक्तिरनयोरपि समनुवर्तते ॥१६॥

iti ha sma sakala-veda-loka-deva-brāhmaṇa-gavāṁ parama-guror bhagavata ṛṣabhākhyasya viśuddhācaritam īritaṁ puṁsāṁ samasta-duścaritābhiharaṇaṁ parama-mahā-maṅgalāyanam idam anuśraddhayopacitayānuśṛṇoty āśrāvayati vāvahito bhagavati tasmin vāsudeva ekāntato bhaktir anayor api samanuvartate.

iti—thus; *ha sma*—indeed; *sakala*—all; *veda*—of knowledge; *loka*—of people in general; *deva*—of the demigods; *brāhmaṇa*—of the *brāhmaṇas; gavām*—of the cows; *parama*—the supreme; *guroḥ*—master; *bhagavataḥ*—of the Supreme Personality of Godhead; *ṛṣabha-ākhyasya*—whose name was Lord Ṛṣabhadeva; *viśuddha*—pure; *ācaritam*—activities; *īritam*—now explained; *puṁsām*—of every living entity; *samasta*—all; *duścarita*—sinful activities; *abhiharaṇam*—destroying; *parama*—foremost; *mahā*—great; *maṅgala*—of auspiciousness; *ayanam*—the shelter; *idam*—this; *anuśraddhayā*—with faith; *upacitayā*—increasing; *anuśṛṇoti*—hears from the authority; *āśrāvayati*—speaks to others; *vā*—or; *avahitaḥ*—being attentive; *bhagavati*—the Supreme Personality of Godhead; *tasmin*—unto Him; *vāsudeve*—to Lord Vāsudeva, Lord Kṛṣṇa; *eka-antataḥ*—unflinching; *bhaktiḥ*—devotion; *anayoḥ*—of both groups, the listeners and the speakers; *api*—certainly; *samanuvartate*—factually begins.

TRANSLATION

Śukadeva Gosvāmī continued: Lord Ṛṣabhadeva is the master of all Vedic knowledge, human beings, demigods, cows and brāhmaṇas. I have already explained His pure, transcendental activities, which will vanquish the sinful activities of all living entities. This narration of Lord Ṛṣabhadeva's pastimes is the reservoir of all auspicious things. Whoever attentively hears or speaks of them, following in the footsteps of the ācaryas, will

certainly attain unalloyed devotional service at the lotus feet of Lord Vāsudeva, the Supreme Personality of Godhead.

PURPORT

The teachings of Lord Ṛṣabhadeva are for the people of all *yugas*—Satya-yuga, Tretā-yuga, Dvāpara-yuga and especially Kali-yuga. These instructions are so powerful that even in this age of Kali, one can attain perfection simply by explaining the instructions, following in the footsteps of the *ācāryas* or listening to the instructions with great attention. If one does so, one can attain the platform of pure devotional service to Lord Vāsudeva. The pastimes of the Supreme Personality of Godhead and His devotees are recorded in *Śrīmad-Bhāgavatam* so that those who recite these pastimes and listen to them will become purified. *Nityaṁ bhāgavata-sevayā.* As a matter of principle, devotees should read, speak and hear *Śrīmad-Bhāgavatam* persistently, twenty-four hours daily if possible. That is the recommendation of Śrī Caitanya Mahāprabhu. *Kīrtanīyaḥ sadā hariḥ.* One should either chant the Hare Kṛṣṇa *mahā-mantra* or read *Śrīmad-Bhāgavatam* and thereby try to understand the characteristics and instructions of the Supreme Lord, who appeared as Lord Ṛṣabhadeva, Lord Kapila and Lord Kṛṣṇa. In this way one can become fully aware of the transcendental nature of the Supreme Personality of Godhead. As stated in *Bhagavad-gītā,* one who knows the transcendental nature of the Lord's birth and activities attains liberation from material bondage and returns to Godhead.

TEXT 17

यस्यामेव कवय आत्मानमविरतं विविधवृजिनसंसारपरितापोपतप्यमानमनुसवनं
स्नापयन्तस्तयैव परया निर्वृत्या ह्यपवर्गमात्यन्तिकं परमपुरुषार्थमपि स्वयमासादितं
नो एवाद्रियन्ते भगवदीयत्वेनैव परि समाप्तसर्वार्थाः ॥१७॥

yasyām eva kavaya ātmānam aviratam vividha-vṛjina-saṁsāra-
paritāpopatapyamānam anusavanaṁ snāpayantas tayaiva parayā
nirvṛtyā hy apavargam ātyantikaṁ parama-puruṣārtham api svayam
āsāditaṁ no evādriyante bhagavadīyatvenaiva parisamāpta-sarvārthāḥ.

yasyām eva—in which (Kṛṣṇa consciousness or the nectar of devotional service); *kavayaḥ*—the advancement of learned scholars or philosophers in spiritual life; *ātmānam*—the self; *aviratam*—constantly; *vividha*—various; *vṛjina*—full of sins; *saṁsāra*—in material existence; *paritāpa*—from miserable conditions; *upatapyamānam*—suffering; *anusavanam*—without stopping; *snāpayantaḥ*—bathing; *tayā*—by that; *eva*—certainly; *parayā*—great; *nirvṛtyā*—with happiness; *hi*—certainly; *apavargam*—liberation; *ātyantikam*—uninterrupted; *parama-puruṣa-artham*—the best of all human achievements; *api*—although; *svayam*—itself; *āsāditam*—obtained; *no*—not; *eva*—certainly; *ādriyante*—endeavor to achieve; *bhagavadīyatvena eva*—because of a relationship with the Supreme Personality of Godhead; *parisamāpta-sarva-arthāḥ*—those who have ended all kinds of material desires.

TRANSLATION

Devotees always bathe themselves in devotional service in order to be relieved from the various tribulations of material existence. By doing this, the devotees enjoy supreme bliss, and liberation personified comes to serve them. Nonetheless, they do not accept that service, even if it is offered by the Supreme Personality of Godhead Himself. For the devotees, liberation [mukti] is very unimportant because, having attained the Lord's transcendental loving service, they have attained everything desirable and have transcended all material desires.

PURPORT

Devotional service unto the Lord is the highest attainment for anyone desiring liberation from the tribulations of material existence. As stated in *Bhagavad-gītā* (6.22), *yaṁ labdhvā cāparaṁ lābhaṁ manyate nādhikaṁ tataḥ:* "Gaining this, one thinks there is no greater gain." When one attains the service of the Lord, which is non-different from the Lord, one does not desire anything material. *Mukti* means relief from material existence. Bilvamaṅgala Ṭhākura says: *muktiḥ mukulitāñjaliḥ sevate'smān.* For a devotee, *mukti* is not a very great achievement. *Mukti* means being situated in one's constitutional position. The constitutional position of every living being is that of the Lord's servant; therefore when a living entity is engaged in the Lord's loving service, he has already attained *mukti.* Consequently a devotee does not aspire for *mukti,* even if it is offered by the Supreme Lord Himself.

TEXT 18

राजन् पतिर्गुरुरलं भवतां यदूनां
दैवं प्रियः कुलपतिः क्व च किङ्करो वः ।

अस्त्वेवमङ्ग भगवान् भजतां मुकुन्दो
मुक्तिं ददाति कर्हिचित्स्म न भक्तियोगम् ॥१८॥

rājan patir gurur alaṁ bhavatāṁ yadūnāṁ
daivaṁ priyaḥ kula-patiḥ kva ca kiṅkaro vaḥ
astv evam aṅga bhagavān bhajatāṁ mukundo
muktiṁ dadāti karhicit sma na bhakti-yogam

rājan—O my dear King; *patiḥ*—maintainer; *guruḥ*—spiritual master; *alam*—certainly; *bhavatām*—of you; *yadūnām*—the Yadu dynasty; *daivam*—the worshipable Deity; *priyaḥ*—very dear friend; *kula-patiḥ*—the master of the dynasty; *kva ca*—sometimes even; *kiṅkaraḥ*—servant; *vaḥ*—of you (the Pāṇḍavas); *astu*—to be sure; *evam*—thus; *aṅga*—O King; *bhagavān*—the Supreme Personality of Godhead; *bhajatām*—of those devotees engaged in service; *mukundaḥ*—the Lord, the Supreme Personality of Godhead; *muktim*—liberation; *dadāti*—delivers; *karhicit*—at any time; *sma*—indeed; *na*—not; *bhakti-yogam*—loving devotional service.

TRANSLATION

Śukadeva Gosvāmī continued: My dear King, the Supreme Person, Mukunda, is actually the maintainer of all the members of the Pāṇḍava and Yadu dynasties. He is your spiritual master, worshipable Deity, friend, and the director of your activities. To say nothing of this, He sometimes serves your family as a messenger or servant. This means He worked just as ordinary servants do. Those engaged in getting the Lord's favor attain liberation from the Lord very easily, but He does not very easily give the opportunity to render direct service unto Him.

PURPORT

While instructing Mahārāja Parīkṣit, Śukadeva Gosvāmī thought it wise to encourage the King because the King might be thinking of the glorious position of various royal dynasties. Especially glorious is the dynasty of Priyavrata, in which the Supreme Lord Ṛṣabhadeva incarnated. Similarly, the family of Uttānapāda Mahārāja, the father of Mahārāja Dhruva, is also glorious due to King Pṛthu's taking birth in it. The dynasty of Mahārāja Raghu is glorified because Lord Rāmacandra appeared in that family. As far as the Yadu and Kuru dynasties are concerned, they existed simultaneously, but of the two, the Yadu dynasty was more glorious due to the appearance of Lord

Kṛṣṇa. Mahārāja Parīkṣit might have been thinking that the Kuru dynasty was not as fortunate as the others because the Supreme Lord did not appear in that family, neither as Kṛṣṇa, Lord Rāmacandra, Lord Ṛṣabhadeva or Mahārāja Pṛthu. Therefore Parīkṣit Mahārāja was encouraged by Śukadeva Gosvāmī in this particular verse.

The Kuru dynasty may be considered more glorious due to the presence of devotees like the five Pāṇḍavas, who rendered unalloyed devotional service. Although Lord Kṛṣṇa did not appear in the Kuru dynasty, He was so obligated to the Pāṇḍavas' devotional service that He acted as a maintainer of the family and spiritual master of the Pāṇḍavas. Although He took birth in the Yadu dynasty, Lord Kṛṣṇa was more affectionate to the Pāṇḍavas. By His actions, Lord Kṛṣṇa proved that He was more inclined to the Kuru dynasty than the Yadu dynasty. Indeed, Lord Kṛṣṇa, indebted to the Pāṇḍavas' devotional service, sometimes acted as their messenger, and He guided them through many dangerous situations. Therefore Mahārāja Parīkṣit should not have been saddened because Lord Kṛṣṇa did not appear in his family. The Supreme Personality of Godhead is always inclined toward His pure devotees, and by His action it is clear that liberation is not very important for the devotees. Lord Kṛṣṇa easily gives one liberation, but He does not so easily give one the facility to become a devotee. *Muktiṁ dadāti karhicit sma na bhakti-yogam.* Directly or indirectly, it is proved that *bhakti-yoga* is the basis for the supreme relationship with the Supreme Lord. It is far superior to liberation. For a pure devotee of the Lord, *mukti* is automatically attained.

TEXT 19

नित्यानुभूतनिजलाभनिवृत्ततृष्णः
श्रेयस्यतद्रचनया चिरसुप्तबुद्धेः ।
लोकस्य यः करुणयाभयमात्मलोक-
माख्यान्नमो भगवते ऋषभाय तस्मै ॥१९॥

nityānubhūta-nija-lābha-nivṛtta-tṛṣṇaḥ
śreyasy atad-racanayā cira-supta-buddheḥ
lokasya yaḥ karuṇayābhayam ātma-lokam
ākhyān namo bhagavate ṛṣabhāya tasmai

nitya-anubhūta—due to being always conscious of His real identity; *nija-lābha-nivṛtta-tṛṣṇaḥ*—who was complete in Himself and had no other desire to fulfill; *śreyasi*—in life's genuine welfare; *a-tat-racanayā*—by expanding activities in the material field, mistaking the body for the self; *cira*—for a long time; *supta*—sleeping; *buddheḥ*—whose intelligence; *lokasya*—of men; *yaḥ* —who (Lord Ṛṣabhadeva); *karuṇayā*—by His causeless mercy; *abhayam*—fearlessness; *ātma-lokam*—the real identity of the self; *ākhyāt*—instructed; *namaḥ*—respectful obeisances; *bhagavate*—unto the Supreme Personality of Godhead; *ṛṣabhāya*—unto Lord Ṛṣabhadeva; *tasmai*—unto Him.

TRANSLATION

The Supreme Personality of Godhead, Lord Ṛṣabhadeva, was fully aware of His true identity; therefore He was self-sufficient, and He did not desire external gratification. There was no need for Him to aspire for success, since He was complete in Himself. Those who unnecessarily engage in bodily conceptions and create an atmosphere of materialism are always ignorant of their real self-interest. Out of His causeless mercy, Lord Ṛṣabhadeva taught the self's real identity and the goal of life. We therefore offer our respectful obeisances unto the Lord, who appeared as Lord Ṛṣabhadeva.

PURPORT

This is the summary of this chapter, in which the activities of Lord Ṛṣabhadeva are described. Being the Supreme Personality of Godhead Himself, Lord Ṛṣabhadeva is complete in Himself. We living entities, as parts and parcels of the Supreme Lord, should follow the instructions of Lord Ṛṣabhadeva and become self-sufficient. We should not create unnecessary demands due to the bodily conception. When one is self-realized, he is sufficiently satisfied due to being situated in his original spiritual position. As confirmed in *Bhagavad-gītā* (18.54): *Brahma-bhūtaḥ prasannātmā na śocati na kāṅkṣati.* This is the goal of all living entities. Even though one may be situated within this material world, he can become fully satisfied and devoid of hankering and lamentation simply by following the instructions of the Lord as set forth in *Bhagavad-gītā* or *Śrīmad-Bhāgavatam.* Satisfaction through self-realization is called *svarūpānanda.* The conditioned soul, eternally sleeping in darkness, does not understand his self-interest. He simply tries to become happy by making material adjustments, but this is impossible. It is therefore said in *Śrīmad-Bhāgavatam, na te viduḥ svārtha-gatiṁ hi viṣṇum:* due to gross ignorance, the conditioned soul does not know that his real self-interest is to take shelter at the lotus feet of Lord Viṣṇu. To try to become happy by adjusting the material atmosphere is a useless endeavor. Indeed, it is impossible. By His personal behavior and instructions, Lord Ṛṣabhadeva enlightened the conditioned soul and showed him how to become self-sufficient in his spiritual identity.

Thus end the Bhaktivedanta purports of the Fifth Canto, Sixth Chapter, of the Śrīmad-Bhāgavatam, *entitled "The Activities of Lord Ṛṣabhadeva."*

CHAPTER SEVEN

The Activities of King Bharata

In this chapter, the activities of King Bharata Mahārāja, the emperor of the whole world, are described. Bharata Mahārāja performed various ritualistic ceremonies (Vedic *yajñas*) and satisfied the Supreme Lord by his different modes of worship. In due course of time, he left home and resided in Hardwar and passed his days in devotional activities. Being ordered by his father, Lord Ṛṣabhadeva, Bharata Mahārāja married Pañcajanī, the daughter of Viśvarūpa. After this, he ruled the whole world peacefully. Formerly this planet was known as Ajanābha, and after the reign of Bharata Mahārāja it became known as Bhārata-varṣa. Bharata Mahārāja begot five sons in the womb of Pañcajanī, and he named the sons Sumati, Rāṣṭrabhṛta, Sudarśana, Āvaraṇa and Dhūmraketu. Bharata Mahārāja was very rigid in executing religious principles and following in the footsteps of his father. He therefore ruled the citizens very successfully. Because he performed various *yajñas* to satisfy the Supreme Lord, he was personally very satisfied. Being of undisturbed mind, he increased his devotional activities unto Lord Vāsudeva. Bharata Mahārāja was competent in understanding the principles of saintly persons like Nārada, and he followed in the footsteps of the sages. He also kept Lord Vāsudeva constantly within his heart. After finishing his kingly duties, he divided his kingdom among his five sons. He then left home and went to the place of Pulaha known as Pulahāśrama. There he ate forest vegetables and fruits, and worshiped Lord Vāsudeva with everything available. Thus he increased his devotion toward Vāsudeva, and he automatically began to realize further his transcendental, blissful life. Due to his highly advanced spiritual position, there were sometimes visible in his body the *aṣṭa-sāttvika* transformations, such as ecstatic crying and bodily trembling, which are symptoms of love of Godhead. It is understood that Mahārāja Bharata worshiped the Supreme Lord with the *mantras* mentioned in the *Ṛg Veda,* generally known as Gāyatrī *mantra,* which aim at the Supreme Nārāyaṇa situated within the sun.

TEXT 1

श्रीशुक उवाच

भरतस्तु महाभागवतो यदा भगवतावनितलपरिपालनाय सञ्चिन्तितस्तदनु-
शासनपरः पञ्चजनीं विश्वरूपदुहितरमुपयेमे ॥१॥

śrī-śuka uvāca
bharatas tu mahā-bhāgavato yadā bhagavatāvani-tala-paripālanāya sañcintitas tad-anuśāsana-paraḥ pañcajanīṁ viśvarūpa-duhitaram upayeme.

śrī-śukaḥ uvāca—Śukadeva Gosvāmī said; *bharataḥ*—Mahārāja Bharata; *tu*—but; *mahā-bhāgavataḥ*—a *mahā-bhāgavata,* most exalted devotee of the Lord; *yadā*—when; *bhagavatā*—by the order of his father, Lord Ṛṣabhadeva; *avani-tala*—the surface of the globe; *paripālanāya*—for ruling over; *sañcintitaḥ*—made up his mind; *tat-anuśāsana-paraḥ*—engaged in governing the globe; *pañcajanīm*—Pañcajanī; *viśvarūpa-duhitaram*—the daughter of Viśvarūpa; *upayeme*—married.

TRANSLATION

Śukadeva Gosvāmī continued speaking to Mahārāja Parīkṣit: My dear King, Bharata Mahārāja was a topmost devotee. Following the orders of his father, who had already decided to install him on the throne, he began to rule the earth accordingly. When Bharata Mahārāja ruled the entire globe, he followed the orders of his father and married Pañcajanī, the daughter of Viśvarūpa.

TEXT 2

तस्यामु ह वा आत्मजान् कार्त्स्न्येनानुरूपानात्मनः पञ्च जनयामास भूतादिरिव भूतसूक्ष्माणि सुमतिं राष्ट्रभृतं सुदर्शनमावरणं धूम्रकेतुमिति ॥२॥

tasyām u ha vā ātmajān kārtsnyenānurūpān ātmanaḥ pañca janayām āsa bhūtādir iva bhūta-sūkṣmāṇi sumatiṁ rāṣṭrabhṛtaṁ sudarśanam āvaraṇaṁ dhūmraketum iti.

tasyām—in her womb; *u ha vā*—indeed; *ātma-jān*—sons; *kārtsnyena*—entirely; *anurūpān*—exactly like; *ātmanaḥ*—himself; *pañca*—five; *janayām āsa*—begot; *bhūta-ādiḥ iva*—like the false ego; *bhūta-sūkṣmāṇi*—the five subtle objects of sense perception; *su-matim*—Sumatim; *rāṣṭra-bhṛtam*—Rāṣṭrabhṛta; *su-darśanam*—Sudarśana; *āvaraṇam*—Āvaraṇa; *dhūmra-ketum*—Dhūmraketu; *iti*—thus.

TRANSLATION

Just as the false ego creates the subtle sense objects, Mahārāja Bharata created five sons in the womb of Pañcajanī, his wife. These sons were named Sumati, Rāṣṭrabhṛta, Sudarśana, Āvaraṇa and Dhūmraketu.

TEXT 3

अजनाभं नामैतद्वर्षं भारतमिति यत आरभ्य व्यपदिशन्ति ॥३॥

ajanābhaṁ nāmaitad varṣaṁ bhāratam iti yata ārabhya vyapadiśanti.

ajanābham—Ajanābha; *nāma*—by the name; *etat*—this; *varṣam*—island; *bhāratam*—Bhārata; *iti*—thus; *yataḥ*—from whom; *ārabhya*—beginning; *vyapadiśanti*—they celebrate.

TRANSLATION

Formerly this planet was known as Ajanābha-varṣa, but since Mahārāja Bharata's reign, it has become known as Bhārata-varṣa.

PURPORT

This planet was formerly known as Ajanābha because of the reign of King Nābhi. After Bharata Mahārāja ruled the planet, it became celebrated as Bhārata-varṣa.

TEXT 4

स बहुविन्महीपतिः पितृपितामहवदुरुवत्सलतया स्वे स्वे कर्मणि वर्तमानाः प्रजाः स्वधर्ममनुवर्तमानः पर्यपालयत् ॥४॥

sa bahuvin mahī-patiḥ pitṛ-pitāmahavad uru-vatsalatayā sve sve karmaṇi vartamānāḥ prajāḥ sva-dharmam anuvartamānaḥ paryapālayat.

saḥ—that King (Mahārāja Bharata); *bahu-vit*—being very advanced in knowledge; *mahī-patiḥ*—the ruler of the earth; *pitṛ*—father; *pitāmaha*—grandfather; *vat*—exactly like; *uru-vatsalatayā*—with the quality of being very affectionate to the citizens; *sve sve*—in their own respective; *karmaṇi*—duties; *vartamānāḥ*—remaining; *prajāḥ*—the citizens; *sva-dharmam anuvartamānaḥ*—being perfectly situated in his own occupational duty; *paryapālayat*—ruled.

TRANSLATION

Mahārāja Bharata was a very learned and experienced king on this earth. He perfectly ruled the citizens, being himself engaged in his own respective duties. Mahārāja Bharata was as affectionate to the citizens as his father and grandfather had been. Keeping them engaged in their occupational duties, he ruled the earth.

PURPORT

It is most important that the chief executive rules the citizens by keeping them fully engaged in their respective occupational duties. Some of the citizens were *brāhmaṇas,* some were *kṣatriyas,* and some were *vaiśyas* and *śūdras.* It is the duty of the government to see that the citizens act according to these material divisions for their spiritual advancement. No one should remain unemployed or unoccupied in any way. One must work as a *brāhmaṇa, kṣatriya, vaiśya* or *śūdra* on the material path, and on the spiritual path, everyone should act as a *brahmacārī, gṛhastha, vānaprastha* or *sannyāsī.* Although formerly the government was a monarchy, all the kings were very affectionate toward the citizens, and they strictly kept them engaged in their respective duties. Therefore society was very smoothly conducted.

TEXT 5

**ईजे च भगवन्तं यज्ञक्रतुरूपं क्रतुभिरुच्चावचैः श्रद्धयाऽऽहृताग्निहोत्रदर्शपूर्ण-
मासचातुर्मास्यपशुसोमानां प्रकृतिविकृतिभिरनुसवनं चातुर्होत्रविधिना ॥ ५ ॥**

*īje ca bhagavantaṁ yajña-kratu-rūpaṁ kratubhir uccāvacaiḥ
śraddhayāhṛtāgnihotra-darśa-pūrṇamāsa-cāturmāsya-paśu-somānāṁ
prakṛti-vikṛtibhir anusavanaṁ cāturhotra-vidhinā.*

īje—worshiped; *ca*—also; *bhagavantam*—the Supreme Personality of Godhead; *yajña-kratu-rūpam*—having the form of sacrifices without animals and sacrifices with animals; *kratubhiḥ*—by such sacrifices; *uccāvacaiḥ*—very great and very small; *śraddhayā*—with faith; *āhṛta*—being performed; *agni-hotra*—of the *agnihotra-yajña; darśa*—of the *darśa-yajña; pūrṇamāsa*—of the *pūrṇamāsa-yajña; cāturmāsya*—of the *cāturmāsya-yajña; paśu-somānām*—of the *yajña* with animals and the *yajña* with *soma-rasa; prakṛti*—by full performances; *vikṛtibhiḥ*—and by partial performances; *anusavanam*—almost always; *cātuḥ-hotra-vidhinā*—by the regulative principles of sacrifice directed by four kinds of priests.

TRANSLATION

With great faith King Bharata performed various kinds of sacrifice. He performed the sacrifices known as agni-hotra, darśa, pūrṇa-māsa, cātur-māsya, paśu-yajña [wherein a horse is sacrificed] and soma-yajña [wherein a kind of beverage is offered]. Sometimes these sacrifices were performed completely and sometimes partially. In any case, in all the sacrifices the

regulations of cāturhotra were strictly followed. In this way Bharata Mahārāja worshiped the Supreme Personality of Godhead.

PURPORT

Animals like hogs and cows were offered in sacrifice to test the proper execution of the sacrifice. Otherwise, there was no purpose in killing the animal. Actually the animal was offered in the sacrificial fire to get a rejuvenated life. Generally an old animal was sacrificed in the fire, and it would come out again in a youthful body. Some of the rituals however, did not require animal sacrifice. In the present age, animal sacrifices are forbidden. As stated by Śrī Caitanya Mahāprabhu:

aśvamedhaṁ gavālambhaṁ
sannyāsaṁ pala-paitṛkam
devareṇa sutotpattiṁ
kalau pañca vivarjayet

"In this age of Kali, five acts are forbidden: the offering of a horse in sacrifice, the offering of a cow in sacrifice, the acceptance of the order of *sannyāsa,* the offering of oblations of flesh to the forefathers, and a man's begetting children in his brother's wife." (*Cc. Ādi* 17.164) Such sacrifices are impossible in this age due to the scarcity of expert *brāhmaṇas* or *ṛtvijaḥ* who are able to take the responsibility. In the absence of these, the *saṅkīrtana-yajña* is recommended. *Yajñaiḥ saṅkīrtana-prāyair yajanti hi sumedhasaḥ* (*Bhāg.* 11.5.32). After all, sacrifices are executed to please the Supreme Personality of Godhead. *Yajñārtha-karma:* such activities should be carried out for the Supreme Lord's pleasure. In this age of Kali, the Supreme Lord in His incarnation of Śrī Caitanya Mahāprabhu should be worshiped with His associates by performance of *saṅkīrtana-yajña,* the congregational chanting of the Hare Kṛṣṇa *mantra.* This process is accepted by intelligent men. *Yajñaiḥ saṅkīrtana-prāyair yajanti hi sumedhasaḥ.* The word *sumedhasaḥ* refers to intelligent men who possess very good brain substance.

TEXT 6

सम्प्रचरत्सु नानायागेषु विरचिताङ्गक्रियेष्वपूर्वं यत्तत्क्रियाफलं धर्माख्यं परे ब्रह्मणि यज्ञपुरुषे सर्वदेवतालिङ्गानां मन्त्राणामर्थनियामकतया साक्षात्कर्तरि परदेवतायां भगवति वासुदेव एव भावयमान आत्मनैपुण्यमृदितकषायो

हविःष्वध्वर्युभिर्गृह्यमाणेषु स यजमानो यज्ञभाजो देवांस्तान् पुरुषावयवेष्वभ्यध्यायत् ॥६॥

sampracaratsu nānā-yāgeṣu viracitāṅga-kriyeṣv apūrvaṁ yat tat kriyā-phalaṁ dharmākhyaṁ pare brahmaṇi yajña-puruṣe sarva-devatā-liṅgānāṁ mantrāṇām artha-niyāma-katayā sākṣāt-kartari para-devatāyāṁ bhagavati vāsudeva eva bhāvayamāna ātma-naipuṇya-mṛdita-kaṣāyo haviḥṣv adhvaryubhir gṛhyamāṇeṣu sa yajamāno yajña-bhājo devāṁs tān puruṣāvayaveṣv abhyadhyāyat.

sampracaratsu—when beginning to perform; *nānā-yāgeṣu*—various kinds of sacrifice; *viracita-aṅga-kriyeṣu*—in which the supplementary rites were performed; *apūrvam*—remote; *yat*—whatever; *tat*—that; *kriyā-phalam*—the result of such sacrifice; *dharma-ākhyam*—by the name of religion; *pare*—unto the transcendence; *brahmaṇi*—the Supreme Lord; *yajña-puruṣe*—the enjoyer of all sacrifices; *sarva-devatā-liṅgānām*—which manifest all the demigods; *mantrāṇām*—of the Vedic hymns; *artha-niyāma-katayā*—due to being the controller of the objects; *sākṣāt-kartari*—directly the performer; *para-devatāyām*—the origin of all demigods; *bhagavati*—the Supreme Personality of Godhead; *vāsudeve*—unto Kṛṣṇa; *eva*—certainly; *bhāvayamānaḥ*—always thinking; *ātma-naipuṇya-mṛdita-kaṣāyaḥ*—freed from all lust and anger by his expertise in such thinking; *haviḥṣu*—the ingredients to be offered in the sacrifice; *adhvaryubhiḥ*—when the priests expert in the sacrifices mentioned in the *Atharva Veda; gṛhyamāṇeṣu*—taking; *saḥ*—Mahārāja Bharata; *yajamānaḥ*—the sacrificer; *yajña-bhājaḥ*—the recipients of the results of sacrifice; *devān*—all the demigods; *tān*—them; *puruṣa-avayaveṣu*—as different parts and limbs of the body of the Supreme Personality of Godhead, Govinda; *abhyadhyāyat*—he thought.

TRANSLATION

After performing the preliminaries of various sacrifices, Mahārāja Bharata offered the results in the name of religion to the Supreme Personality of Godhead, Vāsudeva. In other words, he performed all the yajñas for the satisfaction of Lord Vāsudeva, Kṛṣṇa. Mahārāja Bharata thought that since the demigods were different parts of Vāsudeva's body, He controls those who are explained in the Vedic mantras. By thinking in this way, Mahārāja Bharata was freed from all material contamination, such as attachment, lust and greed. When the priests were about to offer

the sacrificial ingredients into the fire, Mahārāja Bharata expertly understood how the offering made to different demigods was simply an offering to the different limbs of the Lord. For instance, Indra is the arm of the Supreme Personality of Godhead, and Sūrya [the sun] is His eye. Thus Mahārāja Bharata considered that the oblations offered to different demigods were actually offered unto the different limbs of Lord Vāsudeva.

PURPORT

The Supreme Personality of Godhead says that as long as one does not develop the pure devotional service of *śravaṇaṁ kīrtanam,* hearing and chanting, one must carry out his prescribed duties. Since Bharata Mahārāja was a great devotee, one may ask why he performed so many sacrifices that are actually meant for *karmīs.* The fact is that he was simply following the orders of Vāsudeva. As Kṛṣṇa says in *Bhagavad-gītā, sarva dharmān parityajya mām ekaṁ śaraṇaṁ vraja:* "Abandon all varieties of religion and just surrender unto Me." (Bg. 18.66) Whatever we do, we should constantly remember Vāsudeva. People are generally addicted to offering obeisances to various demigods, but Bharata Mahārāja simply wanted to please Lord Vāsudeva. As stated in *Bhagavad-gītā: bhoktāraṁ yajña-tapasāṁ sarva-loka-maheśvaram* (Bg. 5.29). A *yajña* may be carried out to satisfy a particular demigod, but when the *yajña is* offered to the *yajña-puruṣa,* Nārāyaṇa, the demigods are satisfied. The purpose of performing different *yajñas* is to satisfy the Supreme Lord. One may perform them in the name of different demigods or directly. If we directly offer oblations to the Supreme Personality of Godhead, the demigods are automatically satisfied. If we water the root of a tree, the branches, twigs, fruits and flowers are automatically satisfied. When one offers sacrifices to different demigods, one should remember that the demigods are simply parts of the body of the Supreme. If we worship the hand of a person, we intend to satisfy the person himself. If we massage a person's legs, we do not really serve the legs but the person who possesses the legs. All the demigods are different parts of the Lord, and if we offer service to them, we actually serve the Lord Himself. Demigod worship is mentioned in *Brahma-saṁhitā,* but actually the *ślokas* advocate worship of the Supreme Personality of Godhead, Govinda. For instance, worship of the goddess Durgā is mentioned this way in *Brahma-saṁhitā* (5.44):

sṛṣṭi-sthiti-pralaya-sādhana-śaktir ekā
chāyeva yasya bhuvanāni vibharti durgā

icchānurūpam api yasya ca ceṣṭate sā
govindam ādi-puruṣaṁ tam ahaṁ bhajāmi

Following the orders of Śrī Kṛṣṇa, the goddess Durgā creates, maintains and annihilates. Śrī Kṛṣṇa also confirms this statement in *Bhagavad-gītā. Mayādhyakṣeṇa prakṛtiḥ sūyate sa-carācaram:* "This material nature is working under My direction, O son of Kuntī, and it is producing all moving and unmoving beings." (Bg. 9.10)

We should worship the demigods in that spirit. Because the goddess Durgā satisfies Kṛṣṇa, we should therefore offer respects to Goddess Durgā. Because Lord Śiva is nothing but Kṛṣṇa's functional body, we should therefore offer respects to Lord Śiva. Similarly, we should offer respects to Brahmā, Agni and Sūrya. There are many offerings to different demigods, and one should always remember that these offerings are usually meant to satisfy the Supreme Personality of Godhead. Bharata Mahārāja did not aspire to receive some benediction from demigods. His aim was to please the Supreme Lord. In the *Mahābhārata,* among the thousand names of Viṣṇu, it is said *yajña-bhug yajña-kṛd yajñaḥ.* The enjoyer of *yajña,* the performer of *yajña* and *yajña* itself are the Supreme Lord. The Supreme Lord is the performer of everything, but out of ignorance the living entity thinks that he is the actor. As long as we think we are the actors, we bring about *karma-bandha* (bondage to activity). If we act for *yajña,* for Kṛṣṇa, there is no *karma-bandha. Yajñārthāt karmaṇo'nyatra loko'yaṁ karma-bandhanaḥ:* "Work done as a sacrifice for Viṣṇu has to be performed, otherwise work binds one to this material world." (Bg. 3.9)

Following the instructions of Bharata Mahārāja, we should act not for our personal satisfaction but for the satisfaction of the Supreme Personality of Godhead. In *Bhagavad-gītā* (17.28) it is also stated:

aśraddhayā hutaṁ dattaṁ
tapas taptaṁ kṛtaṁ ca yat
asad ity ucyate pārtha
na ca tat pretya no iha

Sacrifices, austerities and charities performed without faith in the Supreme Personality of Godhead are nonpermanent. Regardless of whatever rituals are performed, they are called *asat,* nonpermanent. They are therefore useless both in this life and the next.

Kings like Mahārāja Ambarīṣa and many other *rājarṣis* who were pure devotees of the Lord simply passed their time in the service of the Supreme Lord. When a pure devotee executes some service through the agency of another person, he should not be criticized, for his activities are meant for the satisfaction of the Supreme Lord. A devotee may have a priest perform some *karma-kāṇḍa,* and the priest may not be a pure Vaiṣṇava, but because the devotee wants to please the Supreme Lord, he should not be criticized. The word *apūrva* is very significant. The resultant actions of *karma* are called *apūrva.* When we act piously or impiously, immediate results do not ensue. We therefore wait for the results, which are called *apūrva.* The results are manifest in the future. Even the *smārtas* accept this *apūrva.* Pure devotees simply act for the pleasure of the Supreme Personality of Godhead; therefore the results of their activities are spiritual, or permanent. They are not like those of the *karmīs,* which are nonpermanent. This is confirmed in *Bhagavad-gītā* (4.23):

gata-saṅgasya muktasya
jñānāvasthita-cetasaḥ
yajñāyācarataḥ karma
samagraṁ pravilīyate

"The work of a man who is unattached to the modes of material nature and who is fully situated in transcendental knowledge merges entirely into transcendence."

A devotee is always free from material contamination. He is fully situated in knowledge, and therefore his sacrifices are intended for the satisfaction of the Supreme Personality of Godhead.

TEXT 7

एवं कर्मविशुद्ध्या विशुद्धसत्त्वस्यान्तर्हृदयाकाशशरीरे ब्रह्मणि भगवति वासुदेवे महापुरुषरूपोपलक्षणे श्रीवत्सकौस्तुभवनमालारिदरगदादिभिरुपलक्षिते निजपुरुषहृल्लिखितेनात्मनि पुरुषरूपेण विरोचमान उच्चैस्तरां भक्तिरनु-दिनमेधमानरयाजायत ॥७॥

evaṁ karma-viśuddhyā viśuddha-sattvasyāntar-hṛdayākāśa-śarīre brahmaṇi bhagavati vāsudeve mahā-puruṣa-rūpopalakṣaṇe śrīvatsa-kaustubha-vana-mālāri-dara-gadādibhir upalakṣite nija-puruṣa-hṛl-likhitenātmani puruṣa-rūpeṇa virocamāna uccaistarāṁ bhaktir anudinam edhamāna-rayājāyata.

evam—thus; *karma-viśuddhyā*—by offering everything for the service of the Supreme Personality of Godhead and not desiring any results of his pious activities; *viśuddha-sattvasya*—of Bharata Mahārāja, whose existence was completely purified; *antaḥ-hṛdaya-ākāśa-śarīre*—the Supersoul within the heart, as meditated on by *yogīs; brahmaṇi*—into impersonal Brahman, which is worshiped by impersonalist *jñānīs; bhagavati*—unto the Supreme Personality of Godhead; *vāsudeve*—the son of Vasudeva, Lord Kṛṣṇa; *mahā-puruṣa*—of the Supreme Person; *rūpa*—of the form; *upalakṣaṇe*—having the symptoms; *śrīvatsa*—the mark on the chest of the Lord; *kaustubha*—the Kaustubha gem used by the Lord; *vana-mālā*—flower garland; *ari-dara*—by the disc and conchshell; *gadā-ādibhiḥ*—by the club and other symbols; *upalakṣite*—being recognized; *nija-puruṣa-hṛt-likhitena*—which is situated in the heart of His own devotee like an engraved picture; *ātmani*—in his own mind; *puruṣa-rūpeṇa*—by His personal form; *virocamāne*—shining; *uccaistarām*—on a very high level; *bhaktiḥ*—devotional service; *anudinam*—day after day; *edhamāna*—increasing; *rayā*—possessing force; *ajāyata*—appeared.

TRANSLATION

In this way, being purified by ritualistic sacrifices, the heart of Mahārāja Bharata was completely uncontaminated. His devotional service unto Vāsudeva, Lord Kṛṣṇa, increased day after day. Lord Kṛṣṇa, the son of Vasudeva, is the original Personality of Godhead manifest as the Supersoul [Paramātmā] as well as the impersonal Brahman. Yogīs meditate upon the localized Paramātmā situated in the heart, jñānīs worship the impersonal Brahman as the Supreme Absolute Truth, and devotees worship Vāsudeva, the Supreme Personality of Godhead, whose transcendental body is described in the śāstras. His body is decorated with the Śrīvatsa, the Kaustubha jewel and a flower garland, and His hands hold a conchshell, disc, club and lotus flower. Devotees like Nārada always think of Him within their hearts.

PURPORT

Lord Vāsudeva, or Śrī Kṛṣṇa, the son of Vasudeva, is the Supreme Personality of Godhead. He is manifest within the hearts of *yogīs* in His Paramātmā feature, and He is worshiped as impersonal Brahman by *jñānīs.* The Paramātmā feature is described in the *śāstras* as having four hands, holding disc, conchshell, lotus flower and club. As confirmed in the *Śrīmad-Bhāgavatam* (2.2.8):

kecit sva-dehāntar-hṛdayāvakāśe
prādeśa-mātraṁ puruṣaṁ vasantam
catur-bhujaṁ kañja-rathāṅga-śaṅkha-
gadā-dharaṁ dhāraṇayā smaranti

Paramātmā is situated in the hearts of all living beings. He has four hands, which hold four symbolic weapons. All devotees who think of the Paramātmā within the heart worship the Supreme Personality of Godhead as the temple Deity. They also understand the impersonal features of the Lord and His bodily rays, the Brahman effulgence.

TEXT 8

एवं वर्षायुतसहस्रपर्यन्तावसितकर्मनिर्वाणावसरोऽधिभुज्यमानं स्वतनयेभ्यो रिक्थं पितृपैतामहं यथादायं विभज्य स्वयं सकलसम्पन्निकेतात्स्वनिकेतात् पुलहाश्रमं प्रवव्राज ॥८॥

evaṁ varṣāyuta-sahasra-paryantāvasita-karma-nirvāṇāvasaro 'dhibhujyamānaṁ sva-tanayebhyo rikthaṁ pitṛ-paitāmahaṁ yathā-dāyaṁ vibhajya svayaṁ sakala-sampan-niketāt sva-niketāt pulahāśramaṁ pravavrāja.

evam—thus being always engaged; *varṣa-ayuta-sahasra*—one thousand times ten thousand years; *paryanta*—until then; *avasita-karma-nirvāṇa-avasaraḥ*—Mahārāja Bharata who ascertained the moment of the end of his royal opulence; *adhibhujyamānam*—being enjoyed in this way for that duration; *sva-tanayebhyaḥ*—unto his own sons; *riktham*—the wealth; *pitṛ-paitāmaham*—which he received from his father and forefathers; *yathā-dāyam*—according to the *dāya-bhāk* laws of Manu; *vibhajya*—dividing; *svayam*—personally; *sakala-sampat*—of all kinds of opulence; *niketāt*—the abode; *sva-niketāt*—from his paternal home; *pulaha-āśramam pravavrāja*—he went to the *āśrama* of Pulaha in Hardwar (where the *śālagrāma-śilās* are obtainable).

TRANSLATION

Destiny fixed the time for Mahārāja Bharata's enjoyment of material opulence at one thousand times ten thousand years. When that period was finished, he retired from family life and divided the wealth he had received from his forefathers among his sons. He left his paternal home,

the reservoir of all opulence, and started for Pulahāśrama, which is situated in Hardwar. The śālagrāma-śilās are obtainable there.

PURPORT

According to the law of *dāya-bhāk,* when one inherits an estate, he must hand it over to the next generation. Bharata Mahārāja did this properly. First he enjoyed his paternal property for one thousand times ten thousand years. At the time of his retirement, he divided this property among his sons and left for Pulaha-āśrama.

TEXT 9

यत्र ह वाव भगवान् हरिरद्यापि तत्रत्यानां निजजनानां वात्सल्येन संनिधाप्यत इच्छारूपेण ॥९॥

yatra ha vāva bhagavān harir adyāpi tatratyānāṁ nija-janānāṁ
vātsalyena sannidhāpyata icchā-rūpeṇa.

yatra—where; *ha vāva*—certainly; *bhagavān*—the Supreme Personality of Godhead; *hariḥ*—the Lord; *adya-api*—even today; *tatratyānām*—residing in that place; *nija-janānām*—for His own devotees; *vātsalyena*—by His transcendental affection; *sannidhāpyate*—becomes visible; *icchā-rūpeṇa*—according to the desire of the devotee.

TRANSLATION

At Pulaha-āśrama, the Supreme Personality of Godhead, Hari, out of His transcendental affection for His devotee, becomes visible to His devotee, satisfying His devotee's desires.

PURPORT

The Lord always exists in different transcendental forms. As stated in *Brahma-saṁhitā* (5.39):

rāmādi-mūrtiṣu kalā-niyamena tiṣṭhan
nānāvatāram akarod bhuvaneṣu kintu
kṛṣṇaḥ svayaṁ samabhavat paramaḥ pumān yo
govindam ādi-puruṣaṁ tam ahaṁ bhajāmi

The Lord is situated as Himself, Lord Kṛṣṇa, the Supreme Personality of Godhead, and He is accompanied by His expansions like Lord Rāma, Baladeva,

Saṅkarṣaṇa, Nārāyaṇa, Mahā-Viṣṇu and so forth. The devotees worship all these forms according to their liking, and the Lord, out of His affection, presents Himself as *arcā-vigraha.* He sometimes presents Himself personally before the devotee out of reciprocation or affection. A devotee is always fully surrendered to the loving service of the Lord, and the Lord is visible to the devotee according to the devotee's desires. He may be present in the form of Lord Rāma, Lord Kṛṣṇa, Lord Nṛsiṁhadeva and so on. Such is the exchange of love between the Lord and His devotees.

TEXT 10

यत्राश्रमपदान्युभयतोनाभिभिर्दृषच्चक्रैश्चक्रनदी नाम सरित्प्रवरा सर्वतः पवित्री-करोति ॥१०॥

yatrāśrama-padāny ubhayato nābhibhir dṛṣac-cakraiś cakra-nadī nāma sarit-pravarā sarvataḥ pavitrī-karoti.

yatra—where; *āśrama-padāni*—all hermitages; *ubhayataḥ*—both on top and below; *nābhibhiḥ*—like the symbolic mark of a navel; *dṛṣat*—visible; *cakraiḥ*—with the circles; *cakra-nadī*—the Cakra-nadī River (generally known as the Gaṇḍakī); *nāma*—of the name; *sarit-pravarā*—the most important river of all; *sarvataḥ*—everywhere; *pavitrī-karoti*—sanctifies.

TRANSLATION

In Pulaha-āśrama is the Gaṇḍakī River, which is the best of all rivers. The śālagrāma-śilā, the marble pebbles, purify all those places. On each and every marble pebble, up and down, circles like navels are visible.

PURPORT

Śālagrāma-śilā refers to pebbles that appear like stones with circles marked up and down. These are available in the river known as Gaṇḍakī-nadī. Wherever the waters of this river flow, the place becomes immediately sanctified.

TEXT 11

तस्मिन् वाव किल स एकलः पुलहाश्रमोपवने विविधकुसुमकिसलयतुल-सिकाम्बुभिः कन्दमूलफलोपहारैश्च समीहमानो भगवत आराधनं विविक्त उपरतविषयाभिलाष उपभृतोपशमः परां निर्वृतिमवाप ॥११॥

tasmin vāva kila sa ekalaḥ pulahāśramopavane vividha-kusuma-kisalaya-tulasikāmbubhiḥ kanda-mūla-phalopahāraiś ca samīhamāno bhagavata ārādhanaṁ vivikta uparata-viṣayābhilāṣa upabhṛtopaśamaḥ parāṁ nirvṛtim avāpa.

tasmin—in that *āśrama; vāva kila*—indeed; *saḥ*—Bharata Mahārāja; *ekalaḥ*—alone, only; *pulaha-āśrama-upavane*—in the gardens situated in Pulaha-āśrama; *vividha-kusuma-kisalaya-tulasikā-ambubhiḥ*—with varieties of flowers, twigs and *tulasī* leaves, as well as with water; *kanda-mūla-phala-upahāraiḥ*—by offerings of roots, bulbs and fruits; *ca*—and; *samīhamānaḥ*—performing; *bhagavataḥ*—of the Supreme Personality of Godhead; *ārādhanam*—worshiping; *viviktaḥ*—purified; *uparata*—being freed from; *viṣaya-abhilāṣaḥ*—desire for material sense enjoyment; *upabhṛta*—increased; *upaśamaḥ*—tranquillity; *parām*—transcendental; *nirvṛtim*—satisfaction; *avāpa*—he obtained.

TRANSLATION

In the gardens of Pulaha-āśrama, Mahārāja Bharata lived alone and collected a variety of flowers, twigs and tulasī leaves. He also collected the water of the Gaṇḍakī River, as well as various roots, fruits and bulbs. With these he offered food to the Supreme Personality of Godhead, Vāsudeva, and, worshiping Him, he remained satisfied. In this way his heart was completely uncontaminated, and he did not have the least desire for material enjoyment. All material desires vanished. In this steady position, he felt full satisfaction and was situated in devotional service.

PURPORT

Everyone is searching after peace of mind. This is obtainable only when one is completely freed from the desire for material sense gratification and is engaged in the devotional service of the Lord. As stated in *Bhagavad-gītā: patraṁ puṣpaṁ phalaṁ toyaṁ yo me bhaktyā prayacchati.* Worship of the Lord is not at all expensive. One can offer the Lord a leaf, a flower, a little fruit and some water. The Supreme Lord accepts these offerings when they are offered with love and devotion. In this way, one can become freed from material desires. As long as one maintains material desires, he cannot be happy. As soon as one engages in the devotional service of the Lord, his mind is purified of all material desires. Then one becomes fully satisfied.

sa vai puṁsāṁ paro dharmo
yato bhaktir adhokṣaje

ahaituky apratihatā
yayātmā suprasīdati

vāsudeve bhagavati
bhakti-yogaḥ prayojitaḥ
janayaty āśu vairāgyaṁ
jñānaṁ ca yad ahaitukam

"The supreme occupation [*dharma*] for all humanity is that by which men can attain to loving devotional service unto the transcendent Lord. Such devotional service must be unmotivated and uninterrupted in order to completely satisfy the self. By rendering devotional service unto the Personality of Godhead, Śrī Kṛṣṇa, one immediately acquires causeless knowledge and detachment from the world." (*Bhāg.* 1.2.6–7)

These are the instructions given in *Śrīmad-Bhāgavatam,* the supreme Vedic literature. One may not be able to go to Pulaha-āśrama, but wherever one is one can happily render devotional service to the Lord by adopting the processes mentioned above.

TEXT 12

तयेत्थमविरतपुरुषपरिचर्यया भगवति प्रवर्धमानानुरागभरद्रुतहृदयशैथिल्यः प्रहर्षवेगेनात्मन्युद्भिद्यमानरोमपुलककुलक औत्कण्ठ्यप्रवृत्तप्रणयबाष्पनिरुद्धावलोकनयन एवं निजरमणारुणचरणारविन्दानुध्यानपरिचितभक्तियोगेन परिप्लुतपरमाह्लादगम्भीरहृदयह्रदावगाढधिषणस्तामपि क्रियमाणां भगवत्सपर्यां न सस्मार ॥१२॥

tayettham avirata-puruṣa-paricaryayā bhagavati pravardhamānā-nurāga-bhara-druta-hṛdaya-śaithilyaḥ praharṣa-vegenātmany udbhidyamāna-roma-pulaka-kulaka autkaṇṭhya-pravṛtta-praṇaya-bāṣpa-niruddhāvaloka-nayana evaṁ nija-ramaṇāruṇa-caraṇāravindānudhyāna-paricita-bhakti-yogena paripluta-paramāhlāda-gambhīra-hṛdaya-hradāvagāḍha-dhiṣaṇas tām api kriyamāṇāṁ bhagavat-saparyāṁ na sasmāra.

tayā—by that; *ittham*—in this manner; *avirata*—constant; *puruṣa*—of the Supreme Lord; *paricaryayā*—by service; *bhagavati*—unto the Supreme Personality of Godhead; *pravardhamāna*—constantly increasing; *anurāga*—of attachment; *bhara*—by the load; *druta*—melted; *hṛdaya*—heart;

śaithilyaḥ—laxity; *praharṣa-vegena*—by the force of transcendental ecstasy; *ātmani*—in his body; *udbhidyamāna-roma-pulaka-kulakaḥ*—standing of the hair on end; *autkaṇṭhya*—because of intense longing; *pravṛtta*—produced; *praṇaya-bāṣpa-niruddha-avaloka-nayanaḥ* awakening of tears of love in the eyes, obstructing the vision; *evam*—thus; *nija-ramaṇa-aruṇa-caraṇa-aravinda*—on the Lord's reddish lotus feet; *anudhyāna*—by meditating; *paricita*—increased; *bhakti-yogena*—by dint of devotional service; *paripluta*—spreading everywhere; *parama*—highest; *āhlāda*—of spiritual bliss; *gambhīra*—very deep; *hṛdaya-hrada*—in the heart, which is compared to a lake; *avagāḍha*—immersed; *dhiṣaṇaḥ*—whose intelligence; *tām*—that; *api*—although; *kriyamāṇām*—executing; *bhagavat*—of the Supreme Personality of Godhead; *saparyām*—the worship; *na*—not; *sasmāra*—remembered.

TRANSLATION

That most exalted devotee, Mahārāja Bharata, in this way engaged constantly in the devotional service of the Lord. Naturally his love for Vāsudeva, Kṛṣṇa, increased more and more and melted his heart. Consequently he gradually lost all attachment for regulative duties. The hairs of his body stood on end, and all the ecstatic bodily symptoms were manifest. Tears flowed from his eyes, so much so that he could not see anything. Thus he constantly meditated on the reddish lotus feet of the Lord. At that time, his heart, which was like a lake, was filled with the water of ecstatic love. When his mind was immersed in that lake, he even forgot the regulative service to the Lord.

PURPORT

When one is actually advanced in ecstatic love for Kṛṣṇa, eight transcendental, blissful symptoms are manifest in the body. Those are the symptoms of perfection arising from loving service to the Supreme Personality of Godhead. Since Mahārāja Bharata was constantly engaged in devotional service, all the symptoms of ecstatic love were manifest in his body.

TEXT 13

इत्थं धृतभगवद्व्रत ऐणेयाजिनवाससानुसवनाभिषेकार्द्रकपिशकुटिलजटा-
कलापेन च विरोचमानः सूर्यर्चा भगवन्तं हिरण्मयं पुरुषमुज्जिहाने सूर्य-
मण्डलेऽभ्युपतिष्ठन्नेतदु होवाच ॥१३॥

itthaṁ dhṛta-bhagavad-vrata aiṇeyājina-vāsasānusavanābhiṣekārdra-kapiśa-kuṭila-jaṭā-kalāpena ca virocamānaḥ sūryarcā bhagavantaṁ hiraṇmayaṁ puruṣam ujjihāne sūrya-maṇḍale'bhyupatiṣṭhann etad u hovāca.

ittham—in this way; *dhṛta-bhagavat-vrataḥ*—having accepted the vow to serve the Supreme Personality of Godhead; *aiṇeya-ajina-vāsasa*—with a dress of a deerskin; *anusavana*—three times in a day; *abhiṣeka*—by a bath; *ardra*—wet; *kapiśa*—tawny; *kuṭila-jaṭā*—of curling and matted hair; *kalāpena*—by masses; *ca*—and; *virocamānaḥ*—being very beautifully decorated; *sūryarcā*—by the Vedic hymns worshiping the expansion of Nārāyaṇa within the sun; *bhagavantam*—unto the Supreme Personality of Godhead; *hiraṇmayam*—the Lord, whose bodily hue is just like gold; *puruṣam*—the Supreme Personality of Godhead; *ujjihāne*—when rising; *sūrya-maṇḍale*—the sun globe; *abhyupatiṣṭhan*—worshiping; *etat*—this; *u ha*—certainly; *uvāca*—he recited.

TRANSLATION

Mahārāja Bharata appeared very beautiful. He had a wealth of curly hair on his head, which was wet from bathing three times daily. He dressed in a deerskin. He worshiped Lord Nārāyaṇa, whose body was composed of golden effulgence and who resided within the sun. Mahārāja Bharata worshiped Lord Nārāyaṇa by chanting the hymns given in the Ṛg Veda, and he recited the following verse as the sun rose.

PURPORT

The predominating Deity within the sun is Hiraṇmaya, Lord Nārāyaṇa. He is worshiped by the Gāyatrī *mantra: oṁ bhūr bhuvaḥ svaḥ tat savitur vareṇyaṁ bhargo devasya dhīmahi.* He is also worshiped by other hymns mentioned in the *Ṛg Veda,* for instance: *dhyeyaḥ sadā savitṛ-maṇḍala-madhya-vartī.* Within the sun, Lord Nārāyaṇa is situated, and He has a golden hue.

TEXT 14

परोरजः सवितुर्जातवेदो
देवस्य भर्गो मनसेदं जजान ।
सुरेतसादः पुनराविश्य चष्टे
हंसं गृध्राणं नृषद्रिङ्गिरामिमः ॥१४॥

paro-rajaḥ savitur jāta-vedo
devasya bhargo manasedaṁ jajāna
suretasādaḥ punar āviśya caṣṭe
haṁsaṁ gṛdhrāṇaṁ nṛṣad-riṅgirām imaḥ

paraḥ-rajaḥ—beyond the mode of passion (situated in the pure mode of goodness); *savituḥ*—of the one who illuminates the whole universe; *jāta-vedaḥ*—from which all the devotee's desires are fulfilled; *devasya*—of the Lord; *bhargaḥ*—the self-effulgence; *manasā*—simply by contemplating; *idam*—this universe; *jajāna*—created; *su-retasā*—by spiritual potency; *adaḥ*—this created world; *punaḥ*—again; *āviśya*—entering; *caṣṭe*—sees or maintains; *haṁsam*—the living entity; *gṛdhrāṇam*—desiring for material enjoyment; *nṛṣat*—to the intelligence; *riṅgirām*—to one who gives motion; *imaḥ*—let me offer my obeisances.

TRANSLATION

"The Supreme Personality of Godhead is situated in pure goodness. He illuminates the entire universe and bestows all benedictions upon His devotees. The Lord has created this universe from His own spiritual potency. According to His desire, the Lord entered this universe as the Supersoul, and by virtue of His different potencies, He is maintaining all living entities desiring material enjoyment. Let me offer my respectful obeisances unto the Lord, who is the giver of intelligence."

PURPORT

The predominating Deity of the sun is another expansion of Nārāyaṇa, who is illuminating the entire universe. The Lord enters the hearts of all living entities as the Supersoul, and He gives them intelligence and fulfills their material desires. This is also confirmed in *Bhagavad-gītā. Sarvasya cāhaṁ hṛdi sanniviṣṭaḥ.* "I am sitting in everyone's heart." (Bg. 15.15)

As the Supersoul, the Lord enters the hearts of all living entities. As stated in *Brahma-saṁhitā* (5.35), *aṇḍāntara-stha-paramāṇu-cayāntara-stham:* "He enters the universe and the atom as well." In the *Ṛg Veda,* the predominating Deity of the sun is worshiped by this mantra: *dhyeyaḥ sadā savitṛ-maṇḍala-madhya-vartī nārāyaṇaḥ sarasijāsana-sanniviṣṭaḥ.* Nārāyaṇa sits on His lotus flower within the sun. By reciting this *mantra,* every living entity should take shelter of Nārāyaṇa just as the sun rises. According to modern scientists, the material world rests on the sun's effulgence. Due to the sunshine, all planets are rotating and vegetables are growing. We also have information that the moonshine helps vegetables and herbs grow. Actually Nārāyaṇa within the sun is maintaining the entire universe; therefore Nārāyaṇa should be worshiped by the Gāyatrī *mantra* or the *Ṛg mantra.*

Thus end the Bhaktivedanta purports of the Fifth Canto, Seventh Chapter, of the Śrīmad-Bhāgavatam, *entitled "The activities of King Bharata."*

CHAPTER EIGHT

A Description of the Character of Bharata Mahārāja

Although Bharata Mahārāja was very elevated, he fell down due to his attachment to a young deer. One day after Bharata Mahārāja had taken his bath as usual in the River Gaṇḍakī and was chanting his *mantra,* he saw a pregnant deer come to the river to drink water. Suddenly there could be heard the thundering roar of a lion, and the deer was so frightened that it immediately gave birth to its calf. It then crossed the river, but died immediately thereafter. Mahārāja Bharata took compassion upon the motherless calf, rescued it from the water, took it to his *āśrama* and cared for it affectionately. He gradually became attached to this young deer and always thought of it affectionately. As it grew up, it became Mahārāja Bharata's constant companion, and he always took care of it. Gradually he became so absorbed in thinking of this deer that his mind became agitated. As he became more attached to the deer, his devotional service slackened. Although he was able to give up his opulent kingdom, he became attached to the deer. Thus he fell down from his mystic *yoga* practice. Once when the deer was absent, Mahārāja Bharata was so disturbed that he began to search for it. While searching and lamenting the deer's absence, Mahārāja Bharata fell down and died. Because his mind was fully absorbed thinking of the deer, he naturally took his next birth from the womb of a deer. However, because he was considerably advanced spiritually, he did not forget his past activities, even though he was in the body of a deer. He could understand how he had fallen down from his exalted position, and remembering this, he left his mother deer and again went to Pulaha-āśrama. He finally ended his fruitive activities in the form of a deer, and when he died he was released from the deer's body.

TEXT 1

श्रीशुक उवाच

एकदा तु महानद्यां कृताभिषेकनैयमिकावश्यको ब्रह्माक्षरमभिगृणानो मुहूर्तत्रयमुदकान्त उपविवेश ॥१॥

śrī-śuka uvāca
ekadā tu mahā-nadyāṁ kṛtābhiṣeka-naiyamikāvaśyako brahmākṣaram abhigṛṇāno muhūrta-trayam udakānta upaviveśa.

śrī-śukaḥ uvāca—Śrī Śukadeva Gosvāmī said; *ekadā*—once upon a time; *tu*—but; *mahā-nadyām*—in the great river known as Gaṇḍakī; *kṛta-abhiṣeka-naiyamika-avaśyakaḥ*—having taken a bath after finishing the daily external duties such as passing stool and urine and brushing the teeth; *brahma-akṣaram*—the *praṇava-mantra* (om); *abhigṛṇānaḥ*—chanting; *muhūrta-trayam*—for three minutes; *udaka-ante*—on the bank of the river; *upaviveśa*—he sat down.

TRANSLATION

Śrī Śukadeva Gosvāmī continued: My dear King, one day, after finishing his morning duties—evacuating, urinating and bathing—Mahārāja Bharata sat down on the bank of the River Gaṇḍakī for a few minutes and began chanting his mantra, beginning with oṁkāra.

TEXT 2

तत्र तदा राजन् हरिणी पिपासया जलाशयाभ्याशमेकैवोपजगाम ॥२॥

tatra tadā rājan hariṇī pipāsayā jalāśayābhyāśam ekaivopajagāma.

tatra—on the bank of the river; *tadā*—at the time; *rājan*—O King; *hariṇī*—a doe; *pipāsayā*—because of thirst; *jalāśaya-abhyāśam*—near the river; *eka*—one; *eva*—certainly; *upajagāma*—arrived.

TRANSLATION

O King, while Bharata Mahārāja was sitting on the bank of that river, a doe, being very thirsty, came there to drink.

TEXT 3

तया पेपीयमान उदके तावदेवाविदूरेण नदतो मृगपतेरुन्नादो लोकभयङ्कर उदपतत् ॥३॥

tayā pepīyamāna udake tāvad evāvidūreṇa nadato mṛga-pater
unnādo loka-bhayaṅkara udapatat.

tayā—by the doe; *pepīyamāne*—being drunk with great satisfaction; *udake*—the water; *tāvat eva*—exactly at that time; *avidūreṇa*—very near;

nadataḥ—roaring; *mṛga-pateḥ*—of one lion; *unnādaḥ*—the tumultuous sound; *loka-bhayam-kara*—very fearful to all living entities; *udapatat*—arose.

TRANSLATION

While the doe was drinking with great satisfaction, a lion, which was very close, roared very loudly. This was frightful to every living entity, and it was heard by the doe.

TEXT 4

तमुपश्रुत्य सा मृगवधूः प्रकृति विक्लवा चकितनिरीक्षणा सुतरामपिहरिभ-
याभिनिवेशव्यग्रहृदया पारिप्लवदृष्टिरगततृषा भयात् सहसैवोच्चक्राम ॥४॥

tam upaśrutya sā mṛga-vadhūḥ prakṛti-viklavā cakita-nirīkṣaṇā
sutarām api hari-bhayābhiniveśa-vyagra-hṛdayā pāriplava-dṛṣṭir
agata-tṛṣā bhayāt sahasaivoccakrāma.

tam upaśrutya—hearing that tumultuous sound; *sā*—that; *mṛga-vadhūḥ*—wife of a deer; *prakṛti-viklavā*—by nature always afraid of being killed by others; *cakita-nirīkṣaṇā*—having wandering eyes; *sutarām api*—almost immediately; *hari*—of the lion; *bhaya*—of fear; *abhiniveśa*—by the entrance; *vyagra-hṛdayā*—whose mind was agitated; *pāriplava-dṛṣṭiḥ*—whose eyes were moving to and fro; *agata-tṛṣā*—without fully satisfying the thirst; *bhayāt*—out of fear; *sahasā*—suddenly; *eva*—certainly; *uccakrāma*—crossed the river.

TRANSLATION

By nature the doe was always afraid of being killed by others, and it was always looking about suspiciously. When it heard the lion's tumultuous roar, it became very agitated. Looking here and there with disturbed eyes, the doe, although it had not fully satisfied itself by drinking water, suddenly leaped across the river.

TEXT 5

तस्या उत्पतन्त्या अन्तर्वत्न्या उरुभयावगलितो योनिनिर्गतो गर्भः स्रोतसि
निपपात ॥५॥

tasyā utpatantyā antarvatnyā uru-bhayāvagalito yoni-nirgato garbhaḥ
srotasi nipapāta.

tasyāḥ—of it; *utpatantyāḥ*—forcefully jumping up; *antarvatnyāḥ*—having a full womb; *uru-bhaya*—due to great fear; *avagalitaḥ*—having slipped out; *yoni-nirgataḥ*—coming out of the womb; *garbhaḥ*—the offspring; *srotasi*—in the flowing water; *nipapāta*—fell down.

TRANSLATION

The doe was pregnant, and when it jumped out of fear, the baby deer fell from its womb into the flowing waters of the river.

PURPORT

There is every chance of a woman's having a miscarriage if she experiences some ecstatic emotion or is frightened. Pregnant women should therefore be spared all these external influences.

TEXT 6

तत्प्रसवोत्सर्पणभयखेदातुरा स्वगणेन वियुज्यमाना कस्याञ्चिद्दर्यां कृष्णसारसती निपपाताथ च ममार ॥६॥

tat-prasavotsarpaṇa-bhaya-khedāturā sva-gaṇena viyujyamānā
kasyāñcid daryāṁ kṛṣṇa-sārasatī nipapātātha ca mamāra.

tat-prasava—from untimely discharge of that (baby deer); *utsarpaṇa*—from jumping across the river; *bhaya*—and from fear; *kheda*—by exhaustion; *āturā*—afflicted; *sva-gaṇena*—from the flock of deer; *viyujyamānā*—being separated; *kasyāñcit*—in some; *daryām*—cave of a mountain; *kṛṣṇa-sārasatī*—the black doe; *nipapāta*—fell down; *atha*—therefore; *ca*—and; *mamāra*—died.

TRANSLATION

Being separated from its flock and distressed by its miscarriage, the black doe, having crossed the river, was very much distressed. Indeed, it fell down in a cave and died immediately.

TEXT 7

तं त्वेणकुणकं कृपणं स्त्रोतसानूह्यमानमभिवीक्ष्यापविद्धं बन्धुरिवानुकम्पया राजर्षिर्भरत आदाय मृतमातरमित्याश्रमपदमनयत् ॥७॥

taṁ tv eṇa-kuṇakaṁ kṛpaṇaṁ srotasānūhyamānam
abhivīkṣyāpaviddhaṁ bandhur ivānukampayā rājarṣir bharata ādāya
mṛta-mātaram ity āśrama-padam anayat.

tam—that; *tu*—but; *eṇa-kuṇakam*—the deer calf; *kṛpaṇam*—helpless; *srotasā*—by the waves; *anūhyamānam*—floating; *abhivīkṣya*—seeing; *apaviddham*—removed from its own kind; *bandhuḥ iva*—just like a friend; *anukampayā*—with compassion; *rāja-ṛṣiḥ bharataḥ*—the great, saintly King Bharata; *ādāya*—taking; *mṛta-mātaram*—who lost its mother; *iti*—thus thinking; *āśrama-padam*—to the *āśrama; anayat*—brought.

TRANSLATION

The great King Bharata, while sitting on the bank of the river, saw the small deer, bereft of its mother, floating down the river. Seeing this, he felt great compassion. Like a sincere friend, he lifted the infant deer from the waves, and, knowing it to be motherless, brought it to his āśrama.

PURPORT

The laws of nature work in subtle ways unknown to us. Mahārāja Bharata was a great king very advanced in devotional service. He had almost reached the point of loving service to the Supreme Lord, but even from that platform he could fall down onto the material platform. In *Bhagavad-gītā* we are therefore warned:

yaṁ hi na vyathayanty ete
puruṣaṁ puruṣarṣabha
sama-duḥkha-sukhaṁ dhīraṁ
so'mṛtatvāya kalpate

"O best among men [Arjuna], the person who is not disturbed by happiness and distress and is steady in both is certainly eligible for liberation." (Bg. 2.15)

Spiritual salvation and liberation from material bondage must be worked out with great caution, otherwise a little discrepancy will cause one to fall down again into material existence. By studying the activities of Mahārāja Bharata, we can learn the art of becoming completely freed from all material attachment. As it will be revealed in later verses, Bharata Mahārāja had to accept the body of a deer due to being overly compassionate for this infant deer. We should be compassionate by raising one from the material platform to the spiritual platform; otherwise at any moment our spiritual advancement may be spoiled, and we may fall down onto the material platform. Mahārāja Bharata's compassion for the deer was the beginning of his falldown into the material world.

TEXT 8

तस्य ह वा एणकुणक उच्चैरेतस्मिन् कृतनिजाभिमानस्याहरहस्तत्पोषण-पालनलालनप्रीणनानुध्यानेनात्मनियमाः सहयमाः पुरुषपरिचर्यादय एकैकशः कतिपयेनाहर्गणेन वियुज्यमानाः किल सर्व एवोदवसन् ॥८॥

tasya ha vā eṇa-kuṇaka uccair etasmin kṛta-nijābhimānasyāhar-ahas tat-poṣaṇa-pālana-lālana-prīṇanānudhyānenātma-niyamāḥ saha-yamāḥ puruṣa-paricaryādaya ekaikaśaḥ katipayenāhar-gaṇena viyujyamānāḥ kila sarva evodavasan.

tasya—of that King; *ha vā*—indeed; *eṇa-kuṇake*—in the deer calf; *uccaiḥ*—greatly; *etasmin*—in this; *kṛta-nija-abhimānasya*—who accepted the calf as his own son; *ahaḥ-ahaḥ*—every day; *tat-poṣaṇa*—maintaining that calf; *pālana*—protecting from dangers; *lālana*—raising it or showing love to it by kissing and so on; *prīṇana*—petting it in love; *anudhyānena*—by such attachment; *ātma-niyamāḥ*—his personal activities for taking care of his body; *saha-yamāḥ*—with his spiritual duties, such as nonviolence, tolerance and simplicity; *puruṣa-paricaryā-ādayaḥ*—worshiping the Supreme Personality of Godhead and performing other duties; *eka-ekaśaḥ*—every day; *katipayena*—with only a few; *ahaḥ-gaṇena*—days of time; *viyujyamānāḥ*—being given up; *kila*—indeed; *sarve*—all; *eva*—certainly; *udavasan*—became destroyed.

TRANSLATION

Gradually Mahārāja Bharata became very affectionate toward the deer. He began to raise it and maintain it by giving it grass. He was always careful to protect it from the attacks of tigers and other animals. When it itched, he petted it, and in this way he always tried to keep it in a comfortable condition. He sometimes kissed it out of love. Being attached to raising the deer, Mahārāja Bharata forgot the rules and regulations for the advancement of spiritual life, and he gradually forgot to worship the Supreme Personality of Godhead. After a few days, he forgot everything about his spiritual advancement.

PURPORT

From this we can understand how we have to be very cautious in executing our spiritual duties by observing the rules and regulations and regularly chanting the Hare Kṛṣṇa *mahā-mantra.* If we neglect doing this, we will eventually fall down. We must rise early in the morning, bathe, attend *maṅgala-ārati,* worship the Deities, chant the Hare Kṛṣṇa *mantra,* study the Vedic literatures and follow all the rules prescribed by the *ācāryas* and the spiritual master. If we deviate from this process, we may fall down, even though we may be very highly advanced. As stated in *Bhagavad-gītā* (18.5):

yajña-dāna-tapaḥ-karma
na tyājyaṁ kāryam eva tat
yajño dānaṁ tapaś caiva
pāvanāni manīṣiṇām

"Acts of sacrifice, charity and penance are not to be given up but should be performed. Indeed, sacrifice, charity and penance purify even the great soul." Even if one is in the renounced order, he should never give up the regulative principles. He should worship the Deity and give his time and life to the service of Kṛṣṇa. He should also continue following the rules and regulations of austerity and penance. These things cannot be given up. One should not think oneself very advanced simply because one has accepted the *sannyāsa* order. The activities of Bharata Mahārāja should be carefully studied for one's spiritual advancement.

TEXT 9

अहो बतायं हरिणकुणकः कृपण ईश्वररथचरणपरिभ्रमणरयेण स्वगणसुहृद्-बन्धुभ्यः परिवर्जितः शरणं च मोपसादितो मामेव मातापितरौ भ्रातृज्ञातीन् यौथिकांश्चैवोपेयाय नान्यं कञ्चन वेद मय्यतिविस्रब्धश्चात एव मया मत्परायणस्य पोषणपालनप्रीणनलालनमनसूयुनानुष्ठेयं शरण्योपेक्षादोषविदुषा ॥९॥

aho batāyaṁ hariṇa-kuṇakaḥ kṛpaṇa īśvara-ratha-caraṇa-paribhramaṇa-rayeṇa sva-gaṇa-suhṛd-bandhubhyaḥ parivarjitaḥ śaraṇaṁ ca mopasādito mām eva mātā-pitarau bhrātṛ-jñātīn yauthikāṁś caivopeyāya nānyaṁ kañcana veda mayy ati-visrabdhaś cāta eva mayā mat-parāyaṇasya poṣaṇa-pālana-prīṇana-lālanam anasūyunānuṣṭheyaṁ śaraṇyopekṣā-doṣa-viduṣā.

aho bata—alas; *ayam*—this; *hariṇa-kuṇakaḥ*—the deer calf; *kṛpaṇaḥ*—helpless; *īśvara-ratha-caraṇa-paribhramaṇa-rayeṇa*—by the force of the rotation of the time agent of the Supreme Personality of Godhead, which is compared to the wheel of His chariot; *sva-gaṇa*—own kinsmen; *suhṛt*—and friends; *bandhubhyaḥ*—relatives; *parivarjitaḥ*—deprived of; *śaraṇam*—as shelter; *ca*—and; *mā*—me; *upasāditaḥ*—having obtained; *mām*—me; *eva*—alone; *mātā-pitarau*—father and mother; *bhrātṛ-jñātīn*—brothers and kinsmen; *yauthikān*—belonging to the herd; *ca*—also; *eva*—certainly; *upeyāya*—having gotten; *na*—not; *anyam*—anyone else; *kañcana*—some person; *veda*—it knows; *mayi*—in me; *ati*—very great; *visrabdhaḥ*—having faith; *ca*—and; *ataḥ eva*—therefore; *mayā*—by me; *mat-parāyaṇasya*—of one who is so dependent upon me; *poṣaṇa-pālana-prīṇana-lālanam*—raising, maintaining, petting and protecting; *anasūyunā*—who am without any grudge; *anuṣṭheyam*—to be executed; *śaraṇya*—the one who has taken shelter; *upekṣā*—of neglecting; *doṣa-viduṣā*—who knows the fault.

TRANSLATION

The great King Mahārāja Bharata began to think: Alas, this helpless young deer, by the force of time, an agent of the Supreme Personality of Godhead, has now lost its relatives and friends and has taken shelter of me. It does not know anyone but me, as I have become its father, mother, brother and relatives. This deer is thinking in this way, and it has full faith in me. It does not know anyone but me; therefore I should not be envious and think that for the deer my own welfare will be destroyed. I should certainly raise, protect, gratify and fondle it. When it has taken shelter with me, how can I neglect it? Even though the deer is disturbing my spiritual life, I realize that a helpless person who has taken shelter cannot be neglected. That would be a great fault.

PURPORT

When a person is advanced in spiritual consciousness or Kṛṣṇa consciousness, he naturally becomes very sympathetic toward all living entities suffering in the material world. Naturally such an advanced person thinks of the suffering of the people in general. However, if one does not know of the material sufferings of fallen souls and becomes sympathetic because of bodily comforts, as in the case of Bharata Mahārāja, such sympathy or compassion is the cause of one's downfall. If one is actually sympathetic to fallen, suffering humanity, he should try to elevate people from material consciousness to spiritual consciousness. As far as the deer was concerned, Bharata Mahārāja became very sympathetic, but he forgot that it was impossible for him to elevate a deer to spiritual consciousness, because, after all, a deer is but an animal. It was very dangerous for Bharata Mahārāja to sacrifice all his regulative principles simply to take care of an animal. The principles enunciated in *Bhagavad-gītā* should be followed. *Yaṁ hi na vyathayanty ete puruṣaṁ puruṣarṣabha.* As far as the material body is concerned, we cannot do anything for anyone. However, by the grace of Kṛṣṇa, we may raise a person to spiritual consciousness if we ourselves follow the rules and regulations. If we give up our own spiritual activities and simply become concerned with the bodily comforts of others, we will fall into a dangerous position.

TEXT 10

नूनं ह्यार्याः साधव उपशमशीलाः कृपणसुहृद एवंविधार्थे स्वार्थानपि गुरुतरानु-
पेक्षन्ते ॥१०॥

nūnaṁ hy āryāḥ sādhava upaśama-śīlāḥ kṛpaṇa-suhṛda evaṁ-
vidhārthe svārthān api gurutarān upekṣante.

nūnam—indeed; *hi*—certainly; *āryāḥ*—those who are advanced in civilization; *sādhavaḥ*—saintly persons; *upaśama-śīlāḥ*—even though completely in the renounced order of life; *kṛpaṇa-suhṛdaḥ*—the friends of the helpless; *evaṁ-vidha-arthe*—to execute such principles; *sva-arthān api*—even their own personal interests; *guru-tarān*—very important; *upekṣante*—neglect.

TRANSLATION

Even though one is in the renounced order, one who is advanced certainly feels compassion for suffering living entities. One should certainly neglect his own personal interests, although they may be very important, to protect one who has surrendered.

PURPORT

Māyā is very strong. In the name of philanthropy, altruism and communism, people are feeling compassion for suffering humanity throughout the world. Philanthropists and altruists do not realize that it is impossible to improve people's material conditions. Material conditions are already established by the superior administration according to one's *karma.* They cannot be changed. The only benefit we can render to suffering beings is to try to raise them to spiritual consciousness. Material comforts cannot be increased or decreased. It is therefore said in *Śrīmad-Bhāgavatam* (1.5.18), *tal labhyate duḥkhavad anyataḥ sukham:* "As far as material happiness is concerned, that comes without effort, just as tribulations come without effort." Material happiness and pain can be attained without endeavor. One should not bother for material activities. If one is at all sympathetic or able to do good to others, he should endeavor to raise people to Kṛṣṇa consciousness. In this way everyone advances spiritually by the grace of the Lord. For our instruction, Bharata Mahārāja acted in such a way. We should be very careful not to be misled by so-called welfare activities conducted in bodily terms. One should not give up his interest in attaining the favor of Lord Viṣṇu at any cost. Generally people do not know this, or they forget it. Consequently they sacrifice their original interest, the attainment of Viṣṇu's favor, and engage in philanthropic activities for bodily comfort.

TEXT 11

इति कृतानुषङ्ग आसनशयनाटनस्नानाशनादिषु सह मृगजहुना स्नेहानुबद्धहृदय
आसीत् ॥११॥

iti kṛtānuṣaṅga āsana-śayanāṭana-snānāśanādiṣu saha mṛga-jahunā
snehānubaddha-hṛdaya āsīt.

iti—thus; *kṛta-anuṣaṅgaḥ*—having developed attachment; *āsana*—sitting; *śayana*—lying down; *aṭana*—walking; *snāna*—bathing; *āśana-ādiṣu*—while eating and so on; *saha mṛga-jahunā*—with the deer calf; *sneha-anubaddha*—captivated by affection; *hṛdayaḥ*—his heart; *āsīt*—became.

TRANSLATION

Due to attachment for the deer, Mahārāja Bharata lay down with it, walked about with it, bathed with it and even ate with it. Thus his heart became bound to the deer in affection.

TEXT 12

कुशकुसुमसमित्पलाशफलमूलोदकान्याहरिष्यमाणो वृकसालावृकादिभ्यो
भयमाशंसमानो यदा सह हरिणकुणकेन वनं समाविशति ॥१२॥

kuśa-kusuma-samit-palāśa-phala-mūlodakāny āhariṣyamāṇo vṛkasālā-
vṛkādibhyo bhayam āśaṁsamāno yadā saha hariṇa-kuṇakena vanaṁ
samāviśati.

kuśa—a kind of grass required for ritualistic ceremonies; *kusuma*—flowers; *samit*—firewood; *palāśa*—leaves; *phala-mūla*—fruits and roots;

udakāni—and water; *āhariṣyamāṇaḥ*—desiring to collect; *vṛkasālā-vṛka*—from wolves and dogs; *ādibhyaḥ*—and other animals, such as tigers; *bhayam*—fear; *āśaṁsamānaḥ*—doubting; *yadā*—when; *saha*—with; *hariṇa-kuṇakena*—the deer calf; *vanam*—the forest; *samāviśati*—enters.

TRANSLATION

When Mahārāja Bharata wanted to enter the forest to collect kuśa grass, flowers, wood, leaves, fruits, roots and water, he would fear that dogs, jackals, tigers and other ferocious animals might kill the deer. He would therefore always take the deer with him when entering the forest.

PURPORT

How Mahārāja Bharata increased his affection for the deer is described herein. Even such an exalted personality as Bharata Mahārāja, who had attained loving affection for the Supreme Personality of Godhead, fell down from his position due to his affection for some animal. Consequently, as will be seen, he had to accept the body of a deer in his next life. Since this was the case with Bharata Mahārāja, what can we say of those who are not advanced in spiritual life but who become attached to cats and dogs? Due to their affection for their cats and dogs, they have to take the same bodily forms in the next life unless they clearly increase their affection and love for the Supreme Personality of Godhead. Unless we increase our faith in the Supreme Lord, we shall be attracted to many other things. That is the cause of our material bondage.

TEXT 13

पथिषु च मुग्धभावेन तत्र तत्र विषक्तमतिप्रणयभरहृदयः कार्पण्यात्स्कन्धेनोद्वहति एवमुत्सङ्ग उरसि चाधायोपलालयन्मुदं परमामवाप ॥१३॥

pathiṣu ca mugdha-bhāvena tatra tatra viṣakta-mati-praṇaya-bhara-
hṛdayaḥ kārpaṇyāt skandhenodvahati evam utsaṅga urasi
cādhāyopalālayan mudaṁ paramām avāpa.

pathiṣu—on the forest paths; *ca*—also; *mugdha-bhāvena*—by the childish behavior of the deer; *tatra tatra*—here and there; *viṣakta-mati*—whose mind was too much attracted; *praṇaya*—with love; *bhara*—loaded; *hṛdayaḥ*—whose heart; *kārpaṇyāt*—because of affection and love; *skandhena*—by the shoulder; *udvahati*—carries; *evam*—in this way; *utsaṅge*—

sometimes on the lap; *urasi*—on the chest while sleeping; *ca*—also; *ādhāya* —keeping; *upalālayan*—fondling; *mudam*—pleasure; *paramām*—very great; *avāpa*—he felt.

TRANSLATION

When entering the forest, the animal would appear very attractive to Mahārāja Bharata due to its childish behavior. Mahārāja Bharata would even take the deer on his shoulders and carry it due to affection. His heart was so filled with great love for the deer that he would sometimes keep it on his lap or, when sleeping, on his chest. In this way he felt great pleasure in fondling the animal.

PURPORT

Mahārāja Bharata left his home, wife, children, kingdom and everything else to advance his spiritual life in the forest, but again he fell victim to material affection due to his attachment to an insignificant pet deer. What, then, was the use of his renouncing his family? One who is serious in advancing his spiritual life should be very cautious not to become attached to anything but Kṛṣṇa. Sometimes, in order to preach, we have to accept many material activities, but we should remember that everything is for Kṛṣṇa. If we remember this, there is no chance of our being victimized by material activities.

TEXT 14

क्रियायां निर्वर्त्यमानायामन्तरालेऽप्युत्थायोत्थाय यदैनमभिचक्षीत तर्हि वाव स वर्षपतिः प्रकृतिस्थेन मनसा तस्मा आशिष आशास्ते स्वस्ति स्ताद्वत्स ते सर्वत इति ॥१४॥

kriyāyāṁ nirvartyamānāyām antarāle'py utthāyotthāya yadainam
abhicakṣīta tarhi vāva sa varṣa-patiḥ prakṛti-sthena manasā tasmā āśiṣa
āśāste svasti stād vatsa te sarvata iti.

kriyāyām—the activities of worshiping the Lord or performing ritualistic ceremonies; *nirvartyamānāyām*—even without finishing; *antarāle*—at intervals in the middle; *api*—although; *utthāya utthāya*—repeatedly getting up; *yadā*—when; *enam*—the deer calf; *abhicakṣīta*—would see; *tarhi vāva* —at that time; *saḥ*—he; *varṣa-patiḥ*—Mahārāja Bharata; *prakṛti-sthena*—happy; *manasā*—within his mind; *tasmai*—unto it; *āśiṣaḥ āśāste*—bestows benedictions; *svasti*—all auspiciousness; *stāt*—let there be; *vatsa*—O my dear calf; *te*—unto you; *sarvataḥ*—in all respects; *iti*—thus.

TRANSLATION

When Mahārāja Bharata was actually worshiping the Lord or was engaged in some ritualistic ceremony, although his activities were unfinished, he would still, at intervals, get up and see where the deer was. In this way he would look for it, and when he could see that the deer was comfortably situated, his mind and heart would be very satisfied, and he would bestow his blessings upon the deer, saying, "My dear calf, may you be happy in all respects."

PURPORT

Because his attraction for the deer was so intense, Bharata Mahārāja could not concentrate upon worshiping the Lord or performing his ritualistic ceremonies. Even though he was engaged in worshiping the Deity, his mind was restless due to his inordinate affection. While trying to meditate, he would simply think of the deer, wondering where it had gone. In other words, if one's mind is distracted from worship, a mere show of worship will not be of any benefit. The fact that Bharata Mahārāja had to get up at intervals to look for the deer was simply a sign that he had fallen down from the spiritual platform.

TEXT 15

अन्यदा भृशमुद्विग्नमना नष्टद्रविण इव कृपणः सकरुणमतितर्षेण हरिणकुणक विरहविह्वलहृदयसन्तापस्तमेवानुशोचन् किल कश्मलं महदभिरम्भित इति होवाच ॥१५॥

anyadā bhṛśam udvigna-manā naṣṭa-draviṇa iva kṛpaṇaḥ
sakaruṇam ati-tarṣeṇa hariṇa-kuṇaka-viraha-vihvala-hṛdaya-santāpas
tam evānuśocan kila kaśmalaṁ mahad abhirambhita iti hovāca.

anyadā—sometimes (not seeing the calf); *bhṛśam*—very much; *udvigna-manāḥ*—his mind full of anxiety; *naṣṭa-draviṇaḥ*—who has lost his riches; *iva*—like; *kṛpaṇaḥ*—a miserly man; *sa-karuṇam*—piteously; *ati-tarṣeṇa*—with great anxiety; *hariṇa-kuṇaka*—from the calf of the deer; *viraha*—by separation; *vihvala*—agitated; *hṛdaya*—in mind or heart; *santāpaḥ*—whose affliction; *tam*—that calf; *eva*—only; *anuśocan*—continuously thinking of; *kila*—certainly; *kaśmalam*—illusion; *mahat*—very great; *abhirambhitaḥ*—obtained; *iti*—thus; *ha*—certainly; *uvāca*—said.

TRANSLATION

If Bharata Mahārāja sometimes could not see the deer, his mind would be very agitated. He would become like a miser, who, having obtained some riches, had lost them and had then become very unhappy. When the deer was gone, he would be filled with anxiety and would lament due to separation. Thus he would become illusioned and speak as follows.

PURPORT

If a poor man loses some money or gold, he at once becomes very agitated. Similarly, the mind of Mahārāja Bharata would become agitated when he did not see the deer. This is an example of how our attachment can be transferred. If our attachment is transferred to the Lord's service, we progress. Śrīla Rūpa Gosvāmī prayed to the Lord that he would be as naturally attracted to the Lord's service as young men and young women are naturally attracted to each other. Śrī Caitanya Mahāprabhu exhibited such attachment to the Lord when He jumped into the ocean or cried at night in separation. However, if our attachment is diverted to material things instead of to the Lord, we will fall down from the spiritual platform.

TEXT 16

अपि बत स वै कृपण एणबालको मृतहरिणीसुतोऽहो ममानार्यस्य शठ-किरातमतेरकृतसुकृतस्य कृतविस्रम्भ आत्मप्रत्ययेन तदविगणयन् सुजन इवागमिष्यति ॥१६॥

api bata sa vai kṛpaṇa eṇa-bālako mṛta-hariṇī-suto'ho mamānāryasya
śaṭha-kirāta-mater akṛta-sukṛtasya kṛta-visrambha ātma-pratyayena
tad avigaṇayan sujana ivāgamiṣyati.

api—indeed; *bata*—alas; *saḥ*—that calf; *vai*—certainly; *kṛpaṇaḥ*—aggrieved; *eṇa-bālakaḥ*—the deer child; *mṛta-hariṇī-sutaḥ*—the calf of the dead doe; *aho*—oh; *mama*—of me; *anāryasya*—the most ill-behaved; *śaṭha*—of a cheater; *kirāta*—or of an uncivilized aborigine; *mateḥ*—whose mind is that; *akṛta-sukṛtasya*—who has no pious activities; *kṛta-visrambhaḥ*—putting all faith; *ātma-pratyayena*—by assuming me to be like himself; *tat avigaṇayan*—without thinking of all these things; *su-janaḥ iva*—like a perfect gentle person; *agamiṣyati*—will he again return.

TRANSLATION

Bharata Mahārāja would think: Alas, the deer is now helpless. I am now very unfortunate, and my mind is like a cunning hunter, for it is always filled with cheating propensities and cruelty. The deer has put its faith in me, just as a good man who has a natural interest in good behavior forgets the misbehavior of a cunning friend and puts his faith in him. Although I have proved faithless, will this deer return and place its faith in me?

PURPORT

Bharata Mahārāja was very noble and exalted, and therefore when the deer was absent from him he thought himself unworthy to give it protection. Due to his attachment for the animal, he thought that the animal was as noble and exalted as he himself was. According to the logic of *ātmavan manyate jagat,* everyone thinks of others according to his own position. Therefore Mahārāja Bharata felt that the deer had left him due to his negligence and that due to the animal's noble heart, it would again return.

TEXT 17

अपि क्षेमेणास्मिन्नाश्रमोपवने शष्पाणि चरन्तं देवगुप्तं द्रक्ष्यामि ॥१७॥

api kṣemeṇāsminn āśramopavane śaṣpāṇi carantaṁ deva-guptaṁ drak-ṣyāmi.

api—it may be; *kṣemeṇa*—with fearlessness because of the absence of tigers and other animals; *asmin*—in this; *āśrama-upavane*—garden of the hermitage; *śaṣpāṇi carantam*—walking and eating the soft grasses; *deva-guptam*—being protected by the demigods; *drakṣyāmi*—shall I see.

TRANSLATION

Alas, is it possible that I shall again see this animal protected by the Lord and fearless of tigers and other animals? Shall I again see him wandering in the garden eating soft grass?

PURPORT

Mahārāja Bharata thought that the animal was disappointed in his protection and had left him for the protection of a demigod. Regardless, he ardently desired to see the animal again within his *āśrama* eating the soft grass and not fearing tigers and other animals. Mahārāja Bharata could think only of the deer and how the animal could be protected from all kinds of inauspicious things. From the materialistic point of view, such kind thoughts may be very laudable, but from the spiritual point of view the King was actually falling from his exalted spiritual position and unnecessarily becoming attached to an animal. Thus degrading himself, he would have to accept an animal body.

TEXT 18

अपि च न वृकः सालावृकोऽन्यतमो वा नैकचर एकचरो वा भक्षयति ॥१८॥

api ca na vṛkaḥ sālā-vṛko'nyatamo vā naika-cara eka-caro vā bhak-ṣayati.

api ca—or; *na*—not; *vṛkaḥ*—a wolf; *sālā-vṛkaḥ*—a dog; *anyatamaḥ*—any one of many; *vā*—or; *na-eka-caraḥ*—the hogs that flock together; *eka-caraḥ*—the tiger that wanders alone; *vā*—or; *bhakṣayati*—is eating (the poor creature).

TRANSLATION

I do not know, but the deer might have been eaten by a wolf or a dog or by the boars that flock together or the tiger who travels alone.

PURPORT

Tigers never wander in the forest in flocks. Each tiger wanders alone, but forest boars keep together. Similarly, hogs, wolves and dogs also do the same. Thus Mahārāja Bharata thought that the deer had been killed by some of the many ferocious animals within the forest.

TEXT 19

निम्लोचति ह भगवान् सकलजगत्क्षेमोदयस्त्रय्यात्माद्यापि मम न मृगव धून्यास आगच्छति ॥१९॥

nimlocati ha bhagavān sakala-jagat-kṣemodayas trayy-ātmādyāpi mama na mṛga-vadhū-nyāsa āgacchati.

nimlocati—sets; *ha*—alas; *bhagavān*—the Supreme Personality of Godhead, represented as the sun; *sakala-jagat*—of all the universe; *kṣema-udayaḥ*—who increases the auspiciousness; *trayī-ātmā*—who consists of the three *Vedas; adya api*—until now; *mama*—my; *na*—not; *mṛga-vadhū-nyāsaḥ*—this baby deer entrusted to me by its mother; *āgacchati*—has come back.

TRANSLATION

Alas, when the sun rises, all auspicious things begin. Unfortunately, they have not begun for me. The sun-god is the Vedas personified, but I am bereft of all Vedic principles. That sun-god is now setting, yet the poor animal who trusted in me since its mother died has not returned.

PURPORT

In the *Brahma-saṁhitā* (5.52), the sun is described as the eye of the Supreme Personality of Godhead.

yac-cakṣur eṣa savitā sakala-grahāṇāṁ
rājā samasta-sura-mūrtir aśeṣa-tejāḥ
yasyājñayā bhramati sambhṛta-kāla-cakro
govindam ādi-puruṣaṁ tam ahaṁ bhajāmi

As the sun arises, one should chant the Vedic *mantra* beginning with the Gāyatrī. The sun is the symbolic representation of the eyes of the Supreme Lord. Mahārāja Bharata lamented that although the sun was going to set, due to the poor animal's absence, he could not find anything auspicious. Bharata Mahārāja considered himself most unfortunate, for due to the animal's absence, there was nothing auspicious for him in the presence of the sun.

TEXT 20

अपिस्विदकृतसुकृतमागत्य मां सुखयिष्यति हरिणराजकुमारो विविधरुचिर-दर्शनीयनिजमृगदारकविनोदैरसन्तोषं स्वानामपनुदन् ॥२०॥

api svid akṛta-sukṛtam āgatya māṁ sukhayiṣyati hariṇa-rāja-kumāro
vividha-rucira-darśanīya-nija-mṛga-dāraka-vinodair asantoṣaṁ
svānām apanudan.

api svit—whether it will; *akṛta-sukṛtam*—who has never executed any pious activities; *āgatya*—coming back; *mām*—to me; *sukhayiṣyati*—give pleasure; *hariṇa-rāja-kumāraḥ*—the deer, who was just like a prince because of my taking care of it exactly like a son; *vividha*—various; *rucira*—very pleasing; *darśanīya*—to be seen; *nija*—own; *mṛga-dāraka*—befitting the calf of the deer; *vinodaiḥ*—by pleasing activities; *asantoṣam*—the unhappiness; *svānām*—of his own kind; *apanudan*—driving away.

TRANSLATION

That deer is exactly like a prince. When will it return? When will it again display its personal activities, which are so pleasing? When will it again pacify a wounded heart like mine? I certainly must have no pious assets, otherwise the deer would have returned by now.

PURPORT

Out of strong affection, the King accepted the small deer as if it were a prince. This is called *moha.* Due to his anxiety over the deer's absence, the King addressed the animal as though it were his son. Out of affection, anyone can be addressed as anything.

TEXT 21

क्ष्वेलिकायां मां मृषासमाधिनाऽऽमीलितदृशं प्रेमसंरम्भेण चकितचकित आगत्य पृषदपरुषविषाणाग्रेण लुठति ॥२१॥

kṣvelikāyāṁ māṁ mṛṣā-samādhināmīlita-dṛśaṁ prema-saṁrambheṇa cakita-cakita āgatya pṛṣad-aparuṣa-viṣāṇāgreṇa luṭhati.

kṣvelikāyām—while playing; *mām*—unto me; *mṛṣā*—feigning; *samādhinā*—by a meditational trance; *āmīlita-dṛśam*—with closed eyes; *prema-saṁrambheṇa*—because of anger due to love; *cakita-cakitaḥ*—with fear; *āgatya*—coming; *pṛṣat*—like drops of water; *aparuṣa*—very soft; *viṣāṇa*—of the horns; *agreṇa*—by the point; *luṭhati*—touches my body.

TRANSLATION

Alas, the small deer, while playing with me and seeing me feigning meditation with closed eyes, would circumambulate me due to anger arising from love, and it would fearfully touch me with the points of its soft horns, which felt like drops of water.

PURPORT

Now King Bharata considers his meditation false. While engaged in meditation, he was actually thinking of his deer, and he would feel great pleasure when the animal pricked him with the points of its horns. Feigning meditation, the King would actually think of the animal, and this was but a sign of his downfall.

TEXT 22

आसादितहविषि बर्हिषि दूषिते मयोपालब्धो भीतभीतः सपद्युपरतरास ऋषिकुमारवदवहितकरणकलाप आस्ते ॥२२॥

āsādita-haviṣi barhiṣi dūṣite mayopālabdho bhīta-bhītaḥ sapady uparata-rāsa ṛṣi-kumāravad avahita-karaṇa-kalāpa āste.

āsādita—placed; *haviṣi*—all the ingredients to be offered in the sacrifice; *barhiṣi*—on the *kuśa* grass; *dūṣite*—when polluted; *mayā upālabdhaḥ*—being scolded by me; *bhīta-bhītaḥ*—in great fear; *sapadi*—immediately; *uparata-rāsaḥ*—stopped its playing; *ṛṣi-kumāravat*—exactly like the son or disciple of a saintly person; *avahita*—completely restrained; *karaṇa-kalāpaḥ*—all the senses; *āste*—sits.

TRANSLATION

When I placed all the sacrificial ingredients on the kuśa grass, the deer, when playing, would touch the grass with its teeth and thus pollute it. When I chastised the deer by pushing it away, it would immediately become fearful and sit down motionless, exactly like the son of a saintly person. Thus it would stop its play.

PURPORT

Bharata Mahārāja was constantly thinking of the activities of the deer, forgetting that such meditation and diversion of attention was killing his progress in spiritual achievement.

TEXT 23

किं वा अरे आचरितं तपस्तपस्विन्यानया यदियमवनिः सविनयकृष्णसारत-नयतनुतरसुभगशिवतमाखरखुरपदपङ्क्तिभिर्द्रविण विधुरातुरस्य कृपणस्य मम द्रविणपदवीं सूचयन्त्यात्मानं च सर्वतः कृतकौतुकं द्विजानां स्वर्गापवर्ग-कामानां देवयजनं करोति ॥२३॥

kiṁ vā are ācaritaṁ tapas tapasvinyānayā yad iyam avaniḥ savinaya-kṛṣṇa-sāra-tanaya-tanutara-subhaga-śivatamākhara-khura-pada-paṅktibhir draviṇa-vidhurāturasya kṛpaṇasya mama draviṇa-padavīṁ sūcayanty ātmānaṁ ca sarvataḥ kṛta-kautukaṁ dvijānāṁ svargāpavarga-kāmānāṁ deva-yajanaṁ karoti.

kim vā—what; *are*—oh; *ācaritam*—practiced; *tapaḥ*—penance; *tapasvinyā*—by the most fortunate; *anayā*—this planet earth; *yat*—since; *iyam*—this; *avaniḥ*—earth; *sa-vinaya*—very mild and well-behaved; *kṛṣṇa-sāra-tanaya*—of the calf of the black deer; *tanutara*—small; *subhaga*—beautiful; *śiva-tama*—most auspicious; *akhara*—soft; *khura*—of the hooves; *pada-paṅktibhiḥ*—by the series of the marks; *draviṇa-vidhura-āturasya*—who is very aggrieved because of loss of wealth; *kṛpaṇasya*—a most unhappy creature; *mama*—for me; *draviṇa-padavīm*—the way to achieve that wealth; *sūcayanti*—indicating; *ātmānam*—her own personal body; *ca*—and; *sarvataḥ*—on all sides; *kṛta-kautukam*—ornamented; *dvijānām*—of the *brāhmaṇas; svarga-apavarga-kāmānām*—who are desirous of achieving heavenly planets or liberation; *deva-yajanam*—a place of sacrifice to the demigods; *karoti*—it makes.

TRANSLATION

After speaking like a madman in this way, Mahārāja Bharata got up and went outside. Seeing the footprints of the deer on the ground, he praised the footprints out of love, saying: O unfortunate Bharata, your austerities and penances are very insignificant compared to the penance and austerity undergone by this earth planet. Due to the earth's severe penances, the footprints of this deer, which are small, beautiful, most auspicious and soft, are imprinted on the surface of this fortunate planet. This series of footprints show a person like me, who am bereaved due to loss of the deer, how the animal has passed through the forest and how I can regain my lost wealth. By these footprints, this land has become a proper place for brāhmaṇas who desire heavenly planets or liberation to execute sacrifices to the demigods.

PURPORT

It is said that when a person becomes overly involved in loving affairs, he forgets himself as well as others, and he forgets how to act and how to speak. It is said that once when a man's son was blind since birth, the father, out of staunch affection for the child, named him Padmalocana, or "lotus-eyed." This is the situation arising from blind love. Bharata Mahārāja gradually fell into this condition due to his material love for the deer. It is said in the *smṛti-śāstra:*

yasmin deśe mṛgaḥ kṛṣṇas
tasmin dharmānn ivodhata

"That tract of land wherein the footprints of a black deer can be seen is to be understood as a suitable place to execute religious rituals."

TEXT 24

अपिस्विदसौ भगवानुडुपतिरेनं मृगपतिभयान्मृतमातरं मृगबालकं स्वाश्रमपरिभ्रष्टमनुकम्पया कृपणजनवत्सलः परिपाति ॥२४॥

api svid asau bhagavān uḍu-patir enaṁ mṛga-pati-bhayān mṛta-mātaraṁ mṛga-bālakaṁ svāśrama-paribhraṣṭam anukampayā kṛpaṇa-jana-vatsalaḥ paripāti.

api svit—can it be; *asau*—that; *bhagavān*—most powerful; *uḍu-patiḥ*—the moon; *enam*—this; *mṛga-pati-bhayāt*—because of fear of the lion; *mṛta-mātaram*—who lost its mother; *mṛga-bālakam*—the son of a deer; *sva-āśrama-paribhraṣṭam*—who strayed from its *āśrama; anukampayā*—out of compassion; *kṛpaṇa-jana-vatsalaḥ*—(the moon) who is very kind to the unhappy men; *paripāti*—now is protecting it.

TRANSLATION

Mahārāja Bharata continued to speak like a madman. Seeing above his head the dark marks on the rising moon, which resembled a deer, he said: Can it be that the moon, who is so kind to an unhappy man, might also be kind upon my deer, knowing that it has strayed from home and has become motherless? This moon has given the deer shelter near itself just to protect it from the fearful attacks of a lion.

TEXT 25

किं वाऽऽत्मजविश्लेषज्वरदवदहनशिखाभिरुपतप्यमानहृदयस्थलनलिनीकं मामुपसृतमृगीतनयं शिशिरशान्तानुरागगुणितनिजवदनसलिलामृतमयगभस्तिभिः स्वधयतीति च ॥२५॥

kiṁ vātmaja-viśleṣa-jvara-dava-dahana-śikhābhir upatapyamāna-hṛdaya-sthala-nalinīkaṁ mām upasṛta-mṛgī-tanayaṁ śiśira-śāntānurāga-guṇita-nija-vadana-salilāmṛtamaya-gabhastibhiḥ svadhayatīti ca.

kim vā—or it may be; *ātma-ja*—from the son; *viśleṣa*—because of separation; *jvara*—the heat; *dava-dahana*—of the forest fire; *śikhābhiḥ*—by the flames; *upatapyamāna*—being burned; *hṛdaya*—the heart; *sthala-nalinīkam*—compared to a red lotus flower; *mām*—unto me; *upasṛta-mṛgī-tanayam*—to whom the son of the deer was so submissive; *śiśira-śānta*—which is so peaceful and cool; *anurāga*—out of love; *guṇita*—flowing; *nija-vadana-salila*—the water from its mouth; *amṛta-maya*—as good as nectar; *gabhastibhiḥ*—by the rays of the moon; *svadhayati*—is giving me pleasure; *iti*—thus; *ca*—and.

TRANSLATION

After perceiving the moonshine, Mahārāja Bharata continued speaking like a crazy person. He said: The deer's son was so submissive and dear to me that due to its separation I am feeling separation from my own son. Due to the burning fever of this separation, I am suffering as if inflamed by a forest fire. My heart, which is like the lily of the land, is now burning. Seeing me so distressed, the moon is certainly splashing its shining nectar upon me—just as a friend throws water on another friend who has a high fever. In this way, the moon is bringing me happiness.

PURPORT

According to Āyurvedic treatment, it is said that if one has a high fever, someone should splash him with water after gargling this water. In this way the fever subsides. Although Bharata Mahārāja was very aggrieved due to the separation of his so-called son, the deer, he thought that the moon was splashing gargled water on him from its mouth and that this water would subdue his high fever, which was raging due to separation from the deer.

TEXT 26

एवमघटमानमनोरथाकुलहृदयो मृगदारकाभासेन स्वारब्धकर्मणा योगारम्भणतो विभ्रंशितः स योगतापसो भगवदाराधनलक्षणाच्च कथमितरथा जात्यन्तर एणकुणक आसङ्गः साक्षान्निःश्रेयसप्रतिपक्षतया प्राक्परित्यक्तदुस्त्यजहृदयाभिजातस्य तस्यैवमन्तरायविहत योगारम्भणस्य राजर्षेर्भरतस्य तावन्मृगार्भकपोषणपालनप्रीणनलालनानुषङ्गेणाविगणयत आत्मानमहिरिवाखुबिलं दुरतिक्रमः कालः करालरभस आपद्यत ॥२६॥

evam aghaṭamāna-manorathākula-hṛdayo mṛga-dārakābhāsena svārabdha-karmaṇā yogārambhaṇato vibhraṁśitaḥ sa yoga-tāpaso bhagavad-ārādhana-lakṣaṇāc ca katham itarathā jāty-antara eṇa-

kuṇaka āsaṅgaḥ sākṣān niḥśreyasa-pratipakṣatayā prāk-parityakta-dustyaja-hṛdayābhijātasya tasyaivam antarāya-vihata-yogārambhaṇasya rājarṣer bharatasya tāvan mṛgārbhaka-poṣaṇa-pālana-prīṇana-lālanānuṣaṅgeṇāvigaṇayata ātmānam ahir ivākhu-bilaṁ duratikramaḥ kālaḥ karāla-rabhasa āpadyata.

evam—in that way; *aghaṭamāna*—impossible to be achieved; *manaḥ-ratha*—by desires, which are like mental chariots; *ākula*—aggrieved; *hṛdayaḥ*—whose heart; *mṛga-dāraka-ābhāsena*—resembling the son of a deer; *sva-ārabdha-karmaṇā*—by the bad results of his unseen fruitive actions; *yoga-ārambhaṇataḥ*—from the activities of *yoga* performances; *vibhraṁśitaḥ*—fallen down; *saḥ*—he (Mahārāja Bharata); *yoga-tāpasaḥ*—executing the activities of mystic *yoga* and austerities; *bhagavat-ārādhana-lakṣaṇāt*—from the activities of devotional service rendered to the Supreme Personality of Godhead; *ca*—and; *katham*—how; *itarathā*—else; *jāti-antare*—belonging to a different species of life; *eṇa-kuṇake*—to the body of a deer calf; *āsaṅgaḥ*—so much affectionate attachment; *sākṣāt*—directly; *niḥśreyasa*—to achieve the ultimate goal of life; *pratipakṣatayā*—with the quality of being an obstacle; *prāk*—who previously; *parityakta*—given up; *dustyaja*—although very difficult to give up; *hṛdaya-abhijātasya*—his sons, born of his own heart; *tasya*—of him; *evam*—thus; *antarāya*—by that obstacle; *vihata*—obstructed; *yoga-ārambhaṇasya*—whose path of executing the mystic *yoga* practices; *rāja-ṛṣeḥ*—of the great saintly King; *bharatasya*—of Mahārāja Bharata; *tāvat*—in that way; *mṛga-arbhaka*—the son of a deer; *poṣaṇa*—in maintaining; *pālana*—in protecting; *prīṇana*—in making happy; *lālana*—in fondling; *anuṣaṅgeṇa*—by constant absorption; *avigaṇayataḥ*—neglecting; *ātmānam*—his own soul; *ahiḥ iva*—like a serpent; *ākhu-bilam*—the hole of a mouse; *duratikramaḥ*—unsurpassable; *kālaḥ*—ultimate death; *karāla*—terrible; *rabhasaḥ*—having speed; *āpadyata*—arrived.

TRANSLATION

Śukadeva Gosvāmī continued: My dear King, in this way Bharata Mahārāja was overwhelmed by an uncontrollable desire which was manifest in the form of the deer. Due to the fruitive results of his past deeds, he fell down from mystic yoga, austerity and worship of the Supreme Personality of Godhead. If it were not due to his past fruitive activity, how could he have been attracted to the deer after giving up the association of his own son and family, considering them stumbling blocks

on the path of spiritual life? How could he show such uncontrollable affection for a deer? This was definitely due to his past karma. The King was so engrossed in petting and maintaining the deer that he fell down from his spiritual activities. In due course of time, insurmountable death, which is compared to a venomous snake that enters the hole created by a mouse, situated itself before him.

PURPORT

As will be seen in later verses, Bharata Mahārāja, at the time of death, would be forced to accept the body of a deer due to his attraction for the deer. In this regard, a question may be raised. How can a devotee be affected by his past misconduct and vicious activities? In *Brahma-saṁhitā* (5.54) it is said, *karmāṇi nirdahati kintu ca bhakti-bhājām:* "For those engaged in devotional service, *bhakti-bhajana,* the results of past deeds are indemnified." According to this, Bharata Mahārāja could not be punished for his past misdeeds. The conclusion must be that Mahārāja Bharata purposefully became over-addicted to the deer and neglected his spiritual advancement. To immediately rectify his mistake, for a short time he was awarded the body of a deer. This was just to increase his desire for mature devotional service. Although Bharata Mahārāja was awarded the body of an animal, he did not forget what had previously happened due to his purposeful mistake. He was very anxious to get out of his deer body, and this indicates that his affection for devotional service was intensified, so much so that he was quickly to attain perfection in a *brāhmaṇa* body in the next life. It is with this conviction that we declare in our *Back to Godhead* magazine that devotees like the *gosvāmīs* living in Vṛndāvana who purposely commit some sinful activity are born in the bodies of dogs, monkeys and tortoises in that holy land. Thus they take on these lower life forms for a short while, and after they give up those animal bodies, they are again promoted to the spiritual world. Such punishment is only for a short period, and it is not due to past *karma.* It may appear to be due to past *karma,* but it is offered to rectify the devotee and bring him to pure devotional service.

TEXT 27

तदानीमपि पार्श्ववर्तिनमात्मजमिवानुशोचन्तमभिवीक्षमाणो मृगएवाभि-निवेशितमना विसृज्य लोकमिमं सह मृगेण कलेवरं मृतमनु न मृतजन्मानु-स्मृतिरितरवन्मृगशरीरमवाप ॥२७॥

tadānīm api pārśva-vartinam ātmajam ivānuśocantam abhivīkṣamāṇo mṛga evābhiniveśita-manā visṛjya lokam imaṁ saha mṛgeṇa kalevaraṁ mṛtam anu na mṛta-janmānusmṛtir itaravan mṛga-śarīram avāpa.

tadānīm—at that time; *api*—indeed; *pārśva-vartinam*—by the side of his deathbed; *ātma-jam*—his own son; *iva*—like; *anuśocantam*—lamenting; *abhivīkṣamāṇaḥ*—seeing; *mṛge*—in the deer; *eva*—certainly; *abhiniveśita-manāḥ*—his mind was absorbed; *visṛjya*—giving up; *lokam*—world; *imam*—this; *saha*—with; *mṛgeṇa*—the deer; *kalevaram*—his body; *mṛtam*—died; *anu*—thereafter; *na*—not; *mṛta*—destroyed; *janma-anusmṛtiḥ*—remembrance of the incident before his death; *itara-vat*—like others; *mṛga-śarīram*—the body of a deer; *avāpa*—got.

TRANSLATION

At the time of death, the King saw that the deer was sitting by his side, exactly like his own son, and was lamenting his death. Actually the mind of the King was absorbed in the body of the deer, and consequently—like those bereft of Kṛṣṇa consciousness—he left the world, the deer, and his material body and acquired the body of a deer. However, there was one advantage. Although he lost his human body and received the body of a deer, he did not forget the incidents of his past life.

PURPORT

There was a difference between Bharata Mahārāja's acquiring a deer body and others' acquiring different bodies according to their mental condition at the time of death. After death, others forget everything that has happened in their past lives, but Bharata Mahārāja did not forget. According to *Bhagavad-gītā:*

yaṁ yaṁ vāpi smaran bhāvaṁ
tyajaty ante kalevaram
taṁ tam evaiti kaunteya
sadā tad-bhāva-bhāvitaḥ

"Whatever state of being one remembers when he quits his body, that state he will attain without fail." (Bg. 8.6)

After quitting his body, a person gets another body according to his mental condition at the time of death. At death, a person always thinks of that subject matter in which he has been engrossed during his life. According to this law, because Bharata Mahārāja was always thinking of the deer and forgetting his worship of the Supreme Lord, he acquired the body of a deer. However, due to his having been elevated to the topmost platform of devotional service, he did not forget the incidents of his past life. This special benediction saved him from further deterioration. Due to his past activities in devotional service, he became determined to finish his devotional service even in the body of a deer. It is therefore said in this verse, *mṛtam,* although he had died, *anu,* afterwards, *na mṛta janmānusmṛtir itaravat,* he did not forget the incidents of his past life as others forget them. As stated in *Brahma-saṁhitā: karmāṇi nirdahati kintu ca bhakti-bhājām (Bs. 5.54).* It is proved herein that due to the grace of the Supreme Lord, a devotee is never vanquished. Due to his willful neglect of devotional service, a devotee may be punished for a short time, but he again revives his devotional service and returns home, back to Godhead.

TEXT 28

तत्रापि ह वा आत्मनो मृगत्वकारणं भगवदाराधनसमीहानुभावेनानुस्मृत्य
भृशमनुतप्यमान आह ॥२८॥

tatrāpi ha vā ātmano mṛgatva-kāraṇaṁ bhagavad-ārādhana-
samīhānubhāvenānusmṛtya bhṛśam anutapyamāna āha.

tatra api—in that birth; *ha vā*—indeed; *ātmanaḥ*—of himself; *mṛgatva-kāraṇam*—the cause of accepting the body of a deer; *bhagavat-ārādhana-samīhā*—of past activities in devotional service; *anubhāvena*—by consequence; *anusmṛtya*—remembering; *bhṛśam*—always; *anutapyamānaḥ*—repenting; *āha*—said.

TRANSLATION

Although in the body of a deer, Bharata Mahārāja, due to his rigid devotional service in his past life, could understand the cause of his birth in that body. Considering his past and present life, he constantly repented his activities, speaking in the following way.

PURPORT

This is a special concession for a devotee. Even if he attains a body that is nonhuman, by the grace of the Supreme Personality of Godhead he advances further in devotional service, whether by remembering his past life or by natural causes. It is not easy for a common man to remember the activities of his past life, but Bharata Mahārāja could remember his past activities due to his great sacrifices and engagement in devotional service.

TEXT 29

अहो कष्टं भ्रष्टोऽहमात्मवतामनुपथाद्यद्विमुक्तसमस्तसङ्गस्य विविक्तपुण्यारण्यशरणस्यात्मवत आत्मनि सर्वेषामात्मनां भगवति वासुदेवे तदनुश्रवणमननसङ्कीर्तनाराधनानुस्मरणाभियोगेनाशून्यसकलयामेन कालेन समावेशितं समाहितं कार्त्स्न्येन मनस्तत्तु पुनर्ममाबुधस्यारान्मृगसुतमनु परिसुस्राव ॥२९॥

aho kaṣṭaṁ bhraṣṭo'ham ātmavatām anupathād yad-vimukta-samasta-saṅgasya vivikta-puṇyāraṇya-śaraṇasyātmavata ātmani sarveṣām ātmanāṁ bhagavati vāsudeve tad-anuśravaṇa-manana-saṅkīrtanārādhanānusmaraṇābhiyogenāśūnya-sakala-yāmena kālena samāveśitaṁ samāhitaṁ kārtsnyena manas tat tu punar mamābudhasyārān mṛga-sutam anu parisusrāva.

aho kaṣṭam—alas, what a miserable condition of life; *bhraṣṭaḥ*—fallen; *aham*—I (am); *ātma-vatām*—of great devotees who have achieved perfection; *anupathāt*—from the way of life; *yat*—from which; *vimukta-samasta-saṅgasya*—although having given up the association of my real sons and home; *vivikta*—solitary; *puṇya-araṇya*—of a sacred forest; *śaraṇasya*—who had taken shelter; *ātma-vataḥ*—of one who had become perfectly situated on the transcendental platform; *ātmani*—in the Supersoul; *sarveṣām*—of all; *ātmanām*—living entities; *bhagavati*—unto the Supreme Personality of Godhead; *vāsudeve*—Lord Vāsudeva; *tat*—of Him; *anuśravaṇa*—constantly hearing; *manana*—thinking; *saṅkīrtana*—chanting; *ārādhana*—worshiping; *anusmaraṇa*—constantly remembering; *abhiyogena*—by absorption in; *aśūnya*—filled; *sakala-yāmena*—in which all the hours; *kālena*—by time; *samāveśitam*—fully established; *samāhitam*—fixed; *kārtsnyena*—totally; *manaḥ*—the mind in such a situation; *tat*—that mind; *tu*—but; *punaḥ*—again; *mama*—of me; *abudhasya*—a great fool; *ārāt*—from a great distance; *mṛga-sutam*—the son of a deer; *anu*—being affected by; *parisusrāva*—fell down.

TRANSLATION

In the body of a deer, Bharata Mahārāja began to lament: What misfortune! I have fallen from the path of the self-realized. I gave up my real sons, wife and home to advance in spiritual life, and I took shelter in a

solitary holy place in the forest. I became self-controlled and self-realized, and I engaged constantly in devotional service—hearing, thinking, chanting, worshiping and remembering the Supreme Personality of Godhead, Vāsudeva. I was successful in my attempt, so much so that my mind was always absorbed in devotional service. However, due to my personal foolishness, my mind again became attached—this time to a deer. Now I have obtained the body of a deer and have fallen far from my devotional practices.

PURPORT

Due to his stringent execution of devotional service, Mahārāja Bharata could remember the activities of his past life and how he was raised to the spiritual platform. Due to his foolishness, he became attached to an insignificant deer and thus fell down and had to accept the body of a deer. This is significant for every devotee. If we misuse our position and think that we are fully engaged in devotional service and can do whatever we like, we have to suffer like Bharata Mahārāja and be condemned to accept the type of body that impairs our devotional service. Only the human form is able to execute devotional service, but if we voluntarily give this up for sense gratification, we certainly have to be punished. This punishment is not exactly like that endured by an ordinary materialistic person. By the grace of the Supreme Lord, a devotee is punished in such a way that his eagerness to attain the lotus feet of Lord Vāsudeva is increased. By his intense desire, he returns home in the next lifetime. Devotional service is very completely described here: *tad-anuśravaṇa-manana-saṅkīrtanārādhanānusmaraṇābhiyogena.* The constant hearing and chanting of the glories of the Lord is recommended in *Bhagavad-gītā: satataṁ kīrtayanto māṁ yatantaś ca dṛḍha-vratāḥ.* Those who have taken to Kṛṣṇa consciousness should be very careful that not a single moment is wasted and that not a single moment is spent without chanting and remembering the Supreme Personality of Godhead and His activities. By His own actions and by the actions of His devotees, Kṛṣṇa teaches us how to become cautious in devotional service. Through the medium of Bharata Mahārāja, Kṛṣṇa teaches us that we must be careful in the discharge of devotional service. If we want to keep our minds completely fixed without deviation, we must engage them in devotional service full time. As far as the members of the International Society for Krishna Consciousness are concerned, they have sacrificed everything to push on this Kṛṣṇa consciousness movement. Yet they must take a lesson from the life of Bharata Mahārāja to be very cautious and to see that not a single moment is wasted in frivolous talk, sleep or voracious eating. Eating is not prohibited, but if we eat voraciously we shall certainly sleep more than required. Sense gratification ensues, and we may be degraded to a lower life form. In that way our spiritual progress may be checked at least for the time being. The best course is to take the advice of Śrīla Rūpa Gosvāmī: *avyartha-kālatvam.* We should see that every moment of our lives is utilized for the rendering of devotional service and nothing else. This is the secure position for one wanting to return home, back to Godhead.

TEXT 30

इत्येवं निगूढनिर्वेदो विसृज्य मृगीं मातरं पुनर्भगवत्क्षेत्रमुपशमशीलमुनि-गणदयितं शालग्रामं पुलस्त्यपुलहाश्रमं कालञ्जरात्प्रत्याजगाम ॥३०॥

ity evaṁ nigūḍha-nirvedo visṛjya mṛgīṁ mātaraṁ punar bhagavat-kṣetram upaśama-śīla-muni-gaṇa-dayitaṁ śālagrāmaṁ pulastya-pulahāśramaṁ kālañjarāt pratyājagāma.

iti—thus; *evam*—in this way; *nigūḍha*—hidden; *nirvedaḥ*—completely unattached to material activities; *visṛjya*—giving up; *mṛgīm*—the deer; *mātaram*—its mother; *punaḥ*—again; *bhagavat-kṣetram*—the place where the Supreme Lord is worshiped; *upaśama-śīla*—completely detached from all material attachments; *muni-gaṇa-dayitam*—which is dear to the great saintly residents; *śālagrāmam*—the village known as Śālagrāma; *pulastya-pulaha-āśramam*—to the *āśrama* conducted by such great sages as Pulastya and Pulaha; *kālañjarāt*—from the Kālañjara Mountain, where he had taken his birth in the womb of a deer; *pratyājagāma*—he came back.

TRANSLATION

Although Bharata Mahārāja received the body of a deer, by constant repentance he became completely detached from all material things. He did not disclose these things to anyone, but he left his mother deer in a place known as Kālañjara Mountain, where he was born. He again went to the forest of Śālagrāma and to the āśrama of Pulastya and Pulaha.

PURPORT

It is significant that Mahārāja Bharata, by the grace of Vāsudeva, remembered his past life. He did not waste a moment; he returned to Pulaha-āśrama to the village known as Śālagrāma. Association is very meaningful; therefore ISKCON tries to perfect one who enters the society. The members of this society should always remember that the society is not like a free hotel. All the members should be very careful to execute their spiritual duties so that whoever comes will automatically become a devotee and will be able to return back to Godhead in this very life. Although Bharata Mahārāja acquired the body of a deer, he again left his hearth and home, in this case the Mountain Kālañjara. No one should be captivated by his birthplace and family; one should take shelter of the association of devotees and cultivate Kṛṣṇa consciousness.

TEXT 31

तस्मिन्नपि कालं प्रतीक्षमाणः सङ्गाच्च भृशमुद्विग्न आत्मसहचरः शुष्कपर्ण-तृणवीरुधा वर्तमानो मृगत्वनिमित्तावसानमेव गणयन्मृगशरीरं तीर्थोदकक्लिन्नमुत्ससर्ज ॥३१॥

tasminn api kālaṁ pratīkṣamāṇaḥ saṅgāc ca bhṛśam udvigna ātma-sahacaraḥ śuṣka-parṇa-tṛṇa-vīrudhā vartamāno mṛgatva-nimittāvasānam eva gaṇayan mṛga-śarīraṁ tīrthodaka-klinnam ut-sasarja.

tasmin api—in that *āśrama* (Pulaha-āśrama); *kālam*—the end of the duration of life in the deer body; *pratīkṣamāṇaḥ*—always waiting for; *saṅgāt*—from association; *ca*—and; *bhṛśam*—constantly; *udvignaḥ*—full of anxiety; *ātma-sahacaraḥ*—having the Supersoul as the only constant companion (no one should think of being alone); *śuṣka-parṇa-tṛṇa-vīrudhā*—by eating only the dry leaves and herbs; *vartamānaḥ*—existing; *mṛgatva-nimitta*—of the cause of a deer's body; *avasānam*—the end; *eva*—only; *gaṇayan*—considering; *mṛga-śarīram*—the body of a deer; *tīrtha-udaka-klinnam*—bathing in the water of that holy place; *utsasarja*—gave up.

TRANSLATION

Remaining in that āśrama, the great King Bharata Mahārāja was now very careful not to fall victim to bad association. Without disclosing his past to anyone, he remained in that āśrama and ate dry leaves only. He was not exactly alone, for he had the association of the Supersoul. In this way he waited for death in the body of a deer. Bathing in that holy place, he finally gave up that body.

PURPORT

Holy places like Vṛndāvana, Hardwar, Prayāga and Jagannātha Purī are especially meant for the execution of devotional service. Vṛndāvana specifically is the most exalted and preferred holy place for Vaiṣṇava devotees of Lord Kṛṣṇa who are aspiring to return back to Godhead, the Vaikuṇṭha planets. There are many devotees in Vṛndāvana who regularly bathe in the Yamunā, and this cleanses all the contamination of the material world. By constantly chanting and hearing the holy names and pastimes of the Supreme Lord, one certainly becomes purified and becomes a fit candidate for liberation. However, if one purposefully falls victim to sense gratification, he has to be punished, at least for one lifetime, like Bharata Mahārāja.

Thus end the Bhaktivedanta purports of the Fifth Canto, Eighth Chapter, of the Śrīmad-Bhāgavatam, *entitled "A Description of the Character of Bharata Mahārāja."*

CHAPTER NINE

The Supreme Character of Jaḍa Bharata

In this chapter Bharata Mahārāja's attainment of the body of a *brāhmaṇa* is described. In this body he remained like one dull, deaf and dumb, so much so that when he was brought before the goddess Kālī to be killed as a sacrifice, he never protested but remained silent. After having given up the body of a deer, he took birth in the womb of the youngest wife of a *brāhmaṇa.* In this life he could also remember the activities of his past life, and in order to avoid the influence of society, he remained like a deaf and dumb person. He was very careful not to fall down again. He did not mix with anyone who was not a devotee. This process should be adopted by every devotee. As advised by Śrī Caitanya Mahāprabhu: *asat-saṅga-tyāga—ei vaiṣṇava-ācāra.* One should strictly avoid the company of nondevotees, even though they may be family members. When Bharata Mahārāja was in the body of a *brāhmaṇa,* the people in the neighborhood thought of him as a crazy, dull fellow, but within he was always chanting and remembering Vāsudeva, the Supreme Personality of Godhead. Although his father wanted to give him an education and purify him as a *brāhmaṇa* by offering him the sacred thread, he remained in such a way that his father and mother could understand that he was crazy and not interested in the reformatory method. Nonetheless, he remained fully Kṛṣṇa conscious, even without undergoing such official ceremonies. Due to his silence, some people who were no better than animals began to tease him in many ways, but he tolerated this. After the death of his father and mother, his stepmother and stepbrothers began to treat him very poorly. They would give him the most condemned food, but still he did not mind; he remained completely absorbed in Kṛṣṇa consciousness. He was ordered by his stepbrothers and mother to guard a paddy field one night, and at that time the leader of a dacoit party took him away and tried to kill him by offering him as a sacrifice before Bhadra Kālī. When the dacoits brought Bharata Mahārāja before the goddess Kālī and raised a chopper to kill him, the goddess Kālī became immediately alarmed due to the mistreatment of a devotee. She came out of the deity and, taking the chopper in her own hands, killed all the dacoits there. Thus a pure devotee of the Supreme Personality of Godhead can remain silent despite the mistreatment of nondevotees. Rogues and dacoits who misbehave toward a devotee are punished at last by the arrangement of the Supreme Personality of Godhead.

TEXTS 1–2

श्रीशुक उवाच

अथ कस्यचिद् द्विजवरस्याङ्गिरःप्रवरस्य शमदमतपः स्वाध्यायाध्ययनत्याग-सन्तोषतितिक्षाप्रश्रयविद्यानसूयात्मज्ञानानन्दयुक्तस्यात्मसदृशश्रुतशीलाचाररू-पौदार्यगुणा नव सोदर्या अङ्गजा बभूवुर्मिथुनं च यवीयस्यां भार्यायाम् ॥१॥ यस्तु तत्र पुमांस्तं परमभागवतं राजर्षिप्रवरं भरतमुत्सृष्टमृगशरीरं चरमशरीरेण विप्रत्वं गतमाहुः ॥२॥

śrī-śuka uvāca
atha kasyacid dvija-varasyāṅgiraḥ-pravarasya śama-dama-tapaḥ-svādhyāyādhyayana-tyāga-santoṣa-titikṣā-praśraya-vidyānasūyātma-jñānānanda-yuktasyātma-sadṛśa-śruta-śīlācāra-rūpaudārya-guṇā nava sodaryā aṅgajā babhūvur mithunaṁ ca yavīyasyāṁ bhāryāyām yas tu tatra pumāṁs taṁ parama-bhāgavataṁ rājarṣi-pravaraṁ bharatam utsṛṣṭa-mṛga-śarīraṁ carama-śarīreṇa vipratvaṁ gatam āhuḥ.

śrī-śukaḥ uvāca—Śukadeva Gosvāmī continued to speak; *atha*—thereafter; *kasyacit*—of some; *dvija-varasya*—*brāhmaṇa; aṅgiraḥ-pravarasya*—who came in the dynasty of the great saint Aṅgirā; *śama*—control of the mind; *dama*—control of the senses; *tapaḥ*—practice of austerities and penances; *svādhyāya*—recitation of the Vedic literatures; *adhyayana*—studying; *tyāga*—renunciation; *santoṣa*—satisfaction; *titikṣā*—tolerance; *praśraya*—very gentle; *vidyā*—knowledge; *anasūya*—without envy; *ātma-jñāna-ānanda*—satisfied in self-realization; *yuktasya*—who was qualified with; *ātma-sadṛśa*—and exactly like himself; *śruta*—in education; *śīla*—in character; *ācāra*—in behavior; *rūpa*—in beauty; *audārya*—in magnanimity; *guṇāḥ*—possessing all these qualities; *nava sa-udaryāḥ*—nine brothers born of the same womb; *aṅga-jāḥ*—sons; *babhūvuḥ*—were born; *mithunam*—a twin brother and sister; *ca*—and; *yavīyasyām*—in the youngest; *bhāryāyām*—wife; *yaḥ*—who; *tu*—but; *tatra*—there; *pumān*—the male child; *tam*—him; *parama-bhāgavatam*—the most exalted devotee; *rāja-ṛṣi*—of saintly kings; *pravaram*—most honored; *bharatam*—Bharata Mahārāja; *utsṛṣṭa*—having given up; *mṛga-śarīram*—the body of a deer; *carama-śarīreṇa*—with the last body; *vipratvam*—being a *brāhmaṇa; gatam*—obtained; *āhuḥ*—they said.

TRANSLATION

Śrīla Śukadeva Gosvāmī continued: My dear King, after giving up the body of a deer, Bharata Mahārāja took birth in a very pure brāhmaṇa family. There was a brāhmaṇa who belonged to the dynasty of Aṅgirā. He was fully qualified with brahminical qualifications. He could control his mind and senses, and he had studied the Vedic literatures and other subsidiary literatures. He was expert in giving charity, and he was always satisfied, tolerant, very gentle, learned and nonenvious. He was self-realized and engaged in the devotional service of the Lord. He remained always in a trance. He had nine equally qualified sons by his first wife, and by his second wife he begot twins—a brother and a sister, of which the male child was said to be the topmost devotee and foremost of saintly kings—Bharata Mahārāja. This, then, is the story of the birth he took after giving up the body of a deer.

PURPORT

Bharata Mahārāja was a great devotee, but he did not attain success in one life. In *Bhagavad-gītā* it is said that a devotee who does not fulfill his devotional duties in one life is given the chance to be born in a fully qualified *brāhmaṇa* family or a rich *kṣatriya* or *vaiśya* family. *Śucīnāṁ śrīmatāṁ gehe* (Bg. 6.41). Bharata Mahārāja was the firstborn son of Mahārāja Ṛṣabha in a rich *kṣatriya* family, but due to his willful negligence of his spiritual duties and his excessive attachment to an insignificant deer, he was obliged to take birth as the son of a deer. However, due to his strong position as a devotee, he was gifted with the remembrance of his past life. Being repentant, he remained in a solitary forest and always thought of Kṛṣṇa. Then he was given the chance to take birth in a very good *brāhmaṇa* family.

TEXT 3

तत्रापि स्वजनसङ्गाच्च भृशमुद्विजमानो भगवतः कर्मबन्धविध्वंसनश्रवणस्मरण-गुणविवरणचरणारविन्दयुगलं मनसा विदधदात्मनः प्रतिघातमाशङ्कमानो भगवदनुग्रहेणानुस्मृतस्वपूर्वजन्मावलिरात्मानमुन्मत्तजडान्धबधिरस्वरूपेण दर्शया-मास लोकस्य ॥ ३ ॥

tatrāpi svajana-saṅgāc ca bhṛśam udvijamāno bhagavataḥ karma-bandha-vidhvaṁsana-śravaṇa-smaraṇa-guṇa-vivaraṇa-caraṇāravinda-yugalaṁ manasā vidadhad ātmanaḥ pratighātam āśaṅkamāno bhagavad-anugraheṇānusmṛta-sva-pūrva-janmāvalir ātmānam unmatta-jaḍāndha-badhira-svarūpeṇa darśayām āsa lokasya.

tatra api—in that *brāhmaṇa* birth also; *sva-jana-saṅgāt*—from association with relatives and friends; *ca*—and; *bhṛśam*—greatly; *udvijamānaḥ*—being always afraid that he would fall down again; *bhagavataḥ*—of the Supreme Personality of Godhead; *karma-bandha*—the bondage of the reactions of fruitive activities; *vidhvaṁsana*—which vanquishes; *śravaṇa*—hearing; *smaraṇa*—remembering; *guṇa-vivaraṇa*—hearing descriptions of the qualities of the Lord; *caraṇa-aravinda*—lotus feet; *yugalam*—the two; *manasā*—with the mind; *vidadhat*—always thinking of; *ātmanaḥ*—of his soul; *pratighātam*—obstruction on the path of devotional service; *āśaṅkamānaḥ*—always fearing; *bhagavat-anugraheṇa*—by the special mercy of the Supreme Personality of Godhead; *anusmṛta*—remembered; *sva-pūrva*—his own previous; *janma-āvaliḥ*—string of births; *ātmānam*—himself; *unmatta*—mad; *jaḍa*—dull; *andha*—blind; *badhira*—and deaf; *svarūpeṇa*—with these features; *darśayām āsa*—he exhibited; *lokasya*—to people in general.

TRANSLATION

Due to his being especially gifted with the Lord's mercy, Bharata Mahārāja could remember the incidents of his past life. Although he received the body of a brāhmaṇa, he was still very much afraid of his relatives and friends who were not devotees. He was always very cautious of such association because he feared that he would again fall down. Consequently he manifested himself before the public eye as a madman—dull, blind and deaf—so that others would not try to talk to him. In this way he saved himself from bad association. Within he was always thinking of the lotus feet of the Lord and chanting the Lord's glories, which save one from the bondage of fruitive action. In this way he saved himself from the onslaught of nondevotee associates.

PURPORT

Every living entity is bound by different activities due to association with the modes of nature. As stated in *Bhagavad-gītā, kāraṇaṁ guṇa-saṅgo'sya sad-asad-yoni-janmasu:* "This is due to his association with that material nature. Thus he meets with good and evil among various species." (Bg. 13.22)

We get different types of bodies among 8,400,000 species according to our *karma. Karmaṇā daiva-netreṇa:* we work under the influence of material nature contaminated by the three modes, and thus we get a certain type of body according to superior order. This is called *karma-bandha.* To get out of this *karma-bandha,* one must engage himself in devotional service. Then one will not be affected by the modes of material nature.

māṁ ca yo'vyabhicāreṇa
bhakti-yogena sevate
sa guṇān samatītyaitān
brahma-bhūyāya kalpate

"One who engages in full devotional service, who does not fall down in any circumstance, at once transcends the modes of material nature and thus comes to the level of Brahman." (Bg. 14.26) To remain immune from the material qualities, one must engage himself in devotional service—*śravaṇaṁ kīrtanaṁ viṣṇoḥ.* That is the perfection of life. When Mahārāja Bharata took birth as a *brāhmaṇa,* he was not very interested in the duties of a *brāhmaṇa,* but within he remained a pure Vaiṣṇava, always thinking of the lotus feet of the Lord. As advised in *Bhagavad-gītā: man-manā bhava mad-bhakto mad-yājī māṁ namaskuru.* This is the only process by which one can be saved from the danger of repeated birth and death.

TEXT 4

तस्यापि ह वा आत्मजस्य विप्रः पुत्रस्नेहानुबद्धमनाआसमावर्तनात्संस्कारान् यथोपदेशं विदधान उपनीतस्य च पुनः शौचाचमनादीन् कर्मनियमाननभिप्रेतानपि समशिक्षयदनुशिष्टेन हि भाव्यं पितुः पुत्रेणेति ॥४॥

tasyāpi ha vā ātmajasya vipraḥ putra-snehānubaddha-manā
āsamāvartanāt saṁskārān yathopadeśaṁ vidadhāna upanītasya ca
punaḥ śaucācamanādīn karma-niyamān anabhipretān api
samaśikṣayad anuśiṣṭena hi bhāvyaṁ pituḥ putreṇeti.

tasya—of him; *api ha vā*—certainly; *ātma-jasya*—of his son; *vipraḥ*—the *brāhmaṇa* father of Jaḍa Bharata (mad, crazy Bharata); *putra-sneha-anubaddha-manāḥ*—who was obliged by affection for his son; *ā-sama-āvartanāt*—until the end of the *brahmacarya-āśrama; saṁskārān*—the purificatory processes; *yathā-upadeśam*—as prescribed in the *śāstras; vidadhānaḥ*—performing; *upanītasya*—of one who has a sacred thread; *ca*—also; *punaḥ*—again; *śauca-ācamana-ādīn*—practice of cleanliness, washing of the mouth, legs and hands, etc.; *karma-niyamān*—the regulative principles of fruitive activities; *anabhipretān api*—although not wanted by Jaḍa Bharata; *samaśikṣayat*—taught; *anuśiṣṭena*—taught to follow the regulative principles; *hi*—indeed; *bhāvyam*—should be; *pituḥ*—from the father; *putreṇa*—the son; *iti*—thus.

TRANSLATION

The brāhmaṇa father's mind was always filled with affection for his son, Jaḍa Bharata [Bharata Mahārāja]. Therefore he was always attached to Jaḍa Bharata. Because Jaḍa Bharata was unfit to enter the gṛhastha-āśrama, he simply executed the purificatory process up to the end of the brahmacarya-āśrama. Although Jaḍa Bharata was unwilling to accept his father's instructions, the brāhmaṇa nonetheless instructed him in how to keep clean and how to wash, thinking that the son should be taught by the father.

PURPORT

Jaḍa Bharata was Bharata Mahārāja in the body of a *brāhmaṇa,* and he outwardly conducted himself as if he were dull, deaf, dumb and blind. Actually he was quite alert within. He knew perfectly well of the results of fruitive activity and the results of devotional service. In the body of a *brāhmaṇa,* Mahārāja Bharata was completely absorbed in devotional service within; therefore it was not at all necessary for him to execute the regulative principles of fruitive activity. As confirmed in *Śrīmad-Bhāgavatam: svanuṣṭhitasya dharmasya saṁsiddhir hari-toṣaṇam* (*Bhāg.* 1.2.13). One has to satisfy Hari, the Supreme Personality of Godhead. That is the perfection of the regulative principles of fruitive activity. Besides that, it is stated in *Śrīmad-Bhāgavatam:*

dharmaḥ svanuṣṭhitaḥ puṁsāṁ
viṣvaksena-kathāsu yaḥ
notpādayed yadi ratiṁ
śrama eva hi kevalam

"Duties [*dharma*] executed by men, regardless of occupation, are only so much useless labor if they do not provoke attraction for the message of the Supreme Lord." (*Bhāg.* 1.2.8) These *karma-kāṇḍa* activities are required as long as one has not developed Kṛṣṇa consciousness. If one is developed in Kṛṣṇa consciousness, there is no need to execute the prior regulative principles of *karma-kāṇḍa.* Śrīla Mādhavendra Purī said, "O regulative principles of *karma-kāṇḍa,* please excuse me. I cannot follow all these regulative principles, for I am fully engaged in devotional service." He expressed the desire to sit somewhere beneath a tree and continue chanting the Hare Kṛṣṇa *mahā-mantra.* Consequently he did not execute all the regulative principles. Similarly, Haridāsa Ṭhākura was born in a Mohammedan family. From the very beginning of his life he was never trained in the *karma-kāṇḍa* system, but because he was always chanting the holy name of the Lord, Śrī Caitanya Mahāprabhu accepted him as *nāmācārya,* the authority in chanting the holy name. As Jaḍa Bharata, Bharata Mahārāja was always engaged in devotional service within his mind. Since he had executed the regulative principles continuously for three lives, he was not interested in continuing to execute them, although his *brāhmaṇa* father wanted him to do so.

TEXT 5

स चापि तदु ह पितृसंनिधावेवासध्रीचीनमिव स्म करोति छन्दांस्यध्यापयिष्यन् सह व्याहृतिभिः सप्रणवशिरस्त्रिपदीं सावित्रीं ग्रैष्मवासन्तिकान्मासानधीयान-मप्यसमवेतरूपं ग्राहयामास ॥ ५ ॥

sa cāpi tad u ha pitṛ-sannidhāv evāsadhrīcīnam iva sma karoti
chandāṁsy adhyāpayiṣyan saha vyāhṛtibhiḥ sapraṇava-śiras tripadīṁ
sāvitrīṁ graiṣma-vāsantikān māsān adhīyānam apy asamaveta-rūpaṁ
grāhayām āsa.

saḥ—he (Jaḍa Bharata); *ca*—also; *api*—indeed; *tat u ha*—that which was instructed by his father; *pitṛ-sannidhau*—in the presence of his father; *eva*—even; *asadhrīcīnam iva*—not correct, as if he could not understand anything; *sma karoti*—used to perform; *chandāṁsi adhyāpayiṣyan*—desiring to teach him Vedic *mantras* during the months beginning with Śrāvaṇa or during the period of Cāturmāsya; *saha*—along with; *vyāhṛtibhiḥ*—the utterance of the names of the heavenly planets (*bhūḥ, bhuvaḥ, svaḥ*); *sa-praṇava-śiraḥ*—headed by *oṁkāra; tri-padīm*—three-footed; *sāvitrīm*—the Gāyatrī *mantra; graiṣma-vāsantikān*—for four months, beginning with Caitra, on the fifteenth of May; *māsān*—the months; *adhīyānam api*—although fully studying; *asamaveta-rūpam*—in an incomplete form; *grāhayām āsa*—he made him learn.

TRANSLATION

Jaḍa Bharata behaved before his father like a fool, despite his father's adequately instructing him in Vedic knowledge. He behaved in that way

so that his father would know that he was unfit for instruction and would abandon the attempt to instruct him further. He would behave in a completely opposite way. Although instructed to wash his hands after evacuating, he would wash them before. Nonetheless, his father wanted to give him Vedic instructions during the spring and summer. He tried to teach him the Gāyatrī mantra along with oṁkāra and vyāhṛti, but after four months, his father still was not successful in instructing him.

TEXT 6

एवं स्वतनुज आत्मन्यनुरागावेशितचित्तः शौचाध्ययनव्रतनियमगुर्वनलशुश्रूषणाद्यौपकुर्वाणककर्माण्यनभियुक्तान्यपि समनुशिष्टेन भाव्यमित्यसदाग्रहः पुत्रमनुशास्य स्वयं तावद् अनधिगतमनोरथः कालेनाप्रमत्तेन स्वयं गृह एव प्रमत्त उपसंहृतः ॥६॥

evaṁ sva-tanuja ātmany anurāgāveśita-cittaḥ śaucādhyayana-vrata-niyama-gurv-anala-śuśrūṣaṇādy-aupakurvāṇaka-karmāṇy anabhiyuktāny api samanuśiṣṭena bhāvyam ity asad-āgrahaḥ putram anuśāsya svayaṁ tāvad anadhigata-manorathaḥ kālenāpramattena svayaṁ gṛha eva pramatta upasaṁhṛtaḥ.

evam—thus; *sva*—own; *tanu-je*—in his son, Jaḍa Bharata; *ātmani*—whom he considered to be himself; *anurāga-āveśita-cittaḥ*—the *brāhmaṇa* who was absorbed in love for his son; *śauca*—cleanliness; *adhyayana*—study of Vedic literature; *vrata*—accepting all the vows; *niyama*—regulative principles; *guru*—of the spiritual master; *anala*—of the fire; *śuśrūṣaṇa-ādi*—the service, etc.; *aupakurvāṇaka*—of the *brahmacarya-āśrama; karmāṇi*—all the activities; *anabhiyuktāni api*—although not liked by his son; *samanuśiṣṭena*—fully instructed; *bhāvyam*—should be; *iti*—thus; *asat-āgrahaḥ*—having unsuitable obstinacy; *putram*—his son; *anuśāsya*—instructing; *svayam*—himself; *tāvat*—in that way; *anadhigata-manorathaḥ*—not having fulfilled his desires; *kālena*—by the influence of time; *apramattena*—which is not forgetful; *svayam*—he himself; *gṛhe*—to his home; *eva*—certainly; *pramattaḥ*—being madly attached; *upasaṁhṛtaḥ*—died.

TRANSLATION

The brāhmaṇa father of Jaḍa Bharata considered his son his heart and soul, and therefore he was very much attached to him. He thought it wise

to educate his son properly, and being absorbed in this unsuccessful endeavor, he tried to teach his son the rules and regulations of brahmacarya—including the execution of the Vedic vows, cleanliness, study of the Vedas, the regulative methods, service to the spiritual master and the method of offering a fire sacrifice. He tried his best to teach his son in this way, but all his endeavors failed. In his heart he hoped that his son would be a learned scholar, but all his attempts were unsuccessful. Like everyone, this brāhmaṇa was attached to his home, and he had forgotten that someday he would die. Death, however, was not forgetful. At the proper time, death appeared and took him away.

PURPORT

Those too attached to family life, who forget that death comes in the future to take them away, become attached and unable to finish their duty as human beings. The duty of human life is to solve all the problems of life, but instead people remain attached to family affairs and duties. Although they forget death, death will not forget them. Suddenly they will be kicked off the platform of a peaceful family life. One may forget that he has to die, but death never forgets. Death comes always at the right time. The *brāhmaṇa* father of Jaḍa Bharata wanted to teach his son the process of *brahmacarya,* but he was unsuccessful due to his son's unwillingness to undergo the process of Vedic advancement. Jaḍa Bharata was simply concerned with returning home, back to Godhead, by executing devotional service through *śravaṇaṁ kīrtanaṁ viṣṇoḥ.* He did not care for the Vedic instructions of his father. When one is fully interested in the service of the Lord, he does not need to follow all the regulative principles enunciated in the *Vedas.* Of course, for an ordinary man, the Vedic principles are imperative. No one can avoid them. But when one has attained the perfection of devotional service, it is not very important to follow the Vedic principles. Lord Kṛṣṇa advised Arjuna to ascend to the platform of *nistraiguṇya,* the transcendental position above the Vedic principles.

traiguṇya-viṣayā vedā
nistraiguṇyo bhavārjuna
nirdvandvo nitya-sattva-stho
niryoga-kṣema ātmavān

"The *Vedas* mainly deal with the subject of the three modes of material nature. Rise above these modes, O Arjuna. Be transcendental to all of them. Be free from all dualities and from all anxieties for gain and safety, and be established in the Self." (Bg. 2.45)

TEXT 7

अथ यवीयसी द्विजसती स्वगर्भजातं मिथुनं सपत्न्या उपन्यस्य स्वयमनुसंस्थया पतिलोकमगात् ॥७॥

atha yavīyasī dvija-satī sva-garbha-jātaṁ mithunaṁ sapatnyā
upanyasya svayam anusaṁsthayā patilokam agāt.

atha—thereafter; *yavīyasī*—the youngest; *dvija-satī*—wife of the *brāhmaṇa; sva-garbha-jātam*—born of her womb; *mithunam*—the twins; *sapatnyai*—unto the co-wife; *upanyasya*—entrusting; *svayam*—personally; *anusaṁsthayā*—by following her husband; *pati-lokam*—the planet named Patiloka; *agāt*—went to.

TRANSLATION

Thereafter, the brāhmaṇa's younger wife, after entrusting her twin children—the boy and girl—to the elder wife, departed for Patiloka, voluntarily dying with her husband.

TEXT 8

पितर्युपरते भ्रातर एनमतत्प्रभावविदस्त्रय्यां विद्यायामेव पर्यवसितमतयो न परविद्यायां जडमतिरिति भ्रातुरनुशासननिर्बन्धान्न्यवृत्सन्त ॥८॥

pitary uparate bhrātara enam atat-prabhāva-vidas trayyāṁ
vidyāyām eva paryavasita-matayo na para-vidyāyāṁ jaḍa-matir iti
bhrātur anuśāsana-nirbandhān nyavṛtsanta.

pitari uparate—after the death of the father; *bhrātaraḥ*—the stepbrothers; *enam*—unto this Bharata (Jaḍa Bharata); *a-tat-prabhāva-vidaḥ*—without understanding his exalted position; *trayyām*—of the three *Vedas; vidyāyām*—in the matter of material ritualistic knowledge; *eva*—indeed; *paryavasita*—settled; *matayaḥ*—whose minds; *na*—not; *para-vidyāyām*—in the transcendental knowledge of spiritual life (devotional service); *jaḍa-matiḥ*—most dull intelligence; *iti*—thus; *bhrātuḥ*—their brother (Jaḍa Bharata); *anuśāsana-nirbandhāt*—from the endeavor to teach; *nyavṛtsanta*—stopped.

TRANSLATION

After the father died, the nine stepbrothers of Jaḍa Bharata, who considered Jaḍa Bharata dull and brainless, abandoned the father's attempt to give Jaḍa Bharata a complete education. The stepbrothers of Jaḍa Bharata were learned in the three Vedas—the Ṛg Veda, Sāma Veda and Yajur Veda—which very much encourage fruitive activity. The nine brothers were not at all spiritually enlightened in devotional service to the Lord. Consequently they could not understand the highly exalted position of Jaḍa Bharata.

TEXTS 9–10

स च प्राकृतैर्द्विपदपशुभिरुन्मत्तजडबधिरमूकेत्यभिभाष्यमाणो यदा तदनुरूपाणि प्रभाषते कर्माणि च कार्यमाणः परेच्छया करोति विष्टितो वेतनतो वा याच्ञया यदृच्छया वोपसादितमल्पं बहु मृष्टं कदन्नं वाभ्यवहरति परं नेन्द्रियप्रीतिनिमित्तम्। नित्यनिवृत्तनिमित्तस्वसिद्धविशुद्धानुभवानन्दस्वात्म-लाभाधिगमः सुखदुःखयोर्द्वन्द्वनिमित्तयोरसम्भावितदेहाभिमानः ॥९॥
शीतोष्णवातवर्षेषु वृष इवानावृताङ्गः पीनः संहननाङ्गः स्थण्डिलसंवेशनानुन्मर्दनामज्जनरजसा महामणिरिवानभिव्यक्तब्रह्मवर्चसः कुपटावृतकटिरुपवीतेनोरुमषिणा द्विजातिरिति ब्रह्मबन्धुरिति संज्ञयातज्ज्ञजनावमतो विचचार ॥१०॥

sa ca prākṛtair dvipada-paśubhir unmatta-jaḍa-badhira-mūkety abhibhāṣyamāṇo yadā tad-anurūpāṇi prabhāṣate karmāṇi ca kāryamāṇaḥ parecchayā karoti viṣṭito vetanato vā yācñayā yadṛcchayā vopasāditam alpaṁ bahu mṛṣṭaṁ kadannaṁ vābhyavaharati paraṁ nendriya-prīti-nimittam. nitya-nivṛtta-nimitta-sva-siddha-viśuddhānubhavānanda-svātma-lābhādhigamaḥ sukha-duḥkhayor dvandva-nimittayor asambhāvita-dehābhimānaḥ; śītoṣṇa-vāta-varṣeṣu vṛṣa ivānāvṛtāṅgaḥ pīnaḥ saṁhananāṅgaḥ sthaṇḍila-saṁveśanānunmardanāmajjana-rajasā mahāmaṇir ivānabhivyakta-brahma-varcasaḥ kupaṭāvṛta-kaṭir upavītenoru-maṣiṇā dvijātir iti brahma-bandhur iti saṁjñayātaj-jñajanāvamato vicacāra.

saḥ ca—he also; *prākṛtaiḥ*—by common persons who have no access to spiritual knowledge; *dvi-pada-paśubhiḥ*—who are nothing but animals with two legs; *unmatta*—mad; *jaḍa*—dull; *badhira*—deaf; *mūka*—dumb; *iti*—thus; *abhibhāṣyamāṇaḥ*—being addressed; *yadā*—when; *tat-anurūpāṇi*—words suitable to reply to theirs; *prabhāṣate*—he used to speak; *karmāṇi*

—activities; *ca*—also; *kāryamāṇaḥ*—being caused to execute; *para-icchayā* —by the order of others; *karoti*—he used to act; *viṣṭitaḥ*—by force; *vetanataḥ*—or by some wages; *vā*—either; *yācñayā*—by begging; *yadṛcchayā*—by its own accord; *vā*—or; *upasāditam*—gotten; *alpam*—a very small quantity; *bahu*—a large quantity; *mṛṣṭam*—very palatable; *kat-annam*—stale, tasteless foods; *vā*—or; *abhyavaharati*—he used to eat; *param*—only; *na*—not; *indriya-prīti-nimittam*—for the satisfaction of the senses; *nitya*—eternally; *nivṛtta*—stopped; *nimitta*—fruitive activity; *sva-siddha*—by self-accomplished; *viśuddha*—transcendental; *anubhava-ānanda*—blissful perception; *sva-ātma-lābha-adhigamaḥ*—who has achieved knowledge of the self; *sukha-duḥkhayoḥ*—in happiness and distress; *dvandva-nimittayoḥ*—in the causes of duality; *asambhāvita-deha-abhimānaḥ*—not identified with the body; *śīta*—in the winter; *uṣṇa*—in the summer; *vāta*—in the wind; *varṣeṣu*—in the rainfall; *vṛṣaḥ*—a bull; *iva*—like; *anāvṛta-aṅgaḥ*—uncovered body; *pīnaḥ*—very strong; *saṁhanana-aṅgaḥ*—whose limbs were firm; *sthaṇḍila-saṁveśana*—from lying down on the ground; *anunmardana*—without any massage; *amajjana* —without bathing; *rajasā*—by dirt; *mahā-maṇiḥ*—highly valuable gem; *iva* —like; *anabhivyakta*—unmanifested; *brahma-varcasaḥ*—spiritual splendor; *ku-paṭa-āvṛta*—covered by a dirty cloth; *kaṭiḥ*—whose loins; *upavītena*—with a sacred thread; *uru-maṣiṇā*—which was highly blackish due to dirt; *dvi-jātiḥ*—born in a *brāhmaṇa* family; *iti*—thus (saying out of contempt); *brahma-bandhuḥ*—a friend of a *brāhmaṇa; iti*—thus; *saṁjñayā*—by such names; *a-tat-jña-jana*—by persons not knowing his real position; *avamataḥ* —being disrespected; *vicacāra*—he wandered.

TRANSLATION

Degraded men are actually no better than animals. The only difference is that animals have four legs and such men have only two. These two-legged, animalistic men used to call Jaḍa Bharata mad, dull, deaf and dumb. They mistreated him, and Jaḍa Bharata behaved for them like a madman who was deaf, blind or dull. He did not protest or try to convince them that he was not so. If others wanted him to do something, he acted according to their desires. Whatever food he could acquire by begging or by wages, and whatever came of its own accord—be it a small quantity, palatable, stale or tasteless—he would accept and eat. He never ate anything for sense gratification because he was already liberated from the bodily conception, which induces one to accept palatable or unpalatable

food. He was full in the transcendental consciousness of devotional service, and therefore he was unaffected by the dualities arising from the bodily conception. Actually his body was as strong as a bull's, and his limbs were very muscular. He didn't care for winter or summer, wind or rain, and he never covered his body at any time. He lay on the ground, and never smeared oil on his body or took a bath. Because his body was dirty, his spiritual effulgence and knowledge were covered, just as the splendor of a valuable gem is covered by dirt. He only wore a dirty loincloth and his sacred thread, which was blackish. Understanding that he was born in a brāhmaṇa family, people would call him a brahma-bandhu and other names. Being thus insulted and neglected by materialistic people, he wandered here and there.

PURPORT

Śrīla Narottama dāsa Ṭhākura has sung: *deha-smṛti nāhi yāra, saṁsāra-bandhana kāhāṅ tāra.* One who has no desire to maintain the body or who is not anxious to keep the body in order and who is satisfied in any condition must be either mad or liberated. Actually Bharata Mahārāja in his birth as Jaḍa Bharata was completely liberated from material dualities. He was a *paramahaṁsa* and therefore did not care for bodily comfort.

TEXT 11

यदा तु परत आहारं कर्मवेतनत ईहमानः स्वभ्रातृभिरपि केदारकर्मणि निरूपितस्तदपि करोति किन्तु न समं विषमं न्यूनमधिकमिति वेद कणपिण्याकफलीकरणकुल्माषस्थालीपुरीषादीन्यप्यमृतवदभ्यवहरति ॥११॥

yadā tu parata āhāraṁ karma-vetanata īhamānaḥ sva-bhrātṛbhir api
kedāra-karmaṇi nirūpitas tad api karoti kintu na samaṁ viṣamaṁ
nyūnam adhikam iti veda kaṇa-piṇyāka-phalī-karaṇa-kulmāṣa-
sthālīpurīṣādīny apy amṛtavad abhyavaharati.

yadā—when; *tu*—but; *parataḥ*—from others; *āhāram*—food; *karma-vetanataḥ*—in exchange for wages from working; *īhamānaḥ*—looking for; *sva-bhrātṛbhiḥ api*—even by his own stepbrothers; *kedāra-karmaṇi*—in working in the field and adjusting the agricultural work; *nirūpitaḥ*—engaged; *tat api*—at that time also; *karoti*—he used to do; *kintu*—but; *na*—not; *samam*—level; *viṣamam*—uneven; *nyūnam*—deficient; *adhikam*—more raised; *iti*—thus; *veda*—he knew; *kaṇa*—broken rice; *piṇyāka*—oil cakes;

phalī-karaṇa—the chaff of rice; *kulmāṣa*—worm-eaten grains; *sthālī-purīṣa-ādīni*—burned rice stuck to the pot and so on; *api*—even; *amṛta-vat*—like nectar; *abhyavaharati*—used to eat.

TRANSLATION

Jaḍa Bharata used to work only for food. His stepbrothers took advantage of this and engaged him in agricultural field work in exchange for some food, but actually he did not know how to work very well in the field. He did not know where to spread dirt or where to make the ground level or uneven. His brothers used to give him broken rice, oil cakes, the chaff of rice, worm-eaten grains and burned grains that had stuck to the pot, but he gladly accepted all this as if it were nectar. He did not hold any grudges and ate all this very gladly.

PURPORT

The platform of *paramahaṁsa* is described in *Bhagavad-gītā* (2.15): *sama-duḥkha-sukhaṁ dhīraṁ so'mṛtatvāya kalpate.* When one is callous to all duality, the happiness and distress of this material world, one is fit for *amṛtatva,* eternal life. Bharata Mahārāja was determined to finish his business in this material world, and he did not at all care for the world of duality. He was complete in Kṛṣṇa consciousness and was oblivious to good and evil, happiness and distress. As stated in *Caitanya-caritāmṛta* (*Cc. Antya* 4.176):

'dvaite' bhadrābhadra-jñāna, saba-'manodharma'
'ei bhāla, ei manda',—saba 'bhrama'

"In the material world, conceptions of good and bad are all mental speculations. Therefore, saying, 'This is good and this is bad,' is all a mistake." One has to understand that in the material world of duality, to think that this is good or that this is bad is simply a mental concoction. However, one should not imitate this consciousness; one should actually be situated on the spiritual platform of neutrality.

TEXT 12

अथ कदाचित्कश्चिद् वृषलपतिर्भद्रकाल्यै पुरुषपशुमालभतापत्यकामः ॥१२॥

atha kadācit kaścid vṛṣala-patir bhadra-kālyai puruṣa-paśum
ālabhatāpatya-kāmaḥ.

atha—thereafter; *kadācit*—at some time; *kaścit*—some; *vṛṣala-patiḥ*—the leader of *śūdras* engaged in plundering the property of others; *bhadra-kālyai*—unto the goddess known as Bhadra Kālī; *puruṣa-paśum*—an animal in the shape of a man; *ālabhata*—started to sacrifice; *apatya-kāmaḥ*—desiring a son.

TRANSLATION

At this time, being desirous of obtaining a son, a leader of dacoits who came from a śūdra family wanted to worship the goddess Bhadra Kālī by offering her in sacrifice a dull man, who is considered no better than an animal.

PURPORT

Low-class men such as *śūdras* worship demigods like Goddess Kālī, or Bhadra Kālī, for the fulfillment of material desires. To this end, they sometimes kill a human being before the deity. They generally choose a person who is not very intelligent—in other words, an animal in the shape of a man.

TEXT 13

तस्य ह दैवमुक्तस्य पशोः पदवीं तदनुचराः परिधावन्तो निशि निशीथसमये तमसाऽऽवृतायामनधिगतपशव आकस्मिकेन विधिना केदारान् वीरासनेन मृगवराहादिभ्यः संरक्षमाणमङ्गिरःप्रवर सुतमपश्यन् ॥१३॥

tasya ha daiva-muktasya paśoḥ padavīṁ tad-anucarāḥ paridhāvanto
niśi niśītha-samaye tamasāvṛtāyām anadhigata-paśava ākasmikena
vidhinā kedārān vīrāsanena mṛga-varāhādibhyaḥ saṁrakṣamāṇam
aṅgiraḥ-pravara-sutam apaśyan.

tasya—of the leader of the dacoits; *ha*—certainly; *daiva-muktasya*—by chance having escaped; *paśoḥ*—of the human animal; *padavīm*—the path; *tat-anucarāḥ*—his followers or assistants; *paridhāvantaḥ*—searching here and there to find; *niśi*—at night; *niśītha-samaye*—at midnight; *tamasā āvṛtāyām*—being covered by darkness; *anadhigata-paśavaḥ*—not catching the man-animal; *ākasmikena vidhinā*—by the unexpected law of providence; *kedārān*—the fields; *vīra-āsanena*—by a seat on a raised place; *mṛga-varāha-ādibhyaḥ*—from the deer, wild pigs and so on; *saṁrakṣamāṇam*—protecting; *aṅgiraḥ-pravara-sutam*—the son of the *brāhmaṇa* descending from the Āṅgirā family; *apaśyan*—they found.

TRANSLATION

The leader of the dacoits captured a man-animal for sacrifice, but he escaped, and the leader ordered his followers to find him. They ran in different directions but could not find him. Wandering here and there in the middle of the night, covered by dense darkness, they came to a paddy field where they saw the exalted son of the Āṅgirā family [Jaḍa Bharata], who was sitting in an elevated place guarding the field against the attacks of deer and wild pigs.

TEXT 14

अथ त एनमनवद्यलक्षणमवमृश्य भर्तृकर्मनिष्पत्तिं मन्यमाना बद्ध्वा रशनया चण्डिकागृहमुपनिन्युर्मुदा विकसितवदनाः ॥१४॥

atha ta enam anavadya-lakṣaṇam avamṛśya bhartṛ-karma-niṣpattiṁ manyamānā baddhvā raśanayā caṇḍikā-gṛham upaninyur mudā vikasita-vadanāḥ.

atha—thereafter; *te*—they (the servants of the leader of the dacoits); *enam*—this (Jaḍa Bharata); *anavadya-lakṣaṇam*—as bearing the characteristics of a dull animal because of a fat body like a bull's and because of being deaf and dumb; *avamṛśya*—recognizing; *bhartṛ-karma-niṣpattim*—the accomplishment of their master's work; *manyamānāḥ*—understanding; *baddhvā*—binding tightly; *raśanayā*—with ropes; *caṇḍikā-gṛham*—to the temple of Goddess Kālī; *upaninyuḥ*—brought; *mudā*—with great happiness; *vikasita-vadanāḥ*—with bright faces.

TRANSLATION

The followers and servants of the dacoit chief considered Jaḍa Bharata to possess qualities quite suitable for a man-animal, and they decided that he was a perfect choice for sacrifice. Their faces bright with happiness, they bound him with ropes and brought him to the temple of the goddess Kālī.

PURPORT

In some parts of India, animalistic men are still sacrificed before the goddess Kālī. However, such a sacrifice is only performed by *śūdras* and dacoits. Their business is to plunder the wealthy, and to become successful they offer an animalistic man before the goddess Kālī. It should be noted that they never sacrifice an intelligent man before the goddess. In the body of a *brāhmaṇa,* Bharata Mahārāja appeared deaf and dumb, yet he was the most intelligent man in the world. Nonetheless, being completely surrendered unto the Supreme Personality of Godhead, he remained in that condition and did not protest being brought before the deity for slaughter. As we have learned from the previous verses, he was very strong and could have very easily avoided being bound with ropes, but he did not do anything. He simply depended on the Supreme Personality of Godhead for his protection. Śrīla Bhaktivinoda Ṭhākura describes surrender unto the Supreme Lord in this way:

mārabi rākhabi—yo icchā tohārā
nitya-dāsa-prati tuyā adhikārā

"My Lord, I am now surrendered unto You. I am Your eternal servant, and if You like You can kill me, or, if You like, You can protect me. In any case, I am fully surrendered unto You."

TEXT 15

अथ पणयस्तं स्वविधिनाभिषिच्याहतेन वाससाऽऽच्छाद्य भूषणालेपस्रक्तिलकादिभिरुपस्कृतं भुक्तवन्तं धूपदीपमाल्यलाजकिसलयाङ्कुरफलोपहारोपेतया वैशससंस्थया महता गीतस्तुतिमृदङ्गपणवघोषेण च पुरुषपशुं भद्रकाल्याः पुरत उपवेशयामासुः ॥१५॥

atha paṇayas taṁ sva-vidhinābhiṣicyāhatena vāsasācchādya bhūṣaṇālepa-srak-tilakādibhir upaskṛtaṁ bhuktavantaṁ dhūpa-dīpa-mālya-lāja-kisalayāṅkura-phalopahāropetayā vaiśasa-saṁsthayā mahatā gīta-stuti-mṛdaṅga-paṇava-ghoṣeṇa ca puruṣa-paśuṁ bhadra-kālyāḥ purata upaveśayām āsuḥ.

atha—thereafter; *paṇayaḥ*—all the followers of the dacoit; *tam*—him (Jaḍa Bharata); *sva-vidhinā*—according to their own ritualistic principles; *abhiṣicya*—bathing; *ahatena*—with new; *vāsasā*—garments; *ācchādya*—covering; *bhūṣaṇa*—ornaments; *ālepa*—smearing the body with sandalwood pulp; *srak*—a flower garland; *tilaka-ādibhiḥ*—with markings on the body and so on; *upaskṛtam*—completely decorated; *bhuktavantam*—having eaten; *dhūpa*—with incense; *dīpa*—lamps; *mālya*—garlands; *lāja*—parched grain; *kisalaya-aṅkura*—twigs and sprouts; *phala*—fruits; *upahāra*—other paraphernalia; *upetayā*—fully equipped; *vaiśasa-saṁsthayā*—with complete arrangements for sacrifice; *mahatā*—great; *gīta-stuti*—of songs and prayers; *mṛdaṅga*—of the drums; *paṇava*—of the bugles; *ghoṣeṇa*—by vibration; *ca*—also; *puruṣa-paśum*—the man-animal; *bhadra-kālyāḥ*—of the goddess Kālī; *purataḥ*—just in front; *upaveśayām āsuḥ*—made him sit down.

TRANSLATION

After this, all the thieves, according to their imaginative ritual for killing animalistic men, bathed Jaḍa Bharata, dressed him in new clothes, decorated him with ornaments befitting an animal, smeared his body with scented oils and decorated him with tilaka, sandalwood pulp and garlands. They fed him sumptuously and then brought him before the goddess Kālī, offering her incense, lamps, garlands, parched grain, newly grown twigs, sprouts, fruits and flowers. In this way they worshiped the deity before killing the man-animal, and they vibrated songs and prayers and played drums and bugles. Jaḍa Bharata was then made to sit down before the deity.

PURPORT

In this verse the word *sva-vidhinā* (according to their own ritualistic principles) is very significant. According to the Vedic *śāstras,* everything must be done according to regulative principles, but here it is stated that the thieves and rogues devised their own process for killing an animalistic man. The tamasic *śāstras* give instructions for the sacrifice of an animal like a goat or buffalo before the goddess Kālī, but there is no mention of killing a man, however dull he may be. This process was manufactured by the dacoits themselves; therefore the word *sva-vidhinā* is used. Even at this time there are many sacrifices being conducted without reference to the Vedic scriptures. For instance, in Calcutta recently a slaughterhouse was being advertised as a temple of the goddess Kālī. Meat-eaters foolishly purchase meat from such shops, thinking it different from ordinary meat and taking it to be the *prasāda* of Goddess Kālī. The sacrifice of a goat or a similar animal before the goddess Kālī is mentioned in *śāstras* just to keep people from eating slaughterhouse meat and becoming responsible for the killing of animals. The conditioned soul has a natural tendency toward sex and meat-eating; consequently the *śāstras* grant them some concessions. Actually the *śāstras* aim at putting an end to these abominable activities, but they impart some regulative principles so that gradually meat-eaters and sex hunters will be rectified.

TEXT 16

अथ वृषलराजपणिः पुरुषपशोरसृगासवेन देवीं भद्रकालीं यक्ष्यमाणस्तद-भिमन्त्रितमसिमतिकरालनिशितमुपाददे ॥१६॥

atha vṛṣala-rāja-paṇiḥ puruṣa-paśor asṛg-āsavena devīṁ bhadra-kālīṁ yakṣyamāṇas tad-abhimantritam asim ati-karāla-niśitam upādade.

atha—thereafter; *vṛṣala-rāja-paṇiḥ*—the so-called priest of the leader of the dacoits (one of the thieves); *puruṣa-paśoḥ*—of the animalistic man for being sacrificed (Bharata Mahārāja); *asṛk-āsavena*—with the liquor of blood; *devīm*—to the deity; *bhadra-kālīm*—the goddess Kālī; *yakṣyamāṇaḥ*—desiring to offer; *tat-abhimantritam*—consecrated by the *mantra* of Bhadra Kālī; *asim*—the sword; *ati-karāla*—very fearful; *niśitam*—finely sharpened; *upādade*—he took up.

TRANSLATION

At this time, one of the thieves, acting as the chief priest, was ready to offer the blood of Jaḍa Bharata, whom they imagined to be an animal-man, to the goddess Kālī to drink as a liquor. He therefore took up a very fearsome sword, which was very sharp and, consecrating it by the mantra of Bhadra Kālī, raised it to kill Jaḍa Bharata.

TEXT 17

इति तेषां वृषलानां रजस्तमःप्रकृतीनां धनमदरजउत्सिक्तमनसां भगवत्कला-वीरकुलं कदर्थीकृत्योत्पथेन स्वैरं विहरतां हिंसाविहाराणां कर्मातिदारुणं यद्ब्रह्मभूतस्य साक्षाद्ब्रह्मर्षिसुतस्य निर्वैरस्य सर्वभूतसुहृदः सूनायामप्यननुमत-मालम्भनं तदुपलभ्य ब्रह्मतेजसातिदुर्विषहेण दन्दह्यमानेन वपुषा सहसोच्चचाट सैव देवी भद्रकाली ॥१७॥

iti teṣāṁ vṛṣalānāṁ rajas-tamaḥ-prakṛtīnāṁ dhana-mada-raja-utsikta-manasāṁ bhagavat-kalā-vīra-kulaṁ kadarthī-kṛtyotpathena svairaṁ viharatāṁ hiṁsā-vihārāṇāṁ karmāti-dāruṇaṁ yad brahma-bhūtasya sākṣād brahmarṣi-sutasya nirvairasya sarva-bhūta-suhṛdaḥ sūnāyām apy ananumatam ālambhanaṁ tad upalabhya brahma-tejasāti-durviṣaheṇa dandahyamānena vapuṣā sahasoccacāṭa saiva devī bhadra-kālī.

iti—thus; *teṣām*—of them; *vṛṣalānām*—the *śūdras,* by whom all religious principles are destroyed; *rajaḥ*—in passion; *tamaḥ*—in ignorance; *prakṛtīnām* —having natures; *dhana-mada*—in the form of infatuation by material wealth; *rajaḥ*—by passion; *utsikta*—puffed up; *manasām*—whose minds; *bhagavat-kalā*—an expansion of the plenary expansion of the Supreme Personality of Godhead; *vīra-kulam*—the group of elevated personalities (the *brāhmaṇas*); *kat-arthī-kṛtya*—disrespecting; *utpathena*—by a wrong path; *svairam*—independently; *viharatām*—who are proceeding; *hiṁsā-vihārāṇām* —whose business is to commit violence against others; *karma*—the activity; *ati-dāruṇam*—very fearful; *yat*—that which; *brahma-bhūtasya*—of a self-realized person born in a *brāhmaṇa* family; *sākṣāt*—directly; *brahma-ṛṣi-sutasya*—of the son born of a *brāhmaṇa* exalted in spiritual consciousness; *nirvairasya*—who had no enemies; *sarva-bhūta-suhṛdaḥ*—a well-wisher to all others; *sūnāyām*—at the last moment; *api*—even though; *ananumatam*—not being sanctioned by law; *ālambhanam*—against the desire of the Lord; *tat*—that; *upalabhya*—perceiving; *brahma-tejasā*—with the effulgence of spiritual bliss; *ati-durviṣaheṇa*—being too bright and unbearable; *dandahyamānena*—burning; *vapuṣā*—with a physical body; *sahasā*—suddenly; *uccacāṭa*—fractured (the deity); *sā*—she; *eva*—indeed; *devī*—the goddess; *bhadra-kālī*—Bhadra Kālī.

TRANSLATION

All the rogues and thieves who had made arrangements for the worship of Goddess Kālī were low minded and bound to the modes of passion and ignorance. They were overpowered by the desire to become very rich; therefore they had the audacity to disobey the injunctions of the Vedas, so much so that they were prepared to kill Jaḍa Bharata, a self-realized soul born in a brāhmaṇa family. Due to their envy, these dacoits brought him before the goddess Kālī for sacrifice. Such people are always addicted to envious activities, and therefore they dared to try to kill Jaḍa Bharata. Jaḍa Bharata was the best friend of all living entities. He was no one's enemy, and he was always absorbed in meditation on the Supreme Personality of Godhead. He was born of a good brāhmaṇa father, and killing him was forbidden, even though he might have been an enemy or aggressive person. In any case, there was no reason to kill Jaḍa Bharata, and the goddess Kālī could not bear this. She could immediately understand that these sinful dacoits were about to kill a great devotee of the Lord. Suddenly the deity's body burst asunder, and the goddess Kālī

personally emerged from it in a body burning with an intense and intolerable effulgence.

PURPORT

According to the Vedic injunctions, only an aggressor can be killed. If a person comes with an intent to kill, one can immediately take action and kill in self-defense. It is also stated that one can be killed if he comes to set fire to the home or to pollute or kidnap one's wife. Lord Rāmacandra killed the entire family of Rāvaṇa because Rāvaṇa kidnapped His wife, Sītādevī. However, killing is not sanctioned in the *śāstras* for other purposes. The killing of animals in sacrifice to the demigods, who are expansions of the Supreme Personality of Godhead, is sanctioned for those who eat meat. This is a kind of restriction for meat-eating. In other words, the slaughter of animals is also restricted by certain rules and regulations in the *Vedas.* Considering these points, there was no reason to kill Jaḍa Bharata, who was born in a respectable, highly exalted *brāhmaṇa* family. He was a God-realized soul and a well-wisher to all living entities. The *Vedas* did not at all sanction the killing of Jaḍa Bharata by rogues and thieves. Consequently the goddess Bhadra Kālī emerged from the deity to give protection to the Lord's devotee. Śrīla Viśvanātha Cakravartī Ṭhākura explains that due to the Brahman effulgence of such a devotee as Jaḍa Bharata, the deity was fractured. Only thieves and rogues in the modes of passion and ignorance and maddened by material opulence offer a man in sacrifice before the goddess Kālī. This is not sanctioned by the Vedic instructions. Presently there are many hundreds and thousands of slaughterhouses throughout the world that are maintained by a puffed-up population mad for material opulence. Such activities are never supported by the *Bhāgavata* school.

TEXT 18

भृशममर्षरोषावेशरभसविलसितभ्रुकुटिविटपकुटिलदंष्ट्रारुणेक्षणाटोपातिभयानक-
वदना हन्तुकामेवेदं महाट्टहासमतिसंरम्भेण विमुञ्चन्ती तत उत्पत्य पापीयसां दुष्टानां
तेनैवासिना विवृक्णशीर्ष्णां गलात्स्रवन्तमसृगासवमत्युष्णं सह गणेन
निपीयातिपानमदविह्वलोच्चैस्तरां स्वपार्षदैः सह जगौ ननर्त च विजहार च
शिरःकन्दुकलीलया ॥१८॥

bhṛśam amarṣa-roṣāveśa-rabhasa-vilasita-bhru-kuṭi-viṭapa-kuṭila-
daṁṣṭrāruṇekṣaṇāṭopāti-bhayānaka-vadanā hantu-kāmevedaṁ

mahāṭṭa-hāsam ati-saṁrambheṇa vimuñcantī tata utpatya pāpīyasāṁ duṣṭānāṁ tenaivāsinā vivṛkṇa-śīrṣṇāṁ galāt sravantam asṛg-āsavam atyuṣṇaṁ saha gaṇena nipīyāti-pāna-mada-vihvaloccaistarāṁ sva-pārṣadaiḥ saha jagau nanarta ca vijahāra ca śiraḥ-kanduka-līlayā.

bhṛśam—very highly; *amarṣa*—in intolerance of the offenses; *roṣa*—in anger; *āveśa*—of her absorption; *rabhasa-vilasita*—expanded by the force; *bhru-kuṭi*—of her eyebrows; *viṭapa*—the branches; *kuṭila*—curved; *daṁṣṭra*—teeth; *aruṇa-īkṣaṇa*—of reddish eyes; *āṭopa*—by the agitation; *ati*—very much; *bhayānaka*—fearful; *vadanā*—having a face; *hantu-kāmā*—desirous to destroy; *iva*—as if; *idam*—this universe; *mahā-aṭṭa-hāsam*—a greatly fearful laugh; *ati*—great; *saṁrambheṇa*—because of anger; *vimuñcantī*—releasing; *tataḥ*—from that altar; *utpatya*—coming forth; *pāpīyasām*—of all the sinful; *duṣṭānām*—great offenders; *tena eva asinā*—by that same chopper; *vivṛkṇa*—separated; *śīrṣṇām*—whose heads; *galāt*—from the neck; *sravantam*—oozing out; *asṛk-āsavam*—the blood, compared to an intoxicating beverage; *ati-uṣṇam*—very hot; *saha*—with; *gaṇena*—her associates; *nipīya*—drinking; *ati-pāna*—from drinking so much; *mada*—by intoxication; *vihvalā*—overwhelmed; *uccaiḥ-tarām*—very loudly; *sva-pārṣadaiḥ*—her own associates; *saha*—with; *jagau*—sang; *nanarta*—danced; *ca*—also; *vijahāra*—played; *ca*—also; *śiraḥ-kanduka*—using the heads as balls; *līlayā*—by sports.

TRANSLATION

Intolerant of the offenses committed, the infuriated Goddess Kālī flashed her eyes and displayed her fierce, curved teeth. Her reddish eyes glowed, and she displayed her fearsome features. She assumed a frightening body, as if she were prepared to destroy the entire creation. Leaping violently from the altar, she immediately decapitated all the rogues and thieves with the very sword with which they had intended to kill Jaḍa Bharata. She then began to drink the hot blood that flowed from the necks of the beheaded rogues and thieves, as if this blood were liquor. Indeed, she drank this intoxicant with her associates, who were witches and female demons. Becoming intoxicated with this blood, they all began to sing very loudly and dance as though prepared to annihilate the entire universe. At the same time, they began to play with the heads of the rogues and thieves, tossing them about as if they were balls.

PURPORT

It is evident from this verse that the devotees of Goddess Kālī are not at all favored by her. It is Goddess Kālī's work to kill and punish the demons. Goddess Kālī (Durgā) engages in decapitating many demons, dacoits and other unwanted elements in society. Neglecting Kṛṣṇa consciousness, foolish people try to satisfy the goddess by offering her many abominable things, but ultimately when there is a little discrepancy in this worship, the goddess punishes the worshiper by taking his life. Demoniac people worship Goddess Kālī to obtain some material benefit, but they are not excused of the sins performed in the name of worship. To sacrifice a man or animal before the deity is specifically forbidden.

TEXT 19

एवमेव खलु महदभिचारातिक्रमः कार्त्स्न्येनात्मने फलति ॥१९॥

evam eva khalu mahad-abhicārāti-kramaḥ kārtsnyenātmane phalati.

evam eva—in this way; *khalu*—indeed; *mahat*—to great personalities; *abhicāra*—in the form of envy; *ati-kramaḥ*—the limit of offense; *kārtsnyena*—always; *ātmane*—unto oneself; *phalati*—gives the result.

TRANSLATION

When an envious person commits an offense before a great personality, he is always punished in the way mentioned above.

TEXT 20

न वा एतद्विष्णुदत्त महदद्भुतं यदसम्भ्रमः स्वशिरश्छेदन आपतितेऽपि विमुक्तदेहाद्यात्मभावसुदृढहृदयग्रन्थीनां सर्वसत्त्वसुहृदात्मनां निर्वैराणां साक्षाद्भगवतानिमिषारिवरायुधेनाप्रमत्तेन तैस्तैर्भावैः परिरक्ष्यमाणानां तत्पादमूलमकुतश्चिद्भयमुपसृतानां भागवतपरमहंसानाम् ॥२०॥

na vā etad viṣṇudatta mahad-adbhutaṁ yad asambhramaḥ sva-śiraś-chedana āpatite'pi vimukta-dehādy-ātma-bhāva-sudṛḍha-hṛdaya-granthīnāṁ sarva-sattva-suhṛd-ātmanāṁ nirvairāṇāṁ sākṣād bhagavatānimiṣāri-varāyudhenāpramattena tais tair bhāvaiḥ parirakṣyamāṇānāṁ tat-pāda-mūlam akutaścid-bhayam upasṛtānāṁ bhāgavata-paramahaṁsānām.

na—not; *vā*—or; *etat*—this; *viṣṇu-datta*—O Mahārāja Parīkṣit, who was protected by Lord Viṣṇu; *mahat*—a great; *adbhutam*—wonder; *yat*—which; *asambhramaḥ*—lack of perplexity; *sva-śiraḥ-chedane*—when the chopping off of the head; *āpatite*—was about to happen; *api*—even though; *vimukta*—completely liberated from; *deha-ādi-ātma-bhāva*—the false bodily concept of life; *su-dṛḍha*—very strong and tight; *hṛdaya-granthīnām*—of those whose knots within the heart; *sarva-sattva-suhṛt-ātmanām*—of persons who in their hearts always wish well to all living entities; *nirvairāṇām*—who do not find anyone as their enemy; *sākṣāt*—directly; *bhagavatā*—by the Supreme Personality of Godhead; *animiṣa*—invincible time; *ari-vara*—and the best of weapons, the Sudarśana *cakra; āyudhena*—by Him who possesses the weapons; *apramattena*—not agitated at any time; *taiḥ taiḥ*—by those respective; *bhāvaiḥ*—moods of the Supreme Personality of Godhead; *parirakṣyamāṇānām*—of persons who are protected; *tat-pāda-mūlam*—at the lotus feet of the Supreme Personality of Godhead; *akutaścit*—from nowhere; *bhayam*—fear; *upasṛtānām*—of those who have taken complete shelter; *bhāgavata*—of devotees of the Lord; *parama-haṁsānām*—of the most liberated persons.

TRANSLATION

Śukadeva Gosvāmī then said to Mahārāja Parīkṣit: O Viṣṇudatta, those who already know that the soul is separate from the body, who are liberated from the invincible knot in the heart, who are always engaged in welfare activities for all living entities and who never contemplate harming anyone are always protected by the Supreme Personality of Godhead, who carries His disc [the Sudarśana cakra] and acts as supreme time to kill the demons and protect His devotees. The devotees always take shelter at the lotus feet of the Lord. Therefore at all times, even if threatened by decapitation, they remain unagitated. For them, this is not at all wonderful.

PURPORT

These are some of the great qualities of a pure devotee of the Supreme Personality of Godhead. First, a devotee is firmly convinced of his spiritual identity. He never identifies with the body; he is firmly convinced that the spirit soul is different from the body. Consequently he fears nothing. Even though his life may be threatened, he is not at all afraid. He does not even treat an enemy like an enemy. Such are the qualifications of devotees. Devotees are always fully dependent on the Supreme Personality of Godhead, and the Lord is always eager to give them all protection in all circumstances.

Thus end the Bhaktivedanta purports of the Fifth Canto, Ninth Chapter, of the Śrīmad-Bhāgavatam, *entitled "The Supreme Character of Jaḍa Bharata."*

CHAPTER TEN

The Discussion Between Jaḍa Bharata and Mahārāja Rahūgaṇa

In this chapter Bharata Mahārāja, now Jaḍa Bharata, was successfully accepted by King Rahūgaṇa, ruler of the states known as Sindhu and Sauvīra. The King forced Jaḍa Bharata to carry his palanquin and chastised him because he did not carry it properly. A carrier of King Rahūgaṇa's palanquin was needed, and to fulfill this need the chief carriers found Jaḍa Bharata as the most likely person to do the work. He was therefore forced to carry the palanquin. Jaḍa Bharata, however, did not protest this proud order, but humbly accepted the job and carried the palanquin. While carrying it, however, he was very careful to see that he did not step on an ant, and whenever he saw one, he would stop until the ant had passed. Because of this, he could not keep pace with the other carriers. The King within the palanquin became very disturbed and chastised Jaḍa Bharata with filthy language, but Jaḍa Bharata, being completely freed from the bodily conception, did not protest; he proceeded carrying the palanquin. When he continued as before, the King threatened him with punishment, and being threatened by the King, Jaḍa Bharata began to talk. He protested against the filthy language used by the King when the King chastised him, and the King, hearing the instructions of Jaḍa Bharata, was awakened to his real knowledge. When he came to his consciousness, he understood that he had offended a great, learned and saintly person. At that time he very humbly and respectfully prayed to Jaḍa Bharata. He now wanted to understand the deep meaning of the philosophical words used by Jaḍa Bharata, and with great sincerity, he begged his pardon. He admitted that if one offends the lotus feet of a pure devotee, he is certainly punished by the trident of Lord Śiva.

TEXT 1

श्रीशुक उवाच

अथ सिन्धुसौवीरपते रहूगणस्य व्रजत इक्षुमत्यास्तटे तत्कुलपतिना शिबिकावाहपुरुषान्वेषण समये दैवेनोपसादितः स द्विजवर उपलब्ध एष पीवा युवा संहननाङ्गो गोखरवद्धुरं वोढुमलमिति पूर्वविष्टिगृहीतैः सह गृहीतः प्रसभमतदर्ह उवाह शिबिकां स महानुभावः ॥१॥

śrī-śuka uvāca
atha sindhu-sauvīra-pate rahūgaṇasya vrajata ikṣumatyās taṭe tat-kula-patinā śibikā-vāha-puruṣānveṣaṇa-samaye daivenopasāditaḥ sa dvija- vara upalabdha eṣa pīvā yuvā saṁhananāṅgo go-kharavad dhuraṁ voḍhum alam iti pūrva-viṣṭi-gṛhītaiḥ saha gṛhītaḥ prasabham atad-arha uvāha śibikāṁ sa mahānubhāvaḥ.

śrī-śukaḥ uvāca—Śukadeva Gosvāmī continued to speak; *atha*—thus; *sindhu-sauvīra-pateḥ*—of the ruler of the states known as Sindhu and Sauvīra; *rahū-gaṇasya*—the King known as Rahūgaṇa; *vrajataḥ*—while going (to the *āśrama* of Kapila); *ikṣu-matyāḥ taṭe*—on the bank of the river known as Ikṣumatī; *tat-kula-patinā*—by the leader of the palanquin carriers; *śibikā-vāha*—to become a carrier of the palanquin; *puruṣa-anveṣaṇa-samaye*—at the time of searching for a man; *daivena*—by chance; *upasāditaḥ*—led near; *saḥ*—that; *dvija-varaḥ*—Jaḍa Bharata, the son of a *brāhmaṇa; upalabdhaḥ*—obtained; *eṣaḥ*—this man; *pīvā*—very strong and stout; *yuvā*—young; *saṁhanana-aṅgaḥ*—having very firm limbs; *go-khara-vat*—like a cow or an ass; *dhuram*—a load; *voḍhum*—to carry; *alam*—able; *iti*—thus thinking; *pūrva-viṣṭi-gṛhītaiḥ*—others who were formerly forced to do the task; *saha*—with; *gṛhītaḥ*—being taken; *prasabham*—by force; *a-tat-arhaḥ*—although not fit for carrying the palanquin; *uvāha*—carried; *śibikām*—the palanquin; *saḥ*—he; *mahā-anubhāvaḥ*—a great soul.

TRANSLATION

Śukadeva Gosvāmī continued: My dear King, after this, King Rahūgaṇa, ruler of the states known as Sindhu and Sauvīra, was going to Kapilāśrama. When the King's chief palanquin carriers reached the banks of the River Ikṣumatī, they needed another carrier. Therefore they began searching for someone, and by chance they came upon Jaḍa Bharata. They considered the fact that Jaḍa Bharata was very young and strong and had firm limbs. Like cows and asses, he was quite fit to carry loads. Thinking in this way, although the great soul Jaḍa Bharata was unfit for such work, they nonetheless unhesitatingly forced him to carry the palanquin.

TEXT 2

यदा हि द्विजवरस्येषुमात्रावलोकानुगतेर्न समाहिता पुरुषगतिस्तदा विषमगतां स्वशिबिकां रहूगण उपधार्य पुरुषानधिवहत आह हे वोढारः साध्वतिक्रमत किमिति विषममुह्यते यानमिति ॥२॥

yadā hi dvija-varasyeṣu-mātrāvalokānugater na samāhitā puruṣa-gatis tadā viṣama-gatāṁ sva-śibikāṁ rahūgaṇa upadhārya puruṣān adhivahata āha he voḍhāraḥ sādhv atikramata kim iti viṣamam uhyate yānam iti.

yadā—when; *hi*—certainly; *dvija-varasya*—of Jaḍa Bharata; *iṣu-mātra*—the measurement of an arrow (three feet) ahead; *avaloka-anugateḥ*—from moving only after glancing; *na samāhitā*—not united; *puruṣa-gatiḥ*—the movement of the carriers; *tadā*—at that time; *viṣama-gatām*—becoming uneven; *sva-śibikām*—his own palanquin; *rahūgaṇaḥ*—King Rahūgaṇa; *upadhārya*—understanding; *puruṣān*—unto the men; *adhivahataḥ*—who were carrying the palanquin; *āha*—said; *he*—oh; *voḍhāraḥ*—carriers of the palanquin; *sādhu atikramata*—please walk evenly so that there will not be bouncing; *kim iti*—for what reason; *viṣamam*—uneven; *uhyate*—is being carried; *yānam*—the palanquin; *iti*—thus.

TRANSLATION

The palanquin, however, was very erratically carried by Jaḍa Bharata due to his sense of nonviolence. As he stepped forward, he checked before him every three feet to see whether he was about to step on ants. Consequently he could not keep pace with the other carriers. Due to this, the palanquin was shaking, and King Rahūgaṇa immediately asked the carriers, "Why are you carrying this palanquin unevenly? Better carry it properly."

PURPORT

Although Jaḍa Bharata was forced to carry the palanquin, he did not give up his sympathetic feelings toward the poor ants passing on the road. A devotee of the Lord does not forget his devotional service and other favorable activities, even when he is in a most distressful condition. Jaḍa Bharata was a qualified *brāhmaṇa,* highly elevated in spiritual knowledge, yet he was forced to carry the palanquin. He did not mind this, but while walking on the road, he could not forget his duty to avoid killing even an ant. A Vaiṣṇava is never envious or unnecessarily violent. There were many ants on the path, but Jaḍa Bharata took care by looking ahead three feet. When the ants were no longer in his way, he would place his foot on the ground. A Vaiṣṇava is always very kind at heart to all living entities. In His *sāṅkhya-yoga,* Lord Kapiladeva explains: *suhṛdaḥ sarva-dehinām.* Living entities assume different bodily forms. Those who are not Vaiṣṇavas consider only human society worthy of their sympathy, but Kṛṣṇa claims to be the supreme father of all life forms. Consequently the Vaiṣṇava takes care not to annihilate untimely or unnecessarily any life form. All living entities have to fulfill a certain duration for being encaged in a particular type of material body. They have to finish the duration allotted a particular body before being promoted or evolved to another body. Killing an animal or any other living being simply places an impediment in the way of his completing his term of imprisonment in a certain body. One should therefore not kill bodies for one's sense gratification, for this will implicate one in sinful activity.

TEXT 3

अथ त ईश्वरवचः सोपालम्भमुपाकर्ण्योपायतुरीयाच्छङ्कितमनसस्तं विज्ञापयांबभूवुः ॥३॥

atha ta īśvara-vacaḥ sopālambham upākarṇyopāya-turīyāc chaṅkita-manasas taṁ vijñāpayāṁ babhūvuḥ.

atha—thus; *te*—they (the carriers of the palanquin); *īśvara-vacaḥ*—the words of the master, King Rahūgaṇa; *sa-upālambham*—with reproach; *upākarṇya*—hearing; *upāya*—the means; *turīyāt*—from the fourth one; *śaṅkita-manasaḥ*—whose minds were afraid; *tam*—him (the King); *vijñāpayām babhūvuḥ*—informed.

TRANSLATION

When the palanquin carriers heard the threatening words of Mahārāja Rahūgaṇa, they became very afraid of his punishment and began to speak to him as follows.

PURPORT

According to political science, a king sometimes tries to pacify his subordinates, sometimes chastises them, sometimes derides them and sometimes rewards them. In this way the king rules his subordinates. The bearers of the palanquin could understand that the King was angry and that he would chastise them.

TEXT 4

न वयं नरदेव प्रमत्ता भवन्नियमानुपथाः साध्वेव वहामः । अयमधुनैव नियुक्तोऽपि न द्रुतं व्रजति नानेन सह वोढुमु ह वयं पारयाम इति ॥४॥

na vayaṁ nara-deva pramattā bhavan-niyamānupathāḥ sādhv eva vahāmaḥ; ayam adhunaiva niyukto'pi na drutaṁ vrajati nānena saha voḍhum u ha vayaṁ pārayāma iti.

na—not; *vayam*—we; *nara-deva*—O lord among human beings (the king is supposed to be the representative of *deva,* the Supreme Personality of Godhead); *pramattāḥ*—neglectful in our duties; *bhavat-niyama-anupathāḥ* —who are always obedient to your order; *sādhu*—properly; *eva*—certainly; *vahāmaḥ*—we are carrying; *ayam*—this man; *adhunā*—just recently; *eva*—indeed; *niyuktaḥ*—being engaged to work with us; *api*—although; *na*—not; *drutam*—very quickly; *vrajati*—works; *na*—not; *anena*—him; *saha*—with; *voḍhum*—to carry; *u ha*—oh; *vayam*—we; *pārayāmaḥ*—are able; *iti*—thus.

TRANSLATION

O lord, please note that we are not at all negligent in discharging our duties. We have been faithfully carrying this palanquin according to your desire, but this man who has been recently engaged to work with us cannot walk very swiftly. Therefore we are not able to carry the palanquin with him.

PURPORT

The other palanquin carriers were *śūdras,* whereas Jaḍa Bharata was not only a high-caste *brāhmaṇa* but also a great devotee. *Śūdras* do not sympathize with other living beings, but a Vaiṣṇava cannot act like a *śūdra.* Whenever a *śūdra* and a *brāhmaṇa* Vaiṣṇava are combined, there will certainly be imbalance in the execution of duties. The *śūdras* were walking with the palanquin without at all caring for the ants on the ground, but Jaḍa Bharata could not act like a *śūdra,* and therefore difficulty arose.

TEXT 5

सांसर्गिको दोष एव नूनमेकस्यापि सर्वेषां सांसर्गिकाणां भवितुमर्हतीति निश्चित्य निशम्य कृपणवचो राजा रहूगण उपासितवृद्धोऽपि निसर्गेण बलात्कृत ईषदुत्थितमन्युरविस्पष्टब्रह्मतेजसं जातवेदसमिव रजसाऽऽवृत मतिराह ॥ ५ ॥

sāṁsargiko doṣa eva nūnam ekasyāpi sarveṣāṁ sāṁsargikāṇāṁ bhavitum arhatīti niścitya niśamya kṛpaṇa-vaco rājā rahūgaṇa upāsita-vṛddho'pi nisargeṇa balāt kṛta īṣad-utthita-manyur avispaṣṭa-brahma-tejasaṁ jāta-vedasam iva rajasāvṛta-matir āha.

sāṁsargikaḥ—resulting from intimate association; *doṣaḥ*—a fault; *eva*—indeed; *nūnam*—certainly; *ekasya*—of one; *api*—although; *sarveṣām*—of all other; *sāṁsargikāṇām*—persons associated with him; *bhavitum*—to become; *arhati*—is able; *iti*—thus; *niścitya*—ascertaining; *niśamya*—by hearing; *kṛpaṇa-vacaḥ*—the words of the poor servants, who were very afraid of being punished; *rājā*—the King; *rahūgaṇaḥ*—Rahūgaṇa; *upāsita-vṛddhaḥ*—having served and heard from many elderly sages; *api*—in spite of; *nisargeṇa*—by his personal nature, which was that of a *kṣatriya; balāt*—by force; *kṛtaḥ*—done; *īṣat*—slightly; *utthita*—awakened; *manyuḥ*—whose anger; *avispaṣṭa*—not being distinctly visible; *brahma-tejasam*—his (Jaḍa Bharata's) spiritual effulgence; *jāta-vedasam*—a fire covered by ashes in Vedic ritualistic ceremonies; *iva*—like; *rajasā āvṛta*—covered by the mode of passion; *matiḥ*—whose mind; *āha*—said.

TRANSLATION

King Rahūgaṇa could understand the speeches given by the carriers, who were afraid of being punished. He could also understand that simply due to the fault of one person, the palanquin was not being carried properly. Knowing this perfectly well and hearing their appeal, he became a little angry, although he was very advanced in political science and was very experienced. His anger arose due to his inborn nature as a king. Actually King Rahūgaṇa's mind was covered by the mode of passion, and he therefore spoke as follows to Jaḍa Bharata, whose Brahman effulgence was not clearly visible, being covered like a fire covered by ashes.

PURPORT

The distinction between *rajo-guṇa* and *sattva-guṇa* is explained in this verse. Although the King was very upright and advanced in political science and governmental management, he was nonetheless in the mode of passion, and therefore, due to a slight agitation, he became angry. Jaḍa Bharata, despite all kinds of injustice endured because of his deaf and dumb display, remained silent by the strength of his spiritual advancement. Nonetheless his *brahma-tejaḥ,* his Brahman effulgence, was indistinctly visible in his person.

TEXT 6

अहो कष्टं भ्रातर्व्यक्तमुरु परिश्रान्तो दीर्घमध्वानमेक एव ऊहिवान् सुचिरं नातिपीवा न संहननाङ्गो जरसा चोपद्रुतो भवान् सखे नो एवापर एते सङ्घट्टिन इति बहु

विप्रलब्धोऽप्यविद्यया रचितद्रव्यगुणकर्माशयस्वचरमकलेवरेऽवस्तुनि संस्थानविशेषेऽहं ममेत्यनध्यारोपितमिथ्याप्रत्ययो ब्रह्मभूतस्तूष्णीं शिबिकां पूर्ववदुवाह ॥६॥

aho kaṣṭaṁ bhrātar vyaktam uru-pariśrānto dīrgham adhvānam eka eva ūhivān suciraṁ nāti-pīvā na saṁhananāṅgo jarasā copadruto bhavān sakhe no evāpara ete saṅghaṭṭina iti bahu-vipralabdho'py avidyayā racita-dravya-guṇa-karmāśaya-sva-carama-kalevare'vastuni saṁsthāna-viśeṣe'haṁ mamety anadhyāropita-mithyā-pratyayo brahma-bhūtas tūṣṇīṁ śibikāṁ pūrvavad uvāha.

aho—alas; *kaṣṭam*—how troublesome it is; *bhrātaḥ*—my dear brother; *vyaktam*—clearly; *uru*—very much; *pariśrāntaḥ*—fatigued; *dīrgham*—a long; *adhvānam*—path; *ekaḥ*—alone; *eva*—certainly; *ūhivān*—you have carried; *su-ciram*—for a long time; *na*—not; *ati-pīvā*—very strong and stout; *na*—nor; *saṁhanana-aṅgaḥ*—having a firm, tolerant body; *jarasā*—by old age; *ca*—also; *upadrutaḥ*—disturbed; *bhavān*—yourself; *sakhe*—my friend; *no eva*—not certainly; *apare*—the other; *ete*—all these; *saṅghaṭṭinaḥ*—co-workers; *iti*—thus; *bahu*—very much; *vipralabdhaḥ*—sarcastically criticized; *api*—although; *avidyayā*—by nescience; *racita*—manufactured; *dravya-guṇa-karma-āśaya*—in a combination of material elements, material qualities, and the results of past activities and desires; *sva-carama-kalevare*—in the body, which is moved by the subtle elements (mind, intelligence and ego); *avastuni*—in such physical things; *saṁsthāna-viśeṣe*—having a particular disposition; *aham mama*—I and mine; *iti*—in this way; *anadhyāropita*—not interposed; *mithyā*—false; *pratyayaḥ*—belief; *brahma-bhūtaḥ*—who was self-realized, standing on the Brahman platform; *tūṣṇīm*—being silent; *śibikām*—the palanquin; *pūrva-vat*—as before; *uvāha*—carried.

TRANSLATION

King Rahūgaṇa told Jaḍa Bharata: How troublesome this is, my dear brother. You certainly appear very fatigued because you have carried this palanquin alone without assistance for a long time and for a long distance. Besides that, due to your old age you have become greatly troubled. My dear friend, I see that you are not very firm, nor very strong and stout. Aren't your fellow carriers cooperating with you?

In this way the King criticized Jaḍa Bharata with sarcastic words, yet despite being criticized in this way, Jaḍa Bharata had no bodily conception

of the situation. He knew that he was not the body, for he had attained his spiritual identity. He was neither fat, lean nor thin, nor had he anything to do with a lump of matter, a combination of the five gross and three subtle elements. He had nothing to do with the material body and its two hands and legs. In other words, he had completely realized his spiritual identity [ahaṁ brahmāsmi]. He was therefore unaffected by this sarcastic criticism from the King. Without saying anything, he continued carrying the palanquin as before.

PURPORT

Jaḍa Bharata was completely liberated. He did not even care when the dacoits attempted to kill his body; he knew that he certainly was not the body. Even if the body were killed, he would not have cared, for he was thoroughly convinced of the proposition found in *Bhagavad-gītā* (2.20): *na hanyate hanyamāne śarīre.* He knew that he could not be killed even if his body were killed. Although he did not protest, the Supreme Personality of Godhead in His agent could not tolerate the injustice of the dacoits; therefore he was saved by the mercy of Kṛṣṇa, and the dacoits were killed. In this case, while carrying the palanquin, he also knew that he was not the body. This body was very strong and stout, in sound condition and quite competent to carry the palanquin. Due to his being freed from the bodily conception, the sarcastic words of the King did not at all affect him. The body is created according to one's *karma,* and material nature supplies the ingredients for the development of a certain type of body. The soul the body covers is different from the bodily construction; therefore anything favorable or mischievous done to the body does not affect the spirit soul. The Vedic injunction is *asaṅgo hy ayaṁ puruṣaḥ:* the spirit soul is always unaffected by material arrangements.

TEXT 7

अथ पुनः स्वशिबिकायां विषमगतायां प्रकुपित उवाच रहूगणः किमिदमरे त्वं जीवन्मृतो मां कदर्थीकृत्य भर्तृशासनमतिचरसि प्रमत्तस्य च ते करोमि चिकित्सां दण्डपाणिरिव जनताया यथा प्रकृतिं स्वां भजिष्यस इति ॥७॥

atha punaḥ sva-śibikāyāṁ viṣama-gatāyāṁ prakupita uvāca rahūgaṇaḥ kim idam are tvaṁ jīvan-mṛto māṁ kadarthī-kṛtya bhartṛ-śāsanam aticarasi pramattasya ca te karomi cikitsāṁ daṇḍa-pāṇir iva janatāyā yathā prakṛtiṁ svāṁ bhajiṣyasa iti.

atha—thereafter; *punaḥ*—again; *sva-śibikāyām*—in his own palanquin; *viṣama-gatāyām*—being unevenly carried because of Jaḍa Bharata's not walking properly; *prakupitaḥ*—becoming very angry; *uvāca*—said; *rahūgaṇaḥ*—King Rahūgaṇa; *kim idam*—what is this nonsense; *are*—O fool; *tvam*—you; *jīvat*—living; *mṛtaḥ*—dead; *mām*—me; *kat-arthī-kṛtya*—neglecting; *bhartṛ-śāsanam*—chastisement by the master; *aticarasi*—you are overstepping; *pramattasya*—who are almost crazy; *ca*—also; *te*—your; *karomi*—I shall do; *cikitsām*—proper treatment; *daṇḍa-pāṇiḥ iva*—like Yamarāja; *janatāyāḥ*—of the people in general; *yathā*—so that; *prakṛtim*—natural position; *svām*—your own; *bhajiṣyase*—you will take to; *iti*—thus.

TRANSLATION

Thereafter, when the King saw that his palanquin was still being shaken by the carriers, he became very angry and said: You rascal, what are you doing? Are you dead despite the life within your body? Do you not know that I am your master? You are disregarding me and are not carrying out my order. For this disobedience I shall now punish you just as Yamarāja, the superintendent of death, punishes sinful people. I shall give you proper treatment so that you will come to your senses and do the correct thing.

TEXT 8

एवं बह्वबद्धमपि भाषमाणं नरदेवाभिमानं रजसा तमसानुविद्धेन मदेन तिरस्कृताशेषभगवत्प्रियनिकेतं पण्डितमानिनं स भगवान् ब्राह्मणो ब्रह्मभूतः सर्वभूतसुहृदात्मा योगेश्वरचर्यायां नातिव्युत्पन्नमतिं स्मयमान इव विगतस्मय इदमाह ॥८॥

evaṁ bahv abaddham api bhāṣamāṇaṁ nara-devābhimānaṁ rajasā
tamasānuviddhena madena tiraskṛtāśeṣa-bhagavat-priya-niketaṁ
paṇḍita-māninaṁ sa bhagavān brāhmaṇo brahma-bhūta-sarva-bhūta-
suhṛd-ātmā yogeśvara-caryāyāṁ nāti-vyutpanna-matiṁ smayamāna
iva vigata-smaya idam āha.

evam—in this way; *bahu*—much; *abaddham*—nonsensical; *api*—although; *bhāṣamāṇam*—talking; *nara-deva-abhimānam*—King Rahūgaṇa, who thought himself the ruler; *rajasā*—by the material mode of passion; *tamasā*—as well as by the mode of ignorance; *anuviddhena*—being increased; *madena*—by madness; *tiraskṛta*—who rebuked; *aśeṣa*—innumerable; *bhagavat-priya-niketam*—devotees of the Lord;

paṇḍita-māninam—considering himself a very learned scholar; *saḥ*—that; *bhagavān*—spiritually most powerful (Jaḍa Bharata); *brāhmaṇaḥ*—a fully qualified *brāhmaṇa; brahma-bhūta*—fully self-realized; *sarva-bhūta-suhṛt-ātmā*—who was thus the friend of all living entities; *yoga-īśvara*—of the most advanced mystic *yogīs; caryāyām*—in the behavior; *na ati-vyutpanna-matim*—unto King Rahūgaṇa, who was not actually experienced; *smayamānaḥ*—slightly smiling; *iva*—like; *vigata-smayaḥ*—who was relieved from all material pride; *idam*—this; *āha*—spoke.

TRANSLATION

Thinking himself a king, King Rahūgaṇa was in the bodily conception and was influenced by material nature's modes of passion and ignorance. Due to madness, he chastised Jaḍa Bharata with uncalled-for and contradictory words. Jaḍa Bharata was a topmost devotee and the dear abode of the Supreme Personality of Godhead. Although considering himself very learned, the King did not know about the position of an advanced devotee situated in devotional service, nor did he know his characteristics. Jaḍa Bharata was the residence of the Supreme Personality of Godhead; he always carried the form of the Lord within his heart. He was the dear friend of all living beings, and he did not entertain any bodily conception. He therefore smiled and spoke the following words.

PURPORT

The distinction between a person in the bodily conception and a person beyond the bodily conception is presented in this verse. In the bodily conception, King Rahūgaṇa considered himself a king and chastised Jaḍa Bharata in so many unwanted ways. Being self-realized, Jaḍa Bharata, who was fully situated on the transcendental platform, did not at all become angry; instead, he smiled and began to deliver his teachings to King Rahūgaṇa. A highly advanced Vaiṣṇava devotee is a friend to all living entities, and consequently he is a friend to his enemies also. In fact, he does not consider anyone to be his enemy. *Suhṛdaḥ sarva-dehinām.* Sometimes a Vaiṣṇava becomes superficially angry at a nondevotee, but this is good for the nondevotee. We have several examples of this in Vedic literature. Once Nārada became angry with the two sons of Kuvera, Nalakūvara and Maṇigrīva, and he chastised them by turning them into trees. The result was that later they were liberated by Lord Śrī Kṛṣṇa. The devotee is situated on the absolute platform, and when he is angry or pleased, there is no difference, for in either case he bestows his benediction.

TEXT 9

ब्राह्मण उवाच
त्वयोदितं व्यक्तमविप्रलब्धं
भर्तुः स मे स्याद्यदि वीर भारः ।
गन्तुर्यदि स्यादधिगम्यमध्वा
पीवेति राशौ न विदां प्रवादः ॥९॥

brāhmaṇa uvāca
tvayoditaṁ vyaktam avipralabdhaṁ
bhartuḥ sa me syād yadi vīra bhāraḥ
gantur yadi syād adhigamyam adhvā
pīveti rāśau na vidāṁ pravādaḥ

brāhmaṇaḥ uvāca—the learned *brāhmaṇa* (Jaḍa Bharata) spoke; *tvayā*—by you; *uditam*—explained; *vyaktam*—very clearly; *avipralabdham*—without contradictions; *bhartuḥ*—of the bearer, the body; *saḥ*—that; *me*—mine; *syāt*—it would have been; *yadi*—if; *vīra*—O great hero (Mahārāja Rahūgaṇa); *bhāraḥ*—a load; *gantuḥ*—of the mover, also the body; *yadi*—if; *syāt*—it had been; *adhigamyam*—the object to be obtained; *adhvā*—the path; *pīvā*—very stout and strong; *iti*—thus; *rāśau*—in the body; *na*—not; *vidām*—of the self-realized persons; *pravādaḥ*—subject matter for discussion.

TRANSLATION

The great brāhmaṇa Jaḍa Bharata said: My dear King and hero, whatever you have spoken sarcastically is certainly true. Actually these are not simply words of chastisement, for the body is the carrier. The load carried by the body does not belong to me, for I am the spirit soul. There is no contradiction in your statements because I am different from the body. I am not the carrier of the palanquin; the body is the carrier. Certainly, as you have hinted, I have not labored carrying the palanquin, for I am detached from the body. You have said that I am not stout and strong, and these words are befitting a person who does not know the distinction between the body and the soul. The body may be fat or thin, but no learned man would say such things of the spirit soul. As far as the spirit soul is concerned, I am neither fat nor skinny; therefore you are correct when you say that I am not very stout. Also, if the object of this journey and the path leading there were mine, there would be many

troubles for me, but because they relate not to me but to my body, there is no trouble at all.

PURPORT

In *Bhagavad-gītā* it is stated that one who is advanced in spiritual knowledge is not disturbed by the pains and pleasures of the material body. The material body is completely separate from the spirit soul, and the pains and pleasures of the body are superfluous. The practice of austerity and penance is meant for understanding the distinction between the body and the soul and how the soul can be unaffected by the pleasures and pains of the body. Jaḍa Bharata was actually situated on the platform of self-realization. He was completely aloof from the bodily conception; therefore he immediately took this position and convinced the King that whatever contradictory things the King had said about his body did not actually apply to him as a spirit soul.

TEXT 10

स्थौल्यं कार्श्यं व्याधय आधयश्च
क्षुत्तृड् भयं कलिरिच्छा जरा च ।
निद्रा रतिर्मन्युरहंमदः शुचो
देहेन जातस्य हि मे न सन्ति ॥१०॥

sthaulyaṁ kārśyaṁ vyādhaya ādhayaś ca
kṣut tṛḍ bhayaṁ kalir icchā jarā ca
nidrā ratir manyur ahaṁ madaḥ śuco
dehena jātasya hi me na santi

sthaulyam—being very stout and strong; *kārśyam*—being skinny and weak; *vyādhayaḥ*—the pains of the body, such as disease; *ādhayaḥ*—the pains of the mind; *ca*—and; *kṣut tṛṭ bhayam*—hunger, thirst and fear; *kaliḥ*—quarrels between two persons; *icchā*—desires; *jarā*—old age; *ca*—and; *nidrā*—sleep; *ratiḥ*—attachment for sense gratification; *manyuḥ*—anger; *aham*—false identification (in the bodily concept of life); *madaḥ*—illusion; *śucaḥ*—lamentation; *dehena*—with this body; *jātasya*—of one who has taken birth; *hi*—certainly; *me*—of me; *na*—not; *santi*—exist.

TRANSLATION

Fatness, thinness, bodily and mental distress, thirst, hunger, fear, disagreement, desires for material happiness, old age, sleep, attachment

for material possessions, anger, lamentation, illusion and identification of the body with the self are all transformations of the material covering of the spirit soul. A person absorbed in the material bodily conception is affected by these things, but I am free from all bodily conceptions. Consequently I am neither fat nor skinny nor anything else you have mentioned.

PURPORT

Śrīla Narottama dāsa Ṭhākura has sung: *deha-smṛti nāhi yāra, saṁsāra-bandhana kāhāṅ tāra.* One who is spiritually advanced has no connection with the body or with the bodily actions and reactions. When one comes to understand that he is not the body and therefore is neither fat nor skinny, one attains the topmost form of spiritual realization. When one is not spiritually realized, the bodily conception entangles one in the material world. At the present moment all human society is laboring under the bodily conception; therefore in the *śāstras* people in this age are referred to as *dvipada-paśu,* two-legged animals. No one can be happy in a civilization conducted by such animals. Our Kṛṣṇa consciousness movement is trying to raise fallen human society to the status of spiritual understanding. It is not possible for everyone to become immediately self-realized like Jaḍa Bharata. However, as stated in *Śrīmad-Bhāgavatam* (1.2.18): *naṣṭa-prāyeṣv abhadreṣu nityaṁ bhāgavata-sevayā.* By spreading the *Bhāgavata* principles, we can raise human society to the platform of perfection. When one is not affected by the bodily conceptions, one can advance to the Lord's devotional service.

naṣṭa-prāyeṣv abhadreṣu
nityaṁ bhāgavata-sevayā
bhagavaty uttamaśloke
bhaktir bhavati naiṣṭhikī

The more we advance our freedom from the bodily conception, the more we are fixed in devotional service, and the more we are happy and peaceful. In this regard, Śrīla Madhvācārya says that those who are too materially affected continue the bodily conception. Such persons are concerned with different bodily symptoms, whereas one freed from bodily conceptions lives without the body even in the material condition.

TEXT 11

जीवन्मृतत्वं नियमेन राजन्
आद्यन्तवद्यद्विकृतस्य दृष्टम् ।

स्वस्वाम्यभावो ध्रुव ईड्य यत्र
तर्ह्युच्यतेऽसौ विधिकृत्ययोगः ॥११॥

jīvan-mṛtatvaṁ niyamena rājan
ādyantavad yad vikṛtasya dṛṣṭam
sva-svāmya-bhāvo dhruva īḍya yatra
tarhy ucyate'sau vidhikṛtya-yogaḥ

jīvat-mṛtatvam—the quality of being dead while living; *niyamena*—by the laws of nature; *rājan*—O King; *ādi-anta-vat*—everything material has a beginning and an end; *yat*—because; *vikṛtasya*—of things that are transformed, such as the body; *dṛṣṭam*—is seen; *sva-svāmya-bhāvaḥ*—the condition of servanthood and mastership; *dhruvaḥ*—unchangeable; *īḍya*—O you who are worshiped; *yatra*—wherein; *tarhi*—then; *ucyate*—it is said; *asau*—that; *vidhi-kṛtya-yogaḥ*—fitness of order and duty.

TRANSLATION

My dear King, you have unnecessarily accused me of being dead though alive. In this regard, I can only say that this is the case everywhere because everything material has its beginning and end. As far as your thinking that you are the king and master and are thus trying to order me, this is also incorrect because these positions are temporary. Today you are a king and I am your servant, but tomorrow the position may be changed, and you may be my servant and I your master. These are temporary circumstances created by providence.

PURPORT

The bodily conception is the basic principle of suffering in material existence. In Kali-yuga especially, people are so uneducated that they cannot even understand that the body is changing at every moment and that the ultimate change is called death. In this life one may be a king, and in the next life one may be a dog, according to *karma.* The spirit soul is in a deep slumber caused by the force of material nature. He is put in one type of condition and again changed into another type. Without self-realization and knowledge, conditional life continues, and one falsely claims himself a king, a servant, a cat or a dog. These are simply different transformations brought about by the supreme arrangement. One should not be misled by such temporary bodily conceptions. Actually no one is master within the material world, for everyone is under the control of material nature, which is under the control of the

Supreme Personality of Godhead. Therefore the Supreme Personality of Godhead, Kṛṣṇa, is the ultimate master. As explained in *Caitanya-caritāmṛta, ekale īśvara kṛṣṇa, āra saba bhṛtya:* the only master is Kṛṣṇa, and everyone else is His servant. Forgetfulness of our relationship with the Supreme Lord brings about our suffering in the material world.

TEXT 12

विशेषबुद्धेर्विवरं मनाक् च
पश्याम यन्न व्यवहारतोऽन्यत् ।
क ईश्वरस्तत्र किमीशितव्यं
तथापि राजन् करवाम किं ते ॥१२॥

viśeṣa-buddher vivaraṁ manāk ca
paśyāma yan na vyavahārato'nyat
ka īśvaras tatra kim īśitavyaṁ
tathāpi rājan karavāma kiṁ te

viśeṣa-buddheḥ—of the conception of the distinction between master and servant; *vivaram*—the scope; *manāk*—a little; *ca*—also; *paśyāmaḥ*—I see; *yat*—which; *na*—not; *vyavahārataḥ*—than the temporary usage or convention; *anyat*—other; *kaḥ*—who; *īśvaraḥ*—the master; *tatra*—in this; *kim*—who; *īśitavyam*—is to be controlled; *tathāpi*—nevertheless; *rājan*—O King (if you still think that you are master and I am servant); *karavāma*—I may do; *kim*—what; *te*—for you.

TRANSLATION

My dear King, if you still think that you are the King and that I am your servant, you should order me, and I should follow your order. I can then say that this differentiation is temporary, and it expands only from usage or convention. I do not see any other cause. In that case, who is the master, and who is the servant? Everyone is being forced by the laws of material nature; therefore no one is master, and no one is servant. Nonetheless, if you think that you are the master and that I am the servant, I shall accept this. Please order me. What can I do for you?

PURPORT

It is said in *Śrīmad-Bhāgavatam, ahaṁ mameti:* One thinks, "I am this body, and in this bodily relationship he is my master, he is my servant, she is my wife, and he is my son." All these conceptions are temporary due to the inevitable change of body and the arrangement of material nature. We are gathered together like straws floating in the waves of an ocean, straws that are inevitably separated by the laws of the waves. In this material world, everyone is floating on the waves of the ocean of nescience. As described by Bhaktivinoda Ṭhākura:

(miche) māyāra vaśe, yāccha bhese',
khāccha hābuḍubu, bhāi
(jīva) kṛṣṇa-dāsa, ei viśvāsa,
karle ta' āra duḥkha nāi

Śrīla Bhaktivinoda Ṭhākura states that all men and women are floating like straws on the waves of material nature. If they come to the understanding that they are the eternal servants of Kṛṣṇa, they will put an end to this floating condition. As stated in *Bhagavad-gītā* (3.37): *kāma eṣa krodha eṣa rajo-guṇa-samudbhavaḥ.* Due to the mode of passion, we desire many things, and according to our desire or anxiety and according to the order of the Supreme Lord, material nature gives us a certain type of body. For some time we play as master or servant, as actors play on the stage under someone else's direction. While we are in the human form, we should put an end to this nonsensical stage performance. We should come to our original constitutional position, known as Kṛṣṇa consciousness. At the present moment, the real master is material nature. *Daivī hy eṣā guṇa-mayī mama māyā duratyayā* (Bg. 7.14). Under the spell of material nature, we are becoming servants and masters, but if we agree to be controlled by the Supreme Personality of Godhead and His eternal servants, this temporary condition ceases to exist.

TEXT 13

उन्मत्तमत्तजडवत्स्वसंस्थां
गतस्य मे वीर चिकित्सितेन ।
अर्थः कियान् भवता शिक्षितेन
स्तब्धप्रमत्तस्य च पिष्टपेषः ॥१३॥

unmatta-matta-jaḍavat sva-saṁsthāṁ
gatasya me vīra cikitsitena
arthaḥ kiyān bhavatā śikṣitena
stabdha-pramattasya ca piṣṭapeṣaḥ

unmatta—madness; *matta*—a drunkard; *jaḍa-vat*—like a dunce; *sva-saṁsthām*—situation in my original constitutional position; *gatasya*—of one who has obtained; *me*—of me; *vīra*—O King; *cikitsitena*—by your chastisement; *arthaḥ*—the meaning or purpose; *kiyān*—what; *bhavatā*—by you; *śikṣitena*—by being instructed; *stabdha*—dull; *pramattasya*—of a crazy man; *ca*—also; *piṣṭa-peṣaḥ*—like grinding flour.

TRANSLATION

My dear King, you have said, "You rascal, you dull, crazy fellow! I am going to chastise you, and then you will come to your senses." In this regard, let me say that although I live like a dull, deaf and dumb man, I am actually a self-realized person. What will you gain by punishing me? If your calculation is true and I am a madman, then your punishment will be like beating a dead horse. There will be no effect. When a madman is punished, he is not cured of his madness.

PURPORT

Everyone in this material world is working like a madman under certain impressions falsely acquired in the material condition. For example, a thief who knows that stealing is not good and who knows that it is followed with punishment by a king or by God, who has seen that thieves are arrested and punished by the police, nonetheless steals again and again. He is obsessed with the idea that by stealing he will be happy. This is a sign of madness. Despite repeated punishment, the thief cannot give up his stealing habit; therefore the punishment is useless.

TEXT 14

श्रीशुक उवाच

एतावदनुवादपरिभाषया प्रत्युदीर्य मुनिवर उपशमशील उपरतानात्म्यनिमित्त उपभोगेन कर्मारब्धं व्यपनयन् राजयानमपि तथोवाह ॥१४॥

śrī-śuka uvāca

etāvad anuvāda-paribhāṣayā pratyudīrya muni-vara upaśama-śīla uparatānātmya-nimitta upabhogena karmārabdhaṁ vyapanayan rāja-yānam api tathovāha.

śrī-śukaḥ uvāca—Śukadeva Gosvāmī continued to speak; *etāvat*—so much; *anuvāda-paribhāṣayā*—by explanatory repetition of words spoken previously by the King; *pratyudīrya*—giving replies one after another; *muni-varaḥ*—great sage Jaḍa Bharata; *upaśama-śīlaḥ*—who was calm and peaceful in character; *uparata*—ceased; *anātmya*—things not related to the soul; *nimittaḥ*—whose cause (ignorance) for identification with things not related to the soul; *upabhogena*—by accepting the consequences of his *karma; karma-ārabdham*—the resultant action now attained; *vyapanayan*—finishing; *rāja-yānam*—the palanquin of the King; *api*—again; *tathā*—as before; *uvāha*—continued to carry.

TRANSLATION

Śukadeva Gosvāmī said: O Mahārāja Parīkṣit, when King Rahūgaṇa chastised the exalted devotee Jaḍa Bharata with harsh words, that peaceful, saintly person tolerated it all and replied properly. Nescience is due to the bodily conception, and Jaḍa Bharata was not affected by this false conception. Out of his natural humility, he never considered himself a great devotee, and he agreed to suffer the results of his past karma. Like an ordinary man, he thought that by carrying the palanquin, he was destroying the reactions of his past misdeeds. Thinking in this way, he began to carry the palanquin as before.

PURPORT

An exalted devotee of the Lord never thinks that he is a *paramahaṁsa* or a liberated person. He always remains a humble servant of the Lord. In all reverse conditions, he agrees to suffer the results of his past life. He never accuses the Lord of putting him into a distressed condition. These are the signs of an exalted devotee. *Tat te'nukampāṁ susamīkṣyamāṇaḥ.* When suffering reversed conditions, the devotee always considers that the reverse conditions are the Lord's concessions. He is never angry with his master; he is always satisfied with the position his master offers. In any case, he continues performing his duty in devotional service. Such a person is guaranteed promotion back home, back to Godhead. As stated in *Śrīmad-Bhāgavatam* (10.14.8):

tat te'nukampāṁ susamīkṣamāṇo
bhuñjāna evātma-kṛtaṁ vipākam
hṛd-vāg-vapurbhir vidadhan namas te
jīveta yo mukti-pade sa dāya-bhāk

"My dear Lord, one who constantly waits for Your causeless mercy to be bestowed upon him and who goes on suffering the reactions of his past misdeeds, offering You respectful obeisances from the core of his heart, is surely eligible for liberation, for it has become his rightful claim."

TEXT 15

स चापि पाण्डवेय सिन्धुसौवीरपतिस्तत्त्वजिज्ञासायां सम्यक् श्रद्धयाधिकृताधिकारस्तद्धृदयग्रन्थिमोचनं द्विजवच आश्रुत्य बहुयोगग्रन्थसम्मतं त्वरयावरुह्य शिरसा पादमूलमुपसृतः क्षमापयन् विगतनृपदेवस्मय उवाच ॥१५॥

sa cāpi pāṇḍaveya sindhu-sauvīra-patis tattva-jijñāsāyāṁ samyak-śraddhayādhikṛtādhikāras tad dhṛdaya-granthi-mocanaṁ dvija-vaca āśrutya bahu-yoga-grantha-sammataṁ tvarayāvaruhya śirasā pāda-mūlam upasṛtaḥ kṣamāpayan vigata-nṛpa-deva-smaya uvāca.

saḥ—he (Mahārāja Rahūgaṇa); *ca*—also; *api*—indeed; *pāṇḍaveya*—O best of the Pāṇḍu dynasty (Mahārāja Parīkṣit); *sindhu-sauvīra-patiḥ*—the King of the states known as Sindhu and Sauvīra; *tattva-jijñāsāyām*—in the matter of inquiring about the Absolute Truth; *samyak-śraddhayā*—by faith consisting of complete control of the senses and the mind; *adhikṛta-adhikāraḥ*—who attained the proper qualification; *tat*—that; *hṛdaya-granthi*—the knot of false conceptions within the heart; *mocanam*—which eradicates; *dvija-vacaḥ*—the words of the *brāhmaṇa* (Jaḍa Bharata); *āśrutya*—hearing; *bahu-yoga-grantha-sammatam*—approved by all yogic processes and their scriptures; *tvarayā*—very hastily; *avaruhya*—getting down (from the palanquin); *śirasā*—by his head; *pāda-mūlam*—at the lotus feet; *upasṛtaḥ*—falling down flat to offer obeisances; *kṣamāpayan*—obtaining pardon for his offense; *vigata-nṛpa-deva-smayaḥ*—giving up the false pride of being the King and therefore being worshipable; *uvāca*—said.

TRANSLATION

Śukadeva Gosvāmī continued: O best of the Pāṇḍu dynasty [Mahārāja Parīkṣit], the King of the Sindhu and Sauvīra states [Mahārāja Rahūgaṇa] had great faith in discussions of the Absolute Truth. Being thus qualified, he heard from Jaḍa Bharata that philosophical presentation which is approved by all scriptures on the mystic yoga process and which slackens the knot in the heart. His material conception of himself as a king was thus destroyed. He immediately descended from his palanquin and fell flat on the ground with his head at the lotus feet of Jaḍa Bharata in such a way that he might be excused for his insulting words against the great brāhmaṇa. He then prayed as follows.

PURPORT

In *Bhagavad-gītā* (4.2) Lord Kṛṣṇa says:

evaṁ paramparā-prāptam
imaṁ rājarṣayo viduḥ
sa kāleneha mahatā
yogo naṣṭaḥ parantapa

"This supreme science was thus received through the chain of disciplic succession, and the saintly kings understood it in that way. But in course of time the succession was broken, and therefore the science as it is appears to be lost."

Through the disciplic succession the royal order was on the same platform as great saintly persons (*rāja-ṛṣis*). Formerly they could understand the philosophy of life and knew how to train the citizens to come to the same standard. In other words, they knew how to deliver the citizens from the entanglement of birth and death. When Mahārāja Daśaratha ruled Ayodhyā, the great sage Viśvāmitra once came to him to take away Lord Rāmacandra and Lakṣmaṇa to the forest to kill a demon. When the saintly person Viśvāmitra came to the court of Mahārāja Daśaratha, the King, in order to receive the saintly person, asked him, *aihiṣṭaṁ yat tat punar janma jayāya.* He asked the sage whether everything was going on well in his endeavor to conquer the repetition of birth and death. The whole process of Vedic civilization is based on this point. We must know how to conquer the repetition of birth and death. Mahārāja Rahūgaṇa also knew the purpose of life; therefore when Jaḍa Bharata put the philosophy of life before him, he immediately appreciated it. This is the foundation of Vedic society. Learned scholars, *brāhmaṇas,* saintly persons and sages who were fully aware of the Vedic purpose advised the royal order how to benefit the general masses, and by their cooperation, the general masses were benefited. Therefore everything was successful. Mahārāja Rahūgaṇa attained this perfection of understanding the value of human life; therefore he regretted his insulting words to Jaḍa Bharata, and he immediately descended from his palanquin and fell down at the lotus feet of Jaḍa Bharata in order to be excused and to hear from him further about the values of life known as *brahma jijñāsā* (inquiry into the Absolute Truth). At the present moment, high government officials are ignorant of the values of life, and when saintly persons endeavor to broadcast the Vedic knowledge, the so-called executives do not offer their respectful obeisances but try to obstruct the spiritual propaganda. Thus one can say that the former kingly government was like heaven and that the present government is like hell.

TEXT 16

कस्त्वं निगूढश्चरसि द्विजानां
बिभर्षि सूत्रं कतमोऽवधूतः ।
कस्यासि कुत्रत्य इहापि कस्मात्
क्षेमाय नश्चेदसि नोत शुक्लः ॥१६॥

kas tvaṁ nigūḍhaś carasi dvijānāṁ
bibharṣi sūtraṁ katamo'vadhūtaḥ
kasyāsi kutratya ihāpi kasmāt
kṣemāya naś ced asi nota śuklaḥ

kaḥ tvam—who are you; *nigūḍhaḥ*—very much covered; *carasi*—you move within this world; *dvijānām*—among the *brāhmaṇas* or saintly persons; *bibharṣi*—you also wear; *sūtram*—the sacred thread belonging to the first-class *brāhmaṇas; katamaḥ*—which; *avadhūtaḥ*—highly elevated person; *kasya asi*—whose are you (whose disciple or son are you); *kutratyaḥ*—from where; *iha api*—here in this place; *kasmāt*—for what purpose; *kṣemāya*—for the benefit; *naḥ*—of us; *cet*—if; *asi*—you are; *na uta*—or not; *śuklaḥ*—the personality of the pure mode of goodness (Kapiladeva).

TRANSLATION

King Rahūgaṇa said: O brāhmaṇa, you appear to be moving in this world very much covered and unknown to others. Who are you? Are you a learned brāhmaṇa and saintly person? I see that you are wearing a sacred thread. Are you one of those exalted, liberated saints such as Dattātreya and other highly advanced, learned scholars? May I ask whose disciple you are? Where do you live? Why have you come to this place? Is your mission in coming here to do good for us? Please let me know who you are.

PURPORT

Mahārāja Rahūgaṇa was very anxious to receive further enlightenment in Vedic knowledge because he could understand that Jaḍa Bharata belonged to a *brāhmaṇa* family either by disciplic succession or by birth in a *brāhmaṇa* dynasty. As stated in the *Vedas: tad vijñānārthaṁ sa gurum evābhigacchet.* Rahūgaṇa was accepting Jaḍa Bharata as a *guru,* but a *guru* must prove his position not only by wearing a sacred thread but by advancing knowledge in spiritual life. It is also significant that Rahūgaṇa asked Jaḍa Bharata which family he belonged to. There are two types of families—one according to dynasty and the other according to disciplic succession. In either way, one can be enlightened. The word *śuklaḥ* refers to a person in the mode of goodness. If one wants to receive spiritual knowledge, he must approach a bona fide *brāhmaṇa-guru,* either in the disciplic succession or in a family of learned *brāhmaṇas.*

TEXT 17

नाहं विशङ्के सुरराजवज्रा-
न्न त्र्यक्षशूलान्न यमस्य दण्डात् ।
नाग्न्यर्कसोमानिलवित्तपास्त्रा-
च्छङ्के भृशं ब्रह्मकुलावमानात् ॥१७॥

nāhaṁ viśaṅke sura-rāja-vajrān
na tryakṣa-śūlān na yamasya daṇḍāt
nāgny-arka-somānila-vittapāstrāc
chaṅke bhṛśaṁ brahma-kulāvamānāt

na—not; *aham*—I; *viśaṅke*—am afraid; *sura-rāja-vajrāt*—from the thunderbolt of the King of heaven, Indra; *na*—nor; *tryakṣa-śūlāt*—from the piercing trident of Lord Śiva; *na*—nor; *yamasya*—of the superintendent of death, Yamarāja; *daṇḍāt*—from the punishment; *na*—nor; *agni*—of fire; *arka*—of the scorching heat of the sun; *soma*—of the moon; *anila*—of the wind; *vitta-pa*—of the owner of riches, Kuvera, the treasurer of the heavenly planets; *astrāt*—from the weapons; *śaṅke*—I am afraid; *bhṛśam*—very much; *brahma-kula*—the group of the *brāhmaṇas; avamānāt*—from offending.

TRANSLATION

My dear sir, I am not at all afraid of the thunderbolt of King Indra, nor am I afraid of the serpentine, piercing trident of Lord Śiva. I do not care about the punishment of Yamarāja, the superintendent of death, nor am I afraid of fire, scorching sun, moon, wind, nor the weapons of Kuvera. Yet I am afraid of offending a brāhmaṇa. I am very much afraid of this.

PURPORT

When Śrī Caitanya Mahāprabhu was instructing Rūpa Gosvāmī at the Daśāśvamedha-ghāṭa in Prayāga, He pointed out very clearly the seriousness of offending a Vaiṣṇava. He compared the *vaiṣṇava-aparādha* to *hātī mātā,* a mad elephant. When a mad elephant enters a garden, it spoils all the fruits and flowers. Similarly, if one offends a Vaiṣṇava, he spoils all his spiritual assets. Offending a *brāhmaṇa* is very dangerous, and this was known to Mahārāja Rahūgaṇa. He therefore frankly admitted his fault. There are many dangerous things—thunderbolts, fire, Yamarāja's punishment, the punishment of Lord Śiva's trident, and so forth—but none is considered as serious as offending a *brāhmaṇa* like Jaḍa Bharata. Therefore Mahārāja Rahūgaṇa immediately descended from his palanquin and fell flat before the lotus feet of the *brāhmaṇa* Jaḍa Bharata just to be excused.

TEXT 18

तद् ब्रूह्यसङ्गो जडवन्निगूढ-
विज्ञानवीर्यो विचरस्यपारः ।
वचांसि योगग्रथितानि साधो
न नः क्षमन्ते मनसापि भेत्तुम् ॥१८॥

tad brūhy asaṅgo jaḍavan nigūḍha-
vijñāna-vīryo vicarasy apāraḥ
vacāṁsi yoga-grathitāni sādho
na naḥ kṣamante manasāpi bhettum

tat—therefore; *brūhi*—please speak; *asaṅgaḥ*—who have no association with the material world; *jaḍa-vat*—appearing like a deaf and dumb man; *nigūḍha*—completely hidden; *vijñāna-vīryaḥ*—who have full knowledge of the spiritual science and are thus very powerful; *vicarasi*—you are moving; *apāraḥ*—who possess unlimited spiritual glories; *vacāṁsi*—the words uttered by you; *yoga-grathitāni*—bearing the complete meaning of mystic *yoga;* *sādho*—O great, saintly person; *na*—not; *naḥ*—of us; *kṣamante*—are able; *manasā api*—even by the mind; *bhettum*—to understand by analytical study.

TRANSLATION

My dear sir, it appears that the influence of your great spiritual knowledge is hidden. Factually you are bereft of all material association and fully absorbed in the thought of the Supreme. Consequently you are unlimitedly advanced in spiritual knowledge. Please tell me why you are wandering around like a dullard. O great, saintly person, you have spoken

words approved by the yogic process, but it is not possible for us to understand what you have said. Therefore kindly explain it.

PURPORT

Saintly people like Jaḍa Bharata do not speak ordinary words. Whatever they say is approved by great *yogīs* and those advanced in spiritual life. That is the difference between ordinary people and saintly people. The listener must also be advanced to understand the words of such exalted, spiritually advanced people as Jaḍa Bharata. *Bhagavad-gītā* was spoken to Arjuna, not to others. Lord Kṛṣṇa especially selected Arjuna for instruction in spiritual knowledge because Arjuna happened to be a great devotee and confidential friend. Similarly, great personalities also speak to the advanced, not to *śūdras, vaiśyas,* women or unintelligent men. Sometimes it is very risky to give great philosophical instructions to ordinary people, but Śrī Caitanya Mahāprabhu, for the benefit of the fallen souls of Kali-yuga, has given us a very nice instrument, the chanting of the Hare Kṛṣṇa *mantra.* The general mass of people, although *śūdras* and less, can be purified by chanting this Hare Kṛṣṇa *mantra.* Then they can understand the exalted philosophical statements of *Bhagavad-gītā* and *Śrīmad-Bhāgavatam.* Our Kṛṣṇa consciousness movement has therefore adopted the chanting of the Hare Kṛṣṇa *mahā-mantra* for the general masses. When people gradually become purified, they are instructed in the lessons of *Bhagavad-gītā* and *Śrīmad-Bhāgavatam.* Materialistic people like *strī, śūdra* and *dvija-bandhu* cannot understand words of spiritual advancement, yet one can take to the shelter of a Vaiṣṇava, for he knows the art of enlightening even *śūdras* in the highly elevated subject matter spoken in *Bhagavad-gītā* and *Śrīmad-Bhāgavatam.*

TEXT 19

अहं च योगेश्वरमात्मतत्त्व-
विदां मुनीनां परमं गुरुं वै ।
प्रष्टुं प्रवृत्तः किमिहारणं तत्
साक्षाद्धरिं ज्ञानकलावतीर्णम् ॥१९॥

ahaṁ ca yogeśvaram ātma-tattva-
vidāṁ munīnāṁ paramaṁ guruṁ vai
praṣṭuṁ pravṛttaḥ kim ihāraṇaṁ tat
sākṣād dhariṁ jñāna-kalāvatīrṇam

aham—I; *ca*—and; *yoga-īśvaram*—the master of all mystic power; *ātma-tattva-vidām*—of the learned scholars who are aware of the spiritual science; *munīnām*—of such saintly persons; *paramam*—the best; *gurum*—the preceptor; *vai*—indeed; *praṣṭum*—to inquire; *pravṛttaḥ*—engaged; *kim*—what; *iha*—in this world; *araṇam*—the most secure shelter; *tat*—that which; *sākṣāt harim*—directly the Supreme Personality of Godhead; *jñāna-kalā-avatīrṇam*—who has descended as the incarnation of complete knowledge in His plenary portion known as Kapiladeva.

TRANSLATION

I consider your good self the most exalted master of mystic power. You know the spiritual science perfectly well. You are the most exalted of all learned sages, and you have descended for the benefit of all human society. You have come to give spiritual knowledge, and you are a direct representative of Kapiladeva, the incarnation of God and the plenary portion of knowledge. I am therefore asking you, O spiritual master, what is the most secure shelter in this world?

PURPORT

As Kṛṣṇa confirms in *Bhagavad-gītā*:

yoginām api sarveṣāṁ
mad-gatenāntarātmanā
śraddhāvān bhajate yo māṁ
sa me yuktatamo mataḥ

"Of all *yogīs,* he who abides in Me with great faith, worshiping Me in transcendental loving service, is most intimately united with Me in *yoga* and is the highest of all." (Bg. 6.47)

Jaḍa Bharata was a perfect *yogī.* He was formerly the emperor Bharata Mahārāja, and he was now the most exalted personality among learned sages and the master of all mystic powers. Although Jaḍa Bharata was an ordinary living entity, he had inherited all the knowledge given by the Supreme Personality of Godhead, Kapiladeva. He could therefore be taken directly as the Supreme Personality of Godhead. As confirmed by Śrīla Viśvanātha Cakravartī Ṭhākura in his stanzas to the spiritual master: *sākṣād-dharitvena samasta-śāstraiḥ.* An exalted personality like Jaḍa Bharata is as good as the Supreme Personality of Godhead because he fully represents the Lord by giving knowledge to others. Jaḍa Bharata is herein accepted as the direct representative of the Supreme Personality of Godhead because he was imparting knowledge on behalf of the Supreme Lord. Therefore Mahārāja Rahūgaṇa concluded that it was appropriate to ask him about *ātma-tattva,* the spiritual science. *Tad-vijñānārthaṁ sa gurum evābhigacchet.* This Vedic injunction is also confirmed herein. If anyone is at all interested in knowing the spiritual science (*brahma jijñāsā*), he must approach a *guru* like Jaḍa Bharata.

TEXT 20

स वै भवाँल्लोकनिरीक्षणार्थ-
मव्यक्तलिङ्गो विचरत्यपिस्वित् ।
योगेश्वराणां गतिमन्धबुद्धिः
कथं विचक्षीत गृहानुबन्धः ॥२०॥

sa vai bhavāl̐ loka-nirīkṣaṇārtham
avyakta-liṅgo vicaraty api svit
yogeśvarāṇāṁ gatim andha-buddhiḥ
kathaṁ vicakṣīta gṛhānubandhaḥ

saḥ—that Supreme Personality of Godhead or His incarnation Kapiladeva; *vai*—indeed; *bhavān*—your good self; *loka-nirīkṣaṇa-artham*—just to study the characteristics of the people of this world; *avyakta-liṅgaḥ*—without manifesting your real identity; *vicarati*—are traveling in this world; *api svit*—whether; *yoga-īśvarāṇām*—of all the advanced *yogīs; gatim*—the characteristics or actual behavior; *andha-buddhiḥ*—who are illusioned and have become blind to spiritual knowledge; *katham*—how; *vicakṣīta*—may know; *gṛha-anubandhaḥ*—I who am bound by attachment to family life, or worldly life.

TRANSLATION

Is it not a fact that your good self is the direct representative of Kapila-deva, the incarnation of the Supreme Personality of Godhead? To examine people and see who is actually a human being and who is not, you have presented yourself to be a deaf and dumb person. Are you not moving this way upon the surface of the world? I am very attached to family life and worldly activities, and I am blind to spiritual knowledge. Nonetheless, I am now present before you and am seeking enlightenment from you. How can I advance in spiritual life?

PURPORT

Although Mahārāja Rahūgaṇa was playing the part of a king, he had been informed by Jaḍa Bharata that he was not a king nor was Jaḍa Bharata deaf and dumb. Such designations were simply coverings of the spirit soul. Everyone must come to this knowledge. As confirmed in *Bhagavad-gītā* (2.13): *dehino'smin yathā dehe.* Everyone is encased within the body. Since the body is never identical with the soul, the bodily activities are simply illusory. In the association of such a *sādhu* as Jaḍa Bharata, Mahārāja Rahūgaṇa came to the awareness that his activities as a royal authority were simply illusory phenomena. He therefore agreed to receive knowledge from Jaḍa Bharata, and that was the beginning of his perfection. *Tad-vijñānārthaṁ sa gurum evābhigacchet.* A person like Mahārāja Rahūgaṇa, who was very inquisitive to know the value of life and the spiritual science, must approach a personality like Jaḍa Bharata. *Tasmād guruṁ prapadyeta jijñāsuḥ śreya uttamam* (*Bhāg.* 11.3.21). One must approach a *guru* like Jaḍa Bharata, a representative of the Supreme Personality of Godhead, to inquire about the goal of human life.

TEXT 21

दृष्टः श्रमः कर्मत आत्मनो वै
भर्तुर्गन्तुर्भवतश्चानुमन्ये ।
यथासतोदानयनाद्यभावात्
समूल इष्टो व्यवहारमार्गः ॥२१॥

dṛṣṭaḥ śramaḥ karmata ātmano vai
bhartur gantur bhavataś cānumanye
yathāsatodānayanādy-abhāvāt
samūla iṣṭo vyavahāra-mārgaḥ

dṛṣṭaḥ—it is experienced by everyone; *śramaḥ*—fatigue; *karmataḥ*—from acting in some way; *ātmanaḥ*—of the soul; *vai*—indeed; *bhartuḥ*—of one who is carrying the palanquin; *gantuḥ*—of one who is moving; *bhavataḥ*—of yourself; *ca*—and; *anumanye*—I guess like that; *yathā*—as much as; *asatā*—with something that is not an actual fact; *uda*—of water; *ānayana-ādi*—of the bringing and other such tasks; *abhāvāt*—from the absence; *sa-mūlaḥ*—based on evidence; *iṣṭaḥ*—respected; *vyavahāra-mārgaḥ*—phenomenon.

TRANSLATION

You have said, "I am not fatigued from labor." Although the soul is different from the body, there is fatigue because of bodily labor, and it appears to be the fatigue of the soul. When you are carrying the palanquin, there is certainly labor for the soul. This is my conjecture. You have also said that the external behavior exhibited between the master and the servant is not factual, but although in the phenomenal world it is not factual, the products of the phenomenal world can actually affect things. That is visible and experienced. As such, even though material activities are impermanent, they cannot be said to be untrue.

PURPORT

This is a discussion on impersonal Māyāvāda philosophy and the practical philosophy of Vaiṣṇavas. The Māyāvāda philosophy explains this phenomenal world to be false, but Vaiṣṇava philosophers do not agree. They know that the phenomenal world is a temporary manifestation, but it is not false. A dream that we see at night is certainly false, but a horrible dream certainly affects the person seeing it. The soul's fatigue is not factual, but as long as one is immersed in the illusory bodily conception, one is affected by such false dreams. When dreaming, it is not possible to avoid the actual facts, and the conditioned soul is forced to suffer due to his dream. A waterpot is made of earth and is temporary. Actually there is no waterpot; there is simply earth. However, as long as the waterpot can contain water, we can use it in that way. It cannot be said to be absolutely false.

TEXT 22

स्थाल्यग्नितापात्पयसोऽभिताप-
स्तत्तापतस्तण्डुलगर्भरन्धिः ।
देहेन्द्रियास्वाशयसन्निकर्षात्
तत्संसृतिः पुरुषस्यानुरोधात् ॥२२॥

sthāly-agni-tāpāt payaso'bhitāpas
tat-tāpatas taṇḍula-garbha-randhiḥ
dehendriyāsvāśaya-sannikarṣāt
tat-saṁsṛtiḥ puruṣasyānurodhāt

sthāli—on the cooking pot; *agni-tāpāt*—because of the heat of fire; *payasaḥ*—the milk put into the pot; *abhitāpaḥ*—becomes hot; *tat-tāpataḥ*

—because of the milk's becoming hot; *taṇḍula-garbha-randhiḥ*—the center of the rice within the milk becomes cooked; *deha-indriya-asvāśaya*—the bodily senses; *sannikarṣāt*—from having connections with; *tat-saṁsṛtiḥ*—the experience of fatigue and other miseries; *puruṣasya*—of the soul; *anurodhāt*—from compliance due to being grossly attached to the body, senses and mind.

TRANSLATION

King Rahūgaṇa continued: My dear sir, you have said that designations like bodily fatness and thinness are not characteristics of the soul. That is incorrect because designations like pain and pleasure are certainly felt by the soul. You may put a pot of milk and rice within fire, and the milk and rice are automatically heated one after the other. Similarly, due to bodily pains and pleasures, the senses, mind and soul are affected. The soul cannot be completely detached from this conditioning.

PURPORT

This argument put forward by Mahārāja Rahūgaṇa is correct from the practical point of view, but it arises from an attachment to the bodily conception. It can be said that a person sitting in his car is certainly different from his car, but if there is damage to the car, the owner of the car, being overly attached to the car, feels pain. Actually, the damage done to the car has nothing to do with the car's proprietor, but because the proprietor has identified himself with the interest of the car, he feels pleasure and pain connected with it. This conditional state can be avoided if attachment is withdrawn from the car. Then the proprietor would not feel pleasure or pain if the car is damaged or whatever. Similarly, the soul has nothing to do with the body and the senses, but due to ignorance, he identifies himself with the body, and he feels pleasure and pain due to bodily pleasure and pain.

TEXT 23

शास्ताभिगोप्ता नृपतिः प्रजानां
यः किङ्करो वै न पिनष्टि पिष्टम् ।
स्वधर्ममाराधनमच्युतस्य
यदीहमानो विजहात्यघौघम् ॥२३॥

śāstābhigoptā nṛpatiḥ prajānāṁ
yaḥ kiṅkaro vai na pinaṣṭi piṣṭam

sva-dharmam ārādhanam acyutasya
yad īhamāno vijahāty aghaugham

śāstā—the governor; *abhigoptā*—a well-wisher of the citizens as a father is the well-wisher of his children; *nṛ-patiḥ*—the king; *prajānām*—of the citizens; *yaḥ*—one who; *kiṅkaraḥ*—order carrier; *vai*—indeed; *na*—not; *pinaṣṭi piṣṭam*—grinds what is already ground; *sva-dharmam*—one's own occupational duty; *ārādhanam*—worshiping; *acyutasya*—of the Supreme Personality of Godhead; *yat*—which; *īhamānaḥ*—performing; *vijahāti*—they are released from; *agha-ogham*—all kinds of sinful activity and faulty action.

TRANSLATION

My dear sir, you have said that the relationship between the king and the subject or between the master and the servant are not eternal, but although such relationships are temporary, when a person takes the position of a king, his duty is to rule the citizens and punish those who are disobedient to the laws. By punishing them, he teaches the citizens to obey the laws of the state. Again, you have said that punishing a person who is deaf and dumb is like chewing the chewed or grinding the pulp; that is to say, there is no benefit in it. However, if one is engaged in his own occupational duty as ordered by the Supreme Lord, his sinful activities are certainly diminished. Therefore if one is engaged in his occupational duty by force, he benefits because he can vanquish all his sinful activities in that way.

PURPORT

This argument offered by Mahārāja Rahūgaṇa is certainly very effective. In his *Bhakti-rasāmṛta-sindhu* (1.2.4), Śrīla Rūpa Gosvāmī says, *tasmāt kenāpy upāyena manaḥ kṛṣṇe niveśayet:* somehow or other, one should engage in Kṛṣṇa consciousness. Actually every living being is an eternal servant of Kṛṣṇa, but due to forgetfulness, a living entity engages himself as an eternal servant of *māyā.* As long as one is engaged in *māyā's* service, he cannot be happy. Our Kṛṣṇa consciousness movement aims at engaging people in Lord Kṛṣṇa's service. That will help them become freed from all material contamination and sinful activity. This is confirmed in *Bhagavad-gītā* (4.10): *vīta-rāga-bhaya-krodhāḥ.* By becoming detached from material activities, we will be freed from fear and anger. By austerity, one becomes purified and eligible to return home, back to Godhead. The duty of the king is to rule his citizens in such a way that they can become Kṛṣṇa conscious. This would be very beneficial for everyone.

Unfortunately the king or president engages people in sense gratification instead of the Lord's service, and such activities are certainly not beneficial for anyone. King Rahūgaṇa tried to engage Jaḍa Bharata in carrying the palanquin, which is a form of sense gratification for the King. However, if one is engaged as a palanquin carrier in the Lord's service, that is certainly beneficial. In this godless civilization, if a president engages people somehow or other in devotional service or the awakening of Kṛṣṇa consciousness, he renders the very best service to the citizens.

TEXT 24

तन्मे भवान्नरदेवाभिमान-
मदेन तुच्छीकृतसत्तमस्य ।
कृषीष्ट मैत्रीदृशमार्तबन्धो
यथा तरे सदवध्यानमंहः ॥२४॥

tan me bhavān nara-devābhimāna-
madena tucchīkṛta-sattamasya
kṛṣīṣṭa maitrī-dṛśam ārta-bandho
yathā tare sad-avadhyānam aṁhaḥ

tat—therefore; *me*—unto me; *bhavān*—your good self; *nara-deva-abhimāna-madena*—by madness due to having the body of a king and thus being proud of it; *tucchīkṛta*—who has insulted; *sat-tamasya*—you who are the best among human beings; *kṛṣīṣṭa*—kindly show; *maitrī-dṛśam*—your causeless mercy upon me like a friend; *ārta-bandho*—O friend of all distressed persons; *yathā*—so; *tare*—I can get relief from; *sat-avadhyānam*—neglecting a great personality like you; *aṁhaḥ*—the sin.

TRANSLATION

Whatever you have spoken appears to me to be contradictory. O best friend of the distressed, I have committed a great offense by insulting you. I was puffed up with false prestige due to possessing the body of a king. For this I have certainly become an offender. Therefore I pray that you kindly glance at me with your causeless mercy. If you do so, I can be relieved from sinful activities brought about by insulting you.

PURPORT

Śrī Caitanya Mahāprabhu has said that by offending a Vaiṣṇava, one finishes all his spiritual activities. Offending a Vaiṣṇava is considered the mad elephant offense. A mad elephant can destroy an entire garden which has been developed with great labor. One may attain the topmost platform of devotional service, but somehow or other if he offends a Vaiṣṇava, the whole structure collapses. Unconsciously, King Rahūgaṇa offended Jaḍa Bharata, but due to his good sense, he asked to be excused. This is the process by which one can be relieved from a *vaiṣṇava-aparādha.* Kṛṣṇa is always very simple and by nature merciful. When one commits an offense at the feet of a Vaiṣṇava, one must immediately apologize to such a personality so that his spiritual advancement may not be hampered.

TEXT 25

न विक्रिया विश्वसुहृत्सखस्य
साम्येन वीताभिमतेस्तवापि ।
महद्विमानात् स्वकृताद्धि माद्दङ्
नङ्क्ष्यत्यदूरादपि शूलपाणिः ॥२५॥

na vikriyā viśva-suhṛt-sakhasya
sāmyena vītābhimates tavāpi
mahad-vimānāt sva-kṛtād dhi mādṛṅ
naṅkṣyaty adūrād api śūlapāṇiḥ

na—not; *vikriyā*—material transformation; *viśva-suhṛt*—of the Supreme Personality of Godhead, who is a friend to everyone; *sakhasya*—of you, the friend; *sāmyena*—because of your mental equilibrium; *vīta-abhimateḥ*—who has completely forsaken the bodily concept of life; *tava*—your; *api*—indeed; *mahat-vimānāt*—of insulting a great devotee; *sva-kṛtāt*—from my own activity; *hi*—certainly; *mādṛk*—a person like me; *naṅkṣyati*—will be destroyed; *adūrāt*—very soon; *api*—certainly; *śūla-pāṇiḥ*—even though as powerful as Lord Śiva (Śūlapāṇi).

TRANSLATION

O my dear lord, you are the friend of the Supreme Personality of Godhead, who is the friend of all living entities. You are therefore equal to everyone, and you are free from the bodily conception. Although I have committed an offense by insulting you, I know that there is no loss or gain for you due to my insult. You are fixed in your determination, but I have committed an offense. Because of this, even though I may be as strong as Lord Śiva, I shall be vanquished without delay due to my offense at the lotus feet of a Vaiṣṇava.

PURPORT

Mahārāja Rahūgaṇa was very intelligent and conscious of the inauspicious effects arising from insulting a Vaiṣṇava. He was therefore very anxious to be excused by Jaḍa Bharata. Following in the footsteps of Mahārāja Rahūgaṇa, everyone should be very cautious not to commit an offense at the lotus feet of a Vaiṣṇava. Śrīla Vṛndāvana dāsa Ṭhākura in the *Caitanya-bhāgavata* (*Madhya* 13) says:

śūlapāṇi-sama yadi bhakta-nindā kare
bhāgavata pramāṇa—tathāpi śīghra mare

hena vaiṣṇavere ninde sarvajña ha-i
se janera adhaḥ-pāta sarva-śāstre ka-i

"Even if one is as strong as Lord Śiva, who carries a trident in his hand, one will nonetheless fall down from his spiritual position if he tries to insult a Vaiṣṇava. That is the verdict of all Vedic scriptures." He also says this in *Caitanya-bhāgavata* (*Madhya* 22):

vaiṣṇavera nindā karibeka yāra gaṇa
tāra rakṣā sāmarthya nāhika kona jana

śūlapāṇi-sama yadi vaiṣṇavere ninde
tathāpiha nāśa yāya—kahe śāstra-vṛnde

ihā nā māniyā ye sujana nindā kare
janme janme se pāpiṣṭha daiva-doṣe mare

"One who blasphemes a Vaiṣṇava cannot be protected by anyone. Even if a person is as strong as Lord Śiva, if he blasphemes a Vaiṣṇava, he is sure to be destroyed. This is the verdict of all *śāstras.* If one does not care for the verdict of the *śāstras* and dares blaspheme a Vaiṣṇava, he suffers life after life because of this."

Thus end the Bhaktivedanta purports of the Fifth Canto, Tenth Chapter, of the Śrīmad-Bhāgavatam, *entitled "The Discussion Between Jaḍa Bharata and Mahārāja Rahūgaṇa."*

CHAPTER ELEVEN

Jaḍa Bharata Instructs King Rahūgaṇa

In this chapter the *brāhmaṇa* Jaḍa Bharata instructs Mahārāja Rahūgaṇa in detail. He tells the King: "You are not very experienced, yet you pose yourself as a learned person because you are very proud of your knowledge. Actually a person who is on the transcendental platform does not care for social behavior that sacrifices spiritual advancement. Social behavior comes within the jurisdiction of *karma-kāṇḍa,* material benefit. No one can spiritually advance by such activities. The conditioned soul is always overpowered by the modes of material nature, and consequently he is simply concerned with material benefits and auspicious and inauspicious material things. In other words, the mind, which is the leader of the senses, is absorbed in material activities life after life. Thus he continuously gets different types of bodies and suffers miserable material conditions. On the basis of mental concoction, social behavior has been formulated. If one's mind is absorbed in these activities, he certainly remains conditioned within the material world. According to different opinions, there are eleven or twelve mental activities, which can be transformed into hundreds and thousands. A person who is not Kṛṣṇa conscious is subjected to all these mental concoctions and is thus governed by the material energy. The living entity who is free from mental concoctions attains the platform of pure spirit soul, devoid of material contamination. There are two types of living entities- *jīvātmā* and *Paramātmā,* the individual soul and the Supreme Soul. That Supreme Soul in His ultimate realization is Lord Vāsudeva, Kṛṣṇa. He enters into everyone's heart and controls the living entity in his different activities. He is therefore the supreme shelter of all living entities. One can understand the Supreme Soul and one's position in relationship with Him when one is completely freed from the unwanted association of ordinary men. In this way one can become fit to cross the ocean of nescience. The cause of conditional life is attachment to the external energy. One has to conquer these mental concoctions: unless one does so, he will never be freed from material anxieties. Although mental concoctions have no value, their influence is still very formidable. No one should neglect to control the mind. If one does, the mind becomes so powerful that one immediately forgets his real position. Forgetting that he is an eternal servant of Kṛṣṇa and that service to Kṛṣṇa is his only business, one is doomed by material nature to serve the objects of the senses. One should kill mental concoctions by the sword of service to the Supreme Personality of Godhead and His devotee (*guru-kṛṣṇa-prasāde pāya bhakti-latā-bīja*)."

TEXT 1

ब्राह्मण उवाच
अकोविदः कोविदवादवादान्
वदस्यथो नातिविदां वरिष्ठः ।
न सूरयो हि व्यवहारमेनं
तत्त्वावमर्शेन सहामनन्ति ॥१॥

brāhmaṇa uvāca
akovidaḥ kovida-vāda-vādān
vadasy atho nāti-vidāṁ variṣṭhaḥ
na sūrayo hi vyavahāram enaṁ
tattvāvamarśena sahāmananti

brāhmaṇaḥ uvāca—the *brāhmaṇa* said; *akovidaḥ*—without having experience; *kovida-vāda-vādān*—words used by experienced persons; *vadasi*—you are speaking; *atho*—therefore; *na*—not; *ati-vidām*—of those who are very experienced; *variṣṭhaḥ*—the most important; *na*—not; *sūrayaḥ*—such intelligent persons; *hi*—indeed; *vyavahāram*—mundane and social behavior; *enam*—this; *tattva*—of the truth; *avamarśena*—fine judgment by intelligence; *saha*—with; *āmananti*—discuss.

TRANSLATION

The brāhmaṇa Jaḍa Bharata said: My dear King, although you are not at all experienced, you are trying to speak like a very experienced man. Consequently you cannot be considered an experienced person. An experienced person does not speak the way you are speaking about the relationship between a master and a servant or about material pains and pleasures. These are simply external activities. Any advanced, experienced man, considering the Absolute Truth, does not talk in this way.

PURPORT

Kṛṣṇa similarly chastised Arjuna. *Aśocyān anvaśocas tvaṁ prajñā-vādāṁś ca bhāṣase:* "While speaking learned words, you are lamenting for what is not worthy of grief." (Bg. 2.11) Similarly, among people in general, 99.9 percent try to talk like experienced advisers, but they are actually devoid of spiritual knowledge and are therefore like inexperienced children speaking nonsensically. Consequently their words cannot be given any importance. One has to learn from Kṛṣṇa or His devotee. If one speaks on the basis of this experience—that is, on the basis of spiritual knowledge—one's words are valuable. At the present moment, the entire world is full of foolish people. *Bhagavad-gītā* describes these people as *mūḍhas.* They are trying to rule human society, but because they are devoid of spiritual knowledge, the entire world is in a chaotic condition. To be released from these miserable conditions, one has to become Kṛṣṇa conscious and take lessons from an exalted personality like Jaḍa Bharata, Lord Kṛṣṇa and Kapiladeva. That is the only way to solve the problems of material life.

TEXT 2

तथैव राजन्नुरुगार्हमेध-
वितानविद्योरुविजृम्भितेषु ।
न वेदवादेषु हि तत्त्ववादः
प्रायेण शुद्धो नु चकास्ति साधुः ॥ २ ॥

tathaiva rājann uru-gārhamedha-
vitāna-vidyoru-vijṛmbhiteṣu
na veda-vādeṣu hi tattva-vādaḥ
prāyeṇa śuddho nu cakāsti sādhuḥ

tathā—therefore; *eva*—indeed; *rājan*—O King; *uru-gārha-medha*—rituals related to material household life; *vitāna-vidyā*—in knowledge that expands; *uru*—very greatly; *vijṛmbhiteṣu*—among those interested; *na*—not; *veda-vādeṣu*—who speak the version of the *Vedas; hi*—indeed; *tattva-vādaḥ*—the spiritual science; *prāyeṇa*—almost always; *śuddhaḥ*—free from all contaminated activities; *nu*—indeed; *cakāsti*—appear; *sādhuḥ*—a person who is advanced in devotional service.

TRANSLATION

My dear King, talks of the relationship between the master and the servant, the king and the subject and so forth are simply talks about material activities. People interested in material activities, which are expounded in the Vedas, are intent on performing material sacrifices and

placing faith in their material activities. For such people, spiritual advancement is definitely not manifest.

PURPORT

In this verse, two words are significant—*veda-vāda* and *tattva-vāda.* According to *Bhagavad-gītā,* those who are simply attached to the *Vedas* and who do not understand the purpose of the *Vedas* or the *Vedānta-sūtra* are called *veda-vāda-ratāḥ.*

yām imāṁ puṣpitāṁ vācaṁ
pravadanty avipaścitaḥ
veda-vāda-ratāḥ pārtha
nānyad astīti vādinaḥ

kāmātmānaḥ svarga-parā
janma-karma-phala-pradām
kriyā-viśeṣa-bahulāṁ
bhogaiśvarya-gatiṁ prati

"Men of small knowledge are very much attached to the flowery words of the *Vedas,* which recommend various fruitive activities for elevation to heavenly planets, resultant good birth, power and so forth. Being desirous of sense gratification and opulent life, they say there is nothing more than this." (*Bg.* 2.42–43)

The *veda-vāda* followers of the *Vedas* are generally inclined to *karma-kāṇḍa,* the performance of sacrifice according to the Vedic injunctions. They are thereby promoted to higher planetary systems. They generally practice the Cātur-māsya system. *Akṣayyaṁ ha vai cātur-māsya-yājinaḥ sukṛtaṁ bhavati:* one who performs the *cātur-māsya-yajña* becomes pious. By becoming pious, one may be promoted to the higher planetary systems (*ūrdhvaṁ gacchanti sattva-sthāḥ*). Some of the followers of the *Vedas* are attached to *karma-kāṇḍa,* the fruitive activities of the *Vedas,* in order to be promoted to a higher standard of life. Others argue that this is not the purpose of the *Vedas. Tad yathaiveha karma jitaḥ lokaḥ kṣīyate evam evam utra puṇya jitaḥ lokaḥ kṣīyate.* In this world someone may become very highly elevated by taking birth in an aristocratic family, by being well educated, beautiful or very rich. These are the gifts for pious activities enacted in the past life. However, these will be finished when the stock of pious activity is finished. If we become attached to pious activities, we may get these various worldly facilities in the next life and may take birth in the heavenly planets. But all this will eventually be finished. *Kṣīṇe puṇye martya-lokaṁ viśanti* (Bg. 9.21): when the stock of pious activity is finished, one again has to come to this *martya-loka.* According to the Vedic injunctions, the performance of pious activity is not really the objective of the *Vedas.* The objective of the *Vedas* is explained in *Bhagavad-gītā. Vedaiś ca sarvair aham eva vedyaḥ:* the objective of the *Vedas* is to understand Kṛṣṇa, the Supreme Personality of Godhead. Those who are *veda-vādīs* are not actually advanced in knowledge, and those who are followers of *jñāna-kāṇḍa* (Brahman understanding) are also not perfect. However, when one comes to the platform of *upāsanā* and accepts the worship of the Supreme Personality of Godhead, he becomes perfect (*ārādhanānāṁ sarveṣāṁ viṣṇor ārādhanaṁ param*). In the *Vedas* the worship of different demigods and the performance of sacrifice are certainly, mentioned, but such worship is inferior because the worshipers do not know that the ultimate goal is Viṣṇu (*na te viduḥ svārtha-gatiṁ hi viṣṇum*). When one comes to the platform of *viṣṇor ārādhanam,* or *bhakti-yoga,* one has attained the perfection of life. Otherwise, as indicated in *Bhagavad-gītā,* one is not a *tattva-vādī* but a *veda-vādī, a* blind follower of the Vedic injunctions. A *veda-vādī* cannot be purified from material contamination unless he becomes a *tattva-vādī,* that is, one who knows *tattva,* the Absolute Truth. *Tattva* is also experienced in three features—*brahmeti paramātmeti bhagavān iti śabdyate.* Even after coming to the platform of understanding *tattva,* one must worship Bhagavān, Viṣṇu and His expansions, or one is not yet perfect. *Bahūnāṁ janmanām ante jñānavān māṁ prapadyate:* after many births, one who is actually in knowledge surrenders unto Kṛṣṇa. The conclusion is that unintelligent men with a poor fund of knowledge cannot understand Bhagavān, Brahman or Paramātmā, but after studying the *Vedas* and attaining the understanding of the Absolute Truth, the Supreme Personality of Godhead, one is supposed to be on the platform of perfect knowledge.

TEXT 3

न तस्य तत्त्वग्रहणाय साक्षाद्
वरीयसीरपि वाचः समासन् ।
स्वप्ने निरुक्त्या गृहमेधिसौख्यं
न यस्य हेयानुमितं स्वयं स्यात् ॥३॥

na tasya tattva-grahaṇāya sākṣād
varīyasīr api vācaḥ samāsan

svapne niruktyā gṛhamedhi-saukhyaṁ
na yasya heyānumitaṁ svayaṁ syāt

na—not; *tasya*—of him (a student studying the *Vedas*); *tattva-grahaṇāya*—for accepting the real purpose of Vedic knowledge; *sākṣāt*—directly; *varīyasīḥ*—very exalted; *api*—although; *vācaḥ*—words of the *Vedas; samāsan*—sufficiently became; *svapne*—in a dream; *niruktyā*—by example; *gṛha-medhi-saukhyam*—happiness within this material world; *na*—not; *yasya*—of him who; *heya-anumitam*—concluded to be inferior; *svayam*—automatically; *syāt*—become.

TRANSLATION

A dream becomes automatically known to a person as false and immaterial, and similarly one eventually realizes that material happiness in this life or the next, on this planet or a higher planet, is insignificant. When one realizes this, the Vedas, although an excellent source, are insufficient to bring about direct knowledge of the truth.

PURPORT

In *Bhagavad-gītā* (2.45), Kṛṣṇa advised Arjuna to become transcendental to the material activities impelled by the three material modes of nature (*traiguṇya-viṣayā vedā nistraiguṇyo bhavārjuna*). The purpose of Vedic study is to transcend the activities of the three modes of material nature. Of course in the material world the mode of goodness is accepted as the best, and one can be promoted to the higher planetary systems by being on the *sattva-guṇa* platform. However, that is not perfection. One must come to the conclusion that even the *sattva-guṇa* platform is also not good. One may dream that he has become a king with a good family, wife and children, but immediately at the end of that dream he comes to the conclusion that it is false. Similarly, all kinds of material happiness are undesirable for a person who wants spiritual salvation. If a person does not come to the conclusion that he has nothing to do with any kind of material happiness, he cannot come to the platform of understanding the Absolute Truth, or *tattva jñāna. Karmīs, jñānīs* and *yogīs* are after some material elevation. The *karmīs* work hard day and night for some bodily comfort, and the *jñānīs* simply speculate about how to get out of the entanglement of *karma* and merge into the Brahman effulgence. The *yogīs* are very much addicted to the acquisition of material perfection and magical powers. All of them are trying to be materially perfect, but a devotee very easily comes to the platform of *nirguṇa* in devotional service, and consequently for the devotee the results of *karma, jñāna* and *yoga* become very insignificant. Therefore only the devotee is on the platform of *tattva jñāna,* not the others. Of course the *jñānī's* position is better than that of the *karmī* but that position is also insufficient. The *jñānī* must actually become liberated, and after liberation he may be situated in devotional service (*mad-bhaktiṁ labhate parām*).

TEXT 4

यावन्मनो रजसा पूरुषस्य
सत्त्वेन वा तमसा वानुरुद्धम् ।
चेतोभिराकूतिभिरातनोति
निरङ्कुशं कुशलं चेतरं वा ॥४॥

yāvan mano rajasā pūruṣasya
sattvena vā tamasā vānuruddham
cetobhir ākūtibhir ātanoti
niraṅkuśaṁ kuśalaṁ cetaraṁ vā

yāvat—as long as; *manaḥ*—the mind; *rajasā*—by the mode of passion; *pūruṣasya*—of the living entity; *sattvena*—by the mode of goodness; *vā*—or; *tamasā*—by the mode of darkness; *vā*—or; *anuruddham*—controlled; *cetobhiḥ*—by the knowledge-acquiring senses; *ākūtibhiḥ*—by the senses of action; *ātanoti*—expands; *niraṅkuśam*—independent like an elephant not controlled by a trident; *kuśalam*—auspiciousness; *ca*—also; *itaram*—other than auspiciousness, sinful activities; *vā*—or.

TRANSLATION

As long as the mind of the living entity is contaminated by the three modes of material nature (goodness, passion and ignorance), his mind is exactly like an independent, uncontrolled elephant. It simply expands its jurisdiction of pious and impious activities by using the senses. The result is that the living entity remains in the material world to enjoy and suffer pleasures and pains due to material activity.

PURPORT

In *Caitanya-caritāmṛta* it is said that material pious and impious activities are both opposed to the principle of devotional service. Devotional service means *mukti,* freedom from material entanglement, but pious and impious activities result in entanglement within this material world. If the mind is captivated by the pious and impious activities mentioned in the *Vedas,* one remains eternally in darkness; one cannot attain the absolute platform. To change the consciousness from ignorance to passion or from passion to goodness does not really solve the problem. As stated in *Bhagavad-gītā* (14.26), *sa guṇān samatītyaitān brahma-bhūyāya kalpate.* One must come to the transcendental platform; otherwise life's mission is never fulfilled.

TEXT 5

स वासनात्मा विषयोपरक्तो
गुणप्रवाहो विकृतः षोडशात्मा ।
बिभ्रत्पृथङ्नामभि रूपभेद-
मन्तर्बहिष्ट्वं च पुरैस्तनोति ॥५॥

sa vāsanātmā viṣayoparakto
guṇa-pravāho vikṛtaḥ ṣoḍaśātmā
bibhrat pṛthaṅ-nāmabhi rūpa-bhedam
antar-bahiṣṭvaṁ ca purais tanoti

saḥ—that; *vāsanā*—endowed with many desires; *ātmā*—the mind; *viṣaya-uparaktaḥ*—attached to material happiness, sense gratification; *guṇa-pravāhaḥ*—driven by the force of either *sattva-guṇa, rajo-guṇa* or *tamo-guṇa; vikṛtaḥ*—transformed by lust and so on; *ṣoḍaśa-ātmā*—the chief of the sixteen material elements (the five gross elements, the ten senses and the mind); *bibhrat*—wandering; *pṛthak-nāmabhiḥ*—with separate names; *rūpa-bhedam*—assuming different forms; *antaḥ-bahiṣṭvam*—the quality of being first-class or last-class; *ca*—and; *puraiḥ*—with different bodily forms; *tanoti*—manifests.

TRANSLATION

Because the mind is absorbed in desires for pious and impious activities, it is naturally subjected to the transformations of lust and anger. In this way, it becomes attracted to material sense enjoyment. In other words, the mind is conducted by the modes of goodness, passion and ignorance. There are eleven senses and five material elements, and out of these sixteen items, the mind is the chief. Therefore the mind brings about birth in different types of bodies among demigods, human beings, animals

and birds. When the mind is situated in a higher or lower position, it accepts a higher or lower material body.

PURPORT

Transmigration among the 8,400,000 species is due to the mind's being polluted by certain material qualities. Due to the mind, the soul is subjected to pious and impious activities. The continuation of material existence is like the waves of material nature. In this regard, Śrīla Bhaktivinoda Ṭhākura says, *māyāra vaśe, yāccha bhese', khāccha hābuḍubu, bhāi:* "My dear brother, the spirit soul is completely under the control of *māyā,* and you are being carried away by its waves." This is also confirmed in *Bhagavad-gītā*:

prakṛteḥ kriyamāṇāni
guṇaiḥ karmāṇi sarvaśaḥ
ahaṅkāra-vimūḍhātmā
kartāham iti manyate

"The bewildered spirit soul, under the influence of the three modes of material nature, thinks himself the doer of activities, which are in actuality carried out by nature." (Bg. 3.27)

Material existence means being fully controlled by material nature. The mind is the center for accepting the dictations of material nature. In this way the living entity is carried away in different types of bodies continuously, millennium after millennium.

kṛṣṇa bhuli' sei jīva anādi-bahirmukha
ataeva māyā tāre deya saṁsāra-duḥkha
(Caitanya-caritāmṛta, Madhya 20.117)

Due to the living entity's forgetfulness of Kṛṣṇa, one is bound by the laws of material nature.

TEXT 6

दुःखं सुखं व्यतिरिक्तं च तीव्रं
कालोपपन्नं फलमाव्यनक्ति ।
आलिङ्ग्य मायारचितान्तरात्मा
स्वदेहिनं संसृतिचक्रकूटः ॥६॥

duḥkhaṁ sukhaṁ vyatiriktaṁ ca tīvraṁ
kālopapannaṁ phalam āvyanakti
āliṅgya māyā-racitāntarātmā
sva-dehinaṁ saṁsṛti-cakra-kūṭaḥ

duḥkham—unhappiness due to impious activities; *sukham*—happiness due to pious activities; *vyatiriktam*—illusion; *ca*—also; *tīvram*—very severe; *kāla-upapannam*—obtained in the course of time; *phalam*—the resultant action; *āvyanakti*—creates; *āliṅgya*—embracing; *māyā-racita*—created by material nature; *antaḥ-ātmā*—the mind; *sva-dehinam*—the living being himself; *saṁsṛti*—of the actions and reactions of material existence; *cakra-kūṭaḥ*—which deceives the living entity into the wheel.

TRANSLATION

The materialistic mind covering the living entity's soul carries it to different species of life. This is called continued material existence. Due to the mind, the living entity suffers or enjoys material distress and happiness. Being thus illusioned, the mind further creates pious and impious activities and their karma, and thus the soul becomes conditioned.

PURPORT

Mental activities under the influence of material nature cause happiness and distress within the material world. Being covered by illusion, the living entity eternally continues conditioned life under different designations. Such living entities are known as *nitya-baddha,* eternally conditioned. On the whole, the mind is the cause of conditioned life; therefore the entire yogic process is meant to control the mind and the senses. If the mind is controlled, the senses are automatically controlled, and therefore the soul is saved from the reactions of pious and impious activity. If the mind is engaged at the lotus feet of Lord Kṛṣṇa (*sa vai manaḥ kṛṣṇa-padāravindayoḥ*), the senses are automatically engaged in the Lord's service. When the mind and senses are engaged in devotional service, the living entity naturally becomes Kṛṣṇa conscious. As soon as one always thinks of Kṛṣṇa, he becomes a perfect *yogī,* as confirmed in *Bhagavad-gītā* (*yoginām api sarveṣāṁ mad-gatenāntarātmanā*). This *antarātmā,* the mind, is conditioned by material nature. As stated here, *māyā-racitāntarātmā sva-dehinaṁ saṁsṛti-cakra-kūṭaḥ:* the mind, being most powerful, covers the living entity and puts him in the waves of material existence.

TEXT 7

तावानयं व्यवहारः सदाविः
क्षेत्रज्ञसाक्ष्यो भवति स्थूलसूक्ष्मः ।
तस्मान्मनो लिङ्गमदो वदन्ति
गुणागुणत्वस्य परावरस्य ॥ ७ ॥

tāvān ayaṁ vyavahāraḥ sadāviḥ
kṣetrajña-sākṣyo bhavati sthūla-sūkṣmaḥ
tasmān mano liṅgam ado vadanti
guṇāguṇatvasya parāvarasya

tāvān—until that time; *ayam*—this; *vyavahāraḥ*—the artificial designations (being fat or skinny, or belonging to the demigods or human beings); *sadā*—always; *āviḥ*—manifesting; *kṣetra-jña*—of the living entity; *sākṣyaḥ*—testimony; *bhavati*—is; *sthūla-sūkṣmaḥ*—fat and skinny; *tasmāt*—therefore; *manaḥ*—the mind; *liṅgam*—the cause; *adaḥ*—this; *vadanti*—they say; *guṇa-aguṇatvasya*—of being absorbed in material qualities or devoid of material qualities; *para-avarasya*—and of lower and higher conditions of life.

TRANSLATION

The mind makes the living entity within this material world wander through different species of life, and thus the living entity experiences mundane affairs in different forms as a human being, demigod, fat person, skinny person and so forth. Learned scholars say that bodily appearance, bondage and liberation are caused by the mind.

PURPORT

Just as the mind is the cause of bondage, it can also be the cause of liberation. The mind is described here as *para-avara. Para* means transcendental, and *avara* means material. When the mind is engaged in the Lord's service (*sa vai manaḥ kṛṣṇa-padāravindayoḥ*), it is called *para,* transcendental. When the mind is engaged in material sense gratification, it is called *avara,* or material. At the present moment, in our conditioned state, our mind is fully absorbed in material sense gratification, but it can be purified and brought to its original Kṛṣṇa consciousness by the process of devotional service. We have often given the example of Ambarīṣa Mahārāja. *Sa vai manaḥ kṛṣṇa-padāravindayor vacāṁsi vaikuṇṭha-guṇānuvarṇane.* The mind must be controlled in Kṛṣṇa consciousness. The tongue can be utilized to spread the message of Kṛṣṇa and glorify the Lord or take *prasāda,* the remnants of food offered to Kṛṣṇa. *Sevonmukhe hi jihvādau:* when one utilizes the tongue in the service of the Lord, the other senses can become purified. As stated in the *Nārada-pañcarātra, sarvopādhi-vinirmuktaṁ tat-paratvena nirmalam:* when the mind and senses are purified, one's total existence is purified, and one's designations are also purified. One no longer considers himself a human being, a demigod, cat, dog, Hindu, Muslim and so forth. When the senses and mind are purified and one is fully engaged in Kṛṣṇa's service, one can be liberated and return home, back to Godhead.

TEXT 8

गुणानुरक्तं व्यसनाय जन्तोः
क्षेमाय नैर्गुण्यमथो मनः स्यात् ।
यथा प्रदीपो घृतवर्तिमश्नन्
शिखाः सधूमा भजति ह्यन्यदा स्वम् ।
पदं तथा गुणकर्मानुबद्धं
वृत्तीर्मनः श्रयतेऽन्यत्र तत्त्वम् ॥८॥

guṇānuraktaṁ vyasanāya jantoḥ
kṣemāya nairguṇyam atho manaḥ syāt
yathā pradīpo ghṛta-vartim aśnan
śikhāḥ sadhūmā bhajati hy anyadā svam
padaṁ tathā guṇa-karmānubaddhaṁ
vṛttīr manaḥ śrayate 'nyatra tattvam

guṇa-anuraktam—being attached to the material modes of nature; *vyasanāya*—for the conditioning in material existence; *jantoḥ*—of the living entity; *kṣemāya*—for the ultimate welfare; *nairguṇyam*—being unaffected by the material modes of nature; *atho*—thus; *manaḥ*—the mind; *syāt*—becomes; *yathā*—as much as; *pradīpaḥ*—a lamp; *ghṛta-vartim*—a wick within clarified butter; *aśnan*—burning; *śikhāḥ*—the flame; *sadhūmāḥ*—with smoke; *bhajati*—enjoys; *hi*—certainly; *anyadā*—otherwise; *svam*—its own original; *padam*—position; *tathā*—so; *guṇa-karma-anubaddham*—bound by the modes of nature and the reactions of material activities; *vṛttīḥ*—various engagements; *manaḥ*—the mind; *śrayate*—takes shelter of; *anyatra*—otherwise; *tattvam*—its original condition.

TRANSLATION

When the living entity's mind becomes absorbed in the sense gratification of the material world, it brings about his conditioned life and suffering within the material situation. However, when the mind becomes unattached to material enjoyment, it becomes the cause of liberation. When the flame in a lamp burns the wick improperly, the lamp is blackened, but when the lamp is filled with ghee and is burning properly, there is bright illumination. Similarly, when the mind is absorbed in material sense gratification, it causes suffering, and when detached from material sense gratification, it brings about the original brightness of Kṛṣṇa consciousness.

PURPORT

It is therefore concluded that the mind is the cause of material existence and liberation also. Everyone is suffering in this material world because of the mind; it is therefore proper to train the mind or to cleanse the mind from material attachment and engage it fully in the Lord's service. This is called spiritual engagement. As confirmed in *Bhagavad-gītā*:

māṁ ca yo'vyabhicāreṇa
bhakti-yogena sevate
sa guṇān samatītyaitān
brahma-bhūyāya kalpate

"One who engages in full devotional service, who does not fall down in any circumstance, at once transcends the modes of material nature and thus comes to the level of Brahman." (Bg. 14.26)

We should engage the mind fully in Kṛṣṇa conscious activities. Then it will be the cause of our liberation, for our returning home, back to Godhead. However, if we keep the mind engaged in material activities for sense gratification, it will cause continuous bondage and will make us remain in this material world in different bodies, suffering the consequences of our different actions.

TEXT 9

एकादशासन्मनसो हि वृत्तय
आकूतयः पञ्च धियोऽभिमानः ।
मात्राणि कर्माणि पुरं च तासां
वदन्ति हैकादश वीर भूमीः ॥९॥

ekādaśāsan manaso hi vṛttaya
ākūtayaḥ pañca dhiyo'bhimānaḥ
mātrāṇi karmāṇi puraṁ ca tāsāṁ
vadanti haikādaśa vīra bhūmīḥ

ekādaśa—eleven; *āsan*—there are; *manasaḥ*—of the mind; *hi*—certainly; *vṛttayaḥ*—activities; *ākūtayaḥ*—senses of action; *pañca*—five; *dhiyaḥ*—senses for gathering knowledge; *abhimānaḥ*—the false ego; *mātrāṇi*—different sense objects; *karmāṇi*—different material activities; *puram ca*—and the body, society, nation, family or place of nativity; *tāsām*—of those functions; *vadanti*—they say; *ha*—oh; *ekādaśa*—eleven; *vīra*—O hero; *bhūmīḥ*—fields of activity.

TRANSLATION

There are five working senses and five knowledge-acquiring senses. There is also the false ego. In this way, there are eleven items for the mind's functions. O hero, the objects of the senses [such as sound and touch], the organic activities [such as evacuation] and the different types of bodies, society, friendship and personality are considered by learned scholars the fields of activity for the functions of the mind.

PURPORT

The mind is the controller of the five knowledge-acquiring senses and the five working senses. Each sense has its particular field of activity. In all cases, the mind is the controller or owner. By the false ego one thinks oneself the body and thinks in terms of "my body, my house, my family, my society, my nation" and so on. These false identifications are due to the expansions of the false ego. Thus one thinks that he is this or that. Thus the living entity becomes entangled in material existence.

TEXT 10

गन्धाकृतिस्पर्शरसश्रवांसि
विसर्गरत्यर्त्यभिजल्पशिल्पाः ।
एकादशं स्वीकरणं ममेति
शय्यामहं द्वादशमेक आहुः ॥१०॥

gandhākṛti-sparśa-rasa-śravāṁsi
visarga-raty-arty-abhijalpa-śilpāḥ

ekādaśaṁ svīkaraṇaṁ mameti
śayyām ahaṁ dvādaśam eka āhuḥ

gandha—smell; *ākṛti*—form; *sparśa*—touch; *rasa*—taste; *śravāṁsi*—and sound; *visarga*—evacuating; *rati*—sexual intercourse; *arti*—movement; *abhijalpa*—speaking; *śilpāḥ*—grasping or releasing; *ekādaśam*—eleventh; *svīkaraṇam*—accepting as; *mama*—mine; *iti*—thus; *śayyām*—this body; *aham*—I; *dvādaśam*—twelfth; *eke*—some; *āhuḥ*—have said.

TRANSLATION

Sound, touch, form, taste and smell are the objects of the five knowledge-acquiring senses. Speech, touch, movement, evacuation and sexual intercourse are the objects of the working senses. Besides this, there is another conception by which one thinks, "This is my body, this is my society, this is my family, this is my nation," and so forth. This eleventh function, that of the mind, is called the false ego. According to some philosophers, this is the twelfth function, and its field of activity is the body.

PURPORT

There are different objects for the eleven items. Through the nose we can smell, by the eyes we can see, by the ears we can hear, and in this way we gather knowledge. Similarly, there are the *karmendriyas,* the working senses —the hands, legs, genitals, rectum, mouth and so forth. When the false ego expands, it makes one think, "This is my body, family, society, country," etc.

TEXT 11

द्रव्यस्वभावाशयकर्मकालै-
रेकादशामी मनसो विकाराः ।
सहस्रशः शतशः कोटिशश्च
क्षेत्रज्ञतो न मिथो न स्वतः स्युः ॥११॥

dravya-svabhāvāśaya-karma-kālair
ekādaśāmī manaso vikārāḥ
sahasraśaḥ śataśaḥ koṭiśaś ca
kṣetrajñato na mitho na svataḥ syuḥ

dravya—by physical objects; *sva-bhāva*—by nature as the cause of development; *āśaya*—by culture; *karma*—by predestined resultant actions;

kālaiḥ—by time; *ekādaśa*—eleven; *amī*—all these; *manasaḥ*—of the mind; *vikārāḥ*—transformations; *sahasraśaḥ*—in thousands; *śataśaḥ*—in hundreds; *koṭiśaḥ ca*—and in millions; *kṣetra-jñataḥ*—from the original Supreme Personality of Godhead; *na*—not; *mithaḥ*—one another; *na*—nor; *svataḥ*—from themselves; *syuḥ*—are.

TRANSLATION

The physical elements, nature, the original cause, culture, destiny and the time element are all material causes. Agitated by these material causes, the eleven functions transform into hundreds of functions and then into thousands and then into millions. But all these transformations do not take place automatically by mutual combination. Rather, they are under the direction of the Supreme Personality of Godhead.

PURPORT

One should not think that all the interactions of the physical elements, gross and subtle, that cause the transformation of mind and consciousness are working independently. They are under the direction of the Supreme Personality of Godhead. In *Bhagavad-gītā* (15.15), Kṛṣṇa says that the Lord is situated in everyone's heart (*sarvasya cāhaṁ hṛdi sanniviṣṭo mattaḥ smṛtir jñānam apohanaṁ ca*). As mentioned herein, Supersoul (*kṣetrajña*) is directing everything. The living entity is also *kṣetrajña,* but the supreme *kṣetrajña* is the Supreme Personality of Godhead. He is the witness and order giver. Under His direction, everything takes place. The different inclinations of the living entity are created by his own nature or his expectations, and he is trained by the Supreme Personality of Godhead through the agency of material nature. The body, nature and the physical elements are under the direction of the Supreme Personality of Godhead. They do not function automatically. Nature is neither independent nor automatic. As confirmed in *Bhagavad-gītā,* the Supreme Personality of Godhead is behind nature.

mayādhyakṣeṇa prakṛtiḥ
sūyate sa-carācaram
hetunānena kaunteya
jagad viparivartate

"This material nature is working under My direction, O son of Kuntī, and it is producing all moving and unmoving beings. By its rule this manifestation is created and annihilated again and again." (Bg. 9.10)

TEXT 12

क्षेत्रज्ञ एता मनसो विभूती-
जींवस्य मायारचितस्य नित्याः ।
आविर्हिताः क्वापि तिरोहिताश्च
शुद्धो विचष्टे ह्यविशुद्धकर्तुः ॥१२॥

kṣetrajña etā manaso vibhūtīr
jīvasya māyā-racitasya nityāḥ
āvirhitāḥ kvāpi tirohitāś ca
śuddho vicaṣṭe hy aviśuddha-kartuḥ

kṣetra-jñaḥ—the individual soul; *etāḥ*—all these; *manasaḥ*—of the mind; *vibhūtīḥ*—different activities; *jīvasya*—of the living entity; *māyā-racitasya*—created by the external, material energy; *nityāḥ*—from time immemorial; *āvirhitāḥ*—sometimes manifested; *kvāpi*—somewhere; *tirohitāḥ ca*—and not manifested; *śuddhaḥ*—purified; *vicaṣṭe*—sees this; *hi*—certainly; *aviśuddha*—unpurified; *kartuḥ*—of the doer.

TRANSLATION

The individual soul bereft of Kṛṣṇa consciousness has many ideas and activities created in the mind by the external energy. They have been existing from time immemorial. Sometimes they are manifest in the wakening state and in the dream state, but during deep sleep [unconsciousness] or trance, they disappear. A person who is liberated in this life [jīvan-mukta] can see all these things vividly.

PURPORT

As stated in *Bhagavad-gītā* (13.3), *kṣetra-jñaṁ cāpi māṁ viddhi sarva-kṣetreṣu bhārata.* There are two kinds of *kṣetrajña,* or living beings. One is the individual living being, and the other is the supreme living being. The ordinary living being knows about his body to some extent, but the Supreme, Paramātmā, knows the condition of all bodies. The individual living being is localized, and the Supreme, Paramātmā, is all-pervading. In this *śloka* the word *kṣetrajña* refers to an ordinary living being, not the supreme living being. This ordinary living being is of two kinds—*nitya-baddha* or *nitya-mukta.* One is eternally conditioned and the other eternally liberated. The eternally liberated living beings are in the Vaikuṇṭha *jagat,* the spiritual world, and they never fall into the material world. Those in the material world are conditioned souls, *nitya-baddha.* The *nitya-baddhas* can become liberated by controlling the mind because the cause of conditioned life is the mind. When the mind is trained and the soul is not under the mind's control, the soul can be liberated even in this material world. When it is liberated, one is called *jīvan-mukta.* A *jīvan-mukta* knows how he has become conditioned; therefore he tries to purify himself and return home, back to Godhead. The eternally conditioned soul is eternally conditioned because he is controlled by the mind. The conditioned state and liberated state are compared to the sleeping, unconscious state and the awakened state. Those who are sleeping and unconscious are eternally conditioned, but those who are awake understand that they are eternally part and parcel of the Supreme Personality of Godhead, Kṛṣṇa. Therefore even in this material world, they engage in Kṛṣṇa's service. As confirmed by Śrīla Rūpa Gosvāmī: *īhā yasya harer dāsye.* If one takes to Kṛṣṇa's service, he is liberated, even though he appears to be a conditioned soul within the material world. *Jīvan-muktaḥ sa ucyate.* In any condition, one is to be considered liberated if his only business is to serve Kṛṣṇa.

TEXTS 13–14

क्षेत्रज्ञ आत्मा पुरुषः पुराणः
साक्षात्स्वयंज्योतिरजः परेशः ।
नारायणो भगवान् वासुदेवः
स्वमाययाऽऽत्मन्यवधीयमानः ॥१३॥

यथानिलः स्थावरजङ्गमाना-
मात्मस्वरूपेण निविष्ट ईशेत् ।
एवं परो भगवान् वासुदेवः
क्षेत्रज्ञ आत्मेदमनुप्रविष्टः ॥१४॥

kṣetrajña ātmā puruṣaḥ purāṇaḥ
sākṣāt svayaṁ jyotir ajaḥ pareśaḥ
nārāyaṇo bhagavān vāsudevaḥ
sva-māyayātmany avadhīyamānaḥ

yathānilaḥ sthāvara-jaṅgamānām
ātma-svarūpeṇa niviṣṭa īśet
evaṁ paro bhagavān vāsudevaḥ
kṣetrajña ātmedam anupraviṣṭaḥ

kṣetra-jñaḥ—the Supreme Personality of Godhead*; *ātmā*—all-pervading, present everywhere; *puruṣaḥ*—the unrestricted controller, who has unlimited power; *purāṇaḥ*—the original; *sākṣāt*—perceivable by hearing from the authorities and by direct perception; *svayam*—personal; *jyotiḥ*—manifesting His bodily rays (the Brahman effulgence); *ajaḥ*—never born; *pareśaḥ*—the Supreme Personality of Godhead; *nārāyaṇaḥ*—the resting place of all living entities; *bhagavān*—the Personality of Godhead with six full opulences; *vāsudevaḥ*—the shelter of everything, manifested and nonmanifest; *sva-māyayā*—by His own potency; *ātmani*—in His own self, or in the ordinary living entities; *avadhīyamānaḥ*—existing as the controller; *yathā*—as much as; *anilaḥ*—the air; *sthāvara*—of nonmoving living entities; *jaṅgamānām*—and of the moving living entities; *ātma-svarūpeṇa*—by His expansion as the Supersoul; *niviṣṭaḥ*—entered; *īśet*—controls; *evam*—thus; *paraḥ*—transcendental; *bhagavān*—the Supreme Personality of Godhead; *vāsudevaḥ*—the shelter of everything; *kṣetra-jñaḥ*—known as *kṣetrajña; ātmā*—the vital force; *idam*—this material world; *anupraviṣṭaḥ*—entered within.

TRANSLATION

There are two kinds of kṣetrajña—the living entity, as explained above, and the Supreme Personality of Godhead, who is explained as follows. He is the all-pervading cause of creation. He is full in Himself and is not dependent on others. He is perceived by hearing and direct perception. He is self-effulgent and does not experience birth, death, old age or disease. He is the controller of all the demigods, beginning with Lord Brahmā. He is called Nārāyaṇa, and He is the shelter of living entities after the annihilation of this material world. He is full of all opulences, and He is the resting place of everything material. He is therefore known as Vāsudeva, the Supreme Personality of Godhead. By His own potency, He is present within the hearts of all living entities, just as the air or vital force is within the bodies of all beings, moving and nonmoving. In this way He controls the body. In His partial feature, the Supreme Personality of Godhead enters all bodies and controls them.

PURPORT

This is confirmed in *Bhagavad-gītā* (15.15). *Sarvasya cāhaṁ hṛdi sanniviṣṭo mattaḥ smṛtir jñānam apohanaṁ ca.* Every living being is controlled by the supreme living being, Paramātmā, who resides within everyone's heart. He is

* In text 12 the word *kṣetrajña* described the living being, but in this verse the word *ksetrajña* indicates the Supreme person.

the *puruṣa,* the *puruṣa-avatāra,* who creates this material world. The first *puruṣa-avatāra* is Mahā-Viṣṇu, and that Mahā-Viṣṇu is the plenary portion of the plenary portion of the Supreme Personality of Godhead, Kṛṣṇa. Kṛṣṇa's first expansion is Baladeva, and His next expansions are Vāsudeva, Saṅkarṣaṇa, Aniruddha and Pradyumna. Vāsudeva is the original cause of the *brahmajyoti,* and the *brahmajyoti* is the expansion of the rays of the body of Vāsudeva.

yasya prabhā prabhavato jagad-aṇḍa-koṭi-
koṭiṣv aśeṣa-vasudhādi-vibhūti-bhinnam
tad brahma niṣkalam anantam aśeṣa-bhūtaṁ
govindam ādi-puruṣaṁ tam ahaṁ bhajāmi

"I worship Govinda, the primeval Lord, who is endowed with great power. The glowing effulgence of His transcendental form is the impersonal Brahman, which is absolute, complete and unlimited and which displays the varieties of countless planets, with their different opulences, in millions and millions of universes." (*Brahma-saṁhitā* 5.40) The Supreme Personality of Godhead is thus described in *Bhagavad-gītā*:

mayā tatam idaṁ sarvaṁ
jagad avyakta-mūrtinā
mat-sthāni sarva-bhūtāni
na cāhaṁ teṣv avasthitaḥ

"By Me, in My unmanifested form, this entire universe is pervaded. All beings are in Me, but I am not in them." (Bg. 9.4)

This is the position of the plenary expansions of Kṛṣṇa as the all-pervading Vāsudeva, Saṅkarṣaṇa, Pradyumna and Aniruddha.

TEXT 15

न यावदेतां तनुभृन्नरेन्द्र
विधूय मायां वयुनोदयेन ।
विमुक्तसङ्गो जितषट्सपत्नो
वेदात्मतत्त्वं भ्रमतीह तावत् ॥१५॥

na yāvad etāṁ tanu-bhṛn narendra
vidhūya māyāṁ vayunodayena
vimukta-saṅgo jita-ṣaṭ-sapatno
vedātma-tattvaṁ bhramatīha tāvat

na—not; *yāvat*—as long as; *etām*—this; *tanu-bhṛt*—one who has accepted a material body; *narendra*—O King; *vidhūya māyām*—washing away the infection accumulated because of contamination by the material world; *vayunā udayena*—by awakening of transcendental knowledge due to good association and study of the Vedic literatures; *vimukta-saṅgaḥ*—free from all material association; *jita-ṣaṭ-sapatnaḥ*—conquering the six enemies (the five knowledge-acquiring senses and the mind); *veda*—knows; *ātma-tattvam*—spiritual truth; *bhramati*—he wanders; *iha*—in this material world; *tāvat*—until that time.

TRANSLATION

My dear King Rahūgaṇa, as long as the conditioned soul accepts the material body and is not freed from the contamination of material enjoyment, and as long as he does not conquer his six enemies and come to the platform of self-realization by awakening his spiritual knowledge, he has to wander among different places and different species of life in this material world.

PURPORT

When one's mind is absorbed in the material conception, he thinks that he belongs to a particular nation, family, country or creed. These are all called *upādhis,* designations, and one has to become freed from them (*sarvopādhi-vinirmuktam*). As long as one is not freed, he has to continue conditioned life in material existence. The human form of life is meant for cleansing away these misconceptions. If this is not done, one has to repeat the cycle of birth and death and thus suffer all material conditions.

TEXT 16

न यावदेतन्मन आत्मलिङ्गं
संसारतापावपनं जनस्य ।
यच्छोकमोहामयरागलोभ-
वैरानुबन्धं ममतां विधत्ते ॥१६॥

na yāvad etan mana ātma-liṅgaṁ
saṁsāra-tāpāvapanaṁ janasya
yac choka-mohāmaya-rāga-lobha-
vairānubandhaṁ mamatāṁ vidhatte

na—not; *yāvat*—as long as; *etat*—this; *manaḥ*—mind; *ātma-liṅgam*—existing as the false designation of the soul; *saṁsāra-tāpa*—of the miseries of this material world; *āvapanam*—the growing ground; *janasya*—of the living being; *yat*—which; *śoka*—of lamentation; *moha*—of illusion; *āmaya*—of disease; *rāga*—of attachment; *lobha*—of greed; *vaira*—of enmity; *anubandham*—the consequence; *mamatām*—the sense of ownership; *vidhatte*—gives.

TRANSLATION

The soul's designation, the mind, is the cause of all tribulations in the material world. As long as this fact is unknown to the conditioned living entity, he has to accept the miserable condition of the material body and wander within this universe in different positions. Because the mind is affected by disease, lamentation, illusion, attachment, greed and enmity, it creates bondage and a false sense of intimacy within this material world.

PURPORT

The mind is the cause of both material bondage and liberation. The impure mind thinks, "I am this body." The pure mind knows that he is not the material body; therefore the mind is considered to be the root of all material designations. Until the living entity is aloof from the association and contaminations of this material world, the mind will be absorbed in such material things as birth, death, disease, illusion, attachment, greed and enmity. In this way the living entity is conditioned, and he suffers material miseries.

TEXT 17

भ्रातृव्यमेनं तददभ्रवीर्य-
मुपेक्षयाध्येधितमप्रमत्तः ।
गुरोर्हरेश्चरणोपासनास्त्रो
जहि व्यलीकं स्वयमात्ममोषम् ॥१७॥

bhrātṛvyam enaṁ tad adabhra-vīryam
upekṣayādhyedhitam apramattaḥ
guror hareś caraṇopāsanāstro
jahi vyalīkaṁ svayam ātma-moṣam

bhrātṛvyam—the formidable enemy; *enam*—this mind; *tat*—that; *adabhra-vīryam*—very, very powerful; *upekṣayā*—by neglecting;

adhyedhitam—unnecessarily increased in power; *apramattaḥ*—one who is without illusion; *guroḥ*—of the spiritual master; *hareḥ*—of the Supreme Personality of Godhead; *caraṇa*—of the lotus feet; *upāsanā-astraḥ*—applying the weapon of worshiping; *jahi*—conquer; *vyalīkam*—false; *svayam*—personally; *ātma-moṣam*—which covers the constitutional position of the living entity.

TRANSLATION

This uncontrolled mind is the greatest enemy of the living entity. If one neglects it or gives it a chance, it will grow more and more powerful and will become victorious. Although it is not factual, it is very strong. It covers the constitutional position of the soul. O King, please try to conquer this mind by the weapon of service to the lotus feet of the spiritual master and of the Supreme Personality of Godhead. Do this with great care.

PURPORT

There is one easy weapon with which the mind can be conquered—neglect. The mind is always telling us to do this or that; therefore we should be very expert in disobeying the mind's orders. Gradually the mind should be trained to obey the orders of the soul. It is not that one should obey the orders of the mind. Śrīla Bhaktisiddhānta Sarasvatī Ṭhākura used to say that to control the mind one should beat it with shoes many times just after awakening and again before going to sleep. In this way one can control the mind. This is the instruction of all the *śāstras.* If one does not do so, one is doomed to follow the dictations of the mind. Another bona fide process is to abide strictly by the orders of the spiritual master and engage in the Lord's service. Then the mind will be automatically controlled. Śrī Caitanya Mahāprabhu has instructed Śrīla Rūpa Gosvāmī:

brahmāṇḍa bhramite kona bhāgyavān jīva
guru-kṛṣṇa-prasāde pāya bhakti-latā-bīja

When one receives the seed of devotional service by the mercy of the *guru* and Kṛṣṇa, the Supreme Personality of Godhead, one's real life begins. If one abides by the orders of the spiritual master, by the grace of Kṛṣṇa he is freed from service to the mind.

Thus end the Bhaktivedanta purports of the Fifth Canto, Eleventh Chapter, of the Śrīmad-Bhāgavatam, *entitled "Jaḍa Bharata Instructs King Rahūgaṇa."*

CHAPTER TWELVE

Conversation Between Mahārāja Rahūgaṇa and Jaḍa Bharata

Because Mahārāja Rahūgaṇa was still doubtful about his enlightenment, he asked the *brāhmaṇa* Jaḍa Bharata to repeat his instructions and clarify ideas he could not understand. In this chapter, Mahārāja Rahūgaṇa offers his respectful obeisances to Jaḍa Bharata, who was concealing his real position. The King could understand by his speech how exalted and advanced he was in spiritual knowledge. He very much regretted his offense against him. Mahārāja Rahūgaṇa was bitten by the serpent of ignorance, but was cured by the nectarean words of Jaḍa Bharata. Later, because he was doubtful about the subjects discussed, he made further inquiries, one question after another. First he wanted to be released from the offense he had committed at the lotus feet of Jaḍa Bharata.

Mahārāja Rahūgaṇa was somewhat unhappy at not being able to grasp Jaḍa Bharata's instructions, which were full of meaning that could not be understood by a materialistic person. Therefore Jaḍa Bharata repeated his instructions more clearly. He said that on the surface of the globe all living entities, moving and unmoving, were but transformations of the earth in different ways. The King was very proud of his king's body, but that body was simply another transformation of the earth. Out of his false prestige, the King was misbehaving toward the palanquin carrier, as a master toward a servant, and he was actually very unkind to other living entities. Consequently King Rahūgaṇa was unfit to give protection to the citizens, and because he was ignorant, he was unfit to be counted among advanced philosophers. Everything in the material world is but a transformation of the earth, although things have different names according to their transformations. Actually the varieties are one and the same, and ultimately all these varieties are vanquished into atoms. Nothing is permanent in this material world. The variety of things and their distinctions are simply mental concoctions. The Absolute Truth is beyond illusion and is manifest in three features—impersonal Brahman, localized Paramātmā and the Supreme Personality of Godhead. Ultimate realization of the Absolute Truth is the Supreme Personality of Godhead, called Vāsudeva by His devotees. Unless one is blessed with the dust from the feet of a pure devotee on his head, one cannot possibly become a devotee of the Supreme Personality of Godhead.

Jaḍa Bharata also told about his own previous birth and informed the King that by the grace of the Lord he still remembered all the incidents of his past life. Due to the activities of his past life, Jaḍa Bharata was being very cautious and was therefore assuming the characteristics of a deaf and dumb man to avoid mingling with the material world. Association with the material modes of nature is very powerful. The bad association of materialistic men can be avoided only in the association of devotees. In the association of devotees, one is given an opportunity to render devotional service in nine different ways—*śravaṇaṁ kīrtanaṁ viṣṇoḥ smaraṇaṁ pāda-sevanam arcanaṁ vandanaṁ dāsyaṁ sakhyam ātma-nivedanam.* In this way, in the association of devotees, one can pass over material association, cross over the ocean of nescience and return home, back to Godhead.

TEXT 1

रहूगण उवाच
नमो नमः कारणविग्रहाय
स्वरूपतुच्छीकृतविग्रहाय ।
नमोऽवधूत द्विजबन्धुलिङ्ग-
निगूढनित्यानुभवाय तुभ्यम् ॥१॥

rahūgaṇa uvāca
namo namaḥ kāraṇa-vigrahāya
svarūpa-tucchīkṛta-vigrahāya
namo'vadhūta dvija-bandhu-liṅga-
nigūḍha-nityānubhavāya tubhyam

rahūgaṇaḥ uvāca—King Rahūgaṇa said; *namaḥ*—my respectful obeisances; *namaḥ*—obeisances; *kāraṇa-vigrahāya*—to one whose body emanates from the Supreme Person, the cause of all causes; *svarūpa-tucchīkṛta-vigrahāya*—who has completely removed all the contradictions of the scriptures by manifesting his true self; *namaḥ*—respectful obeisances; *avadhūta*—O master of all mystic power; *dvija-bandhu-liṅga*—by the characteristics of a person born in a *brāhmaṇa* family but not executing the duties of a *brāhmaṇa; nigūḍha*—covered; *nitya-anubhavāya*—to him whose eternal self-realization; *tubhyam*—to you.

TRANSLATION

King Rahūgaṇa said: O most exalted personality, you are not different from the Supreme Personality of Godhead. By the influence of your true self, all kinds of contradiction in the śāstras have been removed. In the dress of a friend of a brāhmaṇa, you are hiding your transcendental blissful position. I offer my respectful obeisances unto you.

PURPORT

From the *Brahma-saṁhitā* we understand the Supreme Personality of Godhead is the cause of all causes (*sarva-kāraṇa-kāraṇam*). Ṛṣabhadeva was the direct incarnation of the Supreme Personality of Godhead, the cause of all causes. His son, Bharata Mahārāja, who was now acting as the *brāhmaṇa* Jaḍa Bharata, had received his body from the cause of all causes. Therefore he is addressed as *kāraṇa-vigrahāya.*

TEXT 2

ज्वरामयार्तस्य यथागदं सत्
निदाघदग्धस्य यथा हिमाम्भः ।
कुदेहमानाहिविदष्टदृष्टेः
ब्रह्मन् वचस्तेऽमृतमौषधं मे ॥२॥

jvarāmayārtasya yathāgadaṁ sat
nidāgha-dagdhasya yathā himāmbhaḥ
kudeha-mānāhi-vidaṣṭa-dṛṣṭeḥ
brahman vacas te'mṛtam auṣadhaṁ me

jvara—of a fever; *āmaya*—by the disease; *ārtasya*—of a distressed person; *yathā*—just as; *agadam*—the medicine; *sat*—right; *nidāgha-dagdhasya*—of one scorched by the heat of the sun; *yathā*—just as; *hima-ambhaḥ*—very cold water; *ku-deha*—in this body made of matter and full of dirty things such as stool and urine; *māna*—of pride; *ahi*—by the serpent; *vidaṣṭa*—bitten; *dṛṣṭeḥ*—of one whose vision; *brahman*—O best of the *brāhmaṇas; vacaḥ*—words; *te*—your; *amṛtam*—nectar; *auṣadham*—medicine; *me*—for me.

TRANSLATION

O best of the brāhmaṇas, my body is filled with dirty things, and my vision has been bitten by the serpent of pride. Due to my material conceptions, I am diseased. Your nectarean instructions are the proper

medicine for one suffering from such a fever, and they are cooling waters for one scorched by the heat.

PURPORT

The conditioned soul has a body full of dirty things—bones, blood, urine, stool and so forth. Nonetheless, the most intelligent men in this material world think they are these combinations of blood, bone, urine and stool. If this is so, why can't other intelligent men be made with these ingredients, which are so readily available? The entire world is going on under the bodily conception and creating a hellish condition unfit for any gentleman's living. The instructions given to King Rahūgaṇa by Jaḍa Bharata are very valuable. They are like the medicine that can save one from a snakebite. The Vedic instructions are like nectar and cool water for one suffering from scorching heat.

TEXT 3

तस्माद्भवन्तं मम संशयार्थं
प्रक्ष्यामि पश्चादधुना सुबोधम् ।
अध्यात्मयोगग्रथितं तवोक्त-
माख्याहि कौतूहलचेतसो मे ॥३॥

tasmād bhavantaṁ mama saṁśayārthaṁ
prakṣyāmi paścād adhunā subodham
adhyātma-yoga-grathitaṁ tavoktam
ākhyāhi kautūhala-cetaso me

tasmāt—therefore; *bhavantam*—to you; *mama*—of me; *saṁśaya-artham*—the subject matter that is not clear to me; *prakṣyāmi*—I shall submit; *paścāt*—afterwards; *adhunā*—now; *su-bodham*—so that it can be clearly understood; *adhyātma-yoga*—of mystic instruction for self-realization; *grathitam*—as composed; *tava*—your; *uktam*—speech; *ākhyāhi*—please explain again; *kautūhala-cetasaḥ*—whose mind is very inquisitive to understand the mystery of such statements; *me*—to me.

TRANSLATION

Whatever doubts I have about a particular subject matter I shall ask you about later. For the time being, these mysterious yoga instructions you have given me for self-realization appear very difficult to understand.

Please repeat them in a simple way so that I can understand them. My mind is very inquisitive, and I want to understand this clearly.

PURPORT

The Vedic literature instructs: *tasmād guruṁ prapadyeta jijñāsuḥ śreya uttamam.* An intelligent man must be very inquisitive to know the transcendental science deeply. Therefore one must approach a *guru,* a spiritual master. Although Jaḍa Bharata explained everything to Mahārāja Rahūgaṇa, it appears that his intelligence was not perfect enough to understand clearly. He therefore requested a further explanation. As stated in *Bhagavad-gītā* (4.34): *tad viddhi praṇipātena paripraśnena sevayā.* The student must approach a spiritual master and surrender unto him fully (*praṇipātena*). He must also question him in order to understand his instructions (*paripraśnena*). One should not only surrender to the spiritual master but also render loving service unto him (*sevayā*) so that the spiritual master will be pleased with the student and explain the transcendental subject matter more clearly. A challenging spirit before the spiritual master should be avoided if one is at all interested in learning the Vedic instructions in depth.

TEXT 4

यदाह योगेश्वर दृश्यमानं
क्रियाफलं सद्व्यवहारमूलम् ।
न ह्यञ्जसा तत्त्वविमर्शनाय
भवानमुष्मिन् भ्रमते मनो मे ॥४॥

yad āha yogeśvara dṛśyamānaṁ
kriyā-phalaṁ sad-vyavahāra-mūlam
na hy añjasā tattva-vimarśanāya
bhavān amuṣmin bhramate mano me

yat—that which; *āha*—have said; *yoga-īśvara*—O master of mystic power; *dṛśyamānam*—being clearly seen; *kriyā-phalam*—the results of moving the body here and there, such as feeling fatigue; *sat*—existing; *vyavahāra-mūlam*—whose basis is etiquette alone; *na*—not; *hi*—certainly; *añjasā*—on the whole, or in fact; *tattva-vimarśanāya*—for understanding the truth by consultation; *bhavān*—your good self; *amuṣmin*—in that explanation; *bhramate*—is bewildered; *manaḥ*—mind; *me*—my.

TRANSLATION

O master of yogic power, you said that fatigue resulting from moving the body here and there is appreciated by direct perception, but actually there is no fatigue. It simply exists as a matter of formality. By such inquiries and answers, no one can come to the conclusion of the Absolute Truth. Because of your presentation of this statement, my mind is a little disturbed.

PURPORT

Formal inquiries and answers about the bodily conception do not constitute knowledge of the Absolute Truth. Knowledge of the Absolute Truth is quite different from the formal understanding of bodily pains and pleasures. In *Bhagavad-gītā* Lord Kṛṣṇa informs Arjuna that the pains and pleasures experienced in relation to the body are temporary; they come and go. One should not be disturbed by them but should tolerate them and continue with spiritual realization.

TEXTS 5–6

ब्राह्मण उवाच

अयं जनो नाम चलन् पृथिव्यां
यः पार्थिवः पार्थिव कस्य हेतोः ।
तस्यापि चाङ्घ्र्योरधि गुल्फजङ्घा-
जानूरुमध्योरशिरोधरांसाः ॥५॥

अंसेऽधि दार्वी शिबिका च यस्यां
सौवीरराजेत्यपदेश आस्ते ।
यस्मिन् भवान् रूढनिजाभिमानो
राजास्मि सिन्धुष्विति दुर्मदान्धः ॥६॥

brāhmaṇa uvāca
ayaṁ jano nāma calan pṛthivyāṁ
yaḥ pārthivaḥ pārthiva kasya hetoḥ
tasyāpi cāṅghryor adhi gulpha-jaṅghā-
jānūru-madhyora-śirodharāṁsāḥ

aṁse'dhi dārvī śibikā ca yasyāṁ
sauvīra-rājety apadeśa āste
yasmin bhavān rūḍha-nijābhimāno
rājāsmi sindhuṣv iti durmadāndhaḥ

brāhmaṇaḥ uvāca—the *brāhmaṇa* said; *ayam*—this; *janaḥ*—person; *nāma*—celebrated as such; *calan*—moving; *pṛthivyām*—on the earth; *yaḥ*—who; *pārthivaḥ*—a transformation of the earth; *pārthiva*—O King, who possesses a similar earthly body; *kasya*—for what; *hetoḥ*—reason; *tasya api*—of him also; *ca*—and; *aṅghryoḥ*—feet; *adhi*—above; *gulpha*—ankles; *jaṅghā*—calves; *jānu*—knees; *uru*—thighs; *madhyora*—waist; *śiraḥ-dhara*—neck; *aṁsāḥ*—shoulders; *aṁse*—shoulder; *adhi*—upon; *dārvī*—made of wood; *śibikā*—palanquin; *ca*—and; *yasyām*—on which; *sauvīra-rājā*—the King of Sauvīra; *iti*—thus; *apadeśaḥ*—known as; *āste*—there is; *yasmin*—in which; *bhavān*—Your Lordship; *rūḍha*—imposed upon; *nija-abhimānaḥ*—having a conception of false prestige; *rājā asmi*—I am the King; *sindhuṣu*—in the state of Sindhu; *iti*—thus; *durmada-andhaḥ*—captivated by false prestige.

TRANSLATION

The self-realized brāhmaṇa Jaḍa Bharata said: Among the various material combinations and permutations, there are various forms and earthly transformations. For some reason, these move on the surface of the earth and are called palanquin carriers. Those material transformations which do not move are gross material objects like stones. In any case, the material body is made of earth and stone in the form of feet, ankles, calves, knees, thighs, torso, throat and head. Upon the shoulders is the wooden palanquin, and within the palanquin is the so-called King of Sauvīra. The body of the King is simply another transformation of earth, but within that body Your Lordship is situated and falsely thinking that you are the King of the state of Sauvīra.

PURPORT

After analyzing the material bodies of the palanquin carrier and the palanquin passenger, Jaḍa Bharata concludes that the real living force is the living entity. The living entity is the offshoot or offspring of Lord Viṣṇu; therefore within this material world, among moving and nonmoving things, the real principle is Lord Viṣṇu. Due to His presence, everything is working, and there are actions and reactions. One who understands Lord Viṣṇu as the original cause of everything is to be understood to be perfectly situated in knowledge. Although he was falsely proud of being a king, King Rahūgaṇa was not really situated in knowledge. Therefore he was rebuking the palanquin carriers, including the self-realized *brāhmaṇa,* Jaḍa Bharata. This is the first accusation Jaḍa Bharata made against the King, who was daring to talk to a learned *brāhmaṇa* from the flimsy ground of ignorance, identifying everything with matter. King Rahūgaṇa argued that the living entity is within the body and that when the body is fatigued the living entity within must therefore be suffering. It is clearly explained in the following verses that the living entity does not suffer due to the body's fatigue. Śrīla Viśvanātha Cakravartī gives an example of a child heavily decorated with ornaments; although the child's body is very delicate, he does not feel fatigue, nor do the parents think that his ornaments should be taken away. The living entity has nothing to do with bodily pains and pleasures. These are simply mental concoctions. An intelligent man will find the original cause of everything. Material combinations and permutations may be a matter of fact in worldly dealings, but actually the living force, the soul, has nothing to do with them. Those who are materially upset take care of the body and manufacture *daridra-nārāyaṇa* (poor Nārāyaṇa). However, it is not a fact that the soul or Supersoul becomes poor simply because the body is poor. These are the statements of ignorant people. The soul and Supersoul are always apart from bodily pleasure and pain.

TEXT 7

शोच्यानिमांस्त्वमधिकष्टदीनान्
विष्ट्या निगृह्णन्निरनुग्रहोऽसि ।
जनस्य गोप्तास्मि विकत्थमानो
न शोभसे वृद्धसभासु धृष्टः ॥ ७ ॥

śocyān imāṁs tvam adhikaṣṭa-dīnān
viṣṭyā nigṛhṇan niranugraho'si
janasya goptāsmi vikatthamāno
na śobhase vṛddha-sabhāsu dhṛṣṭaḥ

śocyān—lamentable; *imān*—all these; *tvam*—you; *adhi-kaṣṭa-dīnān*—poor persons suffering more pains because of their poverty-stricken position; *viṣṭyā*—by force; *nigṛhṇan*—seizing; *niranugrahaḥ asi*—you have no mercy in your heart; *janasya*—of the people in general; *goptā asmi*—I am the protector (king); *vikatthamānaḥ*—bragging; *na śobhase*—you do not look very good; *vṛddha-sabhāsu*—in the society of learned persons; *dhṛṣṭaḥ*—simply impudent.

TRANSLATION

It is a fact, however, that these innocent people carrying your palanquin without payment are certainly suffering due to this injustice.

Their condition is very lamentable because you have forcibly engaged them in carrying your palanquin. This proves that you are cruel and unkind, yet due to false prestige you were thinking that you were protecting the citizens. This is ludicrous. You were such a fool that you could not have been adored as a great man in an assembly of persons advanced in knowledge.

PURPORT

King Rahūgaṇa was proud of being king, and he felt he had the right to control the citizens as he liked, but actually he was engaging men in carrying his palanquin without payment, and therefore he was causing them trouble without reason. Nonetheless, the King was thinking that he was the protector of the citizens. Actually the king should be the representative of the Supreme Personality of Godhead. For this reason he is called *nara-devatā,* the Lord among human beings. However, when a king thinks that because he is the head of the state, he can utilize the citizens for his sense gratification, he is in error. Such an attitude is not appreciated by learned scholars. According to the Vedic principles, the king should be advised by learned sages, *brāhmaṇas* and scholars, who advise him according to the injunctions given in the *dharma-śāstra.* The duty of the king is to follow these instructions. Learned circles do not appreciate the king's utilizing public endeavor for his own benefit. His duty is to give protection to the citizens instead. The king should not become such a rogue that he exploits the citizens for his own benefit.

It is stated in *Śrīmad-Bhāgavatam* that in Kali-yuga the heads of government will be plunderers and thieves. These thieves and plunderers take the money and property of the public by force or connivance. Therefore it is said in *Śrīmad-Bhāgavatam, rājanyair nirghṛṇair dasyu-dharmabhiḥ.* As Kali-yuga advances, we can see that these characteristics are already visible. We can certainly imagine how deteriorated human civilization will be by the end of Kali-yuga. Indeed, there will no longer be a sane man capable of understanding God and our relationship with Him. In other words, human beings will be just like animals. At that time, in order to reform human society, Lord Kṛṣṇa will come in the form of the Kalki *avatāra.* His business will be to kill all the atheists because ultimately the real protector is Viṣṇu, or Kṛṣṇa.

The Lord incarnates and sets things in order when things are mismanaged by so-called kings and heads of government. As Kṛṣṇa says in *Bhagavad-gītā, yadā yadā hi dharmasya glānir bhavati bhārata.* Of course this takes many years, but the principle is there. When the king or governmental head does not follow the proper principles, nature deals out the punishments in the forms of war, famine and so forth. Therefore if the governmental head is not aware of life's goal, he should not take charge of ruling the people. Actually the supreme proprietor of everything is Lord Viṣṇu. He is the maintainer of everyone. The king, the father, and the guardian are simply representatives of Lord Viṣṇu, empowered by Him to look after the management and maintain things. It is therefore the duty of the head of the state to maintain the general populace in such a way that people will ultimately know the goal of life. *Na te viduḥ svārtha-gatiṁ hi viṣṇum.* Unfortunately the foolish governmental head and the general populace do not know that the ultimate goal of life is to understand and approach Lord Viṣṇu. Without this knowledge, everyone is in ignorance, and all society is crowded with cheaters and cheated.

TEXT 8

यदा क्षितावेव चराचरस्य
विदाम निष्ठां प्रभवं च नित्यम् ।
तन्नामतोऽन्यद् व्यवहारमूलं
निरूप्यतां सत्क्रिययानुमेयम् ॥८॥

yadā kṣitāv eva carācarasya
vidāma niṣṭhāṁ prabhavaṁ ca nityam
tan nāmato'nyad vyavahāra-mūlaṁ
nirūpyatāṁ sat-kriyayānumeyam

yadā—therefore; *kṣitau*—in the earth; *eva*—certainly; *cara-acarasya*—of different bodies, some moving and some not moving; *vidāma*—we know; *niṣṭhām*—annihilation; *prabhavam*—appearance; *ca*—and; *nityam*—regularly by the principles of nature; *tat*—that; *nāmataḥ*—than simply by name; *anyat*—other; *vyavahāra-mūlam*—cause of material activities; *nirūpyatām*—let it be ascertained; *sat-kriyayā*—by actual employment; *anumeyam*—to be inferred.

TRANSLATION

All of us on the surface of the globe are living entities in different forms. Some of us are moving and some not moving. All of us come into existence, remain for some time and are annihilated when the body is again mingled with the earth. We are all simply different transformations of the earth. Different bodies and capacities are simply transformations of the earth

that exist in name only, for everything grows out of the earth and when everything is annihilated it again mingles with the earth. In other words, we are but dust, and we shall but be dust. Everyone can consider this point.

PURPORT

In the *Brahma-sūtra* it is said: *tad-ananyatvam ārabhambhaṇa-śabdādibhyaḥ* (2.1.14). This cosmic manifestation is a mixture of matter and spirit, but the cause is the Supreme Brahman, the Supreme Personality of Godhead. Therefore in *Śrīmad-Bhāgavatam* (1.5.20) it is said: *idaṁ hi viśvaṁ bhagavān ivetaraḥ.* The entire cosmic manifestation is but a transformation of the energy of the Supreme Personality of Godhead, but because of illusion, no one can appreciate that God is nondifferent from the material world. Actually He is not different, but this material world is simply a transformation of His different energies; *parāsya śaktir vividhaiva śrūyate.* There are also other versions of this in the *Vedas: sarvaṁ khalv idaṁ brahma.* Matter and spirit are all nondifferent from the Supreme Brahman, Bhagavān. Lord Śrī Kṛṣṇa confirms this statement in the *Bhagavad-gītā* (7.4): *me bhinnā prakṛtir aṣṭadhā.* The material energy is Kṛṣṇa's energy, but it is separated from Him. The spiritual energy is also His energy, but it is not separated from Him. When the material energy is engaged in the service of the Supreme Spirit, so-called material energy is also transformed into spiritual energy, just as an iron rod becomes fire when placed in contact with fire. When we can understand by an analytical study that the Supreme Personality of Godhead is the cause of all causes, our knowledge is perfect. Simply understanding the transformations of different energies is partial knowledge. We must come to the ultimate cause. *Na te viduḥ svārtha gatiṁ hi viṣṇum.* The knowledge of those who are not interested in knowing the original cause of all emanations is never perfect knowledge. There is nothing in the phenomenal world that is not produced by the supreme energy of the Supreme Personality of Godhead. Aromas from the earth are different scents manufactured and used for different purposes, but the original cause is the earth, nothing else. A waterpot made of earth can be used to carry water for some time, but ultimately the pot is nothing but earth. Therefore there is no difference between the pot and its original ingredient, earth. It is simply a different transformation of the energy. Originally the cause or primary ingredient is the Supreme Personality of Godhead, and the varieties are only by-products. In the *Chāndogya Upaniṣad* it is stated: *yathā saumy ekena mṛt-piṇḍena sarvaṁ mṛnmayaṁ vijñātaṁ syād vācārambhañaṁ vikāro nāmadheyaṁ mṛttikety eva satyam.* If one studies the earth, he naturally understands the by-products of the earth. The *Vedas* therefore enjoin, *kasmin bhagavo vijñāte sarvam idaṁ vijñātaṁ bhavati :* if one simply understands the original cause, Kṛṣṇa, the cause of all causes, then naturally everything else is understood, although it may be presented in different varieties. By understanding the original cause of different varieties, one can understand everything. If we understand Kṛṣṇa, the original cause of everything, we do not need to separately study the subsidiary varieties. Therefore from the very beginning it is said: *satyaṁ paraṁ dhīmahi.* One has to concentrate one's understanding on the Supreme Truth, Kṛṣṇa or Vāsudeva. The word Vāsudeva indicates the Supreme Personality of Godhead, who is the cause of all causes. *Mat-sthāni sarva-bhūtāni na cāhaṁ teṣv avasthitaḥ.* This is a summary of phenomenal and noumenal philosophy. The phenomenal world depends on the noumenal existence; similarly, everything exists by virtue of the potency of the Supreme Lord, although due to our ignorance the Supreme Lord is not perceived in everything.

TEXT 9

एवं निरुक्तं क्षितिशब्दवृत्त-
मसन्निधानात्परमाणवो ये ।
अविद्यया मनसा कल्पितास्ते
येषां समूहेन कृतो विशेषः ॥९॥

evaṁ niruktaṁ kṣiti-śabda-vṛttam
asan nidhānāt paramāṇavo ye
avidyayā manasā kalpitās te
yeṣāṁ samūhena kṛto viśeṣaḥ

evam—thus; *niruktam*—falsely described; *kṣiti-śabda*—of the word "earth"; *vṛttam*—the existence; *asat*—not real; *nidhānāt*—from the dissolution; *parama-aṇavaḥ*—atomic particles; *ye*—all of which; *avidyayā*—because of less intelligence; *manasā*—in the mind; *kalpitāḥ*—imagined; *te*—they; *yeṣām*—of which; *samūhena*—by the aggregate; *kṛtaḥ*—made; *viśeṣaḥ*—the particulars.

TRANSLATION

One may say that varieties arise from the planet earth itself. However, although the universe may temporarily appear to be the truth, it ultimately has no real existence. The earth was originally created by a combination

of atomic particles, but these particles are impermanent. Actually the atom is not the cause of the universe, although some philosophers think so. It is not a fact that the varieties found in this material world simply result from atomic juxtaposition or combination.

PURPORT

Those who follow the atomic theory think that the protons and electrons of atoms combine in such a way as to bring all material existence into being. However, the scientists fail to discover the cause of atomic existence itself. Under these circumstances, we cannot accept that the atom is the cause of the universe. Such theories are advanced by unintelligent people. According to real intelligence, the real cause of the cosmic manifestation is the Supreme Lord. *Janmādy asya yataḥ:* He is the original cause of all creation. As stated in *Bhagavad-gītā* (10.8): *ahaṁ sarvasya prabhavo mattaḥ sarvaṁ pravartate.* Kṛṣṇa is the original cause. *Sarva-kāraṇa-kāraṇam:* He is the cause of all causes. Kṛṣṇa is the cause of atoms, the material energy.

bhūmir āpo'nalo vāyuḥ
khaṁ mano buddhir eva ca
ahaṅkāra itīyaṁ me
bhinnā prakṛtir aṣṭadhā

(Bg. 7.4)

The ultimate cause is the Supreme Personality of Godhead, and only those in ignorance try to find out other causes by posing different theories.

TEXT 10

एवं कृशं स्थूलमणुर्बृहद्यद्
असच्च सज्जीवमजीवमन्यत् ।
द्रव्यस्वभावाशयकालकर्म-
नाम्नाजयावेहि कृतं द्वितीयम् ॥१०॥

evaṁ kṛśaṁ sthūlam aṇur bṛhad yad
asac ca saj jīvam ajīvam anyat
dravya-svabhāvāśaya-kāla-karma-
nāmnājayāvehi kṛtaṁ dvitīyam

evam—thus; *kṛśam*—skinny or short; *sthūlam*—fat; *aṇuḥ*—tiny; *bṛhat*—big; *yat*—which; *asat*—impermanent; *ca*—and; *sat*—existing; *jīvam*—

the living entities; *ajīvam*—inanimate, lifeless matter; *anyat*—other causes; *dravya*—phenomena; *sva-bhāva*—nature; *āśaya*—disposition; *kāla*—time; *karma*—activities; *nāmnā*—only by such names; *ajayā*—by material nature; *avehi*—you should understand; *kṛtam*—done; *dvitīyam*—duality.

TRANSLATION

Since this universe has no real ultimate existence, the things within it—shortness, differences, grossness, skinniness, smallness, bigness, result, cause, living symptoms, and materials—are all imagined. They are all pots made of the same substance, earth, but they are named differently. The differences are characterized by the substance, nature, predisposition, time and activity. You should know that all these are simply mechanical manifestations created by material nature.

PURPORT

The temporary manifestations and varieties within this material world are simply creations of material nature under various circumstances: *prakṛteḥ kriyamāṇāni guṇaiḥ karmāṇi sarvaśaḥ.* The actions and reactions carried out by the material nature are sometimes accepted as our scientific inventions; therefore we want to take credit for them and defy the existence of God. This is described in *Bhagavad-gītā* (3.27), *ahaṅkāra-vimūḍhātmā kartāham iti manyate:* due to being covered by the illusory external energy, the living entity tries to take credit for the differentiated creations within the material world. Actually all these are being created automatically by the material force set in motion by the energy of the Supreme Personality of Godhead. Therefore the ultimate cause is the Supreme Person. As stated in *Brahma-saṁhitā:*

īśvaraḥ paramaḥ kṛṣṇaḥ
sac-cid-ānanda-vigrahaḥ
anādir ādir govindaḥ
sarva-kāraṇa-kāraṇam

He is the cause of all causes, the ultimate cause. In this regard Śrīla Madhvācārya says: *evaṁ sarvaṁ tathā prakṛtvayai kalpitaṁ viṣṇor anyat; evaṁ prakṛtyādhāraḥ svayam ananyādhāro viṣṇur eva. ataḥ sarva-śabdāś ca tasminn eva.* Actually the original cause is Lord Viṣṇu, but out of ignorance people think that matter is the cause of everything.

rājā goptāśrayo bhūmiḥ
śaraṇaṁ ceti laukikaḥ

vyavahāro na tat satyaṁ
tayor brahmāśrayo vibhuḥ

Things are contemplated on the ephemeral or external platform, but actually this is not the truth. The actual protector and shelter of everyone is Brahman, the Supreme, not the king.

goptrī ca tasya prakṛtis
tasyā viṣṇuḥ svayaṁ prabhuḥ
tava goptrī tu pṛthivī
na tvaṁ goptā kṣiteḥ smṛtaḥ

ataḥ sarvāśrayaiś caiva
goptā ca harir īśvaraḥ
sarva-śabdābhidheyaś ca
śabda-vṛtter hi kāraṇam
sarvāntaraḥ sarva-bahir
eka eva janārdanaḥ

The actual protectress is the material nature, but Viṣṇu is her Lord. He is the Lord of everything. Lord Janārdana is the director both externally and internally. He is the cause of the function of words and what is expressed in all sound.

śirasodhāratā yadvad
grīvāyās tadvad eva tu
āśrayatvaṁ ca goptṛtvam
anyeṣām upacārataḥ

Lord Viṣṇu is the resting place of the entire creation: *brahmaṇo hi pratiṣṭhāham* (Bg. 14.27). On Brahman, everything is resting. All the universes are resting on the *brahmajyoti,* and all the planets are resting on the universal atmosphere. In each and every planet there are oceans, hills, states and kingdoms, and each planet is giving shelter to so many living entities. They are all standing on the earth of feet and legs, torso and shoulders, but actually everything is resting ultimately on the potencies of the Supreme Personality of Godhead. Therefore He is known ultimately as *sarva-kāraṇa-kāraṇam,* the cause of all causes.

TEXT 11

ज्ञानं विशुद्धं परमार्थमेक-
मनन्तरं त्वबहिर्ब्रह्म सत्यम् ।

प्रत्यक् प्रशान्तं भगवच्छब्दसंज्ञं
यद्वासुदेवं कवयो वदन्ति ॥११॥

jñānaṁ viśuddhaṁ paramārtham ekam
anantaraṁ tv abahir brahma satyam
pratyak praśāntaṁ bhagavac-chabda-saṁjñaṁ
yad vāsudevaṁ kavayo vadanti

jñānam—the supreme knowledge; *viśuddham*—without contamination; *parama-artham*—giving the ultimate goal of life; *ekam*—unified; *anantaram*—without interior, unbroken; *tu*—also; *abahiḥ*—without exterior; *brahma*—the Supreme; *satyam*—Absolute Truth; *pratyak*—inner; *praśāntam*—the calm and peaceful Supreme Lord, worshiped by the *yogīs; bhagavat-śabda-saṁjñam*—known in the higher sense as Bhagavān, or full of all opulences; *yat*—that; *vāsudevam*—Lord Kṛṣṇa, the son of Vasudeva; *kavayaḥ*—the learned scholars; *vadanti*—say.

TRANSLATION

What, then, is the ultimate truth? The answer is that nondual knowledge is the ultimate truth. It is devoid of the contamination of material qualities. It gives us liberation. It is the one without a second, all-pervading and beyond imagination. The first realization of that knowledge is Brahman. Then Paramātmā, the Supersoul, is realized by the yogīs who try to see Him without grievance. This is the second stage of realization. Finally, full realization of the same supreme knowledge is realized in the Supreme Person. All learned scholars describe the Supreme Person as Vāsudeva, the cause of Brahman, Paramātmā and others.

PURPORT

In *Caitanya-caritāmṛta* it is said: *yad advaitaṁ brahmopaniṣadi tad apy asya tanu-bhā.* The impersonal Brahman effulgence of the Absolute Truth consists of the bodily rays of the Supreme Personality of Godhead. *Ya ātmāntaryāmī puruṣa iti so'syāṁśa-vibhavaḥ.* What is known as *ātmā* and *antaryāmī,* the Supersoul, is but an expansion of the Supreme Personality of Godhead. *Ṣaḍ-aiśvaryaiḥ pūrṇo ya iha bhagavān sa svayam ayam.* What is described as the Supreme Personality of Godhead, complete with all six opulences, is Vāsudeva, and Śrī Caitanya Mahāprabhu is nondifferent from Him. Great learned scholars and philosophers accept this after many, many births. *Vāsudevaḥ sarvam iti sa mahātmā sudurlabhaḥ* (Bg. 7.19). The wise man can understand that ultimately

Vāsudeva, Kṛṣṇa, is the cause of Brahman, and Paramātmā, the Supersoul. Thus Vāsudeva is *sarva-kāraṇa-kāraṇam,* the cause of all causes. This is confirmed in *Śrīmad-Bhāgavatam.* The real *tattva,* Absolute Truth, is Bhagavān, but due to incomplete realization of the Absolute Truth, people sometimes describe the same Viṣṇu as impersonal Brahman or localized Paramātmā.

vadanti tat tattva-vidas
tattvaṁ yaj jñānam advayam
brahmeti paramātmeti
bhagavān iti śabdyate
(*Bhāg.* 1.2.11)

From the very beginning, *Śrīmad-Bhāgavatam* says, *satyaṁ paraṁ dhīmahi:* we meditate on the supreme truth. The supreme truth is explained here as *jñānaṁ viśuddhaṁ satyam.* The Absolute Truth is devoid of material contamination and is transcendental to the material qualities. It gives all spiritual success and liberation from this material world. That Supreme Absolute Truth is Kṛṣṇa, Vāsudeva. There is no difference between Kṛṣṇa's inner self and outward body. Kṛṣṇa is *pūrṇa,* the complete whole. There is no distinction between His body and soul as there is between ours. Sometimes so-called scholars, not knowing the constitutional position of Kṛṣṇa, mislead people by saying that the Kṛṣṇa within is different from the Kṛṣṇa without. When Kṛṣṇa says, *man-manā bhava mad-bhakto mad-yājī māṁ namaskuru,* so-called scholars advise the reader that it is not the person Kṛṣṇa to whom we must surrender but the Kṛṣṇa within. So-called scholars, Māyāvādīs, cannot understand Kṛṣṇa with their poor fund of knowledge. One should therefore approach an authorized person to understand Kṛṣṇa. The spiritual master has actually seen Kṛṣṇa; therefore he can explain Him properly.

tad viddhi praṇipātena
paripraśnena sevayā
upadekṣyanti te jñānaṁ
jñāninas tattva-darśinaḥ
(Bg. 4.34)

Without approaching an authorized person, one cannot understand Kṛṣṇa.

TEXT 12

रहूगणैतत्तपसा न याति
न चेज्यया निर्वपणाद् गृहाद्वा ।

नच्छन्दसा नैव जलाग्निसूर्यै-
र्विना महत्पादरजोऽभिषेकम् ॥१२॥

rahūgaṇaitat tapasā na yāti
na cejyayā nirvapaṇād gṛhād vā
na cchandasā naiva jalāgni-sūryair
vinā mahat-pāda-rajo-'bhiṣekam

rahūgaṇa—O King Rahūgaṇa; *etat*—this knowledge; *tapasā*—by severe austerities and penances; *na yāti*—does not become revealed; *na*—not; *ca*—also; *ijyayā*—by a great arrangement for worshiping the Deity; *nirvapaṇāt*—or from finishing all material duties and accepting *sannyāsa; gṛhāt*—from ideal householder life; *vā*—or; *na*—nor; *chandasā*—by observing celibacy or studying Vedic literature; *na eva*—nor; *jala-agni-sūryaiḥ*—by severe austerities such as keeping oneself in water, in a burning fire or in the scorching sun; *vinā*—without; *mahat*—of the great devotees; *pāda-rajaḥ*—the dust of the lotus feet; *abhiṣekam*—smearing all over the body.

TRANSLATION

My dear King Rahūgaṇa, unless one has the opportunity to smear his entire body with the dust of the lotus feet of great devotees, one cannot realize the Absolute Truth. One cannot realize the Absolute Truth simply by observing celibacy [brahmacarya], strictly following the rules and regulations of householder life, leaving home as a vānaprastha, accepting sannyāsa, or undergoing severe penances in winter by keeping oneself submerged in water or surrounding oneself in summer by fire and the scorching heat of the sun. There are many other processes to understand the Absolute Truth, but the Absolute Truth is only revealed to one who has attained the mercy of a great devotee.

PURPORT

Actual knowledge of transcendental bliss can be bestowed upon anyone by a pure devotee. *Vedeṣu durlabham adurlabham ātma-bhaktau.* One cannot attain the perfection of spiritual life simply by following the directions of the *Vedas.* One has to approach a pure devotee: *anyābhilāṣitā-śūnyaṁ jñāna-karmādy-anāvṛtam.* By the grace of such a devotee, one can understand the Absolute Truth, Kṛṣṇa, and one's relationship with Him. A materialistic person sometimes thinks that simply by executing pious activities and remaining at home one can understand the Absolute Truth. That is denied in this verse. Nor can one understand the Absolute Truth simply by observing the rules and regulations of *brahmacarya* (celibacy). One only has to serve the pure devotee. That will help one understand the Absolute Truth without fail.

TEXT 13

यत्रोत्तमश्लोकगुणानुवादः
प्रस्तूयते ग्राम्यकथाविघातः ।
निषेव्यमाणोऽनुदिनं मुमुक्षो-
र्मतिं सतीं यच्छति वासुदेवे ॥१३॥

yatrottamaśloka-guṇānuvādaḥ
prastūyate grāmya-kathā-vighātaḥ
niṣevyamāṇo'nudinaṁ mumukṣor
matiṁ satīṁ yacchati vāsudeve

yatra—in which place (in the presence of exalted devotees); *uttama-śloka-guṇa-anuvādaḥ*—discussion of the pastimes and glories of the Supreme Personality of Godhead; *prastūyate*—is presented; *grāmya-kathā-vighātaḥ*—due to which there is no chance of talking of worldly matters; *niṣevyamāṇaḥ*—being heard very seriously; *anudinam*—day after day; *mumukṣoḥ*—of persons who are very serious about getting out of material entanglement; *matim*—meditation; *satīm*—pure and simple; *yacchati*—is turned; *vāsudeve*—unto the lotus feet of Lord Vāsudeva.

TRANSLATION

Who are the pure devotees mentioned here? In an assembly of pure devotees, there is no question of discussing material subjects like politics and sociology. In an assembly of pure devotees, there is discussion only of the qualities, forms and pastimes of the Supreme Personality of Godhead. He is praised and worshiped with full attention. In the association of pure devotees, by constantly hearing such topics respectfully, even a person who wants to merge into the existence of the Absolute Truth abandons this idea and gradually becomes attached to the service of Vāsudeva.

PURPORT

The symptoms of pure devotees are described in this verse. The pure devotee is never interested in material topics. Śrī Caitanya Mahāprabhu has strictly prohibited His devotees to talk about worldly matters. *Grāmya-vārtā nā kahibe:* one should not indulge in talking unnecessarily about news of the material world. One should not waste time in this way. This is a very important feature in the life of a devotee. A devotee has no other ambition than to serve Kṛṣṇa, the Supreme Personality of Godhead. This Kṛṣṇa consciousness movement was started to engage people twenty-four hours daily in the service of the Lord and in His glorification. The students in this institution engage in the cultivation of Kṛṣṇa consciousness from five in the morning to ten at night. They actually have no opportunity to waste their time unnecessarily by discussing politics, sociology and current events. These will go their own way. A devotee is concerned only with serving Kṛṣṇa positively and seriously.

TEXT 14

अहं पुरा भरतो नाम राजा
विमुक्तदृष्टश्रुतसङ्गबन्धः ।
आराधनं भगवत ईहमानो
मृगोऽभवं मृगसङ्गाद्धतार्थः ॥१४॥

ahaṁ purā bharato nāma rājā
vimukta-dṛṣṭa-śruta-saṅga-bandhaḥ
ārādhanaṁ bhagavata īhamāno
mṛgo'bhavaṁ mṛga-saṅgād dhatārthaḥ

aham—I; *purā*—formerly (in my previous birth); *bharataḥ nāma rājā*—a King named Mahārāja Bharata; *vimukta*—liberated from; *dṛṣṭa-śruta*—by experiencing personally through direct association, or by getting knowledge from the *Vedas; saṅga-bandhaḥ*—bondage by association; *ārādhanam*—the worship; *bhagavataḥ*—of the Supreme Personality of Godhead, Vāsudeva; *īhamānaḥ*—always performing; *mṛgaḥ abhavam*—I became a deer; *mṛga-saṅgāt*—because of my intimate association with a deer; *hata-arthaḥ*—having neglected the regulative principles in the discharge of devotional service.

TRANSLATION

In a previous birth I was known as Mahārāja Bharata. I attained perfection by becoming completely detached from material activities through direct experience, and through indirect experience I received

understanding from the Vedas. I was fully engaged in the service of the Lord, but due to my misfortune, I became very affectionate to a small deer, so much so that I neglected my spiritual duties. Due to my deep affection for the deer, in my next life I had to accept the body of a deer.

PURPORT

The incident herein described is very significant. In a previous verse it is stated, *vinā mahat-pāda-rajo-'bhiṣekam:* one cannot attain perfection without smearing the dust from the lotus feet of an exalted devotee on his head. If one always follows the orders of the spiritual master, there is no question of falling down. As soon as a foolish disciple tries to overtake his spiritual master and becomes ambitious to occupy his post, he immediately falls down. *Yasya prasādād bhagavat-prasādo yasyāprasādān na gatiḥ kuto'pi.* If the spiritual master is considered an ordinary man, the disciple surely loses his chance to advance further. Despite a very rigid life in devotional service, Bharata Mahārāja did not consult a spiritual master when he became overly attached to a deer. Consequently he became strongly attached to the deer, and, forgetting his spiritual routine, he fell down.

TEXT 15

सा मां स्मृतिर्मृगदेहेऽपि वीर
कृष्णार्चनप्रभवा नो जहाति ।
अथो अहं जनसङ्गादसङ्गो
विशङ्कमानोऽविवृतश्चरामि ॥१५॥

sā māṁ smṛtir mṛga-dehe'pi vīra
kṛṣṇārcana-prabhavā no jahāti
atho ahaṁ jana-saṅgād asaṅgo
viśaṅkamāno 'vivṛtaś carāmi

sā—that; *mām*—me; *smṛtiḥ*—remembrance of the activities of my previous life; *mṛga-dehe*—in the body of a deer; *api*—although; *vīra*—O great hero; *kṛṣṇa-arcana-prabhavā*—which appeared because of the influence of sincere service to Kṛṣṇa; *no jahāti*—did not leave; *atho*—therefore; *aham*—I; *jana-saṅgāt*—from the association of ordinary men; *asaṅgaḥ*—completely detached; *viśaṅkamānaḥ*—being afraid; *avivṛtaḥ*—unobserved by others; *carāmi*—I go here and there.

TRANSLATION

My dear heroic King, due to my past sincere service to the Lord, I could remember everything of my past life even while in the body of a deer. Because I am aware of the falldown in my past life, I always keep myself separate from the association of ordinary men. Being afraid of their bad, materialistic association, I wander alone unnoticed by others.

PURPORT

In *Bhagavad-gītā* it is said: *svalpam apy asya dharmasya (Bg.2.40)*. It is certainly a great fall to go from human life to animal life, but in the case of Bharata Mahārāja or any devotee, devotional service to the Lord never goes in vain. As stated in *Bhagavad-gītā* (8.6): *yaṁ yaṁ vāpi smaran bhāvaṁ tyajaty ante kalevaram.* At the time of death, by nature's law the mind is absorbed in a certain type of thinking. This may lead one to animal life, yet for a devotee there is no loss. Even though Bharata Mahārāja received the body of a deer, he didn't forget his position. Consequently, in the body of a deer he was very careful to remember the cause of his downfall. As a result, he was given a chance to be born in a family of very pure *brāhmaṇas.* Thus his service to the Lord never went in vain.

TEXT 16

तस्मान्नरोऽसङ्गसुसङ्गजात-
ज्ञानासिनेहैव विवृक्णमोहः ।
हरिं तदीहाकथनश्रुताभ्यां
लब्धस्मृतिर्यात्यतिपारमध्वनः ॥१६॥

tasmān naro 'saṅga-susaṅga-jāta-
jñānāsinehaiva vivṛkṇa-mohaḥ
hariṁ tad-īhā-kathana-śrutābhyāṁ
labdha-smṛtir yāty atipāram adhvanaḥ

tasmāt—for this reason; *naraḥ*—every person; *asaṅga*—by detachment from the association of worldly people; *su-saṅga*—by the association of devotees; *jāta*—produced; *jñāna-asinā*—by the sword of knowledge; *iha*—in this material world; *eva*—even; *vivṛkṇa-mohaḥ*—whose illusion is completely cut to pieces; *harim*—the Supreme Personality of Godhead; *tad-īhā*—of His activities; *kathana-śrutābhyām*—by the two processes of hearing and chanting; *labdha-smṛtiḥ*—the lost consciousness is regained; *yāti*—achieves; *atipāram*—the ultimate end; *adhvanaḥ*—of the path back home, back to Godhead.

TRANSLATION

Simply by associating with exalted devotees, anyone can attain perfection of knowledge and with the sword of knowledge can cut to pieces the illusory associations within this material world. Through the association of devotees, one can engage in the service of the Lord by hearing and chanting [śravaṇaṁ kīrtanam]. Thus one can revive his dormant Kṛṣṇa consciousness and, sticking to the cultivation of Kṛṣṇa consciousness, return home, back to Godhead, even in this life.

PURPORT

To become liberated from material bondage, one must give up the association of worldly people and accept the association of devotees. Positive and negative processes are mentioned in this regard. Through the association of devotees, one develops Kṛṣṇa consciousness, which is dormant within. This Kṛṣṇa consciousness movement is giving this chance to everyone. We are giving shelter to everyone who is serious about progressing in Kṛṣṇa consciousness. We arrange for their lodging and board so that they can peacefully cultivate Kṛṣṇa consciousness and return home, back to Godhead, even in this life.

Thus end the Bhaktivedanta purports of the Fifth Canto, Twelfth Chapter, of the Śrīmad-Bhāgavatam, *entitled "The Conversation Between Mahārāja Rahūgaṇa and Jaḍa Bharata."*

CHAPTER THIRTEEN

Further Talks Between King Rahūgaṇa and Jaḍa Bharata

The *brāhmaṇa* Jaḍa Bharata became very kind to King Rahūgaṇa, and to disassociate him from the material world, he spoke figuratively of the forest of the material world. He explained that this material world is like a great forest in which one becomes entangled due to association with material life. In this forest there are plunderers (the six senses) as well as carnivorous animals like jackals, wolves and lions (wife, children and other relatives) who are always anxious to suck the blood from the head of the family. The forest plunderers and the carnivorous blood-sucking animals combine to exploit the energy of a man within this material world. In this forest there is also a black hole, covered by grass, into which one may fall. Coming into the forest and being captivated by so many material attractions, one identifies himself with this material world, society, friendship, love and family. Having lost the path and not knowing where to go, being harassed by animals and birds, one is also victimized by many desires. Thus one works very hard within the forest and wanders here and there. He becomes captivated by temporary happiness and becomes aggrieved by so-called distress. Actually one simply suffers in the forest from so-called happiness and distress. Sometimes he is attacked by a snake (deep sleep), and due to the snakebite he loses consciousness and becomes puzzled and bewildered about discharging his duties. Sometimes he is attracted by women other than his wife, and thus be thinks he enjoys extramarital love with another woman. He is attacked by various diseases, by lamentation and by summer and winter. Thus one within the forest of the material world suffers the pains of material existence. Expecting to become happy, the living entity changes his position from one place to another, but actually a materialistic person within the material world is never happy. Being constantly engaged in materialistic activities, he is always disturbed. He forgets that one day he has to die. Although he suffers severely, being illusioned by the material energy, he still hankers after material happiness. In this way he completely forgets his relationship with the Supreme Personality of Godhead.

By hearing this from Jaḍa Bharata, Mahārāja Rahūgaṇa revived his Kṛṣṇa consciousness and thus benefited from Jaḍa Bharata's association. He could understand that his illusion was over, and he begged pardon from Jaḍa Bharata for his misbehavior. All this was told to Mahārāja Parīkṣit by Śukadeva Gosvāmī.

TEXT 1

ब्राह्मण उवाच
दुरत्ययेऽध्वन्यजया निवेशितो
रजस्तमःसत्त्वविभक्तकर्मदृक् ।
स एष सार्थोऽर्थपरः परिभ्रमन्
भवाटवीं याति न शर्म विन्दति ॥१॥

brāhmaṇa uvāca
duratyaye 'dhvany ajayā niveśito
rajas-tamaḥ-sattva-vibhakta-karmadṛk
sa eṣa sārtho 'rtha-paraḥ paribhraman
bhavāṭavīṁ yāti na śarma vindati

brāhmaṇaḥ uvāca—the *brāhmaṇa* Jaḍa Bharata continued to speak; *duratyaye*—which is very difficult to traverse; *adhvani*—on the path of fruitive activities (performing actions in this life, creating a body in the next life by those actions, and in this way continuously accepting birth and death); *ajayā*—by *māyā,* the external energy of the Supreme Personality of Godhead; *niveśitaḥ*—caused to enter; *rajaḥ-tamaḥ-sattva-vibhakta-karma-dṛk*—a conditioned soul who sees only immediately beneficial fruitive activities and their results, which are divided into three groups by the modes of goodness, passion and ignorance; *saḥ*—he; *eṣaḥ*—this; *sa-arthaḥ*—the living entity falsely seeking sense gratification; *artha-paraḥ*—intent upon gaining wealth; *paribhraman*—wandering all over; *bhava-aṭavīm*—the forest known as *bhava,* which means the repetition of birth and death; *yāti*—enters; *na*—not; *śarma*—happiness; *vindati*—obtains.

TRANSLATION

Jaḍa Bharata, who had fully realized Brahman, continued: My dear King Rahūgaṇa, the living entity wanders on the path of the material world, which is very difficult for him to traverse, and he accepts repeated birth and death. Being captivated by the material world under the influence of the three modes of material nature (sattva-guṇa, rajo-guṇa and tamo-guṇa), the living entity can see only the three fruits of activities under the spell of material nature. These fruits are auspicious, inauspicious and

mixed. He thus becomes attached to religion, economic development, sense gratification and the monistic theory of liberation (merging with the Supreme). He works very hard day and night exactly like a merchant who enters a forest to acquire some articles to sell later for profit. However, he cannot really achieve happiness within this material world.

PURPORT

One can very easily understand how difficult and insurmountable the path of sense gratification is. Not knowing what the path of sense gratification is, one becomes implicated in the repetition of birth and accepts different types of bodies again and again. Thus one suffers in material existence. In this life one may think that he is very happy being an American, Indian, Englishman or German, but in the next life one has to accept another body among 8,400,000 species. The next body has to be immediately accepted according to *karma.* One will be forced to accept a certain type of body, and protesting will not help. That is the stringent law of nature. Due to the living entity's ignorance of his eternal blissful life, he becomes attracted to material activities under the spell of *māyā.* In this world, he can never experience happiness, yet he works very hard to do so. This is called *māyā.*

TEXT 2

यस्यामिमे षण्नरदेव दस्यवः
सार्थं विलुम्पन्ति कुनायकं बलात् ।
गोमायवो यत्र हरन्ति सार्थिकं
प्रमत्तमाविश्य यथोरणं वृकाः ॥२॥

yasyām ime ṣaṇ nara-deva dasyavaḥ
sārthaṁ vilumpanti kunāyakaṁ balāt
gomāyavo yatra haranti sārthikaṁ
pramattam āviśya yathoraṇaṁ vṛkāḥ

yasyām—in which (in the forest of material existence); *ime*—these; *ṣaṭ*—six; *nara-deva*—O King; *dasyavaḥ*—the plunderers; *sa-artham*—the conditioned souls, who are interested in false ideas; *vilumpanti*—plunder, regularly taking away all the possessions; *ku-nāyakam*—who are always misguided by so-called *gurus,* or spiritual masters; *balāt*—by force; *gomāyavaḥ*—exactly like foxes; *yatra*—in which forest; *haranti*—they take away; *sa-arthikam*—the conditioned soul who is seeking material profits to maintain the body and soul; *pramattam*—who is a crazy man not knowing his self-interest; *āviśya*—entering the heart; *yathā*—just as; *uraṇam*—nicely protected lambs; *vṛkāḥ*—the tigers.

TRANSLATION

O King Rahūgaṇa, in this forest of material existence there are six very powerful plunderers. When the conditioned soul enters the forest to acquire some material gain, the six plunderers misguide him. Thus the conditioned merchant does not know how to spend his money, and it is taken away by these plunderers. Like tigers, jackals and other ferocious animals in a forest that are ready to take away a lamb from the custody of its protector, the wife and children enter the heart of the merchant and plunder him in so many ways.

PURPORT

In the forest there are many plunderers, dacoits, jackals and tigers. The jackals are compared to one's wife and children. In the dead of night, jackals cry very loudly, and similarly one's wife and children in this material world also cry like jackals. The children say, "Father, this is wanted; give me this. I am your dear son." Or the wife says, "I am your dear wife. Please give me this. This is now needed." In this way one is plundered by the thieves in the forest. Not knowing the aim of human life, one is constantly being misguided. The aim of life is Viṣṇu (*na te viduḥ svārtha-gatiṁ hi viṣṇum*). Everyone works very hard to earn money, but no one knows that his real self-interest is in serving the Supreme Personality of Godhead. Instead of spending money for advancing the Kṛṣṇa consciousness movement, one spends his hard-earned money on clubs, brothels, liquor, slaughterhouses and so forth. Due to sinful activities, one becomes implicated in the process of transmigration and thus has to accept one body after another. Being thus absorbed in a distressed condition, one never attains happiness.

TEXT 3

प्रभूतवीरुत्तृणगुल्मगह्वरे
कठोरदंशैर्मशकैरुपद्रुतः ।
क्वचित्तु गन्धर्वपुरं प्रपश्यति
क्वचित्क्वचिच्चाशुरयोल्मुकग्रहम् ॥३॥

prabhūta-vīrut-tṛṇa-gulma-gahvare
kaṭhora-daṁśair maśakair upadrutaḥ
kvacit tu gandharva-puraṁ prapaśyati
kvacit kvacic cāśu-rayolmuka-graham

prabhūta—a very large number; *vīrut*—of creepers; *tṛṇa*—of varieties of grass; *gulma*—of thickets; *gahvare*—in bowers; *kaṭhora*—cruel; *daṁśaiḥ*—by bites; *maśakaiḥ*—by mosquitoes; *upadrutaḥ*—disturbed; *kvacit*—sometimes; *tu*—but; *gandharva-puram*—a false palace created by the Gandharvas; *prapaśyati*—be sees; *kvacit*—and sometimes; *kvacit*—sometimes; *ca*—and; *āśu-raya*—very quickly; *ulmuka*—like a meteor; *graham*—a fiend.

TRANSLATION

In this forest there are dense bowers composed of thickets of bushes, grass and creepers. In these bowers the conditioned soul is always disturbed by cruelly biting mosquitoes [envious people]. Sometimes he sees an imaginary palace in the forest, and sometimes he is bewildered by seeing a fleeting fiend or ghost, which appears like a meteor in the sky.

PURPORT

The material household is actually a hole of fruitive activity. To earn a livelihood one engages in different industries and trades, and sometimes one performs great sacrifices to go to higher planetary systems. Apart from this, at least everyone is engaged in earning a livelihood in some profession or occupation. In these dealings, one has to meet many undesirable people, and their behavior is compared to the biting of mosquitoes. This creates very undesirable conditions. Even in the midst of these disturbances, one imagines that he is going to construct a grand house and live there permanently, although he knows that he cannot. Gold is compared to a quickly fleeting fiend, which appears like a meteor in the sky. It displays itself for a moment and is then gone. Generally *karmīs* are attracted to gold or money, but these are compared herein to ghosts and witches.

TEXT 4

निवासतोयद्रविणात्मबुद्धि-
स्ततस्ततो धावति भो अटव्याम् ।
क्वचिच्च वात्योत्थितपांसुधूम्रा
दिशो न जानाति रजस्वलाक्षः ॥४॥

nivāsa-toya-draviṇātma-buddhis
tatas tato dhāvati bho aṭavyām
kvacic ca vātyotthita-pāṁsu-dhūmrā
diśo na jānāti rajas-valākṣaḥ

nivāsa—residential place; *toya*—water; *draviṇa*—wealth; *ātma-buddhiḥ*—who considers these material things the *ātma,* or self; *tataḥ tataḥ*—here and there; *dhāvati*—he runs; *bhoḥ*—O King; *aṭavyām*—on that forest path of material existence; *kvacit ca*—and sometimes; *vātyā*—by the whirlwind; *utthita*—raised; *pāṁsu*—by dust; *dhūmrāḥ*—appear smoke-colored; *diśaḥ*—the directions; *na*—not; *jānāti*—knows; *rajaḥ-vala-akṣaḥ*—whose eyes are covered by the dust of the wind or who is captivated by his wife during her menstrual period.

TRANSLATION

My dear King, the merchant on the forest path of the material world, his intelligence victimized by home, wealth, relatives and so forth, runs from one place to another in search of success. Sometimes his eyes are covered by the dust of a whirlwind—that is to say, in his lust he is captivated by the beauty of his wife, especially during her menstrual period. Thus his eyes are blinded, and he cannot see where to go or what he is doing.

PURPORT

It is said that household attraction resides in the wife because sex is the center of household life: *yan maithunādi-gṛhamedhi-sukhaṁ hi tuccham.* A materialistic person, making his wife the center of attraction, works very hard day and night. His only enjoyment in material life is sexual intercourse. Therefore *karmīs* are attracted to women as friends or wives. Indeed, they cannot work without sex. Under the circumstances the wife is compared to a whirlwind, especially during her menstrual period. Those who strictly follow the rules and regulations of householder life engage in sex only once a month, at the end of the menstrual period. As one looks forward to this opportunity, his eyes are overwhelmed by the beauty of his wife. Thus it is said that the whirlwind covers the eyes with dust. Such a lusty person does not know that all his material activities are being observed by different demigods, especially the sun-god, and are being recorded for the *karma* of one's next body. Astrological calculations are called *jyoti-śāstra.* Because the *jyoti,* or effulgence, in the material world comes from the different stars and planets, the science is called *jyoti-śāstra,* the science of the luminaries. By the calculations of *jyoti,* our future is indicated. In other words, all the luminaries—the stars, sun and moon—witness the activities of the conditioned soul. Thus he is awarded a particular type of body. A lusty person whose eyes are covered by the dust of the whirlwind of material existence does not at all consider that his activities are being observed by different stars and planets and are being recorded. Not knowing this, the conditioned soul commits all kinds of sinful activities for the satisfaction of his lusty desires.

TEXT 5

अदृश्यझिल्लीस्वनकर्णशूल
उलूकवाग्भिर्व्यथितान्तरात्मा ।
अपुण्यवृक्षान् श्रयते क्षुधार्दितो
मरीचितोयान्यभिधावति क्वचित् ॥ ५ ॥

adṛśya-jhillī-svana-karṇa-śūla
ulūka-vāgbhir vyathitāntarātmā
apuṇya-vṛkṣān śrayate kṣudhārdito
marīci-toyāny abhidhāvati kvacit

adṛśya—invisible; *jhillī*—of crickets or a kind of bee; *svana*—by the sounds; *karṇa-śūla*—whose ears are disturbed; *ulūka*—of the owls; *vāgbhiḥ*—by sound vibrations; *vyathita*—very disturbed; *antaḥ-ātmā*—whose mind and heart; *apuṇya-vṛkṣān*—impious trees that have no fruits or flowers; *śrayate*—he takes shelter of; *kṣudha*—from hunger; *arditaḥ*—suffering; *marīci-toyāni*—the waters of a mirage in the desert; *abhidhāvati*—he runs after; *kvacit*—sometimes.

TRANSLATION

Wandering in the forest of the material world, the conditioned soul sometimes hears an invisible cricket making harsh sounds, and his ears become very much aggrieved. Sometimes his heart is pained by the sounds of owls, which are just like the harsh words of his enemies. Sometimes he takes shelter of a tree that has no fruits or flowers. He approaches such a tree due to his strong appetite, and thus he suffers. He would like to acquire water, but he is simply illusioned by a mirage, and he runs after it.

PURPORT

In *Śrīmad-Bhāgavatam* it is said that the *Bhāgavata* philosophy is meant for people who are completely free from envy (*paramo nirmatsarāṇām*). The material world is full of envious people. Even within one's inner circle there is much backbiting, and this is compared to the sound vibration of a cricket in the forest. One cannot see the cricket, but one hears its sounds and thus becomes aggrieved. When one takes to Kṛṣṇa consciousness, one always hears unpalatable words from relatives. This is the nature of the world; one cannot avoid mental distress due to the backbiting of envious people. Being very much aggrieved, sometimes one goes to a sinful person for help, but he has no means to help because he has no intelligence. Thus the living entity is disappointed. This is like running after a mirage in the desert in an effort to find water. Such activities do not produce any tangible results. Due to being directed by the illusory energy, a conditioned soul suffers in so many ways.

TEXT 6

क्वचिद्वितोयाः सरितोऽभियाति
परस्परं चालषते निरन्धः ।
आसाद्य दावं क्वचिदग्नितप्तो
निर्विद्यते क्व च यक्षैर्हृतासुः ॥ ६ ॥

kvacid vitoyāḥ sarito'bhiyāti
parasparaṁ cālaṣate nirandhaḥ
āsādya dāvaṁ kvacid agni-tapto
nirvidyate kva ca yakṣair hṛtāsuḥ

kvacit—sometimes; *vitoyāḥ*—without depth to the water; *saritaḥ*—rivers; *abhiyāti*—he goes to bathe or jumps into; *parasparam*—one another; *ca*—and; *ālaṣate*—desires; *nirandhaḥ*—being with no stock of food; *āsādya*—experiencing; *dāvam*—a forest fire in family life; *kvacit*—sometimes; *agni-taptaḥ*—burned by fire; *nirvidyate*—is despondent; *kva*—somewhere; *ca*—and; *yakṣaiḥ*—by kings resembling rogues and thieves; *hṛta*—taken away; *asuḥ*—wealth, which is as dear as one's life.

TRANSLATION

Sometimes the conditioned soul jumps into a shallow river, or being short of food grains, he goes to beg food from people who are not at all

charitable. Sometimes he suffers from the burning heat of household life, which is like a forest fire, and sometimes he becomes sad to have his wealth, which is as dear as life, plundered by kings in the name of heavy income taxes.

PURPORT

When one is hot due to the scorching sun, one sometimes jumps into a river to gain relief. However, if the river is almost dried up and the water is too shallow, one may break his bones by jumping in. The conditioned soul is always experiencing miserable conditions. Sometimes his efforts to get help from friends are exactly like jumping into a dry river. By such actions, he does not derive any benefit. He only breaks his bones. Sometimes, suffering from a shortage of food, one may go to a person who is neither able to give charity nor willing to do so. Sometimes one is stationed in household life, which is compared to a forest fire (*saṁsāra-dāvānala-līḍha-loka*). When a man is heavily taxed by the government, he becomes very sad. Heavy taxation obliges one to hide his income, but despite this endeavor the government agents are often so vigilant and strong that they take all the money anyway, and the conditioned soul becomes very aggrieved.

Thus people are trying to become happy within the material world, but this is like trying to be happy in a forest fire. No one need go to a forest to set it ablaze: fire takes place automatically. Similarly, no one wants to be unhappy in family life or worldly life, but by the laws of nature unhappiness and distress are forced upon everyone. To become dependent on another's maintenance is very degrading; therefore, according to the Vedic system, everyone should live independently. Only the *śūdras* are unable to live independently. They are obliged to serve someone for maintenance. It is said in the *śāstras: kalau śūdra-sambhavāḥ.* In this age of Kali, everyone is dependent on another's mercy for the maintenance of the body; therefore everyone is classified as a *śūdra.* In the Twelfth Canto of *Śrīmad-Bhāgavatam* it is said that in Kali-yuga the government will levy taxes without reciprocally benefiting the citizens. *Anāvṛṣṭyā vinaṅkṣyanti durbhikṣa-kara-pīḍitāḥ.* In this age there will also be a shortage of rain; therefore a scarcity of food will arise, and the citizens will be very much harassed by government taxation. In this way the citizens will abandon their attempts to lead a peaceful life and will leave their homes and hearths and go to the forest in sheer disappointment.

TEXT 7

शूरैर्हृतस्वः क्व च निर्विण्णचेताः
शोचन् विमुह्यन्नुपयाति कश्मलम् ।
क्वचिच्च गन्धर्वपुरं प्रविष्टः
प्रमोदते निर्वृतवन्मुहूर्तम् ॥ ७ ॥

śūrair hṛta-svaḥ kva ca nirviṇṇa-cetāḥ
śocan vimuhyann upayāti kaśmalam
kvacic ca gandharva-puraṁ praviṣṭaḥ
pramodate nirvṛtavan muhūrtam

śūraiḥ—by very powerful enemies; *hṛta-svaḥ*—all of whose possessions have been stolen; *kva ca*—sometimes; *nirviṇṇa-cetāḥ*—very morose and aggrieved at heart; *śocan*—deeply lamenting; *vimuhyan*—becoming bewildered; *upayāti*—achieves; *kaśmalam*—unconsciousness; *kvacit*—sometimes; *ca*—also; *gandharva-puram*—an imaginary city in the forest; *praviṣṭaḥ*—having entered; *pramodate*—he enjoys; *nirvṛta-vat*—exactly like a person who has achieved success; *muhūrtam*—for a moment only.

TRANSLATION

Sometimes, being defeated or plundered by a superior, powerful agent, a living entity loses all his possessions. He then becomes very morose, and lamenting their loss, he sometimes becomes unconscious. Sometimes he imagines a great palatial city in which he desires to live happily with his family members and riches. He thinks himself fully satisfied if this is possible, but such so-called happiness continues only for a moment.

PURPORT

The word *gandharva-puram* is very significant in this verse. Sometimes in the forest a very big castle appears, and this is called a castle in the air. Actually this castle does not exist anywhere but in one's imagination. This is called *gandharva-pura.* In the material forest, the conditioned soul sometimes contemplates great castles and skyscrapers, and he wastes his energy for such things, hoping to live in them very peacefully with his family forever. However, the laws of nature do not allow this. When he enters such castles, he temporarily thinks that he is very happy, even though his happiness is impermanent. His happiness may last for a few years, but because the owner of the castle has to leave the castle at the time of death, everything is eventually lost. This is the way of worldly transactions. Such happiness is described by Vidyāpati as the happiness one derives upon seeing a drop of water in the desert. The desert is heated by scorching sunshine, and if we want to reduce the desert temperature, we need huge amounts of water—millions and millions of gallons. What effect will one drop have? Water certainly has value, but one drop of water cannot reduce the heat of the desert. In this material world everyone is ambitious, but the heat is very scorching. What will an imaginary castle in the air do to help? Śrīla Vidyāpati has therefore sung: *tāṭala saikate, vāri-bindu-sama, suta-mita-ramaṇi-samāje.* The happiness of family life, friends and society is compared to a drop of water in the scorching desert. The entire material world is busy trying to attain happiness because happiness is the prerogative of the living being. Unfortunately, due to falling in contact with the material world, the living entity simply struggles for existence. Even if one becomes happy for a while, a very powerful enemy may plunder everything. There are many instances in which big businessmen suddenly become paupers in the street. Yet the nature of material existence is such that foolish people are attracted to these transactions and they forget the real business of self-realization.

TEXT 8

चलन् क्वचित्कण्टकशर्कराङ्घ्रि-
नगारुरुक्षुर्विमना इवास्ते ।
पदे पदेऽभ्यन्तरवह्निनार्दितः
कौटुम्बिकः क्रुध्यति वै जनाय ॥ ८ ॥

calan kvacit kaṇṭaka-śarkarāṅghrir
nagārurukṣur vimanā ivāste
pade pade'bhyantara-vahninārditaḥ
kauṭumbikaḥ krudhyati vai janāya

calan—wandering; *kvacit*—sometimes; *kaṇṭaka-śarkara*—pierced by thorns and small stones; *aṅghriḥ*—whose feet; *naga*—the hills; *ārurukṣuḥ*—one desiring to climb; *vimanāḥ*—disappointed; *iva*—like; *āste*—becomes; *pade pade*—step by step; *abhyantara*—within the abdomen; *vahninā*—by the strong fire of appetite; *arditaḥ*—being fatigued and aggrieved; *kauṭumbikaḥ*—a person living with his family members; *krudhyati*—becomes angry; *vai*—certainly; *janāya*—at the family members.

TRANSLATION

Sometimes the merchant in the forest wants to climb the hills and mountains, but due to insufficient footwear, his feet are pricked by small stone fragments and by thorns on the mountain. Being pricked by them, he becomes very aggrieved. Sometimes a person who is very attached to his family becomes overwhelmed with hunger, and due to his miserable condition he becomes furious with his family members.

PURPORT

The ambitious conditioned soul wants to be very happy in this material world with his family, but he is compared to a traveler in the forest who desires to climb a hill full of thorns and small stones. As stated in the previous verse, the happiness derived from society, friendship and love is like a drop of water in the scorching heat of the desert. One may want to become very great and powerful in society, but this is like attempting to climb a hill full of thorns. Śrīla Viśvanātha Cakravartī Ṭhākura compares one's family to high mountains. Becoming happy in their association is like a hungry man's endeavoring to climb a mountain full of thorns. Almost 99.9 percent of the population is unhappy in family life, despite all the attempts being made to satisfy the family members. In the Western countries, due to the dissatisfaction of the family members, there is actually no family life. There are many cases of divorce, and out of dissatisfaction, the children leave the protection of their parents. Especially in this age of Kali, family life is being reduced. Everyone is becoming self-centered because that is the law of nature. Even if one has sufficient money to maintain a family, the situation is such that no one is happy in family life. Consequently according to the *varṇāśrama* institution, one has to retire from family life in middle age: *pañcāśordhvaṁ vanaṁ vrajet.* One should voluntarily retire from family life at the age of fifty and go to Vṛndāvana or a forest. This is recommended by Śrīla Prahlāda Mahārāja (*Bhāg.* 7.5.5):

tat sādhu manye'sura-varya dehināṁ
sadā samudvigna-dhiyām asad-grahāt
hitvātma-pātaṁ gṛham andha-kūpaṁ
vanaṁ gato yad dharim āśrayeta

There is no benefit in transferring from one forest to another. One must go to the Vṛndāvana forest and take shelter of Govinda. That will make one happy. The International Society for Krishna Consciousness is therefore constructing a Kṛṣṇa-Balarāma temple to invite its members as well as outsiders to come and live peacefully in a spiritual atmosphere. That will help one become elevated to the transcendental world and return home, back to Godhead. Another sentence in this verse is very significant: *kauṭumbikaḥ krudhyati vai janāya.* When one's mind is disturbed in so many ways, he satisfies himself by becoming angry with his poor wife and children. The wife and children are naturally dependent on the father, but the father, being unable to maintain the family properly, becomes mentally distressed and therefore chastises the family members unnecessarily. As stated in *Śrīmad-Bhāgavatam* (12.2.9): *ācchinna-dāra-draviṇā yāsyanti giri-kānanam.* Being disgusted with family life, one separates from the family by divorce or some other means. If one has to separate, why not separate willingly? Systematic separation is better than forced separation. Forced separation cannot make anyone happy, but by mutual consent or by the Vedic arrangement one must separate from his family affairs at a certain age and fully depend on Kṛṣṇa. This makes one's life successful.

TEXT 9

क्वचिन्निगीर्णोऽजगराहिना जनो
नावैति किञ्चिद्विपिनेऽपविद्धः ।
दष्टः स्म शेते क्व च दन्दशूकै-
रन्धोऽन्धकूपे पतितस्तमिस्रे ॥९॥

kvacin nigīrṇo'jagarāhinā jano
nāvaiti kiñcid vipine'paviddhaḥ
daṣṭaḥ sma śete kva ca danda-śūkair
andho'ndha-kūpe patitas tamisre

kvacit—sometimes; *nigīrṇaḥ*—being swallowed; *ajagara-ahinā*—by the great snake known as the python; *janaḥ*—the conditioned soul; *na*—not; *avaiti*—understands; *kiñcit*—anything; *vipine*—in the forest; *apaviddhaḥ*—pierced by arrows of suffering; *daṣṭaḥ*—being bitten; *sma*—indeed; *śete*—lies down; *kva ca*—sometimes; *danda-śūkaiḥ*—by other kinds of snakes; *andhaḥ*—blind; *andha-kūpe*—in a blind well; *patitaḥ*—fallen; *tamisre*—in a hellish condition of life.

TRANSLATION

The conditioned soul in the material forest is sometimes swallowed by a python or crushed. At such a time he is left lying in the forest like a dead

person, devoid of consciousness and knowledge. Sometimes other poisonous snakes bite him. Being blind to his consciousness, he falls down into a dark well of hellish life with no hope of being rescued.

PURPORT

When one becomes unconscious due to being bitten by a snake, one cannot understand what is taking place outside the body. This unconscious condition is the condition of deep sleep. Similarly, the conditioned soul is actually sleeping on the lap of the illusory energy. Bhaktivinoda Ṭhākura has sung, *kota nidrā yāo māyā-piśācīra kole:* "O living entity, how long will you sleep in this condition on the lap of the illusory energy?" People do not understand that they are actually sleeping in this material world, being devoid of knowledge of spiritual life. Caitanya Mahāprabhu therefore says:

enechi auṣadhi māyā nāśibāra lāgi'
hari-nāma-mahā-mantra lao tumi māgi'

"I have brought medicine to awaken every living being from perpetual sleep. Please receive the holy name of the Lord, the Hare Kṛṣṇa *mahā-mantra,* and awaken." The *Kaṭha Upaniṣad* (1.3.14) also says, *uttiṣṭha jāgrata prāpya varān nibodhata:* "O living entity, you are sleeping in this material world. Please get up and take advantage of your human form of life." The sleeping condition means loss of all knowledge. In *Bhagavad-gītā* (2.69) it is also said, *yā niśā sarva-bhūtānāṁ tasyāṁ jāgarti saṁyamī:* "What is night for all beings is the time of awakening for the self-controlled." Even in the higher planets, everyone is under the spell of the illusory energy. No one is really interested in the real values of life. The sleeping condition, called *kāla-sarpa* (the time factor), keeps the conditioned soul in a state of ignorance, and therefore pure consciousness is lost. In the forest there are many blind wells, and if one falls down in one there is no chance of being rescued. In a state of sleep, one remains perpetually bitten by some animals, especially snakes.

TEXT 10

कर्हि स्म चित्क्षुद्ररसान् विचिन्वं-
स्तन्मक्षिकाभिर्व्यथितो विमानः ।
तत्रातिकृच्छ्रात्प्रतिलब्धमानो
बलाद्विलुम्पन्त्यथ तं ततोऽन्ये ॥१०॥

karhi sma cit kṣudra-rasān vicinvaṁs
tan-makṣikābhir vyathito vimānaḥ
tatrāti-kṛcchrāt pratilabdhamāno
balād vilumpanty atha taṁ tato 'nye

karhi sma cit—sometimes; *kṣudra*—very insignificant; *rasān*—sexual enjoyment; *vicinvan*—searching for; *tat*—of those women; *makṣikābhiḥ*—by honeybees, or the husbands or family members; *vyathitaḥ*—very much aggrieved; *vimānaḥ*—insulted; *tatra*—in that; *ati*—very much; *kṛcchrāt*—with difficulty because of spending money; *pratilabdhamānaḥ*—obtaining sexual enjoyment; *balāt*—by force; *vilumpanti*—kidnapped; *atha*—thereafter; *tam*—the object of sense enjoyment (the woman); *tataḥ*—from him; *anye*—another debauchee.

TRANSLATION

Sometimes, in order to have a little insignificant sex enjoyment, one searches after debauched women. In this attempt, one is insulted and chastised by the women's kinsmen. This is like going to take honey from a beehive and being attacked by the bees. Sometimes, after spending lots of money, one may acquire another woman for some extra sense enjoyment. Unfortunately, the object of sense enjoyment, the woman, is taken away or kidnapped by another debauchee.

PURPORT

In a great forest, honeycombs are very important. People often go there to collect honey from the combs, and sometimes the bees attack and punish them. In human society, those who are not Kṛṣṇa conscious remain in the forest of material life simply for the honey of sex life. Such debauchees are not at all satisfied with one wife. They want many women. Day after day, with great difficulty, they try to secure such women, and sometimes, while trying to taste this kind of honey, one is attacked by a woman's kinsmen and chastised very heavily. By bribing others, one may secure another woman for enjoyment, yet another debauchee may kidnap her or offer her something better. This woman hunting is going on in the forest of the material world, sometimes legally, and sometimes illegally. Consequently in this Kṛṣṇa consciousness movement the devotees are forbidden to have illicit sex. Thus they avoid so many difficulties. One should remain satisfied with one woman, being duly married. One can satisfy one's lusty desires with his wife without creating disturbances in society and being punished for doing so.

TEXT 11

क्वचिच्च शीतातपवातवर्ष-
प्रतिक्रियां कर्तुमनीश आस्ते ।
क्वचिन्मिथो विपणन् यच्च किञ्चिद्
विद्वेषमृच्छत्युत वित्तशाठ्यात् ॥११॥

kvacic ca śītātapa-vāta-varṣa-
pratikriyāṁ kartum anīśa āste
kvacin mitho vipaṇan yac ca kiñcid
vidveṣam ṛcchaty uta vitta-śāṭhyāt

kvacit—sometimes; *ca*—also; *śīta-ātapa-vāta-varṣa*—of freezing cold, scorching heat, strong wind and excessive rainfall; *pratikriyām*—counteraction; *kartum*—to do; *anīśaḥ*—being unable; *āste*—remains in misery; *kvacit*—sometimes; *mithaḥ*—one another; *vipaṇan*—selling; *yat ca*—whatever; *kiñcit*—a little bit; *vidveṣam*—mutual enmity; *ṛcchati*—obtain; *uta*—it is so said; *vitta-śāṭhyāt*—because of cheating one another merely for money.

TRANSLATION

Sometimes the living entity is busy counteracting the natural disturbances of freezing cold, scorching heat, strong wind, excessive rainfall and so forth. When he is unable to do so, he becomes very unhappy. Sometimes he is cheated in business transactions one after another. In this way, by cheating, living entities create enmity among themselves.

PURPORT

This is an example of the struggle for existence, the attempt to counteract the onslaught of material nature. This creates enmity in society, and consequently society is filled with envious people. One person is envious of another, and this is the way of the material world. The Kṛṣṇa consciousness movement aims at creating an atmosphere of non-envy. Of course it is not possible for everyone to become Kṛṣṇa conscious, but the Kṛṣṇa consciousness movement can create an exemplary society wherein there is no envy.

TEXT 12

क्वचित्क्वचित्क्षीणधनस्तु तस्मिन्
शय्यासनस्थानविहारहीनः ।

याचन् परादप्रतिलब्धकामः
पारक्यदृष्टिर्लभतेऽवमानम् ॥१२॥

kvacit kvacit kṣīṇa-dhanas tu tasmin
śayyāsana-sthāna-vihāra-hīnaḥ
yācan parād apratilabdha-kāmaḥ
pārakya-dṛṣṭir labhate'vamānam

kvacit kvacit—sometimes; *kṣīṇa-dhanaḥ*—becoming bereft of all riches; *tu*—but; *tasmin*—in that forest; *śayyā*—of bedding for lying down; *āsana*—of a sitting place; *sthāna*—of a residential house; *vihāra*—of enjoyment with a family; *hīnaḥ*—being bereft; *yācan*—begging; *parāt*—from others (friends and relatives); *apratilabdha-kāmaḥ*—not getting his desires fulfilled; *pārakya-dṛṣṭiḥ*—becomes greedy for the wealth of others; *labhate*—he obtains; *avamānam*—dishonor.

TRANSLATION

On the forest path of material existence, sometimes a person is without wealth and due to this does not have a proper home, bed or sitting place, nor proper family enjoyment. He therefore goes to beg money from others, but when his desires are not fulfilled by begging, he wants to borrow or steal the property of others. Thus he is insulted in society.

PURPORT

The principles of beg, borrow or steal are very appropriate in this material world. When one is in want, he begs, borrows or steals. If begging is unsuccessful, he borrows. If he cannot pay, he steals, and when he is caught, he is insulted. This is the law of material existence. No one can live here very honestly; therefore by trickery, cheating, begging, borrowing or stealing, one tries to satisfy his senses. Thus no one in this material world is living peacefully.

TEXT 13

अन्योन्यवित्तव्यतिषङ्गवृद्ध-
वैरानुबन्धो विवहन्मिथश्च ।
अध्वन्यमुष्मिन्नुरुकृच्छ्रवित्त-
बाधोपसर्गैर्विहरन् विपन्नः ॥१३॥

anyonya-vitta-vyatiṣaṅga-vṛddha-
vairānubandho vivahan mithaś ca

adhvany amuṣminn uru-kṛcchra-vitta-
bādhopasargair viharan vipannaḥ

anyonya—with one another; *vitta-vyatiṣaṅga*—by monetary transactions; *vṛddha*—increased; *vaira-anubandhaḥ*—one is encumbered by enmity; *vivahan*—sometimes marrying; *mithaḥ*—one another; *ca*—and; *adhvani*—on the path of material existence; *amuṣmin*—that; *uru-kṛcchra*—by great difficulties; *vitta-bādha*—by scarcity of money; *upasargaiḥ*—by diseases; *viharan*—wandering; *vipannaḥ*—one becomes fully embarrassed.

TRANSLATION

Due to monetary transactions, relationships become very strained and end in enmity. Sometimes the husband and wife walk on the path of material progress, and to maintain their relationship they work very hard. Sometimes due to scarcity of money or due to diseased conditions, they are embarrassed and almost die.

PURPORT

In this material world, there are many transactions between peoples and societies as well as between nations, but gradually these end in enmity between the two parties. Similarly, in the marriage relationship, monetary transactions are sometimes overpowered by the dangerous conditions of material life. One then becomes diseased or monetarily embarrassed. In the modern age most countries have developed economically, but due to business exchanges, relationships seem to be strained. Finally wars are declared between nations, and as a result of these upheavals there is destruction all over the world, and people suffer heavily.

TEXT 14

तांस्तान् विपन्नान् स हि तत्र तत्र
विहाय जातं परिगृह्य सार्थः ।
आवर्ततेऽद्यापि न कश्चिदत्र
वीराध्वनः पारमुपैति योगम् ॥१४॥

tāṁs tān vipannān sa hi tatra tatra
vihāya jātaṁ parigṛhya sārthaḥ
āvartate'dyāpi na kaścid atra
vīrādhvanaḥ pāram upaiti yogam

tān tān—all of them; *vipannān*—embarrassed in various ways; *saḥ*—the living being; *hi*—certainly; *tatra tatra*—here and there; *vihāya*—giving up; *jātam*—those who are newly born; *parigṛhya*—taking; *sa-arthaḥ*—the living being searching for his own interest; *āvartate*—wanders in this forest; *adya api*—even until now; *na*—not; *kaścit*—any of them; *atra*—here in this forest; *vīra*—O hero; *adhvanaḥ*—of the path of material life; *pāram*—the ultimate end; *upaiti*—gets; *yogam*—the process of devotional service to the Supreme Personality of Godhead.

TRANSLATION

My dear King, on the forest path of material life, first a person is bereft of his father and mother, and after their death he becomes attached to his newly born children. In this way he wanders on the path of material progress and is eventually embarrassed. Nonetheless, no one knows how to get out of this, even up to the moment of death.

PURPORT

In this material world, family life is an institution of sex. *Yan maithunādi-gṛhamedhi-sukham* (*Bhāg.* 7.9.45). Through sex, the father and mother beget children, and the children get married and go down the same path of sexual life. After the death of the father and mother, the children get married and beget their own children. Thus generation after generation these things go on in the same way without anyone's attaining liberation from the embarrassment of material life. No one accepts the spiritual processes of knowledge and renunciation, which end in *bhakti-yoga.* Actually human life is meant for *jñāna* and *vairāgya,* knowledge and renunciation. Through these one can attain the platform of devotional service. Unfortunately people in this age avoid the association of liberated people (*sādhu-saṅga*) and continue in their stereotyped way of family life. Thus they are embarrassed by the exchange of money and sex.

TEXT 15

मनस्विनो निर्जितदिग्गजेन्द्रा
ममेति सर्वे भुवि बद्धवैराः ।
मृधे शयीरन्न तु तद्व्रजन्ति
यन्न्यस्तदण्डो गतवैरोऽभियाति ॥१५॥

manasvino nirjita-dig-gajendrā
mameti sarve bhuvi baddha-vairāḥ

mṛdhe śayīran na tu tad vrajanti
yan nyasta-daṇḍo gata-vairo 'bhiyāti

manasvinaḥ—very great heroes (mental speculators); *nirjita-dik-gajendrāḥ*—who have conquered many other heroes as powerful as elephants; *mama*—my (my land, my country, my family, my community, my religion); *iti*—thus; *sarve*—all (great political, social and religious leaders); *bhuvi*—in this world; *baddha-vairāḥ*—who have created enmity among themselves; *mṛdhe*—in battle; *śayīran*—fall dead on the ground; *na*—not; *tu*—but; *tat*—the abode of the Supreme Personality of Godhead; *vrajanti*—approach; *yat*—which; *nyasta-daṇḍaḥ*—a *sannyāsī; gata-vairaḥ*—who has no enmity throughout the whole world; *abhiyāti*—attains that perfection.

TRANSLATION

There were and are many political and social heroes who have conquered enemies of equal power, yet due to their ignorance in believing that the land is theirs, they fight one another and lay down their lives in battle. They are not able to take up the spiritual path accepted by those in the renounced order. Although they are big heroes and political leaders, they cannot take to the path of spiritual realization.

PURPORT

Big political leaders might be able to conquer equally powerful political enemies, but unfortunately they cannot subdue their strong senses, the enemies that always accompany them. Not being able to conquer these nearby enemies, they simply try to conquer other enemies, and ultimately they die in the struggle for existence. They do not take to the path of spiritual realization or become *sannyāsīs.* Sometimes these big leaders take up the guise of a *sannyāsī* and call themselves *mahātmās,* but their only business is conquering their political enemies. Because they spoil their lives with the illusion of "this is my land and my family," they cannot progress spiritually and attain liberation from the clutches of *māyā.*

TEXT 16

प्रसज्जति क्वापि लताभुजाश्रय-
स्तदाश्रयाव्यक्तपदद्विजस्पृहः ।
क्वचित्कदाचिद्धरिचक्रतस्त्रसन्
सख्यं विधत्ते बककङ्कगृध्रैः ॥१६॥

prasajjati kvāpi latā-bhujāśrayas
tad-āśrayāvyakta-pada-dvija-spṛhaḥ
kvacit kadācid dhari-cakratas trasan
sakhyaṁ vidhatte baka-kaṅka-gṛdhraiḥ

prasajjati—becomes more and more attached; *kvāpi*—sometimes; *latā-bhuja-āśrayaḥ*—who takes shelter of the soft arms of his beautiful wife which are like creepers; *tat-āśraya*—who are sheltered by such creepers; *avyakta-pada*—who sing unclear songs; *dvija-spṛhaḥ*—desiring to hear birds; *kvacit*—sometimes; *kadācit*—somewhere; *hari-cakrataḥ trasan*—being afraid of the roaring sound of a lion; *sakhyam*—friendship; *vidhatte*—makes; *baka-kaṅka-gṛdhraiḥ*—with cranes, herons and vultures.

TRANSLATION

Sometimes the living entity in the forest of material existence takes shelter of creepers and desires to hear the chirping of the birds in those creepers. Being afraid of roaring lions in the forest, he makes friends with cranes, herons and vultures.

PURPORT

In the forest of the material world there are many animals and birds, trees and creepers. Sometimes the living entity wants to take shelter of the creepers; in other words, he wants to be happy by being embraced by the creeperlike arms of his wife. Within the creepers there are many chirping birds; this indicates that he wants to satisfy himself by hearing the sweet voice of his wife. In old age, however, he sometimes becomes afraid of imminent death, which is compared to a roaring lion. To save himself from the lion's attack, he takes shelter of some bogus *svāmīs, yogīs,* incarnations, pretenders and cheaters. Being misled by the illusory energy in this way, he spoils his life. It is said, *Hariṁ vinā naiva sṛtiṁ taranti:* no one can be saved from the imminent danger of death without taking shelter of the Supreme Personality of Godhead. The word *hari* indicates the lion as well as the Supreme Lord. To be saved from the hands of *Hari,* the lion of death, one must take shelter of the supreme *Hari,* the Supreme Personality of Godhead. People with a poor fund of knowledge take shelter of nondevotee cheaters and pretenders in order to be saved from the clutches of death. In the forest of the material world, the living entity first of all wants to be very happy by taking shelter of the creeperlike arms of his wife and hearing her sweet voice. Later, he sometimes takes shelter of so-called *gurus* and *sādhus* who are like crane, herons and vultures. Thus he is cheated both ways by not taking shelter of the Supreme Lord.

TEXT 17

तैर्वञ्चितो हंसकुलं समाविश-
न्नरोचयन् शीलमुपैति वानरान् ।
तज्जातिरासेन सुनिर्वृतेन्द्रियः
परस्परोद्वीक्षणविस्मृतावधिः ॥१७॥

tair vañcito haṁsa-kulaṁ samāviśann
arocayan śīlam upaiti vānarān
taj-jāti-rāsena sunirvṛtendriyaḥ
parasparodvīkṣaṇa-vismṛtāvadhiḥ

taiḥ—by them (the cheaters and pretenders, the so-called *yogīs, svāmīs,* incarnations and *gurus*); *vañcitaḥ*—being cheated; *haṁsa-kulam*—the association of great *paramahaṁsas,* or devotees; *samāviśan*—contacting; *arocayan*—not being satisfied with; *śīlam*—their behavior; *upaiti*—approaches; *vānarān*—the monkeys, which are all debauchees with no good character; *tat-jāti-rāsena*—by sense gratification in the association of such debauchees; *sunirvṛta-indriyaḥ*—being very satisfied with getting the opportunity of sense gratification; *paraspara*—of one another; *udvīkṣaṇa*—by seeing the faces; *vismṛta*—who has forgotten; *avadhiḥ*—the end of life.

TRANSLATION

Being cheated by them, the living entity in the forest of the material world tries to give up the association of these so-called yogīs, svāmīs and incarnations and come to the association of real devotees, but due to misfortune he cannot follow the instructions of the spiritual master or advanced devotees; therefore he gives up their company and again returns to the association of monkeys who are simply interested in sense gratification and women. He derives satisfaction by associating with sense gratifiers and enjoying sex and intoxication. In this way he spoils his life simply by indulging in sex and intoxication. Looking into the faces of other sense gratifiers, he becomes forgetful and thus approaches death.

PURPORT

Sometimes a foolish person becomes disgusted with bad association and comes to the association of devotees and *brāhmaṇas* and takes initiation from a spiritual master. As advised by the spiritual master, he tries to follow the regulative principles, but due to misfortune he cannot follow the instructions of the spiritual master. He therefore gives up the company of devotees and goes to associate with simian people who are simply interested in sex and intoxication. Those who are so-called spiritualists are compared to monkeys. Outwardly, monkeys sometimes resemble *sādhus* because they live naked in the forest and pick fruits, but their only desire is to keep many female monkeys and enjoy sex life. Sometimes so-called spiritualists seeking a spiritual life come to associate with Kṛṣṇa conscious devotees, but they cannot execute the regulative principles or follow the path of spiritual life. Consequently they leave the association of devotees and go to associate with sense gratifiers, who are compared to monkeys. Again they revive their sex and intoxication, and looking at one another's faces, they are thus satisfied. In this way they pass their lives up to the point of death.

TEXT 18

द्रुमेषु रंस्यन् सुतदारवत्सलो
व्यवायदीनो विवशः स्वबन्धने ।
क्वचित्प्रमादाद्गिरिकन्दरे पतन्
वल्लीं गृहीत्वा गजभीत आस्थितः ॥१८॥

drumeṣu raṁsyan suta-dāra-vatsalo
vyavāya-dīno vivaśaḥ sva-bandhane
kvacit pramādād giri-kandare patan
vallīṁ gṛhītvā gaja-bhīta āsthitaḥ

drumeṣu—in the trees (or in houses standing like trees in which monkeys jump from one branch to another); *raṁsyan*—enjoying; *suta-dāra-vatsalaḥ*—being attached to the children and wife; *vyavāya-dīnaḥ*—who is poor-hearted because of acting on the platform of sex desire; *vivaśaḥ*—unable to give up; *sva-bandhane*—in bondage to the reactions of one's own activities; *kvacit*—sometimes; *pramādāt*—from fear of imminent death; *giri-kandare*—in a cave in a mountain; *patan*—falling down; *vallīm*—the branches of a creeper; *gṛhītvā*—capturing; *gaja-bhītaḥ*—being afraid of the elephant of death; *āsthitaḥ*—remains in that position.

TRANSLATION

When the living entity becomes exactly like a monkey jumping from one branch to another, he remains in the tree of household life without

any profit but sex. Thus he is kicked by his wife just like the he-ass. Unable to gain release, he remains helplessly in that position. Sometimes he falls victim to an incurable disease, which is like falling into a mountain cave. He becomes afraid of death, which is like the elephant in the back of that cave, and he remains stranded, grasping at the twigs and branches of a creeper.

PURPORT

The precarious condition of a householder's life is described herein. A householder's life is full of misery, and the only attraction is sex with the wife who kicks him during sexual intercourse, just as the she-ass does her mate. Due to continuous sex life, he falls victim to many incurable diseases. At that time, being afraid of death, which is like an elephant, he remains hanging from the twigs and branches of the tree, just like a monkey.

TEXT 19

अतः कथञ्चित्स विमुक्त आपदः
पुनश्च सार्थं प्रविशत्यरिन्दम ।
अध्वन्यमुष्मिन्नजया निवेशितो
भ्रमञ्जनोऽद्यापि न वेद कश्चन ॥१९॥

ataḥ kathañcit sa vimukta āpadaḥ
punaś ca sārthaṁ praviśaty arindama
adhvany amuṣminn ajayā niveśito
bhramañ jano'dyāpi na veda kaścana

ataḥ—from this; *kathañcit*—somehow; *saḥ*—he; *vimuktaḥ*—liberated; *āpadaḥ*—from the danger; *punaḥ ca*—again; *sa-artham*—taking interest in that life; *praviśati*—begins; *arim-dama*—O King, killer of the enemies; *adhvani*—on the path of enjoyment; *amuṣmin*—that; *ajayā*—by the influence of the illusory energy; *niveśitaḥ*—being absorbed; *bhraman*—traveling; *janaḥ*—the conditioned soul; *adya api*—even up to death; *na veda*—does not understand; *kaścana*—anything.

TRANSLATION

O killer of enemies, Mahārāja Rahūgaṇa, if the conditioned soul somehow or other gets out of his dangerous position, he again returns to his home to enjoy sex life, for that is the way of attachment. Thus, under

the spell of the Lord's material energy, he continues to loiter in the forest of material existence. He does not discover his real interest even at the point of death.

PURPORT

This is the way of material life. When one is captured by sexual attraction, he becomes implicated in so many ways and cannot understand the real aim of life. Therefore *Śrīmad-Bhāgavatam* (7.5.31) says, *na te viduḥ svārtha-gatiṁ hi viṣṇum:* generally people do not understand the ultimate goal of life. As stated in the *Vedas, oṁ tad viṣṇoḥ paramaṁ padaṁ sadā paśyanti sūrayaḥ:* those who are spiritually advanced simply look to the lotus feet of Viṣṇu. The conditioned soul, however, not being interested in reviving his relationship with Viṣṇu, becomes captivated by material activities and remains in everlasting bondage, being misled by so-called leaders.

TEXT 20

रहूगण त्वमपि ह्यध्वनोऽस्य
संन्यस्तदण्डः कृतभूतमैत्रः ।
असज्जितात्मा हरिसेवया शितं
ज्ञानासिमादाय तरातिपारम् ॥२०॥

rahūgaṇa tvam api hy adhvano'sya
sannyasta-daṇḍaḥ kṛta-bhūta-maitraḥ
asaj-jitātmā hari-sevayā śitaṁ
jñānāsim ādāya tarāti-pāram

rahūgaṇa—O King Rahūgaṇa; *tvam*—you; *api*—also; *hi*—certainly; *adhvanaḥ*—of the path of material existence; *asya*—this; *sannyasta-daṇḍaḥ*—having given up the king's rod for punishing criminals; *kṛta-bhūta-maitraḥ*—having become friendly to everyone; *asat-jita-ātmā*—whose mind is not attracted to the material pleasure of life; *hari-sevayā*—by the means of loving service to the Supreme Lord; *śitam*—sharpened; *jñāna-asim*—the sword of knowledge; *ādāya*—taking in hand; *tara*—cross over; *ati-pāram*—to the ultimate end of spiritual existence.

TRANSLATION

My dear King Rahūgaṇa, you are also a victim of the external energy, being situated on the path of attraction to material pleasure. So that you

may become an equal friend to all living entities, I now advise you to give up your kingly position and the rod by which you punish criminals. Give up attraction to the sense objects and take up the sword of knowledge sharpened by devotional service. Then you will be able to cut the hard knot of illusory energy and cross to the other side of the ocean of nescience.

PURPORT

In *Bhagavad-gītā* Lord Kṛṣṇa compares the material world to a tree of illusion from which one must cut oneself free:

na rūpam asyeha tathopalabhyate
nānto na cādir na ca sampratiṣṭhā
aśvattham enaṁ suvirūḍha-mūlam
asaṅga-śastreṇa dṛḍhena chittvā

tataḥ padaṁ tat parimārgitavyaṁ
yasmin gatā na nivartanti bhūyaḥ
tam eva cādyaṁ puruṣaṁ prapadye
yataḥ pravṛttiḥ prasṛtā purāṇī

"The real form of this tree cannot be perceived in this world. No one can understand where it ends, where it begins, or where its foundation is. But with determination, one must cut down this tree with the weapon of detachment. So doing, one must seek that place from which, having once gone, one never returns, and there surrender to that Supreme Personality of Godhead from whom everything has begun and in whom everything is abiding since time immemorial." (Bg. 15.3–4)

TEXT 21

राजोवाच
अहो नृजन्माखिलजन्मशोभनं
किं जन्मभिस्त्वपरैरप्यमुष्मिन् ।
न यद्धृषीकेशयशःकृतात्मनां
महात्मनां वः प्रचुरः समागमः ॥२१॥

rājovāca
aho nṛ-janmākhila-janma-śobhanaṁ
kiṁ janmabhis tv aparair apy amuṣmin

na yad dhṛṣīkeśa-yaśaḥ-kṛtātmanāṁ
mahātmanāṁ vaḥ pracuraḥ samāgamaḥ

rājā uvāca—King Rahūgaṇa said; *aho*—alas; *nṛ-janma*—you who have taken birth as a human being; *akhila-janma-śobhanam*—the best of all species of life; *kim*—what need; *janmabhiḥ*—with births in a higher species like the demigods in the heavenly planets; *tu*—but; *aparaiḥ*—not superior; *api*—indeed; *amuṣmin*—in the next birth; *na*—not; *yat*—which; *hṛṣīkeśa-yaśaḥ*—by the glories of the Supreme Personality of Godhead, Hṛṣīkeśa, the master of all senses; *kṛta-ātmanām*—of those whose hearts are purified; *mahā-ātmanām*—who are actually great souls; *vaḥ*—of us; *pracuraḥ*—abundant; *samāgamaḥ*—the association.

TRANSLATION

King Rahūgaṇa said: This birth as a human being is the best of all. Even birth among the demigods in the heavenly planets is not as glorious as birth as a human being on this earth. What is the use of the exalted position of a demigod? In the heavenly planets, due to profuse material comforts, there is no possibility of associating with devotees.

PURPORT

Human birth is a great opportunity for self-realization. One may take birth in a high planetary system among the demigods, but due to the profusion of material comforts, one cannot gain release from material bondage. Even on this earth those who are very opulent do not generally care to take to Kṛṣṇa consciousness. An intelligent person actually interested in getting freed from the material clutches must associate with pure devotees. By such association, one can gradually become detached from the material attraction of money and women. Money and women are the basic principles of material attachment. Śrī Caitanya Mahāprabhu therefore advised those who are actually serious about returning back to Godhead to give up money and women in order to be fit to enter the kingdom of God. Money and women can be fully utilized in the service of the Lord, and one who can utilize them in this way can become freed from material bondage. *Satāṁ prasaṅgān mama vīrya-saṁvido bhavanti hṛt-karṇa-rasāyanāḥ kathāḥ* (*Bhāg.* 3.25.25). Only in the association of devotees can one relish the glorification of the Supreme Personality of Godhead. Just through a little association with a pure devotee, one can become successful in his journey back to Godhead.

TEXT 22

न ह्यद्भुतं त्वच्चरणाब्जरेणुभि-
र्हतांहसो भक्तिरधोक्षजेऽमला ।
मौहूर्तिकाद्यस्य समागमाच्च मे
दुस्तर्कमूलोऽपहतोऽविवेकः ॥२२॥

na hy adbhutaṁ tvac-caraṇābja-reṇubhir
hatāṁhaso bhaktir adhokṣaje 'malā
mauhūrtikād yasya samāgamāc ca me
dustarka-mūlo 'pahato 'vivekaḥ

na—not; *hi*—certainly; *adbhutam*—wonderful; *tvat-caraṇa-abja-reṇubhiḥ*—by the dust of your lotus feet; *hata-aṁhasaḥ*—who am completely freed from the reactions of sinful life; *bhaktiḥ*—love and devotion; *adhokṣaje*—unto the Supreme Personality of Godhead, who is beyond the capture of experimental knowledge; *amalā*—completely freed from all material contamination; *mauhūrtikāt*—momentary; *yasya*—of whom; *samāgamāt*—by the visit and association; *ca*—also; *me*—my; *dustarka*—of false arguments; *mūlaḥ*—the root; *apahataḥ*—completely vanquished; *avivekaḥ*—not discriminating.

TRANSLATION

It is not at all wonderful that simply by being covered by the dust of your lotus feet, one immediately attains the platform of pure devotional service to Adhokṣaja, which is not available even to great demigods like Brahmā. By associating with you just for a moment, I am now freed from all argument, false prestige and lack of discrimination, which are the roots of entanglement in the material world. Now I am free from all these problems.

PURPORT

Association with pure devotees certainly frees one from the material clutches. This is certainly true of King Rahūgaṇa's association with Jaḍa Bharata. King Rahūgaṇa was immediately freed from the misgivings of material association. The arguments offered by pure devotees to their disciples are so convincing that even a dull-headed disciple is immediately enlightened with spiritual knowledge.

TEXT 23

नमो महद्भ्योऽस्तु नमः शिशुभ्यो
नमो युवभ्यो नम आवटुभ्यः ।
ये ब्राह्मणा गामवधूतलिङ्गा-
श्चरन्ति तेभ्यः शिवमस्तु राज्ञाम् ॥२३॥

namo mahadbhyo 'stu namaḥ śiśubhyo
namo yuvabhyo nama āvaṭubhyaḥ
ye brāhmaṇā gām avadhūta-liṅgāś
caranti tebhyaḥ śivam astu rājñām

namaḥ—all obeisances; *mahadbhyaḥ*—unto the great personalities; *astu*—let there be; *namaḥ*—my obeisances; *śiśubhyaḥ*—unto those great personalities who appear as boys; *namaḥ*—respectful obeisances; *yuvabhyaḥ*—unto those who appear as young men; *namaḥ*—respectful obeisances; *ā-vaṭubhyaḥ*—unto those who appear as children; *ye*—all those who; *brāhmaṇāḥ*—self-realized in transcendental knowledge; *gām*—the earth; *avadhūta-liṅgāḥ*—who remain hidden under different bodily guises; *caranti*—they traverse; *tebhyaḥ*—from them; *śivam astu*—let there be all good fortune; *rājñām*—unto the royal dynasties or kings (who are always very puffed up).

TRANSLATION

I offer my respectful obeisances unto the great personalities, whether they walk on the earth's surface as children, young boys, avadhūtas or great brāhmaṇas. Even if they are hidden under different guises, I offer my respects to all of them. By their mercy, may there be good fortune in the royal dynasties that are always offending them.

PURPORT

King Rahūgaṇa was very repentant because he had forced Jaḍa Bharata to carry his palanquin. He therefore began offering prayers to all kinds of *brāhmaṇas* and self-realized persons, even though they might be playing like children or hiding in some guises. The four Kumāras walked everywhere in the guise of five-year-old boys, and similarly there are many *brāhmaṇas,* knowers of Brahman, who traverse the globe either as young men, children or *avadhūtas.* Being puffed up due to their position, the royal dynasties generally offend these great personalities. Therefore King Rahūgaṇa began to offer his respectful obeisances unto them so that the offensive royal dynasties might not glide down into a hellish condition. If one offends a great personality, the Supreme Personality of Godhead does not excuse one, although the great personalities themselves might not take offense. Mahārāja Ambarīṣa was offended by Durvāsā, who even approached Lord Viṣṇu for pardon. Lord Viṣṇu would not grant him pardon; therefore he had to fall down at the lotus feet of Mahārāja Ambarīṣa, even though Mahārāja Ambarīṣa was a *kṣatriya-gṛhastha.* One should be very careful not to offend the lotus feet of Vaiṣṇavas and *brāhmaṇas.*

TEXT 24

श्रीशुक उवाच

इत्येवमुत्तरामातः स वै ब्रह्मर्षिसुतः सिन्धुपतय आत्मसतत्त्वं विगणयतः परानुभावः परमकारुणिकतयोपदिश्य रहूगणेन सकरुणमभिवन्दित चरण आपूर्णार्णव इव निभृतकरणोर्म्याशयो धरणिमिमां विचचार ॥२४॥

śrī-śuka uvāca

ity evam uttarā-mātaḥ sa vai brahmarṣi-sutaḥ sindhu-pataya ātma-satattvaṁ vigaṇayataḥ parānubhāvaḥ parama-kāruṇikatayopadiśya rahūgaṇena sakaruṇam abhivandita-caraṇa āpūrṇārṇava iva nibhṛta-karaṇormy-āśayo dharaṇim imāṁ vicacāra.

śrī-śukaḥ uvāca—Śrī Śukadeva Gosvāmī said; *iti evam*—in this way; *uttarā-mātaḥ*—O Mahārāja Parīkṣit, son of mother Uttarā; *saḥ*—that *brāhmaṇa; vai*—indeed; *brahma-ṛṣi-sutaḥ*—Jaḍa Bharata, the son of a highly educated *brāhmaṇa; sindhu-pataye*—unto the king of the province of Sindhu; *ātma-sa-tattvam*—the actual constitutional position of the soul; *vigaṇayataḥ*—although insulting Jaḍa Bharata; *para-anubhāvaḥ*—who was very exalted in spiritual realization; *parama-kāruṇikatayā*—by his quality of being very kind to the fallen souls; *upadiśya*—instructing; *rahūgaṇena*—by King Rahūgaṇa; *sa-karuṇam*—piteously; *abhivandita-caraṇaḥ*—whose lotus feet were worshiped; *āpūrṇa-arṇavaḥ iva*—like the full ocean; *nibhṛta*—completely silenced; *karaṇa*—of the senses; *ūrmi*—the waves; *āśayaḥ*—possessing a heart in which; *dharaṇim*—the earth; *imām*—this; *vicacāra*—continued to roam.

TRANSLATION

Śrīla Śukadeva Gosvāmī continued: My dear King, O son of mother Uttarā, there were some waves of dissatisfaction in the mind of Jaḍa

Bharata due to his being insulted by King Rahūgaṇa, who made him carry his palanquin, but Jaḍa Bharata neglected this, and his heart again became calm and quiet like an ocean. Although King Rahūgaṇa had insulted him, he was a great paramahaṁsa. Being a Vaiṣṇava, he was naturally very kindhearted, and he therefore told the King about the constitutional position of the soul. He then forgot the insult because King Rahūgaṇa pitifully begged pardon at his lotus feet. After this, he began to wander all over the earth, just as before.

PURPORT

In *Śrīmad-Bhāgavatam* (3.25.21), Kapiladeva describes the symptoms of great personalities: *titikṣavaḥ kāruṇikāḥ suhṛdaḥ sarva-dehinām.* A saintly devotee is certainly very tolerant. He is the friend of all living entities, and he does not create enemies within the world. A pure devotee has all the qualities of a *sādhu.* Jaḍa Bharata is an example of this. Due to the material body, his senses were certainly agitated when he was insulted by King Rahūgaṇa, but later, due to the King's humble submission, Jaḍa Bharata excused him. It is the duty of everyone desiring to return to Godhead to become submissive like King Rahūgaṇa and beg pardon of Vaiṣṇavas one may have offended. Vaiṣṇavas are generally very kindhearted; therefore if one immediately submits himself at the lotus feet of a Vaiṣṇava, one is immediately cleared of offensive reactions. If one does not do so, the reactions will remain, and the results will not be very palatable.

TEXT 25

**सौवीरपतिरपि सुजनसमवगतपरमात्मसतत्त्व आत्मन्यविद्याध्यारोपितां च देहा-
त्ममतिं विससर्ज। एवं हि नृप भगवदाश्रिताश्रितानुभावः ॥२५॥**

*sauvīra-patir api sujana-samavagata-paramātma-satattva ātmany
avidyādhyāropitāṁ ca dehātma-matiṁ visasarja; evaṁ hi nṛpa
bhagavad-āśritāśritānubhāvaḥ.*

sauvīra-patiḥ—the King of the state of Sauvīra; *api*—certainly; *su-jana*—from an elevated person; *samavagata*—having completely understood; *paramātma-sa-tattvaḥ*—the truth of the constitutional position of the spirit soul and the Supersoul; *ātmani*—in himself; *avidyā*—by nescience; *adhyāropitām*—erroneously attributed; *ca*—and; *deha*—in the body; *ātma-matim*—the concept of the self; *visasarja*—completely gave up; *evam*—thus;

hi—certainly; *nṛpa*—O King; *bhagavat-āśrita-āśrita-anubhāvaḥ*—the consequence of taking shelter of a devotee who has similarly taken shelter of a spiritual master in the *paramparā* system (one is sure to get out of the great nescience of the bodily concept of life).

TRANSLATION

After receiving lessons from the great devotee Jaḍa Bharata, King Rahūgaṇa of the state of Sauvīra became completely aware of the constitutional position of the soul. He thus gave up the bodily conception completely. My dear King, whoever takes shelter of the servant of the servant of the Lord is certainly glorified because he can without difficulty give up the bodily conception.

PURPORT

As stated in *Caitanya-caritāmṛta* (*Madhya* 22.54):

"sādhu-saṅga", "sādhu-saṅga"—sarva-śāstre kaya
lava-mātra sādhu-saṅge sarva-siddhi haya

It is a fact that if one takes shelter of a pure devotee, one attains all perfection, even if the association is a short one. A *sādhu* is a pure devotee of the Lord. It has been our practical experience that the first instruction of our spiritual master infused us with Kṛṣṇa consciousness so that now we are at least on the path of Kṛṣṇa consciousness and can understand the philosophy. As a result, there are many devotees engaged in this Kṛṣṇa consciousness movement. The whole world is revolving under the bodily conception; therefore there must be devotees all over the world to deliver people from the false bodily conception and fully engage them in Kṛṣṇa consciousness.

TEXT 26

राजोवाच
यो ह वा इह बहुविदा महाभागवत त्वयाभिहितः परोक्षेण वचसा जीवलोक-
भवाध्वा स ह्यार्यमनीषया कल्पितविषयो नाञ्जसाव्युत्पन्नलोकसमधिगमः । अथ
तदेवैतद्दुरवगमं समवेतानुकल्पेन निर्दिश्यतामिति ॥२६॥

rājovāca
yo ha vā iha bahu-vidā mahā-bhāgavata tvayābhihitaḥ parokṣeṇa
vacasā jīva-loka-bhavādhvā sa hy ārya-manīṣayā kalpita-viṣayo

nāñjasāvyutpanna-loka-samadhigamaḥ; atha tad evaitad duravagamaṁ samavetānukalpena nirdiśyatām iti.

rājā uvāca—King Parīkṣit said; *yaḥ*—which; *ha*—certainly; *vā*—or; *iha*—in this narration; *bahu-vidā*—who are aware of many incidents of transcendental knowledge; *mahā-bhāgavata*—O great devotee sage; *tvayā*—by you; *abhihitaḥ*—described; *parokṣeṇa*—figuratively; *vacasā*—by words; *jīva-loka-bhava-adhvā*—the path of material existence of the conditioned soul; *saḥ*—that; *hi*—indeed; *ārya-manīṣayā*—by the intelligence of advanced devotees; *kalpita-viṣayaḥ*—the subject matter is imagined; *na*—not; *añjasā*—directly; *avyutpanna-loka*—of persons who are not very experienced or intelligent; *samadhigamaḥ*—the complete understanding; *atha*—therefore; *tat eva*—because of that; *etat*—this matter; *duravagamam*—which is difficult to understand; *samaveta-anukalpena*—by substituting the direct meaning of such incidents; *nirdiśyatām*—let it be described; *iti*—thus.

TRANSLATION

King Parīkṣit then told Śukadeva Gosvāmī: My dear lord, O great devotee sage, you are omniscient. You have very nicely described the position of the conditioned soul, who is compared to a merchant in the forest. From these instructions intelligent men can understand that the senses of a person in the bodily conception are like rogues and thieves in that forest, and one's wife and children are like jackals and other ferocious animals. However, it is not very easy for the unintelligent to understand the purport of this story because it is difficult to extricate the exact meaning from the allegory. I therefore request Your Holiness to give the direct meaning.

PURPORT

There are many stories and incidents in *Śrīmad-Bhāgavatam* that are described figuratively. Such allegorical descriptions may not be understood by unintelligent men; therefore it is the duty of the student to approach a bona fide spiritual master for the direct explanation.

Thus end the Bhaktivedanta purports of the Fifth Canto, Thirteenth Chapter, of the Śrīmad-Bhāgavatam, *entitled "Further Talks Between King Rahūgaṇa and Jaḍa Bharata."*

CHAPTER FOURTEEN

The Material World as the Great Forest of Enjoyment

The direct meaning of the forest of material existence is given in this chapter. Merchants sometimes enter the forest to collect many rare things and sell them at a good profit in the city, but the forest path is always bedecked with dangers. When the pure soul wants to give up the Lord's service to enjoy the material world, Kṛṣṇa certainly gives him a chance to enter the material world. As stated in the *Prema-vivarta: kṛṣṇa-bahirmukha hañā bhoga vāñchā kare.* This is the reason the pure spirit soul falls down to the material world. Due to his activities under the influence of the three modes of material nature, the living entity takes different positions in different species. Sometimes he is a demigod in the heavenly planets and sometimes a most insignificant creature in the lower planetary systems. In this regard, Śrīla Narottama dāsa Ṭhākura says, *nānā yoni sadā phire:* the living entity passes through various species. *Kardarya bhakṣaṇa kare:* he is obliged to eat and enjoy abominable things. *Tāra janma adhaḥ-pāte yāya:* in this way his whole life is spoiled. Without the protection of an all-merciful Vaiṣṇava. the conditioned soul cannot get out of the clutches of *māyā.* As stated in *Bhagavad-gītā* (*manaḥ ṣaṣṭhānīndriyāṇi prakṛti-sthāni karṣati*), the living entity begins material life with his mind and the five knowledge-acquiring senses, and with these he struggles for existence within the material world. These senses are compared to rogues and thieves within the forest. They take away a man's knowledge and place him in a network of nescience. Thus the senses are like rogues and thieves that plunder his spiritual knowledge. Over and above this, there are family members, wife and children, who are exactly like ferocious animals in the forest. The business of such ferocious animals is to eat a man's flesh. The living entity allows himself to be attacked by jackals and foxes (wife and children), and thus his real spiritual life is finished. In the forest of material life, everyone is envious like mosquitoes, and rats and mice are always creating disturbances. Everyone in this material world is placed in many awkward positions and surrounded by envious people and disturbing animals. The result is that the living entity in the material world is always plundered and bitten by many living entities. Nonetheless, despite these disturbances, he does not want to give up his family life, and he continues his fruitive activities in an attempt to become happy in the future. He thus becomes more and more entangled in the results of *karma,* and thus he is forced to act impiously. His witnesses are the sun during the day and the moon during the night. The demigods also witness, but the conditioned soul thinks that his attempts at sense gratification are not being witnessed by anyone. Sometimes, when he is detected, he temporarily renounces everything, but due to his great attachment for the body, his renunciation is given up before he can attain perfection.

In this material world there are many envious people. There is the tax-exacting government, which is compared to an owl, and there are invisible crickets that create unbearable sounds. The conditioned soul is certainly greatly harassed by the agents of material nature, but his intelligence is lost due to undesirable association. In an attempt to gain relief from the disturbances of material existence, he falls victim to so-called *yogīs, sādhus* and incarnations who can display some magic but who do not understand devotional service. Sometimes the conditioned soul is bereft of all money, and consequently he becomes unkind to his family members. In this material world there is not a pinch of actual happiness, for which the conditioned soul is longing life after life. The government officials are like carnivorous Rākṣasas who exact heavy taxes for the maintenance of the government. The hard-working conditioned soul is very saddened due to these heavy taxes.

The path of fruitive activities leads to difficult mountains, and sometimes the conditioned soul wants to cross these mountains, but he is never successful, and consequently he becomes more and more aggrieved and disappointed. Becoming materially and financially embarrassed, the conditioned soul unnecessarily chastises his family. In the material condition there are four principal needs, out of which sleep is compared to a python. When asleep, the conditioned soul completely forgets his real existence, and in sleep he does not feel the tribulations of material life. Sometimes, being in need of money, the conditioned soul steals and cheats, although he may apparently be associated with devotees for spiritual advancement. His only business is getting out of the clutches of *māyā,* but due to improper guidance he becomes more and more entangled in material dealings. This material world is simply an embarrassment and is composed of tribulations presented as happiness, distress, attachment, enmity and envy. On the whole it is simply full of tribulation and misery. When a person loses his intelligence due to attachment to wife and sex, his entire consciousness becomes polluted. He thus only thinks of the association of women. The time factor, which is like a serpent, takes away everyone's life, including that of Lord Brahmā and the insignificant ant. Sometimes the conditioned soul tries to save himself from inexorable time and thus takes shelter of some bogus savior. Unfortunately, the bogus savior cannot even save himself. How, then, can he protect others? The bogus saviors do not care for bona fide knowledge received from qualified *brāhmaṇas* and Vedic sources. Their only business is indulging in sex and recommending sexual freedom even for widows. Thus they are like monkeys in the forest. Śrīla Śukadeva Gosvāmī thus explains the material forest and its difficult path to Mahārāja Parīkṣit.

TEXT 1

स होवाच

स एष देहात्ममानिनां सत्त्वादिगुणविशेषविकल्पितकुशलाकुशलसम-वहारविनिर्मितविविधदेहावलिभिर्वियोगसंयोगाद्यनादिसंसारानुभवस्य द्वारभूतेन-षडिन्द्रियवर्गेण तस्मिन्दुर्गाध्ववदसुगमेऽध्वन्यापतित ईश्वरस्य भगवतो विष्णोर्वशवर्तिन्या मायया जीवलोकोऽयं यथा वणिक्सार्थोऽर्थपरः स्वदेह-निष्पादितकर्मानुभवः श्मशानवदशिवतमायां संसाराटव्यां गतो नाद्यापि विफल-बहुप्रतियोगेहस्तत्तापोपशमनीं हरिगुरुचरणारविन्दमधुकरानुपदवीमवरुन्धे ॥१॥

sa hovāca

sa eṣa dehātma-māninām sattvādi-guṇa-viśeṣa-vikalpita-kuśalāku-śala-samavahāra-vinirmita-vividha-dehāvalibhir viyoga-saṁyogādy-anādi-saṁsārānubhavasya dvāra-bhūtena ṣaḍ-indriya-vargeṇa tasmin durgādhvavad asugame'dhvany āpatita īśvarasya bhagavato viṣṇor vaśa-vartinyā māyayā jīva-loko'yaṁ yathā vaṇik-sārtho'rtha-paraḥ sva-deha-niṣpādita-karmānubhavaḥ śmaśānavad aśivatamāyāṁ saṁsārāṭavyāṁ gato nādyāpi viphala-bahu-pratiyogehas tat-tāpopaśamanīṁ hari-guru-caraṇāravinda-madhukarānupadavīm avarundhe.

saḥ—the self-realized devotee (Śrī Śukadeva Gosvāmī); *ha*—indeed; *uvāca*—spoke; *saḥ*—he (the conditioned soul); *eṣaḥ*—this one; *deha-ātma-māninām*—of those who foolishly take the body to be the self; *sattva-ādi*—of *sattva, rajaḥ* and *tamaḥ; guṇa*—by the modes; *viśeṣa*—particular; *vikalpita*—falsely constituted; *kuśala*—sometimes by favorable actions; *akuśala*—sometimes by very unfavorable actions; *samavahāra*—by a mixture of both; *vinirmita*—obtained; *vividha*—various types; *deha-āvalibhiḥ*—by the series of bodies; *viyoga-saṁyoga-ādi*—symptomized by giving up one type of body (*viyoga*) and accepting another (*saṁyoga*); *anādi-saṁsāra-anubhavasya*—of the perception of the beginningless process of transmigration; *dvāra-bhūtena*—existing as the doorways; *ṣaṭ-indriya-vargeṇa*—by these six senses (the mind and five knowledge-acquiring senses, namely the eyes, ears, tongue, nose and skin); *tasmin*—on that; *durga-adhva-vat*—like a path that is very difficult to traverse; *asugame*—being difficult to pass through; *adhvani*—on a path in the forest; *āpatitaḥ*—happened; *īśvarasya*—of the controller; *bhagavataḥ*—the Supreme Personality of Godhead; *viṣṇoḥ*—of Lord Viṣṇu; *vaśa-vartinyā*—acting under the control; *māyayā*—by the material energy; *jīva-lokaḥ*—the conditioned living entity; *ayam*—this; *yathā*—exactly like; *vaṇik*—a merchant; *sa-arthaḥ*—having an object; *artha-paraḥ*—who is very attached to money; *sva-deha-niṣpādita*—performed by his own body; *karma*—the fruits of activities; *anubhavaḥ*—who experiences; *śmaśāna-vat aśivatamāyām*—like an inauspicious cemetery or place of burial; *saṁsāra-aṭavyām*—in the forest of material life; *gataḥ*—having entered; *na*—not; *adya api*—until now; *viphala*—unsuccessful; *bahu-pratiyoga*—full of great difficulties and varieties of miserable conditions; *īhaḥ*—whose activities here in this material world; *tat-tāpa-upaśa-manīm*—which pacifies the miseries of the forest of material life; *hari-guru-caraṇa-aravinda*—to the lotus feet of the Lord and His devotee; *madhukara-anupadavīm*—the road followed in pursuance of devotees who are attached like bumblebees; *avarundhe*—gain.

TRANSLATION

When King Parīkṣit asked Śukadeva Gosvāmī about the direct meaning of the material forest, Śukadeva Gosvāmī replied as follows: My dear King, a man belonging to the mercantile community [vaṇik] is always interested in earning money. Sometimes he enters the forest to acquire some cheap commodities like wood and earth and sell them in the city at good prices. Similarly, the conditioned soul, being greedy, enters this material world for some material profit. Gradually he enters the deepest part of the forest, not really knowing how to get out. Having entered the material world, the pure soul becomes conditioned by the material atmosphere, which is created by the external energy under the control of Lord Viṣṇu. Thus the living entity comes under the control of the external energy, daivī māyā. Living independently and bewildered in the forest, he does not attain the association of devotees who are always engaged in the service of the Lord. Once in the bodily conception, he gets different types of bodies one after

the other under the influence of material energy and impelled by the modes of material nature [sattva-guṇa, rajo-guṇa and tamo-guṇa]. In this way the conditioned soul goes sometimes to the heavenly planets, sometimes to the earthly planets and sometimes to the lower planets and lower species. Thus he suffers continuously due to different types of bodies. These sufferings and pains are sometimes mixed. Sometimes they are very severe, and sometimes they are not. These bodily conditions are acquired due to the conditioned soul's mental speculation. He uses his mind and five senses to acquire knowledge, and these bring about the different bodies and different conditions. Using the senses under the control of the external energy, māyā, the living entity suffers the miserable conditions of material existence. He is actually searching for relief, but he is generally baffled, although sometimes he is relieved after great difficulty. Struggling for existence in this way, he cannot get the shelter of pure devotees, who are like bumblebees engaged in loving service at the lotus feet of Lord Viṣṇu.

PURPORT

The most important information in this verse is *hari-guru-caraṇa-aravinda-madhukara-anupadavīm.* In this material world the conditioned souls are baffled by their activities, and sometimes they are relieved after great difficulty. On the whole the conditioned soul is never happy. He simply struggles for existence. Actually his only business is to accept the spiritual master, the *guru,* and through him he must accept the lotus feet or the Lord. This is explained by Śrī Caitanya Mahāprabhu: *guru-kṛṣṇa-prasāde pāya bhakti-latā-bīja.* People struggling for existence in the forests or cities of the material world are not actually enjoying life. They are simply suffering different pains and pleasures, generally pains that are always inauspicious. They try to gain release from these pains, but they cannot due to ignorance. For them it is stated in the *Vedas: tad-vijñānārthaṁ sa gurum evābhigacchet.* When the living entity is lost in the forest of the material world, in the struggle for existence, his first business is to find a bona fide *guru* who is always engaged at the lotus feet of the Supreme Personality of Godhead, Viṣṇu. After all, if he is at all eager to be relieved of the struggle for existence, he must find a bona fide *guru* and take instructions at his lotus feet. In this way he can get out of the struggle.

Since the material world is compared herein to a forest, it may be argued that in Kali-yuga modern civilization is mainly situated in the cities. A great city, however, is like a great forest. Actually city life is more dangerous than life in the forest. If one enters an unknown city without friend or shelter, living in that city is more difficult than living in a forest. There are many big cities all over the surface of the globe, and wherever one looks he sees the struggle for existence going on twenty-four hours a day. People rush about in cars going seventy and eighty miles an hour, constantly coming and going, and this sets the scene of the great struggle for existence. One has to rise early in the morning and travel in that car at breakneck speed. There is always the danger of an accident, and one has to take great care. In his automobile, the living entity is full of anxieties, and his struggle is not at all auspicious. Apart from human beings, other species like cats and dogs are also struggling very hard day and night for existence. Thus the struggle for existence continues, and the conditioned soul changes from one position to another. For a while, he is a child, but he has to become a boy. From a boy, he has to change into a youth, and from youth to manhood and old age. Finally, when the body is no longer workable, he has to accept a new body in a different species. Giving up the body is called death, and accepting another body is called birth. The human form is an opportunity to take shelter of the bona fide spiritual master and, through him, the Supreme Lord. This Kṛṣṇa consciousness movement has been started to give an opportunity to all the members of human society, who are misled by foolish leaders. No one can get out of this struggle for existence, which is full of miseries, without accepting a pure devotee of the Lord. The material attempt changes from one position to another, and no one actually gains relief from the struggle for existence. The only resort is the lotus feet of a bona fide spiritual master, and, through him, the lotus feet of the Lord.

TEXT 2

यस्यामु ह वा एते षडिन्द्रियनामानः कर्मणा दस्यव एव ते। तद्यथा पुरुषस्य धनं यत्किञ्चिद्धर्मौपयिकं बहुकृच्छ्राधिगतं साक्षात्परमपुरुषाराधनलक्षणो योऽसौ धर्मस्तं तु साम्पराय उदाहरन्ति। तद्धर्म्यं धनं दर्शनस्पर्शनश्रवणास्वादनावघ्राणसङ्कल्प-व्यवसायगृहग्राम्योपभोगेन कुनाथस्याजितात्मनो यथा सार्थस्य विलुम्पन्ति ॥२॥

yasyām u ha vā ete ṣaḍ-indriya-nāmānaḥ karmaṇā dasyava eva te; tad yathā puruṣasya dhanaṁ yat kiñcid dharmaupayikaṁ bahu-kṛcchrādhigataṁ sākṣāt parama-puruṣārādhana-lakṣaṇo yo'sau dharmas taṁ tu sāmparāya udāharanti; tad-dharmyaṁ dhanaṁ darśana-sparśana-śravaṇāsvādanāvaghrāṇa-saṅkalpa-vyavasāya-gṛha-grāmyopabhogena kunāthasyājitātmano yathā sārthasya vilum-panti.

yasyām—in which; *u ha*—certainly; *vā*—or; *ete*—all these; *ṣaṭ-indriya-nāmānaḥ*—who are named the six senses (the mind and the five knowledge-acquiring senses); *karmaṇā*—by their activity; *dasyavaḥ*—the plunderers; *eva*—certainly; *te*—they; *tat*—that; *yathā*—as; *puruṣasya*—of a person; *dhanam*—the wealth; *yat*—whatever; *kiñcit*—something; *dharma-aupayikam*—which is a means to religious principles; *bahu-kṛcchra-adhigatam*—earned after much hard labor; *sākṣāt*—directly; *parama-puruṣa-ārādhana-lakṣaṇaḥ*—whose symptoms are worship of the Supreme Lord by performance of sacrifices and so on; *yaḥ*—which; *asau*—that; *dharmaḥ*—religious principles; *tam*—that; *tu*—but; *sāmparāye*—for the benefit of the living entity after death; *udāharanti*—the wise declare; *tat-dharmyam*—religious (relating to the prosecution of the *varṇāśrama-dharma*); *dhanam*—wealth; *darśana*—by seeing; *sparśana*—by touching; *śravaṇa*—by hearing; *āsvādana*—by tasting; *avaghrāṇa*—by smelling; *saṅkalpa*—by determination; *vyavasāya*—by a conclusion; *gṛha*—in the material home; *grāmya-upabhogena*—by material sense gratification; *kunāthasya*—of the misguided conditioned soul; *ajita-ātmanaḥ*—who has not controlled himself; *yathā*—just as; *sārthasya*—of the living entity interested in sense gratification; *vilumpanti*—they plunder.

TRANSLATION

In the forest of material existence, the uncontrolled senses are like plunderers. The conditioned soul may earn some money for the advancement of Kṛṣṇa consciousness, but unfortunately the uncontrolled senses plunder his money through sense gratification. The senses are plunderers because they make one spend his money unnecessarily for seeing, smelling, tasting, touching, hearing, desiring and willing. In this way the conditioned soul is obliged to gratify his senses, and thus all his money is spent. This money is actually acquired for the execution of religious principles, but it is taken away by the plundering senses.

PURPORT

Pūrva jamnārjitā vidyā pūrva janmārjitaṁ dhanaṁ agre dhāvati dhāvati. By following the principles of the *varṇāśrama-dharma,* one attains a better position in the material world. One may be rich, learned, beautiful or highborn. One who has all these assets should know that they are all meant for the advancement of Kṛṣṇa consciousness. Unfortunately, when a person is misguided he misuses his high position for sense gratification. Therefore the uncontrolled senses are considered plunderers. The good position one attains by executing religious principles is wasted as the plundering senses take it away. By executing religious principles under the laws of *varṇāśrama-dharma,* one is placed in a comfortable position. One may very easily use his assets for the further advancement of Kṛṣṇa consciousness. One should understand that the wealth and opportunity one gets in the material world should not be squandered in sense gratification. They are meant for the advancement of Kṛṣṇa consciousness. This Kṛṣṇa consciousness movement is therefore teaching people to control the mind and five knowledge-acquiring senses by a definite process. One should practice a little austerity and not spend money on anything other than the regulative life of devotional service. The senses demand that one see beautiful things; therefore money should be spent for decorating the Deity in the temple. Similarly, the tongue has to taste good food, which should be bought and offered to the Deity. The nose can be utilized in smelling the flowers offered to the Deity, and the hearing can be utilized by listening to the vibration of the Hare Kṛṣṇa *mantra.* In this way the senses can be regulated and utilized to advance Kṛṣṇa consciousness. Thus a good position might not be spoiled by material sense gratification in the form of illicit sex, meat-eating, intoxication and gambling. One spoils an opulent position in the material world by driving cars, spending time in nightclubs or tasting abominable food in restaurants. In these ways, the plundering senses take away all the assets that the conditioned soul has acquired with great difficulty.

TEXT 3

अथ च यत्र कौटुम्बिका दारापत्यादयो नाम्ना कर्मणा वृकसृगाला एवानिच्छतोऽपि कदर्यस्य कुटुम्बिन उरणकवत्संरक्ष्यमाणं मिषतोऽपि हरन्ति ॥३॥

atha ca yatra kauṭumbikā dārāpatyādayo nāmnā karmaṇā vṛka-sṛgālā evānicchato 'pi kadaryasya kuṭumbina uraṇakavat saṁrakṣyamāṇaṁ miṣato 'pi haranti.

atha—in this way; *ca*—also; *yatra*—in which; *kauṭumbikāḥ*—the family members; *dāra-apatya-ādayaḥ*—beginning with the wife and children; *nāmnā*—by name only; *karmaṇā*—by their behavior; *vṛka-sṛgālāḥ*—tigers and jackals; *eva*—certainly; *anicchataḥ*—of one who does not desire to spend his wealth; *api*—certainly; *kadaryasya*—being too miserly; *kuṭumbinaḥ*—who is surrounded by family members; *uraṇaka-vat*—like a lamb;

saṁrakṣyamāṇam—although protected; *miṣataḥ*—of one who is observing; *api*—even; *haranti*—they forcibly take away.

TRANSLATION

My dear King, family members in this material world go under the names of wife and children, but actually they behave like tigers and jackals. A herdsman tries to protect his sheep to the best of his ability, but the tigers and foxes take them away by force. Similarly, although a miserly man wants to guard his money very carefully, his family members take away all his assets forcibly, even though he is very vigilant.

PURPORT

One Hindi poet has sung: *din kā dakinī rāt kā bāghinī pālak pālak rahu cuse.* During the daytime, the wife is compared to a witch, and at night she is compared to a tigress. Her only business is sucking the blood of her husband both day and night. During the day there are household expenditures, and the money earned by the husband at the cost of his blood is taken away. At night, due to sex pleasure, the husband discharges blood in the form of semen. In this way he is bled by his wife both day and night, yet he is so crazy that he very carefully maintains her. Similarly, the children are also like tigers, jackals and foxes. As tigers, jackals and foxes take away lambs despite the herdsman's vigilant protection, children take away the father's money, although the father supervises the money himself. Thus family members may be called wives and children, but actually they are plunderers.

TEXT 4

यथा ह्यनुवत्सरं कृष्यमाणमप्यदग्धबीजं क्षेत्रं पुनरेवावपनकाले गुल्मतृण-वीरुद्भिर्गह्वरमिव भवत्येवमेव गृहाश्रमः कर्मक्षेत्रं यस्मिन्न हि कर्माण्युत्सीदन्ति यदयं कामकरण्ड एष आवसथः ॥४॥

yathā hy anuvatsaraṁ kṛṣyamāṇam apy adagdha-bījaṁ kṣetraṁ punar evāvapana-kāle gulma-tṛṇa-vīrudbhir gahvaram iva bhavaty evam eva gṛhāśramaḥ karma-kṣetraṁ yasmin na hi karmāṇy utsīdanti yad ayaṁ kāma-karaṇḍa eṣa āvasathaḥ.

yathā—just as; *hi*—certainly; *anuvatsaram*—every year; *kṛṣyamāṇam*—being plowed; *api*—although; *adagdha-bījam*—in which the seeds are not burned; *kṣetram*—the field; *punaḥ*—again; *eva*—certainly; *āvapana-kāle*—

at the times for sowing the seeds; *gulma*—by bushes; *tṛṇa*—by grasses; *vīrudbhiḥ*—by the creepers; *gahvaram iva*—like a bower; *bhavati*—becomes; *evam*—thus; *eva*—certainly; *gṛha-āśramaḥ*—family life; *karma-kṣetram*—the field of activities; *yasmin*—in which; *na*—not; *hi*—certainly; *karmāṇi utsīdanti*—fruitive activities disappear; *yat*—therefore; *ayam*—this; *kāma-karaṇḍaḥ*—the storehouse of fruitive desire; *eṣaḥ*—this; *āvasathaḥ*—abode.

TRANSLATION

Every year the plowman plows over his grain field, completely uprooting all weeds. Nonetheless, the seeds lie there and, not being completely burned, again come up with the plants sown in the field. Even after being plowed under, the weeds come up densely. Similarly, the gṛhastha-āśrama [family life] is a field of fruitive activity. Unless the desire to enjoy family life is completely burned out, it grows up again and again. Even though camphor may be removed from a pot, the pot nonetheless retains the aroma of camphor. As long as the seeds of desire are not destroyed, fruitive activities are not destroyed.

PURPORT

Unless one's desires are completely transferred to the service of the Supreme Personality of Godhead, the desire for family life continues, even after one has taken *sannyāsa.* Sometimes in our society, ISKCON, a person out of sentiment may take *sannyāsa,* but because his desires are not burned completely, he again takes to family life, even at the risk of losing his prestige and disgracing his good name. These strong desires can be burned out completely when one fully engages in the service of the Lord in devotional service.

TEXT 5

तत्रगतो दंशमशकसमापसदैर्मनुजैः शलभशकुन्ततस्करमूषकादिभिरुपरुध्यमानबहिःप्राणः क्वचित् परिवर्तमानोऽस्मिन्नध्वन्यविद्याकामकर्मभिरुपरक्तमनसानुपपन्नार्थं नरलोकं गन्धर्वनगरमुपपन्नमिति मिथ्यादृष्टिरनुपश्यति ॥५॥

tatra gato daṁśa-maśaka-samāpasadair manujaiḥ śalabha-śakunta-
taskara-mūṣakādibhir uparudhyamāna-bahiḥ-prāṇaḥ kvacit
parivartamāno'sminn adhvany avidyā-kāma-karmabhir uparakta-
manasānupapannārthaṁ nara-lokaṁ gandharva-nagaram upapannam
iti mithyā-dṛṣṭir anupaśyati.

tatra—to that household life; *gataḥ*—gone; *daṁśa*—gadflies; *maśaka*—mosquitoes; *sama*—equal to; *apasadaiḥ*—who are low-class; *manu-jaiḥ*—by men; *śalabha*—locusts; *śakunta*—a large bird of prey; *taskara*—thieves; *mūṣaka-ādibhiḥ*—by rats and so on; *uparudhyamāna*—being disturbed; *bahiḥ-prāṇaḥ*—the external life air in the form of wealth and so on; *kvacit*—sometimes; *parivartamānaḥ*—wandering; *asmin*—in this; *adhvani*—path of material existence; *avidyā-kāma*—by ignorance and lust; *karmabhiḥ*—and by fruitive activities; *uparakta-manasā*—due to the mind's being influenced; *anupapanna-artham*—in which the desired results are never obtained; *nara-lokam*—this material world; *gandharva-nagaram*—a will-o'-the-wisp city; *upapannam*—existing; *iti*—taking it as; *mithyā-dṛṣṭiḥ*—he whose vision is mistaken; *anupaśyati*—observes.

TRANSLATION

Sometimes the conditioned soul in household life, being attached to material wealth and possessions, is disturbed by gadflies and mosquitoes, and sometimes locusts, birds of prey and rats give him trouble. Nonetheless, he still wanders down the path of material existence. Due to ignorance he becomes lusty and engages in fruitive activity. Because his mind is absorbed in these activities, he sees the material world as permanent, although it is temporary like a phantasmagoria, a house in the sky.

PURPORT

The following song is sung by Narottama dāsa Ṭhākura:

ahaṅkāre matta hañā, nitāi-pada pāsariyā,
asatyere satya kari māni

Due to forgetting the lotus feet of Lord Nityānanda and being puffed up by material possessions, wealth and opulence, one thinks the false, temporary material world to be an actual fact. This is the material disease. The living entity is eternal and blissful, but despite miserable material conditions, he thinks the material world to be real and factual due to his ignorance.

TEXT 6

तत्र च क्वचिदातपोदकनिभान् विषयानुपधावति पानभोजनव्यवाया-
दिव्यसनलोलुपः ॥६॥

tatra ca kvacid ātapodaka-nibhān viṣayān upadhāvati pāna-bhojana-vyavāyādi-vyasana-lolupaḥ.

tatra—there (in this phantom place); *ca*—also; *kvacit*—sometimes; *ātapa-udaka-nibhān*—like the water in a mirage in the desert; *viṣayān*—the objects of sense enjoyment; *upadhāvati*—runs after; *pāna*—to drinking; *bhojana*—to eating; *vyavāya*—to sex life; *ādi*—and so on; *vyasana*—with addiction; *lolupaḥ*—a debauchee.

TRANSLATION

Sometimes in this house in the sky [gandharva-pura] the conditioned soul drinks, eats and has sex. Being overly attached, he chases after the objects of the senses just as a deer chases a mirage in the desert.

PURPORT

There are two worlds—the spiritual and the material. The material world is false like a mirage in the desert. In the desert, animals think they see water, but actually there is none. Similarly, those who are animalistic try to find peace within the desert of material life. It is repeatedly said in different *śāstras* that there is no pleasure in this material world. Furthermore, even if we agree to live without pleasure, we are not allowed to do so. In *Bhagavad-gītā,* Lord Kṛṣṇa says that the material world is not only full of miseries (*duḥkhālayam*) but also temporary (*aśāśvatam*). Even if we want to live here amid miseries, material nature will not allow us to do so. It will oblige us to change bodies and enter another atmosphere full of miserable conditions.

TEXT 7

क्वचिच्चाशेषदोषनिषदनं पुरीषविशेषं तद्वर्णगुणनिर्मितमतिः सुवर्णमुपादित्स-
त्यग्निकामकातर इवोल्मुकपिशाचम् ॥ ७ ॥

kvacic cāśeṣa-doṣa-niṣadanaṁ purīṣa-viśeṣaṁ tad-varṇa-guṇa-nirmita-matiḥ suvarṇam upāditsaty agni-kāma-kātara ivolmuka-piśācam.

kvacit—sometimes; *ca*—also; *aśeṣa*—unlimited; *doṣa*—of faults; *niṣadanam*—the source of; *purīṣa*—of stool; *viśeṣam*—a particular type; *tat-varṇa-guṇa*—whose color is the same as that of the mode of passion (reddish); *nirmita-matiḥ*—whose mind is absorbed in that; *suvarṇam*—gold; *upāditsati*—desiring to get; *agni-kāma*—by the desire for fire; *kātaraḥ*—who is troubled; *iva*—like; *ulmuka-piśācam*—a phosphorescent light known as a will-o'-the-wisp, which is sometimes mistaken for a ghost.

TRANSLATION

Sometimes the living entity is interested in the yellow stool known as gold and runs after it. That gold is the source of material opulence and envy, and it can enable one to afford illicit sex, gambling, meat-eating and intoxication. Those whose minds are overcome by the mode of passion are attracted by the color of gold, just as a man suffering from cold in the forest runs after a phosphorescent light in a marshy land, considering it to be fire.

PURPORT

Parīkṣit Mahārāja told Kali-yuga to leave his kingdom immediately and reside in four places: brothels, liquor shops, slaughterhouses and gambling casinos. However, Kali-yuga requested him to give him only one place where these four places are included, and Parīkṣit Mahārāja gave him the place where gold is stored. Gold encompasses the four principles of sin, and therefore, according to spiritual life, gold should be avoided as far as possible. If there is gold, there is certainly illicit sex, meat-eating, gambling and intoxication. Because people in the Western world have a great deal of gold, they are victims of these four sins. The color of gold is very glittering, and a materialistic person becomes very much attracted by its yellow color. However, this gold is actually a type of stool. A person with a bad liver generally passes yellow stool. The color of this stool attracts a materialistic person, just as the will-o'-the-wisp attracts one who needs heat.

TEXT 8

अथ कदाचिन्निवासपानीयद्रविणाद्यनेकात्मोपजीवनाभिनिवेश एतस्यां संसा-
राटव्यामितस्ततः परिधावति ॥८॥

atha kadācin nivāsa-pānīya-draviṇādy-anekātmopajīvanābhiniveśa etasyāṁ saṁsārāṭavyām itas tataḥ paridhāvati.

atha—in this way; *kadācit*—sometimes; *nivāsa*—residence; *pānīya*—water; *draviṇa*—wealth; *ādi*—and so on; *aneka*—in various items; *ātma-upajīvana*—which are considered necessary to maintain body and soul together; *abhiniveśaḥ*—a person fully absorbed; *etasyām*—in this; *saṁsāra-aṭavyām*—the material world, which is like a great forest; *itaḥ tataḥ*—here and there; *paridhāvati*—runs around.

TRANSLATION

Sometimes the conditioned soul is absorbed in finding residential quarters or apartments and getting a supply of water and riches to maintain his body. Absorbed in acquiring a variety of necessities, he forgets everything and perpetually runs around the forest of material existence.

PURPORT

As originally mentioned, a poor man belonging to the mercantile community goes to the forest to get some cheap goods to bring back to the city to sell at a profit. He is so absorbed in the thought of maintaining body and soul together that he forgets his original relationship with Kṛṣṇa and seeks only the bodily comforts. Thus material activities are the conditioned soul's only engagement. Not knowing the aim of life, the materialist perpetually wanders in material existence, struggling to get the necessities of life. Not understanding the aim of life, even though he acquires sufficient necessities, he manufactures artificial necessities and thus becomes more and more entangled. He creates a mental situation whereby he needs greater and greater comforts. The materialist does not know the secret of nature's ways. As confirmed in *Bhagavad-gītā* (3.27):

prakṛteḥ kriyamāṇāni
guṇaiḥ karmāṇi sarvaśaḥ
ahaṅkāra-vimūḍhātmā
kartāham iti manyate

"The bewildered spirit soul, under the influence of the three modes of material nature, thinks himself to be the doer of activities which are in actuality carried out by nature." Due to lusty desire, the living entity creates a certain mental situation whereby he wants to enjoy this material world. He thus becomes entangled, enters different bodies and suffers in them.

TEXT 9

क्वचिच्च वात्यौपम्यया प्रमदयाऽऽरोहमारोपितस्तत्कालरजसा रजनीभूत इवासाधुमर्यादो रजस्वलाक्षोऽपि दिग्देवता अतिरजस्वलमतिर्न विजानाति ॥९॥

kvacic ca vātyaupamyayā pramadayāroham āropitas tat-kāla-rajasā rajanī-bhūta ivāsādhu-maryādo rajas-valākṣo'pi dig-devatā atirajas-vala-matir na vijānāti.

kvacit—sometimes; *ca*—also; *vātyā aupamyayā*—compared to a whirlwind; *pramadayā*—by a beautiful woman; *āroham āropitaḥ*—raised onto the lap for sex enjoyment; *tat-kāla-rajasā*—by the passion of lusty desires at that moment; *rajanī-bhūtaḥ*—the darkness of night; *iva*—like; *asādhu-maryādaḥ*—who is without proper respect for the higher witnesses; *rajaḥ-vala-akṣaḥ*—blinded by strong lusty desires; *api*—certainly; *dik-devatāḥ*—the demigods in charge of different directions, like the sun and the moon; *atirajaḥ-vala-matiḥ*—whose mind is overcome by lust; *na vijānāti*—he does not know (that witnesses all around take note of his impudent sexual act).

TRANSLATION

Sometimes, as if blinded by the dust of a whirlwind, the conditioned soul sees the beauty of the opposite sex, which is called pramadā. Being thus bewildered, he is raised upon the lap of a woman, and at that time his good senses are overcome by the force of passion. He thus becomes almost blind with lusty desire and disobeys the rules and regulations governing sex life. He does not know that his disobedience is witnessed by different demigods, and he enjoys illicit sex in the dead of night, not seeing the future punishment awaiting him.

PURPORT

In *Bhagavad-gītā* (7.11) it is said: *dharmāviruddho bhūteṣu kāmo'smi bharatarṣabha.* Sex is allowed only for the begetting of children, not for enjoyment. One can indulge in sex to beget a good child for the benefit of the family, society and world. Otherwise, sex is against the rules and regulations of religious life. A materialistic person does not believe that everything is managed in nature, and he does not know that if one does something wrong, he is witnessed by different demigods. A person enjoys illicit sex, and due to his blind, lusty desire, he thinks that no one can see him, but this illicit sex is thoroughly observed by the agents of the Supreme Personality of Godhead. Therefore the person is punished in so many ways. Presently in Kali-yuga there are many pregnancies due to illicit sex, and sometimes abortions ensue. These sinful activities are witnessed by the agents of the Supreme Personality of Godhead, and a man and woman who create such a situation are punished in the future by the stringent laws of material nature (*daivī hy eṣā guṇa-mayī mama māyā duratyayā*). Illicit sex is never excused, and those who indulge in it are punished life after life. As confirmed in *Bhagavad-gītā* (16.20):

āsurīṁ yonim āpannā
mūḍhā janmani janmani
mām aprāpyaiva kaunteya
tato yānty adhamāṁ gatim

"Attaining repeated birth among the species of demoniac life, such persons can never approach Me. Gradually they sink down to the most abominable type of existence."

The Supreme Personality of Godhead does not allow anyone to act against the stringent laws of material nature; therefore illicit sex is punished life after life. Illicit sex creates pregnancies, and these unwanted pregnancies lead to abortion. Those involved become implicated in these sins, so much so that they are punished in the same way the next life. Thus in the next life they also enter the womb of a mother and are killed in the same way. All these things can be avoided by remaining on the transcendental platform of Kṛṣṇa consciousness. In this way one does not commit sinful activity. Illicit sex is the most prominent sin due to lusty desire. When one associates with the mode of passion, he is implicated in suffering life after life.

TEXT 10

क्वचित्सकृदवगतविषयवैतथ्यः स्वयं पराभिध्यानेन विभ्रंशितस्मृतिस्तयैव मरीचितोयप्रायांस्तानेवाभिधावति ॥१०॥

kvacit sakṛd avagata-viṣaya-vaitathyaḥ svayaṁ parābhidhyānena vibhraṁśita-smṛtis tayaiva marīci-toya-prāyāṁs tān evābhidhāvati.

kvacit—sometimes; *sakṛt*—once; *avagata-viṣaya-vaitathyaḥ*—becoming conscious of the uselessness of enjoying material sense gratification; *svayam*—himself; *para-abhidhyānena*—by the bodily concept of the self; *vibhraṁśita*—destroyed; *smṛtiḥ*—whose remembrance; *tayā*—by that; *eva*—certainly; *marīci-toya*—water in a mirage; *prāyān*—similar to; *tān*—those sense objects; *eva*—certainly; *abhidhāvati*—runs after.

TRANSLATION

The conditioned soul sometimes personally appreciates the futility of sense enjoyment in the material world, and he sometimes considers material enjoyment to be full of miseries. However, due to his strong bodily conception, his memory is destroyed, and again and again he runs after material enjoyment, just as an animal runs after a mirage in the desert.

PURPORT

The main disease in material life is the bodily conception. Being baffled again and again in material activity, the conditioned soul temporarily thinks of the futility of material enjoyment, but he again tries the same thing. By the association of devotees, a person may become convinced of the material futility, but he cannot give up his engagement, although he is very eager to return home, back to Godhead. Under these circumstances, the Supreme Personality of Godhead, who is situated in everyone's heart, compassionately takes away all the material possessions of such a devotee. As stated in *Śrīmad-Bhāgavatam* (10.88.8): *yasyāham anugṛhṇāmi hariṣye tad-dhanaṁ śanaiḥ.* Lord Kṛṣṇa says that He takes everything away from the devotee whom He especially favors when that devotee is overly attached to material possessions. When everything is taken away, the devotee feels helpless and frustrated in society, friendship and love. He feels that his family does not care for him any longer, and he therefore completely surrenders unto the lotus feet of the Supreme Lord. This is a special favor granted by the Lord to a devotee who cannot fully surrender to the Lord due to a strong bodily conception. As explained in *Caitanya-caritāmṛta* (*Madhya* 22.39): *āmi—vijña, ei mūrkhe 'viṣaya' kene diba.* The Lord understands the devotee who hesitates to engage in the Lord's service, not knowing whether he should again try to revive his material life. After repeated attempts and failures, he fully surrenders to the lotus feet of the Lord. The Lord then gives him directions, and, attaining happiness, he forgets all material engagement.

TEXT 11

क्वचिदुलूकझिल्लीस्वनवदतिपरुषरभसाटोपं प्रत्यक्षं परोक्षं वा रिपुराज-
कुलनिर्भर्त्सितेनातिव्यथितकर्णमूलहृदयः ॥११॥

kvacid ulūka-jhillī-svanavad ati-paruṣa-rabhasāṭopaṁ pratyakṣaṁ
parokṣaṁ vā ripu-rāja-kula-nirbhartsitenāti-vyathita-karṇa-mūla-
hṛdayaḥ.

kvacit—sometimes; *ulūka*—of the owl; *jhillī*—and the cricket; *svana-vat*—exactly like intolerable sounds; *ati-paruṣa*—extremely piercing; *rabhasa*—by perseverance; *āṭopam*—agitation; *pratyakṣam*—directly; *parokṣam*—indirectly; *vā*—or; *ripu*—of enemies; *rāja-kula*—and of government officers; *nirbhartsitena*—by chastisement; *ati-vyathita*—very aggrieved; *karṇa-mūla-hṛdayaḥ*—whose ear and heart.

TRANSLATION

Sometimes the conditioned soul is very aggrieved by the chastisement of his enemies and government servants, who use harsh words against him directly or indirectly. At that time his heart and ears become very saddened. Such chastisement may be compared to the sounds of owls and crickets.

PURPORT

There are different types of enemies within this material world. The government chastises one due to not paying income taxes. Such criticism, direct or indirect, saddens one, and sometimes the conditioned soul tries to counteract that chastisement. Unfortunately, he cannot do anything.

TEXT 12

स यदा दुग्धपूर्वसुकृतस्तदा कारस्करकाकतुण्डाद्यपुण्यद्रुमलताविषोदपानवदुभ-
यार्थशून्यद्रविणान् जीवन्मृतान् स्वयं जीवन्म्रियमाण उपधावति ॥१२॥

sa yadā dugdha-pūrva-sukṛtas tadā kāraskara-kākatuṇḍādy-apuṇya-
druma-latā-viṣoda-pānavad ubhayārtha-śūnya-draviṇān jīvan-mṛtān
svayaṁ jīvan-mriyamāṇa upadhāvati.

saḥ—that conditioned soul; *yadā*—when; *dugdha*—exhausted; *pūrva*—previous; *sukṛtaḥ*—pious activities; *tadā*—at that time; *kāraskara-kākatuṇḍa-ādi*—named *kāraskara, kākatuṇḍa,* etc.; *apuṇya-druma-latā*—impious trees and creepers; *viṣa-uda-pāna-vat*—like wells with poisonous water; *ubhaya-artha-śūnya*—which cannot give happiness either in this life or in the next; *draviṇān*—those who possess wealth; *jīvat-mṛtān*—who are dead, although apparently alive; *svayam*—he himself; *jīvat*—living; *mriyamāṇaḥ*—being dead; *upadhāvati*—approaches for material acquisition.

TRANSLATION

Due to his pious activities in previous lives, the conditioned soul attains material facilities in this life, but when they are finished, he takes shelter of wealth and riches, which cannot help him in this life or the next. Because of this, he approaches the living dead who possess these things. Such people are compared to impure trees, creepers and poisonous wells.

PURPORT

The wealth and riches acquired through previous pious activities should not be misused for sense gratification. Enjoying them for sense gratification is like enjoying the fruits of a poisonous tree. Such activities will not help the conditioned soul in any way, neither in this life nor the next. However, if one engages his possessions in the service of the Lord under the guidance of a proper spiritual master, he will attain happiness both in this life and the next. Unless he does so, he eats a forbidden apple and thereby loses his paradise. Lord Śrī Kṛṣṇa therefore advises that one's possessions should be given unto Him.

yat karoṣi yad aśnāsi
yaj juhoṣi dadāsi yat
yat tapasyasi kaunteya
tat kuruṣva mad-arpaṇam

"O son of Kuntī, all that you do, all that you eat, all that you offer and give away, as well as all austerities that you may perform, should be done as an offering unto Me." (Bg. 9.27) Material wealth and opulence attained through previous pious activities can be fully utilized for one's benefit in this life and the next if one is Kṛṣṇa conscious. One should not try to possess more than he needs for the bare necessities. If one gets more than is needed, the surplus should be fully engaged in the Lord's service. That will make the conditioned soul, the world and Kṛṣṇa happy, and this is the aim of life.

TEXT 13

एकदासत्प्रसङ्गान्निकृतमतिर्व्युदकस्रोतःस्खलनवदुभयतोऽपि दुःखदं पाखण्डमभियाति ॥१३॥

ekadāsat-prasaṅgān nikṛta-matir vyudaka-srotaḥ-skhalanavad ubhayato'pi duḥkhadaṁ pākhaṇḍam abhiyāti.

ekadā—sometimes; *asat-prasaṅgāt*—by association of nondevotees who are against the Vedic principles and who manufacture different paths of religion; *nikṛta-matiḥ*—whose intelligence has been brought to the abominable status of defying the authority of the Supreme Personality of Godhead; *vyudaka-srotaḥ*—into rivers without sufficient water; *skhalana-vat*—like jumping; *ubhayataḥ*—from both sides; *api*—although; *duḥkha-dam*—giving distress; *pākhaṇḍam*—the atheistic path; *abhiyāti*—he approaches.

TRANSLATION

Sometimes, to mitigate distresses in this forest of the material world, the conditioned soul receives cheap blessings from atheists. He then loses all intelligence in their association. This is exactly like jumping in a shallow river. As a result one simply breaks his head. He is not able to mitigate his sufferings from the heat, and in both ways he suffers. The misguided conditioned soul also approaches so-called sādhus and svāmīs who preach against the principles of the Vedas. He does not receive benefit from them, either in the present or in the future.

PURPORT

Cheaters are always there to manufacture their own way of spiritual realization. To get some material benefit, the conditioned soul approaches these pseudo *sannyāsīs* and *yogīs* for cheap blessings, but he does not receive any benefit from them, either spiritual or material. In this age there are many cheaters who show some jugglery and magic. They even create gold to amaze their followers, and their followers accept them as God. This type of cheating is very prominent in Kali-yuga. Viśvanātha Cakravartī Ṭhākura describes the real *guru* in this way.

saṁsāra-dāvānala-līḍha-loka-
trāṇāya kāruṇya-ghanāghanatvam
prāptasya kalyāṇa-guṇārṇavasya
vande guroḥ śrī-caraṇāravindam

One should approach a *guru* who can extinguish the blazing fire of this material world, the struggle for existence. People want to be cheated, and therefore they go to *yogīs* and *svāmīs* who play tricks, but tricks do not mitigate the miseries of material life. If being able to manufacture gold is a criterion for becoming God, then why not accept Kṛṣṇa, the proprietor of the entire universe, wherein there are countless tons of gold? As mentioned before, the color of gold is compared to the will-o'-the-wisp or yellow stool; therefore one should not be allured by gold-manufacturing *gurus* but should sincerely approach a devotee like Jaḍa Bharata. Jaḍa Bharata instructed Rahūgaṇa Mahārāja so well that the King was relieved from the bodily conception. One cannot become happy by accepting a false *guru.* A *guru* should be accepted as advised in *Śrīmad-Bhāgavatam* (11.3.21). *Tasmād guruṁ prapadyeta jijñāsuḥ śreya uttamam:* One should approach a bona fide *guru* to inquire about the highest benefit of life. Such a *guru* is described as follows: *śābde pare ca niṣṇātam.* Such a *guru* does not manufacture gold or juggle words. He is well versed in the conclusions of Vedic knowledge (*vedaiś ca sarvair aham eva vedyaḥ*). He is freed from all material contamination and is fully engaged in Kṛṣṇa's service. If one is able to obtain the dust of the lotus feet of such a *guru,* his life becomes successful. Otherwise he is baffled both in this life and in the next.

TEXT 14

यदा तु परबाधयान्ध आत्मने नोपनमति तदा हि पितृपुत्रबर्हिष्मतः पितृपुत्रान् वा स खलु भक्षयति ॥१४॥

yadā tu para-bādhayāndha ātmane nopanamati tadā hi pitṛ-putra-barhiṣmataḥ pitṛ-putrān vā sa khalu bhakṣayati.

yadā—when; *tu*—but (because of misfortune); *para-bādhayā*—in spite of exploiting all others; *andhaḥ*—blind; *ātmane*—for himself; *na upanamati*—does not fall into one's share; *tadā*—at that time; *hi*—certainly; *pitṛ-putra*—of the father or sons; *barhiṣmataḥ*—as insignificant as a piece of grass; *pitṛ-putrān*—father or sons; *vā*—or; *saḥ*—he (the conditioned soul); *khalu*—indeed; *bhakṣayati*—gives trouble to.

TRANSLATION

In this material world, when the conditioned soul cannot arrange for his own maintenance, despite exploiting others, he tries to exploit his own father or son, taking away that relative's possessions, although they may be very insignificant. If he cannot acquire things from his father, son or other relatives, he is prepared to give them all kinds of trouble.

PURPORT

Once we actually saw a distressed man steal ornaments from his daughter just to maintain himself. As the English proverb goes, necessity knows no law. When a conditioned soul needs something, he forgets his relationship with his relatives and exploits his own father or son. We also receive information from *Śrīmad-Bhāgavatam* that in this age of Kali the time is quickly approaching when a relative will kill another relative for a small farthing. Without Kṛṣṇa consciousness, people will deteriorate further and further into a hellish condition wherein they will perform abominable acts.

TEXT 15

क्वचिदासाद्य गृहं दाववत्प्रियार्थविधुरमसुखोदर्कं शोकाग्निना दह्यमानो भृशं निर्वेदमुपगच्छति ॥१५॥

kvacid āsādya gṛhaṁ dāvavat priyārtha-vidhuram asukhodarkaṁ
śokāgninā dahyamāno bhṛśaṁ nirvedam upagacchati.

kvacit—sometimes; *āsādya*—experiencing; *gṛham*—the home life; *dāva-vat*—exactly like a blazing fire in the forest; *priya-artha-vidhuram*—without any beneficial object; *asukha-udarkam*—resulting only in more and more unhappiness; *śoka-agninā*—by the fire of lamentation; *dahyamānaḥ*—being burned; *bhṛśam*—very great; *nirvedam*—disappointment; *upagacchati*—he obtains.

TRANSLATION

In this world, family life is exactly like a blazing fire in the forest. There is not the least happiness, and gradually one becomes more and more implicated in unhappiness. In household life, there is nothing favorable for perpetual happiness. Being implicated in home life, the conditioned soul is burned by the fire of lamentation. Sometimes he condemns himself as being very unfortunate, and sometimes he claims that he suffers because he performed no pious activities in his previous life.

PURPORT

In the *Gurv-aṣṭaka,* Śrīla Viśvanātha Cakravartī Ṭhākura has sung:

saṁsāra-dāvānala-līḍha-loka-
trāṇāya kāruṇya-ghanāghanatvam

A life in this material world is exactly like a blazing forest fire. No one goes to set fire to the forest, yet the fire takes place. Similarly, everyone wants to be happy in the material world, but the miserable conditions of material life simply increase. Sometimes a person caught in the blazing fire of material existence condemns himself, but due to his bodily conception he cannot get out of the entanglement, and thus he suffers more and more.

TEXT 16

क्वचित्कालविषमितराजकुलरक्षसापहृतप्रियतमधनासुः प्रमृतक इव विगतजीवलक्षण आस्ते ॥१६॥

kvacit kāla-viṣa-mita-rāja-kula-rakṣasāpahṛta-priyatama-dhanāsuḥ pramṛtaka iva vigata-jīva-lakṣaṇa āste.

kvacit—sometimes; *kāla-viṣa-mita*—made crooked by time; *rāja-kula*—the government men; *rakṣasā*—by those who are like carnivorous human beings; *apahṛta*—being plundered; *priya-tama*—most dear; *dhana*—in the form of wealth; *asuḥ*—whose life air; *pramṛtakaḥ*—dead; *iva*—like; *vigata-jīva-lakṣaṇaḥ*—bereft of all signs of life; *āste*—he remains.

TRANSLATION

Government men are always like carnivorous demons called Rākṣasas [man-eaters]. Sometimes these government men turn against the conditioned soul and take away all his accumulated wealth. Being bereft of his life's reserved wealth, the conditioned soul loses all enthusiasm. Indeed, it is as though he loses his life.

PURPORT

The word *rāja-kula-rakṣasā* is very significant. *Śrīmad-Bhāgavatam* was compiled about five thousand years ago, yet government men are referred to as Rākṣasas, or carnivorous demons. If government men are opposed to a person, that person will be bereft of all his riches, which he has accumulated with great care over a long period of time. Actually no one wants to pay income taxes—even government men themselves try to avoid these taxes—but at unfavorable times income taxes are exacted forcibly, and the taxpayers become very morose.

TEXT 17

कदाचिन्मनोरथोपगतपितृपिता महाद्यसत्सदिति स्वप्ननिर्वृतिलक्षणमनुभवति ॥१७॥

kadācin manorathopagata-pitṛ-pitāmahādy asat sad iti svapna-nirvṛti-lakṣaṇam anubhavati.

kadācit—sometimes; *manoratha-upagata*—obtained by mental concoction; *pitṛ*—the father; *pitā-maha-ādi*—or grandfather and others; *asat*—although long dead (and although no one knows that the soul has gone); *sat*—again the father or grandfather has come; *iti*—thus thinking; *svapna-nirvṛti-lakṣaṇam*—the kind of happiness found in dreams; *anubhavati*—the conditioned soul feels.

TRANSLATION

Sometimes the conditioned soul imagines that his father or grandfather has again come in the form of his son or grandson. In this way he feels the happiness one sometimes feels in a dream, and the conditioned soul sometimes takes pleasure in such mental concoctions.

PURPORT

Due to ignorance of the real existence of the Lord, the conditioned soul imagines many things. Influenced by fruitive activity, he comes together with his relatives, fathers, sons and grandfathers, exactly as straws gather together in a moving stream. In a moment the straws are thrown everywhere, and they lose contact. In conditional life, the living entity is temporarily with many other conditioned souls. They gather together as family members, and the material affection is so strong that even after a father or grandfather passes away, one takes pleasure in thinking that they return to the family in different forms. Sometimes this may happen, but in any case the conditioned soul likes to take pleasure in such concocted thoughts.

TEXT 18

क्वचिद् गृहाश्रमकर्मचोदनातिभरगिरिमारुरुक्षमाणो लोकव्यसनकर्षितमनाः कण्टकशर्कराक्षेत्रं प्रविशन्निव सीदति ॥१८॥

kvacid gṛhāśrama-karma-codanāti-bhara-girim āruruksamāṇo loka-vyasana-karṣita-manāḥ kaṇṭaka-śarkarā-kṣetraṁ praviśann iva sīdati.

kvacit—sometimes; *gṛha-āśrama*—in householder life; *karma-codana*—of the rules of fruitive activity; *ati-bhara-girim*—the big hill; *āruruksamāṇaḥ*—desiring to ascend; *loka*—material; *vyasana*—to pursuits; *karṣita-manāḥ*—whose mind is attracted; *kaṇṭaka-śarkarā-kṣetram*—a field covered with thorns and sharp pebbles; *praviśan*—entering; *iva*—like; *sīdati*—he laments.

TRANSLATION

In household life one is ordered to execute many yajñas and fruitive activities, especially the vivāha-yajña [the marriage ceremony for sons and daughters] and the sacred thread ceremony. These are all the duties of a gṛhastha, and they are very extensive and troublesome to execute. They are compared to a big hill over which one must cross when one is attached to material activities. A person desiring to cross over these ritualistic

ceremonies certainly feels pains like the piercing of thorns and pebbles endured by one attempting to climb a hill. Thus the conditioned soul suffers unlimitedly.

PURPORT

There are many social functions for keeping a prestigious position in society. In different countries and societies there are various festivals and rituals. In India, the father is supposed to get his children married. When he does so, his responsibility to the family is complete. Arranging marriages is very difficult, especially in these days. At the present moment no one can perform the proper ritual of sacrifice, nor can anyone afford to pay for the marriage ceremony of sons and daughters. Therefore householders are very much distressed when they are confronted by these social duties. It is as though they were pierced by thorns and hurt by pebbles. Material attachment is so strong that despite the suffering, one cannot give it up. Prahlāda Mahārāja therefore recommends (*Bhāg.* 7.5.5):

hitvātma-pātaṁ gṛham andha-kūpaṁ
vanaṁ gato yad dharim āśrayeta

The so-called comfortable family position is compared to a dark well in a field. If one falls in a dark well covered by grass, his life is lost, despite his cry for rescue. Highly advanced spiritualists therefore recommend that one should not enter the *gṛhastha-āśrama.* It is better to prepare oneself in the *brahmacarya-āśrama* for austerities and remain a pure *brahmacārī* throughout one's life so that one will not feel the piercing thorns of material life in the *gṛhastha-āśrama.* In the *gṛhastha-āśrama* one has to accept invitations from friends and relatives and perform ritualistic ceremonies. By so doing, one becomes captivated by such things, although he may not have sufficient resources to continue them. To maintain the *gṛhastha* lifestyle, one has to work very hard to acquire money. Thus one is implicated in material life, and he suffers the thorn pricks.

TEXT 19

क्वचिच्च दुःसहेन कायाभ्यन्तरवह्निना गृहीतसारः स्वकुटुम्बाय क्रुध्यति ॥१९॥

kvacic ca duḥsahena kāyābhyantara-vahninā gṛhīta-sāraḥ sva-kuṭumbāya krudhyati.

kvacit ca—and sometimes; *duḥsahena*—unbearable; *kāya-abhyantara-vahninā*—because of the fire of hunger and thirst within the body; *gṛhīta-sāraḥ*—whose patience is exhausted; *sva-kuṭumbāya*—unto his own family members; *krudhyati*—he becomes angry.

TRANSLATION

Sometimes, due to bodily hunger and thirst, the conditioned soul becomes so disturbed that he loses his patience and becomes angry with his own beloved sons, daughters and wife. Thus, being unkind to them, he suffers all the more.

PURPORT

Śrīla Vidyāpati Ṭhākura has sung:

tātala saikate, vāri-bindu-sama,
suta-mita-ramaṇī-samāje

The happiness of family life is compared to a drop of water in the desert. No one can be happy in family life. According to the Vedic civilization, one cannot give up the responsibilities of family life, but today everyone is giving up family life by divorce. This is due to the miserable condition experienced in the family. Sometimes, due to misery, one becomes very hardened toward his affectionate sons, daughters and wife. This is but part of the blazing fire of the forest of material life.

TEXT 20

स एव पुनर्निद्राजगरगृहीतोऽन्धे तमसि मग्नः शून्यारण्य इव शेते नान्यत्किञ्चन वेद शव इवापविद्धः ॥२०॥

sa eva punar nidrājagara-gṛhīto'ndhe tamasi magnaḥ śūnyāraṇya iva
śete nānyat-kiñcana veda śava ivāpaviddhaḥ.

saḥ—that conditioned soul; *eva*—certainly; *punaḥ*—again; *nidrā-ajagara*—by the python of deep sleep; *gṛhītaḥ*—being devoured; *andhe*—in deep darkness; *tamasi*—in ignorance; *magnaḥ*—being absorbed; *śūnya-araṇye*—in the isolated forest; *iva*—like; *śete*—he lies down; *na*—not; *anyat*—else; *kiñcana*—anything; *veda*—knows; *śavaḥ*—a dead body; *iva*—like; *apaviddhaḥ*—thrown away.

TRANSLATION

Śukadeva Gosvāmī continued speaking to Mahārāja Parīkṣit: My dear King, sleep is exactly like a python. Those who wander in the forest of material life are always devoured by the python of sleep. Being bitten by this python, they always remain in the darkness of ignorance. They are like dead bodies thrown in a distant forest. Thus the conditioned souls cannot understand what is going on in life.

PURPORT

Material life means being fully absorbed in eating, sleeping, mating and defending. Out of these, sleep is taken very seriously. While asleep, one completely forgets the object of life and what to do. For spiritual realization, one should try to avoid sleep as much as possible. The Gosvāmīs of Vṛndāvana practically did not sleep at all. Of course, they slept some, for the body requires sleep, but they slept only about two hours, and sometimes not even that. They always engaged in spiritual cultivation. *Nidrāhāra-vihārakādi-vijitau* . Following in the footsteps of the Gosvāmīs, we should try to reduce sleeping, eating, mating and defending.

TEXT 21

कदाचिद्भग्नमानदंष्ट्रो दुर्जनदन्दशूकैरलब्धनिद्राक्षणो व्यथितहृदयेनानुक्षीयमाणविज्ञानोऽन्धकूपेऽन्धवत्पतति ॥२१॥

kadācid bhagna-māna-daṁṣṭro durjana-danda-śūkair alabdha-nidrā-kṣaṇo vyathita-hṛdayenānukṣīyamāṇa-vijñāno'ndha-kūpe 'ndhavat patati.

kadācit—sometimes; *bhagna-māna-daṁṣṭraḥ*—whose teeth of pride are broken; *durjana-danda-śūkaiḥ*—by the envious activities of evil men, who are compared to a kind of serpent; *alabdha-nidrā-kṣaṇaḥ*—who does not get an opportunity to sleep; *vyathita-hṛdayena*—by a disturbed mind; *anukṣīyamāṇa*—gradually being decreased; *vijñānaḥ*—whose real consciousness; *andha-kūpe*—in a blind well; *andha-vat*—like illusion; *patati*—he falls down.

TRANSLATION

In the forest of the material world, the conditioned soul is sometimes bitten by envious enemies, which are compared to serpents and other creatures. Through the tricks of the enemy, the conditioned soul falls from

his prestigious position. Being anxious, he cannot even sleep properly. He thus becomes more and more unhappy, and he gradually loses his intelligence and consciousness. In that state he becomes almost perpetually like a blind man who has fallen into a dark well of ignorance.

TEXT 22

कर्हि स्म चित्काममधुलवान् विचिन्वन् यदा परदारपरद्रव्याण्यवरुन्धानो राज्ञा स्वामिभिर्वा निहतः पतत्यपारे निरये ॥२२॥

karhi sma cit kāma-madhu-lavān vicinvan yadā para-dāra-para-drav-
yāṇy avarundhāno rājñā svāmibhir vā nihataḥ pataty apāre niraye.

karhi sma cit—sometimes; *kāma-madhu-lavān*—little drops of honeylike sense gratification; *vicinvan*—searching after; *yadā*—when; *para-dāra*—another's wife, or a woman other than his own wife; *para-dravyāṇi*—another's money and possessions; *avarundhānaḥ*—taking as his own property; *rājñā*—by the government; *svāmibhiḥ vā*—or by the husband or relatives of the woman; *nihataḥ*—severely beaten; *patati*—he falls down; *apāre*—into unlimitedly; *niraye*—hellish conditions of life (the government's prison for criminal activities like rape, kidnapping or theft of others' property).

TRANSLATION

The conditioned soul is sometimes attracted to the little happiness derived from sense gratification. Thus he has illicit sex or steals another's property. At such a time he may be arrested by the government or chastised by the woman's husband or protector. Thus simply for a little material satisfaction, he falls into a hellish condition and is put into jail for rape, kidnapping, theft and so forth.

PURPORT

Material life is such that due to indulgence in illicit sex, gambling, intoxication and meat-eating, the conditioned soul is always in a dangerous condition. Meat-eating and intoxication excite the senses more and more, and the conditioned soul falls victim to women. In order to keep women, money is required, and to acquire money, one begs, borrows or steals. Indeed, he commits abominable acts that cause him to suffer both in this life and in the next. Consequently illicit sex must be stopped by those who are spiritually inclined or who are on the path of spiritual realization. Many devotees fall down due to illicit sex. They may steal money and even fall down from the highly honored renounced order. Then for a livelihood they accept menial services and become beggars. It is therefore said in the *śāstras, yan maithunādi-gṛhamedhi-sukhaṁ hi tuccham:* materialism is based on sex, whether licit or illicit. Sex is full of dangers even for those who are addicted to household life. Whether one has a license for sex or not, there is great trouble. *Bahu-duḥkha-bhāk:* after one indulges in sex, many volumes of miseries ensue. One suffers more and more in material life. A miserly person cannot properly utilize the wealth he has, and similarly a materialistic person misuses the human form. Instead of using it for spiritual emancipation, he uses the body for sense gratification. Therefore he is called a miser.

TEXT 23

अथ च तस्मादुभयथापि हि कर्मास्मिन्नात्मनः संसारावपनमुदाहरन्ति ॥२३॥

atha ca tasmād ubhayathāpi hi karmāsminn ātmanaḥ saṁsārāvapanam udāharanti.

atha—now; *ca*—and; *tasmāt*—because of this; *ubhayathā api*—both in this life and in the next; *hi*—undoubtedly; *karma*—fruitive activities; *asmin*—on this path of sense enjoyment; *ātmanaḥ*—of the living entity; *saṁsāra*—of material life; *āvapanam*—the cultivation ground or source; *udāharanti*—the authorities of the *Vedas* say.

TRANSLATION

Learned scholars and transcendentalists therefore condemn the materialistic path of fruitive activity because it is the original source and breeding ground of material miseries, both in this life and in the next.

PURPORT

Not knowing the value of life, *karmīs* create situations whereby they suffer in this life and the next. Unfortunately, *karmīs* are very attached to material sense gratification, and they cannot appreciate the miserable condition of material life, neither in this life nor in the next. Therefore the *Vedas* enjoin that one should awaken to spiritual consciousness and utilize all his activities to attain the favor of the Supreme Personality of Godhead. The Lord Himself says in *Bhagavad-gītā* (9.27):

yat karoṣi yad aśnāsi
yaj juhoṣi dadāsi yat

yat tapasyasi kaunteya
tat kuruṣva mad-arpaṇam

"O son of Kuntī, all that you do, all that you eat, all that you offer and give away, as well as all austerities that you may perform, should be done as an offering unto Me."

The results of all one's activities should be utilized not for sense gratification but for the mission of the Supreme Personality of Godhead. The Supreme Lord gives all information in *Bhagavad-gītā* about the aim of life, and at the end of *Bhagavad-gītā* He demands surrender unto Him. People do not generally like this demand, but one who cultivates spiritual knowledge for many births eventually surrenders unto the lotus feet of the Lord (*bahūnāṁ janmanām ante jñānavān māṁ prapadyate*).

TEXT 24

मुक्तस्ततो यदि बन्धाद्देवदत्त उपाच्छिनत्ति तस्मादपि विष्णुमित्र इत्यनवस्थितिः ॥२४॥

muktas tato yadi bandhād devadatta upācchinatti tasmād api viṣṇumitra
ity anavasthitiḥ.

muktaḥ—liberated; *tataḥ*—from that; *yadi*—if; *bandhāt*—from the government imprisonment or being beaten by the protector of the woman; *deva-dattaḥ*—person named Devadatta; *upācchinatti*—takes the money from him; *tasmāt*—from the person named Devadatta; *api*—again; *viṣṇu-mitraḥ*—a person named Viṣṇumitra; *iti*—thus; *anavasthitiḥ*—the riches do not stay in one place but pass from one hand to another.

TRANSLATION

Stealing or cheating another person out of his money, the conditioned soul somehow or other keeps it in his possession and escapes punishment. Then another man, named Devadatta, cheats him and takes the money away. Similarly, another man, named Viṣṇumitra, steals the money from Devadatta and takes it away. In any case, the money does not stay in one place. It passes from one hand to another. Ultimately no one can enjoy the money, and it remains the property of the Supreme Personality of Godhead.

PURPORT

Riches come from Lakṣmī, the goddess of fortune, and the goddess of fortune is the property of Nārāyaṇa, the Supreme Personality of Godhead. The goddess of fortune cannot stay anywhere but by the side of Nārāyaṇa; therefore another of her names is Cañcalā, restless. She cannot be peaceful unless she is in the company of her husband, Nārāyaṇa. For example, Lakṣmī was carried away by the materialistic Rāvaṇa. Rāvaṇa kidnapped Sītā, the goddess of fortune belonging to Lord Rāma. As a result, Rāvaṇa's entire family, opulence and kingdom were smashed, and Sītā, the goddess of fortune, was recovered from his clutches and reunited with Lord Rāma. Thus all property, riches and wealth belong to Kṛṣṇa. As stated in *Bhagavad-gītā* (5.29):

bhoktāraṁ yajña-tapasāṁ
sarva-loka-maheśvaram

"The Supreme Personality of Godhead is the true beneficiary of all sacrifices and austerities, and He is the supreme proprietor of all the planetary systems."

Foolish materialistic people collect money and steal from other thieves, but they cannot keep it. In any case, it must be spent. One person cheats another, and another person cheats someone else; therefore the best way to possess Lakṣmī is to keep her by the side of Nārāyaṇa. This is the point of the Kṛṣṇa consciousness movement. We worship Lakṣmī (Rādhārāṇī) along with Nārāyaṇa (Kṛṣṇa). We collect money from various sources, but that money does not belong to anyone but Rādhā and Kṛṣṇa (Lakṣmī-Nārāyaṇa). If money is utilized in the service of Lakṣmī-Nārāyaṇa, the devotee automatically lives in an opulent way. However, if one wants to enjoy Lakṣmī the way Rāvaṇa did, he will be vanquished by the laws of nature, and whatever few possessions he has will be taken away. Finally death will take everything away, and death is the representative of Kṛṣṇa.

TEXT 25

क्वचिच्च शीतवाताद्यनेकाधिदैविकभौतिकात्मीयानां दशानां प्रतिनिवारणेऽकल्पो दुरन्तचिन्तया विषण्ण आस्ते ॥२५॥

kvacic ca śīta-vātādy-anekādhidaivika-bhautikātmīyānāṁ daśānāṁ pratinivāraṇe'kalpo duranta-cintayā viṣaṇṇa āste.

kvacit—sometimes; *ca*—also; *śīta-vāta-ādi*—such as cold and strong wind; *aneka*—various; *adhidaivika*—created by the demigods; *bhautika*—

adhibhautika, created by other living beings; *ātmīyānām—adhyātmika,* created by the body and mind; *daśānām*—of conditions of misery; *pratinivāraṇe*—in the counteracting; *akalpaḥ*—unable; *duranta*—very severe; *cintayā*—by anxieties; *viṣaṇṇaḥ*—morose; *āste*—he remains.

TRANSLATION

Being unable to protect himself from the threefold miseries of material existence, the conditioned soul becomes very morose and lives a life of lamentation. These threefold miseries are miseries suffered by mental calamity at the hands of the demigods [such as freezing wind and scorching heat], miseries offered by other living entities, and miseries arising from the mind and body themselves.

PURPORT

The so-called happy materialistic person is constantly having to endure the threefold miseries of life, called *adhidaivika, adhyātmika* and *adhibhautika.* Actually no one can counteract these threefold miseries. All three may assail one at one time, or one misery may be absent and the other present. Thus the living entity is full of anxiety, fearing misery from one side or the other. The conditioned soul must be disturbed by at least one of these three miseries. There is no escape.

TEXT 26

क्वचिन्मिथो व्यवहरन् यत्किञ्चिद्धनमन्येभ्यो वा काकिणिकामात्रमप्यपहरन्
यत्किञ्चिद्वा विद्वेषमेति वित्तशाठ्यात् ॥२६॥

kvacin mitho vyavaharan yat kiñcid dhanam anyebhyo vā kākiṇikā-
mātram apy apaharan yat kiñcid vā vidveṣam eti vitta-śāṭhyāt.

kvacit—sometimes; *mithaḥ*—with one another; *vyavaharan*—trading; *yat kiñcit*—whatever little bit; *dhanam*—money; *anyebhyaḥ*—from others; *vā*—or; *kākiṇikā-mātram*—a very small amount (twenty cowries); *api*—certainly; *apaharan*—taking away by cheating; *yat kiñcit*—whatever small amount; *vā*—or; *vidveṣam eti*—creates enmity; *vitta-śāṭhyāt*—because of cheating.

TRANSLATION

As far as transactions with money are concerned, if one person cheats another by a farthing or less, they become enemies.

PURPORT

This is called *saṁsāra-dāvānala.* Even in ordinary transactions between two people, there is invariably cheating because the conditioned soul is defective in four ways—he is illusioned, he commits mistakes, his knowledge is imperfect, and he has a propensity to cheat. Unless one is liberated from material conditioning, these four defects must be there. Consequently every man has a cheating propensity, which is employed in business or money transactions. Although two friends may be living peacefully together, due to their propensity to cheat they become enemies when there is a transaction between them. A philosopher accuses an economist of being a cheater, and an economist may accuse a philosopher of being a cheater when he comes in contact with money. In any case, this is the condition of material life. One may profess a high philosophy, but when one is in need of money, he becomes a cheater. In this material world, so-called scientists, philosophers and economists are nothing but cheaters in one way or another. The scientists are cheaters because they present so many bogus things in the name of science. They propose going to the moon, but actually they end up cheating the entire public of large sums of money for their experiments. They cannot do anything useful. Unless one can find a person transcendental to the four basic defects, one should not accept advice and become a victim of the material condition. The best process is to take the advice and instructions of Śrī Kṛṣṇa or His bona fide representative. In this way one can be happy in this life and the next.

TEXT 27

अध्वन्यमुष्मिन्निम उपसर्गास्तथा सुखदुःखरागद्वेषभयाभिमानप्रमादोन्माद-
शोकमोहलोभमात्सर्येर्ष्यावमानक्षुत्पिपासाधिव्याधिजन्मजरामरणादयः ॥२७॥

adhvany amuṣminn ima upasargās tathā sukha-duḥkha-rāga-dveṣa-
bhayābhimāna-pramādonmāda-śoka-moha-lobha-mātsaryerṣyāva-
māna-kṣut-pipāsādhi-vyādhi-janma-jarā-maraṇādayaḥ.

adhvani—on the path of material life; *amuṣmin*—on that; *ime*—all these; *upasargāḥ*—eternal difficulties; *tathā*—so much also; *sukha*—so-called happiness; *duḥkha*—unhappiness; *rāga*—attachment; *dveṣa*—hate; *bhaya*—fear; *abhimāna*—false prestige; *pramāda*—illusion; *unmāda*—madness; *śoka*—lamentation; *moha*—bewilderment; *lobha*—greed; *mātsarya*—envy; *īrṣya*—enmity; *avamāna*—insult; *kṣut*—hunger; *pipāsā*—thirst; *ādhi*—

tribulations; *vyādhi*—disease; *janma*—birth; *jarā*—old age; *maraṇa*—death; *ādayaḥ*—and so on.

TRANSLATION

In this materialistic life, there are many difficulties, as I have just mentioned, and all of these are insurmountable. In addition, there are difficulties arising from so-called happiness, distress, attachment, hate, fear, false prestige, illusion, madness, lamentation, bewilderment, greed, envy, enmity, insult, hunger, thirst, tribulation, disease, birth, old age and death. All these combine together to give the materialistic conditioned soul nothing but misery.

PURPORT

The conditioned soul has to accept all these conditions simply to enjoy sense gratification in this world. Although people declare themselves great scientists, economists, philosophers, politicians and sociologists, they are actually nothing but rascals. Therefore they have been described as *mūḍhas* and *narādhamas* in *Bhagavad-gītā* (7.15):

na māṁ duṣkṛtino mūḍhāḥ
prapadyante narādhamāḥ
māyayāpahṛta-jñānā
āsuraṁ bhāvam āśritāḥ

"Those miscreants who are grossly foolish, lowest among mankind. whose knowledge is stolen by illusion, and who partake of the atheistic nature of demons, do not surrender unto Me."

Due to their foolishness, all these materialists are described in *Bhagavad-gītā* as *narādhamas.* They have attained the human form in order to get released from material bondage, but instead of doing so, they become further embarrassed amid the miserable material conditions. Therefore they are *narādhamas,* the lowest of men. One may ask whether scientists, philosophers, economists and mathematicians are also *narādhamas,* the lowest of men, and the Supreme Personality of Godhead replies that they are because they have no actual knowledge. They are simply proud of their false prestige and position. Actually they do not know how to get relief from the material condition and renovate their spiritual life of transcendental bliss and knowledge. Consequently they waste time and energy in the search for so-called happiness. These are the qualifications of the demons. In *Bhagavad-gītā* it says that when one has all these demonic qualities, he becomes a *mūḍha.* Due to this, he envies the Supreme Personality of Godhead; therefore birth after birth he is born into a demonic family, and he transmigrates from one demonic body to another. Thus he forgets his relationship with Kṛṣṇa and remains a *narādhama* in an abominable condition life after life.

TEXT 28

क्वापि देवमायया स्त्रिया भुजलतोपगूढः प्रस्कन्नविवेकविज्ञानो यद्विहारगृहारम्भाकुलहृदयस्तदाश्रयावसक्तसुतदुहितृकलत्रभाषितावलोकविचेष्टितापहृतहृदय आत्मानमजितात्मापारेऽन्धे तमसि प्रहिणोति ॥२८॥

kvāpi deva-māyayā striyā bhuja-latopagūḍhaḥ praskanna-viveka-vijñāno
yad-vihāra-gṛhārambhākula-hṛdayas tad-āśrayāvasakta-suta-duhitṛ-
kalatra-bhāṣitāvaloka-viceṣṭitāpahṛta-hṛdaya ātmānam ajitātmāpāre
'ndhe tamasi prahiṇoti.

kvāpi—somewhere; *deva-māyayā*—by the influence of the illusory energy; *striyā*—in the form of one's girlfriend or wife; *bhuja-latā*—by beautiful arms, which are compared to tender creepers in the forest; *upagūḍhaḥ*—being deeply embraced; *praskanna*—lost; *viveka*—all intelligence; *vijñānaḥ*—scientific knowledge; *yat-vihāra*—for the enjoyment of the wife; *gṛha-ārambha*—to find a house or apartment; *ākula-hṛdayaḥ*—whose heart becomes engrossed; *tat*—of that house; *āśraya-avasakta*—who are under the shelter; *suta*—of sons; *duhitṛ*—of daughters; *kalatra*—of the wife; *bhāṣita-avaloka*—by the conversations and by their beautiful glances; *viceṣṭita*—by activities; *apahṛta-hṛdayaḥ*—whose consciousness is taken away; *ātmānam*—himself; *ajita*—uncontrolled; *ātmā*—whose self; *apāre*—in unlimited; *andhe*—blind darkness; *tamasi*—in hellish life; *prahiṇoti*—he hurls.

TRANSLATION

Sometimes the conditioned soul is attracted by illusion personified (his wife or girlfriend) and becomes eager to be embraced by a woman. Thus he loses his intelligence as well as knowledge of life's goal. At that time, no longer attempting spiritual cultivation, he becomes overly attached to his wife or girlfriend and tries to provide her with a suitable apartment. Again, he becomes very busy under the shelter of that home and is captivated by the talks, glances and activities of his wife and children. In

this way he loses his Kṛṣṇa consciousness and throws himself in the dense darkness of material existence.

PURPORT

When the conditioned soul is embraced by his beloved wife, he forgets everything about Kṛṣṇa consciousness. The more he becomes attached to his wife, the more he becomes implicated in family life. One Bengali poet, Bankim Chandra, says that to the eyes of the lover the beloved is always very beautiful, even though ugly. This attraction is called *deva-māyā.* The attraction between man and woman is the cause of bondage for both. Actually both belong to the *parā prakṛti,* the superior energy of the Lord, but both are actually *prakṛti* (female). However, because both want to enjoy one another, they are sometimes described as *puruṣa* (male). Actually neither is *puruṣa,* but both can be superficially described as *puruṣa.* As soon as man and woman are united, they become attached to home, hearth, land, friendship and money. In this way they are both entrapped in material existence. The word *bhuja-latā-upagūḍha,* meaning "being embraced by beautiful arms which are compared to creepers," describes the way the conditioned soul is bound within this material world. The products of sex life—sons and daughters—certainly follow. This is the way of material existence.

TEXT 29

कदाचिदीश्वरस्य भगवतो विष्णोश्चक्रात्परमाण्वादिद्विपरार्धापवर्गकालोपल-
क्षणात्परिवर्तितेन वयसा रंहसा हरत आब्रह्मतृणस्तम्बादीनां भूतानामनिमिषतो
मिषतां वित्रस्तहृदयस्तमेवेश्वरं कालचक्रनिजायुधं साक्षाद्भगवन्तं यज्ञपुरुषमनादृत्य
पाखण्डदेवताः कङ्कगृध्रबककवटप्राया आर्यसमयपरिहृताः साङ्केत्येनाभिधत्ते ॥२९॥

kadācid īśvarasya bhagavato viṣṇoś cakrāt paramāṇv-ādi-dvi-
parārdhāpavarga-kālopalakṣaṇāt parivartitena vayasā raṁhasā harata
ābrahma-tṛṇa-stambādīnāṁ bhūtānām animiṣato miṣatāṁ vitrasta-
hṛdayas tam eveśvaraṁ kāla-cakra-nijāyudhaṁ sākṣād bhagavantaṁ
yajña-puruṣam anādṛtya pākhaṇḍa-devatāḥ kaṅka-gṛdhra-baka-vaṭa-
prāyā ārya-samaya-parihṛtāḥ sāṅketyenābhidhatte.

kadācit—sometimes; *īśvarasya*—of the Supreme Lord; *bhagavataḥ*—of the Supreme Personality of Godhead; *viṣṇoḥ*—of Lord Viṣṇu; *cakrāt*—from the disc; *paramāṇu-ādi*—beginning from the time of minute atoms; *dvi-parārdha*—the duration of the life of Brahmā; *apavarga*—ending; *kāla*—of time; *upalakṣaṇāt*—having the symptoms; *parivartitena*—revolving; *vayasā*

—by the chronological order of ages; *raṁhasā*—swiftly; *harataḥ*—taking away; *ā-brahma*—beginning from Lord Brahmā; *tṛṇa-stamba-ādīnām*—down to the small clumps of grass; *bhūtānām*—of all living entities; *animiṣataḥ*—without blinking the eyes (without fail); *miṣatām*—before the eyes of the living entities (without their being able to stop it); *vitrasta-hṛdayaḥ*—being afraid in the heart; *tam*—Him; *eva*—certainly; *īśvaram*—the Supreme Lord; *kāla-cakra-nija-āyudham*—whose personal weapon is the disc of time; *sākṣāt*—directly; *bhagavantam*—the Supreme Personality of Godhead; *yajña-puruṣam*—who accepts all kinds of sacrificial ceremonies; *anādṛtya*—without caring for; *pākhaṇḍa-devatāḥ*—concocted incarnations of God (man-made gods or demigods); *kaṅka*—buzzards; *gṛdhra*—vultures; *baka*—herons; *vaṭa-prāyāḥ*—like crows; *ārya-samaya-parihṛtāḥ*—who are rejected by authorized Vedic scriptures accepted by the Āryans; *sāṅketyena*—by concoction or with no basis of authority indicated by scripture; *abhidhatte*—he accepts as worshipable.

TRANSLATION

The personal weapon used by Lord Kṛṣṇa, the disc, is called hari-cakra, the disc of Hari. This cakra is the wheel of time. It expands from the beginning of the atoms up to the time of Brahmā's death, and it controls all activities. It is always revolving and spending the lives of the living entities, from Lord Brahmā down to an insignificant blade of grass. Thus one changes from infancy, to childhood, to youth and maturity, and thus one approaches the end of life. It is impossible to check this wheel of time. This wheel is very exacting because it is the personal weapon of the Supreme Personality of Godhead. Sometimes the conditioned soul, fearing the approach of death, wants to worship someone who can save him from imminent danger. Yet he does not care for the Supreme Personality of Godhead, whose weapon is the indefatigable time factor. The conditioned soul instead takes shelter of a man-made god described in unauthorized scriptures. Such gods are like buzzards, vultures, herons and crows. Vedic scriptures do not refer to them. Imminent death is like the attack of a lion, and neither vultures, buzzards, crows nor herons can save one from such an attack. One who takes shelter of unauthorized man-made gods cannot be saved from the clutches of death.

PURPORT

It is stated: *Hariṁ vinā naiva sṛtiṁ taranti.* No one can save himself from the cruel hands of death without being favored by Hari, the Supreme Personality of Godhead. In *Bhagavad-gītā* it is stated, *mām eva ye prapadyante māyām etāṁ taranti te:* whoever fully surrenders unto Kṛṣṇa can be saved from the cruel hands of material nature. The conditioned soul, however, sometimes wants to take shelter of a demigod, man-made god, pseudo incarnation or bogus *svāmī* or *yogī.* All these cheaters claim to follow religious principles, and all this has become very popular in this age of Kali. There are many *pāṣaṇḍīs* who, without referring to the *śāstras,* pose themselves as incarnations, and foolish people follow them. Kṛṣṇa, the Supreme Personality of Godhead, has left behind Him *Śrīmad-Bhāgavatam* and *Bhagavad-gītā.* Not referring to these authorized scriptures, rascals take shelter of man-made scriptures and try to compete with Lord Kṛṣṇa. That is the greatest difficulty one encounters when trying to promote spiritual consciousness in human society. The Kṛṣṇa consciousness movement is trying its best to bring people back to Kṛṣṇa consciousness in its pure form, but the *pāṣaṇḍīs* and atheists, who are cheaters, are so numerous that sometimes we become perplexed and wonder how to push this movement forward. In any case, we cannot accept the unauthorized ways of so-called incarnations, gods, cheaters and bluffers, who are described here as crows, vultures, buzzards and herons.

TEXT 30

यदा पाखण्डिभिरात्मवञ्चितैस्तैरुरु वञ्चितो ब्रह्मकुलं समावसंस्तेषां शील-मुपनयनादिश्रौतस्मार्तकर्मानुष्ठानेन भगवतो यज्ञपुरुषस्याराधनमेव तदरोचयन् शूद्रकुलं भजते निगमाचारेऽशुद्धितो यस्य मिथुनीभावः कुटुम्बभरणं यथा वानरजातेः ॥३०॥

yadā pākhaṇḍibhir ātma-vañcitais tair uru vañcito brahma-kulaṁ
samāvasaṁs teṣāṁ śīlam upanayanādi-śrauta-smārta-karmānuṣṭhā-
nena bhagavato yajña-puruṣasyārādhanam eva tad arocayan śūdra-
kulaṁ bhajate nigamācāre'śuddhito yasya mithunī-bhāvaḥ kuṭumba-
bharaṇaṁ yathā vānara-jāteḥ.

yadā—when; *pākhaṇḍibhiḥ*—by *pāṣaṇḍīs* (godless atheists); *ātma-vañcitaiḥ*—who themselves are cheated; *taiḥ*—by them; *uru*—more and more; *vañcitaḥ*—being cheated; *brahma-kulam*—the bona fide *brāhmaṇas* strictly following the Vedic culture; *samāvasan*—settling among them to advance spiritually; *teṣām*—of them (the *brāhmaṇas* who strictly follow Vedic principles); *śīlam*—the good character; *upanayana-ādi*—beginning with offering the sacred thread or training the conditioned soul to qualify as a bona fide *brāhmaṇa; śrauta*—according to the Vedic principles; *smārta*—according to the authorized scriptures derived from the *Vedas; karma-anuṣṭhānena*—the performance of activities; *bhagavataḥ*—of the Supreme Personality of Godhead; *yajña-puruṣasya*—who is worshiped by Vedic ritualistic ceremonies; *ārādhanam*—the process of worshiping Him; *eva*—certainly; *tat arocayan*—not finding pleasure in it due to its being difficult for unscrupulous persons to perform; *śūdra-kulam*—the society of *śūdras; bhajate*—he turns to; *nigama-ācāre*—in behaving according to Vedic principles; *aśuddhitaḥ*—not purified; *yasya*—of whom; *mithunī-bhāvaḥ*—sex enjoyment or the materialistic way of life; *kuṭumba-bharaṇam*—the maintenance of the family; *yathā*—as it is; *vānara-jāteḥ*—of the society of monkeys, or the descendants of the monkey.

TRANSLATION

The pseudo svāmīs, yogīs and incarnations who do not believe in the Supreme Personality of Godhead are known as pāṣaṇḍīs. They themselves are fallen and cheated because they do not know the real path of spiritual advancement, and whoever goes to them is certainly cheated in his turn. When one is thus cheated, he sometimes takes shelter of the real followers of Vedic principles [brāhmaṇas or those in Kṛṣṇa consciousness], who teach everyone how to worship the Supreme Personality of Godhead according to the Vedic rituals. However, being unable to stick to these principles, these rascals again fall down and take shelter among śūdras who are very expert in making arrangements for sex indulgence. Sex is very prominent among animals like monkeys, and such people who are enlivened by sex may be called descendants of monkeys.

PURPORT

By fulfilling the process of evolution from the aquatics to the animal platform, a living entity eventually reaches the human form. The three modes of material nature are always working in the evolutionary process. Those who come to the human form through the quality of *sattva-guṇa* were cows in their last animal incarnation. Those who come to the human form through the quality of *rajo-guṇa* were lions in their last animal incarnation. And those who come to the human form through the quality of *tamo-guṇa* were monkeys in their last animal incarnation. In this age, those who come through the monkey species are considered by modern anthropologists like Darwin to be descendants of monkeys. We receive information herein that those who are simply interested in sex are actually no better than monkeys. Monkeys are very expert in sexual enjoyment, and sometimes sex glands are taken from monkeys and placed in the human body so that a human being can enjoy sex in old age. In this way modern civilization has advanced. Many monkeys in India were caught and sent to Europe so that their sex glands could serve as replacements for those of old people. Those who actually descend from the monkeys are interested in expanding their aristocratic families through sex. In the *Vedas* there are also certain ceremonies especially meant for sexual improvement and promotion to higher planetary systems, where the demigods are enjoying sex. The demigods are also very much inclined toward sex because that is the basic principle of material enjoyment.

First of all, the conditioned soul is cheated by so-called *svāmīs, yogīs* and incarnations when he approaches them to be relieved of material miseries. When the conditioned soul is not satisfied with them, he comes to devotees and pure *brāhmaṇas* who try to elevate him for final liberation from material bondage. However, the unscrupulous conditioned soul cannot rigidly follow the principles prohibiting illicit sex, intoxication, gambling and meat-eating. Thus he falls down and takes shelter of people who are like monkeys. In the Kṛṣṇa consciousness movement these monkey disciples, being unable to follow the strict regulative principles, sometimes fall down and try to form societies based on sex. This is proof that such people are descendants of monkeys, as confirmed by Darwin. In this verse it is therefore clearly stated: *yathā vānara jāteḥ.*

TEXT 31

तत्रापि निरवरोधः स्वैरेण विहरन्नतिकृपणबुद्धिरन्योन्यमुखनिरीक्षणादिना ग्राम्यकर्मणैव विस्मृतकालावधिः ॥३१॥

tatrāpi niravarodhaḥ svaireṇa viharann ati-kṛpaṇa-buddhir anyonya-mukha-nirīkṣaṇādinā grāmya-karmaṇaiva vismṛta-kālāvadhiḥ.

tatra api—in that condition (in the society of human beings descended from monkeys); *niravarodhaḥ*—without hesitation; *svaireṇa*—independently, without reference to the goal of life; *viharan*—enjoying like monkeys; *ati-kṛpaṇa-buddhiḥ*—whose intelligence is dull because he does not properly utilize his assets; *anyonya*—of one another; *mukha-nirīkṣaṇa-ādinā*—by seeing the faces (when a man sees the beautiful face of a woman and the woman sees the strong build of the man's body, they always desire one another); *grāmya-karmaṇā*—by material activities for sense gratification;

eva—only; *vismṛta*—forgotten; *kāla-avadhiḥ*—the limited span of life (after which one's evolution may be degrading or elevating).

TRANSLATION

In this way the descendants of the monkeys intermingle with each other, and they are generally known as śūdras. Without hesitating, they live and move freely, not knowing the goal of life. They are captivated simply by seeing the faces of one another, which remind them of sense gratification. They are always engaged in material activities, known as grāmya-karma, and they work hard for material benefit. Thus they forget completely that one day their small life spans will be finished and they will be degraded in the evolutionary cycle.

PURPORT

Materialistic people are sometimes called *śūdras,* or descendants of monkeys, due to their monkeylike intelligence. They do not care to know how the evolutionary process is taking place, nor are they eager to know what will happen after they finish their small human life span. This is the attitude of *śūdras.* Śrī Caitanya Mahāprabhu's mission, this Kṛṣṇa consciousness movement, is trying to elevate *śūdras* to the *brāhmaṇa* platform so that they will know the real goal of life. Unfortunately, being overly attached to sense gratification, materialists are not serious in helping this movement. Instead, some of them try to suppress it. Thus it is the business of monkeys to disturb the activities of the *brāhmaṇas.* The descendants of monkeys completely forget that they have to die, and they are very proud of scientific knowledge and the progress of material civilization. The word *grāmya-karmaṇā* indicates activities meant only for the improvement of bodily comforts. Presently all human society is engaged in improving economic conditions and bodily comforts. People are not interested in knowing what is going to happen after death, nor do they believe in the transmigration of the soul. When one scientifically studies the evolutionary theory, one can understand that human life is a junction where one may take the path of promotion or degradation. As stated in *Bhagavad-gītā* (9.25):

yānti deva-vratā devān
pitṝn yānti pitṛ-vratāḥ
bhūtāni yānti bhūtejyā
yānti mad-yājino'pi mām

"Those who worship the demigods will take birth among the demigods; those who worship ghosts and spirits will take birth among such beings; those who worship ancestors go to the ancestors; and those who worship Me will live with Me."

In this life we have to prepare ourselves for promotion to the next life. Those who are in the mode of *rajo-guṇa* are generally interested in being promoted to the heavenly planets. Some, unknowingly, are degraded to lower animal forms. Those in the mode of goodness can engage in devotional service, and after that they can return home, back to Godhead (*yānti mad-yājino'pi mām*). That is the real purpose of human life. This Kṛṣṇa consciousness movement is trying to bring intelligent human beings to the platform of devotional service. Instead of wasting time trying to attain a better position in material life, one should simply endeavor to return home, back to Godhead. Then all problems will be solved. As stated in *Śrīmad-Bhāgavatam* (1.2.17):

śṛṇvatāṁ sva-kathāḥ kṛṣṇaḥ
puṇya-śravaṇa-kīrtanaḥ
hṛdy antaḥ-stho hy abhadrāṇi
vidhunoti su-hṛt-satām

"Śrī Kṛṣṇa, the Personality of Godhead, who is the Paramātmā [Supersoul] in everyone's heart and the benefactor of the truthful devotee, cleanses the desire for material enjoyment from the heart of the devotee who relishes His messages, which are in themselves virtuous when properly heard and chanted."

One simply has to follow the regulative principles, act like a *brāhmaṇa*, chant the Hare Kṛṣṇa *mantra* and read *Bhagavad-gītā* and *Śrīmad-Bhāgavatam.* In this way one purifies himself of the baser material modes (*tamo-guṇa* and *rajo-guṇa*) and, becoming freed from the greed of these modes, can attain complete peace of mind. In this way one can understand the Supreme Personality of Godhead and one's relationship with Him and thus be promoted to the highest perfection (*siddhiṁ paramāṁ gatāḥ*).

TEXT 32

क्वचिद् द्रुमवदैहिकार्थेषु गृहेषु रंस्यन् यथा वानरः सुतदारवत्सलो व्यवायक्षणः ॥३२॥

kvacid drumavad aihikārtheṣu gṛheṣu raṁsyan yathā vānaraḥ suta-dāra-vatsalo vyavāya-kṣaṇaḥ.

kvacit—sometimes; *druma-vat*—like trees (as monkeys jump from one tree to another, the conditioned soul transmigrates from one body to another); *aihika-artheṣu*—simply to bring about better worldly comforts; *gṛheṣu*—in houses (or bodies); *raṁsyan*—delighting (in one body after another, either in animal life, human life or demigod life); *yathā*—exactly as; *vānaraḥ*—the monkey; *suta-dāra-vatsalaḥ*—very affectionate to the children and wife; *vyavāya-kṣaṇaḥ*—whose leisure time is spent in sex pleasure.

TRANSLATION

Just as a monkey jumps from one tree to another, the conditioned soul jumps from one body to another. As the monkey is ultimately captured by the hunter and is unable to get out of captivity, the conditioned soul, being captivated by momentary sex pleasure, becomes attached to different types of bodies and is encaged in family life. Family life affords the conditioned soul a festival of momentary sex pleasure, and thus he is completely unable to get out of the material clutches.

PURPORT

As stated in *Śrīmad-Bhāgavatam* (11.9.29): *viṣayaḥ khalu sarvataḥ syāt.* Bodily necessities—eating, sleeping, mating and defending—are all very easily available in any form of life. It is stated here that the *vānara* (monkey) is very much attracted to sex. Each monkey keeps at least two dozen wives, and he jumps from one tree to another to capture the female monkeys. Thus he immediately engages in sexual intercourse. In this way the monkey's business is to jump from one tree to another and enjoy sex with his wives. The conditioned soul is doing the same thing, transmigrating from one body to another and engaging in sex. He thus completely forgets how to become free from the clutches of material encagement. Sometimes the monkey is captured by a hunter, who sells its body to doctors so that its glands can be removed for the benefit of another monkey. All this is going on in the name of economic development and improved sex life.

TEXT 33

एवमध्वन्यवरुन्धानो मृत्युगजभयात्तमसि गिरिकन्दरप्राये ॥३३॥

evam adhvany avarundhāno mṛtyu-gaja-bhayāt tamasi giri-kandara-prāye.

evam—in this way; *adhvani*—on the path of sense gratification; *avarundhānaḥ*—being confined, he forgets the real purpose of life; *mṛtyu-gaja-bhayāt*—out of fear of the elephant of death; *tamasi*—in the darkness; *giri-kandara-prāye*—similar to the dark caves in the mountains.

TRANSLATION

In this material world, when the conditioned soul forgets his relationship with the Supreme Personality of Godhead and does not care for Kṛṣṇa consciousness, he simply engages in different types of mischievous and sinful activities. He is then subjected to the threefold miseries, and, out of fear of the elephant of death, he falls into the darkness found in a mountain cave.

PURPORT

Everyone is afraid of death, and however strong a materialistic person may be, when there is disease and old age one must certainly accept death's notice. The conditioned soul becomes very morose to receive notice of death. His fear is compared to the fear experienced upon entering a dark mountain cave, and death is compared to a great elephant.

TEXT 34

क्वचिच्छीतवाताद्यनेकदैविकभौतिकात्मीयानां दुःखानां प्रतिनिवारणेऽकल्पो दुरन्तविषयविषण्ण आस्ते ॥३४॥

kvacic chīta-vātādy-aneka-daivika-bhautikātmīyānāṁ duḥkhānāṁ
pratinivāraṇe 'kalpo duranta-viṣaya-viṣaṇṇa āste.

kvacit—sometimes; *śīta-vāta-ādi*—such as extreme cold or wind; *aneka*—many; *daivika*—offered by the demigods or powers beyond our control; *bhautika*—offered by other living entities; *ātmīyānām*—offered by the conditioned material body and mind; *duḥkhānām*—the many miseries; *pratinivāraṇe*—in counteracting; *akalpaḥ*—being unable; *duranta*—insurmountable; *viṣaya*—from connection with sense gratification; *viṣaṇṇaḥ*—morose; *āste*—he remains.

TRANSLATION

The conditioned soul suffers many miserable bodily conditions, such as being affected by severe cold and strong winds. He also suffers due to the activities of other living beings and due to natural disturbances. When he is unable to counteract them and has to remain in a miserable condition, he naturally becomes very morose because he wants to enjoy material facilities.

TEXT 35

क्वचिन्मिथो व्यवहरन् यत्किञ्चिद्धनमुपयाति वित्तशाठ्येन ॥३५॥

kvacin mitho vyavaharan yat kiñcid dhanam upayāti vitta-śāṭhyena.

kvacit—sometimes or somewhere; *mithaḥ vyavaharan*—transacting with each other; *yat*—whatever; *kiñcit*—little bit; *dhanam*—material benefit or wealth; *upayāti*—he obtains; *vitta-śāṭhyena*—by means of cheating someone of his wealth.

TRANSLATION

Sometimes conditioned souls exchange money, but in due course of time, enmity arises because of cheating. Although there may be a tiny profit, the conditioned souls cease to be friends and become enemies.

PURPORT

As stated in *Śrīmad-Bhāgavatam* (5.5.8):

puṁsaḥ striyā mithunī-bhāvam etaṁ
tayor mitho hṛdaya-granthim āhuḥ
ato gṛha-kṣetra-sutāpta-vittair
janasya moho'yam ahaṁ mameti

The monkeylike conditioned soul first becomes attached to sex, and when intercourse actually takes place he becomes more attached. He then requires some material comforts—apartment, house, food, friends, wealth and so on. In order to acquire these things he has to cheat others, and this creates enmity even among the most intimate friends. Sometimes this enmity is created between the conditioned soul and the father or spiritual master. Unless one is firmly fixed in the regulative principles, one may perform mischievous acts, even if one is a member of the Kṛṣṇa consciousness movement. We therefore advise our disciples to strictly follow the regulative principles; otherwise the most important movement for the upliftment of humanity will be hampered due to dissension among its members. Those who are serious about pushing forward this Kṛṣṇa consciousness movement should remember this and strictly follow the regulative principles so that their minds will not be disturbed.

TEXT 36

**क्वचित्क्षीणधनः शय्यासनाशनाद्युपभोगविहीनो यावदप्रतिलब्धमनोरथोपगता-
दानेऽवसितमतिस्ततस्ततोऽवमानादीनि जनादभिलभते ॥ ३६ ॥**

kvacit kṣīṇa-dhanaḥ śayyāsanāśanādy-upabhoga-vihīno yāvad
apratilabdha-manorathopagatādāne'vasita-matis tatas tato
'vamānādīni janād abhilabhate.

kvacit—sometimes; *kṣīṇa-dhanaḥ*—not having sufficient money; *śayyā-āsana-aśana-ādi*—accommodations for sleeping, sitting or eating; *upabhoga*—of material enjoyment; *vihīnaḥ*—being bereft; *yāvat*—as long as; *apratilabdha*—not achieved; *manoratha*—by his desire; *upagata*—obtained; *ādāne*—in seizing by unfair means; *avasita-matiḥ*—whose mind is determined; *tataḥ*—because of that; *tataḥ*—from that; *avamāna-ādīni*—insults and punishment; *janāt*—from the people in general; *abhilabhate*—he gets.

TRANSLATION

Sometimes, having no money, the conditioned soul does not get sufficient accommodations. Sometimes he doesn't even have a place to sit, nor does he have the other necessities. In other words, he falls into scarcity, and at that time, when he is unable to secure the necessities by fair means, he decides to seize the property of others unfairly. When he cannot get the things he wants, he simply receives insults from others and thus becomes very morose.

PURPORT

It is said that necessity knows no law. When the conditioned soul needs money to acquire life's bare necessities, he adopts any means. He begs, borrows or steals. Instead of receiving these things, he is insulted and chastised. Unless one is very well organized, one cannot accumulate riches by unfair means. Even if one acquires riches by unfair means, he cannot avoid punishment and insult from the government or the general populace. There are many instances of important people's embezzling money, getting caught and being put in prison. One may be able to avoid the punishment of prison, but one cannot avoid the punishment of the Supreme Personality of Godhead, who works through the agency of material nature. This is described in *Bhagavad-gītā* (7.14): *daivī hy eṣā guṇa-mayī mama māyā duratyayā.* Nature is very cruel. She does not excuse anyone. When people do not care for nature, they commit all kinds of sinful activities, and consequently they have to suffer.

TEXT 37

एवं वित्तव्यतिषङ्गविवृद्धवैरानुबन्धोऽपि पूर्ववासनया मिथ उद्वहत्यथापवहति ॥३७॥

evaṁ vitta-vyatiṣaṅga-vivṛddha-vairānubandho'pi pūrva-vāsanayā
mitha udvahaty athāpavahati.

evam—in this way; *vitta-vyatiṣaṅga*—because of monetary transactions; *vivṛddha*—increased; *vaira-anubandhaḥ*—having relationships of enmity; *api*—although; *pūrva-vāsanayā*—by the fructifying results of previous impious activities; *mithaḥ*—with each other; *udvahati*—become united by means of the marriage of sons and daughters; *atha*—thereafter; *apavahati*—they give up the marriage or get a divorce.

TRANSLATION

Although people may be enemies, in order to fulfill their desires again and again, they sometimes get married. Unfortunately, these marriages do not last very long, and the people involved are separated again by divorce or other means.

PURPORT

As stated previously, every conditioned soul has the propensity to cheat, even in marriage. Everywhere in this material world, one conditioned soul is envious of another. For the time being, people may remain friends, but eventually they become enemies again and fight over money. Sometimes they marry and then separate by divorce or other means. On the whole, unity is never permanent. Due to the cheating propensity, both parties always remain envious. Even in Kṛṣṇa consciousness, separation and enmity take place due to the prominence of material propensities.

TEXT 38

एतस्मिन् संसाराध्वनि नानाक्लेशोपसर्गबाधित आपन्नविपन्नो यत्र यस्तमु ह वावेतरस्तत्र विसृज्य जातं जातमुपादाय शोचन्मुह्यन् बिभ्यद्विवदन्क्रन्दन् संहृष्यन् गायन्नह्यमानः साधुवर्जितो नैवावर्ततेऽद्यापि यत आरब्ध एष नरलोकसार्थो यमध्वनः पारमुपदिशन्ति ॥३८॥

etasmin saṁsārādhvani nānā-kleśopasarga-bādhita āpanna-vipanno yatra yas tam u ha vāvetaras tatra visṛjya jātaṁ jātam upādāya śocan muhyan bibhyad-vivadan krandan saṁhṛṣyan gāyan nahyamānaḥ sādhu-varjito naivāvartate 'dyāpi yata ārabdha eṣa nara-loka-sārtho yam adhvanaḥ pāram upadiśanti.

etasmin—on this; *saṁsāra*—of miserable conditions; *adhvani*—path; *nānā*—various; *kleśa*—by miseries; *upasarga*—by the troubles of material existence; *bādhitaḥ*—disturbed; *āpanna*—sometimes having gained; *vipannaḥ*—sometimes having lost; *yatra*—in which; *yaḥ*—who; *tam*—him; *u ha vāva*—or; *itaraḥ*—someone else; *tatra*—thereupon; *visṛjya*—giving up; *jātam jātam*—newly born; *upādāya*—accepting; *śocan*—lamenting; *muhyan*—being illusioned; *bibhyat*—fearing; *vivadan*—sometimes exclaiming loudly; *krandan*—sometimes crying; *saṁhṛṣyan*—sometimes being pleased; *gāyan*—singing; *nahyamānaḥ*—being bound; *sādhu-varjitaḥ*—being away from saintly persons; *na*—not; *eva*—certainly; *āvartate*—achieves; *adya api*—even until now; *yataḥ*—from whom; *ārabdhaḥ*—commenced; *eṣaḥ*—this; *nara-loka*—of the material world; *sa-arthaḥ*—the self-interested living entities; *yam*—whom (the Supreme Personality of Godhead); *adhvanaḥ*—of the path of material existence; *pāram*—the other end; *upadiśanti*—saintly persons indicate.

TRANSLATION

The path of this material world is full of material miseries, and various troubles disturb the conditioned souls. Sometimes he loses, and sometimes he gains. In either case, the path is full of danger. Sometimes the conditioned soul is separated from his father by death or other circumstances. Leaving him aside he gradually becomes attached to others, such as his children. In this way, the conditioned soul is sometimes illusioned and afraid. Sometimes he cries loudly out of fear. Sometimes he is happy maintaining his family, and sometimes he is overjoyed and sings

melodiously. In this way he becomes entangled and forgets his separation from the Supreme Personality of Godhead since time immemorial. Thus he traverses the dangerous path of material existence, and on this path he is not at all happy. Those who are self-realized simply take shelter of the Supreme Personality of Godhead in order to get out of this dangerous material existence. Without accepting the devotional path, one cannot get out of the clutches of material existence. The conclusion is that no one can be happy in material life. One must take to Kṛṣṇa consciousness.

PURPORT

By thoroughly analyzing the materialistic way of life, any sane man can understand that there is not the least happiness in this world. However, due to continuing on the path of danger from time immemorial and not associating with saintly persons, the conditioned soul, under illusion, wants to enjoy this material world. Material energy sometimes gives him a chance at so-called happiness, but the conditioned soul is perpetually being punished by material nature. It is therefore said: *daṇḍya-jane rājā yena nadīte cubāya* (*Cc. Madhya* 20.118). Materialistic life means continuous unhappiness, but sometimes we accept happiness as it appears between the gaps. Sometimes a condemned person is submerged in water and hauled out. Actually all of this is meant for punishment, but he feels a little comfort when he is taken out of the water. This is the situation with the conditioned soul. All the *śāstras* therefore advise that one associate with devotees and saintly people.

'sādhu-saṅga', 'sādhu-saṅga'—sarva-śāstre kaya
lava-mātra sādhu-saṅge sarva-siddhi haya
(*Cc. Madhya* 22.54)

Even by a little association with devotees, the conditioned soul can get out of this miserable material condition. This Kṛṣṇa consciousness movement is therefore trying to give everyone a chance to associate with saintly people. Therefore all the members of this Kṛṣṇa consciousness society must themselves be perfect *sādhus* in order to give a chance to fallen conditioned souls. This is the best humanitarian work.

TEXT 39

यदिदं योगानुशासनं न वा एतदवरुन्धते यन्न्यस्तदण्डा मुनय उपशमशीला उपरतात्मानः समवगच्छन्ति ॥३९॥

yad idaṁ yogānuśāsanaṁ na vā etad avarundhate yan nyasta-daṇḍā munaya upaśama-śīlā uparatātmānaḥ samavagacchanti.

yat—which; *idam*—this ultimate abode of the Supreme Personality of Godhead; *yoga-anuśāsanam*—only to be achieved by practicing devotional service; *na*—not; *vā*—either; *etat*—this path of liberation; *avarundhate*—obtain; *yat*—therefore; *nyasta-daṇḍāḥ*—persons who have given up envying others; *munayaḥ*—saintly persons; *upaśama-śīlāḥ*—who are now situated in a most peaceful existence; *uparata-ātmānaḥ*—who have control over the mind and senses; *samavagacchanti*—very easily obtain.

TRANSLATION

Saintly persons, who are friends to all living entities, have a peaceful consciousness. They have controlled their senses and minds, and they easily attain the path of liberation, the path back to Godhead. Being unfortunate and attached to the miserable material conditions, a materialistic person cannot associate with them.

PURPORT

The great saint Jaḍa Bharata described both the miserable condition and the means to get out. The only way out of it is association with devotees, and this association is very easy. Although unfortunate people also get this opportunity, due to their great misfortune they cannot take shelter of pure devotees, and consequently they continuously suffer. Nonetheless, this Kṛṣṇa consciousness movement insists that everyone take to this path by adopting the chanting of the Hare Kṛṣṇa *mahā-mantra.* The preachers of Kṛṣṇa consciousness go from door to door to inform people how they can be relieved from the miserable conditions of material life. As stated by Śrī Caitanya Mahāprabhu, *guru-kṛṣṇa-prasāde pāya bhakti-latā-bīja:* by the mercy of Kṛṣṇa and *guru,* one can get the seed of devotional service. If one is a little intelligent, he can cultivate Kṛṣṇa consciousness and be freed from the miserable conditions of material life.

TEXT 40

यदपि दिगिभजयिनो यज्विनो ये वै राजर्षयः किं तु परं मृधे शयीरन्नस्यामेव ममेयमिति कृतवैरानुबन्धायां विसृज्य स्वयमुपसंहृताः ॥४०॥

yad api dig-ibha-jayino yajvino ye vai rājarṣayaḥ kiṁ tu paraṁ mṛdhe śayīrann asyām eva mameyam iti kṛta-vairānubandhāyāṁ visṛjya svayam upasaṁhṛtāḥ.

yat api—although; *dik-ibha-jayinaḥ*—who are victorious in all directions; *yajvinaḥ*—expert in performing great sacrifices; *ye*—all of whom; *vai*—indeed; *rāja-ṛṣayaḥ*—very great saintly kings; *kim tu*—but; *param*—only this earth; *mṛdhe*—in battle; *śayīran*—lying down; *asyām*—on this (earth); *eva*—indeed; *mama*—mine; *iyam*—this; *iti*—considering in that way; *kṛta*—on which is created; *vaira-anu-bandhāyām*—a relationship of enmity with others; *visṛjya*—giving up; *svayam*—his own life; *upasaṁhṛtāḥ*—being killed.

TRANSLATION

There were many great saintly kings who were very expert in performing sacrificial rituals and very competent in conquering other kingdoms, yet despite their power they could not attain the loving service of the Supreme Personality of Godhead. This is because those great kings could not even conquer the false consciousness of "I am this body, and this is my property." Thus they simply created enmity with rival kings, fought with them and died without having discharged life's real mission.

PURPORT

The real mission of life for the conditioned soul is to reestablish the forgotten relationship with the Supreme Personality of Godhead and engage in devotional service so that he may revive Kṛṣṇa consciousness after giving up the body. One doesn't have to give up his occupation as a *brāhmaṇa, kṣatriya, vaiśya, śūdra* or whatever. In any position, while discharging his prescribed duty, one can develop Kṛṣṇa consciousness simply by associating with devotees who are representatives of Kṛṣṇa and who can teach this science. Regretfully, the big politicians and leaders in the material world simply create enmity and are not interested in spiritual advancement. Material advancement may be very pleasing to an ordinary man, but ultimately he is defeated because he identifies himself with the material body and considers everything related to it to be his property. This is ignorance. Actually nothing belongs to him, not even the body. By one's *karma,* one gets a particular body, and if he does not utilize his body to please the Supreme Personality of Godhead, all his activities are frustrated. The real purpose of life is stated in *Śrīmad-Bhāgavatam* (1.2.13):

ataḥ pumbhir dvija-śreṣṭhā
varṇāśrama-vibhāgaśaḥ
svanuṣṭhitasya dharmasya
saṁsiddhir hari-toṣaṇam

It really doesn't matter what activity a man engages in. If he can simply satisfy the Supreme Lord, his life is successful.

TEXT 41

कर्मवल्लीमवलम्ब्य तत आपदः कथञ्चिन्नरकाद्विमुक्तः पुनरप्येवं संसाराध्वनि वर्तमानो नरलोकसार्थमुपयाति एवमुपरि गतोऽपि ॥४१॥

karma-vallīm avalambya tata āpadaḥ kathañcin narakād vimuktaḥ punar apy evaṁ saṁsārādhvani vartamāno nara-loka-sārtham upayāti evam upari gato 'pi.

karma-vallīm—the creeper of fruitive activities; *avalambya*—taking shelter of; *tataḥ*—from that; *āpadaḥ*—dangerous or miserable condition; *kathañcit*—somehow or other; *narakāt*—from the hellish condition of life; *vimuktaḥ*—being freed; *punaḥ api*—again; *evam*—in this way; *saṁsāra-adhvani*—on the path of material existence; *vartamānaḥ*—existing; *nara-loka-sa-artham*—the field of self-interested material activities; *upayāti*—he enters; *evam*—thus; *upari*—above (in the higher planetary systems); *gataḥ api*—although promoted.

TRANSLATION

When the conditioned soul accepts the shelter of the creeper of fruitive activity, he may be elevated by his pious activities to higher planetary systems and thus gain liberation from hellish conditions, but unfortunately he cannot remain there. After reaping the results of his pious activities, he has to return to the lower planetary systems. In this way he perpetually goes up and comes down.

PURPORT

In this regard Śrī Caitanya Mahāprabhu says:

brahmāṇḍa bhramite kona bhāgyavān jīva
guru-kṛṣṇa-prasāde pāya bhakti-latā-bīja
(*Cc. Madhya* 19.151)

Even if one wanders for many millions of years, from the time of creation until the time of annihilation, one cannot get free from the path of material existence unless one receives shelter at the lotus feet of a pure devotee. As a monkey takes shelter of the branch of a banyan tree and thinks he is enjoying, the conditioned soul, not knowing the real interest of his life, takes shelter of the path of *karma-kāṇḍa,* fruitive activities. Sometimes he is elevated to the heavenly planets by such activities, and sometimes he again descends to earth. This is described by Śrī Caitanya Mahāprabhu as *brahmāṇḍa bhramite.* However, if by Kṛṣṇa's grace one is fortunate enough to come under the shelter of the *guru,* by the mercy of Kṛṣṇa he receives lessons on how to execute devotional service to the Supreme Lord. In this way he receives a clue of how to get out of his continuous struggle up and down within the material world. Therefore the Vedic injunction is that one should approach a spiritual master. The *Vedas* declare: *tad-vijñānārthaṁ sa gurum evābhigacchet* (*Muṇḍaka Upaniṣad* 1.2.12). Similarly in *Bhagavad-gītā* (4.34) the Supreme Personality of Godhead advises:

tad viddhi praṇipātena
paripraśnena sevayā
upadekṣyanti te jñānaṁ
jñāninas tattva-darśinaḥ

"Just try to learn the truth by approaching a spiritual master. Inquire from him submissively and render service unto him. The self-realized soul can impart knowledge unto you because he has seen the truth." *Śrīmad-Bhāgavatam* (11.3.21) gives similar advice:

tasmād guruṁ prapadyeta
jijñāsuḥ śreya uttamam
śābde pare ca niṣṇātaṁ
brahmaṇy upaśamāśrayam

"Any person who seriously desires to achieve real happiness must seek out a bona fide spiritual master and take shelter of him by initiation. The qualification of his spiritual master is that he must have realized the conclusion of the scriptures by deliberation and be able to convince others of these conclusions. Such great personalities, who have taken shelter of the Supreme Godhead, leaving aside all material considerations, are to be understood as bona fide spiritual masters." Similarly, Viśvanātha Cakravartī, a great Vaiṣṇava, also advises, *yasya prasādād bhagavat-prasādaḥ:* "By the mercy of the spiritual master one receives the mercy of Kṛṣṇa." This is the same advice given by Śrī Caitanya Mahāprabhu (*guru-kṛṣṇa-prasāde pāya bhakti-latā-bīja*). This is essential. One must come to Kṛṣṇa consciousness, and therefore one must take shelter of a pure devotee. Thus one can become free from the clutches of matter.

TEXT 42

तस्येदमुपगायन्ति —
आर्षभस्येह राजर्षेर्मनसापि महात्मनः ।
नानुवर्त्मार्हति नृपो मक्षिकेव गरुत्मतः ॥४२॥

tasyedam upagāyanti—
ārṣabhasyeha rājarṣer
manasāpi mahātmanaḥ
nānuvartmārhati nṛpo
makṣikeva garutmataḥ

tasya—of Jaḍa Bharata; *idam*—this glorification; *upagāyanti*—they sing; *ārṣabhasya*—of the son of Ṛṣabhadeva; *iha*—here; *rāja-ṛṣeḥ*—of the great saintly King; *manasā api*—even by the mind; *mahā-ātmanaḥ*—of the great personality Jaḍa Bharata; *na*—not; *anuvartma arhati*—able to follow the path; *nṛpaḥ*—any king; *makṣikā*—a fly; *iva*—like; *garutmataḥ*—of Garuḍa, the carrier of the Supreme Personality of Godhead.

TRANSLATION

Having summarized the teachings of Jaḍa Bharata, Śukadeva Gosvāmī said: My dear King Parīkṣit, the path indicated by Jaḍa Bharata is like the path followed by Garuḍa, the carrier of the Lord, and ordinary kings are just like flies. Flies cannot follow the path of Garuḍa, and to date none of the great kings and victorious leaders could follow this path of devotional service, not even mentally.

PURPORT

As Kṛṣṇa says in *Bhagavad-gītā* (7.3):

manuṣyāṇāṁ sahasreṣu
kaścid yatati siddhaye
yatatām api siddhānāṁ
kaścin māṁ vetti tattvataḥ

"Out of many thousands among men, one may endeavor for perfection, and of those who have achieved perfection, hardly one knows Me in truth." The path of devotional service is very difficult, even for great kings who have conquered many enemies. Although these kings were victorious on the battlefield, they could not conquer the bodily conception. There are many big leaders, *yogīs, svāmīs* and so-called incarnations who are very much addicted to mental speculation and who advertise themselves as perfect personalities, but they are not ultimately successful. The path of devotional service is undoubtedly very difficult to follow, but it becomes very easy if the candidate actually wants to follow the path of the *mahājana.* In this age there is the path of Śrī Caitanya Mahāprabhu, who appeared to deliver all fallen souls. This path is so simple and easy that everyone can take to it by chanting the holy name of the Lord.

harer nāma harer nāma
harer nāmaiva kevalam
kalau nāsty eva nāsty eva
nāsty eva gatir anyathā

We are very satisfied that this path is being opened by this Kṛṣṇa consciousness movement because so many European and American boys and girls are taking this philosophy seriously and gradually attaining perfection.

TEXT 43

यो दुस्त्यजान्दारसुतान् सुहृद्राज्यं हृदिस्पृशः ।
जहौ युवैव मलवदुत्तमश्लोकलालसः ॥४३॥

yo dustyajān dāra-sutān
suhṛd rājyaṁ hṛdi-spṛśaḥ
jahau yuvaiva malavad
uttamaśloka-lālasaḥ

yaḥ—the same Jaḍa Bharata who was formerly Mahārāja Bharata, the son of Mahārāja Ṛṣabhadeva; *dustyajān*—very difficult to give up; *dāra-sutān*—the wife and children or the most opulent family life; *suhṛt*—friends and well-wishers; *rājyam*—a kingdom that extended all over the world; *hṛdi-spṛśaḥ*—that which is situated within the core of one's heart; *jahau*—he gave up; *yuvā eva*—even as a young man; *mala-vat*—like stool; *uttama-śloka-lālasaḥ*—who was so fond of serving the Supreme Personality of Godhead, known as Uttamaśloka.

TRANSLATION

While in the prime of life, the great Mahārāja Bharata gave up everything because he was fond of serving the Supreme Personality of Godhead, Uttamaśloka. He gave up his beautiful wife, nice children, great friends and an enormous empire. Although these things were very difficult to give up, Mahārāja Bharata was so exalted that he gave them up just as one gives up stool after evacuating. Such was the greatness of His Majesty.

PURPORT

The name of God is Kṛṣṇa, because He is so attractive that the pure devotee can give up everything within this material world on His behalf. Mahārāja Bharata was an ideal king, instructor and emperor of the world. He possessed all the opulences of the material world, but Kṛṣṇa is so attractive that He attracted Mahārāja Bharata from all his material possessions. Yet somehow or other, the King became affectionate to a little deer and, falling from his position, had to accept the body of a deer in his next life. Due to Kṛṣṇa's great mercy upon him, he could not forget his position, and he could understand how he had fallen. Therefore in the next life, as Jaḍa Bharata, Mahārāja Bharata was careful not to spoil his energy, and therefore he presented himself as a deaf and dumb person. In this way he could concentrate on his devotional service. We have to learn from the great King Bharata how to become cautious in cultivating Kṛṣṇa consciousness. A little inattention will retard our devotional service for the time being. Yet any service rendered to the Supreme Personality of Godhead is never lost: *svalpam apy asya dharmasya trāyate mahato bhayāt* (Bg. 2.40). A little devotional service rendered sincerely is a permanent asset. As stated in *Śrīmad-Bhāgavatam* (1.5.17):

tyaktvā sva-dharmaṁ caraṇāmbujaṁ harer
bhajann apakvo 'tha patet tato yadi
yatra kva vābhadram abhūd amuṣya kiṁ
ko vārtha āpto 'bhajatāṁ sva-dharmataḥ

Somehow or other, if one is attracted to Kṛṣṇa, whatever he does in devotional service is a permanent asset. Even if one falls down due to immaturity or bad association, his devotional assets are never lost. There are many examples of this—Ajāmila, Mahārāja Bharata, and many others. This Kṛṣṇa consciousness movement is giving everyone a chance to engage in devotional service for at least some time. A little service will give one an impetus to advance and thus make one's life successful.

In this verse the Lord is described as Uttamaśloka. *Uttama* means "the best," and *śloka* means "reputation." Lord Kṛṣṇa is full in six opulences, one of which is reputation. *Aiśvaryasya samagrasya vīryasya yaśasaḥ śriyaḥ*. Kṛṣṇa's reputation is still expanding. We are spreading the glories of Kṛṣṇa by pushing forward this Kṛṣṇa consciousness movement. Kṛṣṇa's reputation, five thousand years after the Battle of Kurukṣetra, is still expanding throughout the world. Every important individual within this world must have heard of Kṛṣṇa, especially at the present moment, due to the Kṛṣṇa consciousness movement. Even people who do not like us and want to suppress the movement are also somehow or other chanting Hare Kṛṣṇa. They say, "The Hare Kṛṣṇa people should be chastised." Such foolish people do not realize the true value of this movement, but the mere fact that they want to criticize it gives them a chance to chant Hare Kṛṣṇa, and this is its success.

TEXT 44

यो दुस्त्यजान् क्षितिसुतस्वजनार्थदारान्
प्रार्थ्यां श्रियं सुरवरैः सदयावलोकाम् ।
नैच्छन्नृपस्तदुचितं महतां मधुद्विट्-
सेवानुरक्तमनसामभवोऽपि फल्गुः ॥४४॥

yo dustyajān kṣiti-suta-svajanārtha-dārān
prārthyāṁ śriyaṁ sura-varaiḥ sadayāvalokām
naicchan nṛpas tad-ucitaṁ mahatāṁ madhudviṭ-
sevānurakta-manasām abhavo 'pi phalguḥ

yaḥ—who; *dustyajān*—very difficult to give up; *kṣiti*—the earth; *suta*—children; *sva-jana-artha-dārān*—relatives, riches and a beautiful wife; *prārthyām*—desirable; *śriyam*—the goddess of fortune; *sura-varaiḥ*—by the best of the demigods; *sa-daya-avalokām*—whose merciful glance; *na*—not; *aicchat*—desired; *nṛpaḥ*—the King; *tat-ucitam*—this is quite befitting him; *mahatām*—of great personalities (*mahātmās*); *madhu-dviṭ*—of Lord Kṛṣṇa, who killed the demon Madhu; *sevā-anurakta*—attracted by the loving service; *manasām*—of those whose minds; *abhavaḥ api*—even the position of liberation; *phalguḥ*—insignificant.

TRANSLATION

Śukadeva Gosvāmī continued: My dear King, the activities of Bharata Mahārāja are wonderful. He gave up everything difficult for others to give

up. He gave up his kingdom, his wife and his family. His opulence was so great that even the demigods envied it, yet he gave it up. It was quite befitting a great personality like him to be a great devotee. He could renounce everything because he was so attracted to the beauty, opulence, reputation, knowledge, strength and renunciation of the Supreme Personality of Godhead, Kṛṣṇa. Kṛṣṇa is so attractive that one can give up all desirable things for His sake. Indeed, even liberation is considered insignificant for those whose minds are attracted to the loving service of the Lord.

PURPORT

This verse confirms Kṛṣṇa's all-attractiveness. Mahārāja Bharata was so attracted to Kṛṣṇa that he gave up all his material possessions. Generally materialistic people are attracted by such possessions.

ato gṛha-kṣetra-sutāpta-vittair
janasya moho'yam ahaṁ mameti
(*Bhāg.* 5.5.8)

"One becomes attracted to his body, home, property, children, relatives and wealth. In this way one increases life's illusions and thinks in terms of 'I and mine.'" The attraction for material things is certainly due to illusion. There is no value in attraction to material things, for the conditioned soul is diverted by them. One's life is successful if he is absorbed in the attraction of Kṛṣṇa's strength, beauty and pastimes as described in the Tenth Canto of *Śrīmad-Bhāgavatam.* The Māyāvādīs are attracted to merging into the existence of the Lord, but Kṛṣṇa is more attractive than the desire to merge. The word *abhavaḥ* means "not to take birth again in this material world." A devotee doesn't care whether he is going to be reborn or not. He is simply satisfied with the Lord's service in any condition. That is real *mukti.*

īhā yasya harer dāsye
karmaṇā manasā girā
nikhilāsv apy avasthāsu
jīvan-muktaḥ sa ucyate

"One who acts to serve Kṛṣṇa with his body, mind, intelligence and words is a liberated person, even within this material world." (*Bhakti-rasāmṛta-sindhu* 1.2.187) A person who always desires to serve Kṛṣṇa is interested in ways to convince people that there is a Supreme Personality of Godhead and that the

Supreme Personality of Godhead is Kṛṣṇa. That is his ambition. It doesn't matter whether he is in heaven or in hell. This is called *uttamaśloka-lālasa.*

TEXT 45

यज्ञाय धर्मपतये विधिनैपुणाय
योगाय सांख्यशिरसे प्रकृतीश्वराय ।
नारायणाय हरये नम इत्युदारं
हास्यन्मृगत्वमपि यः समुदाजहार ॥४५॥

yajñāya dharma-pataye vidhi-naipuṇāya
yogāya sāṅkhya-śirase prakṛtīśvarāya
nārāyaṇāya haraye nama ity udāraṁ
hāsyan mṛgatvam api yaḥ samudājahāra

yajñāya—unto the Supreme Personality of Godhead, who enjoys the results of all great sacrifices; *dharma-pataye*—unto the master or propounder of religious principles; *vidhi-naipuṇāya*—who gives the devotee the intelligence to follow the regulative principles expertly; *yogāya*—the personification of mystic *yoga; sāṅkhya-śirase*—who taught the Sāṅkhya philosophy or who actually gives knowledge of Sāṅkhya to the people of the world; *prakṛti-īśvarāya*—the supreme controller of this cosmic manifestation; *nārāyaṇāya*—the resting place of the innumerable living entities (*nara* means the living entities, and *ayana* means the shelter); *haraye*—unto the Supreme Personality of Godhead, known as Hari; *namaḥ*—respectful obeisances; *iti*—thus; *udāram*—very loudly; *hāsyan*—smiling; *mṛgatvam api*—although in the body of a deer; *yaḥ*—who; *samudājahāra*—chanted.

TRANSLATION

Even though in the body of a deer, Mahārāja Bharata did not forget the Supreme Personality of Godhead; therefore when he was giving up the body of a deer, he loudly uttered the following prayer: "The Supreme Personality of Godhead is sacrifice personified. He gives the results of ritualistic activity. He is the protector of religious systems, the personification of mystic yoga, the source of all knowledge, the controller of the entire creation, and the Supersoul in every living entity. He is beautiful and attractive. I am quitting this body offering obeisances unto Him and hoping that I may perpetually engage in His transcendental loving service." Uttering this, Mahārāja Bharata left his body.

PURPORT

The entire *Vedas* are meant for the understanding of *karma, jñāna* and *yoga*—fruitive activity, speculative knowledge and mystic *yoga.* Whatever way of spiritual realization we accept, the ultimate goal is Nārāyaṇa, the Supreme Personality of Godhead. The living entities are eternally connected with Him via devotional service. As stated in *Śrīmad-Bhāgavatam, ante nārāyaṇa-smṛtiḥ:* the perfection of life is to remember Nārāyaṇa at the time of death. Although Bharata Mahārāja had to accept the body of a deer, he could remember Nārāyaṇa at the time of death. Consequently he took birth as a perfect devotee in a *brāhmaṇa* family. This confirms the statement of *Bhagavad-gītā* (6.41), *śucīnāṁ śrīmatāṁ gehe yoga-bhraṣṭo 'bhijāyate:* "One who falls from the path of self-realization takes birth in a family of *brāhmaṇas* or wealthy aristocrats." Although Mahārāja Bharata appeared in the royal family, he became neglectful and took birth as a deer. Because he was very cautious within his deer body, he took birth in a *brāhmaṇa* family as Jaḍa Bharata. During this lifetime, he remained perfectly Kṛṣṇa conscious and preached the gospel of Kṛṣṇa consciousness directly, beginning with his instructions to Mahārāja Rahūgaṇa. In this regard, the word *yogāya* is very significant. The purpose of *aṣṭāṅga-yoga,* as stated by Madhvācārya, is to link or connect with the Supreme Personality of Godhead. The goal is not to display some material perfections.

TEXT 46

य इदं भागवतसभाजितावदातगुणकर्मणो राजर्षेर्भरतस्यानुचरितं स्वस्त्य-यनमायुष्यं धन्यं यशस्यं स्वर्ग्यापवर्ग्यं वानुशृणोत्याख्यास्यत्यभिनन्दति च सर्वा एवाशिष आत्मन आशास्ते न काञ्चन परत इति ॥४६॥

ya idaṁ bhāgavata-sabhājitāvadāta-guṇa-karmaṇo rājarṣer
bharatasyānucaritaṁ svasty-ayanam āyuṣyaṁ dhanyaṁ yaśasyaṁ
svargyāpavargyaṁ vānuśṛṇoty ākhyāsyaty abhinandati ca sarvā evāśiṣa
ātmana āśāste na kāñcana parata iti.

yaḥ—anyone who; *idam*—this; *bhāgavata*—by exalted devotees; *sabhājita*—greatly worshiped; *avadāta*—pure; *guṇa*—whose qualities; *karmaṇaḥ*—and activities; *rāja-ṛṣeḥ*—of the great saintly King; *bharatasya*—of Bharata Mahārāja; *anucaritam*—the narration; *svasti-ayanam*—the abode of auspiciousness; *āyuṣyam*—which increases one's duration of life; *dhanyam*

—increases one's fortune; *yaśasyam*—bestows reputation; *svargya*—gives promotion to the higher planetary systems (the goal of the *karmīs*); *apavargyam*—gives liberation from this material world and enables one to merge into the Supreme (the goal of the *jñānīs*); *vā*—or; *anuśṛṇoti*—always hears, following the path of devotional service; *ākhyāsyati*—describes for the benefit of others; *abhinandati*—glorifies the characteristics of devotees and the Supreme Lord; *ca*—and; *sarvāḥ*—all; *eva*—certainly; *āśiṣaḥ*—blessings; *ātmanaḥ*—for himself; *āśāste*—he achieves; *na*—not; *kāñcana*—anything; *parataḥ*—from anyone else; *iti*—thus.

TRANSLATION

Devotees interested in hearing and chanting [śravaṇaṁ kīrtanam] regularly discuss the pure characteristics of Bharata Mahārāja and praise his activities. If one submissively hears and chants about the all-auspicious Mahārāja Bharata, one's life span and material opulences certainly increase. One can become very famous and easily attain promotion to the heavenly planets, or attain liberation by merging into the existence of the Lord. Whatever one desires can be attained simply by hearing, chanting and glorifying the activities of Mahārāja Bharata. In this way, one can fulfill all his material and spiritual desires. One does not have to ask anyone else for these things, for simply by studying the life of Mahārāja Bharata, one can attain all desirable things.

PURPORT

The forest of material existence is summarized in this Fourteenth Chapter. The word *bhavāṭavī* refers to the path of material existence. The merchant is the living entity who comes to the forest of material existence to try to make money for sense gratification. The six plunderers are the senses—eyes, ears, nose, tongue, touch and mind. The bad leader is diverted intelligence. Intelligence is meant for Kṛṣṇa consciousness, but due to material existence we divert all our intelligence to achieve material facilities. Everything belongs to Kṛṣṇa, the Supreme Personality of Godhead, but due to our perverted mind and senses, we plunder the property of the Lord and engage in satisfying our senses. The jackals and tigers in the forest are our family members, and the herbs and creepers are our material desires. The mountain cave is our happy home, and the mosquitoes and serpents are our enemies. The rats, beasts and vultures are different types of thieves who take away our possessions, and the *gandharva-pura* is the phantasmagoria of the body and home. The will-o'-the-wisp is our attraction for gold and its color, and material residence and wealth are the ingredients for our material enjoyment. The whirlwind is our attraction for our wife, and the dust storm is our blinding passion experienced during sex. The demigods control the different directions, and the cricket is the harsh words spoken by our enemy during our absence. The owl is the person who directly insults us, and the impious trees are impious men. The waterless river represents atheists who give us trouble in this world and the next. The meat-eating demons are the government officials, and the pricking thorns are the impediments of material life. The little taste experienced in sex is our desire to enjoy another's wife, and the flies are the guardians of women, like the husband, father-in-law, mother-in-law and so forth. The creeper itself is women in general. The lion is the wheel of time, and the herons, crows and vultures are so-called demigods, pseudo *svāmīs, yogīs* and incarnations. All of these are too insignificant to give one relief. The swans are the perfect *brāhmaṇas,* and the monkeys are the extravagant *śūdras* engaged in eating, sleeping, mating and defending. The trees of the monkeys are our households, and the elephant is ultimate death. Thus all the constituents of material existence are described in this chapter.

Thus end the Bhaktivedanta purports of the Fifth Canto, Fourteenth Chapter, of the Śrīmad-Bhāgavatam, *entitled "The Material World as the Great Forest of Enjoyment."*

CHAPTER FIFTEEN

The Glories of the Descendants of King Priyavrata

In this chapter the descendants of Bharata Mahārāja and many other kings are described. The son of Mahārāja Bharata was named Sumati. He followed the path of liberation given by Ṛṣabhadeva. Some people mistakenly thought Sumati to be the direct incarnation of Lord Buddha. The son of Sumati was Devatājit, and his son was Devadyumna. Devadyumna's son was Parameṣṭhī, and his son was Pratīha. Pratīha was a very great devotee of Lord Viṣṇu, and he had three sons, named Pratihartā, Prastotā and Udgātā. Pratihartā had two sons, Aja and Bhūmā. The son of Bhūmā was Udgītha, and the son of Udgītha was Prastāva. The son of Prastāva was Vibhu, and the son of Vibhu was Pṛthuṣeṇa, whose son was Nakta. The wife of Nakta, Druti, gave birth to Gaya, who was a very famous and saintly king. Actually King Gaya was a partial incarnation of Lord Viṣṇu, and because of his great devotion to Lord Viṣṇu he received the title Mahāpuruṣa. King Gaya had sons named Citraratha, Sumati and Avarodhana. The son of Citraratha was the emperor Samrāṭ, and his son was Marīci, whose son was Bindu. Bindu's son was Madhu, and Madhu's son was Vīravrata. Vīravrata's two sons were Manthu and Pramanthu, and the son of Manthu was Bhauvana. The son of Bhauvana was Tvaṣṭā, and the son of Tvaṣṭā was Viraja, who glorified the whole dynasty. Viraja had one hundred sons and one daughter. Of these, the son named Śatajit became very famous.

TEXT 1

श्रीशुक उवाच

भरतस्यात्मजः सुमतिर्नामाभिहितो यमु ह वाव केचित्पाखण्डिन ऋषभपद-वीमनुवर्तमानं चानार्या अवेदसमाम्नातां देवतां स्वमनीषया पापीयस्या कलौ कल्पयिष्यन्ति ॥१॥

śrī-śuka uvāca
bharatasyātmajaḥ sumatir nāmābhihito yam u ha vāva kecit pākhaṇḍina ṛṣabha-padavīm anuvartamānaṁ cānāryā aveda-samāmnātāṁ devatāṁ sva-manīṣayā pāpīyasyā kalau kalpayiṣyanti.

śrī-śukaḥ uvāca—Śrī Śukadeva Gosvāmī continued to speak; *bharatasya*—of Bharata Mahārāja; *ātma-jaḥ*—the son; *sumatiḥ nāma-abhihitaḥ*—named Sumati; *yam*—unto whom; *u ha vāva*—indeed; *kecit*—some; *pākhaṇḍinaḥ*—atheists, men without Vedic knowledge; *ṛṣabha-padavīm*—the path of King Ṛṣabhadeva; *anuvartamānam*—following; *ca*—and; *anāryāḥ*—not belonging to the Āryans who strictly follow the Vedic principles; *aveda-samāmnātām*—not enumerated in the *Vedas; devatām*—to be Lord Buddha or a similar Buddhist deity; *sva-manīṣayā*—by their own mental speculation; *pāpīyasyā*—most sinful; *kalau*—in this age of Kali; *kalpayiṣyanti*—will imagine.

TRANSLATION

Śrīla Śukadeva Gosvāmī continued: The son of Mahārāja Bharata known as Sumati followed the path of Ṛṣabhadeva, but some unscrupulous people imagined him to be Lord Buddha himself. These people, who were actually atheistic and of bad character, took up the Vedic principles in an imaginary, infamous way to support their activities. Thus these sinful people accepted Sumati as Lord Buddhadeva and propagated the theory that everyone should follow the principles of Sumati. In this way they were carried away by mental concoction.

PURPORT

Those who are Āryans strictly follow the Vedic principles, but in this age of Kali a community has sprung up known as the *ārya-samāja,* which is ignorant of the import of the *Vedas* in the *paramparā* system. Their leaders decry all bona fide *ācāryas,* and they pose themselves as the real followers of the Vedic principles. These *ācāryas* who do not follow the Vedic principles are presently known as the *ārya-samājas,* or the Jains. Not only do they not follow the Vedic principles, but they have no relationship with Lord Buddha. Imitating the behavior of Sumati, they claim to be the descendants of Ṛṣabhadeva. Those who are Vaiṣṇavas carefully avoid their company because they are ignorant of the path of the *Vedas.* In *Bhagavad-gītā* (15.15) Kṛṣṇa says, *vedaiś ca sarvair aham eva vedyaḥ:* "The real purpose of the *Vedas* is to understand Me." This is the injunction of all Vedic literatures. One who does not know the greatness of Lord Kṛṣṇa cannot be accepted as an Āryan. Lord Buddha, an incarnation of Lord Kṛṣṇa, adopted a particular means to propagate the philosophy of *bhāgavata-dharma.* He preached almost exclusively among atheists. Atheists do not want any God, and Lord Buddha therefore said that there is no God, but he adopted the means to instruct his followers for their benefit. Therefore he preached in a duplicitous way, saying that there is no God. Nonetheless, he himself was an incarnation of God.

TEXT 2

तस्माद् वृद्धसेनायां देवताजिन्नाम पुत्रोऽभवत् ॥२॥

tasmād vṛddhasenāyāṁ devatājin-nāma putro 'bhavat.

tasmāt—from Sumati; *vṛddha-senāyām*—in the womb of his wife, named Vṛddhasenā; *devatājit-nāma*—named Devatājit; *putraḥ*—a son; *abhavat*—was born.

TRANSLATION

From Sumati, a son named Devatājit was born by the womb of his wife named Vṛddhasenā.

TEXT 3

अथासुर्यां तत्तनयो देवद्युम्नस्ततो धेनुमत्यां सुतः परमेष्ठी तस्य सुवर्चलायां प्रतीह उपजातः ॥३॥

athāsuryāṁ tat-tanayo devadyumnas tato dhenumatyāṁ sutaḥ parameṣṭhī tasya suvarcalāyāṁ pratīha upajātaḥ.

atha—thereafter; *āsuryām*—in the womb of his wife, named Āsurī; *tat-tanayaḥ*—one son of Devatājit; *deva-dyumnaḥ*—named Devadyumna; *tataḥ*—from Devadyumna; *dhenu-matyām*—in the womb of Dhenumatī, the wife of Devadyumna; *sutaḥ*—one son; *parameṣṭhī*—named Parameṣṭhī; *tasya*—of Parameṣṭhī; *suvarcalāyām*—in the womb of his wife, named Suvarcalā; *pratīhaḥ*—the son named Pratīha; *upajātaḥ*—appeared.

TRANSLATION

Thereafter, in the womb of Āsurī, the wife of Devatājit, a son named Devadyumna was begotten. Devadyumna begot in the womb of his wife, Dhenumatī, a son named Parameṣṭhī. Parameṣṭhī begot a son named Pratīha in the womb of his wife, Suvarcalā.

TEXT 4

य आत्मविद्यामाख्याय स्वयं संशुद्धो महापुरुषमनुसस्मार ॥४॥

ya ātma-vidyām ākhyāya svayaṁ saṁśuddho mahā-puruṣam anusasmāra.

yaḥ—who (King Pratīha); *ātma-vidyām ākhyāya*—after instructing many people about self-realization; *svayam*—personally; *saṁśuddhaḥ*—being very advanced and purified in self-realization; *mahā-puruṣam*—the Supreme Personality of Godhead, Viṣṇu; *anusasmāra*—perfectly understood and always remembered.

TRANSLATION

King Pratīha personally propagated the principles of self-realization. In this way, not only was he purified, but he became a great devotee of the Supreme Person, Lord Viṣṇu, and directly realized Him.

PURPORT

The word *anusasmāra* is very significant. God consciousness is not imaginary or concocted. The devotee who is pure and advanced realizes God as He is. Mahārāja Pratīha did so, and due to his direct realization of Lord Viṣṇu, he propagated self-realization and became a preacher. A real preacher cannot be bogus; he must first of all realize Lord Viṣṇu as He is. As confirmed in *Bhagavad-gītā* (4.34), *upadekṣyanti te jñānaṁ jñāninas tattva-darśinaḥ:* "one who has seen the truth can impart knowledge." The word *tattva-darśī* refers to one who has perfectly realized the Supreme Personality of Godhead. Such a person can become a *guru* and propound Vaiṣṇava philosophy all over the world. The paragon of bona fide preachers and *guru* is King Pratīha.

TEXT 5

प्रतीहात्सुवर्चलायां प्रतिहर्त्रादयस्त्रय आसन्निज्याकोविदाः सूनवः प्रतिहर्तुः स्तुत्यामजभूमानावजनिषाताम् ॥५॥

pratīhāt suvarcalāyāṁ pratihartrādayas traya āsann ijyā-kovidāḥ
sūnavaḥ pratihartuḥ stutyām aja-bhūmānāv ajaniṣātām.

pratīhāt—from King Pratīha; *suvarcalāyām*—in the womb of his wife, named Suvarcalā; *pratihartṛ-ādayaḥ trayaḥ*—the three sons Pratihartā, Prastotā and Udgātā; *āsan*—came into being; *ijyā-kovidāḥ*—who were all very expert in the ritualistic ceremonies of the *Vedas; sūnavaḥ*—sons; *pratihartuḥ*—from Pratihartā; *stutyām*—in the womb of Stutī, his wife; *aja-bhūmānau*—the two sons Aja and Bhūmā; *ajaniṣātām*—were brought into existence.

TRANSLATION

In the womb of his wife Suvarcalā, Pratīha begot three sons, named Pratihartā, Prastotā and Udgātā. These three sons were very expert in performing Vedic rituals. Pratihartā begot two sons, named Aja and Bhūmā, in the womb of his wife, named Stutī.

TEXT 6

भूम्न ऋषिकुल्यायामुद्गीथस्ततः प्रस्तावो देवकुल्यायां प्रस्तावान्नियुत्सायां हृदयज आसीद्विभुर्विभो रत्यां च पृथुषेणस्तस्मान्नक्त आकूत्यां जज्ञे नक्ताद् द्रुतिपुत्रो गयो राजर्षिप्रवर उदारश्रवा अजायत साक्षाद्भगवतो विष्णोर्जगद् रिरक्षिषया गृहीतसत्त्वस्य कलाऽऽत्मवत्त्वादिलक्षणेन महापुरुषतां प्राप्तः ॥६॥

bhūmna ṛṣikulyāyām udgīthas tataḥ prastāvo devakulyāyāṁ prastāvān niyutsāyāṁ hṛdayaja āsīd vibhur vibho ratyāṁ ca pṛthuṣeṇas tasmān nakta ākūtyāṁ jajñe naktād druti-putro gayo rājarṣi-pravara udāra-śravā ajāyata sākṣād bhagavato viṣṇor jagad-rirakṣiṣayā gṛhīta-sattvasya kalātmavattvādi-lakṣaṇena mahā-puruṣatāṁ prāptaḥ.

bhūmnaḥ—from King Bhūmā; *ṛṣi-kulyāyām*—in the womb of his wife, named Ṛṣikulyā; *udgīthaḥ*—the son named Udgītha; *tataḥ*—again from King Udgītha; *prastāvaḥ*—the son named Prastāva; *deva-kulyāyām*—his wife, named Devakulyā; *prastāvāt*—from King Prastāva; *niyutsāyām*—in his wife, named Niyutsā; *hṛdaya-jaḥ*—the son; *āsīt*—was begotten; *vibhuḥ*—named Vibhu; *vibhoḥ*—from King Vibhu; *ratyām*—in his wife, named Ratī; *ca*—also; *pṛthu-ṣeṇaḥ*—named Pṛthuṣeṇa; *tasmāt*—from him (King Pṛthuṣeṇa); *naktaḥ*—a son named Nakta; *ākūtyām*—in his wife, named Ākūti; *jajñe*—was begotten; *naktāt*—from King Nakta; *druti-putraḥ*—a son in the womb of Druti; *gayaḥ*—named King Gaya; *rāja-ṛṣi-pravaraḥ*—most exalted among the saintly royal order; *udāra-śravāḥ*—famous as a very pious king; *ajāyata*—was born; *sākṣāt bhagavataḥ*—of the Supreme Personality of Godhead directly; *viṣṇoḥ*—of Lord Viṣṇu; *jagat-rirak-ṣiṣayā*—for the purpose of giving protection to the whole world; *gṛhīta*—who is conceived; *sattvasya*—in the *śuddha-sattva* qualities; *kalā-ātma-vattva-ādi*—of being a direct incarnation of the Lord; *lakṣaṇena*—by symptoms; *mahā-puruṣatām*—the chief quality of being the leader of the human society (exactly like the chief leader of all living beings, Lord Viṣṇu); *prāptaḥ*—achieved.

TRANSLATION

In the womb of his wife, Ṛṣikulyā, King Bhūmā begot a son named Udgītha. From Udgītha's wife, Devakulyā, a son named Prastāva was born, and Prastāva begot a son named Vibhu through his wife, Niyutsā. In the womb of his wife, Ratī, Vibhu begot a son named Pṛthuṣeṇa. Pṛthuṣeṇa begot a son named Nakta in the womb of his wife, named Ākūti. Nakta's wife was Druti, and from her womb the great King Gaya was born. Gaya was very famous and pious; he was the best of saintly kings. Lord Viṣṇu and His expansions, who are meant to protect the universe, are always situated in the transcendental mode of goodness, known as viśuddha-sattva. Being the direct expansion of Lord Viṣṇu, King Gaya was also situated in the viśuddha-sattva. Because of this, Mahārāja Gaya was fully equipped with transcendental knowledge. Therefore he was called Mahāpuruṣa.

PURPORT

From this verse it appears that the incarnations of God are various. Some are part and parcel of the direct expansions, and some are direct expansions of Lord Viṣṇu. A direct incarnation of the Supreme Personality of Godhead is called *aṁśa* or *svāṁśa,* whereas an incarnation from *aṁśa* is called *kalā.* Among the *kalās* there are the *vibhinnāṁśa-jīvas,* or living entities. These are counted among the *jīva-tattvas.* Those who come directly from Lord Viṣṇu are called *viṣṇu-tattva* and are sometimes designated as Mahāpuruṣa. Another name for Kṛṣṇa is Mahāpuruṣa, and a devotee is sometimes called *mahā-pauruṣika.*

TEXT 7

स वै स्वधर्मेण प्रजापालन पोषणप्रीणनोपलालनानुशासनलक्षणेनेज्यादिना च भगवति महापुरुषे परावरे ब्रह्मणि सर्वात्मना र्पितपरमार्थलक्षणेन ब्रह्मविच्चरणानुसेवयाऽऽपादितभगवद्भक्तियोगेन चाभीक्ष्णशः परिभावितातिशुद्ध मतिरुपरतानात्म्य आत्मनि स्वयमुपलभ्यमानब्रह्मात्मानुभवोऽपि निरभिमान एवावनिमजूगुपत् ॥७॥

sa vai sva-dharmeṇa prajā-pālana-poṣaṇa-prīṇanopalālanānuśāsana-
lakṣaṇenejyādinā ca bhagavati mahā-puruṣe parāvare brahmaṇi
sarvātmanārpita-paramārtha-lakṣaṇena brahmavic-
caraṇānusevayāpādita-bhagavad-bhakti-yogena cābhīkṣṇaśaḥ
paribhāvitāti-śuddha-matir uparatānātmya ātmani svayam
upalabhyamāna-brahmātmānubhavo 'pi nirabhimāna evāvanim ajūgupat.

saḥ—that King Gaya; *vai*—indeed; *sva-dharmeṇa*—by his own duty; *prajā-pālana*—of protecting the subjects; *poṣaṇa*—of maintaining them; *prīṇana*—of making them happy in all respects; *upalālana*—of treating them as sons; *anuśāsana*—of sometimes chastising them for their mistakes; *lakṣaṇena*—by the symptoms of a king; *ijyā-ādinā*—by performing the ritualistic ceremonies as recommended in the *Vedas; ca*—also; *bhagavati*—unto the Supreme Personality of Godhead, Viṣṇu; *mahā-puruṣe*—the chief of all living entities; *para-avare*—the source of all living entities, from the highest, Lord Brahmā, to the lowest, like the insignificant ants; *brahmaṇi*—unto Parabrahman, the Supreme Personality of Godhead, Vāsudeva; *sarva-ātmanā*—in all respects; *arpita*—of being surrendered; *parama-artha-lakṣaṇena*—with spiritual symptoms; *brahma-vit*—of self-realized, saintly devotees; *caraṇa-anusevayā*—by the service of the lotus feet; *āpādita*—achieved; *bhagavat-bhakti-yogena*—by the practice of devotional service to the Lord; *ca*—also; *abhīkṣṇaśaḥ*—continuously; *paribhāvita*—saturated; *ati-śuddha-matiḥ*—whose completely pure consciousness (full realization that the body and mind are separate from the soul); *uparata-anātmye*—wherein identification with material things was stopped; *ātmani*—in his own self; *svayam*—personally; *upalabhyamāna*—being realized; *brahma-ātma-anubhavaḥ*—perception of his own position as the Supreme Spirit; *api*—although; *nirabhimānaḥ*—without false prestige; *eva*—in this way; *avanim*—the whole world; *ajūgupat*—ruled strictly according to the Vedic principles.

TRANSLATION

King Gaya gave full protection and security to the citizens so that their personal property would not be disturbed by undesirable elements. He also saw that there was sufficient food to feed all the citizens. [This is called poṣaṇa.] He would sometimes distribute gifts to the citizens to satisfy them. [This is called prīṇana.] He would sometimes call meetings and satisfy the citizens with sweet words. [This is called upalālana.] He would also give them good instructions on how to become first-class citizens. [This is called anuśāsana.] Such were the characteristics of King Gaya's royal order. Besides all this, King Gaya was a householder who strictly observed the rules and regulations of household life. He performed sacrifices and was an unalloyed pure devotee of the Supreme Personality of Godhead. He was called Mahāpuruṣa because as a king he gave the citizens all facilities, and as a householder he executed all his duties so that at the end he became a strict devotee of the Supreme Lord. As a devotee,

he was always ready to give respect to other devotees and to engage in the devotional service of the Lord. This is the bhakti-yoga process. Due to all these transcendental activities, King Gaya was always free from the bodily conception. He was full in Brahman realization, and consequently he was always jubilant. He did not experience material lamentation. Although he was perfect in all respects, he was not proud, nor was he anxious to rule the kingdom.

PURPORT

As Lord Kṛṣṇa states in *Bhagavad-gītā,* when He descends on earth, He has two types of business—to give protection to the faithful and annihilate the demons (*paritrāṇāya sādhūnāṁ vināśāya ca duṣkṛtām*). Since the king is the representative of the Supreme Personality of Godhead, he is sometimes called *nara-deva,* that is, the Lord as a human being. According to the Vedic injunctions, he is worshiped as God on the material platform. As a representative of the Supreme Lord, the king had the duty to protect the citizens in a perfect way so that they would not be anxious for food and protection and so that they would be jubilant. The king would supply everything for their benefit, and because of this he would levy taxes. If the king or government otherwise levies taxes on the citizens, he becomes responsible for the sinful activities of the citizens. In Kali-yuga, monarchy is abolished because the kings themselves are subjected to the influence of Kali-yuga. It is understood from the *Rāmāyaṇa* that when Bibhīṣaṇa became friends with Lord Rāmacandra, he promised that if by chance or will he broke the laws of friendship with Lord Rāmacandra, he would become a *brāhmaṇa* or a king in Kali-yuga. In this age, as Bibhīṣaṇa indicated, both *brāhmaṇas* and kings are in a wretched condition. Actually there are no kings or *brāhmaṇas* in this age, and due to their absence the whole world is in a chaotic condition and is always in distress. Compared to present standards, Mahārāja Gaya was a true representative of Lord Viṣṇu; therefore he was known as Mahāpuruṣa.

TEXT 8

तस्येमां गाथां पाण्डवेय पुराविद उपगायन्ति ॥८॥

tasyemāṁ gāthāṁ pāṇḍaveya purāvida upagāyanti.

tasya—of King Gaya; *imām*—these; *gāthām*—poetic verses of glorification; *pāṇḍaveya*—O Mahārāja Parīkṣit; *purā-vidaḥ*—those learned in the historical events of the *Purāṇas; upagāyanti*—sing.

TRANSLATION

My dear King Parīkṣit, those who are learned scholars in the histories of the Purāṇas eulogize and glorify King Gaya with the following verses.

PURPORT

The historical references to exalted kings serve as a good example for present rulers. Those who are ruling the world at the present moment should take lessons from King Gaya, King Yudhiṣṭhira and King Pṛthu and rule the citizens so that they will be happy. Presently the governments are levying taxes without improving the citizens in any cultural, religious, social or political way. According to the *Vedas,* this is not recommended.

TEXT 9

गयं नृप: क: प्रतियाति कर्मभि-
र्यज्वाभिमानी बहुविद्धर्मगोप्ता ।
समागतश्री: सदसस्पति: सतां
सत्सेवकोऽन्यो भगवत्कलामृते ॥ ९ ॥

gayaṁ nṛpaḥ kaḥ pratiyāti karmabhir
yajvābhimānī bahuvid dharma-goptā
samāgata-śrīḥ sadasas-patiḥ satāṁ
sat-sevako'nyo bhagavat-kalām ṛte

gayam—King Gaya; *nṛpaḥ*—king; *kaḥ*—who; *pratiyāti*—is a match for; *karmabhiḥ*—by his execution of ritualistic ceremonies; *yajvā*—who performed all sacrifices; *abhimānī*—so widely respected all over the world; *bahu-vit*—fully aware of the conclusion of Vedic literature; *dharma-goptā*—protector of the occupational duties of everyone; *samāgata-śrīḥ*—possessing all kinds of opulence; *sadasaḥ-patiḥ satām*—the dean of the assembly of great persons; *sat-sevakaḥ*—servant of the devotees; *anyaḥ*—anyone else; *bhagavat-kalām*—the plenary incarnation of the Supreme Personality of Godhead; *ṛte*—besides.

TRANSLATION

The great King Gaya used to perform all kinds of Vedic rituals. He was highly intelligent and expert in studying all the Vedic literatures. He maintained the religious principles and possessed all kinds of opulence. He was a leader among gentlemen and a servant of the devotees. He was

a totally qualified plenary expansion of the Supreme Personality of Godhead. Therefore who could equal him in the performance of gigantic ritualistic ceremonies?

TEXT 10

यमभ्यषिञ्चन् परया मुदा सतीः
सत्याशिषो दक्षकन्याः सरिद्भिः ।
यस्य प्रजानां दुदुहे धराऽऽशिषो
निराशिषो गुणवत्सस्नुतोधाः ॥१०॥

yam abhyaṣiñcan parayā mudā satīḥ
satyāśiṣo dakṣa-kanyāḥ saridbhiḥ
yasya prajānāṁ duduhe dharāśiṣo
nirāśiṣo guṇa-vatsa-snutodhāḥ

yam—whom; *abhyaṣiñcan*—bathed; *parayā*—with great; *mudā*—satisfaction; *satīḥ*—all chaste and devoted to their husbands; *satya*—true; *āśiṣaḥ*—whose blessings; *dakṣa-kanyāḥ*—the daughters of King Dakṣa; *saridbhiḥ*—with sanctified water; *yasya*—whose; *prajānām*—of the citizens; *duduhe*—fulfilled; *dharā*—the planet earth; *āśiṣaḥ*—of all desires; *nirāśiṣaḥ*—although personally having no desire; *guṇa-vatsa-snuta-udhāḥ*—earth becoming like a cow whose udders flowed upon seeing Gaya's qualities in ruling over the citizens.

TRANSLATION

All the chaste and honest daughters of Mahārāja Dakṣa, such as Śraddhā, Maitrī and Dayā, whose blessings were always effective, bathed Mahārāja Gaya with sanctified water. Indeed, they were very satisfied with Mahārāja Gaya. The planet earth personified came as a cow, and, as though she saw her calf, she delivered milk profusely when she saw all the good qualities of Mahārāja Gaya. In other words, Mahārāja Gaya was able to derive all benefits from the earth and thus satisfy the desires of his citizens. However, he personally had no desire.

PURPORT

The earth over which Mahārāja Gaya ruled is compared to a cow. The good qualities whereby he maintained and ruled the citizens are compared to the calf. A cow delivers milk in the presence of her calf; similarly the cow, or earth, fulfilled the desires of Mahārāja Gaya, who was able to utilize all the resources of the earth to benefit his citizens. This was possible because he was bathed in sanctified water by the honest daughters of Dakṣa. Unless a king or ruler is blessed by authorities, he cannot rule the citizens very satisfactorily. Through the good qualities of the ruler, the citizens become very happy and well qualified.

TEXT 11

छन्दांस्यकामस्य च यस्य कामान्
दुदूहुराजह्रुरथो बलिं नृपाः ।
प्रत्यञ्चिता युधि धर्मेण विप्रा
यदाशिषां षष्ठमंशं परेत्य ॥११॥

chandāṁsy akāmasya ca yasya kāmān
dudūhur ājahrur atho baliṁ nṛpāḥ
pratyañcitā yudhi dharmeṇa viprā
yadāśiṣāṁ ṣaṣṭham aṁśaṁ paretya

chandāṁsi—all the different parts of the *Vedas; akāmasya*—of one who has no desire for personal sense gratification; *ca*—also; *yasya*—whose; *kāmān*—all desirables; *dudūhuḥ*—yielded; *ājahruḥ*—offered; *atho*—thus; *balim*—presentation; *nṛpāḥ*—all the kings; *pratyañcitāḥ*—being satisfied by his fighting in opposition; *yudhi*—in the war; *dharmeṇa*—by religious principles; *viprāḥ*—all the *brāhmaṇas; yadā*—when; *āśiṣām*—of blessings; *ṣaṣṭham aṁśam*—one sixth; *paretya*—in the next life.

TRANSLATION

Although King Gaya had no personal desire for sense gratification, all his desires were fulfilled by virtue of his performance of Vedic rituals. All the kings with whom Mahārāja Gaya had to fight were forced to fight on religious principles. They were very satisfied with his fighting, and they would present all kinds of gifts to him. Similarly, all the brāhmaṇas in his kingdom were very satisfied with King Gaya's munificent charities. Consequently the brāhmaṇas contributed a sixth of their pious activities for King Gaya's benefit in the next life.

PURPORT

As a *kṣatriya* or emperor, Mahārāja Gaya sometimes had to fight with subordinate kings to maintain his government, but the subordinate kings were not dissatisfied with him because they knew that he fought for religious principles. Consequently they accepted their subordination and offered all kinds of gifts to him. Similarly, the *brāhmaṇas* who performed Vedic rituals were so satisfied with the King that they very readily agreed to part with a sixth of their pious activities for his benefit in the next life. Thus the *brāhmaṇas* and *kṣatriyas* were all satisfied with Mahārāja Gaya because of his proper administration. In other words, Mahārāja Gaya satisfied the *kṣatriya* kings by his fighting and satisfied the *brāhmaṇas* by his charities. The *vaiśyas* were also encouraged by kind words and affectionate dealings, and due to Mahārāja Gaya's constant sacrifices, the *śūdras* were satisfied by sumptuous food and charity. In this way Mahārāja Gaya kept all the citizens very satisfied. When *brāhmaṇas* and saintly persons are honored, they part with their pious activities, giving them to those who honor them and render them service. Therefore, as stated in *Bhagavad-gītā* (4.34), *tad viddhi praṇipātena paripraśnena sevayā:* one should try to approach a spiritual master submissively and render service unto him.

TEXT 12

यस्याध्वरे भगवानध्वरात्मा
मघोनि माद्यत्युरुसोमपीथे ।
श्रद्धाविशुद्धाचलभक्तियोग-
समर्पितेज्याफलमाजहार ॥१२॥

yasyādhvare bhagavān adhvarātmā
maghoni mādyaty uru-soma-pīthe
śraddhā-viśuddhācala-bhakti-yoga-
samarpitejyā-phalam ājahāra

yasya—of whom (King Gaya); *adhvare*—in his different sacrifices; *bhagavān*—the Supreme Personality of Godhead; *adhvara-ātmā*—the supreme enjoyer of all sacrifices, the *yajña-puruṣa; maghoni*—when King Indra; *mādyati*—intoxicated; *uru*—greatly; *soma-pīthe*—drinking the intoxicant called *soma; śraddhā*—by devotion; *viśuddha*—purified; *acala*—and steady; *bhakti-yoga*—by devotional service; *samarpita*—offered; *ijyā*—of worshiping; *phalam*—the result; *ājahāra*—accepted personally.

TRANSLATION

In Mahārāja Gaya's sacrifices, there was a great supply of the intoxicant known as soma. King Indra used to come and become intoxicated by

drinking large quantities of soma-rasa. Also, the Supreme Personality of Godhead, Lord Viṣṇu [the yajña-puruṣa] also came and personally accepted all the sacrifices offered unto Him with pure and firm devotion in the sacrificial arena.

PURPORT

Mahārāja Gaya was so perfect that he satisfied all the demigods, who were headed by the heavenly King Indra. Lord Viṣṇu Himself also personally came to the sacrificial arena to accept the offerings. Although Mahārāja Gaya did not want them, he received all the blessings of the demigods and the Supreme Lord Himself.

TEXT 13

यत्प्रीणनाद्बर्हिषि देवतिर्यङ्-
मनुष्यवीरुत्तृणमाविरिञ्चात् ।
प्रीयेत सद्यः स ह विश्वजीवः
प्रीतः स्वयं प्रीतिमगाद्गयस्य ॥१३॥

yat-prīṇanād barhiṣi deva-tiryaṅ-
manuṣya-vīrut-tṛṇam āviriñcāt
prīyeta sadyaḥ sa ha viśva-jīvaḥ
prītaḥ svayaṁ prītim agād gayasya

yat-prīṇanāt—because of pleasing the Supreme Personality of Godhead; *barhiṣi*—in the sacrificial arena; *deva-tiryak*—the demigods and lower animals; *manuṣya*—human society; *vīrut*—the plants and trees; *tṛṇam*—the grass; *ā-viriñcāt*—beginning from Lord Brahmā; *prīyeta*—becomes satisfied; *sadyaḥ*—immediately; *saḥ*—that Supreme Personality of Godhead; *ha*—indeed; *viśva-jīvaḥ*—maintains the living entities all over the universe; *prītaḥ*—although naturally satisfied; *svayam*—personally; *prītim*—satisfaction; *agāt*—he obtained; *gayasya*—of Mahārāja Gaya.

TRANSLATION

When the Supreme Lord is pleased by a person's actions, automatically all the demigods, human beings, animals, birds, bees, creepers, trees, grass and all other living entities, beginning with Lord Brahmā, are pleased. The Supreme Personality of Godhead is the Supersoul of everyone, and He is by nature fully pleased. Nonetheless, He came to the arena of Mahārāja Gaya and said, "I am fully pleased."

PURPORT

It is explicitly stated herein that simply by satisfying the Supreme Personality of Godhead, one satisfies the demigods and all other living entities without differentiation. If one pours water on the root of a tree, all the branches, twigs, flowers and leaves are nourished. Although the Supreme Lord is self-satisfied, He was so pleased with the behavior of Mahārāja Gaya that He personally came to the sacrificial arena and said, "I am fully satisfied." Who can compare to Mahārāja Gaya?

TEXTS 14–15

गयाद्गयन्त्यां चित्ररथः सुगतिरवरोधन इति त्रयः पुत्रा बभूवुश्चित्ररथादूर्णायां सम्राडजनिष्ट तत उत्कलायां मरीचिर्मरीचे ॥ १४ ॥
र्बिन्दुमत्यां बिन्दुमानुदपद्यत तस्मात्सरघायां मधुर्नामाभवन्मधोः सुमनसि वीरव्रतस्ततो भोजायां मन्थुप्रमन्थू जज्ञाते मन्थोः सत्यायां भौवनस्ततो दूषणायां त्वष्टाजनिष्ट त्वष्टुर्विरोचनायां विरजो विरजस्य शतजित्प्रवरं पुत्रशतं कन्या च विषूच्यां किल जातम् ॥ १५ ॥

gayād gayantyāṁ citrarathaḥ sugatir avarodhana iti trayaḥ putrā babhūvuś citrarathād ūrṇāyāṁ samrāḍ ajaniṣṭa; tata utkalāyāṁ marīcir marīcer bindumatyāṁ bindum ānudapadyata tasmāt saraghāyāṁ madhur nāmābhavan madhoḥ sumanasi vīravratas tato bhojāyāṁ manthu-pramanthū jajñāte manthoḥ satyāyāṁ bhauvanas tato dūṣaṇāyāṁ tvaṣṭājaniṣṭa tvaṣṭur virocanāyāṁ virajo virajasya śatajit-pravaraṁ putra-śataṁ kanyā ca viṣūcyāṁ kila jātam.

gayāt—from Mahārāja Gaya; *gayantyām*—in his wife, named Gayantī; *citra-rathaḥ*—named Citraratha; *sugatiḥ*—named Sugati; *avarodhanaḥ*—named Avarodhana; *iti*—thus; *trayaḥ*—three; *putrāḥ*—sons; *babhūvuḥ*—were born; *citrarathāt*—from Citraratha; *ūrṇāyām*—in the womb of Ūrṇā; *samrāṭ*—named Samrāṭ; *ajaniṣṭa*—was born; *tataḥ*—from him; *utkalāyām*—in his wife named Utkalā; *marīciḥ*—named Marīci; *marīceḥ*—from Marīci; *bindu-matyām*—in the womb of his wife Bindumatī; *bindum*—a son named Bindu; *ānudapadyata*—was born; *tasmāt*—from him; *saraghāyām*—in the womb of his wife Saraghā; *madhuḥ*—Madhu; *nāma*—named; *abhavat*—was born; *madhoḥ*—from Madhu; *sumanasi*—in the womb of his wife, Sumanā; *vīra-vrataḥ*—a son named Vīravrata; *tataḥ*—from Vīravrata; *bhojāyām*—in the womb of his wife Bhojā;

manthu-pramanthū—two sons named Manthu and Pramanthu; *jajñāte*—were born; *manthoḥ*—from Manthu; *satyāyām*—in his wife, Satyā; *bhauvanaḥ*—a son named Bhauvana; *tataḥ*—from him; *dūṣaṇāyām*—in the womb of his wife Dūṣaṇā; *tvaṣṭā*—one son named Tvaṣṭā; *ajaniṣṭa*—was born; *tvaṣṭuḥ*—from Tvaṣṭā; *virocanāyām*—in his wife named Virocanā; *virajaḥ*—a son named Viraja; *virajasya*—of King Viraja; *śatajit-pravaram*—headed by Śatajit; *putra-śatam*—one hundred sons; *kanyā*—a daughter; *ca*—also; *viṣūcyām*—in his wife Viṣūcī; *kila*—indeed; *jātam*—took birth.

TRANSLATION

In the womb of Gayantī, Mahārāja Gaya begot three sons, named Citraratha, Sugati and Avarodhana. In the womb of his wife Ūrṇā, Citraratha begot a son named Samrāṭ. The wife of Samrāṭ was Utkalā, and in her womb Samrāṭ begot a son named Marīci. In the womb of his wife Bindumatī, Marīci begot a son named Bindu. In the womb of his wife Saraghā, Bindu begot a son named Madhu. In the womb of his wife named Sumanā, Madhu begot a son named Vīravrata. In the womb of his wife Bhojā, Vīravrata begot two sons named Manthu and Pramanthu. In the womb of his wife Satyā, Manthu begot a son named Bhauvana, and in the womb of his wife Dūṣaṇā, Bhauvana begot a son named Tvaṣṭā. In the womb of his wife Virocanā, Tvaṣṭā begot a son named Viraja. The wife of Viraja was Viṣūcī, and in her womb Viraja begot one hundred sons and one daughter. Of all these sons, the son named Śatajit was predominant.

TEXT 16

तत्रायं श्लोकः —
प्रैयव्रतं वंशमिमं विरजश्चरमोद्भवः ।
अकरोदत्यलं कीर्त्या विष्णुः सुरगणं यथा ॥१६॥

tatrāyaṁ ślokaḥ—
praiyavrataṁ vaṁśam imaṁ
virajaś caramodbhavaḥ
akarod aty-alaṁ kīrtyā
viṣṇuḥ sura-gaṇaṁ yathā

tatra—in that connection; *ayam ślokaḥ*—there is this famous verse; *praiyavratam*—coming from King Priyavrata; *vaṁśam*—the dynasty; *imam*—this; *virajaḥ*—King Viraja; *carama-udbhavaḥ*—the source of one hundred sons (headed by Śatajit); *akarot*—decorated; *ati-alam*—very greatly; *kīrtyā* —by his reputation; *viṣṇuḥ*—Lord Viṣṇu, the Supreme Personality of Godhead; *sura-gaṇam*—the demigods; *yathā*—just as.

TRANSLATION

There is a famous verse about King Viraja. "Because of his high qualities and wide fame, King Viraja became the jewel of the dynasty of King Priyavrata, just as Lord Viṣṇu, by His transcendental potency, decorates and blesses the demigods."

PURPORT

Within a garden, a flowering tree attains a good reputation because of its fragrant flowers. Similarly, if there is a famous man in a family, he is compared to a fragrant flower in a forest. Because of him, an entire family can become famous in history. Because Lord Kṛṣṇa took birth in the Yadu dynasty, the Yadu dynasty and the Yādavas have remained famous for all time. Because of King Viraja's appearance, the family of Mahārāja Priyavrata has remained famous for all time.

Thus end the Bhaktivedanta purports of the Fifth Canto, Fifteenth Chapter, of the Śrīmad-Bhāgavatam, *entitled "The Glories of the Descendants of King Priyavrata."*

CHAPTER SIXTEEN

A Description of Jambūdvīpa

While describing the character of Mahārāja Priyavrata and his descendants, Śukadeva Gosvāmī also described Meru Mountain and the planetary system known as Bhū-maṇḍala. Bhū-maṇḍala is like a lotus flower, and its seven islands are compared to the whorl of the lotus. The place known as Jambūdvīpa is in the middle of that whorl. In Jambūdvīpa there is a mountain known as Sumeru, which is made of solid gold. The height of this mountain is 84,000 *yojanas,* of which 16,000 *yojanas* are below the earth. Its width is estimated to be 32,000 *yojanas* at its summit and 16,000 *yojanas* at its foot. (One *yojana* equals approximately eight miles.) This king of mountains, Sumeru, is the support of the planet earth.

On the southern side of the land known as Ilāvṛta-varṣa are the mountains known as Himavān, Hemakūṭa and Niṣadha, and on the northern side are the mountains Nīla, Śveta and Śṛṅga. Similarly, on the eastern and western side there are Mālyavān and Gandhamādana, two large mountains. Surrounding Sumeru Mountain are four mountains known as Mandara, Merumandara, Supārśva and Kumuda, each 10,000 *yojanas* long and 10,000 *yojanas* high. On these four mountains there are trees 1,100 *yojanas* high—a mango tree, a rose apple tree, a *kadamba* tree and a banyan tree. There are also lakes full of milk, honey, sugarcane juice and pure water. These lakes can fulfill all desires. There are also gardens named Nandana, Citraratha, Vaibhrājaka and Sarvatobhadra. On the side of Supārśva Mountain is a *kadamba* tree with streams of honey flowing from its hollows, and on Kumuda Mountain there is a banyan tree named Śatavalśa, from whose roots flow rivers containing milk, yogurt and many other desirable things. Surrounding Sumeru Mountain like filaments of the whorl of a lotus are twenty mountain ranges such as Kuraṅga, Kurara, Kusumbha, Vaikaṅka and Trikūṭa. To the east of Sumeru are the mountains Jaṭhara and Devakūṭa, to the west are Pavana and Pāriyātra, to the south are Kailāsa and Karavīra, and to the north are Triśṛṅga and Makara. These eight mountains are about 18,000 *yojanas* long, 2,000 *yojanas* wide and 2,000 *yojanas* high. On the summit of Mount Sumeru is Brahmapurī, the residence of Lord Brahmā. Each of its four sides is 10,000 *yojanas* long. Surrounding Brahmapurī are the cities of King Indra and seven other demigods. These cities are one fourth the size of Brahmapurī.

TEXT 1

राजोवाच

उक्तस्त्वया भूमण्डलायामविशेषो यावदादित्यस्तपति यत्र चासौ ज्योतिषां गणैश्चन्द्रमा वा सह दृश्यते ॥१॥

rājovāca
uktas tvayā bhū-maṇḍalāyāma-viśeṣo yāvad ādityas tapati yatra cāsau jyotiṣāṁ gaṇaiś candramā vā saha dṛśyate.

rājā uvāca—Mahārāja Parīkṣit said; *uktaḥ*—already been said; *tvayā*—by you; *bhū-maṇḍala*—of the planetary system known as Bhū-maṇḍala; *āyāma-viśeṣaḥ*—the specific length of the radius; *yāvat*—as far as; *ādityaḥ*—the sun; *tapati*—heats; *yatra*—wherever; *ca*—also; *asau*—that; *jyotiṣām*—of the luminaries; *gaṇaiḥ*—with hordes; *candramā*—the moon; *vā*—either; *saha*—with; *dṛśyate*—is seen.

TRANSLATION

King Parīkṣit said to Śukadeva Gosvāmī: O brāhmaṇa, you have already informed me that the radius of Bhū-maṇḍala extends as far as the sun spreads its light and heat and as far as the moon and all the stars can be seen.

PURPORT

In this verse it is stated that the planetary system known as Bhū-maṇḍala extends to the limits of the sunshine. According to modern science, the sunshine reaches earth from a distance of 93,000,000 miles. If we calculate according to this modern information, 93,000,000 miles can be considered the radius of Bhū-maṇḍala. In the Gāyatrī *mantra,* we chant *oṁ bhūr bhuvaḥ svaḥ.* The word *bhūr* refers to Bhū-maṇḍala. *Tat savitur vareṇyam:* the sunshine spreads throughout Bhū-maṇḍala. Therefore the sun is worshipable. The stars, which are known as *nakṣatra,* are not different suns, as modern astronomers suppose. From *Bhagavad-gītā* (10.21) we understand that the stars are similar to the moon (*nakṣatrāṇām ahaṁ śaśī*). Like the moon, the stars reflect the sunshine. Apart from our modern distinguished estimations of where the planetary systems are located, we can understand that the sky and its various planets were studied long, long before *Śrīmad-Bhāgavatam* was compiled. Śukadeva Gosvāmī explained the location of the planets, and this indicates that the information was known long, long before Śukadeva

Gosvāmī related it to Mahārāja Parīkṣit. The location of the various planetary systems was not unknown to the sages who flourished in the Vedic age.

TEXT 2

तत्रापि प्रियव्रतरथचरणपरिखातैः सप्तभिः सप्त सिन्धव उपक्लृप्ता यत एतस्याः सप्तद्वीपविशेषविकल्पस्त्वया भगवन् खलु सूचित एतदेवाखिलमहं मानतो लक्षणतश्च सर्वं विजिज्ञासामि ॥२॥

tatrāpi priyavrata-ratha-caraṇa-parikhātaiḥ saptabhiḥ sapta sindhava
upakḷptā yata etasyāḥ sapta-dvīpa-viśeṣa-vikalpas tvayā bhagavan
khalu sūcita etad evākhilam ahaṁ mānato lakṣaṇataś ca sarvaṁ vi-
jijñāsāmi.

tatra api—in that Bhū-maṇḍala; *priyavrata-ratha-caraṇa-parikhātaiḥ*—by the ditches made by the wheels of the chariot used by Priyavrata Mahārāja while circumambulating Sumeru behind the sun; *saptabhiḥ*—by the seven; *sapta*—seven; *sindhavaḥ*—oceans; *upakḷptāḥ*—created; *yataḥ*—because of which; *etasyāḥ*—of this Bhū-maṇḍala; *sapta-dvīpa*—of the seven islands; *viśeṣa-vikalpaḥ*—the mode of the construction; *tvayā*—by you; *bhagavan*—O great saint; *khalu*—indeed; *sūcitaḥ*—described; *etat*—this; *eva*—certainly; *akhilam*—whole subject; *aham*—I; *mānataḥ*—from the point of view of measurement; *lakṣaṇataḥ*—and from symptoms; *ca*—also; *sarvam*—everything; *vijijñāsāmi*—wish to know.

TRANSLATION

My dear Lord, the rolling wheels of Mahārāja Priyavrata's chariot created seven ditches, in which the seven oceans came into existence. Because of these seven oceans, Bhū-maṇḍala is divided into seven islands. You have given a very general description of their measurement, names and characteristics. Now I wish to know of them in detail. Kindly fulfill my desire.

TEXT 3

भगवतो गुणमये स्थूलरूप आवेशितं मनो ह्यगुणेऽपि सूक्ष्मतम आत्मज्योतिषि परे ब्रह्मणि भगवति वासुदेवाख्ये क्षममावेशितुं तदु हैतद् गुरोऽर्हस्यनुवर्णयितु-मिति ॥३॥

bhagavato guṇamaye sthūla-rūpa āveśitaṁ mano hy aguṇe 'pi
sūkṣmatama ātma-jyotiṣi pare brahmaṇi bhagavati vāsudevākhye
kṣamam āveśituṁ tad u haitad guro 'rhasy anuvarṇayitum iti.

bhagavataḥ—of the Supreme Personality of Godhead; *guṇa-maye*—into the external features, consisting of the three modes of material nature; *sthūla-rūpe*—the gross form; *āveśitam*—entered; *manaḥ*—the mind; *hi*—indeed; *aguṇe*—transcendental; *api*—although; *sūkṣmatame*—in His smaller form as Paramātmā within the heart; *ātma-jyotiṣi*—who is full of Brahman effulgence; *pare*—the supreme; *brahmaṇi*—spiritual entity; *bhagavati*—the Supreme Personality of Godhead; *vāsudeva-ākhye*—known as Bhagavān Vāsudeva; *kṣamam*—suitable; *āveśitum*—to absorb; *tat*—that; *u ha*—indeed; *etat*—this; *guro*—O my dear spiritual master; *arhasi anuvarṇayitum*—please describe factually; *iti*—thus.

TRANSLATION

When the mind is fixed upon the Supreme Personality of Godhead in His external feature made of the material modes of nature—the gross universal form—it is brought to the platform of pure goodness. In that transcendental position, one can understand the Supreme Personality of Godhead, Vāsudeva, who in His subtler form is self-effulgent and beyond the modes of nature. O my lord, please describe vividly how that form, which covers the entire universe, is perceived.

PURPORT

Mahārāja Parīkṣit had already been advised by his spiritual master, Śukadeva Gosvāmī, to think of the universal form of the Lord, and therefore, following the advice of his spiritual master, he continuously thought of that form. The universal form is certainly material, but because everything is an expansion of the energy of the Supreme Personality of Godhead, ultimately nothing is material. Therefore Parīkṣit Mahārāja's mind was saturated with spiritual consciousness. Śrīla Rūpa Gosvāmī has stated:

prāpañcikatayā buddhyā
hari-sambandhi-vastunaḥ
mumukṣubhiḥ parityāgo
vairāgyaṁ phalgu kathyate

Everything, even that which is material, is connected with the Supreme Personality of Godhead. Therefore everything should be engaged in the service of the Lord. Śrīla Bhaktisiddhānta Sarasvatī Ṭhākura translates this verse as follows:

hari-sevāya yāhā haya anukūla
viṣaya baliyā tāhāra tyāge haya bhula

"One should not give up anything connected with the Supreme Personality of Godhead, thinking it material or enjoyable for the material senses." Even the senses, when purified, are spiritual. When Mahārāja Parīkṣit was thinking of the universal form of the Lord, his mind was certainly situated on the transcendental platform. Therefore although he might not have had any reason to be concerned with detailed information of the universe, he was thinking of it in relationship with the Supreme Lord, and therefore such geographical knowledge was not material but transcendental. Elsewhere in *Śrīmad-Bhāgavatam* (1.5.20) Nārada Muni has said, *idaṁ hi viśvaṁ bhagavān ivetaraḥ:* the entire universe is also the Supreme Personality of Godhead, although it appears different from Him. Therefore although Parīkṣit Mahārāja had no need for geographical knowledge of this universe, that knowledge was also spiritual and transcendental because he was thinking of the entire universe as an expansion of the energy of the Lord.

In our preaching work also, we deal with so much property and money and so many books bought and sold, but because these dealings all pertain to the Kṛṣṇa consciousness movement, they should never be considered material. That one is absorbed in thoughts of such management does not mean that he is outside of Kṛṣṇa consciousness. If one rigidly observes the regulative principle of chanting sixteen rounds of the *mahā-mantra* every day, his dealings with the material world for the sake of spreading the Kṛṣṇa consciousness movement are not different from the spiritual cultivation of Kṛṣṇa consciousness.

TEXT 4

ऋषिरुवाच
न वै महाराज भगवतो मायागुणविभूतेः काष्ठां मनसा वचसा वाधिगन्तुमलं विबुधायुषापि पुरुषस्तस्मात्प्राधान्येनैव भूगोलकविशेषं नामरूप मानलक्षणतो व्याख्यास्यामः ॥४॥

ṛṣir uvāca
na vai mahārāja bhagavato māyā-guṇa-vibhūteḥ kāṣṭhāṁ manasā vacasā vādhigantum alaṁ vibudhāyuṣāpi puruṣas tasmāt prādhān-yenaiva bhū-golaka-viśeṣaṁ nāma-rūpa-māna-lakṣaṇato vyākhyāsyāmaḥ.

ṛṣiḥ uvāca—Śrī Śukadeva Gosvāmī continued to speak; *na*—not; *vai*—indeed; *mahā-rāja*—O great King; *bhagavataḥ*—of the Supreme Personality of Godhead; *māyā-guṇa-vibhūteḥ*—of the transformation of the qualities of the material energy; *kāṣṭhām*—the end; *manasā*—by the mind; *vacasā*—by words; *vā*—either; *adhigantum*—to understand fully; *alam*—capable; *vibudha-āyuṣā*—with a duration of life like that of Brahmā; *api*—even; *puruṣaḥ*—a person; *tasmāt*—therefore; *prādhānyena*—by a general description of the chief places; *eva*—certainly; *bhū-golaka-viśeṣam*—the particular description of Bhūloka; *nāma-rūpa*—names and forms; *māna*—measurements; *lakṣaṇataḥ*—according to symptoms; *vyākhyāsyāmaḥ*—I shall try to explain.

TRANSLATION

The great ṛṣi Śukadeva Gosvāmī said: My dear King, there is no limit to the expansion of the Supreme Personality of Godhead's material energy. This material world is a transformation of the material qualities [sattva-guṇa, rajo-guṇa and tamo-guṇa], yet no one could possibly explain it perfectly, even in a lifetime as long as that of Brahmā. No one in the material world is perfect, and an imperfect person could not describe this material universe accurately, even after continued speculation. O King, I shall nevertheless try to explain to you the principal regions, such as Bhū-goloka [Bhūloka], with their names, forms, measurements and various symptoms.

PURPORT

The material world is only one fourth of the Supreme Personality of Godhead's creation, but it is unlimited and impossible for anyone to know or describe, even with the qualification of a life as long as that of Brahmā, who lives for millions and millions of years. Modern scientists and astronomers try to explain the cosmic situation and the vastness of space, and some of them believe that all the glittering stars are different suns. From *Bhagavad-gītā,* however, we understand that all these stars (*nakṣatras*) are like the moon, in that they reflect the sunshine. They are not independent luminaries. Bhūloka is explained to be that portion of outer space through which the heat and light of the sun extend. Therefore it is natural to conclude that this universe extends in space as far as we can see and encompasses the glittering stars. Śrīla Śukadeva Gosvāmī admitted that to give full details of this expansive material universe would be impossible, but nevertheless he wanted to give the King as much knowledge as he had received through the *paramparā* system. We should conclude that if one cannot comprehend the material expansions of the Supreme Personality of Godhead, one certainly cannot estimate the expansiveness of the spiritual world. The *Brahma-saṁhitā* (5.33) confirms this:

advaitam acyutam anādim ananta-rūpam
ādyaṁ purāṇa-puruṣaṁ nava-yauvanaṁ ca

The limits of the expansions of Govinda, the Supreme Personality of Godhead, cannot be estimated by anyone, even a person as perfect as Brahmā, not to speak of tiny scientists whose senses and instruments are all imperfect and who cannot give us information of even this one universe. We should therefore be satisfied with the information obtainable from Vedic sources as spoken by authorities like Śukadeva Gosvāmī.

TEXT 5

यो वायं द्वीपः कुवलयकमलकोशाभ्यन्तरकोशो नियुतयोजन विशालः समवर्तुलो यथा पुष्करपत्रम् ॥५॥

yo vāyaṁ dvīpaḥ kuvalaya-kamala-kośābhyantara-kośo niyuta-yojana-viśālaḥ samavartulo yathā puṣkara-patram.

yaḥ—which; *vā*—either; *ayam*—this; *dvīpaḥ*—island; *kuvalaya*—the Bhūloka; *kamala-kośa*—of the whorl of a lotus flower; *abhyantara*—inner; *kośaḥ*—whorl; *niyuta-yojana-viśālaḥ*—one million *yojanas* (eight million miles) wide; *samavartulaḥ*—equally round, or having a length and breadth of the same measurement; *yathā*—like; *puṣkara-patram*—a lotus leaf.

TRANSLATION

The planetary system known as Bhū-maṇḍala resembles a lotus flower, and its seven islands resemble the whorl of that flower. The length and breadth of the island known as Jambūdvīpa, which is situated in the middle of the whorl, are one million yojanas [eight million miles]. Jambūdvīpa is round like the leaf of a lotus flower.

TEXT 6

यस्मिन्नव वर्षाणि नवयोजनसहस्रायामान्यष्टभिर्मर्यादागिरिभिः सुविभक्तानि भवन्ति ॥६॥

yasmin nava varṣāṇi nava-yojana-sahasrāyāmāny aṣṭabhir maryādā-giribhiḥ suvibhaktāni bhavanti.

yasmin—in that Jambūdvīpa; *nava*—nine; *varṣāṇi*—divisions of land; *nava-yojana-sahasra*—72,000 miles in length; *āyāmāni*—measuring; *aṣṭabhiḥ*—by eight; *maryādā*—indicating the boundaries; *giribhiḥ*—by mountains; *suvibhaktāni*—nicely divided from one another; *bhavanti*—are.

TRANSLATION

In Jambūdvīpa there are nine divisions of land, each with a length of 9,000 yojanas [72,000 miles]. There are eight mountains that mark the boundaries of these divisions and separate them nicely.

PURPORT

Śrīla Viśvanātha Cakravartī Ṭhākura gives the following quotation from the *Vāyu Purāṇa,* wherein the locations of the various mountains, beginning with the Himalayas, are described.

dhanurvat saṁsthite jñeye dve varṣe dakṣiṇottare; dīrghāṇi tatra catvāri caturasram ilāvṛtam iti dakṣiṇottare bhāratottara-kuru-varṣe catvāri kiṁpuruṣa-harivarṣa-ramyaka-hiraṇmayāni varṣāṇi nīla-niṣadhayos tiraścinībhūya samudra-praviṣṭayoḥ saṁlagnatvam aṅgīkṛtya bhadrāśva-ketumālayor api dhanur-ākṛtitvam; atas tayor dairghyata eva madhye saṅkucitatvena nava-sahasrāyāmatvam; ilāvṛtasya tu meroḥ sakāśāt catur-dikṣu nava-sahasrāyāmatvaṁ saṁbhavet vastutas tv ilāvṛta-bhadrāśva-ketumālānāṁ catus-triṁśat-sahasrāyāmatvaṁ jñeyam.

TEXT 7

एषां मध्ये इलावृतं नामाभ्यन्तरवर्षं यस्य नाभ्यामवस्थितः सर्वतः सौवर्णः कुलगिरिराजो मेरुर्द्वीपायामसमुन्नाहः कर्णिकाभूतः कुवलयकमलस्य मूर्धनि द्वात्रिंशत् सहस्रयोजनविततो मूले षोडशसहस्रं तावतान्तर्भूम्यां प्रविष्टः ॥७॥

eṣāṁ madhye ilāvṛtaṁ nāmābhyantara-varṣaṁ yasya nābhyām avasthitaḥ sarvataḥ sauvarṇaḥ kula-giri-rājo merur dvīpāyāma-samunnāhaḥ karṇikā-bhūtaḥ kuvalaya-kamalasya mūrdhani dvā-triṁśat sahasra-yojana-vitato mūle ṣoḍaśa-sahasraṁ tāvat āntar-bhūmyāṁ praviṣṭaḥ.

eṣām—all these divisions of Jambūdvīpa; *madhye*—among; *ilāvṛtam nāma*—named Ilāvṛta-varṣa; *abhyantara-varṣam*—the inner division; *yasya*—of which; *nābhyām*—in the navel; *avasthitaḥ*—situated; *sarvataḥ*—entirely; *sauvarṇaḥ*—made of gold; *kula-giri-rājaḥ*—the most famous among famous mountains; *meruḥ*—Mount Meru; *dvīpa-āyāma-samunnāhaḥ*—whose height is the same measurement as the width of Jambūdvīpa; *karṇikā-bhūtaḥ*—existing as the pericarp; *kuvalaya*—of this planetary system; *kamalasya*—like a lotus flower; *mūrdhani*—on the top; *dvā-triṁśat*—thirty-two; *sahasra*—thousand; *yojana*—*yojanas* (eight miles each); *vitataḥ*—expanded; *mūle*—at the base; *ṣoḍaśa-sahasram*—sixteen thousand *yojanas; tāvat*—so much; *āntaḥ-bhūmyām*—within the earth; *praviṣṭaḥ*—entered.

TRANSLATION

Amidst these divisions, or varṣas, is the varṣa named Ilāvṛta, which is situated in the middle of the whorl of the lotus. Within Ilāvṛta-varṣa is Sumeru Mountain, which is made of gold. Sumeru Mountain is like the pericarp of the lotuslike Bhū-maṇḍala planetary system. The mountain's height is the same as the width of Jambūdvīpa—or, in other words, 100,000 yojanas [800,000 miles]. Of that, 16,000 yojanas [128,000 miles] are within the earth, and therefore the mountain's height above the earth is 84,000 yojanas [672,000 miles]. The mountain's width is 32,000 yojanas [256,000 miles] at its summit and 16,000 yojanas at its base.

TEXT 8

उत्तरोत्तरेणेलावृतं नीलः श्वेतः शृङ्गवानिति त्रयो रम्यकहिरण्मयकुरूणां वर्षाणां मर्यादागिरयः प्रागायता उभयतः क्षारोदावधयो द्विसहस्रपृथव एकैकशः पूर्वस्मात्पूर्वस्मादुत्तर उत्तरो दशांशाधिकांशेन दैर्घ्य एव ह्रसन्ति ॥८॥

uttarottareṇelāvṛtaṁ nīlaḥ śvetaḥ śṛṅgavān iti trayo ramyaka-
hiraṇmaya-kurūṇāṁ varṣāṇāṁ maryādā-girayaḥ prāg-āyatā
ubhayataḥ kṣārodāvadhayo dvi-sahasra-pṛthava ekaikaśaḥ pūrvasmāt
pūrvasmād uttara uttaro daśāṁśādhikāṁśena dairghya eva hrasanti.

uttara-uttareṇa ilāvṛtam—further and further north of Ilāvṛta-varṣa; *nīlaḥ*—Nīla; *śvetaḥ*—Śveta; *śṛṅgavān*—Śṛṅgavān; *iti*—thus; *trayaḥ*—three mountains; *ramyaka*—Ramyaka; *hiraṇmaya*—Hiraṇmaya; *kurūṇām*—of the Kuru division; *varṣāṇām*—of the *varṣas; maryādā-girayaḥ*—the mountains marking the borders; *prāk-āyatāḥ*—extended on the eastern side; *ubhayataḥ*—to the east and the west; *kṣāroda*—the ocean of salt water; *avadhayaḥ*—extending to; *dvi-sahasra-pṛthavaḥ*—which are two thousand *yojanas* wide; *eka-ekaśaḥ*—one after another; *pūrvasmāt*—than the former; *pūrvasmāt*—than the former; *uttaraḥ*—further north; *uttaraḥ*—further north; *daśa-aṁśa-adhika-aṁśena*—by one tenth of the former; *dairghyaḥ*—in length; *eva*—indeed; *hrasanti*—become shorter.

TRANSLATION

Just north of Ilāvṛta-varṣa—and going further northward, one after another—are three mountains named Nīla, Śveta and Śṛṅgavān. These mark the borders of the three varṣas named Ramyaka, Hiraṇmaya and Kuru and separate them from one another. The width of these mountains is 2,000 yojanas [16,000 miles]. Lengthwise, they extend east and west to the beaches of the ocean of salt water. Going from south to north, the length of each mountain is one tenth that of the previous mountain, but the height of them all is the same.

PURPORT

In this regard, Madhvācārya quotes the following verses from the *Brahmāṇḍa Purāṇa:*

yathā bhāgavate tūktaṁ
bhauvanaṁ kośa-lakṣaṇam
tasyāvirodhato yojyam
anya-granthāntare sthitam

maṇḍode puraṇaṁ caiva
vyatyāsaṁ kṣīra-sāgare
rāhu-soma-ravīṇāṁ ca
maṇḍalād dvi-guṇoktitām
vinaiva sarvam unneyaṁ
yojanābhedato'tra tu

It appears from these verses that aside from the sun and moon, there is an invisible planet called Rāhu. The movements of Rāhu cause both solar and lunar eclipses. We suggest that the modern expeditions attempting to reach the moon are mistakenly going to Rāhu.

TEXT 9

एवं दक्षिणेनेलावृतं निषधो हेमकूटो हिमालय इति प्रागायता यथा नीलादयो-ऽयुतयोजनोत्सेधा हरिवर्षकिम्पुरुषभारतानां यथासंख्यम् ॥९॥

evaṁ dakṣiṇenelāvṛtaṁ niṣadho hemakūṭo himālaya iti prāg-āyatā yathā nīlādayo 'yuta-yojanotsedhā hari-varṣa-kimpuruṣa-bhāratānāṁ yathā-saṅkhyam.

evam—thus; *dakṣiṇena*—by degrees to the southern side; *ilāvṛtam*—of Ilāvṛta-varṣa; *niṣadhaḥ hema-kūṭaḥ himālayaḥ*—three mountains named Niṣadha, Hemakūṭa and Himālaya; *iti*—thus; *prāk-āyatāḥ*—extended to the east; *yathā*—just as; *nīla-ādayaḥ*—the mountains headed by Nīla; *ayuta-yojana-utsedhāḥ*—ten thousand *yojanas* high; *hari-varṣa*—the division named Hari-varṣa; *kimpuruṣa*—the division named Kimpuruṣa; *bhāratānām*—the division named Bhārata-varṣa; *yathā-saṅkhyam*—according to number.

TRANSLATION

Similarly, south of Ilāvṛta-varṣa and extending from east to west are three great mountains named (from north to south) Niṣadha, Hemakūṭa and Himālaya. Each of them is 10,000 yojanas [80,000 miles] high. They mark the boundaries of the three varṣas named Hari-varṣa, Kimpuruṣa-varṣa and Bhārata-varṣa [India].

TEXT 10

तथैवेलावृतमपरेण पूर्वेण च माल्यवद्गन्धमादनावानीलनिषधायतौ द्विसहस्रं पप्रथतुः केतुमालभद्राश्वयोः सीमानं विदधाते ॥१०॥

tathaivelāvṛtam apareṇa pūrveṇa ca mālyavad-gandhamādanāv ānīla-niṣadhāyatau dvi-sahasraṁ paprathatuḥ ketumāla-bhadrāśvayoḥ sīmānaṁ vidadhāte.

tathā eva—exactly like that; *ilāvṛtam apareṇa*—on the western side of Ilāvṛta-varṣa; *pūrveṇa ca*—and on the eastern side; *mālyavad-gandha-mādanau*—the demarcation mountains of Mālyavān on the west and Gandhamādana on the east; *ā-nīla-niṣadha-āyatau*—on the northern side up to the mountain known as Nīla and on the southern side up to the mountain known as Niṣadha; *dvi-sahasram*—two thousand *yojanas; paprathatuḥ*—they extend; *ketumāla-bhadrāśvayoḥ*—of the two *varṣas* named Ketumāla and Bhadrāśva; *sīmānam*—the border; *vidadhāte*—establish.

TRANSLATION

In the same way, west and east of Ilāvṛta-varṣa are two great mountains named Mālyavān and Gandhamādana respectively. These two mountains, which are 2,000 yojanas [16,000 miles] high, extend as far as Nīla Mountain in the north and Niṣadha in the south. They indicate the borders of Ilāvṛta-varṣa and also the varṣas known as Ketumāla and Bhadrāśva.

PURPORT

There are so many mountains, even on this planet earth. We do not think that the measurements of all of them have actually been calculated. While passing over the mountainous region from Mexico to Caracas, we actually saw so many mountains that we doubt whether their height, length and breadth have been properly measured. Therefore, as indicated in *Śrīmad-Bhāgavatam* by Śukadeva Gosvāmī, we should not try to comprehend the greater mountainous areas of the universe merely by our calculations. Śukadeva Gosvāmī has already stated that such calculations would be very difficult even if one had a duration of life like that of Brahmā. We should simply be satisfied with the statements of authorities like Śukadeva Gosvāmī and appreciate how the entire cosmic manifestation has been made possible by the external energy of the Supreme Personality of Godhead. The measurements given herein, such as 10,000 *yojanas* or 100,000 *yojanas,* should be considered correct because they have been given by Śukadeva Gosvāmī. Our experimental knowledge can neither verify nor disprove the statements of *Śrīmad-Bhāgavatam.* We should simply hear these statements from the authorities. If we can appreciate the extensive energy of the Supreme Personality of Godhead, that will benefit us.

TEXT 11

मन्दरो मेरुमन्दरः सुपार्श्वः कुमुद इत्ययुतयोजनविस्तारोन्नाहा मेरो-
श्चतुर्दिशमवष्टम्भगिरय उपक्लृप्ताः ॥११॥

mandaro merumandaraḥ supārśvaḥ kumuda ity ayuta-yojana-
vistāronnāhā meroś catur-diśam avaṣṭambha-giraya upakḷptāḥ.

mandaraḥ—the mountain named Mandara; *meru-mandaraḥ*—the mountain named Merumandara; *supārśvaḥ*—the mountain named Supārśva; *kumudaḥ*—the mountain named Kumuda; *iti*—thus; *ayuta-yojana-vistāra-*

unnāhāḥ—which measure ten thousand *yojanas* high and wide; *meroḥ*—of Sumeru; *catuḥ-diśam*—the four sides; *avaṣṭambha-girayaḥ*—mountains that are like the belts of Sumeru; *upakḷptāḥ*—situated.

TRANSLATION

On the four sides of the great mountain known as Sumeru are four mountains—Mandara, Merumandara, Supārśva and Kumuda—which are like its belts. The length and height of these mountains are calculated to be 10,000 yojanas [80,000 miles].

TEXT 12

चतुर्ष्वेतेषु चूतजम्बूकदम्बन्यग्रोधाश्चत्वारः पादप प्रवराः पर्वतकेतव इवाधिसहस्रयोजनोन्नाहास्तावद् विटपविततयः शतयोजनपरिणाहाः ॥१२॥

caturṣv eteṣu cūta-jambū-kadamba-nyagrodhāś catvāraḥ pādapa-pravarāḥ parvata-ketava ivādhi-sahasra-yojanonnāhās tāvad viṭapa-vitatayaḥ śata-yojana-pariṇāhāḥ.

caturṣu—on the four; *eteṣu*—on these mountains, beginning with Mandara; *cūta-jambū-kadamba*—of trees such as the mango, rose apple and *kadamba; nyagrodhāḥ*—and the banyan tree; *catvāraḥ*—four kinds; *pādapa-pravarāḥ*—the best of trees; *parvata-ketavaḥ*—the flagstaffs on the mountains; *iva*—like; *adhi*—over; *sahasra-yojana-unnāhāḥ*—one thousand *yojanas* high; *tāvat*—so much also; *viṭapa-vitatayaḥ*—the length of the branches; *śata-yojana*—one hundred *yojanas; pariṇāhāḥ*—wide.

TRANSLATION

Standing like flagstaffs on the summits of these four mountains are a mango tree, a rose apple tree, a kadamba tree and a banyan tree. Those trees are calculated to have a width of 100 yojanas [800 miles] and a height of 1,100 yojanas [8,800 miles]. Their branches also spread to a radius of 1,100 yojanas.

TEXTS 13–14

ह्रदाश्चत्वारः पयोमध्विक्षुरसमृष्टजला यदुपस्पर्शिन उपदेवगणा योगैश्वर्याणि स्वाभाविकानि भरतर्षभ धारयन्ति ॥१३॥ देवो द्यानानि च भवन्ति चत्वारि नन्दनं चैत्ररथं वैभ्राजकं सर्वतोभद्रमिति ॥१४॥

hradāś catvāraḥ payo-madhv-ikṣurasa-mṛṣṭa-jalā yad-upasparśina upadeva-gaṇā yogaiśvaryāṇi svābhāvikāni bharatarṣabha dhārayanti; devodyānāni ca bhavanti catvāri nandanaṁ caitrarathaṁ vaibhrājakaṁ sarvatobhadram iti.

hradāḥ—lakes; *catvāraḥ*—four; *payaḥ*—milk; *madhu*—honey; *ikṣu-rasa*—sugarcane juice; *mṛṣṭa-jalāḥ*—filled with pure water; *yat*—of which; *upasparśinaḥ*—those who use the liquids; *upadeva-gaṇāḥ*—the demigods; *yoga-aiśvaryāṇi*—all the perfections of mystic *yoga; svābhāvikāni*—without being tried for; *bharata-ṛṣabha*—O best of the Bharata dynasty; *dhārayanti*—possess; *deva-udyānāni*—celestial gardens; *ca*—also; *bhavanti*—there are; *catvāri*—four; *nandanam*—of the Nandana garden; *caitra-ratham*—Caitraratha garden; *vaibhrājakam*—Vaibhrājaka garden; *sarvataḥ-bhadram*—Sarvatobhadra garden; *iti*—thus.

TRANSLATION

O Mahārāja Parīkṣit, best of the Bharata dynasty, between these four mountains are four huge lakes. The water of the first tastes just like milk; the water of the second, like honey; and that of the third, like sugarcane juice. The fourth lake is filled with pure water. The celestial beings such as the Siddhas, Cāraṇas and Gandharvas, who are also known as demigods, enjoy the facilities of those four lakes. Consequently they have the natural perfections of mystic yoga, such as the power to become smaller than the smallest or greater than the greatest. There are also four celestial gardens named Nandana, Caitraratha, Vaibhrājaka and Sarvatobhadra.

TEXT 15

येष्वमर परिवृढाः सह सुरललनाललामयूथपतय उपदेवगणैरुपगीयमानमहिमानः किल विहरन्ति ॥१५॥

yeṣv amara-parivṛḍhāḥ saha sura-lalanā-lalāma-yūtha-pataya upadeva-gaṇair upagīyamāna-mahimānaḥ kila viharanti.

yeṣu—in which; *amara-parivṛḍhāḥ*—the best of the demigods; *saha*—with; *sura-lalanā*—of the wives of all the demigods and semi-demigods; *lalāma*—of those women who are like ornaments; *yūtha-patayaḥ*—the husbands; *upadeva-gaṇaiḥ*—by the semi-demigods (the Gandharvas); *upagīyamāna*—being chanted; *mahimānaḥ*—whose glories; *kila*—indeed; *viharanti*—they enjoy sports.

TRANSLATION

The best of the demigods, along with their wives, who are like ornaments of heavenly beauty, meet together and enjoy within those gardens, while their glories are sung by lesser demigods known as Gandharvas.

TEXT 16

मन्दरोत्सङ्ग एकादशशतयोजनोत्तुङ्गदेवचूतशिरसो गिरिशिखरस्थूलानि फलान्यमृतकल्पानि पतन्ति ॥१६॥

mandarotsaṅga ekādaśa-śata-yojanottuṅga-devacūta-śiraso giri-śikhara-sthūlāni phalāny amṛta-kalpāni patanti.

mandara-utsaṅge—on the lower slopes of Mandara Mountain; *ekādaśa-śata-yojana-uttuṅga*—1,100 *yojanas* high; *devacūta-śirasaḥ*—from the top of a mango tree named Devacūta; *giri-śikhara-sthūlāni*—which are as fat as mountain peaks; *phalāni*—fruit; *amṛta-kalpāni*—as sweet as nectar; *patanti*—fall down.

TRANSLATION

On the lower slopes of Mandara Mountain is a mango tree named Devacūta. It is 1,100 yojanas high. Mangoes as big as mountain peaks and as sweet as nectar fall from the top of this tree for the enjoyment of the denizens of heaven.

PURPORT

In the *Vāyu Purāṇa* there is also a reference to this tree by great learned sages:

aratnīnāṁ śatāny aṣṭāv
eka-ṣaṣṭy-adhikāni ca
phala-pramāṇam ākhyātam
ṛṣibhis tattva-darśibhiḥ

TEXT 17

तेषां विशीर्यमाणानामतिमधुरसुरभिसुगन्धिबहुलारुणरसोदेनारुणोदा नाम नदी मन्दरगिरिशिखरान्निपतन्ती पूर्वेणेलावृतमुपप्लावयति ॥१७॥

teṣāṁ viśīryamāṇānām ati-madhura-surabhi-sugandhi-bahulāruṇa-rasodenāruṇodā nāma nadī mandara-giri-śikharān nipatantī pūrveṇelāvṛtam upaplāvayati.

teṣām—of all the mangoes; *viśīryamāṇānām*—being broken because of falling from the top; *ati-madhura*—very sweet; *surabhi*—fragrant; *sugandhi*—scented with other aromas; *bahula*—large quantities; *aruṇa-rasa-udena*—by reddish juice; *aruṇodā*—Aruṇodā; *nāma*—named; *nadī*—the river; *mandara-giri-śikharāt*—from the top of Mandara Mountain; *nipatantī*—falling down; *pūrveṇa*—on the eastern side; *ilāvṛtam*—through Ilāvṛta-varṣa; *upaplāvayati*—flows.

TRANSLATION

When all those solid fruits fall from such a height, they break, and the sweet, fragrant juice within them flows out and becomes increasingly more fragrant as it mixes with other scents. That juice cascades from the mountain in waterfalls and becomes a river called Aruṇodā, which flows pleasantly through the eastern side of Ilāvṛta.

TEXT 18

यदुपजोषणाद्भवान्या अनुचरीणां पुण्यजनवधूनामवयवस्पर्शसुगन्धवातो दशयोजनं समन्तादनुवासयति ॥१८॥

yad-upajoṣaṇād bhavānyā anucarīṇāṁ puṇya-jana-vadhūnām avayava-sparśa-sugandha-vāto daśa-yojanaṁ samantād anuvāsayati.

yat—of which; *upajoṣaṇāt*—because of using the fragrant water; *bhavānyāḥ*—of Bhavānī, the wife of Lord Śiva; *anucarīṇām*—of attendant maidservants; *puṇya-jana-vadhūnām*—who are wives of the most pious Yakṣas; *avayava*—of the bodily limbs; *sparśa*—from contact; *sugandha-vātaḥ*—the wind, which becomes fragrant; *daśa-yojanam*—up to ten *yojanas* (about eighty miles); *samantāt*—all around; *anuvāsayati*—makes fragrant.

TRANSLATION

The pious wives of the Yakṣas act as personal maidservants to assist Bhavānī, the wife of Lord Śiva. Because they drink the water of the River Aruṇodā, their bodies become fragrant, and as the air carries away that fragrance, it perfumes the entire atmosphere for eighty miles around.

TEXT 19

एवं जम्बूफलानामत्युच्चनिपातविशीर्णानामनस्थिप्रायाणामिभकायनिभानां रसेन जम्बू नाम नदी मेरुमन्दरशिखरादयुतयोजनादवनितले निपतन्ती दक्षिणेनात्मानं यावदिलावृतमुपस्यन्दयति ॥१९॥

evaṁ jambū-phalānām atyucca-nipāta-viśīrṇānām anasthi-prāyāṇām ibha-kāya-nibhānāṁ rasena jambū nāma nadī meru-mandara-śikharād ayuta-yojanād avani-tale nipatantī dakṣiṇenātmānaṁ yāvad ilāvṛtam upasyandayati.

evam—similarly; *jambū-phalānām*—of the fruits called *jambū* (the rose apple); *ati-ucca-nipāta*—because of falling from a great height; *viśīrṇānām*—which are broken to pieces; *anasthi-prāyāṇām*—having very small seeds; *ibha-kāya-nibhānām*—and which are as large as the bodies of elephants; *rasena*—by the juice; *jambū nāma nadī*—a river named Jambū-nadī; *meru-mandara-śikharāt*—from the top of Merumandara Mountain; *ayuta-yojanāt*—ten thousand *yojanas* high; *avani-tale*—on the ground; *nipatantī*—falling; *dakṣiṇena*—on the southern side; *ātmānam*—itself; *yāvat*—the whole; *ilāvṛtam*—Ilāvṛta-varṣa; *upasyandayati*—flows through.

TRANSLATION

Similarly, the fruits of the jambū tree, which are full of pulp and have very small seeds, fall from a great height and break to pieces. Those fruits are the size of elephants, and the juice gliding from them becomes a river named Jambū-nadī. This river falls a distance of 10,000 yojanas, from the summit of Merumandara to the southern side of Ilāvṛta, and floods the entire land of Ilāvṛta with juice.

PURPORT

We can only imagine how much juice there might be in a fruit that is the size of an elephant but has a very tiny seed. Naturally the juice from the broken *jambū* fruits forms waterfalls and floods the entire land of Ilāvṛta. That juice produces an immense quantity of gold, as will be explained in the next verses.

TEXTS 20–21

तावदुभयोरपि रोधसोर्या मृत्तिका तद्रसेनानुविध्यमाना वाय्वर्कसंयोगविपाकेन सदामरलोकाभरणं जाम्बूनदं नाम सुवर्णं भवति ॥२०॥ यदु ह वाव विबुधादयः सह युवतिभिर्मुकुटकटककटिसूत्राद्याभरणरूपेण खलु धारयन्ति ॥२१॥

tāvad ubhayor api rodhasor yā mṛttikā tad-rasenānuvidhyamānā vāyv-arka-saṁyoga-vipākena sadāmara-lokābharaṇaṁ jāmbū-nadaṁ nāma suvarṇaṁ bhavati; yad u ha vāva vibudhādayaḥ saha yuvatibhir mukuṭa-kaṭaka-kaṭi-sūtrādy-ābharaṇa-rūpeṇa khalu dhārayanti.

tāvat—entirely; *ubhayoḥ api*—of both; *rodhasoḥ*—of the banks; *yā*—which; *mṛttikā*—the mud; *tat-rasena*—with the juice of the *jambū* fruits that flows in the river; *anuvidhyamānā*—being saturated; *vāyu-arka-saṁyoga-vipākena*—because of a chemical reaction with the air and sunshine; *sadā*—always; *amara-loka-ābharaṇam*—which is used for the ornaments of the demigods, the denizens of the heavenly planets; *jāmbū-nadam nāma*—named Jāmbū-nada; *suvarṇam*—gold; *bhavati*—becomes; *yat*—which; *u ha vāva*—indeed; *vibudha-ādayaḥ*—the great demigods; *saha*—with; *yuvatibhiḥ*—their everlastingly youthful wives; *mukuṭa*—crowns; *kaṭaka*—bangles; *kaṭi-sūtra*—belts; *ādi*—and so on; *ābharaṇa*—of all kinds of ornaments; *rūpeṇa*—in the form; *khalu*—indeed; *dhārayanti*—they possess.

TRANSLATION

The mud on both banks of the River Jambū-nadī, being moistened by the flowing juice and then dried by the air and the sunshine, produces huge quantities of gold called Jāmbū-nada. The denizens of heaven use this gold for various kinds of ornaments. Therefore all the inhabitants of the heavenly planets and their youthful wives are fully decorated with golden helmets, bangles and belts, and thus they enjoy life.

PURPORT

By the arrangement of the Supreme Personality of Godhead, the rivers on some planets produce gold on their banks. The poor inhabitants of this earth, because of their incomplete knowledge, are captivated by a so-called *bhagavān* who can produce a small quantity of gold. However, it is understood that in a higher planetary system in this material world, the mud on the banks of the Jambū-nadī mixes with *jambū* juice, reacts with the sunshine in the air, and automatically produces huge quantities of gold. Thus the men and women are decorated there by various golden ornaments, and they look very nice. Unfortunately, on earth there is such a scarcity of gold that the governments of the world try to keep it in reserve and issue paper currency. Because that currency is not backed up by gold, the paper they distribute as money is worthless, but nevertheless the people on earth are very proud of material advancement. In modern times, girls and ladies have ornaments made of plastic instead of gold, and plastic utensils are used instead of golden ones, yet people are very proud of their material wealth. Therefore the people of this age are described as *mandāḥ sumanda-matayo manda-bhāgyā hy upadrutāḥ* (*Bhāg.* 1.1.10). In other words, they are extremely bad and slow to understand the opulence of the Supreme Personality of Godhead. They have been described as *sumanda-matayaḥ* because their conceptions are so crippled that they accept a bluffer who produces a little gold to be God. Because they have no gold in their possession, they are actually poverty-stricken, and therefore they are considered unfortunate.

Sometimes these unfortunate people want to be promoted to the heavenly planets to achieve fortunate positions, as described in this verse, but pure devotees of the Lord are not at all interested in such opulence. Indeed, devotees sometimes compare the color of gold to that of bright golden stool. Śrī Caitanya Mahāprabhu has instructed devotees not to be allured by golden ornaments and beautifully decorated women. *Na dhanaṁ na janaṁ na sundarīm:* a devotee should not be allured by gold, beautiful women or the prestige of having many followers. Śrī Caitanya Mahāprabhu, therefore, confidentially prayed, *mama janmani janmanīśvare bhavatād bhaktir ahaitukī tvayi:* "My Lord, please bless Me with Your devotional service. I do not want anything else." A devotee may pray to be delivered from this material world. That is his only aspiration.

ayi nanda-tanuja kiṅkaraṁ
patitaṁ māṁ viṣame bhavāmbudhau
kṛpayā tava pāda-paṅkaja-
sthita-dhūlī-sadṛśaṁ vicintaya

The humble devotee simply prays to the Lord, "Kindly pick me up from the material world, which is full of varieties of material opulence, and keep me under the shelter of Your lotus feet."

Śrīla Narottama dāsa Ṭhākura prays:

hā hā prabhu nanda-suta, vṛṣabhānu-sutā-yuta,
karuṇā karaha ei-bāra
narottama-dāsa kaya, nā ṭheliha rāṅgā-pāya,
tomā vine ke āche āmāra

"O my Lord, O son of Nanda Mahārāja, now You are standing before me with Your consort, the daughter of Vṛṣabhānu, Śrīmatī Rādhārāṇī. Kindly accept me as the dust of Your lotus feet. Please do not kick me away, for I have no other shelter."

Similarly, Prabodhānanda Sarasvatī indicates that the position of the demigods, who are decorated with golden helmets and other ornaments, is no better than a phantasmagoria (*tri-daśa-pūr ākāśa-puṣpāyate*). A devotee is never allured by such opulences. He simply aspires to become the dust of the lotus feet of the Lord.

TEXT 22

यस्तु महाकदम्बः सुपार्श्वनिरूढो यास्तस्य कोटरेभ्यो विनिःसृताः पञ्चायामपरिणाहाः पञ्च मधुधाराः सुपार्श्वशिखरात्पतन्त्योऽपरेणात्मानमिलावृत-मनुमोदयन्ति ॥२२॥

yas tu mahā-kadambaḥ supārśva-nirūḍho yās tasya koṭarebhyo
viniḥsṛtāḥ pañcāyāma-pariṇāhāḥ pañca madhu-dhārāḥ supārśva-
śikharāt patantyo'pareṇātmānam ilāvṛtam anumodayanti.

yaḥ—which; *tu*—but; *mahā-kadambaḥ*—the tree named Mahākadamba; *supārśva-nirūḍhaḥ*—which stands on the side of the mountain known as Supārśva; *yāḥ*—which; *tasya*—of that; *koṭarebhyaḥ*—from the hollows; *viniḥsṛtāḥ*—flowing; *pañca*—five; *āyāma*—*vyāma,* a unit of measurement of about eight feet; *pariṇāhāḥ*—whose measurement; *pañca*—five; *madhu-dhārāḥ*—flows of honey; *supārśva-śikharāt*—from the top of Supārśva Mountain; *patantyaḥ*—flowing down; *apareṇa*—on the western side of Sumeru Mountain; *ātmānam*—the whole of; *ilāvṛtam*—Ilāvṛta-varṣa; *anumodayanti*—make fragrant.

TRANSLATION

On the side of Supārśva Mountain stands a big tree called Mahākadamba, which is very celebrated. From the hollows of this tree flow five rivers of honey, each about five vyāmas wide. This flowing honey falls incessantly from the top of Supārśva Mountain and flows all around Ilāvṛta-varṣa, beginning from the western side. Thus the whole land is saturated with the pleasing fragrance.

PURPORT

The distance between one hand and another when one spreads both his arms is called a *vyāma.* This comes to about eight feet. Thus each of the rivers was about forty feet wide, making a total of about two hundred feet.

TEXT 23

या ह्युपयुञ्जानानां मुखनिर्वासितो वायुः समन्ताच्छतयोजनमनुवासयति ॥२३॥

yā hy upayuñjānānāṁ mukha-nirvāsito vāyuḥ samantāc chata-yojanam anuvāsayati.

yāḥ—which (those flows of honey); *hi*—indeed; *upayuñjānānām*—of those who drink; *mukha-nirvāsitaḥ vāyuḥ*—the air emanating from the mouths; *samantāt*—all around; *śata-yojanam*—up to one hundred *yojanas* (eight hundred miles); *anuvāsayati*—makes sweetly flavored.

TRANSLATION

The air carrying the scent from the mouths of those who drink that honey perfumes the land for a hundred yojanas around.

TEXT 24

एवं कुमुदनिरूढो यः शतवल्शो नाम वटस्तस्य स्कन्धेभ्यो नीचीनाः पयोदधिमधुघृतगुडान्नाद्यम्बरशय्यासनाभरणादयः सर्व एव कामदुघा नदाः कुमुदाग्रात्पतन्तस्तमुत्तरेणेलावृतमुपयोजयन्ति ॥२४॥

evaṁ kumuda-nirūḍho yaḥ śatavalśo nāma vaṭas tasya skandhebhyo nīcīnāḥ payo-dadhi-madhu-ghṛta-guḍānnādy-ambara-śayyāsanābharaṇādayaḥ sarva eva kāma-dughā nadāḥ kumudāgrāt patantas tam uttareṇelāvṛtam upayojayanti.

evam—thus; *kumuda-nirūḍhaḥ*—having grown on Kumuda Mountain; *yaḥ*—that; *śata-valśaḥ nāma*—the tree named Śatavalśa (because of having hundreds of trunks); *vaṭaḥ*—a banyan tree; *tasya*—of it; *skandhebhyaḥ*—from the thick branches; *nīcīnāḥ*—flowing down; *payaḥ*—milk; *dadhi*—yogurt; *madhu*—honey; *ghṛta*—clarified butter; *guḍa*—molasses; *anna*—food grains; *ādi*—and so on; *ambara*—clothing; *śayyā*—bedding; *āsana*—sitting places; *ābharaṇa-ādayaḥ*—carrying ornaments and so on; *sarve*—everything; *eva*—certainly; *kāma-dughāḥ*—fulfilling all desires; *nadāḥ*—big rivers; *kumuda-agrāt*—from the top of Kumuda Mountain; *patantaḥ*—flowing; *tam*—to that; *uttareṇa*—on the northern side; *ilāvṛtam*—the land known as Ilāvṛta-varṣa; *upayojayanti*—give happiness.

TRANSLATION

Similarly, on Kumuda Mountain there is a great banyan tree, which is called Śatavalśa because it has a hundred main branches. From those branches come many roots, from which many rivers are flowing. These rivers flow down from the top of the mountain to the northern side of Ilāvṛta-varṣa for the benefit of those who live there. Because of these flowing rivers, all the people have ample supplies of milk, yogurt, honey, clarified butter [ghee], molasses, food grains, clothes, bedding, sitting places and ornaments. All the objects they desire are sufficiently supplied for their prosperity, and therefore they are very happy.

PURPORT

The prosperity of humanity does not depend on a demoniac civilization that has no culture and no knowledge but has only gigantic skyscrapers and huge automobiles always rushing down the highways. The products of nature are sufficient. When there is a profuse supply of milk, yogurt, honey, food grains, ghee, molasses, dhotis, saris, bedding, sitting places and ornaments, the residents are actually opulent. When a profuse supply of water from the river inundates the land, all these things can be produced, and there will not be scarcity. This all depends, however, on the performance of sacrifice as described in the Vedic literature.

annād bhavanti bhūtāni
parjanyād anna-sambhavaḥ
yajñād bhavati parjanyo
yajñaḥ karma-samudbhavaḥ

"All living bodies subsist on food grains, which are produced from rains. Rains are produced by performance of *yajña* [sacrifice], and *yajña* is born of prescribed duties." These are the prescriptions given in *Bhagavad-gītā* (3.14). If people follow these principles in full Kṛṣṇa consciousness, human society will be prosperous, and they will be happy both in this life and in the next.

TEXT 25

यानुपजुषाणानां न कदाचिदपि प्रजानां वलीपलितक्लमस्वेददौर्गन्ध्यजरामय-
मृत्युशीतोष्णवैवर्ण्योपसर्गादयस्तापविशेषा भवन्ति यावज्जीवं सुखं निरतिशयमेव
॥२५॥

yān upajuṣāṇānāṁ na kadācid api prajānāṁ valī-palita-klama-sveda-daurgandhya-jarāmaya-mṛtyu-śītoṣṇa-vaivarṇyopasargādayas tāpa-viśeṣā bhavanti yāvaj jīvaṁ sukhaṁ niratiśayam eva.

yān—which (all the products produced because of the flowing rivers mentioned above); *upajuṣāṇānām*—of persons who are fully utilizing; *na*—not; *kadācit*—at any time; *api*—certainly; *prajānām*—of the citizens; *valī*—wrinkles; *palita*—grey hair; *klama*—fatigue; *sveda*—perspiration; *daurgandhya*—bad odors because of unclean perspiration; *jarā*—old age; *āmaya*—disease; *mṛtyu*—untimely death; *śīta*—severe cold; *uṣṇa*—scorching heat; *vaivarṇya*—fading of the luster of the body; *upasarga*—troubles; *ādayaḥ*—and so on; *tāpa*—of sufferings; *viśeṣāḥ*—varieties; *bhavanti*—are; *yāvat*—as long as; *jīvam*—life; *sukham*—happiness; *niratiśayam*—unlimited; *eva*—only.

TRANSLATION

The residents of the material world who enjoy the products of these flowing rivers have no wrinkles on their bodies and no grey hair. They never feel fatigue, and perspiration does not give their bodies a bad odor. They are not afflicted by old age, disease or untimely death, they do not suffer from chilly cold or scorching heat, nor do their bodies lose their luster. They all live very happily, without anxieties, until death.

PURPORT

This verse hints at the perfection of human society even within this material world. The miserable conditions of this material world can be corrected by a sufficient supply of milk, yogurt, honey, ghee, molasses, food grains, ornaments, bedding, sitting places and so on. This is human civilization. Ample food grains can be produced through agricultural enterprises, and profuse supplies of milk, yogurt and ghee can be arranged through cow protection. Abundant honey can be obtained if the forests are protected. Unfortunately, in modern civilization, men are busy killing the cows that are the source of yogurt, milk and ghee, they are cutting down all the trees that supply honey, and they are opening factories to manufacture nuts, bolts, automobiles and wine instead of engaging in agriculture. How can the people be happy? They must suffer from all the misery of materialism. Their bodies become wrinkled and gradually deteriorate until they become almost like dwarves, and a bad odor emanates from their bodies because of unclean perspiration resulting from eating all kinds of nasty things. This is not human civilization. If people actually want happiness in this life and want to prepare for the best in the next life, they must adopt a Vedic civilization. In a Vedic civilization, there is a full supply of all the necessities mentioned above.

TEXT 26

कुरङ्गकुररकुसुम्भवैकङ्कत्रिकूटशिशिरपतङ्गरुचकनिषधशिनीवासकपिलशङ्खवैदूर्यजारुधिहंसर्षभनागकालञ्जरनारदादयो विंशतिगिरयो मेरोः कर्णिकाया इव केसरभूता मूलदेशे परित उपक्लृप्ताः ॥२६॥

kuraṅga-kurara-kusumbha-vaikaṅka-trikūṭa-śiśira-pataṅga-rucaka-niṣadha-śinīvāsa-kapila-śaṅkha-vaidūrya-jārudhi-haṁsa-ṛṣabha-nāga-kālañjara-nāradādayo viṁśati-girayo meroḥ karṇikāyā iva kesara-bhūtā mūla-deśe parita upakḷptāḥ.

kuraṅga—Kuraṅga; *kurara*—Kurara; *kusumbha-vaikaṅka-trikūṭa-śiśira-pataṅga-rucaka-niṣadha-śinīvāsa-kapila-śaṅkha-vaidūrya-jārudhi-haṁsa-ṛṣabha-nāga-kālañjara-nārada*—the names of mountains; *ādayaḥ*—and so on; *viṁśati-girayaḥ*—twenty mountains; *meroḥ*—of Sumeru Mountain; *karṇikāyāḥ*—of the whorl of the lotus; *iva*—like; *kesara-bhūtāḥ*—as filaments; *mūla-deśe*—at the base; *paritaḥ*—all around; *upakḷptāḥ*—arranged by the Supreme Personality of Godhead.

TRANSLATION

There are other mountains beautifully arranged around the foot of Mount Meru like the filaments around the whorl of a lotus flower. Their names are Kuraṅga, Kurara, Kusumbha, Vaikaṅka, Trikūṭa, Śiśira, Pataṅga, Rucaka, Niṣadha, Sinīvāsa, Kapila, Śaṅkha, Vaidūrya, Jārudhi, Haṁsa, Ṛṣabha, Nāga, Kālañjara and Nārada.

TEXT 27

जठरदेवकूटौ मेरुं पूर्वेणाष्टादशयोजनसहस्रमुदगायतौ द्विसहस्रं पृथुतुङ्गौ भवतः। एवमपरेण पवनपारियात्रौ दक्षिणेन कैलासकरवीरौ प्रागायतावेवमुत्तरतस्त्रिशृङ्गमकरावष्टभिरेतैः परिसृतोऽग्निरिव परितश्चकास्ति काञ्चनगिरिः ॥२७॥

jaṭhara-devakūṭau meruṁ pūrveṇāṣṭādaśa-yojana-sahasram udagāyatau dvi-sahasraṁ pṛthu-tuṅgau bhavataḥ; evam apareṇa pavana-pāriyātrau dakṣiṇena kailāsa-karavīrau prāg-āyatāv evam uttaratas triśṛṅga-makarāv aṣṭabhir etaiḥ parisṛto'gnir iva paritaś cakāsti kāñcana-giriḥ.

jaṭhara-devakūṭau—two mountains named Jaṭhara and Devakūṭa; *merum*—Sumeru Mountain; *pūrveṇa*—on the eastern side; *aṣṭādaśa-yojana-sahasram*—eighteen thousand *yojanas; udagāyatau*—stretching from north to south; *dvi-sahasram*—two thousand *yojanas; pṛthu-tuṅgau*—in width and height; *bhavataḥ*—there are; *evam*—similarly; *apareṇa*—on the western side; *pavana-pāriyātrau*—two mountains named Pavana and Pāriyātra; *dakṣiṇena*—on the southern side; *kailāsa-karavīrau*—two mountains named Kailāsa and Karavīra; *prāk-āyatau*—expanding east and west; *evam*—similarly; *uttarataḥ*—on the northern side; *triśṛṅga-makarau*—two mountains named Triśṛṅga and Makara; *aṣṭabhiḥ etaiḥ*—by these eight mountains; *parisṛtaḥ*—surrounded; *agniḥ iva*—like fire; *paritaḥ*—all over; *cakāsti*—brilliantly shines; *kāñcana-giriḥ*—the golden mountain named Sumeru, or Meru.

TRANSLATION

On the eastern side of Sumeru Mountain are two mountains named Jaṭhara and Devakūṭa, which extend to the north and south for 18,000 yojanas [144,000 miles]. Similarly, on the western side of Sumeru are two mountains named Pavana and Pāriyātra, which also extend north and south for the same distance. On the southern side of Sumeru are two mountains named Kailāsa and Karavīra, which extend east and west for 18,000 yojanas, and on the northern side of Sumeru, extending for the same distance east and west, are two mountains named Triśṛṅga and Makara. The width and height of all these mountains is 2,000 yojanas [16,000 miles]. Sumeru, a mountain of solid gold shining as brilliantly as fire, is surrounded by these eight mountains.

TEXT 28

मेरोर्मूर्धनि भगवत आत्मयोनेर्मध्यत उपक्लृप्तां पुरीमयुतयोजनसाहस्रीं समचतुरस्रां शातकौम्भीं वदन्ति ॥२८॥

meror mūrdhani bhagavata ātma-yoner madhyata upakḷptāṁ purīm ayuta-yojana-sāhasrīṁ sama-caturasrāṁ śātakaumbhīṁ vadanti.

meroḥ—of Sumeru Mountain; *mūrdhani*—on the head; *bhagavataḥ*—of the most powerful being; *ātma-yoneḥ*—of Lord Brahmā; *madhyataḥ*—in the middle; *upakḷptām*—situated; *purīm*—the great township; *ayuta-yojana*—

ten thousand *yojanas; sāhasrīm*—one thousand; *sama-caturasrām*—of the same length on all sides; *śāta-kaumbhīm*—made entirely of gold; *vadanti*—the great learned sages say.

TRANSLATION

In the middle of the summit of Meru is the township of Lord Brahmā. Each of its four sides is calculated to extend for ten million yojanas [eighty million miles]. It is made entirely of gold, and therefore learned scholars and sages call it Śātakaumbhī.

TEXT 29

तामनुपरितो लोकपालानामष्टानां यथादिशं यथारूपं तुरीयमानेन पुरोऽष्टा-
वुपक्लृप्ताः ॥२९॥

tām anuparito loka-pālānām aṣṭānāṁ yathā-diśaṁ yathā-rūpaṁ turīya-mānena puro'ṣṭāv upakḷptāḥ.

tām—that great township named Brahmapurī; *anuparitaḥ*—surrounding; *loka-pālānām*—of the governors of the planets; *aṣṭānām*—eight; *yathā-diśam*—according to the directions; *yathā-rūpam*—in exact conformity with the township of Brahmapurī; *turīya-mānena*—by measurement only one fourth; *puraḥ*—townships; *aṣṭau*—eight; *upakḷptāḥ*—situated.

TRANSLATION

Surrounding Brahmapurī in all directions are the residences of the eight principal governors of the planetary systems, beginning with King Indra. These abodes are similar to Brahmapurī but are one fourth the size.

PURPORT

Śrīla Viśvanātha Cakravartī Ṭhākura confirms that the townships of Lord Brahmā and the eight subordinate governors of the planetary systems, beginning with Indra, are mentioned in other *Purāṇas.*

merau nava-pūrāṇi syur
manovaty amarāvatī
tejovatī saṁyamanī
tathā kṛṣṇāṅganā parā
śraddhāvatī gandhavatī
tathā cānyā mahodayā

yaśovatī ca brahmendra
bahyādīnāṁ yathā-kramam

Brahmā's township is known as Manovatī, and those of his assistants such as Indra and Agni are known as Amarāvatī, Tejovatī, Saṁyamanī, Kṛṣṇāṅganā, Śraddhāvatī, Gandhavatī, Mahodayā and Yaśovatī. Brahmapurī is situated in the middle, and the other eight *purīs* surround it in all directions.

Thus end the Bhaktivedanta purports of the Fifth Canto, Sixteenth Chapter, of the Śrīmad-Bhāgavatam, *entitled "A Description of Jambūdvīpa."*

CHAPTER SEVENTEEN

The Descent of the River Ganges

The Seventeenth Chapter describes the origin of the Ganges River and how it flows in and around Ilāvṛta-varṣa. There is also a description of the prayers Lord Śiva offers to Lord Saṅkarṣaṇa, part of the quadruple expansions of the Supreme Personality of Godhead. Lord Viṣṇu once approached Bali Mahārāja while the King was performing a sacrifice. The Lord appeared before him as Trivikrama, or Vāmana, and begged alms from the King in the form of three steps of land. With two steps, Lord Vāmana covered all three planetary systems and pierced the covering of the universe with the toes of His left foot. A few drops of water from the Causal Ocean leaked through this hole and fell on the head of Lord Śiva, where they remained for one thousand millenniums. These drops of water are the sacred Ganges River. It first flows onto the heavenly planets, which are located on the soles of Lord Viṣṇu's feet. The Ganges River is known by many names, such as the Bhāgīrathī and the Jāhnavī. It purifies Dhruvaloka and the planets of the seven sages because both Dhruva and the sages have no other desire than to serve the Lord's lotus feet.

The Ganges River, emanating from the lotus feet of the Lord, inundates the heavenly planets, especially the moon, and then flows through Brahmapurī atop Mount Meru. Here the river divides into four branches (known as Sītā, Alakanandā, Cakṣu and Bhadrā), which then flow down to the ocean of salt water. The branch known as Sītā flows through Śekhara-parvata and Gandhamādana-parvata and then flows down to Bhadrāśva-varṣa, where it mixes with the ocean of salt water in the West. The Cakṣu branch flows through Mālyavān-giri and, after reaching Ketumāla-varṣa, mixes with the ocean of salt water in the West . The branch known as Bhadrā flows onto Mount Meru, Mount Kumuda, and the Nīla, Śveta and Śṛṅgavān mountains before it reaches Kuru-deśa, where it flows into the ocean of salt water in the north. The Alakanandā branch flows through Brahmālaya, crosses over many mountains, including Hemakūṭa and Himakūṭa, and then reaches Bhārata-varṣa, where it flows into the southern side of the ocean of salt water. Many other rivers and their branches flow through the nine *varṣas.*

The tract of land known as Bhārata-varṣa is the field of activities, and the other eight *varṣas* are for persons who are meant to enjoy heavenly comfort. In each of these eight beautiful provinces, the celestial denizens enjoy various standards of material comfort and pleasure. A different incarnation of the Supreme Personality of Godhead distributes His mercy in each of the nine *varṣas* of Jambūdvīpa.

In the Ilāvṛta-varṣa, Lord Śiva is the only male. There he lives with his wife, Bhavānī, who is attended by many maidservants. If any other male enters that province, Bhavānī curses him to become a woman. Lord Śiva worships Lord Saṅkarṣaṇa by offering various prayers, one of which is as follows: "My dear Lord, please liberate all Your devotees from material life and bind all the nondevotees to the material world. Without Your mercy, no one can be released from the bondage of material existence."

TEXT 1

श्रीशुक उवाच

तत्र भगवतः साक्षाद्यज्ञलिङ्गस्य विष्णोर्विक्रमतो वामपादाङ्गुष्ठनखनिर्भिन्नोर्ध्वाण्डकटाहविवरेणान्तःप्रविष्टा या बाह्यजलधारा तच्चरणपङ्कजावनेजनारुणकिञ्जल्कोपरञ्जिताखिलजगदघमलापहोपस्पर्शनामला साक्षाद्भगवत्पदीत्यनुपलक्षितवचोऽभिधीयमानातिमहता कालेन युगसहस्रोपलक्षणेन दिवो मूर्धन्यवततार यत्तद्विष्णुपदमाहुः ॥१॥

śrī-śuka uvāca
tatra bhagavataḥ sākṣād yajña-liṅgasya viṣṇor vikramato vāma-pādāṅguṣṭha-nakha-nirbhinnordhvāṇḍa-kaṭāha-vivareṇāntaḥ-praviṣṭā yā bāhya-jala-dhārā tac-caraṇa-paṅkajāvanejanāruṇa-kiñjalkoparañjitākhila-jagad-agha-malāpahopasparśanāmalā sākṣād bhagavat-padīty anupalakṣita-vaco'bhidhīyamānāti-mahatā kālena yuga-sahasropalakṣaṇena divo mūrdhany avatatāra yat tad viṣṇu-padam āhuḥ.

śrī-śukaḥ uvāca—Śrī Śukadeva Gosvāmī said; *tatra*—at that time; *bhagavataḥ*—of the incarnation of the Supreme Personality of Godhead; *sākṣāt*—directly; *yajña-liṅgasya*—the enjoyer of the results of all sacrifices; *viṣṇoḥ*—of Lord Viṣṇu; *vikramataḥ*—while taking His second step; *vāma-pāda*—of His left leg; *aṅguṣṭha*—of the big toe; *nakha*—by the nail; *nirbhinna*—pierced; *ūrdhva*—upper; *aṇḍa-kaṭāha*—the covering of the universe (consisting of seven layers—earth, water, fire, etc.); *vivareṇa*—through the hole; *antaḥ-praviṣṭā*—having entered the universe; *yā*—which; *bāhya-jala-dhārā*—the flow of water from the Causal Ocean outside the universe; *tat*—of

Him; *caraṇa-paṅkaja*—of the lotus feet; *avanejana*—by the washing; *aruṇa-kiñjalka*—by reddish powder; *uparañjitā*—being colored; *akhila-jagat*—of the whole world; *agha-mala*—the sinful activities; *apahā*—destroys; *upasparśana*—the touching of which; *amalā*—completely pure; *sākṣāt*—directly; *bhagavat-padī*—emanating from the lotus feet of the Supreme Personality of Godhead; *iti*—thus; *anupalakṣita*—described; *vacaḥ*—by the name; *abhidhīyamānā*—being called; *ati-mahatā kālena*—after a long time; *yuga-sahasra-upalakṣaṇena*—consisting of one thousand millenniums; *divaḥ*—of the sky; *mūrdhani*—on the head (Dhruvaloka); *avatatāra*—descended; *yat*—which; *tat*—that; *viṣṇu-padam*—the lotus feet of Lord Viṣṇu; *āhuḥ*—they call.

TRANSLATION

Śukadeva Gosvāmī said: My dear King, Lord Viṣṇu, the enjoyer of all sacrifices, appeared as Vāmanadeva in the sacrificial arena of Bali Mahārāja. Then He extended His left foot to the end of the universe and pierced a hole in its covering with the nail of His big toe. Through the hole, the pure water of the Causal Ocean entered this universe as the Ganges River. Having washed the lotus feet of the Lord, which are covered with reddish powder, the water of the Ganges acquired a very beautiful pink color. Every living being can immediately purify his mind of material contamination by touching the transcendental water of the Ganges, yet its waters remain ever pure. Because the Ganges directly touches the lotus feet of the Lord before descending within this universe, she is known as Viṣṇupadī. Later she received other names like Jāhnavī and Bhāgīrathī. After one thousand millenniums, the water of the Ganges descended on Dhruvaloka, the topmost planet in this universe. Therefore all learned sages and scholars proclaim Dhruvaloka to be Viṣṇupada ["situated on Lord Viṣṇu's lotus feet"].

PURPORT

In this verse, Śukadeva Gosvāmī describes the glories of the Ganges River. The water of the Ganges is called *patita-pāvanī,* the deliverer of all sinful living beings. It is a proven fact that a person who regularly bathes in the Ganges is purified both externally and internally. Externally his body becomes immune to all kinds of disease, and internally he gradually develops a devotional attitude toward the Supreme Personality of Godhead. Throughout India, many thousands of people live on the banks of the Ganges, and by regularly bathing in her waters, they are undoubtedly being purified both spiritually and materially. Many sages, including Śaṅkarācārya, have composed prayers in praise of the Ganges, and the land of India itself has become glorious because such rivers as the Ganges, Yamunā, Godāvarī, Kāverī, Kṛṣṇā and Narmadā flow there. Anyone living on the land adjacent to these rivers is naturally advanced in spiritual consciousness. Śrīla Madhvācārya says:

vārāhe vāma-pādaṁ tu
tad-anyeṣu tu dakṣiṇam
pādaṁ kalpeṣu bhagavān
ujjahāra trivikramaḥ

Standing on His right foot and extending His left to the edge of the universe, Lord Vāmana became known as Trivikrama, the incarnation who performed three heroic deeds.

TEXT 2

यत्र ह वाव वीरव्रत औत्तानपादिः परमभागवतोऽस्मत्कुलदेवताचरणा-
रविन्दोदकमिति यामनुसवनमुत्कृष्यमाणभगवद्भक्तियोगेन दृढं क्लिद्यमाना-
न्तर्हृदयऔत्कण्ठ्यविवशामीलितलोचनयुगलकुड्मलविगलितामलबाष्पकलयाभि
व्यज्यमानरोमपुलककुलकोऽधुनापि परमादरेण शिरसा बिभर्ति ॥२॥

yatra ha vāva vīra-vrata auttānapādiḥ parama-bhāgavato'smat-kula-devatā-caraṇāravindodakam iti yām anusavanam utkṛṣyamāṇa-bhagavad-bhakti-yogena dṛḍhaṁ klidyamānāntar-hṛdaya autkaṇṭhya-vivaśāmīlita-locana-yugala-kuḍmala-vigalitāmala-bāṣpa-kalayābhivyajyamāna-roma-pulaka-kulako'dhunāpi paramādareṇa śirasā bibharti.

yatra ha vāva—in Dhruvaloka; *vīra-vrataḥ*—firmly determined; *auttānapādiḥ*—the famous son of Mahārāja Uttānapāda; *parama-bhāgavataḥ*—the most exalted devotee; *asmat*—our; *kula-devatā*—of the family Deity; *caraṇa-aravinda*—of the lotus feet; *udakam*—in the water; *iti*—thus; *yām*—which; *anusavanam*—constantly; *utkṛṣyamāṇa*—being increased; *bhagavat-bhakti-yogena*—by devotional service unto the Lord; *dṛḍham*—greatly; *klidyamāna-antaḥ-hṛdayaḥ*—being softened within the core of his heart; *autkaṇṭhya*—by great anxiety; *vivaśa*—spontaneously; *amīlita*—slightly open; *locana*—of eyes; *yugala*—pair; *kuḍmala*—from the flowerlike;

vigalita—emanating; *amala*—uncontaminated; *bāṣpa-kalayā*—with tears; *abhivyajyamāna*—being manifested; *roma-pulaka-kulakaḥ*—whose symptoms of ecstasy on the body; *adhunā api*—even now; *parama-ādareṇa*—with great reverence; *śirasā*—by the head; *bibharti*—he bears.

TRANSLATION

Dhruva Mahārāja, the famous son of Mahārāja Uttānapāda, is known as the most exalted devotee of the Supreme Lord because of his firm determination in executing devotional service. Knowing that the sacred Ganges water washes the lotus feet of Lord Viṣṇu, Dhruva Mahārāja, situated on his own planet, to this very day accepts that water on his head with great devotion. Because he constantly thinks of Kṛṣṇa very devoutly within the core of his heart, he is overcome with ecstatic anxiety. Tears flow from his half-open eyes, and eruptions appear on his entire body.

PURPORT

When a person is firmly fixed in devotional service to the Supreme Personality of Godhead, he is described as *vīra-vrata,* fully determined. Such a devotee increases his ecstasy in devotional service more and more. Thus as soon as he remembers Lord Viṣṇu, his eyes fill with tears. This is a symptom of a *mahā-bhāgavata.* Dhruva Mahārāja maintained himself in that devotional ecstasy, and Śrī Caitanya Mahāprabhu also gave us a practical example of transcendental ecstasy when He lived at Jagannātha Purī. His pastimes there are fully narrated in *Caitanya-caritāmṛta.*

TEXT 3

ततः सप्त ऋषयस्तत्प्रभावाभिज्ञा यां ननु तपसआत्यन्तिकी सिद्धिरेतावती भगवति सर्वात्मनि वासुदेवेऽनुपरतभक्तियोगलाभेनैवोपेक्षितान्यार्थात्मगतयो मुक्ति मिवागतां मुमुक्षव इव सबहुमानमद्यापि जटाजूटैरुद्वहन्ति ॥३॥

tataḥ sapta ṛṣayas tat prabhāvābhijñā yāṁ nanu tapasa ātyantikī
siddhir etāvatī bhagavati sarvātmani vāsudeve'nuparata-bhakti-yoga-
lābhenaivopekṣitānyārthātma-gatayo muktim ivāgatāṁ mumukṣava iva
sabahu-mānam adyāpi jaṭā-jūṭair udvahanti.

tataḥ—thereafter; *sapta ṛṣayaḥ*—the seven great sages (beginning with Marīci); *tat prabhāva-abhijñāḥ*—who knew very well the influence of the Ganges River; *yām*—this Ganges water; *nanu*—indeed; *tapasaḥ*—of our austerities; *ātyantikī*—the ultimate; *siddhiḥ*—perfection; *etāvatī*—this much; *bhagavati*—the Supreme Personality of Godhead; *sarva-ātmani*—in the all-pervading; *vāsudeve*—Kṛṣṇa; *anuparata*—continuous; *bhakti-yoga*—of the mystic process of devotional service; *lābhena*—simply by achieving this platform; *eva*—certainly; *upekṣita*—neglected; *anya*—other; *artha-ātma-gatayaḥ*—all other means of perfection (namely religion, economic development, sense gratification and liberation); *muktim*—liberation from material bondage; *iva*—like; *āgatām*—obtained; *mumukṣavaḥ*—persons desiring liberation; *iva*—like; *sa-bahu-mānam*—with great honor; *adya api*—even now; *jaṭā-jūṭaiḥ*—with matted locks of hair; *udvahanti*—they carry.

TRANSLATION

The seven great sages [Marīci, Vasiṣṭha, Atri and so on] reside on planets beneath Dhruvaloka. Well aware of the influence of the water of the Ganges, to this day they keep Ganges water on the tufts of hair on their heads. They have concluded that this is the ultimate wealth, the perfection of all austerities, and the best means of prosecuting transcendental life. Having obtained uninterrupted devotional service to the Supreme Personality of Godhead, they neglect all other beneficial processes like religion, economic development, sense gratification and even merging into the Supreme. Just as jñānīs think that merging into the existence of the Lord is the highest truth, these seven exalted personalities accept devotional service as the perfection of life.

PURPORT

Transcendentalists are divided into two primary groups: the *nirviśeṣa-vādīs,* or impersonalists, and the *bhaktas,* or devotees. The impersonalists do not accept spiritual varieties of life. They want to merge into the existence of the Supreme Lord in His Brahman feature (the *brahmajyoti*). The devotees, however, desire to take part in the transcendental activities of the Supreme Lord. In the upper planetary system, the topmost planet is Dhruvaloka, and beneath Dhruvaloka are the seven planets occupied by the great sages, beginning with Marīci, Vasiṣṭha and Atri. All these sages regard devotional service as the highest perfection of life. Therefore they all carry the holy water of the Ganges on their heads. This verse proves that for one who has achieved the platform of pure devotional service, nothing else is important, even so-called liberation (*kaivalya*). Śrīla Śrīdhara Svāmī states that only by achieving pure devotional service of the Lord can one give up all other engagements as insignificant. Prabodhānanda Sarasvatī confirms his statement as follows:

kaivalyaṁ narakāyate tri-daśa-pūr ākāśa-puṣpāyate
durdāntendriya-kāla-sarpa-paṭalī protkhāta-daṁṣṭrāyate
viśvaṁ pūrṇa-sukhāyate vidhi-mahendrādiś ca kīṭāyate
yat kāruṇya-kaṭākṣa-vaibhavavatāṁ taṁ gauram eva stumaḥ

Śrī Caitanya Mahāprabhu has perfectly enunciated and broadcast the process of *bhakti-yoga.* Consequently, for one who has taken shelter at the lotus feet of Śrī Caitanya Mahāprabhu, the highest perfection of the Māyāvādīs, *kaivalya,* or becoming one with the Supreme, is considered hellish, to say nothing of the *karmīs'* aspiration to be promoted to the heavenly planets. Devotees consider such goals to be worthless phantasmagoria. There are also *yogīs,* who try to control their senses, but they can never succeed without coming to the stage of devotional service. The senses are compared to poisonous snakes, but the senses of a *bhakta* engaged in the service of the Lord are like snakes with their poisonous fangs removed. The *yogī* tries to suppress his senses, but even great mystics like Viśvāmitra fail in the attempt. Viśvāmitra was conquered by his senses when he was captivated by Menakā during his meditation. She later gave birth to Śakuntalā. The wisest persons in the world, therefore, are the *bhakti-yogīs,* as Lord Kṛṣṇa confirms in *Bhagavad-gītā* (6.47):

yoginām api sarveṣāṁ
mad-gatenāntarātmanā
śraddhāvān bhajate yo māṁ
sa me yuktatamo mataḥ

"Of all *yogīs,* he who always abides in Me with great faith, worshiping Me in transcendental loving service, is most intimately united with Me in *yoga* and is the highest of all."

TEXT 4

ततोऽनेकसहस्रकोटिविमानानीकसङ्कुलदेवयानेनावतरन्तीन्दुमण्डलमावार्य ब्रह्मसदने निपतति ॥४॥

tato 'neka-sahasra-koṭi-vimānānīka-saṅkula-deva-yānenāvatar-antīndu maṇḍalam āvārya brahma-sadane nipatati.

tataḥ—after purifying the seven planets of the seven great sages; *aneka*—many; *sahasra*—thousands; *koṭi*—of millions; *vimāna-anīka*—with contingents of airplanes; *saṅkula*—congested; *deva-yānena*—by the spaceways of the demigods; *avatarantī*—descending; *indu-maṇḍalam*—the moon planet; *āvārya*—inundated; *brahma-sadane*—to the abode of Lord Brahmā atop Sumeru-parvata; *nipatati*—falls down.

TRANSLATION

After purifying the seven planets near Dhruvaloka [the polestar], the Ganges water is carried through the spaceways of the demigods in billions of celestial airplanes. Then it inundates the moon [Candraloka] and finally reaches Lord Brahmā's abode atop Mount Meru.

PURPORT

We should always remember that the Ganges River comes from the Causal Ocean, beyond the covering of the universe. After the water of the Causal Ocean leaks through the hole created by Lord Vāmanadeva, it flows down to Dhruvaloka (the polestar) and then to the seven planets beneath Dhruvaloka. Then it is carried to the moon by innumerable celestial airplanes, and then it falls to the top of Mount Meru, which is known as Sumeru-parvata. In this way, the water of the Ganges finally reaches the lower planets and the peaks of the Himalayas, and from there it flows through Hardwar and throughout the plains of India, purifying the entire land. How the Ganges water reaches the various planets from the top of the universe is explained herein. Celestial airplanes carry the water from the planets of the sages to other planets. So-called advanced scientists of the modern age are trying to go to the higher planets, but at the same time they are experiencing a power shortage on earth. If they were actually capable scientists, they could personally go by airplane to other planets, but this they are unable to do. Having now given up their moon excursions, they are attempting to go to other planets, but without success.

TEXT 5

तत्र चतुर्धा भिद्यमाना चतुर्भिर्नामभिश्चतुर्दिशमभिस्पन्दन्ती नदनदीपतिमेवा-भिनिविशति सीतालकनन्दा चक्षुर्भद्रेति ॥५॥

tatra caturdhā bhidyamānā caturbhir nāmabhiś catur-diśam abhispandantī nada-nadī-patim evābhiniviśati sītālakanandā cakṣur bhadreti.

tatra—there (on top of Mount Meru); *caturdhā*—into four branches; *bhidyamānā*—being divided; *caturbhiḥ*—with four; *nāmabhiḥ*—names; *catuḥ-diśam*—the four directions (east, west, north and south); *abhispandantī*—profusely flowing; *nada-nadī-patim*—the reservoir of all great rivers (the ocean); *eva*—certainly; *abhiniviśati*—enters; *sītā-alakanandā*—Sītā and Alakanandā; *cakṣuḥ*—Cakṣu; *bhadrā*—Bhadrā; *iti*—known by these names.

TRANSLATION

On top of Mount Meru, the Ganges divides into four branches, each of which gushes in a different direction [east, west, north and south]. These branches, known by the names Sītā, Alakanandā, Cakṣu and Bhadrā, flow down to the ocean.

TEXT 6

सीता तु ब्रह्मसदनात्केसराचलादिगिरिशिखरेभ्योऽधोऽधः प्रस्रवन्ती गन्ध-
मादनमूर्धसु पतित्वान्तरेण भद्राश्ववर्षं प्राच्यां दिशि क्षारसमुद्रमभिप्रविशति ॥६॥

sītā tu brahma-sadanāt kesarācalādi-giri-śikharebhyo'dho'dhaḥ
prasravantī gandhamādana-mūrdhasu patitvāntareṇa bhadrāśva-
varṣaṁ prācyāṁ diśi kṣāra-samudram abhipraviśati.

sītā—the branch known as Sītā; *tu*—certainly; *brahma-sadanāt*—from Brahmapurī; *kesarācala-ādi*—of Kesarācala and of other great mountains; *giri*—hills; *śikharebhyaḥ*—from the tops; *adhaḥ adhaḥ*—downward; *prasravantī*—flowing; *gandhamādana*—of Gandhamādana Mountain; *mūrdhasu*—on the top; *patitvā*—falling down; *antareṇa*—within; *bhadrāśva-varṣam*—the province known as Bhadrāśva; *prācyām*—in the western; *diśi*—direction; *kṣāra-samudram*—the ocean of salt water; *abhipraviśati*—enters.

TRANSLATION

The branch of the Ganges known as the Sītā flows through Brahmapurī atop Mount Meru, and from there it runs down to the nearby peaks of the Kesarācala Mountains, which stand almost as high as Mount Meru itself. These mountains are like a bunch of filaments around Mount Meru. From the Kesarācala Mountains, the Ganges falls to the peak of Gandhamādana Mountain and then flows into the land of Bhadrāśva-varṣa. Finally it reaches the ocean of salt water in the west.

TEXT 7

एवं माल्यवच्छिखरान्निष्पतन्ती ततोऽनुपरतवेगा केतुमालमभि चक्षुः प्रतीच्यां दिशि सरित्पतिं प्रविशति ॥७॥

evaṁ mālyavac-chikharān niṣpatantī tato'nuparata-vegā ketumālam abhi cakṣuḥ pratīcyāṁ diśi sarit-patiṁ praviśati.

evam—in this way; *mālyavat-śikharāt*—from the top of Mālyavān Mountain; *niṣpatantī*—falling down; *tataḥ*—thereafter; *anuparata-vegā*—whose force is uninterrupted; *ketumālam abhi*—into the land known as Ketumāla-varṣa; *cakṣuḥ*—the branch known as Cakṣu; *pratīcyām*—in the west; *diśi*—direction; *sarit-patim*—the ocean; *praviśati*—enters into.

TRANSLATION

The branch of the Ganges known as Cakṣu falls onto the summit of Mālyavān Mountain and from there cascades onto the land of Ketumāla-varṣa. The Ganges flows incessantly through Ketumāla-varṣa and in this way also reaches the ocean of salt water in the west.

TEXT 8

भद्रा चोत्तरतो मेरुशिरसो निपतिता गिरिशिखराद्गिरिशिखरमतिहाय शृङ्गवतः शृङ्गादवस्यन्दमाना उत्तरांस्तु कुरूनभित उदीच्यां दिशि जलधिमभिप्रविशति ॥८॥

bhadrā cottarato meru-śiraso nipatitā giri-śikharād giri-śikharam atihāya śṛṅgavataḥ śṛṅgād avasyandamānā uttarāṁs tu kurūn abhita udīcyāṁ diśi jaladhim abhipraviśati.

bhadrā—the branch known as Bhadrā; *ca*—also; *uttarataḥ*—to the northern side; *meru-śirasaḥ*—from the top of Mount Meru; *nipatitā*—having fallen; *giri-śikharāt*—from the peak of Kumuda Mountain; *giri-śikharam*—to the peak of Nīla Mountain; *atihāya*—passing over as if not touching; *śṛṅgavataḥ*—of the mountain known as Śṛṅgavān; *śṛṅgāt*—from the peak; *avasyandamānā*—flowing; *uttarān*—the northern; *tu*—but; *kurūn*—the land known as Kuru; *abhitaḥ*—on all sides; *udīcyām*—in the northern; *diśi*—direction; *jaladhim*—the ocean of salt water; *abhipraviśati*—enters into.

TRANSLATION

The branch of the Ganges known as Bhadrā flows from the northern side of Mount Meru. Its waters fall onto the peaks of Kumuda Mountain,

Mount Nīla, Śveta Mountain and Śṛṅgavān Mountain in succession. Then it runs down into the province of Kuru and, after crossing through that land, flows into the saltwater ocean in the north.

TEXT 9

तथैवालकनन्दा दक्षिणेन ब्रह्मसदनाद्बहूनि गिरिकूटान्यतिक्रम्य हेमकूटाद्धैमकूटान्यतिरभसतररंहसा लुठयन्ती भारतमभिवर्षं दक्षिणस्यां दिशि जलधिमभिप्रविशति यस्यां स्नानार्थं चागच्छतः पुंसः पदे पदेऽश्वमेधराजसूयादीनां फलं न दुर्लभमिति ॥९॥

tathaivālakanandā dakṣiṇena brahma-sadanād bahūni giri-kūṭāny
atikramya hemakūṭād dhaimakūṭāny ati-rabhasatara-raṁhasā
luṭhayantī bhāratam abhivarṣaṁ dakṣiṇasyāṁ diśi jaladhim
abhipraviśati yasyāṁ snānārthaṁ cāgacchataḥ puṁsaḥ pade pade
'śvamedha-rājasūyādīnāṁ phalaṁ na durlabham iti.

tathā eva—similarly; *alakanandā*—the branch known as Alakanandā; *dakṣiṇena*—by the southern side; *brahma-sadanāt*—from the city known as Brahmapurī; *bahūni*—many; *giri-kūṭāni*—the tops of mountains; *atikramya*—crossing over; *hemakūṭāt*—from Hemakūṭa Mountain; *haimakūṭāni*—and Himakūṭa; *ati-rabhasatara*—more fiercely; *raṁhasā*—with great force; *luṭhayantī*—plundering; *bhāratam abhivarṣam*—on all sides of Bhārata-varṣa; *dakṣiṇasyām*—in the southern; *diśi*—direction; *jaladhim*—the ocean of salt water; *abhipraviśati*—enters into; *yasyām*—in which; *snāna-artham*—for bathing; *ca*—and; *āgacchataḥ*—of one who is coming; *puṁsaḥ*—a person; *pade pade*—at every step; *aśvamedha-rājasūya-ādīnām*—of great sacrifices like the Aśvamedha-*yajña* and Rājasūya *yajña*; *phalam*—the result; *na*—not; *durlabham*—very difficult to obtain; *iti*—thus.

TRANSLATION

Similarly, the branch of the Ganges known as Alakanandā flows from the southern side of Brahmapurī [Brahma-sadana]. Passing over the tops of mountains in various lands, it falls down with fierce force upon the peaks of the mountains Hemakūṭa and Himakūṭa. After inundating the tops of those mountains, the Ganges falls down onto the tract of land known as Bhārata-varṣa, which she also inundates. Then the Ganges flows into the ocean of salt water in the south. Persons who come to bathe in this river are fortunate. It is not very difficult for them to achieve

with every step the results of performing great sacrifices like the Rājasūya and Aśvamedha yajñas.

PURPORT

The place where the Ganges flows into the salt water of the Bay of Bengal is still known as Gaṅgā-sāgara, or the meeting place of the Ganges and the Bay of Bengal. On Makara-saṅkrānti, in the month of January–February, thousands of people still go there to bathe, hoping to be liberated. That they can actually be liberated in this way is confirmed herein. For those who bathe in the Ganges at any time, the results of great sacrifices like the Aśvamedha and Rājasūya *yajñas* are not at all difficult to achieve. Most people in India are still inclined to bathe in the Ganges, and there are many places where they can do so. At Prayāga (Allahabad), many thousands of people gather during the month of January to bathe in the confluence of the Ganges and Yamunā. Afterward, many of them go to the confluence of the Bay of Bengal and the Ganges to take bath there. Thus it is a special facility for all the people of India that they can bathe in the water of the Ganges at so many places of pilgrimage.

TEXT 10

अन्ये च नदा नद्यश्च वर्षे वर्षे सन्ति बहुशो मेर्वादिगिरिदुहितरः शतशः ॥१०॥

anye ca nadā nadyaś ca varṣe varṣe santi bahuśo merv-ādi-giri-
duhitaraḥ śataśaḥ.

anye—many others; *ca*—also; *nadāḥ*—rivers; *nadyaḥ*—small rivers; *ca*—and; *varṣe varṣe*—in each tract of land; *santi*—are; *bahuśaḥ*—of many varieties; *meru-ādi-giri-duhitaraḥ*—daughters of the mountains beginning with Meru; *śataśaḥ*—in the hundreds.

TRANSLATION

Many other rivers, both big and small, flow from the top of Mount Meru. These rivers are like daughters of the mountain, and they flow to the various tracts of land in hundreds of branches.

TEXT 11

तत्रापि भारतमेव वर्षं कर्मक्षेत्रमन्यान्यष्ट वर्षाणि स्वर्गिणां पुण्यशेषोप-
भोगस्थानानि भौमानि स्वर्गपदानि व्यपदिशन्ति ॥११॥

tatrāpi bhāratam eva varṣaṁ karma-kṣetram anyāny aṣṭa varṣāṇi svargiṇāṁ puṇya-śeṣopabhoga-sthānāni bhaumāni svarga-padāni vyapadiśanti.

tatra api—out of all of them; *bhāratam*—known as Bhārata-varṣa; *eva*—certainly; *varṣam*—the tract of land; *karma-kṣetram*—the field of activities; *anyāni*—the others; *aṣṭa varṣāṇi*—eight tracts of land; *svargiṇām*—of the living entities elevated to the heavenly planets by extraordinary pious activities; *puṇya*—of the results of pious activities; *śeṣa*—of the remainder; *upabhoga-sthānāni*—the places for material enjoyment; *bhaumāni svarga-padāni*—as the heavenly places on earth; *vyapadiśanti*—they designate.

TRANSLATION

Among the nine varṣas, the tract of land known as Bhārata-varṣa is understood to be the field of fruitive activities. Learned scholars and saintly persons declare the other eight varṣas to be meant for very highly elevated pious persons. After returning from the heavenly planets, they enjoy the remaining results of their pious activities in these eight earthly varṣas.

PURPORT

The heavenly places of enjoyment are divided into three groups: the celestial heavenly planets, the heavenly places on earth, and the *bila* heavenly places, which are found in the lower regions. Among these three classes of heavenly places (*bhauma-svarga-padāni*), the heavenly places on earth are the eight *varṣas* other than Bhārata-varṣa. In *Bhagavad-gītā* (9.21) Kṛṣṇa says, *kṣīṇe puṇye martya-lokaṁ viśanti:* when the persons living in the heavenly planets exhaust the results of their pious activities, they return to this earth. In this way, they are elevated to the heavenly planets, and then they again fall to the earthly planets. This process is known as *brahmāṇḍa bhramaṇa,* wandering up and down throughout the universes. Those who are intelligent —in other words, those who have not lost their intelligence—do not involve themselves in this process of wandering up and down. They take to the devotional service of the Lord so that they can ultimately penetrate the covering of this universe and enter the spiritual kingdom. Then they are situated on one of the planets known as Vaikuṇṭhaloka or, still higher, Kṛṣṇaloka (Goloka Vṛndāvana). A devotee is never caught in the process of being promoted to the heavenly planets and again coming down. Therefore Śrī Caitanya Mahāprabhu says:

ei rūpe brahmāṇḍa bhramite kona bhāgyavān jīva
guru-kṛṣṇa-prasāde pāya bhakti-latā-bīja

Among all the living entities wandering throughout the universe, one who is most fortunate comes in contact with a representative of the Supreme Personality of Godhead and thus gets the opportunity to execute devotional service. Those who are sincerely seeking the favor of Kṛṣṇa come in contact with a *guru,* a bona fide representative of Kṛṣṇa. The Māyāvādīs indulging in mental speculation and the *karmīs* desiring the results of their actions cannot become *gurus.* A *guru* must be a direct representative of Kṛṣṇa who distributes the instructions of Kṛṣṇa without any change. Thus only the most fortunate persons come in contact with the *guru.* As confirmed in the Vedic literatures, *tad-vijñānārthaṁ sa gurum evābhigacchet:* one has to search out a *guru* to understand the affairs of the spiritual world. *Śrīmad-Bhāgavatam* also confirms this point. *Tasmād guruṁ prapadyeta jijñāsuḥ śreya uttamam:* one who is very interested in understanding the activities in the spiritual world must search out a *guru*—a bona fide representative of Kṛṣṇa. From all angles of vision, therefore, the word *guru* is especially meant for the bona fide representative of Kṛṣṇa and no one else. *Padma Purāṇa* states, *avaiṣṇavo gurur na syāt:* one who is not a Vaiṣṇava, or who is not a representative of Kṛṣṇa, cannot be a *guru.* Even the most qualified *brāhmaṇa* cannot become a *guru* if he is not a representative of Kṛṣṇa. *Brāhmaṇas* are supposed to acquire six kinds of auspicious qualifications: they become very learned scholars (*paṭhana*) and very qualified teachers (*pāṭhana*); they become expert in worshiping the Lord or the demigods (*yajana*), and they teach others how to execute this worship (*yājana*); they qualify themselves as bona fide persons to receive alms from others (*pratigraha*), and they distribute the wealth in charity (*dāna*). Yet even a *brāhmaṇa* possessing these qualifications cannot become a *guru* unless he is the representative of Kṛṣṇa (*gurur na syāt*). *Vaiṣṇavaḥ śva-paco guruḥ:* but a Vaiṣṇava, a bona fide representative of the Supreme Personality of Godhead, Viṣṇu, can become a *guru,* even if he is *śva-paca,* a member of a family of dog-eaters. Of the three divisions of heavenly planets (*svarga-loka*), *bhauma-svarga* is sometimes accepted as the tract of land in Bhārata-varṣa known as Kashmir. In this region there are certainly good facilities for material sense enjoyment, but this is not the business of a pure transcendentalist. Rūpa Gosvāmī describes the engagement of a pure transcendentalist as follows:

anyābhilāṣitā-śūnyaṁ
jñāna-karmādy-anāvṛtam
ānukūlyena kṛṣṇānu-
śīlanaṁ bhaktir uttamā

"One should render transcendental loving service to the Supreme Lord Kṛṣṇa favorably and without desire for material profit or gain through fruitive activities or philosophical speculation. That is called pure devotional service." Those who fully engage in devotional service to Kṛṣṇa just to please Him are not interested in the three divisions of heavenly places, namely, *divya-svarga, bhauma-svarga* and *bila-svarga.*

TEXT 12

एषु पुरुषाणामयुतपुरुषायुर्वर्षाणां देवकल्पानां नागायुतप्राणानां वज्रसंह-ननबलवयोमोदप्रमुदितमहासौरतमिथुनव्यवायापवर्गवर्षधृतैकगर्भ कलत्राणां तत्र तु त्रेतायुगसमः कालो वर्तते ॥१२॥

eṣu puruṣāṇām ayuta-puruṣāyur-varṣāṇāṁ deva-kalpānāṁ nāgāyuta-prāṇānāṁ vajra- saṁhanana-bala-vayo-moda-pramudita- mahā-saurata-mithuna-vyavāyāpavarga-varṣa-dhṛtaika-garbha-kalatrāṇāṁ tatra tu tretā-yuga-samaḥ kālo vartate.

eṣu—in these (eight) *varṣas,* or tracts of land; *puruṣāṇām*—of all the men; *ayuta*—ten thousand; *puruṣa*—by the measure of men; *āyuḥ-varṣāṇām*—of those whose years of life; *deva-kalpānām*—who are like the demigods; *nāga-ayuta-prāṇānām*—having the strength of ten thousand elephants; *vajra-saṁhanana*—by bodies as solid as thunderbolts; *bala*—by bodily strength; *vayaḥ*—by youth; *moda*—by abundant sense enjoyment; *pramudita*—being excited; *mahā-saurata*—a great deal of sexual; *mithuna*—combinations of man and woman; *vyavāya-apavarga*—at the end of their period of sexual enjoyment; *varṣa*—in the last year; *dhṛta-eka-garbha*—who conceive one child; *kalatrāṇām*—of those who have wives; *tatra*—there; *tu*—but; *tretā-yuga-samaḥ*—exactly like the Tretā-yuga (when there is no tribulation); *kālaḥ*—time; *vartate*—exists.

TRANSLATION

In these eight varṣas, or tracts of land, human beings live ten thousand years according to earthly calculations. All the inhabitants are almost like

demigods. They have the bodily strength of ten thousand elephants. Indeed, their bodies are as sturdy as thunderbolts. The youthful duration of their lives is very pleasing, and both men and women enjoy sexual union with great pleasure for a long time. After years of sensual pleasure—when a balance of one year of life remains—the wife conceives a child. Thus the standard of pleasure for the residents of these heavenly regions is exactly like that of the human beings who lived during Tretā-yuga.

PURPORT

There are four *yugas:* Satya-yuga, Tretā-yuga, Dvāpara-yuga and Kali-yuga. During the first *yuga,* Satya-yuga, people were very pious. Everyone practiced the mystic *yoga* system for spiritual understanding and realization of God. Because everyone was always absorbed in *samādhi,* no one was interested in material sense enjoyment. During Tretā-yuga, people enjoyed sense pleasure without tribulations. Material miseries began in Dvāpara-yuga, but they were not very stringent. Stringent material miseries really began from the advent of Kali-yuga.

Another point in this verse is that in all eight of these heavenly *varṣas,* although men and women enjoy sex pleasure, there is no pregnancy. Pregnancy takes place only in lower-grade life. For example, animals like dogs and hogs become pregnant twice a year, and each time they beget at least half a dozen offspring. Even lower species of life such as snakes give birth to hundreds of young at one time. This verse informs us that in grades of life higher than ours, pregnancy occurs once in a lifetime. People still have sex life, but there is no pregnancy. In the spiritual world, people are not very attracted to sex life, due to their exalted devotional attitude. Practically speaking, there is no sex life in the spiritual world, but even if sometimes it does occur, there is no pregnancy at all. On the planet earth, however, human beings do become pregnant, although the tendency is to avoid having children. In this sinful age of Kali, people have even taken to the process of killing the child in the womb. This is the most degraded practice; it can only perpetuate the miserable material conditions of those who perform it.

TEXT 13

यत्र ह देवपतयः स्वैः स्वैर्गणनायकैर्विहितमहार्हणाः सर्वर्तुकुसुमस्तबक-
फलकिसलयश्रियाऽऽनम्यमानविटपलता विटपिभिरुपशुम्भमानरुचिरकानना-
श्रमायतनवर्षगिरिद्रोणीषु तथा चामलजलाशयेषु विकचविविधनववनरुहामोद -

मुदितराजहंसजलकुक्कुटकारण्डवसारसचक्रवाकादिभिर्मधुकरनिकराकृतिभिरु -
पकूजितेषु जलक्रीडादिभिर्विचित्रविनोदैः सुललितसुरसुन्दरीणां कामकलिल -
विलासहासलीलावलोकाकृष्टमनोदृष्टयः स्वैरं विहरन्ति ॥१३॥

yatra ha deva-patayaḥ svaiḥ svair gaṇa-nāyakair vihita-mahārhaṇāḥ sarvartu-kusuma-stabaka-phala-kisalaya-śriyānamyamāna-viṭapa-latā-viṭapibhir upaśumbhamāna-rucira-kānanāśramāyatana-varṣa-giri-droṇīṣu tathā cāmala-jalāśayeṣu vikaca-vividha-nava-vanaruhāmoda-mudita-rāja-haṁsa-jala-kukkuṭa-kāraṇḍava-sārasa-cakravākādibhir madhukara-nikarākṛtibhir upakūjiteṣu jala-krīḍādibhir vicitra-vinodaiḥ sulalita-sura-sundarīṇāṁ kāma-kalila-vilāsa-hāsa-līlāvalokākṛṣṭa-mano-dṛṣṭayaḥ svairaṁ viharanti.

yatra ha—in those eight tracts of land; *deva-patayaḥ*—the lords of the demigods, such as Lord Indra; *svaiḥ svaiḥ*—by their own respective; *gaṇa-nāyakaiḥ*—leaders of the servants; *vihita*—furnished with; *mahā-arhaṇāḥ*—valuable gifts, such as sandalwood pulp and garlands; *sarva-ṛtu*—in all seasons; *kusuma-stabaka*—of bunches of flowers; *phala*—of fruits; *kisalaya-śriyā*—by the opulences of shoots; *ānamyamāna*—being bent down; *viṭapa*—whose branches; *latā*—and creepers; *viṭapibhiḥ*—by many trees; *upaśumbhamāna*—being fully decorated; *rucira*—beautiful; *kānana*—gardens; *āśrama-āyatana*—and many hermitages; *varṣa-giri-droṇīṣu*—the valleys between the mountains designating the borders of the tracts of land; *tathā*—as well as; *ca*—also; *amala-jala-āśayeṣu*—in lakes with clear water; *vikaca*—just fructified; *vividha*—varieties; *nava-vanaruha-āmoda*—by the fragrance of lotus flowers; *mudita*—enthused; *rāja-haṁsa*—great swans; *jala-kukkuṭa*—water fowl; *kāraṇḍava*—aquatic birds called *kāraṇḍavas; sārasa*—cranes; *cakravāka-ādibhiḥ*—by birds known as *cakravākas* and so on; *madhukara-nikara-ākṛtibhiḥ*—by the bumblebees; *upakūjiteṣu*—which were made to resound; *jala-krīḍā-ādibhiḥ*—such as water sports; *vicitra*—various; *vinodaiḥ*—by pastimes; *su-lalita*—attractive; *sura-sundarīṇām*—of the women of the demigods; *kāma*—from lust; *kalila*—born; *vilāsa*—pastimes; *hāsa*—smiling; *līlā-avaloka*—by playful glances; *ākṛṣṭa-manaḥ*—whose minds are attracted; *dṛṣṭayaḥ*—and whose vision is attracted; *svairam*—very freely; *viharanti*—engage in sportive enjoyment.

TRANSLATION

In each of those tracts of land, there are many gardens filled with flowers and fruits according to the season, and there are beautifully decorated

hermitages as well. Between the great mountains demarcating the borders of those lands lie enormous lakes of clear water filled with newly grown lotus flowers. Aquatic birds such as swans, ducks, water chickens, and cranes become greatly excited by the fragrance of lotus flowers, and the charming sound of bumblebees fills the air. The inhabitants of those lands are important leaders among the demigods. Always attended by their respective servants, they enjoy life in gardens alongside the lakes. In this pleasing situation, the wives of the demigods smile playfully at their husbands and look upon them with lusty desires. All the demigods and their wives are constantly supplied with sandalwood pulp and flower garlands by their servants. In this way, all the residents of the eight heavenly varṣas enjoy, attracted by the activities of the opposite sex.

PURPORT

Here is a description of the lower heavenly planets. The inhabitants of those planets enjoy life in a pleasing atmosphere of clear lakes filled with newly grown lotus flowers and gardens filled with fruits, flowers, various kinds of birds and humming bees. In that atmosphere they enjoy life with their very beautiful wives, who are always sexually stimulated. Nonetheless, they are all devotees of the Supreme Personality of Godhead, as will be explained in subsequent verses. The inhabitants of this earth also desire such heavenly enjoyment, but when they somehow or other achieve imitation pleasures like sex and intoxication, they completely forget the service of the Supreme Lord. In the heavenly planets, however, although the residents enjoy superior sense gratification, they never forget their positions as eternal servants of the Supreme Being.

TEXT 14

नवस्वपि वर्षेषु भगवान्नारायणो महापुरुषः पुरुषाणां तदनुग्रहायात्मतत्त्व-
व्यूहेनात्मनाद्यापि संनिधीयते ॥१४॥

navasv api varṣeṣu bhagavān nārāyaṇo mahā-puruṣaḥ puruṣāṇāṁ tad-anugrahāyātma-tattva-vyūhenātmanādyāpi sannidhīyate.

navasu—in the nine; *api*—certainly; *varṣeṣu*—tracts of land known as *varṣas; bhagavān*—the Supreme Personality of Godhead; *nārāyaṇaḥ*—Lord Viṣṇu; *mahā-puruṣaḥ*—the Supreme Person; *puruṣāṇām*—unto His various devotees; *tat-anugrahāya*—to show His mercy; *ātma-tattva-vyūhena*—by expansions of Himself in the quadruple forms Vāsudeva, Saṅkarṣaṇa, Pradyumna and Aniruddha; *ātmanā*—personally; *adya api*—until now; *sannidhīyate*—is near the devotees for accepting their services.

TRANSLATION

To show mercy to His devotees in each of these nine tracts of land, the Supreme Personality of Godhead known as Nārāyaṇa expands Himself in His quadruple principles of Vāsudeva, Saṅkarṣaṇa, Pradyumna and Aniruddha. In this way He remains near His devotees to accept their service.

PURPORT

In this connection, Viśvanātha Cakravartī Ṭhākura informs us that the demigods worship the Supreme Lord in His various Deity forms (*arcā-vigraha*) because except in the spiritual world, the Supreme Personality of Godhead cannot be directly worshiped in person. In the material world, the Lord is always worshiped as the *arcā-vigraha,* or Deity in the temple. There is no difference between the *arcā-vigraha* and the original person, and therefore those who are engaged in worshiping the Deity in the temple in full opulence, even on this planet, should be understood to be directly in touch with the Supreme Personality of Godhead without a doubt. As enjoined in the *śāstras, arcye viṣṇau śilā-dhīr guruṣu nara-matiḥ:* "No one should treat the Deity in the temple as stone or metal, nor should one think that the spiritual master is an ordinary human being." One should strictly follow this śāstric injunction and worship the Deity, the Supreme Personality of Godhead, without offenses. The spiritual master is the direct representative of the Lord, and no one should consider him an ordinary human being. By avoiding offenses against the Deity and the spiritual master, one can advance in spiritual life, or Kṛṣṇa consciousness.

In this regard, the following quotation appears in the *Laghu-bhāgavatāmṛta:*

pādme tu parama-vyomnaḥ
pūrvādye dik-catuṣṭaye
vāsudevādayo vyūhaś
catvāraḥ kathitāḥ kramāt

tathā pāda-vibhūtau ca
nivasanti kramādi me
jalāvṛti-stha-vaikuṇṭha-
sthita vedavatī-pure

satyordhve vaiṣṇave loke
nityākhye dvārakā-pure
śuddhodād uttare śveta-
dvīpe cairāvatī-pure

kṣīrāmbudhi-sthitānte
kroḍa-paryaṅka-dhāmani
sātvatīye kvacit tantre
nava vyūhāḥ prakīrtitāḥ

catvāro vāsudevādyā
nārāyaṇa-nṛsiṁhakau

hayagrīvo mahā-kroḍo
brahmā ceti navoditāḥ
tatra brahmā tu vijñeyaḥ
pūrvokta-vidhayā hariḥ

"In the *Padma Purāṇa* it is said that in the spiritual world the Lord personally expands in all directions and is worshiped as Vāsudeva, Saṅkarṣaṇa, Pradyumna and Aniruddha. The same God is represented by the Deity in this material world, which is only one quarter of His creation. Vāsudeva, Saṅkarṣaṇa, Pradyumna and Aniruddha are also present in the four directions of this material world. There is a Vaikuṇṭhaloka covered with water in this material world, and on that planet is a place called Vedavatī, where Vāsudeva is located. Another planet known as Viṣṇuloka is situated above Satyaloka, and there Saṅkarṣaṇa is present. Similarly, in Dvārakā-purī, Pradyumna is the predominator. On the island known as Śvetadvīpa, there is an ocean of milk, and in the midst of that ocean is a place called Airāvatī-pura, where Aniruddha lies on Ananta. In some of the *sātvata-tantras,* there is a description of the nine *varṣas* and the predominating Deity worshiped in each: (1) Vāsudeva, (2) Saṅkarṣaṇa, (3) Pradyumna, (4) Aniruddha, (5) Nārāyaṇa, (6) Nṛsiṁha, (7) Hayagrīva, (8) Mahāvarāha, and (9) Brahmā." The Lord Brahmā mentioned in this connection is the Supreme Personality of Godhead. When there is no fit human being to empower as Lord Brahmā, the Lord Himself takes the position of Lord Brahmā. *Tatra brahmā tu vijñeyaḥ pūrvokta-vidhayā hariḥ.* That Brahmā mentioned here is Hari Himself.

TEXT 15

इलावृते तु भगवान् भव एक एव पुमान्न ह्यन्यस्तत्रापरो निर्विशति भवान्याः शापनिमित्तज्ञो यत्प्रवेक्ष्यतः स्त्रीभावस्तत्पश्चाद्वक्ष्यामि ॥१५॥

ilāvṛte tu bhagavān bhava eka eva pumān na hy anyas tatrāparo nirviśati bhavānyāḥ śāpa-nimitta-jño yat-pravekṣyataḥ strī-bhāvas tat paścād vakṣyāmi.

ilāvṛte—in the tract of land known as Ilāvṛta-varṣa; *tu*—but; *bhagavān*—the most powerful; *bhavaḥ*—Lord Śiva; *eka*—only; *eva*—certainly; *pumān*—male person; *na*—not; *hi*—certainly; *anyaḥ*—any other; *tatra*—there; *aparaḥ*—besides; *nirviśati*—enters; *bhavānyāḥ śāpa-nimitta-jñaḥ*—who knows the cause of the curse by Bhavānī, the wife of Lord Śiva; *yat-pravekṣyataḥ*—of one who forcibly enters that tract of land; *strī-bhāvaḥ*—transformation into a female; *tat*—that; *paścāt*—later; *vakṣyāmi*—I shall explain.

TRANSLATION

Śukadeva Gosvāmī said: In the tract of land known as Ilāvṛta-varṣa, the only male person is Lord Śiva, the most powerful demigod. Goddess Durgā, the wife of Lord Śiva, does not like any man to enter that land. If any foolish man dares to do so, she immediately turns him into a woman. I shall explain this later [in the Ninth Canto of Śrīmad-Bhāgavatam].

TEXT 16

भवानीनाथैः स्त्रीगणार्बुदसहस्रै रवरुध्यमानो भगवतश्चतुर्मूर्तेर्महापुरुषस्य तुरीयां तामसीं मूर्तिं प्रकृतिमात्मनः सङ्कर्षणसंज्ञामात्मसमाधिरूपेण संनिधाप्यैत-दभिगृणन् भव उपधावति ॥१६॥

bhavānī-nāthaiḥ strī-gaṇārbuda-sahasrair avarudhyamāno bhagavataś catur-mūrter mahā-puruṣasya turīyāṁ tāmasīṁ mūrtiṁ prakṛtim ātmanaḥ saṅkarṣaṇa-saṁjñām ātma-samādhi-rūpeṇa sannidhāpyaitad abhigṛṇan bhava upadhāvati.

bhavānī-nāthaiḥ—by the company of Bhavānī; *strī-gaṇa*—of females; *arbuda-sahasraiḥ*—by ten billion; *avarudhyamānaḥ*—always being served; *bhagavataḥ catuḥ-mūrteḥ*—the Supreme Personality of Godhead, who is expanded in four; *mahā-puruṣasya*—of the Supreme Person; *turīyām*—the fourth expansion; *tāmasīm*—related to the mode of ignorance; *mūrtim*—the form; *prakṛtim*—as the source; *ātmanaḥ*—of himself (Lord Śiva); *saṅkarṣaṇa-saṁjñām*—known as Saṅkarṣaṇa; *ātma-samādhi-rūpeṇa*—by meditating upon Him in trance; *sannidhāpya*—bringing Him near; *etat*—this; *abhigṛṇan*—clearly chanting; *bhavaḥ*—Lord Śiva; *upadhāvati*—worships.

TRANSLATION

In Ilāvṛta-varṣa, Lord Śiva is always encircled by ten billion maidservants of Goddess Durgā, who minister to him. The quadruple expansion of the Supreme Lord is composed of Vāsudeva, Pradyumna, Aniruddha and Saṅkarṣaṇa. Saṅkarṣaṇa, the fourth expansion, is certainly transcendental, but because his activities of destruction in the material world are in the mode of ignorance, He is known as tāmasī, the Lord's form in the mode of ignorance. Lord Śiva knows that Saṅkarṣaṇa is the original cause of his own existence, and thus he always meditates upon Him in trance by chanting the following mantra.

PURPORT

Sometimes we see a picture of Lord Śiva engaged in meditation. This verse explains that Lord Śiva is always meditating upon Lord Saṅkarṣaṇa in trance. Lord Śiva is in charge of the destruction of the material world. Lord Brahmā creates the material world, Lord Viṣṇu maintains it, and Lord Śiva destroys it. Because destruction is in the mode of ignorance, Lord Śiva and his worshipable Deity, Saṅkarṣaṇa, are technically called *tāmasī.* Lord Śiva is the incarnation of *tamo-guṇa.* Since both Lord Śiva and Saṅkarṣaṇa are always enlightened and situated in the transcendental position, they have nothing to do with the modes of material nature—goodness, passion and ignorance—but because their activities involve them with the mode of ignorance, they are sometimes called *tāmasī.*

TEXT 17

श्रीभगवानुवाच

ॐ नमो भगवते महापुरुषाय सर्वगुणसङ्ख्यानायानन्तायाव्यक्ताय नम इति ॥१७॥

śrī-bhagavān uvāca

oṁ namo bhagavate mahā-puruṣāya sarva-guṇa-
saṅkhyānāyānantāyāvyaktāya nama iti.

śrī-bhagavān uvāca—the most powerful Lord Śiva says; *om namo bhagavate*—O Supreme Personality of Godhead, I offer my respectful obeisances unto You; *mahā-puruṣāya*—who are the Supreme person; *sarva-guṇa-saṅkhyānāya*—the reservoir of all transcendental qualities; *anantāya*—the unlimited; *avyaktāya*—not manifested within the material world; *namaḥ*—my respectful obeisances; *iti*—thus.

TRANSLATION

The most powerful Lord Śiva says: O Supreme Personality of Godhead, I offer my respectful obeisances unto You in Your expansion as Lord Saṅkarṣaṇa. You are the reservoir of all transcendental qualities. Although You are unlimited, You remain unmanifest to the nondevotees.

TEXT 18

भजे भजन्यारणपादपङ्कजं
भगस्य कृत्स्नस्य परं परायणम् ।
भक्तेष्वलं भावितभूतभावनं
भवापहं त्वा भवभावमीश्वरम् ॥१८॥

bhaje bhajanyāraṇa-pāda-paṅkajaṁ
bhagasya kṛtsnasya paraṁ parāyaṇam
bhakteṣv alaṁ bhāvita-bhūta-bhāvanaṁ
bhavāpahaṁ tvā bhava-bhāvam īśvaram

bhaje—I worship; *bhajanya*—O worshipable Lord; *araṇa-pāda-paṅkajam*—whose lotus feet protect His devotees from all fearful situations; *bhagasya*—of opulences; *kṛtsnasya*—of all different varieties (wealth, fame, strength, knowledge, beauty and renunciation); *param*—the best; *parāyaṇam*—the ultimate shelter; *bhakteṣu*—to the devotees; *alam*—beyond value; *bhāvita-bhūta-bhāvanam*—who manifests His different forms for the satisfaction of His devotees; *bhava-apaham*—who stops the devotees' repetition of birth and death; *tvā*—unto You; *bhava-bhāvam*—who is the origin of the material creation; *īśvaram*—the Supreme Personality of Godhead.

TRANSLATION

O my Lord, You are the only worshipable person, for You are the Supreme Personality of Godhead, the reservoir of all opulences. Your secure lotus feet are the only source of protection for all Your devotees,

whom You satisfy by manifesting Yourself in various forms. O my Lord, You deliver Your devotees from the clutches of material existence. Nondevotees, however, remain entangled in material existence by Your will. Kindly accept me as Your eternal servant.

TEXT 19

न यस्य मायागुणचित्तवृत्तिभि-
निरीक्षतो ह्यण्वपि दृष्टिरज्यते ।
ईशे यथा नोऽजितमन्युरंहसां
कस्तं न मन्येत जिगीषुरात्मनः ॥१९॥

na yasya māyā-guṇa-citta-vṛttibhir
nirīkṣato hy aṇv api dṛṣṭir ajyate
īśe yathā no'jita-manyu-raṁhasāṁ
kas taṁ na manyeta jigīṣur ātmanaḥ

na—never; *yasya*—whose; *māyā*—of the illusory energy; *guṇa*—in the qualities; *citta*—of the heart; *vṛttibhiḥ*—by the activities (thinking, feeling and willing); *nirīkṣataḥ*—of Him who is glancing; *hi*—certainly; *aṇu*—slightly; *api*—even; *dṛṣṭiḥ*—vision; *ajyate*—is affected; *īśe*—for the purpose of regulating; *yathā*—as; *naḥ*—of us; *ajita*—who have not conquered; *manyu*—of anger; *raṁhasām*—the force; *kaḥ*—who; *tam*—unto Him (the Supreme Lord); *na*—not; *manyeta*—would worship; *jigīṣuḥ*—aspiring to conquer; *ātmanaḥ*—the senses.

TRANSLATION

We cannot control the force of our anger. Therefore when we look at material things, we cannot avoid feeling attraction or repulsion for them. But the Supreme Lord is never affected in this way. Although He glances over the material world for the purpose of creating, maintaining and destroying it, He is not affected, even to the slightest degree. Therefore, one who desires to conquer the force of the senses must take shelter of the lotus feet of the Lord. Then he will be victorious.

PURPORT

The Supreme Personality of Godhead is always equipped with inconceivable potencies. Although creation takes place by His glancing over the material energy, He is not affected by the modes of material nature. Because of His eternally transcendental position, when the Supreme

Personality of Godhead appears in this material world, the modes of material nature cannot affect Him. Therefore the Supreme Lord is called Transcendence, and anyone who wants to be secure from the influence of the modes of material nature must take shelter of Him.

TEXT 20

असदृशो यः प्रतिभाति मायया
क्षीबेव मध्वासवताम्रलोचनः ।
न नागवध्वोऽर्हण ईशिरे ह्रिया
यत्पादयोः स्पर्शनधर्षितेन्द्रियाः ॥२०॥

asad-dṛśo yaḥ pratibhāti māyayā
kṣībeva madhv-āsava-tāmra-locanaḥ
na nāga-vadhvo 'rhaṇa īśire hriyā
yat-pādayoḥ sparśana-dharṣitendriyāḥ

asat-dṛśaḥ—for a person with polluted vision; *yaḥ*—who; *pratibhāti*—appears; *māyayā*—the influence of *māyā; kṣībaḥ*—one who is inebriated or angry; *iva*—like; *madhu*—by honey; *āsava*—and liquor; *tāmra-locanaḥ*—having eyes reddish like copper; *na*—not; *nāga-vadhvaḥ*—the wives of the serpent demon; *arhaṇe*—in worshiping; *īśire*—were unable to proceed; *hriyā*—because of bashfulness; *yat-pādayoḥ*—of whose lotus feet; *sparśana*—by the touching; *dharṣita*—agitated; *indriyāḥ*—whose senses.

TRANSLATION

For persons with impure vision, the Supreme Lord's eyes appear like those of someone who indiscriminately drinks intoxicating beverages. Thus bewildered, such unintelligent persons become angry at the Supreme Lord, and due to their angry mood the Lord Himself appears angry and very fearful. However, this is an illusion. When the wives of the serpent demon were agitated by the touch of the Lord's lotus feet, due to shyness they could proceed no further in their worship of Him. Yet the Lord remained unagitated by their touch, for He is equipoised in all circumstances. Therefore who will not worship the Supreme Personality of Godhead?

PURPORT

Anyone who remains unagitated, even in the presence of cause for agitation, is called *dhīra,* or equipoised. The Supreme Personality of Godhead, being always in a transcendental position, is never agitated by anything. Therefore someone who wants to become *dhīra* must take shelter of the lotus feet of the Lord. In *Bhagavad-gītā* (2.13) Kṛṣṇa says, *dhīras tatra na muhyati:* a person who is equipoised in all circumstances is never bewildered. Prahlāda Mahārāja is a perfect example of a *dhīra.* When the fierce form of Nṛsiṁhadeva appeared in order to kill Hiraṇyakaśipu, Prahlāda was unagitated. He remained calm and quiet, whereas others, including even Lord Brahmā, were frightened by the features of the Lord.

TEXT 21

यमाहुरस्य स्थितिजन्मसंयमं
त्रिभिर्विहीनं यमनन्तमृषयः ।
न वेद सिद्धार्थमिव क्वचित्स्थितं
भूमण्डलं मूर्धसहस्रधामसु ॥२१॥

yam āhur asya sthiti-janma-saṁyamaṁ
tribhir vihīnaṁ yam anantam ṛṣayaḥ
na veda siddhārtham iva kvacit sthitaṁ
bhū-maṇḍalaṁ mūrdha-sahasra-dhāmasu

yam—whom; *āhuḥ*—they said; *asya*—of the material world; *sthiti*—the maintenance; *janma*—creation; *saṁyamam*—annihilation; *tribhiḥ*—these three; *vihīnam*—without; *yam*—which; *anantam*—unlimited; *ṛṣayaḥ*—all the great sages; *na*—not; *veda*—feels; *siddha-artham*—a mustard seed; *iva*—like; *kvacit*—where; *sthitam*—situated; *bhū-maṇḍalam*—the universe; *mūrdha-sahasra-dhāmasu*—on the hundreds and thousands of hoods of the Lord.

TRANSLATION

Lord Śiva continued: All the great sages accept the Lord as the source of creation, maintenance and destruction, although He actually has nothing to do with these activities. Therefore the Lord is called unlimited. Although the Lord in His incarnation as Śeṣa holds all the universes on His hoods, each universe feels no heavier than a mustard seed to Him. Therefore, what person desiring perfection will not worship the Lord?

PURPORT

The incarnation of the Supreme Personality of Godhead known as Śeṣa or Ananta has unlimited strength, fame, wealth, knowledge, beauty and renunciation. As described in this verse, Ananta's strength is so great that the innumerable universes rest on His hoods. He has the bodily features of a snake with thousands of hoods, and since His strength is unlimited, all the universes resting on His hoods feel no heavier than mustard seeds. We can just imagine how insignificant a mustard seed is on the hood of a serpent. In this connection, the reader is referred to *Śrī Caitanya-caritāmṛta, Ādi-līlā,* Chapter Five, verses 117–125. There it is stated that Lord Viṣṇu's incarnation as the serpentine Ananta Śeṣa Nāga supports all the universes on His hoods. By our calculation, a universe may be very, very heavy, but because the Lord is *ananta* (unlimited), He feels the weight to be no heavier than a mustard seed.

TEXTS 22–23

यस्याद्य आसीद् गुणविग्रहो महान्
विज्ञानधिष्ण्यो भगवानजः किल ।
यत्सम्भवोऽहं त्रिवृता स्वतेजसा
वैकारिकं तामसमैन्द्रियं सृजे ॥२२॥
एते वयं यस्य वशे महात्मनः
स्थिताः शकुन्ता इव सूत्रयन्त्रिताः ।
महानहं वैकृततामसेन्द्रियाः
सृजाम सर्वे यदनुग्रहादिदम् ॥२३॥

yasyādya āsīd guṇa-vigraho mahān
vijñāna-dhiṣṇyo bhagavān ajaḥ kila
yat-sambhavo 'haṁ tri-vṛtā sva-tejasā
vaikārikaṁ tāmasam aindriyaṁ sṛje

ete vayaṁ yasya vaśe mahātmanaḥ
sthitāḥ śakuntā iva sūtra-yantritāḥ
mahān ahaṁ vaikṛta-tāmasendriyāḥ
sṛjāma sarve yad-anugrahād idam

yasya—from whom; *ādyaḥ*—the beginning; *āsīt*—there was; *guṇa-vigrahaḥ*—the incarnation of the material qualities; *mahān*—the total material energy; *vijñāna*—of full knowledge; *dhiṣṇyaḥ*—the reservoir; *bhagavān*—the most powerful; *ajaḥ*—Lord Brahmā; *kila*—certainly; *yat*—from whom; *sambhavaḥ*—born; *aham*—I; *tri-vṛtā*—having three varieties according to the three modes of nature; *sva-tejasā*—by my material strength;

vaikārikam—all the demigods; *tāmasam*—material elements; *aindriyam*—the senses; *sṛje*—I create; *ete*—all of these; *vayam*—we; *yasya*—of whom; *vaśe*—under the control; *mahā-ātmanaḥ*—great personalities; *sthitāḥ*—situated; *śakuntāḥ*—vultures; *iva*—like; *sūtra-yantritāḥ*—bound by rope; *mahān*—the *mahat-tattva; aham*—I; *vaikṛta*—the demigods; *tāmasa*—the five material elements; *indriyāḥ*—senses; *sṛjāmaḥ*—we create; *sarve*—all of us; *yat*—of whom; *anugrahāt*—by the mercy; *idam*—this material world.

TRANSLATION

From that Supreme Personality of Godhead appears Lord Brahmā, whose body is made from the total material energy, the reservoir of intelligence predominated by the passionate mode of material nature. From Lord Brahmā, I myself am born as a representation of false ego known as Rudra. By my own power I create all the other demigods, the five elements and the senses. Therefore, I worship the Supreme Personality of Godhead, who is greater than any of us and under whose control are situated all the demigods, material elements and senses, and even Lord Brahmā and I myself, like birds bound by a rope. Only by the Lord's grace can we create, maintain and annihilate the material world. Therefore I offer my respectful obeisances unto the Supreme Being.

PURPORT

A summary of creation is given in this verse. From Saṅkarṣaṇa, Mahā-Viṣṇu expands, and from Mahā-Viṣṇu, Garbhodakaśāyī Viṣṇu expands. Lord Brahmā, who was born of Garbhodakaśāyī Viṣṇu, fathers Lord Śiva, from whom all the other demigods gradually evolve. Lord Brahmā, Lord Śiva and Lord Viṣṇu are incarnations of the different material qualities. Lord Viṣṇu is actually above all material qualities, but He accepts control of *sattva-guṇa* (the mode of goodness) to maintain the universe. Lord Brahmā is born from the *mahat-tattva.* Brahmā creates the entire universe, Lord Viṣṇu maintains it, and Lord Śiva annihilates it. The Supreme Personality of Godhead controls all the most important demigods—especially Lord Brahmā and Lord Śiva—exactly as the owner of a bird controls it by binding it with a rope. Sometimes vultures are controlled in this way.

TEXT 24

यन्निर्मितां कर्ह्यपि कर्मपर्वणीं
मायां जनोऽयं गुणसर्गमोहितः ।

न वेद निस्तारणयोगमञ्जसा
तस्मै नमस्ते विलयोदयात्मने ॥२४॥

yan-nirmitāṁ karhy api karma-parvaṇīṁ
māyāṁ jano'yaṁ guṇa-sarga-mohitaḥ
na veda nistāraṇa-yogam añjasā
tasmai namas te vilayodayātmane

yat—by whom; *nirmitām*—created; *karhi api*—at any time; *karma-parvaṇīm*—which ties the knots of fruitive activity; *māyām*—the illusory energy; *janaḥ*—a person; *ayam*—this; *guṇa-sarga-mohitaḥ*—bewildered by the three modes of material nature; *na*—not; *veda*—knows; *nistāraṇa-yogam*—the process of getting out of material entanglement; *añjasā*—soon; *tasmai*—unto Him (the Supreme); *namaḥ*—respectful obeisances; *te*—unto You; *vilaya-udaya-ātmane*—in whom everything is annihilated and from whom everything is again manifested.

TRANSLATION

The illusory energy of the Supreme Personality of Godhead binds all of us conditioned souls to this material world. Therefore, without being favored by Him, persons like us cannot understand how to get out of that illusory energy. Let me offer my respectful obeisances unto the Lord, who is the cause of creation and annihilation.

PURPORT

Kṛṣṇa clearly states in *Bhagavad-gītā* (7.14):

daivī hy eṣā guṇa-mayī
mama māyā duratyayā
mām eva ye prapadyante
māyām etāṁ taranti te

"This divine energy of Mine, consisting of the three modes of material nature, is difficult to overcome. But those who have surrendered unto Me can easily cross beyond it." All conditioned souls working within the illusory energy of the Lord consider the body to be the self, and thus they continuously wander throughout the universe, taking birth in different species of life and creating more and more problems. Sometimes they become disgusted with the problems and seek out a process by which they can get out of this entanglement. Unfortunately, such so-called research workers are unaware of the Supreme Personality of Godhead and His illusory energy, and thus all of them work only in darkness, never finding a way out. So-called scientists and advanced research scholars are ludicrously trying to find the cause of life. They take no notice of the fact that life is already being produced. What will be their credit if they find out the chemical composition of life? All their chemicals are nothing but different transformations of the five elements—earth, water, fire, air and ether. As stated in *Bhagavad-gītā* (2.20), the living entity is never created (*na jāyate mriyate vā kadācin*). There are five gross material elements and three minor material elements (mind, intelligence and ego), and there are eternal living entities. The living entity desires a certain type of body, and by the order of the Supreme Personality of Godhead, that body is created from material nature, which is nothing but a kind of machine handled by the Supreme Lord. The Lord gives the living entity a particular type of mechanical body, and the living entity must work with it according to the law of fruitive activities. Fruitive activities are described in this verse: *karma-parvanīṁ māyām.* The living entity is seated on a machine (the body), and according to the order of the Supreme Lord, he operates the machine. This is the secret of transmigration of the soul from one body to another. The living entity thus becomes entangled in fruitive activities in this material world. As confirmed in *Bhagavad-gītā* (15.7), *manaḥ ṣaṣṭhānīndriyāṇi prakṛti-sthāni karṣati:* the living entity is struggling very hard against the six senses, which include the mind.

In all the activities of creation and annihilation, the living entity is entangled in fruitive activities, which are executed by the illusory energy, *māyā.* He is exactly like a computer handled by the Supreme Personality of Godhead. The so-called scientists say that nature acts independently, but they cannot explain what nature is. Nature is nothing but a machine operated by the Supreme Personality of Godhead. When one understands the operator, his problems of life are solved. As Kṛṣṇa says in *Bhagavad-gītā* (7.19):

bahūnāṁ janmanām ante
jñānavān māṁ prapadyate
vāsudevaḥ sarvam iti
sa mahātmā sudurlabhaḥ

"After many births and deaths, he who is actually in knowledge surrenders unto Me, knowing Me to be the cause of all causes and all that is. Such a great soul is very rare." A sane man, therefore, surrenders to the Supreme Personality of Godhead and thus gets out of the clutches of the illusory energy, *māyā.*

Thus end the Bhaktivedanta purports of the Fifth Canto, Seventeenth Chapter, of the Śrīmad-Bhāgavatam, *entitled "The Descent of the River Ganges."*

CHAPTER EIGHTEEN

The Prayers Offered to the Lord by the Residents of Jambūdvīpa

In this chapter Śukadeva Gosvāmī describes the different *varṣas* of Jambūdvīpa and the incarnation of the Supreme Lord worshiped in each. The predominating ruler of Bhadrāśva-varṣa is Bhadraśravā. He and his many servants always worship the incarnation known as Lord Hayagrīva. At the end of each *kalpa,* when the demon Ajñāna steals the Vedic knowledge, Lord Hayagrīva appears and preserves it. Then He delivers it to Lord Brahmā. In the land known as Hari-varṣa, the exalted devotee Prahlāda Mahārāja worships Lord Nṛsiṁhadeva. (The appearance of Lord Nṛsiṁhadeva is described in the Seventh Canto of *Śrīmad-Bhāgavatam.*) Following in the footsteps of Prahlāda Mahārāja, the inhabitants of Hari-varṣa always worship Lord Nṛsiṁhadeva to receive from Him the benediction of being engaged in His loving service. In the tract of land known as Ketumāla-varṣa, the Supreme Personality of Godhead (Lord Hṛṣīkeśa) appears in the form of Cupid. The goddess of fortune and the demigods living there engage in His service day and night. Manifesting Himself in sixteen parts, Lord Hṛṣīkeśa is the source of all encouragement, strength and influence. The conditioned living entity has the defect of being always fearful, but simply by the mercy of the Supreme Personality of Godhead, he can rid himself of this defect of material life. Therefore the Lord alone can be addressed as master. In the tract of land known as Ramyaka-varṣa, Manu and all the inhabitants worship Matsyadeva to this very day. Matsyadeva, whose form is pure goodness, is the ruler and maintainer of the whole universe, and as such He is the director of all the demigods, headed by King Indra. In Hiraṇmaya-varṣa Lord Viṣṇu has assumed the form of a tortoise (Kūrma *mūrti*) and is worshiped there by Aryamā, along with all the other residents. Similarly, in the tract of land known as Uttarakuru-varṣa, Lord Śrī Hari has assumed the form of a boar, and in that form He accepts service from all the inhabitants living there.

All the information in this chapter can be fully realized by one who associates with devotees of the Lord. Therefore in the *śāstras* it is recommended that one associate with devotees. This is better than residing on the banks of the Ganges. In the hearts of pure devotees reside all good sentiments as well as all the superior qualities of the demigods. In the hearts of nondevotees, however, there cannot be any good qualities, for such people are simply enchanted by the external, illusory energy of the Lord. Following in the footsteps of devotees, one should know that the Supreme Personality of Godhead is the only worshipable Deity. Everyone should accept this proposal and worship the Lord. As stated in *Bhagavad-gītā* (15.15), *vedaiś ca sarvair aham eva vedyaḥ:* the purpose of studying all Vedic literature is to worship the Supreme Personality of Godhead, Kṛṣṇa. If after studying all the Vedic literature, one does not awaken his dormant love for the Supreme Lord, it is to be understood that he has labored for nothing. He has simply wasted his time. Lacking attachment for the Supreme Personality of Godhead, he remains attached to family life in this material world. Thus the lesson of this chapter is that one should get out of family life and completely take shelter of the lotus feet of the Lord.

TEXT 1

श्रीशुक उवाच

तथा च भद्रश्रवा नाम धर्मसुतस्तत्कुलपतयः पुरुषा भद्राश्ववर्षे साक्षाद्भगवतो वासुदेवस्य प्रियां तनुं धर्ममयीं हयशीर्षाभिधानां परमेण समाधिना संनिधाप्येदमभिगृणन्त उपधावन्ति ॥१॥

śrī-śuka uvāca
tathā ca bhadraśravā nāma dharma-sutas tat-kula-patayaḥ puruṣā
bhadrāśva-varṣe sākṣād bhagavato vāsudevasya priyāṁ tanuṁ
dharmamayīṁ hayaśīrṣābhidhānāṁ parameṇa samādhinā
sannidhāpyedam abhigṛṇanta upadhāvanti.

śrī-śukaḥ uvāca—Śukadeva Gosvāmī said; *tathā ca*—similarly (just as Lord Śiva worships Saṅkarṣaṇa in Ilāvṛta-varṣa); *bhadra-śravā*—Bhadraśravā; *nāma*—known as; *dharma-sutaḥ*—the son of Dharmarāja; *tat*—of him; *kula-patayaḥ*—the chiefs of the dynasty; *puruṣāḥ*—all the residents; *bhadrāśva-varṣe*—in the land known as Bhadrāśva-varṣa; *sākṣāt*—directly; *bhagavataḥ*—of the Supreme Personality of Godhead; *vāsudevasya*—of Lord Vāsudeva; *priyām tanum*—very dear form; *dharma-mayīm*—the director of all religious principles; *hayaśīrṣa-abhidhānām*—the Lord's incarnation named Hayaśīrṣa (also called Hayagrīva); *parameṇa samādhinā*—with the highest form of trance; *sannidhāpya*—coming near; *idam*—this; *abhigṛṇantaḥ*—chanting; *upadhāvanti*—they worship.

TRANSLATION

Śrī Śukadeva Gosvāmī said: Bhadraśravā, the son of Dharmarāja, rules the tract of land known as Bhadrāśva-varṣa. Just as Lord Śiva worships Saṅkarṣaṇa in Ilāvṛta-varṣa, Bhadraśravā, accompanied by his intimate servants and all the residents of the land, worships the plenary expansion of Vāsudeva known as Hayaśīrṣa. Lord Hayaśīrṣa is very dear to the devotees, and He is the director of all religious principles. Fixed in the topmost trance, Bhadraśravā and his associates offer their respectful obeisances to the Lord and chant the following prayers with careful pronunciation.

TEXT 2

भद्रश्रवस ऊचुः
ॐ नमो भगवते धर्मायात्मविशोधनाय नम इति ॥ २ ॥

bhadraśravasa ūcuḥ
oṁ namo bhagavate dharmāyātma-viśodhanāya nama iti.

bhadraśravasaḥ ūcuḥ—the ruler Bhadraśravā and his intimate associates said; *om*—O Lord; *namaḥ*—respectful obeisances; *bhagavate*—unto the Supreme Personality of Godhead; *dharmāya*—the source of all religious principles; *ātma-viśodhanāya*—who purifies us of material contamination; *namaḥ*—our obeisances; *iti*—thus.

TRANSLATION

The ruler Bhadraśravā and his intimate associates utter the following prayer: We offer our respectful obeisances unto the Supreme Personality of Godhead, the reservoir of all religious principles, who cleanses the heart of the conditioned soul in this material world. Again and again we offer our respectful obeisances unto Him.

PURPORT

Foolish materialistic persons do not know how they are being controlled and punished at every step by the laws of nature. They think they are very happy in the conditioned state of material life, not knowing the purpose of repeated birth, death, old age and disease. Therefore in *Bhagavad-gītā* (7.15) Lord Kṛṣṇa describes such materialistic persons as *mūḍhas* (rascals): *na māṁ duṣkṛtino mūḍhāḥ prapadyante narādhamāḥ*. These *mūḍhas* do not know that if they want to purify themselves, they must worship Lord Vāsudeva (Kṛṣṇa) by performing penances and austerities. This purification is the aim of human life. This life is not meant for blind indulgence in sense gratification. In the human form, the living being must engage himself in Kṛṣṇa consciousness to purify his existence: *tapo divyaṁ putrakā yena sattvaṁ śuddhyet.* This is the instruction of King Ṛṣabhadeva to His sons. In the human form of life, one must undergo all kinds of austerities to purify his existence. *Yasmād brahma-saukhyaṁ tv anantam.* We are all seeking happiness, but because of our ignorance and foolishness, we cannot know what unobstructed happiness really is. Unobstructed happiness is called *brahma-saukhya,* spiritual happiness. Although we may get some so-called happiness in this material world, that happiness is temporary. The foolish materialists cannot understand this. Therefore Prahlāda Mahārāja points out, *māyā-sukhāya bharam udvahato vimūḍhān:* merely for temporary materialistic happiness, these rascals are making huge arrangements, and thus they are baffled life after life.

TEXT 3

अहो विचित्रं भगवद्विचेष्टितं
घ्नन्तं जनोऽयं हि मिषन्न पश्यति ।
ध्यायन्नसद्यर्हि विकर्म सेवितुं
निर्हृत्य पुत्रं पितरं जिजीविषति ॥३॥

aho vicitraṁ bhagavad-viceṣṭitaṁ
ghnantaṁ jano'yaṁ hi miṣan na paśyati
dhyāyann asad yarhi vikarma sevituṁ
nirhṛtya putraṁ pitaraṁ jijīviṣati

aho—alas; *vicitram*—wonderful; *bhagavat-viceṣṭitam*—the pastimes of the Lord; *ghnantam*—death; *janaḥ*—a person; *ayam*—this; *hi*—certainly; *miṣan*—although seeing; *na paśyati*—does not see; *dhyāyan*—thinking about; *asat*—material happiness; *yarhi*—because; *vikarma*—forbidden activities; *sevitum*—to enjoy; *nirhṛtya*—burning; *putram*—sons; *pitaram*—the father; *jijīviṣati*—desires a long life.

TRANSLATION

Alas! How wonderful it is that the foolish materialist does not heed the great danger of impending death! He knows that death will surely come, yet he is nevertheless callous and neglectful. If his father dies, he wants to

enjoy his father's property, and if his son dies, he wants to enjoy his son's possessions as well. In either case, he heedlessly tries to enjoy material happiness with the acquired money.

PURPORT

Material happiness means to have good facilities for eating, sleeping, sexual intercourse and defense. Within this world, the materialistic person lives only for these four principles of sense gratification, not caring for the impending danger of death. After his father's death, a son tries to inherit his money and use it for sense gratification. Similarly, one whose son dies tries to enjoy the possessions of his son. Sometimes the father of a dead son even enjoys his son's widow. Materialistic persons behave in this way. Thus Śukadeva Gosvāmī says, "How wonderful are these pastimes of material happiness transacted by the will of the Supreme Personality of Godhead!" In other words, materialistic persons want to commit all kinds of sinful activities, but without the sanction of the Supreme Personality of Godhead, no one can do anything. Why does the Supreme Personality of Godhead permit sinful activities? The Supreme Lord does not want any living being to act sinfully, and He begs him through his good conscience to refrain from sin. But when someone insists upon acting sinfully, the Supreme Lord gives him the sanction to act at his own risk (*mattaḥ smṛtir jñānam apohanaṁ ca*). No one can do anything without the sanction of the Lord, but He is so kind that when the conditioned soul persists in doing something, the Lord permits the individual soul to act at his own risk.

According to Śrīla Viśvanātha Cakravartī Ṭhākura, sons always outlive their fathers in other planetary systems and other lands in this universe, especially on Svargaloka. However, on this planet earth a son often dies before his father, and the materialistic father is pleased to enjoy the possessions of his son. Neither the father nor the son can see the reality—that both of them are awaiting death. When death comes, however, all their plans for material enjoyment are finished.

TEXT 4

वदन्ति विश्वं कवयः स्म नश्वरं
पश्यन्ति चाध्यात्मविदो विपश्चितः ।
तथापि मुह्यन्ति तवाज मायया
सुविस्मितं कृत्यमजं नतोऽस्मि तम् ॥४॥

vadanti viśvaṁ kavayaḥ sma naśvaraṁ
paśyanti cādhyātmavido vipaścitaḥ
tathāpi muhyanti tavāja māyayā
suvismitaṁ kṛtyam ajaṁ nato 'smi tam

vadanti—they say authoritatively; *viśvam*—the entire material creation; *kavayaḥ*—great learned sages; *sma*—certainly; *naśvaram*—perishable; *paśyanti*—they see in trance; *ca*—also; *adhyātma-vidaḥ*—who have realized spiritual knowledge; *vipaścitaḥ*—very learned scholars; *tathā api*—still; *muhyanti*—become illusioned; *tava*—your; *aja*—O unborn one; *māyayā*—by the illusory energy; *su-vismitam*—most wonderful; *kṛtyam*—activity; *ajam*—unto the supreme unborn one; *nataḥ asmi*—I offer my obeisances; *tam*—unto Him.

TRANSLATION

O unborn one, learned Vedic scholars who are advanced in spiritual knowledge certainly know that this material world is perishable, as do other logicians and philosophers. In trance they realize the factual position of this world, and they preach the truth as well. Yet even they are sometimes bewildered by Your illusory energy. This is Your own wonderful pastime. Therefore, I can understand that Your illusory energy is very wonderful, and I offer my respectful obeisances unto You.

PURPORT

Not only does the illusory energy of the Supreme Personality of Godhead act on the conditioned soul within this material world, but sometimes it also acts on the most advanced learned scholars, who factually know the constitutional position of this material world through realization. As soon as someone thinks, "I am this material body (*ahaṁ mameti*) and everything in relationship with this material body is mine," he is in illusion (*moha*). This illusion caused by the material energy acts especially on the conditioned souls, but it sometimes also acts on liberated souls as well. A liberated soul is a person who has sufficient knowledge of this material world and is therefore unattached to the bodily conception of life. But because of association with the modes of material nature for a very long time, even liberated souls sometimes become captivated by the illusory energy due to inattentiveness in the transcendental position. Therefore Lord Kṛṣṇa says in *Bhagavad-gītā* (7.14), *mām eva ye prapadyante māyām etāṁ taranti te:* "Only those who surrender unto Me can overcome the influence of the material energy."

Therefore no one should think of himself as a liberated person immune to the influence of *māyā.* Everyone should very cautiously execute devotional service by rigidly following regulative principles. Thus he will remain fixed at the lotus feet of the Lord. Otherwise, a little inattention will create havoc. We have already seen an example of this in the case of Mahārāja Bharata. Mahārāja Bharata was undoubtedly a great devotee, but because he turned his attention slightly toward a small deer, he had to suffer two more births, one as a deer and another as the *brāhmaṇa* Jaḍa Bharata. Afterward he was liberated and went back home, back to Godhead.

The Lord is always prepared to excuse His devotee, but if a devotee takes advantage of the Lord's leniency and purposefully commits mistakes again and again, the Lord will certainly punish him by letting him fall down into the clutches of the illusory energy. In other words, theoretical knowledge acquired by studying the *Vedas* is insufficient to protect one from the clutches of *māyā.* One must strongly adhere to the lotus feet of the Lord in devotional service. Then one's position is secure.

TEXT 5

विश्वोद्भवस्थाननिरोधकर्म ते
ह्यकर्तुरङ्गीकृतमप्यपावृतः ।
युक्तं न चित्रं त्वयि कार्यकारणे
सर्वात्मनि व्यतिरिक्ते च वस्तुतः ॥५॥

viśvodbhava-sthāna-nirodha-karma te
hy akartur aṅgīkṛtam apy apāvṛtaḥ
yuktaṁ na citraṁ tvayi kārya-kāraṇe
sarvātmani vyatirikte ca vastutaḥ

viśva—of the whole universe; *udbhava*—of the creation; *sthāna*—of the maintenance; *nirodha*—of the annihilation; *karma*—these activities; *te*—of You (O dear Lord); *hi*—indeed; *akartuḥ*—aloof; *aṅgīkṛtam*—still accepted by the Vedic literature; *api*—although; *apāvṛtaḥ*—untouched by all these activities; *yuktam*—befitting; *na*—not; *citram*—wonderful; *tvayi*—in You; *kārya-kāraṇe*—the original cause of all effects; *sarva-ātmani*—in all respects; *vyatirikte*—set apart; *ca*—also; *vastutaḥ*—the original substance.

TRANSLATION

O Lord, although You are completely detached from the creation, maintenance and annihilation of this material world and are not directly

affected by these activities, they are all attributed to You. We do not wonder at this, for Your inconceivable energies perfectly qualify You to be the cause of all causes. You are the active principle in everything, although You are separate from everything. Thus we can realize that everything is happening because of Your inconceivable energy.

TEXT 6

वेदान् युगान्ते तमसा तिरस्कृतान्
रसातलाद्यो नृतुरङ्गविग्रहः ।
प्रत्याददे वै कवयेऽभियाचते
तस्मै नमस्तेऽवितथेहिताय इति ॥६॥

vedān yugānte tamasā tiraskṛtān
rasātalād yo nṛ-turaṅga-vigrahaḥ
pratyādade vai kavaye'bhiyācate
tasmai namas te 'vitathehitāya iti

vedān—the four *Vedas; yuga-ante*—at the end of the millennium; *tamasā*—by the demon of ignorance personified; *tiraskṛtān*—stolen away; *rasātalāt*—from the lowest planetary system (Rasātala); *yaḥ*—who (the Supreme Personality of Godhead); *nṛ-turaṅga-vigrahaḥ*—assuming the form of half-horse, half-man; *pratyādade*—returned; *vai*—indeed; *kavaye*—to the supreme poet (Lord Brahmā); *abhiyā-cate*—when he asked for them; *tasmai*—unto Him (the form of Hayagrīva); *namaḥ*—my respectful obeisances; *te*—to You; *avitatha-īhitāya*—whose resolution never fails; *iti*—thus.

TRANSLATION

At the end of the millennium, ignorance personified assumed the form of a demon, stole all the Vedas and took them down to the planet of Rasātala. The Supreme Lord, however, in His form of Hayagrīva retrieved the Vedas and returned them to Lord Brahmā when he begged for them. I offer my respectful obeisances unto the Supreme Lord, whose determination never fails.

PURPORT

Although Vedic knowledge is imperishable, within this material world it is sometimes manifest and sometimes not. When the people of this material world become too absorbed in ignorance, the Vedic knowledge disappears.

Lord Hayagrīva or Lord Matsya, however, always protects the Vedic knowledge, and in due course of time it is again distributed through the medium of Lord Brahmā. Brahmā is the trustworthy representative of the Supreme Lord. Therefore when he again asked for the treasure of Vedic knowledge, the Lord fulfilled his desire.

TEXT 7

हरिवर्षे चापि भगवान्नरहरिरूपेणास्ते। तद्रूपग्रहणनिमित्तमुत्तरत्राभिधास्ये। तद्दयितं रूपं महापुरुषगुणभाजनो महाभागवतो दैत्यदानवकुलतीर्थीकरणशीलाचरितः प्रह्लादोऽव्यवधानानन्यभक्तियोगेन सह तद्वर्षपुरुषैरुपास्ते इदं चोदाहरति ॥७॥

hari-varṣe cāpi bhagavān nara-hari-rūpeṇāste. tad-rūpa-grahaṇa-
nimittam uttaratrābhidhāsye. tad dayitaṁ rūpaṁ mahā-puruṣa-guṇa-
bhājano mahā-bhāgavato daitya-dānava-kula-tīrthīkaraṇa-śīlā-caritaḥ
prahlādo'vyavadhānānanya-bhakti-yogena saha tad-varṣa-puruṣair
upāste idaṁ codāharati.

hari-varṣe—in the tract of land known as Harivarṣa; *ca*—also; *api*—indeed; *bhagavān*—the Supreme Personality of Godhead; *nara-hari-rūpeṇa*—His form of Nṛsiṁhadeva; *āste*—is situated; *tat-rūpa-grahaṇa-nimittam*—the reason why Lord Kṛṣṇa (Keśava) assumed the form of Nṛsiṁha; *uttaratra*—in later chapters; *abhidhāsye*—I shall describe; *tat*—that; *dayitam*—most pleasing; *rūpam*—form of the Lord; *mahā-puruṣa-guṇa-bhājanaḥ*—Prahlāda Mahārāja, who is the abode of all the good qualities of great personalities; *mahā-bhāgavataḥ*—the topmost devotee; *daitya-dānava-kula-tīrthī-karaṇa-śīlā-caritaḥ*—whose activities and character were so exalted that he delivered all the *daityas* (demons) born in his family; *prahlādaḥ*—Mahārāja Prahlāda; *avyavadhāna-ananya-bhakti-yogena*—by uninterrupted and unflinching devotional service; *saha*—with; *tat-varṣa-puruṣaiḥ*—the inhabitants of Hari-varṣa; *upāste*—offers obeisances to and worships; *idam*—this; *ca*—and; *udāharati*—chants.

TRANSLATION

Śukadeva Gosvāmī continued: My dear King, Lord Nṛsiṁhadeva resides in the tract of land known as Hari-varṣa. In the Seventh Canto of Śrīmad-Bhāgavatam, I shall describe to you how Prahlāda Mahārāja caused the Lord to assume the form of Nṛsiṁhadeva. Prahlāda Mahārāja, the topmost

devotee of the Lord, is a reservoir of all the good qualities of great personalities. His character and activities have delivered all the fallen members of his demoniac family. Lord Nṛsiṁhadeva is very dear to this exalted personality. Thus Prahlāda Mahārāja, along with his servants and all the denizens of Hari-varṣa, worships Lord Nṛsiṁhadeva by chanting the following mantra.

PURPORT

Jayadeva Gosvāmī's ten prayers worshiping the incarnations of Lord Kṛṣṇa (Keśava) contain His name in every stanza. For example, *keśava dhṛta-nara-hari-rūpa jaya jagad-īśa hare, keśava dhṛta-mīna-śarīra jaya jagad-īśa hare,* and *keśava dhṛta-vāmana-rūpa jaya jagad-īśa hare.* The word *jagad-īśa* refers to the proprietor of all the universes. His original form is the two-handed form of Lord Kṛṣṇa, standing with a flute in His hands and engaged in tending the cows. As stated in *Brahma-saṁhitā:*

cintāmaṇi-prakara-sadmasu kalpa-vṛkṣa-
lakṣāvṛteṣu surabhīr abhipālayantam
lakṣmī-sahasra-śata-sambhrama-sevyamānaṁ
govindam ādi-puruṣaṁ tam ahaṁ bhajāmi

"I worship Govinda, the primeval Lord, the first progenitor, who is tending the cows, yielding all desires, in abodes built with spiritual gems and surrounded by millions of purpose trees. He is always served with great reverence and affection by hundreds and thousands of goddesses of fortune." From this verse we learn that Govinda, or Kṛṣṇa, is the *ādi-puruṣa* (the original person). The Lord has innumerable incarnations, exactly like the innumerable waves of a flowing river, but the original form is Kṛṣṇa, or Keśava.

Śukadeva Gosvāmī refers to Nṛsiṁhadeva because of Prahlāda Mahārāja. Prahlāda Mahārāja was put into great distress by his powerful father, the demon Hiraṇyakaśipu. Apparently helpless before him, Prahlāda Mahārāja called on the Lord, who immediately assumed the gigantic form of Nṛsiṁha-deva, half-lion and half-man, to kill the gigantic demon. Although Kṛṣṇa is the original person, one without a second, He assumes different forms just to satisfy His devotees or to execute a specific purpose. Therefore Jayadeva Gosvāmī always repeats the name of Keśava, the original Personality of Godhead, in his prayers describing the Lord's different incarnations for different purposes.

TEXT 8

ॐ नमो भगवते नरसिंहाय नमस्तेजस्तेजसे आविराविर्भव वज्रनख वज्रदंष्ट्र कर्माशयान् रन्धय रन्धय तमो ग्रस ग्रस ॐ स्वाहा। अभयमभयमात्मनि भूयिष्ठा ॐ क्ष्रौम् ॥८॥

oṁ namo bhagavate narasiṁhāya namas tejas-tejase āvir-āvirbhava vajra-nakha vajra-daṁṣṭra karmāśayān randhaya randhaya tamo grasa grasa oṁ svāhā; abhayam abhayam ātmani bhūyiṣṭhā oṁ kṣraum.

om—O Lord; *namaḥ*—my respectful obeisances; *bhagavate*—unto the Supreme Personality of Godhead; *nara-siṁhāya*—known as Lord Nṛsiṁha; *namaḥ*—obeisances; *tejaḥ-tejase*—the power of all power; *āviḥ-āvirbhava*—please be fully manifest; *vajra-nakha*—O You who possess nails like thunderbolts; *vajra-daṁṣṭra*—O You who possess teeth like thunderbolts; *karma-āśayān*—demoniac desires to be happy by material activities; *randhaya randhaya*—kindly vanquish; *tamaḥ*—ignorance in the material world; *grasa*—kindly drive away; *grasa*—kindly drive away; *om*—O my Lord; *svāhā*—respectful oblations; *abhayam*—fearlessness; *abhayam*—fearlessness; *ātmani*—in my mind; *bhūyiṣṭhāḥ*—may You appear; *om*—O Lord; *kṣraum*—the *bīja,* or seed, of *mantras* offering prayers to Lord Nṛsiṁha.

TRANSLATION

I offer my respectful obeisances unto Lord Nṛsiṁhadeva, the source of all power. O my Lord who possesses nails and teeth just like thunderbolts, kindly vanquish our demonlike desires for fruitive activity in this material world. Please appear in our hearts and drive away our ignorance so that by Your mercy we may become fearless in the struggle for existence in this material world.

PURPORT

In *Śrīmad-Bhāgavatam* (4.22.39) Sanat-kumāra speaks the following words to Mahārāja Pṛthu:

yat-pāda-paṅkaja-palāśa-vilāsa-bhaktyā
karmāśayaṁ grathitam udgrathayanti santaḥ
tadvan na rikta-matayo yatayo'pi ruddha-
srotogaṇās tam araṇaṁ bhaja vāsudevam

"Devotees always engaged in the service of the toes of the Lord's lotus feet can very easily become free from hard-knotted desires for fruitive activities. Because this is very difficult, the nondevotees—the *jñānīs* and *yogīs*—cannot stop the waves of sense gratification, although they try to do so. Therefore you are advised to engage in the devotional service of Kṛṣṇa, the son of Vasudeva."

Every living being within this material world has a strong desire to enjoy matter to his fullest satisfaction. For this purpose, the conditioned soul must accept one body after another, and thus his strongly fixed fruitive desires continue. One cannot stop the repetition of birth and death without being completely desireless. Therefore Śrīla Rūpa Gosvāmī describes pure *bhakti* (devotional service) as follows:

anyābhilāṣitā-śūnyaṁ
jñāna-karmādy-anāvṛtam
ānukūlyena kṛṣṇānu-
śīlanaṁ bhaktir uttamā

"One should render transcendental loving service to the Supreme Lord Kṛṣṇa favorably and without desire for material profit or gain through fruitive activities or philosophical speculation. That is called pure devotional service." Unless one is completely freed of all material desires, which are caused by the dense darkness of ignorance, one cannot fully engage in the devotional service of the Lord. Therefore we should always offer our prayers to Lord Nṛsiṁhadeva, who killed Hiraṇyakaśipu, the personification of material desire. *Hiraṇya* means "gold," and *kaśipu* means "a soft cushion or bed." Materialistic persons always desire to make the body comfortable, and for this they require huge amounts of gold. Thus Hiraṇyakaśipu was the perfect representative of materialistic life. He was therefore the cause of great disturbance to the topmost devotee, Prahlāda Mahārāja, until Lord Nṛsiṁhadeva killed him. Any devotee aspiring to be free of material desires should offer his respectful prayers to Nṛsiṁhadeva as Prahlāda Mahārāja did in this verse.

TEXT 9

स्वस्त्यस्तु विश्वस्य खलः प्रसीदतां
ध्यायन्तु भूतानि शिवं मिथो धिया ।
मनश्च भद्रं भजतादधोक्षजे
आवेश्यतां नो मतिरप्यहैतुकी ॥९॥

svasty astu viśvasya khalaḥ prasīdatāṁ
dhyāyantu bhūtāni śivaṁ mitho dhiyā
manaś ca bhadraṁ bhajatād adhokṣaje
āveśyatāṁ no matir apy ahaitukī

svasti—auspiciousness; *astu*—let there be; *viśvasya*—of the entire universe; *khalaḥ*—the envious (almost everyone); *prasīdatām*—let them be pacified; *dhyāyantu*—let them consider; *bhūtāni*—all the living entities; *śivam*—auspiciousness; *mithaḥ*—mutual; *dhiyā*—by their intelligence; *manaḥ*—the mind; *ca*—and; *bhadram*—calmness; *bhajatāt*—let it experience; *adhokṣaje*—in the Supreme Personality of Godhead, who is beyond the perception of mind, intelligence and senses; *āveśyatām*—let it be absorbed; *naḥ*—our; *matiḥ*—intelligence; *api*—indeed; *ahaitukī*—without any motive.

TRANSLATION

May there be good fortune throughout the universe, and may all envious persons be pacified. May all living entities become calm by practicing bhakti-yoga, for by accepting devotional service they will think of each other's welfare. Therefore let us all engage in the service of the supreme transcendence, Lord Śrī Kṛṣṇa, and always remain absorbed in thought of Him.

PURPORT

The following verse describes a Vaiṣṇava:

vāñchā-kalpa-tarubhyaś ca
kṛpā-sindhubhya eva ca
patitānāṁ pāvanebhyo
vaiṣṇavebhyo namo namaḥ

Just like a desire tree, a Vaiṣṇava can fulfill all the desires of anyone who takes shelter of his lotus feet. Prahlāda Mahārāja is a typical Vaiṣṇava. He prays not for himself but for all living entities—the gentle, the envious and the mischievous. He always thought of the welfare of mischievous persons like his father, Hiraṇyakaśipu. Prahlāda Mahārāja did not ask for anything for himself; rather, he prayed for the Lord to excuse his demoniac father. This is the attitude of a Vaiṣṇava, who always thinks of the welfare of the entire universe.

Śrīmad-Bhāgavatam and *bhāgavata-dharma* are meant for persons who are completely free of envy (*parama-nirmatsarāṇām*). Therefore Prahlāda

Mahārāja prays in this verse, *khalaḥ prasīdatām:* "May all the envious persons be pacified." The material world is full of envious persons, but if one frees himself of envy, he becomes liberal in his social dealings and can think of others' welfare. Anyone who takes up Kṛṣṇa consciousness and engages himself completely in the service of the Lord cleanses his mind of all envy (*manaś ca bhadraṁ bhajatād adhokṣaje*). Therefore we should pray to Lord Nṛsiṁhadeva to sit in our hearts. We should pray, *bahir nṛsiṁho hṛdaye nṛsiṁhaḥ:* "Let Lord Nṛsiṁhadeva sit in the core of my heart, killing all my bad propensities. Let my mind become clean so that I may peacefully worship the Lord and bring peace to the entire world."

Śrīla Viśvanātha Cakravartī Ṭhākura has given us a very fine purport in this regard. Whenever one offers a prayer to the Supreme Personality of Godhead, one always requests some benediction from Him. Even pure (*niṣkāma*) devotees pray for some benediction, as instructed by Lord Śrī Caitanya Mahāprabhu in His *Śikṣāṣṭaka:*

ayi nanda-tanuja kiṅkaraṁ
patitaṁ māṁ viṣame bhavāmbudhau
kṛpayā tava pāda-paṅkaja-
sthita-dhūlī-sadṛśaṁ vicintaya

"O son of Mahārāja Nanda [Kṛṣṇa], I am Your eternal servitor, yet somehow or other I have fallen into the ocean of birth and death. Please pick Me up from the ocean of death and place Me as one of the atoms at Your lotus feet." In another prayer Lord Caitanya says, *mama janmani janmanīśvare bhavatād bhaktir ahaitukī tvayi:* "Life after life, kindly let Me have unalloyed love and devotion at Your Lordship's lotus feet." When Prahlāda Mahārāja chants *oṁ namo bhagavate narasiṁhāya,* he prays for a benediction from the Lord, but because he is also an exalted Vaiṣṇava, he wants nothing for his personal sense gratification. The first desire expressed in his prayer is *svasty astu viśvasya:* "Let there be good fortune throughout the entire universe." Prahlāda Mahārāja thus requested the Lord to be merciful to everyone, including his father, a most envious person. According to Cāṇakya Paṇḍita, there are two kinds of envious living entities: one is a snake, and the other is the man like Hiraṇyakaśipu, who is by nature envious of everyone, even of his father or son. Hiraṇyakaśipu was envious of his little son Prahlāda, but Prahlāda Mahārāja asked a benediction for the benefit of his father. Hiraṇyakaśipu was very envious of devotees, but Prahlāda wished that his father and other demons like him would give up their envious nature by the grace of the Lord and stop harassing the devotees (*khalaḥ prasīdatām*). The difficulty is that the *khala* (envious living entity) is rarely pacified. One kind of *khala,* the snake, can be pacified simply by *mantras* or by the action of a particular herb (*mantrauṣadhi-vaśaḥ sarpaḥ khalakena nivāryate*). An envious person, however, cannot be pacified by any means. Therefore Prahlāda Mahārāja prays that all envious persons may undergo a change of heart and think of the welfare of others.

If the Kṛṣṇa consciousness movement spreads all over the world, and if by the grace of Kṛṣṇa everyone accepts it, the thinking of envious people will change. Everyone will think of the welfare of others. Therefore Prahlāda Mahārāja prays, *śivaṁ mitho dhiyā.* In material activities, everyone is envious of others, but in Kṛṣṇa consciousness, no one is envious of anyone else; everyone thinks of the welfare of others. Therefore Prahlāda Mahārāja prays that everyone's mind may become gentle by being fixed at the lotus feet of Kṛṣṇa (*bhajatād adhokṣaje*). As indicated elsewhere in *Śrīmad-Bhāgavatam* (*sa vai manaḥ kṛṣṇa-padāravindayoḥ*) and as advised by Lord Kṛṣṇa in *Bhagavad-gītā* (18.65), *man-manā bhava mad-bhaktaḥ,* one should constantly think of the lotus feet of Lord Kṛṣṇa. Then one's mind will certainly be cleansed (*ceto-darpaṇa-mārjanam*). Materialists always think of sense gratification, but Prahlāda Mahārāja prays that the Lord's mercy will change their minds and they will stop thinking of sense gratification. If they think of Kṛṣṇa always, everything will be all right. Some people argue that if everyone thought of Kṛṣṇa in that way, the whole universe would be vacated because everyone would go back home, back to Godhead. However, Śrīla Viśvanātha Cakravartī Ṭhākura says that this is impossible because the living entities are innumerable. If one set of living entities is actually delivered by the Kṛṣṇa consciousness movement, another set will fill the entire universe.

TEXT 10

मागारदारात्मजवित्तबन्धुषु
सङ्गो यदि स्याद्भगवत्प्रियेषु नः ।
यः प्राणवृत्त्या परितुष्ट आत्मवान्
सिद्ध्यत्यदूरान्न तथेन्द्रियप्रियः ॥१०॥

māgāra-dārātmaja-vitta-bandhuṣu
saṅgo yadi syād bhagavat-priyeṣu naḥ
yaḥ prāṇa-vṛttyā parituṣṭa ātmavān
siddhyaty adūrān na tathendriya-priyaḥ

mā—not; *agāra*—house; *dāra*—wife; *ātma-ja*—children; *vitta*—bank balance; *bandhuṣu*—among friends and relatives; *saṅgaḥ*—association or attachment; *yadi*—if; *syāt*—there must be; *bhagavat-priyeṣu*—among persons to whom the Supreme Personality of Godhead is very dear; *naḥ*—of us; *yaḥ*—anyone who; *prāṇa-vṛttyā*—by the bare necessities of life; *parituṣṭaḥ*—satisfied; *ātma-vān*—who has controlled his mind and realized his self; *siddhyati*—becomes successful; *adūrāt*—very soon; *na*—not; *tathā*—so much; *indriya-priyaḥ*—a person attached to sense gratification.

TRANSLATION

My dear Lord, we pray that we may never feel attraction for the prison of family life, consisting of home, wife, children, friends, bank balance, relatives and so on. If we do have some attachment, let it be for devotees, whose only dear friend is Kṛṣṇa. A person who is actually self-realized and who has controlled his mind is perfectly satisfied with the bare necessities of life. He does not try to gratify his senses. Such a person quickly advances in Kṛṣṇa consciousness, whereas others, who are too attached to material things, find advancement very difficult.

PURPORT

When Śrī Kṛṣṇa Caitanya Mahāprabhu was requested to explain the duty of a Vaiṣṇava, a Kṛṣṇa conscious person, He immediately said, *asat-saṅga-tyāga—ei vaiṣṇava-ācāra.* The first business of a Vaiṣṇava is to give up the association of persons who are not devotees of Kṛṣṇa and who are too attached to material things—wife, children, bank balance and so on. Prahlāda Mahārāja also prays to the Personality of Godhead that he may avoid the association of nondevotees attached to the materialistic way of life. If he must be attached to someone, he prays to be attached only to a devotee.

A devotee is not interested in unnecessarily increasing the demands of the senses for gratification. Of course, as long as one is in this material world, one must have a material body, and it must be maintained for executing devotional service. The body can be maintained very easily by eating *kṛṣṇa-prasāda.* As Kṛṣṇa says in *Bhagavad-gītā* (9.26):

patraṁ puṣpaṁ phalaṁ toyaṁ
yo me bhaktyā prayacchati
tad ahaṁ bhakty-upahṛtam
aśnāmi prayatātmanaḥ

"If one offers Me with love and devotion a leaf, a flower, fruit or water, I will accept it." Why should the menu be unnecessarily increased for the satisfaction of the tongue? Devotees should eat as simply as possible. Otherwise, attachment for material things will gradually increase, and the senses, being very strong, will soon require more and more material enjoyment. Then the real business of life—to advance in Kṛṣṇa consciousness—will stop.

TEXT 11

यत्सङ्गलब्धं निजवीर्यवैभवं
तीर्थं मुहुः संस्पृशतां हि मानसम् ।
हरत्यजोऽन्तः श्रुतिभिर्गतोऽङ्गजं
को वै न सेवेत मुकुन्दविक्रमम् ॥११॥

yat-saṅga-labdhaṁ nija-vīrya-vaibhavaṁ
tīrthaṁ muhuḥ saṁspṛśatāṁ hi mānasam
haraty ajo 'ntaḥ śrutibhir gato 'ṅgajaṁ
ko vai na seveta mukunda-vikramam

yat—of whom (the devotees); *saṅga-labdham*—achieved by the association; *nija-vīrya-vaibhavam*—whose influence is uncommon; *tīrtham*—holy places like the Ganges; *muhuḥ*—repeatedly; *saṁspṛśatām*—of those touching; *hi*—certainly; *mānasam*—the dirty things in the mind; *harati*—vanquishes; *ajaḥ*—the supreme unborn one; *antaḥ*—in the core of the heart; *śrutibhiḥ*—by the ears; *gataḥ*—entered; *aṅga-jam*—dirty things or infections of the body; *kaḥ*—who; *vai*—indeed; *na*—not; *seveta*—would serve; *mukunda-vikramam*—the glorious activities of Mukunda, the Supreme Personality of Godhead.

TRANSLATION

By associating with persons for whom the Supreme Personality of Godhead, Mukunda, is the all in all, one can hear of His powerful activities and soon come to understand them. The activities of Mukunda are so potent that simply by hearing of them one immediately associates with the Lord. For a person who constantly and very eagerly hears narrations of the Lord's powerful activities, the Absolute Truth, the Personality of Godhead in the form of sound vibrations, enters within his heart and cleanses it of all contamination. On the other hand, although bathing in

the Ganges diminishes bodily contaminations and infections, this process and the process of visiting holy places can cleanse the heart only after a long time. Therefore who is the sane man who will not associate with devotees to quickly perfect his life?

PURPORT

Bathing in the Ganges can certainly cure one of many infectious diseases, but it cannot cleanse one's materially attached mind, which creates all kinds of contaminations in material existence. However, one who directly associates with the Supreme Lord by hearing of His activities cleanses the dirt from his mind and very soon comes to Kṛṣṇa consciousness. Sūta Gosvāmī confirms this in *Śrīmad-Bhāgavatam* (1.2.17):

śṛṇvatāṁ sva-kathāḥ kṛṣṇaḥ
puṇya-śravaṇa-kīrtanaḥ
hṛdy antaḥ-stho hy abhadrāṇi
vidhunoti suhṛt-satām

The Supreme Lord within everyone's heart becomes very pleased when a person hears narrations of His activities, and He personally cleanses the dirt from the mind of the listener. *Hṛdy antaḥ-stho hy abhadrāṇi vidhunoti:* He washes off all dirt from the mind. Material existence is caused by dirty things within the mind. If one can cleanse his mind, he immediately comes to his original position of Kṛṣṇa consciousness, and thus his life becomes successful. Therefore all the great saints in the devotional line very strongly recommend the process of hearing. Śrī Caitanya Mahāprabhu introduced the congregational chanting of the Hare Kṛṣṇa *mantra* to give everyone a chance to hear Kṛṣṇa's holy name, for simply by hearing Hare Kṛṣṇa, Hare Kṛṣṇa, Kṛṣṇa Kṛṣṇa, Hare Hare/ Hare Rāma, Hare Rāma, Rāma Rāma, Hare Hare, one becomes purified (*ceto-darpaṇa-mārjanam*). Therefore our Kṛṣṇa consciousness movement is chiefly engaged in chanting the Hare Kṛṣṇa *mantra* all over the world.

After one's mind becomes cleansed by chanting Hare Kṛṣṇa, one gradually comes to the platform of Kṛṣṇa consciousness and then reads books like *Bhagavad-gītā, Śrīmad-Bhāgavatam, Caitanya-caritāmṛta* and *The Nectar of Devotion.* In this way, one becomes more and more purified of material contamination. As stated in *Śrīmad-Bhāgavatam* (1.2.18):

naṣṭa-prāyeṣv abhadreṣu
nityaṁ bhāgavata-sevayā

bhagavaty uttama-śloke
bhaktir bhavati naiṣṭhikī

"By regularly hearing the *Bhāgavatam* and rendering service unto the pure devotee, all that is troublesome to the heart is practically destroyed, and loving service unto the glorious Lord, who is praised with transcendental songs, is established as an irrevocable fact." In this way, simply by hearing of the powerful activities of the Lord, the devotee's heart becomes almost completely cleansed of material contamination, and thus his original position as an eternal servant who is part and parcel of the Lord becomes manifest. While the devotee engages in devotional service, the passionate and ignorant modes of material nature are gradually vanquished, and then he acts only in the mode of goodness. At that time he becomes happy and gradually advances in Kṛṣṇa consciousness.

All the great *ācāryas* strongly recommend that people be given a chance to hear about the Supreme Lord. Then success is assured. The more we cleanse the dirt of material attachment from our hearts, the more we will be attracted by Kṛṣṇa's name, form, qualities, paraphernalia and activities. This is the sum and substance of the Kṛṣṇa consciousness movement.

TEXT 12

यस्यास्ति भक्तिर्भगवत्यकिञ्चना
सर्वैर्गुणैस्तत्र समासते सुराः ।
हरावभक्तस्य कुतो महद्गुणा
मनोरथेनासति धावतो बहिः ॥१२॥

yasyāsti bhaktir bhagavaty akiñcanā
sarvair guṇais tatra samāsate surāḥ
harāv abhaktasya kuto mahad-guṇā
manorathenāsati dhāvato bahiḥ

yasya—of whom; *asti*—there is; *bhaktiḥ*—devotional service; *bhagavati*—to the Supreme Personality of Godhead; *akiñcanā*—without any motive; *sarvaiḥ*—with all; *guṇaiḥ*—good qualities; *tatra*—there (in that person); *samāsate*—reside; *surāḥ*—all the demigods; *harau*—unto the Supreme Personality of Godhead; *abhaktasya*—of a person who is not devoted; *kutaḥ*—where; *mahat-guṇāḥ*—good qualities; *manorathena*—by mental speculation; *asati*—in the temporary material world; *dhāvataḥ*—who is running; *bahiḥ*—outside.

TRANSLATION

All the demigods and their exalted qualities, such as religion, knowledge and renunciation, become manifest in the body of one who has developed unalloyed devotion for the Supreme Personality of Godhead, Vāsudeva. On the other hand, a person devoid of devotional service and engaged in material activities has no good qualities. Even if he is adept at the practice of mystic yoga or the honest endeavor of maintaining his family and relatives, he must be driven by his own mental speculations and must engage in the service of the Lord's external energy. How can there be any good qualities in such a man?

PURPORT

As explained in the next verse, Kṛṣṇa is the original source of all living entities. This is confirmed in *Bhagavad-gītā* (15.7), wherein Kṛṣṇa says:

mamaivāṁśo jīva-loke
jīva-bhūtaḥ sanātanaḥ
manaḥ ṣaṣṭhānīndriyāṇi
prakṛti-sthāni karṣati

"The living entities in this conditioned world are My eternal, fragmental parts. Due to conditioned life, they are struggling very hard with the six senses, which include the mind." All living entities are part and parcel of Kṛṣṇa, and therefore when they revive their original Kṛṣṇa consciousness, they possess all the good qualities of Kṛṣṇa in a small quantity. When one engages himself in the nine processes of devotional service (*śravaṇaṁ kīrtanaṁ viṣṇoḥ smaraṇaṁ pāda-sevanam/ arcanaṁ vandanaṁ dāsyaṁ sakhyam ātma-nivedanam*), one's heart becomes purified, and he immediately understands his relationship with Kṛṣṇa. He then revives his original quality of Kṛṣṇa consciousness.

In the *Ādi-līlā* of *Caitanya-caritāmṛta,* Chapter Eight, there is a description of some of the qualities of devotees. For example, Śrī Paṇḍita Haridāsa is described as being very well-behaved, tolerant, peaceful, magnanimous and grave. In addition, he spoke very sweetly, his endeavors were very pleasing, he was always patient, he respected everyone, he always worked for everyone's benefit, his mind was free of duplicity, and he was completely devoid of all malicious activities. These are all originally qualities of Kṛṣṇa, and when one becomes a devotee they automatically become manifest. Śrī Kṛṣṇadāsa Kavirāja, the author of *Caitanya-caritāmṛta,* says that all good qualities become manifest in the body of a Vaiṣṇava and that only by the presence of these good qualities can one distinguish a Vaiṣṇava from a non-Vaiṣṇava. Kṛṣṇadāsa Kavirāja lists the following twenty-six good qualities of a Vaiṣṇava: (1) He is very kind to everyone. (2) He does not make anyone his enemy. (3) He is truthful. (4) He is equal to everyone. (5) No one can find any fault in him. (6) He is magnanimous. (7) He is mild. (8) He is always clean. (9) He is without possessions. (10) He works for everyone's benefit. (11) He is very peaceful. (12) He is always surrendered to Kṛṣṇa. (13) He has no material desires. (14) He is very meek. (15) He is steady. (16) He controls his senses. (17) He does not eat more than required. (18) He is not influenced by the Lord's illusory energy. (19) He offers respect to everyone. (20) He does not desire any respect for himself. (21) He is very grave. (22) He is merciful. (23) He is friendly. (24) He is poetic. (25) He is expert. (26) He is silent.

TEXT 13

हरिर्हि साक्षाद्भगवान् शरीरिणा-
मात्मा झषाणामिव तोयमीप्सितम् ।
हित्वा महांस्तं यदि सज्जते गृहे
तदा महत्त्वं वयसा दम्पतीनाम् ॥१३॥

harir hi sākṣād bhagavān śarīriṇām
ātmā jhaṣāṇām iva toyam īpsitam
hitvā mahāṁs taṁ yadi sajjate gṛhe
tadā mahattvaṁ vayasā dampatīnām

hariḥ—the Lord; *hi*—certainly; *sākṣāt*—directly; *bhagavān*—the Supreme Personality of Godhead; *śarīriṇām*—of all living entities who have accepted material bodies; *ātmā*—the life and soul; *jhaṣāṇām*—of the aquatics; *iva*—like; *toyam*—the vast water; *īpsitam*—is desired; *hitvā*—giving up; *mahān*—a great personality; *tam*—Him; *yadi*—if; *sajjate*—becomes attached; *gṛhe*—to household life; *tadā*—at that time; *mahattvam*—greatness; *vayasā*—by age; *dam-patīnām*—of the husband and wife.

TRANSLATION

Just as aquatics always desire to remain in the vast mass of water, all conditioned living entities naturally desire to remain in the vast existence of the Supreme Lord. Therefore if someone very great by material calculations fails to take shelter of the Supreme Soul but instead becomes

attached to material household life, his greatness is like that of a young, low-class couple. One who is too attached to material life loses all good spiritual qualities.

PURPORT

Although crocodiles are very fierce animals, they are powerless when they venture out of the water onto land. When they are out of the water, they cannot exhibit their original power. Similarly, the all-pervading Supersoul, Paramātmā, is the source of all living entities, and all living entities are part and parcel of Him. When the living entity remains in contact with the all-pervading Vāsudeva, the Personality of Godhead, he manifests his spiritual power, exactly as the crocodile exhibits its strength in the water. In other words, the greatness of the living entity can be perceived when he is in the spiritual world, engaged in spiritual activities. Many householders, although well-educated in the knowledge of the *Vedas,* become attached to family life. They are compared herein to crocodiles out of water, for they are devoid of all spiritual strength. Their greatness is like that of a young husband and wife who, though uneducated, praise one another and become attracted to their own temporary beauty. This kind of greatness is appreciated only by low-class men with no qualifications.

Everyone should therefore seek the shelter of the Supreme Soul, the source of all living entities. No one should waste his time in the so-called happiness of materialistic household life. In the Vedic civilization, this type of crippled life is allowed only until one's fiftieth year, when one must give up family life and enter either the order of *vānaprastha* (independent retired life for cultivation of spiritual knowledge) or *sannyāsa* (the renounced order, in which one completely takes shelter of the Supreme Personality of Godhead).

TEXT 14

तस्माद्रजोरागविषादमन्यु-
मानस्पृहाभयदैन्याधिमूलम् ।
हित्वा गृहं संसृतिचक्रवालं
नृसिंहपादं भजताकुतोभयमिति ॥१४॥

tasmād rajo-rāga-viṣāda-manyu-
māna-spṛhā-bhayadainyādhimūlam
hitvā gṛhaṁ saṁsṛti-cakravālaṁ
nṛsiṁha-pādaṁ bhajatākutobhayam iti

tasmāt—therefore; *rajaḥ*—of passion or material desires; *rāga*—attachment for material things; *viṣāda*—then disappointment; *manyu*—anger; *māna-spṛhā*—the desire to be respectable in society; *bhaya*—fear; *dainya*—of poverty; *adhimūlam*—the root cause; *hitvā*—giving up; *gṛham*—household life; *saṁsṛti-cakravālam*—the cycle of repeated birth and death; *nṛsiṁha-pādam*—the lotus feet of Lord Nṛsiṁhadeva; *bhajata*—worship; *akutaḥ-bhayam*—the shelter of fearlessness; *iti*—thus.

TRANSLATION

Therefore, O demons, give up the so-called happiness of family life and simply take shelter of the lotus feet of Lord Nṛsiṁhadeva, which are the actual shelter of fearlessness. Entanglement in family life is the root cause of material attachment, indefatigable desires, moroseness, anger, despair, fear and the desire for false prestige, all of which result in the repetition of birth and death.

TEXT 15

केतुमालेऽपि भगवान् कामदेवस्वरूपेण लक्ष्म्याः प्रियचिकीर्षया प्रजापतेर्दुहितॄणां पुत्राणां तद्वर्षपतीनां पुरुषायुषाहोरात्रपरिसंख्यानानां यासां गर्भा महापुरुषमहास्त्रतेजसोद्वेजितमनसां विध्वस्ता व्यसवः संवत्सरान्ते विनिपतन्ति ॥१५॥

ketumāle 'pi bhagavān kāmadeva-svarūpeṇa lakṣmyāḥ priya-
cikīrṣayā prajāpater duhitṝṇāṁ putrāṇāṁ tad-varṣa-patīnāṁ
puruṣāyuṣāho-rātra-parisaṅkhyānānāṁ yāsāṁ garbhā mahā-puruṣa-
mahāstra-tejasodvejita-manasāṁ vidhvastā vyasavaḥ saṁvatsarānte
vinipatanti.

ketumāle—in the tract of land known as Ketumāla-varṣa; *api*—also; *bhagavān*—the Supreme Personality of Godhead, Lord Viṣṇu; *kāmadeva-svarūpeṇa*—in the form of Kāmadeva (Cupid or Pradyumna); *lakṣmyāḥ*—of the goddess of fortune; *priya-cikīrṣayā*—with a desire to bring about the satisfaction; *prajāpateḥ*—of Prajāpati; *duhitṝṇām*—of the daughters; *putrāṇām*—of the sons; *tat-varṣa-patīnām*—the ruler of that land; *puruṣa-āyuṣā*—in a human lifetime (about one hundred years); *ahaḥ-rātra*—the days and nights; *parisaṅkhyānānām*—which equal in number; *yāsām*—of whom (the daughters); *garbhāḥ*—fetuses; *mahā-puruṣa*—of the Supreme Personality of Godhead; *mahā-astra*—of the great weapon (the disc); *tejasā*

—by the effulgence; *udvejita-manasām*—whose minds are agitated; *vidhvastāḥ*—ruined; *vyasavaḥ*—dead; *saṁvatsara-ante*—at the end of the year; *vinipatanti*—fall down.

TRANSLATION

Śukadeva Gosvāmī continued: In the tract of land called Ketumāla-varṣa, Lord Viṣṇu lives in the form of Kāmadeva, only for the satisfaction of His devotees. These include Lakṣmījī [the goddess of fortune], the Prajāpati Saṁvatsara and all of Saṁvatsara's sons and daughters. The daughters of Prajāpati are considered the controlling deities of the nights, and his sons are considered the controllers of the days. The Prajāpati's offspring number 36,000, one for each day and each night in the lifetime of a human being. At the end of each year, the Prajāpati's daughters become very agitated upon seeing the extremely effulgent disc of the Supreme Personality of Godhead, and thus they all suffer miscarriages.

PURPORT

This Kāmadeva, who appears as Kṛṣṇa's son named Pradyumna, is *viṣṇu-tattva.* How this is so is explained by Madhvācārya, who quotes from the *Brahmāṇḍa Purāṇa: kāmadeva-sthitaṁ viṣṇum upāste.* Although this Kāmadeva is *viṣṇu-tattva,* His body is not spiritual but material. Lord Viṣṇu as Pradyumna or Kāmadeva accepts a material body, but He still acts spiritually. It does not make any difference whether He accepts a spiritual or a material body; He can act spiritually in any condition of existence. Māyāvādī philosophers regard even Lord Kṛṣṇa's body as material, but their opinions cannot impede the spiritual activity of the Lord.

TEXT 16

अतीव सुललितगतिविलासविलसितरुचिरहासलेशावलोकलीलया
किञ्चिदुत्तम्भितसुन्दरभ्रूमण्डलसुभगवदनारविन्दश्रिया रमां
रमयन्निन्द्रियाणि रमयते ॥१६॥

atīva sulalita-gati-vilāsa-vilasita-rucira-hāsa-leśāvaloka-līlayā kiñcid-
uttambhita-sundara-bhrū-maṇḍala-subhaga-vadanāravinda-śriyā
ramāṁ ramayann indriyāṇi ramayate.

atīva—very much; *su-lalita*—beautiful; *gati*—with movements; *vilāsa*—by pastimes; *vilasita*—manifested; *rucira*—pleasing; *hāsa-leśa*—mild smiling; *avaloka-līlayā*—by playful glancing; *kiñcit-uttambhita*—slightly raised; *sundara*—beautiful; *bhrū-maṇḍala*—by the eyebrows; *subhaga*—auspicious; *vadana-aravinda-śriyā*—with His beautiful lotuslike face; *ramām*—the goddess of fortune; *ramayan*—pleasing; *indriyāṇi*—all the senses; *ramayate*—He pleases.

TRANSLATION

In Ketumāla-varṣa, Lord Kāmadeva [Pradyumna] moves very graciously. His mild smile is very beautiful, and when He increases the beauty of His face by slightly raising His eyebrows and glancing playfully, He pleases the goddess of fortune. Thus He enjoys His transcendental senses.

TEXT 17

तद्भगवतो मायामयं रूपं परमसमाधियोगेन रमा देवी संवत्सरस्य रात्रिषु प्रजापतेर्दुहितृभिरुपेताहःसु च तद्भर्तृभिरुपास्ते इदं चोदाहरति ॥१७॥

tad bhagavato māyāmayaṁ rūpaṁ parama-samādhi-yogena ramā devī
saṁvatsarasya rātriṣu prajāpater duhitṛbhir upetāhaḥsu ca tad-
bhartṛbhir upāste idaṁ codāharati.

tat—that; *bhagavataḥ*—of the Supreme Personality of Godhead; *māyā-mayam*—full of affection for the devotees; *rūpam*—form; *parama*—highest; *samādhi-yogena*—by absorption of the mind in the service of the Lord; *ramā*—the goddess of fortune; *devī*—divine woman; *saṁvatsarasya*—known as Saṁvatsara; *rātriṣu*—during the nights; *prajāpateḥ*—of Prajāpati; *duhitṛbhiḥ*—with the daughters; *upeta*—combined; *ahaḥsu*—during the days; *ca*—also; *tat-bhartṛbhiḥ*—with the husbands; *upāste*—worships; *idam*—this; *ca*—also; *udāharati*—chants.

TRANSLATION

Accompanied during the daytime by the sons of the Prajāpati [the predominating deities of the days] and accompanied at night by his daughters [the deities of the nights], Lakṣmīdevī worships the Lord during the period known as the Saṁvatsara in His most merciful form as Kāmadeva. Fully absorbed in devotional service, she chants the following mantras.

PURPORT

The word *māyāmayam* used in this verse should not be understood according to the interpretations of the Māyāvādīs. *Māyā* means affection as well as illusion. When a mother deals with her child affectionately, she is called *māyāmaya.* In whatever form the Supreme Lord Viṣṇu appears, He is always affectionate toward His devotees. Thus the word *māyāmayam* is used here to mean "very affectionate toward the devotees." Śrīla Jīva Gosvāmī writes in this regard that *māyāmayam* can also mean *kṛpā-pracuram,* deeply merciful. Similarly, Śrīla Vīrarāghava says, *māyā-pracuranātmīya-saṅkalpena parigṛhītam ity arthaḥ jñāna-paryāyo 'tra māyā-śabdaḥ:* when one is very affectionate due to an intimate relationship, one is described as *māyāmaya.* Śrīla Viśvanātha Cakravartī Ṭhākura explains *māyāmayam* by dividing it into the words *māyā* and *āmayam.* He explains these words to indicate that because the living entity is covered by the disease of illusion, the Lord is always eager to deliver His devotee from the clutches of *māyā* and cure him of the disease caused by the illusory energy.

TEXT 18

ॐ ह्रां ह्रीं ह्रूं ॐ नमो भगवते हृषीकेशाय सर्वगुणविशेषैर्विलक्षितात्मने आकूतीनां चित्तीनां चेतसां विशेषाणां चाधिपतये षोडशकलायच्छन्दोमया-यान्नमयायामृतमयाय सर्वमयाय सहसे ओजसे बलाय कान्ताय कामाय नमस्ते उभयत्र भूयात् ॥१८॥

oṁ hrāṁ hrīṁ hrūṁ oṁ namo bhagavate hṛṣīkeśāya sarva-guṇa-viśeṣair
vilakṣitātmane ākūtīnāṁ cittīnāṁ cetasāṁ viśeṣāṇāṁ cādhipataye
ṣoḍaśa-kalāya cchando-mayāyānna-mayāyāmṛta-mayāya sarva-
mayāya sahase ojase balāya kāntāya kāmāya namas te ubhayatra bhūyāt.

om—O Lord; *hrām hrīm hrūm*—the seeds of the *mantra,* chanted for a successful result; *om*—O Lord; *namaḥ*—respectful obeisances; *bhagavate*—unto the lotus feet of the Supreme Personality of Godhead; *hṛṣīkeśāya*—unto Hṛṣīkeśa, the Lord of the senses; *sarva-guṇa*—with all transcendental qualities; *viśeṣaiḥ*—with all varieties; *vilakṣita*—particularly observed; *ātmane*—unto the soul of all living entities; *ākūtīnām*—of all kinds of activity; *cittīnām*—of all kinds of knowledge; *cetasām*—of the functions of the mind, such as determination and mental effort; *viśeṣāṇām*—of their respective objects; *ca*—and; *adhipataye*—unto the master; *ṣoḍaśa-kalāya*—whose parts are the sixteen original ingredients of creation (namely the five objects of the senses and the eleven senses, including the mind); *chandaḥ-mayāya*—unto the enjoyer of all ritualistic ceremonies; *anna-mayāya*—who maintains all living entities by supplying the necessities of life; *amṛta-mayāya*—who awards eternal life; *sarva-mayāya*—who is all-pervading; *sahase*—the powerful; *ojase*—who supplies strength to the senses; *balāya*—who supplies strength to the body; *kāntāya*—the supreme husband or master of all living entities; *kāmāya*—who supplies all necessities for the devotees; *namaḥ*—respectful obeisances; *te*—unto You; *ubhayatra*—always (during both day and night, or both in this life and the next); *bhūyāt*—may there be all good fortune.

TRANSLATION

Let me offer my respectful obeisances unto the Supreme Personality of Godhead, Lord Hṛṣīkeśa, the controller of all my senses and the origin of everything. As the supreme master of all bodily, mental and intellectual activities, He is the only enjoyer of their results. The five sense objects and eleven senses, including the mind, are His partial manifestations. He supplies all the necessities of life, which are His energy and thus nondifferent from Him, and He is the cause of everyone's bodily and mental prowess, which is also nondifferent from Him. Indeed, He is the husband and provider of necessities for all living entities. The purpose of all the Vedas is to worship Him. Therefore let us all offer Him our respectful obeisances. May He always be favorable toward us in this life and the next.

PURPORT

In this verse the word *māyāmaya* is further explained in regard to how the Lord expands His mercy in different ways. *Parāsya śaktir vividhaiva śrūyate:* the energies of the Supreme Lord are understood in different ways. In this verse He is described as the original source of everything, even our body, senses, mind, activities, prowess, bodily strength, mental strength and determination for securing the necessities of life. Indeed, the Lord's energies can be perceived in everything. As stated in *Bhagavad-gītā* (7.8), *raso'ham apsu kaunteya:* the taste of water is also Kṛṣṇa. Kṛṣṇa is the active principle of everything we need for our maintenance.

This verse offering respectful obeisances unto the Lord was composed by Ramā, the goddess of fortune, and is full of spiritual power. Under the guidance of a spiritual master, everyone should chant this *mantra* and thus become a complete and perfect devotee of the Lord. One may chant this *mantra* for complete liberation from material bondage, and after liberation one may continue to chant it while worshiping the Supreme Lord in Vaikuṇṭhaloka. All *mantras,* of course, are meant for this life and the next life, as Kṛṣṇa Himself confirms in *Bhagavad-gītā* (9.14):

satataṁ kīrtayanto māṁ
yatantaś ca dṛḍha-vratāḥ
namasyantaś ca māṁ bhaktyā
nitya-yuktā upāsate

"Always chanting My glories, endeavoring with great determination, bowing down before Me, the great souls perpetually worship Me with devotion." A devotee who both in this life and the next chants the *mahā-mantra,* or any *mantra,* is called *nitya-yuktopāsaka.*

TEXT 19

स्त्रियो व्रतैस्त्वा हृषिकेश्वरं स्वतो
ह्याराध्य लोके पतिमाशासतेऽन्यम् ।
तासां न ते वै परिपान्त्यपत्यं
प्रियं धनायूंषि यतोऽस्वतन्त्राः ॥१९॥

striyo vratais tvā hṛṣīkeśvaraṁ svato
hy ārādhya loke patim āśāsate 'nyam
tāsāṁ na te vai paripānty apatyaṁ
priyaṁ dhanāyūṁṣi yato 'sva-tantrāḥ

striyaḥ—all women; *vrataiḥ*—by observing fasting and other vows; *tvā*—you; *hṛṣīkeśvaram*—the Supreme Personality of Godhead, master of the senses; *svataḥ*—of your own accord; *hi*—certainly; *ārādhya*—worshiping; *loke*—in the world; *patim*—a husband; *āśāsate*—ask for; *anyam*—another; *tāsām*—of all those women; *na*—not; *te*—the husbands; *vai*—indeed; *paripānti*—able to protect; *apatyam*—the children; *priyam*—very dear; *dhana*—the wealth; *āyūṁṣi*—or the duration of life; *yataḥ*—because; *asva-tantrāḥ*—dependent.

TRANSLATION

My dear Lord, You are certainly the fully independent master of all the senses. Therefore all women who worship You by strictly observing vows because they wish to acquire a husband to satisfy their senses are surely under illusion. They do not know that such a husband cannot actually give protection to them or their children. Nor can he protect their wealth or duration of life, for he himself is dependent on time, fruitive results and the modes of nature, which are all subordinate to You.

PURPORT

In this verse, Lakṣmīdevī (Ramā) shows compassion toward women who worship the Lord for the benediction of possessing a good husband. Although such women desire to be happy with children, wealth, a long duration of life and everything dear to them, they cannot possibly do so. In the material world, a so-called husband is dependent on the control of the Supreme Personality of Godhead. There are many examples of a woman whose husband, being dependent on the result of his own fruitive actions, cannot maintain his wife, her children, her wealth or her duration of life. Therefore, factually the only real husband of all women is Kṛṣṇa, the supreme husband. Because the *gopīs* were liberated souls, they understood this fact. Therefore they rejected their material husbands and accepted Kṛṣṇa as their real husband. Kṛṣṇa is the real husband not only of the *gopīs,* but of every living entity. Everyone should perfectly understand that Kṛṣṇa is the real husband of all living entities, who are described in the *Bhagavad-gītā* as *prakṛti* (female), not *puruṣa* (male). In *Bhagavad-gītā* (10.12), only Kṛṣṇa is addressed as *puruṣa:*

paraṁ brahma paraṁ dhāma
pavitraṁ paramaṁ bhavān
puruṣaṁ śāśvataṁ divyam
ādi-devam ajaṁ vibhum

"You are the Supreme Brahman, the ultimate, the supreme abode and purifier, the Absolute Truth and the eternal divine person. You are the primal God, transcendental and original, and You are the unborn and all-pervading beauty."

Kṛṣṇa is the original *puruṣa,* and the living entities are *prakṛti.* Thus Kṛṣṇa is the enjoyer, and all living entities are meant to be enjoyed by Him. Therefore any woman who seeks a material husband for her protection, or any man who desires to become the husband of a woman, is under illusion. To become a husband means to maintain a wife and children nicely by supplying wealth and security. However, a material husband cannot possibly do this, for he is dependent on his *karma. Karmaṇā-daiva-netreṇa:* his circumstances are determined by his past fruitive activities. Therefore if one proudly thinks he can protect his wife, he is under illusion. Kṛṣṇa is the only husband, and therefore the relationship between a husband and wife in this material world cannot be absolute. Because we have the desire to marry, Kṛṣṇa mercifully allows the so-called husband to possess a wife, and the wife to possess a so-called husband, for mutual satisfaction. In the *Īśopaniṣad* it is said, *tena tyaktena bhuñjīthā:* the Lord provides everyone with his quota. Actually, however, every living entity is *prakṛti,* or female, and Kṛṣṇa is the only husband.

ekale īśvara kṛṣṇa, āra saba bhṛtya
yāre yaiche nācāya, se taiche kare nṛtya
(*Cc. Ādi* 5.142)

Kṛṣṇa is the original master or husband of everyone, and all other living entities, having taken the form of so-called husbands, or wives, are dancing according to His desire. A so-called husband may unite with his wife for sense gratification, but his senses are conducted by Hṛṣīkeśa, the master of the senses, who is therefore the actual husband.

TEXT 20

स वै पतिः स्यादकुतोभयः स्वयं
समन्ततः पाति भयातुरं जनम् ।
स एक एवेतरथा मिथो भयं
नैवात्मलाभादधि मन्यते परम् ॥२०॥

sa vai patiḥ syād akutobhayaḥ svayaṁ
samantataḥ pāti bhayāturaṁ janam
sa eka evetarathā mitho bhayaṁ
naivātmalābhād adhi manyate param

saḥ—he; *vai*—indeed; *patiḥ*—a husband; *syāt*—would be; *akutaḥ-bhayaḥ*—who is not fearful of anyone; *svayam*—self-sufficient; *samantataḥ*—entirely; *pāti*—maintains; *bhaya-āturam*—who is very afraid; *janam*—a person; *saḥ*—therefore he; *ekaḥ*—one; *eva*—only; *itarathā*—otherwise; *mithaḥ*—from one another; *bhayam*—fear; *na*—not; *eva*—indeed; *ātma-lābhāt*—than the attainment of You; *adhi*—greater; *manyate*—is accepted; *param*—other thing.

TRANSLATION

He alone who is never afraid but who, on the contrary, gives complete shelter to all fearful persons can actually become a husband and protector. Therefore, my Lord, You are the only husband, and no one else can claim this position. If You were not the only husband, You would be afraid of

others. Therefore persons learned in all Vedic literature accept only Your Lordship as everyone's master, and they think no one else a better husband and protector than You.

PURPORT

Here the meaning of husband or guardian is clearly explained. People want to become a husband, a guardian, a governor or a political leader without knowing the actual meaning of such a superior position. There are many people all over the world—indeed, throughout the universe—who claim for some time that they are husbands, political leaders or guardians, but in due course of time the Supreme Lord desires their removal from their posts, and their careers are immediately finished. Therefore those who are actually learned and advanced in spiritual life do not accept any leader, husband or maintainer other than the Supreme Personality of Godhead.

Lord Kṛṣṇa personally states in *Bhagavad-gītā* (18.66), *ahaṁ tvāṁ sarva-pāpebhyo mokṣayiṣyāmi:* "I shall deliver you from all sinful reactions." Kṛṣṇa is not afraid of anyone. On the contrary, everyone is afraid of Kṛṣṇa. Therefore He can actually give protection to a subordinate living entity. Since so-called leaders or dictators are completely under the control of material nature, they can never give complete protection to others, although they claim this ability due to false prestige. *Na te viduḥ svārtha-gatiṁ hi viṣṇum:* people do not know that real advancement in life consists of accepting the Supreme Personality of Godhead as one's master. Instead of deceiving themselves and others by pretending to be all-powerful, all political leaders, husbands and guardians should spread the Kṛṣṇa consciousness movement so that everyone can learn how to surrender to Kṛṣṇa, the supreme husband.

TEXT 21

या तस्य ते पादसरोरुहार्हणं
निकामयेत्साखिलकामलम्पटा ।
तदेव रासीप्सितमीप्सितोऽर्चितो
यद्भग्नयाच्ञा भगवन् प्रतप्यते ॥२१॥

yā tasya te pāda-saroruhārhaṇaṁ
nikāmayet sākhila-kāma-lampaṭā
tad eva rāsīpsitam īpsito 'rcito
yad-bhagna-yācñā bhagavan pratapyate

yā—a woman who; *tasya*—of Him; *te*—of You; *pāda-saroruha*—of the lotus feet; *arhaṇam*—the worship; *nikāmayet*—fully desires; *sā*—such a woman; *akhila-kāma-lampaṭā*—although maintaining all kinds of material desire; *tat*—that; *eva*—only; *rāsi*—You award; *īpsitam*—some other desired benediction; *īpsitaḥ*—being looked to for; *arcitaḥ*—worshiped; *yat*—from which; *bhagna-yācñā*—one who desires objects other than Your lotus feet and who thus becomes broken; *bhagavan*—O my Lord; *pratapyate*—is pained.

TRANSLATION

My dear Lord, You automatically fulfill all the desires of a woman who worships Your lotus feet in pure love. However, if a woman worships Your lotus feet for a particular purpose, You also quickly fulfill her desires, but in the end she becomes broken-hearted and laments. Therefore one need not worship Your lotus feet for some material benefit.

PURPORT

Śrīla Rūpa Gosvāmī describes pure devotional service as *anyābhilāṣitā-śūnyaṁ jñāna-karmādy-anāvṛtam.* One should not worship the Supreme Personality of Godhead to fulfill some material desire for success in fruitive activities or mental speculation. To serve the lotus feet of the Lord means to serve Him exactly as He desires. The neophyte devotee is therefore ordered to worship the Lord strictly according to the regulative principles given by the spiritual master and the *śāstras.* By executing devotional service in that way, he gradually becomes attached to Kṛṣṇa, and when his original dormant love for the Lord becomes manifest, he spontaneously serves the Lord without any motive. This condition is the perfect stage of one's relationship with the Lord. The Lord then looks after the comfort and security of His devotee without being asked. Kṛṣṇa promises in *Bhagavad-gītā* (9.22):

ananyāś cintayanto māṁ
ye janāḥ paryupāsate
teṣāṁ nityābhiyuktānāṁ
yoga-kṣemaṁ vahāmy aham

The Supreme Lord personally takes care of anyone who is completely engaged in His devotional service. Whatever he has, the Lord protects, and whatever he needs, the Lord supplies. Therefore why should one bother the Lord for something material? Such prayers are unnecessary.

Śrīla Viśvanātha Cakravartī Ṭhākura explains that even if a devotee wishes the Lord to fulfill a particular desire, the devotee should not be considered a *sakāma-bhakta* (a devotee with some motive). In the *Bhagavad-gītā* (7.16) Kṛṣṇa says:

catur-vidhā bhajante māṁ
janāḥ sukṛtino'rjuna
ārto jijñāsur arthārthī
jñānī ca bharatarṣabha

"O best among the Bharatas [Arjuna], four kinds of pious men render devotional service unto Me—the distressed, the desirer of wealth, the inquisitive and he who is searching for knowledge of the Absolute." The *ārta* and the *arthārthī,* who approach the Supreme Personality of Godhead for relief from misery or for some money, are not *sakāma-bhaktas,* although they appear to be. Being neophyte devotees, they are simply ignorant. Later in *Bhagavad-gītā* the Lord says, *udārāḥ sarva evaite:* they are all magnanimous (*udārāḥ*). Although in the beginning a devotee may harbor some desire, in due course of time it will vanish. Therefore the *Śrīmad-Bhāgavatam* enjoins:

akāmaḥ sarva-kāmo vā
mokṣa-kāma udāra-dhīḥ
tīvreṇa bhakti-yogena
yajeta puruṣaṁ param

"A person who has broader intelligence, whether he is full of all material desire, is free from material desire, or has a desire for liberation, must by all means worship the supreme whole, the Personality of Godhead." (*Bhāg.* 2.3.10)

Even if one wants something material, he should pray to no one but the Lord to fulfill his desire. If one approaches a demigod for the fulfillment of his desires, he is to be considered *naṣṭa-buddhi,* bereft of all good sense. Kṛṣṇa says in *Bhagavad-gītā* (7.20):

kāmais tais tair hṛta-jñānāḥ
prapadyante'nya-devatāḥ
taṁ taṁ niyamam āsthāya
prakṛtyā niyatāḥ svayā

"Those whose minds are distorted by material desires surrender unto demigods and follow the particular rules and regulations of worship according to their own natures."

Lakṣmīdevī advises all devotees who approach the Lord with material desires that according to her practical experience, the Lord is Kāmadeva, and thus there is no need to ask Him for anything material. She says that everyone should simply serve the Lord without any motive. Since the Supreme Personality of Godhead is sitting in everyone's heart, He knows everyone's thoughts, and in due course of time He will fulfill all desires. Therefore let us completely depend on the service of the Lord without bothering Him with our material requests.

TEXT 22

मत्प्राप्तयेऽजेशसुरासुरादय-
स्तप्यन्त उग्रं तप ऐन्द्रियेधियः ।
ऋते भवत्पादपरायणान्न मां
विन्दन्त्यहं त्वद्धृदया यतोऽजित ॥२२॥

mat-prāptaye 'jeśa-surāsurādayas
tapyanta ugraṁ tapa aindriye dhiyaḥ
ṛte bhavat-pāda-parāyaṇān na mām
vindanty ahaṁ tvad-dhṛdayā yato 'jita

mat-prāptaye—to obtain my mercy; *aja*—Lord Brahmā; *īśa*—Lord Śiva; *sura*—the other demigods, headed by King Indra, Candra and Varuṇa; *asura-ādayaḥ*—as well as the demons; *tapyante*—undergo; *ugram*—severe; *tapaḥ*—austerity; *aindriye dhiyaḥ*—whose minds are absorbed in thoughts of superior sense gratification; *ṛte*—unless; *bhavat-pāda-parāyaṇāt*—one who is wholly and solely engaged in the service of the Supreme Lord's lotus feet; *na*—not; *mām*—me; *vindanti*—obtain; *aham*—I; *tvat*—in You; *hṛdayāḥ*—whose hearts; *yataḥ*—therefore; *ajita*—O unconquerable one.

TRANSLATION

O supreme unconquerable Lord, when they become absorbed in thoughts of material enjoyment, Lord Brahmā and Lord Śiva, as well as other demigods and demons, undergo severe penances and austerities to receive my benedictions. But I do not favor anyone, however great he may be; unless he is always engaged in the service of Your lotus feet. Because I always keep You within my heart, I cannot favor anyone but a devotee.

PURPORT

In this verse the goddess of fortune, Lakṣmīdevī, clearly states that she does not bestow her favor on any materialistic person. Although sometimes a materialist becomes very opulent in the eyes of another materialist, such opulence is bestowed upon him by the goddess Durgādevī, a material expansion of the goddess of fortune, not by Lakṣmīdevī herself. Those who desire material wealth worship Durgādevī with the following *mantra: dhanaṁ dehi rūpaṁ dehi rūpapati-bhājaṁ dehi.* "O worshipable mother Durgādevī, please give me wealth, strength, fame, a good wife and so on." By pleasing Goddess Durgā one can obtain such benefits, but since they are temporary, they result only in *māyā-sukha* (illusory happiness). As stated by Prahlāda Mahārāja, *māyā-sukhāya bharam udvahato vimūḍhān:* those who work very hard for material benefits are *vimūḍhas,* foolish rascals, because such happiness will not endure. On the other hand, devotees like Prahlāda and Dhruva Mahārāja achieved extraordinary material opulences, but such opulences were not *māyā-sukha.* When a devotee acquires unparalleled opulences, they are the direct gifts of the goddess of fortune, who resides in the heart of Nārāyaṇa.

The material opulences a person obtains by offering prayers to the goddess Durgā are temporary. As described in *Bhagavad-gītā* (7.23), *antavat tu phalaṁ teṣāṁ tad bhavaty alpa-medhasām:* men of meager intelligence desire temporary happiness. We have actually seen that one of the disciples of Bhaktisiddhānta Sarasvatī Ṭhākura wanted to enjoy the property of his spiritual master, and the spiritual master, being merciful toward him, gave him the temporary property, but not the power to preach the cult of Caitanya Mahāprabhu all over the world. That special mercy of the power to preach is given to a devotee who does not want anything material from his spiritual master but wants only to serve him. The story of the demon Rāvaṇa illustrates this point. Although Rāvaṇa tried to abduct the goddess of fortune Sītādevī from the custody of Lord Rāmacandra, he could not possibly do so. The Sītādevī he forcibly took with him was not the original Sītādevī, but an expansion of *māyā,* or Durgādevī. As a result, instead of winning the favor of the real goddess of fortune, Rāvaṇa and his whole family were vanquished by the power of Durgādevī (*sṛṣṭi-sthiti-pralaya-sādhana-śaktir ekā*).

TEXT 23

स त्वं ममाप्यच्युत शीर्ष्णि वन्दितं
कराम्बुजं यत्त्वदधायि सात्वताम् ।

बिभर्षि मां लक्ष्म वरेण्य मायया
क ईश्वरस्येहितमूहितुं विभुरिति ॥२३॥

sa tvaṁ mamāpy acyuta śīrṣṇi vanditaṁ
karāmbujaṁ yat tvad-adhāyi sātvatām
bibharṣi māṁ lakṣma vareṇya māyayā
ka īśvarasyehitam ūhituṁ vibhur iti

saḥ—that; *tvam*—You; *mama*—of me; *api*—also; *acyuta*—O infallible one; *śīrṣṇi*—on the head; *vanditam*—worshiped; *kara-ambujam*—Your lotus hand; *yat*—which; *tvat*—by You; *adhāyi*—placed; *sātvatām*—on the head of the devotees; *bibharṣi*—You maintain; *mām*—me; *lakṣma*—as an insignia on Your chest; *vareṇya*—O worshipable one; *māyayā*—with deceit; *kaḥ*—who; *īśvarasya*—of the supremely powerful controller; *īhitam*—the desires; *ūhitum*—to understand by reason and argument; *vibhuḥ*—is able; *iti*—thus.

TRANSLATION

O infallible one, Your lotus palm is the source of all benediction. Therefore Your pure devotees worship it, and You very mercifully place Your hand on their heads. I wish that You may also place Your hand on My head, for although You already bear my insignia of golden streaks on Your chest, I regard this honor as merely a kind of false prestige for me. You show Your real mercy to Your devotees, not to me. Of course, You are the supreme absolute controller, and no one can understand Your motives.

PURPORT

In many places, the *śāstras* describe the Supreme Personality of Godhead as being more inclined toward His devotees than toward His wife, who always remains on His chest. In *Śrīmad-Bhāgavatam* (11.14.15) it is stated:

na tathā me priyatama
ātma-yonir na śaṅkaraḥ
na ca saṅkarṣaṇo na śrīr
naivātmā ca yathā bhavān

Here Kṛṣṇa plainly says that His devotees are more dear to Him than Lord Brahmā, Lord Śiva, Lord Saṅkarṣaṇa (the original cause of creation), the goddess of fortune or even His own Self. Elsewhere in *Śrīmad-Bhāgavatam* (10.9.20) Śukadeva Gosvāmī says:

nemam viriñco na bhavo
na śrīr apy aṅga saṁśrayā
prasādaṁ lebhire gopī
yat tat prāpa vimuktidāt

The Supreme Lord, who can award liberation to anyone, showed more mercy toward the *gopīs* than to Lord Brahmā, Lord Śiva or even the goddess of fortune, who is His own wife and is associated with His body. Similarly, *Śrīmad-Bhāgavatam* (10.47.60) also states:

nāyaṁ śriyo 'ṅga u nitānta-rateḥ prasādaḥ
svar-yoṣitāṁ nalina-gandha-rucāṁ kuto 'nyāḥ
rāsotsave 'sya bhuja-daṇḍa-gṛhīta-kaṇṭha-
labdhāśiṣāṁ ya udagād vraja-sundarīṇām

"The *gopīs* received benedictions from the Lord that neither Lakṣmīdevī nor the most beautiful dancers in the heavenly planets could attain. In the *rāsa* dance, the Lord showed His favor to the most fortunate *gopīs* by placing His arms on their shoulders and dancing with each of them individually. No one can compare with the *gopīs,* who received the causeless mercy of the Lord."

In the *Caitanya-caritāmṛta* it is said that no one can receive the real favor of the Supreme Personality of Godhead without following in the footsteps of the *gopīs.* Even the goddess of fortune could not receive the same favor as the *gopīs,* although she underwent severe austerities and penances for many years. Lord Śrī Caitanya Mahāprabhu discusses this point with Vyeṅkaṭa Bhaṭṭa in *Caitanya-caritāmṛta* (*Madhya* 9.111–131): "The Lord inquired from Vyeṅkaṭa Bhaṭṭa,'Your worshipable goddess of fortune, Lakṣmī, always remains on the chest of Nārāyaṇa, and she is certainly the most chaste woman in the creation. However, My Lord is Lord Śrī Kṛṣṇa, a cowherd boy engaged in tending cows. Why is it that Lakṣmī, being such a chaste wife, wants to associate with My Lord? Just to associate with Kṛṣṇa, Lakṣmī abandoned all transcendental happiness in Vaikuṇṭha and for a long time accepted vows and regulative principles and performed unlimited austerities."

"Vyeṅkaṭa Bhaṭṭa replied,'Lord Kṛṣṇa and Lord Nārāyaṇa are one and the same, but the pastimes of Kṛṣṇa are more relishable due to their sportive nature. They are very pleasing for Kṛṣṇa's *śaktis.* Since Kṛṣṇa and Nārāyaṇa are both the same personality, Lakṣmī's association with Kṛṣṇa did not break her vow of chastity. Rather, it was in great fun that the goddess of fortune wanted to associate with Lord Kṛṣṇa. The goddess of fortune considered that her vow of chastity would not be damaged by her relationship with Kṛṣṇa. Rather, by associating with Kṛṣṇa she could enjoy the benefit of the *rāsa* dance. If she wanted to enjoy herself with Kṛṣṇa what fault is there? Why are you joking so about this?"

"Lord Caitanya Mahāprabhu replied,'I know that there is no fault in the goddess of fortune, but still she could not enter into the *rāsa* dance. We hear this from revealed scriptures. The authorities of Vedic knowledge met Lord Rāmacandra in Daṇḍakāraṇya, and by their penances and austerities, they were allowed to enter into the *rāsa* dance. But can you tell me why the goddess of fortune, Lakṣmī, could not get that opportunity?"

"To this Vyeṅkaṭa Bhaṭṭa replied,'I cannot enter into the mystery of this incident. I am an ordinary living being. My intelligence is limited, and I am always disturbed. How can I understand the pastimes of the Supreme Lord? They are deeper than millions of oceans."

"Lord Caitanya replied,'Lord Kṛṣṇa has a specific characteristic. He attracts everyone's heart by the mellow of His personal conjugal love. By following in the footsteps of the inhabitants of the planet known as Vrajaloka or Goloka Vṛndāvana, one can attain the shelter of the lotus feet of Śrī Kṛṣṇa. However, the inhabitants of that planet do not know that Lord Kṛṣṇa is the Supreme Personality of Godhead. Unaware that Kṛṣṇa is the Supreme Lord, the residents of Vṛndāvana like Nanda Mahārāja, Yaśodādevī and the *gopīs* treat Kṛṣṇa as their beloved son or lover. Mother Yaśodā accepts Him as her son and sometimes binds Him to a grinding mortar. Kṛṣṇa's cowherd boyfriends think He is an ordinary boy and get up on His shoulders. In Goloka Vṛndāvana no one has any desire other than to love Kṛṣṇa.'"

The conclusion is that one cannot associate with Kṛṣṇa unless he has fully received the favor of the inhabitants of Vrajabhūmi. Therefore if one wants to be delivered by Kṛṣṇa directly, he must take to the service of the residents of Vṛndāvana, who are unalloyed devotees of the Lord.

TEXT 24

रम्यके च भगवतः प्रियतमं मात्स्यमवताररूपं तद्वर्षपुरुषस्य मनोः प्राक्प्रदर्शितं स इदानीमपि महता भक्तियोगेनाराधयतीदं चोदाहरति ॥२४॥

ramyake ca bhagavataḥ priyatamaṁ mātsyam avatāra-rūpaṁ tad-varṣa-puruṣasya manoḥ prāk-pradarśitaṁ sa idānīm api mahatā bhakti-yogenārādhayatīdaṁ codāharati.

ramyake ca—also in Ramyaka-varṣa; *bhagavataḥ*—of the Supreme Personality of Godhead; *priya-tamam*—the foremost; *mātsyam*—fish; *avatāra-rūpam*—the form of the incarnation; *tat-varṣa-puruṣasya*—of the ruler of that land; *manoḥ*—Manu; *prāk*—previously (at the end of the Cākṣuṣa-manvantara); *pradarśitam*—exhibited; *saḥ*—that Manu; *idānīm api*—even until now; *mahatā bhakti-yogena*—by dint of advanced devotional service; *ārādhayati*—worships the Supreme Personality of Godhead; *idam*—this; *ca*—and; *udāharati*—chants.

TRANSLATION

Śukadeva Gosvāmī continued: In Ramyaka-varṣa, where Vaivasvata Manu rules, the Supreme Personality of Godhead appeared as Lord Matsya at the end of the last era [the Cākṣuṣa-manvantara]. Vaivasvata Manu now worships Lord Matsya in pure devotional service and chants the following mantra.

TEXT 25

ॐ नमो भगवते मुख्यतमाय नमः सत्त्वाय प्राणायौजसे सहसे बलाय महामत्स्याय
नम इति ॥२५॥

oṁ namo bhagavate mukhyatamāya namaḥ sattvāya prāṇāyaujase sahase
balāya mahā-matsyāya nama iti.

om—O my Lord; *namaḥ*—respectful obeisances; *bhagavate*—unto the Supreme Personality of Godhead; *mukhya-tamāya*—the first incarnation to appear; *namaḥ*—my respectful obeisances; *sattvāya*—unto the pure transcendence; *prāṇāya*—the origin of life; *ojase*—the source of the potency of the senses; *sahase*—the origin of all mental power; *balāya*—the origin of bodily strength; *mahā-matsyāya*—unto the gigantic fish incarnation; *namaḥ*—respectful obeisances; *iti*—thus.

TRANSLATION

I offer my respectful obeisances unto the Supreme Personality of Godhead, who is pure transcendence. He is the origin of all life, bodily strength, mental power and sensory ability. Known as Matsyāvatāra, the gigantic fish incarnation, He appears first among all the incarnations. Again I offer my obeisances unto Him.

PURPORT

Śrīla Jayadeva Gosvāmī sings:

pralayo payodhi-jale dhṛtavān asi vedaṁ
vihita-vahitra-caritram akhedam
keśava dhṛta-mīna-śarīra jaya jagad-īśa hare

Soon after the cosmic creation, the entire universe was inundated with water. At that time Lord Kṛṣṇa (Keśava) incarnated as a gigantic fish to protect the *Vedas.* Therefore Manu addresses Lord Matsya as *mukhyatama,* the first incarnation to appear. Fish are generally considered a mixture of the modes of ignorance and passion, but we must understand that every incarnation of the Supreme Personality of Godhead is completely transcendental. There is never any deterioration of the Supreme Lord's original transcendental quality. Therefore the word *sattvāya* is used here, meaning pure goodness on the transcendental platform. There are many incarnations of the Supreme Lord: Varāha *mūrti* (the boar form), Kūrma *mūrti* (the tortoise form), Hayagrīva *mūrti* (the form of a horse) and so on. Yet we should never think any of Them material. They are always situated on the platform of *śuddha-sattva,* pure transcendence.

TEXT 26

अन्तर्बहिश्चाखिललोकपालकै-
रदृष्टरूपो विचरस्युरुस्वनः ।
स ईश्वरस्त्वं य इदं वशेऽनय-
न्नाम्ना यथा दारुमयीं नरः स्त्रियम् ॥२६॥

antar bahiś cākhila-loka-pālakair
adṛṣṭa-rūpo vicarasy uru-svanaḥ
sa īśvaras tvaṁ ya idaṁ vaśe 'nayan
nāmnā yathā dārumayīṁ naraḥ striyam

antaḥ—within; *bahiḥ*—without; *ca*—also; *akhila-loka-pālakaiḥ*—by the leaders of the different planets, societies, kingdoms and so on; *adṛṣṭa-rūpaḥ*—not seen; *vicarasi*—You wander; *uru*—very great; *svanaḥ*—whose sounds (Vedic *mantras*); *saḥ*—He; *īśvaraḥ*—the supreme controller; *tvam*—You; *yaḥ*—who; *idam*—this; *vaśe*—under control; *anayat*—has brought; *nāmnā*—by different names like *brāhmaṇa, kṣatriya, vaiśya* and *śūdra; yathā*—exactly like; *dārumayīm*—made of wood; *naraḥ*—a man; *striyam*—a doll.

TRANSLATION

My dear Lord, just as a puppeteer controls his dancing dolls and a husband controls his wife, Your Lordship controls all the living entities in the universe, such as the brāhmaṇas, kṣatriyas, vaiśyas and śūdras. Although You are in everyone's heart as the supreme witness and commander and are outside everyone as well, the so-called leaders of societies, communities and countries cannot realize You. Only those who hear the vibration of the Vedic mantras can appreciate You.

PURPORT

The Supreme Personality of Godhead is *antarbahiḥ,* present within and without everything. One must overcome the delusion caused by the Lord's external energy and realize His presence both externally and internally. In *Śrīmad-Bhāgavatam* (1.8.19) Śrīmatī Kuntīdevī has explained that Kṛṣṇa appears in this world *naṭo nāṭyadharo yathā,* "exactly like an actor dressed as a player." In *Bhagavad-gītā* (18.61) Kṛṣṇa says, *īśvaraḥ sarva-bhūtānāṁ hṛd-deśe'rjuna tiṣṭhati:* "The Supreme Lord is situated in everyone's heart, O Arjuna." The Lord is situated within everyone's heart, and outside as well. Within the heart He is the Supersoul, the incarnation who acts as the adviser and witness. Yet although God is residing within their hearts, foolish people say, "I cannot see God. Please show Him to me."

Everyone is under the control of the Supreme Personality of Godhead, exactly like dancing dolls controlled by a puppeteer or a woman controlled by her husband. A woman is compared to a doll (*dārumayī*) because she has no independence. She should always be controlled by a man. Still, due to false prestige, a class of women wants to remain independent. What to speak of women, all living entities are *prakṛti* (female) and therefore dependent on the Supreme Lord, as Kṛṣṇa Himself explains in *Bhagavad-gītā* (*apareyam itas tv anyāṁ prakṛtiṁ viddhi me parām*). The living entity is never independent. Under all circumstances, he is dependent on the mercy of the Lord. The Lord creates the social divisions of human society—*brāhmaṇas, kṣatriyas, vaiśyas* and *śūdras*—and ordains that they follow rules and regulations suited to their particular position. In this way, all members of society remain always under the Supreme Lord's control. Still, some people foolishly deny the existence of God.

Self-realization means to understand one's subordinate position in relation to the Lord. When one is thus enlightened, he surrenders to the Supreme Personality of Godhead and is liberated from the clutches of the material energy. In other words, unless one surrenders to the lotus feet of the Lord, the material energy in its many varieties will continue to control him. No one in the material world can deny that he is under control. The Supreme Lord, Nārāyaṇa, who is beyond this material existence, controls everyone. The following Vedic *mantra* confirms this point: *eko ha vai nārāyaṇa āsīt.* Foolish persons think Nārāyaṇa to be on the platform of ordinary material existence. Because they do not realize the natural constitutional position of the living entity, they concoct names like *daridra-nārāyaṇa, svāmi-nārāyaṇa* or *mithyā-nārāyaṇa.* However, Nārāyaṇa is actually the supreme controller of everyone. This understanding is self-realization.

TEXT 27

यं लोकपालाः किल मत्सरज्वरा
हित्वा यतन्तोऽपि पृथक समेत्य च ।
पातुं न शेकुर्द्विपदश्चतुष्पदः
सरीसृपं स्थाणु यदत्र दृश्यते ॥२७॥

yaṁ loka-pālāḥ kila matsara-jvarā
hitvā yatanto 'pi pṛthak sametya ca
pātuṁ na śekur dvi-padaś catuṣ-padaḥ
sarīsṛpaṁ sthāṇu yad atra dṛśyate

yam—whom (You); *loka-pālāḥ*—the great leaders of the universe, beginning with Lord Brahmā; *kila*—what to speak of others; *matsara-jvarāḥ*—who are suffering from the fever of envy; *hitvā*—leaving aside; *yatantaḥ*—endeavoring; *api*—although; *pṛthak*—separately; *sametya*—combined; *ca*—also; *pātum*—to protect; *na*—not; *śekuḥ*—able; *dvi-padaḥ*—two-legged; *catuḥ-padaḥ*—four-legged; *sarīsṛpam*—reptiles; *sthāṇu*—not moving; *yat*—whatever; *atra*—within this material world; *dṛśyate*—is visible.

TRANSLATION

My Lord, from the great leaders of the universe, such as Lord Brahmā and other demigods, down to the political leaders of this world, all are envious of Your authority. Without Your help, however, they could neither separately nor concertedly maintain the innumerable living entities within the universe. You are actually the only maintainer of all human beings, of animals like cows and asses, and of plants, reptiles, birds, mountains and whatever else is visible within this material world.

PURPORT

It is fashionable for materialistic persons to compete with the power of God. When so-called scientists try to manufacture living entities in their laboratories, their only purpose is to defy the talent and ability of the Supreme Personality of Godhead. This is called illusion. It exists even in the higher planetary systems, where great demigods like Lord Brahmā, Lord Śiva and others reside. In this world everyone is puffed up with false prestige despite the failure of all his endeavors. When so-called philanthropists, who supposedly want to help the poor, are approached by members of the Kṛṣṇa consciousness movement, they say, "You are simply wasting your time, while I am feeding vast masses of starving people." Unfortunately, their meager efforts, either singly or together, do not solve anyone's problems.

Sometimes so-called *svāmīs* are very eager to feed poor people, thinking them to be *daridra-nārāyaṇa,* the Lord's incarnations as beggars. They prefer to serve the manufactured *daridra-nārāyaṇa* than the original, supreme Nārāyaṇa. They say, "Don't encourage service to Lord Nārāyaṇa. It is better to serve the starving people of the world." Unfortunately such materialists, either singly or combined in the form of the United Nations, cannot fulfill their plans. The truth is that the many millions of human beings, animals, birds and trees —indeed, all living entities—are maintained solely by the Supreme Personality of Godhead. *Eko bahūnāṁ yo vidadhāti kāmān:* one person, the Supreme Lord, is supplying the necessities of life for all other living entities. To challenge the authority of Nārāyaṇa, the Supreme Personality of Godhead, is the business of *asuras* (demons). Yet sometimes *suras,* or devotees, are also bewildered by the illusory energy and falsely claim to be the maintainer of the entire universe. Such incidents are described in the Tenth Canto of *Śrīmad-Bhāgavatam,* where Śukadeva Gosvāmī tells how Lord Brahmā and King Indra became puffed up and were eventually chastised by Kṛṣṇa.

TEXT 28

भवान् युगान्तार्णव ऊर्मिमालिनि
क्षोणीमिमामोषधिवीरुधां निधिम् ।
मया सहोरु क्रमतेऽज ओजसा
तस्मै जगत्प्राणगणात्मने नम इति ॥२८॥

bhavān yugāntārṇava ūrmi-mālini
kṣoṇīm imām oṣadhi-vīrudhāṁ nidhim

mayā sahoru kramate 'ja ojasā
tasmai jagat-prāṇa-gaṇātmane nama iti

bhavān—Your Lordship; *yuga-anta-arṇave*—in the water of devastation at the end of the millennium; *ūrmi-mālini*—possessing rows of big waves; *kṣoṇīm*—the planet earth; *imām*—this; *oṣadhi-vīrudhām*—of all kinds of herbs and drugs; *nidhim*—the storehouse; *mayā*—me; *saha*—with; *uru*—great; *kramate*—You roamed; *aja*—O unborn one; *ojasā*—with speed; *tasmai*—unto Him; *jagat*—of the entire universe; *prāṇa-gaṇa-ātmane*—the ultimate source of life; *namaḥ*—my respectful obeisances; *iti*—thus.

TRANSLATION

O almighty Lord, at the end of the millennium this planet earth, which is the source of all kinds of herbs, drugs and trees, was inundated by water and drowned beneath the devastating waves. At that time, You protected me along with the earth and roamed the sea with great speed. O unborn one, You are the actual maintainer of the entire universal creation, and therefore You are the cause of all living entities. I offer my respectful obeisances unto You.

PURPORT

Envious persons cannot appreciate how wonderfully the Lord creates, maintains and annihilates the universe, but devotees of the Lord can understand this perfectly well. Devotees can see how the Lord is acting behind the wonderful workings of the material nature. In *Bhagavad-gītā* (9.10) the Lord says:

mayādhyakṣeṇa prakṛtiḥ
sūyate sa-carācaram
hetunānena kaunteya
jagad viparivartate

"This material nature is working under My direction, O son of Kuntī, and it is producing all moving and unmoving beings. By its rule this manifestation is created and annihilated again and again." All the wonderful transformations of nature are happening under the superintendence of the Supreme Personality of Godhead. Envious persons cannot see this, but a devotee, even though very humble and even if uneducated, knows that behind all the activities of nature is the supreme hand of the Supreme Being.

TEXT 29

हिरण्मयेऽपि भगवान्निवसति कूर्मतनुं बिभ्राणस्तस्य तत्प्रियतमां तनुमर्यमा सह वर्षपुरुषैः पितृगणाधिपतिरुपधावति मन्त्रमिमं चानुजपति ॥२९॥

hiraṇmaye 'pi bhagavān nivasati kūrma-tanuṁ bibhrāṇas tasya tat priyatamāṁ tanum aryamā saha varṣa-puruṣaiḥ pitṛ-gaṇādhipatir upadhāvati mantram imaṁ cānujapati.

hiraṇmaye—in Hiraṇmaya-varṣa; *api*—indeed; *bhagavān*—the Supreme Personality of Godhead; *nivasati*—resides; *kūrma-tanum*—the body of a tortoise; *bibhrāṇaḥ*—manifesting; *tasya*—of the Supreme Personality of Godhead; *tat*—that; *priya-tamām*—dearmost; *tanum*—body; *aryamā*—Aryamā, the chief resident of Hiraṇmaya-varṣa; *saha*—with; *varṣa-puruṣaiḥ*—the people of that tract of land; *pitṛ-gaṇa-adhipatiḥ*—who is the chief of the *pitās; upadhāvati*—worships in devotional service; *mantram*—hymn; *imam*—this; *ca*—also; *anujapati*—chants.

TRANSLATION

Śukadeva Gosvāmī continued: In Hiraṇmaya-varṣa, the Supreme Lord, Viṣṇu, lives in the form of a tortoise [kūrma-śarīra]. This most dear and beautiful form is always worshiped there in devotional service by Aryamā, the chief resident of Hiraṇmaya-varṣa, along with the other inhabitants of that land. They chant the following hymns.

PURPORT

The word *priyatama* (dearmost) is very significant in this verse. Each devotee regards a particular form of the Lord as most dear. Because of an atheistic mentality, some people think that the tortoise, boar and fish incarnations of the Lord are not very beautiful. They do not know that any form of the Lord is always the fully opulent Personality of Godhead. Since one of His opulences is infinite beauty, all the Lord's incarnations are very beautiful and are appreciated as such by devotees. Nondevotees, however, think that Lord Kṛṣṇa's incarnations are ordinary material creatures, and therefore they distinguish between the beautiful and the not beautiful. A certain form of the Lord is worshiped by a particular devotee because he loves to see that form of the Lord. As stated in *Brahma-saṁhitā* (5.33): *advaitam acyutam anādim ananta-rūpam ādyaṁ purāṇa-puruṣaṁ nava-yauvanaṁ ca.* The very beautiful form of the Lord is always youthful. Sincere servants of a particular form of the

Lord always see that form as very beautiful, and thus they engage in constant devotional service to Him.

TEXT 30

ॐ नमो भगवते अकूपाराय सर्वसत्त्वगुणविशेषणायानुपलक्षितस्थानाय नमो वर्ष्मणे नमो भूम्ने नमो नमोऽवस्थानाय नमस्ते ॥३०॥

oṁ namo bhagavate akūpārāya sarva-sattva-guṇa-viśeṣaṇāyānu-
palakṣita-sthānāya namo varṣmaṇe namo bhūmne namo namo
'vasthānāya namas te.

om—O my Lord; *namaḥ*—respectful obeisances; *bhagavate*—unto You, the Supreme Personality of Godhead; *akūpārāya*—in the form of a tortoise; *sarva-sattva-guṇa-viśeṣaṇāya*—whose form consists of *śuddha-sattva,* transcendental goodness; *anupalakṣita-sthānāya*—unto You, whose position is not discernible; *namaḥ*—my respectful obeisances; *varṣmaṇe*—unto You who, although the oldest, are unaffected by time; *namaḥ*—my respectful obeisances; *bhūmne*—to the great one who can go everywhere; *namaḥ namaḥ*—repeated obeisances; *avasthānāya*—the shelter of everything; *namaḥ*—respectful obeisances; *te*—unto You.

TRANSLATION

O my Lord, I offer my respectful obeisances unto You, who have assumed the form of a tortoise. You are the reservoir of all transcendental qualities, and being entirely untinged by matter, You are perfectly situated in pure goodness. You move here and there in the water, but no one can discern Your position. Therefore I offer my respectful obeisances unto You. Because of Your transcendental position, You are not limited by past, present and future. You are present everywhere as the shelter of all things, and therefore I offer my respectful obeisances unto You again and again.

PURPORT

In the *Brahma-saṁhitā* it is said, *goloka eva nivasaty akhilātma-bhūtaḥ:* the Lord always remains in Goloka, the topmost planet in the spiritual world. At the same time, He is all-pervading. This paradox is only possible for the Supreme Personality of Godhead, who is full of all opulences. The Lord's all-pervasiveness is confirmed in *Bhagavad-gītā* (18.61) where Kṛṣṇa states, *īśvaraḥ sarva-bhūtānāṁ hṛd-deśe'rjuna tiṣṭhati:* "The Supreme Lord is seated in everyone's heart, O Arjuna." Elsewhere in *Bhagavad-gītā* (15.15) the Lord says, *sarvasya cāhaṁ hṛdi sanniviṣṭo mattaḥ smṛtir jñānam apohanaṁ ca:* "I am seated in everyone's heart, and from Me come remembrance, knowledge and forgetfulness." Therefore, although the Lord is present everywhere, He cannot be seen with ordinary eyes. As Aryamā says, the Lord is *anupalakṣita-sthāna:* no one can locate Him. This is the greatness of the Supreme Personality of Godhead.

TEXT 31

यद्रूपमेतन्निजमाययार्पित-
मर्थस्वरूपं बहुरूपरूपितम् ।
संख्या न यस्यास्त्ययथोपलम्भनात्-
तस्मै नमस्तेऽव्यपदेशरूपिणे ॥३१॥

yad-rūpam etan nija-māyayārpitam
artha-svarūpaṁ bahu-rūpa-rūpitam
saṅkhyā na yasyāsty ayathopalambhanāt
tasmai namas te 'vyapadeśa-rūpiṇe

yat—of whom; *rūpam*—the form; *etat*—this; *nija-māyayā arpitam*—manifested by Your personal potency; *artha-svarūpam*—this entire visible cosmic manifestation; *bahu-rūpa-rūpitam*—manifested in various forms; *saṅkhyā*—the measurement; *na*—not; *yasya*—of which; *asti*—there is; *ayathā*—falsely; *upalambhanāt*—from perceiving; *tasmai*—unto Him (the Supreme Lord); *namaḥ*—my respectful obeisances; *te*—unto You; *avyapadeśa*—cannot be ascertained by mental speculation; *rūpiṇe*—whose real form.

TRANSLATION

My dear Lord, this visible cosmic manifestation is a demonstration of Your own creative energy. Since the countless varieties of forms within this cosmic manifestation are simply a display of Your external energy, this virāṭ-rūpa [universal body] is not Your real form. Except for a devotee in transcendental consciousness, no one can perceive Your actual form. Therefore I offer my respectful obeisances unto You.

PURPORT

Māyāvādī philosophers think the universal form of the Lord to be real and His personal form illusory. We can understand their mistake by a simple example. A fire consists of three elements: heat and light, which are the energy of the fire, and the fire itself. Anyone can understand that the original fire is the reality and that the heat and light are simply the fire's energy. Heat and light are the formless energies of fire, and in that sense they are unreal. Only the fire has form, and therefore it is the real form of the heat and light. As Kṛṣṇa states in *Bhagavad-gītā* (9.4), *mayā tatam idaṁ sarvaṁ jagad avyakta-mūrtinā:* "By Me, in My unmanifested form, this entire universe is pervaded." Thus the impersonal conception of the Lord is like the expansion of heat and light from a fire. In *Bhagavad-gītā* the Lord also says, *mat-sthāni sarva-bhūtāni na cāhaṁ teṣv avasthitaḥ:* the entire material creation is resting on Kṛṣṇa's energy, either material, spiritual or marginal, but because His form is absent from the expansion of His energy, He is not personally present. This inconceivable expansion of the Supreme Lord's energy is called *acintya-śakti.* Therefore no one can understand the real form of the Lord without becoming His devotee.

TEXT 32

जरायुजं स्वेदजमण्डजोद्भिदं
चराचरं देवर्षिपितृभूतमैन्द्रियम् ।
द्यौः खं क्षितिः शैलसरित्समुद्र-
द्वीपग्रहर्क्षेत्यभिधेय एकः ॥३२॥

jarāyujaṁ svedajam aṇḍajodbhidaṁ
carācaraṁ devarṣi-pitṛ-bhūtam aindriyam
dyauḥ khaṁ kṣitiḥ śaila-sarit-samudra-
dvīpa-graharkṣety abhidheya ekaḥ

jarāyu-jam—one born from a womb; *sveda-jam*—one born from perspiration; *aṇḍa-ja*—one born from an egg; *udbhidam*—one born of the earth; *cara-acaram*—the moving and the stationary; *deva*—the demigods; *ṛṣi*—the great sages; *pitṛ*—the inhabitants of Pitṛloka; *bhūtam*—the material elements air, fire, water and earth; *aindriyam*—all the senses; *dyauḥ*—the higher planetary systems; *kham*—the sky; *kṣitiḥ*—the earthly planets; *śaila*—the hills and mountains; *sarit*—the rivers; *samudra*—the oceans; *dvīpa*—the islands; *graha-ṛkṣa*—the stars and planets; *iti*—thus; *abhidheyaḥ*—to be variously named; *ekaḥ*—one.

TRANSLATION

My dear Lord, You manifest Your different energies in countless forms: as living entities born from wombs, from eggs and from perspiration; as

plants and trees that grow out of the earth; as all living entities, both moving and standing, including the demigods, the learned sages and the pitās; as outer space, as the higher planetary system containing the heavenly planets, and as the planet earth with its hills, rivers, seas, oceans and islands. Indeed, all the stars and planets are simply manifestations of Your different energies, but originally You are one without a second. Therefore there is nothing beyond You. This entire cosmic manifestation is therefore not false but is simply a temporary manifestation of Your inconceivable energy.

PURPORT

This verse completely rejects the theory of *brahma satyaṁ jagan mithyā,* which states that spirit, or Brahman, is real, whereas the manifested material world, with its great variety of things, is false. Nothing is false. One thing may be permanent and another temporary, but both the permanent and the temporary are facts. For example, if someone becomes angry for a certain period, no one can say that his anger is false. It is simply temporary. Everything we experience in our daily lives is of this same character; it is temporary but real.

The different kinds of living entities coming from various sources are very clearly described in this verse. Some are born from a womb and some (like certain insects) from human perspiration. Others hatch from eggs, and still others sprout from the earth. A living entity takes birth under different circumstances according to his past activities (*karma*). Although the body of the living entity is material, it is never false. No one will accept the argument that since a person's material body is false, murder has no repercussions. Our temporary bodies are given to us according to our *karma,* and we must remain in our given bodies to enjoy the pains and pleasures of life. Our bodies cannot be called false; they are only temporary. In other words, the energy of the Supreme Lord is as permanent as the Lord Himself, although His energy is sometimes manifest and sometimes not. As summarized in the *Vedas, sarvaṁ khalv idaṁ brahma:* "Everything is Brahman."

TEXT 33

यस्मिन्नसंख्येयविशेषनाम-
रूपाकृतौ कविभिः कल्पितेयम् ।
संख्या यया तत्त्वदृशापनीयते
तस्मै नमः सांख्यनिदर्शनाय ते इति ॥३३॥

yasminn asaṅkhyeya-viśeṣa-nāma-
rūpākṛtau kavibhiḥ kalpiteyam
saṅkhyā yayā tattva-dṛśāpanīyate
tasmai namaḥ sāṅkhya-nidarśanāya te iti

yasmin—in You (the Supreme Personality of Godhead); *asaṅkhyeya*—innumerable; *viśeṣa*—particular; *nāma*—names; *rūpa*—forms; *ākṛtau*—possessing bodily features; *kavibhiḥ*—by great learned persons; *kalpitā*—imagined; *iyam*—this; *saṅkhyā*—number; *yayā*—by whom; *tattva*—of the truth; *dṛśā*—by knowledge; *apanīyate*—is extracted; *tasmai*—unto Him; *namaḥ*—respectful obeisances; *sāṅkhya-nidarśanāya*—who is the revealer of this numerical knowledge; *te*—unto You; *iti*—thus.

TRANSLATION

O my Lord, Your name, form and bodily features are expanded in countless forms. No one can determine exactly how many forms exist, yet You Yourself, in Your incarnation as the learned scholar Kapiladeva, have analyzed the cosmic manifestation as containing twenty-four elements. Therefore if one is interested in Sāṅkhya philosophy, by which one can enumerate the different truths, he must hear it from You. Unfortunately, nondevotees simply count the different elements and remain ignorant of Your actual form. I offer my respectful obeisances unto You.

PURPORT

Philosophers and scientists have been trying to study the entire cosmic situation and have been theorizing and calculating in different ways for millions and millions of years. However, the speculative research work of a so-called scientist or philosopher is always interrupted when he dies, and the laws of nature go on without regard for his work.

For billions of years changes take place in the material creation, until at last the whole universe is dissolved and remains in an unmanifested state. Constant change and destruction (*bhūtvā bhūtvā pralīyate*) is perpetually going on in nature, yet the material scientists want to study natural laws without knowing the Supreme Personality of Godhead, who is the background of nature. As Kṛṣṇa states in *Bhagavad-gītā* (9.10):

mayādhyakṣeṇa prakṛtiḥ
sūyate sa-carācaram
hetunānena kaunteya
jagad viparivartate

"This material nature is working under My direction, O son of Kuntī, and it is producing all moving and unmoving beings. By its rule this manifestation is created and annihilated again and again."

Now the material creation is manifest, eventually it will be annihilated and remain for many millions of years in a dormant state, and finally it will again be created. This is the law of nature.

TEXT 34

उत्तरेषु च कुरुषु भगवान् यज्ञपुरुषः कृतवराहरूप आस्ते तं तु देवी हैषा भूः सह कुरुभिरस्खलितभक्तियोगेनोपधावति इमां च परमामुपनिषदमावर्तयति ॥३४॥

uttareṣu ca kuruṣu bhagavān yajña-puruṣaḥ kṛta-varāha-rūpa āste taṁ tu devī haiṣā bhūḥ saha kurubhir askhalita-bhakti-yogenopadhāvati imāṁ ca paramām upaniṣadam āvartayati.

uttareṣu—on the northern side; *ca*—also; *kuruṣu*—in the tract of land known as Kuru; *bhagavān*—the Supreme Personality of Godhead; *yajña-puruṣaḥ*—who accepts all results of sacrifices; *kṛta-varāha-rūpaḥ*—having accepted the form of a boar; *āste*—exists eternally; *tam*—Him; *tu*—certainly; *devī*—the goddess; *ha*—certainly; *eṣā*—this; *bhūḥ*—planet earth; *saha*—along with; *kurubhiḥ*—the inhabitants of the land known as Kuru; *askhalita*—unfailing; *bhakti-yogena*—by devotional service; *upadhāvati*—worship; *imām*—this; *ca*—also; *paramām upaniṣadam*—the supreme *Upaniṣad* (the process by which one can approach the Lord); *āvartayati*—chants again and again for the purpose of practice.

TRANSLATION

Śukadeva Gosvāmī said: Dear King, the Supreme Lord in His boar incarnation, who accepts all sacrificial offerings, lives in the northern part of Jambūdvīpa. There, in the tract of land known as Uttarakuru-varṣa, mother earth and all the other inhabitants worship Him with unfailing devotional service by repeatedly chanting the following Upaniṣad mantra.

TEXT 35

ॐ नमो भगवते मन्त्रतत्त्वलिङ्गाय यज्ञक्रतवे महाध्वरावयवाय महापुरुषाय नमः कर्मशुक्लाय त्रियुगाय नमस्ते ॥३५॥

oṁ namo bhagavate mantra-tattva-liṅgāya yajña-kratave mahā-dhvarāvayavāya mahā-puruṣāya namaḥ karma-śuklāya tri-yugāya namas te.

om—O Lord; *namaḥ*—respectful obeisances; *bhagavate*—unto the Supreme Personality of Godhead; *mantra-tattva-liṅgāya*—who is understood in truth by different *mantras; yajña*—in the form of animal sacrifices; *kratave*—and animal sacrifice; *mahā-dhvara*—great sacrifices; *avayavāya*—whose limbs and bodily parts; *mahā-puruṣāya*—unto the Supreme Person; *namaḥ*—respectful obeisances; *karma-śuklāya*—who purifies the fruitive activities of the living entities; *tri-yugāya*—unto the Supreme Personality of Godhead, who is full with six opulences and who appears in three *yugas* (remaining concealed in the fourth *yuga*); *namaḥ*—my respectful obeisances; *te*—unto You.

TRANSLATION

O Lord, we offer our respectful obeisances unto You as the gigantic person. Simply by chanting mantras, we shall be able to understand You fully. You are yajña [sacrifice], and You are the kratu [ritual]. Therefore all the ritualistic ceremonies of sacrifice are part of Your transcendental body, and You are the only enjoyer of all sacrifices. Your form is composed of transcendental goodness. You are known as tri-yuga because in Kali-yuga You appeared as a concealed incarnation and because You always fully possess the three pairs of opulences.

PURPORT

Śrī Caitanya Mahāprabhu is the incarnation for this age of Kali, as confirmed in many places throughout the *Purāṇas*, the *Mahābhārata, Śrīmad-Bhāgavatam* and the *Upaniṣads.* The summary of His appearance is given in *Caitanya-caritāmṛta* (*Madhya* 6.99) as follows:

kali-yuge līlāvatāra nā kare bhagavān
ataeva 'tri-yuga' kari' kahi tāra nāma

In this age of Kali, the Supreme Personality of Godhead (Bhagavān) does not appear as a *līlāvatāra,* an incarnation to display pastimes. Therefore He is known as *tri-yuga.* Unlike other incarnations, Lord Śrī Caitanya Mahāprabhu appears in this age of Kali as a devotee of the Lord. Therefore He is called a concealed incarnation (*channāvatāra*).

TEXT 36

यस्य स्वरूपं कवयो विपश्चितो
गुणेषु दारुष्विव जातवेदसम् ।
मथ्नन्ति मथ्ना मनसा दिदृक्षवो
गूढं क्रियार्थैर्नम ईरितात्मने ॥३६॥

yasya svarūpaṁ kavayo vipaścito
guṇeṣu dāruṣv iva jāta-vedasam
mithnanti mathnā manasā didṛkṣavo
gūḍhaṁ kriyārthair nama īritātmane

yasya—whose; *sva-rūpam*—form; *kavayaḥ*—the greatly learned sages; *vipaścitaḥ*—expert in ascertaining the Absolute Truth; *guṇeṣu*—in the material manifestation, consisting of the three modes of nature; *dāruṣu*—in wood; *iva*—like; *jāta*—manifested; *vedasam*—fire; *mithnanti*—stir; *mathnā*—with a piece of wood used for producing fire; *manasā*—by the mind; *didṛkṣavaḥ*—who are inquisitive; *gūḍham*—hidden; *kriyā-arthaiḥ*—by fruitive activities and their results; *namaḥ*—respectful obeisances; *īrita-ātmane*—unto the Lord, who is manifested.

TRANSLATION

By manipulating a fire-generating stick, great saints and sages can bring forth the fire lying dormant within wood. In the same way, O Lord, those expert in understanding the Absolute Truth try to see You in everything—even in their own bodies. Yet You remain concealed. You are not to be understood by indirect processes involving mental or physical activities. Because You are self-manifested, only when You see that a person is wholeheartedly engaged in searching for You do You reveal Yourself. Therefore I offer my respectful obeisances unto You.

PURPORT

The word *kriyārthaiḥ* means "by performing ritualistic ceremonies to satisfy the demigods." The word *vipaścitaḥ* is explained in the *Taittirīya Upaniṣad* as follows: *satyaṁ jñānam anantaṁ brahma; yo veda nihitaṁ guhāyāṁ parame vyoman; so'śnute sarvān kāmān saha brahmaṇā vipaściteti.* As Kṛṣṇa states in *Bhagavad-gītā* (7.19), *bahūnāṁ janmanām ante jñānavān māṁ prapadyate*: "After many births and deaths, he who is actually in knowledge surrenders unto

Me." When one understands that the Lord is situated in everyone's heart and actually sees the Lord present everywhere, he has perfect knowledge. The word *jāta-vedaḥ* means "fire which is produced by rubbing wood." In Vedic times, learned sages could bring forth fire from wood. *Jāta-vedaḥ* also indicates the fire in the stomach, which digests everything we eat and which produces an appetite. The word *gūḍha* is explained in the *Śvetāśvatara Upaniṣad. Eko devaḥ sarva-bhūteṣu gūḍhaḥ*: The Supreme Personality of Godhead is understood by chanting the Vedic *mantras. Sarva-vyāpī sarva-bhūtāntar-ātmā* : He is all-pervading, and He is within the heart of living entities. *Karmādhyakṣaḥ sarva-bhūtādhivāsaḥ* : He witnesses all activities of the living entity. *Sākṣī cetā kevalo nirguṇaś ca*: The Supreme Lord is the witness as well as the living force, yet He is transcendental to all material qualities.

TEXT 37

द्रव्यक्रियाहेत्वयनेशकर्तृभि-
मायागुणैर्वस्तुनिरीक्षितात्मने ।
अन्वीक्षयाङ्गातिशयात्मबुद्धिभि-
र्निरस्तमायाकृतये नमो नमः ॥३७॥

dravya-kriyā-hetv-ayaneśa-kartṛbhir
māyā-guṇair vastu-nirīkṣitātmane
anvīkṣayāṅgātiśayātma-buddhibhir
nirasta-māyākṛtaye namo namaḥ

dravya—by the objects of sense enjoyment; *kriyā*—the activities of the senses; *hetu*—the predominating deities of sensory activities; *ayana*—the body; *īśa*—the predominating time; *kartṛbhiḥ*—by false egotism; *māyā-guṇaiḥ*—by the modes of material nature; *vastu*—as a fact; *nirīkṣita*—being observed; *ātmane*—unto the Supreme Soul; *anvīkṣayā*—by careful consideration; *aṅga*—by the limbs of yogic practice; *atiśaya-ātma-buddhibhiḥ*—by those whose intelligence has become fixed; *nirasta*—completely freed from; *māyā*—the illusory energy; *ākṛtaye*—whose form; *namaḥ*—all respectful obeisances; *namaḥ*—respectful obeisances.

TRANSLATION

The objects of material enjoyment [sound, form, taste, touch and smell], the activities of the senses, the controllers of sensory activities [the demigods], the body, eternal time and egotism are all creations of Your

material energy. Those whose intelligence has become fixed by perfect execution of mystic yoga can see that all these elements result from the actions of Your external energy. They can also see Your transcendental form as Supersoul in the background of everything. Therefore I repeatedly offer my respectful obeisances unto You.

PURPORT

The objects of material enjoyment, the sensory activities, attachment to sensual pleasure, the body, false egotism and so on are produced by the Lord's external energy, *māyā.* The background of all these activities is the living being, and the director of the living beings is the Supersoul. The living being is not the all in all. He is directed by the Supersoul. In *Bhagavad-gītā* (15.15) Kṛṣṇa confirms this:

sarvasya cāhaṁ hṛdi sanniviṣṭo
mattaḥ smṛtir jñānam apohanaṁ ca

"I am seated in everyone's heart, and from Me come remembrance, knowledge and forgetfulness." The living entity depends on the Supersoul for directions. A person advanced in spiritual knowledge, or a person expert in the practice of mystic *yoga* (*yama, niyama, āsana* and so on) can understand transcendence either as Paramātmā or as the Supreme Personality of Godhead. The Supreme Lord is the original cause of all natural events. Therefore He is described as *sarva-kāraṇa-kāraṇam,* the cause of all causes. Behind everything visible to our material eyes is some cause, and one who can see the original cause of all causes, Lord Kṛṣṇa, can actually see. Kṛṣṇa, the *sac-cid-ānanda-vigraha,* is the background of everything, as He Himself confirms in *Bhagavad-gītā* (9.10):

mayādhyakṣeṇa prakṛtiḥ
sūyate sa-carācaram
hetunānena kaunteya
jagad viparivartate

"This material nature is working under My direction, O son of Kuntī, and it is producing all moving and unmoving beings. By its rule this manifestation is created and annihilated again and again."

TEXT 38

करोति विश्वस्थितिसंयमोदयं
यस्येप्सितं नेप्सितमीक्षितुर्गुणैः ।

माया यथायो भ्रमते तदाश्रयं
ग्राव्णो नमस्ते गुणकर्मसाक्षिणे ॥ ३८ ॥

karoti viśva-sthiti-saṁyamodayaṁ
yasyepsitaṁ nepsitam īkṣitur guṇaiḥ
māyā yathāyo bhramate tad-āśrayaṁ
grāvṇo namas te guṇa-karma-sākṣiṇe

karoti—performing; *viśva*—of the universe; *sthiti*—the maintenance; *saṁyama*—winding up; *udayam*—creation; *yasya*—of whom; *īpsitam*—desired; *na*—not; *īpsitam*—desired; *īkṣituḥ*—of the one glancing over; *guṇaiḥ*—with the modes of material nature; *māyā*—the material energy; *yathā*—as much as; *ayaḥ*—iron; *bhramate*—moves; *tat-āśrayam*—placed near that; *grāvṇaḥ*—a magnetic stone; *namaḥ*—my respectful obeisances; *te*—unto You; *guṇa-karma-sākṣiṇe*—the witness of the actions and reactions of material nature.

TRANSLATION

O Lord, You do not desire the creation, maintenance or annihilation of this material world, but You perform these activities for the conditioned souls by Your creative energy. Exactly as a piece of iron moves under the influence of a lodestone, inert matter moves when You glance over the total material energy.

PURPORT

Sometimes the question arises why the Supreme Lord has created this material world, which is so full of suffering for the living entities entrapped in it. The answer given herein is that the Supreme Personality of Godhead does not wish to create this material world just to inflict suffering on the living entities. The Supreme Lord creates this world only because the conditioned souls want to enjoy it.

The workings of nature are not going on automatically. It is only because the Lord glances over the material energy that it acts in wonderful ways, just as a lodestone causes a piece of iron to move here and there. Because materialistic scientists and so-called Sāṅkhya philosophers do not believe in God, they think that material nature is working without supervision. But that is not the fact. In *Caitanya-caritāmṛta* (*Ādi* 6.18–19) the creation of the material world is explained as follows:

yadyapi sāṅkhya māne 'pradhāna'—kāraṇa
jaḍa ha-ite kabhu nahe jagat-sṛjana

nija-sṛṣṭi-śakti prabhu sañcāre pradhāne
īśvarera śaktye tabe haye ta' nirmāṇe

"Atheistic Sāṅkhya philosophers think that the total material energy causes the cosmic manifestation, but they are wrong. Dead matter has no moving power, and therefore it cannot act independently. The Lord infuses the material ingredients with His own creative potency. Then, by the power of the Lord, matter moves and interacts." Sea waves are moved by the air, the air is created from ether, the ether is produced by the agitation of the three modes of material nature, and the three modes of material nature interact due to the Supreme Lord's glance over the total material energy. Therefore the background of all natural occurrences is the Supreme Personality of Godhead, as confirmed in *Bhagavad-gītā* (*mayādhyakṣeṇa prakṛtiḥ sūyate sa-carācaram*). This is also further explained in *Caitanya-caritāmṛta* (*Ādi* 5.59–61):

jagat-kāraṇa nahe prakṛti jaḍa-rūpā
śakti sañcāriyā tāre kṛṣṇa kare kṛpā

kṛṣṇa-śaktye prakṛti haya gauṇa kāraṇa
agni-śaktye lauha yaiche karaye jāraṇa

ataeva kṛṣṇa mūla-jagat-kāraṇa
prakṛti—kāraṇa yaiche ajā-gala-stana

"Because *prakṛti* [material nature] is dull and inert, it cannot actually be the cause of the material world. Lord Kṛṣṇa shows His mercy by infusing His energy into the dull, inert material nature. Thus *prakṛti*, by the energy of Lord Kṛṣṇa, becomes the secondary cause, just as iron becomes red-hot by the energy of fire. Therefore Lord Kṛṣṇa is the original cause of the cosmic manifestation. *Prakṛti* is like the nipples on the neck of a goat, for they cannot give any milk." Thus it is a great mistake on the part of the material scientists and philosophers to think that matter moves independently.

TEXT 39

प्रमथ्य दैत्यं प्रतिवारणं मृधे
यो मां रसाया जगदादिसूकरः ।

कृत्वाग्रदंष्ट्रे निरगादुदन्वतः
क्रीडन्निवेभः प्रणतास्मि तं विभुमिति ॥३९॥

pramathya daityaṁ prativāraṇaṁ mṛdhe
yo māṁ rasāyā jagad-ādi-sūkaraḥ
kṛtvāgra-daṁṣṭre niragād udanvataḥ
krīḍann ivebhaḥ praṇatāsmi taṁ vibhum iti

pramathya—after killing; *daityam*—the demon; *prativāraṇam*—most formidable opponent; *mṛdhe*—in the fight; *yaḥ*—He who; *mām*—me (the earth); *rasāyāḥ*—fallen to the bottom of the universe; *jagat*—in this material world; *ādi-sūkaraḥ*—the original form of a boar; *kṛtvā*—keeping it; *agra-daṁṣṭre*—on the end of the tusk; *niragāt*—came out of the water; *udanvataḥ*—from the Garbhodaka Ocean; *krīḍan*—playing; *iva*—like; *ibhaḥ*—elephant; *praṇatā asmi*—I bow down; *tam*—to Him; *vibhum*—the Supreme Lord; *iti*—thus.

TRANSLATION

My Lord, as the original boar within this universe, You fought and killed the great demon Hiraṇyakṣa. Then You lifted me [the earth] from the Garbhodaka Ocean on the end of Your tusk, exactly as a sporting elephant plucks a lotus flower from the water. I bow down before You.

Thus end the Bhaktivedanta purports of the Fifth Canto, Eighteenth Chapter, of the Śrīmad-Bhāgavatam, *entitled "The Prayers Offered to the Lord by the Residents of Jambūdvīpa."*

CHAPTER NINETEEN

A Description of the Island of Jambūdvīpa

This chapter describes the glories of Bhārata-varṣa, and it also describes how Lord Rāmacandra is being worshiped in the tract of land known as Kimpuruṣa-varṣa. The inhabitants of Kimpuruṣa-varṣa are fortunate because they worship Lord Rāmacandra with His faithful servant Hanumān. Lord Rāmacandra exemplifies an incarnation of Godhead who descends for the mission of *paritrāṇāya sādhūnāṁ vināśāya ca duṣkṛtām*—protecting the devotees and destroying the miscreants. Lord Rāmacandra exhibits the actual purpose of an incarnation of the Supreme Personality of Godhead, and the devotees take the opportunity to offer loving transcendental service to Him. One should surrender fully to the Lord, forgetting one's so-called material happiness, opulence and education, which are not at all useful for pleasing the Lord. The Lord is pleased only by the process of surrender unto Him.

When Devarṣi Nārada descended to instruct Sārvaṇi Manu, he described the opulence of Bhārata-varṣa, India. Sārvaṇi Manu and the inhabitants of Bhārata-varṣa engage in devotional service to the Supreme Personality of Godhead, who is the origin of creation, maintenance and annihilation and who is always worshiped by self-realized souls. In the planet known as Bhārata-varṣa there are many rivers and mountains, as there are in other tracts of land, yet Bhārata-varṣa has special significance because in this tract of land there exists the Vedic principle of *varṇāśrama-dharma,* which divides society into four *varṇas* and four *āśramas.* Furthermore, Nārada Muni's opinion is that even if there is some temporary disturbance in the execution of the *varṇāśrama-dharma* principles, they can be revived at any moment. The effect of adhering to the institution of *varṇāśrama* is gradual elevation to the spiritual platform and liberation from material bondage. By following the principles of *varṇāśrama-dharma,* one gets the opportunity to associate with devotees. Such association gradually awakens one's dormant propensity to serve the Supreme Personality of Godhead and frees one from all the basic principles of sinful life. One then gets the opportunity to offer unalloyed devotional service to the Supreme Lord, Vāsudeva. Because of this opportunity, the inhabitants of Bhārata-varṣa are praised even in the heavenly planets. Even in the topmost planet of this universe, Brahmaloka, the position of Bhārata-varṣa is discussed with great relish.

All the conditioned living entities are evolving within the universe in different planets and different species of life. Thus one may be elevated to Brahmaloka, but then one must again descend to earth, as confirmed in *Śrīmad Bhagavad-gītā* (*ābrahma-bhuvanāl lokāḥ punar āvartino'rjuna*). If those who live in Bhārata-varṣa rigidly follow the principles of *varṇāśrama-dharma* and develop their dormant Kṛṣṇa consciousness, they need not return to this material world after death. Any place where one cannot hear about the Supreme Personality of Godhead from realized souls, even if it be Brahmaloka, is not very congenial to the living entity. If one who has taken birth in the land of Bhārata-varṣa as a human being does not take advantage of the opportunity for spiritual elevation, his position is certainly the most miserable. In the land known as Bhāratavarṣa, even if one is a *sarva-kāma-bhakta,* a devotee seeking the fulfillment of some material desire, he is freed from all material desires by his association with devotees, and ultimately he becomes a pure devotee and returns home, back to Godhead, without difficulty.

At the end of this chapter, Śrī Śukadeva Gosvāmī describes to Mahārāja Parīkṣit the eight sub-islands within the island of Jambūdvīpa.

TEXT 1

श्रीशुक उवाच

किम्पुरुषे वर्षे भगवन्तमादिपुरुषं लक्ष्मणाग्रजं सीताभिरामं रामं तच्चरणसं-
निकर्षाभिरतः परमभागवतो हनुमान् सह किम्पुरुषैरविरतभक्तिरुपास्ते ॥१॥

śrī-śuka uvāca

kimpuruṣe varṣe bhagavantam ādi-puruṣaṁ lakṣmaṇāgrajaṁ
sītābhirāmaṁ rāmaṁ tac-caraṇa-sannikarṣābhirataḥ parama-
bhāgavato hanumān saha kimpuruṣair avirata-bhaktir upāste.

śrī-śukaḥ uvāca—Śrī Śukadeva Gosvāmī continued to speak; *kimpuruṣe varṣe*—the tract of land known as Kimpuruṣa; *bhagavantam*—the Supreme Personality of Godhead; *ādi-puruṣam*—the original cause of all causes; *lakṣmaṇa-agra-jam*—the elder brother of Lakṣmaṇa; *sītā-abhirāmam*—who is very pleasing to mother Sītā, or who is the husband of Sītādevī; *rāmam*—Lord Rāmacandra; *tat-caraṇa-sannikarṣa-abhirataḥ*—one always engaged in service at the lotus feet of Lord Rāmacandra; *parama-bhāgavataḥ*—the great devotee celebrated throughout the universe; *hanumān*—His Grace

Hanumānjī; *saha*—with; *kimpuruṣaiḥ*—the inhabitants of the tract of land known as Kimpuruṣa; *avirata*—continuous; *bhaktiḥ*—who possesses devotional service; *upāste*—worships.

TRANSLATION

Śrīla Śukadeva Gosvāmī said: My dear King, in Kimpuruṣa-varṣa the great devotee Hanumān is always engaged with the inhabitants of that land in devotional service to Lord Rāmacandra, the elder brother of Lakṣmaṇa and dear husband of Sītādevī.

TEXT 2

आर्ष्टिषेणेन सह गन्धर्वैरनुगीयमानां परमकल्याणीं भर्तृभगवत्कथां समुपशृणोति स्वयं चेदं गायति ॥२॥

ārṣṭiṣeṇena saha gandharvair anugīyamānāṁ parama-kalyāṇīṁ bhartṛ-bhagavat-kathāṁ samupaśṛṇoti svayaṁ cedaṁ gāyati.

ārṣṭi-ṣeṇena—Ārṣṭiṣeṇa, the chief personality of Kimpuruṣa-varṣa; *saha*—with; *gandharvaiḥ*—by a company of Gandharvas; *anugīyamānām*—being chanted; *parama-kalyāṇīm*—most auspicious; *bhartṛ-bhagavat-kathām*—the glories of his master, who is also the Supreme Personality of Godhead; *samupaśṛṇoti*—he hears with great attention; *svayam ca*—and personally; *idam*—this; *gāyati*—chants.

TRANSLATION

A host of Gandharvas is always engaged in chanting the glories of Lord Rāmacandra. That chanting is always extremely auspicious. Hanumānjī and Ārṣṭiṣeṇa, the chief person in Kimpuruṣa-varṣa, constantly hear those glories with complete attention. Hanumān chants the following mantras.

PURPORT

In the *Purāṇas* there are two different opinions concerning Lord Rāmacandra. In the *Laghu-bhāgavatāmṛta* (5.34–36) this is confirmed in the description of the incarnation of Manu.

vāsudevādi-rūpāṇām
avatārāḥ prakīrtitāḥ
viṣṇu-dharmottare rāma-
lakṣmaṇādyāḥ kramādamī

pādme tu rāmo bhagavān
nārāyaṇa itīritaḥ
śeṣaś cakraṁ ca śaṅkhaś ca
kramāt syur lakṣmaṇādayaḥ

madhya-deśa-sthitāyodhyā-
pure'sya vasatiḥ smṛtā
mahā-vaikuṇṭhaloke ca
rāghavedrasya kīrtitā

The *Viṣṇu-dharmottara* describes that Lord Rāmacandra and His brothers—Lakṣmaṇa, Bharata and Śatrughna—are incarnations of Vāsudeva, Saṅkarṣaṇa, Pradyumna and Aniruddha respectively. The *Padma Purāṇa,* however, says that Lord Rāmacandra is an incarnation of Nārāyaṇa and that the other three brothers are incarnations of Śeṣa, Cakra and Śaṅkha. Therefore Śrīla Baladeva Vidyābhūṣaṇa has concluded, *tad idaṁ kalpa-bhedenaiva sambhāvyam.* In other words, these opinions are not contradictory. In some millenniums Lord Rāmacandra and His brothers appear as incarnations of Vāsudeva, Saṅkarṣaṇa, Pradyumna and Aniruddha, and in other millenniums They appear as incarnations of Nārāyaṇa, Śeṣa, Cakra and Śaṅkha. The residence of Lord Rāmacandra on this planet is Ayodhyā. Ayodhyā City is still existing in the district of Hyderabad, which is situated on the northern side of Uttar Pradesh.

TEXT 3

ॐ नमो भगवते उत्तमश्लोकाय नम आर्यलक्षणशीलव्रताय नम उपशिक्षितात्मन उपासितलोकाय नमः साधुवादनिकषणाय नमो ब्रह्मण्यदेवाय महापुरुषाय महाराजाय नम इति ॥३॥

oṁ namo bhagavate uttamaślokāya nama ārya-lakṣaṇa-śīla-vratāya nama upaśikṣitātmana upāsita-lokāya namaḥ sādhu-vāda-nikaṣaṇāya namo brahmaṇya-devāya mahā-puruṣāya mahā-rājāya nama iti.

om—O my Lord; *namaḥ*—my respectful obeisances; *bhagavate*—unto the Supreme Personality of Godhead; *uttama-ślokāya*—who is always worshiped with selected verses; *namaḥ*—my respectful obeisances; *ārya-lakṣaṇa-śīla-vratāya*—who possesses all the good qualities of advanced personalities; *namaḥ*—my respectful obeisances; *upaśikṣita-ātmane*—unto

You whose senses are under control; *upāsita-lokāya*—who is always remembered and worshiped by all the different classes of living entities; *namaḥ*—my respectful obeisances; *sādhu-vāda-nikaṣaṇāya*—to the Lord, who is like a stone for examining all the good qualities of a *sādhu; namaḥ*—my respectful obeisances; *brahmaṇya-devāya*—who is worshiped by the most qualified *brāhmaṇas; mahā-puruṣāya*—unto the Supreme Lord, who is worshiped by the *Puruṣa-sūkta* because of being the cause of this material creation; *mahā-rājāya*—unto the supreme king, or the king of all kings; *namaḥ* —my respectful obeisances; *iti*—thus.

TRANSLATION

Let me please Your Lordship by chanting the bīja-mantra oṁkāra. I wish to offer my respectful obeisances unto the Personality of Godhead, who is the best among the most highly elevated personalities. Your Lordship is the reservoir of all the good qualities of Āryans, people who are advanced. Your character and behavior are always consistent, and You always control Your senses and mind. Acting just like an ordinary human being, You exhibit exemplary character to teach others how to behave. There is a touchstone that can be used to examine the quality of gold, but You are like a touchstone that can verify all good qualities. You are worshiped by brāhmaṇas who are the foremost of all devotees. You, the Supreme Person, are the King of kings, and therefore I offer my respectful obeisances unto You.

TEXT 4

यत्तद्विशुद्धानुभवमात्रमेकं
स्वतेजसा ध्वस्तगुणव्यवस्थम् ।
प्रत्यक् प्रशान्तं सुधियोपलम्भनं
ह्यनामरूपं निरहं प्रपद्ये ॥ ४ ॥

yat tad viśuddhānubhava-mātram ekaṁ
sva-tejasā dhvasta-guṇa-vyavastham
pratyak praśāntaṁ sudhiyopalambhanaṁ
hy anāma-rūpaṁ nirahaṁ prapadye

yat—which; *tat*—to that supreme truth; *viśuddha*—transcendentally pure, without contamination by material nature; *anubhava*—experience; *mātram*—that *sac-cid-ānanda* transcendental body; *ekam*—the one; *sva-*

tejasā—by His own spiritual potency; *dhvasta*—vanquished; *guṇa-vyavastham*—the influence of the modes of material nature; *pratyak*—transcendental, not to be seen with material eyes; *praśāntam*—undisturbed by material agitation; *sudhiyā*—by Kṛṣṇa consciousness, or purified consciousness, uncontaminated by material desires, fruitive activities and speculative philosophy; *upalambhanam*—who can be achieved; *hi*—indeed; *anāma-rūpam*—without a material name and form; *niraham*—without a material ego; *prapadye*—let me offer my respectful obeisances.

TRANSLATION

The Lord, whose pure form [sac-cid-ānanda-vigraha] is uncontaminated by the modes of material nature, can be perceived by pure consciousness. In the Vedānta He is described as being one without a second. Because of His spiritual potency, He is untouched by the contamination of material nature, and because He is not subjected to material vision, He is known as transcendental. He has no material activities, nor has He a material form or name. Only in pure consciousness, Kṛṣṇa consciousness, can one perceive the transcendental form of the Lord. Let us be firmly fixed at the lotus feet of Lord Rāmacandra, and let us offer our respectful obeisances unto those transcendental lotus feet.

PURPORT

The Supreme Personality of Godhead, Kṛṣṇa, appears in various expansions, as stated in the *Brahma-saṁhitā* (5.39):

rāmādi-mūrtiṣu kalā-niyamena tiṣṭhan
nānāvatāram akarod bhuvaneṣu kintu
kṛṣṇaḥ svayaṁ samabhavat paramaḥ pumān yo
govindam ādi-puruṣaṁ tam ahaṁ bhajāmi

"I worship the Supreme Personality of Godhead, Govinda, who is always situated in various incarnations such as Rāma, Nṛsiṁha and many subincarnations as well, but who is the original Personality of Godhead known as Kṛṣṇa and who incarnates personally also." Kṛṣṇa, who is *viṣṇu-tattva,* has expanded Himself in many Viṣṇu forms, of which Lord Rāmacandra is one. We know that the *viṣṇu-tattva* is carried by the transcendental bird Garuḍa and is equipped with different types of weapons in four hands. Therefore we may doubt whether Lord Rāmacandra could be in the same category, since He was carried by Hanumān, not by Garuḍa, and had neither four hands nor the *śaṅkha, cakra, gadā* and *padma.* Consequently this verse clarifies that Rāmacandra is as good as Kṛṣṇa (*rāmādi-mūrtiṣu kalā*). Although Kṛṣṇa is the original Supreme Personality of Godhead, Rāmacandra is not different from Him. Rāmacandra is unaffected by the modes of material nature, and therefore He is *praśānta,* never disturbed by those modes.

Unless one is saturated with love for the Supreme Personality of Godhead, one cannot appreciate the transcendental value of Lord Rāmacandra; one cannot see Him with material eyes. Because demons like Rāvaṇa have no spiritual vision, they consider Lord Rāmacandra an ordinary *kṣatriya* king. Rāvaṇa therefore attempted to kidnap Lord Rāmacandra's eternal consort, Sītādevī. Actually, however, Rāvaṇa could not carry off Sītādevī in her original form. As soon as she was touched by Rāvaṇa's hands, she gave him a material form, but she maintained her original form beyond his vision. Therefore in this verse the words *pratyak praśāntam* indicate that Lord Rāmacandra and His potency, the goddess Sītā, keep themselves aloof from the influence of the material energy.

In the *Upaniṣads* it is said: *yam evaiṣa vṛṇute tena labhyaḥ* (*Kaṭha Upaniṣad* 1.2.23.) The Supreme Lord, Paramātmā, the Personality of Godhead, can be seen or perceived only by persons who are saturated with devotional service. As stated in the *Brahma-saṁhitā* (5.38):

premāñjana-cchurita-bhakti-vilocanena
santaḥ sadaiva hṛdayeṣu vilokayanti
yaṁ śyāmasundaram acintya-guṇa-svarūpaṁ
govindam ādi-puruṣaṁ tam ahaṁ bhajāmi

"I worship the primeval Lord, Govinda, who is always seen by the devotee whose eyes are anointed with the pulp of love. He is seen in His eternal form of Śyāmasundara, situated within the heart of the devotee." Similarly, in the *Chāndogya Upaniṣad* it is stated, *etās tisro devatā anena jīvena.* In this verse of the *Chāndogya Upaniṣad* the word *anena* is used to distinguish the *ātmā* and Paramātmā as two separate identities. The words *tisro devatā* indicate that the body of the living entity is made of three material elements—fire, earth and water. Although the Paramātmā enters the heart of the *jīvātmā,* who is influenced and designated by a material body, the Paramātmā has nothing to do with the *jīvātmā's* body. Because the Paramātmā has no material connections, He is described here as *anāma-rūpaṁ niraham.* The Paramātmā has no material identity, whereas the *jīvātmā* does. The *jīvātmā* may introduce himself as an Indian, American, German and so on, but the Paramātmā has no such material designations, and therefore He has no material name. The *jīvātmā* is different from his name, but the Paramātmā is not; His name and He Himself are one and the same. This is the meaning of *niraham,* which means "without material designations." This word cannot possibly be twisted to mean that the Paramātmā has no *ahaṅkāra,* no "I-ness" or identity. He has His transcendental identity as the Supreme. This is the explanation given by Śrīla Jīva Gosvāmī. According to another interpretation, given by Viśvanātha Cakravartī Ṭhākura, *niraham* means *nirniścayena aham. Niraham* does not mean that the Supreme Lord has no identity. Rather, the stress given by the word *aham* proves strongly that He does have His personal identity because *nir* not only means "negative" but also means "strong ascertainment."

TEXT 5

मर्त्यावतारस्त्विह मर्त्यशिक्षणं
रक्षोवधायैव न केवलं विभोः ।
कुतोऽन्यथा स्याद्रमतः स्व आत्मनः
सीताकृतानि व्यसनानीश्वरस्य ॥५॥

martyāvatāras tv iha martya-śikṣaṇaṁ
rakṣo-vadhāyaiva na kevalaṁ vibhoḥ
kuto 'nyathā syād ramataḥ sva ātmanaḥ
sītā-kṛtāni vyasanānīśvarasya

martya—as a human being; *avatāraḥ*—whose incarnation; *tu*—however; *iha*—in the material world; *martya-śikṣaṇam*—for teaching all the living entities, especially human beings; *rakṣaḥ-vadhāya*—to kill the demon Rāvaṇa; *eva*—certainly; *na*—not; *kevalam*—only; *vibhoḥ*—of the Supreme Personality of Godhead; *kutaḥ*—from where; *anyathā*—otherwise; *syāt*—there would be; *ramataḥ*—of one enjoying; *sve*—in Himself; *ātmanaḥ*—the spiritual identity of the universe; *sītā*—of the wife of Lord Rāmacandra; *kṛtāni*—appearing due to the separation; *vyasanāni*—all the miseries; *īśvarasya*—of the Supreme Personality of Godhead.

TRANSLATION

It was ordained that Rāvaṇa, chief of the Rākṣasas, could not be killed by anyone but a man, and for this reason Lord Rāmacandra, the Supreme Personality of Godhead, appeared in the form of a human being. Lord

Rāmacandra's mission, however, was not only to kill Rāvaṇa but also to teach mortal beings that material happiness centered around sex life or centered around one's wife is the cause of many miseries. He is the self-sufficient Supreme Personality of Godhead, and nothing is lamentable for Him. Therefore why else could He be subjected to tribulations by the kidnapping of mother Sītā?

PURPORT

When the Lord appears in this universe in the form of a human being, He has two purposes, as stated in *Bhagavad-gītā* (4.9) —*paritrāṇāya sādhūnāṁ vināśāya ca duṣkṛtām:* to destroy the demons and protect the devotees. To protect the devotees, the Lord not only satisfies them by His personal presence but also teaches them so that they will not fall down from devotional service. By His personal example, Lord Rāmacandra taught the devotees that it is better not to enter married life, which is certainly followed by many tribulations. As confirmed in *Śrīmad-Bhāgavatam* (7.9.45):

yan maithunādi-gṛhamedhi-sukhaṁ hi tucchaṁ
kaṇḍūyanena karayor iva duḥkha-duḥkham
tṛpyanti neha kṛpaṇā bahu-duḥkha-bhājaḥ
kaṇḍūtivan manasijaṁ viṣaheta-dhīraḥ

Kṛpaṇas, those who are not advanced in spiritual knowledge and who are therefore just the opposite of *brāhmaṇas,* generally take to family life, which is a concession for sex. Thus they enjoy sex again and again, although that sex is followed by many tribulations. This is a warning to devotees. To teach this lesson to devotees and to human society in general, Lord Śrī Rāmacandra, although the Supreme Personality of Godhead Himself, underwent a series of tribulations because He accepted a wife, mother Sītā. Lord Rāmacandra underwent these austerities, of course, only to instruct us; actually He never has any reason to lament for anything.

Another aspect of the Lord's instructions is that one who accepts a wife must be a faithful husband and give her full protection. Human society is divided into two classes of men—those who strictly follow the religious principles and those who are devotees. By His personal example, Lord Rāmacandra wanted to instruct both of them how to fully adopt the discipline of the religious system and how to be a beloved and dutiful husband. Otherwise He had no reason to undergo apparent tribulations. One who strictly follows religious principles must not neglect to provide all facilities for the complete protection of his wife. There may be some suffering because of this, but one must nevertheless endure it. That is the duty of a faithful husband. By His personal example, Lord Rāmacandra demonstrated this duty. Lord Rāmacandra could have produced hundreds and thousands of Sītās from His pleasure energy, but just to show the duty of a faithful husband, He not only rescued Sītā from the hands of Rāvaṇa but also killed Rāvaṇa and all the members of his family.

Another aspect of the teachings of Lord Rāmacandra is that although Lord Viṣṇu, the Supreme Personality of Godhead, and His devotees may apparently suffer from material tribulations, they have nothing to do with such tribulations. They are *mukta-puruṣas,* liberated persons, under all circumstances. It is therefore said in the *Caitanya-bhāgavata:*

yata dekha vaiṣṇavera vyavahāra duḥkha
niścaya jāniha tāhā paramānanda-sukha

A Vaiṣṇava is always firmly situated in transcendental bliss because of engagement in devotional service. Although he may appear to suffer material pains, his position is called transcendental bliss in separation (*viraha*). The emotions a lover and beloved feel when separated from one another are actually very blissful, although apparently painful. Therefore the separation of Lord Rāmacandra from Sītādevī, as well as the consequent tribulation they suffered, is but another display of transcendental bliss. That is the opinion of Śrīla Viśvanātha Cakravartī Ṭhākura.

TEXT 6

न वै स आत्माऽऽत्मवतां सुहृत्तमः
सक्तस्त्रिलोक्यां भगवान् वासुदेवः ।
न स्त्रीकृतं कश्मलमश्नुवीत
न लक्ष्मणं चापि विहातुमर्हति ॥६॥

na vai sa ātmātmavatāṁ suhṛttamaḥ
saktas tri-lokyāṁ bhagavān vāsudevaḥ
na strī-kṛtaṁ kaśmalam aśnuvīta
na lakṣmaṇaṁ cāpi vihātum arhati

na—not; *vai*—indeed; *saḥ*—He; *ātmā*—the Supreme Soul; *ātmavatām*—of the self-realized souls; *suhṛt-tamaḥ*—the best friend; *saktaḥ*—attached; *tri-lokyām*—to anything within the three worlds; *bhagavān*—the

Supreme Personality of Godhead; *vāsudevaḥ*—the all-pervading Lord; *na*—not; *strī-kṛtam*—obtained because of His wife; *kaśmalam*—sufferings of separation; *aśnuvīta*—would obtain; *na*—not; *lakṣmaṇam*—His younger brother Lakṣmaṇa; *ca*—also; *api*—certainly; *vihātum*—to give up; *arhati*—be able.

TRANSLATION

Since Lord Śrī Rāmacandra is the Supreme Personality of Godhead, Vāsudeva, He is not attached to anything in this material world. He is the most beloved Supersoul of all self-realized souls, and He is their very intimate friend. He is full of all opulences. Therefore He could not possibly have suffered because of separation from His wife, nor could He have given up His wife and Lakṣmaṇa, His younger brother. To give up either would have been absolutely impossible.

PURPORT

In defining the Supreme Personality of Godhead, we say that He is full in all six opulences—wealth, fame, strength, influence, beauty and renunciation. He is called renounced because He is not attached to anything in this material world; He is specifically attached to the spiritual world and the living entities there. The affairs of the material world take place under the superintendence of Durgādevī (*sṛṣṭi-sthiti-pralaya-sādhana-śaktir ekā/ chāyeva yasya bhuvanāni bibharti durgā*). Everything is going on under the strict rules and regulations of the material energy, represented by Durgā. Therefore the Lord is completely detached and need not give attention to the material world. Sītādevī belongs to the spiritual world. Similarly, Lord Lakṣmaṇa, Rāmacandra's younger brother, is a manifestation of Saṅkarṣaṇa, and Lord Rāmacandra Himself is Vāsudeva, the Supreme Personality of Godhead.

Since the Lord is always spiritually qualified, He is attached to servants who always render transcendental loving service unto Him. He is attached to the truth in life, not to brahminical qualities. Indeed, He is never attached to any material qualities. Although He is the Supersoul of all living entities, He is specifically manifest to those who are self-realized, and He is especially dear to the hearts of His transcendental devotees. Because Lord Rāmacandra descended to teach human society how dutiful a king should be, He apparently gave up the company of mother Sītā and Lakṣmaṇa. Factually, however, He could not have given them up. One should therefore learn about the activities of Lord Rāmacandra from a self-realized soul. Then one can understand the transcendental activities of the Lord.

TEXT 7

न जन्म नूनं महतो न सौभगं
न वाङ् न बुद्धिर्नाकृतिस्तोषहेतुः ।
तैर्यद्विसृष्टानपि नो वनौकस-
श्चकार सख्ये बत लक्ष्मणाग्रजः ॥ ७ ॥

na janma nūnaṁ mahato na saubhagaṁ
na vāṅ na buddhir nākṛtis toṣa-hetuḥ
tair yad visṛṣṭān api no vanaukasaś
cakāra sakhye bata lakṣmaṇāgrajaḥ

na—not; *janma*—birth in a very polished, aristocratic family; *nūnam*—indeed; *mahataḥ*—of the Supreme Personality of Godhead; *na*—nor; *saubhagam*—great fortune; *na*—nor; *vāk*—an elegant manner of speaking; *na*—nor; *buddhiḥ*—sharpness of intelligence; *na*—not; *ākṛtiḥ*—features of the body; *toṣa-hetuḥ*—the cause of pleasure to the Lord; *taiḥ*—by all those above-mentioned qualities; *yat*—because; *visṛṣṭān*—rejected; *api*—although; *naḥ*—us; *vana-okasaḥ*—the inhabitants of the forest; *cakāra*—accepted; *sakhye*—in friendship; *bata*—alas; *lakṣmaṇa-agra-jaḥ*—Lord Śrī Rāmacandra, the elder brother of Lakṣmaṇa.

TRANSLATION

One cannot establish a friendship with the Supreme Lord Rāmacandra on the basis of material qualities such as one's birth in an aristocratic family, one's personal beauty, one's eloquence, one's sharp intelligence or one's superior race or nation. None of these qualifications is actually a prerequisite for friendship with Lord Śrī Rāmacandra. Otherwise how is it possible that although we uncivilized inhabitants of the forest have not taken noble births, although we have no physical beauty and although we cannot speak like gentlemen, Lord Rāmacandra has nevertheless accepted us as friends?

PURPORT

In a prayer to Kṛṣṇa expressing her feelings, Śrīmatī Kuntīdevī called Him *akiñcana-gocara.* The prefix *a* means "not," and *kiñcana* "something of this material world." One may be very proud of his prestigious position, material wealth, beauty, education and so on, but although these are certainly good qualifications in material dealings, they are not necessary for achieving friendship with the Supreme Personality of Godhead. One who possesses all these material qualities is expected to become a devotee, and when he actually does, the qualities are properly utilized. Those who are puffed up by a high birth, wealth, education and personal beauty (*janmaiśvarya-śruta-śrī*) unfortunately do not care for developing Kṛṣṇa consciousness, nor does the Supreme Personality of Godhead care about all these material qualifications. The Supreme Lord is achieved by devotion (*bhaktyā mām abhijānāti*). One's devotion and sincere desire to serve the Supreme Personality of Godhead are the only qualifications. Rūpa Gosvāmī has also said that the price for achieving God's favor is simply one's sincere eagerness to have it (*laulyam ekaṁ mūlyam*). In the *Caitanya-bhāgavata* it is said:

kholāvecā sevakera dekha bhāgya-sīmā
brahmā śiva kāṅde yāra dekhiyā mahimā

dhane jane pāṇḍitye kṛṣṇa nāhi pāi
kevala bhaktira vaśa caitanya-gosāñi

"Behold the great fortune of the devotee Kholāvecā. Lord Brahmā and Śiva shed tears upon seeing his greatness. One cannot attain Lord Kṛṣṇa by any amount of wealth, followers, or learning. Śrī Caitanya Mahāprabhu is controlled only by pure devotion." Lord Śrī Caitanya Mahāprabhu had a very sincere devotee whose name was Kholāvecā Śrīdhara and whose only business was to sell pots made of the skin of banana trees. Whatever income he had, he used fifty percent for the worship of mother Ganges, and with the other fifty percent he provided for his necessities. On the whole, he was so very poor that he lived in a cottage that had a broken roof with many holes in it. He could not afford brass utensils, and therefore he drank water from an iron pot. Nevertheless, he was a great devotee of Lord Śrī Caitanya Mahāprabhu. He is a typical example of how a poor man with no material possessions can become a most exalted devotee of the Lord. The conclusion is that one cannot attain shelter at the lotus feet of Lord Kṛṣṇa or Śrī Caitanya Gosāñi through material opulence; that shelter is attainable only by pure devotional service.

anyābhilāṣitā-śūnyaṁ
jñāna-karmādy-anāvṛtam
ānukūlyena kṛṣṇānu-
śīlanaṁ bhaktir uttamā

"One should render transcendental loving service to the Supreme Lord Kṛṣṇa favorably and without desire for material profit or gain through fruitive activities or philosophical speculation. That is called pure devotional service."

TEXT 8

सुरोऽसुरो वाप्यथ वानरो नरः
सर्वात्मना यः सुकृतज्ञमुत्तमम् ।
भजेत रामं मनुजाकृतिं हरिं
य उत्तराननयत्कोसलान्दिवमिति ॥ ८ ॥

suro 'suro vāpy atha vānaro naraḥ
sarvātmanā yaḥ sukṛtajñam uttamam
bhajeta rāmaṁ manujākṛtiṁ hariṁ
ya uttarān anayat kosalān divam iti

suraḥ—demigod; *asuraḥ*—demon; *vā api*—or; *atha*—therefore; *vā*—or; *anaraḥ*—other than a human being (bird, beast, animal and so on); *naraḥ*—a human being; *sarva-ātmanā*—wholeheartedly; *yaḥ*—who; *su-kṛtajñam*—easily made grateful; *uttamam*—most highly elevated; *bhajeta*—should worship; *rāmam*—Lord Rāmacandra; *manuja-ākṛtim*—appearing as a human being; *harim*—the Supreme Personality of Godhead; *yaḥ*—who; *uttarān*—of northern India; *anayat*—brought back; *kosalān*—the inhabitants of Kosala-deśa, Ayodhyā; *divam*—to the spiritual world, Vaikuṇṭha; *iti*—thus.

TRANSLATION

Therefore, whether one is a demigod or a demon, a man or a creature other than man, such as a beast or bird, everyone should worship Lord Rāmacandra, the Supreme Personality of Godhead, who appears on this earth just like a human being. There is no need of great austerities or penances to worship the Lord, for He accepts even a small service offered by His devotee. Thus He is satisfied, and as soon as He is satisfied, the devotee is successful. Indeed, Lord Śrī Rāmacandra brought all the devotees of Ayodhyā back home, back to Godhead [Vaikuṇṭha].

PURPORT

Lord Śrī Rāmacandra is so kind and merciful to His devotees that He is very easily satisfied by a little service rendered by anyone, human or not. This is the special advantage of worshiping Lord Rāmacandra, and there is the same advantage in worshiping Lord Śrī Caitanya Mahāprabhu. Lord Kṛṣṇa and Lord Rāmacandra, in the manner of *kṣatriyas,* sometimes showed Their mercy by killing *asuras,* but Lord Śrī Caitanya Mahāprabhu awarded love of God without difficulty even to the *asuras.* All the incarnations of the Supreme Personality of Godhead—but especially Lord Rāmacandra, Lord Kṛṣṇa and, later, Lord Śrī Caitanya Mahāprabhu—delivered many of the living entities present before Them, indeed almost all of them. Śrī Caitanya Mahāprabhu is therefore represented in the six-armed form of *ṣaḍ-bhūja-mūrti,* which is a combination of Lord Rāmacandra, Lord Kṛṣṇa and Lord Śrī Caitanya Mahāprabhu. The best purpose of human life can be fulfilled by worshiping the *ṣaḍ-bhūja-mūrti,* the form of the Lord with six arms—two arms of Rāmacandra, two arms of Kṛṣṇa and two arms of Śrī Caitanya Mahāprabhu.

TEXT 9

भारतेऽपि वर्षे भगवान्नरनारायणाख्य आकल्पान्तमुपचितधर्मज्ञानवैराग्यै-
श्वर्योपशमोपरमात्मोपलम्भनमनुग्रहायात्मवतामनुकम्पया तपोऽव्यक्तगतिश्चरति ॥९॥

bhārate 'pi varṣe bhagavān nara-nārāyaṇākhya ākalpāntam upacita-
dharma-jñāna-vairāgyaiśvaryopaśamoparamātmopalambhanam
anugrahāyātmavatām anukampayā tapo 'vyakta-gatiś carati.

bhārate—in Bhārata; *api*—also; *varṣe*—the tract of land; *bhagavān*—the Supreme Personality of Godhead; *nara-nārāyaṇa-ākhyaḥ*—known as Nara-Nārāyaṇa; *ā-kalpa-antam*—up to the end of the millennium; *upacita*—increasing; *dharma*—religion; *jñāna*—knowledge; *vairāgya*—renunciation or nonattachment; *aiśvarya*—mystic opulences; *upaśama*—control of the senses; *uparama*—freedom from false ego; *ātma-upalambhanam*—self-realization; *anugrahāya*—to show favor; *ātma-vatām*—unto persons interested in self-realization; *anukampayā*—by causeless mercy; *tapaḥ*—austerities; *avyakta-gatiḥ*—whose glories are inconceivable; *carati*—executes.

TRANSLATION

[Śukadeva Gosvāmī continued:] The glories of the Supreme Personality of Godhead are inconceivable. He has appeared in the form of Nara-Nārāyaṇa in the land of Bhārata-varṣa, at the place known as Badarikāśrama, to favor His devotees by teaching them religion, knowledge, renunciation, spiritual power, sense control and freedom from false ego. He is advanced in the opulence of spiritual assets, and He

engages in executing austerity until the end of this millennium. This is the process of self-realization.

PURPORT

People in India may visit the temple of Nara-Nārāyaṇa at Badarikāśrama just to learn how the Supreme Personality of Godhead in His incarnation as Nara-Nārāyaṇa engages in austerities to teach the people of the world how to achieve self-realization. It is impossible to realize oneself simply by absorbing oneself in speculation and material activities. One must be very serious about self-realization and the practice of austerity. Unfortunately, the people of this age of Kali do not even know the meaning of austerity. Under these circumstances, the Lord has appeared as Śrī Caitanya Mahāprabhu to bestow upon the fallen souls the easiest method of self-realization, technically called *ceto-darpaṇa-mārjanam,* cleansing of the dirt from the core of one's heart. This method is extremely simple. Anyone can chant the glorious *kṛṣṇa-saṅkīrtana*—Hare Kṛṣṇa, Hare Kṛṣṇa, Kṛṣṇa Kṛṣṇa, Hare Hare/ Hare Rāma, Hare Rāma, Rāma Rāma, Hare Hare. In this age there are different forms of so-called advanced scientific knowledge, such as anthropology, Marxism, Freudianism, nationalism and industrialism, but if we work very hard under their guidance instead of adopting the process practiced by Nara-Nārāyaṇa, we shall waste our valuable human form of life. Thus we shall certainly be cheated and misled.

TEXT 10

तं भगवान्नारदो वर्णाश्रमवतीभिर्भारतीभिः प्रजाभिर्भगवत्प्रोक्ताभ्यां सांख्य-योगाभ्यां भगवदनुभावोपवर्णनं सावर्णेरुपदेक्ष्यमाणः परमभक्तिभावेनोपसरति इदं चाभिगृणाति ॥१०॥

taṁ bhagavān nārado varṇāśramavatībhir bhāratībhiḥ prajābhir
bhagavat-proktābhyāṁ sāṅkhya-yogābhyāṁ bhagavad-
anubhāvopavarṇanaṁ sāvarṇer upadekṣyamāṇaḥ parama-bhakti-
bhāvenopasarati idaṁ cābhigṛṇāti.

tam—Him (Nara-Nārāyaṇa); *bhagavān*—the most powerful saintly person; *nāradaḥ*—the great sage Nārada; *varṇa-āśrama-vatībhiḥ*—by followers of the institution of the four *varṇas* and four *āśramas; bhāratībhiḥ* —of the land known as Bhārata-varṣa (India); *prajābhiḥ*—who are the inhabitants; *bhagavat-proktābhyām*—which was stated by the Supreme Personality of Godhead; *sāṅkhya*—by the *sāṅkhya-yoga* system (the analytical study of material conditions); *yogābhyām*—by practice of the *yoga* system; *bhagavat-anubhāva-upavarṇanam*—which describes the process of God realization; *sāvarṇeḥ*—unto Sāvarṇi Manu; *upadekṣyamāṇaḥ*—instructing; *parama-bhakti-bhāvena*—in greatly ecstatic loving service to the Lord; *upasarati*—serves the Lord; *idam*—this; *ca*—and; *abhigṛṇāti*—chants.

TRANSLATION

In his own book, known as Nārada Pañcarātra, Bhagavān Nārada has very vividly described how to work to achieve the ultimate goal of life—devotion—through knowledge and through execution of the mystic yoga system. He has also described the glories of the Lord, the Supreme Personality of Godhead. The great sage Nārada instructed the tenets of this transcendental literature to Sāvarṇi Manu in order to teach those inhabitants of Bhārata-varṣa who strictly follow the principles of varṇāśrama-dharma how to achieve the devotional service of the Lord. Thus Nārada Muni, along with the other inhabitants of Bhārata-varṣa, always engages in the service of Nara-Nārāyaṇa, and he chants as follows.

PURPORT

Śrī Caitanya Mahāprabhu has clearly declared:

bhārata-bhūmite haila manuṣya-janma yāra
janma sārthaka kari' kara para-upakāra

The real success or fulfillment of the mission of human life can be achieved in India, Bhārata-varṣa, because in Bhārata-varṣa the purpose of life and the method for achieving success are evident. People should take advantage of the opportunity afforded by Bhārata-varṣa, and this is especially so for those who are following the principles of *varṇāśrama-dharma.* If we do not take to the principles of *varṇāśrama-dharma* by accepting the four social orders (*brāhmaṇa, kṣatriya, vaiśya* and *śūdra*) and the four orders of spiritual life (*brahmacārī, gṛhastha, vānaprastha* and *sannyāsa*), there can be no question of success in life. Unfortunately, because of the influence of Kali-yuga, everything is now being lost. The inhabitants of Bhārata-varṣa are gradually becoming degraded *mlecchas* and *yavanas.* How then will they teach others? Therefore, this Kṛṣṇa consciousness movement has been started not only for the inhabitants of Bhārata-varṣa but for all the people of the world, as announced by Śrī Caitanya Mahāprabhu. There is still time, and if the inhabitants of Bhārata-varṣa take this movement of Kṛṣṇa consciousness seriously, the entire world will be saved from gliding down to a hellish condition. The Kṛṣṇa consciousness movement follows the process of *pañcarātrika-vidhi* and that of *bhāgavata-vidhi* simultaneously, so that people can take advantage of the movement and make their lives successful.

TEXT 11

ॐ नमो भगवते उपशमशीलायोपरतानात्म्याय नमोऽकिञ्चनवित्ताय ऋषिऋषभाय नरनारायणाय परमहंसपरमगुरवे आत्मारामाधिपतये नमो नम इति ॥११॥

oṁ namo bhagavate upaśama-śīlāyoparatānātmyāya namo 'kiñcana-vittāya ṛṣi-ṛṣabhāya nara-nārāyaṇāya paramahaṁsa-parama-gurave ātmārāmādhipataye namo nama iti.

om—O Supreme Lord; *namaḥ*—my respectful obeisances; *bhagavate*—unto the Supreme Personality of Godhead; *upaśama-śīlāya*—who has mastered the senses; *uparata-anātmyāya*—having no attachment for this material world; *namaḥ*—my respectful obeisances; *akiñcana-vittāya*—unto the Supreme Personality of Godhead, who is the only asset of persons who have no material possessions; *ṛṣi-ṛṣabhāya*—the most exalted of saintly persons; *nara-nārāyaṇāya*—Nara-Nārāyaṇa; *paramahaṁsa-parama-gurave*—the most exalted spiritual master of all *paramahaṁsas,* liberated persons; *ātmārāma-adhipataye*—the best of self-realized persons; *namaḥ namaḥ*—my respectful obeisances again and again; *iti*—thus.

TRANSLATION

Let me offer my respectful obeisances unto Nara-Nārāyaṇa, the best of all saintly persons, the Supreme Personality of Godhead. He is the most self-controlled and self-realized, He is free from false prestige, and He is the asset of persons who have no material possessions. He is the spiritual master of all paramahaṁsas, who are the most exalted human beings, and He is the master of the self-realized. Let me offer my repeated obeisances at His lotus feet.

TEXT 12

गायति चेदम् :

कर्तास्य सर्गादिषु यो न बध्यते
न हन्यते देहगतोऽपि दैहिकैः ।

द्रष्टुर्न दृग्यस्य गुणैर्विदूष्यते
तस्मै नमोऽसक्तविविक्तसाक्षिणे ॥१२॥

gāyati cedam—
kartāsya sargādiṣu yo na badhyate
na hanyate deha-gato 'pi daihikaiḥ
draṣṭur na dṛg yasya guṇair vidūṣyate
tasmai namo 'sakta-vivikta-sākṣiṇe

gāyati—he sings; *ca*—and; *idam*—this; *kartā*—the executor; *asya*—of this cosmic manifestation; *sarga-ādiṣu*—of the creation, maintenance and destruction; *yaḥ*—one who; *na badhyate*—is not attached as the creator, master or proprietor; *na*—not; *hanyate*—is victimized; *deha-gataḥ api*—although appearing as a human being; *daihikaiḥ*—by bodily tribulations such as hunger, thirst and fatigue; *draṣṭuḥ*—of Him who is the seer of everything; *na*—not; *dṛk*—the power of vision; *yasya*—of whom; *guṇaiḥ*—by the material qualities; *vidūṣyate*—is polluted; *tasmai*—unto Him; *namaḥ*—my respectful obeisances; *asakta*—unto the Supreme Person, who is unattached; *vivikta*—without affection; *sākṣiṇe*—the witness of everything.

TRANSLATION

Nārada, the most powerful saintly sage, also worships Nara-Nārāyaṇa by chanting the following mantra: The Supreme Personality of Godhead is the master of the creation, maintenance and annihilation of this visible cosmic manifestation, yet He is completely free from false prestige. Although to the foolish He appears to have accepted a material body like us, He is unaffected by bodily tribulations like hunger, thirst and fatigue. Although He is the witness who sees everything, His senses are unpolluted by the objects He sees. Let me offer my respectful obeisances unto that unattached, pure witness of the world, the Supreme Soul, the Personality of Godhead.

PURPORT

The Supreme Personality of Godhead, Kṛṣṇa, is described as *sac-cid-ānanda-vigraha,* the body of eternity, transcendental bliss and full knowledge. Now in this verse He is more fully described. Kṛṣṇa is the creator of the entire cosmic manifestation, yet He is unattached to it. If we were to construct a very tall skyscraper, we would be very attached to it, but Kṛṣṇa is so renounced that although He has created everything, He is not attached to anything (*na badhyate*). Furthermore, although Kṛṣṇa has His transcendental form, *sac-cid-ānanda-vigraha,* He is not disturbed by the bodily necessities of life, which are called *daihika;* for example, He is never hungry, thirsty or fatigued (*na hanyate deha-gato'pi daihikaiḥ*). Then again, since everything is Kṛṣṇa's property, He sees everything and is present everywhere, but because His body is transcendental, He is above vision, the objects of vision and the process of vision. When we see someone beautiful, we are attracted. The sight of a beautiful woman immediately attracts a man, and the sight of a man naturally attracts a woman. Kṛṣṇa, however, is transcendental to all these faults. Although He is the seer of everything, He is not afflicted with faulty vision (*na dṛg yasya guṇair vidūṣyate*). Therefore, although He is the witness and seer, He is aloof from all affection for the activities He sees. He is always unattached and separate; He is only a witness.

TEXT 13

इदं हि योगेश्वर योगनैपुणं
हिरण्यगर्भो भगवाञ्जगाद यत् ।
यदन्तकाले त्वयि निर्गुणे मनो
भक्त्या दधीतोज्झितदुष्कलेवरः ॥१३॥

idaṁ hi yogeśvara yoga-naipuṇaṁ
hiraṇyagarbho bhagavāñ jagāda yat
yad anta-kāle tvayi nirguṇe mano
bhaktyā dadhītojjhita-duṣkalevaraḥ

idam—this; *hi*—certainly; *yoga-īśvara*—O my Lord, master of all mystic power; *yoga-naipuṇam*—the expert process of executing yogic principles; *hiraṇya-garbhaḥ*—Lord Brahmā; *bhagavān*—the most powerful; *jagāda*—spoke; *yat*—which; *yat*—which; *anta-kāle*—at the time of death; *tvayi*—in You; *nirguṇe*—the transcendence; *manaḥ*—the mind; *bhaktyā*—with a devotional attitude; *dadhīta*—one should place; *ujjhita-duṣkalevaraḥ*—having given up his identification with the material body.

TRANSLATION

O my Lord, master of all mystic yoga, this is the explanation of the yogic process spoken of by Lord Brahmā [Hiraṇyagarbha], who is self-realized. At the time of death, all yogīs give up the material body with full

detachment simply by placing their minds at Your lotus feet. That is the perfection of yoga.

PURPORT

Śrīla Madhvācārya says:

yasya samyag bhagavati
jñānaṁ bhaktis tathaiva ca
niścintas tasya mokṣaḥ syāt
sarva-pāpa-kṛto'pi tu

"For one who very seriously practices devotional service during his lifetime in order to understand the constitutional position of the Supreme Personality of Godhead, liberation from this material world is guaranteed, even if he has previously been addicted to sinful habits." This is also confirmed in *Bhagavad-gītā*:

api cet su-durācāro
bhajate mām ananya-bhāk
sādhur eva sa mantavyaḥ
samyag vyavasito hi saḥ

"Even if one commits the most abominable actions, if he is engaged in devotional service he is to be considered saintly because he is properly situated." (Bg. 9.30) The only purpose of life is to be fully absorbed in thoughts of Kṛṣṇa and His form, pastimes, activities and qualities. If one is able to think of Kṛṣṇa in this way, twenty-four hours a day, he is already liberated (*svarūpeṇa vyavasthitiḥ*). Whereas materialists are absorbed in material thoughts and activities, devotees, on the contrary, are always absorbed in thoughts of Kṛṣṇa and Kṛṣṇa's activities. Therefore they are already on the platform of liberation. One has to think of Kṛṣṇa with full absorption at the time of death. Then he will certainly return home, back to Godhead, without a doubt.

TEXT 14

यथैहिकामुष्मिककामलम्पटः
सुतेषु दारेषु धनेषु चिन्तयन् ।
शङ्केत विद्वान् कुकलेवरात्ययाद्
यस्तस्य यत्नः श्रम एव केवलम् ॥१४॥

yathaihikāmuṣmika-kāma-lampaṭaḥ
suteṣu dāreṣu dhaneṣu cintayan
śaṅketa vidvān kukalevarātyayād
yas tasya yatnaḥ śrama eva kevalam

yathā—as; *aihika*—in the present life; *amuṣmika*—in the expected future life; *kāma-lampaṭaḥ*—a person who is very attached to lusty desires for bodily enjoyment; *suteṣu*—children; *dāreṣu*—wife; *dhaneṣu*—wealth; *cintayan*—thinking about; *śaṅketa*—is afraid; *vidvān*—a person advanced in spiritual knowledge; *ku-kalevara*—of this body, which is full of stool and urine; *atyayāt*—because of loss; *yaḥ*—anyone; *tasya*—his; *yatnaḥ*—endeavors; *śramaḥ*—a waste of time and energy; *eva*—certainly; *kevalam*—only.

TRANSLATION

Materialists are generally very attached to their present bodily comforts and to the bodily comforts they expect in the future. Therefore they are always absorbed in thoughts of their wives, children and wealth and are afraid of giving up their bodies, which are full of stool and urine. If a person engaged in Kṛṣṇa consciousness, however, is also afraid of giving up his body, what is the use of his having labored to study the śāstras? It was simply a waste of time.

PURPORT

At the time of death a materialist thinks of his wife and children. He is absorbed in thinking of how they will live and who will take care of them after he leaves. Consequently he is never prepared to give up his body; rather, he wants to continue to live in his body to serve his society, family, friends and so on. Therefore by practicing the mystic *yoga* system one must become detached from bodily relationships. If despite practicing *bhakti-yoga* and studying all the Vedic literature, one is afraid of giving up his bad body, which is the cause of all his suffering, what is the use of his attempts to advance in spiritual life? The secret of success in practicing *yoga* is to become free from bodily attachments. Śrīla Narottama dāsa Ṭhākura says, *deha-smṛti nāhi yāra, saṁsāra-bandhana kāhāṅ tāra:* one whose practice has freed him from the anxieties of bodily needs is no longer in conditional life. Such a person is freed from conditional bondage. A person in Kṛṣṇa consciousness must fully discharge his devotional duties without material attachment. Then his liberation is guaranteed.

TEXT 15

तन्नः प्रभो त्वं कुकलेवरार्पितां
त्वन्माययाहंममतामधोक्षज ।
भिन्द्याम येनाशु वयं सुदुर्भिदां
विधेहि योगं त्वयि नः स्वभावमिति ॥१५॥

tan naḥ prabho tvaṁ kukalevarārpitāṁ
tvan-māyayāhaṁ-mamatām adhokṣaja
bhindyāma yenāśu vayaṁ sudurbhidāṁ
vidhehi yogaṁ tvayi naḥ svabhāvam iti

tat—therefore; *naḥ*—our; *prabho*—O my Lord; *tvam*—You; *ku-kalevara-arpitām*—invested in this bad body full of stool and urine; *tvat-māyayā*—by Your illusory energy; *aham-mamatām*—the conception of "I and my"; *adhokṣaja*—O Transcendence; *bhindyāma*—may give up; *yena*—by which; *āśu*—very soon; *vayam*—we; *sudurbhidām*—which is very difficult to give up; *vidhehi*—please give; *yogam*—the mystic process; *tvayi*—unto You; *naḥ*—our; *svabhāvam*—which is symptomized by a steady mind; *iti*—thus.

TRANSLATION

Therefore, O Lord, O Transcendence, kindly help us by giving us the power to execute bhakti-yoga so that we can control our restless minds and fix them upon You. We are all infected by Your illusory energy; therefore we are very attached to the body, which is full of stool and urine, and to anything related with the body. Except for devotional service, there is no way to give up this attachment. Therefore kindly bestow upon us this benediction.

PURPORT

The Lord advises in *Bhagavad-gītā: man-manā bhava mad-bhakto mad-yājī māṁ namaskuru.* The perfect *yoga* system consists of always thinking of Kṛṣṇa, always engaging in devotional service, always worshiping Kṛṣṇa and always offering obeisances unto Him. Unless we practice this *yoga* system, our illusory attachment for this bad body, which is full of stool and urine, is impossible to give up. The perfection of *yoga* consists of giving up attachment for this body and bodily relationships and transferring that attachment to Kṛṣṇa. We are very attached to material enjoyment, but when we transfer that same attachment to Kṛṣṇa, we traverse the path of liberation. One has to practice this *yoga* system and none other.

TEXT 16

भारतेऽप्यस्मिन् वर्षे सरिच्छैलाः सन्ति बहवो मलयो मङ्गलप्रस्थो मैनाकस्त्रिकूट ऋषभः कूटकः कोल्लकः सह्यो देवगिरिर्ऋष्यमूकः श्रीशैलो वेङ्कटो महेन्द्रो वारिधारो विन्ध्यः शुक्तिमानृक्षगिरिः पारियात्रो द्रोणश्चित्रकूटो गोवर्धनो रैवतकः ककुभो नीलो गोकामुख इन्द्रकीलः कामगिरिरिति चान्ये च शतसहस्रशः शैलास्तेषां नितम्बप्रभवा नदा नद्यश्च सन्त्यसङ्ख्याताः ॥१६॥

bhārate'py asmin varṣe saric-chailāḥ santi bahavo malayo maṅgala-prastho mainākas trikūṭa ṛṣabhaḥ kūṭakaḥ kollakaḥ sahyo devagirir ṛṣyamūkaḥ śrī-śailo veṅkaṭo mahendro vāridhāro vindhyaḥ śuktimān ṛkṣagiriḥ pāriyātro droṇaś citrakūṭo govardhano raivatakaḥ kakubho nīlo gokāmukha indrakīlaḥ kāmagirir iti cānye ca śata-sahasraśaḥ śailās teṣāṁ nitamba-prabhavā nadā nadyaś ca santy asaṅkhyātāḥ.

bhārate—in the land of Bhārata-varṣa; *api*—also; *asmin*—in this; *varṣe*—tract of land; *sarit*—rivers; *śailāḥ*—mountains; *santi*—there are; *bahavaḥ*—many; *malayaḥ*—Malaya; *maṅgala-prasthaḥ*—Maṅgala-prastha; *mainākaḥ*—Maināka; *tri-kūṭaḥ*—Trikūṭa; *ṛṣabhaḥ*—Ṛṣabha; *kūṭakaḥ*—Kūṭaka; *kollakaḥ*—Kollaka; *sahyaḥ*—Sahya; *devagiriḥ*—Devagiri; *ṛṣya-mūkaḥ*—Ṛṣyamūka; *śrī-śailaḥ*—Śrī-śaila; *veṅkaṭaḥ*—Veṅkaṭa; *mahendraḥ*—Mahendra; *vāri-dhāraḥ*—Vāridhāra; *vindhyaḥ*—Vindhya; *śuktimān*—Śuktimān; *ṛkṣa-giriḥ*—Ṛkṣagiri; *pāriyātraḥ*—Pāriyātra; *droṇaḥ*—Droṇa; *citra-kūṭaḥ*—Citrakūṭa; *govardhanaḥ*—Govardhana; *raivatakaḥ*—Raivataka; *kakubhaḥ*—Kakubha; *nīlaḥ*—Nīla; *gokāmukhaḥ*—Gokāmukha; *indrakīlaḥ*—Indrakīla; *kāma-giriḥ*—Kāmagiri; *iti*—thus; *ca*—and; *anye*—others; *ca*—also; *śata-sahasraśaḥ*—many hundreds and thousands; *śailāḥ*—mountains; *teṣām*—of them; *nitamba-prabhavāḥ*—born of the slopes; *nadāḥ*—big rivers; *nadyaḥ*—small rivers; *ca*—and; *santi*—there are; *asaṅkhyātāḥ*—innumerable.

TRANSLATION

In the tract of land known as Bhārata-varṣa, as in Ilāvṛta-varṣa, there are many mountains and rivers. Some of the mountains are known as Malaya, Maṅgala-prastha, Maināka, Trikūṭa, Ṛṣabha, Kūṭaka, Kollaka,

Sahya, Devagiri, Ṛṣyamūka, Śrī-śaila, Veṅkaṭa, Mahendra, Vāridhāra, Vindhya, Śuktimān, Ṛkṣagiri, Pāriyātra, Droṇa, Citrakūṭa, Govardhana, Raivataka, Kakubha, Nīla, Gokāmukha, Indrakīla and Kāmagiri. Besides these, there are many other hills, with many large and small rivers flowing from their slopes.

TEXTS 17–18

एतासामपो भारत्यः प्रजा नामभिरेव पुनन्तीनामात्मना चोपस्पृशन्ति ॥१७॥
चन्द्रवसा ताम्रपर्णी अवटोदा कृतमाला वैहायसी कावेरी वेणी पयस्विनी शर्करावर्ता तुङ्गभद्रा कृष्णा वेण्या भीमरथी गोदावरी निर्विन्ध्या पयोष्णी तापी रेवा सुरसा नर्मदा चर्मण्वती सिन्धुरन्धः शोणश्च नदौ महानदी वेदस्मृतिर्ऋषिकुल्या त्रिसामा कौशिकी मन्दाकिनी यमुना सरस्वती दृषद्वती गोमती सरयू रोधस्वती सप्तवती सुषोमा शतद्रूश्चन्द्रभागा मरुद्वृधा वितस्ता असिक्नी विश्वेति महानद्यः ॥१८॥

etāsām apo bhāratyaḥ prajā nāmabhir eva punantīnām ātmanā copaspṛśanti; candravasā tāmraparṇī avaṭodā kṛtamālā vaihāyasī kāverī veṇī payasvinī śarkarāvartā tuṅgabhadrā kṛṣṇāveṇyā bhīmarathī godāvarī nirvindhyā payoṣṇī tāpī revā surasā narmadā carmaṇvatī sindhur andhaḥ śoṇaś ca nadau mahānadī vedasmṛtir ṛṣikulyā trisāmā kauśikī mandākinī yamunā sarasvatī dṛṣadvatī gomatī sarayū rodhasvatī saptavatī suṣomā śatadrūś candrabhāgā marudvṛdhā vitastā asiknī viśveti mahā-nadyaḥ.

etāsām—of all these; *apaḥ*—water; *bhāratyaḥ*—of Bhārata-varṣa (India); *prajāḥ*—the residents; *nāmabhiḥ*—by the names; *eva*—only; *punantīnām*—are purifying; *ātmanā*—by the mind; *ca*—also; *upaspṛśanti*—touch; *candra-vasā*—Candravasā; *tāmra-parṇī*—Tāmraparṇī; *avaṭodā*—Avaṭodā; *kṛta-mālā*—Kṛtamālā; *vaihāyasī*—Vaihāyasī; *kāverī*—Kāverī; *veṇī*—Veṇī; *payasvinī*—Payasvinī; *śarkarāvartā*—Śarkarāvartā; *tuṅga-bhadrā*—Tuṅgabhadrā; *kṛṣṇā-veṇyā*—Kṛṣṇāveṇyā; *bhīma-rathī*—Bhīmarathī; *godāvarī*—Godāvarī; *nirvindhyā*—Nirvindhyā; *payoṣṇī*—Payoṣṇī; *tāpī*—Tāpī; *revā*—Revā; *surasā*—Surasā; *narmadā*—Narmadā; *carmaṇvatī*—Carmaṇvatī; *sindhuḥ*—Sindhu; *andhaḥ*—Andha; *śoṇaḥ*—Śoṇa; *ca*—and; *nadau*—two rivers; *mahā-nadī*—Mahānadī; *veda-smṛtiḥ*—Vedasmṛti; *ṛṣi-kulyā*—Ṛṣikulyā; *tri-sāmā*—Trisāmā; *kauśikī*—Kauśikī; *mandākinī*—Mandākinī; *yamunā*—Yamunā; *sarasvatī*—Sarasvatī; *dṛṣadvatī*—Dṛṣadvatī; *gomatī*—Gomatī; *sarayū*—Sarayū; *rodhasvatī*—Rodhasvatī;

saptavatī—Saptavatī; *suṣomā*—Suṣomā; *śata-drūḥ*—Śatadrū; *candrabhāgā*—Candrabhāgā; *marudvṛdhā*—Marudvṛdhā; *vitastā*—Vitastā; *asiknī*—Asiknī; *viśvā*—Viśvā; *iti*—thus; *mahā-nadyaḥ*—big rivers.

TRANSLATION

Two of the rivers—the Brahmaputra and the Śoṇa—are called nadas, or main rivers. These are other great rivers that are very prominent: Candravasā, Tāmraparṇī, Avaṭodā, Kṛtamālā, Vaihāyasī, Kāverī, Veṇī, Payasvinī, Śarkarāvartā, Tuṅgabhadrā, Kṛṣṇāveṇyā, Bhīmarathī, Godāvarī, Nirvindhyā, Payoṣṇī, Tāpī, Revā, Surasā, Narmadā, Carmaṇvatī, Mahānadī, Vedasmṛti, Ṛṣikulyā, Trisāmā, Kauśikī, Mandākinī, Yamunā, Sarasvatī, Dṛṣadvatī, Gomatī, Sarayū, Rodhasvatī, Saptavatī, Suṣomā, Śatadrū, Candrabhāgā, Marudvṛdhā, Vitastā, Asiknī and Viśvā. The inhabitants of Bhārata-varṣa are purified because they always remember these rivers. Sometimes they chant the names of these rivers as mantras, and sometimes they go directly to the rivers to touch them and bathe in them. Thus the inhabitants of Bhārata-varṣa become purified.

PURPORT

All these rivers are transcendental. Therefore one can be purified by remembering them, touching them or bathing in them. This practice is still going on.

TEXT 19

अस्मिन्नेव वर्षे पुरुषैर्लब्धजन्मभिः शुक्ललोहितकृष्णवर्णेन स्वारब्धेन कर्मणा
दिव्यमानुषनारकगतयो बह्व्य आत्मन आनुपूर्व्येण सर्वा ह्येव सर्वेषां विधीयन्ते
यथावर्णविधानमपवर्गश्चापि भवति ॥१९॥

asminn eva varṣe puruṣair labdha-janmabhiḥ śukla-lohita-kṛṣṇa-
varṇena svārabdhena karmaṇā divya-mānuṣa-nāraka-gatayo bahvya
ātmana ānupūrvyeṇa sarvā hy eva sarveṣāṁ vidhīyante yathā-varṇa-
vidhānam apavargaś cāpi bhavati.

asmin eva varṣe—in this tract of land (Bhārata-varṣa); *puruṣaiḥ*—by the people; *labdha-janmabhiḥ*—who have taken birth; *śukla*—of the mode of goodness; *lohita*—of the mode of passion; *kṛṣṇa*—of the mode of ignorance; *varṇena*—according to the division; *sva*—by himself; *ārabdhena*—begun; *karmaṇā*—by activities; *divya*—divine; *mānuṣa*—human; *nāraka*—hellish;

gatayaḥ—goals; *bahvyaḥ*—many; *ātmanaḥ*—of his own; *ānupūrvyeṇa*—according to acts performed previously; *sarvāḥ*—all; *hi*—certainly; *eva*—indeed; *sarveṣām*—of all of them; *vidhīyante*—are allotted; *yathā-varṇa-vidhānam*—in terms of different castes; *apavargaḥ*—the path of liberation; *ca*—and; *api*—also; *bhavati*—is possible.

TRANSLATION

The people who take birth in this tract of land are divided according to the qualities of material nature—the modes of goodness [sattva-guṇa], passion [rajo-guṇa], and ignorance [tamo-guṇa]. Some of them are born as exalted personalities, some are ordinary human beings, and some are extremely abominable, for in Bhārata-varṣa one takes birth exactly according to one's past karma. If one's position is ascertained by a bona fide spiritual master and one is properly trained to engage in the service of Lord Viṣṇu according to the four social divisions [brāhmaṇa, kṣatriya, vaiśya and śūdra] and the four spiritual divisions [brahmacārī, gṛhastha, vānaprastha and sannyāsa], one's life becomes perfect.

PURPORT

For further information, one should refer to *Bhagavad-gītā* (14.18 and 18.42–45). Śrīla Rāmānujācārya writes in his book *Vedānta-saṅgraha:*

evaṁ-vidha-parābhakti-svarūpa-jñāna-viśeṣasyotpādakaḥ pūrvoktāharahar upacīyamāna-jñāna-pūrvaka-karmānugṛhīta-bhakti-yoga eva; yathoktaṁ bhagavatā parāśareṇa—varṇāśrameti. nikhila-jagad-uddhāraṇāyāvanitale 'vatīrṇaṁ para-brahma-bhūtaḥ puruṣottamaḥ svayam etad uktavān—"svakarma-nirataḥ siddhiṁ yathā vindati tac chṛṇu" "yataḥ pravṛttir bhūtānāṁ yena sarvam idaṁ tatam/ svakarmaṇā tam abhyarcya siddhiṁ vindati mānavaḥ."

Quoting from the *Viṣṇu Purāṇa* (389), the great sage Parāśara Muni has recommended:

varṇāśramācāravatā
puruṣeṇa paraḥ pumān
viṣṇur ārādhyate panthā
nānyat tat-toṣa-kāraṇam

"The Supreme Personality of Godhead, Lord Viṣṇu, is worshiped by the proper execution of prescribed duties in the system of *varṇa* and *āśrama.* There is no other way to satisfy the Lord." In the land of Bhārata-varṣa, the institution of *varṇāśrama-dharma* may be easily adopted. At the present moment, certain demoniac sections of the population of Bhārata-varṣa are disregarding the system of *varṇāśrama-dharma.* Because there is no institution to teach people how to become *brāhmaṇas, kṣatriyas, vaiśyas* and *śūdras* or *brahmacārīs, gṛhasthas, vānaprasthas* and *sannyāsīs,* these demons want a classless society. This is resulting in chaotic conditions. In the name of secular government, unqualified people are taking the supreme governmental posts. No one is being trained to act according to the principles of *varṇāśrama-dharma,* and thus people are becoming increasingly degraded and are heading in the direction of animal life. The real aim of life is liberation, but unfortunately the opportunity for liberation is being denied to people in general, and therefore their human lives are being spoiled. The Kṛṣṇa consciousness movement, however, is being propagated all over the world to reestablish the *varṇāśrama-dharma* system and thus save human society from gliding down to hellish life.

TEXT 20

योऽसौ भगवति सर्वभूतात्मन्यनात्म्येऽनिरुक्तेऽनिलयने परमात्मनि वासुदेवेऽनन्यनिमित्तभक्तियोगलक्षणो नानागतिनिमित्ताविद्याग्रन्थिरन्धनद्वारेण यदा हि महापुरुषपुरुषप्रसङ्गः ॥२०॥

yo 'sau bhagavati sarva-bhūtātmany anātmye 'nirukte 'nilayane paramātmani vāsudeve 'nanya-nimitta-bhakti-yoga-lakṣaṇo nānā-gati-nimittāvidyā-granthi-randhana-dvāreṇa yadā hi mahā-puruṣa- puruṣa-prasaṅgaḥ.

yaḥ—anyone who; *asau*—that; *bhagavati*—unto the Supreme Personality of Godhead; *sarva-bhūta-ātmani*—the Supersoul of all living entities; *anātmye*—having no attachment; *anirukte*—who is beyond the mind and speech; *anilayane*—not dependent on anything else; *parama-ātmani*—unto the Supreme Soul; *vāsudeve*—Lord Vāsudeva, the son of Vasudeva; *ananya*—without any other; *nimitta*—cause; *bhakti-yoga-lakṣaṇaḥ*—having symptoms of pure devotional service; *nānā-gati*—of varied destinations; *nimitta*—the cause; *avidyā-granthi*—the bondage of ignorance; *randhana*—of cutting; *dvāreṇa*—by means; *yadā*—when; *hi*—indeed; *mahā-puruṣa*—of the Supreme Personality of Godhead; *puruṣa*—with the devotee; *prasaṅgaḥ*—an intimate relationship.

TRANSLATION

After many, many births, when the results of one's pious activities mature, one gets an opportunity to associate with pure devotees. Then one is able to cut the knot of bondage to ignorance, which bound him because of varied fruitive activities. As a result of associating with devotees, one gradually renders service to Lord Vāsudeva, who is transcendental, free from attachment to the material world, beyond the mind and words, and independent of everything else. That bhakti-yoga, devotional service to Lord Vāsudeva, is the real path of liberation.

PURPORT

Brahman realization is the beginning of liberation, and Paramātmā realization is still further advancement toward the realm of liberation, but one achieves real liberation when he understands his position as an eternal servant of the Supreme Personality of Godhead (*muktir hitvānyathā rūpaṁ svarūpeṇa vyavasthitiḥ*). In the material world, in the bodily concept of life, everyone is working in the wrong direction. When one becomes *brahma-bhūta,* spiritually realized, one understands that he is not the body and that working in the bodily concept of life is useless and misdirected. Then his devotional service begins. As Kṛṣṇa says in *Bhagavad-gītā* (18.54):

brahma-bhūtaḥ prasannātmā
na śocati na kāṅkṣati
samaḥ sarveṣu bhūteṣu
mad-bhaktiṁ labhate parām

"One who is thus transcendentally situated realizes the Supreme Brahman and becomes fully joyful. He never laments or desires to have anything. He is equally disposed to every living entity. In that state he attains pure devotional service unto Me." Devotional service is actual liberation. When one is attracted by the beauty of the Supreme Personality of Godhead and his mind is always engaged at the Lord's lotus feet, he is no longer interested in subjects that do not help him in self-realization. In other words, he loses all attraction for material activities. In the *Taittirīya Upaniṣad* (2.7) it is said: *eṣa hy evānandayati; yadā hy evaiṣa etasmin na dṛśye'nātmye anirukte'nilayane 'bhayaṁ pratiṣṭhāṁ vindate'tha so'bhayaṁ gato bhavati.* A living entity becomes established in spiritual, blissful life when he fully understands that his happiness depends on spiritual self-realization, which is the basic principle of *ānanda* (bliss), and when he is eternally situated in the service of the Lord, who has no other lord above Him.

TEXT 21

एतदेव हि देवा गायन्ति —
अहो अमीषां किमकारि शोभनं
प्रसन्न एषां स्विदुत स्वयं हरिः ।
यैर्जन्म लब्धं नृषु भारताजिरे
मुकुन्दसेवौपयिकं स्पृहा हि नः ॥२१॥

etad eva hi devā gāyanti—
aho amīṣāṁ kim akāri śobhanaṁ
prasanna eṣāṁ svid uta svayaṁ hariḥ
yair janma labdhaṁ nṛṣu bhāratājire
mukunda-sevaupayikaṁ spṛhā hi naḥ

etat—this; *eva*—indeed; *hi*—certainly; *devāḥ*—all the demigods; *gāyanti*—chant; *aho*—oh; *amīṣām*—of these inhabitants of Bhāratavarṣa; *kim*—what; *akāri*—was done; *śobhanam*—pious, beautiful activities; *prasannaḥ*—pleased; *eṣām*—upon them; *svit*—or; *uta*—it is said; *svayam*—personally; *hariḥ*—the Supreme Personality of Godhead; *yaiḥ*—by whom; *janma*—birth; *labdham*—obtained; *nṛṣu*—in human society; *bhārata-ajire*—in the courtyard of Bhārata-varṣa; *mukunda*—the Supreme Personality of Godhead, who can offer liberation; *sevā-aupayikam*—which is the means of serving; *spṛhā*—desire; *hi*—indeed; *naḥ*—our.

TRANSLATION

Since the human form of life is the sublime position for spiritual realization, all the demigods in heaven speak in this way: How wonderful it is for these human beings to have been born in the land of Bhārata-varṣa. They must have executed pious acts of austerity in the past, or the Supreme Personality of Godhead Himself must have been pleased with them. Otherwise, how could they engage in devotional service in so many ways? We demigods can only aspire to achieve human births in Bhārata-varṣa to execute devotional service, but these human beings are already engaged there.

PURPORT

These facts are further explained in *Caitanya-caritāmṛta* (*Ādi* 9.41):

bhārata-bhūmite haila manuṣya-janma yāra
janma sārthaka kari' kara para-upakāra

"One who has taken his birth as a human being in the land of India [Bhārata-varṣa] should make his life successful and work for the benefit of all other people."

There are many facilities in India, Bhārata-varṣa, for executing devotional service. In Bhārata-varṣa, all the *ācāryas* contributed their experience, and Śrī Caitanya Mahāprabhu personally appeared to teach the people of Bhārata-varṣa how to progress in spiritual life and be fixed in devotional service to the Lord. From all points of view, Bhārata-varṣa is the special land where one can very easily understand the process of devotional service and adopt it to make his life successful. If one makes his life successful in devotional service and then preaches devotional service in other parts of the world, people throughout the world will actually benefit.

TEXT 22

किं दुष्करैर्नः क्रतुभिस्तपोव्रतै-
दानादिभिर्वा द्युजयेन फल्गुना ।
न यत्र नारायणपादपङ्कज-
स्मृतिः प्रमुष्टातिशयेन्द्रियोत्सवात् ॥२२॥

kiṁ duṣkarair naḥ kratubhis tapo-vratair
dānādibhir vā dyujayena phalgunā
na yatra nārāyaṇa-pāda-paṅkaja-
smṛtiḥ pramuṣṭātiśayendriyotsavāt

kim—what is the value; *duṣkaraiḥ*—very difficult to perform; *naḥ*—our; *kratubhiḥ*—with performances of sacrifice; *tapaḥ*—with austerities; *vrataiḥ*—vows; *dāna-ādibhiḥ*—with executing charitable activities and so on; *vā*—or; *dyujayena*—with achieving the heavenly kingdom; *phalgunā*—which is insignificant; *na*—no; *yatra*—where; *nārāyaṇa-pāda-paṅkaja*—of the lotus feet of Lord Nārāyaṇa; *smṛtiḥ*—the remembrance; *pramuṣṭa*—lost; *atiśaya*—excessive; *indriya-utsavāt*—due to material sense gratification.

TRANSLATION

The demigods continue: After performing the very difficult tasks of executing Vedic ritualistic sacrifices, undergoing austerities, observing vows and giving charity, we have achieved this position as inhabitants of the heavenly planets. But what is the value of this achievement? Here we are certainly very engaged in material sense gratification, and therefore

we can hardly remember the lotus feet of Lord Nārāyaṇa. Indeed, because of our excessive sense gratification, we have almost forgotten His lotus feet.

PURPORT

The land of Bhārata-varṣa is so exalted that by taking birth there one can not only attain the heavenly planets but also go directly back home, back to Godhead. As Kṛṣṇa says in *Bhagavad-gītā* (9.25):

yānti deva-vratā devān
pitṝn yānti pitṛ-vratāḥ
bhūtāni yānti bhūtejyā
yānti mad-yājino'pi mām

"Those who worship the demigods will take birth among the demigods; those who worship ghosts and spirits will take birth among such beings; those who worship ancestors go to the ancestors; and those who worship Me will live with Me." People in the land of Bhārata-varṣa generally follow the Vedic principles and consequently perform great sacrifices by which they can be elevated to the heavenly planets. However, what is the use of such great attainments? As stated in *Bhagavad-gītā* (9.21), *kṣīṇe puṇye martya-lokaṁ viśanti:* after the results of one's sacrifices, charity and other pious activities expire, one must return to the lower planetary systems and again feel the pangs of birth and death. However, one who becomes Kṛṣṇa conscious can go back to Kṛṣṇa (*yānti-mad-yājino'pi mām*). Therefore the demigods even regret having been elevated to the higher planetary systems. The denizens of the heavenly planets regret that they could not take full advantage of being born in the land of Bhārata-varṣa. Instead, they became captivated by a higher standard of sense gratification, and therefore they forgot the lotus feet of Lord Nārāyaṇa at the time of death. The conclusion is that one who has taken birth in the land of Bhārata-varṣa must follow the instructions given personally by the Supreme Personality of Godhead. *Yad gatvā na nivartante tad dhāma paramaṁ mama.* One should try to return home, back to Godhead, to the Vaikuṇṭha planets—or to the topmost Vaikuṇṭha planet, Goloka Vṛndāvana—to live eternally in full, blissful knowledge in the company of the Supreme Personality of Godhead.

TEXT 23

कल्पायुषां स्थानजयात्पुनर्भवात्
क्षणायुषां भारतभूजयो वरम् ।

क्षणेन मर्त्येन कृतं मनस्विनः
संन्यस्य संयान्त्यभयं पदं हरेः ॥२३॥

kalpāyuṣāṁ sthānajayāt punar-bhavāt
kṣaṇāyuṣāṁ bhārata-bhūjayo varam
kṣaṇena martyena kṛtaṁ manasvinaḥ
sannyasya saṁyānty abhayaṁ padaṁ hareḥ

kalpa-āyuṣām—of those who have a life duration of many millions of years, like Lord Brahmā; *sthāna-jayāt*—than achievement of the place or planetary systems; *punaḥ-bhavāt*—which is liable to birth, death and old age; *kṣaṇa-āyuṣām*—of persons who have only one hundred years of life; *bhārata-bhū-jayaḥ*—a birth in the land of Bhārata-varṣa; *varam*—more valuable; *kṣaṇena*—for such a short life; *martyena*—by the body; *kṛtam*—the work executed; *manasvinaḥ*—those actually understanding the value of life; *sannyasya*—surrendering unto the lotus feet of Kṛṣṇa; *saṁyānti*—they achieve; *abhayam*—where there is no anxiety; *padam*—the abode; *hareḥ*—of the Supreme Personality of Godhead.

TRANSLATION

A short life in the land of Bharata-varṣa is preferable to a life achieved in Brahmaloka for millions and billions of years because even if one is elevated to Brahmaloka, he must return to repeated birth and death. Although life in Bhārata-varṣa, in a lower planetary system, is very short, one who lives there can elevate himself to full Kṛṣṇa consciousness and achieve the highest perfection, even in this short life, by fully surrendering unto the lotus feet of the Lord. Thus one attains Vaikuṇṭhaloka, where there is neither anxiety nor repeated birth in a material body.

PURPORT

This is further confirmation of the statement given by Lord Caitanya Mahāprabhu:

bhārata-bhūmite haila manuṣya-janma yāra
janma sārthaka kari' kara para-upakāra

One who has taken birth in the land of Bhārata-varṣa has a full opportunity to study the direct instructions given by Kṛṣṇa in *Bhagavad-gītā* and thus finally decide what to do in his human form of life. One should certainly give up all other propositions and surrender to Kṛṣṇa. Kṛṣṇa will then immediately take charge and relieve one of the results of past sinful life (*ahaṁ tvāṁ sarva-pāpebhyo mokṣayiṣyāmi mā śucaḥ*). Therefore one should take to Kṛṣṇa consciousness, as Kṛṣṇa Himself recommends. *Man-manā bhava mad-bhakto mad-yājī māṁ namaskuru:* "Always think of Me, become My devotee, worship Me and offer Me obeisances." This is very easy, even for a child. Why not take this path? One should try to follow the instructions of Kṛṣṇa exactly and thus become fully eligible to be promoted to the kingdom of God (*tyaktvā dehaṁ punar janma naiti mām eti so 'rjuna*). One should go directly to Kṛṣṇa and engage in His service. This is the best opportunity offered to the inhabitants of Bhārata-varṣa. One who is fit to return home, back to Godhead, is no longer liable to the results of *karma,* good or bad.

TEXT 24

न यत्र वैकुण्ठकथासुधापगा
न साधवो भागवतास्तदाश्रयाः ।
न यत्र यज्ञेशमखा महोत्सवाः
सुरेशलोकोऽपि न वै स सेव्यताम् ॥२४॥

na yatra vaikuṇṭha-kathā-sudhāpagā
na sādhavo bhāgavatās tadāśrayāḥ
na yatra yajñeśa-makhā mahotsavāḥ
sureśa-loko 'pi na vai sa sevyatām

na—not; *yatra*—where; *vaikuṇṭha-kathā-sudhā-āpagāḥ*—the nectarean rivers of discussions about the Supreme Personality of Godhead, who is called Vaikuṇṭha, or one who drives away all anxiety; *na*—nor; *sādhavaḥ*—devotees; *bhāgavatāḥ*—always engaged in the service of the Lord; *tat-āśrayāḥ*—who are sheltered by the Supreme Personality of Godhead; *na*—nor; *yatra*—where; *yajña-īśa-makhāḥ*—the performance of devotional service to the Lord of sacrifices; *mahā-utsavāḥ*—which are actual festivals; *sureśa-lokaḥ*—a place inhabited by the denizens of heaven; *api*—although; *na*—not; *vai*—certainly; *saḥ*—that; *sevyatām*—be frequented.

TRANSLATION

An intelligent person does not take interest in a place, even in the topmost planetary system, if the pure Ganges of topics concerning the Supreme Lord's activities does not flow there, if there are not devotees

engaged in service on the banks of such a river of piety, or if there are no festivals of saṅkīrtana-yajña to satisfy the Lord [especially since saṅkīrtana-yajña is recommended in this age].

PURPORT

Śrī Caitanya Mahāprabhu appeared in the land of Bhārata-varṣa, specifically in Bengal, in the district of Nadia, where Navadvīpa is situated. It is therefore to be concluded, as stated by Śrīla Bhaktivinoda Ṭhākura, that within this universe, this earth is the best planet, and on this planet the land of Bhārata-varṣa is the best; in the land of Bhārata-varṣa, Bengal is still better, in Bengal the district of Nadia is still better, and in Nadia the best place is Navadvīpa because Śrī Caitanya Mahāprabhu appeared there to inaugurate the performance of the sacrifice of chanting the Hare Kṛṣṇa *mahā-mantra.* The *śāstras* recommend:

kṛṣṇa-varṇaṁ tviṣākṛṣṇaṁ
sāṅgopāṅgāstra-pārṣadam
yajñaiḥ saṅkīrtana-prāyair
yajanti hi sumedhasaḥ

Lord Śrī Caitanya Mahāprabhu is always accompanied by His very confidential associates such as Śrī Nityānanda, Śrī Gadādhara and Śrī Advaita and by many devotees like Śrīvāsa. They are always engaged in chanting the name of the Lord and are always describing Lord Kṛṣṇa. Therefore this is the best among all the places in the universe. The Kṛṣṇa consciousness movement has established its center in Māyāpur, the birthsite of Lord Śrī Caitanya Mahāprabhu, to give men the great opportunity to go there and perform a constant festival of *saṅkīrtana-yajña,* as recommended herein (*yajñeśa-makhā mahotsavāḥ*) and to distribute *prasāda* to millions of hungry people hankering for spiritual emancipation. This is the mission of the Kṛṣṇa consciousness movement. *Caitanya-bhāgavata* confirms this as follows: "One should not desire to be elevated even to a place in the heavenly planetary systems if it has no propaganda to expand the glories of the Supreme Personality of Godhead, no trace of Vaiṣṇavas, pure devotees of the Lord, and no festivals for spreading Kṛṣṇa consciousness. It would be better to live perpetually cramped within the airtight bag of a mother's womb, where one can at least remember the lotus feet of the Lord, than to live in a place where there is no opportunity to remember His lotus feet. I pray not to be allowed to take birth in such a condemned place."

Similarly, in *Caitanya-caritāmṛta,* Kṛṣṇadāsa Kavirāja Gosvāmī says that since Śrī Caitanya Mahāprabhu is the inaugurator of the *saṅkīrtana* movement, anyone who performs *saṅkīrtana* to please the Lord is very, very glorious. Such a person has perfect intelligence, whereas others are in the ignorance of material existence. Of all the sacrifices mentioned in the Vedic literatures, the performance of *saṅkīrtana-yajña* is the best. Even the performance of one hundred *aśvamedha* sacrifices cannot compare to the sacrifice of *saṅkīrtana.* According to the author of *Śrī Caitanya-caritāmṛta,* if one compares *saṅkīrtana-yajña* to other *yajñas,* he is a *pāṣaṇḍī,* an infidel, and is liable to be punished by Yamarāja. There are many Māyāvādīs who think that the performance of *saṅkīrtana-yajña* is a pious activity similar to the performance of the *aśvamedha-yajña* and other such pious functions, but this is a *nāma-aparādha.* Chanting of the holy name of Nārāyaṇa and chanting of other names are never equal, despite what Māyāvādīs think.

TEXT 25

प्राप्ता नृजातिं त्विह ये च जन्तवो
ज्ञानक्रियाद्रव्यकलापसम्भृताम् ।
न वै यतेरन्नपुनर्भवाय ते
भूयो वनौका इव यान्ति बन्धनम् ॥२५॥

prāptā nṛ-jātiṁ tv iha ye ca jantavo
jñāna-kriyā-dravya-kalāpa-sambhṛtām
na vai yaterann apunar-bhavāya te
bhūyo vanaukā iva yānti bandhanam

prāptāḥ—who have obtained; *nṛ-jātim*—a birth in human society; *tu*—certainly; *iha*—in this land of Bhārata-varṣa; *ye*—those who; *ca*—also; *jantavaḥ*—the living beings; *jñāna*—with knowledge; *kriyā*—with activities; *dravya*—of ingredients; *kalāpa*—with a collection; *sambhṛtām*—full; *na*—not; *vai*—certainly; *yateran*—endeavor; *apunaḥ-bhavāya*—for the position of immortality; *te*—such persons; *bhūyaḥ*—again; *vanaukāḥ*—birds; *iva*—like; *yānti*—go; *bandhanam*—to bondage.

TRANSLATION

Bhārata-varṣa offers the proper land and circumstances in which to execute devotional service, which can free one from the results of jñāna and karma. If one obtains a human body in the land of Bhārata-varṣa, with

clear sensory organs with which to execute the saṅkīrtana-yajña, but in spite of this opportunity he does not take to devotional service, he is certainly like liberated forest animals and birds that are careless and are therefore again bound by a hunter.

PURPORT

In the land of Bhārata-varṣa one can very easily perform the *saṅkīrtana-yajña,* which consists of *śravaṇaṁ kīrtanaṁ viṣṇoḥ,* or one can perform other methods of devotional service, such as *smaraṇaṁ vandanaṁ arcanaṁ dāsyaṁ sakhyam* and *ātma-nivedanam.* In Bhārata-varṣa one has the opportunity to visit many holy places, especially Lord Caitanya's birthsite and Lord Kṛṣṇa's birthsite—Navadvīpa and Vṛndāvana—where there are many pure devotees who have no desire other than to execute devotional service (*anyābhilāṣitā-śūnyaṁ jñāna-karmādy-anāvṛtam*), and one may thus become free from the bondage of material conditions. Other paths, such as the path of *jñāna* and the path of *karma,* are not very profitable. Pious activities can elevate one to the higher planetary systems, and by speculative knowledge one can merge into the Brahman existence, but that is not real profit, for one has to come down again even from the liberated condition of being merged in Brahman, and certainly one must come down from the heavenly kingdom. One should endeavor to go back home, back to Godhead (*yānti mad-yājino'pi mām*). Otherwise there is no difference between human life and the lives of jungle animals and birds. Animals and birds also have freedom, but because of their lower birth, they cannot use it. Taking advantage of all the facilities offered him , a human being who has taken birth in the land of Bhārata-varṣa should become a fully enlightened devotee and go back home, back to Godhead. This is the subject matter of the Kṛṣṇa consciousness movement. The inhabitants of places other than Bhārata-varṣa have facilities for material enjoyment, but they do not have the same facility to take to Kṛṣṇa consciousness. Therefore Śrī Caitanya Mahāprabhu has advised that one who has taken birth as a human being in Bhārata-varṣa must first realize himself as a part and parcel of Kṛṣṇa, and after taking to Kṛṣṇa consciousness, he must distribute this knowledge all over the world.

TEXT 26

यैः श्रद्धया बर्हिषि भागशो हवि-
र्निरुप्तमिष्टं विधिमन्त्रवस्तुतः ।

एकः पृथङ्नामभिराहुतो मुदा
गृह्णाति पूर्णः स्वयमाशिषां प्रभुः ॥२६॥

yaiḥ śraddhayā barhiṣi bhāgaśo havir
niruptam iṣṭaṁ vidhi-mantra-vastutaḥ
ekaḥ pṛthaṅ-nāmabhir āhuto mudā
gṛhṇāti pūrṇaḥ svayam āśiṣāṁ prabhuḥ

yaiḥ—by whom (the inhabitants of Bhārata-varṣa); *śraddhayā*—faith and confidence; *barhiṣi*—in the performance of Vedic ritualistic sacrifices; *bhāgaśaḥ*—by division; *haviḥ*—oblations; *niruptam*—offered; *iṣṭam*—to the desired deity; *vidhi*—by the proper method; *mantra*—by reciting *mantras; vastutaḥ*—with the proper ingredients; *ekaḥ*—that one Supreme Personality of Godhead; *pṛthak*—separate; *nāmabhiḥ*—by names; *āhutaḥ*—called; *mudā*—with great happiness; *gṛhṇāti*—He accepts; *pūrṇaḥ*—the Supreme Lord. who is full in Himself; *svayam*—personally; *āśiṣām*—of all benedictions; *prabhuḥ*—the bestower.

TRANSLATION

In India [Bhārata-varṣa], there are many worshipers of the demigods, the various officials appointed by the Supreme Lord, such as Indra, Candra and Sūrya, all of whom are worshiped differently. The worshipers offer the demigods their oblations, considering the demigods part and parcel of the whole, the Supreme Lord. Therefore the Supreme Personality of Godhead accepts these offerings and gradually raises the worshipers to the real standard of devotional service by fulfilling their desires and aspirations. Because the Lord is complete, He offers the worshipers the benedictions they desire even if they worship only part of His transcendental body.

PURPORT

In *Bhagavad-gītā* (9.13) Lord Kṛṣṇa says:

mahātmānas tu māṁ pārtha
daivīṁ prakṛtim āśritāḥ
bhajanty ananya-manaso
jñātvā bhūtādim avyayam

"O son of Pṛthā, those who are not deluded, the great souls, are under the protection of the divine nature. They are fully engaged in devotional service because they know Me as the Supreme Personality of Godhead, original and inexhaustible." *Mahātmās,* advanced devotees, worship only the Supreme Personality of Godhead. Others, however, who are also sometimes called *mahātmās,* worship the Lord as *ekatvena pṛthaktvena.* In other words, they accept the demigods as different parts of Kṛṣṇa and worship them for various benedictions. Although the devotees of the demigods thus achieve the desired results offered by Kṛṣṇa, they have been described in *Bhagavad-gītā* as *hṛta-jñānah,* not very intelligent. Kṛṣṇa does not desire to be worshiped indirectly through the different parts of His body; Kṛṣṇa wants direct devotional worship. Therefore a devotee who directly worships Lord Kṛṣṇa through staunch devotional service, as recommended in *Śrīmad-Bhāgavatam,* (*tīvreṇa bhakti-yogena yajeta puruṣaṁ param*), is very quickly elevated to the transcendental position. Nevertheless, devotees who worship the demigods, the different parts of the Lord, receive the benedictions they desire because the Lord is the original master of all benedictions. If anyone wants a particular benediction, for the Lord to award it is not at all difficult.

TEXT 27

सत्यं दिशत्यर्थितमर्थितो नृणां
नैवार्थदो यत्पुनरर्थिता यतः ।
स्वयं विधत्ते भजतामनिच्छता-
मिच्छापिधानं निजपादपल्लवम् ॥२७॥

satyaṁ diśaty arthitam arthito nṛṇāṁ
naivārthado yat punar arthitā yataḥ
svayaṁ vidhatte bhajatām anicchatām
icchāpidhānaṁ nija-pāda-pallavam

satyam—certainly; *diśati*—He offers; *arthitam*—the object prayed for; *arthitaḥ*—being prayed to; *nṛṇām*—by the human beings; *na*—not; *eva*—indeed; *artha-daḥ*—the bestower of benedictions; *yat*—which; *punaḥ*—again; *arthitā*—a demand for a benediction; *yataḥ*—from which; *svayam*—personally; *vidhatte*—He gives; *bhajatām*—unto those engaged in His service; *anicchatām*—although not desiring it; *icchā-pidhānam*—which covers all desirable things; *nija-pāda-pallavam*—His own lotus feet.

TRANSLATION

The Supreme Personality of Godhead fulfills the material desires of a devotee who approaches Him with such motives, but He does not bestow

benedictions upon the devotee that will cause him to demand more benedictions again. However, the Lord willingly gives the devotee shelter at His own lotus feet, even though such a person does not aspire for it, and that shelter satisfies all his desires. That is the Supreme Personality's special mercy.

PURPORT

The devotees mentioned in the previous verse approach the Supreme Personality of Godhead with material motives, but this verse explains how such devotees are saved from those desires. *Śrīmad-Bhāgavatam* (2.3.10) advises:

akāmaḥ sarva-kāmo vā
mokṣa-kāma udāra-dhīḥ
tīvreṇa bhakti-yogena
yajeta puruṣaṁ param

"Whether one is freed from all material desires, is full of material desires, or desires to become one with the Supreme, he should engage in devotional service." In this way, not only will the devotee's desires be fulfilled, but the day will come when he will have no other desire than to serve the lotus feet of the Lord. One who engages in the service of the Lord with some motive is called a *sakāma-bhakta,* and one who serves the Lord without any motives is called an *akāma-bhakta.* Kṛṣṇa is so merciful that He turns a *sakāma-bhakta* into an *akāma-bhakta.* A pure devotee, an *akāma-bhakta,* who has no material motives, is satisfied simply to serve the lotus feet of the Lord. This is confirmed in *Bhagavad-gītā* (6.22). *Yaṁ labdhvā cāparaṁ lābhaṁ manyate nādhikaṁ tataḥ:* if one engages in the service of the lotus feet of the Lord, he does not want anything more. This is the highest stage of devotional service. The Lord is so kind even to a *sakāma-bhakta,* a motivated devotee, that He satisfies his desires in such a way that one day he becomes an *akāma-bhakta.* Dhruva Mahārāja, for example, became a *bhakta* with the motive of getting a better kingdom than that of his father, but finally he became an *akāma-bhakta* and said to the Lord, *svāmin kṛtārtho 'smi varaṁ na yāce:* "My dear Lord, I am very satisfied simply to serve Your lotus feet. I do not want any material benefits." Sometimes it is found that a small child eats dirty things, but his parents take away the dirty things and offer him a *sandeśa* or some other sweetmeat. Devotees who aspire for material benedictions are compared to such children. The Lord is so kind that He takes away their material desires and gives them the highest benediction. Therefore, even for material motives, one should not worship anyone other than the Supreme Personality of Godhead; one must fully engage himself in the devotional service of the Lord so that all his desires will be fulfilled and at the end he can go back home, back to Godhead. This is explained in *Caitanya-caritāmṛta* (*Madhya* 22.37–39, 41) as follows.

Anyakāmī—a devotee may desire something other than service to the lotus feet of the Lord; *yadi kare kṛṣṇera bhajana*—but if he engages in Lord Kṛṣṇa's service; *nā māgiteha kṛṣna tāre dena sva-caraṇa*—Kṛṣṇa gives him shelter at His lotus feet, even though he does not aspire for it. *Kṛṣṇa kahe*—the Lord says; *āmā bhaje*—"He is engaged in My service"; *māge viṣaya-sukha*—"but he wants the benefits of material sense gratification." *Amṛta chāḍi' viṣa māge:*—"Such a devotee is like a person who asks for poison instead of nectar." *Ei baḍa mūrkha:* "That is his foolishness." *Ami—vijña:* "But I am experienced." *Ei mūrkhe 'viṣaya' kene diba:* "Why should I give such a foolish person the dirty things of material enjoyment?" *Sva-caraṇāmṛta:* "It would be better for Me to give him shelter at My lotus feet." *'Viṣaya' bhulāiba:* "I shall cause him to forget all material desires." *Kāma lāgi' kṛṣṇa bhaje*—if one engages in the service of the Lord for sense gratification; *paya kṛṣṇa-rase*—the result is that he ultimately gets a taste for serving the lotus feet of the Lord. *Kāma chāḍi" dāsa' haite haya abhilāṣe:* He then gives up all material desires and wants to become an eternal servant of the Lord.

TEXT 28

यद्यत्र नः स्वर्गसुखावशेषितं
स्विष्टस्य सूक्तस्य कृतस्य शोभनम् ।
तेनाजनाभे स्मृतिमज्जन्म नः स्याद्
वर्षे हरिर्यद्भजतां शं तनोति ॥२८॥

yady atra naḥ svarga-sukhāvaśeṣitaṁ
sviṣṭasya sūktasya kṛtasya śobhanam
tenājanābhe smṛtimaj janma naḥ syād
varṣe harir yad-bhajatāṁ śaṁ tanoti

yadi—if; *atra*—in this heavenly planet; *naḥ*—of us; *svarga-sukha-avaśeṣitam*—whatever remains after the enjoyment of heavenly happiness; *su-iṣṭasya*—of a perfect sacrifice; *su-uktasya*—of diligently studying the Vedic literature; *kṛtasya*—of having performed a kind act; *śobhanam*—the resultant actions; *tena*—by such a resultant action; *ajanābhe*—in the land of Bhārata-varṣa; *smṛti-mat janma*—a birth enabling one to remember the lotus feet of the Lord; *naḥ*—of us; *syāt*—let there be; *varṣe*—in the land; *hariḥ*—the Supreme Personality of Godhead; *yat*—wherein; *bhajatām*—of the devotees; *śam tanoti*—expands the auspiciousness.

TRANSLATION

We are now living in the heavenly planets, undoubtedly as a result of our having performed ritualistic ceremonies, pious activities and yajñas and having studied the Vedas. However, our lives here will one day be finished. We pray that at that time, if any merit remains from our pious activities, we may again take birth in Bhārata-varṣa as human beings able to remember the lotus feet of the Lord. The Lord is so kind that He personally comes to the land of Bhārata-varṣa and expands the good fortune of its people.

PURPORT

It is certainly as a result of pious activities that one takes birth in the heavenly planets, but from those planets one must nevertheless come down again to earth, as stated in *Bhagavad-gītā* (*kṣīṇe puṇye martya-lokaṁ viśanti*). Even the demigods must return to earth to work like ordinary men when the results of their pious activities expire. Nevertheless, the demigods desire to come to the land of Bhārata-varṣa if even a small portion of the merits of their pious activities remains. In other words, to take birth in Bhārata-varṣa, one must perform more pious activities than the demigods. In Bhārata-varṣa one is naturally Kṛṣṇa conscious, and if one further cultivates his Kṛṣṇa consciousness, by the grace of Kṛṣṇa he certainly expands his good fortune by becoming perfect in Kṛṣṇa consciousness and very easily going back home, back to Godhead. In many other places in the Vedic literature it is found that even the demigods want to come to this land of Bhārata-varṣa. A foolish person may desire to be promoted to the heavenly planets as a result of his pious activities, but even the demigods from the heavenly planets want to come to Bhārata-varṣa and achieve bodies that may be very easily used to cultivate Kṛṣṇa consciousness. Therefore Śrī Caitanya Mahāprabhu repeatedly says:

bhārata-bhūmite haila manuṣya-janma yāra
janma sārthaka kari' kara para-upakāra

A human being born in the land of Bhārata-varṣa has the special prerogative to develop Kṛṣṇa consciousness. Therefore those already born in Bhārata-varṣa should take lessons from the *śāstras* and *guru* and should fully take advantage of the mercy of Śrī Caitanya Mahāprabhu in order to be fully equipped with Kṛṣṇa consciousness. By taking full advantage of Kṛṣṇa consciousness, one goes back home, back to Godhead (*yānti mad-yājino'pi mām*). The Kṛṣṇa consciousness movement is therefore spreading this facility to human society by opening many, many centers all over the world so that people may associate with the pure devotees of the Kṛṣṇa consciousness movement, understand the science of Kṛṣṇa consciousness and ultimately go back home, back to Godhead.

TEXTS 29–30

श्रीशुक उवाच

जम्बूद्वीपस्य च राजन्नुपद्वीपानष्टौ हैक उपदिशन्ति सगरात्मजैरश्वान्वेषण इमां महीं परितो निखनद्भिरुपकल्पितान् ॥ २९ ॥ तद्यथा स्वर्णप्रस्थश्चन्द्रशुक्ल आवर्तनो रमणको मन्दरहरिणः पाञ्चजन्यः सिंहलो लङ्केति ॥ ३० ॥

śrī-śuka uvāca
jambūdvīpasya ca rājann upadvīpān aṣṭau haika upadiśanti sagarātmajair aśvānveṣaṇa imāṁ mahīṁ parito nikhanadbhir upakalpitān. tad yathā svarṇaprasthaś candraśukla āvartano ramaṇako mandarahariṇaḥ pāñcajanyaḥ siṁhalo laṅketi.

śrī-śukaḥ uvāca—Śrī Śukadeva Gosvāmī continued to speak; *jambūdvīpasya*—of the island known as Jambūdvīpa; *ca*—also; *rājan*—O King; *upadvīpān aṣṭau*—eight subordinate islands; *ha*—certainly; *eke*—some; *upadiśanti*—learned scholars describe; *sagara-ātma-jaiḥ*—by the sons of Mahārāja Sagara; *aśva-anveṣaṇe*—while trying to find their lost horse; *imām*—this; *mahīm*—tract of land; *paritaḥ*—all around; *nikhanadbhiḥ*—digging; *upakalpitān*—created; *tat*—that; *yathā*—as follows; *svarṇa-prasthaḥ*—Svarṇaprastha; *candra-śuklaḥ*—Candraśukla; *āvartanaḥ*—Āvartana; *ramaṇakaḥ*—Ramaṇaka; *mandara-hariṇaḥ*—Mandarahariṇa; *pāñcajanyaḥ*—Pāñcajanya; *siṁhalaḥ*—Siṁhala; *laṅkā*—Laṅkā; *iti*—thus.

TRANSLATION

Śrī Śukadeva Gosvāmī said: My dear King, in the opinion of some learned scholars, eight smaller islands surround Jambūdvīpa. When the sons of Mahārāja Sagara were searching all over the world for their lost horse, they dug up the earth, and in this way eight adjoining islands came

into existence. The names of these islands are Svarṇaprastha, Candraśukla, Āvartana, Ramaṇaka, Mandarahariṇa, Pāñcajanya, Siṁhala and Laṅkā.

PURPORT

In the *Kūrma Purāṇa* there is this statement about the desires of the demigods:

anadhikāriṇo devāḥ
svarga-sthā bhāratodbhavam
vāñchanty ātma-vimokṣārtha-
mudrekārthe'dhikāriṇaḥ

Although the demigods are situated in exalted positions in the heavenly planets, they nevertheless desire to descend to the land of Bhārata-varṣa on the planet earth. This indicates that even the demigods are unfit to reside in Bhārata-varṣa. Therefore if persons already born in Bhāratavarṣa live like cats and dogs, not taking full advantage of their birth in this land, they are certainly unfortunate.

TEXT 31

एवं तव भारतोत्तम जम्बूद्वीपवर्षविभागो यथोपदेशमुपवर्णित इति ॥३१॥

evaṁ tava bhāratottama jambūdvīpa-varṣa-vibhāgo yathopadeśam upavarṇita iti.

evam—thus; *tava*—unto you; *bhārata-uttama*—O best of the descendents of Bharata; *jambūdvīpa-varṣa-vibhāgaḥ*—the divisions of the island of Jambūdvīpa; *yathā-upadeśam*—as much as I am instructed by the authorities; *upavarṇitaḥ*—explained; *iti*—thus.

TRANSLATION

My dear King Parīkṣit, O best of the descendants of Bharata Mahārāja, I have thus described to you, as I myself have been instructed, the island of Bhārata-varṣa and its adjoining islands. These are the islands that constitute Jambūdvīpa.

Thus end the Bhaktivedanta purports of the Fifth Canto, Nineteenth Chapter, of the Śrīmad-Bhāgavatam, *entitled "A Description of the Island of Jambūdvīpa."*

CHAPTER TWENTY

Studying the Structure of the Universe

In this chapter there is a description of various islands, beginning with Plakṣadvīpa, and the oceans that surround them. There is also a description of the location and dimensions of the mountain known as Lokāloka. The island of Plakṣadvīpa, which is twice as broad as Jambūdvīpa, is surrounded by an ocean of salt water. The master of this island is Idhmajihva, one of the sons of Mahārāja Priyavrata. The island is divided into seven regions, each with a mountain and a large river.

The second island is called Śālmalīdvīpa. It is surrounded by an ocean of liquor and is 3,200,000 miles wide, twice as wide as Plakṣadvīpa. The master of this island is Yajñabāhu, one of the sons of Mahārāja Priyavrata. Like Plakṣadvīpa, this island is also divided into seven regions, each with a mountain and a very large river. The inhabitants of this island worship the Supreme Personality of Godhead in the form of Candrātmā.

The third island, which is surrounded by an ocean of clarified butter and is also divided into seven regions, is called Kuśadvīpa. Its master is Hiraṇyaretā, another son of Mahārāja Priyavrata, and its inhabitants worship the Supreme Personality of Godhead in the form of Agni, the fire-god. The width of this island is 6,400,000 miles, or, in other words, twice the width of Śālmalīdvīpa.

The fourth island, Krauñcadvīpa, which is surrounded by an ocean of milk, is 12,800,000 miles wide and is also divided, like the others, into seven regions, each with a large mountain and a large river. The master of this island is Ghṛtapṛṣṭha, another son of Mahārāja Priyavrata. The inhabitants of this island worship the Supreme Personality of Godhead in the form of water.

The fifth island, Śākadvīpa, which is 25,600,000 miles wide, is surrounded by an ocean of yogurt. Its master is Medhātithi, another son of Mahārāja Priyavrata. It is also divided into seven regions, each with a large mountain and a large river. Its inhabitants worship the Supreme Personality of Godhead in the form of Vāyu, air.

The sixth island, Puṣkaradvīpa, which is twice as wide as the previous island, is surrounded by an ocean of clear water. Its master is Vītihotra, another son of Mahārāja Priyavrata. The island is divided in two by a large mountain named Mānasottara. The inhabitants of this island worship Svayambhū, another feature of the Supreme Personality of Godhead. Beyond Puṣkaradvīpa there are two islands, one always lit by the sunshine and the other always dark. Between them is a mountain called Lokāloka, which is situated one billion miles from the edge of the universe. Lord Nārāyaṇa, expanding His opulence, resides upon this mountain. The area beyond Lokāloka Mountain is called Aloka-varṣa, and beyond Aloka-varṣa is the pure destination of persons who desire liberation.

Vertically, the sun globe is situated just in the middle of the universe, in Antarikṣa, the space between Bhūrloka and Bhuvarloka. The distance between the sun and the circumference of Aṇḍa-golaka, the globe of the universe, is estimated to be twenty-five *koṭi yojanas* (two billion miles). Because the sun enters the universe and divides the sky, it is known as Mārtaṇḍa, and because it is produced from Hiraṇyagarbha, the body of the *mahat-tattva,* it is also called Hiraṇyagarbha.

TEXT 1

श्रीशुक उवाच

अतः परं प्लक्षादीनां प्रमाणलक्षणसंस्थानतो वर्षविभाग उपवर्ण्यते ॥१॥

śrī-śuka uvāca

ataḥ paraṁ plakṣādīnāṁ pramāṇa-lakṣaṇa-saṁsthānato varṣa-vibhāga upavarṇyate.

śrī-śukaḥ uvāca—Śukadeva Gosvāmī said; *ataḥ param*—after this; *plakṣa-ādīnām*—of the island named Plakṣa and others; *pramāṇa- lakṣaṇa-saṁsthānataḥ*—from the angle of dimensions, particular characteristics and form; *varṣa-vibhāgaḥ*—the division of the island; *upavarṇyate*—is described.

TRANSLATION

The great sage Śukadeva Gosvāmī said: Hereafter I shall describe the dimensions, characteristics and forms of the six islands beginning with the island of Plakṣa.

TEXT 2

जम्बूद्वीपोऽयं यावत्प्रमाणविस्तारस्तावता क्षारोदधिना परिवेष्टितो यथा मेरुर्जम्ब्वाख्येन लवणोदधिरपि ततो द्विगुणविशालेन प्लक्षाख्येन परिक्षिप्तो यथा परिखा बाह्योपवनेन। प्लक्षो जम्बूप्रमाणो द्वीपाख्याकरो हिरण्मय उत्थितो यत्राग्निरुपास्ते सप्तजिह्वस्तस्याधिपतिः प्रियव्रतात्मज इध्मजिह्वः स्वं द्वीपं सप्तवर्षाणि विभज्य सप्तवर्षनामभ्य आत्मजेभ्य आकलय्य स्वयमात्मयोगेनोपरराम ॥२॥

jambūdvīpo 'yaṁ yāvat-pramāṇa-vistāras tāvatā kṣārodadhinā pariveṣṭito yathā merur jambv-ākhyena lavaṇodadhir api tato dvi-guṇa-viśālena plakṣākhyena parikṣipto yathā parikhā bāhyopavanena; plakṣo jambū-pramāṇo dvīpākhyākaro hiraṇmaya utthito yatrāgnir upāste sapta-jihvas tasyādhipatiḥ priyavratātmaja idhmajihvaḥ svaṁ dvīpaṁ sapta-varṣāṇi vibhajya sapta-varṣa-nāmabhya ātmajebhya ākalayya svayam ātma-yogenopararāma.

jambū-dvīpaḥ—Jambūdvīpa, the island named Jambū; *ayam*—this; *yāvat-pramāṇa-vistāraḥ*—as much as the measure of its width, namely 100,000 *yojanas* (one *yojana* equals eight miles); *tāvatā*—so much; *kṣāra-udadhinā*—by the ocean of salt water; *pariveṣṭitaḥ*—surrounded; *yathā*—just as; *meruḥ*—Sumeru Mountain; *jambū-ākhyena*—by the island named Jambū; *lavaṇa-udadhiḥ*—the ocean of salt water; *api*—certainly; *tataḥ*—thereafter; *dvi-guṇa-viśālena*—which is twice as wide; *plakṣa-ākhyena*—by the island named Plakṣa; *parikṣiptaḥ*—surrounded; *yathā*—like; *parikhā*—a moat; *bāhya*—external; *upavanena*—by a gardenlike forest; *plakṣaḥ*—a *plakṣa* tree; *jambū-pramāṇaḥ*—having the height of the *jambū* tree; *dvīpa-ākhyā-karaḥ*—causing the name of the island; *hiraṇmayaḥ*—magnificently splendorous; *utthitaḥ*—rising; *yatra*—where; *agniḥ*—a fire; *upāste*—is situated; *sapta-jihvaḥ*—having seven flames; *tasya*—of that island; *adhipatiḥ*—the king or master; *priyavrata-ātmajaḥ*—the son of King Priyavrata; *idhma-jihvaḥ*—named Idhmajihva; *svam*—own; *dvīpam*—island; *sapta*—seven; *varṣāṇi*—tracts of land; *vibhajya*—dividing into; *sapta-varṣa-nāmabhyaḥ*—for whom the seven tracts of land were named; *ātmajebhyaḥ*—to his own sons; *ākalayya*—offering; *svayam*—personally; *ātma-yogena*—by the devotional service of the Lord; *upararāma*—he retired from all material activities.

TRANSLATION

As Sumeru Mountain is surrounded by Jambūdvīpa, Jambūdvīpa is also surrounded by an ocean of salt water. The breadth of Jambūdvīpa is 100,000 yojanas [800,000 miles], and the breadth of the saltwater ocean is the same. As a moat around a fort is sometimes surrounded by gardenlike forest, the saltwater ocean surrounding Jambūdvīpa is itself surrounded by Plakṣadvīpa. The breadth of Plakṣadvīpa is twice that of the saltwater ocean—in other words 200,000 yojanas [1,600,000 miles]. On Plakṣadvīpa there is a tree shining like gold and as tall as the jambū tree on Jambūdvīpa. At its root is a fire with seven flames. It is because this tree

is a plakṣa tree that the island is called Plakṣadvīpa. Plakṣadvīpa was governed by Idhmajihva, one of the sons of Mahārāja Priyavrata. He endowed the seven islands with the names of his seven sons, divided the islands among the sons, and then retired from active life to engage in the devotional service of the Lord.

TEXTS 3–4

शिवं यवसं सुभद्रं शान्तं क्षेमममृतमभयमिति वर्षाणि तेषु गिरयो नद्यश्च सप्तैवाभिज्ञाताः ॥ ३ ॥ मणिकूटो वज्रकूट इन्द्रसेनो ज्योतिष्मान् सुपर्णो हिरण्यष्ठीवो मेघमाल इति सेतुशैलाः। अरुणा नृम्णाऽऽङ्गिरसी सावित्री सुप्तभाता ऋतम्भरा सत्यम्भरा इति महानद्यः। यासां जलोपस्पर्शनविधूतरजस्तमसो हंसपतङ्गो-र्ध्वायनसत्याङ्गसंज्ञाश्चत्वारो वर्णाः सहस्रायुषो विबुधोपमसन्दर्शनप्रजननाः स्वर्गद्वारं त्रय्या विद्यया भगवन्तं त्रयीमयं सूर्यमात्मानं यजन्ते ॥ ४ ॥

śivaṁ yavasaṁ subhadraṁ śāntaṁ kṣemam amṛtam abhayam iti varṣāṇi teṣu girayo nadyaś ca saptaivābhijñātāḥ; maṇikūṭo vajrakūṭa indraseno jyotiṣmān suparṇo hiraṇyaṣṭhīvo meghamāla iti setu-śailāḥ aruṇā nṛmṇāṅgirasī sāvitrī suptabhātā ṛtambharā satyambharā iti mahā-nadyaḥ; yāsāṁ jalopasparśana-vidhūta-rajas-tamaso haṁsa-pataṅgordhvāyana-satyāṅga-saṁjñāś catvāro varṇāḥ sahasrāyuṣo vibudhopama-sandarśana-prajananāḥ svarga-dvāraṁ trayyā vidyayā bhagavantaṁ trayīmayaṁ sūryam ātmānaṁ yajante.

śivam—Śiva; *yavasam*—Yavasa; *subhadram*—Subhadra; *śāntam*—Śānta; *kṣemam*—Kṣema; *amṛtam*—Amṛta; *abhayam*—Abhaya; *iti*—thus; *varṣāṇi*—the tracts of land according to the names of the seven sons; *teṣu*—in them; *girayaḥ*—mountains; *nadyaḥ ca*—and rivers; *sapta*—seven; *eva*—indeed; *abhijñātāḥ*—are known; *maṇi-kūṭaḥ*—Maṇikūṭa; *vajra-kūṭaḥ*—Vajrakūṭa; *indra-senaḥ*—Indrasena; *jyotiṣmān*—Jyotiṣmān; *suparṇaḥ*—Suparṇa; *hiraṇya-ṣṭhīvaḥ*—Hiraṇyaṣṭhīva; *megha-mālaḥ*—Meghamāla; *iti*—thus; *setu-śailāḥ*—the ranges of mountains marking the borders of the *varṣas; aruṇā*—Aruṇā; *nṛmṇā*—Nṛmṇā; *āṅgirasī*—Āṅgirasī; *sāvitrī*—Sāvitrī; *supta-bhātā*—Suptabhātā; *ṛtambharā*—Ṛtambharā; *satyambharā*—Satyambharā; *iti*—thus; *mahā-nadyaḥ*—very large rivers; *yāsām*—of which; *jala-upasparśana*—simply by touching the water; *vidhūta*—washed off; *rajaḥ-tamasaḥ*—whose modes of passion and ignorance; *haṁsa*—Haṁsa; *pataṅga*—Pataṅga; *ūrdhvāyana*—Ūrdhvāyana; *satyāṅga*—Satyāṅga; *saṁjñāḥ*—

named; *catvāraḥ*—four; *varṇāḥ*—castes or divisions of men; *sahasra-āyuṣaḥ* —living for one thousand years; *vibudha-upama*—similar to the demigods; *sandarśana*—in having very beautiful forms; *prajananāḥ*—and in producing children; *svarga-dvāram*—the gateway to the heavenly planets; *trayyā vidyayā* —by performing ritualistic ceremonies according to Vedic principles; *bhagavantam*—the Supreme Personality of Godhead; *trayī-mayam*—established in the *Vedas; sūryam ātmānam*—the Supersoul, represented by the sun-god; *yajante*—they worship.

TRANSLATION

The seven islands [varṣas] are named according to the names of those seven sons—Śiva, Yavasa, Subhadra, Śānta, Kṣema, Amṛta and Abhaya. In those seven tracts of land, there are seven mountains and seven rivers. The mountains are named Maṇikūṭa, Vajrakūṭa, Indrasena, Jyotiṣmān, Suparṇa, Hiraṇyaṣṭhīva and Meghamāla, and the rivers are named Aruṇā, Nṛmṇā, Āṅgirasī, Sāvitrī, Suptabhātā, Ṛtambharā and Satyambharā. One can immediately be free from material contamination by touching or bathing in those rivers, and the four castes of people who live in Plakṣadvīpa—the Haṁsas, Pataṅgas, Ūrdhvāyanas and Satyāṅgas—purify themselves in that way. The inhabitants of Plakṣadvīpa live for one thousand years. They are beautiful like the demigods, and they also beget children like the demigods. By completely performing the ritualistic ceremonies mentioned in the Vedas and by worshiping the Supreme Personality of Godhead as represented by the sun-god, they attain the sun, which is a heavenly planet.

PURPORT

According to general understanding, there are originally three deities—Lord Brahmā, Lord Viṣṇu and Lord Śiva—and people with a poor fund of knowledge consider Lord Viṣṇu no better than Lord Brahmā or Lord Śiva. This conclusion, however, is invalid. As stated in the *Vedas, iṣṭāpūrtaṁ bahudhā jāyamānaṁ viśvaṁ bibharti bhuvanasya nābhiḥ tad evāgnis tad vāyus tat sūryas tad u candramāḥ agniḥ sarvadaivataḥ.* This means that the Supreme Lord, who accepts and enjoys the results of Vedic ritualistic ceremonies (technically called *iṣṭāpūrta*), who maintains the entire creation, who supplies the necessities of all living entities (*eko bahūnāṁ yo vidadhāti kāmān*) and who is the central point of all creation, is Lord Viṣṇu. Lord Viṣṇu expands as the demigods known as Agni, Vāyu, Sūrya and Candra, who are simply parts and parcels of His body. Lord Kṛṣṇa says in *Śrīmad Bhagavad-gītā* (9.23):

ye'py anya-devatā-bhaktā
yajante śraddhayānvitāḥ
te'pi mām eva kaunteya
yajanty avidhi-pūrvakam

"Devotees who worship the demigods with firm faith worship Me also, but not according to regulative principles." In other words, if one worships the demigods but does not understand the relationship between the demigods and the Supreme Personality of Godhead, his worship is irregular. Kṛṣṇa also says in *Bhagavad-gītā* (9.24), *ahaṁ hi sarva-yajñānāṁ bhoktā ca prabhur eva ca:* "I am the only enjoyer of ritualistic ceremonies."

It may be argued that the demigods are as important as Lord Viṣṇu because the names of the demigods are different names of Viṣṇu. This, however, is not a sound conclusion, for it is contradicted in the Vedic literatures. The *Vedas* declare:

candramā manaso jātaś cakṣoḥ sūryo ajāyata; śrotrādayaś ca prāṇaś ca mukhād agnir ajāyata; nārāyaṇād brahmā, nārāyaṇād rudro jāyate, nārāyaṇāt prajāpatiḥ jāyate, nārāyaṇād indro jāyate, nārāyaṇād aṣṭau vasavo jāyante, nārāyaṇād ekādaśa rudrā jāyante.

"The demigod of the moon, Candra, came from the mind of Nārāyaṇa, and the sun-god came from His eyes. The controlling deities of hearing and the life air came from Nārāyaṇa, and the controlling deity of fire was generated from His mouth. Prajāpati, Lord Brahmā, came from Nārāyaṇa, Indra came from Nārāyaṇa, and the eight Vasus, the eleven expansions of Lord Śiva and the twelve Ādityas also came from Nārāyaṇa." In the *smṛti* Vedic literature it is also said:

brahmā śambhus tathaivārkaś
candramāś ca śatakratuḥ
evam ādyās tathaivānye
yuktā vaiṣṇava-tejasā

jagat-kāryāvasāne tu
viyujyante ca tejasā
vitejaś ca te sarve
pañcatvam upayānti te

"Brahmā, Śambhu, Sūrya and Indra are all merely products of the power of the Supreme Personality of Godhead. This is also true of the many other demigods whose names are not mentioned here. When the cosmic manifestation is annihilated, these different expansions of Nārāyaṇa's potencies will merge into Nārāyaṇa. In other words, all these demigods will die. Their living force will be withdrawn, and they will merge into Nārāyaṇa."

Therefore it should be concluded that Lord Viṣṇu, not Lord Brahmā or Lord Śiva, is the Supreme Personality of Godhead. As a government officer is sometimes accepted as the entire government although he is actually but a departmental manager, so the demigods, having achieved power of attorney from Viṣṇu, act on His behalf, although they are not as powerful as He. All the demigods must work under the orders of Viṣṇu. Therefore it is said, *ekale īśvara kṛṣṇa, āra saba bhṛtya.* The only master is Lord Kṛṣṇa, or Lord Viṣṇu, and all others are His obedient servants, who act exactly according to His orders. The distinction between Lord Viṣṇu and the demigods is also expressed in *Bhagavad-gītā* (9.25). *yānti deva-vratā devān...yānti mad-yājino'pi mām:* those who worship the demigods go to the planets of the demigods, whereas the worshipers of Lord Kṛṣṇa and Lord Viṣṇu go to the planets in Vaikuṇṭha. These are the statements of the *smṛti.* Therefore the idea that Lord Viṣṇu is on the same level as the demigods is in contradiction to the *śāstras.* The demigods are not supreme. The supremacy of the demigods is dependent on the mercy of Lord Nārāyaṇa (Viṣṇu, or Kṛṣṇa).

TEXT 5

प्रत्नस्य विष्णो रूपं यत्सत्यस्यर्तस्य ब्रह्मणः ।
अमृतस्य च मृत्योश्च सूर्यमात्मानमीमहीति ॥ ५ ॥

pratnasya viṣṇo rūpaṁ yat
satyasyartasya brahmaṇaḥ
amṛtasya ca mṛtyoś ca
sūryam ātmānam īmahīti

pratnasya—of the oldest person; *viṣṇoḥ*—Lord Viṣṇu; *rūpam*—the form; *yat*—which; *satyasya*—of the Absolute Truth; *ṛtasya*—of *dharma; brahmaṇaḥ*—of the Supreme Brahman; *amṛtasya*—of the auspicious result; *ca*—and; *mṛtyoḥ*—of death (the inauspicious result); *ca*—and; *sūryam*—the demigod Sūrya; *ātmānam*—the Supersoul or origin of all souls; *īmahi*—we approach for shelter; *iti*—thus.

TRANSLATION

[This is the mantra by which the inhabitants of Plakṣadvīpa worship the Supreme Lord.] Let us take shelter of the sun-god, who is a reflection

of Lord Viṣṇu, the all-expanding Supreme Personality of Godhead, the oldest of all persons. Viṣṇu is the only worshipable Lord. He is the Vedas, He is religion, and He is the origin of all auspicious and inauspicious results.

PURPORT

Lord Viṣṇu is even the Supreme Lord of death, as confirmed in *Bhagavad-gītā* (*mṛtyuḥ sarva-haraś cāham*). There are two kinds of activity—auspicious and inauspicious—and both are controlled by Lord Viṣṇu. Inauspicious activities are said to be behind Lord Viṣṇu, whereas auspicious activities stand before Him. The auspicious and the inauspicious exist throughout the entire world, and Lord Viṣṇu is the controller of them both.

In regard to this verse, Śrīla Madhvācārya says:

sūrya-somāgni-vārīśa-
vidhātṛṣu yathā-kramam
plakṣādi-dvīpa-saṁsthāsu
sthitaṁ harim upāsate

There are many lands, fields, mountains and oceans throughout the creation, and everywhere the Supreme Personality of Godhead is worshiped by His different names.

Śrīla Vīrarāghava Ācārya explains this verse of *Śrīmad-Bhāgavatam* as follows. The original cause of the cosmic manifestation must be the oldest person and must therefore be beyond material transformations. He is the enjoyer of all auspicious activities and is the cause of conditional life and also liberation. The demigod Sūrya, who is categorized as a very powerful *jīva,* or living entity, is a representation of one of the parts of His body. We are naturally subordinate to powerful living entities, and therefore we can worship the various demigods as living beings who are powerful representatives of the Supreme Personality of Godhead. Although the worship of the sun-god is recommended in this *mantra,* He is worshiped not as the Supreme Personality of Godhead but as His powerful representative.

In the *Kaṭha Upaniṣad* (1.3.1) it is said:

ṛtaṁ pibantau sukṛtasya loke
guhāṁ praviṣṭau parame parārdhe
chāyātapau brahmavido vadanti
pañcāgnayo ye ca tri-ṇāciketāḥ

"O Nāciketā, the expansions of Lord Viṣṇu as the tiny living entity and the Supersoul are both situated within the cave of the heart of this body. Having entered that cavity, the living entity, resting on the chief of the life airs, enjoys the results of activities, and the Supersoul, acting as witness enables him to enjoy them. Those who are well-versed in knowledge of Brahman and those householders who carefully follow the Vedic regulations say that the difference between the two is like the difference between a shadow and the sun."

In the *Śvetāśvatara Upaniṣad* (6.16) it is said:

sa viśvakṛd viśvavidātmayoniḥ
jñaḥ kālākāro guṇī sarvavid yaḥ
pradhāna-kṣetrajña-patir guṇeśaḥ
saṁsāra-mokṣa-sthiti-bandha-hetuḥ

"The Supreme Lord, the creator of this cosmic manifestation, knows every nook and corner of His creation. Although He is the cause of creation, there is no cause for His appearance. He is fully aware of everything. He is the Supersoul, the master of all transcendental qualities, and He is the master of this cosmic manifestation in regard to bondage to the conditional state of material existence and liberation from that bondage."

Similarly, in the *Taittirīya Upaniṣad* (2.8) it is said:

bhīṣāsmād vātaḥ pavate
bhīṣodeti sūryaḥ
bhīṣāsmād agniś candraś ca
mṛtyur dhāvati pañcamaḥ

"It is out of fear of the Supreme Brahman that the wind is blowing, out of fear of Him that the sun regularly rises and sets, and out of fear of Him that fire acts. It is only due to fear of Him that death and Indra, the King of heaven, perform their respective duties."

As described in this chapter, the inhabitants of the five islands beginning with Plakṣadvīpa worship the sun-god, the moon-god, the fire-god, the air-god and Lord Brahmā respectively. Although they engage in the worship of these five demigods, however, they actually worship Lord Viṣṇu, the Supersoul of all living entities, as indicated in this verse by the words *pratnasya viṣṇo rūpam.* Viṣṇu is *brahma, amṛta, mṛtyu*—the Supreme Brahman and the origin of everything, auspicious and inauspicious. He is situated in the heart of everyone, including all the demigods. As stated in *Bhagavad-gītā* (7.20), *kāmais tais tair hṛta-jñānāḥ prapadyante'nya devatāḥ:* those whose minds are distorted by material desires surrender unto the demigods. People who are almost blind because of lusty desires are recommended to worship the demigods to have their material desires fulfilled, but actually those desires are not fulfilled by the material demigods. Whatever the demigods do is done with the sanction of Lord Viṣṇu. People who are too lusty worship various demigods instead of worshiping Lord Viṣṇu, the Supersoul of all living entities, but ultimately it is Lord Viṣṇu they worship because He is the Supersoul of all demigods.

TEXT 6

प्लक्षादिषु पञ्चसु पुरुषाणामायुरिन्द्रियमोजः सहो बलं बुद्धिर्विक्रम इति च सर्वेषामौत्पत्तिकी सिद्धिरविशेषेण वर्तते ॥६॥

plakṣādiṣu pañcasu puruṣāṇām āyur indriyam ojaḥ saho balaṁ buddhir vikrama iti ca sarveṣām autpattikī siddhir aviśeṣeṇa vartate.

plakṣa-ādiṣu—in the islands headed by Plakṣa; *pañcasu*—five; *puruṣāṇām*—of the inhabitants; *āyuḥ*—long duration of life; *indriyam*—soundness of the senses; *ojaḥ*—bodily strength; *sahaḥ*—mental strength; *balam*—physical strength; *buddhiḥ*—intelligence; *vikramaḥ*—bravery; *iti*—thus; *ca*—also; *sarveṣām*—of all of them; *autpattikī*—inborn; *siddhiḥ*—perfection; *aviśeṣeṇa*—without distinction; *vartate*—exists.

TRANSLATION

O King, longevity, sensory prowess, physical and mental strength, intelligence and bravery are naturally and equally manifested in all the inhabitants of the five islands headed by Plakṣadvīpa.

TEXT 7

प्लक्षः स्वसमानेनेक्षुरसोदेनावृतो यथा तथा द्वीपोऽपि शाल्मलो द्विगुणविशालः समानेन सुरोदेनावृतः परिवृङ्क्ते ॥७॥

plakṣaḥ sva-samānenekṣu-rasodenāvṛto yathā tathā dvīpo'pi śālmalo dvi-guṇa-viśālaḥ samānena surodenāvṛtaḥ parivṛṅkte.

plakṣaḥ—the land known as Plakṣadvīpa; *sva-samānena*—equal in width; *ikṣu-rasa*—of sugarcane juice; *udena*—by an ocean; *āvṛtaḥ*—surrounded; *yathā*—just as; *tathā*—similarly; *dvīpaḥ*—another island; *api*—also;

śālmalaḥ—known as Śālmala; *dvi-guṇa-viśālaḥ*—twice as big; *samānena*—equal in width; *surā-udena*—by an ocean of liquor; *āvṛtaḥ*—surrounded; *parivṛṅkte*—exists.

TRANSLATION

Plakṣadvīpa is surrounded by an ocean of sugarcane juice, equal in breadth to the island itself. Similarly, there is then another island—Śālmalīdvīpa—twice as broad as Plakṣadvīpa [400,000 yojanas, or 3,200,000 miles] and surrounded by an equally broad body of water called Surāsāgara, the ocean that tastes like liquor.

TEXT 8

यत्र ह वै शाल्मली प्लक्षायामा यस्यां वाव किल निलयमाहुर्भगवतश्छन्दःस्तुतः पतत्त्रिराजस्य सा द्वीपहूतये उपलक्ष्यते ॥८॥

yatra ha vai śālmalī plakṣāyāmā yasyāṁ vāva kila nilayam āhur
bhagavataś chandaḥ-stutaḥ patattri-rājasya sā dvīpa-hūtaye upalakṣyate.

yatra—where; *ha vai*—certainly; *śālmalī*—a *śālmalī* tree; *plakṣa-āyāmā*—as big as the *plakṣa* tree (one hundred *yojanas* broad and eleven hundred *yojanas* high); *yasyām*—in which; *vāva kila*—indeed; *nilayam*—rest or living place; *āhuḥ*—they say; *bhagavataḥ*—of the most powerful; *chandaḥ-stutaḥ*—who worships the Lord by Vedic prayers; *patattri-rājasya*—of Garuḍa, the carrier of Lord Viṣṇu; *sā*—that tree; *dvīpa-hūtaye*—for the name of the island; *upalakṣyate*—is distinguished.

TRANSLATION

On Śālmalīdvīpa there is a śālmalī tree, from which the island takes its name. That tree is as broad and tall as the plakṣa tree—in other words 100 yojanas [800 miles] broad and 1,100 yojanas [8,800 miles] tall. Learned scholars say that this gigantic tree is the residence of Garuḍa, the king of all birds and carrier of Lord Viṣṇu. In that tree, Garuḍa offers Lord Viṣṇu his Vedic prayers.

TEXT 9

तद्द्वीपाधिपतिः प्रियव्रतात्मजो यज्ञबाहुः स्वसुतेभ्यः सप्तभ्यस्तन्नामानि सप्तवर्षाणि व्यभजत्सुरोचनं सौमनस्यं रमणकं देववर्षं पारिभद्रमाप्यायनमविज्ञातमिति ॥९॥

tad-dvīpādhipatiḥ priyavratātmajo yajñabāhuḥ sva-sutebhyaḥ
saptabhyas tan-nāmāni sapta-varṣāṇi vyabhajat surocanaṁ
saumanasyaṁ ramaṇakaṁ deva-varṣaṁ pāribhadram āpyāyanam
avijñātam iti.

tat-dvīpa-adhipatiḥ—the master of that island; *priyavrata-ātmajaḥ*—the son of Mahārāja Priyavrata; *yajña-bāhuḥ*—named Yajñabāhu; *sva-sutebhyaḥ*—unto his sons; *saptabhyaḥ*—seven in number; *tat-nāmāni*—having names according to their names; *sapta-varṣāṇi*—seven tracts of land; *vyabhajat*—divided; *surocanam*—Surocana; *saumanasyam*—Saumanasya; *ramaṇakam*—Ramaṇaka; *deva-varṣam*—Deva-varṣa; *pāribhadram*—Pāribhadra; *āpyāyanam*—Āpyāyana; *avijñātam*—Avijñāta; *iti*—thus.

TRANSLATION

The son of Mahārāja Priyavrata named Yajñabāhu, the master of Sālmalīdvīpa, divided the island into seven tracts of land, which he gave to his seven sons. The names of those divisions, which correspond to the names of the sons, are Surocana, Saumanasya, Ramaṇaka, Deva-varṣa, Pāribhadra, Āpyāyana and Avijñāta.

TEXT 10

तेषु वर्षाद्रयो नद्यश्च सप्तैवाभिज्ञाताः स्वरसः शतशृङ्गो वामदेवः कुन्दो मुकुन्दः पुष्पवर्षः सहस्रश्रुतिरिति। अनुमतिः सिनीवाली सरस्वती कुहू रजनी नन्दा राकेति ॥१०॥

teṣu varṣādrayo nadyaś ca saptaivābhijñātāḥ svarasaḥ śataśṛṅgo
vāmadevaḥ kundo mukundaḥ puṣpa-varṣaḥ sahasra-śrutir iti; anumatiḥ
sinīvālī sarasvatī kuhū rajanī nandā rāketi.

teṣu—in those tracts of land; *varṣa-adrayaḥ*—mountains; *nadyaḥ ca*—as well as rivers; *sapta eva*—seven in number; *abhijñātāḥ*—understood; *svarasaḥ*—Svarasa; *śata-śṛṅgaḥ*—Śataśṛṅga; *vāma-devaḥ*—Vāmadeva; *kundaḥ*—Kunda; *mukundaḥ*—Mukunda; *puṣpa-varṣaḥ*—Puṣpa-varṣa; *sahasra-śrutiḥ*—Sahasra-śruti; *iti*—thus; *anumatiḥ*—Anumati; *sinīvālī*—Sinīvālī; *sarasvatī*—Sarasvatī; *kuhū*—Kuhū; *rajanī*—Rajanī; *nandā*—Nandā; *rākā*—Rākā; *iti*—thus.

TRANSLATION

In those tracts of land there are seven mountains—Svarasa, Śataśṛṅga, Vāmadeva, Kunda, Mukunda, Puṣpa-varṣa and Sahasra-śruti. There are

also seven rivers—Anumati, Sinīvālī, Sarasvatī, Kuhū, Rajanī, Nandā and Rākā. They are still existing.

TEXT 11

तद्वर्षपुरुषाः श्रुतधरवीर्यधरवसुन्धरेषन्धरसंज्ञा भगवन्तं वेदमयं सोममात्मानं वेदेन यजन्ते ॥११॥

tad-varṣa-puruṣāḥ śrutadhara-vīryadhara-vasundhareṣandhara-saṁjñā bhagavantaṁ vedamayaṁ somam ātmānaṁ vedena yajante.

tat-varṣa-puruṣāḥ—the residents of those tracts of land; *śrutadhara*—Śrutadhara; *vīryadhara*—Vīryadhara; *vasundhara*—Vasundhara; *iṣandhara*—Iṣandhara; *saṁjñāḥ*—known as; *bhagavantam*—the Supreme Personality of Godhead; *veda-mayam*—fully conversant with the Vedic knowledge; *somam ātmānam*—represented by the living entity known as Soma; *vedena*—by following the Vedic rules and regulations; *yajante*—they worship.

TRANSLATION

Strictly following the cult of varṇāśrama-dharma, the inhabitants of those islands, who are known as Śrutidharas, Vīryadharas, Vasundharas and Iṣandharas, all worship the expansion of the Supreme Personality of Godhead named Soma, the moon-god.

TEXT 12

स्वगोभिः पितृदेवेभ्यो विभजन् कृष्णशुक्लयोः ।
प्रजानां सर्वासां राजान्धः सोमो न आस्त्विति ॥१२॥

sva-gobhiḥ pitṛ-devebhyo
vibhajan kṛṣṇa-śuklayoḥ
prajānāṁ sarvāsāṁ rājā-
ndhaḥ somo na āstv iti

sva-gobhiḥ—by expansion of his own illuminating rays; *pitṛ-devebhyaḥ*—unto the *pitās* and the demigods; *vibhajan*—dividing; *kṛṣṇa-śuklayoḥ*—into the two fortnights, dark and light; *prajānām*—of the citizens; *sarvāsām*—of all; *rājā*—the king; *andhaḥ*—food grains; *somaḥ*—the moon god; *naḥ*—toward us; *āstu*—let him remain favorable; *iti*—thus.

TRANSLATION

[The inhabitants of Śālmalīdvīpa worship the demigod of the moon in the following words.] By his own rays, the moon-god has divided the month into two fortnights, known as śukla and kṛṣṇa, for the distribution of food grains to the pitās and the demigods. The demigod of the moon is he who divides time, and he is the king of all the residents of the universe. We therefore pray that he may remain our king and guide, and we offer him our respectful obeisances.

TEXT 13

एवं सुरोदाद्बहिस्तद्द्विगुणः समानेनावृतो घृतोदेन यथापूर्वः कुशद्वीपो यस्मिन् कुशस्तम्बो देवकृतस्तद्द्वीपाख्याकरो ज्वलन इवापरः स्वशष्परोचिषा दिशो विराजयति ॥१३॥

evaṁ surodād bahis tad-dvi-guṇaḥ samānenāvṛto ghṛtodena yathā-pūrvaḥ kuśa-dvīpo yasmin kuśa-stambo deva-kṛtas tad-dvīpākhyākaro jvalana ivāparaḥ sva-śaṣpa-rociṣā diśo virājayati.

evam—thus; *surodāt*—from the ocean of liquor; *bahiḥ*—outside; *tat-dvi-guṇaḥ*—twice that; *samānena*—equal in width; *āvṛtaḥ*—surrounded; *ghṛta-udena*—an ocean of clarified butter; *yathā-pūrvaḥ*—as previously with Sālmalīdvīpa; *kuśa-dvīpa*—the island called Kuśadvīpa; *yasmin*—in which; *kuśa-stambaḥ*—*kuśa* grass; *deva-kṛtaḥ*—created by the supreme will of the Supreme Personality of Godhead; *tat-dvīpa-ākhyā-karaḥ*—giving the island its name; *jvalanaḥ*—fire; *iva*—like; *aparaḥ*—another; *sva-śaṣpa-rociṣā*—by the effulgence of the young sprouting grass; *diśaḥ*—all directions; *virājayati*—illuminates.

TRANSLATION

Outside the ocean of liquor is another island, known as Kuśadvīpa, which is 800,000 yojanas [6,400,000 miles] wide, twice as wide as the ocean of liquor. As Śālmalīdvīpa is surrounded by a liquor ocean, Kuśadvīpa is surrounded by an ocean of liquid ghee as broad as the island itself. On Kuśadvīpa there are clumps of kuśa grass, from which the island takes its name. This kuśa grass, which was created by the demigods by the will of the Supreme Lord, appears like a second form of fire, but with very mild and pleasing flames. Its young shoots illuminate all directions.

PURPORT

From the descriptions in this verse, we can make an educated guess about the nature of the flames on the moon. Like the sun, the moon must also be full of flames because without flames there cannot be illumination. The flames on the moon, however, unlike those on the sun, must be mild and pleasing. This is our conviction. The modern theory that the moon is full of dust is not accepted in the verses of *Śrīmad-Bhāgavatam.* In regard to this verse, Śrīla Viśvanātha Cakravartī Ṭhākura says, *suśaṣpāṇi sukomala-śikhās teṣāṁ rociṣā:* the *kuśa* grass illuminates all directions, but its flames are very mild and pleasing. This gives some idea of the flames existing on the moon.

TEXT 14

तदद्द्वीपपतिः प्रैयव्रतो राजन् हिरण्यरेता नाम स्वं द्वीपं सप्तभ्यः स्वपुत्रेभ्यो यथाभागं विभज्य स्वयं तप आतिष्ठत वसुवसुदानदृढरुचिनाभिगुप्तस्तुत्यव्रतविविक्तवाम-देवनामभ्यः ॥१४॥

tad-dvīpa-patiḥ praiyavrato rājan hiraṇyaretā nāma svaṁ dvīpaṁ
saptabhyaḥ sva-putrebhyo yathā-bhāgaṁ vibhajya svayaṁ tapa
ātiṣṭhata vasu-vasudāna-dṛḍharuci-nābhigupta-stutyavrata-vivikta-
vāmadeva-nāmabhyaḥ.

tat-dvīpa-patiḥ—the master of that island; *praiyavrataḥ*—the son of Mahārāja Priyavrata; *rājan*—O King; *hiraṇyaretā*—Hiraṇyaretā; *nāma*—named; *svam*—his own; *dvīpam*—island; *saptabhyaḥ*—unto seven; *sva-putrebhyaḥ*—his own sons; *yathā-bhāgam*—according to division; *vibhajya*—dividing; *svayam*—himself; *tapaḥ ātiṣṭhata*—engaged in austerities; *vasu*—unto Vasu; *vasudāna*—Vasudāna; *dṛḍharuci*—Dṛḍharuci; *nābhi-gupta*—Nābhigupta; *stutya-vrata*—Stutyavrata; *vivikta*—Vivikta; *vāma-deva*—Vāmadeva; *nāmabhyaḥ*—named.

TRANSLATION

O King, another son of Mahārāja Priyavrata, Hiraṇyaretā, was the king of this island. He divided it into seven parts, which he delivered to his seven sons according to the rights of inheritance. The King then retired from family life to engage in austerities. The names of those sons are Vasu, Vasudāna, Dṛḍharuci, Stutyavrata, Nābhigupta, Vivikta and Vāmadeva.

TEXT 15

तेषां वर्षेषु सीमागिरयो नद्यश्चाभिज्ञाताः सप्त सप्तैव चक्रश्चतुःशृङ्गः कपिलश्चित्रकूटो देवानीक ऊर्ध्वरोमा द्रविण इति रसकुल्या मधुकुल्या मित्रविन्दा श्रुतविन्दा देवगर्भा घृतच्युता मन्त्रमालेति ॥१५॥

teṣāṁ varṣeṣu sīmā-girayo nadyaś cābhijñātāḥ sapta saptaiva cakraś catuḥśṛṅgaḥ kapilaś citrakūṭo devānīka ūrdhvaromā draviṇa iti rasakulyā madhukulyā mitravindā śrutavindā devagarbhā ghṛtacyutā mantramāleti.

teṣām—all those sons; *varṣeṣu*—in the tracts of land; *sīmā-girayaḥ*—border mountains; *nadyaḥ ca*—as well as rivers; *abhijñātāḥ*—known; *sapta*—seven; *sapta*—seven; *eva*—certainly; *cakraḥ*—Cakra; *catuḥ-śṛṅgaḥ*—Catuḥ-śṛṅga; *kapilaḥ*—Kapila; *citra-kūṭaḥ*—Citrakūṭa; *devānīkaḥ*—Devānīka; *ūrdhva-romā*—Ūrdhvaromā; *draviṇaḥ*—Draviṇa; *iti*—thus; *rasa-kulyā*—Ramakulyā; *madhu-kulyā*—Madhukulyā; *mitra-vindā*—Mitravindā; *śruta-vindā*—Śrutavindā; *deva-garbhā*—Devagarbhā; *ghṛta-cyutā*—Ghṛtacyutā; *mantra-mālā*—Mantramālā; *iti*—thus.

TRANSLATION

In those seven islands there are seven boundary mountains, known as Cakra, Catuḥśṛṅga, Kapila, Citrakūṭa, Devānīka, Ūrdhvaromā and Draviṇa. There are also seven rivers, known as Ramakulyā, Madhukulyā, Mitravindā, Śrutavindā, Devagarbhā, Ghṛtacyutā and Mantramālā.

TEXT 16

यासां पयोभिः कुशद्वीपौकसः कुशलकोविदाभियुक्तकुलकसंज्ञा भगवन्तं जातवेदसरूपिणं कर्मकौशलेन यजन्ते ॥१६॥

yāsāṁ payobhiḥ kuśadvīpaukasaḥ kuśala-kovidābhiyukta-kulaka-saṁjñā bhagavantaṁ jātaveda-sarūpiṇaṁ karma-kauśalena yajante.

yāsām—of which; *payobhiḥ*—by the water; *kuśa-dvīpa-okasaḥ*—the inhabitants of the island known as Kuśadvīpa; *kuśala*—Kuśala; *kovida*—Kovida; *abhiyukta*—Abhiyukta; *kulaka*—Kulaka; *saṁjñāḥ*—named; *bhagavantam*—unto the Supreme Personality of Godhead; *jātaveda*—the demigod of fire; *sa-rūpiṇam*—manifesting the form; *karma-kauśalena*—by expertise in ritualistic ceremonies; *yajante*—they worship.

TRANSLATION

The inhabitants of the island of Kuśadvīpa are celebrated as the Kuśalas, Kovidas, Abhiyuktas and Kulakas. They are like the brāhmaṇas, kṣatriyas, vaiśyas and śūdras respectively. By bathing in the waters of those rivers, they all become purified. They are expert in performing ritualistic ceremonies according to the orders of the Vedic scriptures. Thus they worship the Lord in His aspect as the demigod of fire.

TEXT 17

परस्य ब्रह्मणः साक्षाज्जातवेदोऽसि हव्यवाट् ।
देवानां पुरुषाङ्गानां यज्ञेन पुरुषं यजेति ॥१७॥

parasya brahmaṇaḥ sākṣāj
jāta-vedo 'si havyavāṭ
devānāṁ puruṣāṅgānāṁ
yajñena puruṣaṁ yajeti

parasya—of the Supreme; *brahmaṇaḥ*—Brahman; *sākṣāt*—directly; *jāta-vedaḥ*—O fire-god; *asi*—you are; *havyavāṭ*—the carrier of Vedic offerings of grains and ghee; *devānām*—of all the demigods; *puruṣa-aṅgānām*—who are limbs of the Supreme Person; *yajñena*—by performing the ritualistic sacrifices; *puruṣam*—to the Supreme Person; *yaja*—please carry oblations; *iti*—thus.

TRANSLATION

[This is the mantra by which the inhabitants of Kuśadvīpa worship the fire-god.] O fire-god, you are a part of the Supreme Personality of Godhead, Hari, and you carry to Him all the offerings of sacrifices. Therefore we request you to offer to the Supreme Personality of Godhead the yajñic ingredients we are offering the demigods, for the Lord is the real enjoyer.

PURPORT

The demigods are servants who assist the Supreme Personality of Godhead. If one worships the demigods, the demigods, as servants of the Supreme, carry the sacrificial offerings to the Lord, like tax collectors collecting revenue from the citizens and bringing it to the government's treasury. The demigods cannot accept the sacrificial offerings; they simply carry the offerings to the Supreme Personality of Godhead. As stated by Śrīla Viśvanātha

Cakravartī Ṭhākura, *yasya prasādād bhagavat-prasādaḥ:* since the *guru* is a representative of the Supreme Personality of Godhead, he carries to the Lord whatever is offered to him. Similarly, all the demigods, as faithful servants of the Supreme Lord, hand over to the Supreme Lord whatever is offered to them in sacrificial performances. There is no fault in worshiping the demigods with this understanding, but to think that the demigods are independent of the Supreme Personality of Godhead and equal to Him is called *hṛta-jñāna,* a loss of intelligence (*kāmais tais tair hṛta jñānāḥ*). One who thinks that the demigods themselves are the actual benefactors is mistaken.

TEXT 18

तथा घृतोदाद्बहिः क्रौञ्चद्वीपो द्विगुणः स्वमानेन क्षीरोदेन परित उपक्लृप्तो वृतो यथा कुशद्वीपो घृतोदेन यस्मिन् क्रौञ्चो नाम पर्वतराजो द्वीपनामनिर्वर्तक आस्ते ॥१८॥

tathā ghṛtodād bahiḥ krauñcadvīpo dvi-guṇaḥ sva-mānena kṣīrodena
parita upakḷpto vṛto yathā kuśadvīpo ghṛtodena yasmin krauñco nāma
parvata-rājo dvīpa-nāma-nirvartaka āste.

tathā—so also; *ghṛta-udāt*—from the ocean of clarified butter; *bahiḥ*—outside; *krauñca-dvīpaḥ*—another island, known as Krauñcadvīpa; *dvi-guṇaḥ*—twice as big; *sva-mānena*—as the same measurement; *kṣīra-udena*—by an ocean of milk; *paritaḥ*—all around; *upakḷptaḥ*—surrounded; *vṛtaḥ*—surrounded; *yathā*—like; *kuśa-dvīpaḥ*—the island known as Kuśadvīpa; *ghṛta-udena*—by an ocean of clarified butter; *yasmin*—in which; *krauñcaḥ nāma*—named Krauñca; *parvata-rājaḥ*—a king of mountains; *dvīpa-nāma*—the name of the island; *nirvartakaḥ*—bringing about; *āste*—exists.

TRANSLATION

Outside the ocean of clarified butter is another island, known as Krauñcadvīpa, which has a width of 1,600,000 yojanas [12,800,000 miles], twice the width of the ocean of clarified butter. As Kuśadvīpa is surrounded by an ocean of clarified butter, Krauñcadvīpa is surrounded by an ocean of milk as broad as the island itself. On Krauñcadvīpa there is a great mountain known as Krauñca, from which the island takes its name.

TEXT 19

योऽसौ गुहप्रहरणोन्मथितनितम्बकुञ्जोऽपि क्षीरोदेनासिच्यमानो भगवता वरुणेनाभिगुप्तो विभयो बभूव ॥१९॥

yo 'sau guha-praharaṇonmathita-nitamba-kuñjo 'pi kṣīrodenā-sicyamāno bhagavatā varuṇenābhigupto vibhayo babhūva.

yaḥ—which; *asau*—that (mountain); *guha-praharaṇa*—by the weapons of Kārttikeya, the son of Lord Śiva; *unmathita*—shaken; *nitamba-kuñjaḥ*—whose trees and vegetables along the slopes; *api*—although; *kṣīra-udena*—by the ocean of milk; *āsicyamānaḥ*—being always bathed; *bhagavatā*—by the greatly powerful; *varuṇena*—the demigod known as Varuṇa; *abhiguptaḥ*—protected; *vibhayaḥ babhūva*—has become fearless.

TRANSLATION

Although the vegetables living on the slopes of Mount Krauñca were attacked and devastated by the weapons of Kārttikeya, the mountain has become fearless because it is always bathed on all sides by the ocean of milk and protected by Varuṇadeva.

TEXT 20

तस्मिन्नपि प्रैयव्रतो घृतपृष्ठो नामाधिपतिः स्वे द्वीपे वर्षाणि सप्त विभज्य तेषु पुत्रनामसु सप्त रिक्थादान् वर्षपान्निवेश्य स्वयं भगवान् भगवतः परमकल्याणयशस आत्मभूतस्य हरेश्चरणारविन्दमुपजगाम ॥२०॥

tasminn api praiyavrato ghṛtapṛṣṭho nāmādhipatiḥ sve dvīpe varṣāṇi sapta vibhajya teṣu putra-nāmasu sapta rikthādān varṣapān niveśya svayaṁ bhagavān bhagavataḥ parama-kalyāṇa-yaśasa ātma-bhūtasya hareś caraṇāravindam upajagāma.

tasmin—in that island; *api*—also; *praiyavrataḥ*—the son of Mahārāja Priyavrata; *ghṛta-pṛṣṭhaḥ*—Ghṛtapṛṣṭha; *nāma*—named; *adhipatiḥ*—the king of that island; *sve*—his own; *dvīpe*—in the island; *varṣāṇi*—tracts of land; *sapta*—seven; *vibhajya*—dividing; *teṣu*—in each of them; *putra-nāmasu*—possessing the names of his sons; *sapta*—seven; *rikthā-dān*—sons; *varṣa-pān*—the masters of the *varṣas; niveśya*—appointing; *svayam*—himself; *bhagavān*—very powerful; *bhagavataḥ*—of the Supreme Personality of Godhead; *parama-kalyāṇa-yaśasaḥ*—whose glories are so auspicious; *ātma-bhūtasya*—the soul of all souls; *hareḥ caraṇa-aravindam*—the lotus feet of the Lord; *upajagāma*—took shelter at.

TRANSLATION

The ruler of this island was another son of Mahārāja Priyavrata. His name was Ghṛtapṛṣṭha, and he was a very learned scholar. He also divided his own island among his seven sons. After dividing the island into seven parts, named according to the names of his sons, Ghṛtapṛṣṭha Mahārāja completely retired from family life and took shelter at the lotus feet of the Lord, the soul of all souls, who has all auspicious qualities. Thus he attained perfection.

TEXT 21

आमो मधुरुहो मेघपृष्ठः सुधामा भ्राजिष्ठो लोहितार्णो वनस्पतिरिति घृतपृष्ठसुतास्तेषां वर्षगिरयः सप्त सप्तैव नद्यश्चाभिख्याताः शुक्लो वर्धमानो भोजन उपबर्हिणो नन्दो नन्दनः सर्वतोभद्र इति अभया अमृतौघा आर्यका तीर्थवती रूपवती पवित्रवती शुक्लेति ॥२१॥

āmo madhuruho meghapṛṣṭhaḥ sudhāmā bhrājiṣṭho lohitārṇo vanaspatir iti ghṛtapṛṣṭha-sutās teṣāṁ varṣa-girayaḥ sapta saptaiva nadyaś cābhikhyātāḥ śuklo vardhamāno bhojana upabarhiṇo nando nandanaḥ sarvatobhadra iti abhayā amṛtaughā āryakā tīrthavatī rūpavatī pavitravatī śukleti.

āmaḥ—Āma; *madhu-ruhaḥ*—Madhuruha; *megha-pṛṣṭhaḥ*—Meghapṛṣṭha; *sudhāmā*—Sudhāmā; *bhrājiṣṭhaḥ*—Bhrājiṣṭha; *lohitārṇaḥ*—Lohitārṇa; *vanaspatiḥ*—Vanaspati; *iti*—thus; *ghṛtapṛṣṭha-sutāḥ*—the sons of Ghṛtapṛṣṭha; *teṣām*—of those sons; *varṣa-girayaḥ*—boundary hills of the tracts of land; *sapta*—seven; *sapta*—seven; *eva*—also; *nadyaḥ*—rivers; *ca*—and; *abhikhyātāḥ*—celebrated; *śuklaḥ vardhamānaḥ*—Śukla and Vardhamāna; *bhojanaḥ*—Bhojana; *upabarhiṇaḥ*—Upabarhiṇa; *nandaḥ*—Nanda; *nandanaḥ*—Nandana; *sarvataḥ-bhadraḥ*—Sarvatobhadra; *iti*—thus; *abhayā*—Abhayā; *amṛtaughā*—Amṛtaughā; *āryakā*—Āryakā; *tīrthavatī*—Tīrthavatī; *rūpavatī*—Rūpavatī; *pavitravatī*—Pavitravatī; *śuklā*—Śuklā; *iti*—thus.

TRANSLATION

The sons of Mahārāja Ghṛtapṛṣṭha were named Āma, Madhuruha, Meghapṛṣṭha, Sudhāmā, Bhrājiṣṭha, Lohitārṇa and Vanaspati. In their island there are seven mountains, which indicate the boundaries of the seven tracts of land, and there are also seven rivers. The mountains are named Śukla, Vardhamāna, Bhojana, Upabarhiṇa, Nanda, Nandana and

Sarvatobhadra. The rivers are named Abhayā, Amṛtaughā, Āryakā, Tīrthavatī, Rūpavatī, Pavitravatī and Śuklā.

TEXT 22

यासामम्भः पवित्रममलमुपयुञ्जानाः पुरुषऋषभद्रविणदेवकसंज्ञा वर्षपुरुषा आपोमयं देवमपां पूर्णेनाञ्जलिना यजन्ते ॥२२॥

yāsām ambhaḥ pavitram amalam upayuñjānāḥ puruṣa-ṛṣabha-draviṇa-devaka-saṁjñā varṣa-puruṣā āpomayaṁ devam apāṁ pūrṇenāñjalinā yajante.

yāsām—of all the rivers; *ambhaḥ*—the water; *pavitram*—very sanctified; *amalam*—very clean; *upayuñjānāḥ*—using; *puruṣa*—Puruṣa; *ṛṣabha*—Ṛṣabha; *draviṇa*—Draviṇa; *devaka*—Devaka; *saṁjñāḥ*—endowed with the names; *varṣa-puruṣāḥ*—the inhabitants of those *varṣas; āpaḥ-mayam*—Varuṇa, the lord of water; *devam*—as the worshipable deity; *apām*—of water; *pūrṇena*—with full; *añjalinā*—folded palms; *yajante*—do worship.

TRANSLATION

The inhabitants of Krauñcadvīpa are divided into four castes, called the Puruṣas, Ṛṣabhas, Draviṇas and Devakas. Using the waters of those sanctified rivers, they worship the Supreme Personality of Godhead by offering a palmful of water at the lotus feet of Varuṇa, the demigod who has a form of water.

PURPORT

Viśvanātha Cakravartī Ṭhākura says, *āpomayaḥ asmayam:* with joined palms the inhabitants of the various sections of Krauñcadvīpa offer the sanctified waters of the rivers to a deity made of stone or iron.

TEXT 23

आपः पुरुषवीर्याः स्थ पुनन्तीर्भूर्भुवःसुवः ।
ता नः पुनीतामीवघ्नीः स्पृशतामात्मना भुव इति ॥२३॥

āpaḥ puruṣa-vīryāḥ stha
punantīr bhūr-bhuvaḥ-suvaḥ
tā naḥ punītāmīva-ghnīḥ
spṛśatām ātmanā bhuva iti

āpaḥ—O water; *puruṣa-vīryāḥ*—endowed with the energy of the Supreme Personality of Godhead; *stha*—you are; *punantīḥ*—sanctifying; *bhūḥ*—of the planetary system known as Bhūḥ; *bhuvaḥ*—of the Bhuvaḥ planetary system; *suvaḥ*—of the Svaḥ planetary system; *tāḥ*—that water; *naḥ*—of us; *punīta*—purify; *amīva-ghnīḥ*—who destroys sin; *spṛśatām*—of those touching; *ātmanā*—by your constitutional position; *bhuvaḥ*—the bodies; *iti*—thus.

TRANSLATION

[The inhabitants of Krauñcadvīpa worship with this mantra.] O water of the rivers, you have obtained energy from the Supreme Personality of Godhead. Therefore you purify the three planetary systems, known as Bhūloka, Bhuvarloka and Svarloka. By your constitutional nature, you take away sins, and that is why we are touching you. Kindly continue to purify us.

PURPORT

Kṛṣṇa says in *Bhagavad-gītā* (7.4):

bhūmir āpo'nalo vāyuḥ
khaṁ mano buddhir eva ca
ahaṅkāra itīyaṁ me
bhinnā prakṛtir aṣṭadhā

"Earth, water, fire, air, ether, mind, intelligence and false ego—all together these eight comprise My separated material energies."

The energy of the Lord acts throughout the creation, just as heat and light, the energies of the sun, act within the universe and make everything work. The specific rivers mentioned in the *śāstras* are also energies of the Supreme Personality of Godhead, and people who regularly bathe in them are purified. It can actually be seen that many people are cured of diseases simply by bathing in the Ganges. Similarly, the inhabitants of Krauñcadvīpa purify themselves by bathing in the rivers there.

TEXT 24

एवं पुरस्तात्क्षीरोदात्परित उपवेशितः शाकद्वीपो द्वात्रिंशल्लक्षयोजनायामः समानेन च दधिमण्डोदेन परीतो यस्मिन् शाको नाम महीरुहः स्वक्षेत्रव्यपदेशको यस्य ह महासुरभिगन्धस्तं द्वीपमनुवासयति ॥२४॥

evaṁ purastāt kṣīrodāt parita upaveśitaḥ śākadvīpo dvātriṁśal-lakṣa-yojanāyāmaḥ samānena ca dadhi-maṇḍodena parīto yasmin śāko nāma mahīruhaḥ sva-kṣetra-vyapadeśako yasya ha mahā-surabhi-gandhas taṁ dvīpam anuvāsayati.

evam—thus; *purastāt*—beyond; *kṣīra-udāt*—from the ocean of milk; *paritaḥ*—all around; *upaveśitaḥ*—situated; *śāka-dvīpaḥ*—another island, known as Śākadvīpa; *dvā-triṁśat*—thirty-two; *lakṣa*—100,000; *yojana*—yojanas; *āyāmaḥ*—whose measure; *samānena*—of equal length; *ca*—and; *dadhi-maṇḍa-udena*—by an ocean containing water resembling churned yogurt; *parītaḥ*—surrounded; *yasmin*—in which land; *śākaḥ*—*śāka; nāma*—named; *mahīruhaḥ*—a fig tree; *sva-kṣetra-vyapadeśakaḥ*—giving the island its name; *yasya*—of which; *ha*—indeed; *mahā-surabhi*—a greatly fragrant; *gandhaḥ*—aroma; *tam dvīpam*—that island; *anuvāsayati*—makes fragrant.

TRANSLATION

Outside the ocean of milk is another island, Śākadvīpa, which has a width of 3,200,000 yojanas [25,600,000 miles]. As Krauñcadvīpa is surrounded by its own ocean of milk, Śākadvīpa is surrounded by an ocean of churned yogurt as broad as the island itself. In Śākadvīpa there is a big śāka tree, from which the island takes its name. This tree is very fragrant. Indeed, it lends its scent to the entire island.

TEXT 25

तस्यापि प्रैयव्रत एवाधिपतिर्नाम्ना मेधातिथिः सोऽपि विभज्य सप्त वर्षाणि पुत्रनामानि तेषु स्वात्मजान् पुरोजवमनोजवपवमानधूम्रानीकचित्ररेफबहुरूप-विश्वधारसंज्ञान्निधाप्याधिपतीन् स्वयं भगवत्यनन्त आवेशितमतिस्तपोवनं प्रविवेश ॥२५॥

tasyāpi praiyavrata evādhipatir nāmnā medhātithiḥ so 'pi vibhajya sapta varṣāṇi putra-nāmāni teṣu svātmajān purojava-manojava-pavamāna-dhūmrānīka-citrarepha-bahurūpa-viśvadhāra-saṁjñān nidhāpyādhipatīn svayaṁ bhagavaty ananta ā-veśita-matis tapovanaṁ praviveśa.

tasya api—of that island also; *praiyavrataḥ*—a son of Mahārāja Priyavrata; *eva*—certainly; *adhipatiḥ*—the ruler; *nāmnā*—by the name; *medhā-tithiḥ*—

Medhātithi; *saḥ api*—he also; *vibhajya*—dividing; *sapta varṣāṇi*—seven divisions of the island; *putra-nāmāni*—possessing the names of his sons; *teṣu*—in them; *sva-ātmajān*—his own sons; *purojava*—Purojava; *manojava*—Manojava; *pavamāna*—Pavamāna; *dhūmrānīka*—Dhūmrānīka; *citra-repha*—Citrarepha; *bahu-rūpa*—Bahurūpa; *viśvadhāra*—Viśvadhāra; *saṁjñān*—having as names; *nidhāpya*—establishing as; *adhipatīn*—the rulers; *svayam*—himself; *bhagavati*—in the Supreme Personality of Godhead; *anante*—in the unlimited; *āveśita-matiḥ*—whose mind was fully absorbed; *tapaḥ-vanam*—in the forest where meditation is performed; *praviveśa*—he entered.

TRANSLATION

The master of this island, also one of the sons of Priyavrata, was known as Medhātithi. He also divided his island into seven sections, named according to the names of his own sons, whom he made the kings of that island. The names of those sons are Purojava, Manojava, Pavamāna, Dhūmrānīka, Citrarepha, Bahurūpa and Viśvadhāra. After dividing the island and situating his sons as its rulers, Medhātithi personally retired, and to fix his mind completely upon the lotus feet of the Supreme Personality of Godhead, he entered a forest suitable for meditation.

TEXT 26

एतेषां वर्षमर्यादागिरयो नद्यश्च सप्त सप्तैव ईशान उरुशृङ्गो बलभद्रः शतकेसरः सहस्रस्रोतो देवपालो महानस इति अनघाऽऽयुर्दा उभयस्पृष्टिरपराजिता पञ्चपदी सहस्रस्रुतिर्निजधृतिरिति ॥२६॥

eteṣāṁ varṣa-maryādā-girayo nadyaś ca sapta saptaiva īśāna uruśṛṅgo
balabhadraḥ śatakesaraḥ sahasrasroto devapālo mahānasa iti
anaghāyurdā ubhayaspṛṣṭir aparājitā pañcapadī sahasrasrutir nijadhṛtir
iti.

eteṣām—of all these divisions; *varṣa-maryādā*—acting as the boundary limits; *girayaḥ*—the big hills; *nadyaḥ ca*—and the rivers also; *sapta*—seven; *sapta*—seven; *eva*—indeed; *īśānaḥ*—Īśāna; *uruśṛṅgaḥ*—Uruśṛṅga; *bala-bhadraḥ*—Balabhadra; *śata-kesaraḥ*—Śatakesara; *sahasra-srotaḥ*—Sahasrasrota; *deva-pālaḥ*—Devapāla; *mahānasaḥ*—Mahānasa; *iti*—thus; *anaghā*—Anaghā; *āyurdā*—Āyurdā; *ubhayaspṛṣṭiḥ*—Ubhayaspṛṣṭi; *aparājitā*—Aparājitā; *pañcapadī*—Pañcapadī; *sahasra-srutiḥ*—Sahasrasruti; *nija-dhṛtiḥ*—Nijadhṛti; *iti*—thus.

TRANSLATION

For these lands also, there are seven boundary mountains and seven rivers. The mountains are Īśāna, Uruśṛṅga, Balabhadra, Śatakesara, Sahasrasrota, Devapāla and Mahānasa. The rivers are Anaghā, Āyurdā, Ubhayaspṛṣṭi, Aparājitā, Pañcapadī, Sahasrasruti and Nijadhṛti.

TEXT 27

तद्वर्षपुरुषा ऋतव्रतसत्यव्रतदानव्रतानुव्रतनामानो भगवन्तं वाय्वात्मकं प्राणायामविधूतरजस्तमसः परमसमाधिना यजन्ते ॥२७॥

tad-varṣa-puruṣā ṛtavrata-satyavrata-dānavratānuvrata-nāmāno bhagavantaṁ vāyv-ātmakaṁ prāṇāyāma-vidhūta-rajas-tamasaḥ parama-samādhinā yajante.

tat-varṣa-puruṣāḥ—the inhabitants of those tracts of land; *ṛta-vrata*—Ṛtavrata; *satya-vrata*—Satyavrata; *dāna-vrata*—Dānavrata; *anuvrata*—Anuvrata; *nāmānaḥ*—having the four names; *bhagavantam*—the Supreme Personality of Godhead; *vāyu-ātmakam*—represented by the demigod Vāyu; *prāṇāyāma*—by the practice of regulating the airs within the body; *vidhūta*—cleansed away; *rajaḥ-tamasaḥ*—whose passion and ignorance; *parama*—sublime; *samādhinā*—by trance; *yajante*—they worship.

TRANSLATION

The inhabitants of those islands are also divided into four castes—Ṛtavrata, Satyavrata, Dānavrata and Anuvrata—which exactly resemble brāhmaṇa, kṣatriya, vaiśya and śūdra. They practice prāṇāyāma and mystic yoga, and in trance they worship the Supreme Lord in the form of Vāyu.

TEXT 28

अन्तःप्रविश्य भूतानि यो बिभर्त्यात्मकेतुभिः ।
अन्तर्यामीश्वरः साक्षात्पातु नो यद्वशे स्फुटम् ॥२८॥

antaḥ-praviśya bhūtāni
yo bibharty ātma-ketubhiḥ
antaryāmīśvaraḥ sākṣāt
pātu no yad-vaśe sphuṭam

antaḥ-praviśya—entering within; *bhūtāni*—all living entities; *yaḥ*—who; *bibharti*—maintains; *ātma-ketubhiḥ*—by the functions of the inner airs (*prāṇa, apāna,* etc.); *antaryāmī*—the Supersoul within; *īśvaraḥ*—the Supreme Person; *sākṣāt*—directly; *pātu*—please maintain; *naḥ*—us; *yat-vaśe* —under whose control; *sphuṭam*—the cosmic manifestation.

TRANSLATION

[The inhabitants of Śākadvīpa worship the Supreme Personality of Godhead in the form of Vāyu in the following words.] O Supreme Person, situated as the Supersoul within the body, You direct the various actions of the different airs, such as prāṇa, and thus You maintain all living entities. O Lord, O Supersoul of everyone, O controller of the cosmic manifestation under whom everything exists, may You protect us from all dangers.

PURPORT

Through the mystic *yoga* practice called *prāṇāyāma,* the *yogī* controls the airs within the body to maintain the body in a healthy condition. In this way, the *yogī* comes to the point of trance and tries to see the Supersoul within the core of his heart. *Prāṇāyāma* is the means to attain *samādhi,* trance, in order to fully absorb oneself in seeing the Supreme Lord as *antaryāmī,* the Supersoul within the core of the heart.

TEXT 29

एवमेव दधिमण्डोदात्परतः पुष्करद्वीपस्ततो द्विगुणायामः समन्तत उपकल्पितः समानेन स्वादूदकेन समुद्रेण बहिरावृतो यस्मिन् बृहत्पुष्करं ज्वलनशिखा-मलकनकपत्रायुतायुतं भगवतः कमलासनस्याध्यासनं परिकल्पितम् ॥२९॥

evam eva dadhi-maṇḍodāt parataḥ puṣkaradvīpas tato dvi-
guṇāyāmaḥ samantata upakalpitaḥ samānena svādūdakena samudreṇa
bahir āvṛto yasmin bṛhat-puṣkaraṁ jvalana-śikhāmala-kanaka-
patrāyutāyutaṁ bhagavataḥ kamalāsanasyādhyāsanaṁ parikalpitam.

evam eva—thus; *dadhi-maṇḍa-udāt*—the ocean of yogurt; *parataḥ*—beyond; *puṣkara-dvīpaḥ*—another island, named Puṣkaradvīpa; *tataḥ*—than that (Śākadvīpa); *dvi-guṇa-āyāmaḥ*—whose measurement is twice as great; *samantataḥ*—on all sides; *upakalpitaḥ*—surrounded; *samānena*—equal in width; *svādu-udakena*—possessing sweet water; *samudreṇa*—by an ocean; *bahiḥ*—outside; *āvṛtaḥ*—surrounded; *yasmin*—in which; *bṛhat*—very big;

puṣkaram—lotus flower; *jvalana-śikhā*—like the flames of a blazing fire; *amala*—pure; *kanaka*—gold; *patra*—leaves; *ayuta-ayutam*—possessing 100,000,000; *bhagavataḥ*—greatly powerful; *kamala āsanasya*—of Lord Brahmā, whose sitting place is on the lotus flower; *adhyāsanam*—sitting place; *parikalpitam*—considered.

TRANSLATION

Outside the ocean of yogurt is another island, known as Puṣkaradvīpa, which is 6,400,000 yojanas [51,200,000 miles] wide, twice as wide as the ocean of yogurt. It is surrounded by an ocean of very tasteful water as broad as the island itself. On Puṣkaradvīpa there is a great lotus flower with 100,000,000 pure golden petals, as effulgent as the flames of fire. That lotus flower is considered the sitting place of Lord Brahmā, who is the most powerful living being and who is therefore sometimes called bhagavān.

TEXT 30

तदद्वीपमध्ये मानसोत्तरनामैक एवार्वाचीनपराचीनवर्षयोर्मर्यादाचलोऽयुत-योजनोच्छ्रायायामो यत्र तु चतसृषु दिक्षु चत्वारि पुराणि लोकपालानामिन्द्रादीनां यदुपरिष्टात्सूर्यरथस्य मेरुं परिभ्रमतः संवत्सरात्मकं चक्रं देवानामहोरात्राभ्यां परिभ्रमति ॥३०॥

tad-dvīpa-madhye mānasottara-nāmaika evārvācīna-parācīna-varṣayor
maryādācalo'yuta-yojanocchrāyāyāmo yatra tu catasṛṣu dikṣu catvāri
purāṇi loka-pālānām indrādīnāṁ yad-upariṣṭāt sūrya-rathasya meruṁ
paribhramataḥ saṁvatsarātmakaṁ cakraṁ devānām aho-rātrābhyāṁ
paribhramati.

tat-dvīpa-madhye—within that island; *mānasottara*—Mānasottara; *nāma*—named; *ekaḥ*—one; *eva*—indeed; *arvācīna*—on this side; *parācīna*—and beyond, or outside; *varṣayoḥ*—of tracts of land; *maryādā*—indicating the boundary; *acalaḥ*—a great mountain; *ayuta*—ten thousand; *yojana*—eight miles; *ucchrāya-āyāmaḥ*—whose height and width; *yatra*—where; *tu*—but; *catasṛṣu*—in the four; *dikṣu*—directions; *catvāri*—four; *purāṇi*—cities; *loka-pālānām*—of the directors of planetary systems; *indra-ādīnām*—headed by Indra; *yat*—of which; *upariṣṭāt*—on the top; *sūrya-rathasya*—of the chariot of the sun-god; *merum*—Meru Mountain; *paribhramataḥ*—while circumambulating; *saṁvatsara-ātmakam*—consisting of one *saṁvatsara;* *cakram*—wheel or orbit; *devānām*—of the demigods; *ahaḥ-rātrābhyām*—by the day and night; *paribhramati*—moves around.

TRANSLATION

In the middle of that island is a great mountain named Mānasottara, which forms the boundary between the inner side and the outer side of the island. Its breadth and height are 10,000 yojanas [80,000 miles]. On that mountain, in the four directions, are the residential quarters of demigods such as Indra. In the chariot of the sun-god, the sun travels on the top of the mountain in an orbit called the Saṁvatsara, encircling Mount Meru. The sun's path on the northern side is called Uttarāyaṇa, and its path on the southern side is called Dakṣiṇāyana. One side represents a day for the demigods, and the other represents their night.

PURPORT

The movement of the sun is confirmed in the *Brahma-saṁhitā* (5.52): *yasyājñāya bhramati saṁbhṛta-kāla-cakraḥ.* The sun orbits around Mount Sumeru, for six months on the northern side and for six months on the southern. This adds up to the duration of a day and night of the demigods in the upper planetary systems.

TEXT 31

तद्द्वीपस्याप्यधिपतिः प्रैयव्रतो वीतिहोत्रो नामैतस्यात्मजौ रमणकधातकिनामानौ
वर्षपती नियुज्य स स्वयं पूर्वजवद्भगवत्कर्मशील एवास्ते ॥३१॥

tad-dvīpasyāpy adhipatiḥ praiyavrato vītihotro nāmaitasyātmajau
ramaṇaka-dhātaki-nāmānau varṣa-patī niyujya sa svayaṁ pūrvajavad-
bhagavat-karma-śīla evāste.

tat-dvīpasya—of that island; *api*—also; *adhipatiḥ*—the ruler; *praiyavrataḥ*—a son of Mahārāja Priyavrata; *vītihotraḥ nāma*—named Vītihotra; *etasya*—of him; *ātma-jau*—unto the two sons; *ramaṇaka*—Ramaṇaka; *dhātaki*—and Dhātaki; *nāmānau*—having the names; *varṣa-patī*—the rulers of the two tracts of land; *niyujya*—appointing; *saḥ svayam*—himself; *pūrvaja-vat*—like his other brothers; *bhagavat-karma-śīlaḥ*—being absorbed in activities to satisfy the Supreme Personality of Godhead; *eva*—indeed; *āste*—remains.

TRANSLATION

The ruler of this island, the son of Mahārāja Priyavrata named Vītihotra, had two sons named Ramaṇaka and Dhātaki. He granted the two sides of the island to these two sons and then personally engaged himself in

activities for the sake of the Supreme Personality of Godhead like his elder brother Medhātithi.

TEXT 32

तद्वर्षपुरुषा भगवन्तं ब्रह्मरूपिणं सकर्मकेण कर्मणाऽऽराधयन्तीदं चोदाहरन्ति ॥३२॥

tad-varṣa-puruṣā bhagavantaṁ brahma-rūpiṇaṁ sakarmakeṇa karmaṇārādhayantīdaṁ codāharanti.

tat-varṣa-puruṣāḥ—the inhabitants of that island; *bhagavantam*—the Supreme Personality of Godhead; *brahma-rūpiṇam*—exhibited as Lord Brahmā being seated on the lotus; *sa-karmakeṇa*—for fulfillment of material desires; *karmaṇā*—by performing ritualistic activities according to the *Vedas; ārādhayanti*—worship; *idam*—this; *ca*—and; *udāharanti*—they chant.

TRANSLATION

For the fulfillment of material desires, the inhabitants of this tract of land worship the Supreme Personality of Godhead as represented by Lord Brahmā. They offer prayers to the Lord as follows.

TEXT 33

यत्तत्कर्ममयं लिङ्गं ब्रह्मलिङ्गं जनोऽर्चयेत् ।
एकान्तमद्वयं शान्तं तस्मै भगवते नम इति ॥३३॥

yat tat karmamayaṁ liṅgaṁ
brahma-liṅgaṁ jano 'rcayet
ekāntam advayaṁ śāntaṁ
tasmai bhagavate nama iti

yat—which; *tat*—that; *karma-mayam*—obtainable by the Vedic ritualistic system; *liṅgam*—the form; *brahma-liṅgam*—which makes known the Supreme Brahman; *janaḥ*—a person; *arcayet*—must worship; *ekāntam*—who has full faith in the one Supreme; *advayam*—nondifferent; *śāntam*—peaceful; *tasmai*—unto him; *bhagavate*—the most powerful; *namaḥ*—our respects; *iti*—thus.

TRANSLATION

Lord Brahmā is known as karma-maya, the form of ritualistic ceremonies, because by performing ritualistic ceremonies one may attain his position and because the Vedic ritualistic hymns become manifest from

him. He is devoted to the Supreme Personality of Godhead without deviation, and therefore in one sense he is not different from the Lord. Nevertheless, he should be worshiped not as the monists worship him, but in duality. One should always remain a servitor of the Supreme Lord, the supreme worshipable Deity. We therefore offer our respectful obeisances unto Lord Brahmā, the form of manifest Vedic knowledge.

PURPORT

In this verse, the word *karma-mayam* ("obtainable by the Vedic ritualistic system") is significant. The *Vedas* say, *svadharma-niṣṭhaḥ śata janmabhiḥ pumān viriñcatām eti:* "One who strictly follows the principles of *varṇāśrama-dharma* for at least one hundred births will be rewarded with the post of Lord Brahmā." It is also significant that although Lord Brahmā is extremely powerful, he never thinks himself one with the Supreme Personality of Godhead; he always knows that he is an eternal servitor of the Lord. Because the Lord and the servant are identical on the spiritual platform, Brahmā is herein addressed as *bhagavān.* Bhagavān is the Supreme Personality of Godhead, Kṛṣṇa, but if a devotee serves Him with full faith, the meaning of the Vedic literature is revealed to him. Therefore Brahmā is called *brahma-liṅga,* which indicates that his entire form consists of Vedic knowledge.

TEXT 34

ऋषिरुवाच

ततः परस्ताल्लोकालोकनामाचलो लोकालोकयोरन्तराले परित उपक्षिप्तः ॥३४॥

tataḥ parastāl lokāloka-nāmācalo lokālokayor antarāle parita upakṣiptaḥ.

tataḥ—from that ocean of sweet drinking water; *parastāt*—beyond; *lokāloka-nāma*—named Lokāloka; *acalaḥ*—a mountain; *loka-alokayoḥ antarāle*—between the countries full of sunlight and those without sunlight; *paritaḥ*—all around; *upakṣiptaḥ*—exists.

TRANSLATION

Thereafter, beyond the ocean of sweet water and fully surrounding it, is a mountain named Lokāloka, which divides the countries that are full of sunlight from those not lit by the sun.

TEXT 35

यावन्मानसोत्तरमेर्वोरन्तरं तावती भूमिः काञ्चन्यन्याऽऽदर्शतलोपमा यस्यां प्रहितः पदार्थो न कथञ्चित्पुनः प्रत्युपलभ्यते तस्मात्सर्वसत्त्वपरिहृताऽऽसीत् ॥ ३५ ॥

yāvan mānasottara-mervor antaraṁ tāvatī bhūmiḥ kāñcany anyādarśa-talopamā yasyāṁ prahitaḥ padārtho na kathañcit punaḥ pratyupalabhyate tasmāt sarva-sattva-parihṛtāsīt.

yāvat—as much as; *mānasottara-mervoḥ antaram*—the land between Mānasottara and Meru (beginning from the middle of Mount Sumeru); *tāvatī*—that much; *bhūmiḥ*—land; *kāñcanī*—made of gold; *anyā*—another; *ādarśa-tala-upamā*—whose surface is just like the surface of a mirror; *yasyām*—on which; *prahitaḥ*—dropped; *padārthaḥ*—a thing; *na*—not; *kathañcit*—in any way; *punaḥ*—again; *pratyupalabhyate*—is found; *tasmāt*—therefore; *sarva-sattva*—by all living entities; *parihṛtā*—abandoned; *āsīt*—was.

TRANSLATION

Beyond the ocean of sweet water is a tract of land as broad as the area between the middle of Mount Sumeru and the boundary of Mānasottara Mountain. In that tract of land there are many living beings. Beyond it, extending to Lokāloka Mountain, is another land, which is made of gold. Because of its golden surface, it reflects light like the surface of a mirror, and any physical article that falls on that land can never be perceived again. All living entities, therefore, have abandoned that golden land.

TEXT 36

लोकालोक इति समाख्या यदनेनाचलेन लोकालोकस्यान्तर्वर्तिनावस्थाप्यते ॥ ३६ ॥

lokāloka iti samākhyā yad anenācalena lokālokasyāntarvar-tināvasthāpyate.

loka—with light (or with inhabitants); *alokaḥ*—without light (or without inhabitants); *iti*—in this way; *samākhyā*—designation; *yat*—which; *anena*—by this; *acalena*—mountain; *loka*—of the land inhabited by living entities; *alokasya*—and of the land not inhabited by living entities; *antarvartinā*—which is in the middle; *avasthāpyate*—is established.

TRANSLATION

Between the lands inhabited by living entities and those that are uninhabited stands the great mountain which separates the two and which is therefore celebrated as Lokāloka.

TEXT 37

स लोकत्रयान्ते परित ईश्वरेण विहितो यस्मात्सूर्यादीनां ध्रुवापवर्गाणां ज्योतिर्गणानां गभस्तयोऽर्वाचीनांस्त्रीँल्लोकानावितन्वाना न कदाचित्पराचीना भवितुमुत्सहन्ते तावदुन्नहनायामः ॥३७॥

sa loka-trayānte parita īśvareṇa vihito yasmāt sūryādīnāṁ
dhruvāpavargāṇāṁ jyotir-gaṇānāṁ gabhastayo 'rvācīnāṁs trīl lokān
āvitanvānā na kadācit parācīnā bhavitum utsahante tāvad unnahanāyāmaḥ.

saḥ—that mountain; *loka-traya-ante*—at the end of the three *lokas* (Bhūrloka, Bhuvarloka and Svarloka); *paritaḥ*—all around; *īśvareṇa*—by the Supreme Personality of Godhead, Kṛṣṇa; *vihitaḥ*—created; *yasmāt*—from which; *sūrya-ādīnām*—of the sun planet; *dhruva-apavargāṇām*—up to Dhruvaloka and other, inferior luminaries; *jyotiḥ-gaṇānām*—of all the luminaries; *gabhastayaḥ*—the rays; *arvācīnān*—on this side; *trīn*—the three; *lokān*—planetary systems; *āvitanvānāḥ*—spreading throughout; *na*—not; *kadācit*—at any time; *parācīnāḥ*—beyond the jurisdiction of that mountain; *bhavitum*—to be; *utsahante*—are able; *tāvat*—that much; *unnahana-āyāmaḥ*—the measure of the height of the mountain.

TRANSLATION

By the supreme will of Kṛṣṇa, the mountain known as Lokāloka has been installed as the outer border of the three worlds—Bhūrloka, Bhuvarloka and Svarloka—to control the rays of the sun throughout the universe. All the luminaries, from the sun up to Dhruvaloka, distribute their rays throughout the three worlds, but only within the boundary formed by this mountain. Because it is extremely high, extending even higher than Dhruvaloka, it blocks the rays of the luminaries, which therefore can never extend beyond it.

PURPORT

When we speak of *loka-traya,* we refer to the three primary planetary systems—Bhūḥ, Bhuvaḥ and Svaḥ—into which the universe is divided. Surrounding these planetary systems are the eight directions, namely east, west, north, south, northeast, southeast, northwest and southwest. Lokāloka Mountain has been established as the outer boundary of all the *lokas* to distribute the rays of the sun and other luminaries equally throughout the universe.

This vivid description of how the rays of the sun are distributed throughout the different planetary systems of the universe is very scientific. Śukadeva Gosvāmī described these universal affairs to Mahārāja Parīkṣit as he had heard about them from his predecessor. He explained these facts five thousand years ago, but the knowledge existed long, long before because Śukadeva Gosvāmī received it through disciplic succession. Because this knowledge is accepted through the disciplic succession, it is perfect. The history of modern scientific knowledge, on the contrary, does not go back more than a few hundred years. Therefore, even if modern scientists do not accept the other factual presentations of *Śrīmad-Bhāgavatam,* how can they deny the perfect astronomical calculations that existed long before they could imagine such things? There is so much information to gather from *Śrīmad-Bhāgavatam.* Modern scientists, however, have no information of other planetary systems and, indeed, are hardly conversant with the planet on which we are now living.

TEXT 38

एतावाँल्लोकविन्यासो मानलक्षणसंस्थाभिर्विचिन्तितः कविभिः स तु
पञ्चाशत्कोटिगणितस्य भूगोलस्य तुरीयभागोऽयं लोकालोकाचलः ॥३८॥

etāvāl loka-vinyāso māna-lakṣaṇa-saṁsthābhir vicintitaḥ kavibhiḥ sa
tu pañcāśat-koṭi-gaṇitasya bhū-golasya turīya-bhāgo'yaṁ lokālokācalaḥ.

etāvān—this much; *loka-vinyāsaḥ*—the placing of the different planets; *māna*—with measurements; *lakṣaṇa*—symptoms; *saṁsthābhiḥ*—as well as with their different situations; *vicintitaḥ*—established by scientific calculations; *kavibhiḥ*—by learned scholars; *saḥ*—that; *tu*—but; *pañcāśat-koṭi*—500,000,000 *yojanas; gaṇitasya*—which is measured at; *bhū-golasya*—of the planetary system known as Bhūgolaka; *turīya-bhāgaḥ*—one fourth; *ayam*—this; *lokāloka-acalaḥ*—the mountain known as Lokāloka.

TRANSLATION

Learned scholars who are free from mistakes, illusions and propensities to cheat have thus described the planetary systems and their particular symptoms, measurements and locations. With great deliberation, they have established the truth that the distance between Sumeru and the mountain known as Lokāloka is one fourth of the diameter of the universe —or, in other words, 125,000,000 yojanas [1 billion miles].

PURPORT

Śrīla Viśvanātha Cakravartī Ṭhākura has given accurate astronomical information about the location of Lokāloka Mountain, the movements of the sun globe and the distance between the sun and the circumference of the universe. However, the technical terms used in the astronomical calculations given by the *Jyotir Veda* are difficult to translate into English. Therefore to satisfy the reader, we may include the exact Sanskrit statement given by Śrīla Viśvanātha Cakravartī Ṭhākura, which records exact calculations regarding universal affairs.

sa tu lokālokas tu bhū-golakasya bhū-sambandhāṇḍa-golakasyety arthaḥ; sūryasy eva bhuvo'py aṇḍa-golakayor madhya-vartitvāt kha-golam iva bhū-golam api pañcāśat-koṭi-yojana-pramāṇaṁ tasya turīya-bhāgaḥ sārdha- dvādaśa-koṭi-yojana-vistārocchrāya ity arthaḥ bhūs tu catus-triṁśal-lakṣonapañcāśat-koṭi-pramāṇā jñeyā; yathā meru-madhyān mānasottara-madhya-paryantaṁ sārdha-sapta-pañcāśal-lakṣottara-koṭi-yojana-pramāṇam; mānasottara-madhyāt svādūdaka-samudra-paryantaṁ ṣaṇ-ṇavati-lakṣa-yojana-pramāṇaṁ tataḥ kāñcanī-bhūmiḥ sārdha-sapta-pañcāśal-lakṣottara-koṭi-yojana-pramāṇā evam ekato meru-lokālokayor antarālam ekādaśa-śal-lakṣādhika-catuṣ-koṭi-parimitam anyato'pi tathatyeto lokālokāl loka-paryantaṁ sthānaṁ dvāviṁśati-lakṣottarāṣṭa-koṭi-parimitaṁ lokālokād bahir apy ekataḥ etāvad eva anyato'py etāvad eva yad vakṣyate, yo'ntar-vistāra etena hy aloka-parimāṇaṁ ca vyākhyātaṁ yad-bahir lokālokācalād ity ekato lokālokaḥ sārdha-dvādaśa-koṭi-yojana-parimāṇaḥ anyato'pi sa tathety evaṁ catus-triṁśal-lakṣonapañcāśat-koṭi-pramāṇā bhūḥ sābdhi-dvīpa-parvatā jñeyā; ata evāṇḍa-golakāt sarvato dikṣu sapta-daśa-lakṣa-yojanāvakāśe vartamāne sati pṛthivyāḥ śeṣa-nāgena dhāraṇaṁ dig-gajaiś ca niścalī-karaṇaṁ sārthakaṁ bhaved anyathā tu vyākhyāntare pañcāśat-koṭi-pramāṇatvād aṇḍa-golaka-lagnatve tat tat sarvam akiñcit-karaṁ syāt cākṣuṣe manvantare cākasmāt majjanaṁ śrī-varāha-devenotthāpanaṁ ca durghaṭaṁ syād ity adikaṁ vivecanīyam.

TEXT 39

तदुपरिष्टाच्चतसृष्वाशास्वात्मयोनिनाखिलजगद्गुरुणाधिनिवेशिता ये द्विरदपतय ऋषभः पुष्करचूडो वामनोऽपराजित इति सकललोकस्थितिहेतवः ॥३९॥

tad-upariṣṭāc catasṛṣv āśāsvātma-yoninākhila-jagad-guruṇādhiniveśitā ye dvirada-pataya ṛṣabhaḥ puṣkaracūḍo vāmano 'parājita iti sakala-loka-sthiti-hetavaḥ.

tat-upariṣṭāt—on the top of Lokāloka Mountain; *catasṛṣu āśāsu*—in the four directions; *ātma-yoninā*—by Lord Brahmā; *akhila-jagat-guruṇā*—the spiritual master of the whole universe; *adhiniveśitāḥ*—established; *ye*—all those; *dvirada-patayaḥ*—the best of elephants; *ṛṣabhaḥ*—Ṛṣabha; *puṣkara-cūḍaḥ*—Puṣkaracūḍa; *vāmanaḥ*—Vāmana; *aparājitaḥ*—Aparājita; *iti*—thus; *sakala-loka-sthiti-hetavaḥ*—the causes of the maintenance of the different planets within the universe.

TRANSLATION

On the top of Lokāloka Mountain are the four gaja-patis, the best of elephants, which were established in the four directions by Lord Brahmā, the supreme spiritual master of the entire universe. The names of those elephants are Ṛṣabha, Puṣkaracūḍa, Vāmana and Aparājita. They are responsible for maintaining the planetary systems of the universe.

TEXT 40

तेषां स्वविभूतीनां लोकपालानां च विविधवीर्योपबृंहणाय भगवान् परममहापुरुषो महाविभूतिपतिरन्तर्याम्यात्मनो विशुद्धसत्त्वं धर्मज्ञानवैराग्यैश्वर्याद्यष्टमहासिद्ध्युपलक्षणं विष्वक्सेनादिभिः स्वपार्षदप्रवरैः परिवारितो निजवरायुधोपशोभितैर्निजभुजदण्डैः सन्धारयमाणस्तस्मिन् गिरिवरे समन्तात्सकललोकस्वस्तय आस्ते ॥ ४० ॥

teṣāṁ sva-vibhūtīnāṁ loka-pālānāṁ ca vividha-vīryopabṛṁhaṇāya
bhagavān parama-mahā-puruṣo mahā-vibhūti-patir antaryāmy ātmano
viśuddha-sattvaṁ dharma-jñāna-vairāgyaiśvaryādy-aṣṭa-mahā-siddhy-
upalakṣaṇaṁ viṣvaksenādibhiḥ sva-pārṣada-pravaraiḥ parivārito nija-
varāyudhopaśobhitair nija-bhuja-daṇḍaiḥ sandhārayamāṇas tasmin
giri-vare samantāt sakala-loka-svastaya āste.

teṣām—of all of them; *sva-vibhūtīnām*—who are his personal expansions and assistants; *loka-pālānām*—who are entrusted with looking after the universal affairs; *ca*—and; *vividha*—varieties; *vīrya-upabṛṁhaṇāya*—for expanding the powers; *bhagavān*—the Supreme Personality of Godhead; *parama-mahā-puruṣaḥ*—the foremost master of all kinds of opulence, the Supreme Personality of Godhead; *mahā-vibhūti-patiḥ*—the master of all inconceivable potencies; *antaryāmī*—the Supersoul; *ātmanaḥ*—of Himself; *viśuddha-sattvam*—having an existence without contamination by the material modes of nature; *dharma-jñāna-vairāgya*—

of religion, pure knowledge and renunciation; *aiśvarya-ādi*—of all kinds of opulence; *aṣṭa*—eight; *mahā-siddhi*—and of great mystic perfections; *upalakṣaṇam*—having the characteristics; *viṣvaksena-ādibhiḥ*—by His expansion known as Viṣvaksena and others; *sva-pārṣada-pravaraiḥ*—the best of personal assistants; *parivāritaḥ*—surrounded; *nija*—His own; *vara-āyudha*—by different types of weapons; *upaśobhitaiḥ*—being decorated; *nija*—own; *bhuja-daṇḍaiḥ*—with stout arms; *sandhārayamāṇaḥ*—manifesting this form; *tasmin*—on that; *giri-vare*—great mountain; *samantāt*—all around; *sakala-loka-svastaye*—for the benefit of all the planetary systems; *āste*—exists.

TRANSLATION

The Supreme Personality of Godhead is the master of all transcendental opulences and the master of the spiritual sky. He is the Supreme Person, Bhagavān, the Supersoul of everyone. The demigods, led by Indra, the King of heaven, are entrusted with seeing to the affairs of the material world. To benefit all living beings in all the varied planets and to increase the power of those elephants and of the demigods, the Lord manifests Himself on top of that mountain in a spiritual body, uncontaminated by the modes of material nature. Surrounded by His personal expansions and assistants like Viṣvaksena, He exhibits all His perfect opulences, such as religion and knowledge, and His mystic powers such as aṇimā, laghimā and mahimā. He is beautifully situated, and He is decorated by the different weapons in His four hands.

TEXT 41

आकल्पमेवं वेषं गत एष भगवानात्मयोगमायया विरचितविविधलोक-
यात्रागोपीयायेत्यर्थः ॥४१॥

ākalpam evaṁ veṣaṁ gata eṣa bhagavān ātma-yogamāyayā viracita-
vividha-loka-yātrā-gopīyāyety arthaḥ.

ā-kalpam—for the duration of the time of creation; *evam*—thus; *veṣam*—appearance; *gataḥ*—has accepted; *eṣaḥ*—this; *bhagavān*—the Supreme Personality of Godhead; *ātma-yoga-māyayā*—by His own spiritual potency; *viracita*—perfected; *vividha-loka-yātrā*—the livelihood of the various planetary systems; *gopīyāya*—just to maintain; *iti*—thus; *arthaḥ*—the purpose.

TRANSLATION

The various forms of the Supreme Personality of Godhead, such as Nārāyaṇa and Viṣṇu, are beautifully decorated with different weapons. The Lord exhibits those forms to maintain all the varied planets created by His personal potency, yoga-māyā.

PURPORT

In *Bhagavad-gītā* (4.6) Lord Kṛṣṇa says, *sambhavāmy ātma-māyayā:* "I appear by My internal potency." The word *ātma-māyā* refers to the Lord's personal potency, *yoga-māyā.* After creating both the material world and spiritual world through *yoga-māyā,* the Supreme Personality of Godhead personally maintains them by expanding Himself in different categories as the Viṣṇu *mūrtis* and the demigods. He maintains the material creation from beginning to end, and He personally maintains the spiritual world.

TEXT 42

योऽन्तर्विस्तार एतेन ह्यलोकपरिमाणं च व्याख्यातं यद्बहिर्लोकालोकाचलात्। ततः परस्ताद्योगेश्वरगतिं विशुद्धामुदाहरन्ति ॥४२॥

yo 'ntar-vistāra etena hy aloka-parimāṇaṁ ca vyākhyātaṁ yad bahir lokālokācalāt; tataḥ parastād yogeśvara-gatiṁ viśuddhām udāharanti.

yaḥ—that which; *antaḥ-vistāraḥ*—the distance inside Lokāloka Mountain; *etena*—by this; *hi*—indeed; *aloka-parimāṇam*—the width of the tract of land known as Aloka-varṣa; *ca*—and; *vyākhyātam*—described; *yat*—which; *bahiḥ*—outside; *lokāloka-acalāt*—beyond Lokāloka Mountain; *tataḥ*—that; *parastāt*—beyond; *yogeśvara-gatim*—the path of Yogeśvara (Kṛṣṇa) in penetrating the coverings of the universe; *viśuddhām*—without material contamination; *udāharanti*—they say.

TRANSLATION

My dear King, outside Lokāloka Mountain is the tract of land known as Aloka-varṣa, which extends for the same breadth as the area within the mountain—in other words, 125,000,000 yojanas [one billion miles]. Beyond Aloka-varṣa is the destination of those who aspire for liberation from the material world. It is beyond the jurisdiction of the material modes of nature, and therefore it is completely pure. Lord Kṛṣṇa took Arjuna through this place to bring back the sons of the brāhmaṇa.

TEXT 43

अण्डमध्यगतः सूर्यो द्यावाभूम्योर्यदन्तरम् ।
सूर्याण्डगोलयोर्मध्ये कोट्यः स्युः पञ्चविंशतिः ॥४३॥

aṇḍa-madhya-gataḥ sūryo
dyāv-ābhūmyor yad antaram
sūryāṇḍa-golayor madhye
koṭyaḥ syuḥ pañca-viṁśatiḥ

aṇḍa-madhya-gataḥ—situated in the center of the universe; *sūryaḥ*—the sun globe; *dyāv-ābhūmyoḥ*—the two planetary systems Bhūrloka and Bhuvarloka; *yat*—which; *antaram*—in between; *sūrya*—of the sun; *aṇḍa-golayoḥ*—and the globe of the universe; *madhye*—in the middle; *koṭyaḥ*—groups of ten million; *syuḥ*—are; *pañca-viṁśatiḥ*—twenty-five.

TRANSLATION

The sun is situated [vertically] in the middle of the universe, in the area between Bhūrloka and Bhuvarloka, which is called antarikṣa, outer space. The distance between the sun and the circumference of the universe is twenty-five koṭi yojanas [two billion miles].

PURPORT

The word *koṭi* means ten million, and a *yojana* is eight miles. The diameter of the universe is fifty *koṭi yojanas* (four billion miles). Therefore, since the sun is in the middle of the universe, the distance between the sun and the edge of the universe is calculated to be twenty-five *koṭi yojanas* (two billion miles).

TEXT 44

मृतेऽण्ड एष एतस्मिन् यदभूत्ततो मार्तण्ड इति व्यपदेशः ।
हिरण्यगर्भ इति यद्धिरण्याण्डसमुद्भवः ॥४४॥

mṛte 'ṇḍa eṣa etasmin yad abhūt tato mārtaṇḍa iti vyapadeśaḥ;
hiraṇyagarbha iti yad dhiraṇyāṇḍa-samudbhavaḥ.

mṛte—dead; *aṇḍe*—in the globe; *eṣaḥ*—this; *etasmin*—in this; *yat*—which; *abhūt*—entered personally at the time of creation; *tataḥ*—from that; *mārtaṇḍa*—Mārtaṇḍa; *iti*—thus; *vyapadeśaḥ*—the designation; *hiraṇya-garbhaḥ*—known as Hiraṇyagarbha; *iti*—thus; *yat*—because;

hiraṇya-aṇḍa-samudbhavaḥ—his material body was created from Hiraṇyagarbha.

TRANSLATION

The sun-god is also known as Vairāja, the total material body for all living entities. Because he entered this dull egg of the universe at the time of creation, he is also called Mārtaṇḍa. He is also known as Hiraṇyagarbha because he received his material body from Hiraṇyagarbha [Lord Brahmā].

PURPORT

The post of Lord Brahmā is meant for very highly elevated, spiritually advanced living beings. When such living beings are unavailable, Lord Viṣṇu, the Supreme Personality of Godhead, expands Himself as Lord Brahmā. This takes place very rarely. Consequently there are two kinds of Brahmās. Sometimes Brahmā is an ordinary living entity, and at other times Brahmā is the Supreme Personality of Godhead. The Brahmā spoken of here is an ordinary living being. Whether Brahmā is the Supreme Personality of Godhead or an ordinary living being, he is known as Vairāja Brahmā and Hiraṇyagarbha Brahmā. Therefore the sun-god is also accepted as Vairāja Brahmā.

TEXT 45

सूर्येण हि विभज्यन्ते दिशः खं द्यौर्मही भिदा ।
स्वर्गापवर्गौ नरका रसौकांसि च सर्वशः ॥४५॥

sūryeṇa hi vibhajyante
diśaḥ khaṁ dyaur mahī bhidā
svargāpavargau narakā
rasaukāṁsi ca sarvaśaḥ

sūryeṇa—by the sun-god within the sun planet; *hi*—indeed; *vibhajyante*—are divided; *diśaḥ*—the directions; *kham*—the sky; *dyauḥ*—the heavenly planets; *mahī*—the earthly planets; *bhidā*—other divisions; *svarga*—the heavenly planets; *apavargau*—and the places for liberation; *narakāḥ*—the hellish planets; *rasaukāṁsi*—such as Atala; *ca*—also; *sarvaśaḥ*—all.

TRANSLATION

O King, the sun-god and the sun planet divide all the directions of the universe. It is only because of the presence of the sun that we can

understand what the sky, the higher planets, this world and the lower planets are. It is also only because of the sun that we can understand which places are for material enjoyment, which are for liberation, which are hellish and subterranean.

TEXT 46

देवतिर्यङ्मनुष्याणां सरीसृपसवीरुधाम् ।
सर्वजीवनिकायानां सूर्य आत्मा दृगीश्वरः ॥४६॥

deva-tiryaṅ-manuṣyāṇāṁ
sarīsṛpa-savīrudhām
sarva-jīva-nikāyānāṁ
sūrya ātmā dṛg-īśvaraḥ

deva—of the demigods; *tiryak*—the lower animals; *manuṣyāṇām*—and the human beings; *sarīsṛpa*—the insects and the serpents; *sa-vīrudhām*—and the plants and trees; *sarva-jīva-nikāyānām*—of all groups of living entities; *sūryaḥ*—the –sun-god; *ātmā*—the life and soul; *dṛk*—of the eyes; *īśvaraḥ*—the Personality of Godhead.

TRANSLATION

All living entities, including demigods, human beings, animals, birds, insects, reptiles, creepers and trees, depend upon the heat and light given by the sun-god from the sun planet. Furthermore, it is because of the sun's presence that all living entities can see, and therefore he is called dṛg-īśvara, the Personality of Godhead presiding over sight.

PURPORT

In this regard, Śrīla Viśvanātha Cakravartī Ṭhākura says, *sūrya ātmā ātmatvenopāsyaḥ.* The actual life and soul of all living entities within this universe is the sun. He is therefore *upāsya,* worshipable. We worship the sun-god by chanting the Gāyatrī *mantra* (*oṁ bhūr bhuvaḥ svaḥ tat savitur vareṇyaṁ bhargo devasya dhīmahi*). Sūrya is the life and soul of this universe, and there are innumerable universes for which a sun-god is the life and soul, just as the Supreme Personality of Godhead is the life and soul of the entire creation. We have information that Vairāja, Hiraṇyagarbha, entered the great, dull, material globe called the sun. This indicates that the theory held by so-called scientists that no one lives there is wrong. *Bhagavad-gītā* also says that Kṛṣṇa first instructed *Bhagavad-gītā* to the sun-god (*imaṁ vivasvate yogaṁ proktavān aham avyayam*). Therefore the sun is not vacant. It is inhabited by living entities, and the predominating deity is Vairāja, or Vivasvān. The difference between the sun and earth is that the sun is a fiery planet, but everyone there has a suitable body and can live there without difficulty.

Thus end the Bhaktivedanta purports of the Fifth Canto, Twentieth Chapter, of the Śrīmad-Bhāgavatam, *entitled "Studying the Structure of the Universe."*

CHAPTER TWENTY-ONE

The Movements of the Sun

This chapter informs us of the movements of the sun. The sun is not stationary; it is also moving like the other planets. The sun's movements determine the duration of night and day. When the sun travels north of the equator, it moves slowly during the day and very quickly at night, thus increasing the duration of the daytime and decreasing the duration of night. Similarly, when the sun travels south of the equator, the exact opposite is true—the duration of the day decreases, and the duration of night increases. When the sun enters Karkaṭa-rāśi (Cancer) and then travels to Siṁha-rāśi (Leo) and so on through Dhanuḥ-rāśi (Sagittarius), its course is called Dakṣiṇāyana, the southern way, and when the sun enters Makara-rāśi (Capricorn) and thereafter travels through Kumbharāśi (Aquarius) and so on through Mithuna-rāśi (Gemini), its course is called Uttarāyaṇa, the northern way. When the sun is in Meṣa-rāśi (Aries) and Tulā-rāśi (Libra), the duration of day and night are equal.

On Mānasottara Mountain are the abodes of four demigods. East of Sumeru Mountain is Devadhānī, where King Indra lives, and south of Sumeru is Saṁyamanī, the abode of Yamarāja, the superintendent of death. Similarly, west of Sumeru is Nimlocanī, the abode of Varuṇa, the demigod who controls the water, and north of Sumeru is Vibhāvarī, where the demigod of the moon lives. Sunrise, noon, sunset and midnight occur in all these places because of the movements of the sun. Diametrically opposite the place where the sunrise takes places and the sun is seen by human eyes, the sun will be setting and passing away from human vision. Similarly, the people residing diametrically opposite the point where it is midday will be experiencing midnight. The sun rises and sets with all the other planets, headed by the moon and other luminaries.

The entire *kāla-cakra,* or wheel of time, is established on the wheel of the sun-god's chariot. This wheel is known as Saṁvatsara. The seven horses pulling the chariot of the sun are known as Gāyatrī, Bṛhatī, Uṣṇik, Jagatī, Triṣṭup, Anuṣṭup and Paṅkti. They are harnessed by a demigod known as Aruṇadeva to a yoke 900,000 *yojanas* wide. Thus the chariot carries Ādityadeva, the sun-god. Always staying in front of the sun-god and offering their prayers are sixty thousand sages known as Vālikhilyas. There are fourteen

Gandharvas, Apsarās and other demigods, who are divided into seven parties and who perform ritualistic activities every month to worship the Supersoul through the sun-god according to different names. Thus the sun-god travels through the universe for a distance of 95,100,000 *yojanas* (760,800,000 miles) at a speed of 16,004 miles at every moment.

TEXT 1

श्रीशुक उवाच
एतावानेव भूवलयस्य संनिवेशः प्रमाणलक्षणतो व्याख्यातः ॥१॥

śrī-śuka uvāca
etāvān eva bhū-valayasya sanniveśaḥ pramāṇa-lakṣaṇato vyākhyātaḥ.

śrī-śukaḥ uvāca—Śrī Śukadeva Gosvāmī said; *etāvān*—so much; *eva*—certainly; *bhū-valayasya sanniveśaḥ*—the arrangement of the whole universe; *pramāṇa-lakṣaṇataḥ*—according to measurement (fifty crores of *yojanas,* or four billion miles in width and length) and characteristics; *vyākhyātaḥ*—estimated.

TRANSLATION

Śukadeva Gosvāmī said: My dear King, I have thus far described the diameter of the universe [fifty crores of yojanas, or four billion miles] and its general characteristics, according to the estimations of learned scholars.

TEXT 2

एतेन हि दिवो मण्डलमानं तद्विद उपदिशन्ति यथा द्विदलयोर्निष्पावादीनां ते अन्तरेणान्तरिक्षं तदुभयसन्धितम् ॥२॥

etena hi divo maṇḍala-mānaṁ tad-vida upadiśanti yathā dvi-dalayor
niṣpāvādīnāṁ te antareṇāntarikṣaṁ tad-ubhaya-sandhitam.

etena—by this estimation; *hi*—indeed; *divaḥ*—of the upper planetary system; *maṇḍala-mānam*—the measurement of the globe; *tat-vidaḥ*—the experts who know about it; *upadiśanti*—instruct; *yathā*—just as; *dvi-dalayoḥ*—in the two halves; *niṣpāva-ādīnām*—of grain such as wheat; *te*—of the two divisions; *antareṇa*—in the intervening space; *antarikṣam*—the sky or outer space; *tat*—by the two; *ubhaya*—on both sides; *sandhitam*—where the two parts join.

TRANSLATION

As a grain of wheat is divided into two parts and one can estimate the size of the upper part by knowing that of the lower, so, expert geographers instruct, one can understand the measurements of the upper part of the universe by knowing those of the lower part. The sky between the earthly sphere and heavenly sphere is called antarikṣa, or outer space. It adjoins the top of the sphere of earth and the bottom of that of heaven.

TEXT 3

यन्मध्यगतो भगवांस्तपताम्पतिस्तपन आतपेन त्रिलोकीं प्रतपत्यवभासयत्या-त्मभासा स एष उदगयनदक्षिणायनवैषुवतसंज्ञाभिर्मान्द्यशैघ्र्यसमानाभिर्गति-भिरारोहणावरोहणसमानस्थानेषु यथासवनमभिपद्यमानो मकरादिषु राशिष्वहोरात्राणि दीर्घह्रस्वसमानानि विधत्ते ॥ ३ ॥

yan-madhya-gato bhagavāṁs tapatāṁ patis tapana ātapena tri-lokīṁ
pratapaty avabhāsayaty ātma-bhāsā sa eṣa udagayana-dakṣiṇāyana-
vaiṣuvata-saṁjñābhir māndya-śaighrya-samānābhir gatibhir
ārohaṇāvarohaṇa-samāna-sthāneṣu yathā-savanam abhipadyamāno
makarādiṣu rāśiṣv aho-rātrāṇi dīrgha-hrasva-samānāni vidhatte.

yat—of which (the intermediate space); *madhya-gataḥ*—being situated in the middle; *bhagavān*—the most powerful; *tapatām patiḥ*—the master of those that heat the whole universe; *tapanaḥ*—the sun; *ātapena*—by heat; *tri-lokīm*—the three worlds; *pratapati*—heats; *avabhāsayati*—lights; *ātma-bhāsā*—by its own illuminating rays; *saḥ*—that; *eṣaḥ*—the sun globe; *udagayana*—of passing to the northern side of the equator; *dakṣiṇa-ayana*—of passing to the southern side of the equator; *vaiṣuvata*—or of passing through the equator; *saṁjñābhiḥ*—by different names; *māndya*—characterized by slowness; *śaighrya*—swiftness; *samānābhiḥ*—and by equality; *gatibhiḥ*—by movement; *ārohaṇa*—of rising; *avarohaṇa*—of going down; *samāna*—or of staying in the middle; *sthāneṣu*—in positions; *yathā-savanam*—according to the order of the Supreme Personality of Godhead; *abhipadyamānaḥ*—moving; *makara-ādiṣu*—headed by the sign Makara (Capricorn); *rāśiṣu*—in different signs; *ahaḥ-rātrāṇi*—the days and nights; *dīrgha*—long; *hrasva*—short; *samānāni*—equal; *vidhatte*—makes.

TRANSLATION

In the midst of that region of outer space [antarikṣa] is the most opulent sun, the king of all the planets that emanate heat, such as the moon. By

the influence of its radiation, the sun heats the universe and maintains its proper order. It also gives light to help all living entities see. While passing toward the north, toward the south or through the equator, in accordance with the order of the Supreme Personality of Godhead, it is said to move slowly, swiftly or moderately. According to its movements in rising above, going beneath or passing through the equator—and correspondingly coming in touch with various signs of the zodiac, headed by Makara [Capricorn]—days and nights are short, long or equal to one another.

PURPORT

Lord Brahmā prays in his *Brahma-saṁhitā* (5.52):

yac cakṣur eṣa savitā sakala-grahāṇāṁ
rājā samasta-sura-mūrtir aśeṣa-tejāḥ
yasyājñayā bhramati saṁbhṛta-kāla-cakro
govindam ādi-puruṣaṁ tam ahaṁ bhajāmi

"I worship Govinda, the primeval Lord, the Supreme Personality of Godhead under whose control even the sun, which is considered to be the eye of the Lord, rotates within the fixed orbit of eternal time. The sun is the king of all planetary systems and has unlimited potency in heat and light." Although the sun is described as *bhagavān,* the most powerful, and although it is actually the most powerful planet within the universe, it nevertheless has to carry out the order of Govinda, Kṛṣṇa. The sun-god cannot deviate even an inch from the orbit designated to him. Therefore in every sphere of life, the supreme order of the Supreme Personality of Godhead is carried out. The entire material nature carries out His orders. However, we foolishly see the activities of material nature without understanding the supreme order and Supreme Person behind them. As confirmed in *Bhagavad-gītā, mayādhyakṣeṇa prakṛtiḥ:* material nature carries out the orders of the Lord, and thus everything is maintained in an orderly way.

TEXT 4

यदा मेषतुलयोर्वर्तते तदाहोरात्राणि समानानि भवन्ति यदा वृषभादिषु पञ्चसु च राशिषु चरति तदाहान्येव वर्धन्ते ह्रसति च मासि मास्येकैका घटिका रात्रिषु ॥४॥

yadā meṣa-tulayor vartate tadāho-rātrāṇi samānāni bhavanti yadā vṛṣabhādiṣu pañcasu ca rāśiṣu carati tadāhāny eva vardhante hrasati ca māsi māsy ekaikā ghaṭikā rātriṣu.

yadā—when; *meṣa-tulayoḥ*—in Meṣa (Aries) and Tulā (Libra); *vartate*—the sun exists; *tadā*—at that time; *ahaḥ-rātrāṇi*—the days and nights; *samānāni*—equal in duration; *bhavanti*—are; *yadā*—when; *vṛṣabha-ādiṣu*—headed by Vṛṣabha (Taurus) and Mithuna (Gemini); *pañcasu*—in the five; *ca*—also; *rāśiṣu*—signs; *carati*—moves; *tadā*—at that time; *ahāni*—the days; *eva*—certainly; *vardhante*—increase; *hrasati*—is diminished; *ca*—and; *māsi māsi*—in every month; *eka-ekā*—one; *ghaṭikā*—half hour; *rātriṣu*—in the nights.

TRANSLATION

When the sun passes through Meṣa [Aries] and Tulā [Libra], the durations of day and night are equal. When it passes through the five signs headed by Vṛṣabha [Taurus], the duration of the days increases [until Cancer], and then it gradually decreases by half an hour each month, until day and night again become equal [in Libra].

TEXT 5

यदा वृश्चिकादिषु पञ्चसु वर्तते तदाहोरात्राणि विपर्ययाणि भवन्ति ॥५॥

yadā vṛścikādiṣu pañcasu vartate tadāho-rātrāṇi viparyayāṇi bhavanti.

yadā—when; *vṛścika-ādiṣu*—headed by Vṛścika (Scorpio); *pañcasu*—five; *vartate*—remains; *tadā*—at that time; *ahaḥ-rātrāṇi*—the days and nights; *viparyayāṇi*—the opposite (the duration of the day decreases, and that of night increases); *bhavanti*—are.

TRANSLATION

When the sun passes through the five signs beginning with Vṛścika [Scorpio], the duration of the days decreases [until Capricorn], and then gradually it increases month after month, until day and night become equal [in Aries].

TEXT 6

यावद्दक्षिणायनमहानि वर्धन्ते यावदुदगयनं रात्रयः ॥६॥

yāvad dakṣiṇāyanam ahāni vardhante yāvad udagayanaṁ rātrayaḥ.

yāvat—until; *dakṣiṇa-ayanam*—the sun passes to the southern side; *ahāni*—the days; *vardhante*—increase; *yāvat*—until; *udagayanam*—the sun passes to the northern side; *rātrayaḥ*—the nights.

TRANSLATION

Until the sun travels to the south the days grow longer, and until it travels to the north the nights grow longer.

TEXT 7

एवं नव कोटय एकपञ्चाशल्लक्षाणि योजनानां मानसोत्तरगिरिपरिवर्तनस्योपदिशन्ति तस्मिन्नैन्द्रीं पुरीं पूर्वस्मान्मेरोर्देवधानीं नाम दक्षिणतो याम्यां संयमनीं नाम पश्चाद्वारुणीं निम्लोचनीं नाम उत्तरतः सौम्यां विभावरीं नाम तासूदयमध्याह्नास्तमयनिशीथानीति भूतानां प्रवृत्तिनिवृत्तिनिमित्तानि समयविशेषेण मेरोश्चतुर्दिशम् ॥ ७ ॥

evaṁ nava koṭaya eka-pañcāśal-lakṣāṇi yojanānāṁ mānasottara-giri-parivartanasyopadiśanti tasminn aindrīṁ purīṁ pūrvasmān meror devadhānīṁ nāma dakṣiṇato yāmyāṁ saṁyamanīṁ nāma paścād vāruṇīṁ nimlocanīṁ nāma uttarataḥ saumyāṁ vibhāvarīṁ nāma tāsūdaya-madhyāhnāstamaya-niśīthānīti bhūtānāṁ pravṛtti-nivṛtti-nimittāni samaya-viśeṣeṇa meroś catur-diśam.

evam—thus; *nava*—nine; *koṭayaḥ*—ten millions; *eka-pañcāśat*—fifty-one; *lakṣāṇi*—hundred thousands; *yojanānām*—of the *yojanas; mānasottara-giri*—of the mountain known as Mānasottara; *parivartanasya*—of the circumambulation; *upadiśanti*—they (learned scholars) teach; *tasmin*—on that (Mānasottara Mountain); *aindrīm*—of King Indra; *purīm*—the city; *pūrvasmāt*—on the eastern side; *meroḥ*—of Sumeru Mountain; *devadhānīm*—Devadhānī; *nāma*—of the name; *dakṣiṇataḥ*—on the southern side; *yāmyām*—of Yamarāja; *saṁyamanīm*—Saṁyamanī; *nāma*—named; *paścāt*—on the western side; *vāruṇīm*—of Varuṇa; *nimlocanīm*—Nimlocanī; *nāma*—named; *uttarataḥ*—on the northern side; *saumyām*—of the moon; *vibhāvarīm*—Vibhāvarī; *nāma*—named; *tāsu*—in all of them; *udaya*—rising; *madhyāhna*—midday; *astamaya*—sunset; *niśīthāni*—midnight; *iti*—thus; *bhūtānām*—of the living entities; *pravṛtti*—of activity; *nivṛtti*—and cessation of activity; *nimittāni*—the causes; *samaya-viśeṣeṇa*—by the particular times; *meroḥ*—of Sumeru Mountain; *catuḥ-diśam*—the four sides.

TRANSLATION

Śukadeva Gosvāmī continued; My dear King, as stated before, the learned say that the sun travels over all sides of Mānasottara Mountain in

a circle whose length is 95,100,000 yojanas [760,800,000 miles]. On Mānasottara Mountain, due east of Mount Sumeru, is a place known as Devadhānī, possessed by King Indra. Similarly, in the south is a place known as Saṁyamanī, possessed by Yamarāja, in the west is a place known as Nimlocanī, possessed by Varuṇa, and in the north is a place named Vibhāvarī, possessed by the moon-god. Sunrise, midday, sunset and midnight occur in all those places according to specific times, thus engaging all living entities in their various occupational duties and also making them cease such duties.

TEXTS 8–9

तत्रत्यानां दिवसमध्यङ्गत एव सदाऽऽदित्यस्तपति सव्येनाचलं दक्षिणेन करोति ॥८॥ यत्रोदेति तस्य ह समानसूत्रनिपाते निम्लोचति यत्र क्वचन स्यन्देनाभितपति तस्य हैष समानसूत्रनिपाते प्रस्वापयति तत्र गतं न पश्यन्ति ये तं समनुपश्येरन् ॥९॥

tatratyānāṁ divasa-madhyaṅgata eva sadādityas tapati savyenācalaṁ
dakṣiṇena karoti; yatrodeti tasya ha samāna-sūtra-nipāte nimlocati
yatra kvacana syandenābhitapati tasya haiṣa samāna-sūtra-nipāte
prasvāpayati tatra gataṁ na paśyanti ye taṁ samanupaśyeran.

tatratyānām—for the living entities residing on Mount Meru; *divasa-madhyaṅgataḥ*—being positioned as at midday; *eva*—indeed; *sadā*—always; *ādityaḥ*—the sun; *tapati*—heats; *savyena*—to the left side; *acalam*—Sumeru Mountain; *dakṣiṇena*—to the right (being forced by wind blowing to the right, the sun moves to the right); *karoti*—moves; *yatra*—the point where; *udeti*—it rises; *tasya*—of that position; *ha*—certainly; *samāna-sūtra-nipāte*—at the diametrically opposite point; *nimlocati*—the sun sets; *yatra*—where; *kvacana*—somewhere; *syandena*—with perspiration; *abhitapati*—heats (at midday); *tasya*—of that; *ha*—certainly; *eṣaḥ*—this (the sun); *samāna-sūtra-nipāte*—at the diametrically opposite point; *prasvāpayati*—the sun causes to sleep (as at midnight); *tatra*—there; *gatam*—gone; *na paśyanti*—do not see; *ye*—who; *tam*—the sunset; *samanupaśyeran*—seeing.

TRANSLATION

The living entities residing on Sumeru Mountain are always very warm, as at midday, because for them the sun is always overhead. Although the sun moves counterclockwise, facing the constellations, with Sumeru Mountain on its left, it also moves clockwise and appears to have the

mountain on its right because it is influenced by the dakṣiṇāvarta wind. People living in countries at points diametrically opposite to where the sun is first seen rising will see the sun setting, and if a straight line were drawn from a point where the sun is at midday, the people in countries at the opposite end of the line would be experiencing midnight. Similarly, if people residing where the sun is setting were to go to countries diametrically opposite, they would not see the sun in the same condition.

TEXT 10

यदा चैन्द्र्या पुर्याः प्रचलते पञ्चदशघटिकाभिर्याम्यां सपादकोटिद्वयं योजनानां सार्धद्वादशलक्षाणि साधिकानि चोपयाति ॥१०॥

yadā caindryāḥ puryāḥ pracalate pañcadaśa-ghaṭikābhir yāmyāṁ sapāda-koṭi-dvayaṁ yojanānāṁ sārdha-dvādaśa-lakṣāṇi sādhikāni copayāti.

yadā—when; *ca*—and; *aindryāḥ*—of Indra; *puryāḥ*—from the residence; *pracalate*—it moves; *pañcadaśa*—by fifteen; *ghaṭikābhiḥ*—half hours (actually twenty-four minutes); *yāmyām*—to the residence of Yamarāja; *sapāda-koṭi-dvayam*—two and a quarter *crores* (22,500,000); *yojanānām*—of *yojanas; sārdha*—and one half; *dvādaśa-lakṣāṇi*—twelve hundred thousand; *sādhikāni*—twenty-five thousand more; *ca*—and; *upayāti*—he passes over.

TRANSLATION

When the sun travels from Devadhānī, the residence of Indra, to Saṁyamanī, the residence of Yamarāja, it travels 23,775,000 yojanas [190,200,000 miles] in fifteen ghaṭikās [six hours].

PURPORT

The distance indicated by the word *sādhikāni* is *pañca-viṁśati-sahasrādhikāni,* or 25,000 *yojanas.* That plus two and a half crores and twelve and a half *lakṣa* of *yojanas* is the distance the sun travels between each two cities. This comes to 23,775,000 *yojanas,* or 190,200,000 miles. The total orbit of the sun is four times that distance, or 95,100,000 *yojanas* (760,800,000 miles).

TEXT 11

एवं ततो वारुणीं सौम्यामैन्द्रीं च पुनस्तथान्ये च ग्रहाः सोमादयो नक्षत्रैः सह ज्योतिश्चक्रे समभ्युद्यन्ति सह वा निम्लोचन्ति ॥११॥

evaṁ tato vāruṇīṁ saumyām aindrīṁ ca punas tathānye ca grahāḥ somādayo nakṣatraiḥ saha jyotiś-cakre samabhyudyanti saha vā nimlo-canti.

evam—in this way; *tataḥ*—from there; *vāruṇīm*—to the quarters where Varuṇa lives; *saumyām*—to the quarters where the moon lives; *aindrīṁ ca*—and to the quarters where Indra lives; *punaḥ*—again; *tathā*—so also; *anye*—the others; *ca*—also; *grahāḥ*—planets; *soma-ādayaḥ*—headed by the moon; *nakṣatraiḥ*—all the stars; *saha*—with; *jyotiḥ-cakre*—in the celestial sphere; *samabhyudyanti*—rise; *saha*—along with; *vā*—or; *nimlocanti*—set.

TRANSLATION

From the residence of Yamarāja the sun travels to Nimlocanī, the residence of Varuṇa, from there to Vibhāvarī, the residence of the moon god, and from there again to the residence of Indra. In a similar way, the moon, along with the other stars and planets, becomes visible in the celestial sphere and then sets and again becomes invisible.

PURPORT

In *Bhagavad-gītā* (10.21) Kṛṣṇa says, *nakṣatrāṇām ahaṁ śaśī:* "Of stars I am the moon." This indicates that the moon is similar to the other stars. The Vedic literature informs us that within this universe there is one sun, which is moving. The Western theory that all the luminaries in the sky are different suns is not confirmed in the Vedic literature. Nor can we assume that these luminaries are the suns of other universes, for each universe is covered by various layers of material elements, and therefore although the universes are clustered together, we cannot see from one universe to another. In other words, whatever we see is within this one universe. In each universe there is one Lord Brahmā, and there are other demigods on other planets, but there is only one sun.

TEXT 12

एवं मुहूर्तेन चतुस्त्रिंशल्लक्षयोजनान्यष्टशताधिकानि सौरो रथस्त्रयीमयोऽसौ चतसृषु परिवर्तते पुरीषु ॥१२॥

evaṁ muhūrtena catus-triṁśal-lakṣa-yojanāny aṣṭa-śatādhikāni sauro rathas trayīmayo 'sau catasṛṣu parivartate purīṣu.

evam—thus; *muhūrtena*—in a *muhūrta* (forty-eight minutes); *catuḥ-triṁśat*—thirty-four; *lakṣa*—hundred thousands; *yojanāni*—*yojanas;*

aṣṭa-śatādhikāni—increased by eight hundred; *sauraḥ rathaḥ*—the chariot of the sun-god; *trayī-mayaḥ*—which is worshiped by the Gāyatrī *mantra* (*oṁ bhūr bhuvaḥ svaḥ tat savitur,* etc.); *asau*—that; *catasṛṣu*—to the four; *parivartate*—he moves; *purīṣu*—through different residential quarters.

TRANSLATION

Thus the chariot of the sun-god, which is trayīmaya, or worshiped by the words oṁ bhūr bhuvaḥ svaḥ, travels through the four residences mentioned above at a speed of 3,400,800 yojanas [27,206,400 miles] in a muhūrta.

TEXT 13

यस्यैकं चक्रं द्वादशारं षण्नेमि त्रिणाभि संवत्सरात्मकं समामनन्ति तस्याक्षो मेरोर्मूर्धनि कृतो मानसोत्तरे कृतेतरभागो यत्र प्रोतं रविरथचक्रं तैलयन्त्रचक्रवद् भ्रमन्मानसोत्तरगिरौ परिभ्रमति ॥१३॥

yasyaikaṁ cakraṁ dvādaśāraṁ ṣaṇ-nemi tri-ṇābhi
saṁvatsarātmakaṁ samāmananti tasyākṣo meror mūrdhani kṛto
mānasottare kṛtetara-bhāgo yatra protaṁ ravi-ratha-cakraṁ taila-
yantra-cakravad bhraman mānasottara-girau paribhramati.

yasya—of which; *ekam*—one; *cakram*—wheel; *dvādaśa*—twelve; *aram*—spokes; *ṣaṭ*—six; *nemi*—the segments of the rim; *tri-ṇābhi*—the three pieces of the hub; *saṁvatsara-ātmakam*—whose nature is a *saṁvatsara; samāmananti*—they fully describe; *tasya*—the chariot of the sun-god; *akṣaḥ*—the axle; *meroḥ*—of Sumeru Mountain; *mūrdhani*—on the top; *kṛtaḥ*—fixed; *mānasottare*—on the mountain known as Mānasottara; *kṛta*—fixed; *itara-bhāgaḥ*—the other end; *yatra*—where; *protam*—fixed on; *ravi-ratha-cakram*—the wheel of the chariot of the sun-god; *taila-yantra-cakra-vat*—like the wheel of an oil-pressing machine; *bhramat*—moving; *mānasottara-girau*—on Mānasottara Mountain; *paribhramati*—turns.

TRANSLATION

The chariot of the sun-god has only one wheel, which is known as Saṁvatsara. The twelve months are calculated to be its twelve spokes, the six seasons are the sections of its rim, and the three cātur-māsya periods are its three-sectioned hub. One side of the axle carrying the wheel rests upon the summit of Mount Sumeru, and the other rests upon Mānasottara

Mountain. Affixed to the outer end of the axle, the wheel continuously rotates on Mānasottara Mountain like the wheel of an oil-pressing machine.

TEXT 14

तस्मिन्नक्षे कृतमूलो द्वितीयोऽक्षस्तुर्यमानेन सम्मितस्तैलयन्त्राक्षवद् ध्रुवे कृतोपरिभागः ॥१४॥

tasminn akṣe kṛtamūlo dvitīyo 'kṣas turyamānena sammitas taila-yantrākṣavad dhruve kṛtopari-bhāgaḥ.

tasmin akṣe—in that axle; *kṛta-mūlaḥ*—whose base is fixed; *dvitīyaḥ*—a second; *akṣaḥ*—axle; *turyamānena*—by one fourth; *sammitaḥ*—measured; *taila-yantra-akṣa-vat*—like the axle of an oil-pressing machine; *dhruve*—to Dhruvaloka; *kṛta*—fixed; *upari-bhāgaḥ*—upper portion.

TRANSLATION

As in an oil-pressing machine, this first axle is attached to a second axle, which is one-fourth as long [3,937,500 yojanas, or 31,500,000 miles]. The upper end of this second axle is attached to Dhruvaloka by a rope of wind.

TEXT 15

रथनीडस्तु षट्त्रिंशल्लक्षयोजनायतस्तत्तुरीयभागविशालस्तावान् रविरथयुगो यत्र हयाश्छन्दोनामानः सप्तारुणयोजिता वहन्ति देवमादित्यम् ॥१५॥

ratha-nīḍas tu ṣaṭ-triṁśal-lakṣa-yojanāyatas tat-turīya-bhāga-viśālas tāvān ravi-ratha-yugo yatra hayāś chando-nāmānaḥ saptāruṇa-yojitā vahanti devam ādityam.

ratha-nīḍaḥ—the interior of the chariot; *tu*—but; *ṣaṭ-triṁśat-lakṣa-yojana-āyataḥ*—3,600,000 *yojanas* long; *tat-turīya-bhāga*—one quarter of that measure (900,000 *yojanas*); *viśālaḥ*—having a width; *tāvān*—so much also; *ravi-ratha-yugaḥ*—the yoke for the horses; *yatra*—where; *hayāḥ*—horses; *chandaḥ-nāmānaḥ*—having the different names of Vedic meters; *sapta*—seven; *aruṇa-yojitāḥ*—hooked up by Aruṇadeva; *vahanti*—carry; *devam*—the demigod; *ādityam*—the sun-god.

TRANSLATION

My dear King, the carriage of the sun-god's chariot is estimated to be 3,600,000 yojanas [28,800,000 miles] long and one-fourth as wide

[900,000 yojanas, or 7,200,000 miles]. The chariot's horses, which are named after Gāyatrī and other Vedic meters, are harnessed by Aruṇadeva to a yoke that is also 900,000 yojanas wide. This chariot continuously carries the sun-god.

PURPORT

In the *Viṣṇu Purāṇa* it is stated:

gāyatrī ca bṛhaty uṣṇig
jagatī triṣṭup eva ca
anuṣṭup paṅktir ity uktāś
chandāṁsi harayo raveḥ

The seven horses yoked to the sun-god's chariot are named Gāyatrī, Bṛhati, Uṣṇik, Jagatī, Triṣṭup, Anuṣṭup and Paṅkti. These names of various Vedic meters designate the seven horses that carry the sun-god's chariot.

TEXT 16

पुरस्तात्सवितुररुणः पश्चाच्च नियुक्तः सौत्ये कर्मणि किलास्ते ॥१६॥

purastāt savitur aruṇaḥ paścāc ca niyuktaḥ sautye karmaṇi kilāste.

purastāt—in front; *savituḥ*—of the sun-god; *aruṇaḥ*—the demigod named Aruṇa; *paścāt*—looking backward; *ca*—and; *niyuktaḥ*—engaged; *sautye*—of a charioteer; *karmaṇi*—in the work; *kila*—certainly; *āste*—remains.

TRANSLATION

Although Aruṇadeva sits in front of the sun-god and is engaged in driving the chariot and controlling the horses, he looks backward toward the sun-god.

PURPORT

In the *Vāyu Purāṇa* the position of the horses is described:

saptāśva-rūpa-cchandāṁsī
vahante vāmato ravim
cakra-pakṣa-nibaddhāni
cakre vākṣaḥ samāhitaḥ

Although Aruṇadeva is in the front seat, controlling the horses, he looks back toward the sun-god from his left side.

TEXT 17

तथा वालखिल्या ऋषयोऽङ्गुष्ठपर्वमात्राः षष्टिसहस्राणि पुरतः सूर्यं सूक्तवाकाय नियुक्ताः संस्तुवन्ति ॥१७॥

tathā vālakhilyā ṛṣayo 'ṅguṣṭha-parva-mātrāḥ ṣaṣṭi-sahasrāṇi purataḥ sūryaṁ sūkta-vākāya niyuktāḥ saṁstuvanti.

tathā—there; *vālikhilyāḥ*—Vālikhilyas; *ṛṣayaḥ*—great sages; *aṅguṣṭha-parva-mātrāḥ*—whose size is that of a thumb; *ṣaṣṭi-sahasrāṇi*—sixty thousand; *purataḥ*—in front; *sūryam*—the sun-god; *su-ukta-vākāya*—for speaking eloquently; *niyuktāḥ*—engaged; *saṁstuvanti*—offer prayers.

TRANSLATION

There are sixty thousand saintly persons named Vālikhilyas, each the size of a thumb, who are located in front of the sun-god and who offer him eloquent prayers of glorification.

TEXT 18

तथान्ये च ऋषयो गन्धर्वाप्सरसो नागा ग्रामण्यो यातुधाना देवा इत्येकैकशो गणाः सप्त चतुर्दश मासि मासि भगवन्तं सूर्यमात्मानं नानानामानं पृथङ्नानानामानः पृथक् कर्मभिर्द्वन्द्वश उपासते ॥१८॥

tathānye ca ṛṣayo gandharvāpsaraso nāgā grāmaṇyo yātudhānā devā ity ekaikaśo gaṇāḥ sapta caturdaśa māsi māsi bhagavantaṁ sūryam ātmānaṁ nānā-nāmānaṁ pṛthaṅ-nānā-nāmānaḥ pṛthak-karmabhir dvandvaśa upāsate.

tathā—similarly; *anye*—others; *ca*—also; *ṛṣayaḥ*—saintly persons; *gandharva-apsarasaḥ*—Gandharvas and Apsarās; *nāgāḥ*—Nāga snakes; *grāmaṇyaḥ*—Yakṣas; *yātudhānāḥ*—Rākṣasas; *devāḥ*—demigods; *iti*—thus; *eka-ekaśaḥ*—one by one; *gaṇāḥ*—groups; *sapta*—seven; *caturdaśa*—fourteen in number; *māsi māsi*—in every month; *bhagavantam*—unto the most powerful demigod; *sūryam*—the sun-god; *ātmānam*—the life of the universe; *nānā*—various; *nāmānam*—who possesses names; *pṛthak*—separate; *nānā-nāmānaḥ*—having various names; *pṛthak*—separate;

karmabhiḥ—by ritualistic ceremonies; *dvandvaśaḥ*—in groups of two; *upāsate*—worship.

TRANSLATION

Similarly, fourteen other saints, Gandharvas, Apsarās, Nāgas, Yakṣas, Rākṣasas and demigods, who are divided into groups of two, assume different names every month and continuously perform different ritualistic ceremonies to worship the Supreme Lord as the most powerful demigod Sūryadeva, who holds many names.

PURPORT

In the *Viṣṇu Purāṇa* it is said:

stuvanti munayaḥ sūryaṁ
gandharvair gīyate puraḥ
nṛtyanto'psaraso yānti
sūryasyānu niśācarāḥ

vahanti pannagā yakṣaiḥ
kriyate'bhiṣusaṅgrahaḥ
vālikhilyās tathaivainaṁ
parivārya samāsate

so'yaṁ sapta-gaṇaḥ sūrya-
maṇḍale muni-sattama
himoṣṇa vāri-vṛṣṭīṇāṁ
hetutve samayaṁ gataḥ

Worshiping the most powerful demigod Sūrya, the Gandharvas sing in front of him, the Apsarās dance before the chariot, the Niśācaras follow the chariot, the Pannagas decorate the chariot, the Yakṣas guard the chariot, and the saints called the Vālikhilyas surround the sun-god and offer prayers. The seven groups of fourteen associates arrange the proper times for regular snow, heat and rain throughout the universe.

TEXT 19

लक्षोत्तरं सार्धनवकोटियोजनपरिमण्डलं भूवलयस्य क्षणेन सगव्यूत्युत्तरं द्विसहस्रयोजनानि स भुङ्क्ते ॥१९॥

lakṣottaraṁ sārdha-nava-koṭi-yojana-parimaṇḍalaṁ bhū-valayasya kṣaṇena sagavyūty-uttaraṁ dvi-sahasra-yojanāni sa bhuṅkte.

lakṣa-uttaram—increased by 100,000; *sārdha*—with 5,000,000; *nava-koṭi-yojana*—of 90,000,000 *yojanas; parimaṇḍalam*—circumference; *bhū-valayasya*—of the earthly sphere; *kṣaṇena*—in one moment; *sagavyūti-uttaram*—augmented by two *krośas* (four miles); *dvi-sahasra-yojanāni*—2,000 *yojanas; saḥ*—the sun-god; *bhuṅkte*—traverses.

TRANSLATION

My dear King, in his orbit through Bhū-maṇḍala, the sun-god traverses a distance of 95,100,000 yojanas [760,800,000 miles] at the speed of 2,000 yojanas and two krośas [16,004 miles] in a moment.

Thus end the Bhaktivedanta purports of the Fifth Canto, Twenty-first Chapter, of the Śrīmad-Bhāgavatam, *entitled "The Movements of the Sun."*

CHAPTER TWENTY-TWO

The Orbits of the Planets

In this chapter the orbits of the planets are described. According to the movements of the moon and other planets, all the inhabitants of the universe are prone to auspicious and inauspicious situations. This is referred to as the influence of the stars.

The sun-god, who controls the affairs of the entire universe, especially in regard to heat, light, seasonal changes and so on, is considered an expansion of Nārāyaṇa. He represents the three *Vedas—Ṛg, Yajur* and *Sāma*—and therefore he is known as Trayīmaya, the form of Lord Nārāyaṇa. Sometimes the sun-god is also called Sūrya Nārāyaṇa. The sun-god has expanded himself in twelve divisions, and thus he controls the six seasonal changes and causes winter, summer, rain and so on. *Yogīs* and *karmīs* following the *varṇāśrama* institution, who practice *haṭha* or *aṣṭāṅga-yoga* or who perform *agnihotra* sacrifices, worship Sūrya Nārāyaṇa for their own benefit. The demigod Sūrya is always in touch with the Supreme Personality of Godhead, Nārāyaṇa. Residing in outer space, which is in the middle of the universe, between Bhūloka and Bhuvarloka, the sun rotates through the time circle of the zodiac, represented by twelve *rāśis,* or signs, and assumes different names according to the sign he is in. For the moon, every month is divided into two fortnights. Similarly, according to solar calculations, a month is equal to the time the sun spends in one constellation; two months constitute one season, and there are twelve months in a year. The entire area of the sky is divided into two halves, each representing an *ayana,* the course traversed by the sun within a period of six months. The sun travels sometimes slowly, sometimes swiftly and sometimes at a moderate speed. In this way it travels within the three worlds, consisting of the heavenly planets, the earthly planets and outer space. These orbits are referred to by great learned scholars by the names Saṁvatsara, Parivatsara, Iḍāvatsara, Anuvatsara and Vatsara.

The moon is situated 100,000 *yojanas* above the rays of the sunshine. Day and night on the heavenly planets and Pitṛloka are calculated according to its waning and waxing. Above the moon by a distance of 200,000 *yojanas* are some stars, and above these stars is Śukra-graha (Venus), whose influence is always auspicious for the inhabitants of the entire universe. Above Śukra-graha by 200,000 *yojanas* is Budha-graha (Mercury), whose influence is sometimes auspicious and sometimes inauspicious. Next, above Budha-graha by 200,000 *yojanas,* is Aṅgāraka (Mars), which almost always has an unfavorable influence. Above Aṅgāraka by another 200,000 *yojanas* is the planet called Bṛhaspati-graha (Jupiter), which is always very favorable for qualified *brāhmaṇas.* Above Bṛhaspati-graha is the planet Śanaiścara (Saturn), which is very inauspicious, and above Saturn is a group of seven stars occupied by great saintly persons who are always thinking of the welfare of the entire universe. These seven stars circumambulate Dhruvaloka, which is the residence of Lord Viṣṇu within this universe.

TEXT 1

राजोवाच
यदेतद्भगवत आदित्यस्य मेरुं ध्रुवं च प्रदक्षिणेन परिक्रामतो राशीनामभिमुखं प्रचलितं चाप्रदक्षिणं भगवतोपवर्णितममुष्य वयं कथमनुमिमीमहीति ॥१॥

rājovāca
yad etad bhagavata ādityasya meruṁ dhruvaṁ ca pradakṣiṇena
parikrāmato rāśīnām abhimukhaṁ pracalitaṁ cāpradakṣiṇaṁ
bhagavatopavarṇitam amuṣya vayaṁ katham anumimīmahīti.

rājā uvāca—the King (Mahārāja Parīkṣit) inquired; *yat*—which; *etat*—this; *bhagavataḥ*—of the most powerful; *ādityasya*—of the sun (Sūrya Nārāyaṇa); *merum*—the mountain known as Sumeru; *dhruvam ca*—as well as the planet known as Dhruvaloka; *pradakṣiṇena*—by placing on the right; *parikrāmataḥ*—which is going around; *rāśīnām*—the different signs of the zodiac; *abhimukham*—facing toward; *pracalitam*—moving; *ca*—and; *apradakṣiṇam*—placing on the left; *bhagavatā*—by Your Lordship; *upavarṇitam*—described; *amuṣya*—of that; *vayam*—we (the hearer); *katham*—how; *anumimīmahi*—can accept it by argument and inference; *iti*—thus.

TRANSLATION

King Parīkṣit inquired from Śukadeva Gosvāmī: My dear lord, you have already affirmed the truth that the supremely powerful sun-god travels around Dhruvaloka with both Dhruvaloka and Mount Sumeru on his right. Yet at the same time the sun-god faces the signs of the zodiac and keeps Sumeru and Dhruvaloka on his left. How can we reasonably accept that the sun-god proceeds with Sumeru and Dhruvaloka on both his left and right simultaneously?

TEXT 2

स होवाच

यथा कुलालचक्रेण भ्रमता सह भ्रमतां तदाश्रयाणां पिपीलिकादीनां गतिरन्यैव प्रदेशान्तरेष्वप्युपलभ्यमानत्वादेवं नक्षत्रराशिभिरुपलक्षितेन कालचक्रेण ध्रुवं मेरुं च प्रदक्षिणेन परिधावता सह परिधावमानानां तदाश्रयाणां सूर्यादीनां ग्रहाणां गतिरन्यैव नक्षत्रान्तरे राश्यन्तरे चोपलभ्यमानत्वात् ॥ २ ॥

sa hovāca
yathā kulāla-cakreṇa bhramatā saha bhramatāṁ tad-āśrayāṇāṁ pipīlikādīnāṁ gatir anyaiva pradeśāntareṣv apy upalabhyamānatvād evaṁ nakṣatra-rāśibhir upalakṣitena kāla-cakreṇa dhruvaṁ meruṁ ca pradakṣiṇena paridhāvatā saha paridhāvamānānāṁ tad-āśrayāṇāṁ sūryādīnāṁ grahāṇāṁ gatir anyaiva nakṣatrāntare rāśy-antare copalabhyamānatvāt.

saḥ—Śukadeva Gosvāmī; *ha*—very clearly; *uvāca*—answered; *yathā*—just as; *kulāla-cakreṇa*—a potter's wheel; *bhramatā*—turning around; *saha*—with; *bhramatām*—of those turning around; *tat-āśrayāṇām*—being located on that (wheel); *pipīlika-ādīnām*—of small ants; *gatiḥ*—the motion; *anyā*—other; *eva*—certainly; *pradeśa-antareṣu*—in different locations; *api*—also; *upalabhyamānatvāt*—due to being experienced; *evam*—similarly; *nakṣatra-rāśibhiḥ*—by the stars and signs; *upalakṣitena*—being seen; *kāla-cakreṇa*—with the great wheel of time; *dhruvam*—the star known as Dhruvaloka; *merum*—the mountain known as Sumeru; *ca*—and; *pradakṣiṇena*—on the right; *paridhāvatā*—going around; *saha*—with; *paridhāvamānānām*—of those going around; *tat-āśrayāṇām*—whose shelter is that wheel of time; *sūrya-ādīnām*—headed by the sun; *grahāṇām*—of the planets; *gatiḥ*—the motion; *anyā*—other; *eva*—certainly; *nakṣatra-antare*—in different stars; *rāśi-antare*—in different signs; *ca*—and; *upalabhyamānatvāt*—due to being observed.

TRANSLATION

Śrī Śukadeva Gosvāmī clearly answered: When a potter's wheel is moving and small ants located on that big wheel are moving with it, one can see that their motion is different from that of the wheel because they appear sometimes on one part of the wheel and sometimes on another. Similarly, the signs and constellations, with Sumeru and Dhruvaloka on their right, move with the wheel of time, and the antlike sun and other

planets move with them. The sun and planets, however, are seen in different signs and constellations at different times. This indicates that their motion is different from that of the zodiac and the wheel of time itself.

TEXT 3

स एष भगवानादिपुरुष एव साक्षान्नारायणो लोकानां स्वस्तय आत्मानं त्रयीमयं कर्मविशुद्धि निमित्तं कविभिरपि च वेदेन विजिज्ञास्यमानो द्वादशधा विभज्य षट्सु वसन्तादिष्वृतुषु यथोपजोषमृतुगुणान् विदधाति ॥३॥

sa eṣa bhagavān ādi-puruṣa eva sākṣān nārāyaṇo lokānāṁ svastaya ātmānaṁ trayīmayaṁ karma-viśuddhi-nimittaṁ kavibhir api ca vedena vijijñāsyamāno dvādaśadhā vibhajya ṣaṭsu vasantādiṣv ṛtuṣu yathopa-joṣam ṛtu-guṇān vidadhāti.

saḥ—that; *eṣaḥ*—this; *bhagavān*—the supremely powerful; *ādi-puruṣaḥ*—the original person; *eva*—certainly; *sākṣāt*—directly; *nārāyaṇaḥ*—the Supreme Personality of Godhead, Nārāyaṇa; *lokānām*—of all the planets; *svastaye*—for the benefit; *ātmānam*—Himself; *trayī-mayam*—consisting of the three *Vedas* (*Sāma, Yajur* and *Ṛg*); *karma-viśuddhi*—of purification of fruitive activities; *nimittam*—the cause; *kavibhiḥ*—by great saintly persons; *api*—also; *ca*—and; *vedena*—by Vedic knowledge; *vijijñāsyamānaḥ*—being inquired about; *dvādaśa-dhā*—in twelve divisions; *vibhajya*—dividing; *ṣaṭsu*—in six; *vasanta-ādiṣu*—headed by spring; *ṛtuṣu*—seasons; *yathā-upajoṣam*—according to the enjoyment of their past activities; *ṛtu-guṇān*—the qualities of the different seasons; *vidadhāti*—he arranges.

TRANSLATION

The original cause of the cosmic manifestation is the Supreme Personality of Godhead, Nārāyaṇa. When great saintly persons, fully aware of the Vedic knowledge, offered prayers to the Supreme Person, He descended to this material world in the form of the sun to benefit all the planets and purify fruitive activities. He divided Himself into twelve parts and created seasonal forms, beginning with spring. In this way He created the seasonal qualities, such as heat, cold and so on.

TEXT 4

तमेतमिह पुरुषास्त्रय्या विद्यया वर्णाश्रमाचारानुपथा उच्चावचैः कर्मभिराम्नातैर्योगवितानैश्च श्रद्धया यजन्तोऽञ्जसा श्रेयः समधिगच्छन्ति ॥४॥

tam etam iha puruṣās trayyā vidyayā varṇāśramācārānupathā
uccāvacaiḥ karmabhir āmnātair yoga-vitānaiś ca śraddhayā yajanto
'ñjasā śreyaḥ samadhigacchanti.

tam—Him (the Supreme Personality of Godhead); *etam*—this; *iha*—in this world of mortality; *puruṣāḥ*—all people; *trayyā*—having three divisions; *vidyayā*—by the Vedic knowledge; *varṇa-āśrama-ācāra*—the practices of the *varṇāśrama* system; *anupathāḥ*—following; *ucca-avacaiḥ*—higher or lower according to the different positions in the *varṇāśrama-dharma* (*brāhmaṇa, kṣatriya, vaiśya* and *śūdra*); *karmabhiḥ*—by their respective activities; *āmnātaiḥ*—handed down; *yoga-vitānaiḥ*—by meditation and other yogic processes; *ca*—and; *śraddhayā*—with great faith; *yajantaḥ*—worshiping; *añjasā*—without difficulty; *śreyaḥ*—the ultimate benefit of life; *samadhigacchanti*—they attain.

TRANSLATION

According to the system of four varṇas and four āśramas, people generally worship the Supreme Personality of Godhead, Nārāyaṇa, who is situated as the sun-god. With great faith they worship the Supreme Personality as the Supersoul according to ritualistic ceremonies handed down in the three Vedas, such as agnihotra and similar higher and lower fruitive acts, and according to the process of mystic yoga. In this way they very easily attain the ultimate goal of life.

TEXT 5

अथ स एष आत्मा लोकानां द्यावापृथिव्योरन्तरेण नभोवलयस्य कालचक्रगतो द्वादश मासान् भुङ्क्ते राशिसंज्ञान् संवत्सरावयवान्मासः पक्षद्वयं दिवा नक्तं चेति सपादर्क्षद्वयमुपदिशन्ति यावता षष्ठमंशं भुञ्जीत स वै ऋतुरित्युपदिश्यते संवत्सरावयवः ॥ ५ ॥

atha sa eṣa ātmā lokānāṁ dyāv-āpṛthivyor antareṇa nabho-valayasya
kālacakra-gato dvādaśa māsān bhuṅkte rāśi-saṁjñān
saṁvatsarāvayavān māsaḥ pakṣa-dvayaṁ divā naktaṁ ceti sapādarkṣa-
dvayam upadiśanti yāvatā ṣaṣṭham aṁśaṁ bhuñjīta sa vai ṛtur ity
upadiśyate saṁvatsarāvayavaḥ.

atha—therefore; *saḥ*—He; *eṣaḥ*—this; *ātmā*—the living force; *lokānām*—of all the three worlds; *dyāv-ā-pṛthivyoḥ antareṇa*—between the upper and lower portions of the universe; *nabhaḥ-valayasya*—of outer space; *kāla-cakra-gataḥ*—positioned in the wheel of time; *dvādaśa māsān*—twelve months; *bhuṅkte*—passes; *rāśi-saṁjñān*—named after the zodiac signs; *saṁvatsara-avayavān*—the parts of the whole year; *māsaḥ*—one month; *pakṣa-dvayam*—two fortnights; *divā*—a day; *naktam ca*—and a night; *iti*—thus; *sapāda-ṛkṣa-dvayam*—by stellar calculations, two and a quarter constellations; *upadiśanti*—they instruct; *yāvatā*—by as much time; *ṣaṣṭham aṁśam*—one sixth of his orbit; *bhuñjīta*—pass; *saḥ*—that portion; *vai*—indeed; *ṛtuḥ*—a season; *iti*—thus; *upadiśyate*—is instructed; *saṁvatsara-avayavaḥ*—a part of a year.

TRANSLATION

The sun-god, who is Nārāyaṇa, or Viṣṇu, the soul of all the worlds, is situated in outer space between the upper and lower portions of the universe. Passing through twelve months on the wheel of time, the sun comes in touch with twelve different signs of the zodiac and assumes twelve different names according to those signs. The aggregate of those twelve months is called a saṁvatsara, or an entire year. According to lunar calculations, two fortnights—one of the waxing moon and the other of the waning—form one month. That same period is one day and night for the planet Pitṛloka. According to stellar calculations, a month equals two and one quarter constellations. When the sun travels for two months, a season passes, and therefore the seasonal changes are considered parts of the body of the year.

TEXT 6

अथ च यावतार्धेन नभोवीथ्यां प्रचरति तं कालमयनमाचक्षते ॥६॥

atha ca yāvatārdhena nabho-vīthyāṁ pracarati taṁ kālam ayanam ācakṣate.

atha—now; *ca*—also; *yāvatā*—by as long as; *ardhena*—half; *nabhaḥ-vīthyām*—in outer space; *pracarati*—the sun moves; *tam*—that; *kālam*—time; *ayanam*—*ayana; ācakṣate*—is said.

TRANSLATION

Thus the time the sun takes to rotate through half of outer space is called an ayana, or its period of movement [in the north or in the south].

TEXT 7

अथ च यावन्नभोमण्डलं सह द्यावापृथिव्योर्मण्डलाभ्यां कार्त्स्न्येन स ह भुञ्जीत तं कालं संवत्सरं परिवत्सरमिडावत्सरमनुवत्सरं वत्सरमिति भानोर्मान्द्यशैघ्र्यसमगतिभिः समामनन्ति ॥ ७॥

atha ca yāvan nabho-maṇḍalaṁ saha dyāv-āpṛthivyor maṇḍalābhyāṁ kārtsnyena sa ha bhuñjīta taṁ kālaṁ saṁvatsaraṁ parivatsaram iḍāvatsaram anuvatsaraṁ vatsaram iti bhānor māndya-śaighrya-sama-gatibhiḥ samāmananti.

atha—now; *ca*—also; *yāvat*—as long as; *nabhaḥ-maṇḍalam*—outer space, between the upper and lower world; *saha*—along with; *dyau*—of the upper world; *āpṛthivyoḥ*—of the lower world; *maṇḍalābhyām*—the spheres; *kārtsnyena*—entirely; *saḥ*—he; *ha*—indeed; *bhuñjīta*—may pass through; *tam*—that; *kālam*—time; *saṁvatsaram*—Saṁvatsara; *parivatsaram*—Parivatsara; *iḍāvatsaram*—Iḍāvatsara; *anuvatsaram*—Anuvatsara; *vatsaram*—Vatsara; *iti*—thus; *bhānoḥ*—of the sun; *māndya*—slow; *śaighrya*—speedy; *sama*—and equal; *gatibhiḥ*—by the speeds; *samāmananti*—the experienced scholars describe.

TRANSLATION

The sun-god has three speeds—slow, fast and moderate. The time he takes to travel entirely around the spheres of heaven, earth and space at these three speeds is referred to, by learned scholars, by the five names Saṁvatsara, Parivatsara, Iḍāvatsara, Anuvatsara and Vatsara.

PURPORT

According to solar astronomical calculations, each year extends six days beyond the calendar year, and according to lunar calculations, each year is six days shorter. Therefore, because of the movements of the sun and moon, there is a difference of twelve days between the solar and lunar years. As the Saṁvatsara, Parivatsara, Iḍāvatsara, Anuvatsara and Vatsara pass by, two extra months are added within each five years. This makes a sixth *saṁvatsara,* but because that *saṁvatsara* is extra, the solar system is calculated according to the above five names.

TEXT 8

एवं चन्द्रमा अर्कगभस्तिभ्य उपरिष्टाल्लक्षयोजनत उपलभ्यमानोऽर्कस्य संवत्सरभुक्तिं पक्षाभ्यां मासभुक्तिं सपादर्क्षाभ्यां दिनेनैव पक्षभुक्तिमग्रचारी द्रुततरगमनो भुङ्क्ते ॥८॥

evaṁ candramā arka-gabhastibhya upariṣṭāl lakṣa-yojanata upalabhyamāno'rkasya saṁvatsara-bhuktiṁ pakṣābhyāṁ māsa-bhuktiṁ sapādarkṣābhyāṁ dinenaiva pakṣa-bhuktim agracārī drutatara-gamano bhuṅkte.

evam—thus; *candramā*—the moon; *arka-gabhastibhyaḥ*—from the rays of the sunshine; *upariṣṭāt*—above; *lakṣa-yojanataḥ*—by a measurement of 100,000 *yojanas; upalabhyamānaḥ*—being situated; *arkasya*—of the sun globe; *saṁvatsara-bhuktim*—the passage of one year of enjoyment; *pakṣābhyām*—by two fortnights; *māsa-bhuktim*—the passage of one month; *sapāda-ṛkṣābhyām*—by two and a quarter days; *dinena*—by a day; *eva*—only; *pakṣa-bhuktim*—the passage of a fortnight; *agracārī*—moving impetuously; *druta-tara-gamanaḥ*—passing more speedily; *bhuṅkte*—passes through.

TRANSLATION

Above the rays of the sunshine by a distance of 100,000 yojanas [800,000 miles] is the moon, which travels at a speed faster than that of the sun. In two lunar fortnights the moon travels through the equivalent of a saṁvatsara of the sun, in two and a quarter days it passes through a month of the sun, and in one day it passes through a fortnight of the sun.

PURPORT

When we take into account that the moon is 100,000 *yojanas,* or 800,000 miles, above the rays of the sunshine, it is very surprising that the modern excursions to the moon could be possible. Since the moon is so distant, how space vehicles could go there is a doubtful mystery. Modern scientific calculations are subject to one change after another, and therefore they are uncertain. We have to accept the calculations of the Vedic literature. These Vedic calculations are steady; the astronomical calculations made long ago and recorded in the Vedic literature are correct even now. Whether the Vedic calculations or modern ones are better may remain a mystery for others, but as far as we are concerned, we accept the Vedic calculations to be correct.

TEXT 9

अथ चापूर्यमाणाभिश्च कलाभिरमराणां क्षीयमाणाभिश्च कलाभिः पितॄणामहोरात्राणि पूर्वपक्षापरपक्षाभ्यां वितन्वानः सर्वजीवनिवहप्राणो जीवश्चैकमेकं नक्षत्रं त्रिंशता मुहूर्तैर्भुङ्क्ते ॥९॥

atha cāpūryamāṇābhiś ca kalābhir amarāṇāṁ kṣīyamāṇābhiś ca kalābhiḥ pitṝṇām aho-rātrāṇi pūrva-pakṣāpara-pakṣābhyāṁ vitanvānaḥ sarva-jīva-nivaha-prāṇo jivaś caikam ekaṁ nakṣatraṁ triṁśatā muhūrtair bhuṅkte.

atha—thus; *ca*—also; *āpūryamāṇābhiḥ*—gradually increasing; *ca*—and; *kalābhiḥ*—by the parts of the moon; *amarāṇām*—of the demigods; *kṣīyamāṇābhiḥ*—by gradually decreasing; *ca*—and; *kalābhiḥ*—by parts of the moon; *pitṝṇām*—of those on the planet known as Pitṛloka; *ahaḥ-rātrāṇi*—the days and nights; *pūrva-pakṣa-apara-pakṣābhyām*—by the period of waxing and waning; *vitanvānaḥ*—distributing; *sarva-jīva-nivaha*—of the total living entities; *prāṇaḥ*—the life; *jīvaḥ*—the chief living being; *ca*—also; *ekam ekam*—one after another; *nakṣatram*—a constellation of stars; *triṁśatā*—by thirty; *muhūrtaiḥ—muhūrtas; bhuṅkte*—passes through.

TRANSLATION

When the moon is waxing, the illuminating portions of it increase daily, thus creating day for the demigods and night for the pitās. When the moon is waning, however, it causes night for the demigods and day for the pitās. In this way the moon passes through each constellation of stars in thirty muhūrtas [an entire day]. The moon is the source of nectarean coolness that influences the growth of food grains, and therefore the moon god is considered the life of all living entities. He is consequently called Jīva, the chief living being within the universe.

TEXT 10

य एष षोडशकलः पुरुषो भगवान्मनोमयोऽन्नमयोऽमृतमयो देवपितृमनुष्य-भूतपशुपक्षिसरीसृपवीरुधां प्राणाप्यायनशीलत्वात्सर्वमय इति वर्णयन्ति ॥१०॥

ya eṣa ṣoḍaśa-kalaḥ puruṣo bhagavān manomayo'nnamayo'mṛtamayo deva-pitṛ-manuṣya-bhūta-paśu-pakṣi-sarīsṛpa-vīrudhāṁ prāṇāpy āyana-śīlatvāt sarvamaya iti varṇayanti.

yaḥ—that; *eṣaḥ*—this; *ṣoḍaśa-kalaḥ*—having all sixteen parts (the full moon); *puruṣaḥ*—the person; *bhagavān*—having great power received from the Supreme Personality of Godhead; *manaḥ-mayaḥ*—the predominating deity of the mind; *anna-mayaḥ*—the source of potency for food grains; *amṛta-mayaḥ*—the source of the substance of life; *deva*—of all the demigods; *pitṛ*—of all the inhabitants of Pitṛloka; *manuṣya*—all human beings; *bhūta*—all living entities; *paśu*—of the animals; *pakṣi*—of the birds; *sarīsṛpa*—of the reptiles; *vīrudhām*—of all kinds of herbs and plants; *prāṇa*—life air; *api*—certainly; *āyana-śīlatvāt*—due to refreshing; *sarva-mayaḥ*—all-pervading; *iti*—thus; *varṇayanti*—the learned scholars describe.

TRANSLATION

Because the moon is full of all potentialities, it represents the influence of the Supreme Personality of Godhead. The moon is the predominating deity of everyone's mind, and therefore the moon god is called Manomaya. He is also called Annamaya because he gives potency to all herbs and plants, and he is called Amṛtamaya because he is the source of life for all living entities. The moon pleases the demigods, pitās, human beings, animals, birds, reptiles, trees, plants and all other living entities. Everyone is satisfied by the presence of the moon. Therefore the moon is also called Sarvamaya [all-pervading].

TEXT 11

तत उपरिष्टाद्द्विलक्षयोजनतो नक्षत्राणि मेरुं दक्षिणेनैव कालायन ईश्वरयोजितानि सहाभिजिताष्टाविंशतिः ॥११॥

tata upariṣṭād dvi-lakṣa-yojanato nakṣatrāṇi merum dakṣiṇenaiva
kālāyana īśvara-yojitāni sahābhijitāṣṭā-viṁśatiḥ.

tataḥ—from that region of the moon; *upariṣṭāt*—above; *dvi-lakṣa-yojanataḥ*—200,000 *yojanas; nakṣatrāṇi*—many stars; *merum*—Sumeru Mountain; *dakṣiṇena eva*—to the right side; *kāla-ayane*—in the wheel of time; *īśvara-yojitāni*—attached by the Supreme Personality of Godhead; *saha*—with; *abhijitā*—the star known as Abhijit; *aṣṭā-viṁśatiḥ*—twenty-eight.

TRANSLATION

There are many stars located 200,000 yojanas [1,600,000 miles] above the moon. By the supreme will of the Supreme Personality of Godhead,

they are fixed to the wheel of time, and thus they rotate with Mount Sumeru on their right, their motion being different from that of the sun. There are twenty-eight important stars, headed by Abhijit.

PURPORT

The stars referred to herein are 1,600,000 miles above the sun, and thus they are 4,000,000 miles above the earth.

TEXT 12

तत उपरिष्टादुशना द्विलक्षयोजनत उपलभ्यते पुरतः पश्चात्सहैव वार्कस्य शैघ्र्यमान्द्यसाम्याभिर्गतिभिरर्कवच्चरति लोकानां नित्यदानुकूल एव प्रायेण वर्षयंश्चारेणानुमीयते स वृष्टिविष्टम्भग्रहोपशमनः ॥१२॥

tata upariṣṭād uśanā dvi-lakṣa-yojanata upalabhyate purataḥ paścāt
sahaiva vārkasya śaighrya-māndya-sāmyābhir gatibhir arkavac carati
lokānāṁ nityadānukūla eva prāyeṇa varṣayaṁś cāreṇānumīyate sa
vṛṣṭi-viṣṭambha-grahopaśamanaḥ.

tataḥ—from that bunch of stars; *upariṣṭāt*—above; *uśanā*—Venus; *dvi-lakṣa-yojanataḥ*—200,000 *yojanas* (1,600,000 miles); *upalabhyate*—is experienced; *purataḥ*—in front; *paścāt*—behind; *saha*—along with; *eva*—indeed; *vā*—and; *arkasya*—of the sun; *śaighrya*—speedy; *māndya*—slow; *sāmyābhiḥ*—equal; *gatibhiḥ*—the movements; *arkavat*—exactly like the sun; *carati*—rotates; *lokānām*—of all the planets within the universe; *nityadā*—constantly; *anukūlaḥ*—offering favorable conditions; *eva*—indeed; *prāyeṇa*—almost always; *varṣayan*—causing rainfall; *cāreṇa*—by infusing the clouds; *anumīyate*—is perceived; *saḥ*—he (Venus); *vṛṣṭi-viṣṭambha*—obstacles to rainfall; *graha-upaśamanaḥ*—nullifying planets.

TRANSLATION

Some 1,600,000 miles above this group of stars is the planet Venus, which moves at almost exactly the same pace as the sun according to swift, slow and moderate movements. Sometimes Venus moves behind the sun, sometimes in front of the sun and sometimes along with it. Venus nullifies the influence of planets that are obstacles to rainfall. Consequently its presence causes rainfall, and it is therefore considered very favorable for all living beings within this universe. This has been accepted by learned scholars.

TEXT 13

उशनसा बुधो व्याख्यातस्तत उपरिष्टाद् द्विलक्षयोजनतो बुधः सोमसुत उपलभ्यमानः प्रायेण शुभकृद्यदार्काद् व्यतिरिच्येत तदातिवाताभ्रप्रायानावृष्ट्यादिभयमाशंसते ॥१३॥

uśanasā budho vyākhyātas tata upariṣṭād dvi-lakṣa-yojanato budhaḥ soma-suta upalabhyamānaḥ prāyeṇa śubha-kṛd yadārkād vyatiricyeta tadātivātābhra-prāyānāvṛṣṭy-ādi-bhayam āśaṁsate.

uśanasā—with Venus; *budhaḥ*—Mercury; *vyākhyātaḥ*—explained; *tataḥ*—from that (Venus); *upariṣṭāt*—above; *dvi-lakṣa-yojanataḥ*—1,600,000 miles; *budhaḥ*—Mercury; *soma-sutaḥ*—the son of the moon; *upalabhyamānaḥ*—is situated; *prāyeṇa*—almost always; *śubha-kṛt*—very auspicious to the inhabitants of the universe; *yadā*—when; *arkāt*—from the sun; *vyatiricyeta*—is separated; *tadā*—at that time; *ativāta*—of cyclones and other bad effects; *abhra*—clouds; *prāya*—almost always; *anāvṛṣṭi-ādi*—such as scarcity of rain; *bhayam*—fearful conditions; *āśaṁsate*—expands.

TRANSLATION

Mercury is described to be similar to Venus, in that it moves sometimes behind the sun, sometimes in front of the sun and sometimes along with it. It is 1,600,000 miles above Venus, or 7,200,000 miles above earth. Mercury, which is the son of the moon, is almost always very auspicious for the inhabitants of the universe, but when it does not move along with the sun, it forbodes cyclones, dust, irregular rainfall, and waterless clouds. In this way it creates fearful conditions due to inadequate or excessive rainfall.

TEXT 14

अत ऊर्ध्वमङ्गारकोऽपि योजनलक्षद्वितय उपलभ्यमानस्त्रिभिस्त्रिभिः पक्षैरेकैकशो राशीन्द्वादशानुभुङ्क्ते यदि न वक्रेणाभिवर्तते प्रायेणाशुभग्रहोऽघशंसः ॥१४॥

ata ūrdhvam aṅgārako 'pi yojana-lakṣa-dvitaya upalabhyamānas tribhis tribhiḥ pakṣair ekaikaśo rāśīn dvādaśānubhuṅkte yadi na vakreṇābhivartate prāyeṇāśubha-graho 'gha-śaṁsaḥ.

ataḥ—from this; *ūrdhvam*—above; *aṅgārakaḥ*—Mars; *api*—also; *yojana-lakṣa-dvitaye*—at a distance of 1,600,000 miles; *upalabhyamānaḥ*—is situated; *tribhiḥ tribhiḥ*—with each three and three; *pakṣaiḥ*—fortnights; *eka-ekaśaḥ*—one after another; *rāśīn*—the signs; *dvādaśa*—twelve; *anubhuṅkte*—passes through; *yadi*—if; *na*—not; *vakreṇa*—with a curve; *abhivartate*—approaches; *prāyeṇa*—almost always; *aśubha-grahaḥ*—an unfavorable, inauspicious planet; *agha-śaṁsaḥ*—creating trouble.

TRANSLATION

Situated 1,600,000 miles above Mercury, or 8,800,000 miles above earth, is the planet Mars. If this planet does not travel in a crooked way, it crosses through each sign of the zodiac in three fortnights and in this way travels through all twelve, one after another. It almost always creates unfavorable conditions in respect to rainfall and other influences.

TEXT 15

तत उपरिष्टाद् द्विलक्षयोजनान्तरगता भगवान् बृहस्पतिरेकैकस्मिन् राशौ परिवत्सरं परिवत्सरं चरति यदि न वक्रः स्यात्प्रायेणानुकूलो ब्राह्मणकुलस्य ॥१५॥

tata upariṣṭād dvi-lakṣa-yojanāntara-gatā bhagavān bṛhaspatir
ekaikasmin rāśau parivatsaraṁ parivatsaraṁ carati yadi na vakraḥ syāt
prāyeṇānukūlo brāhmaṇa-kulasya.

tataḥ—that (Mars); *upariṣṭāt*—above; *dvi-lakṣa-yojana-antara-gatāḥ*—situated at a distance of 1,600,000 miles; *bhagavān*—the most powerful planet; *bṛhaspatiḥ*—Jupiter; *eka-ekasmin*—in one after another; *rāśau*—sign; *parivatsaram parivatsaram*—for the period of Parivatsara; *carati*—moves; *yadi*—if; *na*—not; *vakraḥ*—curved; *syāt*—becomes; *prāyeṇa*—almost always; *anukūlaḥ*—very favorable; *brāhmaṇa-kulasya*—to the *brāhmaṇas* of the universe.

TRANSLATION

Situated 1,600,000 miles above Mars, or 10,400,000 miles above earth, is the planet Jupiter, which travels through one sign of the zodiac within the period of a Parivatsara. If its movement is not curved, the planet Jupiter is very favorable to the brāhmaṇas of the universe.

TEXT 16

तत उपरिष्टाद्योजनलक्षद्वयात्प्रतीयमानः शनैश्चर एकैकस्मिन् राशौ त्रिंशन्मासान् विलम्बमानः सर्वानेवानुपर्येति तावद्भिरनुवत्सरैः प्रायेण हि सर्वेषामशान्तिकरः ॥१६॥

tata upariṣṭād yojana-lakṣa-dvayāt pratīyamānaḥ śanaiścara
ekaikasmin rāśau triṁśan māsān vilambamānaḥ sarvān evānuparyeti
tāvadbhir anuvatsaraiḥ prāyeṇa hi sarveṣām aśāntikaraḥ.

tataḥ—that (Jupiter); *upariṣṭāt*—above; *yojana-lakṣa-dvayāt*—by a distance of 1,600,000 miles; *pratīyamānaḥ*—is situated; *śanaiścaraḥ*—the planet Saturn; *eka-ekasmin*—in one after another; *rāśau*—zodiac signs; *triṁśat māsān*—for a period of thirty months in each; *vilam-bamānaḥ*—lingering; *sarvān*—all twelve signs of the zodiac; *eva*—certainly; *anuparyeti*—passes through; *tāvadbhiḥ*—by so many; *anuvatsaraiḥ*—Anuvatsaras; *prāyeṇa*—almost always; *hi*—indeed; *sarveṣām*—to all the inhabitants; *aśāntikaraḥ*—very troublesome.

TRANSLATION

Situated 1,600,000 miles above Jupiter, or 12,000,000 miles above earth, is the planet Saturn, which passes through one sign of the zodiac in thirty months and covers the entire zodiac circle in thirty Anuvatsaras. This planet is always very inauspicious for the universal situation.

TEXT 17

तत उत्तरस्माद्दषय एकादशलक्षयोजनान्तर उपलभ्यन्ते य एव लोकानां
शमनुभावयन्तो भगवतो विष्णोर्यत्परमं पदं प्रदक्षिणं प्रक्रमन्ति ॥१७॥

tata uttarasmād ṛṣaya ekādaśa-lakṣa-yojanāntara upalabhyante ya eva
lokānāṁ śam anubhāvayanto bhagavato viṣṇor yat paramaṁ padaṁ
pradakṣiṇaṁ prakramanti.

tataḥ—the planet Saturn; *uttarasmāt*—above; *ṛṣayaḥ*—great saintly sages; *ekādaśa-lakṣa-yojana-antare*—at a distance of 1,100,000 *yojanas; upalabhyante*—are situated; *ye*—all of them; *eva*—indeed; *lokānām*—for all the inhabitants of the universe; *śam*—the good fortune; *anubhāvayantaḥ*—always thinking of; *bhagavataḥ*—of the Supreme Personality of Godhead; *viṣṇoḥ*—Lord Viṣṇu; *yat*—which; *paramam padam*—the supreme abode; *pradakṣiṇam*—placing on the right; *prakramanti*—circumambulate.

TRANSLATION

Situated 8,800,000 miles above Saturn, or 20,800,000 miles above earth, are the seven saintly sages, who are always thinking of the well-

being of the inhabitants of the universe. They circumambulate the supreme abode of Lord Viṣṇu, known as Dhruvaloka, the polestar.

PURPORT

Śrīla Madhvācārya quotes the following verse from the *Brahmāṇḍa Purāṇa:*

jñānānandātmano viṣṇuḥ
śiśumāra-vapuṣy atha
ūrdhva-lokeṣu sa vyāpta
ādityādyās tad-āśritā

"Lord Viṣṇu, who is the source of knowledge and transcendental bliss, has assumed the form of Śiśumāra in the seventh heaven, which is situated in the topmost level of the universe. All the other planets, beginning with the sun, exist under the shelter of this Śiśumāra planetary system."

Thus end the Bhaktivedanta purports of the Fifth Canto, Twenty-second Chapter, of Śrīmad-Bhāgavatam, *entitled "The Orbits of the Planets."*

CHAPTER TWENTY-THREE

The Śiśumāra Planetary System

This chapter describes how all the planetary systems take shelter of the polestar, Dhruvaloka. It also describes the totality of these planetary systems to be Śiśumāra, another expansion of the external body of the Supreme Personality of Godhead. Dhruvaloka, the abode of Lord Viṣṇu within this universe, is situated 1,300,000 *yojanas* from the seven stars. In the planetary system of Dhruvaloka are the planets of the fire- god, Indra, Prajāpati, Kaśyapa and Dharma, all of whom are very respectful to the great devotee Dhruva, who lives on the polestar. Like bulls yoked to a central pivot, all the planetary systems revolve around Dhruvaloka, impelled by eternal time. Those who worship the *virāṭ-puruṣa,* the universal form of the Lord, conceive of this entire rotating system of planets as an animal known as *śiśumāra.* This imaginary *śiśumāra* is another form of the Lord. The head of the *śiśumāra* form is downward, and its body appears like that of a coiled snake. On the end of its tail is Dhruvaloka, on the body of the tail are Prajāpati, Agni, Indra and Dharma, and on the root of the tail are Dhātā and Vidhātā. On its waist are the seven great sages. The entire body of the *śiśumāra* faces toward its right and appears like a coil of stars. On the right side of this coil are the fourteen prominent stars from Abhijit to Punarvasu, and on the left side are the fourteen prominent stars from Puṣyā to Uttarāṣāḍhā. The stars known as Punarvasu and Puṣyā are on the right and left hips of the *śiśumāra,* and the stars known as Ārdrā and Aśleṣā are on the right and left feet of the *śiśumāra.* Other stars are also fixed on different sides of the Śiśumāra planetary system according to the calculations of Vedic astronomers. To concentrate their minds, *yogīs* worship the Śiśumāra planetary system, which is technically known as the *kuṇḍalini-cakra.*

TEXT 1

श्रीशुक उवाच

अथ तस्मात्परतस्त्रयोदशलक्षयोजनान्तरतो यत्तद्विष्णोः परमं पदमभिवदन्ति यत्र ह महाभागवतो ध्रुव औत्तानपादिरग्निनेन्द्रेण प्रजापतिना कश्यपेन धर्मेण च समकालयुग्भिः सबहुमानं दक्षिणतः क्रियमाण इदानीमपि कल्पजीविनामाजीव्य उपास्ते तस्येहानुभाव उपवर्णितः ॥१॥

śrī-śuka uvāca

atha tasmāt paratas trayodaśa-lakṣa-yojanāntarato yat tad viṣṇoḥ paramaṁ padam abhivadanti yatra ha mahā-bhāgavato dhruva auttānapādir agninendreṇa prajāpatinā kaśyapena dharmeṇa ca samakāla-yugbhiḥ sabahu-mānaṁ dakṣiṇataḥ kriyamāṇa idānīm api kalpa-jīvinām ājīvya upāste tasyehānubhāva upavarṇitaḥ.

śrī-śukaḥ uvāca—Śrī Śukadeva Gosvāmī said; *atha*—thereupon; *tasmāt*—the sphere of the seven stars; *parataḥ*—beyond that; *trayodaśa-lakṣa-yojana-antarataḥ*—another 1,300,000 *yojanas; yat*—which; *tat*—that; *viṣṇoḥ paramam padam*—the supreme abode of Lord Viṣṇu, or the lotus feet of Lord Viṣṇu; *abhivadanti*—the *Ṛg Veda mantras* praise; *yatra*—on which; *ha*—indeed; *mahā-bhāgavataḥ*—the great devotee; *dhruvaḥ*—Mahārāja Dhruva; *auttānapādiḥ*—the son of Mahārāja Uttānapāda; *agninā*—by the fire-god; *indreṇa*—by the heavenly King, Indra; *prajāpatinā*—by the Prajāpati; *kaśyapena*—by Kaśyapa; *dharmeṇa*—by Dharmarāja; *ca*—also; *samakāla-yugbhiḥ*—who are engaged at the time; *sa-bahu-mānam*—always respectfully; *dakṣiṇataḥ*—on the right side; *kriyamāṇaḥ*—being circumambulated; *idānīm*—now; *api*—even; *kalpa-jīvinām*—of the living entities who exist at the end of the creation; *ājīvyaḥ*—the source of life; *upāste*—remains; *tasya*—his; *iha*—here; *anubhāvaḥ*—greatness in discharging devotional service; *upavarṇitaḥ*—already described (in the Fourth Canto of *Śrīmad-Bhāgavatam*).

TRANSLATION

Śukadeva Gosvāmī continued: My dear King, 1,300,000 yojanas [10,400,000 miles] above the planets of the seven sages is the place that learned scholars describe as the abode of Lord Viṣṇu. There the son of Mahārāja Uttānapāda, the great devotee Mahārāja Dhruva, still resides as the life source of all the living entities who live until the end of the creation. Agni, Indra, Prajāpati, Kaśyapa and Dharma all assemble there to offer him honor and respectful obeisances. They circumambulate him with their right sides toward him. I have already described the glorious activities of Mahārāja Dhruva [in the Fourth Canto of Śrīmad-Bhāgavatam].

TEXT 2

स हि सर्वेषां ज्योतिर्गणानां ग्रहनक्षत्रादीनामनिमिषेणाव्यक्तरंहसा भगवता कालेन भ्राम्यमाणानां स्थाणुरिवावष्टम्भ ईश्वरेण विहितः शश्वदवभासते ॥२॥

sa hi sarveṣāṁ jyotir-gaṇānāṁ graha-nakṣatrādīnām animiṣeṇāvyakta-raṁhasā bhagavatā kālena bhrāmyamāṇānāṁ sthāṇur ivāvaṣṭambha īśvareṇa vihitaḥ śaśvad avabhāsate.

saḥ—that planet of Dhruva Mahārāja; *hi*—indeed; *sarveṣām*—of all; *jyotiḥ-gaṇānām*—the luminaries; *graha-nakṣatra-ādīnām*—such as the planets and stars; *animiṣeṇa*—who does not rest; *avyakta*—inconceivable; *raṁhasā*—whose force; *bhagavatā*—the most powerful; *kālena*—by the time factor; *bhrāmyamāṇānām*—being caused to revolve; *sthāṇuḥ iva*—like a post; *avaṣṭambhaḥ*—the pivot; *īśvareṇa*—by the will of the Supreme Personality of Godhead; *vihitaḥ*—established; *śaśvat*—constantly; *avabhāsate*—shines.

TRANSLATION

Established by the supreme will of the Supreme Personality of Godhead, the polestar, which is the planet of Mahārāja Dhruva, constantly shines as the central pivot for all the stars and planets. The unsleeping, invisible, most powerful time factor causes these luminaries to revolve around the polestar without cessation.

PURPORT

It is distinctly stated herein that all the luminaries, the planets and stars, revolve by the influence of the supreme time factor. The time factor is another feature of the Supreme Personality of Godhead. Everyone is under the influence of the time factor, but the Supreme Personality of Godhead is so kind and loves His devotee Mahārāja Dhruva so much that He has placed all the luminaries under the control of Dhruva's planet and has arranged for the time factor to work under him or with his cooperation. Everything is actually done according to the will and direction of the Supreme Personality of Godhead, but to make His devotee Dhruva the most important individual within the universe, the Lord has placed the activities of the time factor under his control.

TEXT 3

यथा मेढीस्तम्भ आक्रमणपशवः संयोजितास्त्रिभिस्त्रिभिः सवनैर्यथास्थानं मण्डलानि चरन्त्येवं भगणा ग्रहादय एतस्मिन्नन्तर्बहिर्योगेन कालचक्र आयोजिता ध्रुवमेवावलम्ब्य वायुनोदीर्यमाणा आकल्पान्तं परिचङ्क्रमन्ति नभसि यथा मेघाः श्येनादयो वायुवशाः कर्मसारथयः परिवर्तन्ते एवं ज्योतिर्गणाः प्रकृतिपुरुषसंयोगानुगृहीताः कर्मनिर्मितगतयो भुवि न पतन्ति ॥३॥

yathā meḍhīstambha ākramaṇa-paśavaḥ saṁyojitās tribhis tribhiḥ savanair yathā-sthānaṁ maṇḍalāni caranty evaṁ bhagaṇā grahādaya etasminn antar-bahir-yogena kāla-cakra āyojitā dhruvam evāvalambya vāyunodīryamāṇā ākalpāntaṁ paricaṅ kramanti nabhasi yathā meghāḥ śyenādayo vāyu-vaśāḥ karma-sārathayaḥ parivartante evaṁ jyotirgaṇāḥ prakṛti-puruṣa-saṁyogānugṛhītāḥ karma-nirmita-gatayo bhuvi na patanti.

yathā—exactly like; *meḍhīstambhe*—to the pivot post; *ākramaṇa-paśavaḥ*—bulls for threshing rice; *saṁyojitāḥ*—being yoked; *tribhiḥ tribhiḥ*—by three; *savanaiḥ*—movements; *yathā-sthānam*—in their proper places; *maṇḍalāni*—orbits; *caranti*—traverse; *evam*—in the same way; *bha-gaṇāḥ*—the luminaries, like the sun, the moon, Venus, Mercury, Mars and Jupiter; *graha-ādayaḥ*—the different planets; *etasmin*—in this; *antaḥ-bahiḥ-yogena*—by connection with the inner or outer circles; *kāla-cakre*—in the wheel of eternal time; *āyojitāḥ*—fixed; *dhruvam*—Dhruvaloka; *eva*—certainly; *avalambya*—taking support of; *vāyunā*—by the wind; *udīryamāṇāḥ*—being propelled; *ā-kalpa-antam*—until the end of the creation; *paricaṅ kramanti*—revolve all around; *nabhasi*—in the sky; *yathā*—exactly like; *meghāḥ*—heavy clouds; *śyena-ādayaḥ*—birds such as the big eagle; *vāyu-vaśāḥ*—controlled by the air; *karma-sārathayaḥ*—whose chariot drivers are the results of their own past activities; *parivartante*—move around; *evam*—in this way; *jyotiḥ-gaṇāḥ*—the luminaries, the planets and stars in the sky; *prakṛti*—of material nature; *puruṣa*—and of the Supreme Personality, Kṛṣṇa; *saṁyoga-anugṛhītāḥ*—supported by the combined efforts; *karma-nirmita*—caused by their own past fruitive activities; *gatayaḥ*—whose movements; *bhuvi*—on the ground; *na*—not; *patanti*—fall down.

TRANSLATION

When bulls are yoked together and tied to a central post to thresh rice, they tread around that pivot without deviating from their proper positions—one bull being closest to the post, another in the middle, and a third on the outside. Similarly, all the planets and all the hundreds and thousands of stars revolve around the polestar, the planet of Mahārāja Dhruva, in their respective orbits, some higher and some lower. Fastened by the Supreme Personality of Godhead to the machine of material nature according to the results of their fruitive acts, they are driven around the polestar by the wind and will continue to be so until the end of creation.

These planets float in the air within the vast sky, just as clouds with hundreds of tons of water float in the air or as the great śyena eagles, due to the results of past activities, fly high in the sky and have no chance of falling to the ground.

PURPORT

According to the description of this verse, the hundreds and thousands of stars and the great planets such as the sun, the moon, Venus, Mercury, Mars and Jupiter are not clustered together because of the law of gravity or any similar idea of the modern scientists. These planets and stars are all servants of the Supreme Personality of Godhead, Govinda or Kṛṣṇa, and according to His order they sit in their chariots and travel in their respective orbits. The orbits in which they move are compared to machines given by material nature to the operating deities of the stars and planets, who carry out the orders of the Supreme Personality of Godhead by revolving around Dhruvaloka, which is occupied by the great devotee Mahārāja Dhruva. This is confirmed in the *Brahma-saṁhitā* (5.52) as follows:

yac-cakṣur eṣa savitā sakala-grahāṇāṁ
rājā samasta-sura-mūrtir aśeṣa-tejāḥ
yasyājñayā bhramati sambhṛta-kāla-cakro
govindam ādi-puruṣaṁ tam ahaṁ bhajāmi

"I worship Govinda, the primeval Lord, the Supreme Personality of Godhead, under whose control even the sun, which is considered to be the eye of the Lord, rotates within the fixed orbit of eternal time. The sun is the king of all planetary systems and has unlimited potency in heat and light." This verse from *Brahma-saṁhitā* confirms that even the largest and most powerful planet, the sun, rotates within a fixed orbit, or *kāla-cakra,* in obedience to the order of the Supreme Personality of Godhead. This has nothing to do with gravity or any other imaginary laws created by the material scientists.

Material scientists want to avoid the ruling government of the Supreme Personality of Godhead, and therefore they imagine different conditions under which they suppose the planets move. The only condition, however, is the order of the Supreme Personality of Godhead. All the various predominating deities of the planets are persons, and the Supreme Personality of Godhead is also a person. The Supreme Personality orders the subordinate persons, the demigods of various names, to carry out His supreme will. This fact is also confirmed in *Bhagavad-gītā* (9.10), wherein Kṛṣṇa says:

mayādhyakṣeṇa prakṛtiḥ
sūyate sa-carācaram
hetunānena kaunteya
jagad viparivartate

"This material nature is working under My direction, O son of Kuntī, and it is producing all moving and unmoving beings. By its rule this manifestation is created and annihilated again and again."

The orbits of the planets resemble the bodies in which all living entities are seated because they are both machines controlled by the Supreme Personality of Godhead. As Kṛṣṇa says in *Bhagavad-gītā* (18.61):

īśvaraḥ sarva-bhūtānāṁ
hṛd-deśe'rjuna tiṣṭhati
bhrāmayan sarva-bhūtāni
yantrārūḍhāni māyayā

"The Supreme Lord is situated in everyone's heart, O Arjuna, and is directing the wanderings of all living entities, who are seated as on a machine, made of the material energy." The machine given by material nature—whether the machine of the body or the machine of the orbit, or *kāla-cakra*—works according to the orders given by the Supreme Personality of Godhead. The Supreme Personality of Godhead and material nature work together to maintain this great universe, and not only this universe but also the millions of other universes beyond this one.

The question of how the planets and stars are floating is also answered in this verse. It is not because of the laws of gravity. Rather, the planets and stars are enabled to float by manipulations of the air. It is due to such manipulations that big, heavy clouds float and big eagles fly in the sky. Modern airplanes like the 747 jet aircraft work in a similar way: by controlling the air, they float high in the sky, resisting the tendency to fall to earth. Such adjustments of the air are all made possible by the cooperation of the principles of *puruṣa* (male) and *prakṛti* (female). By the cooperation of material nature, which is considered to be *prakṛti,* and the Supreme Personality of Godhead, who is considered the *puruṣa,* all the affairs of the universe are going on nicely in their proper order. *Prakṛti,* material nature, is also described in the *Brahma-saṁhitā* (5.44) as follows:

sṛṣṭi-sthiti-pralaya-sādhana-śaktir ekā
chāyeva yasya bhuvanāni bibharti durgā

icchānurūpam api yasya ca ceṣṭate sā
govindam ādi-puruṣaṁ tam ahaṁ bhajāmi

"The external potency, *māyā,* who is of the nature of the shadow of the *cit* [spiritual] potency, is worshiped by all people as Durgā, the creating, preserving and destroying agency of this mundane world. I adore the primeval Lord Govinda, in accordance with whose will Durgā conducts herself." Material nature, the external energy of the Supreme Lord, is also known as Durgā, or the female energy that protects the great fort of this universe. The word *Durgā* also means fort. This universe is just like a great fort in which all the conditioned souls are kept, and they cannot leave it unless they are liberated by the mercy of the Supreme Personality of Godhead. The Lord Himself declares in *Bhagavad-gītā* (4.9):

janma karma ca me divyam
evaṁ yo vetti tattvataḥ
tyaktvā dehaṁ punar janma
naiti mām eti so'rjuna

"One who knows the transcendental nature of My appearance and activities does not, upon leaving the body, take his birth again in this material world, but attains My eternal abode, O Arjuna." Thus simply by Kṛṣṇa consciousness, by the mercy of the Supreme Personality of Godhead, one can be liberated, or, in other words, one can be released from the great fort of this universe and go outside it to the spiritual world.

It is also significant that the predominating deities of even the greatest planets have been offered their exalted posts because of the very valuable pious activities they performed in previous births. This is indicated herein by the words *karma-nirmita-gatayaḥ.* For example, as we have previously discussed, the moon is called *jīva,* which means that he is a living entity like us, but because of his pious activities he has been appointed to his post as the moon god. Similarly, all the demigods are living entities who have been appointed to their various posts as the masters of the moon, the earth, Venus and so on because of their great service and pious acts. Only the predominating deity of the sun, Sūrya Nārāyaṇa, is an incarnation of the Supreme Personality of Godhead. Mahārāja Dhruva, the predominating deity of Dhruvaloka, is also a living entity. Thus there are two kinds of entities—the supreme entity, the Supreme Personality of Godhead, and the ordinary living entity, the *jīva* (*nityo nityānāṁ cetanaś cetanānām*). All the demigods are engaged in the service of the Lord, and only by such an arrangement are the affairs of the universe going on.

Regarding the great eagles mentioned in this verse, it is understood that there are eagles so big that they can prey on big elephants. They fly so high that they can travel from one planet to another. They start flying in one planet and land in another, and while in flight they lay eggs that hatch into other birds while falling through the air. In Sanskrit such eagles are called *śyena.* Under the present circumstances, of course, we cannot see such huge birds, but at least we know of eagles that can capture monkeys and then throw them down to kill and eat them. Similarly, it is understood that there are gigantic birds that can carry off elephants, kill them and eat them.

The two examples of the eagle and the cloud are sufficient to prove that flying and floating can be made possible through adjustments of the air. The planets, in a similar way, are floating because material nature adjusts the air according to the orders of the Supreme Lord. It could be said that these adjustments constitute the law of gravity, but in any case, one must accept that these laws are made by the Supreme Personality of Godhead. The so-called scientists have no control over them. The scientists can falsely, improperly declare that there is no God, but this is not a fact.

TEXT 4

केचनैतज्ज्योतिरनीकं शिशुमारसंस्थानेन भगवतो वासुदेवस्य योगधारणा-
यामनुवर्णयन्ति ॥४॥

kecanaitaj jyotir-anīkaṁ śiśumāra-saṁsthānena bhagavato
vāsudevasya yoga-dhāraṇāyām anuvarṇayanti.

kecana—some *yogīs* or learned scholars of astronomy; *etat*—this; *jyotiḥ-anīkam*—great wheel of planets and stars; *śiśumāra-saṁsthānena*—imagine this wheel to be a *śiśumāra* (dolphin); *bhagavataḥ*—of the Supreme Personality of Godhead; *vāsudevasya*—Lord Vāsudeva (the son of Vasudeva), Kṛṣṇa; *yoga-dhāraṇāyām*—in absorption in worship; *anuvarṇayanti*—describe.

TRANSLATION

This great machine, consisting of the stars and planets, resembles the form of a śiśumāra [dolphin] in the water. It is sometimes considered an incarnation of Kṛṣṇa, Vāsudeva. Great yogīs meditate upon Vāsudeva in this form because it is actually visible.

PURPORT

Transcendentalists such as *yogīs* whose minds cannot accommodate the form of the Lord prefer to visualize something very great, such as the *virāṭa-puruṣa.* Therefore some *yogīs* contemplate this imaginary *śiśumāra* to be swimming in the sky the way a dolphin swims in water. They meditate upon it as the *virāṭa-rūpa,* the gigantic form of the Supreme Personality of Godhead.

TEXT 5

यस्य पुच्छाग्रेऽवाक्शिरसः कुण्डलीभूतदेहस्य ध्रुव उपकल्पितस्तस्य लाङ्गूले प्रजापतिरग्निरिन्द्रो धर्म इति पुच्छमूले धाता विधाता च कट्यां सप्तर्षयः। तस्य दक्षिणावर्तकुण्डलीभूतशरीरस्य यान्युदगयनानि दक्षिणपार्श्वे तु नक्षत्राण्युपकल्पयन्ति दक्षिणायनानि तु सव्ये। यथा शिशुमारस्य कुण्डलाभोगसन्निवेशस्य पार्श्वयोरुभयोरप्यवयवाः समसंख्या भवन्ति। पृष्ठे त्वजवीथी आकाशगङ्गा चोदरतः ॥५॥

yasya pucchāgre 'vākśirasaḥ kuṇḍalī-bhūta-dehasya dhruva
upakalpitas tasya lāṅgūle prajāpatir agnir indro dharma iti puccha-
mūle dhātā vidhātā ca kaṭyāṁ saptarṣayaḥ; tasya dakṣiṇāvarta-
kuṇḍalī-bhūta-śarīrasya yāny udagayanāni dakṣiṇa-pārśve tu
nakṣatrāṇy upakalpayanti dakṣiṇāyanāni tu savye; yathā śiśumārasya
kuṇḍalā-bhoga-sanniveśasya pārśvayor ubhayor apy avayavāḥ
samasaṅkhyā bhavanti; pṛṣṭhe tv ajavīthī ākāśa-gaṅgā codarataḥ.

yasya—of which; *puccha-agre*—at the end of the tail; *avākśirasaḥ*—whose head is downward; *kuṇḍalī-bhūta-dehasya*—whose body, which is coiled; *dhruvaḥ*—Mahārāja Dhruva on his planet, the polestar; *upakalpitaḥ*—is situated; *tasya*—of that; *lāṅgūle*—on the tail; *prajāpatiḥ*—of the name Prajāpati; *agniḥ*—Agni; *indraḥ*—Indra; *dharmaḥ*—Dharma; *iti*—thus; *puccha-mūle*—at the base of the tail; *dhātā vidhātā*—the demigods known as Dhātā and Vidhātā; *ca*—also; *kaṭyām*—on the hip; *sapta-ṛṣayaḥ*—the seven saintly sages; *tasya*—of that; *dakṣiṇa-āvarta-kuṇḍalī-bhūta-śarīrasya*—whose body is like a coil turning toward the right side; *yāni*—which; *udagayanāni*—marking the northern courses; *dakṣiṇa-pārśve*—on the right side; *tu*—but; *nakṣatrāṇi*—constellations; *upakalpayanti*—are situated; *dakṣiṇa-āyanāni*—the fourteen stars, from Puṣyā to Uttarāṣāḍhā, marking the northern course; *tu*—but; *savye*—on the left side; *yathā*—just like; *śiśumārasya*—of the dolphin; *kuṇḍalā-bhoga-sanniveśasya*—whose body appears like a coil; *pārśvayoḥ*—

on the sides; *ubhayoḥ*—both; *api*—certainly; *avayavāḥ*—the limbs; *samasaṅkhyāḥ*—of equal number (fourteen); *bhavanti*—are; *pṛṣṭhe*—on the back; *tu*—of course; *ajavīthī*—the first three stars marking the southern route (Mūlā, Pūrvaṣāḍhā and Uttarāṣāḍhā); *ākāśa-gaṅgā*—the Ganges in the sky (the Milky Way); *ca*—also; *udarataḥ*—on the abdomen.

TRANSLATION

This form of the śiśumāra has its head downward and its body coiled. On the end of its tail is the planet of Dhruva, on the body of its tail are the planets of the demigods Prajāpati, Agni, Indra and Dharma, and at the base of its tail are the planets of the demigods Dhātā and Vidhātā. Where the hips might be on the śiśumāra are the seven saintly sages like Vasiṣṭha and Aṅgirā. The coiled body of the Śiśumāra-cakra turns toward its right side, on which the fourteen constellations from Abhijit to Punarvasu are located. On its left side are the fourteen stars from Puṣyā to Uttarāṣāḍhā. Thus its body is balanced because its sides are occupied by an equal number of stars. On the back of the śiśumāra is the group of stars known as Ajavīthī, and on its abdomen is the Ganges that flows in the sky [the Milky Way].

TEXT 6

पुनर्वसुपुष्यौ दक्षिणवामयोः श्रोण्योरार्द्राश्लेषे च दक्षिणवामयोः पश्चिमयोः पादयोरभिजिदुत्तराषाढे दक्षिणवामयोर्नासिकयोर्यथासंख्यं श्रवणपूर्वाषाढे दक्षिणवामयोर्लोचनयोर्धनिष्ठा मूलं च दक्षिणवामयोः कर्णयोर्मघादीन्यष्ट नक्षत्राणि दक्षिणायनानि वामपार्श्ववङ्क्रिषु युञ्जीत तथैव मृगशीर्षादीन्युदगयनानि दक्षिणपार्श्ववङ्क्रिषु प्रातिलोम्येन प्रयुञ्जीत शतभिषाज्येष्ठे स्कन्धयोर्दक्षिणवामयोर्न्यसेत् ॥६॥

punarvasu-puṣyau dakṣiṇa-vāmayoḥ śroṇyor ārdrāśleṣe ca dakṣiṇa-
vāmayoḥ paścimayoḥ pādayor abhijid-uttarāṣāḍhe dakṣiṇa-vāmayor
nāsikayor yathā-saṅkhyaṁ śravaṇa-pūrvāṣāḍhe dakṣiṇa-vāmayor
locanayor dhaniṣṭhā mūlaṁ ca dakṣiṇa-vāmayoḥ karṇayor maghādīny aṣṭa
nakṣatrāṇi dakṣiṇāyanāni vāma-pārśva-vaṅkriṣu yuñjīta tathaiva mṛga-
śīrṣādīny udagayanāni dakṣiṇa-pārśva-vaṅkriṣu prātilomyena prayuñjīta
śatabhiṣā-jyeṣṭhe skandhayor dakṣiṇa-vāmayor nyaset.

punarvasu—the star named Punarvasu; *puṣyau*—and the star named Puṣyā; *dakṣiṇa-vāmayoḥ*—on the right and left; *śroṇyoḥ*—loins; *ārdrā*—the star named Ārdrā; *aśleṣe*—the star named Aśleṣā; *ca*—also; *dakṣiṇa-vāmayoḥ*

—at the right and left; *paścimayoḥ*—behind; *pādayoḥ*—feet; *abhijit-uttarāṣāḍhe*—the stars named Abhijit and Uttarāṣāḍhā; *dakṣiṇa-vāmayoḥ*—on the right and left; *nāsikayoḥ*—nostrils; *yathā-saṅkhyam*—according to numerical order; *śravaṇa-pūrvāṣāḍhe*—the stars named Śravaṇā and Pūrvāṣāḍhā; *dakṣiṇa-vāmayoḥ*—at the right and left; *locanayoḥ*—eyes; *dhaniṣṭhā mūlam ca*—and the stars named Dhaniṣṭhā and Mūlā; *dakṣiṇa-vāmayoḥ*—at the right and left; *karṇayoḥ*—ears; *maghā-ādīni*—the stars such as Maghā; *aṣṭa nakṣatrāṇi*—eight stars; *dakṣiṇa-āyanāni*—which mark the southern course; *vāma-pārśva*—of the left side; *vaṅkriṣu*—at the ribs; *yuñjīta*—may place; *tathā eva*—similarly; *mṛga-śīrṣā-ādīni*—such as Mṛgaśīrṣā; *udagayanāni*—marking the northern course; *dakṣiṇa-pārśva-vaṅkriṣu*—on the right side; *prātilomyena*—in the reverse order; *prayuñjīta*—may place; *śatabhiṣā*—Śatabhiṣā; *jyeṣṭhe*—Jyeṣṭhā; *skandhayoḥ*—on the two shoulders; *dakṣiṇa-vāmayoḥ*—right and left; *nyaset*—should place.

TRANSLATION

On the right and left sides of where the loins might be on the Śiśumāra-cakra are the stars named Punarvasu and Puṣyā. Ārdrā and Aśleṣā are on its right and left feet, Abhijit and Uttarāṣāḍhā are on its right and left nostrils, Śravaṇā and Pūrvāṣāḍhā are at its right and left eyes, and Dhaniṣṭhā and Mūla are on its right and left ears. The eight stars from Maghā to Anurādhā, which mark the southern course, are on the ribs of the left of its body, and the eight stars from Mṛgaśīrṣā to Pūrvabhādra, which mark the northern course, are on the ribs on the right side. Śatabhiṣā and Jyeṣṭhā are on the right and left shoulders.

TEXT 7

उत्तराहनावगस्तिरधराहनौ यमो मुखेषु चाङ्गारकः शनैश्चर उपस्थे बृहस्पतिः ककुदि वक्षस्यादित्यो हृदये नारायणो मनसि चन्द्रो नाभ्यामुशना स्तनयोरश्विनौ बुधः प्राणापानयो राहुर्गले केतवः सर्वाङ्गेषु रोमसु सर्वे तारागणाः ॥७॥

uttarā-hanāv agastir adharā-hanau yamo mukheṣu cāṅgārakaḥ
śanaiścara upasthe bṛhaspatiḥ kakudi vakṣasy ādityo hṛdaye nārāyaṇo
manasi candro nābhyām uśanā stanayor aśvinau budhaḥ prāṇāpānayo
rāhur gale ketavaḥ sarvāṅgeṣu romasu sarve tārā-gaṇāḥ.

uttarā-hanau—on the upper jaw; *agastiḥ*—the star named Agasti; *adharā-hanau*—on the lower jaw; *yamaḥ*—Yamarāja; *mukhe*—on the mouth; *ca*

—also; *aṅgārakaḥ*—Mars; *śanaiścaraḥ*—Saturn; *upasthe*—on the genitals; *bṛhaspatiḥ*—Jupiter; *kakudi*—on the back of the neck; *vakṣasi*—on the chest; *ādityaḥ*—the sun; *hṛdaye*—within the heart; *nārāyaṇaḥ*—Lord Nārāyaṇa; *manasi*—in the mind; *candraḥ*—the moon; *nābhyām*—on the navel; *uśanā*—Venus; *stanayoḥ*—on the two breasts; *aśvinau*—the two stars named Aśvin; *budhaḥ*—Mercury; *prāṇāpānayoḥ*—in the inner airs known as *prāṇa* and *apāna; rāhuḥ*—the planet Rāhu; *gale*—on the neck; *ketavaḥ*—comets; *sarva-aṅgeṣu*—all over the body; *romasu*—in the pores of the body; *sarve*—all; *tārā-gaṇāḥ*—the numerous stars.

TRANSLATION

On the upper chin of the śiśumāra is Agasti; on its lower chin, Yamarāja; on its mouth, Mars; on its genitals, Saturn; on the back of its neck, Jupiter; on its chest, the sun; and within the core of its heart, Nārāyaṇa. Within its mind is the moon; on its navel, Venus; and on its breasts, the Aśvinī-kumāras. Within its life air, which is known as prāṇāpāna, is Mercury, on its neck is Rāhu, all over its body are comets, and in its pores are the numerous stars.

TEXT 8

एतदु हैव भगवतो विष्णोः सर्वदेवतामयं रूपमहरहः सन्ध्यायां प्रयतो वाग्यतो निरीक्षमाण उपतिष्ठेत नमो ज्योतिर्लोकाय कालायनायानिमिषां पतये महापुरुषायाभिधीमहीति ॥८॥

etad u haiva bhagavato viṣṇoḥ sarva-devatāmayaṁ rūpam aharahaḥ
sandhyāyāṁ prayato vāgyato nirīkṣamāṇa upatiṣṭheta namo jyotir-lokāya
kālāyanāyānimiṣāṁ pataye mahā-puruṣāyābhidhīmahīti.

etat—this; *u ha*—indeed; *eva*—certainly; *bhagavataḥ*—of the Supreme Personality of Godhead; *viṣṇoḥ*—of Lord Viṣṇu; *sarva-devatā-mayam*—consisting of all the demigods; *rūpam*—form; *ahaḥ-ahaḥ*—always; *sandhyāyām*—in the morning, noon and evening; *prayataḥ*—meditating upon; *vāgyataḥ*—controlling the words; *nirīkṣamāṇaḥ*—observing; *upatiṣṭheta*—one should worship; *namaḥ*—respectful obeisances; *jyotiḥ-lokāya*—unto the resting place of all the planetary systems; *kālāyanāya*—in the form of supreme time; *animiṣām*—of the demigods; *pataye*—unto the master; *mahā-puruṣāya*—unto the Supreme person; *abhidhīmahi*—let us meditate; *iti*—thus.

TRANSLATION

My dear King, the body of the śiśumāra, as thus described, should be considered the external form of Lord Viṣṇu, the Supreme Personality of Godhead. Morning, noon and evening, one should silently observe the form of the Lord as the Śiśumāra-cakra and worship Him with this mantra: "O Lord who has assumed the form of time! O resting place of all the planets moving in different orbits! O master of all demigods, O Supreme Person, I offer my respectful obeisances unto You and meditate upon You."

TEXT 9

ग्रहर्क्षतारामयमाधिदैविकं
पापापहं मन्त्रकृतां त्रिकालम् ।
नमस्यतः स्मरतो वा त्रिकालं
नश्येत तत्कालजमाशु पापम् ॥९॥

graharkṣatārāmayam ādhidaivikaṁ
pāpāpahaṁ mantra-kṛtāṁ tri-kālam
namasyataḥ smarato vā tri-kālaṁ
naśyeta tat-kālajam āśu pāpam

graha-ṛkṣa-tārā-mayam—consisting of all the planets and stars; *ādhidaivikam*—the leader of all the demigods; *pāpa-apaham*—the killer of sinful reactions; *mantra-kṛtām*—of those who chant the *mantra* mentioned above; *tri-kālam*—three times; *namasyataḥ*—offering obeisances; *smarataḥ*—meditating; *vā*—or; *tri-kālam*—three times; *naśyeta*—destroys; *tat-kāla-jam*—born at that time; *āśu*—very quickly; *pāpam*—all sinful reactions.

TRANSLATION

The body of the Supreme Lord, Viṣṇu, which forms the Śiśumāra-cakra, is the resting place of all the demigods and all the stars and planets. One who chants this mantra to worship that Supreme Person three times a day—morning, noon and evening—will surely be freed from all sinful reactions. If one simply offers his obeisances to this form or remembers this form three times a day, all his recent sinful activities will be destroyed.

PURPORT

Summarizing the entire description of the planetary systems of the universe, Śrīla Viśvanātha Cakravartī Ṭhākura says that one who is able to meditate upon this arrangement as the *virāṭa-rūpa,* or *viśva-rūpa,* the external body of the Supreme Personality of Godhead, and worship Him three times a day by meditation will always be free from all sinful reactions. Viśvanātha Cakravartī Ṭhākura estimates that Dhruvaloka, the polestar, is 3,800,000 *yojanas* above the sun. Above Dhruvaloka by 10,000,000 *yojanas* is Maharloka, above Maharloka by 20,000,000 *yojanas* is Janaloka, above Janaloka by 80,000,000 *yojanas* is Tapoloka, and above Tapoloka by 120,000,000 *yojanas* is Satyaloka. Thus the distance from the sun to Satyaloka is 233,800,000 *yojanas,* or 1,870,400,000 miles. The Vaikuṇṭha planets begin 26,200,000 *yojanas* (209,600,000 miles) above Satyaloka. Thus the *Viṣṇu Purāṇa* describes that the covering of the universe is 260,000,000 *yojanas* (2,080,000,000 miles) away from the sun. The distance from the sun to the earth is 100,000 yojanas, and below the earth by 70,000 yojanas are the seven lower planetary systems called Atala, Vitala, Sutala, Talātala, Mahātala, Rasātala and Pātāla. Below these lower planets by 30,000 *yojanas,* Śeṣa Nāga is lying on the Garbhodaka Ocean. That ocean is 249,800,000 *yojanas* deep. Thus the total diameter of the universe is approximately 500,000,000 *yojanas,* or 4,000,000,000 miles.

Thus end the Bhaktivedanta purports to the Fifth Canto, Twenty-third Chapter, of the Śrīmad-Bhāgavatam, *entitled "The Śiśumāra Planetary System."*

CHAPTER TWENTY-FOUR

The Subterranean Heavenly Planets

This chapter describes the planet Rāhu, which is 10,000 *yojanas* (80,000 miles) below the sun, and it also describes Atala and the other lower planetary systems. Rāhu is situated below the sun and moon. It is between these two planets and the earth. When Rāhu conceals the sun and moon, eclipses occur, either total or partial, depending on whether Rāhu moves in a straight or curving way.

Below Rāhu by another 1,000,000 *yojanas* are the planets of the Siddhas, Cāraṇas and Vidyādharas, and below these are planets such as Yakṣaloka and Rakṣaloka. Below these planets is the earth, and 70,000 *yojanas* below the earth are the lower planetary systems—Atala, Vitala, Sutala, Talātala, Mahātala, Rasātala and Pātāla. Demons and Rakṣasas live in these lower planetary systems with their wives and children, always engaged in sense gratification and not fearing their next births. The sunshine does not reach these planets, but they are illuminated by jewels fixed upon the hoods of snakes. Because of these shining gems there is practically no darkness. Those living in these planets do not become old or diseased, and they are not afraid of death from any cause but the time factor, the Supreme Personality of Godhead.

In the planet Atala, the yawning of a demon has produced three kinds of women, called *svairiṇī* (independent), *kāmiṇī* (lusty) and *puṁścalī* (very easily subdued by men). Below Atala is the planet Vitala, wherein Lord Śiva and his wife Gaurī reside. Because of their presence, a kind of gold is produced called *hāṭaka.* Below Vitala is the planet Sutala, the abode of Bali Mahārāja, the most fortunate king. Bali Mahārāja was favored by the Supreme Personality of Godhead, Vāmanadeva, because of his intense devotional service. The Lord went to the sacrificial arena of Bali Mahārāja and begged him for three paces of land, and on this plea the Lord took from him all his possessions. When Bali Mahārāja agreed to all this, the Lord was very pleased, and therefore the Lord serves as his doorkeeper. The description of Bali Mahārāja appears in the Eighth Canto of *Śrīmad-Bhāgavatam.*

When the Supreme Personality of Godhead offers a devotee material happiness, this is not His real favor. The demigods, who are very puffed up by their material opulence, pray to the Lord only for material happiness, not knowing anything better. Devotees like Prahlāda Mahārāja, however, do not want material happiness. Not to speak of material happiness, they do not want even liberation from material bondage, although one can achieve this liberation simply by chanting the holy name of the Lord, even with improper pronunciation.

Below Sutala is the planet Talātala, the abode of the demon Maya. This demon is always materially happy because he is favored by Lord Śiva, but he cannot achieve spiritual happiness at any time. Below Talātala is the planet Mahātala, where there are many snakes with hundreds and thousands of hoods. Below Mahātala is Rasātala, and below that is Pātāla, where the serpent Vasukī lives with his associates.

TEXT 1

श्रीशुक उवाच

अधस्तात्सवितुर्योजनायुते स्वर्भानुर्नक्षत्रवच्चरतीत्येके योऽसावमरत्वं ग्रहत्वं चालभत भगवदनुकम्पया स्वयमसुरापसदः सैंहिकेयो ह्यतदर्हस्तस्य तात जन्म कर्माणि चोपरिष्टाद्वक्ष्यामः ॥१॥

śrī-śuka uvāca

adhastāt savitur yojanāyute svarbhānur nakṣatravac caratīty eke yo 'sāv amaratvaṁ grahatvaṁ cālabhata bhagavad-anukampayā svayam asurāpasadaḥ saiṁhikeyo hy atad-arhas tasya tāta janma karmāṇi copariṣṭād vakṣyāmaḥ.

śrī-śukaḥ uvāca—Śrī Śukadeva Gosvāmī said; *adhastāt*—below; *savituḥ*—the sun globe; *yojana*—a measurement equal to eight miles; *ayute*—ten thousand; *svarbhānuḥ*—the planet known as Rāhu; *nakṣatra-vat*—like one of the stars; *carati*—is rotating; *iti*—thus; *eke*—some who are learned in the *Purāṇas; yaḥ*—which; *asau*—that; *amaratvam*—a lifetime like those of the demigods; *grahatvam*—a position as one of the chief planets; *ca*—and; *alabhata*—obtained; *bhagavat-anukampayā*—by the compassion of the Supreme Personality of Godhead; *svayam*—personally; *asura-apasadaḥ*—the lowest of the *asuras; saiṁhikeyaḥ*—being the son of Siṁhikā; *hi*—indeed; *a-tat-arhaḥ*—not qualified for that position; *tasya*—his; *tāta*—O my dear King; *janma*—birth; *karmāṇi*—activities; *ca*—also; *upariṣṭāt*—later; *vakṣyāmaḥ*—I shall explain.

TRANSLATION

Śrī Śukadeva Gosvāmī said: My dear King, some historians, the speakers of the Purāṇas, say that 10,000 yojanas [80,000 miles] below the sun is the planet known as Rāhu, which moves like one of the stars. The presiding deity of that planet, who is the son of Siṁhikā, is the most abominable of all asuras, but although he is completely unfit to assume the position of a demigod or planetary deity, he has achieved that position by the grace of the Supreme Personality of Godhead. Later I shall speak further about him.

TEXT 2

यददस्तरणेर्मण्डलं प्रतपतस्तद्विस्तरतो योजनायुतमाचक्षते द्वादशसहस्रं सोमस्य त्रयोदशसहस्रं राहोर्यः पर्वणि तद्व्यवधानकृद्वैरानुबन्धः सूर्याचन्द्रमसाव- भिधावति ॥२॥

yad adas taraṇer maṇḍalaṁ pratapatas tad vistarato yojanāyutam
ācakṣate dvādaśa-sahasraṁ somasya trayodaśa-sahasraṁ rāhor yaḥ
parvaṇi tad-vyavadhāna-kṛd vairānubandhaḥ sūryā-candramasāv
abhidhāvati.

yat—which; *adaḥ*—that; *taraṇeḥ*—of the sun; *maṇḍalam*—globe; *pratapataḥ*—which is always distributing heat; *tat*—that; *vistarataḥ*—in terms of width; *yojana*—a distance of eight miles; *ayutam*—ten thousand; *ācakṣate*—they estimate; *dvādaśa-sahasram*—20,000 *yojanas* (160,000 miles); *somasya*—of the moon; *trayodaśa*—thirty; *sahasram*—one thousand; *rāhoḥ*—of the planet Rāhu; *yaḥ*—which; *parvaṇi*—on occasion; *tat-vyavadhāna-kṛt*—who created an obstruction to the sun and moon at the time of the distribution of nectar; *vaira-anubandhaḥ*—whose intentions are inimical; *sūryā*—the sun; *candramasau*—and the moon; *abhidhāvati*—runs after them on the full-moon night and the dark-moon day.

TRANSLATION

The sun globe, which is a source of heat, extends for 10,000 yojanas [80,000 miles]. The moon extends for 20,000 yojanas [160,000 miles], and Rāhu extends for 30,000 yojanas [240,000 miles]. Formerly, when nectar was being distributed, Rāhu tried to create dissension between the sun and moon by interposing himself between them. Rāhu is inimical toward both the sun and the moon, and therefore he always tries to cover the sunshine and moonshine on the dark-moon day and full-moon night.

PURPORT

As stated herein, the sun extends for 10,000 *yojanas,* and the moon extends for twice that, or 20,000 *yojanas.* The word *dvādaśa* should be understood to mean twice as much as ten, or twenty. In the opinion of Vijayadhvaja, the extent of Rāhu should be twice that of the moon, or 40,000 yojanas. However, to reconcile this apparent contradiction to the text of the *Bhāgavatam,* Vijayadhvaja cites the following quotation concerning Rāhu; *rāhu-soma-ravīṇāṁ tu maṇḍalā dvi-guṇoktitām.* This means that Rāhu is twice as large as the moon, which is twice as large as the sun. This is the conclusion of the commentator Vijayadhvaja.

TEXT 3

तन्निशम्योभयत्रापि भगवता रक्षणाय प्रयुक्तं सुदर्शनं नाम भागवतं दयितमस्त्रं तत्तेजसा दुर्विषहं मुहुः परिवर्तमानमभ्यवस्थितो मुहूर्तमुद्विजमानश्चकितहृदय आरादेव निवर्तते तदुपरागमिति वदन्ति लोकाः ॥३॥

tan niśamyobhayatrāpi bhagavatā rakṣaṇāya prayuktaṁ sudarśanaṁ
nāma bhāgavataṁ dayitam astraṁ tat tejasā durviṣahaṁ muhuḥ
parivartamānam abhyavasthito muhūrtam udvijamānaś cakita-hṛdaya
ārād eva nivartate tad uparāgam iti vadanti lokāḥ.

tat—that situation; *niśamya*—hearing; *ubhayatra*—around both the sun and moon; *api*—indeed; *bhagavatā*—by the Supreme Personality of Godhead; *rakṣaṇāya*—for their protection; *prayuktam*—engaged; *sudarśanam*—the wheel of Kṛṣṇa; *nāma*—named; *bhāgavatam*—the most confidential devotee; *dayitam*—the most favorite; *astram*—weapon; *tat*—that; *tejasā*—by its effulgence; *durviṣaham*—unbearable heat; *muhuḥ*—repeatedly; *parivartamānam*—moving around the sun and moon; *abhyavasthitaḥ*—situated; *muhūrtam*—for a *muhūrta* (forty-eight minutes); *udvijamānaḥ*—whose mind was full of anxieties; *cakita*—frightened; *hṛdayaḥ*—the core of whose heart; *ārāt*—to a distant place; *eva*—certainly; *nivartate*—flees; *tat*—that situation; *uparāgam*—an eclipse; *iti*—thus; *vadanti*—they say; *lokāḥ*—the people.

TRANSLATION

After hearing from the sun and moon demigods about Rāhu's attack, the Supreme Personality of Godhead, Viṣṇu, engages His disc, known as the Sudarśana cakra, to protect them. The Sudarśana cakra is the Lord's

most beloved devotee and is favored by the Lord. The intense heat of its effulgence, meant for killing non-Vaiṣṇavas, is unbearable to Rāhu, and he therefore flees in fear of it. During the time Rāhu disturbs the sun or moon, there occurs what people commonly know as an eclipse.

PURPORT

The Supreme Personality of Godhead, Viṣṇu, is always the protector of His devotees, who are also known as demigods. The controlling demigods are most obedient to Lord Viṣṇu, although they also want material sense enjoyment, and that is why they are called demigods, or almost godly. Although Rāhu attempts to attack both the sun and the moon, they are protected by Lord Viṣṇu. Being very afraid of Lord Viṣṇu's *cakra,* Rāhu cannot stay in front of the sun or moon for more than a *muhūrta* (forty-eight minutes). The phenomenon that occurs when Rāhu blocks the light of the sun or moon is called an eclipse. The attempt of the scientists of this earth to go to the moon is as demoniac as Rāhu's attack. Of course. their attempts will be failures because no one can enter the moon or sun so easily. Like the attack of Rāhu, such attempts will certainly be failures.

TEXT 4

ततोऽधस्तात्सिद्धचारणविद्याधराणां सदनानि तावन्मात्र एव ॥४॥

tato 'dhastāt siddha-cāraṇa-vidyādharāṇāṁ sadanāni tāvan mātra eva.

tataḥ—the planet Rāhu; *adhastāt*—below; *siddha-cāraṇa*—of the planets known as Siddhaloka and Cāraṇaloka; *vidyādharāṇām*—and the planets of the Vidyādharas; *sadanāni*—the residential places; *tāvat mātra*—only that much distance (eighty thousand miles); *eva*—indeed.

TRANSLATION

Below Rāhu by 10,000 yojanas [80,000 miles] are the planets known as Siddhaloka, Cāraṇaloka and Vidyādhara-loka.

PURPORT

It is said that the residents of Siddhaloka, being naturally endowed with the powers of *yogīs,* can go from one planet to another by their natural mystic powers without using airplanes or similar machines.

TEXT 5

ततोऽधस्ताद्यक्षरक्षःपिशाचप्रेतभूतगणानां विहाराजिरमन्तरिक्षं यावद्वायुः प्रवाति यावन्मेघा उपलभ्यन्ते ॥५॥

tato 'dhastād yakṣa-rakṣaḥ-piśāca-preta-bhūta-gaṇānāṁ vihārājiram antarikṣaṁ yāvad vāyuḥ pravāti yāvan meghā upalabhyante.

tataḥ adhastāt—beneath the planets occupied by the Siddhas, Cāraṇas and Vidyādharas; *yakṣa-rakṣaḥ-piśāca-preta-bhūta-gaṇānām*—of Yakṣas, Rākṣasas, Piśācas, ghosts and so on; *vihāra-ajiram*—the place of sense gratification; *antarikṣam*—in the sky or outer space; *yāvat*—as far as; *vāyuḥ*—the wind; *pravāti*—blows; *yāvat*—as far as; *meghāḥ*—the clouds; *upalabhyante*—are seen.

TRANSLATION

Beneath Vidyādhara-loka, Cāraṇaloka and Siddhaloka, in the sky called antarikṣa, are the places of enjoyment for the Yakṣas, Rākṣasas, Piśācas, ghosts and so on. Antarikṣa extends as far as the wind blows and the clouds float in the sky. Above this there is no more air.

TEXT 6

ततोऽधस्ताच्छतयोजनान्तर इयं पृथिवी यावद्धंसभासश्येनसुपर्णादयः पतत्त्रिप्रवरा उत्पतन्तीति ॥६॥

tato 'dhastāc chata-yojanāntara iyaṁ pṛthivī yāvad dhaṁsa-bhāsa-śyena-suparṇādayaḥ patattri-pravarā utpatantīti.

tataḥ adhastāt—beneath that; *śata-yojana*—of one hundred *yojanas; antare*—by an interval; *iyam*—this; *pṛthivī*—planet earth; *yāvat*—as high as; *haṁsa*—swans; *bhāsa*—vultures; *śyena*—eagles; *suparṇa-ādayaḥ*—and other birds; *patattri-pravarāḥ*—the chief among birds; *utpatanti*—can fly; *iti*—thus.

TRANSLATION

Below the abodes of the Yakṣas and Rākṣasas by a distance of 100 yojanas [800 miles] is the planet earth. Its upper limits extend as high as swans, hawks, eagles and similar large birds can fly.

TEXT 7

उपवर्णितं भूमेर्यथासंनिवेशावस्थानमवनेरप्यधस्तात् सप्त भूविवरा एकैकशो योजनायुतान्तरेणायामविस्तारेणोपक्लृप्ता अतलं वितलं सुतलं तलातलं महातलं रसातलं पातालमिति ॥७॥

upavarṇitaṁ bhūmer yathā-sanniveśāvasthānam avaner apy adhastāt sapta bhū-vivarā ekaikaśo yojanāyutāntareṇāyāma-vistāreṇopakḷptā atalaṁ vitalaṁ sutalaṁ talātalaṁ mahātalaṁ rasātalaṁ pātālam iti.

upavarṇitam—stated previously; *bhūmeḥ*—of the planet earth; *yathā-sanniveśa-avasthānam*—according to the arrangement of the different places; *avaneḥ*—the earth; *api*—certainly; *adhastāt*—beneath; *sapta*—seven; *bhū-vivarāḥ*—other planets; *eka-ekaśaḥ*—in succession, up to the outer limit of the universe; *yojana-ayuta-antareṇa*—with an interval of ten thousand *yojanas* (eighty thousand miles); *āyāma-vistāreṇa*—by width and length; *upakḷptāḥ*—situated; *atalam*—named Atala; *vitalam*—Vitala; *sutalam*—Sutala; *talātalam*—Talātala; *mahātalam*—Mahātala; *rasātalam*—Rasātala; *pātālam*—Pātāla; *iti*—thus.

TRANSLATION

My dear King, beneath this earth are seven other planets, known as Atala, Vitala, Sutala, Talātala, Mahātala, Rasātala and Pātāla. I have already explained the situation of the planetary systems of earth. The width and length of the seven lower planetary systems are calculated to be exactly the same as those of earth.

TEXT 8

एतेषु हि बिलस्वर्गेषु स्वर्गादप्यधिककामभोगैश्वर्यानन्दभूतिविभूतिभिः सुसमृद्धभवनोद्यानाक्रीडविहारेषु दैत्यदानवकाद्रवेया नित्यप्रमुदितानुरक्तकलत्रापत्यबन्धुसुहृदनुचरा गृहपतय ईश्वरादप्यप्रतिहतकामा मायाविनोदा निवसन्ति ॥८॥

eteṣu hi bila-svargeṣu svargād apy adhika-kāma-bhogaiśvaryānanda-bhūti-vibhūtibhiḥ susamṛddha-bhavanodyānākrīḍa-vihāreṣu daitya-dānava-kādraveyā nitya-pramuditānurakta-kalatrāpatya-bandhu-suhṛd-anucarā gṛha-pataya īśvarād apy apratihata-kāmā māyā-vinodā nivasanti.

eteṣu—in these; *hi*—certainly; *bila-svargeṣu*—known as the heavenly subterranean worlds; *svargāt*—than the heavenly planets; *api*—even; *adhika*—a greater quantity; *kāma-bhoga*—enjoyment of sense gratification; *aiśvarya-ānanda*—bliss due to opulence; *bhūti*—influence; *vibhūtibhiḥ*—by those things and wealth; *su-samṛddha*—improved; *bhavana*—houses; *udyāna*—gardens; *ākrīḍa-vihāreṣu*—in places for different types of sense gratification; *daitya*—the demons; *dānava*—ghosts; *kādraveyāḥ*—snakes; *nitya*—who are always; *pramudita*—overjoyed; *anurakta*—because of attachment; *kalatra*—to wife; *apatya*—children; *bandhu*—family relations; *suhṛt*—friends; *anucarāḥ*—followers; *gṛha-patayaḥ*—the heads of the households; *īśvarāt*—than those more capable, like the demigods; *api*—even; *apratihata-kāmāḥ*—whose fulfillment of lusty desires is unimpeded; *māyā*—illusory; *vinodāḥ*—who feel happiness; *nivasanti*—live.

TRANSLATION

In these seven planetary systems, which are also known as the subterranean heavens [bila-svarga], there are very beautiful houses, gardens and places of sense enjoyment, which are even more opulent than those in the higher planets because the demons have a very high standard of sensual pleasure, wealth and influence. Most of the residents of these planets, who are known as Daityas, Dānavas and Nāgas, live as householders. Their wives, children, friends and society are all fully engaged in illusory, material happiness. The sense enjoyment of the demigods is sometimes disturbed, but the residents of these planets enjoy life without disturbances. Thus they are understood to be very attached to illusory happiness.

PURPORT

According to the statements of Prahlāda Mahārāja, material enjoyment is *māyā-sukha,* illusory enjoyment. A Vaiṣṇava is full of anxieties for the deliverance of all living entities from such false enjoyment. Prahlāda Mahārāja says, *māyā-sukhāya bharam udvahato vimūḍhān:* these fools (*vimūḍhas*) are engaged in material happiness, which is surely temporary. Whether in the heavenly planets, the lower planets or the earthly planets, people are engrossed in temporary, material happiness, forgetting that in due course of time they have to change their bodies according to the material laws and suffer the repetition of birth, death, old age and disease. Not caring what will happen in the next birth, gross materialists are simply busy enjoying during the present short span of life. A Vaiṣṇava is always anxious to give all such bewildered materialists the real happiness of spiritual bliss.

TEXT 9

येषु महाराज मयेन मायाविना विनिर्मिताः पुरो नानामणिप्रवर-प्रवेकविरचितविचित्रभवनप्राकारगोपुरसभाचैत्यचत्वरायतनादिभिर्नागासुरमिथुनपारावतशुकसारिकाकीर्णकृत्रिमभूमिभिर्विवरेश्वरगृहोत्तमैः समलङ्कृताश्चकासति ॥९॥

yeṣu mahārāja mayena māyāvinā vinirmitāḥ puro nānā-maṇi-pravara-praveka-viracita-vicitra-bhavana-prākāra-gopura-sabhā-caitya-catvarāyatanādibhir nāgāsura-mithuna-pārāvata-śuka-sārikākīrṇa-kṛtrima-bhūmibhir vivareśvara-gṛhottamaiḥ samalaṅkṛtāś cakāsati.

yeṣu—in those lower planetary systems; *mahā-rāja*—O my dear King; *mayena*—by the demon named Maya; *māyā-vinā*—possessing advanced knowledge in the construction of material comforts; *vinirmitāḥ*—constructed; *puraḥ*—cities; *nānā-maṇi-pravara*—of valuable gems; *praveka*—with excellent; *viracita*—constructed; *vicitra*—wonderful; *bhavana*—houses; *prākāra*—walls; *gopura*—gates; *sabhā*—legislative meeting rooms; *caitya*—temples; *catvara*—schools; *āyatana-ādibhiḥ*—with hotels or recreation halls and so on; *nāga*—of living entities with snakelike bodies; *asura*—of demons, or godless persons; *mithuna*—by couples; *pārāvata*—pigeons; *śuka*—parrots; *sārikā*—mynas; *ākīrṇa*—crowded; *kṛtrima*—artificial; *bhūmibhiḥ*—possessing areas; *vivara-īśvara*—of the leaders of the planets; *gṛha-uttamaiḥ*—with first-class houses; *samalaṅkṛtāḥ*—decorated; *cakāsati*—shine magnificently.

TRANSLATION

My dear King, in the imitation heavens known as bila-svarga there is a great demon named Maya Dānava, who is an expert artist and architect. He has constructed many brilliantly decorated cities. There are many wonderful houses, walls, gates, assembly houses, temples, yards and temple compounds, as well as many hotels serving as residential quarters for foreigners. The houses for the leaders of these planets are constructed with the most valuable jewels, and they are always crowded with living entities known as Nāgas and Asuras, as well as many pigeons, parrots and similar birds. All in all, these imitation heavenly cities are most beautifully situated and attractively decorated.

TEXT 10

उद्यानानि चातितरां मनइन्द्रियानन्दिभिः कुसुमफलस्तबकसुभगकिसलया-
वनतरुचिरविटपविटपिनां लताङ्गालिङ्गितानां श्रीभिः समिथुनविविधविह-
ङ्गमजलाशयानाममलजलपूर्णानां झषकुलोल्लङ्घनक्षुभितनीरनीरजकुमुदकु -
वलयकह्लारनीलोत्पल लोहितशतपत्रादिवनेषु कृतनिकेतनानामेकविहारा-
कुलमधुरविविधस्वनादिभिरिन्द्रियोत्सवैरमरलोकश्रियमतिशयितानि ॥१०॥

udyānāni cātitarāṁ mana-indriyānandibhiḥ kusuma-phala-stabaka-subhaga-kisalayāvanata-rucira-viṭapa-viṭapināṁ latāṅgāliṅgitānāṁ śrībhiḥ samithuna-vividha-vihaṅgama-jalāśayānām amala-jala-pūrṇānāṁ jhaṣakulollaṅghana-kṣubhita-nīra-nīraja-kumuda-kuva-laya-kahlāra-nīlotpala-lohita-śatapatrādi-vaneṣu kṛta-niketanānām eka-vihārākula-madhura-vividha-svanādibhir indriyotsavair amara-loka-śriyam atiśayitāni.

udyānāni—the gardens and parks; *ca*—also; *atitarām*—greatly; *manaḥ*—to the mind; *indriya*—and to the senses; *ānandibhiḥ*—which cause pleasure; *kusuma*—by flowers; *phala*—of fruits; *stabaka*—bunches; *subhaga*—very beautiful; *kisalaya*—new twigs; *avanata*—bent low; *rucira*—attractive; *viṭapa*—possessing branches; *viṭapinām*—of trees; *latā-aṅga-āliṅgitānām*—which are embraced by the limbs of creepers; *śrībhiḥ*—by the beauty; *sa-mithuna*—in pairs; *vividha*—varieties; *vihaṅgama*—frequented by birds; *jala-āśayānām*—of reservoirs of water; *amala-jala-pūrṇānām*—full of clear and transparent water; *jhaṣa-kula-ullaṅghana*—by the jumping of different fish; *kṣubhita*—agitated; *nīra*—in the water; *nīraja*—of lotus flowers; *kumuda*—lilies; *kuvalaya*—flowers named *kuvalaya; kahlāra-kahlāra* flowers; *nīla-utpala*—blue lotus flowers; *lohita*—red; *śata-patra-ādi*—lotus flowers with a hundred petals and so on; *vaneṣu*—in forests; *kṛta-niketanānām*—of birds that have made their nests; *eka-vihāra-ākula*—full of uninterrupted enjoyment; *madhura*—very sweet; *vividha*—varieties; *svana-ādibhiḥ*—by vibrations; *indriya-utsavaiḥ*—invoking sense enjoyment; *amara-loka-śriyam*—the beauty of the residential places of the demigods; *atiśayitāni*—surpassing.

TRANSLATION

The parks and gardens in the artificial heavens surpass in beauty those of the upper heavenly planets. The trees in those gardens, embraced by

creepers, bend with a heavy burden of twigs with fruits and flowers, and therefore they appear extraordinarily beautiful. That beauty could attract anyone and make his mind fully blossom in the pleasure of sense gratification. There are many lakes and reservoirs with clear, transparent water, agitated by jumping fish and decorated with many flowers such as lilies, kuvalayas, kahlāras and blue and red lotuses. Pairs of cakravākas and many other water birds nest in the lakes and always enjoy in a happy mood, making sweet, pleasing vibrations that are very satisfying and conducive to enjoyment of the senses.

TEXT 11

यत्र ह वाव न भयमहोरात्रादिभिः कालविभागैरुपलक्ष्यते ॥११॥

yatra ha vāva na bhayam aho-rātrādibhiḥ kāla-vibhāgair upalakṣyate.

yatra—where; *ha vāva*—certainly; *na*—not; *bhayam*—fearfulness; *ahaḥ-rātra-ādibhiḥ*—because of days and nights; *kāla-vibhāgaiḥ*—the divisions of time; *upalakṣyate*—is experienced.

TRANSLATION

Since there is no sunshine in those subterranean planets, time is not divided into days and nights, and consequently fear produced by time does not exist.

TEXT 12

यत्र हि महाहिप्रवरशिरोमणयः सर्वं तमः प्रबाधन्ते ॥१२॥

yatra hi mahāhi-pravara-śiro-maṇayaḥ sarvaṁ tamaḥ prabādhante.

yatra—where; *hi*—indeed; *mahā-ahi*—of great serpents; *pravara*—of the best; *śiraḥ-maṇayaḥ*—the gems on the hoods; *sarvam*—all; *tamaḥ*—darkness; *prabādhante*—drive away.

TRANSLATION

Many great serpents reside there with gems on their hoods, and the effulgence of these gems dissipates the darkness in all directions.

TEXT 13

न वा एतेषु वसतां दिव्यौषधिरसरसायनान्नपानस्नानादिभिराधयो व्याधयो वलीपलितजरादयश्च देहवैवर्ण्यदौर्गन्ध्यस्वेदक्लमग्लानिरिति वयोऽवस्थाश्च भवन्ति ॥१३॥

na vā eteṣu vasatāṁ divyauṣadhi-rasa-rasāyanānna-pāna-snānādibhir ādhayo vyādhayo valī-palita-jarādayaś ca deha-vaivarṇya-daurgandhya-sveda-klama-glānir iti vayo 'vasthāś ca bhavanti.

na—not; *vā*—either; *eteṣu*—in these planets; *vasatām*—of those residing; *divya*—wonderful; *auṣadhi*—of herbs; *rasa*—the juices; *rasāyana*—and elixirs; *anna*—by eating; *pāna*—drinking; *snāna-ādibhiḥ*—by bathing in and so on; *ādhayaḥ*—mental troubles; *vyādhayaḥ*—diseases; *valī*—wrinkles; *palita*—grey hair; *jarā*—old age; *ādayaḥ*—and so on; *ca*—and; *deha-vaivarṇya*—the fading of bodily luster; *daurgandhya*—bad odor; *sveda*—perspiration; *klama*—fatigue; *glāniḥ*—lack of energy; *iti*—thus; *vayaḥ avasthāḥ*—miserable conditions due to increasing age; *ca*—and; *bhavanti*—are.

TRANSLATION

Since the residents of these planets drink and bathe in juices and elixirs made from wonderful herbs, they are freed from all anxieties and physical diseases. They have no experience of grey hair, wrinkles or invalidity, their bodily lusters do not fade, their perspiration does not cause a bad smell, and they are not troubled by fatigue or by lack of energy or enthusiasm due to old age.

TEXT 14

न हि तेषां कल्याणानां प्रभवति कुतश्चन मृत्युर्विना भगवत्तेजसश्चक्रापदेशात् ॥१४॥

na hi teṣāṁ kalyāṇānāṁ prabhavati kutaścana mṛtyur vinā bhagavat-tejasaś cakrāpadeśāt.

na hi—not; *teṣām*—of them; *kalyāṇānām*—who are by nature auspicious; *prabhavati*—able to influence; *kutaścana*—from anywhere; *mṛtyuḥ*—death; *vinā*—except; *bhagavat-tejasaḥ*—of the energy of the Supreme Personality of Godhead; *cakra-apadeśāt*—from that weapon named the Sudarśana *cakra.*

TRANSLATION

They live very auspiciously and do not fear death from anything but death's established time, which is the effulgence of the Sudarśana cakra of the Supreme Personality of Godhead.

PURPORT

This is the defect of material existence. Everything in the subterranean heavens is very nicely arranged. There are well situated residential quarters, there is a pleasing atmosphere, and there are no bodily inconveniences or mental anxieties, but nevertheless those who live there have to take another birth according to *karma.* Persons whose minds are dull cannot understand this defect of a materialistic civilization aiming at material comforts. One may make his living conditions very pleasing for the senses, but despite all favorable conditions, one must in due course of time meet death. The members of a demoniac civilization endeavor to make their living conditions very comfortable, but they cannot check death. The influence of the Sudarśana *cakra* will not allow their so-called material happiness to endure.

TEXT 15

यस्मिन् प्रविष्टेऽसुरवधूनां प्रायः पुंसवनानि भयादेव स्रवन्ति पतन्ति च ॥१५॥

yasmin praviṣṭe 'sura-vadhūnāṁ prāyaḥ puṁsavanāni bhayād eva sravanti patanti ca.

yasmin—where; *praviṣṭe*—when entered; *asura-vadhūnām*—of the wives of those demons; *prāyaḥ*—almost always; *puṁsavanāni*—fetuses; *bhayāt*—because of fear; *eva*—certainly; *sravanti*—slip out; *patanti*—fall down; *ca*—and.

TRANSLATION

When the Sudarśana disc enters those provinces, the pregnant wives of the demons all have miscarriages due to fear of its effulgence.

TEXT 16

अथातले मयपुत्रोऽसुरो बलो निवसति येन ह वा इह सृष्टाः षण्णवतिर्मायाः काश्चनाद्यापि मायाविनो धारयन्ति यस्य च जृम्भमाणस्य मुखतस्त्रयः स्त्रीगणा उदपद्यन्त स्वैरिण्यः कामिन्यः पुंश्चल्य इति या वै बिलायनं प्रविष्टं पुरुषं रसेन हाटकाख्येन साधयित्वा स्वविलासावलोकनानुरागस्मितसंलापोपगूहनादिभिः स्वैरं किल रमयन्ति यस्मिन्नुपयुक्ते पुरुष ईश्वरोऽहं सिद्धोऽहमित्ययुत-महागजबलमात्मानमभिमन्यमानः कत्थते मदान्ध इव ॥१६॥

athātale maya-putro 'suro balo nivasati yena ha vā iha sṛṣṭāḥ ṣaṇ-ṇavatir māyāḥ kāścanādyāpi māyāvino dhārayanti yasya ca jṛmbhamāṇasya mukhatas trayaḥ strī-gaṇā udapadyanta svairiṇyaḥ kāminyaḥ puṁścalya iti yā vai bilāyanaṁ praviṣṭaṁ puruṣaṁ rasena hāṭakākhyena sādhayitvā sva-vilāsāvalokanānurāga-smita-saṁlāpopagūhanādibhiḥ svairaṁ kila ramayanti yasminn upayukte puruṣa īśvaro'haṁ siddho 'ham ity ayuta-mahā-gaja-balam ātmānam abhimanyamānaḥ katthate madāndha iva.

atha—now; *atale*—on the planet named Atala; *maya-putraḥ asuraḥ*—the demon son of Maya; *balaḥ*—Bala; *nivasati*—resides; *yena*—by whom; *ha vā*—indeed; *iha*—in this; *sṛṣṭāḥ*—propagated; *ṣaṭ-ṇavatiḥ*—ninety-six; *māyāḥ*—varieties of illusion; *kāścana*—some; *adya api*—even today; *māyā-vinaḥ*—those who know the art of magical feats (like manufacturing gold); *dhārayanti*—utilize; *yasya*—of whom; *ca*—also; *jṛmbhamāṇasya*—while yawning; *mukhataḥ*—from the mouth; *trayaḥ*—three; *strī-gaṇāḥ*—varieties of women; *udapadyanta*—were generated; *svairiṇyaḥ*—*svairiṇī* (one who only marries in her same class); *kāminyaḥ*—*kāmiṇī* (one who, being lusty, marries men from any group); *puṁścalyaḥ*—*puṁścalī* (one who wants to go from one husband to another); *iti*—thus; *yāḥ*—who; *vai*—certainly; *bila-ayanam*—the subterranean planets; *praviṣṭam*—entering; *puruṣam*—a male; *rasena*—by a juice; *hāṭaka-ākhyena*—made from an intoxicating herb known as *hāṭaka; sādhayitvā*—making sexually fit; *sva-vilāsa*—for their personal sense gratification; *avalokana*—by glances; *anurāga*—lustful; *smita*—by smiling; *saṁlāpa*—by talking; *upagūhana-ādibhiḥ*—and by embracing; *svairam*—according to their own desire; *kila*—indeed; *ramayanti*—enjoy sex pleasure; *yasmin*—which; *upayukte*—when used; *puruṣaḥ*—a man; *īśvaraḥ aham*—I am the most powerful person; *siddhaḥ aham*—I am the greatest and most elevated person; *iti*—thus; *ayuta*—ten thousand; *mahā-gaja*—of big elephants; *balam*—the strength; *ātmānam*—himself; *abhimanyamānaḥ*—being full of pride; *katthate*—they say; *mada-andhaḥ*—blinded by false prestige; *iva*—like.

TRANSLATION

My dear King, now I shall describe to you the lower planetary systems, one by one, beginning from Atala. In Atala there is a demon, the son of Maya Dānava named Bala, who created ninety-six kinds of mystic power. Some so-called yogīs and svāmīs take advantage of this mystic power to

cheat people even today. Simply by yawning, the demon Bala created three kinds of women, known as svairiṇī, kāmiṇī and puṁścalī. The svairiṇīs like to marry men from their own group, the kāmiṇīs marry men from any group, and the puṁścalīs change husbands one after another. If a man enters the planet of Atala, these women immediately capture him and induce him to drink an intoxicating beverage made with a drug known as hāṭaka [cannabis indica]. This intoxicant endows the man with great sexual prowess, of which the women take advantage for enjoyment. A woman will enchant him with attractive glances, intimate words, smiles of love and then embraces. In this way she induces him to enjoy sex with her to her full satisfaction. Because of his increased sexual power, the man thinks himself stronger than ten thousand elephants and considers himself most perfect. Indeed, illusioned and intoxicated by false pride, he thinks himself God, ignoring impending death.

TEXT 17

ततोऽधस्ताद्वितले हरो भगवान् हाटकेश्वरः स्वपार्षदभूतगणावृतः प्रजापतिसर्गोपबृंहणाय भवो भवान्या सह मिथुनीभूत आस्ते यतः प्रवृत्ता सरित्प्रवरा हाटकी नाम भवयोर्वीर्येण यत्र चित्रभानुर्मातरिश्वना समिध्यमान ओजसा पिबति तन्निष्ठ्यूतं हाटकाख्यं सुवर्णं भूषणेनासुरेन्द्रावरोधेषु पुरुषाः सह पुरुषीभिर्धारयन्ति ॥१७॥

tato 'dhastād vitale haro bhagavān hāṭakeśvaraḥ sva-pārṣada-bhūta-gaṇāvṛtaḥ prajāpati-sargopabṛṁhaṇāya bhavo bhavānyā saha mithunī-bhūta āste yataḥ pravṛttā sarit-pravarā hāṭakī nāma bhavayor vīryeṇa yatra citrabhānur mātariśvanā samidhyamāna ojasā pibati tan niṣṭhyūtaṁ hāṭakākhyaṁ suvarṇaṁ bhūṣaṇenāsurendrāvarodheṣu puruṣāḥ saha puruṣībhir dhārayanti.

tataḥ—the planet Atala; *adhastāt*—beneath; *vitale*—on the planet; *haraḥ*—Lord Śiva; *bhagavān*—the most powerful personality; *hāṭakeśvaraḥ*—the master of gold; *sva-pārṣada*—by his own associates; *bhūta-gaṇa*—who are ghostly living beings; *āvṛtaḥ*—surrounded; *prajāpati-sarga*—of the creation of Lord Brahmā; *upabṛṁhaṇāya*—to increase the population; *bhavaḥ*—Lord Śiva; *bhavānyā saha*—with his wife, Bhavānī; *mithunī-bhūtaḥ*—being united in sex; *āste*—remains; *yataḥ*—from that planet (Vitala); *pravṛttā*—being emanated; *sarit-pravarā*—the great river; *hāṭakī*—Hāṭakī; *nāma*—named; *bhavayoḥ vīryeṇa*—due to the semina and ovum of Lord Śiva and Bhavānī;

yatra—where; *citra-bhānuḥ*—the fire-god; *mātariśvanā*—by the wind; *samidhyamānaḥ*—being brightly inflamed; *ojasā*—with great strength; *pibati*—drinks; *tat*—that; *niṣṭhyūtam*—spit out with a hissing sound; *hāṭaka-ākhyam*—named Hāṭaka; *suvarṇam*—gold; *bhūṣaṇena*—by different types of ornaments; *asura-indra*—of the great *asuras; avarodheṣu*—in the homes; *puruṣāḥ*—the males; *saha*—with; *puruṣībhiḥ*—their wives and women; *dhārayanti*—wear.

TRANSLATION

The next planet below Atala is Vitala, wherein Lord Śiva, who is known as the master of gold mines, lives with his personal associates, the ghosts and similar living entities. Lord Śiva, as the progenitor, engages in sex with Bhavānī, the progenitress, to produce living entities, and from the mixture of their vital fluid the river named Hāṭakī is generated. When fire, being made to blaze by the wind, drinks of this river and then sizzles and spits it out, it produces gold called Hāṭaka. The demons who live on that planet with their wives decorate themselves with various ornaments made from that gold, and thus they live there very happily.

PURPORT

It appears that when Bhava and Bhavānī, Lord Śiva and his wife, unite sexually, the emulsification of their secretions creates a chemical which when heated by fire can produce gold. It is said that the alchemists of the medieval age tried to prepare gold from base metal, and Śrīla Sanātana Gosvāmī also states that when bell metal is treated with mercury, it can produce gold. Śrīla Sanātana Gosvāmī mentions this in regard to the initiation of low-class men to turn them into *brāhmaṇas.* Sanātana Gosvāmī said:

yathā kāñcanatāṁ yāti
kāṁsyaṁ rasa-vidhānataḥ
tathā dīkṣā-vidhānena
dvijatvaṁ jāyate nṛṇām

"As one can transform *kaṁsa,* or bell metal, into gold by treating it with mercury, one can also turn a lowborn man into a *brāhmaṇa* by initiating him properly into Vaiṣṇava activities." The International Society for Krishna Consciousness is trying to turn *mlecchas* and *yavanas* into real *brāhmaṇas* by properly initiating them and stopping them from engaging in meat-eating, intoxication, illicit sex and gambling. One who stops these four principles of sinful activity and chants the Hare Kṛṣṇa *mahā-mantra* can certainly become a pure *brāhmaṇa* through the process of bona fide initiation, as suggested by Śrīla Sanātana Gosvāmī.

Apart from this, if one takes a hint from this verse and learns how to mix mercury with bell metal by properly heating and melting them, one can get gold very cheaply. The alchemists of the medieval age tried to manufacture gold, but they were unsuccessful, perhaps because they did not follow the right instructions.

TEXT 18

ततोऽधस्तात्सुतले उदारश्रवाः पुण्यश्लोको विरोचनात्मजो बलिर्भगवता महेन्द्रस्य प्रियं चिकीर्षमाणेनादितेर्लब्धकायो भूत्वा वटुवामनरूपेण पराक्षिप्तलोकत्रयो भगवदनुकम्पयैव पुनः प्रवेशित इन्द्रादिष्वविद्यमानया सुसमृद्धया श्रियाभिजुष्टः स्वधर्मेणाराधयंस्तमेव भगवन्तमाराधनीयमपगतसाध्वस आस्तेऽधुनापि ॥१८॥

tato 'dhastāt sutale udāra-śravāḥ puṇya-śloko virocanātmajo balir
bhagavatā mahendrasya priyaṁ cikīrṣamāṇenāditer labdha-kāyo
bhūtvā vaṭu-vāmana-rūpeṇa parākṣipta-loka-trayo bhagavad-
anukampayaiva punaḥ praveśita indrādiṣv avidyamānayā
susamṛddhayā śriyābhijuṣṭaḥ sva-dharmeṇārādhayaṁs tam eva
bhagavantam ārādhanīyam apagata-sādhvasa āste 'dhunāpi.

tataḥ adhastāt—beneath the planet known as Vitala; *sutale*—on the planet known as Sutala; *udāra-śravāḥ*—very greatly celebrated; *puṇya-ślokaḥ*—very pious and advanced in spiritual consciousness; *virocana-ātmajaḥ*—the son of Virocana; *baliḥ*—Bali Mahārāja; *bhagavatā*—by the Supreme Personality of Godhead; *mahā-indrasya*—of the King of heaven, Indra; *priyam*—the welfare; *cikīrṣamāṇena*—desiring to perform; *āditeḥ*—from Āditi; *labdha-kāyaḥ*—having obtained His body; *bhūtvā*—appearing; *vaṭu*—*brahmacāri; vāmana-rūpeṇa*—in the form of a dwarf; *parākṣipta*—wrested away; *loka-trayaḥ*—the three worlds; *bhagavat-anukampayā*—by the causeless mercy of the Supreme Personality of Godhead; *eva*—certainly; *punaḥ*—again; *praveśitaḥ*—caused to enter; *indra-ādiṣu*—even among the demigods like the King of heaven; *avidyamānayā*—not existing; *susamṛddhayā*—much enriched by such exalted opulence; *śriyā*—by good fortune; *abhijuṣṭaḥ*—being blessed; *sva-dharmeṇa*—by discharging devotional service; *ārādhayan*—worshiping; *tam*—Him; *eva*—certainly; *bhagavantam*—the Supreme Personality of Godhead; *ārādhanīyam*—who is most worshipable; *apagata-sādhvasaḥ*—without fear; *āste*—remains; *adhunā api*—even today.

TRANSLATION

Below the planet Vitala is another planet, known as Sutala, where the great son of Mahārāja Virocana, Bali Mahārāja, who is celebrated as the most pious king, resides even now. For the welfare of Indra, the King of heaven, Lord Viṣṇu appeared in the form of a dwarf brahmacārī as the son of Āditi and tricked Bali Mahārāja by begging for only three paces of land but taking all the three worlds. Being very pleased with Bali Mahārāja for giving all his possessions, the Lord returned his kingdom and made him richer than the opulent King Indra. Even now, Bali Mahārāja engages in devotional service by worshiping the Supreme Personality of Godhead in the planet of Sutala.

PURPORT

The Supreme Personality of Godhead is described as Uttamaśloka, "He who is worshiped by the best of selected Sanskrit verses," and His devotees such as Bali Mahārāja are also worshiped by *puṇya-śloka,* verses that increase one's piety. Bali Mahārāja offered everything to the Lord—his wealth, his kingdom and even his own body (*sarvātma-nivedane baliḥ*). The Lord appeared before Bali Mahārāja as a *brāhmaṇa* beggar, and Bali Mahārāja gave Him everything he had. However, Bali Mahārāja did not become poor; by donating all his possessions to the Supreme Personality of Godhead, he became a successful devotee and got everything back again with the blessings of the Lord. Similarly, those who give contributions to expand the activities of the Kṛṣṇa consciousness movement and to accomplish its objectives will never be losers; they will get their wealth back with the blessings of Lord Kṛṣṇa. On the other side, those who collect contributions on behalf of the International Society for Krishna Consciousness should be very careful not to use even a farthing of the collection for any purpose other than the transcendental loving service of the Lord.

TEXT 19

नो एवैतत्साक्षात्कारो भूमिदानस्य यत्तद्भगवत्यशेषजीवनिकायानां जीवभूतात्मभूते
परमात्मनि वासुदेवे तीर्थतमे पात्र उपपन्ने परया श्रद्धया परमादरसमाहितमनसा
सम्प्रतिपादितस्य साक्षादपवर्गद्वारस्य यद्बिलनिलयैश्वर्यम् ॥१९॥

no evaitat sākṣātkāro bhūmi-dānasya yat tad bhagavaty aśeṣa-jīva-
nikāyānāṁ jīva-bhūtātma-bhūte paramātmani vāsudeve tīrthatame pātra
upapanne parayā śraddhayā paramādara-samāhita-manasā
sampratipāditasya sākṣād apavarga-dvārasya yad bila-nilayaiśvaryam.

no—not; *eva*—indeed; *etat*—this; *sākṣātkāraḥ*—the direct result; *bhūmi-dānasya*—of contribution of land; *yat*—which; *tat*—that; *bhagavati*—unto the Supreme Personality of Godhead; *aśeṣa-jīva-nikāyānām*—of unlimited numbers of living entities; *jīva-bhūta-ātma-bhūte*—who is the life and the Supersoul; *parama-ātmani*—the supreme regulator; *vāsudeve*—Lord Vāsudeva (Kṛṣṇa); *tīrtha-tame*—who is the best of all places of pilgrimage; *pātre*—the most worthy recipient; *upapanne*—having approached; *parayā*—by the topmost; *śraddhayā*—faith; *parama-ādara*—with great respect; *samāhita-manasā*—with an attentive mind; *sampratipāditasya*—which was given; *sākṣāt*—directly; *apavarga-dvārasya*—the gate of liberation; *yat*—which; *bila-nilaya*—of *bila-svarga,* the imitation heavenly planets; *aiśvaryam*—the opulence.

TRANSLATION

My dear King, Bali Mahārāja donated all his possessions to the Supreme Personality of Godhead, Vāmanadeva, but one should certainly not conclude that he achieved his great worldly opulence in bila-svarga as a result of his charitable disposition. The Supreme Personality of Godhead, who is the source of life for all living entities, lives within everyone as the friendly Supersoul, and under His direction a living entity enjoys or suffers in the material world. Greatly appreciating the transcendental qualities of the Lord, Bali Mahārāja offered everything at His lotus feet. His purpose, however, was not to gain anything material, but to become a pure devotee. For a pure devotee, the door of liberation is automatically opened. One should not think that Bali Mahārāja was given so much material opulence merely because of his charity. When one becomes a pure devotee in love, he may also be blessed with a good material position by the will of the Supreme Lord. However, one should not mistakenly think that the material opulence of a devotee is the result of his devotional service. The real result of devotional service is the awakening of pure love for the Supreme Personality of Godhead, which continues under all circumstances.

TEXT 20

यस्य ह वाव क्षुतपतनप्रस्खलनादिषु विवशः सकृन्नामाभिगृणन् पुरुषः कर्मबन्धनमञ्जसा विधुनोति यस्य हैव प्रतिबाधनं मुमुक्षवोऽन्यथैवोपलभन्ते ॥२०॥

yasya ha vāva kṣuta-patana-praskhalanādiṣu vivaśaḥ sakṛn
nāmābhigṛṇan puruṣaḥ karma-bandhanam añjasā vidhunoti yasya
haiva pratibādhanaṁ mumukṣavo 'nyathaivopalabhante.

yasya—of whom; *ha vāva*—indeed; *kṣuta*—when in hunger; *patana*—falling down; *praskhalana-ādiṣu*—stumbling and so on; *vivaśaḥ*—being helpless; *sakṛt*—once; *nāma abhigṛṇan*—chanting the holy name of the Lord; *puruṣaḥ*—a person; *karma-bandhanam*—the bondage of fruitive activity; *añjasā*—completely; *vidhunoti*—washes away; *yasya*—of which; *ha*—certainly; *eva*—in this way; *pratibādhanam*—the repulsion; *mumukṣavaḥ*—persons desiring liberation; *anyathā*—otherwise; *eva*—certainly; *upalabhante*—are trying to realize.

TRANSLATION

If one who is embarrassed by hunger or who falls down or stumbles chants the holy name of the Lord even once, willingly or unwillingly, he is immediately freed from the reactions of his past deeds. Karmīs entangled in material activities face many difficulties in the practice of mystic yoga and other endeavors to achieve that same freedom.

PURPORT

It is not a fact that one has to offer his material possessions to the Supreme Personality of Godhead and be liberated before he can engage in devotional service. A devotee automatically attains liberation without separate endeavors. Bali Mahārāja did not get back all his material possessions merely because of his charity to the Lord. One who becomes a devotee, free from material desires and motives, regards all opportunities, both material and spiritual, as benedictions from the Lord, and in this way his service to the Lord is never hampered. *Bhukti,* material enjoyment, and *mukti,* liberation, are only by-products of devotional service. A devotee need not work separately to attain *mukti.* Śrīla Bilvamaṅgala Ṭhākura said, *muktiḥ svayaṁ mukulitāñjaliḥ sevate'smān:* a pure devotee of the Lord does not have to endeavor separately for *mukti,* because *mukti* is always ready to serve him.

In this regard, *Caitanya-caritāmṛta* (*Antya* 3.177–188) describes Haridāsa Ṭhākura's confirmation of the effect of chanting the holy name of the Lord.

keha bale—'nāma haite haya pāpa-kṣaya'
keha bale—'nāma haite jīvera mokṣa haya'

Some say that by chanting the holy name of the Lord one is freed from all the reactions of sinful life, and others say that by chanting the holy name of the Lord one attains liberation from material bondage.

haridāsa kahena,—"nāmera ei dui phala naya
nāmera phale kṛṣṇa-pade prema upajaya

Haridāsa Ṭhākura, however, said that the desired result of chanting the holy name of the Lord is not that one is liberated from material bondage or freed from the reactions of sinful life. The actual result of chanting the holy name of the Lord is that one awakens his dormant Kṛṣṇa consciousness, his loving service to the Lord.

ānuṣaṅgika phala nāmera—'mukti', 'pāpa-nāśa'
tāhāra dṛṣṭānta yaiche sūryera prakāśa

Haridāsa Ṭhākura said that liberation and freedom from the reactions of sinful activities are only by-products of chanting the holy name of the Lord. If one chants the holy name of the Lord purely, he attains the platform of loving service to the Supreme Personality of Godhead. In this regard Haridāsa Ṭhākura gave an example comparing the power of the holy name to sunshine.

ei ślokera artha kara paṇḍitera gaṇa"
sabe kahe,—'tumi kaha artha-vivaraṇa'

He placed a verse before all the learned scholars present, but the learned scholars asked him to state the purport of the verse.

haridāsa kahena,—"yaiche sūryera udaya
udaya nā haite ārambhe tamera haya kṣaya

Haridāsa Ṭhākura said that as the sun begins to rise, it dissipates the darkness of night, even before the sunshine is visible.

caura-preta-rākṣasādira bhaya haya nāśa
udaya haile dharma-karma-ādi parakāśa

Before the sunrise even takes place, the light of dawn destroys the fear of the dangers of the night, such as disturbances by thieves, ghosts and Rākṣasas, and when the sunshine actually appears, one engages in his duties.

aiche nāmodayārambhe pāpa-ādira kṣaya
udaya kaile kṛṣṇa-pade haya premodaya

Similarly, even before one's chanting of the holy name is pure, one is freed from all sinful reactions, and when he chants purely he becomes a lover of Kṛṣṇa.

'mukti' tuccha-phala haya nāmābhāsa haite
ye mukti bhakta nā laya, se kṛṣṇa cāhe dite"

A devotee never accepts *mukti,* even if Kṛṣṇa offers it. *Mukti,* freedom from all sinful reactions, is obtained even by *nāmābhāsa,* or a glimpse of the light of the holy name before its full light is perfectly visible.

The *nāmābhāsa* stage is between that of *nāma-aparādha,* or chanting of the holy name with offenses, and pure chanting. There are three stages in chanting the holy name of the Lord. In the first stage, one commits ten kinds of offenses while chanting. In the next stage, *nāmābhāsa,* the offenses have almost stopped, and one is coming to the platform of pure chanting. In the third stage, when one chants the Hare Kṛṣṇa *mantra* without offenses, his dormant love for Kṛṣṇa immediately awakens. This is the perfection.

TEXT 21

तद्भक्तानामात्मवतां सर्वेषामात्मन्यात्मद आत्मतयैव ॥२१॥

tad bhaktānām ātmavatāṁ sarveṣām ātmany ātmada ātmatayaiva.

tat—that; *bhaktānām*—of great devotees; *ātma-vatām*—of self-realized persons like Sanaka and Sanātana; *sarveṣām*—of all; *ātmani*—to the Supreme Personality of Godhead, who is the soul; *ātma-de*—who gives Himself without hesitation; *ātmatayā*—who is the Supreme Soul, Paramātmā; *eva*—indeed.

TRANSLATION

The Supreme Personality of Godhead, who is situated in everyone's heart as the Supersoul, sells Himself to His devotees such as Nārada Muni. In other words, the Lord gives pure love to such devotees and gives Himself to those who love Him purely. Great, self-realized mystic yogīs such as the

four Kumāras also derive great transcendental bliss from realizing the Supersoul within themselves.

PURPORT

The Lord became Bali Mahārāja's doorkeeper not because of his giving everything to the Lord, but because of his exalted position as a lover of the Lord.

TEXT 22

न वै भगवान्नूनममुष्यानुजग्राह यदुत पुनरात्मानुस्मृतिमोषणं मायामय-
भोगैश्वर्यमेवातनुतेति ॥२२॥

na vai bhagavān nūnam amuṣyānujagrāha yad uta punar ātmānusmṛti-
moṣaṇaṁ māyāmaya-bhogaiśvaryam evātanuteti.

na—not; *vai*—indeed; *bhagavān*—the Supreme Personality of Godhead; *nūnam*—certainly; *amuṣya*—unto Bali Mahārāja; *anujagrāha*—showed His favor; *yat*—because; *uta*—certainly; *punaḥ*—again; *ātma-anusmṛti*—of remembrance of the Supreme Personality of Godhead; *moṣaṇam*—which robs one; *māyā-maya*—an attribute of Māyā; *bhoga-aiśvaryam*—the material opulence; *eva*—certainly; *ātanuta*—extended; *iti*—thus.

TRANSLATION

The Supreme Personality of Godhead did not award His mercy to Bali Mahārāja by giving him material happiness and opulence, for these make one forget loving service to the Lord. The result of material opulence is that one can no longer absorb his mind in the Supreme Personality of Godhead.

PURPORT

There are two kinds of opulence. One, which results from one's *karma,* is material, whereas the other is spiritual. A surrendered soul who fully depends upon the Supreme Personality of Godhead does not want material opulence for sense gratification. Therefore when a pure devotee is seen to possess exalted material opulence, it is not due to his *karma.* Rather, it is due to his *bhakti.* In other words, he is in that position because the Supreme Lord wants him to execute service to Him very easily and opulently. The special mercy of the Lord for the neophyte devotee is that he becomes materially poor. This is the Lord's mercy because if a neophyte devotee becomes materially opulent, he forgets the service of the Lord. However, if an advanced devotee is favored by the Lord with opulence, it is not material opulence but a spiritual opportunity. Material opulence offered to the demigods causes forgetfulness of the Lord, but opulence was given to Bali Mahārāja for continuing service to the Lord, which was free from any touch of *māyā.*

TEXT 23

यत्तद्भगवतानधिगतान्योपायेन याच्ञाच्छलेनापहृतस्वशरीरावशेषितलोकत्रयो वरुणपाशैश्च सम्प्रतिमुक्तो गिरिदर्यां चापविद्ध इति होवाच ॥२३॥

yat tad bhagavatānadhigatānyopāyena yācñā-cchalenāpahṛta-sva-śarīrāvaśeṣita-loka-trayo varuṇa-pāśaiś ca sampratimukto giri-daryāṁ cāpaviddha iti hovāca.

yat—which; *tat*—that; *bhagavatā*—by the Supreme Personality of Godhead; *anadhigata-anya-upāyena*—who is not perceived by other means; *yācñā-chalena*—by a trick of begging; *apahṛta*—taken away; *sva-śarīra-avaśeṣita*—with only his own body remaining; *loka-trayaḥ*—the three worlds; *varuṇa-pāśaiḥ*—by the ropes of Varuṇa; *ca*—and; *sampratimuktaḥ*—completely bound; *giri-daryām*—in a cave in a mountain; *ca*—and; *apaviddhaḥ*—being detained; *iti*—thus; *ha*—indeed; *uvāca*—said.

TRANSLATION

When the Supreme Personality of Godhead could see no other means of taking everything away from Bali Mahārāja, He adopted the trick of begging from him and took away all the three worlds. Thus only his body was left, but the Lord was still not satisfied. He arrested Bali Mahārāja, bound him with the ropes of Varuṇa and threw him in a cave in a mountain. Nevertheless, although all his property was taken and he was thrown into a cave, Bali Mahārāja was such a great devotee that he spoke as follows.

TEXT 24

नूनं बतायं भगवानर्थेषु न निष्णातो योऽसाविन्द्रो यस्य सचिवो मन्त्राय वृत एकान्ततो बृहस्पतिस्तमतिहाय स्वयमुपेन्द्रेणात्मानमयाचतात्मनश्चाशिषो नो एव तद्दास्यमतिगम्भीरवयसः कालस्य मन्वन्तरपरिवृत्तं कियल्लोकत्रयमिदम् ॥२४॥

nūnaṁ batāyaṁ bhagavān artheṣu na niṣṇāto yo 'sāv indro yasya sacivo mantrāya vṛta ekāntato bṛhaspatis tam atihāya svayam upendreṇātmānam ayācatātmanaś cāśiṣo no eva tad-dāsyam ati-gambhīra-vayasaḥ kālasya manvantara-parivṛttaṁ kiyal loka-trayam idam.

nūnam—certainly; *bata*—alas; *ayam*—this; *bhagavān*—very learned; *artheṣu*—in self-interest; *na*—not; *niṣṇātaḥ*—very experienced; *yaḥ*—who; *asau*—the King of heaven; *indraḥ*—Indra; *yasya*—of whom; *sacivaḥ*—the prime minister; *mantrāya*—for giving instructions; *vṛtaḥ*—chosen; *ekāntataḥ*—alone; *bṛhaspatiḥ*—named Bṛhaspati; *tam*—him; *atihāya*—ignoring; *svayam*—personally; *upendreṇa*—by means of Upendra (Lord Vāmanadeva); *ātmānam*—myself; *ayācata*—requested; *ātmanaḥ*—for himself; *ca*—and; *āśiṣaḥ*—blessings (the three worlds); *no*—not; *eva*—certainly; *tat-dāsyam*—the loving service of the Lord; *ati*—very; *gambhīra-vayasaḥ*—having an insurmountable duration; *kālasya*—of time; *manvantara-parivṛttam*—changed by the end of a life of a Manu; *kiyat*—what is the value of; *loka-trayam*—three worlds; *idam*—these.

TRANSLATION

Alas, how pitiable it is for Indra, the King of heaven, that although he is very learned and powerful and although he chose Bṛhaspati as his prime minister to instruct him, he is completely ignorant concerning spiritual advancement. Bṛhaspati is also unintelligent because he did not properly instruct his disciple Indra. Lord Vāmanadeva was standing at Indra's door, but King Indra, instead of begging Him for an opportunity to render transcendental loving service, engaged Him in asking me for alms to gain the three worlds for his sense gratification. Sovereignty over the three worlds is very insignificant because whatever material opulence one may possess lasts only for an age of Manu, which is but a tiny fraction of endless time.

PURPORT

Bali Mahārāja was so powerful that he fought with Indra and took possession of the three worlds. Indra was certainly very advanced in knowledge, but instead of asking Vāmanadeva for engagement in His service, he used the Lord to beg for material possessions that would be finished at the end of one age of Manu. An age of Manu, which is the duration of Manu's life, is calculated to last seventy-two *yugas*. One *yuga* consists of 4,300,000 years, and therefore the duration of Manu's life is 309,600,000 years. The demigods possess their material opulence only until the end of the life of Manu. Time is insurmountable. The time one is allotted, even if it be millions of years, is quickly gone. The demigods own their material possessions only within the limits of time. Therefore Bali Mahārāja lamented that although Indra was very learned, he did not know how to use his intelligence properly, for instead of asking Vāmanadeva to allow him to engage in His service, Indra used Him to beg Bali Mahārāja for material wealth. Although Indra was learned and his prime minister, Bṛhaspati, was also learned, neither of them begged to be able to render loving service to Lord Vāmanadeva. Therefore Bali Mahārāja lamented for Indra.

TEXT 25

यस्यानुदास्यमेवास्मत्पितामहः किल वव्रे न तु स्वपित्र्यं यदुताकुतोभयं पदं दीयमानं भगवतः परमिति भगवतोपरते खलु स्वपितरि ॥२५॥

yasyānudāsyam evāsmat-pitāmahaḥ kila vavre na tu sva-pitryaṁ yad
utākutobhayaṁ padaṁ dīyamānaṁ bhagavataḥ param iti
bhagavatoparate khalu sva-pitari.

yasya—of whom (the Supreme Personality of Godhead); *anudāsyam*—the service; *eva*—certainly; *asmat*—our; *pitā-mahaḥ*—grandfather; *kila*—indeed; *vavre*—accepted; *na*—not; *tu*—but; *sva*—own; *pitryam*—paternal property; *yat*—which; *uta*—certainly; *akutaḥ-bhayam*—fearlessness; *padam*—position; *dīyamānam*—being offered; *bhagavataḥ*—than the Supreme Personality of Godhead; *param*—other; *iti*—thus; *bhagavatā*—by the Supreme Personality of Godhead; *uparate*—when killed; *khalu*—indeed; *sva-pitari*—his own father.

TRANSLATION

Bali Mahārāja said: My grandfather Prahlāda Mahārāja is the only person who understood his own self-interest. Upon the death of Prahlāda's father, Hiraṇyakaśipu, Lord Nṛsiṁhadeva wanted to offer Prahlāda his father's kingdom and even wanted to grant him liberation from material bondage, but Prahlāda accepted neither. Liberation and material opulence, he thought, are obstacles to devotional service, and therefore such gifts from the Supreme Personality of Godhead are not His actual mercy. Consequently, instead of accepting the results of karma and jñāna,

Prahlāda Mahārāja simply begged the Lord for engagement in the service of His servant.

PURPORT

Śrī Caitanya Mahāprabhu has instructed that an unalloyed devotee should consider himself a servant of the servant of the servant of the Supreme Lord (*gopī-bhartuḥ pāda-kamalayor dāsa-dāsānudāsaḥ*). In Vaiṣṇava philosophy, one should not even become a direct servant. Prahlāda Mahārāja was offered all the blessings of an opulent position in the material world and even the liberation of merging into Brahman, but he refused all this. He simply wanted to engage in the service of the servant of the servant of the Lord. Therefore Bali Mahārāja said that because his grandfather Prahlāda Mahārāja had rejected the blessings of the Supreme Personality of Godhead in terms of material opulence and liberation from material bondage, he truly understood his self-interest.

TEXT 26

तस्य महानुभावस्यानुपथममृजितकषायः को वास्मद्विधः परिहीणभगवदनुग्रह उपजिगमिषतीति ॥२६॥

tasya mahānubhāvasyānupatham amṛjita-kaṣāyaḥ ko vāsmad-vidhaḥ parihīṇa-bhagavad-anugraha upajigamiṣatīti.

tasya—of Prahlāda Mahārāja; *mahā-anubhāvasya*—who was an exalted devotee; *anupatham*—the path; *amṛjita-kaṣāyaḥ*—a person who is materially contaminated; *kaḥ*—what; *vā*—or; *asmat-vidhaḥ*—like us; *parihīṇa-bhagavat-anugrahaḥ*—being without the favor of the Supreme Personality of Godhead; *upajigamiṣati*—desires to follow; *iti*—thus.

TRANSLATION

Bali Mahārāja said: Persons like us, who are still attached to material enjoyment, who are contaminated by the modes of material nature and who lack the mercy of the Supreme Personality of Godhead, cannot follow the supreme path of Prahlāda Mahārāja, the exalted devotee of the Lord.

PURPORT

It is said that for spiritual realization one must follow great personalities like Lord Brahmā, Devarṣi Nārada, Lord Śiva and Prahlāda Mahārāja. The path of *bhakti* is not at all difficult if we follow in the footsteps of previous *ācāryas* and authorities, but those who are too materially contaminated by the modes of material nature cannot follow them. Although Bali Mahārāja was actually following the path of his grandfather, because of his great humility he thought that he was not. It is characteristic of advanced Vaiṣṇavas following the principles of *bhakti* that they think themselves ordinary human beings. This is not an artificial exhibition of humility; a Vaiṣṇava sincerely thinks this way and therefore never admits his exalted position.

TEXT 27

तस्यानुचरितमुपरिष्टाद्विस्तरिष्यते यस्य भगवान् स्वयमखिलजगद्गुरुर्नारायणो द्वारि गदापाणिरवतिष्ठते निजजनानुकम्पितहृदयो येनाङ्गुष्ठेन पदा दशकन्धरो योजनायुतायुतं दिग्विजय उच्चाटितः ॥२७॥

tasyānucaritam upariṣṭād vistariṣyate yasya bhagavān svayam akhila-
jagad-gurur nārāyaṇo dvāri gadā-pāṇir avatiṣṭhate nija-
janānukampita-hṛdayo yenāṅguṣṭhena padā daśa-kandharo
yojanāyutāyutaṁ dig-vijaya uccāṭitaḥ.

tasya—of Bali Mahārāja; *anucaritam*—the narration; *upariṣṭāt*—later (in the Eighth Canto); *vistariṣyate*—will be explained; *yasya*—of whom; *bhagavān*—the Supreme Personality of Godhead; *svayam*—personally; *akhila-jagat-guruḥ*—the master of all the three worlds; *nārāyaṇaḥ*—the Supreme Lord, Nārāyaṇa Himself; *dvāri*—at the gate; *gadā-pāṇiḥ*—bearing the club in His hand; *avatiṣṭhate*—stands; *nija-jana-anukampita-hṛdayaḥ*—whose heart is always filled with mercy for His devotees; *yena*—by whom; *aṅguṣṭhena*—by the big toe; *padā*—of His foot; *daśa-kandharaḥ*—Rāvaṇa, who had ten heads; *yojana-ayuta-ayutam*—a distance of eighty thousand miles; *dik-vijaye*—for the purpose of gaining victory over Bali Mahārāja; *uccāṭitaḥ*—driven away.

TRANSLATION

Śukadeva Gosvāmī continued: My dear King, how shall I glorify the character of Bali Mahārāja? The Supreme Personality of Godhead, the master of the three worlds, who is most compassionate to His own devotee, stands with club in hand at Bali Mahārāja's door. When Rāvaṇa, the powerful demon, came to gain victory over Bali Mahārāja, Vāmanadeva kicked him a distance of eighty thousand miles with His big toe. I shall

explain the character and activities of Bali Mahārāja later [in the Eighth Canto of Śrīmad-Bhāgavatam].

TEXT 28

ततोऽधस्तात्तलातले मयो नाम दानवेन्द्रस्त्रिपुराधिपतिर्भगवता पुरारिणा त्रिलोकीशं चिकीर्षुणा निर्दग्धस्वपुरत्रयस्तत्प्रसादाल्लब्धपदो मायाविनामाचार्यो महादेवेन परिरक्षितो विगतसुदर्शनभयो महीयते ॥२८॥

tato 'dhastāt talātale mayo nāma dānavendras tri-purādhipatir bhagavatā purāriṇā tri-lokī-śaṁ cikīrṣuṇā nirdagdha-sva-pura-trayas tat-prasādāl labdha-pado māyāvinām ācāryo mahādevena parirakṣito vigata-sudarśana-bhayo mahīyate.

tataḥ—the planet known as Sutala; *adhastāt*—below; *talātale*—in the planet known as Talātala; *mayaḥ*—Maya; *nāma*—named; *dānava-indraḥ*—the king of the Dānava demons; *tri-pura-adhipatiḥ*—the Lord of the three cities; *bhagavatā*—by the most powerful; *purāriṇā*—Lord Śiva, who is known as Tripurāri; *tri-lokī*—of the three worlds; *śam*—the good fortune; *cikīrṣuṇā*—who was desiring; *nirdagdha*—burned; *sva-pura-trayaḥ*—whose three cities; *tat-prasādāt*—by Lord Śiva's mercy; *labdha*—obtained; *padaḥ*—a kingdom; *māyā-vinām ācāryaḥ*—who is the *ācārya,* or master, of all the conjurers; *mahā-devena*—by Lord Śiva; *parirakṣitaḥ*—protected; *vigata-sudarśana-bhayaḥ*—who is not afraid of the Supreme Personality of Godhead and His Sudarśana *cakra; mahīyate*—is worshiped.

TRANSLATION

Beneath the planet known as Sutala is another planet, called Talātala, which is ruled by the Dānava demon named Maya. Maya is known as the ācārya [master] of all the māyāvīs, who can invoke the powers of sorcery. For the benefit of the three worlds, Lord Śiva, who is known as Tripurāri, once set fire to the three kingdoms of Maya, but later, being pleased with him, he returned his kingdom. Since that time, Maya Dānava has been protected by Lord Śiva, and therefore he falsely thinks that he need not fear the Sudarśana cakra of the Supreme Personality of Godhead.

TEXT 29

ततोऽधस्तान्महातले काद्रवेयाणां सर्पाणां नैकशिरसां क्रोधवशो नाम गणः कुहकतक्षककालियसुषेणादिप्रधाना महाभोगवन्तः पतत्त्रिराजाधिपतेः

पुरुषवाहादनवरतमुद्विजमानाः स्वकलत्रापत्यसुहृत्कुटुम्बसङ्गेन क्वचित्प्रमत्ता विहरन्ति ॥२९॥

tato 'dhastān mahātale kādraveyāṇāṁ sarpāṇāṁ naika-śirasāṁ krodhavaśo nāma gaṇaḥ kuhaka-takṣaka-kāliya-suṣeṇādi-pradhānā mahā-bhogavantaḥ patattri-rājādhipateḥ puruṣa-vāhād anavaratam udvijamānāḥ sva-kalatrāpatya-suhṛt-kuṭumba-saṅgena kvacit pramattā viharanti.

tataḥ—the planet Talātala; *adhastāt*—beneath; *mahātale*—in the planet known as Mahātala; *kādraveyāṇām*—of the descendants of Kadrū; *sarpāṇām*—who are big snakes; *na eka-śirasām*—who have many hoods; *krodha-vaśaḥ*—always subject to anger; *nāma*—named; *gaṇaḥ*—the group; *kuhaka*—Kuhaka; *takṣaka*—Takṣaka; *kāliya*—Kāliya; *suṣeṇa*—Suṣeṇa; *ādi*—and so on; *pradhānāḥ*—who are the prominent ones; *mahā-bhogavantaḥ*—addicted to all kinds of material enjoyment; *patattri-rāja-adhipateḥ*—from the king of all birds, Garuḍa; *puruṣa-vāhāt*—who carries the Supreme Personality of Godhead; *anavaratam*—constantly; *udvijamānāḥ*—afraid; *sva*—of their own; *kalatra-apatya*—wives and children; *suhṛt*—friends; *kuṭumba*—relatives; *saṅgena*—in the association; *kvacit*—sometimes; *pramattāḥ*—infuriated; *viharanti*—they sport.

TRANSLATION

The planetary system below Talātala is known as Mahātala. It is the abode of many-hooded snakes, descendants of Kadrū, who are always very angry. The great snakes who are prominent are Kuhaka, Takṣaka, Kāliya and Suṣeṇa. The snakes in Mahātala are always disturbed by fear of Garuḍa, the carrier of Lord Viṣṇu, but although they are full of anxiety, some of them nevertheless sport with their wives, children, friends and relatives.

PURPORT

It is stated here that the snakes who live in the planetary system known as Mahātala are very powerful and have many hoods. They live with their wives and children and consider themselves very happy, although they are always full of anxiety because of Garuḍa, who comes there to destroy them. This is the way of material life. Even if one lives in the most abominable condition, he still thinks himself happy with his wife, children, friends and relatives.

TEXT 30

ततोऽधस्ताद्रसातले दैतेया दानवाः पणयो नाम निवातकवचाः कालेया हिरण्यपुरवासिन इति विबुधप्रत्यनीका उत्पत्त्या महौजसो महासाहसिनो भगवतः सकललोकानुभावस्य हरेरेव तेजसा प्रतिहतबलावलेपा बिलेशया इव वसन्ति ये वै सरमयेन्द्रदूत्या वाग्भिर्मन्त्रवर्णाभिरिन्द्राद्बिभ्यति ॥३०॥

tato 'dhastād rasātale daiteyā dānavāḥ paṇayo nāma nivāta-kavacāḥ kāleyā hiraṇya-puravāsina iti vibudha-pratyanīkā utpattyā mahaujaso mahā-sāhasino bhagavataḥ sakala-lokānubhāvasya harer eva tejasā pratihata-balāvalepā bileśayā iva vasanti ye vai saramayendra-dūtyā vāgbhir mantra-varṇābhir indrād bibhyati.

tataḥ adhastāt—below the planetary system Mahātala; *rasātale*—on the planet called Rasātala; *daiteyāḥ*—the sons of Diti; *dānavāḥ*—the sons of Danu; *paṇayaḥ nāma*—named Paṇis; *nivāta-kavacāḥ*—Nivāta-kavacas; *kāleyāḥ*—Kāleyas; *hiraṇya-puravāsinaḥ*—Hiraṇya-puravāsīs; *iti*—thus; *vibudha-pratyanīkāḥ*—enemies of the demigods; *utpattyāḥ*—from birth; *mahā-ojasaḥ*—very powerful; *mahā-sāhasinaḥ*—very cruel; *bhagavataḥ*—of the Personality of Godhead; *sakala-loka-anubhāvasya*—who is auspicious for all planetary systems; *hareḥ*—of the Supreme Personality of Godhead; *eva*—certainly; *tejasā*—by the Sudarśana *cakra; pratihata*—defeated; *bala*—strength; *avalepāḥ*—and pride (because of bodily strength); *bila-īśayāḥ*—the snakes; *iva*—like; *vasanti*—they live; *ye*—who; *vai*—indeed; *saramayā*—by Saramā; *indra-dūtyā*—the messenger of Indra; *vāgbhiḥ*—by the words; *mantra-varṇābhiḥ*—in the form of a *mantra; indrāt*—from King Indra; *bibhyati*—are afraid.

TRANSLATION

Beneath Mahātala is the planetary system known as Rasātala, which is the abode of the demoniac sons of Diti and Danu. They are called Paṇis, Nivāta-kavacas, Kāleyas and Hiraṇya-puravāsīs [those living in Hiraṇya-pura]. They are all enemies of the demigods, and they reside in holes like snakes. From birth they are extremely powerful and cruel, and although they are proud of their strength, they are always defeated by the Sudarśana cakra of the Supreme Personality of Godhead, who rules all the planetary systems. When a female messenger from Indra named Saramā chants a particular curse, the serpentine demons of Mahātala become very afraid of Indra.

PURPORT

It is said that there was a great fight between these serpentine demons and Indra, the King of heaven. When the defeated demons met the female messenger Saramā, who was chanting a *mantra,* they became afraid, and therefore they are living in the planet called Rasātala.

TEXT 31

ततोऽधस्तात्पाताले नागलोकपतयो वासुकिप्रमुखाः शङ्खकुलिकमहाशङ्खश्वेतधनञ्जयधृतराष्ट्रशङ्खचूडकम्बलाश्वतरदेवदत्तादयो महाभोगिनो महामर्षा निवसन्ति येषामु ह वै पञ्चसप्तदशशतसहस्रशीर्षाणां फणासु विरचिता महामणयो रोचिष्णवः पातालविवरतिमिरनिकरं स्वरोचिषा विधमन्ति ॥३१॥

tato 'dhastāt pātāle nāga-loka-patayo vāsuki-pramukhāḥ śaṅkha-kulika-mahāśaṅkha-śveta-dhanañjaya-dhṛtarāṣṭra-śaṅkhacūḍa-kambalāśvatara-devadattādayo mahā-bhogino mahāmarṣā nivasanti yeṣām u ha vai pañca-sapta-daśa-śata-sahasra-śīrṣāṇāṁ phaṇāsu viracitā mahā-maṇayo rociṣṇavaḥ pātāla-vivara-timira-nikaraṁ sva-rociṣā vidhamanti.

tataḥ adhastāt—beneath that planet Rasātala; *pātāle*—on the planet known as Pātāla; *nāga-loka-patayaḥ*—the masters of the Nāgalokas; *vāsuki*—by Vāsuki; *pramukhāḥ*—headed; *śaṅkha*—Śaṅkha; *kulika*—Kulika; *mahā-śaṅkha*—Mahāśaṅkha; *śveta*—Śveta; *dhanañjaya*—Dhanañjaya; *dhṛtarāṣṭra*—Dhṛtarāṣṭra; *śaṅkha-cūḍa*—Śaṅkhacūḍa; *kambala*—Kambala; *aśvatara*—Aśvatara; *deva-datta*—Devadatta; *ādayaḥ*—and so on; *mahā-bhoginaḥ*—very addicted to material happiness; *mahā-amarṣāḥ*—greatly envious by nature; *nivasanti*—live; *yeṣām*—of all of them; *u ha*—certainly; *vai*—indeed; *pañca*—five; *sapta*—seven; *daśa*—ten; *śata*—one hundred; *sahasra*—one thousand; *śīrṣāṇām*—of those possessing hoods; *phaṇāsu*—on those hoods; *viracitāḥ*—fixed; *mahā-maṇayaḥ*—very valuable gems; *rociṣṇavaḥ*—full of effulgence; *pātāla-vivara*—the caves of the Pātāla planetary system; *timira-nikaram*—the mass of darkness; *sva-rociṣā*—by the effulgence of their hoods; *vidhamanti*—disperse.

TRANSLATION

Beneath Rasātala is another planetary system, known as Pātāla or Nāgaloka, where there are many demoniac serpents, the masters of

Nāgaloka, such as Śaṅkha, Kulika, Mahāśaṅkha, Śveta, Dhanañjaya, Dhṛtarāṣṭra, Śaṅkhacūḍa, Kambala, Aśvatara and Devadatta. The chief among them is Vāsuki. They are all extremely angry, and they have many, many hoods—some snakes five hoods, some seven, some ten, others a hundred and others a thousand. These hoods are bedecked with valuable gems, and the light emanating from the gems illuminates the entire planetary system of bila-svarga.

Thus end the Bhaktivedanta purports of the Fifth Canto, Twenty-fourth Chapter of Śrīmad-Bhāgavatam, *entitled "The Subterranean Heavenly Planets."*

CHAPTER TWENTY FIVE

The Glories of Lord Ananta

In this chapter, Śukadeva Gosvāmī describes Ananta, the source of Lord Śiva. Lord Ananta, whose body is completely spiritual, resides at the root of the planet Pātāla. He always lives in the core of Lord Śiva's heart, and He helps him destroy the universe. Ananta instructs Lord Śiva how to destroy the cosmos, and thus He is sometimes called *tāmasī*, or "one who is in the mode of darkness." He is the original Deity of material consciousness, and because He attracts all living entities, He is sometimes known as Saṅkarṣaṇa. The entire material world is situated on the hoods of Lord Saṅkarṣaṇa. From His forehead He transmits to Lord Śiva the power to destroy this material world. Because Lord Saṅkarṣaṇa is an expansion of the Supreme Personality of Godhead, many devotees offer Him prayers, and in the planetary system of Pātāla, all the *suras, asuras,* Gandharvas, Vidyādharas and learned sages offer Him their respectful obeisances. The Lord talks with them in a sweet voice. His bodily construction is completely spiritual and very, very beautiful. Anyone who hears about Him from a proper spiritual master becomes free from all material conceptions of life. The entire material energy is working according to the plans of Anantadeva. Therefore we should regard Him as the root cause of the material creation. There is no end to His strength, and no one can fully describe Him, even with countless mouths. Therefore He is called Ananta (unlimited). Being very merciful toward all living entities, He has exhibited His spiritual body. Śukadeva Gosvāmī describes the glories of Anantadeva to Mahārāja Parīkṣit in this way.

TEXT 1

श्रीशुक उवाच

तस्य मूलदेशे त्रिंशद्योजनसहस्रान्तर आस्ते या वै कला भगवतस्तामसी समाख्यातानन्त इति सात्वतीया द्रष्टृदृश्ययोः सङ्कर्षणमहमित्यभिमानलक्षणं यं सङ्कर्षणमित्याचक्षते ॥१॥

śrī-śuka uvāca

tasya mūla-deśe triṁśad-yojana-sahasrāntara āste yā vai kalā bhagavatas tāmasī samākhyātānanta iti sātvatīyā draṣṭṛ-dṛśyayoḥ saṅkarṣaṇam aham ity abhimāna-lakṣaṇaṁ yaṁ saṅkarṣaṇam ity ācakṣate.

śrī-śukaḥ uvāca—Śrī Śukadeva Gosvāmī said; *tasya*—of the planet Pātāla; *mūla-deśe*—in the region beneath the base; *triṁśat*—thirty; *yojana*—eight-mile units of measurement; *sahasra-antare*—at an interval of one thousand; *āste*—remains; *yā*—which; *vai*—indeed; *kalā*—an expansion of an expansion; *bhagavataḥ*—of the Supreme Personality of Godhead; *tāmasī*—related to darkness; *samākhyātā*—called; *anantaḥ*—Ananta; *iti*—thus; *sātvatīyāḥ*—the devotees; *draṣṭṛ-dṛśyayoḥ*—of matter and spirit; *saṅkarṣaṇam*—the drawing together; *aham*—I; *iti*—thus; *abhimāna*—by self-conception; *lakṣaṇam*—symptomized; *yam*—whom; *saṅkarṣaṇam*—Saṅkarṣaṇa; *iti*—thus; *ācakṣate*—learned scholars describe.

TRANSLATION

Śrī Śukadeva Gosvāmī said to Mahārāja Parīkṣit: My dear King, approximately 240,000 miles beneath the planet Pātāla lives another incarnation of the Supreme Personality of Godhead. He is the expansion of Lord Viṣṇu known as Lord Ananta or Lord Saṅkarṣaṇa. He is always in the transcendental position, but because He is worshiped by Lord Śiva, the deity of tamo-guṇa or darkness, He is sometimes called tāmasī. Lord Ananta is the predominating Deity of the material mode of ignorance as well as the false ego of all conditioned souls. When a conditioned living being thinks, "I am the enjoyer, and this world is meant to be enjoyed by me," this conception of life is dictated to him by Saṅkarṣaṇa. Thus the mundane conditioned soul thinks himself the Supreme Lord.

PURPORT

There is a class of men akin to Māyāvādī philosophers who misinterpret the *ahaṁ brahmāsmi* and *so 'ham* Vedic *mantras* to mean, "I am the Supreme Brahman" and "I am identical with the Lord." This kind of false conception, in which one thinks himself the supreme enjoyer, is a kind of illusion. It is described elsewhere in *Śrīmad-Bhāgavatam* (5.5.8): *janasya moho'yam ahaṁ mameti.* As explained in the above verse, Lord Saṅkarṣaṇa is the predominating Deity of this false conception. Kṛṣṇa confirms this in *Bhagavad-gītā* (15.15):

sarvasya cāhaṁ hṛdi sanniviṣṭo
mattaḥ smṛtir jñānam apohanaṁ ca

"I am seated in everyone's heart, and from Me come remembrance, knowledge and forgetfulness." The Lord is situated in everyone's heart as Saṅkarṣaṇa, and when a demon thinks himself one with the Supreme Lord, the Lord keeps him in that darkness. Although such a demoniac living entity is only an insignificant part of the Supreme Lord, he forgets his true position and thinks he is the Supreme Lord. Because this forgetfulness is created by Saṅkarṣaṇa, He is sometimes called *tāmasī*. The name *tāmasī* does not indicate that He has a material body. He is always transcendental, but because He is the Supersoul of Lord Śiva, who must perform tamasic activities, Saṅkarṣaṇa is sometimes called *tāmasī*.

TEXT 2

यस्येदं क्षितिमण्डलं भगवतोऽनन्तमूर्तेः सहस्रशिरस एकस्मिन्नेव शीर्षणि ध्रियमाणं सिद्धार्थ इव लक्ष्यते ॥२॥

yasyedaṁ kṣiti-maṇḍalaṁ bhagavato 'nanta-mūrteḥ sahasra-śirasa
ekasminn eva śīrṣaṇi dhriyamāṇaṁ siddhārtha iva lakṣyate.

yasya—of whom; *idam*—this; *kṣiti-maṇḍalam*—universe; *bhagavataḥ*—of the Supreme Personality of Godhead; *ananta-mūrteḥ*—in the form of Anantadeva; *sahasra-śirasaḥ*—who has thousands of hoods; *ekasmin*—on one; *eva*—only; *śīrṣaṇi*—hood; *dhriyamāṇam*—is being sustained; *siddhārthaḥ iva*—and like a white mustard seed; *lakṣyate*—is seen.

TRANSLATION

Śukadeva Gosvāmī continued: This great universe, situated on one of Lord Anantadeva's thousands of hoods, appears just like a white mustard seed. It is infinitesimal compared to the hood of Lord Ananta.

TEXT 3

यस्य ह वा इदं कालेनोपसञ्जिहीर्षतोऽमर्षविरचितरुचिरभ्रमद्भ्रुवोरन्तरेण साङ्कर्षणो नाम रुद्र एकादशव्यूहस्त्र्यक्षस्त्रिशिखं शूलमुत्तम्भयन्नुदतिष्ठत् ॥३॥

yasya ha vā idaṁ kālenopasañjihīrṣato 'marṣa-viracita-rucira-
bhramad-bhruvor antareṇa sāṅkarṣaṇo nāma rudra ekādaśa-vyūhas
try-akṣas tri-śikhaṁ śūlam uttambhayann udatiṣṭhat.

yasya—of whom; *ha vā*—indeed; *idam*—this (material world); *kālena*—in due course of time; *upasañjihīrṣataḥ*—desiring to destroy; *amarṣa*—by anger; *viracita*—formed; *rucira*—very beautiful; *bhramat*—moving; *bhruvoḥ* —the two eyebrows; *antareṇa*—from between; *sāṅkarṣaṇaḥ nāma*—named Sāṅkarṣaṇa; *rudraḥ*—an incarnation of Lord Śiva; *ekādaśa-vyūhaḥ*—who has eleven expansions; *tri-akṣaḥ*—three eyes; *tri-śikham*—having three points; *śūlam*—a trident; *uttambhayan*—raising; *udatiṣṭhat*—arose.

TRANSLATION

At the time of devastation, when Lord Anantadeva desires to destroy the entire creation, He becomes slightly angry. Then from between His two eyebrows appears three-eyed Rudra, carrying a trident. This Rudra, who is known as Sāṅkarṣaṇa, is the embodiment of the eleven Rudras, or incarnations of Lord Śiva. He appears in order to devastate the entire creation.

PURPORT

In each creation, the living entities are given a chance to close their business as conditioned souls. When they misuse this opportunity and do not go back home, back to Godhead, Lord Saṅkarṣaṇa becomes angry. The eleven Rudras, expansions of Lord Śiva, come out of Lord Saṅkarṣaṇa's eyebrows due to His angry mood, and all of them together devastate the entire creation.

TEXT 4

यस्याङ्घ्रिकमलयुगलारुणविशदनखमणिषण्डमण्डलेष्वहिपतयः सह सात्वतर्षभैरेकान्तभक्तियोगेनावनमन्तः स्ववदनानि परिस्फुरत्कुण्डलप्रभामण्डितगण्डस्थलान्यतिमनोहराणि प्रमुदितमनसः खलु विलोकयन्ति ॥४॥

yasyāṅghri-kamala-yugalāruṇa-viśada-nakha-maṇi-ṣaṇḍa-maṇḍaleṣv
ahi-patayaḥ saha sātvatarṣabhair ekānta-bhakti-yogenāvanamantaḥ
sva-vadanāni parisphurat-kuṇḍala-prabhā-maṇḍita-gaṇḍa-sthalāny
ati-manoharāṇi pramudita-manasaḥ khalu vilokayanti.

yasya—of whom; *aṅghri-kamala*—of lotus feet; *yugala*—of the pair; *aruṇa-viśada*—brilliant pink; *nakha*—of the nails; *maṇi-ṣaṇḍa*—like gems; *maṇḍaleṣu*—on the round surfaces; *ahi-patayaḥ*—the leaders of the snakes; *saha*—with; *sātvata-ṛṣabhaiḥ*—the best devotees; *ekānta-bhakti-yogena*—with unalloyed devotional service; *avanamantaḥ*—offering obeisances; *sva-vadanāni*—their own faces; *parisphurat*—glittering; *kuṇḍala*—of the earrings; *prabhā*—by the effulgence; *maṇḍita*—decorated; *gaṇḍa-sthalāni*

—whose cheeks; *ati-manoharāṇi*—very beautiful; *pramudita-manasaḥ*—their minds refreshed; *khalu*—indeed; *vilokayanti*—they see.

TRANSLATION

The pink, transparent toenails on the Lord's lotus feet are exactly like valuable gems polished to a mirror finish. When the unalloyed devotees and the leaders of the snakes offer their obeisances to Lord Saṅkarṣaṇa with great devotion, they become very joyful upon seeing their own beautiful faces reflected in His toenails. Their cheeks are decorated with glittering earrings, and the beauty of their faces is extremely pleasing to see.

TEXT 5

यस्यैव हि नागराजकुमार्य आशिष आशासानाश्चार्वङ्गवलयविलसित विशद विपुलधवलसुभगरुचिरभुजरजतस्तम्भेष्वगुरुचन्दनकुङ्कुमपङ्कानुलेपे-नावलिम्पमानास्तदभिमर्शनोन्मथितहृदयमकरध्वजावेशरुचिरललितस्मितास्तद-नुरागमदमुदितमदविघूर्णितारुणकरुणावलोकनयनवदनारविन्दं सव्रीडं किल विलोकयन्ति ॥५॥

yasyaiva hi nāga-rāja-kumārya āśiṣa āśāsānāś cārv-aṅga-valaya-
vilasita-viśada-vipula-dhavala-subhaga-rucira-bhuja-rajata-stambheṣv
aguru-candana-kuṅkuma-paṅkānulepenāvalimpamānās tad-
abhimarśanonmathita-hṛdaya-makara-dhvajāveśa-rucira-lalita-smitās
tad-anurāgamada-mudita-mada-vighūrṇitāruṇa-karuṇāvaloka-
nayana-vadanāravindaṁ savrīḍaṁ kila vilokayanti.

yasya—of whom; *eva*—certainly; *hi*—indeed; *nāga-rāja-kumāryaḥ*—the unmarried princesses of the serpent kings; *āśiṣaḥ*—blessings; *āśāsānāḥ*—hoping for; *cāru*—beautiful; *aṅga-valaya*—on the sphere of His body; *vilasita*—gleaming; *viśada*—spotless; *vipula*—long; *dhavala*—white; *subhaga*—indicating good fortune; *rucira*—beautiful; *bhuja*—on His arms; *rajata-stambheṣu*—like columns of silver; *aguru*—of aloe; *candana*—of sandalwood; *kuṅkuma*—of saffron; *paṅka*—from the pulp; *anulepena*—with an ointment; *avalimpamānāḥ*—smearing; *tat-abhimarśana*—by contact with His limbs; *unmathita*—agitated; *hṛdaya*—in their hearts; *makara-dhvaja*—of Cupid; *āveśa*—due to the entrance; *rucira*—very beautiful; *lalita*—delicate; *smitāḥ*—whose smiling; *tat*—of Him; *anurāga*—of attachment; *mada*—by the intoxication; *mudita*—delighted; *mada*—due to intoxication with kindness; *vighūrṇita*—rolling; *aruṇa*—pink; *karuṇa-avaloka*—glancing with kindness; *nayana*—eyes; *vadana*—and face; *aravindam*—like lotus flowers; *sa-vrīḍam*—with bashfulness; *kila*—indeed; *vilokayanti*—they see.

TRANSLATION

Lord Ananta's arms are attractively long, beautifully decorated with bangles and completely spiritual. They are white, and so they appear like silver columns. When the beautiful princesses of the serpent kings, hoping for the Lord's auspicious blessing, smear His arms with aguru pulp, sandalwood pulp and kuṅkuma, the touch of His limbs awakens lusty desires within them. Understanding their minds, the Lord looks at the princesses with a merciful smile, and they become bashful, realizing that He knows their desires. Then they smile beautifully and look upon the Lord's lotus face, which is beautified by reddish eyes rolling slightly from intoxication and delighted by love for His devotees.

PURPORT

When males and females touch each other's bodies, their lusty desires naturally awaken. It appears from this verse that there are similar sensations in spiritual bodies. Both Lord Ananta and the women giving Him pleasure had spiritual bodies. Thus all sensations originally exist in the spiritual body. This is confirmed in the *Vedānta-sūtra: janmādy asya yataḥ.* Śrīla Viśvanātha Cakravartī Ṭhākura has commented in this connection that the word *ādi* means *ādi-rasa,* the original lusty feeling, which is born from the Supreme. However, spiritual lust and material lust are as completely different as gold and iron. Only one who is very highly elevated in spiritual realization can understand the lusty feelings exchanged between Rādhā and Kṛṣṇa, or between Kṛṣṇa and the damsels of Vraja. Therefore, unless one is very experienced and advanced in spiritual realization, he is forbidden to discuss the lusty feelings of Kṛṣṇa and the *gopīs.* However, if one is a sincere and pure devotee, the material lust in his heart is completely vanquished as he discusses the lusty feelings between the *gopīs* and Kṛṣṇa, and he makes quick progress in spiritual life.

TEXT 6

स एव भगवाननन्तो ऽनन्तगुणार्णव आदिदेव उपसंहृतामर्षरोषवेगो लोकानां स्वस्तय आस्ते ॥६॥

sa eva bhagavān ananto 'nanta-guṇārṇava ādi-deva upasaṁhṛtāmarṣa-roṣa-vego lokānāṁ svastaya āste.

saḥ—that; *eva*—certainly; *bhagavān*—the Supreme Personality of Godhead; *anantaḥ*—Anantadeva; *ananta-guṇa-arṇavaḥ*—the reservoir of unlimited transcendental qualities; *ādi-devaḥ*—the original Lord, or nondifferent from the original Supreme Personality of Godhead; *upasaṁhṛta*—who has restrained; *amarṣa*—of His intolerance; *roṣa*—and wrath; *vegaḥ*—the force; *lokānām*—of all people on all planets; *svastaye*—for the welfare; *āste*—remains.

TRANSLATION

Lord Saṅkarṣaṇa is the ocean of unlimited spiritual qualities, and thus He is known as Anantadeva. He is nondifferent from the Supreme Personality of Godhead. For the welfare of all living entities within this material world, He resides in His abode, restraining His anger and intolerance.

PURPORT

Anantadeva's main mission is to dissolve this material creation, but He checks His anger and intolerance. This material world is created to give the conditioned souls another chance to go back home, back to Godhead, but most of them do not take advantage of this facility. After the creation, they again exercise their old propensity for lording it over the material world. These activities of the conditioned souls anger Anantadeva, and He desires to destroy the entire material world. Yet, because He is the Supreme Personality of Godhead, He is kind toward us and checks His anger and intolerance. Only at certain times does He express His anger and destroy the material world.

TEXT 7

ध्यायमानः सुरासुरोरगसिद्धगन्धर्वविद्याधरमुनिगणैरनवरतमदमुदितविकृ-
तविह्वललोचनः सुललितमुखरिकामृतेनाप्यायमानः स्वपार्षदविबुधयूथपती-
नपरिम्लानरागनवतुलसिकामोदमध्वासवेन माद्यन्मधुकरव्रातमधुरगीतश्रियं
वैजयन्तीं स्वां वनमालां नीलवासा एककुण्डलो हलककुदि कृतसुभगसुन्दरभुजो
भगवान्महेन्द्रो वारणेन्द्र इव काञ्चनीं कक्षामुदारलीलो बिभर्ति ॥७॥

dhyāyamānaḥ surāsuroraga-siddha-gandharva-vidyādhara-muni-
gaṇair anavarata-mada-mudita-vikṛta-vihvala-locanaḥ sulalita-
mukharikāmṛtenāpyāyamānaḥ sva-pārṣada-vibudha-yūtha-patīn
aparimlāna-rāga-nava-tulasikāmoda-madhv-āsavena mādyan
madhukara-vrāta-madhura-gīta-śriyaṁ vaijayantīṁ svāṁ vanamālāṁ

nīla-vāsā eka-kuṇḍalo hala-kakudi kṛta-subhaga-sundara-bhujo bhagavān mahendro vāraṇendra iva kāñcanīṁ kakṣām udāra-līlo bibharti.

dhyāyamānaḥ—being meditated upon; *sura*—of demigods; *asura*—demons; *uraga*—snakes; *siddha*—inhabitants of Siddhaloka; *gandharva*—inhabitants of Gandharvaloka; *vidyādhara*—Vidyādharas; *muni*—and of great sages; *gaṇaiḥ*—by groups; *anavarata*—constantly; *mada-mudita*—delighted by intoxication; *vikṛta*—moving to and fro; *vihvala*—rolling; *locanaḥ*—whose eyes; *su-lalita*—excellently composed; *mukharika*—of speech; *amṛtena*—by the nectar; *āpyāyamānaḥ*—pleasing; *sva-pārṣada*—His own associates; *vibudha-yūtha-patīn*—the heads of the different groups of demigods; *aparimlāna*—never faded; *rāga*—whose luster; *nava*—ever fresh; *tulasikā*—of the *tulasī* blossoms; *āmoda*—by the fragrance; *madhu-āsavena*—and the honey; *mādyan*—being intoxicated; *madhukara-vrāta*—of the bees; *madhura-gīta*—by the sweet singing; *śrīyam*—which is made more beautiful; *vaijayantīm*—the garland named *vaijayantī; svām*—His own; *vanamālām*—garland; *nīla-vāsāḥ*—covered with blue garments; *eka-kuṇḍalaḥ*—wearing only one earring; *hala-kakudi*—on the handle of a plow; *kṛta*—placed; *subhaga*—auspicious; *sundara*—beautiful; *bhujaḥ*—hands; *bhagavān*—the Supreme Personality of Godhead; *mahā-indraḥ*—the King of heaven; *vāraṇa-indraḥ*—the elephant; *iva*—like; *kāñcanīm*—golden; *kakṣām*—belt; *udāra-līlaḥ*—engaged in transcendental pastimes; *bibharti*—wears.

TRANSLATION

Śukadeva Gosvāmī continued: The demigods, the demons, the Uragas [serpentine demigods], the Siddhas, the Gandharvas, the Vidyādharas and many highly elevated sages constantly offer prayers to the Lord. Because He is intoxicated, the Lord looks bewildered, and His eyes, appearing like flowers in full bloom, move to and fro. He pleases His personal associates, the heads of the demigods, by the sweet vibrations emanating from His mouth. Dressed in bluish garments and wearing a single earring, He holds a plow on His back with His two beautiful and well-constructed hands. Appearing as white as the heavenly King Indra, He wears a golden belt around His waist and a vaijayantī garland of ever-fresh tulasī blossoms around His neck. Bees intoxicated by the honeylike fragrance of the tulasī flowers hum very sweetly around the garland, which thus becomes more and more beautiful. In this way, the Lord enjoys His very magnanimous pastimes.

TEXT 8

य एष एवमनुश्रुतो ध्यायमानो मुमुक्षूणामनादिकालकर्मवासनाग्रथितमविद्यामयं हृदयग्रन्थिं सत्त्वरजस्तमोमयमन्तर्हृदयं गत आशु निर्भिनत्ति तस्यानुभावान् भगवान् स्वायम्भुवो नारदः सह तुम्बुरुणा सभायां ब्रह्मणः संश्लोकयामास ॥ ८ ॥

ya eṣa evam anuśruto dhyāyamāno mumukṣūṇām anādi-kāla-karma-vāsanā-grathitam avidyāmayaṁ hṛdaya-granthiṁ sattva-rajas-tamomayam antar-hṛdayaṁ gata āśu nirbhinatti tasyānubhāvān bhagavān svāyambhuvo nāradaḥ saha tumburuṇā sabhāyāṁ brahmaṇaḥ saṁślokayām āsa.

yaḥ—who; *eṣaḥ*—this one; *evam*—thus; *anuśrutaḥ*—being heard from a bona fide spiritual master; *dhyāyamānaḥ*—being meditated upon; *mumukṣūṇām*—of persons desiring liberation from conditioned life; *anādi*—from immemorial; *kāla*—time; *karma-vāsanā*—by the desire for fruitive activities; *grathitam*—tied tightly; *avidyā-mayam*—consisting of the illusory energy; *hṛdaya-granthim*—the knot within the heart; *sattva-rajaḥ-tamaḥ-mayam*—made of the three modes of material nature; *antaḥ-hṛdayam*—in the core of the heart; *gataḥ*—situated; *āśu*—very soon; *nirbhinatti*—cuts; *tasya*—of Saṅkarṣaṇa; *anubhāvān*—the glories; *bhagavān*—the greatly powerful; *svāyambhuvaḥ*—the son of Lord Brahmā; *nāradaḥ*—the sage Nārada; *saha*—along with; *tumburuṇā*—the stringed instrument called a Tumburu; *sabhāyām*—in the assembly; *brahmaṇaḥ*—of Lord Brahmā; *saṁślokayām āsa*—described in verses.

TRANSLATION

If persons who are very serious about being liberated from material life hear the glories of Anantadeva from the mouth of a spiritual master in the chain of disciplic succession, and if they always meditate upon Saṅkarṣaṇa, the Lord enters the cores of their hearts, vanquishes all the dirty contamination of the material modes of nature, and cuts to pieces the hard knot within the heart, which has been tied tightly since time immemorial by the desire to dominate material nature through fruitive activities. Nārada Muni, the son of Lord Brahmā, always glorifies Anantadeva in his father's assembly. There he sings blissful verses of his own composition, accompanied by his stringed instrument [or a celestial singer] known as Tumburu.

PURPORT

None of these descriptions of Lord Anantadeva are imaginary. They are all transcendentally blissful and full of actual knowledge. However, unless one hears them directly from a bona fide spiritual master in the line of disciplic succession, one cannot understand them. This knowledge is delivered to Nārada by Lord Brahmā, and the great saint Nārada, along with his companion, Tumburu, distributes it all over the universe. Sometimes the Supreme Personality of Godhead is described as Uttamaśloka, one who is praised by beautiful poetry. Nārada composes various poems to glorify Lord Ananta, and therefore the word *saṁślokayām āsa* (praised by selected poetry) is used in this verse.

The Vaiṣṇavas in the Gauḍīya-sampradāya belong to the disciplic succession stemming from Lord Brahmā. Lord Brahmā is the spiritual master of Nārada, Nārada is the spiritual master of Vyāsadeva, and Vyāsadeva wrote the *Śrīmad-Bhāgavatam* as a commentary on the *Vedānta-sūtra.* Therefore all devotees in the Gauḍīya-sampradāya accept the activities of Lord Ananta related in the *Śrīmad-Bhāgavatam* as authentic, and they are thus benefited by going back home, back to Godhead. The contamination in the heart of a conditioned soul is like a huge accumulation of garbage created by the three modes of material nature, especially the modes of *rajas* (passion) and *tamas* (ignorance). This contamination becomes manifest in the form of lusty desires and greed for material possessions. As confirmed herein, unless one receives transcendental knowledge in disciplic succession, there is no question of his becoming purified of this contamination.

TEXT 9

उत्पत्तिस्थितिलयहेतवोऽस्य कल्पाः
सत्त्वाद्याः प्रकृतिगुणा यदीक्षयाऽऽसन् ।
यद्रूपं ध्रुवमकृतं यदेकमात्मन्
नानाधात्कथमु ह वेद तस्य वर्त्म ॥९॥

utpatti-sthiti-laya-hetavo 'sya kalpāḥ
sattvādyāḥ prakṛti-guṇā yad-īkṣayāsan
yad-rūpaṁ dhruvam akṛtaṁ yad ekam ātman
nānādhāt katham u ha veda tasya vartma

utpatti—of creation; *sthiti*—maintenance; *laya*—and dissolution; *hetavaḥ*—the original causes; *asya*—of this material world; *kalpāḥ*—capable of acting; *sattva-ādyāḥ*—headed by the *sattva-guṇa; prakṛti-guṇāḥ*—the modes of material nature; *yat*—of whom; *īkṣayā*—by the glance; *āsan*—became; *yat-rūpam*—the form of whom; *dhruvam*—unlimited; *akṛtam*—uncreated; *yat*—who; *ekam*—one; *ātman*—in Himself; *nānā*—variously; *adhāt*—has manifested; *katham*—how; *u ha*—certainly; *veda*—can understand; *tasya*—His; *vartma*—path.

TRANSLATION

By His glance, the Supreme Personality of Godhead enables the modes of material nature to act as the causes of universal creation, maintenance and destruction. The Supreme Soul is unlimited and beginningless, and although He is one, He has manifested Himself in many forms. How can human society understand the ways of the Supreme?

PURPORT

From Vedic literature we learn that when the Supreme Lord glances (*sa aikṣata*) over the material energy, the three modes of material nature become manifest and create material variety. Before He glances over the material energy, there is no possibility of the creation, maintenance and annihilation of the material world. The Lord existed before the creation, and consequently He is eternal and unchanging. Therefore how can any human being, however great a scientist or philosopher he may be, understand the ways of the Supreme Personality of Godhead?

The following quotations from *Caitanya-bhāgavata* (*Ādi-khaṇḍa,* 1.48–52 and 1.58–69) tell of the glories of Lord Ananta:

ki brahmā, ki śiva, ki sanakādi 'kumāra'
vyāsa, śuka, nāradādi, 'bhakta' nāma yāṅra

"Lord Brahmā, Lord Śiva, the four Kumāras [Sanaka, Sanātana, Sanandana and Sanāt-kumāra], Vyāsadeva, Śukadeva Gosvāmī and Nārada are all pure devotees, eternal servants of the Lord."

sabāra pūjita śrī-ananta-mahāśaya
sahasra-vadana prabhu—bhakti-rasamaya

"Lord Śrī Ananta is worshiped by all the uncontaminated devotees mentioned above. He has thousands of hoods and is the reservoir of all devotional service."

ādideva, mahā-yogī, 'īśvara', 'vaiṣṇava'
mahimāra anta iṅhā nā jānaye saba

"Lord Ananta is the original person and the great mystic controller. At the same time, He is a servant of God, a Vaiṣṇava. Since there is no end to His glories, no one can understand Him fully."

sevana śunilā, ebe śuna ṭhākurāla
ātma-tantre yena-mate vaisena pātāla

"I have already spoken to you of His service to the Lord. Now hear how the self-sufficient Anantadeva exists in the lower planetary system of Pātāla."

śrī-nārada-gosāñi 'tumburu' kari' saṅge
se yaśa gāyena brahmā-sthāne śloka-vandhe

"Bearing his stringed instrument, the *tumburu,* on his shoulders, the great sage Nārada Muni always glorifies Lord Ananta. Nārada Muni has composed many transcendental verses in praise of the Lord."

sṛṣṭi, sthiti, pralaya, sattvādi yata guṇa
yāṅra dṛṣṭi-pāte haya, yāya punaḥ punaḥ

"Simply due to the glance of Lord Ananta, the three material modes of nature interact and produce creation, maintenance and annihilation. These modes of nature appear again and again."

advitīya-rūpa, satya anādi mahattva
tathāpi 'ananta' haya, ke bujhe se tattva?

"The Lord is glorified as one without a second and as the supreme truth who has no beginning. Therefore He is called Anantadeva [unlimited]. Who can understand Him?"

śuddha-sattva-mūrti prabhu dharena karuṇāya
ye-vigrahe sabāra prakāśa sulīlāya

"His form is completely spiritual, and He manifests it only by His mercy. All the activities in this material world are conducted only in His form."

yāṅhāra taraṅga śikhi' siṁha mahāvalī
nija-jana-mano rañje hañā kutūhalī

"He is very powerful and always prepared to please His personal associates and devotees."

ye ananta-nāmera śravaṇa-saṅkīrtane
ye-te mate kene nāhi bole ye-te jane

aśeṣa-janmera bandha chiṇḍe sei-kṣaṇe
ataeva vaiṣṇava nā chāḍe kabhu tāne

"If we simply try to engage in the congregational chanting of the glories of Lord Anantadeva, the dirty things in our hearts, accumulated during many births, will immediately be washed away. Therefore a Vaiṣṇava never loses an opportunity to glorify Anantadeva."

'śeṣa' ba-i saṁsārera gati nāhi āra
anantera nāme sarva-jīvera uddhāra

"Lord Anantadeva is known as Śeṣa [the unlimited end] because He ends our passage through this material world. Simply by chanting His glories, everyone can be liberated."

ananta pṛthivī-giri samudra-sahite
ye-prabhu dharena gire pālana karite

"On His head, Anantadeva sustains the entire universe, with its millions of planets containing enormous oceans and mountains."

sahasra phaṇāra eka-phaṇe 'bindu' yena
ananta vikrama, nā jānena, 'āche' hena

"He is so large and powerful that this universe rests on one of His hoods just like a drop of water. He does not know where it is."

sahasra-vadane kṛṣṇa-yaśa nirantara
gāite āchena ādi-deva mahī-dhara

"While bearing the universe on one of His hoods, Anantadeva chants the glories of Kṛṣṇa with each of His thousands of mouths."

gāyena ananta, śrī-yaśera nāhi anta
jaya-bhaṅga nāhi kāru, doṅhe—balavanta

"Although He has been chanting the glories of Lord Kṛṣṇa since time immemorial, He has still not come to their end."

Adyāpiha 'śeṣa'-deva sahasra-śrī-mukhe
gāyena caitanya-yaśa anta nāhi dekhe

"To this very day, Lord Ananta continues to chant the glories of Śrī Caitanya Mahāprabhu, and still He finds no end to them."

TEXT 10

मूर्तिं नः पुरुकृपया बभार सत्त्वं
संशुद्धं सदसदिदं विभाति तत्र ।
यल्लीलां मृगपतिराददेऽनवद्या-
मादातुं स्वजनमनांस्युदारवीर्यः ॥१०॥

mūrtiṁ naḥ puru-kṛpayā babhāra sattvaṁ
saṁśuddhaṁ sad-asad idaṁ vibhāti tatra
yal-līlāṁ mṛga-patir ādade 'navadyām
ādātuṁ svajana-manāṁsy udāra-vīryaḥ

mūrtim—different forms of the Supreme Personality of Godhead; *naḥ*—unto us; *puru-kṛpayā*—because of great mercy; *babhāra*—exhibited; *sattvam*—existence; *saṁśuddham*—completely transcendental; *sat-asat idam*—this material manifestation of cause and effect; *vibhāti*—shines; *tatra*—in whom; *yat-līlām*—the pastimes of whom; *mṛga-patiḥ*—the master of all living beings, who is exactly like a lion (the master of all other animals); *ādade*—taught; *anavadyām*—without material contamination; *ādātum*—to conquer; *sva-jana-manāṁsi*—the minds of His devotees; *udāra-vīryaḥ*—who is most liberal and powerful.

TRANSLATION

This manifestation of subtle and gross matter exists within the Supreme Personality of Godhead. Out of causeless mercy toward His devotees, He exhibits various forms, which are all transcendental. The Supreme Lord is most liberal, and He possesses all mystic power. To conquer the minds of His devotees and give pleasure to their hearts, He appears in different incarnations and manifests many pastimes.

PURPORT

Śrīla Jīva Gosvāmī has translated this verse as follows. "The Supreme Personality of Godhead is the cause of all causes. It is by His will that gross and subtle ingredients interact. He appears in various incarnations just to please the hearts of His pure devotees." For example, the Supreme Lord appeared in the transcendental incarnation of Lord Varāha (the boar) just to please His devotees by lifting the planet earth from the Garbhodaka Ocean.

TEXT 11

यन्नाम श्रुतमनुकीर्तयेदकस्मा-
दार्तो वा यदि पतितः प्रलम्भनाद्वा ।
हन्त्यंहः सपदि नृणामशेषमन्यं
कं शेषाद्भगवत आश्रयेन्मुमुक्षुः ॥११॥

yan-nāma śrutam anukīrtayed akasmād
ārto vā yadi patitaḥ pralambhanād vā
hanty aṁhaḥ sapadi nṛṇām aśeṣam anyaṁ
kaṁ śeṣād bhagavata āśrayen mumukṣuḥ

yat—of whom; *nāma*—the holy name; *śrutam*—heard; *anukīrtayet*—may chant or repeat; *akasmāt*—by accident; *ārtaḥ*—a distressed person; *vā*—or; *yadi*—if; *patitaḥ*—a fallen person; *pralambhanāt*—out of joking; *vā*—or; *hanti*—destroys; *aṁhaḥ*—sinful; *sapadi*—that instant; *nṛṇām*—of human society; *aśeṣam*—unlimited; *anyam*—of other; *kam*—what; *śeṣāt*—than Lord Śeṣa; *bhagavataḥ*—the Supreme Personality of Godhead; *āśrayet*—should take shelter of; *mumukṣuḥ*—anyone desiring liberation.

TRANSLATION

Even if he be distressed or degraded, any person who chants the holy name of the Lord, having heard it from a bona fide spiritual master, is immediately purified. Even if he chants the Lord's name jokingly or by chance, he and anyone who hears him are freed from all sins. Therefore how can anyone seeking disentanglement from the material clutches avoid chanting the name of Lord Śeṣa? Of whom else should one take shelter?

TEXT 12

मूर्धन्यर्पितमणुवत्सहस्रमूर्ध्नो
भूगोलं सगिरिसरित्समुद्रसत्त्वम् ।
आनन्त्यादनिमितविक्रमस्य भूम्नः
को वीर्याण्यधिगणयेत्सहस्रजिह्वः ॥१२॥

mūrdhany arpitam aṇuvat sahasra-mūrdhno
bhū-golaṁ sagiri-sarit-samudra-sattvam
ānantyād animita-vikramasya bhūmnaḥ
ko vīryāṇy adhi gaṇayet sahasra-jihvaḥ

mūrdhani—on a hood or head; *arpitam*—fixed; *aṇu-vat*—just like an atom; *sahasra-mūrdhnaḥ*—of Ananta, who has thousands of hoods; *bhū-golam*—this universe; *sa-giri-sarit-samudra-sattvam*—with many mountains, trees, oceans and living entities; *ānantyāt*—due to being unlimited; *animita-vikramasya*—whose power is immeasurable; *bhūmnaḥ*—the Supreme Lord; *kaḥ*—who; *vīryāṇi*—potencies; *adhi*—indeed; *gaṇayet*—can count; *sahasra-jihvaḥ*—although having thousands of tongues.

TRANSLATION

Because the Lord is unlimited, no one can estimate His power. This entire universe, filled with its many great mountains, rivers, oceans, trees and living entities, is resting just like an atom on one of His many thousands of hoods. Is there anyone, even with thousands of tongues, who can describe His glories?

TEXT 13

एवम्प्रभावो भगवाननन्तो
दुरन्तवीर्योरुगुणानुभावः ।
मूले रसायाः स्थित आत्मतन्त्रो
यो लीलया क्ष्मां स्थितये बिभर्ति ॥ १३ ॥

evam-prabhāvo bhagavān ananto
duranta-vīryoru-guṇānubhāvaḥ
mūle rasāyāḥ sthita ātma-tantro
yo līlayā kṣmāṁ sthitaye bibharti

evam-prabhāvaḥ—who is so powerful; *bhagavān*—the Supreme Personality of Godhead; *anantaḥ*—Ananta; *duranta-vīrya*—insurmountable prowess; *uru*—great; *guṇa-anubhāvaḥ*—possessing transcendental qualities and glories; *mūle*—at the base; *rasāyāḥ*—of the lower planetary systems; *sthitaḥ*—existing; *ātma-tantraḥ*—completely self-sufficient; *yaḥ*—who; *līlayā*—easily; *kṣmām*—the universe; *sthitaye*—for its maintenance; *bibharti*—sustains.

TRANSLATION

There is no end to the great and glorious qualities of that powerful Lord Anantadeva. Indeed, His prowess is unlimited. Though self-sufficient, He Himself is the support of everything. He resides beneath the lower planetary systems and easily sustains the entire universe.

TEXT 14

एता ह्येवेह नृभिरुपगन्तव्या गतयो यथाकर्मविनिर्मिता यथोपदेशमनुवर्णिताः कामान् कामयमानैः ॥१४॥

etā hy eveha nṛbhir upagantavyā gatayo yathā-karma-vinirmitā yathopadeśam anuvarṇitāḥ kāmān kāmayamānaiḥ.

etāḥ—all these; *hi*—indeed; *eva*—certainly; *iha*—in this universe; *nṛbhiḥ*—by all living entities; *upagantavyāḥ*—achievable; *gatayaḥ*—destinations; *yathā-karma*—according to one's past activities; *vinirmitāḥ*—created; *yathā-upadeśam*—as instructed; *anuvarṇitāḥ*—described accordingly; *kāmān*—material enjoyment; *kāmayamānaiḥ*—by those who are desiring.

TRANSLATION

My dear King, as I heard of it from my spiritual master, I have fully described to you the creation of this material world according to the fruitive activities and desires of the conditioned souls. Those conditioned souls, who are full of material desires, achieve various situations in different planetary systems, and in this way they live within this material creation.

PURPORT

In this regard, Śrīla Bhaktivinoda Ṭhākura sings,

anādi karama-phale,
paḍi' bhavārṇava-jale, taribāre nā dekhi upāya

"My Lord, I do not know when I commenced my material life, but I can certainly experience that I have fallen in the deep ocean of nescience. Now I can also see that there is no other way to get out of it than to take shelter of Your lotus feet." Similarly, Śrī Caitanya Mahāprabhu offers the following prayer:

ayi nanda-tanuja kiṅkaraṁ
patitaṁ māṁ viṣame bhavāmbudhau
kṛpayā tava pāda-paṅkaja-
sthita-dhūlī-sadṛśaṁ vicintaya

"My dear Lord, son of Nanda Mahārāja, I am Your eternal servant. Somehow or other, I have fallen into this ocean of nescience. Kindly, therefore, save me from this horrible condition of materialistic life."

TEXT 15

एतावतीर्हि राजन् पुंसः प्रवृत्तिलक्षणस्य धर्मस्य विपाकगतय उच्चावचा विसदृशा यथाप्रश्नं व्याचख्ये किमन्यत्कथयाम इति ॥१५॥

etāvatīr hi rājan puṁsaḥ pravṛtti-lakṣaṇasya dharmasya vipāka-gataya uccāvacā visadṛśā yathā-praśnaṁ vyācakhye kim anyat kathayāma iti.

etāvatīḥ—of such a kind; *hi*—certainly; *rājan*—O King; *puṁsaḥ*—of the human being; *pravṛtti-lakṣaṇasya*—symptomized by inclinations; *dharmasya*—of the execution of duties; *vipāka-gatayaḥ*—the resultant destinations; *ucca-avacāḥ*—high and low; *visadṛśāḥ*—different; *yathā-praśnam*—as you inquired; *vyācakhye*—I have described; *kim anyat*—what else; *kathayāma*—shall I speak; *iti*—thus.

TRANSLATION

My dear King, I have thus described how people generally act according to their different desires and, as a result, get different types of bodies in higher or lower planets. You inquired of these things from me, and I have explained to you whatever I have heard from authorities. What shall I speak of now?

Thus end the Bhaktivedanta purports of the Fifth Canto, Twenty-fifth Chapter, of the Śrīmad-Bhāgavatam, *entitled "The Glories of Lord Ananta."*

CHAPTER TWENTY-SIX

A Description of the Hellish Planets

The Twenty-sixth Chapter describes how a sinful man goes to different hells, where he is punished in various ways by the assistants of Yamarāja. As stated in the *Bhagavad-gītā* (3.27):

prakṛteḥ kriyamāṇāni
guṇaiḥ karmāṇi sarvaśaḥ
ahaṅkāra-vimūḍhātmā
kartāham iti manyate

"The bewildered spirit soul, under the influence of the three modes of material nature, thinks himself to be the doer of activities, which are in actuality carried out by nature." The foolish person thinks he is independent of any law. He thinks there is no God or regulative principle and that he can do whatever he likes. Thus he engages in different sinful activities, and as a result, he is put into different hellish conditions life after life, to be punished by the laws of nature. The basic principle of his suffering is that he foolishly thinks himself independent, although he is strictly under the control of the laws of material nature. These laws act due to the influence of the three modes of nature, and therefore each human being also works under three different types of influence. According to how he acts, he suffers different reactions in his next life or in this life. Religious persons act differently from atheists, and therefore they suffer different reactions.

Śukadeva Gosvāmī describes the following twenty-eight hells: Tāmisra, Andhatāmisra, Raurava, Mahāraurava, Kumbhīpāka, Kālasūtra, Asi-patravana, Sūkaramukha, Andhakūpa, Kṛmibhojana, Sandaṁśa, Taptasūrmi, Vajrakaṇṭaka-śālmalī, Vaitaraṇī, Pūyoda, Prāṇarodha, Viśasana, Lālābhakṣa, Sārameyādana, Avīci, Ayaḥpāna, Kṣārakardama, Rakṣogaṇa-bhojana, Śūlaprota, Dandaśūka, Avaṭa-nirodhana, Paryāvartana and Sūcīmukha.

A person who steals another's money, wife or possessions is put into the hell known as Tāmisra. A man who tricks someone and enjoys his wife is put into the extremely hellish condition known as Andhatāmisra. A foolish person absorbed in the bodily concept of life, who on the basis of this principle maintains himself or his wife and children by committing violence against other living entities, is put into the hell known as Raurava. There the animals he killed take birth as creatures called *rurus* and cause great suffering for him. Those who kill different animals and birds and then cook them are put by the agents of Yamarāja into the hell known as Kumbhīpāka, where they are boiled in oil. A person who kills a *brāhmaṇa* is put into the hell known as Kālasūtra, where the land, perfectly level and made of copper, is as hot as an oven. The killer of a *brāhmaṇa* burns in that land for many years. One who does not follow scriptural injunctions but who does everything whimsically or follows some rascal is put into the hell known as Asi-patravana. A government official who poorly administers justice, or who punishes an innocent man, is taken by the assistants of Yamarāja to the hell known as Sūkaramukha, where he is mercilessly beaten.

God has given advanced consciousness to the human being. Therefore he can feel the suffering and happiness of other living beings. The human being bereft of his conscience, however, is prone to cause suffering for other living beings. The assistants of Yamarāja put such a person into the hell known as Andhakūpa, where he receives proper punishment from his victims. Any person who does not receive or feed a guest properly but who personally enjoys eating is put into the hell known as Kṛmibhojana. There an unlimited number of worms and insects continuously bite him.

A thief is put into the hell known as Sandaṁśa. A person who has sexual relations with a woman who is not to be enjoyed is put into the hell known as Taptasūrmi. A person who enjoys sexual relations with animals is put into the hell known as Vajrakaṇṭaka-śālmalī. A person born into an aristocratic or highly placed family but who does not act accordingly is put into the hellish trench of blood, pus and urine called the Vaitaraṇī River. One who lives like an animal is put into the hell called Pūyoda. A person who mercilessly kills animals in the forest without sanction is put into the hell called Prāṇarodha. A person who kills animals in the name of religious sacrifice is put into the hell named Viśasana. A man who forces his wife to drink his semen is put into the hell called Lālābhakṣa. One who sets a fire or administers poison to kill someone is put into the hell known as Sārameyādana. A man who earns his livelihood by bearing false witness is put into the hell known as Avīci.

A person addicted to drinking wine is put into the hell named Ayaḥpāna. One who violates etiquette by not showing proper respect to superiors is put into the hell known as Kṣārakardama. A person who sacrifices human beings to Bhairava is put into the hell called Rakṣogaṇa-bhojana. A person who kills pet animals is put into the hell called Śūlaprota. A person who gives trouble to others is put into the hell known as Dandaśūka. One who imprisons a living entity within a cave is put into the hell known as Avaṭa-nirodhana. A person who shows unwarranted wrath toward a guest in his house is put into the hell called Paryāvartana. A person maddened by possessing riches and thus deeply absorbed in thinking of how to collect money is put into the hell known as Sūcīmukha.

After describing the hellish planets, Śukadeva Gosvāmī describes how pious persons are elevated to the highest planetary system, where the demigods live, and how they then come back again to this earth when the results of their pious activities are finished. Finally he describes the universal form of the Lord and glorifies the Lord's activities.

TEXT 1

राजोवाच
महर्ष एतद्वैचित्र्यं लोकस्य कथमिति ॥१॥

rājovāca
maharṣa etad vaicitryaṁ lokasya katham iti.

rājā uvāca—the King said; *maharṣe*—O great saint (Śukadeva Gosvāmī); *etat*—this; *vaicitryam*—variegatedness; *lokasya*—of the living entities; *katham*—how; *iti*—thus.

TRANSLATION

King Parīkṣit inquired from Śukadeva Gosvāmī: My dear sir, why are the living entities put into different material situations? Kindly explain this to me.

PURPORT

Śrīla Viśvanātha Cakravartī Ṭhākura explains that the different hellish planets within this universe are held slightly above the Garbhodaka Ocean and remain situated there. This chapter describes how all sinful persons go to these hellish planets and how they are punished there by the assistants of Yamarāja. Different individuals with different bodily features enjoy or suffer various reactions according to their past deeds.

TEXT 2

ऋषिरुवाच
त्रिगुणत्वात्कर्तुः श्रद्धया कर्मगतयः पृथग्विधाः सर्वा एव सर्वस्य तारतम्येन भवन्ति ॥२॥

ṛṣir uvāca
tri-guṇatvāt kartuḥ śraddhayā karma-gatayaḥ pṛthag-vidhāḥ sarvā eva sarvasya tāratamyena bhavanti.

ṛṣiḥ uvāca—the great saint (Śukadeva Gosvāmī) said; *tri-guṇatvāt*—because of the three modes of material nature; *kartuḥ*—of the worker; *śraddhayā*—because of the attitudes; *karma-gatayaḥ*—destinations resulting from activity; *pṛthak*—different; *vidhāḥ*—varieties; *sarvāḥ*—all; *eva*—thus; *sarvasya*—of all of them; *tāratamyena*—in different degrees; *bhavanti*—become possible.

TRANSLATION

The great sage Śukadeva Gosvāmī said: My dear King, in this material world there are three kinds of activities—those in the mode of goodness, the mode of passion and the mode of ignorance. Because all people are influenced by the three modes of material nature, the results of their activities are also divided into three. One who acts in the mode of goodness is religious and happy, one who acts in passion achieves mixed misery and happiness, and one who acts under the influence of ignorance is always unhappy and lives like an animal. Because of the varying degrees to which the living entities are influenced by the different modes of nature, their destinations are also of different varieties.

TEXT 3

अथेदानीं प्रतिषिद्धलक्षणस्याधर्मस्य तथैव कर्तुः श्रद्धाया वैसादृश्यात्कर्मफलं विसदृशं भवति या ह्यनाद्यविद्यया कृतकामानां तत्परिणामलक्षणाः सृतयः सहस्रशः प्रवृत्तास्तासां प्राचुर्येणानुवर्णयिष्यामः ॥३॥

athedānīṁ pratiṣiddha-lakṣaṇasyādharmasya tathaiva kartuḥ
śraddhāyā vaisādṛśyāt karma-phalaṁ visadṛśaṁ bhavati yā hy anādy-
avidyayā kṛta-kāmānāṁ tat-pariṇāma-lakṣaṇāḥ sṛtayaḥ sahasraśaḥ
pravṛttās tāsāṁ prācuryeṇānuvarṇayiṣyāmaḥ.

atha—thus; *idānīm*—now; *pratiṣiddha*—by what is forbidden; *lakṣaṇasya*—symptomized; *adharmasya*—of impious activities; *tathā*—so also; *eva*—certainly; *kartuḥ*—of the performer; *śraddhāyāḥ*—of faith; *vaisādṛśyāt*—by the difference; *karma-phalam*—the reaction of fruitive activities; *visadṛśam*—different; *bhavati*—is; *yā*—which; *hi*—indeed; *anādi*—from time immemorial; *avidyayā*—by ignorance; *kṛta*—performed; *kāmānām*—of persons possessing many lusty desires; *tat-pariṇāma-lakṣaṇāḥ*—the symptoms of the results of such impious desires; *sṛtayaḥ*—hellish conditions of life; *sahasraśaḥ*—by thousands upon thousands; *pravṛttāḥ*—resulted; *tāsām*—them; *prācuryeṇa*—very widely; *anuvarṇayiṣyāmaḥ*—I shall explain.

TRANSLATION

Just as by executing various pious activities one achieves different positions in heavenly life, by acting impiously one achieves different positions in hellish life. Those who are activated by the material mode of ignorance engage in impious activities, and according to the extent of their ignorance, they are placed in different grades of hellish life. If one acts in the mode of ignorance because of madness, his resulting misery is the least severe. One who acts impiously but knows the distinction between pious and impious activities is placed in a hell of intermediate severity. And for one who acts impiously and ignorantly because of atheism, the resultant hellish life is the worst. Because of ignorance, every living entity has been carried by various desires into thousands of different hellish planets since time immemorial. I shall try to describe them as far as possible.

TEXT 4

राजोवाच

नरका नाम भगवन् किं देशविशेषा अथवा बहिस्त्रिलोक्या आहोस्विदन्तराल इति ॥४॥

rājovāca

narakā nāma bhagavan kiṁ deśa-viśeṣā athavā bahis tri-lokyā āhosvid antarāla iti.

rājā uvāca—the King said; *narakāḥ*—the hellish regions; *nāma*—named; *bhagavan*—O my Lord; *kim*—whether; *deśa-viśeṣāḥ*—a particular country; *athavā*—or; *bahiḥ*—outside; *tri-lokyāḥ*—the three worlds (the universe); *āhosvit*—or; *antarāle*—in the intermediate spaces within the universe; *iti*—thus.

TRANSLATION

King Parīkṣit inquired from Śukadeva Gosvāmī: My dear lord, are the hellish regions outside the universe, within the covering of the universe, or in different places on this planet?

TEXT 5

ऋषिरुवाच

अन्तराल एव त्रिजगत्यास्तु दिशि दक्षिणस्यामधस्ताद्भूमेरुपरिष्टाच्च जलाद्य-स्यामग्निष्वात्तादयः पितृगणा दिशि स्वानां गोत्राणां परमेण समाधिना सत्या एवाशिष आशासाना निवसन्ति ॥५॥

ṛṣir uvāca
antarāla eva tri-jagatyās tu diśi dakṣiṇasyām adhastād bhūmer
upariṣṭāc ca jalād yasyām agniṣvāttādayaḥ pitṛ-gaṇā diśi svānāṁ
gotrāṇāṁ paramena samādhinā satyā evāśiṣa āśāsānā nivasanti.

ṛṣiḥ uvāca—the great sage replied; *antarāle*—in the intermediate space; *eva*—certainly; *tri-jagatyāḥ*—of the three worlds; *tu*—but; *diśi*—in the direction; *dakṣiṇasyām*—southern; *adhastāt*—beneath; *bhūmeḥ*—on the earth; *upariṣṭāt*—a little above; *ca*—and; *jalāt*—the Garbhodaka Ocean; *yasyām*—in which; *agniṣvāttā-ādayaḥ*—headed by Agniṣvāttā; *pitṛ-gaṇāḥ*—the persons known as *pitās; diśi*—direction; *svānām*—their own; *gotrāṇām*—of the families; *paramena*—with great; *samādhinā*—absorption in thoughts of the Lord; *satyāḥ*—in truth; *eva*—certainly; *āśiṣaḥ*—blessings; *āśāsānāḥ*—desiring; *nivasanti*—they live.

TRANSLATION

The great sage Śukadeva Gosvāmī answered: All the hellish planets are situated in the intermediate space between the three worlds and the Garbhodaka Ocean. They lie on the southern side of the universe, beneath Bhū-maṇḍala, and slightly above the water of the Garbhodaka Ocean. Pitṛloka is also located in this region between the Garbhodaka Ocean and the lower planetary systems. All the residents of Pitṛloka, headed by Agniṣvāttā, meditate in great samādhi on the Supreme Personality of Godhead and always wish their families well.

PURPORT

As previously explained, below our planetary system are seven lower planetary systems, the lowest of which is called Pātālaloka. Beneath Pātālaloka are other planets, known as Narakaloka, or the hellish planets. At the bottom of the universe lies the Garbhodaka Ocean. Therefore the hellish planets lie between Pātālaloka and the Garbhodaka Ocean.

TEXT 6

यत्र ह वाव भगवान् पितृराजो वैवस्वतः स्वविषयं प्रापितेषु स्वपुरुषैर्जन्तुषु सम्परेतेषु यथाकर्मावद्यं दोषमेवानुल्लङ्घितभगवच्छासनः सगणो दमं धारयति ॥६॥

yatra ha vāva bhagavān pitṛ-rājo vaivasvataḥ sva-viṣayaṁ prāpiteṣu
sva-puruṣair jantuṣu sampareteṣu yathā-karmāvadyaṁ doṣam
evānullaṅghita-bhagavac-chāsanaḥ sagaṇo damaṁ dhārayati.

yatra—where; *ha vāva*—indeed; *bhagavān*—the most powerful; *pitṛ-rājaḥ*—Yamarāja, the king of the *pitās; vaivasvataḥ*—the son of the sun-god; *sva-viṣayam*—his own kingdom; *prāpiteṣu*—when caused to reach; *sva-puruṣaiḥ*—by his own messengers; *jantuṣu*—the human beings; *sampareteṣu*—dead; *yathā-karma-avadyam*—according to how much they have violated the rules and regulations of conditional life; *doṣam*—the fault; *eva*—certainly; *anullaṅghita-bhagavat-śāsanaḥ*—who never oversteps the Supreme Personality of Godhead's order; *sagaṇaḥ*—along with his followers; *damam*—punishment; *dhārayati*—executes.

TRANSLATION

The King of the pitās is Yamarāja, the very powerful son of the sun-god. He resides in Pitṛloka with his personal assistants and, while abiding by the rules and regulations set down by the Supreme Lord, has his agents, the Yamadūtas, bring all the sinful men to him immediately upon their death. After bringing them within his jurisdiction, he properly judges them according to their specific sinful activities and sends them to one of the many hellish planets for suitable punishments.

PURPORT

Yamarāja is not a fictitious or mythological character; he has his own abode, Pitṛloka, of which he is king. Agnostics may not believe in hell, but Śukadeva Gosvāmī affirms the existence of the Naraka planets, which lie between the Garbhodaka Ocean and Pātālaloka. Yamarāja is appointed by the Supreme Personality of Godhead to see that the human beings do not violate His rules and regulations. As confirmed in *Bhagavad-gītā* (4.17):

karmaṇo hy api boddhavyaṁ
boddhavyaṁ ca vikarmaṇaḥ
akarmaṇaś ca boddhavyaṁ
gahanā karmaṇo gatiḥ

"The intricacies of action are very hard to understand. Therefore one should know properly what action is, what forbidden action is, and what inaction is." One should understand the nature of *karma, vikarma* and *akarma,* and one must act accordingly. This is the law of the Supreme Personality of Godhead. The conditioned souls, who have come to this material world for sense gratification, are allowed to enjoy their senses under certain regulative principles. If they violate these regulations, they are judged and punished by Yamarāja. He brings them to the hellish planets and properly chastises them to bring them back to Kṛṣṇa consciousness. By the influence of *māyā,* however, the conditioned souls remain infatuated with the mode of ignorance. Thus in spite of repeated punishment by Yamarāja, they do not come to their senses, but continue to live within the material condition, committing sinful activities again and again.

TEXT 7

तत्र हैके नरकानेकविंशतिं गणयन्ति अथ तांस्ते राजन्नामरूपलक्षणतोऽनुक्रमिष्यामस्तामिस्रोऽन्धतामिस्रो रौरवो महारौरवः कुम्भीपाकः कालसूत्रमसिपत्रवनं सूकरमुखमन्धकूपः कृमिभोजनः सन्दंशस्तप्तसूर्मिर्वज्रकण्टकशाल्मली वैतरणी पूयोदः प्राणरोधो विशसनं लालाभक्षः सारमेयादनमवीचिरयःपानमिति। किञ्च क्षारकर्दमो रक्षोगणभोजनः शूलप्रोतो दन्दशूकोऽवटनिरोधनः पर्यावर्तनः सूचीमुखमित्यष्टाविंशतिर्नरका विविधयातनाभूमयः ॥७॥

tatra haike narakān eka-viṁśatiṁ gaṇayanti atha tāṁs te rājan nāma-rūpa-lakṣaṇato 'nukramiṣyāmas tāmisro 'ndhatāmisro rauravo mahārauravaḥ kumbhīpākaḥ kālasūtram asipatravanaṁ sūkaramukham andhakūpaḥ kṛmibhojanaḥ sandaṁśas taptasūrmir vajrakaṇṭaka-śālmalī vaitaraṇī pūyodaḥ prāṇarodho viśasanaṁ lālābhakṣaḥ sārameyādanam avīcir ayaḥpānam iti; kiñca kṣārakardamo rakṣogaṇa-bhojanaḥ śūlaproto dandaśūko 'vaṭa-nirodhanaḥ paryāvartanaḥ sūcīmukham ity aṣṭā-viṁśatir narakā vividha-yātanā-bhūmayaḥ.

tatra—there; *ha*—certainly; *eke*—some; *narakān*—the hellish planets; *eka-viṁśatim*—twenty-one; *gaṇayanti*—count; *atha*—therefore; *tān*—them; *te*—unto you; *rājan*—O King; *nāma-rūpa-lakṣaṇataḥ*—according to their names, forms and symptoms; *anukramiṣyāmaḥ*—we shall outline one after another; *tāmisraḥ*—Tāmisra; *andha-tāmisraḥ*—Andhatāmisra; *rauravaḥ* —Raurava; *mahā-rauravaḥ*—Mahāraurava; *kumbhī-pākaḥ*—Kumbhīpāka; *kāla-sūtram*—Kālasūtra; *asi-patravanam*—Asi-patravana; *sūkara-mukham* —Sūkaramukha; *andha-kūpaḥ*—Andhakūpa; *kṛmi-bhojanaḥ*—Kṛmibhojana; *sandaṁśaḥ*—Sandaṁśa; *tapta-sūrmiḥ*—Taptasūrmi; *vajra-kaṇṭaka-śālmalī* —Vajrakaṇṭaka-śālmalī; *vaitaraṇī*—Vaitaraṇī; *pūyodaḥ*—Pūyoda; *prāṇa-rodhaḥ*—Prāṇarodha; *viśasanam*—Viśasana; *lālā-bhakṣaḥ*—Lālābhakṣa; *sārameyādanam*—Sārameyādana; *avīciḥ*—Avīci; *ayaḥ-pānam*—Ayaḥpāna; *iti*—thus; *kiñca*—some more; *kṣāra-kardamaḥ*—Kṣārakardama; *rakṣaḥ-gaṇa-bhojanaḥ*—Rakṣogaṇa-bhojana; *śūla-protaḥ*—Śūlaprota; *danda-śūkaḥ* —Dandaśūka; *avaṭa-nirodhanaḥ*—Avaṭa-nirodhana; *paryāvartanaḥ*—Paryāvartana; *sūcī-mukham*—Sūcīmukha; *iti*—in this way; *aṣṭā-viṁśatiḥ* —twenty-eight; *narakāḥ*—hellish planets; *vividha*—various; *yātanā-bhūmayaḥ*—lands of suffering in hellish conditions.

TRANSLATION

Some authorities say that there is a total of twenty-one hellish planets, and some say twenty-eight. My dear King, I shall outline all of them according to their names, forms and symptoms. The names of the different hells are as follows: Tāmisra, Andhatāmisra, Raurava, Mahāraurava, Kumbhīpāka, Kālasūtra, Asipatravana, Sūkaramukha, Andhakūpa, Kṛmibhojana, Sandaṁśa, Taptasūrmi, Vajrakaṇṭaka-śālmalī, Vaitaraṇī, Pūyoda, Prāṇarodha, Viśasana, Lālābhakṣa, Sārameyādana, Avīci, Ayaḥpāna, Kṣārakardama, Rakṣogaṇa-bhojana, Śūlaprota, Dandaśūka, Avaṭa-nirodhana, Paryāvartana and Sūcīmukha. All these planets are meant for punishing the living entities.

TEXT 8

तत्र यस्तु परवित्तापत्यकलत्राण्यपहरति स हि कालपाशबद्धो यमपुरुषैरतिभयानकैस्तामिस्रे नरके बलान्निपात्यते अनशनानुदपानदण्डताडनसंतर्जनादिभिर्यातनाभिर्यात्यमानो जन्तुर्यत्र कश्मलमासादित एकदैव मूर्च्छामुपयाति तामिस्रप्राये ॥८॥

tatra yas tu para-vittāpatya-kalatrāṇy apaharati sa hi kāla-pāśa-baddho yama-puruṣair ati-bhayānakais tāmisre narake balān nipātyate anaśanānudapāna-daṇḍa-tāḍana-santarjanādibhir yātanābhir yātyamāno jantur yatra kaśmalam āsādita ekadaiva mūrcchām upayāti tāmisra-prāye.

tatra—in those hellish planets; *yaḥ*—a person who; *tu*—but; *para-vitta-apatya-kalatrāṇi*—the money, wife and children of another; *apaharati*—takes away; *saḥ*—that person; *hi*—certainly; *kāla-pāśa-baddhaḥ*—being bound by the ropes of time or Yamarāja; *yama-puruṣaiḥ*—by the assistants of Yamarāja; *ati-bhayānakaiḥ*—who are very fearful; *tāmisre narake*—into the hell known as Tāmisra; *balāt*—by force; *nipātyate*—is thrown; *anaśana*—starvation; *anudapāna*—without water; *daṇḍa-tāḍana*—beaten with rods; *santarjana-ādibhiḥ*—by scolding and so on; *yātanābhiḥ*—by severe punishments; *yātyamānaḥ*—being punished; *jantuḥ*—the living entity; *yatra*—where; *kaśmalam*—misery; *āsāditaḥ*—obtained; *ekadā*—sometimes; *eva*—certainly; *mūrcchām*—fainting; *upayāti*—obtains; *tāmisra-prāye*—in that condition, which is almost entirely dark.

TRANSLATION

My dear King, a person who appropriates another's legitimate wife, children or money is arrested at the time of death by the fierce Yamadūtas, who bind him with the rope of time and forcibly throw him into the hellish planet known as Tāmisra. On this very dark planet, the sinful man is chastised by the Yamadūtas, who beat and rebuke him. He is starved, and he is given no water to drink. Thus the wrathful assistants of Yamarāja cause him severe suffering, and sometimes he faints from their chastisement.

TEXT 9

एवमेवान्धतामिस्रे यस्तु वञ्चयित्वा पुरुषं दारादीनुपयुङ्क्ते यत्र शरीरी निपात्यमानो यातनास्थो वेदनया नष्टमतिर्नष्टदृष्टिश्च भवति यथा वनस्पतिर्वृश्च्यमानमूलस्तस्मादन्धतामिस्रं तमुपदिशन्ति ॥९॥

evam evāndhatāmisre yas tu vañcayitvā puruṣaṁ dārādīn upayuṅkte yatra śarīrī nipātyamāno yātanā-stho vedanayā naṣṭa-matir naṣṭa-dṛṣṭiś ca bhavati yathā vanaspatir vṛścyamāna-mūlas tasmād andhatāmisraṁ tam upadiśanti.

evam—in this way; *eva*—certainly; *andhatāmisre*—in the hellish planet known as Andhatāmisra; *yaḥ*—the person who; *tu*—but; *vañcayitvā*—

cheating; *puruṣam*—another person; *dāra-ādīn*—the wife and children; *upayuṅkte*—enjoys; *yatra*—where; *śarīrī*—the embodied person; *nipātyamānaḥ*—being forcibly thrown; *yātanā-sthaḥ*—always situated in extremely miserable conditions; *vedanayā*—by such suffering; *naṣṭa*—lost; *matiḥ*—whose consciousness; *naṣta*—lost; *dṛṣṭiḥ*—whose sight; *ca*—also; *bhavati*—becomes; *yathā*—as much as; *vanaspatiḥ*—the trees; *vṛścyamāna*—being cut; *mūlaḥ*—whose root; *tasmāt*—because of this; *andhatāmisram*—Andhatāmisra; *tam*—that; *upadiśanti*—they call.

TRANSLATION

The destination of a person who slyly cheats another man and enjoys his wife and children is the hell known as Andhatāmisra. There his condition is exactly like that of a tree being chopped at its roots. Even before reaching Andhatāmisra, the sinful living being is subjected to various extreme miseries. These afflictions are so severe that he loses his intelligence and sight. It is for this reason that learned sages call this hell Andhatāmisra.

TEXT 10

यस्त्विह वा एतदहमिति ममेदमिति भूतद्रोहेण केवलं स्वकुटुम्बमेवानुदिनं प्रपुष्णाति स तदिह विहाय स्वयमेव तदशुभेन रौरवे निपतति ॥१०॥

yas tv iha vā etad aham iti mamedam iti bhūta-droheṇa kevalaṁ sva-
kuṭumbam evānudinaṁ prapuṣṇāti sa tad iha vihāya svayam eva
tad-aśubhena raurave nipatati.

yaḥ—one who; *tu*—but; *iha*—in this life; *vā*—or; *etat*—this body; *aham*—I; *iti*—thus; *mama*—mine; *idam*—this; *iti*—thus; *bhūta-droheṇa*—by envy of other living entities; *kevalam*—alone; *sva-kuṭumbam*—his family members; *eva*—only; *anudinam*—day to day; *prapuṣṇāti*—supports; *saḥ*—such a person; *tat*—that; *iha*—here; *vihāya*—giving up; *svayam*—personally; *eva*—certainly; *tat*—of that; *aśubhena*—by the sin; *raurave*—in Raurava; *nipatati*—he falls down.

TRANSLATION

A person who accepts his body as his self works very hard day and night for money to maintain his own body and the bodies of his wife and children. While working to maintain himself and his family, he may

commit violence against other living entities. Such a person is forced to give up his body and his family at the time of death, when he suffers the reaction for his envy of other creatures by being thrown into the hell called Raurava.

PURPORT

In *Śrīmad-Bhāgavatam* it is said:

yasyātma-buddhiḥ kuṇape tri-dhātuke
sva-dhīḥ kalatrādiṣu bhauma-ijya-dhīḥ
yat-tīrtha-buddhiḥ salile na karhicij
janeṣv abhijñeṣu sa eva go-kharaḥ

"One who accepts this bodily bag of three elements [bile, mucus and air] as his self, who has an affinity for an intimate relationship with his wife and children, who considers his land worshipable, who takes bath in the waters of the holy places of pilgrimage but never takes advantage of those persons who are in actual knowledge—he is no better than an ass or a cow." (*Bhāg.* 10.84.13) There are two classes of men absorbed in the material concept of life. Out of ignorance, a man in the first class thinks his body to be his self, and therefore he is certainly like an animal (*sa eva go-kharaḥ*). The person in the second class, however, not only thinks his material body to be his self, but also commits all kinds of sinful activities to maintain his body. He cheats everyone to acquire money for his family and his self, and he becomes envious of others without reason. Such a person is thrown into the hell known as Raurava. If one simply considers his body to be his self, as do the animals, he is not very sinful. However, if one needlessly commits sins to maintain his body, he is put into the hell known as Raurava. This is the opinion of Śrīla Viśvanātha Cakravartī Ṭhākura. Although animals are certainly in the bodily concept of life, they do not commit any sins to maintain their bodies, mates or offspring. Therefore animals do not go to hell. However, when a human being acts enviously and cheats others to maintain his body, he is put into a hellish condition.

TEXT 11

ये त्विह यथैवामुना विहिंसिता जन्तवः परत्र यमयातनामुपगतं त एव रुरवो भूत्वा तथा तमेव विहिंसन्ति तस्माद्रौरवमित्याहू रुरुरिति सर्पादतिक्रूरसत्त्वस्यापदेशः ॥११॥

ye tv iha yathaivāmunā vihiṁsitā jantavaḥ paratra yama-yātanām upagataṁ ta eva ruravo bhūtvā tathā tam eva vihiṁsanti tasmād rauravam ity āhū rurur iti sarpād ati-krūra-sattvasyāpadeśaḥ.

ye—those who; *tu*—but; *iha*—in this life; *yathā*—as much as; *eva*—certainly; *amunā*—by him; *vihiṁsitāḥ*—who were hurt; *jantavaḥ*—the living entities; *paratra*—in the next life; *yama-yātanām upagatam*—being subjected to miserable conditions by Yamarāja; *te*—those living entities; *eva*—indeed; *ruravaḥ*—*rurus* (a kind of envious animal); *bhūtvā*—becoming; *tathā*—that much; *tam*—him; *eva*—certainly; *vihiṁsanti*—they hurt; *tasmāt*—because of this; *rauravam*—Raurava; *iti*—thus; *āhuḥ*—learned scholars say; *ruruḥ*—the animal known as *ruru; iti*—thus; *sarpāt*—than the snake; *ati-krūra*—much more cruel and envious; *sattvasya*—of the entity; *apadeśaḥ*—the name.

TRANSLATION

In this life, an envious person commits violent acts against many living entities. Therefore after his death, when he is taken to hell by Yamarāja, those living entities who were hurt by him appear as animals called rurus to inflict very severe pain upon him. Learned scholars call this hell Raurava. Not generally seen in this world, the ruru is more envious than a snake.

PURPORT

According to Śrīdhara Svāmī, the ruru is also known as the *bhāra-śṛṅga* (*ati-krūrasya bhāra-śṛṅgākhya-sattvasya apadeśaḥ saṁjñā*). Śrīla Jīva Gosvāmī confirms this in his Sandarbha: *ruru-śabdasya svayaṁ muninaiva ṭīkā-vidhānāl lokeṣv aprasiddha evāyaṁ jantu-viśeṣaḥ.* Thus although *rurus* are not seen in this world, their existence is confirmed in the *śāstras.*

TEXT 12

एवमेव महारौरवो यत्र निपतितं पुरुषं क्रव्यादा नाम रुरवस्तं क्रव्येण घातयन्ति यः केवलं देहम्भरः ॥१२॥

evam eva mahārauravo yatra nipatitaṁ puruṣaṁ kravyādā nāma ruravas taṁ kravyeṇa ghātayanti yaḥ kevalaṁ dehambharaḥ.

evam—thus; *eva*—certainly; *mahā-rauravaḥ*—the hell known as Mahāraurava; *yatra*—where; *nipatitam*—being thrown; *puruṣam*—a person; *kravyādāḥ nāma*—named *kravyāda; ruravaḥ*—the *ruru* animals; *tam*

—him (the condemned person); *kravyeṇa*—for eating his flesh; *ghātayanti* —kill; *yaḥ*—who; *kevalam*—only; *dehambharaḥ*—intent upon maintaining his own body.

TRANSLATION

Punishment in the hell called Mahāraurava is compulsory for a person who maintains his own body by hurting others. In this hell, ruru animals known as kravyāda torment him and eat his flesh.

PURPORT

The animalistic person who lives simply in the bodily concept of life is not excused. He is put into the hell known as Mahāraurava and attacked by *ruru* animals known as *kravyādas.*

TEXT 13

यस्त्विह वा उग्रः पशून् पक्षिणो वा प्राणत उपरन्धयति तमपकरुणं पुरुषादैरपि विगर्हितममुत्र यमानुचराः कुम्भीपाके तप्ततैले उपरन्धयन्ति ॥१३॥

yas tv iha vā ugraḥ paśūn pakṣiṇo vā prāṇata uparandhayati tam
apakaruṇaṁ puruṣādair api vigarhitam amutra yamānucarāḥ
kumbhīpāke tapta-taile uparandhayanti.

yaḥ—a person who; *tu*—but; *iha*—in this life; *vā*—or; *ugraḥ*—very cruel; *paśūn*—animals; *pakṣiṇaḥ*—birds; *vā*—or; *prāṇataḥ*—in a live condition; *uparandhayati*—cooks; *tam*—him; *apakaruṇam*—very cruel-hearted; *puruṣa-ādaiḥ*—by those who eat human flesh; *api*—even; *vigarhitam*—condemned; *amutra*—in the next life; *yama-anucarāḥ*—the servants of Yamarāja; *kumbhīpāke*—in the hell known as Kumbhīpāka; *tapta-taile*—in boiling oil; *uparandhayanti*—cook.

TRANSLATION

For the maintenance of their bodies and the satisfaction of their tongues, cruel persons cook poor animals and birds alive. Such persons are condemned even by man-eaters. In their next lives they are carried by the Yamadūtas to the hell known as Kumbhīpāka, where they are cooked in boiling oil.

TEXT 14

यस्त्विह ब्रह्मध्रुक् स कालसूत्रसंज्ञके नरके अयुतयोजनपरिमण्डले ताम्रमये तप्तखले उपर्यधस्तादग्न्यर्काभ्यामतितप्यमानेऽभिनिवेशितः क्षुत्पिपासाभ्यां च

दह्यमानान्तर्बहिःशरीर आस्ते शेते चेष्टतेऽवतिष्ठति परिधावति च यावन्ति पशुरोमाणि तावद्वर्षसहस्राणि ॥१४॥

yas tv iha brahma-dhruk sa kālasūtra-saṁjñake narake ayuta-yojana-parimaṇḍale tāmramaye tapta-khale upary-adhastād agny-arkābhyām ati-tapyamāne'bhiniveśitaḥ kṣut-pipāsābhyāṁ ca dahyamānāntar-bahiḥ-śarīra āste śete ceṣṭate 'vatiṣṭhati paridhāvati ca yāvanti paśu-romāṇi tāvad varṣa-sahasrāṇi.

yaḥ—anyone who; *tu*—but; *iha*—in this life; *brahma-dhruk*—the killer of a *brāhmaṇa; saḥ*—such a person; *kālasūtra-saṁjñake*—named Kālasūtra; *narake*—in the hell; *ayuta-yojana-parimaṇḍale*—having a circumference of eighty thousand miles; *tāmra-maye*—made of copper; *tapta*—heated; *khale*—in a level place; *upari-adhastāt*—above and beneath; *agni*—by fire; *arkābhyām*—and by the sun; *ati-tapyamāne*—which is being heated; *abhiniveśitaḥ*—being made to enter; *kṣut-pipāsābhyām*—by hunger and thirst; *ca*—and; *dahyamāna*—being burned; *antaḥ*—internally; *bahiḥ*—externally; *śarīraḥ*—whose body; *āste*—remains; *śete*—sometimes lies; *ceṣṭate*—sometimes moves his limbs; *avatiṣṭhati*—sometimes stands; *paridhāvati*—sometimes runs here and there; *ca*—also; *yāvanti*—as many; *paśu-romāṇi*—hairs on the body of an animal; *tāvat*—that long; *varṣa-sahasrāṇi*—thousands of years.

TRANSLATION

The killer of a brāhmaṇa is put into the hell known as Kālasūtra, which has a circumference of eighty thousand miles and which is made entirely of copper. Heated from below by fire and from above by the scorching sun, the copper surface of this planet is extremely hot. Thus the murderer of a brāhmaṇa suffers from being burned both internally and externally. Internally he is burning with hunger and thirst, and externally he is burning from the scorching heat of the sun and the fire beneath the copper surface. Therefore he sometimes lies down, sometimes sits, sometimes stands up and sometimes runs here and there. He must suffer in this way for as many thousands of years as there are hairs on the body of an animal.

TEXT 15

यस्त्विह वै निजवेदपथादनापद्यपगतः पाखण्डं चोपगतस्तमसिपत्रवनं प्रवेश्य कशया प्रहरन्ति तत्र हासावितस्ततो धावमान उभयतोधारैस्ता-

लवनासिपत्रैश्छिद्यमानसर्वाङ्गो हा हतोऽस्मीति परमया वेदनया मूर्च्छितः पदे पदे निपतति स्वधर्महा पाखण्डानुगतं फलं भुङ्क्ते ॥१५॥

yas tv iha vai nija-veda-pathād anāpady apagataḥ pākhaṇḍaṁ copagatas tam asi-patravanaṁ praveśya kaśayā praharanti tatra hāsāv itas tato dhāvamāna ubhayato dhārais tāla-vanāsi-patraiś chidyamāna-sarvāṅgo hā hato 'smīti paramayā vedanayā mūrcchitaḥ pade pade nipatati sva-dharmahā pākhaṇḍānugataṁ phalaṁ bhuṅkte.

yaḥ—anyone who; *tu*—but; *iha*—in this life; *vai*—indeed; *nija-veda-pathāt*—from his own path, recommended by the *Vedas; anāpadi*—even without an emergency; *apagataḥ*—deviated; *pākhaṇḍam*—a concocted, atheistic system; *ca*—and; *upagataḥ*—gone to; *tam*—him; *asi-patravanam*—the hell known as Asi-patravana; *praveśya*—making enter; *kaśayā*—with a whip; *praharanti*—they beat; *tatra*—there; *ha*—certainly; *asau*—that; *itaḥ tataḥ*—here and there; *dhāvamānaḥ*—running; *ubhayataḥ*—on both sides; *dhāraiḥ*—by the edges; *tāla-vana-asi-patraiḥ*—by the swordlike leaves of palm trees; *chidyamāna*—being cut; *sarva-aṅgaḥ*—whose entire body; *hā*—alas; *hataḥ*—killed; *asmi*—I am; *iti*—thus; *paramayā*—with severe; *vedanayā*—pain; *mūrcchitaḥ*—fainted; *pade pade*—at every step; *nipatati*—falls down; *sva-dharma-hā*—the killer of his own principles of religion; *pākhaṇḍa-anugatam phalam*—the result of accepting an atheistic path; *bhuṅkte*—he suffers.

TRANSLATION

If a person deviates from the path of the Vedas in the absence of an emergency, the servants of Yamarāja put him into the hell called Asi-patravana, where they beat him with whips. When he runs hither and thither, fleeing from the extreme pain, on all sides he runs into palm trees with leaves like sharpened swords. Thus injured all over his body and fainting at every step, he cries out, "Oh, what shall I do now! How shall I be saved!" This is how one suffers who deviates from the accepted religious principles.

PURPORT

There is actually only one religious principle: *dharmaṁ tu sākṣād bhagavat-praṇītam.* The only religious principle is to follow the orders of the Supreme Personality of Godhead. Unfortunately, especially in this age of Kali, everyone is an atheist. People do not even believe in God, what to speak of following His words. The words *nija-veda-patha* can also mean "one's own set of religious principles." Formerly there was only one *veda-patha,* or set of religious principles. Now there are many. It doesn't matter which set of religious principles one follows: the only injunction is that he must follow them strictly. An atheist, or *nāstika,* is one who does not believe in the *Vedas.* However, even if one takes up a different system of religion, according to this verse he must follow the religious principles he has accepted. Whether one is a Hindu, or a Mohammedan or a Christian, he should follow his own religious principles. However, if one concocts his own religious path within his mind, or if one follows no religious principles at all, he is punished in the hell known as Asi-patravana. In other words, a human being must follow some religious principles. If he does not follow any religious principles, he is no better than an animal. As Kali-yuga advances, people are becoming godless and taking up so-called secularism. They do not know the punishment awaiting them in Asi-patravana, as described in this verse.

TEXT 16

यस्त्विह वै राजा राजपुरुषो वा अदण्ड्ये दण्डं प्रणयति ब्राह्मणे वा शरीरदण्डं स पापीयान्नरकेऽमुत्र सूकरमुखे निपतति तत्रातिबलैर्विनिष्पिष्यमाणावयवो यथैवेहेक्षुखण्ड आर्तस्वरेण स्वनयन् क्वचिन्मूर्च्छितः कश्मलमुपगतो यथैवेहादृष्टदोषा उपरुद्धाः ॥१६॥

yas tv iha vai rājā rāja-puruṣo vā adaṇḍye daṇḍaṁ praṇayati brāhmaṇe vā śarīra-daṇḍaṁ sa pāpīyān narake'mutra sūkaramukhe nipatati tatrātibalair viniṣpiṣyamāṇāvayavo yathaivehekṣukhaṇḍa ārta-svareṇa svanayan kvacin mūrcchitaḥ kaśmalam upagato yathaivehā-dṛṣṭa-doṣā uparuddhāḥ.

yaḥ—anyone who; *tu*—but; *iha*—in this life; *vai*—indeed; *rājā*—a king; *rāja-puruṣaḥ*—a king's man; *vā*—or; *adaṇḍye*—unto one not punishable; *daṇḍam*—punishment; *praṇayati*—inflicts; *brāhmaṇe*—unto a *brāhmaṇa; vā*—or; *śarīra-daṇḍam*—corporal punishment; *saḥ*—that person, king or government officer; *pāpīyān*—the most sinful; *narake*—in the hell; *amutra*—in the next life; *sūkaramukhe*—named Sūkharamukha; *nipatati*—falls down; *tatra*—there; *ati-balaiḥ*—by very strong assistants of Yamarāja; *viniṣpiṣyamāṇa*—being crushed; *avayavaḥ*—the different parts of whose body; *yathā*—like; *eva*—certainly; *iha*—here; *ikṣu-khaṇḍaḥ*—sugarcane; *ārta-svareṇa*—with a pitiable sound; *svanayan*—crying; *kvacit*—sometimes; *mūrcchitaḥ*—fainted; *kaśmalam upagataḥ*—becoming illusioned; *yathā*—just like; *eva*—indeed; *iha*—here; *adṛṣṭa-doṣāḥ*—who is not at fault; *uparuddhāḥ*—arrested for punishment.

TRANSLATION

In his next life, a sinful king or governmental representative who punishes an innocent person, or who inflicts corporal punishment upon a brāhmaṇa, is taken by the Yamadūtas to the hell named Sūkharamukha, where the most powerful assistants of Yamarāja crush him exactly as one crushes sugarcane to squeeze out the juice. The sinful living entity cries very pitiably and faints, just like an innocent man undergoing punishments. This is the result of punishing a faultless person.

TEXT 17

यस्त्विह वै भूतानामीश्वरोपकल्पितवृत्तीनामविविक्तपरव्यथानां स्वयं पुरुषोपकल्पितवृत्तिर्विविक्तपरव्यथो व्यथामाचरति स परत्रान्धकूपे तदभिद्रोहेण निपतति तत्र हासौ तैर्जन्तुभिः पशुमृगपक्षिसरीसृपैर्मशकयूका-मत्कुणमक्षिकादिभिर्ये के चाभिद्रुग्धास्तैः सर्वतोऽभिद्रुह्यमाणस्तमसि विहतनिद्रानिर्वृतिरलब्धावस्थानः परिक्रामति यथा कुशरीरे जीवः ॥१७॥

yas tv iha vai bhūtānām īśvaropakalpita-vṛttīnām avivikta-para-vyathānāṁ svayaṁ puruṣopakalpita-vṛttir vivikta-para-vyatho vyathām ācarati sa paratrāndhakūpe tad-abhidroheṇa nipatati tatra hāsau tair jantubhiḥ paśu-mṛga-pakṣi-sarīsṛpair maśaka-yūkā-matkuṇa-makṣikādibhir ye ke cābhidrugdhās taiḥ sarvato 'bhidruhyamāṇas tamasi vihata-nidrā-nirvṛtir alabdhāvasthānaḥ parikrāmati yathā kuśarīre jīvaḥ.

yaḥ—any person who; *tu*—but; *iha*—in this life; *vai*—indeed; *bhūtānām*—to some living entities; *īśvara*—by the supreme controller; *upakalpita*—designed; *vṛttīnām*—whose means of livelihood; *avivikta*—not understanding; *para-vyathānām*—the pain of others; *svayam*—himself; *puruṣa-upakalpita*—designed by the Supreme Personality of Godhead; *vṛttiḥ*—whose livelihood; *vivikta*—understanding; *para-vyathaḥ*—the painful conditions of others; *vyathām ācarati*—but still causes pain; *saḥ*—such a person; *paratra*—in his next life; *andhakūpe*—to the hell named Andhakūpa;

tat—to them; *abhidroheṇa*—by the sin of malice; *nipatati*—falls down; *tatra*—there; *ha*—indeed; *asau*—that person; *taiḥ jantubhiḥ*—by those respective living entities; *paśu*—animals; *mṛga*—wild beasts; *pakṣi*—birds; *sarīsṛpaiḥ*—snakes; *maśaka*—mosquitoes; *yūkā*—lice; *matkuṇa*—worms; *makṣika-ādibhiḥ*—flies and so on; *ye ke*—whoever else; *ca*—and; *abhidrugdhāḥ*—persecuted; *taiḥ*—by them; *sarvataḥ*—everywhere; *abhidruhyamāṇaḥ*—being injured; *tamasi*—in the darkness; *vihata*—disturbed; *nidrā-nirvṛtiḥ*—whose resting place; *alabdha*—not being able to obtain; *avasthānaḥ*—a resting place; *parikrāmati*—wanders; *yathā*—just as; *ku-śarīre*—in a low-grade body; *jīvaḥ*—a living entity.

TRANSLATION

By the arrangement of the Supreme Lord, low-grade living beings like bugs and mosquitoes suck the blood of human beings and other animals. Such insignificant creatures are unaware that their bites are painful to the human being. However, first-class human beings—brāhmaṇas, kṣatriyas and vaiśyas—are developed in consciousness, and therefore they know how painful it is to be killed. A human being endowed with knowledge certainly commits sin if he kills or torments insignificant creatures, who have no discrimination. The Supreme Lord punishes such a man by putting him into the hell known as Andhakūpa, where he is attacked by all the birds and beasts, reptiles, mosquitoes, lice, worms, flies, and any other creatures he tormented during his life. They attack him from all sides, robbing him of the pleasure of sleep. Unable to rest, he constantly wanders about in the darkness. Thus in Andhakūpa his suffering is just like that of a creature in the lower species.

PURPORT

From this very instructive verse we learn that lower animals, created by the laws of nature to disturb the human being, are not subjected to punishment. Because the human being has developed consciousness, however, he cannot do anything against the principles of *varṇāśrama-dharma* without being condemned. Kṛṣṇa states in *Bhagavad-gītā* (4.13), *cātur-varṇyaṁ mayā sṛṣṭaṁ guṇa-karma-vibhāgaśaḥ:* "According to the three modes of material nature and the work ascribed to them, the four divisions of human society were created by Me." Thus all men should be divided into four classes—*brāhmaṇas, kṣatriyas, vaiśyas* and *śūdras*—and they should act according to their ordained regulations. They cannot deviate from their prescribed rules and regulations. One of these states that they should never trouble any animal, even those that disturb human beings. Although a tiger is not sinful if he attacks another animal and eats its flesh, if a man with developed consciousness does so, he must be punished. In other words, a human being who does not use his developed consciousness but instead acts like an animal surely undergoes punishment in many different hells.

TEXT 18

यस्त्विह वा असंविभज्याश्नाति यत्किञ्चनोपनतमनिर्मितपञ्चयज्ञो वायससंस्तुतः स परत्र कृमिभोजने नरकाधमे निपतति तत्र शतसहस्रयोजने कृमिकुण्डे कृमिभूतः स्वयं कृमिभिरेव भक्ष्यमाणः कृमिभोजनो यावत्तदप्रत्ता-प्रहूतादोऽनिर्वेशमात्मानं यातयते ॥१८॥

yas tv iha vā asaṁvibhajyāśnāti yat kiñcanopanatam anirmita-pañca-yajño vāyasa-saṁstutaḥ sa paratra kṛmibhojane narakādhame nipatati tatra śata-sahasra-yojane kṛmi-kuṇḍe kṛmi-bhūtaḥ svayaṁ kṛmibhir eva bhakṣyamāṇaḥ kṛmi-bhojano yāvat tad aprattāprahūtādo'nirveśam ātmānaṁ yātayate.

yaḥ—any person who; *tu*—but; *iha*—in this life; *vā*—or; *asaṁ-vibhajya*—without dividing; *aśnāti*—eats; *yat kiñcana*—whatever; *upanatam*—obtained by Kṛṣṇa's grace; *anirmita*—not performing; *pañca-yajñaḥ*—the five kinds of sacrifice; *vāyasa*—with the crows; *saṁstutaḥ*—who is described as equal; *saḥ*—such a person; *paratra*—in the next life; *kṛmibhojane*—named Kṛmibhojana; *naraka-adhame*—into the most abominable of all hells; *nipatati*—falls down; *tatra*—there; *śata-sahasra-yojane*—measuring 100,000 *yojanas* (800,000 miles); *kṛmi-kuṇḍe*—in a lake of worms; *kṛmi-bhūtaḥ*—becoming one of the worms; *svayam*—he himself; *kṛmibhiḥ*—by the other worms; *eva*—certainly; *bhakṣyamāṇaḥ*—being eaten; *kṛmi-bhojanaḥ*—eating worms; *yāvat*—as long as; *tat*—that lake is wide; *apratta-aprahūta*—unshared and unoffered food; *adaḥ*—one who eats; *anirveśam*—who has not performed atonement; *ātmānam*—to himself; *yātayate*—gives pain.

TRANSLATION

A person is considered no better than a crow if after receiving some food, he does not divide it among guests, old men and children, but simply eats it himself, or if he eats it without performing the five kinds of sacrifice. After death he is put into the most abominable hell, known as

Kṛmibhojana. In that hell is a lake 100,000 yojanas [800,000 miles] wide and filled with worms. He becomes a worm in that lake and feeds on the other worms there, who also feed on him. Unless he atones for his actions before his death, such a sinful man remains in the hellish lake of Kṛmibhojana for as many years as there are yojanas in the width of the lake.

PURPORT

As stated in *Bhagavad-gītā* (3.13):

yajña-śiṣṭāśinaḥ santo
mucyante sarva-kilbiṣaiḥ
bhuñjate te tv agham pāpā
ya pacanty ātma-kāraṇāt

"The devotees of the Lord are released from all kinds of sins because they eat food which is first offered for sacrifice. Others, who prepare food for personal sense enjoyment, verily eat only sin." All food is given to us by the Supreme Personality of Godhead. *Eko bahūnāṁ yo vidadhāti kāmān:* the Lord supplies everyone with the necessities of life. Therefore we should acknowledge His mercy by performing *yajña* (sacrifice). This is the duty of everyone. Indeed, the sole purpose of life is to perform *yajña.* According to Kṛṣṇa (Bg. 3.9):

yajñārthāt karmaṇo'nyatra
loko'yam karma-bandhanaḥ
tad-arthaṁ karma kaunteya
mukta-saṅgaḥ samācara

"Work done as a sacrifice for Viṣṇu has to be performed, otherwise work binds one to this material world. Therefore, O son of Kuntī, perform your prescribed duties for His satisfaction, and in that way you will always remain unattached and free from bondage." If we do not perform *yajña* and distribute *prasāda* to others, our lives are condemned. Only after performing *yajña* and distributing the *prasāda* to all dependents—children, *brāhmaṇas* and old men—should one eat. However, one who cooks only for himself or his family is condemned, along with everyone he feeds. After death he is put into the hell known as Kṛmibhojana.

TEXT 19

यस्त्विह वै स्तेयेन बलाद्वा हिरण्यरत्नादीनि ब्राह्मणस्य वापहरत्यन्यस्य वानापदि
पुरुषस्तममुत्र राजन् यमपुरुषा अयस्मयैरग्निपिण्डैः सन्दंशैस्त्वचि निष्कुषन्ति ॥१९॥

yas tv iha vai steyena balād vā hiraṇya-ratnādīni brāhmaṇasya vāpaharaty anyasya vānāpadi puruṣas tam amutra rājan yama-puruṣā ayasmayair agni-piṇḍaiḥ sandaṁśais tvaci niṣkuṣanti.

yaḥ—any person who; *tu*—but; *iha*—in this life; *vai*—indeed; *steyena*—by thievery; *balāt*—by force; *vā*—or; *hiraṇya*—gold; *ratna*—gems; *ādīni*—and so on; *brāhmaṇasya*—of a *brāhmaṇa; vā*—or; *apaharati*—steals; *anyasya*—of others; *vā*—or; *anāpadi*—not in a calamity; *puruṣaḥ*—a person; *tam*—him; *amutra*—in the next life; *rājan*—O King; *yama-puruṣāḥ*—the agents of Yamarāja; *ayaḥ-mayaiḥ*—made of iron; *agni-piṇḍaiḥ*—balls heated in fire; *sandaṁśaiḥ*—with tongs; *tvaci*—on the skin; *niṣkuṣanti*—tear to pieces.

TRANSLATION

My dear King, a person who in the absence of an emergency robs a brāhmaṇa—or, indeed, anyone else—of his gems and gold is put into a hell known as Sandaṁśa. There his skin is torn and separated by red-hot iron balls and tongs. In this way, his entire body is cut to pieces.

TEXT 20

यस्त्विह वा अगम्यां स्त्रियमगम्यं वा पुरुषं योषिदभिगच्छति तावमुत्र कशया ताडयन्तस्तिग्मया सूर्म्या लोहमय्या पुरुषमालिङ्गयन्ति स्त्रियं च पुरुषरूपया सूर्म्या ॥२०॥

yas tv iha vā agamyāṁ striyam agamyaṁ vā puruṣaṁ yoṣid abhigacchati tāv amutra kaśayā tāḍayantas tigmayā sūrmyā lohamayyā puruṣam āliṅgayanti striyaṁ ca puruṣa-rūpayā sūrmyā.

yaḥ—any person who; *tu*—but; *iha*—in this life; *vā*—or; *agamyām*—unsuitable; *striyam*—a woman; *agamyam*—unsuitable; *vā*—or; *puruṣam*—a man; *yoṣit*—a woman; *abhigacchati*—approaches for sexual intercourse; *tau*—both of them; *amutra*—in the next life; *kaśayā*—by whips; *tāḍayantaḥ*—beating; *tigmayā*—very hot; *sūrmyā*—by an image; *loha-mayyā*—made of iron; *puruṣam*—the man; *āliṅgayanti*—they embrace; *striyam*—the woman; *ca*—also; *puruṣa-rūpayā*—in the form of a man; *sūrmyā*—by an image.

TRANSLATION

A man or woman who indulges in sexual intercourse with an unworthy member of the opposite sex is punished after death by the assistants of Yamarāja in the hell known as Taptasūrmi. There such men and women

are beaten with whips. The man is forced to embrace a red-hot iron form of a woman, and the woman is forced to embrace a similar form of a man. Such is the punishment for illicit sex.

PURPORT

Generally a man should not have sexual relations with any woman other than his wife. According to Vedic principles, the wife of another man is considered one's mother, and sexual relations are strictly forbidden with one's mother, sister and daughter. If one indulges in illicit sexual relations with another man's wife, that activity is considered identical with having sex with one's mother. This act is most sinful. The same principle holds for a woman also; if she enjoys sex with a man other than her husband, the act is tantamount to having sexual relations with her father or son. Illicit sex life is always forbidden, and any man or woman who indulges in it is punished in the manner described in this verse.

TEXT 21

यस्त्विह वै सर्वाभिगमस्तममुत्र निरये वर्तमानं वज्रकण्टकशाल्मलीमारोप्य निष्कर्षन्ति ॥२१॥

yas tv iha vai sarvābhigamas tam amutra niraye vartamānaṁ
vajrakaṇṭaka-śālmalīm āropya niṣkarṣanti.

yaḥ—anyone who; *tu*—but; *iha*—in this life; *vai*—indeed; *sarva-abhigamaḥ*—indulges in sex life indiscriminately, with both men and animals; *tam*—him; *amutra*—in the next life; *niraye*—in the hell; *vartamānam*—existing; *vajrakaṇṭaka-śālmalīm*—a silk-cotton tree with thorns like thunderbolts; *āropya*—mounting him on; *niṣkarṣanti*—they pull him out.

TRANSLATION

A person who indulges in sex indiscriminately—even with animals—is taken after death to the hell known as Vajrakaṇṭaka-śālmalī. In this hell there is a silk-cotton tree full of thorns as strong as thunderbolts. The agents of Yamarāja hang the sinful man on that tree and pull him down forcibly so that the thorns very severely tear his body.

PURPORT

The sexual urge is so strong that sometimes a man indulges in sexual relations with a cow, or a woman indulges in sexual relations with a dog. Such men and women are put into the hell known as Vajrakaṇṭaka-śālmalī. The Kṛṣṇa consciousness movement forbids illicit sex. From the description of these verses, we can understand what an extremely sinful act illicit sex is. Sometimes people disbelieve these descriptions of hell, but whether one believes or not, everything must be carried out by the laws of nature, which no one can avoid.

TEXT 22

ये त्विह वै राजन्या राजपुरुषा वा अपाखण्डा धर्मसेतून् भिन्दन्ति ते सम्परेत्य वैतरण्यां निपतन्ति भिन्नमर्यादास्तस्यां निरयपरिखाभूतायां नद्यां यादोगणैरितस्ततो भक्ष्यमाणा आत्मना न वियुज्यमानाश्चासुभिरुह्यमानाः स्वाघेन कर्मपाकमनुस्मरन्तो विण्मूत्रपूयशोणितकेशनखास्थिमेदोमांसवसावाहिन्यामुपतप्यन्ते ॥२२॥

ye tv iha vai rājanyā rāja-puruṣā vā apākhaṇḍā dharma-setūn
bhindanti te samparetya vaitaraṇyāṁ nipatanti bhinna-maryādās
tasyāṁ niraya-parikhā-bhūtāyāṁ nadyāṁ yādo-gaṇair itas tato
bhakṣyamāṇā ātmanā na viyujyamānāś cāsubhir uhyamānāḥ svāghena
karma-pākam anusmaranto viṇ-mūtra-pūya-śoṇita-keśa-nakhāsthi-
medo-māṁsa-vasā-vāhinyām upatapyante.

ye—persons who; *tu*—but; *iha*—in this life; *vai*—indeed; *rājanyāḥ*—members of the royal family, or *kṣatriyas; rāja-puruṣāḥ*—government servants; *vā*—or; *apākhaṇḍāḥ*—although born in responsible families; *dharma-setūn*—the bounds of prescribed religious principles; *bhindanti*—transgress; *te*—they; *samparetya*—after dying; *vaitaraṇyām*—named Vaitaraṇī; *nipatanti*—fall down; *bhinna-maryādāḥ*—who have broken the regulative principles; *tasyām*—in that; *niraya-parikhā-bhūtāyām*—the moat surrounding hell; *nadyām*—in the river; *yādaḥ-gaṇaiḥ*—by ferocious aquatic animals; *itaḥ tataḥ*—here and there; *bhakṣyamāṇāḥ*—being eaten; *ātmanā*—with the body; *na*—not; *viyujyamānāḥ*—being separated; *ca*—and; *asubhiḥ*—the life airs; *uhyamānāḥ*—being carried; *sva-aghena*—by his own sinful activities; *karma-pākam*—the result of his impious activities; *anusmarantaḥ*—remembering; *viṭ*—of stool; *mūtra*—urine; *pūya*—pus; *śoṇita*—blood; *keśa*—hair; *nakha*—nails; *asthi*—bones; *medaḥ*—marrow; *māṁsa*—flesh; *vasā*—fat; *vāhinyām*—in the river; *upatapyante*—are afflicted with pain.

TRANSLATION

A person who is born into a responsible family—such as a kṣatriya, a member of royalty or a government servant—but who neglects to execute

his prescribed duties according to religious principles, and who thus becomes degraded, falls down at the time of death into the river of hell known as Vaitaraṇī. This river, which is a moat surrounding hell, is full of ferocious aquatic animals. When a sinful man is thrown into the River Vaitaraṇī, the aquatic animals there immediately begin to eat him, but because of his extremely sinful life, he does not leave his body. He constantly remembers his sinful activities and suffers terribly in that river, which is full of stool, urine, pus, blood, hair, nails, bones, marrow, flesh and fat.

TEXT 23

ये त्विह वै वृषलीपतयो नष्टशौचाचारनियमास्त्यक्तलज्जाः पशुचर्यां चरन्ति ते चापि प्रेत्य पूयविण्मूत्रश्लेष्ममलापूर्णार्णवे निपतन्ति तदेवातिबीभत्सितमश्नन्ति ॥ २३ ॥

ye tv iha vai vṛṣalī-patayo naṣṭa-śaucācāra-niyamās tyakta-lajjāḥ paśu-caryāṁ caranti te cāpi pretya pūya-viṇ-mūtra-śleṣma-malā-pūrṇārṇave nipatanti tad evātibībhatsitam aśnanti.

ye—persons who; *tu*—but; *iha*—in this life; *vai*—indeed; *vṛṣalī-patayaḥ*—the husbands of the *śūdras*; *naṣṭa*—lost; *śauca-ācāra-niyamāḥ*—whose cleanliness, good behavior and regulated life; *tyakta-lajjāḥ*—without shame; *paśu-caryām*—the behavior of animals; *caranti*—they execute; *te*—they; *ca*—also; *api*—indeed; *pretya*—dying; *pūya*—of pus; *viṭ*—stool; *mūtra*—urine; *śleṣma*—mucus; *malā*—saliva; *pūrṇa*—full; *arṇave*—in an ocean; *nipatanti*—fall; *tat*—that; *eva*—only; *atibībhatsitam*—extremely disgusting; *aśnanti*—they eat.

TRANSLATION

The shameless husbands of lowborn śūdra women live exactly like animals, and therefore they have no good behavior, cleanliness or regulated life. After death, such persons are thrown into the hell called Pūyoda, where they are put into an ocean filled with pus, stool, urine, mucus, saliva and similar things. Śūdras who could not improve themselves fall into that ocean and are forced to eat those disgusting things.

PURPORT

Śrīla Narottama dāsa Ṭhākura has sung,

karma-kāṇḍa, jñāna-kāṇḍa, kevala viṣera bāṇḍa,
amṛta baliyā yebā khāya

nānā yoni sadā phire, kadarya bhakṣaṇa kare,
tāra janma adaḥ-pate yāya

He says that persons following the paths of *karma-kāṇḍa* and *jñāna-kāṇḍa* (fruitive activities and speculative thinking) are missing the opportunities for human birth and gliding down into the cycle of birth and death. Thus there is always the chance that he may be put into the Pūyoda Naraka, the hell named Pūyoda, where one is forced to eat stool, urine, pus, mucus, saliva and other abominable things. It is significant that this verse is spoken especially about *śūdras.* If one is born a *śūdra,* he must continually return to the ocean of Pūyoda to eat horrible things. Thus even a born *śūdra* is expected to become a *brāhmaṇa;* that is the meaning of human life. Everyone should improve himself. Kṛṣṇa says in *Bhagavad-gītā* (4.13), *cātur-varṇyaṁ mayā sṛṣṭaṁ guṇa-karma-vibhāgaśaḥ:* "According to the three modes of material nature and the work ascribed to them, four divisions of human society were created by Me." Even if one is by qualification a *śūdra,* he must try to improve his position and become a *brāhmaṇa.* No one should try to check a person, no matter what his present position is, from coming to the platform of a *brāhmaṇa* or a Vaiṣṇava. Actually, one must come to the platform of a Vaiṣṇava. Then he automatically becomes a *brāhmaṇa.* This can be done only if the Kṛṣṇa consciousness movement is spread, for we are trying to elevate everyone to the platform of Vaiṣṇava. As Kṛṣṇa says in *Bhagavad-gītā* (18.66), *sarva-dharmān parityajya mām ekaṁ śaraṇaṁ vraja:* "Abandon all other duties and simply surrender unto Me." One must give up the occupational duties of a *śūdra, kṣatriya* or *vaiśya* and adopt the occupational duties of a Vaiṣṇava, which include the activities of a *brāhmaṇa.* Kṛṣṇa explains this in *Bhagavad-gītā* (9.32):

māṁ hi pārtha vyapāśritya
ye'pi syuḥ pāpa-yonayaḥ
striyo vaiśyās tathā śūdrās
te'pi yānti parāṁ gatim

"O son of Pṛthā, those who take shelter in Me, though they be of lower birth —women, *vaiśyas* [merchants], as well as *śūdras* [workers]—can approach the supreme destination." Human life is specifically meant for going back home, back to Godhead. That facility should be given to everyone, whether one be a *śūdra,* a *vaiśya,* a woman or a *kṣatriya.* This is the purpose of the Kṛṣṇa consciousness movement. However, if one is satisfied to remain a *śūdra,* he must suffer as described in this verse: *tad evātibībhatsitam aśnanti.*

TEXT 24

ये त्विह वै श्वगर्दभपतयो ब्राह्मणादयो मृगयाविहारा अतीर्थे च मृगान्निघ्नन्ति तानपि सम्परेतांल्लक्ष्यभूतान् यमपुरुषा इषुभिर्विध्यन्ति ॥ २४ ॥

ye tv iha vai śva-gardabha-patayo brāhmaṇādayo mṛgayā vihārā atīrthe ca mṛgān nighnanti tān api samparetāl̐ lakṣya-bhūtān yama-puruṣā iṣubhir vidhyanti.

ye—those who; *tu*—but; *iha*—in this life; *vai*—or; *śva*—of dogs; *gardabha*—and asses; *patayaḥ*—maintainers; *brāhmaṇa-ādayaḥ*—*brāhmaṇas, kṣatriyas* and *vaiśyas; mṛgayā vihārāḥ*—taking pleasure in hunting animals in the forest; *atīrthe*—other than prescribed; *ca*—also; *mṛgān*—animals; *nighnanti*—kill; *tān*—them; *api*—indeed; *samparetān*—having died; *lakṣya-bhūtān*—becoming the targets; *yama-puruṣāḥ*—the assistants of Yamarāja; *iṣubhiḥ*—by arrows; *vidhyanti*—pierce.

TRANSLATION

If in this life a man of the higher classes [brāhmaṇa, kṣatriya and vaiśya] is very fond of taking his pet dogs, mules or asses into the forest to hunt and kill animals unnecessarily, he is placed after death into the hell known as Prāṇarodha. There the assistants of Yamarāja make him their targets and pierce him with arrows.

PURPORT

In the Western countries especially, aristocrats keep dogs and horses to hunt animals in the forest. Whether in the West or the East, aristocratic men in the Kali-yuga adopt the fashion of going to the forest and unnecessarily killing animals. Men of the higher classes (the *brāhmaṇas, kṣatriyas* and *vaiśyas*) should cultivate knowledge of Brahman, and they should also give the *śūdras* a chance to come to that platform. If instead they indulge in hunting, they are punished as described in this verse. Not only are they pierced with arrows by the agents of Yamarāja, but they are also put into the ocean of pus, urine and stool described in the previous verse.

TEXT 25

ये त्विह वै दाम्भिका दम्भयज्ञेषु पशून् विशसन्ति तानमुष्मिँल्लोके वैशसे नरके पतितान्निरयपतयो यातयित्वा विशसन्ति ॥ २५ ॥

ye tv iha vai dāmbhikā dambha-yajñeṣu paśūn viśasanti tān amuṣmiṁ
loke vaiśase narake patitān niraya-patayo yātayitvā viśasanti.

ye—persons who; *tu*—but; *iha*—in this life; *vai*—indeed; *dāmbhikāḥ*—very proud of wealth and a prestigious position; *dambha-yajñeṣu*—in a sacrifice performed to increase prestige; *paśūn*—animals; *viśasanti*—kill; *tān*—them; *amuṣmin loke*—in the next world; *vaiśase*—Vaiśasa or Viśasana; *narake*—into the hell; *patitān*—fallen; *niraya-patayaḥ*—assistants of Yamarāja; *yātayitvā*—causing sufficient pain; *viśasanti*—kill.

TRANSLATION

A person who in this life is proud of his eminent position, and who heedlessly sacrifices animals simply for material prestige, is put into the hell called Viśasana after death. There the assistants of Yamarāja kill him after giving him unlimited pain.

PURPORT

In *Bhagavad-gītā* (6.41) Kṛṣṇa says, *śucīnāṁ śrīmatāṁ gehe yoga-bhraṣṭo'bhijāyate:* "Because of his previous connection with *bhakti-yoga,* a man is born into a prestigious family of *brāhmaṇas* or aristocrats." Having taken such a birth, one should utilize it to perfect *bhakti-yoga.* However, due to bad association one often forgets that his prestigious position has been given to him by the Supreme Personality of Godhead, and he misuses it by performing various kinds of so-called *yajñas* like *kālī-pūjā* or *durgā-pūjā,* in which poor animals are sacrificed. How such a person is punished is described herein. The word *dambha-yajñeṣu* in this verse is significant. If one violates the Vedic instructions while performing *yajña* and simply makes a show of sacrifice for the purpose of killing animals, he is punishable after death. In Calcutta there are many slaughterhouses where animal flesh is sold that has supposedly been offered in sacrifice before the goddess Kālī. The *śāstras* enjoin that one can sacrifice a small goat before the goddess Kālī once a month. Nowhere is it said that one can maintain a slaughterhouse in the name of temple worship and daily kill animals unnecessarily. Those who do so receive the punishments described herein.

TEXT 26

यस्त्विह वै सवर्णां भार्यां द्विजो रेतः पाययति काममोहितस्तं पापकृतममुत्र
रेतःकुल्यायां पातयित्वा रेतः सम्पाययन्ति ॥२६॥

yas tv iha vai savarṇāṁ bhāryāṁ dvijo retaḥ pāyayati kāma-mohitas
taṁ pāpa-kṛtam amutra retaḥ-kulyāyāṁ pātayitvā retaḥ sampāyayanti.

yaḥ—any person who; *tu*—but; *iha*—in this life; *vai*—indeed; *savarṇām*—of the same caste; *bhāryām*—his wife; *dvijaḥ*—a person of a higher caste (such as a *brāhmaṇa, kṣatriya* or *vaiśya*); *retaḥ*—the semen; *pāyayati*—causes to drink; *kāma-mohitaḥ*—being deluded by lusty desires; *tam*—him; *pāpa-kṛtam*—performing sin; *amutra*—in the next life; *retaḥ-kulyāyām*—in a river of semen; *pātayitvā*—throwing; *retaḥ*—semen; *sampāyayanti*—force to drink.

TRANSLATION

If a foolish member of the twice-born classes [brāhmaṇa, kṣatriya and vaiśya] forces his wife to drink his semen out of a lusty desire to keep her under control, he is put after death into the hell known as Lālābhakṣa. There he is thrown into a flowing river of semen, which he is forced to drink.

PURPORT

The practice of forcing one's wife to drink one's own semen is a black art practiced by extremely lusty persons. Those who practice this very abominable activity say that if a wife is forced to drink her husband's semen, she remains very faithful to him. Generally only low-class men engage in this black art, but if a man born in a higher class does so, after death he is put into the hell known as Lālābhakṣa. There he is immersed in the river known as Śukra-nadī and forced to drink semen.

TEXT 27

ये त्विह वै दस्यवोऽग्निदा गरदा ग्रामान् सार्थान् वा विलुम्पन्ति राजानो राजभटा वा तांश्चापि हि परेत्य यमदूता वज्रदंष्ट्राः श्वानः सप्तशतानि विंशतिश्च सरभसं खादन्ति ॥२७॥

ye tv iha vai dasyavo 'gnidā garadā grāmān sārthān vā vilumpanti
rājāno rāja-bhaṭā vā tāṁś cāpi hi paretya yamadūtā vajra-daṁṣṭrāḥ
śvānaḥ sapta-śatāni viṁśatiś ca sarabhasaṁ khādanti.

ye—persons who; *tu*—but; *iha*—in this life; *vai*—indeed; *dasyavaḥ*—thieves and plunderers; *agni-dāḥ*—who set fire; *garadāḥ*—who administer poison; *grāmān*—villages; *sārthān*—the mercantile class of men; *vā*—or;

vilumpanti—plunder; *rājānaḥ*—kings; *rāja-bhaṭāḥ*—government officials; *vā*—or; *tān*—them; *ca*—also; *api*—indeed; *hi*—certainly; *paretya*—having died; *yamadūtāḥ*—the assistants of Yamarāja; *vajra-daṁṣṭrāḥ*—having mighty teeth; *śvānaḥ*—dogs; *sapta-śatāni*—seven hundred; *viṁśatiḥ*—twenty; *ca*—and; *sarabhasam*—voraciously; *khādanti*—devour.

TRANSLATION

In this world, some persons are professional plunderers who set fire to others' houses or administer poison to them. Also, members of the royalty or government officials sometimes plunder mercantile men by forcing them to pay income tax and by other methods. After death such demons are put into the hell known as Sārameyādana. On that planet there are 720 dogs with teeth as strong as thunderbolts. Under the orders of the agents of Yamarāja, these dogs voraciously devour such sinful people.

PURPORT

In the Twelfth Canto of *Śrīmad-Bhāgavatam,* it is said that in this age of Kali everyone will be extremely disturbed by three kinds of tribulations: scarcity of rain, famine, and heavy taxation by the government. Because human beings are becoming more and more sinful, there will be a scarcity of rain, and naturally no food grains will be produced. On the plea of relieving the suffering caused by the ensuing famine, the government will impose heavy taxes, especially on the wealthy mercantile community. In this verse, the members of such a government are described as *dasyu,* thieves. Their main activity will be to plunder the wealth of the people. Whether a highway robber or a government thief, such a man will be punished in his next life by being thrown into the hell known as Sārameyādana, where he will suffer greatly from the bites of ferocious dogs.

TEXT 28

यस्त्विह वा अनृतं वदति साक्ष्ये द्रव्यविनिमये दाने वा कथञ्चित्स वै प्रेत्य नरकेऽवीचिमत्यधःशिरा निरवकाशे योजनशतोच्छ्रायाद् गिरिमूर्ध्नः सम्पात्यते यत्र जलमिव स्थलमश्मपृष्ठमवभासते तदवीचिमत्तिलशो विशीर्यमाणशरीरो न म्रियमाणः पुनरारोपितो निपतति ॥२८॥

yas tv iha vā anṛtaṁ vadati sākṣye dravya-vinimaye dāne vā kathañcit
sa vai pretya narake 'vīcimaty adhaḥ-śirā niravakāśe yojana-
śatocchrāyād giri-mūrdhnaḥ sampātyate yatra jalam iva sthalam aśma-

pṛṣṭham avabhāsate tad avīcimat tilaśo viśīryamāṇa-śarīro na mriyamāṇaḥ punar āropito nipatati.

yaḥ—anyone who; *tu*—but; *iha*—in this life; *vā*—or; *anṛtam*—a lie; *vadati*—speaks; *sākṣye*—giving witness; *dravya-vinimaye*—in exchange for goods; *dāne*—in giving charity; *vā*—or; *kathañcit*—somehow; *saḥ*—that person; *vai*—indeed; *pretya*—after dying; *narake*—in the hell; *avīcimati*—named Avīcimat (having no water); *adhaḥ-śirāḥ*—with his head downward; *niravakāśe*—without support; *yojana-śata*—of eight hundred miles; *ucchrāyāt*—having a height; *giri*—of a mountain; *mūrdhnaḥ*—from the top; *sampātyate*—is thrown; *yatra*—where; *jalam iva*—like water; *sthalam*—land; *aśma-pṛṣṭham*—having a surface of stone; *avabhāsate*—appears; *tat*—that; *avīcimat*—having no water or waves; *tilaśaḥ*—in pieces as small as seeds; *viśīryamāṇa*—being broken; *śarīraḥ*—the body; *na mriyamāṇaḥ*—not dying; *punaḥ*—again; *āropitaḥ*—raised to the top; *nipatati*—falls down.

TRANSLATION

A person who in this life bears false witness or lies while transacting business or giving charity is severely punished after death by the agents of Yamarāja. Such a sinful man is taken to the top of a mountain eight hundred miles high and thrown headfirst into the hell known as Avīcimat. This hell has no shelter and is made of strong stone resembling the waves of water. There is no water there, however, and thus it is called Avīcimat [waterless]. Although the sinful man is repeatedly thrown from the mountain and his body broken to tiny pieces, he still does not die but continuously suffers chastisement.

TEXT 29

यस्त्विह वै विप्रो राजन्यो वैश्यो वा सोमपीथस्तत्कलत्रं वा सुरां व्रतस्थोऽपि वा पिबति प्रमादतस्तेषां निरयं नीतानामुरसि पदाऽऽक्रम्यास्ये वह्निना द्रवमाणं कार्ष्णायसं निषिञ्चन्ति ॥२९॥

yas tv iha vai vipro rājanyo vaiśyo vā soma-pīthas tat-kalatraṁ vā surāṁ vrata-stho'pi vā pibati pramādatas teṣāṁ nirayaṁ nītānām urasi padākramyāsye vahninā dravamāṇaṁ kārṣṇāyasaṁ niṣiñcanti.

yaḥ—anyone who; *tu*—but; *iha*—in this life; *vai*—indeed; *vipraḥ*—a learned *brāhmaṇa; rājanyaḥ*—a *kṣatriya; vaiśyaḥ*—a *vaiśya; vā*—or; *soma-*

pīthaḥ—drink *soma-rasa; tat*—his; *kalatram*—wife; *vā*—or; *surām*—liquor; *vrata-sthaḥ*—being situated in a vow; *api*—certainly; *vā*—or; *pibati*—drinks; *pramādataḥ*—out of illusion; *teṣām*—of all of them; *nirayam*—to hell; *nītānām*—being brought; *urasi*—on the chest; *padā*—with the foot; *ākramya* —stepping; *asye*—in the mouth; *vahninā*—by fire; *dravamāṇam*—melted; *kārṣṇāyasam*—iron; *niṣiñcanti*—they pour into.

TRANSLATION

Any brāhmaṇa or brāhmaṇa's wife who drinks liquor is taken by the agents of Yamarāja to the hell known as Ayaḥpāna. This hell also awaits any kṣatriya, vaiśya, or person under a vow who in illusion drinks soma-rasa. In Ayaḥpāna the agents of Yamarāja stand on their chests and pour hot melted iron into their mouths.

PURPORT

One should not be a *brāhmaṇa* in name only and engage in all kinds of sinful activities, especially drinking liquor. *Brāhmaṇas, kṣatriyas* and *vaiśyas* must behave according to the principles of their order. If they fall down to the level of *śūdras,* who are accustomed to drink liquor, they will be punished as described herein.

TEXT 30

अथ च यस्त्विह वा आत्मसम्भावनेन स्वयमधमो जन्मतपोविद्याचारवर्णाश्रमवतो वरीयसो न बहु मन्येत स मृतक एव मृत्वा क्षारकर्दमे निरयेऽवाक् शिरा निपातितो दुरन्ता यातना ह्यश्नुते ॥३०॥

atha ca yas tv iha vā ātma-sambhāvanena svayam adhamo janma-tapo-
vidyācāra-varṇāśramavato varīyaso na bahu manyeta sa mṛtaka eva
mṛtvā kṣārakardame niraye 'vāk-śirā nipātito durantā yātanā hy aśnute.

atha—furthermore; *ca*—also; *yaḥ*—anyone who; *tu*—but; *iha*—in this life; *vā*—or; *ātma-sambhāvanena*—by false prestige; *svayam*—himself; *adhamaḥ*—very degraded; *janma*—good birth; *tapaḥ*—austerities; *vidyā*—knowledge; *ācāra*—good behavior; *varṇa-āśrama-vataḥ*—in terms of strictly following the principles of *varṇāśrama; varīyasaḥ*—of one who is more honorable; *na*—not; *bahu*—much; *manyeta*—respects; *saḥ*—he; *mṛtakaḥ* —a dead body; *eva*—only; *mṛtvā*—after dying; *kṣārakardame*—named Kṣārakardama; *niraye*—in the hell; *avāk-śirā*—with his head downward;

nipātitaḥ—thrown; *durantāḥ yātanāḥ*—severe painful conditions; *hi*—indeed; *aśnute*—suffers.

TRANSLATION

A lowborn and abominable person who in this life becomes falsely proud, thinking "I am great," and who thus fails to show proper respect to one more elevated than he by birth, austerity, education, behavior, caste or spiritual order, is like a dead man even in this lifetime, and after death he is thrown headfirst into the hell known as Kṣārakardama. There he must suffer great tribulation at the hands of the agents of Yamarāja.

PURPORT

One should not become falsely proud. One must be respectful toward a person more elevated than he by birth, education, behavior, caste or spiritual order. If one does not show respect to such highly elevated persons but indulges in false pride, he receives punishment in Kṣārakardama.

TEXT 31

ये त्विह वै पुरुषाः पुरुषमेधेन यजन्ते याश्च स्त्रियो नृपशून् खादन्ति तांश्च ते पशव इव निहता यमसदने यातयन्तो रक्षोगणाः सौनिका इव स्वधितिनावदायासृक् पिबन्ति नृत्यन्ति च गायन्ति च हृष्यमाणा यथेह पुरुषादाः ॥३१॥

ye tv iha vai puruṣāḥ puruṣa-medhena yajante yāś ca striyo nṛ-paśūn khādanti tāṁś ca te paśava iva nihatā yama-sadane yātayanto rakṣo-gaṇāḥ saunikā iva svadhitināvadāyāsṛk pibanti nṛtyanti ca gāyanti ca hṛṣyamāṇā yatheha puruṣādāḥ.

ye—persons who; *tu*—but; *iha*—in this life; *vai*—indeed; *puruṣāḥ*—men; *puruṣa-medhena*—by sacrifice of a man; *yajante*—worship (the goddess Kālī or Bhadra Kālī); *yāḥ*—those who; *ca*—and; *striyaḥ*—women; *nṛ-paśūn*—the men used as sacrifice; *khādanti*—eat; *tān*—them; *ca*—and; *te*—they; *paśavaḥ iva*—like the animals; *nihatāḥ*—being slain; *yama-sadane*—in the abode of Yamarāja; *yātayantaḥ*—punishing; *rakṣaḥ-gaṇāḥ*—being Rākṣasas; *saunikāḥ*—the killers; *iva*—like; *svadhitinā*—by a sword; *avadāya*—cutting to pieces; *asṛk*—the blood; *pibanti*—drink; *nṛtyanti*—dance; *ca*—and; *gāyanti*—sing; *ca*—also; *hṛṣyamāṇāḥ*—being delighted; *yathā*—just like; *iha*—in this world; *puruṣa-adāḥ*—the man-eaters.

TRANSLATION

There are men and women in this world who sacrifice human beings to Bhairava or Bhadra Kālī and then eat their victims' flesh. Those who perform such sacrifices are taken after death to the abode of Yamarāja, where their victims, having taken the form of Rākṣasas, cut them to pieces with sharpened swords. Just as in this world the man-eaters drank their victims' blood, dancing and singing in jubilation, their victims now enjoy drinking the blood of the sacrificers and celebrating in the same way.

TEXT 32

ये त्विह वा अनागसोऽरण्ये ग्रामे वा वैश्रम्भकैरुपसृतानुपविश्रम्भय्य जिजीविषून् शूलसूत्रादिषूपप्रोतान् क्रीडनकतया यातयन्ति तेऽपि च प्रेत्य यमयातनासु शूलादिषु प्रोतात्मानः क्षुत्तृड्भ्यां चाभिहताः कङ्कवटादिभिश्चेतस्ततस्तिग्मतुण्डैराहन्यमाना आत्मशमलं स्मरन्ति ॥३२॥

ye tv iha vā anāgaso 'raṇye grāme vā vaiśrambhakair upasṛtān
upaviśrambhayya jijīviṣūn śūla-sūtrādiṣūpaprotān krīḍanakatayā
yātayanti te 'pi ca pretya yama-yātanāsu śūlādiṣu protātmānaḥ kṣut-
tṛḍbhyāṁ cābhihatāḥ kaṅka-vaṭādibhiś cetas tatas tigma-tuṇḍair
āhanyamānā ātma-śamalaṁ smaranti.

ye—persons who; *tu*—but; *iha*—in this life; *vā*—or; *anāgasaḥ*—who are faultless; *araṇye*—in the forest; *grāme*—in the village; *vā*—or; *vaiśrambhakaiḥ*—by means of good faith; *upasṛtān*—brought near; *upaviśrambhayya*—inspiring with confidence; *jijīviṣūn*—who want to be protected; *śūla-sūtra-ādiṣu*—on a lance, thread, and so on; *upaprotān*—fixed; *krīḍanakatayā*—like a plaything; *yātayanti*—cause pain; *te*—those persons; *api*—certainly; *ca*—and; *pretya*—after dying; *yama-yātanāsu*—the persecutions of Yamarāja; *śūla-ādiṣu*—on lances and so on; *prota-ātmānaḥ*—whose bodies are fixed; *kṣut-tṛḍbhyām*—by hunger and thirst; *ca*—also; *abhihatāḥ*—overwhelmed; *kaṅka-vaṭa-ādibhiḥ*—by birds such as herons and vultures; *ca*—and; *itaḥ tataḥ*—here and there; *tigma-tuṇḍaiḥ*—having pointed beaks; *āhanyamānāḥ*—being tortured; *ātma-śamalam*—own sinful activities; *smaranti*—they remember.

TRANSLATION

In this life some people give shelter to animals and birds that come to them for protection in the village or forest, and after making them believe

that they will be protected, such people pierce them with lances or threads and play with them like toys, giving them great pain. After death such people are brought by the assistants of Yamarāja to the hell known as Śūlaprota, where their bodies are pierced with sharp, needlelike lances. They suffer from hunger and thirst, and sharp-beaked birds such as vultures and herons come at them from all sides to tear at their bodies. Tortured and suffering, they can then remember the sinful activities they committed in the past.

TEXT 33

ये त्विह वै भूतान्युद्वेजयन्ति नरा उल्बणस्वभावा यथा दन्दशूकास्तेऽपि प्रेत्य नरके दन्दशूकाख्ये निपतन्ति यत्र नृप दन्दशूकाः पञ्चमुखाः सप्तमुखा उपसृत्य ग्रसन्ति यथा बिलेशयान् ॥३३॥

ye tv iha vai bhūtāny udvejayanti narā ulbaṇa-svabhāvā yathā dandaśūkās te 'pi pretya narake dandaśūkākhye nipatanti yatra nṛpa dandaśūkāḥ pañca-mukhāḥ sapta-mukhā upasṛtya grasanti yathā bileśayān.

ye—persons who; *tu*—but; *iha*—in this life; *vai*—indeed; *bhūtāni*—to living entities; *udvejayanti*—cause unnecessary pain; *narāḥ*—men; *ulbaṇa-svabhāvāḥ*—angry by nature; *yathā*—just like; *dandaśūkāḥ*—snakes; *te*—they; *api*—also; *pretya*—after dying; *narake*—in the hell; *dandaśūka-ākhye*—named Dandaśūka; *nipatanti*—fall down; *yatra*—where; *nṛpa*—O King; *dandaśūkāḥ*—serpents; *pañca-mukhāḥ*—having five hoods; *sapta-mukhāḥ*—having seven hoods; *upasṛtya*—reaching up; *grasanti*—eat; *yathā*—just like; *bileśayān*—mice.

TRANSLATION

Those who in this life are like envious serpents, always angry and giving pain to other living entities, fall after death into the hell known as Dandaśūka. My dear King, in this hell there are serpents with five or seven hoods. These serpents eat such sinful persons just as snakes eat mice.

TEXT 34

ये त्विह वा अन्धावटकुसूलगुहादिषु भूतानि निरुन्धन्ति तथामुत्र तेष्वेवोपवेश्य सगरेण वह्निना धूमेन निरुन्धन्ति ॥३४॥

ye tv iha vā andhāvaṭa-kusūla-guhādiṣu bhūtāni nirundhanti tathāmutra teṣv evopaveśya sagareṇa vahninā dhūmena nirundhanti.

ye—persons who; *tu*—but; *iha*—in this life; *vā*—or; *andha-avaṭa*—a blind well; *kusūla*—granaries; *guha-ādiṣu*—and in caves; *bhūtāni*—the living entities; *nirundhanti*—confine; *tathā*—similarly; *amutra*—in the next life; *teṣu*—in those same places; *eva*—certainly; *upaveśya*—causing to enter; *sagareṇa*—with poisonous fumes; *vahninā*—with fire; *dhūmena*—with smoke; *nirundhanti*—confine.

TRANSLATION

Those who in this life confine other living entities in dark wells, granaries or mountain caves are put after death into the hell known as Avaṭa-nirodhana. There they themselves are pushed into dark wells, where poisonous fumes and smoke suffocate them and they suffer very severely.

TEXT 35

यस्त्विह वा अतिथीनभ्यागतान् वा गृहपतिरसकृदुपगतमन्युर्दिधक्षुरिव पापेन चक्षुषा निरीक्षते तस्य चापि निरये पापदृष्टेरक्षिणी वज्रतुण्डा गृध्राः कङ्ककाकवटादयः प्रसह्योरुबलादुत्पाटयन्ति ॥३५॥

yas tv iha vā atithīn abhyāgatān vā gṛha-patir asakṛd upagata-manyur didhakṣur iva pāpena cakṣuṣā nirīkṣate tasya cāpi niraye pāpa-dṛṣṭer akṣiṇī vajra-tuṇḍā gṛdhrāḥ kaṅka-kāka-vaṭādayaḥ prasahyoru-balād utpāṭayanti.

yaḥ—a person who; *tu*—but; *iha*—in this life; *vā*—or; *atithīn*—guests; *abhyāgatān*—visitors; *vā*—or; *gṛha-patiḥ*—a householder; *asakṛt*—many times; *upagata*—obtaining; *manyuḥ*—anger; *didhakṣuḥ*—one desiring to burn; *iva*—like; *pāpena*—sinful; *cakṣuṣā*—with eyes; *nirīkṣate*—looks at; *tasya*—of him; *ca*—and; *api*—certainly; *niraye*—in hell; *pāpa-dṛṣṭeḥ*—of he whose vision has become sinful; *akṣiṇī*—the eyes; *vajra-tuṇḍāḥ*—those who have powerful beaks; *gṛdhrāḥ*—vultures; *kaṅka*—herons; *kāka*—crows; *vaṭa-ādayaḥ*—and other birds; *prasahya*—violently; *uru-balāt*—with great force; *utpāṭayanti*—pluck out.

TRANSLATION

A householder who receives guests or visitors with cruel glances, as if to burn them to ashes, is put into the hell called Paryāvartana, where he is

gazed at by hard-eyed vultures, herons, crows and similar birds, which suddenly swoop down and pluck out his eyes with great force.

PURPORT

According to the Vedic etiquette, even an enemy who comes to a householder's home should be received in such a gentle way that he forgets that he has come to the home of an enemy. A guest who comes to one's home should be received very politely. If he is unwanted, the householder should not stare at him with blinking eyes, for one who does so will be put into the hell known as Paryāvartana after death, and there many ferocious birds like vultures, crows, and coknis will suddenly come upon him and pluck out his eyes.

TEXT 36

यस्त्विह वा आढ्याभिमतिरहङ्कृतिस्तिर्यक्प्रेक्षणः सर्वतोऽभिविशङ्की अर्थव्ययनाशचिन्तया परिशुष्यमाणहृदयवदनो निर्वृतिमनवगतो ग्रह इवार्थमभिरक्षति स चापि प्रेत्य तदुत्पादनोत्कर्षणसंरक्षणशमलग्रहः सूचीमुखे नरके निपतति यत्र ह वित्तग्रहं पापपुरुषं धर्मराजपुरुषा वायका इव सर्वतोऽङ्गेषु सूत्रैः परिवयन्ति ॥३६॥

yas tv iha vā āḍhyābhimatir ahaṅkṛtis tiryak-prekṣaṇaḥ sarvato 'bhiviśaṅkī artha-vyaya-nāśa-cintayā pariśuṣyamāṇa-hṛdaya-vadano nirvṛtim anavagato graha ivārtham abhirakṣati sa cāpi pretya tad-utpādanotkarṣaṇa-saṁrakṣaṇa-śamala-grahaḥ sūcīmukhe narake nipatati yatra ha vitta-grahaṁ pāpa-puruṣaṁ dharmarāja-puruṣā vāyakā iva sarvato 'ṅgeṣu sūtraiḥ parivayanti.

yaḥ—any person who; *tu*—but; *iha*—in this world; *vā*—or; *āḍhya-abhimatiḥ*—proud because of wealth; *ahaṅkṛtiḥ*—egotistic; *tiryak-prekṣaṇaḥ*—whose vision is crooked; *sarvataḥ abhiviśaṅkī*—always fearful of being cheated by others, even by superiors; *artha-vyaya-nāśa-cintayā*—by the thought of expenditure and loss; *pariśuṣyamāṇa*—dried up; *hṛdaya-vadanaḥ*—his heart and face; *nirvṛtim*—happiness; *anavagataḥ*—not obtaining; *grahaḥ*—a ghost; *iva*—like; *artham*—wealth; *abhirakṣati*—protects; *saḥ*—he; *ca*—also; *api*—indeed; *pretya*—after dying; *tat*—of those riches; *utpādana*—of the earning; *utkarṣaṇa*—increasing; *saṁrakṣaṇa*—protecting; *śamala-grahaḥ*—accepting the sinful activities; *sūcīmukhe*—named Sūcīmukha; *narake*—in the hell; *nipatati*—falls down; *yatra*—where; *ha*—indeed; *vitta-graham*—as a money-grabbing ghost; *pāpa-puruṣam*—very sinful man; *dharmarāja-puruṣāḥ*—the commanding men of Yamarāja; *vāyakāḥ iva*—like expert weavers; *sarvataḥ*—all over; *aṅgeṣu*—on the limbs of the body; *sūtraiḥ*—by threads; *parivayanti*—stitch.

TRANSLATION

One who in this world or this life is very proud of his wealth always thinks, "I am so rich. Who can equal me?" His vision is twisted, and he is always afraid that someone will take his wealth. Indeed, he even suspects his superiors. His face and heart dry up at the thought of losing his wealth, and therefore he always looks like a wretched fiend. He is not in any way able to obtain actual happiness, and he does not know what it is to be free from anxiety. Because of the sinful things he does to earn money, augment his wealth and protect it, he is put into the hell called Sūcīmukha, where the officials of Yamarāja punish him by stitching thread through his entire body like weavers manufacturing cloth.

PURPORT

When one possesses more wealth than necessary, he certainly becomes very proud. This is the situation of men in modern civilization. According to the Vedic culture, *brāhmaṇas* do not possess anything, whereas *kṣatriyas* possess riches, but only for performing sacrifices and other noble activities as prescribed in the Vedic injunctions. A *vaiśya* also earns money honestly through agriculture, cow protection and some trade. If a *śūdra* gets money, however, he will spend it lavishly, without discrimination, or simply accumulate it for no purpose. Because in this age there are no qualified *brāhmaṇas, kṣatriyas* or *vaiśyas,* almost everyone is a *śūdra* (*kalau śūdra-sambhavaḥ*). Therefore the *śūdra* mentality is causing great harm to modern civilization. A *śūdra* does not know how to use money to render transcendental loving service to the Lord. Money is also called *lakṣmī,* and Lakṣmī is always engaged in the service of Nārāyaṇa. Wherever there is money, it must be engaged in the service of Lord Nārāyaṇa. Everyone should use his money to spread the great transcendental movement of Kṛṣṇa consciousness. If one does not spend money for this purpose but accumulates more than necessary, he will certainly become proud of the money he illegally possesses. The money actually belongs to Kṛṣṇa, who says in *Bhagavad-gītā* (5.29), *bhoktāraṁ yajña-tapasāṁ sarva-loka-maheśvaram:* "I am the true enjoyer of sacrifices and penances, and I am the owner of all the planets." Therefore nothing belongs to anyone but Kṛṣṇa. One who possesses more money than he needs should spend it for Kṛṣṇa. Unless one does so, he will become puffed up because of his false possessions, and therefore he will be punished in the next life, as described herein.

TEXT 37

एवंविधा नरका यमालये सन्ति शतशः सहस्रशस्तेषु सर्वेषु च सर्व एवाधर्मवर्तिनो ये केचिदिहोदिता अनुदिताश्चावनिपते पर्यायेण विशन्ति तथैव धर्मानुवर्तिन इतरत्र इह तु पुनर्भवे त उभयशेषाभ्यां निविशन्ति ॥३७॥

evaṁ-vidhā narakā yamālaye santi śataśaḥ sahasraśas teṣu sarveṣu ca sarva evādharma-vartino ye kecid ihoditā anuditāś cāvani-pate paryāyeṇa viśanti tathaiva dharmānuvartina itaratra iha tu punar-bhave ta ubhaya-śeṣābhyāṁ niviśanti.

evam-vidhāḥ—of this sort; *narakāḥ*—the many hells; *yama-ālaye*—in the province of Yamarāja; *santi*—are; *śataśaḥ*—hundreds; *sahasraśaḥ*—thousands; *teṣu*—in those hellish planets; *sarveṣu*—all; *ca*—also; *sarve*—all; *eva*—indeed; *adharma-vartinaḥ*—persons not following the Vedic principles or regulative principles; *ye kecit*—whosoever; *iha*—here; *uditāḥ*—mentioned; *anuditāḥ*—not mentioned; *ca*—and; *avani-pate*—O King; *paryāyeṇa*—according to the degree of different kinds of sinful activity; *viśanti*—they enter; *tathā eva*—similarly; *dharma-anuvartinaḥ*—those who are pious and act according to the regulative principles or Vedic injunctions; *itaratra*—elsewhere; *iha*—on this planet; *tu*—but; *punaḥ-bhave*—into another birth; *te*—all of them; *ubhaya-śeṣābhyām*—by the remainder of the results of piety or vice; *niviśanti*—they enter.

TRANSLATION

My dear King Parīkṣit, in the province of Yamarāja there are hundreds and thousands of hellish planets. The impious people I have mentioned—and also those I have not mentioned—must all enter these various planets according to the degree of their impiety. Those who are pious, however, enter other planetary systems, namely the planets of the demigods. Nevertheless, both the pious and impious are again brought to earth after the results of their pious or impious acts are exhausted.

PURPORT

This corresponds to the beginning of Lord Kṛṣṇa's instructions in *Bhagavad-gītā. Tathā dehāntara-prāptiḥ:* within this material world, one is simply meant to change from one body to another in different planetary systems. *Ūrdhvaṁ gacchanti sattva-sthā:* those in the mode of goodness are elevated to the heavenly planets. *Adho gacchanti tāmasāḥ:* similarly, those too engrossed in ignorance enter the hellish planetary systems. Both of them, however, are subjected to the repetition of birth and death. In *Bhagavad-gītā* it is stated that even one who is very pious returns to earth after his enjoyment in the higher planetary systems is over (*kṣīṇe puṇye martya-lokaṁ viśanti*). Therefore, going from one planet to another does not solve the problems of life. The problems of life will only be solved when we no longer have to accept a material body. This can be possible if one simply becomes Kṛṣṇa conscious. As Kṛṣṇa says in *Bhagavad-gītā* (4.9):

janma karma ca me divyam
evaṁ yo vetti tattvataḥ
tyaktvā dehaṁ punar janma
naiti mām eti so'rjuna

"One who knows the transcendental nature of My appearance and activities does not, upon leaving the body, take his birth again in this material world, but attains My eternal abode, O Arjuna." This is the perfection of life and the real solution to life's problems. We should not be eager to go to the higher, heavenly planetary systems, nor should we act in such a way that we have to go to the hellish planets. The complete purpose of this material world will be fulfilled when we resume our spiritual identities and go back home, back to Godhead. The very simple method for doing this is prescribed by the Supreme Personality of Godhead. *Sarva-dharmān parityajya mām ekaṁ śaraṇaṁ vraja.* One should be neither pious nor impious. One should be a devotee and surrender to the lotus feet of Kṛṣṇa. This surrendering process is also very easy. Even a child can perform it. *Man-manā bhava mad-bhakto mad-yājī māṁ namaskuru.* One must always simply think of Kṛṣṇa by chanting Hare Kṛṣṇa, Hare Kṛṣṇa, Kṛṣṇa Kṛṣṇa, Hare Hare/ Hare Rāma, Hare Rāma, Rāma Rāma, Hare Hare. One should become Kṛṣṇa's devotee, worship Him and offer obeisances to Him. Thus one should engage all the activities of his life in the service of Lord Kṛṣṇa.

TEXT 38

निवृत्तिलक्षणमार्ग आदावेव व्याख्यातः ॥ एतावानेवाण्डकोशो यश्चतुर्दशधा पुराणेषु विकल्पित उपगीयते यत्तद्भगवतो नारायणस्य साक्षान्महापुरुषस्य स्थविष्ठं

रूपमात्ममायागुणमयमनुवर्णितमादृतः पठति शृणोति श्रावयति स उपगेयं भगवतः परमात्मनोऽग्राह्यमपि श्रद्धाभक्तिविशुद्धबुद्धिर्वेद ॥३८॥

nivṛtti-lakṣaṇa-mārga ādāv eva vyākhyātaḥ; etāvān evāṇḍa-kośo yaś caturdaśadhā purāṇeṣu vikalpita upagīyate yat tad bhagavato nārāyaṇasya sākṣān mahā-puruṣasya sthaviṣṭhaṁ rūpam ātmamāyā-guṇamayam anuvarṇitam ādṛtaḥ paṭhati śṛṇoti śrāvayati sa upageyaṁ bhagavataḥ paramātmano'grāhyam api śraddhā-bhakti-viśuddha-buddhir veda.

nivṛtti-lakṣaṇa-mārgaḥ—the path symptomized by renunciation, or the path of liberation; *ādau*—in the beginning (the Second and Third Cantos); *eva*—indeed; *vyākhyātaḥ*—described; *etāvān*—this much; *eva*—certainly; *aṇḍa-kośaḥ*—the universe, which resembles a big egg; *yaḥ*—which; *caturdaśa-dhā*—in fourteen parts; *purāṇeṣu*—in the *Purāṇas; vikalpitaḥ*—divided; *upagīyate*—is described; *yat*—which; *tat*—that; *bhagavataḥ*—of the Supreme Personality of Godhead; *nārāyaṇasya*—of Lord Nārāyaṇa; *sākṣāt*—directly; *mahā-puruṣasya*—of the Supreme Person; *sthaviṣṭham*—the gross; *rūpam*—form; *ātma-māyā*—of His own energy; *guṇa*—of the qualities; *mayam*—consisting; *anuvarṇitam*—described; *ādṛtaḥ*—venerating; *paṭhati*—one reads; *śṛṇoti*—or hears; *śrāvayati*—or explains; *saḥ*—that person; *upageyam*—song; *bhagavataḥ*—of the Supreme Personality of Godhead; *paramātmanaḥ*—of the Supersoul; *agrāhyam*—difficult to understand; *api*—although; *śraddhā*—by faith; *bhakti*—and devotion; *viśuddha*—purified; *buddhiḥ*—whose intelligence; *veda*—understands.

TRANSLATION

In the beginning [the Second and Third Cantos of Śrīmad-Bhāgavatam] I have already described how one can progress on the path of liberation. In the Purāṇas the vast universal existence, which is like an egg divided into fourteen parts, is described. This vast form is considered the external body of the Lord, created by His energy and qualities. It is generally called the virāṭa-rūpa. If one reads the description of this external form of the Lord with great faith, or if one hears about it or explains it to others to propagate bhāgavata-dharma, or Kṛṣṇa consciousness, his faith and devotion in spiritual consciousness, Kṛṣṇa consciousness, will gradually increase. Although developing this consciousness is very difficult, by this process one can purify himself and gradually come to an awareness of the Supreme Absolute Truth.

PURPORT

The Kṛṣṇa consciousness movement is pushing forward the publication of *Śrīmad-Bhāgavatam,* as explained especially for the understanding of the modern civilized man, to awaken him to his original consciousness. Without this consciousness, one melts into complete darkness. Whether one goes to the upper planetary systems or the hellish planetary systems, he simply wastes his time. Therefore one should hear of the universal position of the *virāṭa* form of the Lord as described in *Śrīmad-Bhāgavatam.* That will help one save himself from material conditional life and gradually elevate him to the path of liberation so that he can go back home, back to Godhead.

TEXT 39

श्रुत्वा स्थूलं तथा सूक्ष्मं रूपं भगवतो यतिः ।
स्थूले निर्जितमात्मानं शनैः सूक्ष्मं धिया नयेदिति ॥३९॥

śrutvā sthūlaṁ tathā sūkṣmaṁ
rūpaṁ bhagavato yatiḥ
sthūle nirjitam ātmānaṁ
śanaiḥ sūkṣmaṁ dhiyā nayed iti

śrutvā—after hearing of (from the disciplic succession); *sthūlam*—gross; *tathā*—as well as; *sūkṣmam*—subtle; *rūpam*—form; *bhagavataḥ*—of the Supreme Personality of Godhead; *yatiḥ*—a *sannyāsī* or devotee; *sthūle*—the gross form; *nirjitam*—conquered; *ātmānam*—the mind; *śanaiḥ*—gradually; *sūkṣmam*—the subtle, spiritual form of the Lord; *dhiyā*—by intelligence; *nayet*—one should lead it to; *iti*—thus.

TRANSLATION

One who is interested in liberation, who accepts the path of liberation and is not attracted to the path of conditional life, is called yati, or a devotee. Such a person should first control his mind by thinking of the virāṭa-rūpa, the gigantic universal form of the Lord, and then gradually think of the spiritual form of Kṛṣṇa [sac-cid-ānanda-vigraha] after hearing of both forms. Thus one's mind is fixed in samādhi. By devotional service one can then realize the spiritual form of the Lord, which is the destination of devotees. Thus his life becomes successful.

PURPORT

It is said, *mahat-sevāṁ dvāram āhur vimukteḥ:* if one wants to progress on the path of liberation, he should associate with *mahātmās,* or liberated devotees, because in such association there is a full chance for hearing, describing and chanting about the name, form, qualities and paraphernalia of the Supreme Personality of Godhead, all of which are described in *Śrīmad-Bhāgavatam.* On the path of bondage, one eternally undergoes the repetition of birth and death. One who desires liberation from such bondage should join the International Society for Krishna Consciousness and thus take advantage of the opportunity to hear *Śrīmad-Bhāgavatam* from devotees and also explain it to propagate Kṛṣṇa consciousness.

TEXT 40

भूद्वीपवर्षसरिदद्रिनभःसमुद्र-
पातालदिङ्नरकभागणलोकसंस्था ।
गीता मया तव नृपाद्भुतमीश्वरस्य
स्थूलं वपुः सकलजीवनिकायधाम ॥४०॥

bhū-dvīpa-varṣa-sarid-adri-nabhaḥ-samudra-
pātāla-diṅ-naraka-bhāgaṇa-loka-saṁsthā
gītā mayā tava nṛpādbhutam īśvarasya
sthūlaṁ vapuḥ sakala-jīva-nikāya-dhāma

bhū—of this planet earth; *dvīpa*—and other different planetary systems; *varṣa*—of tracts of land; *sarit*—rivers; *adri*—mountains; *nabhaḥ*—the sky; *samudra*—oceans; *pātāla*—lower planets; *dik*—directions; *naraka*—the hellish planets; *bhāgaṇa-loka*—the luminaries and higher planets; *saṁsthā*—the situation; *gītā*—described; *mayā*—by me; *tava*—for you; *nṛpa*—O King; *adbhutam*—wonderful; *īśvarasya*—of the Supreme Personality of Godhead; *sthūlam*—gross; *vapuḥ*—body; *sakala-jīva-nikāya*—of all the masses of living entities; *dhāma*—which is the place of repose.

TRANSLATION

My dear King, I have now described for you this planet earth, other planetary systems, and their lands [varṣas], rivers and mountains. I have also described the sky, the oceans, the lower planetary systems, the directions, the hellish planetary systems and the stars. These constitute

the virāṭa-rūpa, the gigantic material form of the Lord, on which all living entities repose. Thus I have explained the wonderful expanse of the external body of the Lord.

Thus end the Bhaktivedanta purports of the Fifth Canto, Twenty-sixth Chapter, of Śrīmad-Bhāgavatam, *entitled "A Description of the Hellish Planets."*

—Completed in the Honolulu temple of the Pañca-tattva, June 5, 1975.

There is a supplementary note written by His Divine Grace Bhaktisiddhānta Sarasvatī Gosvāmī Mahārāja Prabhupāda in his *Gauḍīya-bhāṣya.* Its translation is as follows. Learned scholars who have full knowledge of all the Vedic scriptures agree that the incarnations of the Supreme Personality of Godhead are innumerable. These incarnations are classified into two divisions, called *prābhava* and *vaibhava.* According to the scriptures, *prābhava* incarnations are also classified in two divisions—those which are called eternal and those which are not vividly described. In this Fifth Canto of *Śrīmad-Bhāgavatam,* in Chapters Three through Six, there is a description of Ṛṣabhadeva, but there is not an expanded description of His spiritual activities. Therefore He is considered to belong to the second group of *prābhava* incarnations. In *Śrīmad-Bhāgavatam,* First Canto, Chapter Three, verse 13, it is said:

aṣṭame merudevyāṁ tu
nābher jāta urukramaḥ
darśayan vartma dhīrāṇāṁ
sarvāśrama-namaskṛtam

"Lord Viṣṇu appeared in the eighth incarnation as the son of Mahārāja Nābhi [the son of Āgnīdhra] and his wife Merudevī. He showed the path of perfection, the *paramahaṁsa* stage of life, which is worshiped by all the followers of *varṇāśrama-dharma.*" Ṛṣabhadeva is the Supreme Personality of Godhead, and His body is spiritual (*sac-cid-ānanda-vigraha*). Therefore one might ask how it might be possible that he passed stool and urine. The Gauḍīya *vedānta ācārya* Baladeva Vidyābhūṣaṇa has replied to this question in his book known as *Siddhānta-ratna* (First Portion, texts 65–68). Imperfect men call attention to Ṛṣabhadeva's passing stool and urine as a subject matter for the study of nondevotees, who do not understand the spiritual position of a transcendental body. In this Fifth Canto of *Śrīmad-Bhāgavatam* (5.6.11) the illusioned and bewildered state of the materialists of this age is fully described. Elsewhere in Fifth Canto (5.5.19) Ṛṣabhadeva stated, *idaṁ śarīram mama durvibhāvyam:* "This body of Mine is inconceivable for materialists." This is also confirmed by Lord Kṛṣṇa in *Bhagavad-gītā* (9.11):

avajānanti māṁ mūḍhā
mānuṣīṁ tanum āśritam
paraṁ bhāvam ajānanto
mama bhūta-maheśvaram

"Fools deride Me when I descend in the human form. They do not know My transcendental nature and My supreme dominion over all that be." The human form of the Supreme Personality of Godhead is extremely difficult to understand, and, in fact, for a common man it is inconceivable. Therefore Ṛṣabhadeva has directly explained that His own body belongs to the spiritual platform. This being so, Ṛṣabhadeva did not actually pass stool and urine. Even though He superficially seemed to pass stool and urine, that was also transcendental and cannot be imitated by any common man. It is also stated in *Śrīmad-Bhāgavatam* that the stool and urine of Ṛṣabhadeva were full of transcendental fragrance. One may imitate Ṛṣabhadeva, but he cannot imitate Him by passing stool that is fragrant.

The activities of Ṛṣabhadeva, therefore, do not support the claims of a certain class of men known as *arhat,* who sometimes advertise that they are followers of Ṛṣabhadeva. How can they be followers of Ṛṣabhadeva while they act against the Vedic principles? Śukadeva Gosvāmī has related that after hearing about the characteristics of Lord Ṛṣabhadeva, the King of Koṅka, Veṅka and Kuṭaka initiated a system of religious principles known as *arhat.* These principles were not in accord with Vedic principles, and therefore they are called *pāṣaṇḍa-dharma.* The members of the *arhat* community considered Ṛṣabhadeva's activities material. However, Ṛṣabhadeva is an incarnation of the Supreme Personality of Godhead. Therefore He is on the transcendental platform, and no one can compare to Him.

Ṛṣabhadeva personally exhibited the activities of the Supreme Personality of Godhead. As stated in *Śrīmad-Bhāgavatam* (5.6.8), *dāvānalas tad vanam ālelihānaḥ saha tena dadāha:* at the conclusion of Ṛṣabhadeva's pastimes, an entire forest and the Lord's body were burned to ashes in a great forest fire. In the same way, Ṛṣabhadeva burned people's ignorance to ashes. He exhibited the characteristics of a *paramahaṁsa* in His instructions to His sons. The principles of the *arhat* community, however, do not correspond to the teachings of Ṛṣabhadeva.

Śrīla Baladeva Vidyābhūṣaṇa remarks that in the Eighth Canto of *Śrīmad-Bhāgavatam* there is another description of Ṛṣabhadeva, but that Ṛṣabhadeva is different from the one described in this canto.

END OF THE FIFTH CANTO

Appendixes

About the Author

His Divine Grace A.C. Bhaktivedanta Swami Prabhupāda appeared in this world in 1896 in Calcutta, India. He first met his spiritual master, Śrīla Bhaktisiddhānta Sarasvatī Gosvāmi, in Calcutta in 1922. Śrīla Bhaktisiddhānta Sarasvatī, a prominent religious scholar and the founder of sixty-four Gauḍīya Maṭhas (Vedic institutes) in India, liked this educated young man and convinced him to dedicate his life to teaching Vedic knowledge. Śrīla Prabhupāda became his student and, in 1933, his formally initiated disciple.

At their first meeting, Śrīla Bhaktisiddhānta Sarasvatī requested Śrīla Prabhupāda to broadcast Vedic knowledge in English. In the years that followed, Śrīla Prabhupāda wrote a commentary on the *Bhagavad-gītā,* assisted the Gauḍīya Maṭha in its work, and, in 1944, started *Back to Godhead,* an English fortnightly magazine. Single-handedly, Śrīla Prabhupāda edited it, typed the manuscripts, checked the galley proofs, and even distributed the individual copies. The magazine is now being continued by his disciples all over the world.

In 1950 Śrīla Prabhupāda retired from married life, adopting the *vānaprastha* (retired) order to devote more time to his studies and writing. He traveled to the holy city of Vṛndāvana, where he lived in humble circumstances in the historic temple of Rādhā-Dāmodara. There he engaged for several years in deep study and writing. He accepted the renounced order of life (*sannyāsa*) in 1959. At Rādhā-Dāmodara, Śrīla Prabhupāda began work on his life's masterpiece: a multivolume commentated translation of the eighteen-thousand-verse *Śrīmad-Bhāgavatam* (*Bhāgavata Purāṇa*). He also wrote *Easy Journey to Other Planets.*

After publishing three volumes of the *Bhāgavatam,* Śrīla Prabhupāda came to the United States, in September 1965, to fulfill the mission of his spiritual master. Subsequently, His Divine Grace wrote more than sixty volumes of authoritative commentated translations and summary studies of the philosophical and religious classics of India.

When he first arrived by freighter in New York City, Śrīla Prabhupāda was practically penniless. It was after almost a year of great difficulty that he established the International Society for Krishna Consciousness in July of 1966. Before he passed away on November 14, 1977, he had guided the Society and seen it grow to a worldwide confederation of more than one hundred *ashrams,* schools, temples, institutes, and farm communities.

In 1972 His Divine Grace introduced the Vedic system of primary and secondary education in the West by founding the *gurukula* school in Dallas, Texas. Since then his disciples have established similar schools throughout the United States and the rest of the world.

Śrīla Prabhupāda also inspired the construction of several large international cultural centers in India. The center at Śrīdhāma Māyāpur is the site for a planned spiritual city, an ambitious project for which construction will extend over many years to come. In Vṛndāvana are the magnificent Kṛṣṇa-Balarāma Temple and International Guesthouse, *gurukula* school, and Śrīla Prabhupāda Memorial and Museum. There is also a major cultural and educational center in Mumbai. There are beautiful temples in Delhi, Bangalore, Ahmedabad and Vadodara besides many other centers throughout India.

Śrīla Prabhupāda's most significant contribution, however, is his books. Highly respected by scholars for their authority, depth, and clarity, they are used as textbooks in numerous college courses. His writings have been translated into over fifty languages. The Bhaktivedanta Book Trust, established in 1972 exclusively to publish the works of His Divine Grace, has thus become the world's largest publisher of books in the field of Indian religion and philosophy.

In just twelve years, despite his advanced age, Śrīla Prabhupāda circled the globe fourteen times on lecture tours that took him to six continents. In spite of such a vigorous schedule, Śrīla Prabhupāda continued to write prolifically. His writings constitute a veritable library of Vedic philosophy, religion, literature, and culture.

References

The purports of *Śrīmad-Bhāgavatam* are all confirmed by standard Vedic authorities. The following authentic scriptures are cited in this volume. For specific page references, consult the general index.

Bhagavad-gītā

Bhakti-rasāmṛta-sindhu

Brahmāṇḍa Purāṇa

Brahma-saṁhitā

Bṛhan-nāradīya Purāṇa

Caitanya-bhāgavata

Caitanya-candrāmṛta

Caitanya-caritāmṛta

Chāndogya Upaniṣad

Garga Upaniṣad

Gautamīya-tantra

Hari-bhakti-vilāsa

Īśopaniṣad

Jyotir Veda

Kaṭha Upaniṣad

Kūrma Purāṇa

Laghu-bhāgavatāmṛta

Mahābhārata

Manu-saṁhitā

Muṇḍaka Upaniṣad

Nārada-pañcarātra

Padma Purāṇa

Satya-saṁhitā

Skanda Purāṇa

Śrīmad-Bhāgavatam

Śvetāśvatara Upaniṣad

Taittirīya Upaniṣad

Vāyu Purāṇa

Vedānta-saṅgraha

Vedānta-sūtra

Viṣṇu-dharmottara

Viṣṇu Purāṇa

Glossary

A

Ācārya—a spiritual master who teaches by his own example, and who sets the proper religious example for all human beings.

Acintya-śakti—the inconceivable energy of the Supreme Lord.

Adhibhautika—(misery) caused by other living beings.

Adhidaivika—(misery) caused by nature.

Adhokṣaja—a name for the Supreme Personality of Godhead, who is beyond material sense perception, who is not perceivable by impure material senses; revealed knowledge. The fourth of the five stages of Vedic knowledge.

Ādhyātmika—miseries arising from one's own body and mind.

Ādi-puruṣa—the Supreme Lord, Kṛṣṇa, the original person.

Ahaṁ brahmāsmi—the Vedic aphorism "I am spirit."

Ahaṁ mameti—the false conception of "I" and "mine" arising from identification of the self with the body.

Ahaṅkāra—false ego, by which the soul misidentifies with the material body.

Akāma—free from material desire.

Akāma-bhakta—one who serves the Lord without material motive.

Akarma (naiṣkarma)—action for which one suffers no reaction because it is performed in Kṛṣṇa consciousness; free from material desire.

Akiñcana-gocara—Lord Kṛṣṇa, who is easily approached by those who are materially exhausted.

Aṁśa—an expansion of the Supreme Lord.

Ānanda—spiritual, transcendental bliss.

Aṇimā-siddhi—mystic power by which one can become as small as an atom.

Antarikṣa—outer space.

Apavarga—liberation from *pavarga*, the miseries of material existence.

Aprākṛta—spiritual, or anti-material, transcendental to material nature; the fifth of the five stages of Vedic knowledge.

Aprameya—immeasurable.

Apsarā—a heavenly courtesan. The most beautiful women in the heavenly planets, who are expert at dancing.

Arcā-vigraha(Arcā-mūrti)—an authorized form of God manifested through material elements, as in a painting or statue of Kṛṣṇa worshiped in a temple or home. Actually present in this form, the Lord accepts worship from His devotees.

Arcana—the procedures followed for worshiping the *arcā-vigraha,* the Deity in the temple; engaging all the senses in the service of the Lord.

Asat—not eternal, temporary.

Āśrama—a spiritual order of life. The four *āśramas* are *brahmacārī* or student life, *gṛhastha* or married life, *vānaprastha* or retired life, and *sannyāsa* or the renounced order of life; the home of the spiritual master, a place where spiritual practices are executed.

Asura—demon, one who does not follow the principles of scripture, an atheist, a gross materialist. One who is envious of God, and is averse to the supremacy and service of the Supreme Lord, Viṣṇu.

Ātmā—the self (refers sometimes to the body, sometimes to the soul, and sometimes to the senses).

Ātma-nivedana—the devotional process of surrendering everything to the Lord.

Ātma-tattva—spiritual science.

Avadhūta—a very saintly and renounced person who is above all rules and regulations having surpassed the need for them.

Avara—material.

Avatāra—literally "one who descends." A partially or fully empowered incarnation of Lord Kṛṣṇa who descends from the spiritual sky to the material universe with a particular mission described in scriptures. Lord Śrī Kṛṣṇa is the original Personality of Godhead from whom all *avatāras* originate. There are two broad categories of *avatāras.* Some, like Śrī Kṛṣṇa, Śrī Rāma and Śrī Nṛsiṁha, are Viṣṇu-tattva, i.e. direct forms of God Himself, the source of all power. Others are ordinary souls (*jīva-tattva*) who are called *śaktyāveśa avatāras,* and are empowered by the Lord to execute a certain purpose.

B

Bhagavad-bhakti—*bhakti-yoga,* devotional service to the Supreme Lord.

Bhagavān—the Supreme Personality of Godhead, an epithet of the Supreme Person; the Personality of Godhead, the possessor (*vān*) of six opulences (*bhaga*) in unlimited fullness: wealth (*aiśvarya*), strength (*vīrya*), fame (*yaśaḥ*), beauty (*śriyaḥ*), knowledge (*jñāna*) and renunciation (*vairāgya*).

Bhāgavata-dharma—the science of devotional service to the Supreme Lord; the religious principles enunciated by the Lord; the eternal function of the living being.

Bhakta—a devotee of the Lord; one who performs devotional service (*bhakti*).

Bhakti—devotional service to the Supreme Lord; purified service of the senses of the Lord by one's own senses; love and devotion to the Supreme Personality of Godhead, Lord Kṛṣṇa. The formal systematization of devotion is called *bhakti-yoga*.

Bhakti-yoga—the system of cultivation of pure devotional service to the Supreme Personality of Godhead, Lord Kṛṣṇa, which is not tinged by sense gratification or philosophical speculation. It consists of nine *aṅgas* or parts: (1) *śravaṇaṁ*–hearing about the transcendental holy name, form, and other qualities of the Lord (2) *kīrtanaṁ*– chanting about these qualities, (3) *viṣṇoḥ smaraṇaṁ*–remembering them, (4) *pāda-sevanam*–serving the lotus feet of the Lord, (5) *arcanaṁ*–worshipping the Deity of the Lord, (6) *vandanaṁ*–offering prayers to the Lord, (7) *dāsyaṁ*–serving His mission, (8) *sakhyam*–making friends with the Lord, and (9) *ātma-nivedanam*–surrendering everything unto Him.

Bhukti—material enjoyment.

Bila-svarga—the subterranean heavens.

Brahma-bandhu—one born in a *brāhmaṇa* family but lacking brahminical qualification.

Brahma-bhūta—the joyful state of being freed from material contamination. One in this state is characterized by transcendental happiness, and he engages in the service of the Supreme Lord; liberation.

Brahmacārī—a celibate student in the first order or *āśrama* of Vedic spiritual life, staying under the care of a spiritual master. They accepted a strict vow of celibacy up to the age of twenty-five, at which time they could marry or continue the life of celibacy.

Brahmacarya—celibate student life, the first order of Vedic spiritual life; the vow of strict abstinence from sex indulgence.

Brahma-jijñāsā—inquiry into the Absolute Truth; spiritual inquiry into one's own identity.

Brahmajyoti—the impersonal bodily effulgence emanating from the transcendental body of the Supreme Lord Kṛṣṇa, which constitutes the brilliant illumination of the spiritual sky; From Kṛṣṇa's transcendental personal form of eternity, knowledge and bliss emanates a shining effulgence called the *brahmajyoti* (light of Brahman). The material *prakṛti*, the souls or *jīvas* who desire to enjoy matter, and *kāla* (time), are situated within this *brahmajyoti*, which is pure existence devoid of difference and activity. It is the impersonal Brahman of the Mayavādīs, and the Clear Light of some Buddhist sects. For many mystics and philosophers the world over, the *brahmajyoti* is the indefinable One from which all things emerge in the beginning and merge into at the end. The *brahmajyoti* is Kṛṣṇa's feature of *sat* (eternality) separated from *cit* (knowledge) and *ānanda* (bliss).

Brāhmaṇa—a member of the intellectual, priestly class; a person wise in Vedic knowledge, fixed in goodness and knowledge of Brahman, the Absolute Truth; one of the four orders of Vedic society. Their occupation consists of learning and teaching Vedic literature, learning and teaching Deity worship, and receiving and giving charity.

Brahmāṇḍa-bhramaṇa—wandering up and down throughout the universe.

Brahma-satra—always meditating on the Supreme Lord.

Brahma-saukhya—spiritual happiness, which is unobstructed and eternal.

C

Caṇḍāla—an outcaste or untouchable; dog-eater, the lowest class of human beings.

Channāvatāra—a concealed incarnation in disguise.

D

Daihika—the bodily necessities of life.

Daiva-varṇāśrama—the social system given by God for the upliftment of mankind. *See:* Varṇāśrama-dharma.

Daivīmāyā—the Lord's divine deluding potency, the material energy.

Dama—controlling the senses, and not deviating from the Lord's service.

Daṇḍavats—respectful prostrated obeisances offered to an elevated personality, such as one's spiritual master or the Supreme Personality of Godhead. The word literally means falling flat like a rod.

Dāsya—the devotional process of rendering service to the Lord in the mood of servitude.

Dasyu-dharma—the occupational duty of rogues and thieves.

Demigods—universal controllers and residents of the higher planets, also known as *devas* or *devatas*. Demigods are *jīvas* or souls whom the Supreme Lord Kṛṣṇa or Viṣṇu empowers to represent Him in the management of the universe. The first of the demigods is Brahmā. Some of the principal demigods are Indra—demigod of rain, Sūrya—of sunshine, Vāyu—of wind, Candra—of moonshine and Varuṇa—of water. There are thirty-three million demigods in all. Demigods live in the upper regions of the universe called *svarga*, or heaven. Less intelligent people worship the demigods through *karma-kāṇḍa* rituals to get material blessings in this life, and to be granted entrance into *svarga* in the next life. In the *Bhagavad-gītā*, Lord Kṛṣṇa condemns demigod worship as being *avidhi-pūrvaka*, against the true purpose of the *Vedas*.

Deva—a demigod or godly person.

Dharā-maṇḍala—the earth planet.

Dharma—religious principles; one's natural occupation; the quality of rendering service, which is the essential, eternal quality of the soul, regarded as inseparable from it. The Sanskrit term *dharma* is variously translated as duty, virtue, morality, righteousness, or religion, but no single English word conveys the actual import of *dharma*. *Dharma* ultimately means to surrender to the Supreme Lord, as Lord Kṛṣṇa commands Arjuna in the *Gīta*.

Dharmānvekṣamāṇah—strictly according to religious principles.

Dhīra—one who is undisturbed by the material energy in all circumstances; ecstasy of sober love for Kṛṣṇa.

Dvija—a *brāhmaṇa*, or twice-born person.

Dvija-bandhus—unworthy sons of the twice-born.

G

Garbhādhāna-saṁskāra—the Vedic ceremony of purification to be performed by parents before conceiving a child.

Govinda—a name of the Supreme Lord Kṛṣṇa meaning "one who gives pleasure to the land, the cows and the senses."

Grāmya-karma—mundane activities.

Gṛha-vrata—one who is attached to living in a comfortable home although it is actually miserable; one attached to the material duties of family life.

Gṛhastha—regulated householder life. One who leads a God conscious married life and raises a family in Kṛṣṇa consciousness according to the Vedic social system; the second order of Vedic spiritual life.

Guṇas—there are three *guṇas*, or modes of material nature: goodness (*sattva-guṇa*), passion (*rajo-guṇa*) and ignorance (*tamo-guṇa*). The modes are three measures of interaction between conscious spirit and unconscious matter. The modes may be compared to the three primary colors, yellow, red and blue, and consciousness may be compared to clear light. The color yellow symbolizes *sattva-guṇa*, the mode of goodness. This mode is pure, illuminating, and sinless. The color red symbolizes *rajo-guṇa*, the mode of passion, full of longings and desires. The color blue symbolizes *tamo-guṇa*, the mode of ignorance, which binds the soul to madness, indolence and sleep. The three modes combine to produce the vast spectrum of states of conditioned consciousness that encompasses all living entities within the universe.

Guru—spiritual master; one of the three spiritual authorities for a Vaiṣṇava. Literally, this term means heavy. The spiritual master is heavy with knowledge.

Guru-dakṣiṇā—a disciple's gift to his spiritual master, collected by begging and given as a token of gratitude.

Gurukula—a school of Vedic learning. Boys begin at five years old and live as celibate students, guided by a spiritual master.

H

Hari—the Supreme Lord, who removes all obstacles to spiritual progress; Lord Viṣṇu.

Hari-cakra—Kṛṣṇa's Sudarśana weapon, the wheel.

Harināma-saṅkīrtana—*See:* Harināma-yajña

Harināma-yajña—congregational chanting of the holy names of the Supreme Lord, the recommended sacrifice for this age.

Hṛdaya-granthi—the hard knot of material attachment in the heart.

Hṛta-jñāna—bereft of intelligence.

I

Īṣitva—in mystic yoga, the perfection of control over others.

J

Jagadīśa—the Supreme Lord, who is the proprietor of all the universes.

Jitendriya—one who has conquered the senses.

Jīva (jīvātmā)—the living entity, vital force in the body who is an eternal individual soul, part and parcel of the Supreme Lord; one of the five *tattvas* or Vedic ontological truths.

Jīvan-mukta—a person who is already liberated even while living in his present body

Jñāna—knowledge. Material *jñāna* does not go beyond the material body and its expansions. Transcendental *jñāna* discriminates between matter and spirit. Perfect *jñāna* is knowledge of the body, the soul and the Supreme Lord.

Jñāna-kāṇḍa—One of the three divisions of the *Vedas* which deals with empirical speculation in pursuit of truth; also such speculation itself; the portions of the *Vedas* containing knowledge of Brahman or spirit.

Jñānī—one who is engaged in the cultivation of knowledge (especially by philosophical speculation). Upon attaining perfection, a *jñānī* surrenders to Kṛṣṇa;

Jyotiḥ-śāstra—the Vedic science of astronomy.

K

Kaitava-dharma—cheating religion.

Kaivalya—the impersonal liberation of merging into the spiritual effulgence of Brahman emanating from the Lord.

Kāla-sarpa—the snake of time.

Kāma—lust; the desire to gratify one's own senses; desire, especially material desire and sexual desire; lust, as opposed to *prema*, or love of God.

Karma—1. material action performed according to scriptural regulations; 2. action pertaining to the development of the material body; 3. any material action which will incur a subsequent reaction and 4. the material reaction one incurs due to fruitive activities. The soul receives due reaction to work by taking his next birth in a lower species, or the human species, or a higher species. Or the soul may be liberated from birth and death altogether. All this depends upon whether the *karma* performed within this lifetime is ignorant, passionate, good or transcendental.

Karma-bandhana—bondage to the reactions of fruitive activities.

Karma-kāṇḍa—the division of the *Vedas* which deals with fruitive activities performed for the purpose of gradual purification of the grossly entangled materialist; the path of fruitive work.

Karmātmaka—one whose mind is colored with fruitive activity.

Karmendriya—The five working senses or organs of action: the mouth (with the double function of speaking and eating), the hands, the legs, the genitalia and the anus.

Karmī—a fruitive laborer, one who is attached to the fruits of work, a materialist who works hard to enjoy material life.

Kīrtana—glorification of the Supreme Lord; narrating or singing the glories of the Supreme Personality of Godhead and His Holy Names; the devotional process of chanting the names and glories of the Supreme Lord.

Koṭī—ten million.

Krpā-siddihi—perfection attained simply by the blessings of a great devotee or transcendentalist.

Kṛpaṇa—a miserly man who wastes his life by not striving for spiritual realization.

Kṛṣṇa-prasādam—*See:* Prasāda.

Kṣatriya—second of the four social orders of the *varṇāśrama* system; a warrior who is inclined to fight and lead others; the administrative or protective occupation.

Kuṅkuma—a sweetly-flavored reddish cosmetic powder which is thrown on the bodies of worshipable persons, also used by married women to decorate their foreheads.

L

Laghima-siddhi—mystic ability to make one's body very light.

Līla-avatāras—innumerable incarnations of the Supreme Lord who descend to the material world to display spiritual pastimes.

M

Mahābhāgavata—a pure devotee of the Supreme Lord in the highest stage of devotional life; the Sanskrit term *bhagavata* refers to a devotee of the Supreme Lord Śrī Kṛṣṇa.

Mahā-mantra— *See:* Hare Kṛṣṇa *mantra*

Mahātmā—a "great soul," an exalted devotee of Lord Kṛṣṇa, free from material contamination. He factually understands that Kṛṣṇa is everything, and therefore surrenders unto Him.

Manīṣā—intelligence.

Mantra—a transcendental sound or Vedic hymn, a prayer or chant; a pure sound vibration when repeated over and over delivers the mind from its material inclinations and illusion. The Vedic scriptures are composed of many thousands of *mantras.*

Martyaloka—the "world of death," the earth.

Māyā—Māyāvāda philosophy. Māyāvāda in Sanskrit means doctrine of illusion. In India, the philosophies of the Buddha and of Śaṅkarācārya are called Māyāvāda. The second grew out of the first. The fundamental principles accepted by both are the following: (1) name, form, individuality, thoughts, desires and words arise from *māyā* or illusion, not God; (2) *māyā* cannot be rationally explained, since the very idea that anything needs explaining is itself *māyā*; (3) the individual self or soul is not eternal, because upon liberation it ceases to exist; (4) like *māyā*, the state of liberation is beyond all explanation. The main difference between the two is that Śaṅkarācārya's Māyāvāda asserts that beyond *māyā* is an eternal impersonal monistic reality, Brahman, the nature of which is the self. Buddhism, however, aims at extinction (*nirodha*) as the final goal. Of the two, Śaṅkarācārya's Māyāvāda is more dangerous, as it apparently derives its authority from the *Vedas*. Much word-jugglery is employed to defend the Vedic origins of Śaṅkarācārya's Māyāvāda. But ultimately Māyāvādīs dispense with Vedic authority by concluding that the Supreme cannot be known through *śabda*, that the name of Kṛṣṇa is a material vibration, that the form of Kṛṣṇa is illusion, and so on. The Śaṅkarites agree with the Buddhists that *nāma-rūpa* (name and form) must always be *māyā*. Therefore Vaiṣṇavas reject both kinds of Māyāvāda as atheism. Buddhists generally do not deny that they are atheists, whereas the Śaṅkarite Māyāvādīs claim to be theists. But actually they are monists and pantheists. Their claim to theism is refuted by their belief that the Supreme Self is overcome by *māyā* and becomes the bound soul. Śaṅkarācārya's Māyāvāda is similar in significant ways to the Western doctrine of solipsism. Like solipsism, it arrives at a philosophical dead end. The questions that remain unanswered are: If my consciousness is the only reality, why can't I change the universe at will, simply by thought? And if my own self is the only reality, why am I dependent for my life, learning and happiness upon a world full of living entities that refuse to acknowledge this reality?

Māyā—illusion; an energy of Krṣna's which deludes the living entity into forgetfulness of the Supreme Lord. That which is not, unreality, deception, forgetfulness, material illusion. Under illusion a man thinks he can be happy in this temporary material world. The nature of the material world is that the more a man tries to exploit the material situation, the more he is bound by *māyā's* complexities; This is a Sanskrit term of many meanings. It may mean energy; *yoga-māyā* is the spiritual energy sustaining the transcendental manifestation of the spiritual Vaikuṇṭha world, while the reflection, *mahā-māyā*, is the energy of the material world. The Lord's twofold *māyā* bewilders the jīva, hence *māyā* also means bewilderment or illusion. Transcendental bewilderment is in love, by which the devotee sees God as his master, friend, dependent or amorous beloved. The material bewilderment of the living entity begins with his attraction to the glare of the brahmajyoti. That attraction leads to his entanglement in the modes of material nature. According to Bhaktisiddhānta Sarasvatī Ṭhākura, *māyā* also means that which can be measured. This is the feature of Lord Kṛṣṇa's *prakṛti* that captures the minds of scientific materialists. The Vaiṣṇava and Māyāvāda explanations of *māyā* are not the same.

Māyā-sukha—material happiness, which is illusory and temporary.

Mleccha—uncivilized humans, outside the Vedic system of society, who are generally meat-eaters, and whose consciousness is lower than a *śūdra*.

Moha—bewilderment, a *vyabhicāri-bhāva*; illusion.

Mokṣa—liberation from material bondage.

Mūḍha—a fool or rascal; ass-like person.

Muhūrta—a period of forty-eight minutes.

Mukta-puruṣa—a liberated soul.

Mukti—liberation of a conditioned soul from material consciousness and bondage.

Muni—a sage or self-realized soul.

Muni-putra—the son of a sage.

N

Naiṣṭhika-brahmacārī—one who has been celibate since birth.

Nakṣatra—a star or constellation through which the moon passes; a lunar mansion, *nakṣatras* mark the daily positions of the moon as it completes its orbit. The *nakṣatra* intervals are associated with star constellations, and one can see what *nakṣatra* the moon is in by observing the stars near the moon.

Nāma-aparādha—an offense against the holy name of the Lord.

Naradeva—the king, who is an earthly god.

Narādhama—the lowest of mankind, those who are socially and politically developed but have no religious principles.

Naṣṭa-buddhi—bereft of all good sense.

Nirguṇa—without material qualities; uncontaminated by the three modes of material nature.

Nirviśeṣa-vādīs—impersonalists who accept an Absolute but deny that He has any qualities of His own.

Niṣkāma—free from material desires.

Niṣkiñcana—free from all material possessions; having nothing; a renunciant.
Nistraiguṇya—the transcendental position above the three modes of nature.
Nitya-baddha—the eternally conditioned soul, bound in the material world.
Nitya-muktas—Nitya-siddhas, eternally liberated souls, associates of the Lord who never come in contact with the external energy, and who never forget Kṛṣṇa at any time.
Nivṛtti-mārga—the path of renunciation, which leads to liberation; directions for giving up the material world for higher spiritual understanding.

O

Oṁkāra—*oṁ*, the root of Vedic knowledge; known as the *mahā-vākya*, the supreme sound; the transcendental syllable which represents Kṛṣṇa, and which is vibrated by transcendentalists for attainment of the Supreme while undertaking sacrifices, charities and penances; it denotes the Personality of Godhead as the root of the creation, maintenance and destruction of the cosmic manifestation.

P

Pañcarātrika-vidhi—the devotional process of Deity worship and *mantra* meditation as found in the Pañcarātra literature.
Para—transcendental.
Parā-prakṛti—the superior, spiritual energy or nature of the Lord.
Paramahaṁsa—a topmost, God-realized, swanlike devotee of the Supreme Lord; the highest stage of *sannyāsa*.
Paramātmā—*See:* Supersoul.
Paramparā—the disciplic succession, beginning with Kṛṣṇa, through which spiritual knowledge is transmitted by bonafide spiritual masters; literally, one after the other.
Pāṣaṇḍī—an offender or atheist; a non-believer who thinks God and the demigods are on the same level, or who considers devotional activities to be material.
Piṇḍa—an offering made to departed ancestors.
Pitās—forefathers; especially those departed ancestors who have been promoted to one of the higher planets.
Pitṛloka—the planet of the ancestors, a heavenly planet.
Prajāpatis—the progenitors of living entities, chief of whom is Lord Brahmā; the demigods in charge of populating the universe.
Prākāmya—the mystic ability to fulfill any of one's desires.

Prakṛti—material nature, the energy of the Supreme (literally that which is predominated); the female principle enjoyed by the male *puruṣa.* There are two *prakṛtis—apara-prakṛti* or the material nature, and *para-prakṛti* or the spiritual nature (living entities)—which are both predominated over by the Supreme Personality of Godhead; one of the five *tattvas* or Vedic ontological truths.

Pramāda—inattention or misunderstanding of reality; a woman to whom a man becomes madly attached.

Pramatta—one who is crazy because he cannot control his senses

Prāpti-siddhi—mystic perfection of acquisition by which the *yogī* can reach his hand anywhere and obtain any material object.

Prasāda, or prasādam—"the mercy of Lord Kṛṣṇa." Food spiritualized by being prepared for the pleasure of Kṛṣṇa, and by offering with love and devotion. Ordinary food subjects one to karmic reactions, one of the reasons being the many living entities that gave up their lives during the preparation. But food offered to Kṛṣṇa is freed of sin and invokes an attraction to Him.

Praśānta—undisturbed by the modes of nature.

Pravṛtti-mārga—the path of sense enjoyment in accordance with Vedic regulations.

Priyatama—dear most.

Puṁścalī—a harlot, or unchaste woman.

Puṇya-śloka—verses that increase one's piety; one who is glorified by such verses, refers to Lord Kṛṣṇa.

Pūrṇa—the complete whole, Lord Kṛṣṇa.

Puruṣa—the enjoyer, or male; the living entity or the Supreme Lord; Viṣṇu, the incarnation of the Lord for material creation; the male or controlling principle. This term may be applied to both, the individual living being and the Supreme Personality of Godhead.

Puruṣa-avatāras—the primary expansions of Lord Viṣṇu who effect the creation, maintenance and destruction of the material universes.

Puruṣottama—Lord Kṛṣṇa, who is the Supreme Person, meaning "the most exalted person."

R

Rājarṣi—a great saintly king.

Rajoguṇa—the mode of passion of material nature.

Rākṣasa—a class of *asura* or ungodly people. The *rākṣasas* are always opposed to God's will. Generally, they are man-eaters and have grotesque forms.

S

Śabda-brahma—transcendental sound vibration; the injunctions of the *Vedas* and *Upaniṣads*.

Sac-cid-ānanda-vigraha—the Lord's transcendental form, which is eternal and full of knowledge and bliss; the eternal transcendental form of the living entity.

Ṣaḍ-bhūja-mūrti—the form of the Lord with six arms—two arms of Rāmacandra, two arms of Kṛṣṇa and two arms of Śrī Caitanya Mahāprabhu.

Sādhu—a saint or Krishna conscious devotee, or Vaiṣṇava. A wandering holy man; a saintly person, one of the three authorities for a Vaiṣṇava. *See:* Guru, Śāstra.

Sadhu-saṅga—the association of saintly persons.

Sakāma-bhakta—a devotee with material desires.

Sakhya-rasa—a relationship with the Supreme Lord in devotional friendship.

Śālagrāma-śilā—the worshipable Deity of the Lord Nārāyaṇa in the form of a round stone. It is described in detail in the final canto of the *Padma Purāṇa*.

Sama—control of the mind.

Sama-darśī—one who sees with equal vision; one who has knowledge of the soul and does not give undue consideration to the body, which is nothing but a dress for the soul.

Samādhi—total absorption, and trance of the mind and senses in consciousness of the Supreme Godhead and service to Him. Also refers to the tomb where a great soul's body is laid after his departure from this world.

Samprekṣya nāsikāgram—keeping one's eyes half-open in the practice of *yoga*.

Saṁsāra—the cycle of repeated birth and death in the material world. The conditioned soul, captivated by the modes of material nature, is moved as if on a wheel through 8,400,000 kinds of births, lifetime after lifetime. Impelled by material nature, time and its own activities, the soul is forced into various wombs, until it surrenders to the Supreme Īśvara, Kṛṣṇa, the controller of the wheel of *saṁsāra*.

Saṅkīrtana—congregational or public glorification of the Supreme Lord Kṛṣṇa through chanting of His holy names, and glorification of His fame and pastimes.

Sannyāsa—the renounced order, the fourth stage of Vedic spiritual life in the Vedic system of *varṇāsrama-dharma*, which is free from family relationships, and in which all activities are completely dedicated to Kṛṣṇa. It is the order of ascetics who travel and constantly preach the message of Godhead for the benefit of all. It is usually accepted at age fifty, after a man has fulfilled his household responsibilities.

Sannyāsī—one in the *sannyāsa* (renounced) order.

Śānta—peaceful.

Sarva-kāraṇa-kāraṇam—Kṛṣṇa, the cause of all causes.

Śāstra—the revealed scriptures, obeyed by all those who follow the Vedic teachings. Śās means "to regulate and direct" and tra means "an instrument"; Vedic literature; The Vedic scriptures; one of the three authorities for a Vaiṣṇava. In his purport to *Cc., Ādi-līlā* 17.157, Śrīla Prabhupāda writes: The word *śāstra* is derived from the dhātu, or verbal root, śas. *Sas-dhātu* pertains to controlling or ruling. A government's ruling through force or weapons is called *śastra*. Thus whenever there is ruling, either by weapons or by injunctions, the *śas-dhātu* is the basic principle. Between *śastra* (ruling through weapons) and *śāstra* (ruling through the injunctions of the scriptures), the better is *śāstra*. Our Vedic scriptures are not ordinary law books of human common sense; they are the statements of factually liberated persons unaffected by the imperfectness of the senses. *Śāstra* must be correct always, not sometimes correct and sometimes incorrect. In the Vedic scriptures, the cow is described as a mother. Therefore she is a mother for all time; it is not, as some rascals say, that in the Vedic age she was a mother but she is not in this age. If *śāstra* is an authority, the cow is a mother always; she was a mother in the Vedic age, and she is a mother in this age also. If one acts according to the injunctions of *śāstra*, he is freed from the reactions of sinful activity. For example, the propensities for eating flesh, drinking wine and enjoying sex life are all natural to the conditioned soul. The path of such enjoyment is called *pravṛtti-mārga*. The *śāstra* says, *pravṛttir eṣāṁ bhūtānāṁ nivṛttis tu mahā-phalā:* one should not be carried away by the propensities of defective conditioned life; one should be guided by the principles of the *śāstras*. A child's propensity is to play all day long, but it is the injunction of the *śāstras* that the parents should take care to educate him. The *śāstras* are there just to guide the activities of human society.

But because people do not refer to the instructions of *śāstras*, which are free from defects and imperfections, they are therefore misguided by so-called educated teachers and leaders who are full of the deficiencies of conditioned life.

Sattva-guṇa—the mode of material goodness, predominated by Lord Viṣṇu.

Satya—truthfulness.

Satya-kāma—directing all of one's desires to the Supreme Truth.

Sevā—devotional service.

Sevaka—a servant.

Sevya—one who is served.

Siddhis—mystic perfections which are usually acquired by yoga practice, but natural to residents of Siddhaloka: becoming small like a particle (*aṇimā-siddhi*), or lighter than a soft feather (*laghimā-siddhi*), getting anything from everywhere (*prāpti-siddhi*), becoming heavier than the heaviest (*mahimā-siddhi*), create something wonderful or annihilate anything at will (*īśitva-siddhi*), to control all material elements (*vaśitva-siddhi*), possessing such power as will never be frustrated in any desire (*prākāmya-siddhi*), assuming any shape or form one may desire (*kāmāvasāyitā-siddhi*).

Śivatama—the most auspicious.

Smaraṇam—the devotional process of remembering the Supreme Lord; constant thinking of Kṛṣṇa (one of the nine methods of devotional service).

Smṛti—remembrance, a *vyabhicāri-bhāva*; revealed scriptures supplementary to the *śruti*, or original Vedic scriptures, which are the *Vedas* and *Upaniṣads*; scriptures compiled by living entities under transcendental direction; the corollaries of the *Vedas*; one of the five functions of *buddhi*.

Soma-rasa—a life-extending heavenly beverage available on the moon to demigods on the higher planets.

Śrāddha—the ceremony of making offerings to one's ancestors to free them from suffering.

Śravaṇam—the devotional process of hearing about the Supreme Lord.

Sravaṇam kīrtanaṁ viṣṇoḥ—the devotional process of hearing and chanting about Lord Viṣṇu, or Kṛṣṇa.

Śrīvatsa—the sign on the chest of Lord Viṣṇu and Nārāyaṇa, indicating the goddess of fortune, Lakṣmī.

Śruti—knowledge via hearing; the original Vedic scriptures (the *Vedas* and *Upaniṣads*), given directly by the Supreme Lord.

Strī—women.

Śuddha-sattva—the spiritual platform of pure goodness; the transcendental mode of purified goodness. *See:* Kṛṣṇa, Modes of nature.

Śūdra—a member of the fourth social order, laborer class, in the traditional Vedic social system. They render service to the three higher classes, namely the *brāhmaṇas*, the *kṣatriyas*, and the *vaiśyas*.

Śukla—a person in the mode of goodness; also, a name for Lord Viṣṇu.

Sukṛti—auspicious activity; pious persons.

Suras—demigods, devotees.

Svāṁśa—Kṛṣṇa's plenary portion.

Svargaloka—the heavenly planets or abodes of the demigods in the material world.

Svarūpa-vismṛti—forgetting one's real constitutional position.

T

Tamo-guṇa—the mode of ignorance, or darkness of material nature. It is controlled by Lord Śiva.

Tapasya—austerity; voluntary acceptance of some material trouble for progress in spiritual life.

Tattva-darśī—one who has seen the truth.

Tilaka—sacred clay markings placed on the forehead and other parts of the body to designate one as a follower of Viṣṇu, Rāma, Śiva etc.

Titikṣā—tolerance; endurance of unhappiness.

Trivikrama—a name for the Supreme Lord Vāmanadeva. indicating His incarnation as the dwarf *brāhmaṇa* Vāmanadeva. Meaning literally "He who took three big steps." this name stands for the Lord's pastime of begging land measuring three steps of His own feet as a charity from Mahārāja Balī, in the process covering the entire universe with His two steps, and extending His foot through the coverings of the material universe and into the Causal Ocean.

Tulasī—a pure devotee of Kṛṣṇa in the form of a basil plant, worshipped by Vaiṣṇavas and other followers of Vedic culture, and very dear to Lord Kṛṣṇa. Its leaves and *mañjarīs* (buds) are always offered to His lotus feet.

U

Udāra—magnanimous.

Ugra-karma—unnecessary, evil activities, not sanctioned by the scriptures.

Upādhis—material designations.

Upāsanā-kāṇḍa—portions of the *Vedas* dealing with ceremonies of worship, especially demigod worship; one of the three departments of Vedic knowledge.

Upāsya—worshipable.

Urukrama—the Supreme Lord, who takes wonderful steps (especially as the dwarf-*brāhmaṇa* incarnation, Vāmanadeva).

Uttamaśloka—the Supreme Lord, Kṛṣṇa, who is worshiped by the choicest verses and the best poetry.

V

Vaikuṇṭha—the eternal planets of the spiritual world, the abode of Lord Nārāyaṇa, which lies beyond the coverings of the material universe. Literally, "the place with no anxiety."

Vairāgya—renunciation; detachment from matter and engagement of the mind in spirit.

Vaiṣṇava—a devotee of the Supreme Lord, Viṣṇu, or Kṛṣṇa.

Vaiṣṇava-aparādha—an offense to the devotee of Kṛṣṇa.

Vaiśya—member of the mercantile or agricultural class, according to the system of four social orders and four spiritual orders.

Vānaprastha—A retired householder, a member of the third Vedic spiritual order or *āśrama*, who quits home to cultivate renunciation and travels to holy places, in preparation for the renounced order of life.

Vandana—the devotional process of offering prayers to the Lord.

Vaṇik—a merchant.

Varṇa—the four socio-occupational divisions of Vedic society. Contrary to popular misconception, *varṇas* are nor fixed by birth, but are determined by a person's inclination toward different types of work and his psychological qualities. The four *varṇas* are *brāhmaṇas*, *kṣatriyas*, *vaiśyas* and *śūdras*.

Varṇa-śaṅkara—children conceived without regard for Vedic religious principles; thus unwanted population.

Varṇāśrama-dharma—the system of four social and four spiritual orders of Vedic society, based on the individual's psycho-physical qualities and tendencies toward particular types of work.

Vibhinnāṁśa—the separated expansions of the Supreme Lord, the minute living entities, who are part and parcel of Kṛṣṇa.

Vidagdha—one who is expert in the art of attracting women.

Vidūra-vigata—a *caṇḍāla*. *See:* Caṇḍāla.

Vijara—not subjected to the miseries of old age.

Vijighatsa—free from desire for material enjoyment.

Vijñāna—the practical realization of spiritual knowledge. *See: Jñāna.*

Vikarma—unauthorized or sinful work, performed against the injunctions of revealed scriptures.

Vimūḍhas—foolish rascals.

Viraha—transcendental bliss in separation from the Lord.

Virāṭ-rupa—the universal form of the Supreme Lord containing the totality of the entire material manifestation.

Vīra-vrata—fully determined.

Viṣaya—the object of worship; an object of material sense gratification.

Viṣaya-taraṅga—the waves of material existence.

Viṣṇu tattva—a primary expansion of Kṛṣṇa having full status as Godhead. The term also applies to primary expansions of the Supreme Lord such as Rāma, Nṛsiṁha etc.

Viśoka—callous to material distress and happiness; the charioteer of Bhīma.

Vivāha-yajña—the sacrifice of marriage.

Y

Yajña—a Vedic sacrifice; also a name for the Supreme Lord meaning "the personification of sacrifice"; the goal and enjoyer of all sacrifices.

Yajña-puruṣa—the supreme enjoyer of all sacrifices.

Yamadūtas—the messengers of Yamarāja, the lord of death.

Yoga—Literally, connection; the discipline of self-realization. a spiritual discipline meant for linking one's consciousness with the Supreme Lord, Kṛṣṇa; one of the six systems of Vedic philosophy, taught by Patañjali. Through the process of *bhakti-yoga*, the consciousness of the individual soul connects with its source, Kṛṣṇa.

Yogamāyā—the internal, spiritual energy of the Supreme Lord, to which the external energy, *mahāmayā*, is subordinate, and which hides Him from non-devotees.

Yogeśvara—the supreme master of all mystic powers, Kṛṣṇa.

Yojana—a standard Vedic measurement of distance, equal to eight miles.

Yuga—one of the four ages of the universe; they differ in length and rotate like calendar months.

Sanskrit Pronunciation Guide

Throughout the centuries, the Sanskrit language has been written in a variety of alphabets. The mode of writing most widely used throughout India, however, is called *devanāgarī*, which means, literally, the writing used in "the cities of the demigods." The *devanāgarī* alphabet consists of forty-eight characters: thirteen vowels and thirty-five consonants. Ancient Sanskrit grammarians arranged this alphabet according to practical linguistic principles, and this order has been accepted by all Western scholars. The system of transliteration used in this book conforms to a system that scholars have accepted to indicate the pronunciation of each Sanskrit sound.

Vowels

अ a आ ā इ i ई ī उ u ऊ ū ऋ ṛ ॠ ṝ ऌ ḷ

ए e ऐ ai ओ o औ au

Consonants

Guttarals:	क ka	ख kha	ग ga	घ gha	ङ ṅa
Palatals:	च ca	छ cha	ज ja	झ jha	ञ ña
Cerebrals:	ट ṭa	ठ ṭha	ड ḍa	ढ ḍha	ण ṇa
Dentals:	त ta	थ tha	द da	ध dha	न na
Labials:	प pa	फ pha	ब ba	भ bha	म ma
Semivowels:	य ya	र ra	ल la	व va	
Sibilants:	श śa	ष ṣa	स sa		
Aspirate :	ह ha	Anusvāra : ं ṁ	Visarga : ः ḥ		

Numerals

०–0 १–1 २–2 ३–3 ४–4 ५–5 ६–6 ७–7 ८–8 ९–9

The vowels are written as follows after a consonant:

ा ā ि i ी ī ु u ू ū ृ ṛ ॄ ṝ े e ै ai ो o ौ au

For example: क ka का kā कि ki की kī कु ku कू kū
कृ kṛ कॄ kṝ के ke कै kai को ko कौ kau

Generally two or more consonants in conjunction are written together in a special form, as for example: **क्ष kṣa** **त्र tra**

The vowel "a" is implied after a consonant with no vowel symbol.

The symbol virāma (्) indicates that there is no final vowel: क्

The vowels are pronounced as follows:.

a — as in b**u**t
ā — as in f**a**r but held twice as long as **a**
ai — as in **ai**sle
au — as in h**ow**
e — as in th**ey**
i — as in p**i**n
ī — as in p**i**que but held twice as long as **i**
ḷ — as in **lree**
o — as in **go**
ṛ — as in **ri**m
ṝ — as in **ree**d but held twice as long as **ṛ**
u — as in p**u**sh
ū — as in r**u**le but held twice as long as **u**

The consonants are pronounced as follows:

Gutterals
(pronounced from the throat)
k — as in **k**ite
kh — as in Ec**kh**art
g — as in **g**ive
gh — as in di**g-h**ard
ṅ — as in si**ng**

Cerebrals
(pronounced with the tip of the tongue against the roof of the mouth)
ṭ — as in **t**ub
ṭh — as in ligh**t-h**eart
ḍ — as in **d**ove
ḍh — as in re**d-h**ot
ṇ — as in si**n**g

Labials
(pronounced with the lips)
p — as in **p**ine
ph — as in u**p-h**ill
b — as in **b**ird
bh — as in ru**b-h**ard
m — as in **m**other

Palatals
(pronounced with the middle of the tongue against the palate)
c — as in **ch**air
ch — as in staun**ch-h**eart
j — as in **j**oy
jh — as in he**dgeh**og
ñ — as in ca**ny**on

Dentals
(pronounced like the cerebrals but with the tongue against the teeth)

t	—	as in **t**ub
th	—	as in ligh**t-h**eart
d	—	as in **d**ove
dh	—	as in re**d-h**ot
n	—	as in **n**ut

Semivowels

y	—	as in **y**es
r	—	as in **r**un
l	—	as in **l**ight
v	—	as in **v**ine, except when preceded in the same syllable by a consonant, then like in s**w**an

Sibilants

ś	—	as in the German word *sprechen*
ṣ	—	as in **sh**ine
s	—	as in **s**un

Aspirate

h	—	as in **h**ome

Anusvāra

ṁ	—	a resonant nasal sound as in the French word *bon*

Visarga

ḥ	—	a final **h**-sound: **aḥ** is pronounced like **aha**; **iḥ** like **ihi**.

There is no strong accentuation of syllables in Sanskrit, or pausing between words in a line, only a flowing of short and long syllables (the long twice as long as the short). A long syllable is one whose vowel is long (**ā, ai, au, e , ī, o, ṝ, ū**) or whose short vowel is followed by more than one consonant (including **ḥ** and **ṁ**). Aspirated consonants (consonants followed by an **h**) count as single consonants.

Index of Sanskrit Verses

This index constitutes a complete listing of the first and third lines of each of the Sanskrit poetry verses of this volume of *Śrīmad-Bhāgavatam*, arranged in English alphabetical order. The first column gives the Sanskrit transliteration; the second, the chapter-verse reference. Apostrophes are alphabetized as a's.

A

O

P

R

Index of Verses Quoted

This index lists the verses quoted in the purports of this volume of *Śrīmad-Bhāgavatam*. Numerals in boldface type refer to the first or third lines of verses quoted in full; numerals in roman type refer to partially quoted verses.

General Index

The references to the translations and purports of the verses of *Śrīmad-Bhāgavatam* are presented in the following format: "xx.yy (para n)", where 'xx' is the chapter number, 'yy' is the verse number (text number) and 'n' is the paragraph number in the purport. Numerals in the boldface type indicate the translations and those in regular type indicate the purports. Numerals in the mixed type indicate both translation and purports. While counting the paragraphs in the purports, please remember that, the new paragraph begins (in the purport) only where the first word is indented.

A

Abhavaḥ defined, 14.44
Abhaya, **20.3–4**
Abhayā River, **20.21**
Abhijit star
  location of, on Śiśumāra, **23.5**, **23.6**
  stars headed by, **22.11**
Abortion, 14.9 (para 1), 17.12 (para 2)
Absolute Truth
  devotees reveal, **12.12**
  features of, three, 11.2, **12.11**
  Kṛṣṇa as, 12.11, 18.19 (para 1)
  liberation via, 12.11
  Rahūgaṇa's faith in discussions about, **10.15**
  as transcendental to material qualities, 12.11
  Vedic study does not reveal, 12.12
  See also: Kṛṣṇa; Supreme Lord
Ācārya. See: Spiritual master; *specific* ācāryas
Acintya-śakti, 18.31
Activities
  association with nature's modes &, 9.3 (para 2)
  bondage via material, 11.4
  contaminated by nature's modes, 4.6
  of devotees meant to satisfy Lord, 7.6 (para 4)
  devotional service opposed by material, 11.4
  freedom from reactions via, 1.16
  fruitive. *See:* Fruitive activities
  Lord's satisfaction &, 3.8
  material, as conditioned soul's only engagement, 14.8
  mind expands material, **11.4**
  pious. *See:* Pious activities
  pure & contaminated, 4.6
Activities (*Continued*)
  reactions via, 1.16
  for senses, **5.27**
Adāhyo 'yam, 6.8
A defined, 19.7
Adharma defined, **5.19**
Adhipuṇyam explained, 6.13
Adhokṣaja explained, 3.4–5
Adhyātma cited on proper action, 5.10–13 (para 3)
Ādi-puruṣa defined, 18.7 (para 1)
Ādityas, 20.3–4 (para 2)
Advaita, Śrī, 19.24
Agasti star, **23.6**
Agni
  Dhruva honored by, **23.1**
  Kuśadvīpa's inhabitants worship, **20.16**
  Lord receives sacrificial ingredients from, **20.17**
  planet of, on Śiśumāra's tail, **23.5**
  Priyavrata's sons named after, **1.25**
  Viṣṇu expands as, 20.3–4 (para 1)
Āgnīdhra, King
  birth of, 2.2 (para 2)
  Brahmā worshiped by, **2.2**
  demigoddess wife desired by, 2.2 (para 3)
  flattery art known by, **2.17**
  as handsome, 2.5 (para 2)
  intelligence lost by, 2.7 (para 1)
  Jambūdvīpa residents protected by, **2.1**
  material attraction &, 2.17
  Pitṛloka attained by, **2.22**
  Pitṛloka residence desired by, **2.2**
  Priyavrata gives sovereignty to, **1.33**
  Priyavrata's order followed by, **2.1**
  Pūnacitti proposed to by, **2.15**

Body, material (*Continued*)
karma designates type of, 9.3 (para 2)
liberated persons &, **1.16**
living entity living force of, 12. 5–6
Lord's body perceived as, 5.19 (para 1), 18.15
via Lord's direction, **1.15**, 10.12
material nature source of, 17.24 (para 1)
Māyāvādīs regard Kṛṣṇa's body as, 18.15
via mind, **11.5**
as misery's source, **5.4**
murder &, 18.32 (para 2)
number of different forms of, 1.13
purpose for accepting, 18.8 (para 2)
via sense gratification, **5.4**
sense gratification available through, **5.4**
soul different from, 10.9, 10.20
soul present in, 5.19 (para 1)
in subterranean heavens, **24.13**
subtle body's role in changing, 1.35 (para 3)
suffering from, 5.1 (para 1), 5.10–13 (para 2), 19.14
on sun planet, 20.46
as temporary but not false, 18.32 (para 2)
tolerance of pains & pleasures of, 5.30 (para 1)
See also: Tolerance
transformations of, **10.10**
Viṣṇu accepts, 18.15
See also: Bodily conception of life
Body, spiritual
Lord's body as, **5.19**
Ṛṣabha-deva's body as, **4.14**, **5.19**, 5.30 (para 2), 5.34, **6.7**, Endnote Pr1 (para 1)
Vaikuṇṭha's residents possess, 5.19 (para 2)
Bondage, material
via attraction to women, 2.6
via bodily conception, **11.15**
chanting Lord's glories saves one from, **9.3**
via family life, 1.1 (para 1), **14.32**
via forgetfulness, 11.5
freedom from. *See:* Liberation
via fruitive activity, 5.6, **19.20**
liberation from. *See:* Liberation
Lord master of, 20.5 (para 3)
male-female attachment cause of, 14.28
material attraction cause of, 8.12
Bondage, material (*Continued*)
via material enjoyment, desire for, **11.15**
mind cause of, **6.5**, **11.7**, 11.16
remembrance of Lord saves one from, **9.3**
via sense gratification, 1.1 (para 1)
via sinful activities, 13.2
Brahmacārī-āśrama
Absolute Truth not understood by observing vows of, 12.12
compared with *gṛhastha-āśrama,* 14.18
Jaḍa Bharata instructed in rules of, **9.6**
principles of, 1.1 (para 1)
Priyavrata gives up vow of, 1.21 (para 1)
Priyavrata trained in principles of, 1.1 (para 1)
Ṛṣabha-deva enters, **4.8**
Brahmacārī-bhūta defined, 1.16, 5.14 (para 1), 19.20
Brahma defined, 4.16
Brahma-jijñāsā defined, 5.14 (para 1), 10.15 (para 2), 10.19 (para 2)
Brahma-jyoti
jñānīs satisfied by merging into, 1.1 (para 2)
Kṛṣṇa source of, 11.13–14 (para 1)
as Lord's bodily rays, 12.11
universes rest on, 12.10
Vāsudeva cause of, 11.13–14 (para 1)
See also: Brahman, impersonal
Brahmaloka
Bhārata-varṣa compared with, **19.23**
as Brahman effulgence, 1.21 (para 2)
as Brahmā's abode, 1.7 (para 3)
as spiritual world, 1.7 (para 3)
See also: Satyaloka
Brahmā, Lord
abode of. *See:* Brahmaloka; Satyaloka
Āgnīdhra worships, **2.2**
Apsarās descend on order of, 2.20
as *ātma-yonī,* 1.7 (para 1)
benedictions in family life awarded by, 2.15
as *bhagavān,* 1.7 (para 1), 2.3
birth from Lord by, **1.7**
brāhmaṇas worship, **2.16**
carrier of, **1.8–9**
compared with Viṣṇu, 2.3
as conditioned souls' well-wisher, 1.7 (para 1)

C

F

H

I

J

K

M

N

O

P

Q

R

S

Scientists, modern (*Continued*)
as cheaters, 14.26
ignorance by, 1.13
Lord challenged by, 18.27 (para 1)
material nature studied by, 18.33 (para 1)
narādhamas, 14.27 (para 1–2)
Rāhu compared with, 24.3
shortcomings of, 17.4, 17.24 (para 1)
speculation by, 16.4
theory of, about sunshine, 7.14 (para 2)
Scorpio, **21.5**
Scripture(s). *See:* Vedic literatures; *specific scriptures*
Self-realization
via devotional service, 1.27 (para 2)
ignorance of, defeats human life, 1.1 (para 1)
as life's mission, 1.1 (para 1)
Nara-Nārāyaṇa teaches process of, **19.9**
via *varṇāśrama-dharma,* 1.29 (para 1)
Semen, punishment for forcing wife to drink, **26.26**
Sense gratification
activities for, as contaminated, 4.6
attachment to. *See:* Attachment, material
bondage via, 1.1 (para 1)
as dangerous, 5.25
detachment from. *See:* Detachment
by devotees in lower stage, 5.7
dogs & hogs experience, **5.1**
family life &, 1.1 (para 1), 1.4
four principles of, 18.3 (para 1)
human life not meant for, **5.1–1**
jñānīs & *yogīs* fail to overcome, 18.8 (para 1)
karmīs strive for, 1.19 (para 1)
king engages citizens in, 10.23
living entity becomes attached to, **13.1**
living entity connected to material world by, 5.4
material body awards, **5.4**
material body via, **5.4**
materialists absorbed in, 18.3 (para 1), 18.9 (para 4)
purification from desire for. *See:* Purification
regulative principles govern, 26.6
sinful activity via, **5.4**
spiritualists can't give up, **13.17**
Sense gratification (*Continued*)
in subterranean heavens, **24.8**
time wasted by endeavor for, **5.7**
wealth misused for, 14.12
See also: Material enjoyment
Senses
compared to plunderers, **14.2**
compared to serpents, 1.17 (para 2), 2.5 (para 2), 17.3
as conditioned soul's "co-wives," **1.17**
control of
by Āgnīdhra, 2.5 (para 2)
by *brāhmaṇas,* **5.24**
by devotees, **1.35**, 2.5 (para 2)
via devotional service, 1.17 (para 1), 2.5 (para 2)
family life &, **1.17**, **1.18**
fear &, **1.17**
by Jaḍa Bharata's father, **9.1–2**
by *jñānīs,* 1.19 (para 1)
Kṛṣṇa consciousness movement teaches, 14.2
by Lord, **19.3**
via Lord's shelter, **17.19**
via mind control, 11.6
necessity of, 6.3
by political leaders, 13.15
by Priyavrata's sons, **1.27**
renunciation &, 1.17 (para 1)
by Ṛṣabha-deva, 4.2
by saintly persons, **14.39**
sannyāsa-āśrama &, 1.18
vānaprastha-āśrama &, 1.18
varṇāśrama trains one in, 1.18
& *yoga* practice, 2.5 (para 2), 11.6
devotional service engagement for, 1.17 (para 1), 1.17 (para 2)
as enemies, 1.17 (para 2)
jñānīs try to conquer, 1.19 (para 1)
knowledge acquired by, **14.1**
living entities struggle with, 17.24 (para 1), 18.12 (para 1)
Lord master of, **17.22–23**, **18.19**
Lord not understood by material, 1.11 (para 2)
as Lord's partial manifestations, **18.18**
Lord's, unpolluted by objects, **19.12**

Senses (*Continued*)
mind uses, to expand material activities, **11.4**
money plundered by, **14.2**
nature's laws superior to, 1.12 (para 1)
objects of
compared to mirage in desert, **14.6**
listed, **11.10**
proper engagement for, **5.27**, 14.2
purification of. *See:* Purification
Śiva creates, **17.22–23**
suffering due to, 6.3
working, listed, 11.10
yogīs conquerors of, 1.19 (para 1)
Śeṣa defined, 25.9
Śeṣa, Lord. *See:* Ananta; Saṅkarṣaṇa
Sevā defined, 5.19 (para 2)
Sevaka defined, 5.19 (para 2)
Sevayā explained, 12.3
Sevya defined, 5.19 (para 2)
Sex
association with people fond of, **5.2**
in Atala, **24.16**
attraction to, in spiritual world, 17.12 (para 2)
as basis of material life, 14.22, 14.30 (para 1)
as *brahmacarya,* 5.10–13 (para 2)
conditioned soul bewildered by attraction to, **14.9**
conditioned souls have tendency for, 9.15
in eight earthly *varṣas,* **17.12**
family life affords pleasure of, **14.32**
family life based on, **5.7**, 13.4
family life concession for, 19.5 (para 1)
family life institution of, 13.14
illicit
abortion result of, 14.9 (para 1–2)
demigods witness, **14.9**
devotees fall down due to, 14.22
Kṛṣṇa consciousness movement forbids, 13.10, 26.21
as most prominent sin, 14.9 (para 1–2)
punishment for, **14.9**, **26.20**–21
as sinful, 4.5 (para 2), 14.9 (para 1–2)
spiritual advancement hampered by, 5.10–13 (para 2), 14.22
illusion expanded by attraction to, **5.8**
Sex (*Continued*)
intoxication enhances desire for, 14.22
in Kali-yuga, 2.2 (para 2)
material life expanded by, 14.35
meat-eating enhances desire for, 14.22
as modern man's only happiness, 5.1 (para 2)
& monkeylike humans, **14.30**
by monkeys, 14.32
pleasure of, compared to hunter, **14.32**
purpose for, 14.9 (para 1)
rules & regulations governing, 13.4
spiritual understanding & attraction to, 13.19
suffering via, **13.10**, 14.22, 19.5 (para 1)
Siddhaloka
Brahmā received by residents of, **1.8**
Rāhu's distance from, **24.4**
residents of, powers possessed by, 1.8, 24.4
Siddhas
Ananta offered prayers by, **25.7**
celestial lakes & gardens enjoyed by, **16.13–14**
Gandharvas inferior to, **5.21–22**
Kinnaras superior to, **5.21–22**
mystic perfection enjoyed by, **16.13–14**
Siddhis defined, 5.35, 6.15
Śikṣāṣṭaka, quotation from
on benediction desired by devotee, 18.9 (para 3)
See also: Caitanya Mahāprabhu quoted
Siṁhala, **19.29**
Siṁhikā, **24.1**
Sindhu, **10.1**
Sinful activity (activities)
bondage via, 13.2
by Durgā's worshipers, 9.18
eradication of, **3.4–5**, 3.12, **6.16**, **23.9**
four, listed, 4.5 (para 2), 5.4
freedom from reactions to, & chanting Lord's names, 24.20 (para 2)
gold facilitates, **14.7**
government leaders responsible for citizens', 15.7
hellish life via, **26.3**
illicit sex most prominent, 14.9 (para 2)
in India, 2.1 (para 2)
killing as, 10.2

T

Z